STRING MUSIC IN PRINT

A Guide to Music for

VIOLIN

VIOLA

VIOLONCELLO

DOUBLE-BASS

String Music IN PRINT

BY MARGARET K. FARISH

R. R. BOWKER COMPANY, 1965 *New York*

Table of Contents

STRING MUSIC IN PRINT is a guide to published music for the violin, viola, violoncello and double-bass. It contains information on solo music, accompanied and unaccompanied; chamber music, including combinations of stringed instruments with wind instruments, keyboard instruments, harp, guitar, percussion and voice; methods and studies. To my best knowledge, all music listed was available on July 1, 1964.

This book is intended primarily for those who wish to obtain music. Editorial decisions have been based upon the desire to provide a practical and convenient tool for the use of performers, teachers, librarians, music dealers and distributors. The material in STRING MUSIC IN PRINT was compiled from catalogues and lists provided by the publishers of the music or their representatives. Although bibliographies and reference works were frequently consulted for verification and amplification of information sent by publishers, no listings were made from these sources, with the few exceptions noted under literature in Section XV. At times the temptation to break this rule was great. Some catalogues are notoriously incomplete, but, even so, publishers are the only proper source of information for a book such as this one. Responsibility here is shared by the editor and the publishers, and any errors are our own.

STRING MUSIC IN PRINT was designed to provide a complete list of all music for stringed instruments published in the United States. A request for information was sent in September, 1963, to all known music publishers. Second letters were sent when necessary, and an announcement of the closing date was mailed in May, 1964. All of the large and most of the small publishers of string music contributed listings. No selection was made on any basis other than that of appropriate instrumentation, as defined in the first paragraph of this preface. Omissions are due entirely to failure to obtain information and are believed to be few in number.

Information on music published abroad was obtained in two ways. First, U.S. publishers were invited to list music offered by them as exclusive representatives of foreign publishers. All these publications are included, but there was a great difference in the amount of material submitted. Some companies handle the complete catalogue of a foreign affiliate, while others stock and promote a small selection. After this information had been received, letters of enquiry were sent directly to foreign publishers without a sole agent in this country. This group of publishers was chosen with the assistance of European associations of composers and publishers. Selections were made from the catalogues of publishers responding in order to include important works without duplicating listings obtained in the U.S.A.

The publisher of each composition listed is given, and the address of either the publisher or selling agent is provided. Representatives of foreign firms were repeatedly requested to indicate the actual publisher of every title submitted, and doubtful cases were checked. All addresses in the List of Publishers are believed to be correct as of June, 1964.

Plainly STRING MUSIC IN PRINT could not have come into existence without the cooperation of music publishers. I wish to thank all who contributed listings to this book. In most cases this entailed a considerable amount of correspondence, and the provision of more information than is customarily included in a catalogue. I am deeply indebted to the president, Bernard Kohn, and the members of the Music Publishers' Association of the United States, particularly Arnold Broido and Walter Hinrichsen, for invaluable support and encouragement.

In preparing the form of the entries, searching for the full names of composers and complete identification of titles, I depended largely upon the resources of two libraries and the help offered by Donald Krummel of the Newberry Library and Jean Kauffman of the Northwestern University Music Library.

The spelling of names and the dates of composers have been taken in large part from Baker's Biographical Dictionary of Musicians, fifth edition (G. Schirmer, 1958). Of the other reference works consulted the following were especially helpful: Wilhelm Altmann, Kammermusik-Katalog (F. Hofmeister, 1945); Cobbett's Cyclopedic Survey of Chamber Music, second edition (Oxford University Press, 1963); Murray Grodner, Comprehensive Catalogue of Literature for the String Bass, 1958; Johannes F. Richter, Kammermusik-Katalog (F. Hofmeister, 1960); Bruno Weigl, Handbuch der Violoncell-Literatur (Universal Edition, 1929); Franz Zeyringer, Literatur für Viola (J. Schönwetter, 1963).

In 1963 a preliminary manuscript, VIOLIN MUSIC IN PRINT, was published by the R.R. Bowker Company with a request for comments and criticism. I am most grateful to all who wrote and returned the questionnaire. It was the response of these violinists, librarians, publishers and music dealers that encouraged us to continue with plans for this book. Every suggestion offered was carefully considered, and many were adopted. I hope STRING MUSIC IN PRINT will meet the expectations of all these persons and others who have felt the need for a book to help them find the music they want for study, performance and pleasure.

Margaret K. Farish

Evanston, Illinois
January, 1965

How to use this book

The 15 sections of this book include:

Solo Music

Concert music for one stringed instrument unaccompanied: Section I

Music for one stringed instrument with piano or other accompanying instrument: Section II

Music for one or more solo stringed instruments with orchestral accompaniment: Section XIII

Chamber Music

Ensemble music for 2 to 10 instruments: Sections II-IX
All music is published in parts for performance unless otherwise indicated.

Trio Sonatas: Section IV
Written in 3 parts, intended for 4 players, most trio sonatas can be performed with 2 violins or other treble instruments, a keyboard instrument, and cello or gamba. Because the bass stringed instrument doubles the bass line of the keyboard instrument, it may be omitted. An edition offering only 3 parts is indicated by the notation, "no separate bass part." If the upper parts are not suitable for violins, instrumentation is given immediately after the title.

Music suitable for several combinations of instruments and collections containing music for more than one instrumental group: Section X

Chamber music for voice and instruments: Section XI

Chamber music scores: Section XII
Scores are listed by composer, irrespective of the number or type of instruments required. If score and parts are published as a unit for one price, the notation "score included" follows the listing of parts in the instrumental sections (Sections II-XI), and cross-reference is made in Section XII. No special mention is made of keyboard scores customarily included in compositions for piano and other instruments. Music published in score form only is listed in Section XII and also in the appropriate instrumental section with the notation, "score only."

Orchestral Music for Solo Stringed Instruments

Music for one or more solo stringed instruments with orchestral accompaniment: Section XIII
This section has been included for the use of the soloist. STRING MUSIC IN PRINT is not an orchestral catalogue and does not contain information on orchestral instrumentation.

Concerti grossi of the Baroque period are listed by some publishers as works for chamber orchestra and by others as compositions for soloists and orchestra. A case can be made for either point of view, depending upon the examples cited. Concerti for one solo instrument and orchestra are listed in this book. Concerti grossi for two or more solo instruments are considered works for chamber orchestra and are not included, with the exception of a very few works, notably the Bach double and triple concerti. This is an arbitrary division made to define the limits of this section and to conform as closely as possible to practices of publishers and performers. It should not be interpreted as a musical classification based upon differences in form.

Orchestral scores: Section XIV
Scores of compositions for solo stringed instruments are listed if they are described by the publishers as study, pocket or miniature scores. This listing is offered as an aid for the soloist rather than the conductor.

Study Material

Methods, etudes, exercises: Section XV
Textbooks and treatises on playing and teaching stringed instruments are also included.

Within each section or sectional subdivision, as listed in the Table of Contents, entries are arranged alphabetically by composer, with the exception of folk songs, which are listed by title, and collections of music by more than one composer, which are listed by title and editor, if known. All music is for sale unless otherwise stated.

<u>Example</u>   Violin, Piano

BRAHMS, JOHANNES (1833-1897)
   Sonata No. 3 in d, Op. 108
     (Auer-Ganz) CF 03774
     (Corti) Ric ER1446
     (Flesch-Schnabel) CF 03716
     (Jacobsen) Aug 4763
     (Kneisel-Bauer) GS L1303
     (Schnirlin) SCH
     BRH
   Sonatensatz. Scherzo
     Int
     SIM "Sonata Movement"

The composer is Johannes Brahms. Sonata No. 3 in d minor (indicated by small d), Op. 108, for violin and piano (instrumentation is given at the top of the page) is available in 7 editions. Auer and Ganz are the editors of the first publication listed. It is published by Carl Fischer (CF). 03774 is the number given in the publisher's catalog for this title. Corti is the editor of the Ricordi (Ric) publication, ER1446. Flesch and Schnabel edited a second publication offered by Carl Fischer, 03716. Jacobsen is the editor for Augener (Aug), 4763. Kneisel and Bauer edited the G. Schirmer (GS) edition, L1303. Schnirlin is editor for Schott's Söhne (SCH). No editor is given by Breitkopf and Härtel for their publication.

Sonatensatz, also by Brahms, is published by International (Int) and by Simrock (SIM). The Simrock edition is listed in U.S. catalogs under a slightly different title which is shown, "Sonata Movement." Neither publisher lists an editor.

<u>Composers</u> are identified by full names and dates whenever possible. Brackets enclose editorial additions believed to be correct, but not corroborated. In many cases only the last name has been provided by the publisher. As a result of this practice, it is sometimes impossible to determine whether the composer listed in one catalog is the same as one with the identical surname listed by another publisher. In these circumstances the name is repeated and works from different catalogs are listed separately.

<u>Titles</u> usually are given in the form and language used by the publisher. The title of a composition available in a number of editions appears only once, followed by a list of publishers offering the work. The exact title used by an individual publisher is added, enclosed in quotation marks, if it differs sufficiently from the listed title. General titles without identifying numbers, such as Sonata in D, are repeated if there is no way to tell from the publishers' listings whether several sonatas or several editions of one sonata are available.

Excerpts are usually listed by individual title, followed by the title of the complete work when known. Pieces which are part of a set, but are published separately, are treated in the same way.

The original instrumentation may follow the title of a transcription, for example: Spanish Dance No. 5, orig for pno. This information has been added whenever possible in response to requests from users of VIOLIN MUSIC IN PRINT. It must <u>not</u> be assumed that the omission of this notation necessarily means that the work is not an arrangement. Information on the original form of a composition is rarely provided by publishers. It can be found in reference sources only for a relatively well-known work published under the original title. It was not considered necessary to indicate the original instrumentation for an excerpt if the title of the complete work was given, nor for concertos published with a piano reduction of the original orchestral accompaniment.

<u>Editors</u>' names are always given in parentheses.

<u>Publishers</u> are indicated below titles, immediately following the editor if one is listed. Full names are given in the LIST OF PUBLISHERS.

<u>Collections</u> of music by more than one composer will be found under the title of the collection and also under the name of the editor, if known. Publishers were requested to list the contents of collections and this information is included if it was provided. Important works found only in collections have been listed individually, with reference to the collection. Familiar songs and popular transcriptions have not been given separate listings but can usually be found in collections with titles beginning with words such as Classical, Christmas, Easy, Favorite, Violin.

Abbreviations and Symbols

Abbreviations

acc	accompanied
accomp	accompaniment
arr	arranged
Bc	basso continuo
bsn	bassoon
clar	clarinet
d-b	double-bass (string bass, contrabass)
fl	flute
harm	harmonium
horn	French horn
mvt	movement
ob	oboe
orch	orchestra
orig	originally
pno	pianoforte
rec	recorder
simpl	simplified
str	string
unacc	unaccompanied
V	volume
vcl	violoncello
vla	viola
vln	violin

Key to the abbreviations for publishers will be found in the LIST OF PUBLISHERS

Symbols

*   score available, see Section XII for chamber music scores or Section XIV for orchestral scores

[ ]   editorial additions believed to be correct, but not corroborated

Keys

Major keys are indicated by capital letters.
Minor keys are given in small letters.

Foreign terms

ut, do	C
re	D
mi	E
fa	F
sol	G
la	A
si	B

Dur, maggiore, majeur	Major
Moll, minore, mineur	Minor
bémol, bemolle	flat
dièse, diesis	sharp

STRING MUSIC IN PRINT

MUSIC FOR
ONE INSTRUMENT

Violin Unaccompanied

AMRAM, DAVID (1930-   )
Sonata
  Pet 6687
ARNELL, RICHARD (1917-   )
Passacaglia
  Hin (Pet No. H1301)
ARRIEU, [CLAUDE (1903-   )]
Cadences. Concerto in sol di Mozart, K.216
  Ric R1449
AUER, LEOPOLD (1845-1930)
Cadenza for Brahms Concerto in D,
  Op. 77
  CF B52
BACH, JOHANN SEBASTIAN (1685-1750)
Chaconne
  (Flesch) Curci
  (Tertis) Aug 5641
Siciliano, BWV1063
  (Cazden) Jack Spratt
*Sonatas and Partitas, 6, S.1001-6[1]
  (Anzoletti) Ric ER227
  (Auer) CF L788
  (Busch) SIM
  (Capet) Senart
  (Davisson) BRH
  (Flesch) Pet 4308   urtext included
  (Hambourg) Oxf 23.370
  (Hausswald) Baer 5116
  (Hellmesberger) Int
  (Hermann) BRH
  (Herrmann) GS L221
  (Joachim) Int   urtext included
  (Joachim-Moser) BB   2V
  (Maglioni) Ric ER2477
  (Nachèz) Aug 7943
  (Polo) Ric ER1618
  (Wessely) JWL (Mil No. W1375)
    published separately
  SCH
Sonatas and Partitas, facsimile,
  see literature under study material
Suites, 6, S. 1007-12,[1] orig for vcl
  (David-Altmann) BRH
  (Polo) Ric ER784
BADINGS, HENK (1907-   )
Sonata No. 2
  DN (Pet No. D149)
Sonata No. 3
  SCH
BADURA-SKODA, PAUL (1927-   )
Cadenzas for Mozart Concerto No. 3
  in G, K. 216
  DOB

Cadenzas for Mozart Concerto No. 4
  in D, K. 218
  DOB
Cadenzas for Mozart Concerto No. 5
  in A, K. 219
  DOB
BALLER, ADOLPH
Cadenza for Paganini Concerto No. 2 in b,
  Op. 7
  (Menuhin) CF B3292
BARTÓK, BÉLA (1881-1945)
Sonata
  (Menuhin) BH
BAUMANN, MAX (1917-   )
Sonate
  Sirius
BEN-HAIM, PAUL (1897-   )
Sonata in G
  (Menuhin) IMP
BERKELEY, LENNOX (1903-   )
Introduction and Allegro, Op. 24
  Ches
Theme and Variations, Op. 33, No. 1
  Ches
(BERTON, ROLAND DE)
Wizard Violinist
  CF 0585
BIBER, HEINRICH IGNAZ FRANZ VON
    (1644-1704)
Passacaglia
  (Rostal) Ches
  see also Solo Violin Music of the Earliest
  Period, under vln and pno
BLACHER, BORIS (1903-   )
Sonata, Op. 40
  BB
BLOCH, ERNEST (1880-1959)
Suite No. 1
  Broude
Suite No. 2
  Broude
BLOCH, WALDEMAR
Sonata
  DOB
BORRIS, SIEGFRIED (1906-   )
Partita, Op. 102, No. 3
  Sirius
BRÜN, HERBERT (1918-   )
Sonatina
  IMP
BRUSTAD, BJARNE (1895-   )
Eventyrsuite
  Norsk
CAMPAGNOLI, [BARTOLOMMEO (1751-1827)]
Fugues, 6
  HL
CAPRI, G.
Cadenzas for Concerti by Tartini, Viotti,

---

[1] S. number is from the thematic catalogue by W. Schmieder:
Thematisch-systematisch Verzeichnis der musikalischen
Werke von Johann Sebastian Bach. Leipzig, 1950.

CAPRI, G. (cont.)
  Nardini, Paganini and "Devil's Trill"
  Sonata
  Carisch
CHAUMONT
  Partita en mi mineur
  Senart
CHOPIN, FRÉDÉRIC (1810-1849)
  Mazurkas, 4, orig for pno
    (Huberman) CF B2661
    Op. 67, No. 2; Op. 68, Nos. 1, 2, 3
COBB, SCRIBNER
  Sonatina
  MPH 1432 for violins in unison
CRUFT, ADRIAN (1921-   )
  Homage to J.S. Bach
  Leng (Mil No. L1130)
DANCLA, CHARLES (1817-1907)
  Cadenza for Viotti Concerto No. 24,
    see Dancla: Etudes brillantes, Op. 20
    under vln study
DAVID, JOHANN NEPOMUK (1895-   )
  Partita, Op. 37, No. 1
  BRH
  Sonata, Op. 31, No. 2
  BRH
DI BIASE, EDOARDO
  Suite
  Mercury
DUNHAM, MELLIE
  Fiddlin' Dance Tunes, 50
  CF 01453
EHRLICH, ABEL
  Bashrav
  IMP
ENESCO, GEORGES (1881-1955)
  Cadenzas for Mozart Concerto No. 7
    in D, K. 271a
  BRH
ENGELBRECHT, RICHARD (1907-   )
  Obra para Violin Solo
  ECIC
FARINA, CARLO (1595- ?)
  Capriccio stravagante, see Solo Violin
    Music of the Earliest Period, under vln
    and pno
FINNEY, ROSS LEE (1906-   )
  Fantasy in 2 Movements
  Pet 6063
FOLK-SONGS AND FIDDLE TUNES OF THE
    U.S.A.
    (Kinscella) CF 04075
FRANCO, JOHAN (1908-   )
  Miniatures, 5, and Encore
  CFE
  Sonata, 1944
  CFE
FRENCH HYMN
  (Ludlow) CF B2090
FRIEDMAN, E.
  Cadenza for Paganini Concerto No. 1
    in D, Op. 6
  CF B3357
FRISCHENSCHLAGER, FRIEDRICH (1885-   )
  Suite, Op. 26
  Krenn
GEMINIANI, FRANCESCO (1687-1762)
  Adagio e Allegro, from Sonata, see Solo
    Violin Music of the Earliest Period, un-
    der vln and pno
  Sonata in B flat
    (Corti) Carisch
    (Corti) Ches

GERHARD, ROBERTO (1896-   )
  Chaconne
  Kuhl (Mil No. K103)
GERSCHEFSKI, EDWIN (1909-   )
  Variations, 100, Op. 38
  CFE
GIACOBBE
  Concertino criollo, Op. 45
    (Pessina) Ric BA10581
GOEB, ROGER (1914-   )
  Sonata
  CFE
GRAETZER, GUILLERMO (1914-   )
  Grave
  SMP
HALFFTER, CHR.
  Sonata, Op. 20
  UE 13425
HALVORSEN, JOHAN (1864-1935)
  Slatter, Norwegian Peasant Dances
  Pet 3083
HEIFETZ, JASCHA (1901-   )
  Cadenza for Brahms Concerto, Op. 77
  CF B2797
  Cadenzas for Mozart Concerto No. 4
    in D, K. 218
  CF B2414
HINDEMITH, PAUL (1895-1963)
  Sonata, Op. 31, No. 1
  SCH
  Sonata, Op. 31, No. 2
  SCH
HONEGGER, ARTHUR (1892-1955)
  Sonate
  Sal
HOPKINS, ANTONY (1921-   )
  Partita in g
  Ches
HOVHANESS, ALAN (1911-   )
  Yeraz
  Mil
JACOB, GORDON (1895-   )
  Sonatina
  JWL (Mil No. W1224)
JARNACH, PHILIPP (1892-   )
  Sonata in a, Op. 8
  LN (Pet No. R59)
JELINEK, HANNS (1901-   )
  Sonate
  EDW
JOACHIM, JOSEPH (1831-1907)
  Cadenzas for Beethoven Concerto, Op. 61
  Int
  Cadenza for Brahms Concerto, Op. 77
  Int
  SIM
JONGEN, JOSEPH (1873-1953)
  Sonata
  CBDM
KAHN, ERICH ITOR (1905-1956)
  Sonata
  CFE
KERR, HARRISON (1897-   )
  Sonata
  CFE
(KINSCELLA, HAZEL GERTRUDE)
  Folk-Songs and Fiddle Tunes of the U.S.A.
  CF 04075
KLEBE, GISELHER (1925-   )
  Sonata, Op. 8
    (Akos) BB
  Sonata No. 2, Op. 20
  BB

KLINGENDE HEIMAT
Sik 222
KNAB, [ARMIN (1881-1951)]
Variations on a Folk Song
SCH
KNEISEL, FRANZ (1865-1926)
Cadenza for Brahms Concerto, Op. 77
CF B2002
KÖLZ, ERNST
Sonatas in the Ancient Style, 2
DOB
KREISLER, FRITZ (1875-1962)
Cadenzas, 3, for Beethoven Concerto,
Op. 61
Fol 1012
Cadenza for Brahms Concerto, Op. 77
Fol 1013
Cadenzas, 3 for Mozart Concerto
No. 3 in G
Fol 1001
Cadenzas, 3, for Mozart Concerto No. 4
in D
Fol 1004
Cadenzas, 2, for Mozart Concerto No. 5
in A, and cadenza for Mozart Concerto
No. 6 in E flat
Fol 1005
Recitativo and Scherzo Caprice
Fol 1046
Study on a choral, in the style of Stamitz
Fol 1058
KURKA, ROBERT (1921-1957)
Sonata, Op. 5
Weintraub
LEONARD, HUBERT (1819-1890)
Cadence pour le concerto de Beethoven
Billaudot
LOUCHEUR, R.
Sonatine
Sal
LOURIÉ, ARTHUR (1892-   )
Sonata
Rongwen
LUENING, OTTO (1900-   )
Elegy for Maurice Wilk
CFE
LUTYENS, ELIZABETH (1906-   )
Aptote
Leng (Mil No. L1122)
MACKERRAS, G.
Cadenzas for Mozart Concerto in G
EKN
MAEGAARD, JAN (1926-   )
Preludes, 5
Dansk 222
MARQUE
Air varié en la
Gaudet
MARTINO, DONALD (1931-   )
Fantasy Variations
CFE
MARTINON, JEAN (1910-   )
Sonatina No. 6, Op. 49, No. 2
SCH
MASCAGNI, PIETRO (1863-1945)
Assolo, from L'Amico Fritz
SON
MASON, LOWELL (1792-1872)
Nearer, My God, to Thee; with Last Hope by
Gottschalk for vln and pno
(Lehrer) Fill
MAYER, JOHN
Sonate
Leng (Mil No. L1135)

MENUHIN, YEHUDI (1916-   )
Cadenzas for Mozart Concerto No. 4
in D, K. 218
CF B2486
MERSMANN, HANS (1891-   )
Kleine Suite, see Musik für eine und zwei
Geigen, under 2 vln
MEULEMANS, ARTHUR (1884-   )
Sonata
CBDM
MIHALOVICI, MARCEL (1898-   )
Sonata, Op. 59
Heugel
MILLS, CHARLES (1914-   )
Stanzas, 4
CFE
MILSTEIN, NATHAN (1904-   )
Paganiniana
GS
MINETTI, E.
Prelude, Improvisation and Caprice
SZ
MOLLIER, P.
Gerbe mélodique. 10 Morceaux brilliants
Gaudet   published separately
NIELSEN, CARL (1865-1931)
Prelude and Theme with Variations, Op. 48
Pet 3817
NOWAK, LIONEL (1911-   )
Sonata
Pr
Toccata
CFE
OISTRAKH, DAVID (1908-   )
Cadenza for Khachaturian Concerto
MZK
ORGAD, B. Z.
Ballade
Mercury
OSTROVSKY, FREDY
Pieces for Solo Violin, 3
Paragon
PAGANINI, NICCOLÒ (1782-1840)
Caprices, 24, Op. 1
(Abbado) SZ
(Berkley) GS L1663
(David) BRH
(Dounis) CF 03667
(Flesch) Int
(Flesch) Pet 1984
(Kross) CF 03224; with Moto Perpetuo and
Duo Merveille
(Marchet) Senart 5280
(Polo) Ric ER226
(Sauret) Aug 7930
(Schmidtner) Sik 189
Caprice No. 2 in b
(Szigeti) CF B2427
Etudes, 60, in Variation Form on the Genoese
air "Barucaba", Op. 14
(Black) CF 04280
(Black) Omega
(Schmidtner) Sik 296
Hin (Pet Nos. H597A, B, C) 3V "Varia-
tions"
Nel cor più non mi sento, Capriccio on theme
by Paisiello
ZM (Pet No. ZM294)
PAZ, JUAN CARLOS (1897-   )
Cuarta Composicion en los Doce Tonos
ECIC
PERGAMENT, MOSES (1893-   )
Sonata
Nordiska

PERLE, GEORGE (1915-   )
Sonata, Op. 40
CFE
PERSICHETTI, VINCENT (1915-   )
Sonata
EV
PICHL, WENZEL (1741-1804)
Fugues, 6, on a Prelude Fugato
Artia
Fugues, 6
HL
PIJPER, WILLEM (1894-1947)
Sonata
DN (Pet No. D120)
PINTO, F.
Sonata in Re
Curci
PISENDEL, JOHANN GEORG (1687-1755)
Sonata
(Hausswald) Baer HM91
PISK, PAUL (1893-   )
Sonata, Op. 16, No. 2
CFE
POLYPHONE MUSIK FÜR VIOLINE ALLEIN
(Spindler) Hof; Bk. 4 of
Violinetüden aus 3 Jahrhunderten
POSER, HANS (1907-   )
Suite in the old manner, Op. 5
Sik 399
PROKOFIEV, SERGEY (1891-1953)
Sonata, Op. 115
(Persinger) Leeds
Int
PRUME, [FRANCOIS JEHIN (1839-1899)]
Etudes de Concert, 6, Op. 14
Lit (Pet No. L1118)
PURCELL, HENRY (c.1659-1695)
Sonatas, 2, in 3 parts
(Solly) Ches
QUIROGA, [MANUEL (1890-   )]
Cadence pour le Concerto de Beethoven
Sal
Cadence pour le Concerto de Brahms
Sal
Cadences, 5, pour les Concertos Nos. 3, 4, 5,
6, 7 de Mozart
Sal
Cadence pour le Concerto en sol de Mozart
Sal
Cadence pour le Concerto en ré de Paganini
Sal
Caprichos, 3
Sal
RAFTER, LEONARD (1911-   )
Prelude, Scherzo and Passacaglia
(East) Bosw
REGER, MAX (1873-1916)
Chaconne in g
BB
Praeludium in e, Op. posth.
(Busch) Pet 3968D
Preludes and Fugues, Op. 117, Nos. 1-8
BB   published separately
Sonatas, 7, Op. 91, Nos. 1-7
BB   published separately
RIBAUPIERRE, MILTON DE
Swiss Lullaby
CF B1862
ROSENBERG, HILDING (1892-   )
Sonata
Nordiska
ROSTAL, MAX (1905-   )
Cadenzas for Beethoven Concerto
Nov

RUST, FRIEDRICH WILHELM (1739-1796)
Sonata No. 2 in B flat
Pet 1472
SAINT-SAENS, CAMILLE (1835-1921)
Cadences pour le Concerto, Op. 61
de Beethoven
Dur
SANTORO, CLAUDIO (1919-   )
Sonata
ECIC
SAPP, ALLEN (1922-   )
Sonata No. 2
CFE
SAURET, EMILE (1852-1920)
Cadenza for Paganini Concerto No. 1
in D, Op. 6
FR (Pet No. F57)
MK
SCHISKE, KARL (1916-   )
Pieces for Gloria, 3, Op. 32
DOB
SCHMIDT, WILLIAM
Variations on a folk hymn, "Mississippi"
Avant
(SEKLES, B.)
Violin-Baukasten, Der
SCH   2nd vln, pno ad lib
10 folk songs
SERLY, TIBOR (1900-   )
Sonata in Modus Lascivus
SMP
SESSIONS, ROGER (1896-   )
Sonata
MK
SHIFRIN, SEYMOUR (1926-   )
Concert Piece
Pet 5874
SPALDING, ALBERT (1888-1953)
Cadenza for Brahms Concerto
VL
Cadenzas for Mozart Concerto in D
VL
Sonata in E
VL
(SPINDLER, FR.)
Polyphone Musik für Violine allein, Bk
4 of Violinetüden aus 3 Jahrhunderten
Hof
STAMITZ, JOHANN (1717-1757)
Divertimenti, 2
(Zetlin) MM
STEIN, LEON (1910-   )
Sonata
CFE
STOUT, ALAN (1932-   )
Construction, Op. 17
CFE
STRAVINSKY, IGOR (1882-   )
Elegie
AMP
SWIFT, RICHARD
Sonata, Op. 15
CFE
SZABO, FERENC (1902-   )
Sonatas, 2
Kul
SZELENYI, [ISTVAN (1904-   )]
Sonata
Kul
SZIGETI, JOSEPH (1892-   )
Cadenza for first movement of Mozart
Concerto No. 3 in G, K. 216
CF B2403

SZOKOLAY, S.
  Sonata
    Kul
TELEMANN, GEORG PHILIPP (1681-1767)
  Fantasien, 12
    (Hausswald) Baer 2972
THILMAN, JOHANNES PAUL (1906-   )
  Kleine Suite
    Hof
TOVEY, DONALD FRANCIS (1875-1940)
  Cadenzas for Beethoven Concerto, Op. 61
    Oxf 23.010
TRETICK, SIDNEY
  Toccata
    CF B3258
TWA, ANDY (1919-   )
  Sonata
    CL
(TZIGANOV)
  Violin Cadenzas, Vol. I
    MZK
VERESS, SÁNDOR (1907-   )
  Sonata
    SZ
VIOLIN-BAUKASTEN, DER
  (Sekles) SCH   2nd vln, pno ad lib
    10 folk songs
VIOLIN CADENZAS, VOL. I
  (Tziganov) MZK
WEINER, S.
  Caprices, 7. Homage to Violinists
    SCH
WELLESZ, EGON (1885-   )
  Sonata, Op. 72
    Rongwen
WILLAUME, C.
  Noce bretonne, La
    Sal
WINKLER, JULIUS
  Cadenza for Beethoven Concerto, Op. 61
    DOB
  Cadenza for Brahms Concerto, Op. 77
    DOB
  Cadenza for Paganini Concerto No. 1, Op. 6
    DOB
  Cadenza for Viotti Concerto No. 22 in a
    DOB
WIZARD VIOLINIST
  (Berton) CF 0585
YARDUMIAN, RICHARD (1917-   )
  Monologue
    EV
YSAŸE, EUGÈNE (1858-1931)
  Cadences du Concerto de Beethoven
    Cinedisc
  Cadence du Concerto de Brahms[2]
    SF
  Cadences du Concerto K. 216 de Mozart
    Cinedisc
  Cadences du Concerto No. 22 de Viotti
    SF (Pet No. SCH14)
  Preludes, see vln study
  Sonatas, 6, Op. 27
    GS
ZIMMERMANN, BERND ALOIS (1918-   )
  Sonata
    SCH

[2] This publication is not listed in current U.S. catalogues.
Information was received from Fondation Eugène Ysaÿe

Viola Unaccompanied

ANGERER, PAUL (1927-   )
  Musik
    DOB
ARNELL, RICHARD (1917-   )
  Partita
    (Forbes) Hin (Pet No. H721)
BACH, JOHANN SEBASTIAN (1685-1750)
  Chaconne
    (Tertis) Aug 5568
  Siciliano, BWV1063
    (Cazden) Jack Spratt
  Sonatas and Partitas, 6, orig for vln
    (Forbes) Pet 7035A, b, C   3V
    (Polo) Ric ER2208
    Int
  Suites, 6, orig for vcl
    (Forbes) Ches
    (Lifschey) GS L1564
    (Polo) Ric ER1022
    (Svecenski) GS L1278
    Sik 316
BIBER, HEINRICH IGNAZ FRANZ VON
    (1644-1704)
  Passacaglia, orig for vln
    (Rostal) Ches
BLOCH, ERNEST (1880-1959)
  Suite
    Broude
BRÜN, HERBERT (1918-   )
  Sonatina
    IMP
BRUNSWICK, MARK (1902-   )
  Fantasia
    Val
BURKHARD, WILLY (1900-1955)
  Sonate, Op. 59
    Baer 2094
CAZDEN, NORMAN (1914-   )
  Chamber Sonata, Op. 17, No. 2
    CFE
CHILDS, BARNEY
  Sonata
    CFE
COOLEY, C.
  Etude Suite
    H Elkan
DAVID, JOHANN NEPOMUK (1895-   )
  Sonata, Op. 31, No. 3
    BRH
DUKE, JOHN (1899-   )
  Suite for Viola alone
    (Rood) Val
FRANCO, JOHAN (1908-   )
  Sonata
    CFE
FUCHS, LILLIAN
  Sonata Pastorale
    AMP
GEIER, OSKAR
  Suite
    Hof
GENZMER, HARALD (1909-   )
  Sonata
    Pet 5860
GROSS, ROBERT
  Sonatina
    CFE

HAMPE, CHARLOTTE (1910-   )
  Short Baroque Dances, 7
    RE (Pet No. RE5)
HANESYAN, H.
  Cadenzas for Handel Concerto in b and
      Telemann Concerto in G
    ESC
  Cadenzas for Stamitz Concerto in D
    ESC
  Cadenzas for Zelter Concerto in E flat
      and Dittersdorf Concerto in F
    ESC
HINDEMITH, PAUL (1895-1963)
  Sonata, Op. 11, No. 5
    SCH
  Sonata, Op. 25, No. 1
    SCH
HOESL, ALBERT
  Suite
    Cor ST5
HOVHANESS, ALAN (1911-   )
  Chahagir, Op. 56a
    Broude
JEMNITZ, ALEXANDER (1890-   )
  Sonata, Op. 46
    Kul
KAMINSKI, HEINRICH (1886-1946)
  Prelude and Fugue
    Pet 4446
KRENEK, ERNST (1900-   )
  Sonata, Op. 92, No. 3
    BMP
LAKNER, YEHOSHUA (1924-   )
  Improvisation
    IMP
LEVY, F.
  Sonata
    Cor ST1
LUENING, OTTO (1900-   )
  Sonata
    CFE
LUTYENS, ELIZABETH (1906-   )
  Sonata, Op. 5, No. 4
    Leng (Mil No. L2007)
PAGANINI, NICCOLÒ (1782-1840)
  Caprices, 24, Op. 1, orig for vln
    (Raby) Int
  Capricci, 6, from Op. 1
    (Ferraguzzi) Ric ER2526
PERLE, GEORGE (1915-   )
  Sonata
    ECIC
POLO, ENRICO
  Studi-Sonate, 3
    SZ
PORTER, QUINCY (1897-   )
  Suite for Viola alone
    Val
REGER, MAX (1873-1916)
  Suites, 3, Op. 131d
    Int
    Pet 3971
ROLLA, ANTONIO (1798-1837)
  Idylles, 6
    Ed M
SCHROEDER, HANNING (1904-   )
  Music in 5 movements
    LN (Pet No. R58b)
SHULMAN, ALAN (1915-   )
  Suite
    Templ
SMITH, LELAND
  Suite
    CFE

STADLMAIR, HANS (1929-   )
  Sonata
    BRH
STRAVINSKY, IGOR (1882-   )
  Elegie
    AMP
TELEMANN, GEORG PHILIPP (1681-1767)
  Fantasias, 12, orig for vln
    (Rood) MM   2V
VOSS, FRIEDRICH
  Variations for Viola
    BRH
WELLESZ, EGON (1885-   )
  Rhapsody, Op. 87
    DOB
ZIMMERMANN, BERND ALOIS (1918-   )
  Sonata
    SCH

Cello Unaccompanied

AMES, WILLIAM (1901-   )
  Sonata, 1951
    CFE
ANDRIESSEN, HENDRIK (1892-   )
  Sonata
    DN (Pet No. D236)
ARBATSKY, [YURY (1911-   )]
  Sonata
    ZM (Pet No. ZM331)
ARNELL, RICHARD (1917-   )
  Suite
    Hin (Pet No. H722)
BACH, JOHANN SEBASTIAN (1685-1750)
  Siciliano, BWV1063
    (Cazden) Jack Spratt
  *Suites, 6, S. 1007-12[3]
    (Alexanian) Mathot   reproduction of orig
      manuscript by Bach included
    (Bazelaire) ESC
    (Becker) Int
    (Dotzauer- Magrini) Ric ER70
    (Francesconi) SZ
    (Gaillard) GS L1565
    (Grümmer) DOB
    (Klengel) BRH
    (Mainardi) SCH
    (Malkin) CF 03439
    (Such) Aug 7663
    (Wenzinger) Baer 320
    Pet 238
  Sonata No. 5 in c
    (Such) Aug
  Suites, facsimile, see literature
BADINGS, HENK (1907-   )
  Sonata No. 2
    DN (Pet No. D6)
BANTOCK, GRANVILLE (1868-1946)
  Sonata in g
    Ches
BJERRE, JENS (1903-   )
  Sonate
    (Bengtsson) Dansk 217
BLOCH, ERNEST (1880-1959)
  Suite No. 1
    Broude
  Suite No. 2
    Broude
  Suite No. 3
    Broude

---

[3] S. number is from the thematic catalogue by W. Schmieder: Thematisch-systematisch Verzeichnis der musikalischen Werke von Johann Sebastian Bach. Leipzig, 1950.

CHOPIN, FRÉDÉRIC (1810-1849)
Etude in A flat, Op. 27, No. 1, orig for pno
(Cassado) Int
COWELL, HENRY (1897-   )
Gravely and Vigorously
AMP
CRUFT, ADRIAN (1921-   )
Homage to J.S. Bach
Leng (Mil No. L3002)
CRUMB, GEORGE (1929-   )
Sonata
Pet 6056
DALLAPICCOLA, LUIGI (1904-   )
Ciaccona, Intermezzo e Adagio
UE 11686
DAVID, JOHANN NEPOMUK (1895-   )
Sonata, Op. 31, No. 4
BRH
DICK, MARCEL (1898-   )
Elegies, 4, and an Epilogue
H Elkan
DOW, JOHN
Prelude and Scherzo
Hin (Pet No. H560A)
FELDMAN, MORTON (1926-   )
Projection I
Pet 6945   graph
FITELBERG, [JERZY (1903-1951)]
Sonata
(Piatigorsky) Omega
FORTNER, WOLFGANG (1907-   )
Suite
SCH
FRANCO, JOHAN (1908-   )
Sonata
CFE
Sonata No. 2
CFE
FRIEDLANDER, ERNST
Little Fantasy on a Folk Tune
CL
GABRIELI, DOMENICO (c.1650-1690)
Ricercare No. 1
(Shuman) SMP
GAGNEBIN, [HENRI (1886-   )]
Suite
Senart
GAILLARD, MARIUS-FRANCOIS (1900-   )
Cadenza
ESC
GERSCHEFSKI, EDWIN (1909-   )
Variations, 24, Op. 50
CFE
GROSS, ROBERT
Epode
CFE
HANDEL, GEORG FRIEDRICH (1685-1759)
Fugue in C
(Cassado) Int
Harmonious Blacksmith, orig for harpsichord
(Cassado) Int
HEISS, HERMANN (1897-   )
Solo-Suite
BRH
HENZE, HANS WERNER (1926-   )
Serenade
SCH
HINDEMITH, PAUL (1895-1963)
Sonata, Op. 25, No. 3
SCH
HOLST, IMOGEN (1907-   )
Fall of the Leaf
Oxf

HUGUET Y TAGELL, R.
Hallucinations
Sal
Suite Espagnole No. 1
Sal
Suite Espagnole No. 2
Sal
JACOB, GORDON (1895-   )
Divertimento
JWL (Mil No. W1507)
JULLIEN, R.
Cadenzas, 2, for Haydn Concerto in D
ESC
KARDOS, I.
Capriccio
Artia
KERR, HARRISON (1897-   )
Study
Pr
KLENGEL, [JULIUS (1859-1933)]
Caprice in the Form of a Chaconne, Op. 43
BRH
KODÁLY, ZOLTÁN (1882-   )
Sonata, Op. 8
UE 6650
KÓSA, [GYÖRGY (1897-   )]
Sonatina
UE 9710
KOSTEK
Dutch Phantasy
Broe (Pet No. B783)
KRENEK, ERNST (1900-   )
Suite, Op. 84
GS
LEVY, F.
Sonata
Cor ST2
LUENING, OTTO (1900-   )
Sonata Composed in 2 Dayturns
CFE
Sonata
CFE
LUTYENS, ELIZABETH (1906-   )
Prelude and Capriccio, Op. 29
Leng (Mil No. L3012)
MACONCHY, ELIZABETH (1907-   )
Variations on a theme from Job by
Vaughan Williams
Leng (Mil No. L3019)
MAINARDI, ENRICO (1897-   )
Sonata
SCH
Sonata Breve
SCH
see also vcl study material
MAMANGAKIS, NIKOS (1929-   )
Monolog
EDW
MAMLOK, URSULA
Composition, 1962
CFE
MAYUZUMI, TOSHIRO (1929-   )
Bunraku
Pet 6356
MEULEMANS, ARTHUR (1884-   )
Sonata
CBDM
MIHALOVICI, MARCEL (1898-   )
Sonata, Op. 60
Heugel
MORITZ, EDVARD (1891-   )
Suite, Op. 20
Birnbach

MORTARI, VIRGILIO (1902-   )
  Piccolo Serenata
    Carisch
NEUKOMM
  Aria
    (Kaplan) Jack Spratt
NEWSON, GEORGE
  Variations
    UE 12952
NOWAK, LIONEL (1911-   )
  Night Lyric
    CFE
PAGANINI, NICCOLÒ (1782-1840)
  Capricci, 24, orig for vln
    (Silva) FC 1428
PARRIS, ROBERT (1924-   )
  Fantasy and Fugue
    Pet 6837
PEKKER
  Cadenzas for Haydn Concerto No. 3
    MZK
PELEMANS, WILLEM (1901-   )
  Sonata
    CBDM
PERLE, GEORGE (1915-   )
  Sonata, Op. 22
    CFE
PIATTI, ALFREDO, see vcl study material
PROKOFIEV, SERGEY (1891-1953)
  March, from Music for Children, Op. 65,
    orig for pno
    (Piatigorsky) Int
REGER, MAX (1873-1916)
  Suites, 3, Op. 131c
    Int
    Pet 3970
SAUGUET, [HENRI (1901-   )]
  Sonate
    Ric R1561
SAYGUN, A. ADNAN (1907-   )
  Partita
    SMP
SCHILLINGER, JOSEPH (1895-1943)
  Dance Suite, Op. 20
    Leeds
SCHMIDT, FRANZ
  Cadenza for 1st mvt of Haydn Concerto in D
    DOB
SCHNABEL, A.
  Sonata
    BH
SCHOEMAKER, MAURICE (1890-   )
  Sonata
    CBDM
SCHROEDER, HANNING (1904-   )
  Music in Five Movements
    LN (Pet No. R58A)
SCHULLER, GUNTHER (1925-   )
  Fantasy, Op. 19
    Broude
SELMI
  Cadenza for Schumann Concerto
    Carisch
SERVAIS, ADRIEN-FRANCOIS
  see vcl study material
SHULMAN, ALAN (1915-   )
  Suite
    Templ
SILWEDEL, G.
  Cadenzas, 3, for Haydn Concerto in D
    BRH
STEVENS, HALSEY (1908-   )
  Sonata
    CFE

STRAUSS, RICHARD (1864-1949)
  Don Quixote, Op. 35, for vcl and orch; vcl
    solo part only
    (Rose) Int
    Pet 4197A
SWIFT, RICHARD
  Study, Op. 7
    CFE
TCHEREPNINE, ALEXANDER (1899-   )
  Suite
    Dur
TELEMANN, GEORG PHILIPP (1681-1767)
  Sonate en ré
    (Ruyssen) Delrieu
  Suite, orig for gamba
    (Bazelaire) Leduc
TORTELIER, [PAUL (1914-   )]
  Cadences, 6, pour les Concertos de C.P.E.
    Bach, Boccherini, Haydn, Schumann
    Delrieu
  Suite en Ré mineur
    Sal
VAN DE VYVÈRE, see vcl study material
VAUGHAN WILLIAMS
  Variations on a theme from Job, see
    Maconchy
VERMAAK, E.
  Sonata
    Wagenaar
VOSS, FRIEDRICH
  Variations for Cello
    BRH
WEBER, BEN (1916-   )
  Dance
    CFE
WELLESZ, EGON (1885-   )
  Sonata, Op. 31
    UE 7257
  Suite, Op. 39
    UE 8881
YSAŸE, EUGÈNE (1858-1931)
  Sonate, Op. 28[4]
    (Fournier) SF
ZILLIG, WINFRIED (1905-   )
  Sonate
    Baer 3961
ZIMMERMANN, BERND ALOIS (1918-   )
  Sonate
    (Palm) EDW

Double-Bass Unaccompanied

BACH, JOHANN SEBASTIAN (1685-1750)
  Sonatas, 6, orig for vcl
    (Sterling) Pet 238b,C,D   3V
    Vol 1: Nos. 1-3
    Vol 2: Nos. 4-5
    Vol 3: No. 6
BITSCH, [MARCEL (1921-   )]
  Suite
    Leduc
CHILDS, BARNEY
  Sonata
    MM
CRUFT, ADRIAN (1921-   )
  Homage to J.S. Bach
    Leng (Mil No. L3050)
DRAGONETTI, DOMENICO (1763-1846)
  Waltzes, 6
    (Turetzky) MM

---

[4] This publication is not listed in current U.S. catalogues.
Information was received from Fondation Eugene Ysaÿe.

LUENING, OTTO (1900-   )
  Sonata
    CFE
MOULAERT, RAYMOND (1875-   )
  Passacaglia
    CBDM
RATIGLIA, LUIGI
  Nostalgia
    Carisch
SALZA
  Improvviso
    Carisch
  Sarabanda
    Carisch
SYDEMAN, WILLIAM (1928-   )
  For Double Bass Alone
    MM
WUORINEN, CHARLES (1938-   )
  Concert
    CFE

Gamba Unaccompanied

ABEL, KARL FRIEDRICH (1723-1787)
  Sonata and 2 Minuets
    (Lefkovitch) SCH
COLIN
  Fantasy, see 8 Instrumental Fantasies
    under 4 viols

Unspecified String Instrument

CAGE, JOHN (1912-   )
  26'1.1499'' for a string player
    Pet 6779
  59 $\frac{1}{2}$'' for a string player
    Pet 6776

MUSIC FOR
TWO INSTRUMENTS

Duos: 2 Violins

(ABEL & MARTEAU)
  Violin-Duette älterer Meister
    Steingräber   2V; for contents see title
ALARD, JEAN-DELPHIN (1815-1888)
  Collection Progressive de Duos
    HL   11V
      Op. 22. Elémentaire   4V
      Op. 23. Facile   3V
      Op. 27. Brillant   4V
AMBROSIUS, HERMANN (1897-   )
  Sonatine
    Moeck 2039
(APPLEBAUM, SAMUEL)
  Beautiful Music for Two Violins
    Bel EL1323-26   4V
ARCHER, VIOLET (1913-   )
  Duets, 3
    Peer
ARDÉVOL, JOSÉ (1911-   )
  Preludio y Allegro
    SMP
(ARMA)
  Little Old-French Dances
    SCH
ARRIEU, CLAUDE (1903-   )
  Sonatine
    Amphion 164
(AUER, LEOPOLD)
  Fiddlers Two
    (Saenger) CF 01425; Vol 2 of Graded
      Course of Ensemble Playing
BACH, JOHANN CHRISTIAN (1735-1782)
  Duets, 6
    (Friedrich) Int   2V
    (Friedrich) NAG   2V
BACH, JOHANN SEBASTIAN (1685-1750)
  Chaconne, from Partita No. 2 in d, orig
    for vln unacc
    (Applebaum) CF B2692
  Little Pieces
    (Lenzewski) SCH
  Sonatas, 6, orig for vln unacc
    VW (Pet No. V31)
BACH, KARL PHILIPP EMANUEL (1714-1788)
  Duets, 2
    (Stephan) NAG
  Duet in G
    Int
  Little Pieces, 12, Wotquenne No. 81[5]
      6 pieces for 2 fl or 2 vln
      6 pieces for 2 fl or 2 vln and pno
    MT (Pet No. MV1205)
    VW (Pet No. V28)   score included
    ZM (Pet No. ZM126)

BACH, WILHELM FRIEDEMANN (1710-1784)
  Duo Sonata
    Ed M
  Sonata in E flat
    (Glöder) NAG
BARTOK, BELA (1881-1945)
  Duets, 44
    BH   2V
  see also Spielmusik, Vols 3 and 4
BEAUTIFUL MUSIC FOR TWO VIOLINS
    (Applebaum) Bel EL1323-26   4V
BECK, CONRAD (1901-   )
  Duo
    SCH
  Sonatina
    ESC
BEGLARIAN, GRANT
  Violin Duets in Contemporary Style
    CF 04046
BENDL, [KARL (1838-1897)]
  Duetta, Op. 117
    Artia
(BERAN, J.)
  Minuets of the Old Masters
    Artia
BERIOT, CHARLES DE (1802-1870)
  Duos concertants, 3, Op. 57
    (Herrmann-Mittell) GS L957
    CF L426
    Pet 3061A
  Short Easy Duets, 12, Op. 87
    Pet 3061b
BICINIEN
    (Doflein) SCH
      20 fantasies by 16th century masters
BLUM, ROBERT (1900-   )
  Duett
    EDW
BOCCHERINI, LUIGI (1743-1805)
  Duos, 3, Op. 5
    (Sitt) Pet 3338
  Duets, 2, Op. 5
    Int
  Duet in G
    (Bormann) Sik 263
BODNAR, I.
  Little Suite
    Kul
BORGHI, LUIGI (18th century)
  Duets, 3
    (Bonelli) ZA 3627
(BORMANN)
  Early Classical Duets
    SCH   2V   for contents see title
  Eighteenth Century Violin Duet
    Sik 290-2   3V   for contents see title
BORRIS, SIEGFRIED (1906-   )
  Partita
    Hof

---

[5] Thematic catalogue by A. Wotquenne. Leipzig, 1905.

BRUNI, ANTONIO BARTOLOMEO (1751-1821)
Duets, 6, Op. 34
Int
Pet 2536
BUCQUET, P.
Suite No. 1
(Bouvet) ESC
Suite No. 2
(Bouvet) ESC
BURKHARD, WILLY (1900-1955)
Suite, Op. 48
Baer 2108
BUTTERWORTH, [ARTHUR (1923-   )]
Dialogues, 3
Hin (Pet No. H695)
CAMPAGNOLI, BARTOLOMMEO (1751-1827)
Duets, 6, Op. 14
(De Guarnieri) Ric ER175
(Hermann) Pet 2506
BRH
(CAREMBAT)
Duos
Jobert   2V   for contents see title
CARLSTEDT, JAN (1926-   )
Sonata, Op. 7
Gehrmans
CARSE, ADAM (1878-1958)
Easy Duets, 3
Aug 5635
CHAGRIN, FRANCIS (1905-   )
Prelude and Fugue
Aug
CHEDEVILLE, NICOLAS (1705-1782)
Pastoral Sonatas, 2
(Upmeyer) NAG
Sonatas, 2
(Upmeyer) Int
CLASSIC PIECES
(Hermann) Pet 2685
12 Pieces by Bach, Beethoven, Gluck,
Handel, Hummel, Mozart, Schumann,
Tartini, Weber.
COBURN
Duet Album for Two Violins
Bel
COUPERIN, FRANCOIS (1668-1733)
Suite No. 1
Mercury
DANCLA, CHARLES (1817-1907)
Duos, 3, Op. 23
Pet 1081A
DAVID, JOHANN NEPOMUK (1895-   )
Sonata, Op. 32, No. 3.
BRH
DEGEN, HELMUT (1911-   )
Stykker, 15
WH
(DISCHNER)
West-Oestliches Liederspiel
BRH   2V
(DOFLEIN)
Bicinien
SCH
20 fantasies by 16th century masters
Frohes Duospiel
SCH
Old-French Duets
SCH   2V   for contents see title
Spielmusik
SCH   for contents see title
DOMERC, J.
Duos concertants, 8
HL

DONIZETTI, GAETANO (1797-1848)
Sextet, from Lucia
CF C44
DRIESSLER, JOHANNES (1921-   )
Duos
Tonger
DUANE, VICTOR
Little Duets, 12
JWL (Mil No. W1377)
Violin Duets, 6
JWL (Mil No. W1376)
DUET ALBUM OF 10 CLASSICAL COMPOSI-
TIONS
(Stouffer) H Elkan
Compositions by Boismortier, Bach,
Handel, Mozart, Peuerl, Purcell,
Telemann
DUET BOOKLET OF THE MASTERS
(Engels) SCH
27 duets by Telemann, Handel, Bach
and L. Mozart
DUOS
(Carembat) Jobert   2V
Vol 1: Duos d'apres Bach, Handel,
Couperin, Rameau, Hummel, Valensin
Vol 2: Duos d'apres Mozart, Pugnani,
Leclair, Destouches
DUOS, 18TH CENTURY
(Rosenthal) MK   for 2 clar or 2 vln
Bach: Bourrée, from English Suite
No. 1
Couperin: Rondeau, "La Badine",
from Pièces de Clavecin
Couperin: 2 Menuets, from Pièces
de Clavecin
Handel: Aria, from Suite No. 14
Handel: Gavotte, from Suite No. 14
Rameau: Rondeau l'Indiscrète
Scarlatti: Grave, from Sonata No. 271
for Clavicembalo
Telemann: Duo, from Suite for flute
and strings
DUOS OF ENGLISH MASTERS
(Giesbert) NAG
43 dance movements by Eccles, Finger,
Gasparini, King, Paisible, Purcell and
others
EARLY CLASSICAL DUETS
(Bormann) SCH   2V
Works by Neubaur, Nardini, Boccherini,
Borghi, Stamitz, and Gossec
EASY VIOLIN DUETS, 38
(Fortunatov) MZK
ECKHARDT-GRAMATTÉ, SOPHIE C.
(1902-   )
Duo
OBV
EICHMANN, ARNOLD HEINZ
Children's Suite
Big 3
EIGHTEENTH CENTURY VIOLIN DUET
(Bormann) Sik 290-2   3V
Vol 1: duets by Barbella, Boccherini,
Geminiani, Gossec, Nardini, Stamitz
Vol 2: duets by J.C. Bach, Boccherini,
Borghi, Gossec, Stamitz
Vol 3: duets by J.C. Bach, Boccherini,
Leclair, Pichl, Stamitz
(ENGELS)
Duet Booklet of the Masters
SCH   for contents see title
FESCH, WILLEM DE (1687-1761)
Sonatas, 6, Op. 9
WM (Pet WM27)

FESCH, WILLEM DE (cont.)
  Sonatas, 3 Easy
    (Doflein) SCH
FIDDLE SESSIONS
  (Gearhart & Green) Shawnee
    for 2, 3, or 4 vln
    Bach, J.S: Canon
    Bach, J.S: Chorale
    Bach, J.S: Preludulerp
    Baltazarini: Ballet
    Beethoven: Minuet
    Brahms: Round for four
    Caldara: Count me in
    Couperin: Air for two viols
    Deep river
    Devil's dream
    Dobon: Zowie! goes the weasel
    Franck: Prayer
    Gearhart: After you, my dear Gaston
    Gearhart: Close quarters
    Gearhart: Mixed metre
    Gearhart: More mixed metre
    Gearhart: Sky blue
    Haydn: Fugue
    Haydn: Minuet
    Hayes: Follow the leader
    Lassus: Anticipation
    Leopold I: Sarabande
    Mendelssohn: Lift thine eyes, from
      Elijah
    Mendelssohn: Theme from Italian
      Symphony
    Moussorgsky: Hopak
    Mozart, L: Etude
    Mozart, W.A: Duet
    Muffat: Gavotte
    Pleyel: Rondo
    Purcell: Madrigal
    Purcell: Round for three
    Quantz: Rigadoon
    Ravel: Pavane
    Round in three styles
    Schubert: Lacrymosa
    Stravinsky: Berceuse, from Firebird
    Sweelinck: Double canon
    Tchaikovsky: Meditation
    Tchaikovsky: Polka
    Volga Boatmen
    Wagner: Chorale, from Meistersinger
    Weber: Ariette
FIDDLERS TWO
  (Auer-Saenger) CF 01425; Vol 2 of
    Graded Course of Ensemble Playing
FIRST DUET ALBUM
  (Whistler & Hummel) Ru
FITELBERG, [JERZY (1903-1951)]
  Sonatina
  Omega
FORTNER, see Spielmusik, Vol. 6
(FORTUNÁTOV)
  Easy Violin Duets, 38
    MZK
  Pieces, 7
    MZK
FROHES DUOSPIEL
  (Doflein) SCH
FUGUES, 15, BY RUSSIAN COMPOSERS
  (Mostras) MZK
GARDONYI, Z.
  Easy Pieces
    BH
GAY DANCES OF OLD MASTERS
  (Hoffmann) SCH
    25 dances for 2-4 violins by M. Franck,

Haussmann, Fischer, Krieger and
    Schmikerer
(GEARHART, LIVINGSTON & GREEN, ELIZA-
    BETH)
  Fiddle Sessions
    Shawnee for contents see title
GEBAUER, MICHAEL JOSEPH (1763-1812)
  Easy Duets, 12, Op. 10
    (Ambrosio) CF L300
    (Hermann-Mittell) GS L956
    (Marchet) Senart 5238
    Pet 1986
GEMINIANI, FRANCESCO (1687-1762)
  Duet, see String Quartet Starts Rehearsing,
    under more than 1 instrumental com-
    bination
GEUSS (18th century)
  Duets, 8
    (Birkner) Moeck 1044
GIARDINI, FELICE DE (1716-1796)
  Sonatas, 6
    (Bonelli) ZA 4104
(GIESBERT)
  Duos of English Masters
    NAG for contents see title
GOEHR, RUDOLPH (1910-   )
  Concerto Cancrizante
    Rongwen
GRADED COURSE OF ENSEMBLE PLAYING,
    VOL 2
  (Auer-Saenger) CF 01425; for complete
    contents see title under more than
    1 instrumental combination
GRANGER, J.
  Délices d'une journée, Les
    Gaudet
GREEN, ELIZABETH, see Gearhart & Green
HALVORSEN, JOHAN (1864-1935)
  Koncert caprice over norske melodier
    Norsk
HANDEL, GEORG FRIEDRICH (1685-1759)
  Easy Duets
    (Twarz-Vieland) Int
HAYDN, JOSEPH (1732-1809)
  Duets, 3, Op. 99
    (Adler) UE 7590
    (Sitt) Pet 3303
    Int
  Duet in D, Op. 102
    Int
  Petit Menuet; with Rondo a la Turque by
    Mozart
    BH
  Sonatas, 6, Op. 6
    (Hoffmann) SCH
HERMANN, F.
  First Ensemble Exercises, Op. 21
    BRH 2V
(HERMANN)
  Classic Pieces
    Pet 2685 for contents see title
HINDEMITH, PAUL (1895-1963)
  Pieces, 9, Op. 44, No. 1
    SCH
  See also Spielmusik, Vols. 1, 2 and 6
(HOFFMANN)
  Gay Dances Of Old Masters
    SCH for contents see title
  Little Dance Book
    SCH
  Volkslied-Spielbuch
    SCH
HONEGGER, ARTHUR (1892-1955)
  Sonatina
    ESC

HUBEAU, JEAN (1917-   )
  Sonatine Caprice
  Dur
HUMMEL, HERMAN A., see Whistler & Hummel
JANSA, LEOPOLD (1795-1875)
  Duos, 6, Op. 46
  Pet 1083A
JEMNITZ, see Spielmusik, Vol. 4
JULIEN-ROUSSEAU, L.
  Berceuse, from 6 Little Duets
  ESC
  Chinoiserie, from 6 Little Duets
  ESC
  Choral, from 6 Little Duets
  ESC
  Duo sentimental, from 6 Little Duets
  ESC
  Petite Gavotte, from 6 Little Duets
  ESC
  Sur le Yacht, from 6 Little Duets
  ESC
JUSEK, V.
  Easy Chamber Music
  Artia
KADOSA, see Spielmusik, Vols 3 and 4
KALLIWODA, JOHANN WENZEL (1801-1866)
  Duos Concertants, 2, Op. 70
    (Hermann) Pet 2518A
  Duos Concertants, 3, Op. 116
    (Hermann) Pet 2518b
  Duos, 3, Op. 178
    (Hermann) Pet 1084A
    (Quesnot) Senart 5181
  Duos, 3, Op. 179
    (Hermann) Pet 1084b
    (Quesnot) Senart 5182
  Duos, 3, Op. 180
    (Hermann) Pet 1084C
    (Quesnot) Senart 5183
  Duos, 3, Op. 181
    (Hermann) Pet 1084D
    (Quesnot) Senart 5184
    CF 03454
KAUFMANN, ARMIN (1902-   )
  Duets, 8, Op. 76
  DOB
KLINGSOR, T.
  Petite Suite
  Senart
KONT, P.
  Erinnerungen, 3
  DOB
KROLL, WILLIAM (1901-   )
  Contra Dance; Donkey Doodle; Peter Rabbit;
    Polka; see vln and pno
KROMMER, FRANZ (1759-1831)
  Duet in A
  (Nemeth) OBV
KUBIZEK, AUGUSTIN (1918-   )
  Musik
  BRH
LAVAGNINO, ANGELO FRANCESCO
    (1909-   )
  Sette Invenzioni in forma di Canone
  Carisch
LECLAIR, JEAN MARIE (1697-1764)
  Sonates, 6
    (Pincherle) Senart 5388, 5395   2V
    Noet (Pet No. N6006)
  Sonatas, 3, Op. 2, Nos. 2, 4, 6
    Hin (Pet No. H15)
LECLAIR, JEAN MARIE (1703-1777)
  Sonate No. 6
    (Vallas-Capelle) Senart 5361

LECLERC, J.N. (c.1700-1765)
  Contradances and Minuets
  Hug (Pet No. A3)
LEDUC, SIMON (1748-1777)
  Little Sonatas, 3
    (Doflein) SCH
LITTLE DANCE BOOK
  (Hoffmann) SCH
LITTLE OLD-FRENCH DANCES
  (Arma) SCH
MARTEAU, H., see Abel & Marteau
MARTINU, BOHUSLAV (1890-1959)
  Etudes faciles
  Leduc
(MAYER)
  Volksweisen
  DOB
MAZAS, JACQUES-FÉRÉOL (1782-1849)
  Duets, 12, Op. 38
    (Corti) Ric ER78-80   3V
    (Quesnot) Senart 5175-76   2V
    (Schradieck) GS L331-332   2V
    CF L130-131   2V
    Pet 1955A, b   2V
    SCH   2V
    UE 240-1   2V
  Duets, 6, Op. 38
    Aug 5708a
  Duets, 6, Op. 39
    (Schradieck) GS L333-334   2V
    CF L148-9   2V
    Pet 1956A, b   2V
    UE 242-3   2V
  Duets, 6, Op. 40
    CF 03514-5   2V
  Duets, 3, Op. 41, Bk. 2
    GS L1748
  Duets, 6, Op. 46
    (Mittell) GS L1250
    CF L619
    Pet 2528
  Duets, 6, Op. 60
    (Quesnot) Senart 5180
    Pet 1957
  Duets 6, Op. 61
    CF L620
    Pet 1958
    UE 253
  Duets, 12, Op. 70
    (Herrmann) GS L446-447   2V
    "School of the violinist"
    Pet 2521A, b   2V
  Duets, 6, Op. 71
    Pet 2522A, b   2V
  Duets, Op. 71, Bk. 1
    CF L151
  Duos abécédaires, 15, Op. 85
    (Quesnot) Senart 5177-79   3V
    CF 02645-02647   3V
    Pet 2166A, b, C   3V
    UE 254-5   2V
  Duos élémentaires, 15, Op. 86
    Pet 2598A, b, C   3V
MENDELSSOHN, FELIX (1809-1847)
  Wedding March
    (Weiss) CF
MERSMANN, HANS (1891-   )
  Musik für eine und zwei Geigen
  Schwann
    Festliches Praeludium I
    Kleine Suite, for vln unacc
    Festliches Praeludium II
  Musik für zwei Geigen
  Schwann

MEYERBEER, GIACOMO (1791-1864)
Coronation March
(Weiss) CF
MIGOT, GEORGES (1891-   )
Petits Prêludes, 6
Leduc   2V
MILHAUD, DARIUS (1892-   )
Duo
Heugel
Sonatine
Heugel
MINUETS OF THE OLD MASTERS
(Beran) Artia
MONTECLAIR, [MICHEL (1667-1737)]
Concerto No. 3, for 2 fl or 2 vln
Noet (Pet No. N1044)
MORLEY, THOMAS (1557-1602)
Fantasies, 9, for 2 viols
STB
MOSTRAS, K.
Etudes and Duets for 2 Violins, Bk. 2
MZK
(MOSTRAS)
Fugues, 15, by Russian Composers
MZK
MOULAERT, RAYMOND (1875-   )
Bagatelles
CBDM
MOZART, LEOPOLD (1719-1787)
Duets, 12
(Hoffmann) Baer HM78
Spielstücke, 12
(Valentin) SCH
MOZART, WOLFGANG AMADEUS (1756-1791)
Duets, 16
Kul
Duets, 12, Op. 70, K. 152
Lit (Pet Nos. L2111A, b, C)   3V
Duets, 12 Easy, K.487
Pet 4518
Duet in A, K.331
Int
German Dances
(Kaempfert) SCH   2V
Laendlerische Taenze, 6, for 2 or 3 vln
Noet (Pet No. N200) pno ad lib
Rondo a la Turque, see Haydn: Petit
Menuet
Viennese Sonatinas, 6
(Kaempfert) SCH
NAUDOT, J, C,
Sonatas, 6
(W. & H. Höckner) SIM   2V
NAUMANN, JOHANN GOTTLIEB (1741-1801)
Leichte Duette, 6
(Bormann) Baer HM90
OLD-FRENCH DUETS
(Doflein) SCH   2V
Duets by de Boismortier, Corrette,
Leclair, Aubert and others
ORFF, CARL
Geigen-übung, see vln study material
see also Spielmusik, Vol. 7, for 2 vln
PEPPING, see Spielmusik, Vol. 8
PIECES, 7
(Fortunatov) MZK
PLEYEL, IGNAZ (1757-1831)
Duets, 6, Op. 8
(Dessauer) SCH
(Hermann) Aug 7597
(Maglioni) Ric ER2457
(Nowotny) UE 156
(Quesnot) Senart 5185
CF L147

GS L297
Pet 1085A
Duets, 6, Op. 23
CF 03481
Pet 1085D
Duets, 6, Op. 24
CF 03261
Pet 1085E
Duets, 3, Op. 44
(Hermann) Aug 5628
Duets, 6, Op. 48
(Dessauer) SCH "Duos-Sonatinas"
(Hermann) Aug 7598 "Sonatinas"
(Marchet) Senart 5248
(Polo) Ric ER1016
CF L157
GS L298
Pet 1085b
Duets, 6, Op. 59
(David) GS L448
Pet 1085C
Duets, 3, Op. 61
Pet 1085F
Duets, 3, Op. 69
Pet 1085H "Grand Duos"
Duets, 3, Op. posth.
(Centano) CF L741 "Grand Duos"
Duets, 3 Easy
(Hermann) Pet 1085G
PRESSER, WILLIAM (1916-   )
Duet
Tritone   printed with Musicwriter
PROKOFIEV, SERGEY (1891-1953)
Sonata, Op. 56
(Oistrakh) Int
BH
MZK
PUGNANI, [GAETANO (1731-1798)]
Duos, 3
Haml
QUIROGA, [MANUEL (1890-   )]
Bruissement d'Ailes
Sal
RAPHAEL, GÜNTHER (1903-   )
Dialogue
Pet 4634
RAWSTHORNE, ALAN (1905-   )
Theme and Variations
Oxf 26.801
REGER, MAX (1873-1916)
Canons and Fugues in Old Style, Op. 131b
Pet 3969D, E, F   published separately
No. 1 in e
No. 2 in d
No. 3 in A
REIN, WALTER (1893-1955)
Spielbuch
SCH
RICHARDS, KATHLEEN (1895-   )
Divertimento No. 1 in G
Oxf 26.104
Divertimento No. 2 in D
Oxf 26.105
RIMMER, FREDERICK (1914-   )
Five Tempers
Hin (Pet No. H1402)
ROESELING, KASPAR (1894-   )
Little Pieces, 5
SCH
ROLLA, ALESSANDRO (1757-1841)
Duetti, Tre, Op. 6
MM   photolith reproduction from orig-
inal edition; published separately

(ROSENTHAL)
  Duos, 18th Century
    MK   for contents see title
RÓZSA, MIKLÓS (1907-   )
  Sonata, Op. 15
    AMP
RUST, FRIEDRICH WILHELM (1739-1796)
  Duet in E flat
    (Bormann) Sik 264
SAEVERUD, HARALD (1897-   )
  Small Violinduets, 20, Op. 32
    Musikk-Huset
(SCHÄFER)
  Volkstänze aus Deutschland und
      Österreich
    DOB   4V
(SCHEUMANN)
  Tanz Mägdlein Tanz
    SCH   for 2 or 3 vln
SCHNEIDER, L. (1765-1847)
  Duos, 3, Op. 4
    VW (Pet No. V47)
SCHUBERT, FRANZ (1797-1828)
  Marche Militaire, Op. 51, No. 1, orig for
      pno duet
    (Weiss) CF
  Songs, 12
    (Hermann) Pet 2205
SECHTER, [SIMON (1788-1867)]
  Fugues and Canons
    (Nowotny) Cranz
SEIBER, MATYAS (1905-1960)
  Easy Dances, Vol. I
    SCH
  Hungarian Folk Songs, 4
    Oxf 26.502
  Studies, 4, in contemporary idioms
    UE 12795
  See also Spielmusik, Vol. 3.
SELECTED DUETS
    (Whistler & Hummel) Ru   2V
SETER, M.
  Sonata
    IMI
SEYBOLD, ARTHUR (1868-1948)
  Recreation, Op. 246
    Pet 3966
SITT, [HANS (1850-1922)]
  Easy Duets, 3, Op. 117
    Pet 3390A
  Easy Duets, 3, Op. 118
    Pet 3390b
SKLENKA, JOHANN
  Fiedelbüchlein
    DOB
SKORZENY, FRITZ (1900-   )
  Divertimento
    DOB   score included
SOKOLOVSKY, [NIKOLAI (1859-1922)]
  Selected Etudes
    MZK
SPIELMUSIK
    (Doflein) SCH
      Vol 1: Hindemith: 14 Easy Duets
      Vol 2: Hindemith: 2 Canonic Duets
      Vol 3: Compositions by Bartok,
        Kadosa and Seiber
      Vol 4: Compositions by Bartok,
        Kadosa and Jemnitz
      Vol 6: Inventions and Fugues by Borne-
        feld, Doflein, Katz, Zuckmayer, Hinde-
        mith, Van Leyden, W. Maler, Weismann
        and Fortner

Vol 7: Suites and Studies by Orff,
    Hindemith, Reutter and Bornefeld
Vol 8: Pepping: Variations and Suite
SPINDLER, FR
  Duett-Schulwerk
    Hof   5V
SPOHR, LUDWIG (1784-1859)
  Duets, 3, Op. 3
    (David) CF L230
    (David-Svecenski) GS L1394
    Pet 1086A
  Duets, 2, Op. 9
    Pet 1086b
  Duets, 3, Op. 39
    Pet 1086C
STAMITZ, KARL (1745-1801
  Duets, Op. 27, Nos. 1-6
    (Bormann) NAG   2V
  Duets, 3, Op. 27
    Int
  Duet in B flat
    (Bormann) Sik 265
STETKA, FRANZ (1899-   )
  Suites, 2
    DOB
(STOUFFER, P.)
  Duet Album of 10 Classical Compositions
    H Elkan   for contents see title
STÜRMER, BRUNO (1892-1958)
  Preludes and Fugues, 5
    Pet 5845
SZELENYI, ISTVAN (1904-   )
  Small Duets, 8. Sonatina
    (Sandor) Kul
SZERVANSZKY, ENDRE (1912-   )
  Duos, 25, on Hungarian Themes
    Kul
  Easy Pieces, 20
    Kul
TANSMAN, ALEXANDER (1897-   )
  Air a Bercer, from Nous jouons pour Maman
    ESC
  Barcarolle, from Nous jouons pour Maman
    ESC
  Chasse, from Nous jouons pour Maman
    ESC
  Danse, from Nous jouons pour Maman
    ESC
  Duos, 8
    ESC
  Poursuite, from Nous jouons pour Maman
    ESC
  Promenade, from Nous jouons pour Maman
    ESC
TANZ MÄGDLEIN TANZ
    (Scheumann) SCH; for 2 or 3 vln
TELEMANN, GEORG PHILIPP (1681-1767)
  Little Pieces, 16
    SCH
  Sonatas, 6, Op. 2, for 2 fl or 2 vln
    Baer 2979-80   2V
  Sonatas in Canon Form, 6, Op. 5, for
      2 fl or 2 vln
    (Hermann) Int
    Baer 2981-2   2V
    Pet 4394
  Sonata in Canon
    OBV
THORNE, FRANCIS
  Sonatina
    AME
TOCH, ERNST (1887-   )
  Duos
    Mil

TWINN, SYDNEY
  English Folk Songs, 12
    Nov
  Old English Songs, 12
    Aug
  Old Irish Songs, 12
    Aug
  Old Scottish Songs, 12
    Aug
  Old Welsh Songs, 12
    Hin (Pet No. H427)
URAY, ERNST LUDWIG (1906-   )
  Variations on an old melody
    DOB
VALENTINE-GLAZER
  Sonatas, 4
    CF 03681
VIARDOT, PAUL (1857-1941)
  Duettini, 6
    Senart
VIOLIN-DUETTE ÄLTERER MEISTER
  (Abel-Marteau) Steingräber   2V
    Vol 1: 9 duets by Wanhall, Bruni,
      Pleyel
    Vol 2: 5 duets by Mazas, Campagnoli
VIOLIN MASTERS' DUET REPERTOIRE
  (Whistler & Hummel) Ru
VIOTTI, GIOVANNI BATTISTA (1755-1824)
  Duets, 3, Op. 9, Bk. 3 of Duos Concertants
    (Lichtenberg) GS L520
  Duets, 6, Op. 20, Bk. 2 of Duos
      Concertants
    (Corti) Ric ER845
    (Gruenwald) CF B3338
    (Lichtenberg) GS L519
  Duets, 3, Op. 29, Bk. 1 of Duos
      Concertants
    (Corti) Ric ER844
    (Gruenwald) CF B3327
    (Lichtenberg) GS L518
    Pet 1087A
  Duos, 3, Op. 30
    Dur
VIVALDI, ANTONIO (c.1669-1741)
  Sonata in F
    Int   vcl and pno ad lib
VOLKSLIED-SPIELBUCH
  (Hoffmann) SCH
VOLKSTÄNZE AUS DEUTSCHLAND UND
      ÖSTERREICH
  (Schäfer) DOB   4V
VOLKSWEISEN
  (Mayer) DOB
WEBBER, LLOYD
  Suite in D
    Aug
WEBER, CARL MARIA VON (1786-1826)
  Invitation to the Dance, orig for pno
    (Weiss-Saenger) CF
WEST-OESTLICHES LIEDERSPIEL
  (Dischner) BRH   2V
(WHISTLER, HARVEY S. & HUMMEL, HER-
    MAN A.)
  First Duet Album
    Ru
  Selected Duets
    Ru
  Violin Masters' Duet Repertoire
    Ru
WILDGANS, FRIEDRICH (1913-   )
  Little Duo
    DOB
WOLFF, CHRISTIAN (1934-   )
  Duo
    Pet 6495

YSAŸE, EUGÈNE (1858-1931)
  Sonate
    (Kogan) Cinedisc

Duos: 2 Violas

BACH, WILHELM FRIEDEMANN (1710-1784)
  Duets, 3
    (Altemark) BRH
    Int
  Duet No. 1 in G
    Hin (Pet No. H83)
  Duets Nos. 2 in C and 3 in g
    Hin (Pet No. H84)
CHERUBINI, [LUIGI (1760-1842)]
  Fugues, 2
    (Twinn) Aug
MAZAS, JACQUES-FÉRÉOL (1782-1849)
  Duos Concertante, Op. 71, orig for 2 vln
    Cranz   2V
STAMITZ, KARL (1745-1801)
  Duets, 3
    (Lebermann) SCH
STERKEL, JOHANN FRANZ XAVER
    (1750-1817)
  Duets, 3
    Hof
TOWNSEND, DOUGLAS (1921-   )
  Duo, Op. 5
    Pet 6038

Duos: 2 Cellos

A DEUX VIOLONCELLES
  (Feuillard-Ruyssen) Delrieu   8V
    contents same as Le Jeune
    Violoncelliste for vcl and pno
ANTONIOTTI, GIORGIO
  Sonata, see Cello Duets
(ARNOLD-ALSHIN)
  Easy Ensembles
    AMP   for 2-4 vcl
BARRIERE, JEAN
  Sonata
    Int
BARTOK, BELA (1881-1945)
  Duos, 18, from 44 Duets, orig for 2 vln
    (Kurz) BH
BASS CLEF SESSIONS
  (Gearhart, Cassel & Hornibrook) Shawnee
    for 2, 3, or 4 vcl
    Arkansas traveler
    Auld lang syne
    Bach, J.S: Now thank we all our God
    Bach, J.S: O sacred Head, now
      wounded
    Bach, J.S: Preludulerp
    Barnby; Now the day is over
    Barnby: Sweet and low
    Beethoven: Andante, from Sonata, Op. 26
    Beethoven: Equali No. 1
    Beethoven: Round on the name B-A-C-H
    Brahms: Hunting song
    Brahms: Round for four
    Chateau: Jazz on rye
    Chinese lullaby
    Chopin: Marche funebre
    Couperin: Air for two viols
    Debussy: Fanfare for a procession
    Fattorini: Ricercare
    Franck: Prayer
    Gearhart: Base, vile blues
    Gearhart: Fanfare for the hunt

BASS CLEF SESSIONS (cont.)
    (Gearhart, Cassel & Hornibrook) Shawnee
      for 2, 3 or 4 vcl (cont.)
      Gearhart: Fugue on A B-A-D E-G-G
      Gearhart: Gavotte
      Gearhart: Habanera
      Gearhart: Hare and tortoise
      Gearhart: Minueteunim
      Gearhart: Passacaglia
      Gearhart: Riffin' a'round
      Gearhart: Roundhouse blues
      Gearhart: Sinfonia
      Gearhart: Waltz glissando
      Good King Wenceslas
      Handel: March
      Haydn: Presto
      Hopkins: We three kings of Orient are
      Hornibrook: Little brown jug
      In the cool cellar
      Kuhnan: Gagliarda
      Massenet: Elegie
      Mendelssohn: Hark, the herald angels
        sing
      Mendelssohn: Nocturne, from Midsum-
        mer Night's Dream
      Misspelled music
      Mozart: Andante, from Sonata K.292
      Mozart: Mixed metre
      Mozart: Rondo, from Sonata K.292
      Palestrina: Madrigal
      Prokofieff: March, from Love for
        3 Oranges
      Prokofieff: Phantasm, from Visions
        Fugitives
      Purcell: Under this stone lies
        Gabriel John
      Sarabande
      Schubert: In memoriam
      Schubert: Lacrimosa
      Schumann: Etude
      Schumann: Northern song
      Schumann: Wild horsemen
      Sicilienne
      Song of the vulgar boatmen
(BENDIK-STORCK)
    Easy Cello Duets
      SCH   2V   for contents see title
BIJVANCK, HENK (1909-   )
    Serenade
      DOB   score included
BOCCHERINI, LUIGI (1743-1805)
    Duetti, Quattro, Op. 10
      Carisch
    Sonata in C
      (Bazelaire) Int
BOISMORTIER, JOSEPH BODIN DE
    (c.1691-1755)
    Sonata No. 1 in G
      (Ruyssen) Delrieu
    Sonata No. 2 in d
      (Ruyssen) Delrieu
    Sonata No. 4
      (Chaigneau) ESC
BORRIS, SIEGFRIED (1906-   )
    Partita, Op. 102, No. 2
      Sirius
BREVAL, JEAN-BAPTISTE (1756-1825)
    Duos, 6
      (Ruyssen) Delrieu   3V
    see also Cello Duets
CAIX D'HERVELOIS, LOUIS DE
    (c.1670-c.1760)
    Pieces, 2
      ESC

CASELLA, C.A.
    Grandes Etudes, 6
      Billaudot
CASSEL, DON, see Gearhart, Cassel &
    Hornibrook
CATELINET, PHILIP (1910-   )
    Suite in Miniature
      Hin (Pet No. H139)
CELLO DUETS, Vol 1
    (Koch) SCH
      Antoniotti: Sonata No. 9 in c, Op. 1
      Breval: Duetto No. 5 in F, Op. 25
      Cervetto: Divertimento No. 1 in g,
        Op. 4
      Giordani: Sonata No. 6 in A, Op. 18
      Neubauer: Duetto No. 1 in B flat,
        Op. 10
CERVETTO, GIACOMO (c.1682-1783)
    Divertimento, see Cello Duets
CHAPMAN, ROGER (1916-   )
    Music for 2 cellos
      Pet 6130
COUPERIN
    Concert
      (Bazelaire) Leduc
DAVID, THOMAS CHRISTIAN (1925-   )
    Sonatina
      DOB   score included
DEVIENNE, FRANCOIS (1759-1803)
    Duos Concertants, 3, Op. 3, for 2 bsn or vcl
      KN (Pet No. K29)
DOTZAUER, J.J. FRIEDRICH (1783-1860)
    Sonatas, 3, Op. 103
      (Schroeder) Int
      Pet 2533
DUETS, 6
    (Ticciati) Oxf 21.023
      Exaudet: Minuet
      Lully: Ariette
      Purcell: Air in d
      Ticciati: Berceuse
      Ticciati: Fughetta
      Ticciati: March
EASY CELLO DUETS
    (Bendik-Storck) SCH   2V
      Vol 1: Old Masters
      Vol 2: Classical to Contemporary
EASY ENSEMBLES
    (Arnold-Alshin) AMP   for 2-4 vcl
(EDELSTEIN)
    Rokoko-Duette
      Moeck 1039, 1045   2V   for contents
        see title
FELDMAN, MORTON (1926-   )
    Extensions V
      Pet 6933
FESCH, WILLEM DE (1687-1761)
    Sonatas, 6
      (Schäffler) Moeck 1019-20   2V
      Vol 1: Op. 8, Nos. 7, 8, 9
      Vol 2: Op. 8, Nos. 10, 11, 12
    Sonata in C, Op. 4, No. 7
      Hin (Pet No. H379)
    Sonata in D
      (Chaigneau) ESC
(FEUILLARD & RUYSSEN)
    A Deux Violoncelles
      Delrieu   8V; contents same as Le Jeune
        Violoncelliste for vcl and pno
FRANCHOMME, see vcl study material
(GEARHART, CASSEL & HORNIBROOK)
    Bass Clef Sessions
      Shawnee   for contents see title

GIARDINI, FELICE DE (1716-1796)
Pieces, 3
  ESC
GIORDANI, TOMMASO (c.1730-1806)
Duos, 6, Op. 4
  (Schultz-Hauser) SCH
Sonata, see Cello Duets
GLIERE, REINHOLD (1875-1956)
Duets, 10, Op. 53
  Int 2V
HOCHSTETTER, ARMIN C. (1899-   )
Duo
  Krenn
HORNIBROOK, WALLACE, see Gearhart,
    Cassel, and Hornibrook
KARJINSKY, N.
Concerto
  ESC
KLEIN, JACOB
Suites, 3
  (Hoffmann) BRH
KLENGEL, JULIUS (1859-1933)
Suite in d, Op. 22
  Int
(KOCH)
Cello Duets, Vol 1
  SCH for contents see title
KUMMER, FRIEDRICH AUGUST (1797-1879)
Duets, 3, Op. 22
  (Klengel) Int
Duos, 6, et un caprice
  Billaudot
LEE, SEBASTIAN (1805-1887)
Duets, 3, Op. 36
  Int
Duets, 3, Op. 37
  Int
Duets, 3, Op. 38
  Int
Duets, 6, Op. 60
  Int 2V
Progressive Melodic Studies, 24, Op. 131
  (Becker) SCH
MENDOZA-NAVA, JAIME (1925-   )
Estampas y Estampillas
  Rongwen
MOZART, WOLFGANG AMADEUS (1756-1791)
Sonata in B flat, K.292, orig for bsn and vcl
  (Werner) Int
  OBV
Variations on a theme by, see Ticciati
NEDBAL, MANFRED JOSEF MARIA
    (1902-   )
Sonatina, Op. 5
  DOB
NEUBAUER, FRANZ CHRISTOPH (1760-1795)
Duetto, see Cello Duets
OFFENBACH, JACQUES (1819-1880)
Duos, 6, Op. 49
  (Such) SCH 2V
  HL 2V "Duos très faciles"
Duos faciles, 6, Op. 50
  HL 2V
Duos moyenne force, 3, Op. 51
  HL 3V
Duos brillants, 3, Op. 52
  HL 3V
Duos difficiles, 3, Op. 53
  HL 3V
Duos très difficiles, 3, Op. 54
  HL 3V
OLD ENGLISH SONGS, 12
  (Twinn) Aug for 2 bsn or 2 vcl
    Arethusa

Black-eyed Susan
Down among the dead men
Girl I left behind me
Here's to the maiden
Leather Bottel
Near Woodstock Town
Simon the cellarer
There was a jolly miller
Thorn
Three Ravens
Tom Bowling
PFEIFFER, [GEORGES-JEAN (1835-1908)]
Musette
  RL
POPPER, DAVID (1843-1913)
Suite, Op. 16
  Int
Tempo alla Marcia
  Int
REINAGLE, JOSEPH (1762-1836)
Leichte Violoncelli-Duette, 12
  (Huttenbach) Moeck 1048-9 2V
ROENTGEN, J.
Duet
  AL (Pet No. AL10)
Rhapsody on American Negro Songs, No. 1
  AL (Pet No. AL8)
Rhapsody on American Negro Songs, No. 2
  AL (Pet No. AL9)
ROKOKO-DUETTE
  (Edelstein) Moeck 1039, 1045 2V
  Vol 1. Boismortier: 3 Sonaten
  Vol 2. Boismortier: 2 Sonaten
    Corette: Sonate
ROMBERG, BERNHARD (1767-1841)
Duet No. 1 in D, Op. 9
  Int
Duet No. 2 in F, Op. 9
  Int
Duet No. 3 in e, Op. 9
  Int
Sonatas, 3, Op. 43
  (Gruetzmacher) Pet 2169
Sonata in B flat, Op. 43, No. 1
  Int
RONCHINI, F.
Polonaise
  Senart
RUYSSEN
  see also Feuillard & Ruyssen
SCHETKY, CHRISTOPH (1740-1773)
Violoncello-Duette, 12
  Moeck 1070-71 2V
SERVAIS, F.
  see vcl study material
SHULMAN, ALAN (1915-   )
Duos, 5, for student and teacher
  Weintraub
SKLENKA, JOHANN
Violoncellobüchlein
  DOB
STEVENS, HALSEY (1908-   )
Duos, 5
  Pet 6028
TELEMANN, GEORG PHILIPP (1681-1767)
Canonic Sonatas, 6, orig for 2 fl
  (Ticciati) Hin (Pet No. H1444)
Sonata No. 4, orig for 2 fl
  MM
Sonata in B flat
  ZA 4268
TICCIATI, NISO (1924-   )
Suite in G
  (Tortelier) Hin (Pet No. H1440)

TICCIATI, NISO (cont.)
Variations on a theme by Mozart
Hin (Pet No. H1445)
(TICCIATI, NISO)
Duets, 6
Oxf 21.023   for contents see title
TREW, ARTHUR
Duets and Trios for Unaccompanied Cellos
Oxf 21.005
(TWINN, SYDNEY)
Old English Songs, 12
Aug   for contents see title
VIOTTI, GIOVANNI BATTISTA (1755-1824)
Duos Concertants, 3, Op. 29
Int

Duos: 2 Double-Basses

CLASSICAL AND MODERN DUETS
(Zimmermann) Int
ROMBERG, BERNHARD (1767-1841)
Sonata No. 1 in B flat, Op. 43,
(Simandl) Int
SCHNEIDER, J.C.
Duette für tiefe Instrumente
Hof

Duos: 2 Viols

COPERARIO, GIOVANNI (c.1575-1626)
Fantasias, 2
(Dolmetsch) SCH
EASY ENSEMBLES
(Arnold-Alshin) AMP   for 2-4 viols
JENKINS, JOHN (1592-1678)
Lady Katherine Audley's Bells and an
Ayre, for treble and bass viols
SCH
LOCKE, MATTHEW (c.1630-1677)
Duos, 12, for 2 gamba
(Dolmetsch) Baer HM167
MORLEY, THOMAS (1557-1602)
Fantasies, 9
STB
ROKOKO-DUETTE, see 2 vcl
SUITE (c.1650)
(A. & N. Dolmetsch) SCH

Duos: Violin, Viola

ALBUM OF CLASSICAL AND MODERN COM-
POSITIONS
(Elkan) H Elkan
ALBUM OF SIX CLASSICAL PIECES
(Hussonmorel) Int
ANDERSEN, KARL (1903-   )
En spillmannstube
Norsk
BACH, JOHANN SEBASTIAN (1685-1750)
Art of Fugue: Canon alla decima (in
contrapunto alla terza) and Canon
all'ottava
Pet 218b
Duets, 15, from Two-Part Inventions,
S.772-786,[6] orig for clavier
(David) BRH
(David) Int

Duets, 4, from Clavier-Übung, S.802-5[6]
(Davisson) BRH
Duets, 4[7]
(David) Int
Duets, 4
(Kortschak) UE 10468
Preludes and Fugues, 20
(Hermann) Aug 5593
BARRIERE, JEAN
Duet No. 4
Int
BECK, CONRAD (1901-   )
Duo
SCH
BEETHOVEN, LUDWIG VAN (1770-1827)
Duets, 3[8]
(Hermann-Pagels) Int
BERNIER, RENÉ (1905-   )
Sonatina
Cranz
BOUCHERIT-LE-FAURÉ
Légende
Sal
BRUNI, ANTONIO BARTOLOMEO (1751-1821)
Duos Concertants, 6
Int   2V
Duos Concertants, 3, Op. 25
Int
BRUSTAD, BJARNE (1895-   )
Capricci
Norsk
CANNIBICH, CHRISTIAN (1731-1798)
Duets, 6
(Höckner-Twarz) SIM   2V
CASTELNUOVO-TEDESCO, MARIO (1895-   )
Sonata
Mercury
CHAILLEY, JACQUES (1910-   )
Improvisation a deux
Leduc
COLLINGS, G.A.
Sonatina
Ches
COPERARIO, GIOVANNI (c.1575-1626)
Fantasias, 2, for 2 viols or vln and vla
(Dolmetsch) SCH
EICHNER, ERNST (1740-1777)
Duets, 6, Op. 10, Vol. 1
NAG
Duets, 3, Op. 10
(Altmann) Int
(ELKAN, H.)
Album of Classical and Modern Compositions
H Elkan
FRANCO, JOHAN (1908-   )
Sonatina
CFE   score only
GABURO, K.
Ideas and Transformations No. 1
Pr
GERSTER, OTTMAR (1897-   )
Divertimento
SCH
HALL, RICHARD (1903-   )
Suite
Hin (Pet No. H274)
HALVORSEN, JOHAN (1864-1935)
Passacaglia, see Handel

---

[6] S. number is from the thematic catalogue by W. Schmieder:
Thematisch-systematisch Verzeichnis der musikalischen
Werke von Johann Sebastian Bach. Leipzig, 1950.

[7] Probably the same as the duets arranged by Davisson.

[8] Probably the duets originally written for clarinet and bassoon.

HALVORSEN, JOHAN (cont.)
  Sarabande con Variazioni, on a theme of
    Handel
    Int   score included
    WH 508
HANDEL, GEORG FRIEDRICH (1685-1759)
  Passacaglia
    (Halvorsen) Int   score included
    (Halvorsen) WH 507
  Sarabande con Variazioni, see Halvorsen
HARDING, K.
  Scherzo
    Ches
HAYDN, JOSEPH (1732-1809)
  Sonatas, 6, Hob. VI: 1-6[9]
    (Bonelli) ZA 4112
  Sonata in F, Hob. VI: 1
    (Zatschek) DOB
  Sonata in A, Hob. VI: 2
    (Zatschek) DOB
  Sonata in B flat, Hob. VI: 3
    (Zatschek) DOB
  Sonata in D, Hob. VI: 4
    (Zatschek) DOB
  Sonata in E flat, Hob. VI: 5
    (Zatschek) DOB
  Sonata in C, Hob. VI; 6
    (Zatschek) DOB
HAYDN, MICHAEL (1737-1806)
  Duos, 4
    (Altmann) BRH   2V "Sonatas"
  Duo No. 1 in C
    (Siderits) OBV
  Duo No. 2 in E
    (Siderits) OBV
  Duo No. 3 in F
    (Siderits) OBV
  Duo No. 4 in D
    (Siderits) OBV
HAYDN
  Sonates, 3
    Ed M
HOFFMEISTER, FRANZ ANTON (1754-1812)
  Duet in D
    (Primrose) Int
HUMMEL, HERMAN A., see Whistler & Hum-
  mel
(HUSSONMOREL, V.)
  Album of 6 Classical Pieces
    Int
JACOB, GORDON (1895-   )
  *Prelude, Passacaglia and Fugue
    JWL (Mil No. W2100)
JANSA, LEOPOLD (1795-1875)
  Duets, 3, Op. 70
    Int
JONGEN, JOSEPH (1873-1953)
  Adagio No. 1, Op. 22
    CBDM
KALLIWODA, JOHANN WENZEL (1801-1866)
  Duets, 2, Op. 208
    Int
    Pet 2105
KOECHLIN, CHARLES (1867-1950)
  Idylle, orig for 2 clar
    Chant du Monde
KUBIZEK, AUGUSTIN (1918-   )
  Little Suite
    DOB,
LUENING, OTTO (1900-   )
  Duo
    CFE   score only

LUTZ, OSWALD (1908-   )
  Kleine Musik, Op. 81
    DOB
MARTINU, BOHUSLAV (1890-1959)
  Duo No. 2
    ESC
  Madrigals, 3
    BH
MILHAUD, DARIUS (1892-   )
  Sonatine
    Heugel
MOZART, WOLFGANG AMADEUS (1756-1791)
  Duets, 12, K.487, orig for 2 basset horns
    BRH
    Int
  Duets, 2, K.423 and K.424
    (Gingold-Katims) Int
    BRH
    Pet 1414
    UE 39
  Duo in G, K. 423
    (Rohm) OBV
  Duo in B flat, K. 424
    (Rohm) OBV
NEUBAUR, FRANZ (1760-1795)
  Duets, 3, Op. 10
    (Altmann) Int
ORE, [HARRY (1911-   )]
  Four Temperaments, Op. 31
    Paxton (Mil No. P557)
PHILLIPS, BURRILL (1907-   )
  Conversations
    SMP
  Dialogues
    SMP
PICHL, WENZEL (1741-1804)
  Duet, see String Quartet Starts Rehearsing,
    under more than 1 instrumental com-
    bination
PLEYEL, IGNAZ (1757-1831)
  Duets, 3, Op. 44
    Aug   vcl ad lib
  Duets, 3, Op. 69
    Int
    Lit (Pet No. L1972)
PONCE, MANUEL MARÍA (1882-1948)
  Sonate en Duo
    Senart
PORTER, QUINCY (1897-   )
  Duo
    Val
RIEGGER, WALLINGFORD (1885-1961)
  Variations, Op. 57
    AMP
ROLLA, ALESSANDRO (1757-1841)
  Duo Concertant
    Ed M
SCHMÄLZLE, GERHARD (1930-   )
  Stücke, Vier
    Sirius
SCHOEN, MORITZ
  Easy and Melodic Duettinos, 6, Op. 37
    CF 02983
SHEBALIN, VISSARION (1902-   )
  Sonata, Op. 35
    (Fuchs) Leeds
SIEGL, OTTO (1896-   )
  Duo-Sonatina, Op. 138
    OBV
SKALKOTTAS, NIKOS (1904-1949)
  Duo
    UE 13266
SKORZENY, FRITZ (1900-   )
  Duo-Studien, 5
    DOB

---

[9] Hob. refers to the thematic catalogue by Anthony van Hoboken.

SPOHR, LUDWIG (1784-1859)
  Duo, Op. 13
    (Doflein) Baer 2316
    Lit (Pet No. L1918)
STAMITZ, KARL (1745-1801)
  Duets, 6, Op. 18
    (Ott) LEU   2V
  Duet, Op. 10, No. 1
    (Doktor) DOB
  Duet, Op. 10, No. 2
    (Doktor) DOB
  Duet, Op. 12, No. 2
    Int
  Grand Duo in G
    (Ott) LEU
STARER, ROBERT (1924-   )
  Duo
    SMP
STRING COMPANIONS
    (Whistler & Hummel) Ru   2V
SZÖNYI, E.
  Duet
    Kul
TOCH, ERNST (1887-   )
  Divertimento, Op. 37, No. 2
    SCH
TWINN, SYDNEY
  Student Songs, 12
    JWL (Mil No. W2302)
VILLA-LOBOS, HEITOR (1887-1959)
  Duo
    Mercury
WEINER, LEO (1885-1960)
  Duet
    Kul
(WHISTLER, HARVEY S. & HUMMEL, HER-
    MAN A.)
  String Companions
    Ru   2V
WISHART, PETER (1921-   )
  Cassation
    Oxf 26.102
WOHLFAHRT, ROBERT
  Little Easy Duets, 28, Op. 191
    Int
YSAŸE, EUGÈNE (1858-1931)
  Cadences du Symphonie Concertante
    de Mozart
    Cinedisc

Duos: Violin, Cello

ABACO, EVARISTO FELICE DALL'
    (1675-1742)
  Solo Sonatas, Op. 1 and Op. 4
    BRH
  Sonata da Camera No. 1 in d
    OBV
  Sonata da Camera No. 2 in g
    OBV
ALBUM OF SIX CLASSICAL PIECES
    (Hussonmorel) Int
ANDRIESSEN, HENDRIK (1892-   )
  Inventions, 3
    DN (Pet No. D235)
BACH, JOHANN SEBASTIAN (1685-1750)
  Art of Fugue: Canon alla duodecima
    (in contrapunto alla quinta) and
    2 Canons per augmentationem (in
    contrario motu)
    Pet 218D

Duets, 4, orig for pno[10]
    (Stutchevsky) Int
    (Stutchevsky) Pet 4285
Duets, 4[11]
    (Kortschak) UE 10468
Duets, 2, from the Clavier-Übung S. 802
    (Aronson) AMP
Gavotte and Musette, from English Suite
    No. 3, orig for clavier
    (Hodgson) JWL (Mil No. W2304)
BAZELAIRE, [PAUL (1886-1958)]
  Cache-Cache
    Sal
BEETHOVEN, LUDWIG VAN (1770-1827)
  Duets, 3, orig for clar and bsn
    (Hermann) Int
    (Hermann) Pet 2523
  Duos, 3
    Jack Spratt
BENTZON, JORGEN (1897-1951)
  Expressive Skizzen, 3, Op. 16
    WH 3165
BOCCHERINI, LUIGI (1743-1805)
  Sonate
    (Bazelaire) Leduc
BORGHI, LUIGI (18th century)
  Duet, Op. 5, No. 3
    Int
  Duet, see also String Quartet Starts Re-
    hearsing, under more than 1 instru-
    mental combination
BORRIS, SIEGFRIED (1906-   )
  Partita, Op. 27, No. 3
    Sirius
BRÉVAL, JEAN-BAPTISTE (1756-1825)
  Duet No. 3 in D
    Int
CAPDEVIELLE, PIERRE (1906-   )
  Sonata da camera
    RL
CERVETTO, JAMES [GIACOMO (1747-1837)]
  Duet, Op. 5, No. 3
    Int
CIRRY, see Duets from the 18th Century
CLARKE, HENRY L. (1907-   )
  Game that two can play
    CFE   score only
DALL'ABACO, see Abaco
DAVID, JOHANN NEPOMUK (1895-   )
  Duo Concertante, Op. 19
    BRH
DOTZAUER, J.J. FRIEDRICH (1783-1860)
  Duet in G, Op. 4, No. 2
    FR (Pet No. F2)
    Int
DRIESSLER, JOHANNES (1921-   )
  Duo, Op. 1, No. 1
    Baer 2690
DUET ALBUM IN SCORE FORM
    (Elkan) H Elkan
    9 compositions by Bach, Beethoven,
    Fiocco, Grazioli, Handel, Martini,
    Scarlatti, Telemann
DUETS FROM THE 18TH CENTURY
    (Feinland) Broe (Pet No. B738A)
    Cirry: Op. 5
    Lidel: Op. 3d
    Salomon: Op. 1

---

[10] Probably S.802-5
S. number is from the thematic catalogue by W. Schmieder:
Thematisch-systematisch Verzeichnis der musikalischen
Werke von Johann Sebastian Bach. Leipzig, 1950.
[11] Probably the same as those arranged by Stutchevsky.

DUOS
  (Hussonmorel) Jobert 2V
    Vol 1: Duos d'apres Bach, Handel,
      Couperin, Rameau, Hummel, Valensin
    Vol 2: Duos d'apres Mozart, Pugnani,
      Leclair, Destouches
EISLER, HANNS (1898-   )
  Duo, Op. 7
    UE 8130
(ELKAN, H.)
  Duet Album in Score Form
    H Elkan for contents see title
EVETT, ROBERT (1922-   )
  Duo
    CFE score only
(FEINLAND)
  Duets, 3, from the 18th century
    Broe (Pet No. B738A) for contents
    see title
FIORILLO, FEDERIGO (1755- ?)
  Duet in C, Op. 31, No. 1
    (Altmann) FR (Pet No. F3)
    Int
FITELBERG, [JERZY (1903-1951)]
  Duo
    Omega
FRANCO, JOHAN (1908-   )
  Inventions, 3, 1937
    CFE score only
GHEDINI, GIORGIO FEDERICO (1892-   )
  Canons, 3
    SZ
GIANNINI, WALTER
  Sonata
    AME
GLIERE, REINHOLD (1875-1956)
  Duets, 8, Op. 39
    Int
GUERRA PEIXE, CÉSAR (1914-   )
  Pequena Duo
    ECIC
HANDEL, GEORG FRIEDRICH (1685-1759)
  Passacaglia
    (Halvorsen) Int score included
    (Halvorsen) WH 1227
HARSÁNYI, TIBOR (1898-1954)
  Duo
    Senart
HAYDN, JOSEPH (1732-1809)
  Duet in D
    FR (Pet No. F15)
    Int
  Duet
    Ed M
HOFFMEISTER, FRANZ ANTON (1754-1812)
  Duet in D
    Int
HONEGGER, ARTHUR (1892-1955)
  Sonatine
    Senart
(HUSSONMOREL, V.)
  Album of 6 Classical Pieces
    Int
  Duos
    Jobert 2V for contents see title
JONGEN, JOSEPH (1873-1953)
  Sonata Duo, Op. 109
    ÇBDM
KODÁLY, ZOLTÁN (1882-   )
  Duo, Op. 7
    UE 7089
KROEGER, KARL
  Duo Concertante
    CFE score only

LIDEL, see Duets from the 18th Century
MCBRIDE, ROBERT (1911-   )
  Take-off
    CFE score only
MACONCHY, ELIZABETH (1907-   )
  Theme and Variations
    Leng (Mil No. L3075)
MAGANINI, [QUINTO (1897-   )]
  Canonic Espressivo
    Ed M
MARCKHL, [ERICH (1902-   )]
  Duo-Sonata No. 1
    DOB score included
  Duo-Sonata No. 2
    DOB score included
MARTINU, BOHUSLAV (1890-1959)
  Duo
    ESC
  Duo No. 2
    ESC
MIGOT, GEORGES (1891-   )
  Suite en 3 mouvements
    Leduc
MIHALOVICI, MARCEL (1898-   )
  Sonate
    Amphion 125
MILHAUD, DARIUS (1892-   )
  Sonatine
    Heugel
NARDINI, PIETRO (1722-1793)
  Duet No. 6 in B flat
    Int
PERGAMENT, MOSES (1893-   )
  Duo, Op. 28
    Nordiska
PFEIFFER, [GEORGES-JEAN (1835-1908)]
  Musette
    RL
PINKHAM, DANIEL (1923-   )
  Duo
    CFE score only
PISK, PAUL (1893-   )
  Variations and Fugue on an American Theme
    CFE score included
PLEYEL, IGNAZ (1757-1831)
  Duets, 3, Op. 30
    Int
  Duets
    Sik 544a,b 2V
RAVEL, MAURICE (1875-1937)
  Sonata
    Dur
RIVIER, JEAN (1896-   )
  Sonatine
    Senart
ROCHBERG, GEORGE (1918-   )
  Duo Concertante
    Pr
ROLLA, ALESSANDRO (1757-1841)
  Duo No. 1 in B flat
    SCH
  Duo No. 2 in C
    SCH
  Duo No. 3 in A
    SCH
SALOMON, see Duets from the 18th Century
SEIBER, MÁTYÁS (1905-   )
  Sonata da Camera
    Ches
SIEGL, OTTO (1896-   )
  Gartenmusik, Op. 19
    DOB
SPRONGL, NORBERT (1892-   )
  Duo No. 1, Op. 101, No. 3
    DOB

STAMITZ, KARL (1745-1801)
  Duos, 6, Op. 19
    (Altmann) Lit (Pet No. L2452)
    Int
SWIFT, RICHARD
  Elegy
    CFE   score only
TANSMAN, ALEXANDER (1897-   )
  Air Russe, from Nous jouons pour Maman
    ESC
  Automne, from Nous jouons pour Maman
    ESC
  Été, from Nous jouons pour Maman
    ESC
  Hiver, from Nous jouons pour Maman
    ESC
  Mazurka, from Nous jouons pour Maman
    ESC
  Printemps, from Nous jouons pour Maman
    ESC
TOCH, ERNST (1887-   )
  Divertimento, Op. 37, No. 1
    SCH
VILLA-LOBOS, HEITOR (1887-1959)
  Chôros No. 2
    ESC
WILDGANS, FRIEDRICH (1913-   )
  Duo-Sonatina
    DOB
WOLF-FERRARI, ERMANNO (1876-1948)
  Duo in g, Op. 33b
    LEU
  Introduction and Balletto, Op. 35
    LEU
ZBINDEN, JULIEN-FRANCOIS (1917-   )
  Partita, Op. 21
    BRH

Duos: Viola, Cello

BEETHOVEN, LUDWIG VAN (1770-1827)
  Duet, "With 2 Eyeglasses Obbligato"
    (Stein) Pet 3375A
    Int
  Minuetto
    (Haas) Pet 3375b
BORRIS, SIEGFRIED (1906-   )
  Partita, Op. 4
    Sirius
BUTTERWORTH, ARTHUR (1923-   )
  Suite
    Hin (Pet No. H394)
CASTELNUOVO-TEDESCO, MARIO (1895-   )
  Sonata
    Mil
DANZI, FRANZ (1763-1826)
  Duos, 2
    KN (Pet No. K23)
DOWLAND, JOHN (1562-1626)
  Elizabethan Melody
    (Tertis) Bosw
HINDEMITH, PAUL (1895-1963)
  Duet
    SCH
MILHAUD, DARIUS (1892-   )
  Sonatine
    Heugel
OLIVIER, FRANCOIS (1907-   )
  Suite
    UE 12079
PISTON, WALTER (1894-   )
  Duo
    AMP

SCHROEDER, HANNING (1904-   )
  Variations on the folksong, "Ach bittrer
    Winter"
    LN (Pet No. R57)
SIEGL, OTTO (1896-   )
  Duo Sonata in G, Op. 139
    DOB
WALSWORTH, IVOR
  Suite
    Oxf 20.012
WALZEL, LEOPOLD MATTHIAS (1902-   )
  Duo, Op. 31
    DOB

Duos: Double-Bass, 1 other String Instrument

DRAGONETTI, DOMENICO (1763-1846)
  Duo, for vcl and d-b
    (Turetzky) MM
NERO, PAUL
  Pitzi-Cats, Duet for fiddle and bass
    CF B2777
WALZEL, LEOPOLD M. (1902-   )
  Bagatelles, 5, for vla and d-b
    DOB   score included

Duos: String-Wind

ABENDROTH, WALTER (1896-   )
  Divertimento, Op. 5, for fl and vla
    WM (Pet No. WM45)
ALBUM OF CLASSICAL AND MODERN COM-
    POSITIONS
    (Elkan) H Elkan; for fl and vla
AMRAM, DAVID (1930-   )
  Three Songs for Marlboro, for horn and vcl
    Pet 6689
(ARX)
  Easy Duets by German Masters
    Noet (Pet No. N3015)   for contents see
      title
BACH, KARL PHILIPP EMANUEL (1714-1788)
  Duos, 2, for fl and vln
    (Stephan) NAG
  Duets, 2, for ob and vln
    Mercury
BAEYENS, AUGUST (1895-   )
  Piranesi Suite, for fl and vcl
    Metr
BECK, CONRAD (1901-   )
  Sonatina, for fl and vln
    ESC
BEETHOVEN, LUDWIG VAN (1770-1827)
  Duos, 3, for vln and bsn[12]
    Jack Spratt
BENTZON, JORGEN (1897-1951)
  Intermezzo, Op. 24, for clar and vln
    WH 3332
BERG, GUNNAR (1909-   )
  Pour Clarinette et Violon
    Dansk 216
CAMPAGNOLI, [BARTOLOMMEO (1751-1827)]
  Duet in D, for fl and vln
    Broe (Pet No. B331)
CAZDEN, NORMAN (1914-   )
  Chamber Sonata, Op. 17, No. 3, for clar and
    vla
    CFE   score only

---

[12] No doubt these are the duos originally for clarinet and bassoon.

DAVID, JOHANN NEPOMUK (1895-   )
Sonata, Op. 32, No. 1, for fl and vla
BRH
Sonata, Op. 32, No. 4, for clar and vla
BRH
DAVID, THOMAS CHRISTIAN (1925-   )
Sonata, for fl and vla
DOB
DEGEN, HELMUT (1911-   )
Sonata for fl and vla
SIM
DUET ALBUM OF 10 CLASSICAL COMPO-
SITIONS
(Stouffer) H Elkan; for 2 vln; or fl, vln; or
vln, ob
Compositions by Bach, Boismortier,
Handel, Mozart, Peuerl, Purcell, Tele-
mann
DUET ALBUM OF 9 CLASSICAL COMPOSI-
TIONS
(Elkan) H Elkan; for fl and vcl
DUKELSKY, VLADIMIR (1903-   )
Etude, for vln and bsn
Leeds
EASY DUETS BY GERMAN MASTERS
(Arx) Noet (Pet No. N3015)
for soprano rec and vln
11 duets by K.P.E. Bach, J.S. Bach,
W.F. Bach, Handel, Haydn, Mozart,
Telemann
EDER, HELMUT (1916-   )
Duo, for fl and vln
BRH
(ELKAN, H.)
Album of Classical & Modern Compositions
H Elkan; for fl and vla
Duet Album of 9 Classical Compositions
H Elkan; for fl and vcl
ETLER, ALVIN (1913-   )
Duo, for ob or vln or fl and vla or clar
Val
FELDMAN, MORTON (1926-   )
Two Instruments, for vcl and horn
Pet 6938
FINE, VIVIAN (1913-   )
Iconomachy. Duo for fl and vla
CFE   score only
FRANCO, JOHAN (1908-   )
Sonatina, for fl and vla
CFE   score only
GENZMER, HARALD (1909-   )
Divertissement, for fl and vln
Pet 5971
HINDEMITH, PAUL (1895-1963)
Abendkonzert No. 3, from Plöner
Musiktag, for vln and clar
SCH
HONEGGER, ARTHUR (1892-1955)
Prélude à 2 voix, from Trois Contrepoints[13],
for ob and vcl
WH 2692
HUYBRECHTS, ALBERT (1899-1938)
Sonatina, for fl and vla
CBDM
HYE-KNUDSEN, JOHAN (1896-   )
Kammerduetter, 2, Op. 4, for fl and vcl
WH 2663
KRAUS, JOSEPH MARTIN (1756-1792)
Sonata, for fl and vla
NAG

LESSARD, JOHN (1920-   )
Music for the occasion of the wedding of
Lydia Huntington and Edward Sparrow,
for fl and vln
CFE   score only
LUENING, OTTO (1900-   )
Short Phantasy, for vln and horn
CFE   score only
MAES, JEF (1905-   )
Sonatina, for fl and vla
CBDM
MOYSE, LOUIS
Dances, 4, for fl and vln
MM
MOZART, WOLFGANG AMADEUS (1756-1791)
Sonata in B flat, K.292, for bsn and vcl
BRH
OBV
PERLE, GEORGE (1915-   )
Slow Piece, Op. 18, for clar and vla
CFE   score only
PRESSER, W.
Serenade, for fl and vla
CP
RAPHAEL, GÜNTHER (1903-   )
Divertimento, Op. 74, for alto sax and vcl
BRH
ROSEN, JEROME (1921-   )
Sonata, for clar and vcl
BH
SCHRÖDER, HANNING (1904-   )
Duo-Sonate, for fl and vla
Hof
SMIT, LEO (1921-   )
Suite for ob and vcl
DN (Pet No. D296)
SMITH, WILLIAM OVERTON
Suite, for clar and vln
Oxf
SPISAK, MICHAL (1914-   )
Duetto concertante, for vla and bsn
Ric R1546
(STOUFFER, P.)
Duet Album of 10 Classical Compositions
H Elkan   for contents see title
TATE, PHYLLIS (1911-   )
Sonata, for clar and vcl
Oxf 07.001
TELEMANN, GEORG PHILIPP (1681-1767)
Duet in G, for fl and vln
NAG
THOMSON, VIRGIL (1896-   )
Serenade, for fl and vln
SMP
VILLA-LOBOS, HEITOR (1887-1959)
Assobio a Jato, for fl and vcl
SMP
WEISS, ADOLPH (1891-   )
Passacaglia, for vla and horn
CFE   score only

Duos: Violin, Piano

ABACO, EVARISTO FELICE DALL' (1675-1742)
Gigue, see Marcello: Scherzando
Sonatas, 6, Op. 1
(Kolneder) SCH   gamba or vcl ad lib
BRH   vcl ad lib
Sonatas, 6, Op. 4
BRH   vcl ad lib
Sonatas, 2
MZK

---

[13] Trois Contrepoints: 1. Prélude à 2 voix; 2. Choral à 3 voix,
for vln, vcl, English horn; 3. Canon sur basse obstinée à
4 voix, for vln, vcl, piccolo, English horn.

ABACO, EVARISTO FELICE DALL' (cont.)
Sonata in fa
(Salmon) Ric R354
ABBADO, MARCELLO (1926-   )
Lento and Rondo
SZ
ABEL, [KARL FRIEDRICH (1723-1787)]
Sonata in G
Broe (Pet No. B330)
Sonatinas, 2
Hin (Pet No. H16)
ABENDROTH, [WALTER (1896-   )]
Sonata, Op. 26
SIM
ABSIL, JEAN (1893-   )
Roumanian Rhapsody, Op. 56, orig for vln
and orch
UE 11965
ACCOLAY, J.B.
Concerto No. 1 in a
(Gingold) Int
(Perlman) CF L518
GS L905
ACHRON, ISIDOR (1892-1948)
Improvisation, Op. 11
CF B2791
ACHRON, JOSEPH (1886-1943)
From the Children's Suite
(Heifetz) CF B2361
Hebrew Dance
(Heifetz) CF B2334
Hebrew Lullaby
(Heifetz) CF B2335
Hebrew Melody
(Auer) CF B1293
(Heifetz) CF B2444
(Zimbalist) GS
Pastel in a, Op. 44, No. 1
CF B2239
Pastel in e, Op. 44, No. 2
CF B2240
ACHRON, [JOSEPH (1886-1943)]
Love Offering, Op. 51
UE 7585
Pensée de L. Auer
UE 8270
Suite No. 2, Op. 22
UE 7692
ACKROYD, W.
At Eventide, from 12 Small Pieces
Aug
Autumn Song, from 12 Small Pieces
Aug
Dancing Peasants, from 12 Small Pieces
Aug
Little Dance, from 12 Small Pieces
Aug
Minuet, from 12 Small Pieces
Aug
Romance, from 12 Small Pieces
Aug
Soldiers' March, from 12 Small Pieces
Aug
Spring Song, from 12 Small Pieces
Aug
Waltz, from 12 Small Pieces
Aug
Winter Tale, from 12 Small Pieces
Aug
ACOCK, GWENDOLYN
Serenade
Paterson (CF No. PT2720)
ADAM, ADOLPHE (1803-1856)
Cantique de Noel
Ru   2nd vln ad lib

ADAMS, S.
Holy City
(Henley) BH
Bel
ADESTE FIDELES
(DeLamater) Ru   2nd vln ad lib
(Harvey) VL 112   2nd vln ad lib
(Herfurth-Streitel) Willis
ADLER, L.
Valse Hongroise
Senart
AERTS
Air varié brillant
Gaudet
Fantaisie brillante
Gaudet
(AGARKOV)
Music for Leisure Hours
MZK
Pieces, 6, by Russian and Soviet Composers
MZK
AGAZHNOV, A.
Miniature on an Armenian Folk Theme
MZK
d'AGREVES, E.
Menuet
Cranz
Toccatella
Cranz
AGUIRRE, JULIÁN (1868-1924)
Aire criollo No. 1
(Tonini) Ric BA10723
Aire criollo No. 2
(Tonini) Ric BA10829
Cueca, Op. 61
(Napolitano) Ric BA11310
Huella, Op. 49, orig for pno
(Heifetz) CF B2608
(Schiuma) Ric BA10854
AIQOUNI, K.H.
Morning Prayer, Op. 5, No. 1
CF B1998
AIRS AND GRACES
(Müller) BH
Corelli: Grave
Corelli: Jig
Corelli: Prelude and Allegro
Dall'Abaco: Allegro
Handel: Gavotte
Handel: March
Handel: Minuet
Handel: Sarabande
Telemann: Allegro
Telemann: Allegro
AIVAZIAN
Song; with Kirghiz March by Vlasov
MZK
AKIMENKO, T
Berceuse de Noël No. 1
Senart
Berceuse de Noël No. 2
Senart
ALARD, JEAN-DELPHIN (1815-1888)
Berceuse and Tyrolienne
CF B2999
Brindisi
CF B2602
Faust, Fantaisie de Concert, Op. 47
CF B3278
ALBENIZ, ISAAC (1860-1909)
Cadiz, orig for pno
(Stoessel) BMC
Jota Aragonesa, orig for pno
(Dushkin) SCH

ALBENIZ, ISAAC (cont.)
  Malaguena, orig for pno
    (Kreisler) Fol 1137
  Navarra, orig for pno
    (Heifetz) CF B2248
  Puerto, El, from Iberia, orig for pno
    (Heifetz) CF B2360
  Sevilla, orig for pno
    (Godowsky) JWL (Mil No. W1267)
    (Heifetz) CF B2234
    (Spalding) CF B2218 "Sevillana"
  Tango in D, Op. 165, No. 2, orig for pno
    (Dushkin) SCH
    (Forbes) Oxf 20.112
    (Sylvain) BMC
  Tango
    (Elman) CF B361
  Tango
    (Kreisler) Fol 1192
  Triana, orig for pno
    MZK
d'ALBERT, F.
  Suite
    STB
ALBINONI, [TOMASO (1671-1750)]
  Sonatas, 3, Op. 6, Nos. 4, 5, 7
    (Reinhart) Hug (Pet No. A26)
    vcl ad lib
  Sonatas, 2 Chamber, Op. 6
    (Upmeyer) NAG vcl ad lib
  Sonata in a, Op. 6, No. 6
    (Paumgartner) Hug (Pet No. A28)
  Sonata in a
    (Schäffler) NAG vcl ad lib
ALBRECHT, VON
  Lieder und Tanze der Randvolker Russlands
    Belaieff
ALBU, SANDU
  Mélodies populaires roumaines
    Ric 128977
ALBUM CLÁSICO DEL JOVEN VIOLINISTA
    (Weil) Ric BA10442, 10892 2V
ALBUM HONGROIS
    (Schermann) CF 04
ALBUM OF CLASSICAL SONATINAS
    (Seitz) BMC
      Beethoven: Sonatinas in D and G
      Clementi: Sonatinas Op. 36, Nos. 1, 3,
        5, 6
ALBUM OF FAVORITE VIOLIN SOLOS
    (Isaac) Cole 218
      Annie Laurie
      Auld lang syne
      Ay, Ay, Ay
      Bach: Ave Maria
      Bach: Come, sweet death
      Balfe: Killarney
      Believe me if all those endearing
        young charms
      Bizet: Agnus Dei
      Bland: Carry me back to old Virginny
      Bohm: Still as the night
      Capua: Beneath thy window
      Capua: Maria, mari
      Capua: O sole mio
      Carey: America
      Chiara: La Spagnola
      Cucaracha
      Debussy: Reverie
      Debussy: Romance
      Deep River
      Denza: Funiculi, Funicula
      Drink to me only with thine eyes
      Dvorak: Songs my mother taught me

      Dykes: Holy, Holy, Holy
      Eli, Eli
      Emmett: Dixie
      Fernandez: Cielito Lindo
      Flotow: Ah, so pure
      Foster: My old Kentucky home
      Foster: Oh, Susanna
      Foster: Old black Joe
      Foster: Old folks at home
      Godard: Berceuse, from Jocelyn
      Gounod: Ave Maria
      Grieg: I love thee
      Grieg: Solvejg's song
      Gruber: Silent night
      Halevy: Call me thine own
      Handel: Largo
      Handel: Wher'er you walk
      How can I leave thee
      Humperdinck: Evening prayer
      Iljinsky: Cradle song
      Irish washerwoman
      Karganoff: Souvenir
      Lehar: Merry Widow waltz
      Lehar: Vilia
      Little man
      Liszt: Liebestraum
      Loch Lomond
      Londonderry air
      Nessler: Young Werner's parting song
      Nobody knows the trouble I've seen
      Offenbach: Barcarolle
      Polly Wolly Doodle
      Reading: Adeste Fideles
      Reichardt: When roses bloom
      Robin Adair
      Rubinstein: Melody in F
      Saint-Saens: My heart at thy sweet
        voice
      Schubert: By the sea
      Schubert: Cradle song
      Schubert: Serenade
      Schubert: Trout
      Schubert: Who is Sylvia
      Schumann: Traumerei
      Seeing Nellie home
      Serradell: La Golondrina
      Sinding: Characteristic
      Steal away
      Sullivan: Lost chord
      Sullivan: Onward, Christian soldiers
      Tchaikovsky: None but the lonely heart
      Verdi: Heavenly Aida
      Wagner: Evening star
      Ward: America the beautiful
      Wearing of the green
      When love is kind
      Work: Marching through Georgia
ALBUM OF VIOLIN PIECES
    Amsco 6
ALBUM OF WALTZES
    CF 01009-10
ALBUM RICORDI. CELEBRI PEZZI CLASSICI
    Ric 127540
      Beethoven: Minuetto, dalla Sonata
        Op. 49 n. 2
      Boccherini: Celebre minuetto, dal
        Quintetto, Op. 2 n. 6
      Brahms: Valzer, Op. 39 n. 15
      Ciakovski: Canzone triste, Op. 40 n. 2
      Chopin: Studio, Op. 10 n. 3
      Handel: Largo, dal Serse
      Lulli: Gavotta
      Mendelssohn: Canto de primavera,
        Op. 62 n. 6
      Mozart: Marcia turca, dalla Sonata in la

ALBUM RICORDI. CELEBRI PEZZI
   CLASSICI (cont.)
   Ric 127540 (cont.)
     Schubert: Memento musicale, Op. 94 n. 3
     Schubert: Serenata
     Schumann: Rêverie
ALBUM RICORDI. CELEBRI PEZZI D'OPERA
   Ric 127539
     Bellini: Casta diva, che inargenti, dalla
       Norma
     Donizetti: Una furtiva lagrima, da
       l'Elisir d'amore
     Ponchielli: Danza delle ore, da La
       Gioconda
     Puccini: Quando men vo soletta per
       la via, da La Bohème
     Puccini: O dolci baci, o languide
       carezze, dalla Tosca
     Rossini: Dal tuo stellato soglio, dal
       Mosè
     Verdi: La donna è mobile, dal Rigoletto
     Verdi: Preludio atto I, da La Traviata
ALBUM RICORDI. CELEBRI PEZZI SCELTI
   Ric 127538
     Bolzoni: Minuetto
     Catalani: A sera. Preludio atto III da
       La Wally
     Denza: Funiculi-funiculà
     Matos Rodriguez: La Cumparsita
     Monti: Czardas
     Simonetti: Madrigale
     Strauss: Sulle reve del Danubio
     Tosti: Marechiare
ALETTER, W.
   Chanson Populaire
     CF B19
   Petite Gavotte
     CF B18
   Rendezvous
     Bosw
ALEXANDRE-GEORGES
   Vénus et Adonis
     Gaudet
ALEXANDROV, A.
   Aria, From Classical Suite, Op. 32
     MZK
   Aria; with Gavotte from Classical Symphony
     by Prokofiev
     MZK
ALEXANDROV, Y.
   Russian Rhapsody
     MZK
ALEXANIAN, D.
   Chant d'Emigré
     Mathot
   Horourt Horinn, from Petites Pièces
     Arméniennes
     Mathot
   Hovarek, from Petites Pièces Arméniennes
     Mathot
   Oror and Alaguias, from Petites Pièces
     Arméniennes
     Mathot
ALFANO, [FRANCO (1876-1954)]
   Nenia e scherzino
     Ric 123711
   Sonata in ré
     Ric 123400
ALFVÉN, HUGO (1872-1960)
   Elegi
     Gehrmans
ALIABIEV, ALEXANDER (1787-1851)
   Dance, see Kozlovsky: Piece

   Introduction: Theme and Variations
     MZK
   Nightingale; with Red Sarafan by Varlamov
     MZK
   Sonata
     MZK
   Variations
     MZK
ALL THROUGH THE NIGHT
   (Harvey) VL 61   2nd vln ad lib
(ALLEN)
   Canadian Fiddle Tunes
     CL   2V
ALPHERAKY, A.
   Sérénade Lévantine
     (Hartmann) AMP
ALTMAN, ARTHUR, see Deutsch & Altman
AMALIE, PRINCESS OF PRUSSIA (1723-1787)
   Sonata in F
     VW (Pet No. V108)
AMANI, N.
   Orientale
     (Elman) CF B23
AMBROSE, R.S.
   One Sweetly Solemn Thought
     VL 44   2nd vln ad lib
d'AMBROSIO, ALFREDO (1871-1914)
   Canzonetta, Op. 6
     GS
   Chanson Napolitaine, Op. 37, No. 1
     JWL (Mil No. W1251)
   Petite Chanson
     (Simon) CF B2103
   Romance, Op. 9
     GS
   Sonnet Allègre, Op. 35, No. 1
     SCH
d'AMBROSIO, LUIGI (1885-   )
   Pagine raccolte
     Ric 129504
AMBROSIO, W.F.
   Alice, where art thou. Fantasy
     CF B2984
   Believe me if all those endearing young
     charms. Fantasy
     CF B3296
   Ben Bolt. Fantasy
     CF B3297
   Dixie's land. Fantasy
     CF B3301
   Drink to me only. Fantasy
     CF B3181
   Minuet, from Suite of Graceful Dances,
     Op. 18
     CF B31
   Mocking bird. Fantasy
     CF B3307
   My old Kentucky home. Fantasy
     CF B3308
   Old black Joe. Fantasy
     CF B3309
   Polka Gracieuse, from Suite of Graceful
     Dances, Op. 18
     CF B29
   Wearing of the green. Fantasy
     CF B3315
(AMBROSIO, W.F.)
   Encore
     CF 03563   for contents see title
   Miniature Masterpieces
     CF 02647, 02638, 02648   3V
     for contents see title
   Religious Meditations
     CF 02585   for contents see title

AMES, WILLIAM (1901-   )
  Dust of Snow
    CP
  Sonata
    CFE
AMFITEATROF, DANIELE (1901-   )
  Melodia
    Santis 213
AMRAM, DAVID (1930-   )
  Sonata
    Pet 6686
(ANDERSEN)
  Mein Heimatland
    SCH
ANDERSON, LEROY (1908-   )
  Belle of the Ball
    Mil
  Blue Tango
    Mil
  Fiddle-Faddle
    Mil
  Jazz Legato
    Mil
  Jazz Pizzicato
    Mil
  Plink, Plank, Plunk
    Mil
  Promenade
    Mil
  Saraband
    Mil
  Serenata
    (Edwards) Mil
  Syncopated Clock
    (Edwards) Mil
  Waltzing Cat
    Mjl
ANDRE, J.
  Cantilena in G
    CF B3003
ANDRIESSEN, JURRIAAN (1925-   )
  Sonata
    DN (Pet No. D115)
d'ANDRIEU, see Dandrieu
ANDY DE JARLIS' CANADIAN FIDDLE TUNES
    CL
ANGERER, [PAUL (1927-   )]
  Technical and Musical Etude
    UE 12651
ANNIE LAURIE
    (Franz) VL 23
ANNUNZIATA
  Enchanted April
    Willis
(ANROLD, MAURICE)
  Tunes from everywhere
    Willis
ANTOLOGIA VIOLINISTICA
    (Maglioni) Ric ER2651
ANTONII, PIETRO DEGLI (1648-1720)
  Sonatas, 3
    Hug (Pet No. A42)
(APPLEBAUM, SAMUEL)
  Building Technic with Beautiful Music
    Bel EL1057-58   2V
  First Solos from the Classics
    GS   for contents see title
(APPLEBAUM & STEINER)
  Masterworks for the Young Violinist
    GS   for contents see title
ARENSKY, ANTON (1861-1906)
  Forget-Me-Not; Fugue
    MZK
  Pieces, 4, Op. 30
    MZK

Serenade
  Aug
Tempo di Valse
  (Heifetz) CF B2222
d'ARGOEUVES, MICHEL
  Fantaisie in D
    Dur
ARIOSTI, ATTILIO (1666-c.1740)
  Sonatas 1 and 2, from 6 Sonatas for
    vla d'amore
    (Sabatini Renzo) Santis 982
  Sonata in mi min.
    (Salmon) Ric R346
  Sonata in sol
    (Salmon) Ric R347
ARMENIAN FOLK SONG; UZBEK FOLK SONG
    (Pobachev-Mostras) MZK
ARNE, THOMAS (1710-1778)
  Sonata in B flat
    (Craxton) Oxf 20.007
ARNELL, RICHARD (1917-   )
  Concerto, Op. 9
    SCH
  Sonata No. 2, Op. 55
    SCH
ARNOLD, MALCOLM (1921-   )
  Sonata
    Leng (Mil No. L1110)
  Sonata No. 2, Op. 43
    Paterson (CF No. PT2654)
ARRIEU, CLAUDE (1903-   )
  Concerto in E
    Amphion 137
  Concerto No. 2 in d
    Heugel
  Mouvement perpétuel
    Amphion 152
  Sonate
    Leduc
  Valse, from Fête galante
    Amphion 132
ARTOT, JOSEPH M.
  Souvenir de Bellini. Fantaisie brillante,
    Op. 4
    CF B2512
ARUTUNIAN, A.
  Dance
    MZK
ASAFIEV, BORIS (1884-1949)
  Caucasian Prisoner
    MZK
ASCHER, JOSEPH (1829-1869)
  Alice Where Art Thou
    VL 49   2nd vln ad lib
    see also Ambrosio
ASHTON, A.T.L.
  Arietta
    STB
  Siciliano
    STB
ATREK, F.H.
  Hasret
    UE 11162
ATTERBERG, KURT (1887-   )
  Concerto, Op. 7
    BRH
AUBERT, JACQUES (1689-1753)
  Air
    (Barrère) GS   for fl or vln and pno
  Concerto No. 3
    (Borrel) Senart 5363
  Sonate en fa majeur
    HL

AUBERT, LOUIS
  Sonate en la mineur
    HL
AUBERT, LOUIS & JACQUES
  Pieces Anciennes, Deux
    HL
AUBERT, LOUIS-FRANCOIS-MARIE
    (1877-   )
  Aubade
    Dur
  Sonate
    Dur
AULIN, TOR (1866-1914)
  Berceuse
    CF S3079
AURIC, GEORGES (1899-   )
  Sonata
    Chant du Monde
AUSERLESENE MELODIEN
    (Piechler) SCH   vln and pno or organ
      Abaco: Pastorale
      J.S. Bach: Air
      Beethoven: Elegischer Gesang
      Corelli: Largo; Sarabande
      Giordani: Aria, "Caro mio ben"
      Handel: Arioso, "Dank sei dir, Herr"
      Handel: Larghetto und Allegro
      Handel: Largo, from Xerxes
      Krebs: Vater unser
      Lotti: Aria, "Pur dicesti"
      Lully: Aria
      Mozart: Ave Verum
      Purcell: Air
      Smith: Pastorale
      Tartini: Sarabande
d'AUVERGNE, ANTOINE (1713-1797)
  Sonate en sol majeur
    HL
d'AUVERGNE
  Ballata d'une Serenade
    (Moffat) JWL (Mil No. W1230)
AVIDOM, MENAHEM (1908-   )
  Concertino
    (Heifetz) IMP
AVILES, J.
  Media Noche, La
    (Stoessel) CF B1113
AVON, A.
  Reels and Jigs de chez-nous
    CL
BABELL, WILLIAM (? -1723)
  Sonata in g
    (Tilmouth) Oxf
BABIN, VICTOR (1908-   )
  Konzertstück, orig for vln and orch
    Aug   arr for vln and pno by composer
BACH, C.P.E,, see Bach, Karl Philipp Emanuel
BACH, JOHANN CHRISTIAN (1735-1782)
  Concerto en Ut mineur
    (Casadesus) Senart 5457B
  Sonatas, 5
    (Landshoff) Hin (Pet Nos. H17A,b)   2V
  Sonatas, 2, Op. 16, Nos. 1 and 2
    (Küster) NAG
  Sonata in A, Op. 16, No. 4
    (Küster) NAG
  Sonata in E flat
    SCH
BACH, JOHANN CHRISTOPH FRIEDRICH
    (1732-1795)
  Sonata in A, Op. 10, No. 4
    (Piersig) BRH
  Sonata in D, Op. 16, No. 1
    (Piersig) BRH

Sonata in F
  (Hinnenthal) BRH
BACH, JOHANN SEBASTIAN (1685-1750)
  Adagios, 4, from Cantatas
    (Frotscher) MT (Pet No. MV1046)
  Adagio, from Goldberg Variations, orig
    for clavier
    (Brearley) Hin (Pet No. H284)
  Adagio, from Toccata in C, orig for organ
    (Murdoch) SCH
    (Siloti-Kochanski) CF B1945
  Affettuoso in E flat, S. 1024[14]
    (Herrmann) ESC
  Air from Orchestral Suite in D. "Air on the
    G string"
    (Burmester) GS
    (Heifetz) CF B2737
    (Wilhelmj) CF S3019
    (Wilhelmj) GS
    (Wilhelmj) SCH
    (Wilhelmj-Corti) Ric 127923 "Aria"
    (Windsperger) SCH
    ABRS (Mil No. A238)
    Aug 11320 "Aria"
    VL 93
  Air and Gavotte
    (Ries) SCH
  Allegro in D, from a Lute Suite
    (Klengel) Pet 4160
  Allegro, from Suite in e
    (Schwartzenstein) Paragon
  Andante, from Italian Concerto, orig for
    clavier
    (Ronchini) ESC
  Andante, from Organ Concerto by Vivaldi-
    Bach
    (Pochon) CF B1835
  Anna Magdalena Bach's Music Book
    LN (Pet No. R95)   vcl ad lib
  Aria. Erbarme dich, from St. Matthew
    Passion
    (Murdoch) SCH
  Aria
    Paxton (Mil No. P519)
  Aria, see also Air, Arioso
  Arioso, from Cantata No. 156 and Clavier
    Concerto in f
    (Isaac) CF B2495
    (Szigeti) CF B2372
    ABRS (Mil No. A244) "Aria"
    GS   for vln or vcl and pno
  Arioso
    Leng (Mil No. L1143)
  Ave Maria, see Gounod, Charles
  Bach for beginners
    (Liepmann) GS
      2 little preludes
      3 minuets
      Theme and variations
      Musette
      Bourree
      Polonaise
  Bouree, see Handel: Larghetto
  Chaconne, from Partita in d, orig for vln
    unacc; with pno accomp by Mendelssohn
    and Schumann
    (Anzoletti) Ric ER558
    (Musin) CF 03498
    Pet 2474
    SCH

---

[14] S. number is from the thematic catalogue by W. Schmieder: Thematisch-systematisch Verzeichnis der musikalischen Werke von Johann Sebastian Bach. Leipzig, 1950.

BACH, JOHANN SEBASTIAN (cont.)
  Concerto No. 1 in a, S. 1041[14]
    (Chaumont) Senart 5331
    (Flesch-Weiner) Kul
    (Galamian) Int
    (Herrmann) GS L1401
    (Joachim-Schnirlin) SIM
    (Klengel-Davisson) BRH
    (Maglioni) Ric ER531
    (Oistrach) Pet 4996
    (Spiering) CF L800
    Pet 229
  Concerto No. 2 in E, S. 1042[14]
    (Chaumont) Senart 5330
    (Flesch-Weiner) Kul
    (Galamian) Int
    (Herrmann) GS L1111
    (Klengel-Davisson) BRH
    (Maglioni) Ric ER555
    (Sauret) Aug 7941
    (Spiering) CF L803
    Pet 230
  Concerto No. 3 in D, S. 1045[14], Fragment
    (Saran) BRH
  Concerto in d, S. 1052[15]
    (Dahl-Szigeti) BH
    (Frotscher) Pet 5609
    (LaFuente-Sladek) VL
    (Reitz-Mostrass) Int
  Concerto No. 3 in d
    (Sauret) Aug 7944
  Concerto in g, S. 1056,[14] orig for clavier in f
    (Abbado) SZ
    (Szigeti) Pet 3069A
  Concerto in g
    (Nachez) GS L1601
  Erbarme dich, see Aria
  Fuga Canonica, from Musical Offering
    VW (Pet No. V29)
  Fugue in g; with Sonata in e and Suite in A
    Pet 236
  Gavottes, 2, from English Suite No. 6,
    orig for clavier
    (Heifetz) CF B2402
  Gavotte in D
    (David) CF B2643
  Gavotte in E
    (Kreisler) Fol 1110
  Gavotte and Musette
    (Heifetz) CF B2311
  Improvisation on Prelude No. 2 from Well-
    Tempered Clavichord, see Benoist
  Jesu, joy of man's desiring
    (Grace) Oxf 20.004
  Komm, süsser Tod
    (Tertis) GS for vln or vla or vcl and pno
  Largo, dalla Cantata "Gottes Zeit ist die
    allerbeste Zeit"
    (Janigro) Ric 127917
  Little Classics, 10
    (Seely-Brown) CF 029
  Loure
    CF B3043
  Lute Prelude
    (Kodaly) Kul
  Minuets, 2
    (Harris) Lud S-1570
  Minuet, from French Suite No. 3, orig for
    clavier
    (Singer) BMC

Minuet in G
  Kjos S-5010
Minuet
  (Benoist-Sladek) VL
Now the sheep secure are grazing, from
    Birthday Cantata
  (Forbes) Oxf 23.416 "Sheep may safely
    graze"
  (La Forge) CF B2676
  (Kramer) SMP "Sheep may safely graze"
Nun Danket Alle Gott
  (Norden) Templ
Partita in e[16]
  (Kochanski-Siloti) CF B2029
Praeludium, see Bové
Prelude, from Partita No. 3
  (Heifetz) CF B2478
Prelude in E
  (Kreisler) Fol 1163
Prelude No. 8, from Well-Tempered
    Clavichord
  (Heifetz) CF B2689
Prelude in f sharp, from Well-Tempered
    Clavichord
  (Spalding) VL
Sarabande, from English Suite No. 3, orig
    for clavier
  (Heifetz) CF B2310
Sarabande, from English Suite No. 6, orig
    for clavier
  (Heifetz) CF B2401
Sarabande, from French Suite No. 4, orig
    for clavier
  (Klengel) Pet 4165
Sarabande
  (Phillips) Oxf 23.020
Sarabande and Loure
  (Herrmann) GS
Sheep may safely graze, see Now the sheep
    secure are grazing
Sicilienne, from Sonata No. 2 in E flat,
    orig for fl and cembalo
  (Auer) BMC
  (Barrère) GS
Sonatas, 9
  (Schleifer-Stiehler) Pet 4591A,b
  (Keller) Pet 4591C
    vcl or gamba ad lib
    Vol 1: Sonatas in b,A,E
    Vol 2: Sonatas in c,f,G
    Vol 3: Sonatas in G,e,c
*Sonatas, 6, in b,A,E,c,f,G
    S. 1014-19[14]
  (Bouvet) Senart 5154, 5159 2V
  (David) Int 2V
  (David) Pet 232-3 2V
  (Debussy) Dur 2V
  (De Guarnieri) Ric ER176
  (Gerber) Baer 5118-9 2V
    gamba ad lib
  (Jacobsen) Pet 232-3C 2V
  (Naumann) BRH 2V
  UE 2841-42 2V
Sonatas, 6, orig for fl and clavier
  Pet 4461A,b 2V vcl ad lib
Sonatas and Partitas, 6, orig for vln unacc;
    with pno accomp by Schumann
  Pet 228C,D 2V pno part only
Sonata No. 1 in b, S. 1014
  (Dyke) JWL (Mil No. W1252)
  (Kortschak-Hughes) GS L1503
Sonata No. 2 in A, S. 1015
  (Dyke) JWL (Mil No. W1253)
  (Korschak-Hughes) GS L1507

---

[15] This is the Clavier Concerto in d. It is possible that it was originally written for the violin and later transcribed by Bach for the clavier.

[16] This may be Sonata in e, S.1023.

BACH, JOHANN SEBASTIAN (cont.)
  Sonata No. 3 in E, S. 1016
    (Dyke) JWL (Mil No. W1254)
    (Kortschak-Hughes) GS L1487
  Sonata No. 4 in c, S. 1017
    (Kortschak-Hughes) GS L1516
  Sonata No. 5 in f, S. 1018
    (Kortschak-Hughes) GS L1525
  Sonata No. 6, in G, S. 1019
    (Kortschak-Hughes) GS L1533
  Sonata in G, S. 1021
    (Blume-Busch) BRH
    BRH
  Sonata in e, S. 1023
    (Ferguson) SCH
  Sonata in e[17]
    Pet 236A
  Sonata in e; with Fugue in g and Suite in A
    Pet 236
  Sonata in c, S. 1024
    RH (Pet No. ER2) Bach's authorship
      uncertain
    see also Affettuoso in E flat and
      Toccata in c
  Sonata in F
    Pet 4460   Bach's arrangement of his
      Trio in G
  Sonata in F, orig for fl and clavier
    Noet (Pet No. N3037)
  Sonata movement in G
    (Duck-Mackerness) Francis Day & Hunter
  Suite in A; with Fugue in g and Sonata in e
    Pet 236
  Suite for string orchestra
    (Sontag) GS   arr for vln and pno
  Toccata in c, S. 1024
    (Hermann) ESC   vcl ad lib
  see also Violinist's Introduction to Bach
BACH, KARL PHILIPP EMANUEL (1714-1788)
  Arioso in a
    (Ruf) Ric SY578
  Awakening of Spring
    (Palaschko) SCH
  Graceful Dance
    (Applebaum) Mil
  Sonata in b
    (Sitt) Pet 3619A
  Sonata in B flat
    (Ruf) Ric SY576
  Sonata in C, orig for gamba
    (Klengel) BRH
  Sonata in C
    (Ruf) Ric SY572
  Sonata in c
    (Sitt) Pet 3619b
  Sonata in D, orig for gamba
    (Klengel) BRH
  Sonata in D
    (Ruf) Ric SY570
  Sonata in d
    (Ruf) Ric SY571
BACH, WILHELM FRIEDEMANN (1710-1784)
  Grave
    (Kreisler) Fol 1025
  Largo
    (Hartmann) AMP
BACHMANN, [ALBERTO (1875-   )]
  Pour mes jeunes amis, Nos. 1-6
    Gaudet   published separately
BACICH, ANTHONY P.
  Tone Poems
    Willis

_____
[17] This is probably S.1023.

BACON, ERNST (1898-   )
  Buncombe County, N.C. (of an afternoon)
    AMP
  Holbert's cove
    GS
BADARZEWSKA, THEKLA (1838-1861)
  Maiden's Prayer, orig for pno
    CF B3180
BADINGS, HENK (1907-   )
  Cavatina
    DN (Pet No. D7)
  Sonata No. 3
    DN (Pet No. D5)
BAEYENS, AUGUST (1895-   )
  Sonata
    CBDM
BAIN, J. M.
  Brother James's Air
    Oxf 23.413
BAKLANOVA, N.
  Allegro, Sonatina
    MZK
  Etude Staccato, see Sulimov: Etude-March
  Etudes, 2
    MZK
  Pieces, 3
    (Levy-Zeitlin) Leeds
BALAKIREV, [MILY (1837-1910)]
  Chant du Pêcheur
    (Hartmann) AMP
  Impromptu
    MZK
BALAZS, FREDERICK (1920-   )
  Capriccio Dies Irae
    CFE
  Kentuckia
    CFE
BALFE, MICHAEL (1808-1870)
  Bohemian Girl. Airs
    VL 65
  Bohemian Girl. Selections
    (Wichtl-Centano) CF S3105
  Bohemian Girl. Transcription
    (Ambrosio) CF B3298
  I dreamt I dwelt in marble halls, from
      Bohemian Girl
    (Halle) Bel 705
  Then you'll remember me, from Bohemian
      Girl
    (Halle) Bel 704
BALKASHIN, Y.
  Sonata
    MZK
BALLARD
  Fiddle Dance
    Mil
  Gypsy Serenade
    Mil
BALLIF, [CLAUDE (1924-   )]
  Sonata, Op. 17
    BB
BALLOU, ESTHER W.
  Capriccio
    CFE
BALOGH, ERNÖ (1897-   )
  Caprice Antique
    (Kreisler) CF B1898
BALSIS, E.
  Concerto No. 2
    MZK
BAMFORD, LESLEY
  In a Coracle
    ABRS (Mil No. A255)

BANG, MAIA
  Gingham Books, see violin study
BANKS, DON (1923-   )
  Sonata
    SCH
BANTOCK, GRANVILLE (1868-1946)
  Sonata No. 2 in D[18]
    GT
BARATI, GEORGE (1913-   )
  Dances, 2
    Peer
  Sonata, 1956
    CFE
BARBARA
  (Maresh) VL 90   2nd vln ad lib
BARBELLA
  Larghetto in g
    (Klengel) Pet 4162
BARBER, SAMUEL (1910-   )
  Canzone, transcribed from 2nd mvt of
    Piano Concerto, Op. 38
    GS
  Concerto, Op. 14
    GS
BARBERA, GIUSEPPE
  Canto di trovatore
    Ric 129074
BARBIER, RENÉ (1890-   )
  Concert Piece, Op. 95
    CBDM
BARBILLION, JEANNE (1895-   )
  Sonate en ré majeur
    Senart
BARBIROLLI, JOHN (1899-   )
  Airs, 6
    Oxf 20.003
BARDOS, LAJOS (1899-   )
  Hungarian Folk Songs, 3
    Oxf 23.024
BARISON, CESARE (1887-   )
  Canzonetta
    Carisch
  Notturno
    Carisch
  Preghiera
    Carisch
BARLOW, DAVID
  Theme and Variations
    Nov
BARLOW, F.
  Sonate
    RL
BARNES, CLIFF
  Very Easy String Book
    Jack Spratt
BARNS, ETHEL (1880-1948)
  Escarpolette, L'
    CF B83
  Faun, Le
    SCH
BARRAINE, ELSA (1910-   )
  Suite Juive
    SCH
BARRATT, E.
  Coronach
    STB
BARRAUD, HENRY (1900-   )
  Sonatine
    Amphion 102
BARTH, JOHN F.
  School Days March
    VL 41   2nd vln ad lib

Sorority March
  VL 73   2nd vln ad lib
BARTHELEMON
  Sonata, Op. 10, No. 2
    (Jensen) Aug 7421
BARTÓK, BÉLA (1881-1945)
  Burlesque, Op. 8c, No. 2
    (Urai) SZ
  Concerto No. 1
    BH
  Concerto No. 2
    BH
  Evening in the country
    (Harris) Lud S-15A3
  Evening in the Village
    Kul
  Hungarian Folk Songs
    Kul
  Hungarian Folk Tunes
    (Szigeti) BH
  Pour les enfants
    (Zathureczky) Kul
  Rhapsody No. 1
    BH
  Rhapsody No. 2
    BH   revised by composer, 1944
  Roumanian Folk Dances
    (Szekely) BH
  Sonata No. 1
    BH
  Sonata No. 2
    BH
  Sonatina, orig for pno
    (Gertler) Kul
BARTOLOZZI, BRUNO
  Concerto
    SZ
BASNER, V.
  Poem, Op. 7, No. 1
    MZK
  Scherzo
    MZK
BASSANI, GIOVANNI BATTISTA (c.1657-1716)
  Balletto, see Solo Violin Music of the Earli-
    est Period
BASSETT, LESLIE (1923-   )
  Sonata
    CFE
BASTON, J.
  Concertino in D
    (Dinn-Bergmann) SCH
BATE, STANLEY (1911-   )
  Sonata No. 1
    Leng (Mil No. L1103)
BATH, S.
  Evening Meditation
    Paxton (Mil No. P510)
BAUMANN, MAX (1917-   )
  Drei Radierungen
    Sirius
BAX, ARNOLD (1883-1953)
  Ballad
    Chap-L
  Concerto
    Chap-L
  Legend
    Aug
  Mediterranean
    (Heifetz) CF B2298
  Sonata No. 1 in E
    Chap-L
  Sonata No. 2 in D
    Chap-L
  Sonata No. 3
    Chap-L

---

[18] In the U.S.A. this publication can be obtained through Mills.

BAYLY, THOMAS H. (1797-1839)
Long, Long Ago
(Gernert) VL 98   2nd vln ad lib
BAYNON, ARTHUR
Twilight-Berceuse
STB
BAZELAIRE, P.
Funérailles
Sal
BAZZINI, ANTONIO (1818-1897)
Allegro de concert, Op. 15
(Auer) GS L1445
Élégie, Op. 35, No. 1
Ric 31866
Ronde des lutins, Op. 25
(Auer) GS
(Pollitzer) CF B3281
(Polo) Ric 128848
(Wilhelmj) SCH
BEALE, JAMES (1924-   )
Sonata
CFE
BEAUMONT, PAUL
Slumber Sweetly
(Saenger) CF B98
VL 9   2nd vln ad lib
BECK, CONRAD (1901-   )
Chamber Concerto
SCH
Sonatina No. 2
Heugel
BECKER, JOHN
Soundpiece No. 3, Sonata
CFE
BECKER
Reverie
(Musin) MK
(BECKER)
Paganini Album
Pet 1990   for contents see title
BECKERATH, ALFRED VON (1901-   )
Weisen-Sonate
Moeck 1104
(BEELER, WALTER)
Christmas Favorites
GS   for contents see title
BEER, L. J.
Concertino in e, Op. 47
Bosw (Bel No. 13)
Concertino in d, Op. 81
Bosw (Bel No. 18)
(BEER, LEOPOLD)
Master Melodies from the Classics
Bel   3V
BEETHOVEN, LUDWIG VAN (1770-1827)
Adagio cantabile, from Sonata, Op. 13,
orig for pno
(Del Maglio) Ric 125601
(Palaschko) SCH
Adagio sostenuto, from Sonata, Op. 27,
No. 2, orig for pno
(Del Maglio) Ric 125602
(Ludlow) CF B2089
Bagatelle
(Hanson) Lud S-15A15
Chorus of Dervishes, from Ruins of Athens
(Auer) CF B49
Concerto in D, Op. 61
(Auer) CF L793
(Dessauer) CF L311
(Flesch) Int   with cadenzas
(Flesch) Pet 189   with cadenzas
(Hubay) Kul

(Jacobsen) UE 310   with cadenzas
by Leonard Jacobsen
(Joachim) SIM
(Parent) Senart 5323
(Polo) Ric ER1866
(Sauret) Aug 7945
(Sauret) SCH
(Schradieck) GS L233   with cadenzas
(Szigeti) Curci   with cadenza by Busoni
cadenzas published separately, see under
vln unacc: Joachim, Kreisler, Leonard,
Quiroga, Rostal, Saint-Saens, Tovey,
Winkler, Ysaÿe
Concerto in C. Fragment
Kal   completed by Hellmesberger
Contra Dance No. 1, orig for orch
(Heifetz) CF B2704
Folk Dance
(Heifetz) CF B2649
For Elise, orig for pno
(Ambrosio) CF B2580
German Dances, 6
BRH
Gertrude's Dream Waltz
(Applebaum) Bel SI18
Marches, 6
(Hermann) Aug 9492
Menuet in D
(Heifetz) CF B2688
Minuet in E flat
(Burmester) SCH
Minuet in G, No. 2 of 6 Minuets, orig for pno
(Ambrosio) CF B2566   simpl
(Burmester) GS
(Elman) CF S3317
(Halle) Bel 671
(Palaschko) SCH
(Powell) AMP
(Trinkaus) Fill
ABRS (Mil No. A221)
Ric 127749
VL 51   2nd vln ad lib
Minuet
BMC
Overtures by Beethoven, Mozart, Weber
Pet 3299A
Romances, 2, orig for vln and orch
No. 1 in G, Op. 40
No. 2 in F, Op. 50
(Anzoletti) Ric ER422
(Auer) CF 04132
(Davisson) BRH
(Flesch) Pet 3393
(Jensen) Aug 7331
(Joachim-Schnirlin) SIM
(Meyer-Wilhelmj) SCH
(Polo) SZ
(Prill) UE 306
(Schradieck) GS L234
Rondino on a theme of, see Kreisler
Rondo in A; with 12 Variations in F on "Se
vuol ballare", from Marriage of Figaro
by Mozart
(David) Pet 13b
Serenade, Op. 8, orig. for vln, vla, vcl
(Hermann) Pet 2174
Serenade in D, Op. 41, arr by composer from
Op. 25
Pet 4663
*Sonatas, 10
Op. 12, Nos. 1-3; Op. 23; Op. 24;
Op. 30, Nos. 1-3; Op. 47; Op. 96
(Auer-Ganz) CF L789

BEETHOVEN, LUDWIG VAN (cont.)
*Sonatas, 10 (cont.)
(Brodsky-Vogrich) GS L232
(Capet-Loyonnet) Senart 5326
(Fischer-Kulenkampff) Ric ER2295-6   2V
(Joachim) Int
(Joachim) Pet 3031
(Kreisler) Aug 8670
(Kreisler) Int
(Lampe-Schäffer) Henle   2V
(Weiner) Kul   2V
Sonata in D, Op. 12, No. 1
(Kreisler) Aug
Sonata in A, Op. 12, No. 2
(Kreisler) Aug
Sonata in E flat, Op. 12, No. 3
(Kreisler) Aug
Sonata in a, Op. 23
(Kreisler) Aug
Sonata in F, Op. 24, "Spring"
(Auer-Ganz) CF 03385
(Brodsky-Vogrich) GS L468
(Kreisler) Aug
(Kreisler) SCH
(Principe-Vitali) Ric ER1475
Pet 4066
Sonata in A, Op. 30, No. 1
(Kreisler) Aug
Sonata in c, Op. 30, No. 2
(Brodsky-Vogrich) GS L467
(Kreisler) Aug
Sonata in G, Op. 30, No. 3
(Kreisler) Aug
Sonata in A, Op. 47, "Kreutzer"
(Auer-Ganz) CF 03758
(Brodsky-Vogrich) GS L74
(Fischer-Kulenkampff) Ric ER2506
(Kreisler) Aug
(Kreisler) SCH
Sonata in G, Op. 96
(Kreisler) Aug
Sonata, Op. 10, No. 3, orig for pno
Aug 7330b
Sonata in F, Op. 17, orig for horn and pno
(Hermann) Pet 149
String Quartets, Op. 18, Nos. 1-3, arr for
vln and pno
Pet 1336A
Symphony No. 5 in c, Op. 67
CF L99
Turkish March, from Ruins of Athens
(Auer) CF B48
(Nagy) Lud-S1570
Variations on "Se vuol ballare", see
Rondo in A
Variierte Themen, 10, Op. 107
BRH   2V
BEHR, FRANZ (1837-1898)
Day with the gypsies
(Applebaum) Bel SI26
In May
Bel
BELETZKY, VALENTIN
Melody, Op. 7
(Hartmann) MZK
BELIEVE ME IF ALL THOSE ENDEARING
YOUNG CHARMS
(Harvey) VL 62   2nd vln ad lib
(Masten) Lud S-1508
BELISI, F.C. (ca.1700)
Sonata in C
(Briner) Hug (Pet No. A34)
BELL, RICHARD
Fantasie
Chap-L

BELLA ROSA
(Moffat) JWL (Mil No. W1231)
BELLINI, VINCENZO (1801-1835)
Fantaisie, see Artot
Overtures by Bellini and Rossini
Pet 494
Variations on a theme of, see Dancla,
Charles: Air Variés, Op. 89, No. 3
and Op. 118, Nos. 1-5
BELLIS, ENZO DE
Sonata in G
ZA 3752
BENARY
Nocturne
Mil
BENDA, [FRANZ (1709-1786)]
Scherzando
(Chaumont) Senart 5401
Sonata No. 8 in a
(Jensen) Aug 7433
Sonata No. 26
(Chaumont) Senart 5396
BENDA, JAN JIRI (1715-1752)
Concerto in G
(Dushkin) SCH
BENDA
Caprice; with Etude by Fiorillo and Bee
by Schubert
MZK
BENDIX, THEODORE
Twilight
Chap-L
BEN-HAIM, PAUL (1897-   )
Songs Without Words, 3
IMP
BENJAMIN, ARTHUR (1893-1960)
Arabesque
STB
Carnavalesque
STB
Concerto
BH
From San Domingo
BH
Humoresque
STB
Jamaican Rumba
(Primrose) BH
Negro Spirituals, 5
(Primrose) BH
Sonatina
BH
Tune and Variations for Little People
BH
BENNARD, GEORGE
Old Rugged Cross
VL 152   2nd vln ad lib
BENNETT, ROBERT RUSSELL (1894-   )
Hexapoda
Chap
Song Sonata
Chap
BENOIST, ANDRÉ (1879-1953)
Improvisation on Prelude No. 2 from Well-
Tempered Clavichord by Bach
CF B2420
(BENOY, A.W.)
Violinist's Books of Carols
Oxf 23.113-32; 23.114-32   2V
BENTZ, J.
Première Position, La
RL   2V
BENTZON, NIELS VIGGO (1919-   )
Capriccietta, Op. 28
WH 3420

BENTZON, NIELS VIGGO (cont.)
  Kvadratrod 3, Op. 35
    WH
BERG, ALBAN (1885-1935)
  Chamber Concerto
    UE 8439
  Concerto
    UE 10903
BERG, NATANAEL (1879-1957)
  Violinkoncert
    Nordiska
BERIO, LUCIANO (1925-   )
  Pieces, 2
    SZ
BÉRIOT, CHARLES DE (1802-1870)
  Airs Variés
    (Sitt) Pet 2637b,C   2V
      Vol 1: Op. 5 in B flat; Op. 7 in E
      Vol 2: Op. 12 in A; Op. 15 in E;
        Op. 42 in D
  Air Varié No. 1 in d, Op. 1
    (Pollitzer) CF B2784
    (Pollitzer) SCH
  Air Varié No. 6 in A, Op. 12
    (Schradieck) GS L409
  Air Varié No. 7 in E, Op. 15
    (Schradieck) GS L410
  Air Varié No. 14 in G
    (Pollitzer) CF L38
  Concerto No. 1 in D, Op. 16, "Military"
    (Saenger) CF L80
    (Schradieck) GS L781
    Pet 2989A
  Concerto No. 2 in b, Op. 32
    (Schradieck) GS L229
    Pet 2989b
  Concerto No. 3 in e, Op. 44
    Pet 2989E
  Concerto No. 4 in d, Op. 46
    Pet 2989F
  Concerto No. 5 in D, Op. 55
    Pet 2989G
  Concerto No. 6 in A, Op. 70
    (Schradieck) GS L215
    Pet 2989H
  Concerto No. 7 in G, Op. 76
    (Fael) Ric ER1783
    (Quesnot) Senart 5289
    (Saenger) CF L82
    (Schradieck) GS L216
    Pet 2989C
  Concerto No. 8 in D, Op. 99
    Pet 2989i
  Concerto No. 9 in a, Op. 104
    (Quesnot) Senart 5288
    (Saenger) CF L83
    (Schradieck) GS L782
    Pet 2989D
    Ric ER2286
  Concerto No. 10 in a, Op. 127
    Pet 2989K
  Scène de Ballet, Op. 100
    (Ambrosio) CF B2540   simpl
    (Centano) CF L64
    (Hermann) Pet 2990
    (Lutz) SCH
    GS L675
    Ric 107917 "Fantaisie ou scene de ballet"
  Variations on a Song of Dargomizhsky
    MZK
(BÉRIOT, CHARLES DE)
  Melodies Italiennes, 12
    (Sitt) Pet 2991

BERKELEY, LENNOX (1903-   )
  Concerto
    Ches   in preparation
  Elegy, Op. 33, No. 2
    Ches
  Pieces, 5, orig for vln and orch
    Ches   in preparation
  Sonatine
    (Rostal) Ches
  Toccata, Op. 33, No. 3
    Ches
BERKLEY, HAROLD
  Sketches, 10, in first position
    CF 03676-7   2V
BERLINSKI, HERMAN (1910-   )
  Sonata in d
    CFE
BERMEISER, V.
  Little Pieces, 3
    OBV   published separately
  Little Suite
    DOB
BERNSTEIN, LEONARD (1918-   )
  Serenade
    (Stern) GS   pno reduction by composer
BERTÉ, EMIL
  Serenade
    (Saenger) CF B2129
BERTHET, FR.
  Berceuse
    RL   for vln or vcl and pno
BERTON, ROLAND DE
  Frolic of the Clowns
    CF B2231
  Mocking bird. Variations, Op. 35
    CF B117
BERTOUILLE, GÉRARD (1898-   )
  Sonata No. 1
    CBDM
  Sonata No. 3
    CBDM
BERWALD, FRANZ (1796-1868)
  Duo
    Gehrmans
BESEKIRSKY, V.
  Sarabande
    MZK
BEST, AGNES, see Palmer & Best
BEZANSON, PHILIP (1916-   )
  Sonata No. 2
    CFE
BEZOLD, E.
  Easy Sketches, 6
    Cranz
BIALAS, GUENTER (1907-   )
  Sonata piccola
    Baer 3471
BIANCHI, GABRIELE (1901-   )
  Concerto
    Ric 124328
BIBER, HEINRICH IGNAZ FRANZ VON
    (1644-1704)
  Mysteries, 15
    (Reitz) UE 7283-84   2V
  Sonata in c
    Pet 4344
BIENE, AUGUST VAN
  Broken Melody
    CF S3112
    Deiss
BIG NOTES FOR LITTLE VIOLINISTS
    (Severn) Willis
BIGAGLIA, DIOGENIO
  Sonate en si bemol majeur
    HL

BILLI
  Bébé s'endort. Ninna-nanna
    Ric 116743
BINA
  Gavotta
    Carisch
  Piccola Marcia
    Carisch
BINDER, CHRISTLIEB SIEGMUND (1723-1789)
  Sonata in G
    (Hausswald) Baer HM62
BINET, [JEAN (1893-1960)]
  Sonata breve
    Ric SY377
BIRCKENSTOCK, JOHANN ADAM (1687-1733)
  Allegro in A, from Sonata Op. 1, No. 3
    (Jacobsen) Pet 4225
  Sonata No. 2 in B flat
    (Woehl) NAG   vcl ad lib
BIRCKENSTOCK
  Sonata in mi min.
    (Salmon) Ric R348
BISHOP, HENRY (1786-1855)
  Home sweet home
    (Franz) VL 21
    (Strietel) Willis
    Fantasia, see, Harris;
      Kron-Saenger
BISSELL, K.W.
  Ballad
    CL
BISTRITZKY, ZINOVI
  Viennese Silhouettes, 2
    Omega
BITSCH, [MARCEL (1921-   )]
  Sonate
    Leduc
BIZET, GEORGES (1838-1875)
  Agnus Dei
    (Ambrosio) CF B2577   simpl
  Andantino quasi Allegretto, from
      L'Arlésienne
    (Dushkin) SCH
  Arioso
    (Linz) SCH
  Carmen. Fantaisie, see Sarasate
  Carmen. Transcription
    (Ambrosio) CF B3299
  Pearl Fishers
    (Halle) Bel 694
  Toreador Song, from Carmen
    (Roberts) CF S3881
    VL 146
BLACHER, BORIS (1903-   )
  Concerto, Op. 29
    BB
  Sonata, Op. 18
    BB
BLACKWOOD, EASLEY (1933-   )
  Sonata
    GS
BLAIR, ARTHUR
  Reveries of Spring
    Mil
BLAKE, HOWARD
  Burlesca
    Chap-L
BLANC DE FONTBELLE, C.
  Sonate
    Senart
BLANCAFORT, [MANUEL (1897-   )]
  Pastorella
    Senart

BLANCHET, G.
  Easy Pieces, 2
    ESC   published separately
  Very Easy Little Pieces, 5
    ESC   published separately
BLAND, JAMES (1854-1911)
  Carry Me Back To Old Virginny
    (Eckstein) CF M309
    VL 150   2nd vln ad lib
BLISS, ARTHUR (1891-   )
  Concerto
    Nov
BLOCH, ERNEST (1880-1959)
  Abodah
    CF B2178
  Baal Shem, see Vidui, Nigun, Simchas
    Torah
  Concerto
    BH
  Mélodie
    CF B1859
  Nigun, from Baal Shem
    CF B1857
  Nuit Exotique
    CF B1967
  Poème Mystique
    LEU
  Simchas Torah, from Baal Shem
    CF B1858
  Sonata
    GS
  Suite Hébraïque, orig for vla and orch
    GS
  Vidui, from Baal Shem
    CF B1856
BLOCH, JOSEPH
  Conte, Op. 48, No. 3
    CF B3008
  Historiette in C, Op. 48, No. 2
    CF B3030
  March, Op. 48, No. 12
    CF B3044
  Romance, Op. 48, No. 6
    CF B3073
  Souvenir, Op. 48, No. 9
    CF B3071
  Valsette, Op. 48, No. 7
    CF B3084
BLOCH, W.
  Sonatina in C
    DOB
BLOK, V.
  Little Suite
    MZK
  Slovak Lullaby; with 3 Slovak Dances
    by Feigin
    MZK
BLON, see Von Blon
BOCCHERINI, LUIGI (1743-1805)
  Canzonetta, from Violin Concerto
    (Dushkin) SCH
  Concerto in D
    (Dushkin) SCH
  Minuet, from Quintet, Op. 13, No. 5
    (Haddock) CF S3318 "Celebrated Minuet"
    (Palaschko) SCH "Celebrated Minuet"
  Minuet in A
    (Musin) MK
  Minuet, see Marcello: Scherzando
  Rondo
    (Willeke) CF B1181
  Sonata in E flat
    (Bonelli) ZA 3555

BOGOSLOVSKY, N.
Easy Pieces, 11
(Levy-Zeitlin) MZK
Pieces, 3
MZK
BOHM, CARL
Bee. Capriccio from Suite in e
(Perlman) CF B2779
Bolero in a, from Album Leaves
CF B2685
Canzonetta in G
CF B3265
Cavatina in D, Op. 314, No. 2
(Ambrosio) CF B2555 simpl
(Centano) CF S3133
Danse Hongroise, Op. 102 La Zingara
(Saenger) CF B3138
Gavotte in G, Op. 314, No. 3
CF S3217
Gondellied in g
CF B3028
Intermezzo in A, from 6 Little Concert
Numbers
CF B3034
Intermezzo in A, from Miniatures, Op. 187
(Saenger) CF B3263
Introduction and Polonaise, from Ara-
besques
CF B2699
Italian Romance in D
CF B3035
Légende in c, Op. 314, No. 7
CF B3039
Moto Perpetuo, from Third Suite, No. 6
BMC
CF B2765
Perpetuo Mobile, from Little Suite, No. 6
(Saenger) CF B2686
(Severn) BMC
Perpetuum Mobile, from Miniatures, Op. 187,
No. 4, "Rain"
(Saenger) CF S3361
Perpetuum Mobile, Op. 380, No. 6
(Saenger) CF B159
Praeludium in C
CF B3069
Sarabande in g, from Album Leaves
CF B2750
Sarabande
(Mittell) GS
Zingara, La, see Danse Hongroise
BOIELDIEU, FRANCOIS-ADRIEN (1775-1834)
Kalif von Bagdad Overture
(Draths) SCH
BOIKO, R.
Sonata
MZK
BOISDEFFRE, RENÉ DE (1838-1906)
Au Bord d'un Ruisseau, Op. 52
CF S3586
BOLDI, J.
Romance Bohémienne
Gaudet
BOLZONI, [GIOVANNI (1841-1919)]
Minuetto
(Danbé) Ric 101965
BOND, CARRIE JACOBS (1862-1946)
I Love You Truly
BMC
Perfect Day
BMC
(BONELLI)
Classici del Violini
ZA 2V for contents see title

BONPORTI, FRANCESCO ANTONIO (1672-1749)
Inventions, 10, Op. 10. "La Pace"
(Giegling) Baer HM44, 45, 77 3V;
vcl ad lib
Vol 1: Inventions in A,b,F
Vol 2: Inventions in g,B flat, c
Vol 3: Inventions in D,e,A,E
Inventions, 4
(Grueters) Pet 2957
BORDES, H.
Sonatina in G
ESC
BOREL-CLERC, CHARLES (1879-   )
Mattchiche, La
Deiss
BORGHI, LUIGI (18th century)
Rondo
(Corti) Carisch
Sonata in A
(Bonelli) ZA
Sonata No. 4 in g, Op. 4
Aug 7414
BORISSOFF, JOSEF (1889-   )
Humoresque Orientale, Op. 11
CF B752
Poème du Nord, Op. 2
CF B753
BORKOVEC, [PAVEL (1894-   )]
Sonata No. 2
Artia
BORNOFF'S FIDDLER'S HOLIDAY
(Bornoff-Wilson) CF 04246-7
(BORNOFF, GEORGE)
Fun for Fiddle Fingers
Gordon V. Thompson
Violin Sings
CF 03615 pno accomp by Don Wilson
for contents see title
BORODIN, ALEXANDER (1833-1887)
Peasants' Chorus, from Prince Igor
(Mitnitzky) AMP
Sérénade, from Piano Suite
(Heifetz) CF B2687
Serenade, see Glinka: Remembrances of a
Mazurka
BOROWSKI, FELIX (1872-1956)
Adoration
(Perlman) CF B3358
Pr
Canzonetta
CF B2730
Valsette
(Ambrosio) CF B2583 simpl
BØRRESEN, HAKON (1876-   )
Konzert in G, Op. 11
WH 1205
BORRIS, SIEGFRIED (1906-   )
Intonation und Capriccio, Op. 62
Sirius
Sonate No. 2, Op. 30, No. 2
Sirius
Sonate No. 3, Op. 30, No. 3
Sirius
Sonatine, Op. 65, No. 2
Sirius
BORTKIEWICZ
In 3/4 Time, Op. 45, No. 5
Lit (Pet L2837)
BORZO-BIHARI
Borzo Csardas
(Orszagh) Kul
BOSSI, RENZO (1883-   )
Momenti agresti, orig for vln and orch
Ric 121772

(BOSTELMANN, LOUIS J.)
Classics, 12, introducing the third
position
GS   for contents see title
BOUGHTON, RUTLAND (1878-   )
Sonata in D
Curwen
BOULANGER, G.
Avant de Mourir, Op. 17
(Schneider) BB
BOULANGER, LILI (1893-1918)
Cortège
Ric R531
D'un matin de Printemps, orig for orch
Dur
Nocturne
Ric R532
BOULNOIS, JOSEPH (1884-1918)
Noël
Senart
BOURGAULT-DUCOUDRAY, LOUIS-ALBERT
(1840-1910)
Bergers à la Crêche, Les
RL
BOURGUIGNON, FRANCIS DE (1890-   )
Ballade, Op. 81
CBDM
BOUSQUET, M.
Vacances, Les
Gaudet
BOUVARD, FRANCOIS
Sonate en fa majeur
ḤL
BOVE, J. HENRY
Praeludium, based on a prelude by Bach
CF W1490
BOWEN, YORK (1884-1961)
Albumleaf
ABRS (Mil No. A247)
Sonata, Op. 112
Ches
BOZZA, [EUGÈNE (1905-   )]
Fantaisie romantique
Senart
Nocturne sur le Lac du Bourget
Senart
Pièces, 6, pour les Enfants
Ricard   published separately
BRACESCO
Canto Incaico
Ric BA11252
BRAGA, GAETANO (1829-1907)
Angel's Serenade. Leggenda valacca,
orig for vcl
(Ambrosio) CF B2533   simpl
(Bellenghi) Ric 98182 "Serenata"
(Halle) Bel 687
(Lutz) SCH "La Serenata"
(Pollitzer-Mittell) GS
(Pollitzer-Saenger) CF B3293
BRAHMS, JOHANNES (1833-1897)
Chorale Prelude "Es ist ein Ros' ent-
sprungen" Op. 122, No. 8, orig for organ
(Kramer) AMP.
Concerto in D, Op. 77
(Auer) CF L779
(Busch) BRH
(Jacobsen) Aug 7975
(Joachim) SIM
(Polo) Ric ER2057
(Zimbalist) GS L1395
Int   with cadenzas by Joachim and Auer
Pet 3893   with cadenza

cadenzas published separately, see under
vln unacc: Auer, Heifetz, Joachim,
Kneisel, Kreisler, Quiroga, Spalding,
Winkler, Ysaÿe
Contemplation
(Heifetz) CF B2432
Cradle Song, Op. 49, No. 4
(Eckstein) CF M320
(Herfurth) BMC
(Hermann) SCH
(Hermann-Mittell) GS
(Hermann-Saenger) CF S3154
(Kramer) CF B541
(Kvelve) VL 162   2nd vln ad lib
(Petroni) Ric 128000 "Ninna-nanna"
(Spalding) CF B2213
Hungarian Dances, 12, orig for pno duet
(Klengel) Pet 3894A
Hungarian dances, 9
(Joachim-Auer) GS L1452-3   2V
Hungarian Dances
(Hubay) Aug 8688a,b   2V
Hungarian Dances Nos. 1-5
(Joachim-Saenger) CF L890
Hungarian Dances Nos. 1, 3, 5
(Hermann) CF S3247
Hungarian Dances Nos. 5 and 6
(Joachim) SIM
Hungarian Dance No. 1
(Joachim-Saenger) CF B2654
Hungarian Dance No. 2
(Kvelve) VL
Hungarian Dance No. 4
(Joachim-Saenger) CF B2638
(Kvelve) VL
Hungarian Dance No. 5
(Abbado) Ric 128088 "Danza ungherese"
(Ambrosio-Perlman) CF B2522   simpl
(Joachim) CF B2757
(Joachim) SCH
(Joachim-Mittell) GS
(Schenkman) GS
VL 156
Hungarian Dance No. 6
(Abbado) Ric ER1936 "Danza ungherese"
(Ambrosio) CF B2551   simpl
(Joachim) CF B3148
(Joachim) SCH
Hungarian Dance No. 7
(Joachim) CF B2694
(Joachim-Heifetz) CF B2437
Hungarian Dance No. 20
(Kvelve) VL
Hungarian Dance
(Kreisler) Fol 1113
Intermezzo, Op. 117, No. 1, orig for pno
(Castelnuovo-Tedesco) Mil
Intermezzo, Op. 117, No. 2, orig for pno
(Castelnuovo-Tedesco) Mil
Intermezzo, Op. 117, No. 3, orig for pno
(Castelnuovo-Tedesco) Mil
Intermezzo in C, Op. 119, No. 3, orig for pno
(Spalding) CF B2365
Intermezzo
Cor ST12
*Sonatas, 3
Int
Op. 78 in G; Op. 100 in A; Op. 108 in d
Sonata No. 1 in G, Op. 78
(Auer-Ganz) CF 03772
(Corti) Ric ER1444
(Flesch-Schnabel) CF 03715
(Jacobsen) Aug 4761

BRAHMS, JOHANNES (cont.)
  Sonata, No. 1 in G, Op. 78 (cont.)
    (Kneisel-Bauer) GS L1301
    (Schnirlin) SCH
    BRH
  Sonata No. 2 in A, Op. 100
    (Auer-Ganz) CF 03773
    (Corti) Ric ER1445
    (Flesch-Schnabel) CF L910
    (Jacobsen) Aug 4762
    (Kneisel-Bauer) GS L1302
    (Schnirlin) SCH
    BRH
  Sonata No. 3 in d, Op. 108
    (Auer-Ganz) CF 03774
    (Corti) Ric ER1446
    (Flesch-Schnabel) CF 03716
    (Jacobsen) Aug 4763
    (Kneisel-Bauer) GS L1303
    (Schnirlin) SCH
    BRH
  Sonatas, 2, Op. 120, orig for clar
    Pet 3896b
  Sonatensatz.[19] Scherzo
    Int
    SIM "Sonata Movement"
  Waltzes, Op. 39, orig for pno duet
    (Abbado) Ric ER2009
    (Klengel) Pet 3668
    Aug 9402
  Waltz, Op. 39, No. 2, orig for pno duet
    (Grunes) Omega
  Waltz, Op. 39, No. 15, orig for pno duet
    (Abbado) Ric ER1937
    (Hochstein) CF B517 "Waltz in A"
    (Kuechler) Hin (Pet No. H14)
    (Willms) SCH
    Hin (Pet No. H29) simpl.
    VL 155 2nd vln ad lib
  Waltz, Famous
    (Perlman-Ambrosio) CF B1937 simpl
  Wiegenlied, see Cradle Song
BRAHMS-DIETRICH-SCHUMANN
  F-A-E Sonata[20]
    Pet 6083
BRANCHE
  Sonate en sol mineur
    HL
BRANDTS-BUYS, [JAN (1868-1933)]
  Suite in D, Op. 43
    DOB
BRANDVIG, HERBERT
  Barn Dance, No. 3 of Suite in Double
    Stops, Op. 9
    CF B2285
  Waltzers, No. 1 of Suite in Double
    Stops, Op. 9
    CF B2278
(BRAYLEY-STEIN-HARRIS)
  Old Treasures, Vol I
    CF
(BRECK, E.S)
  Christmas Joys
    CF 03171 for contents see title
BREESKIN, ELIAS
  Hills of Home
    (Fox) CF B2308
BREIL, JOSEPH CARL (1870-1926)
  Perfect Song
    (Langey) Chap-L with vcl obligato

BRÉVAL, [JEAN-BAPTISTE (1756-1825)]
  Sonata in sol
    (Salmon) Ric R808
BRÉVILLE, PIERRE-ONFROY DE (1861-1949)
  Prière
    RL
  Sonate No. 1 en ut dièze mineur
    RL
  Sonate No. 2 en forme de Rondeau
    RL
  Sonatine
    RL
BRICKEN, CARL (1898-   )
  Sonata No. 1
    CFE
  Sonata No. 2
    CFE
BRIDGE, FRANK (1879-1941)
  Country Dance, from 4 Short Pieces
    for Beginners
    Aug
  Cradle Song
    Aug
  Gondoliera
    Aug
  Heart's Ease
    Aug
  Lullaby, from 4 Short Pieces for Beginners
    Aug
  Meditation, from 4 Short Pieces for Beginners
    Aug
  Melodie
    Aug
  Moto Perpetuo
    Aug
  Sonata
    Aug
  Spring Song, from 4 Short Pieces for Beginners
    Aug
BRIDGEWATER, LESLIE (1893-   )
  Prunella
    Paxton (Mil No. P500)
BRIGHT, D.
  Fischermädchen, Das
    STB
  Polka à la Strauss
    STB
BRINDLE, REGINALD SMITH (1917-   )
  Cloud's Music, Suite
    SZ
BRITISH AIRS: RULE BRITANNIA & ROBIN
    ADAIR
    (Heim) Aug
BRITTEN, BENJAMIN (1913-   )
  Concerto, Op. 15
    BH
  Suite, Op. 6
    BH
BROWN, JAMES
  Hampshire Dumplings
    STB
  Jolly Boy's Dance
    STB
  Little Black Sambo
    STB
  Mantilla Dance
    STB
  Miniature Dance Tunes, 36
    STB
  Neapolitan Tarantella
    STB
  Osterley Violin Book
    STB

---

[19] For complete sonata see Brahms-Dietrich-Schumann:
F-A-E Sonata.
[20] Sonata composed in honor of Joachim. Each composer
wrote one movement.

BROWN, JAMES (cont.)
  Passepied
    STB
  Pastoral Dance
    STB
  Rondo Gavotte
    STB
  Slow Minuet and Cebell
    STB
  Spanish Lady
    STB
  Surrey Roundelay
    STB
  Swing Tune
    STB
  Tambourin
    STB
  Trip it on the green
    STB
BROWN, J. HULLAH
  Bow Craft Series. Contrasted Graded and
    Progressive Solos for Young Performers
    JWL (Mil No. W1220) 12V
      Vol 1: Honeysuckle; Postman's knock
      Vol 2: Lily pond; Woodpecker
      Vol 3: Sand castles; Shells and seaweed
      Vol 4: In the cornfield; Snowdrop time
      Vol 5: Green glades; Highland heather
      Vol 6: Many happy returns; Moonlight
      Vol 7: Merry peasant; Pensive lily
      Vol 8: Fair isle; Fuzzy Wuzzy
      Vol 9: Suavitor in modo; Fortiter in re
      Vol 10: Breakspear; Hullabaloo
      Vol 11: Winding brook; Spring flowers
      Vol 12: Con grazia; Happy-go-lucky
  Oxford Passacaglia
    JWL (Mil No. W1203)
  Students Concertino No. 1 in G
    JWL (Mil No. W1200)
  Students Concertino No. 2 in D
    JWL (Mil No. W1201)
  Students Concertino No. 3 in G
    JWL (Mil No. W1202)
(BROWN, J. HULLAH)
  Welsh Airs
    JWL (Mil No. 1801A,B) 2V
BRUCH, MAX (1838-1920)
  Concerto No. 1 in g, Op. 26
    (Auer) CF L873
    (Francescatti) Int
    (Joachim) Pet 1494
    (Menuhin) Pet 1494A
    (Schradieck) GS L217
    Dur
  Concerto No. 2 in d, Op. 44
    (Auer) CF 03495
    SIM
  Kol Nidre, Op. 47, orig for vcl and orch
    (Ambrosio) CF B2595 simpl.
    (Lehmann) CF S3232
  Romance in a, Op. 42
    (Mlynarczyk) SIM
  Romance in F, Op. 85, orig for vla and orch
    SCH
  Scottish Fantasy, Op. 46, orig for vln and
    orch
    (Spiering) CF L784 "Fantasia on
      Scottish Folk-Melodies"
    (Zimbalist) GS L1398
    SIM
  Swedish Dances, Op. 63
    SIM 2V
BRUNETTE
  (Moffat) JWL (Mil No. W1232)

BRUNNER, ADOLF (1901-   )
  Sonate
    Baer 2691
BRUSH, R.
  Valse joyeuse
    CP
BRUSSELMANS, MICHEL (1886-   )
  Sérénade
    Sal
  Sonate en si mineur
    Senart
BRYDSON, JOHN C. (1900-   )
  Pieces, 2
    Nov
  Summer Idyll
    Leng (Mil No. L1100)
BUCHTEL, FORREST L.
  Ambition Waltz
    Kjos S-5000
  Fiddler's First March
    Kjos S-5001
  Gliding Waltz
    Kjos S-5002
  Happy Days
    Kjos S-5007
  Jiggly Bow
    Kjos S-5015
  Jolly Fellows
    Kjos S-5009
  With Graceful Step
    Kjos S-5008
BUCK, PERCY CARTER (1871-1947)
  Romance in a
    ABRS (Mil No. A222)
BUESSER, HENRI-PAUL (1872-   )
  Sommeil de l'enfant Jésus
    CH (Pet No. C99) vln and pno or harp
BUESST, [VICTOR (1885-   )]
  Concerto
    Ches
BUILDING TECHNIC WITH BEAUTIFUL
    MUSIC, VOLS. 1 and 2
    (Applebaum) Bel EL1057-58 2V
BULL, OLE (1810-1880)
  Saeterjentens Sondag
    (Svendsen-Saenger) CF S3037
BURKHARD, WILLY (1900-1955)
  Sonate
    Baer 2238
  Suite en minature
    Baer 2107
BURLEIGH, CECIL (1885-   )
  Concerto No. 2, Op. 43
    CF 093
  Concerto No. 3, Op. 60
    CF 01667
  Fairy Sailing
    BMC
  Hills, Op. 30, No. 4
    CF B198
  Imps, from Two Humoreskes, Op. 35
    CF B2811
  In Haunted Shadows, from Boyhood Recol-
    lections, Op. 28
    CF B2808
  Of Witches, from Two Humoreskes, Op. 35
    CF B2810
  Sonata, Op. 29. From the life of St. Paul
    CF 01494
  Winter Fun, from Under the Open Sky, Op. 7
    CF B2803
(BURMESTER, WILLY)
  Dances By Old Masters, 12
    BMC for contents see title

(BURMESTER, WILLY) (cont.)
  Old Airs
    SCH 4V
BURTON, ELDIN
  Fiddlestick
    BMC
  Sonatina
    CF 03731
BUSCH, CARL
  Melodic Suite
    CF AA1
BUSH, ALAN (1900-   )
  Concerto
    JWL (Mil No. W1204) pno reduction
      by Rostal
  Lyric Interlude, Op. 26
    JWL (Mil No. W1217)
  Meditation on a German song of 1848, Op. 22
    JWL (Mil No. W1218)
BUSONI, FERRUCCIO BENVENUTO
    (1866-1924)
  Concerto in D, Op. 35a
    BRH
  Sonata, Op. 29
    SIM
  Sonata No. 2, Op. 36a
    BRH
BUTTERFIELD, JAMES A.
  When You and I Were Young, Maggie
    (Saenger) CF B3222
BUTTING, MAX (1888-   )
  Duo, Op. 32
    UE 8785
BYELI, V.
  Sonata
    MZK
CACERES, EMILIO
  Jig in G
    Mutual
CAGE, JOHN (1912-   )
  Melodies, 6, for vln and keyboard
    Pet 6748
  Nocturne
    Pet 6740
CALDARA, [ANTONIO (1670-1736)]
  Canto
    (Rostal) Ches
CALL, AUDREY
  Serenade to a Cornstalk Fiddle
    CF B2417
  Streamline
    CF B2418
  Witch of Harlem
    CF B2419
CALL
  Bishop Check-Mates
    Mil
  Canterbury Tales
    Mil
  Duke Takes A Train
    Mil
  To A Lady From Baltimore
    Mil
CALUDI
  Czardas No. 1
    Liber-S
  Czardas No. 2
    Liber-S
CAMPAGNOLI, BARTOLOMEO (1751-1827)
  Romance
    (Pochon) CF B1276
CAMPAGNOLI
  Andantino con variazioni
    (Corti) Carisch

CAMPOS-PARSI, HECTOR
  Sonatina No. 2
    SMP
CANADIAN FIDDLE TUNES
  (Allen) CL 2V
CANALOS
  Let's Play the Violin
    Mil
CANTALUPI
  Melodia in sol
    Ric BA11520
CANTELOUBE, [JOSEPH (1879-1957)]
  Dans la Montagne
    RL
      1. En plein vent
      2. Le soir
      3. Jour de Fête
      4. Dans les Bois au Printemps
CAPET, LUCIEN (1873-1928)
  Poème
    Mathot
  Sonate
    Mathot
CAPUA, see Di Capua
CARMAN, M.
  Berceuse
    RL
CARMAN-DORSON
  Conte de Noël
    Deiss
CARNIVAL OF VENICE
  (Harvey) VL 144 2nd vln ad lib
CAROLA, HELEN COHAN
  Tears
    BMC
CARPENTER, JOHN ALDEN (1876-1951)
  Concerto
    GS
  Sonata in G
    GS
CARSE, ADAM (1878-1958)
  Alla Minuetta, from First Year Pieces
    JWL (Mil No. W1221A)
  Aria, from Suite in olden style
    Aug
  Berceuse
    Aug
  Bouree, from First Year Pieces
    JWL (Mil No. W1221-4)
  Concertino in D
    Aug
  Dance Scherzo, from First Year Pieces
    JWL (Mil No. W1221-6)
  Day-Dreams, from First Year Pieces
    JWL (Mil No. W1221-2)
  Fiddle Dances
    Aug A.S.85
  Fiddle Fancies
    Aug A.S.92
  Fiddle Tune
    Aug
  Fiddler's Nursery
    Aug A.S.84
  First String Tunes
    Aug A.S.21
  Frog Dance
    Aug
  Gavotte in D, from First Year Pieces
    Mil
  Gavotte in D, from 5 Easy Pieces
    Aug
  Gavotte in D, from Suite in olden style
    Aug
  Gavotte in g, from Sonatina in D
    Aug

CARSE, ADAM (cont.)
Gently Swaying, from 2 Easy Pieces
Aug
Lullaby
Aug
Meditation
Aug
Minuet, from Sonatina in G
Aug
Minuet, from Suite in olden style
Aug
Minuet and Trio
Aug
On the River, from First Year Pieces
JWL (Mil No. W1221-3)
Prelude, from Suite in olden style
Aug
Rigaudon, from Suite in olden style
Aug
Sonatina in A
Aug 11308
Sonatina in D
Aug 11306
Sonatina in g
Aug 11307
Suite in the olden style
Aug A.S.94
Valse, Premiere
BMC
Valse-Rondino, from 2 Easy Pieces
Aug
(CARSE, ADAM)
Minuets by 18th Century Composers
Aug for contents see title
Old English Violin Album
Aug A.S.83
CARULLI, FERDINANDO (1770-1841)
Sonata in A, Op. 21, No. 1, orig for
vln and guitar
ZM (Pet No. ZM244)
Sonata in D, Op. 21, No. 2, orig for
vln and guitar
ZM (Pet No. ZM245)
CASADESUS, [ROBERT (1899-   )]
Sonata No. 2, Op. 32
Dur
CASINIÈRE
Sonatine
RL
CASSADO, GASPAR (1897-   )
Sonata
UE 8567
CASSADO
Flores de Triana
Mathot
CASTELNUOVO-TEDESCO, MARIO (1895-   )
Cherubino, from Marriage of Figaro by
Mozart
Mil
Concerto Italiano in sol min.
Ric 119998
Concerto No. 2, "I Profeti"
Ric 122607   reduction by composer
Figaro, from Barber of Seville by
Rossini
(Heifetz) CF B2669
Ritmo di Tango
(Heifetz) CF B3252
Romance. Fantasy on themes from Fille du
Regiment by Donizetti
Leeds
Rosina, from Barber of Seville by Rossini
(Milstein) CF B2817

Sea-Murmurs
(Heifetz) CF B2303
Tango
(Heifetz) CF B2304
Valse on themes from Daughter of the
Regiment by Donizetti
Mil
Violetta, from La Traviata by Verdi
Mil
CASTÉRA, RENÉ DE (1873-1955)
Sonate en mi mineur
RL
CASTEREDE, J.
Capriccio
Sal
CASTILLON, ALEXIS DE (1838-1873)
Sonate, Op. 6
Heugel
CASTRO, JUAN JOSÉ (1895-   )
Intrata Y Danza Rustica
SMP
CATALANI, ALFREDO (1854-1893)
A sera, from Suite No. 1
Ric 53497
(CATHCART)
Classical Album
BH for contents see title
CATURLA, ALEJANDRO GARCIA (1906-1940)
Danza del Tambor
Senart
CAVERLY, AMICE
Abydos Air
(Willan) Oxf 23.809
CAZDEN, NORMAN (1914-   )
Old Time Dances, Op. 57. 142 Tunes
CFE score only
Presentations, 4, Op. 45
CFE
Reels, Jigs and Squares. 200 Dance Tunes
CFE score only
Suite, Op. 43
CFE
Traditional Dances, Op. 56. 200 Tunes
CFE score only
CECE, ALFREDO
Sonata in D
ZA 3827
CELLIER, [ALEXANDRE (1883-   )]
Berceuse-Fantaisie
Senart
CERHA, FRIEDRICH (1926-   )
Deux éclats
EDW
Formations et solutions
EDW
CERVETTO, [GIACOMO (1747-1837)]
Sonata in do
(Salmon) Ric R70
CHABRIER, EMMANUEL (1841-1894)
Joyeuse Marche, orig for orch
(Dushkin) SCH
CHAGRIN, FRANCIS (1905-   )
Romanian Fantasy
Mil-L 42a
CHALLAN, [HENRI (1910-   )]
Sonate
Leduc
CHALLAN, RENÉ
Concerto in d
CH (Pet No. C358)
CHAMBERLAIN, AILSA
One, Two, Three
Chap-L

CHAMINADE, CÉCILE (1857-1944)
Scarf Dance
(Rosey) MK
Serenade
Kjos S-5018
Sérénade Espagnole
(Kreisler) CF B1308
CHAMP, STEPHEN
Scherzino
Aug
CHAPUIS, AUGUSTE (1858-1933)
Sonate
Dur
CHARPENTIER, A.
Petites Pieces, 4
RL
1. En vacances
2. Berceuse
3. Prière
4. Pastorale
CHAUMONT, E.
Burlesque
Senart
Fox-Trot
Senart
Sunflower
Senart
CHAUSSON, ERNEST (1855-1899)
Interlude du Poème de l'Amour et de la Mer,
orig for voice and orch
RL
Pièce
RL
Poème, Op. 25, orig for vln and orch
(Berkley) CF B2516
(Flesch) Pet 4169
(Francescatti) Int
BRH
GS L1782
SCH
CHENOWETH, WILBUR (1899-   )
In a patio
GS
CHERUBINI, [LUIGI (1760-1842)]
Melody in D
(Dyke) JWL (Mil No. W1283)
CHESTERIAN SERIES OF GRADED VIOLIN
MUSIC
(Radmall) Ches   8V
CHEVAILLIER, L.
Fox-trot, Tango and Finale
ESC
CHEVILLARD, CAMILLE (1859-1923)
Sonate
Dur
CHEVREUILLE, RAYMOND (1901-   )
Concerto No. 2, Op. 56
CBDM
Little Music for Mozart, Op. 64
CBDM
Sonata, Op. 57
CBDM
Variations, Op. 36
CBDM
CHIABRANO
Caccia, La
(Corti) Carisch
CHIARA, V.
Spagnola, La, see Capua: Maria, Mari
CHILDS, BARNEY
Sonata No. 2
CFE
CHOP STICKS
(Applebaum) Bel SI16
(Harvey) VL 148   2nd vln ad lib

CHOPIN, FRÉDÉRIC (1810-1849)[21]
Etude Op. 10, No. 2
(Spivakovsky) GS
Etude Op. 10, No. 6
(Spivakovsky) GS
Etude in f, Op. 25, No. 2
(Dounis) Mil
Etude, Op. 25, No. 6
(Dounis) Mil   in thirds
(Dounis) Mil   in tenths
Etude in D flat, Op. 25, No. 8
(Dounis) Mil
Etude, Op. 27, No. 3
(Spivakovsky) GS
Etude No. 3
(Stone-Seidel) MK
Funeral March, from Sonata in b flat, Op. 35
CF B3024
Maiden's Wish, Waltz
(MacMillen) CF B710
Mazurka in A, Op. 33, No. 2
(Kreisler) Fol 1141
Mazurka
(Francescatti) Mil
Nocturne in E flat, Op. 9, No. 2
(Ambrosio) CF B2541   simpl
(Del Maglio) Ric 125603
(Hermann) SCH   transposed to D
(Sarasate) CF B2641
(Sarasate) GS
(Wilhelmj) CF B3337   transposed to A
(Wilhelmj-Corti) Ric 127895
Nocturne, Op. 15, No. 1
(D'Ambrosio) Ric 129414
Nocturne in D flat, Op. 27, No. 2
(Wilhelmj) CF S3340
Nocturne in E flat, Op. 55, No. 2
(Heifetz) CF B2662
Nocturne in B, Op. 62, No. 1
(Kochanski) CF B1825
Nocturne in e, Op. 72
(Auer) CF B765
Nocturne in c sharp, Op. posth.
(Poltronieri) Ric 128556
Polonaise Militaire in A, Op. 40, No. 1
(Ambrosio) CF S3371
(Dounis) Mil
Polonaise, Op. 53
(Edwards) Mil
Preludio, Op. 28, No. 12
(D'Ambrosio) Ric 129415
Tarantelle
(Francescatti) Mil
Waltzes, 6
Pet 1915
Op. 34, No. 3; Op. 64, Nos. 1, 2;
Op. 69, No. 1; Op. 70, Nos. 1, 2
Waltz in a, Op. 34, No. 2
(Sarasate-Mlynarczyk) SIM
Waltz, Op. 64, No. 1, "Minute Waltz"
(Applebaum) Bel SI30
CHOVEAUX, NICHOLAS (1904-   )
Pieces, 3
Leng (Mil No. L1121)
CHRISTMAS ALBUM
Pet 2800A
24 carols, folk songs and chorales arr
for vln and pno or vln, vcl and pno
CHRISTMAS CAROLS, 25
(Clarke) BMC
Although You Are So Tiny
Away in a manger

---

[21] All compositions listed were written originally for piano
solo, except the song, "Maiden's Wish".

CHRISTMAS CAROLS, 25 (cont.)
  (Clarke) BMC (cont.)
    Bring a Torch, Jeanette, Isabella
    Coventry Carol
    First Nowell
    Gloria In Excelsis Deo
    God Rest You Merry, Gentlemen
    Good King Wenceslas
    Hark! the Herald Angels Sing
    Here in a Stable
    It Came Upon the Midnight Clear
    Joseph, Dearest Joseph
    Joy to the world
    Lay Down your Staffs, O Shepherds
    Let Our Gladness Know No End
    Lo, How a Rose E'er Blooming
    March of the Kings
    O Come, All Ye Faithful
    O Little Town of Bethlehem
    O Sanctissima
    Seven Joys of Mary
    Silent Night
    Sleep Little Dove
    Song of the Bagpipers
    We Three Kings of Orient Are
CHRISTMAS CAROLS
  (Herfurth) BMC
    Angels, From the Realms of Glory
    Angels, We Have Heard On High
    Away in a Manger
    Cantique de Noel
    Deck the Halls
    First Nowell
    God Rest You Merry, Gentlemen
    Good King Wenceslas
    Hark! the Herald Angels Sing
    I Heard the Bells on Christmas Day
    I Saw Three Ships
    It Came Upon the Midnight Clear
    Jingle Bells
    Joy To the World
    O Come All Ye Faithful
    O Little Town of Bethlehem
    O Sanctissima
    Silent Night, Holy Night
    We Three Kings of Orient Are
    What Child Is This
CHRISTMAS CAROLS
  (Martin) Aug
CHRISTMAS FAVORITES
  (Beeler) GS
    Angels we have heard on high
    Away in a Manger
    Deck the halls
    Fairest Lord Jesus
    First Nowell
    God rest you merry, gentlemen
    Good King Wenceslaus
    Hark the herald angels sing
    I heard the bells on Christmas day
    I saw three ships
    It came upon the midnight clear
    Jingle bells
    Joy to the world
    Lullaby
    O come all ye faithful
    O little town of Bethlehem
    Silent night
    We three kings of orient are
CHRISTMAS FESTIVAL
  (DeLamater) Ru vcl ad lib
CHRISTMAS JOYS
  (Breck) CF 03171
    Angels from the realms of glory
    Away in a manger

    Boar's head carol
    Bring a torch
    Cherry tree carol
    Christians, awake
    Christmas song
    Coventry carol
    Deck the halls
    First Nowell
    Glory to God in the highest
    God rest you merry, gentlemen
    Good Christian men, rejoice
    Good King Wenceslas
    Hallelujah
    Hark! the herald angels sing
    Holly and the ivy
    I saw three ships
    It came upon a midnight clear
    Jingle bells
    Joy to the world
    Lo, how a rose e'er blooming
    March of three kings
    O come all ye faithful
    O little town of Bethlehem
    O Sanctissima
    Shepherds, shake off your drowsy sleep
    Silent Night
    Sleep, holy Babe
    Sleep of the child Jesus
    Wassail song
    We three kings of Orient are
    What child is this
    While shepherds watched
CHRISTMAS TIME
  (Whistler) Ru
CHULAKI, M.
  Song
  MZK
CIAKOVSKI, see Tchaikovsky
CILÈA, FRANCESCO (1866-1950)
  Canto, dal Vocalizzo da concerto No. 2
    in re min.
  Ric 122635
  Lamento di Federico, from L'Arlesiana
    (Farinelli) SON
  Suite in mi, orig for vln and orch
  Ric 123871
CIMA, GIOVANNI PAOLO (c.1570- ?)
  Sonatas, 3
    (Grebe) Sik 472
      1. Sonata in g for vln and basso
        continuo
      2. Sonata in d for ob or vln and basso
        continuo
      3. Sonata in a for ob or vln and basso
        continuo
CIRY, MICHEL
  Ballade
  Dur
CLAFLIN, AVERY (1898-)
  Sonata
  CFE
CLARKE, HENRY L. (1907-)
  Rondo
  CFE
(CLARKE, IRMA)
  Christmas Carols, 25
  BM for contents see title
CLARKE, S.H.
  Canzonetta
  STB
CLASSIC PIECES
  (Hermann) Pet 1413A,b,C,D 4V
    Vol 1: 11 pieces by Bach, Beethoven
      Field, Gluck, Handel, Hummel,
      Mozart, Tartini

CLASSIC PIECES (cont.)
  (Hermann) Pet 1413A,b,C,D 4V (cont.)
    Vol 2: 12 pieces by C.P.E. Bach,
      Beethoven, Campagnoli, Field,
      Hummel, Mozart, Schubert, Weber
    Vol 3: 12 pieces by Beethoven
    Vol 4: 9 pieces by Bach, Corelli,
      Handel, Hasse, Leclair, Lotti,
      Nardini, Tartini
CLASSIC PIECES. NEW SERIES
  (Klengel) Pet 3855
    10 pieces by Aubert, J.S. Bach, Handel,
      Leclair, Manfredi, Méhul, Pugnani,
      Tartini
CLASSICAL ALBUM
  (Cathcart) BH
    Gounod: Serenade
    Handel: Largo
    Mendelssohn; Spring Song
    Schubert: Ave Maria
    Schumann: Slumber Song
    Tchaikovsky: Chanson Triste
CLASSICAL ALBUM OF EARLY GRADE
    PIECES BY FAMOUS COMPOSERS
  (Herfurth) BMC
    Bach: March in D
    Bach: Polonaise in C
    Beethoven: Schottische in G
    Beethoven: Two Moods in B flat and g
    Händel: Minuet in d
    Händel: Minuet in F
    Haydn: Allegro in C
    Mozart: Allegro in B flat
    Mozart: Andantino in G
    Mozart: Minuet in F
    Mozart: Minuet in G
    Schubert: Impromptu in G
    Schubert: Landler in G
CLASSICAL AND MODERN
  Artia
CLASSICAL AND MODERN
  (Mlynarczyk) BRH
CLASSICAL AND ROMANTIC PIECES
  (Forbes) Oxf 23.811-14 4V
    Vol 1
      Bach: Minuet, from Flute Sonata
        No. 4 in C
      Brahms: March in B flat
      Chopin: Choral, from Op. 37, No. 1
      Gluck: Little Dance, in G
      Handel: Gavotte in F
      Mattheson: Sarabande in d
      Mozart: Folk Tune
      Mozart: Minuet in G
      Purcell: Ayre, in d
      Purcell: Rigaudon, in C
      Schubert: Berceuse, from 3 pieces,
        1828
      Schumann: Humming Song,
        Op. 68, No. 3
      Schumann: Little Piece, Op. 68, No. 5
      Steibelt: Russian Dance
      Tchaikovsky: Funeral March,
        Op. 39, No. 7
      Weber: Theme, in C
    Vol 2
      Bach: March in D, from Anna
        Magdalena Büchlein
      Bach: Minuet in A, from Anna
        Magdalena Büchlein
      Beethoven: Adagio and Allegro,
        from Serenade, Op. 8
      Brahms: 2 Dances, from Nursery
        Rhymes

Chopin: Prelude in E flat,
  Op. 28, No. 7
Gluck: Gavotte, from Orpheo
Grieg: Norwegian Folk Tune,
  Op. 66, No. 14
Handel: Musette in G, from
  Terpsichore
Haydn: Allegretto in F, from "Clock"
  Symphony
Morley: Ayre, "It was a lover and
  his lass"
Mozart: Polonaise, from Duets for
  2 violins
Purcell: Irish Tune, Lilliburlero
Purcell: Scottish Tune, from
  Musick's Handmaid
Schumann: Album Leaf, Op. 99, No. 6
Schumann: Choral, Op. 68, No. 4
Vol 3
  Bach: Bourree, from French Suite
    No. 6
  Couperin: La Lutine, from the
    harpsichord pieces
  Dvorak: Slavonic Dance, from
    Op. 46, No. 7
  Mendelssohn: Christmas Piece,
    Op. 72, No. 2
  Mozart: Minuet, from Viennese
    Sonatas
  Schubert: Adagio, from Arpeggione
    Sonata
  Schumann: Piece in the style of a folk
    tune, Op. 102, No. 2
  Shield: Theme and Variations, from
    Trio No. 1 in E flat
  Tchaikovsky: Waltz, Op. 39
  Weber: Romance, from Op. 13, No. 1
Vol 4
  Beethoven: Minuet, from Sonatina
    in G and Septet, Op. 20
  Brahms: Hungarian Dance, Bk. 1,
    No. 5
  Corelli: Prelude and Allegro, from
    Sonata in A
  Haydn: Serenata, from String
    Quartet, Op. 3, No. 1
  Rachmaninoff: Melody. Vocalise,
    Op. 34, No. 14
  Rimsky-Korsakov: Melody and
    Dance from Scheherazade
  Schubert: Moment Musical,
    Op. 94, No. 3
CLASSICAL PIECES, 12
  (Moffat) Aug 7526a,b 2V
CLASSICAL PIECES
  (Moffat) SCH 2V
    12 Pieces by Bach, Handel, Veracini,
      Corelli, Boyce and others
CLASSICAL VIOLIN
  (Palaschko) SCH
CLASSICI DEL VIOLINO
  (Bonelli) ZA 2V
    Vol 1
      Allegretto grazioso
      Andante
      Borghi: Adagio
      Campagnoli: Andante and Presto
      Giardini: Rondo
      Largo and Allegro assai
      Nardini: Adagio
      Pugnani: Adagio
      Somis: Allegretto
      Tartini: Andante affettuoso

CLASSICI DEL VIOLINO (cont.)
  (Bonelli) ZA   2V (cont.)
    Vol 2
      Adagio
      Borghi: Rondo
      Giardini: Siciliano
      Largo, Andante, Allegro assai
      Locatelli: Adagio
      Lolli: Adagio affettuoso
      Porpora: Allegretto grazioso
      Tartini: Andante con variazioni
      Veracini: Largo and Rondo
      Viotti: Allegro
CLASSICS, 12, INTRODUCING THE THIRD
    POSITION
  (Bostelmann) GS
    Chopin: The maiden's wish
    Dvořák: Songs my mother taught me
    Martini: Andantino
    Mozart: Aria from Don Juan
    Mozart: Aria from The Magic Flute
    Musette
    Schubert: The heather rose
    Schubert: I heard a rushing brooklet
    Schubert: Singing on the water
    Schumann: Cradle Song
    Spohr: Festpolonaise
    Tchaikovsky: March of the tin soldiers
CLEMENTI, MUZIO (1752-1832)
  Sonatinas, 6, Op. 36
    (Reger) SCH   vln part only, to be used
      with pno sonatinas
CLÉRAMBAULT, LOUIS NICOLAS (1676-1749)
  Largo in c
    (Dandelot) ESC
  Prelude and Allegro in G
    (Dandelot) ESC
CLEVE, HALFDAN (1879-   )
  Sonata in e, Op. 21
    Musikk-Huset
CLIMAX ALBUM NO. 14
  (Sachse) Paxton (Mil No. P516)
    2nd and 3rd vlns, vcl ad lib
CLUTSAM, [GEORGE H. (1866-1951)]
  April Night
    Chap-L
COATES, ERIC (1886-   )
  First Meeting
    Chap-L
  Mirage
    Chap-L
  Under The Stars
    Chap-L
COBURN
  Solo Album
    Bel
(COCKBURN, NOWELL)
  Liederland
    BH   for contents see title
COCKSHOTT, GERALD WILFRED (1915-   )
  Past Three O'Clock
    Oxf 23.300
COERNE, LOUIS ADOLPHE (1870-1922)
  Concertino in D, Op. 63
    Bosw (Bel No. 19)
COLE, ULRIC (1905-   )
  Sonata
    SPAM
COLERIDGE-TAYLOR, SAMUEL (1875-1912)
  African Dances, 4, Op. 58
    Aug 11342
  Ballade in c, Op. 73, orig for vln and orch
    Aug 11343
  Gipsy Dance, Op. 20, No. 3
    Aug

  Romance, Op. 59, orig for vln and orch
    Aug 11341
  Three-fours, Op. 71. Valse suite
    Aug
COLLET, HENRI (1885-1951)
  Pena, La
    (Aghazarian) Sal
  Poème
    Mathot
  Primavera
    Mathot
  Rhapsodie Castillane, orig for vla and orch
    Senart
  Sonate Castillane
    Mathot
COLLETT
  Sonata in A
    (Moffat) Nov
COLLINS, ANTHONY (1893-   )
  Concerto, Op. 48
    Francis Day & Hunter
  Raisins and Almonds
    (Kaufman) CF B3256
COLMAN, TAPIA
  Suite Espanola
    EMM
COLOMBI, GIUSEPPE
  Ciaccona
    (Roncaglia) Ric 128571   realized by
      E. Orlandi
COMPAGNONI, LORNA
  Legend
    Chap-L
CONCERT PIECES, 6
  (Kreitner) MZK
CONTÉ, JEAN
  Marche Militaire in D
    CF B3221
  Romance sans paroles
    CF B3214
  Valse in C
    CF B3092
CONTET & DURAND
  Habanera
    (Edwards) Mil
CONUS, JULES (1869-1942)
  Concerto in e
    (Auer) CF 03478
    (Zimbalist) GS L1635
COOKE, ARNOLD (1906-   )
  Sonata No. 2 in A
    Nov
COOKE, GREVILLE
  High Marley Rest
    JWL (Mil No. W1205)
COOLEY, C.
  Song and Dance
    Senart
COPLAND, AARON (1900-   )
  Hoe Down, from Rodeo
    BH   arr for vln and pno by composer
  Nocturne
    SCH
  Sonata
    BH
  Ukelele Serenade
    SCH
  Waltz and Celebration, from Billy the Kid
    BH   arr for vln and pno by composer
COPPOLA, P.
  Poema Appassionata
    Senart
CORBRIDGE, JAMES B.
  Moto Perpetuo
    VL 126

CORDERO, ROQUE (1917-   )
Short Pieces, 2
Peer
Sonatina
Peer
CORELLI, ARCANGELO (1653-1713)
Adagio in F
(Busch) BRH
Adagio
(Corti) Carisch
Adagio and Allegro
MZK
Chaconne upon the sarabande theme from
Violin Sonata, Op. 5, No. 7, see
Geminiani
Folia, Follia, Folies d'Espagne, see
Sonata in d, Op. 5, No. 12
Introduzione e Giga da Camera
(Moffat) CF B740
Sarabande and Allegretto
(Kreisler) Fol 1172
Sonatas, 12, Op. 5
(Abbado) Ric ER2660-1[22]   2V
(Jensen) SCH   2V
(Paumgartner-Kehr) SCH   2V   vcl ad lib
(Polo) Ric ER1749-50   2V
Aug 7354a,b   2V
Nov   4V
Sonatas, Op. 5, Nos. 1-6
(Jensen) Int   2V
Sonatas, 6, from Op. 5
(Klengel) Pet 3836A,b   2V
Vol 1: Nos. 1, 4, 8
Vol 2: Nos. 3, 5, 9
Sonatas, 3, Op. 5, Nos. 8, 9, 11
(Jensen) Aug 7406
(Jensen) Int
Sonata in A, Op. 5, No. 6
(Jensen) Aug 11356
(Spalding) CF 01939
Sonata in A
MZK
Sonata in C
(Ries-Franko) GS L9
Sonata in D
(Dessoff-Franko) GS L8   with cadenza
by J. Hellmesberger
Sonata in D
ZA 3625
Sonata in d, Op. 5, No. 12, "La Follia"
(Chaumont) Senart 5372
(David-Auer) CF 03719
(David-Petri) BRH "Folies d'Espagne"
(Kreisler) Fol 1127
(Léonard) CF B3288   with cadenza
(Léonard-Anzoletti) Ric ER559
(Léonard-Jacobsen) Pet 2846A
(Léonard-Marteau) SCH   2nd vln ad lib
(Léonard-Thibaud) CF B2134
(Lichtenberg) GS L525   pno accomp and
cadenza by H. Léonard
(Meyer) SCH
(Salmon) Ric R720
(Spalding) CF B2705
Aug 7419
Carisch
MZK
Sonata in d
(Salmon) Ric R353
Sonata in d
MZK

[22] "revisione sulla prima edizione, 1700, con la realizzazione
del basso desunta dai Concerti Grossi di Geminiani. Londra,
1726".

Sonata in e, Op. 5, No. 8
(Moffat) SIM
Aug 11358
Sonata in e
MZK
Sonata in F
(Salmon) Ric R722
Sonata in F
HL
Sonata in g, Op. 5, No. 5
Aug 11355
Sonata in g
(Salmon) Ric R721
Variations on a theme of, see Tartini
CORRETTE
Suite in do
(Ruf) Ric SY641
CORTES, RAMIRO (1933-   )
Elegy
EV
CORTESE, LUIGI (1899-   )
Canto Notturno, Op. 17 bis, orig for vln
and orch
SZ
Sonatina, Op. 9
SZ
COSTA, MICHAEL (1806-1884)
Italian March
VL 85   2nd vln ad lib
COULTHARD, JEAN
Duo Sonata
CL
COUNTRY GARDENS
(Ambrosio) CF B2586
see also Ghys: Amaryllis
COUPERIN, FRANCOIS (1668-1733)
Chérubins, Les
(Salmon) Ric R84
Concert No. 5
Dur
Concert No. 6
Dur
Concert No. 7
Dur
Concert No. 9
Dur
COUPERIN
Grâces Naturelles, Les
(Klengel) Pet 4161
COWELL, HENRY DIXON (1897-   )
Homage to Iran
Pet 6114
Set of 2
CFE   score only
Sonata
AMP
Suite
AMP
COWLES
Forgotten
Pr
CRAS, JEAN (1879-1932)
Air varié
Senart
Églogue
Senart
Évocation
Senart
Habanera
Senart
Interlude, from Polyphème
Senart
Suite en Duo
Senart

CRAWFORD, ROBERT (1899-   )
  U.S. Air Force
    (Kent) CF W1851
CRAXTON, HAROLD (1885-   )
  Alman
    Oxf 20.109
CRESTON, PAUL (1906-   )
  Suite, Op. 18
    GS
CREVECOEUR
  Vignettes romantiques, 3
    Senart
CRIPPS, HENRY
  Melody
    Chap-L
  Romanesque
    Chap-L
CRIST, BAINBRIDGE (1883-   )
  Abhisárika
    CF B1291
  Evening Song
    CF B2063
  Intermezzo, from "Pragiwa's Marriage"
    CF B1381
CROCAMO, A.N.
  Omar
    VL 102
CROSFIELD, A.H.
  Air
    STB
  Ballet No. 1, from Suite
    STB
  Chanson sans paroles
    STB
  Minuetto e Trio
    STB
  Recitative and Aria
    STB
  Rigaudon
    STB
CROUCH, F.W.N.
  Kathleen Mavourneen. Fantasy, see Herman
CROWTHER, JOHN
  Gweedore Brae
    CF B2736
CRUZ, IVO (1901-   )
  Sonata
    Mercury
CSENKI, IMRE
  Gipsy Wedding
    Kul
(CSOKA)
  Rumanian Violin Soli, 3
    DOB
CUI, CESAR (1835-1918)
  Bagpipes, see Mussorgsky: Tears
  Berceuse, Op. 20, No. 8, orig for pno
    (Carse) Aug
  Lettre d'amour, from Kaleidoscope,
    Op. 50, No. 21
    (Elman) CF B2028
  Lullaby; Oriental Melody; Perpetual Motion
    MZK
  Orientale, from Kaleidoscope, Op. 50, No. 9
    (Saenger) CF S3354
  Pieces, 7, Op. 74
    MZK
  Scherzetto, see Tchaikovsky: Song without
    words
CUPIS
  Galant coureur, Le
    (Moffat) JWL (Mil No. W1236)
CURCI, A.
  Ciarda
    Curci

Concertino in La min.
  Curci
Concerto romantico
  Curci
Filatrici, Le
  Curci
Mattinata andalusa
  Curci
Mazurca brillante, Op. 26
  Curci
Pastorale
  Curci
Piccola Suite
  Curci
Polacca
  Curci
Ricreazioni Violinistiche
  Curci   3V
Sognando un Valzer
  Curci
Tarantella
  Curci
CURTIS, ERNESTO DE
  Come back to Sorrento
    (Ambrosio) CF B2585
    VL 153   2nd vln ad lib
CZECH CLASSICAL MASTERS
  Artia
    Benda, F: Presto
    Benda, Jan: Grave
    Benda, Jiri: Andante grazioso
    Dusik, J: Allegro
    Myslivecek: Minuette
    Vanhal, J: Rondo
    Vorisek: Andante sostenuto
CZERWONKY, RICHARD (1886-1949)
  Konzert
    CF 02128
CZIBULKA, [ALPHONS (1842-1894)]
  Stephanie-Gavotte, Op. 312
    (Palaschko) SCH
DACRE, HENRY
  Bicycle Built for Two
    (Eckstein) CF M307
D'AGREVES, see Agreves, d'
D'ALBERT, see Albert, d'
DALE, BENJAMIN
  Ballade, Op. 15
    JWL (Mil No. W1245)
  Holiday Tune
    ABRS (Mil No. A246)
DALE, B.J.
  Prunella
    Aug
DALL'ABACO, see Abaco
DALLAM, HELEN
  Valsette
    CF B2021
DALLAPICCOLA, LUIGI (1904-   )
  Studies, 2
    SZ
  Tartiniana, Divertimento on themes of
    Tartini, orig for vln and orch
    SZ
  Tartiniana seconda
    SZ
DAMASE, [JEAN-MICHEL (1928-   )]
  Concerto
    HL
  Sarabande
    Sal
D'AMBROSIO, see Ambrosio, d'
DAMME, P. VAN
  Melody
    ESC

DANBÉ, JULES (1840-1905)
  Cantabile et Allegro, Op. 30, No. 1; with
    Menuet, Op. 30, No. 2
    CF B3216
  Cantabile et Bolero, Op. 22, No. 6
    (Saenger) CF B3000
  Menuet, Op. 30, No. 2, see Cantabile et
    Allegro
  Nocturne, Op. 20, No. 6, see Romance
  Oberon. Fantaisie, Op. 21, No. 5
    (Saenger) CF B3060
  Petite Gavotte, Op. 20, No. 3; with Petite
    Valse lente, Op. 20, No. 4
    (Saenger) CF B3152
  Romance, Op. 20, No. 5; with Nocturne,
    Op. 20, No. 6
    (Saenger) CF B3235
  Romance et Tyrolienne, Op. 21, No. 1
    (Saenger) CF B3075
DANCES, VOL 1: MOZART AND BEETHOVEN
  (Gehrkens) BMC includes several for
    2, 3, 4 vln
    Beethoven: Musical Joke; Canary Bird;
      Folk Dance; Quadrille; Contre-Dance;
      German Dance
    Mozart: Trio from Menuet; 2 German
      Dances
DANCES BY OLD MASTERS, 12
  (Burmester) BMC
    Clementi: Waltz
    Dussek: Dance In Olden Style
    Field: Waltz
    Händel: Gavotte
    Haydn: Minuet
    Hummel: Waltz
    Martini: Minuet
    Schubert: Round Dance
    Weber: Country Dance
    Weber: Waltz No. 1
DANCLA, CHARLES (1817-1907)
  Airs Variés, 6, Op. 89. Series I
    Variations on themes by Pacini,
    Rossini, Bellini, Donizetti, Weigl,
    Mercandante
    (Svecenski) GS L785
    CF L125
    SCH "Little Melodies with Variations"
  Airs Variés, 6, Op. 118. Series II
    Variations on 5 themes by Bellini
    Variations on Carnevale di Venezia
    (Svecenski) GS L1431
    CF L126
  Air Varié on a theme by Weigl, Op. 89, No. 5
    (Svecenski) GS
    CF B3276
    VL 91
  Air Varié on a theme by Mercandante,
    Op. 89, No. 6
    CF B3340
  Air Varié, Op. 118, No. 1. Il Montecchi
    ed i Capuletti
    CF B3032
  Air with variations, Op. 123, No. 7
    CF B2637
  Allegretto in D, Op. 167, No. 5
    CF B3174
  Bluettes, Op. 48
    Lit (Pet No. L2696)
  Concert Solos, 3, Op. 77
    (Svecenski) GS L1400
    CF L452
    Pet 2819
  Concert Solo No. 4, Op. 93
    Billaudot

Concert Solo No. 5, Op. 94
  Billaudot
Concert Solo No. 6, Op. 95
  Billaudot
Concert Solo No. 7, Op. 224
  Billaudot
Dernière Pensée de Weber, from Easy
  Fantasias, Op. 86
  CF B3012
Donna del Lago, from Easy Fantasias, Op. 86
  CF B3169
Easy Fantasias, 12, on celebrated melodies,
  Op. 86
  (Saenger) CF 03506
Easy Little Fantasies, 6, Op. 126
  CF 03696
Easy Melodies, 24, Op. 115
  CF L578
Easy School of Melody, Op. 123
  SCH 3V
Easy School of Melody, Op. 123.
  Suite No. 1
  (Saenger) CF B3273 "Easy Pieces,
    Op. 123"
Freischütz, Der, from Easy Fantasias,
  Op. 86
  CF B3022
Petites Bluettes, 3, Op. 189
  Lit (Pet No. L2002)
Résignation, Op. 59
  (Saenger) CF B3072
Romance, Op. 187
  CF S3391
Sérénade, Op. 170
  Billaudot
DANCLA, LÉOPOLD (1823-1895)
  Petite Valse, Op. 48, No. 4
    CF B2987
DANDRIEU, JEAN FRANCOIS (1682-1738)
  Sonate en sol majeur
    HL
  see also Easy Sonatas of Old-French
    Masters
DANERI, TULLIO
  Concertino
    Ric 129030
DANKEVICH, K.
  Song and Dance
    MZK
DANKS, HART (1834-1903)
  Silver threads among the gold
    (Halle) Bel 692
    VL 121
DARE, MARIE
  Lac, Le
    Ches
D'ARGOEUVES, see Argoeuves, d'
DARK EYES
  (Ambrosio) CF B2587   simpl
  (Ludlow) CF B2119
DARNTON, CHRISTIAN (1905-   )
  Epic Suite
    Leng (Mil No. L1123)
DAUVERGNE, see Auvergne, d'
DAVAINE, P.
  Libellules, Les
    Gaudet
DAVICO, [VINCENZO (1889-   )]
  Sonatina Rustica
    RL
DAVID, FERDINAND (1810-1873)
  Andante and scherzo capriccioso, Op. 16
    (Schradieck) GS L237

DAVID, FERDINAND (cont.)
Etude, Op. 30, No. 16
CF B3067
Introduction and Variations on "Je suis le
petit tambour", Op. 5
Pet 3074
(DAVID, FERDINAND)
High School of Violin Playing
Pet 3076A,b 2V for contents see title
DAVID, JOHANN NEPOMUK (1895-   )
Concerto, Op. 45
BRH
Concerto No. 2, Op. 50
BRH
DAVID, JOSÉ (1913-   )
Sonate
Dur
DAVID, THOMAS CHRISTIAN (1925-   )
Konzert
DOB
DAVIDOV, KARL (1838-1889)
At the Fountain, Op. 20, No. 2, orig for
vcl and pno
CF B2989
DE BERIOT, see Beriot
DE BOURGUIGNON, see Bourguignon
DEBUSMAN, EMIL
Sonata No. 1
AME
DEBUSSY, CLAUDE (1862-1918)
Après-Midi d'un Faune, L', orig for orch
(Heifetz) CF B2241
Arabesque No. 1, orig for pno
(Choisnel) Dur
Arabesque No. 2, orig for pno
(Choisnel) Dur
Beau Soir, orig for voice and pno
(Bachmann) Jobert
(Heifetz) CF B2331
Chevelure, La, orig for voice and pno
(Heifetz) CF B2799
Clair de lune, from Suite Bergamasque,
orig for pno
(Roelens) Jobert
Danses. Danse Sacrée and Danse Profane,
orig for harp and strings
(Roques) Dur
En bateau, from Petite Suite, orig for
pno duet
(Choisnel) Dur
Fille aux cheveux de lin, from Douze
Préludes, orig for pno
(Hartmann) Dur
Girl with the flaxen hair, see Fille
aux cheveux de lin
Golliwogg's cake-walk, from Children's
Corner, orig for pno
(Choisnel) Dur
(Heifetz) CF B2610
Il pleure dans mon coeur, from Ariettes
Oubliées, orig for voice and pno
(Hartmann) Jobert
Little Shepherd, see Petit berger
Menuet, from Petite Suite, orig for pno duet
(Dushkin) Dur
Minstrels, from Douze Préludes
Dur transcription by composer
Nocturne in D flat, orig for pno
ESC
Petit berger, Le, from Children's Corner,
orig for pno
(Durand) Dur
Plus que lent, La, orig for pno
(Roques) Dur

Prélude, cortège et air de danse, from
L'Enfant Prodigue
(Roques) Dur
Reverie, orig for pno
(Bachmann) Jobert
(Engel) BMC
VL 157
Sonata in g
Dur
DEEP RIVER
(Ambrosio) CF B2525 simpl
(Heifetz) CF B2479
DE FESCH, see Fesch
DEFOSSE, H.
Berceuse
RL
DEFOSSEZ, RENÉ (1905-   )
Impromptu
CBDM
DEGEN, HELMUT (1911-   )
Little Concerto
SCH
DEITZ, ERNEST
World Is Waiting for the Sunrise
Chap-L
DELABRE, L.G.
Colombinella
Sal
DELACHI
Sonata
Carisch
DELAFORET, J.
Douce Mélodie
Gaudet
(DELAMATER, E.)
Christmas Festival
Ru vcl ad lib
DELANNOY, MARCEL (1898-   )
Danse des Maraîchers
ESC
Danse des Négrillons from "La Pantoufle
de Vair"
ESC
Serenade
ESC
DEL CROEBELIS, D.
New Dutch Playhouse
Wagenaar
DELDEN, LEX VAN (1919-   )
Pieces, 2, Op. 17
DN (Pet No. D238)
DELIBES, LEO (1836-1891)
Ballet Music, from Coppélia
(Tolhurst) Paxton (Mil No. P515)
Barcarolle and Pizzicati, from Sylvia
(Marsick) CF B2521
Pas des fleurs, from Naila
(Ambrosio) CF B2547 simpl.
Valse in A, from Coppélia
(Saenger) CF B3175
Valse lente, from Coppélia
(Sieg-Frödner) SCH
DELIUS, FREDERICK (1862-1934)
Concerto
Aug pno part arr by Heseltine
Serenade, from Hassan
(Tertis) BH
Sonata No. 1
(Forsyth) BH
Sonata No. 2
BH
Sonata No. 3
BH

DELLO JOIO, C.
  Canzonetta Appassionata
    CF B532
DELLO JOIO, NORMAN (1913-   )
  Fantasia on a Gregorian Theme
    CF B2976
  Variations and Capriccio
    CF B3257
DELMAR, DEZSO
  Sonata
    CP
DELMAS, [MARC (1885-1931)]
  Sonate
    HL
DELVAUX, [ALBERT (1913-   )]
  Sonata
    CBDM
  Sonatina
    CBDM
DELVINCOURT, [CLAUDE (1888-1954)]
  Sonate
    Senart
DEMARQUEZ, SUZANNE (1899-   )
  Petite Suite
    Sal
DE MAURIZI
  Dan Romania
    Liber-S
  Doina Voda
    Liber-S
DE MEIS
  Parnassos. Danza greca
    Ric 123203
DENIS
  Sonate en la mineur
    HL
DEPLAN
  Entrada; with Gavotte by Lully and Minuet
      by Porpora
    MZK
DÉRÉ, JEAN (1886-   )
  Sonate No. 1
    Senart
  Sonate No. 2
    Senart
  Sonatine No. 1
    Leduc
  Sonatine No. 2
    Leduc
  Sonatine No. 3
    Leduc
DERENDORF, H.
  Poeme
    Metr
DE ROYE, E.
  Canzonetta
    Metr
DESPLANES, J.A.P.
  Intrada
    (Nachèz) SIM
DESTOUCHES, ANDRÉ (1672-1749)
  Four Pipers
    (Applebaum) Bel SI17
DEUTSCH, EMERY & ALTMAN, ARTHUR
  Play Fiddle Play
    (Deutsch) MK
DÉVREESE, GODEFROID (1893-   )
  Capriccio
    CBDM
  Sonate
    Senart
DE WANDEL
  Foolish Strings
    (Paige) Metr

DIAMOND, DAVID (1915-   )
  Chaconne
    SMP
  Perpetual Motion
    EV
  Sonata
    GS
DI BIASE, EDOARDO
  Reverie
    CF B2975
DI CAPUA, EDUARDO (1864-1917)
  Maria, Mari; with La Spagnola by Chiara
      (Saenger) CF B3125
  O Sole Mio
    (Ambrosio) CF B2575   simpl
    VL 40   2nd vln ad lib
DIETRICH
  F-A-E Sonata, see Brahms-Dietrich-
      Schumann
DILLON, [HENRI (1912-   )]
  Sonata
    Haml
D'INDY, see Indy, d'
DINICU
  Hora Staccato
    (Heifetz) CF B2224
    Kul
    MZK
DITTERSDORF, KARL DITTERS VON
      (1739-1799)
  Concerto in C
    (Lebermann) SCH
  Concerto in C
    Noet (Pet No. N3299)   with cadenzas
  Concerto in G
    Hof
  Sonata in B flat
    Hof
  Sonata in G
    Hof
DOBROWEN, ISSAY (1893-1953)
  Ballade, Op. 17
    UE 8602
  Märchen, Op. 16
    UE 7220
  Sonata in f sharp, Op. 15
    UE 7219
(DOFLEIN)
  Leichte Hausmusik
    SCH
      6 easy little suites from an old collec-
      tion, ca. 1740
DOHNÁNYI, ERNST (1877-1960)
  Concerto, Op. 27
    Kul
  Concerto No. 2, Op. 43
    AMP
  Ruralia Hungarica, Op. 32c
    CF B2161
    Kul
  Sonata, Op. 21
    SIM
DOIRE, R.
  Sonate
    Senart
D'OLLONE, see Ollone
DOMINCHEN, K.
  Poem
    MZK
DONATI, PINO (1907-   )
  Intermezzo e romanza
    Ric 125333
DONATO, ANTHONY (1909-   )
  Precipitations
    Mercury

DONATONI, [FRANCO (1927-   )]
  Divertimento, orig for vln and orch
    SCH
DONIZETTI, GAETANO (1797-1848)
  Favorita, La. Fantasia, see Singelée
  Lucia di Lammermoor. Transcription
    (Ambrosio) CF B3303
  Romance. Fantasy on themes from Daugh-
    ter of the Regiment, see Castelnuovo-
    Tedesco
  Sextet, from Lucia di Lammermoor
    (Saenger) CF C44
    VL 6   2nd vln ad lib
  Valse on themes from Daughter of the
    Regiment, see Castelnuovo-Tedesco
  Variations on a theme of, see Dancla,
    Charles: Air Varié, Op. 89, No. 4
DONNER, MAX
  Sonate, Op. 40
    CF P165
DONT, JAKOB (1815-1888)
  Agité
    (Auer) CF B1248
  Concert Etude, Op. 35, No. 16
    (Schwartzenstein) Paragon
  Étincelles
    (Auer) CF B1247
DORATI, ANTAL (1906-   )
  Hungarian Peasant Tunes, 2
    Mil
DORET, [GUSTAVE (1866-1943)]
  Air
    RL
DORSON, C.
  Chanson du vent
    Deiss
  Scherzo-Tarentelle
    Deiss
DOWLAND
  Fantasia on a theme of, see Stevens
DRDLA, FRANZ (1868-1944)
  Ariel
    Sal
  Chanson Vénitienne
    Sal
  Concertino in a, Op. 225
    Bosw (Bel No. 16)
  Humming Bird, Op. 125
    BMC
  Illusion, Op. 48
    UE 6459
  Meditation
    Bosw
  Papillons
    Sal
  Romance Bergère
    Sal
  Serenade No. 1 in A
    (Ambrosio) CF B2553   simpl and trans-
      posed into F
    CF S3426
    VL 56
  Slumber Song
    Bosw
  Souvenir
    (Ambrosio) CF B2552   simpl
    (Halle) Bel 654
    (Mittell) GS
    CF S3458
    VL 55
  Tarentelle
    Sal
DRIESSLER, JOHANNES (1921-   )
  Fantasie, Op. 24, No. 1
    Baer 2695

  Kleine Stücke, 3
    Baer 2536
DRIGO, RICHARD (1846-1930)
  Heart of Harlequin. Serenade
    (Ambrosio) CF B1865   simpl
    (Auer) CF B1850
  Serenade, from ballet, Les Millions
    d'Arlequin
    (Ambrosio) CF B2568   simpl
    (Auer) CF B3259
    (Auer) ZM (Pet No. ZM209)
    (Auer-Zimbalist) GS
    (Halle) Bel 656
    (Hofmann-Saenger) CF S3797
  Serenade
    Kjos S-5020
  Valse Bluette
    (Ambrosio) CF B2571
    (Auer) GS
    (Heifetz) CF B2439
    (Saenger) CF B1767
DRINK TO ME ONLY WITH THINE EYES
    (Harvey) VL 60   2nd vln ad lib
DRIVER, F. PERCIVAL
  Fiddle Tune
    ABRS (Mil No. A254)
DUBAS, R.
  Czardas
    Metr
DUBENSKI, LEONE (1915-   )
  Concerto in ré min.
    Ric 127930
DUBOIS, P.M.
  Capriccio, orig for vln and orch
    Leduc
  Concerto
    Leduc
DUCK, LEONARD
  Eclogue
    Aug
DUKELSKY, VLADIMIR (1903-   )
  Capriccio Mexicano
    Leeds
  Concerto
    CF 03363
DUNHILL, THOMAS F. (1877-1946)
  Meadow-Fairies, Op. 72, No. 4[23]
    GT
  Pastoral, Op. 72, No. 1,[23] from 3 Pieces
    GT
  Playfellows, Op. 72, No. 2,[23] from 3 Pieces
    GT
  Polacaprice, from 4 Pieces
    SCH
  Sailor Dance
    JWL (Mil No. W1260)
  Shepherdess, from 5 Lyrical Pieces
    JWL (Mil No. W1250)
DUPIN, PAUL (1865-1949)
  Sonate en la mineur
    Dur
DUPRADEAU, J.
  Barcarolle
    Mathot
  Douleur
    Mathot
DUPUIS, ALBERT (1877-   )
  Sonate
    Senart
DUPUIS, SYLVAIN (1856-1931)
  Prelude et Danse
    Bosw

---

[23] In the U.S.A. this publication can be obtained through Mills.

DUPUIS, [SYLVAIN]
Invocation
Senart
DUPUITS, JEAN-BAPTISTE
Sonate en ré majeur
HL
Sonata in ré
(Salmon) Ric R355
DURAND, AUGUSTE (1830-1909)
Chaconne in a, Op. 62
(Saenger) CF B3109
DURAND, [EMILE (1830-1903)]
Biniou, Le
RL
DURAND
Song of the Rain
Mil
DURAND, see Contet & Durand
DURANDY & FAUSTIN
Calvacade
Sal
DUSIK, see Dussek
DUSSEK, JOHANN LADISLAUS (1760-1812)
Sonatas, Op. 69, Nos. 1 and 2
Artia
DUVAL, FRANCOIS (c.1673-1728)
Sonatas, 2
(Ruf) SCH   vcl or gamba ad lib
Sonata in A
HL
Sonata in g
(Ruf) Ric SY632
DVARIONAS, B.
Concerto
MZK
Pezzo Elegiaco
MZK
DVOŘÁK, ANTONIN (1841-1904)
Bagatelle, Op. 47, No. 3, orig for 2 vlns,
vcl, and harm.
(Forbes) Hin (Pet No. H626A)
Ballad, Op. 15
(Feld) Artia
Ballad, Op. 15; with Nocturne, Op. 40
Artia
Capriccio
(Raphael) BRH
Concerto in a, Op. 53
Artia
Int
MZK
SIM
Gypsy Melody, see Songs my mother
taught me
Humoresque, Op. 101, No. 7
(Ambrosio) CF B2569   simpl
(Halle) Bel 663
(Heifetz) CF B2406
(Kreisler) SIM
(Langey) GS
(Linz) SCH
(Saenger) CF S3241
(Stoessel) BMC
(Wilhelmj) SIM
Artia
VL 5   2nd vln ad lib; simpl
Indian Lament, 2nd mvt of Sonatina,
Op. 100
(Kreisler) Fol 1120
Largo, from "New World" Symphony
(Ambrosio) CF B1938   simpl
Mazurka in e, Op. 49
Artia
Nocturne, Op. 40, see Ballad

Polonaise in E flat, orig for orch
(Leopold) Pet 4525
Romance, Op. 11, orig for vln and orch
Artia
SIM
Romantic Pieces, Op. 75
SIM
Slavonic Dances, 14, orig for pno duet
MZK
Slavonic Dance No. 1 in g, Op. 46, No. 2
(Kreisler) Fol 1175
Slavonic Dance No. 2 in e, Op. 72, No. 2;
orig No. 10
(Kreisler) Fol 1179
(Linz) SCH
Slavonic Dance No. 3 in G, Op. 72, No. 16
(Kreisler) Fol 1180
Slavonic Fantaisie in b
(Kreisler) Fol 1181
Sonata, Op. 57
Artia
SIM
Sonatina in G, Op. 100
(Kehr-Lechner) SCH
(Stoessel) BMC
Artia
CF 03214
SIM
Songs my mother taught me, Op. 55, No. 4
from 7 Gypsy Songs
(Adler) BMC
(Ambrosio) CF B2572   simpl
(Eckstein) CF M315
(Halle) Bel 701
(Kreisler) Fol 1183
(Persinger) CF B800
AMP "Gypsy Melody"
DYCK, V.
Berceuse Hébraique
Sal
Kadisch
Sal
Voix aimée, La
Gaudet
DYSON, GEORGE (1883-   )
Concerto
Nov
In Pixieland
JWL (Mil No. W1206)
Melody and Intermezzo
STB
Revery in D
ABRS (Mil No. A245)
DZEGELENEK, A.
Pieces, 2, Op. 21
MZK
DZHERBASHIAN, S.
Festival Concert Piece
MZK
EASY MARCH BOOK
(Lechner) SCH
EASY PIECES
(Fortunatov) MZK
EASY PIECES BY OLD COMPOSERS
(Fortunatov) MZK
EASY PIECES BY RUSSIAN COMPOSERS
(Mostras) MZK
EASY PIECES FOR THE VIOLIN
Amsco 12
Bach, J.S.: Minuet
Balfe: I Dreamt I Dwelt in Marble
Halls
Balfe: Then You'll Remember Me
Beethoven: Minuet in G

EASY PIECES FOR THE VIOLIN (cont.)
Amsco 12 (cont.)
Blon: Serenade
Boccherini: Menuett
Bohm: Laendler
Dancla: Novellette
David: Scherzo
Drigo: Serenade
Dvorak: Humoresque
Elgar: Salut d'Amour
Faure: Palm Branches
Flotow: Ah! So Pure, from Martha
Gillet: Loin Du Bal
Giordani: Caro Mio Ben
Godard: Berceuse, from Jocelyn
Gossec: Gavotte
Gounod: Ave Maria
Grieg: To Spring
Halevy: Call Me Thine Own
Handel: Largo
Hauser: Cradle Song
Haydn: Serenade
Jacobowski: Lullaby, from Erminie
Marie: Cinquantaine, La
Marie: Serenade Badine
Mascagni: Intermezzo, from Caval-
leria Rusticana
Mendelssohn: Consolation
Mendelssohn: Intermezzo, from Mid-
summer Night's Dream
Mendelssohn: Nocturne, from Midsum-
mer Night's Dream
Mendelssohn: Spring Song
Moszkowski: Melodie
Mozart: Menuetto
Mozart: Rondo
Neruda: Berceuse Slave
Pergolesi: Siciliana, from Nina
Pierne: Serenade
Ries: Gondoliera
Rubinstein: Melody in F
Rubinstein: Romance
Saint-Saens: Swan
Schmidt: Cavatine
Schubert: Ave Maria
Schubert: Moment Musical
Schumann: Abendlied
Schumann: Traumerei
Simonetti: Madrigale
Tartini: Larghetto
Thome: Simple Aveu
Tschaikowsky: Chanson Triste
Verdi: Celeste Aida
Wagner: Tannhauser March
EASY SONATAS OF OLD-FRENCH MASTERS
(Herrmann) SCH   vcl ad lib
Sonatas by Aubert, Dandrieu,
Senaillé
EASY VIOLIN PIECES
Consolidated 6; 2nd vln ad lib
Beethoven: Menuet in G
Blue Bells of Scotland
Boatmen's Song of the Volga
Boccherini: Minuet
Braga: Angel's Serenade
Brahms: Cradle Song
Dark Eyes
De Curtis: Come Back To Sorrento
Drink To Me Only With Thine Eyes
Dvorak: Humoresque
Dvorak: Largo, from New World Sym-
phony
Fernandez: Cielito Lindo
Foster: Beautiful Dreamer

Khatchaturian: Saber Dance, from
Gayne Ballet
Liszt: Liebestraum
Londonderry Air
Mascagni: Intermezzo, from Cavalle-
ria Rusticana
Mendelssohn: Spring Song
Molloy: Love's Old Sweet Song
Nevin: Narcissus
Offenbach: Barcarolle, from Tales of
Hoffmann
Paganini: Carnival of Venice
Ponce: Estrellita
Rachmaninoff: Theme from Concerto
No. 2
Rimsky-Korsakoff: Young Prince and the
Young Princess, from Scheherezade
Rossini: William Tell
Schubert: Serenade
Schubert: Theme from Unfinished Sym-
phony
Schumann: Happy Farmer
Serradell: Golondrina, La
Strauss: Blue Danube Waltz
Strauss: Emperor Waltz
Tschaikowsky: Andante, from Symphony
No. 5
Tschaikowsky: Theme from Concerto
No. 1
Two Guitars
Verdi: Ah, I have sighed to rest me
Verdi: Celeste Aida, from Aida
Viennese Refrain
Yradier: Paloma, La
EASY VIOLIN PIECES, 11
(Utkin) MZK
EASY VIOLIN SOLOS
Consolidated 38; 2nd vln ad lib
Arnold: Blues in G
Bach, J.S.: Chorale No. 83
Bach, J.S.: In Dulci Jubilo
Bach, J.S.: Jesu, Joy of Man's Desiring
Beautiful Brown Eyes
Bizet: Toreador Song, from Carmen
Black is the color of my true love's hair
Borodin: Melody, from Prince Igor
Brahms: Cradle Song
Brahms: Moderato con moto, from
Clarinet Sonata, Op. 120
Careless Love
Cohan: Give My Regards to Broadway
Cossack
Daniels: You Tell Me Your Dream
Dresser: On the Banks of the Wabash
Eastburn: Little Brown Jug
Greensleeves
Herbert: Gypsy Love Song
Howard & Emerson: Hello Ma Baby
I Ain't Gonna Study War No More
Lawlor: Sidewalks of New York
Mendelssohn: Nocturne
Metallo: Sharpshooters
Mr. Frog Went A-Courting
Offenbach: Scene from Bluebeard
Old Paint
On Top of Old Smoky
Prokofieff: Theme from Peter and the
Wolf
Rimsky-Korsakoff: Young Prince and
the Young Princess, from Schehe-
rezade
Root: There's Music in the Air
Schubert: Valse Noble, from Op. 77

EASY VIOLIN SOLOS (cont.)
    Consolidated 38; 2nd vln ad lib (cont.)
        Schumann: Scheherezade, from Album
          for the Young
        Smetana: Theme from Moldau
        Sousa: High School Cadets
        Sousa: Manhattan Beach
        Sousa: Rifle Regiment
        Sousa: Stars and Stripes Forever
        Spanish Guitar
        Strauss: Polka
        Strauss: Recruiting Song, from Gypsy
          Baron
        Stravinsky: Berceuse, from L'Oiseau
          de Feu
        Sullivan: Selection from H.M.S. Pinafore
        Thompson: Far Above Cayuga's Waters
        When I Was Single
        When the Saints Go Marching In
        Yellow Rose of Texas
EBERHARDT, GOBY
    Dance of the Elves, Op. 25, No. 2
      (Saenger) CF B3011
    Dance of the Gnomes, Op. 25, No. 1
      (Saenger) CF B3010
    Hobgoblin Dance, Op. 82, No. 1
      (Saenger) CF B2603
ECCLES, HENRY (c.1652-c.1742)
    Corrente in g, from Sonata No. 11
      ABRS (Mil No. A223)
    Sonata in d
      (Moffat) Nov
ECCLES
    Sonata in sol min.
      (Salmon) Ric R67
EDELSTEIN
    Chant Oriental
      Mil
EDER, HELMUT (1916-   )
    Sonatina, Op. 34, No. 1
      DOB
EGGE, KLAUS (1906-   )
    Sonata No. 1, Op. 3
      Musikk-Huset
EGGEN, ARNE (1881-1955)
    Melodi fra Liti Kersti
      Norsk
    Sonata in a
      Norsk
EGIAZARIAN, G
    Nocturne; Dance
      MZK
EGK, WERNER (1901-   )
    Geigenmusik, orig for vln and orch
      SCH
EHRLICH, ABEL
    Andante, from Sonata for Violin and Piano
      Mil
EIGES, O.
    Concerto
      MZK
EILENBERG, R.
    Régiment qui passe, Le
      Deiss
EILI, EILI
    (Ambrosio) CF B2593   simpl.
    (Elman) CF B538
    (Gernert) VL 95
EINEM, GOTTFRIED VON (1918-   )
    Sonata, Op. 11
      UE 11992
EISENSTEIN, ALFRED
    Romance
      Mil

EK, GUNNAR (1900-   )
    Fantasi, orig for vln and orch
      Gehrmans
ELDERS, JOOP
    Spanish Coquette
      (Edwards) Mil
ELGAR, EDWARD (1857-1934)
    Adieu
      (Szigeti) Fox
    Bavarian Dances, 3, orig for orch
      (Henley) JWL (Mil No. W1229)
    Capricieuse, La, Op. 17
      (Heifetz) CF B2443
      BRH
      CF B2758
    Chanson de matin, Op. 15, No. 1
      (Ludwig) Lud S-15A1
      Nov
    Chanson de Nuit, Op. 15, No. 2
      Nov
    Concerto, Op. 61
      Nov
    Land of Hope and Glory, see Pomp and
      Circumstance
    May Song
      EKN
    Mazurka, Op. 10, No. 1, orig for orch
      Nov
    Pastourelle
      Nov
    Pomp and Circumstance, Theme, orig
      for orch
      (Akers) CF
      (Eret) BH "Land of Hope and Glory"
    Romance, from Sonata, Op. 82
      Nov
    Rosemary
      EKN
    Salut d'Amour, Op. 12, orig for orch
      (Ambrosio) CF B2549   simpl
      (Saenger) CF S3273
      (Trinkaus) Fill
      BMC
      GS
      Kjos S-5017
      SCH
      VL 80
    Serenade
      (Szigeti) Fox
    Sighs, Op. 70, orig for orch
      BRH
    Sonata, Op. 82
      Nov
    Very Easy Melodious Studies, Op. 22
      Bosw
    Virelai
      Nov
ELIE, JUSTIN
    Haytian Legend
      CF B1183
ELIZALDE, FEDERICO (1907-   )
    Concerto
      Ches
(ELLERT-HERFURTH)
    Music
      Willis
ELLERTON, GUSTAV
    Barcarolle, Op. 18, No. 5
      Bosw
    Cradle Song
      Bosw
    Melodie
      Bosw

ELLINGTON, EDWARD K. "DUKE" (1899-   )
   Sophisticated Lady
      (Rubinoff) Mil
ELLSTEIN, ABRAHAM
   Haftorah
      Mil
ELMAN, MISCHA (1891-   )
   Tango
      CF B2207
ELMAN CONCERT FOLIO
      (Elman) CF 0186
         Ambrosio, d': Serenade
         Arensky: Serenade
         Aulin: Berceuse
         Beethoven: Contredanses
         Brahms: Hungarian Dance No. 7
         Bruch: Kol Nidrei
         Cui: Lettre d'amour
         Delibes: Passepied
         Faure: Apres un reve
         Fibich: Poem
         Grieg: Nocturne
         MacDowell: Scotch Poem
         Nachez: Evening song
         Rubinstein: Dew is sparkling
         Rubinstein: Polka Boheme
         Schumann: Vogel als prophet
         Stojowski: Melodie
         Tenaglia: Aria
ELMAN FAVORITE ENCORES
      (Elman) CF 0187
         Albeniz: Tango
         Amani: Orientale
         Beethoven: Minuet in G
         Cui: Orientale
         Elman: Romance
         Deep River
         Grieg: Grandmother's minuet
         Monasterio: Adieux a l'Alhambra
         Monasterio: Sierra Morena
         Rachmaninoff: Serenade
         Sarasate: Malaguena
         Sarasate: Habanera
         Sinigaglia: Albumblatt
         Sinigaglia: Bagatelle
         Tchaikovsky: Melodie
         Wagner: Romanze
EMMANUEL, MAURICE (1862-1938)
   Sonate en ré mineur
      Dur
EMMETT, D.
   Dixie's land, see Ambrosio
ENCORE
      (Ambrosio) CF 03563
         d'Ambrosio: Serenade
         Aulin: Berceuse
         Beethoven: Minuet No. 2 in G
         Brahms: Cradle song
         Brahms-Joachim: Hungarian Dance
            No. 7
         Chopin-Sarasate: Nocturne, Op. 9, No. 2
         Cui: Orientale
         Drdla: Souvenir
         Dvorak: Humoresque
         Gossec: Gavotte
         Prince Gustav: Where roses fair
         Kriens: Sons du soir
         Schubert: Ave Maria
         Severn: Romance
         Tchaikovsky: Canzonetta, from
            Violin Concerto
         Tchaikovsky: Melodie
         Wieniawski: Kuiawiak

ENESCO, GEORGES (1881-1955)
   Impressions d'enfance
      Sal
   Languir me fais, Chanson XIII
      (Stoessel) CF B1114
   Rumanian Rhapsody No. 1, orig for orch
      SMP
   Rumanian Rhapsody
      (Goehr) MK
   Sonata No. 2, Op. 6[24]
      ENO
   Sonata No. 3, Op. 25[24]
      ENO
ENGLISH CLASSICAL ALBUM
      (Moffat) Aug 7523
ENGLISH MASTERS (17th and 18th Centuries)
      (Moffat) Aug 7537
ENNA, AUGUST (1860-1939)
   Concert in D
      WH 138
ENRIQUEZ, MANUEL
   Suite
      EMM
ERB, MARIE JOSEPH (1858-1944)
   Angelus
      Senart
   Sonate No. 2
      Senart
   Sonate No. 3
      Senart
ERDNA
   Pièces Swing, 6
      Sal
ERICKSON, R.
   Duo
      Pr
ERKEL, FRANZ (1810-1893)
   Hungarian Hymn
      (Hartmann) AMP
ERNST, HEINRICH WILHELM (1814-1865)
   Concerto in f sharp, Op. 23
      (Auer) CF 03698
      (Quesnot) Senart 5292
      Pet 2850
   Concertino
      (Quesnot) Senart 5311
   Gypsy Dance
      (Perlman) CF B2764
   Hungarian Melodies, Op. 22
      Pet 2849
   Polonaise, Op. 17
      (Sitt) UE 6699
ERPF, HERMANN (1891-   )
   Sonatina
      SCH
ESCÔBAR, A.
   Triptico Gitano
      SZ
ESHPAI, Y.
   Hungarian Melodies
      MZK
   Mari Melodies
      MZK
ESPÉJO, C.
   Airs tziganes, orig for vln and orch
      HL
   Prélude ibérique
      HL
ESPOSITO, MICHELE (1855-1929)
   Coulin, from Irish Melodies, Op. 56
      Pigott (Mil No. PT401)

[24] In the U.S.A. this publication can be obtained through Associated Music Publishers.

ESPOSITO, MICHELE (cont.)
Fly not yet, from Irish Melodies, Op. 56
Pigott (Mil No. PT403)
Rich and Rare, from Irish Melodies, Op. 56
Pigott (Mil No. PT400)
Silent, O Moyle, from Irish Melodies,
Op. 56
Pigott (Mil No. PT402)
When through life, from Irish Melodies,
Op. 56
Pigott (Mil No. PT404)
ESSEK, P.
Concertino in G, Op. 4
Bosw (Bel No. 14)
EVANS, D.M.
Simple Tunes, 6
STB
EVANS, EVERETT J.
Sweet and Dainty
CF B2407
EVETT, ROBERT (1922-   )
Sonata
CFE
EXAUDET, JOSEPH
Sonate en ut mineur
HL
FABIANI, ANTONIO
Piccolo Violinista, I1
Carisch
FAIRCHILD, BLAIR (1877-1933)
Etude symphonique, Op. 45, orig for
vln and orch
Dur
Mélodie
Senart
Mosquitos
(Dushkin) SCH
Sonata in e, Op. 43
Dur
FAIRCHILD, WILLIAM
Irish Medley
VL 11
FALLA, MANUEL DE (1876-1946)
Danse de la Frayeur, from El Amor
Brujo
(Kochanski) Ches
Danse du Meunier, from Ballet, El
Sombrero de Tres Picos
(Szigeti) CF B2482
Danse Espagnole, from La Vida Breve
(Kreisler) CF B2048
Danse Rituelle du Feu, from El Amor Brujo
(Kochanski) Ches
Jota, from Suite Populaire Espagnole
CF B2194
Pantomime, from El Amor Brujo
(Kochanski) Ches
Suite Populaire Espagnole
(Kochanski) CF 02429
FAREWELL TO CUCULLAIN, see Londonderry
Air
FARKAS, FERENC (1905-   )
Danses Hongroises du XVIIe Siecle
Kul
Danza Alla Ungherese
Kul
Rumanian Folk Dances
Kul
Sonatinas, 2
Kul
FARKAS
Rondo Capriccio
Mil-L 143

FARMER, HENRY
Blue bells of Scotland. Fantasia
CF B2640
Swiss Air and Gentle Zitella. Fantasia
CF B3104
FARNABY, GILES
Variations on La Spagnoletta, see
Montsalvatge
FARRAR, ERNEST (1885-1918)
Celtic Suite, Op. 11
Nov
FASANO, A.
Evening Chant
BMI
FASSIO, A.
Solitude
MK
FASTOFSKY, S.
Greensleeves
CP
FAUCHEY, [PAUL (1858-1936)]
Hymne aux Fleurs
Sal
Invocation à Zeus
Sal
FAUCONIER, B.C.
Rêverie in G, Op. 114, No. 1
(Saenger) CF B3342
FAURE, GABRIEL (1845-1924)
Andantino
(Barrère) GS for fl or vln and pno
Après un Rêve, orig for voice and pno
(Elman) CF B1301
Haml
Berceuse, Op. 16
GS
Haml
Sonata in A, Op. 13
(Francescatti-Casadesus) Int
(Loeffler) BMC
BRH
Sonata No. 2 in e, Op. 108
Dur
FAURE, JEAN-BAPTISTE (1830-1914)
Palms, orig for voice and pno
(Ambrosio) CF B2538   simpl
(Ritter) CF B2782
VL 53   2nd vln ad lib
FAUST, J.
Little Concertinos, 2
Artia
FAVORITE PIECES, 3
Pet 3383
Raff: Cavatina
Vieuxtemps: Reverie
Wieniawski: Legend
FAVORITE VIOLIN SOLOS, 17
GS
Bizet: Habanera, from Carmen
De Koven: Oh, promise me
Donizetti: Sextet, from Lucia di
Lammermoor
Dvorak: Humoreske, Op. 101, No. 7
Elgar: Salut d'amour, Op. 12
Gillet: Passepied
Hauser: Chanson de berceau,
Op. 11, No. 2
Labitzky: The Alp maid's dream, Op. 45
Lange: Flower-song, Op. 39
Langer: Grandmama, Op. 20
Mascagni: Intermezzo sinfonico, from
Cavalleria Rusticana
Mendelssohn: Spring song

FAVORITE VIOLIN SOLOS, 17 (cont.)
GS (cont.)
Offenbach: Belle nuit. Barcarolle,
from Les Contes d'Hoffmann
Schubert: Serenade
Schumann: Träumerei
Wagner: To the evening star, from
Tannhäuser
Wieniawski: Kujawiak
FAVRE, [GEORGES (1905-   )]
Sonate
Dur
FEIGIN, L.
Indian Songs, Op. 11
MZK
Slovak Dances, 3, see Blok: Slovak Lullaby
FELDMAN, MORTON (1926-   )
Extensions I
Pet 6911
Piece for vln and pno
Pet 6944
Projection IV
Pet 6913   graph
Vertical Thoughts 2
Pet 6953
FÉLINE, J.
Serenade
ESC
FERENC, K.
Gypsy Music Album
Metr
FERGUSON, HOWARD (1908-   )
Sonata No. 1
BH
Sonata No. 2
BH
FERNANDEZ, C.
Cielito Lindo
(Ambrosio) CF B2584
FERNANDEZ, OSCAR L. (1897-1948)
Romance
SMP
FERRARI-TRECATE, LUIGI (1884-   )
Il Canto dell'esule
Ric 123920
FERRARIS, A.
Black Eyes
Liber-S
Caprice Hongrois
Liber-S
Echoes from the Puszta
Liber-S
Gipsy Idyll
Liber-S
Russian Pedlar
Liber-S
Souvenir d'Ukraine
Liber-S
Two Guitars
Liber-S
FERRARIS
Pezzi, 4, Op. 3
Ric 127586
FERROUD, PIERRE-OCTAVE (1900-1936)
Sonate
Dur
FESCH, WILLEM DE (1687-1761)
Short Pieces, 3
STB
Sonaten, 6
(Woehl) Baer HM127-8   2V; vcl ad lib
Sonata in sol
(Salmon) Ric R60

FESTING, MICHAEL CHRISTIAN (c.1680-1752)
Sonata in b
HL
Sonata in D, Op. 8, No. 5
(Bergmann) SCH
FETLER, PAUL (1920-   )
Pieces, 3
SPAM
FÉVRIER, [HENRI (1875-1957)]
Sonate
Leduc
FIBICH, ZDENKO (1850-1900)
Bagatelles
Artia
Poème, Op. 41, No. 6, orig for pno
(Ambrosio) CF B2591   simpl
(Berton) CF B3155
(Kubelik) Artia
(Kvelve) VL 160
(Linz) SCH
(Musin) MK "Poetic Souvenir"
(Schindler) GS "Souvenir poétique"
Poem; with Polish Song by Wieniawski
MZK
Romanza, Op. 10
Artia
Sonata in D
Artia
Sonatina in d, Op. 27
Artia
BMC
FICHER, JACOBO (1896-   )
Piezas, Tres
SMP
FIEBIG, KURT (1908-   )
Sonatina
Pet 5627
FIETTER, C.
Apaisement
Sal
Rêverie au Clair de Lune
Sal
FIEVET, C.
Calme du soir
Gaudet
FINE, VIVIAN (1913-   )
Sonata
CFE
FINNEY, ROSS LEE (1906-   )
Concerto
Pet 6668a
Fiddle-doodle-ad
GS
Sonata No. 2
AME
Sonata No. 3
Val
FIOCCO, JOSEPH-HECTOR (1703-1741)
Allegro
(Gingold) Int
SCH
Allegro, see Pugnani: Largo
FIORILLO, FEDERIGO (1755- ?)
Air for the G String
(Vidas) CF B1279
Capriccio in ré
(D'Ambrosio) Ric 129410
Caprice No. 28
(Idle) JWL (Mil No. 1243)
(Sladek) VL
Caprice, see also Musin: Caprice in D and
Funeral March
Etude, see Benda: Caprice

FIRST POSITION VIOLIN PIECES
  Amsco 24
    Adam: Allegretto, from Si j'etais roi
    Albeniz: Tango
    Arne: Drink to Me Only With Thine Eyes
    Bach: My Heart That Believest
    Beethoven: Minuet in G
    Bizet: Aria, from Pearl Fishers
    Bizet: Habanera, from Carmen
    Brahms: Cradle Song
    Brahms: Hungarian Dance
    Brahms: Waltz
    Chopin: Nocturne
    Cielito Lindo
    Dixie
    Dussek: Old Dance
    Dvorak: Slavonic Dance
    Fibich: Poeme
    A Frangesa
    Gounod: Duet, from Faust
    Gounod: Waltz, from Faust
    Grieg: I Love Thee
    Grieg: Solvejg's Song
    Gypsy Melody
    Handel: Arioso
    Lehar: Gold and Silver Waltz
    Lehar: Merry Widow Waltz
    Londonderry Air
    Luigini: Ballet Egyptien
    Mascagni: Intermezzo, from Cavalleria
      Rusticana
    Mendelssohn: Andante, from the Violin
      Concerto. Excerpt
    Mendelssohn: On Wings of Song
    Mozart: Lullaby
    Mozart: Minuet
    O Sole Mio
    Offenbach: Barcarolle, from Tales of
      Hoffman
    Offenbach: Melody, from Orpheus
    Oh Susanna
    Old Refrain
    Paganini: Melody, from the Violin
      Concerto
    Paganini: Sonatina: Melody and Theme
    Poldini: Waltzing Doll
    Red Sarafan
    Santa Lucia
    Schubert: Ballet Music, from Rosamunde
    Schubert: German Dances
    Schubert: Serenade
    Schumann: First Grief
    Schumann: From Foreign Lands
    Schumann: Merry Peasant
    Schumann: Soldiers' March
    Schumann: Wild Horseman
    Sibelius: Valse Triste
    Smetana: Polka, from Bartered Bride
    Song of the Volga Boatman
    Strauss I: Radetzky March
    Strauss II: On the Beautiful Blue Danube
    Swanee River
    Thomas: Connais-tu le pays, from
      Mignon
    Tschaikowsky: None but the Lonely
      Heart
    Tschaikowsky: Song without Words
    Verdi: Aria, from La Traviata
    Verdi: Donna e mobile, La, from
      Rigoletto
    Verdi: Grand March, from Aida
    Wagner: Bridal Chorus, from Lohen-
      grin

    Wagner: Song to the Evening Star,
      from Tannhauser
    Wieniawski: Mazurka
    Yradier: Paloma, La
FIRST SOLO ALBUM
  (Whistler) Ru
FIRST SOLOS FROM THE CLASSICS
  (Applebaum) GS
    J.S. Bach: Come let us to the
      bagpipes sound
    J.S. Bach: Gavotte, from the French
      Suite No. 5
    Brahms: Waltz, Op. 39
    Ghys: Amaryllis
    Gluck: Air, from Orpheus
    Grieg: Watchman's Song
    Handel: See, the conquering hero comes
    Haydn: Andante, from "Surprise"
      symphony
    Ivanovici: Waves of the Danube
    Offenbach: Barcarolle, from Tales of
      Hoffmann
    Mozart: Minuet in A, K. 439
    Mozart: Minuet in C, K. 439
    Rubinstein: Melody in F
    Schumann: Soldier's March
FISCHER, IRWIN
  Idyll, orig for vln and orch
  CFE
FISCHER, J.
  Divertissement
  (Bergmann) SCH
FISCHER, OTTO
  Wayside Rose
  VL 8   2nd vln ad lib
FITELBERG, JERZY (1903-1951)
  Concerto No. 1
  Omega
  Concertino da Camera
  SMP
  Mazurkas, 3
  (Fraenkel) Sal
  Serenade
  SMP
  Tango
  UE 1117
FITZWILLIAM VIRGINAL BOOK
  Pet 4156b
FLANAGAN, WILLIAM (1928-   )
  Chaconne
  Peer
FLEM, see Le Flem
FLETCHER, STANLEY
  Cornstalk tunes
  GS
FLETCHER, see Rolland & Fletcher
FLOTHUIS, MARIUS (1914-   )
  Partita
  DN (Pet No. D225)
FLOTOW, FRIEDRICH (1812-1883)
  Last Rose of Summer, from Martha
  VL 125   2nd vln ad lib
  Martha. Transcription
  (Ambrosio) CF B3305
FOLK AND MASTER MELODIES FOR THE
  YOUNG VIOLINIST
  (Sontag) GS   3V
FOLK SONGS, 2
  (Komarovsky) MZK
FONTANA, G.B
  Sonatas, 6
  (Cerha) DOB   3V
(FORBES, WATSON)
  Classical and Romantic Pieces
  Oxf 23.811-14   4V   for contents see title

(FORBES-JOHNSON)
  Violin Concertos. The Slow Movements
    Pet 561   for contents see title
FORD, DONALD (1891-   )
  Adagio and Allegretto
    Chap-L
  Ebb-Tide Reverie
    Chap-L
  Simple Pieces, 3
    EKN
FORD, see Merrill & Ford
FORDELL, J.
  To the Mystic Rose
    EKN
FÖRSTER, CHRISTOPH
  Sonatas
    Hof
FORTERRE, H.
  Humoresque
    Gaudet
FORTNER, WOLFGANG (1907-   )
  Concerto
    SCH
(FORTUNATOV)
  Easy Pieces
    MZK
  Easy Pieces by Old Composers
    MZK
  Pieces, 7, by Soviet Composers
    MZK
FOSS, LUKAS (1922-   )
  Composer's holiday
    GS
FOSTER, ARNOLD (1898-   )
  Chanson
    STB
  Conceit
    STB
  Minuet
    STB
FOSTER, STEPHEN COLLINS (1826-1864)
  Beautiful Dreamer
    (Eckstein) CF M305
  Jeanie With the Light Brown Hair
    (Eckstein) CF M302
    (Heifetz) CF B2491
  Massa's in the Cold, Cold Ground
    (Stoessel) BMC
  My Old Kentucky Home
    (Stoessel) BMC
    see also Ambrosio
  Old Black Joe
    (Stoessel) BMC
    VL 88   2nd vln ad lib
    see also Ambrosio
  Old Folks At Home
    (Heifetz) CF B2492
    (Stoessel) BMC
  Old folks at home. Fantasia
    see Kron & Saenger
FOULDS, [JOHN HERBERT (1880-1939)
  Keltic Lament
    BH
FOURDRAIN, H.
  Espoir du Retour
    Deiss
  Pluie de Perles, La
    Deiss
FOURVIÈRES, PAUL
  Méditation Religieuse
    (Ambrosio) CF S3649
FOX, OSCAR J.
  Hills of Home
    (Breeskin) CF B2308

FRANCAIX, JEAN (1912-   )
  Sonatina
    SCH
  Suite
    SCH
FRANCK, CÉSAR (1822-1890)
  Panis Angelicus
    BMC   for vln or vcl and pno
  Sonata in A
    (Busch) BRH
    (Francescatti-Casadesus) Int
    (Lehmann) CF L766
    (Lichtenberg-Adler) GS L1235
    (Polo) Ric ER2068
    (Sauret) SCH
    Dur
    Haml
    Pet 3742
FRANCMESNIL, ROGER DE (1884-   )
  Berceuse
    Mathot
  Sonate
    Mathot
FRANCO, JOHAN (1908-   )
  Suite
    CFE
FRANCOEUR, FRANCOIS (1698-1787)
  Sonata in e
    (Moffat) SIM
  Sonata in e
    HL
  Sonata in g
    HL
FRANCOEUR, [FRANCOIS]
  Sonata in A
    (Salmon) Ric R752
FRANKEL, BENJAMIN (1906-   )
  Concerto, Op. 24
    Aug   pno reduction by P.G. Jones
  Novelette, Op. 16
    Aug
FRANKLIN, HOWARD
  Airs and Graces
    CF B2315   includes 2nd vln part for
    teacher
  Birds' Frolic
    CF B2277   includes 2nd vln part for
    teacher
  Sailor Song
    CF B2299   includes 2nd vln part for
    teacher
FRANKLIN
  Juvenile Violinist
    Pr
FRANKLIN-PIKE, ELEANOR
  Sea Song, Op. 9
    Aug
FRASER, [NORMAN (1904-   )]
  En el tiempo de Chicha
    Ches
FRASER, SHENA
  Pieces in the First Position, 5
    Oxf 23.808
FREIHARDT, G.A.
  Albumblatt
    DOB
FRESCOBALDI, GIROLAMO (1583-1643)
  Toccata
    (Cerha) DOB   vcl ad lib
FRICKER, PETER RACINE (1920-   )
  Concerto, Op. 11
    SCH
  Rapsodia concertante. Concerto
    No. 2, Op. 21
    SCH

FRICKER, PETER RACINE (cont.)
  Sonata, Op. 12
    SCH
FRIED, G.
  Concert Fantasy on Slovak and Moravian
    Themes
    MZK
  Sonata, Op. 27
    MZK
  Sonatina, Op. 32
    MZK
FRIEDMAN
  Tabatière à musique, Op. 33, No. 3
    (Hartmann) UE 8158
FRIML, RUDOLF (1879-   )
  Adieu
    (Borch) BMC
  Amour coquet
    GS
  Berceuse, Op. 50
    GS
  Danse des Demoiselles, Op. 48
    (Kreisler) CF B2091
  Devil's joke
    GS
  Española
    GS
  Giannina mia, from the Firefly
    (Bauerkeller) GS
  Mignonette, Op. 59
    (Rezeda) GS
  Romance, Op. 53, No. 1
    (Hintze) GS
  Spanish serenade
    (Hintze) GS
  Sympathy, from The Firefly
    GS
FRISKIN, JAMES (1886-   )
  Sonata in G
    STB
FRITZ, GASPARD (1716-1782)
  Sonata
    (Grovlez) Ches
FROEHLICH, SEVERIN
  Morceau Diabolique, Op. 14
    CF B403
FROHE RHEINLIEDER-BUCH, DAS
    SCH
FROIDEBISE, PIERRE (1914-   )
  Sonata
    CBDM
FROMM, HERBERT (1905-   )
  Sonata in G
    BH
(FROTSCHER)
  Noels. Old French Christmas Dances
    Noet (Pet Nos. N3228, N3234)   2V
    vcl or gamba ad lib
FRUMERIE, GUNNAR DE (1908-   )
  Sonata
    Nordiska
  Sonata No. 2
    Nordiska
FRYKLÖF, HARALD (1882-1919)
  Sonata alla leggenda
    Nordiska
FUCHS, LILLIAN
  Dances in Olden Style, 2
    Leeds
FUCIK, JULIUS (1872-1916)
  Entrée des Gladiateurs
    Deiss
FUN FOR FIDDLE FINGERS
    (Bornoff-Cooper) Gordon V. Thompson

FUSSAN, WERNER (1912-   )
  Musik
    BRH
GABRIEL MARIE, see Marie, Gabriel
GABUS, M.
  Sonate
    Jobert
GADZHIEV, R.
  Concerto
    MZK
  Scherzo, see Karayev: Lullaby
GAERTNER
  Viennese Melody
    (Kreisler) Fol 1197
GAGNEBIN, HENRI (1886-   )
  Sonate en mi
    RL
GAILLARD, MARIUS-FRANCOIS (1900-   )
  Sonate
    Senart
  Week End
    Heugel
GAITO
  Pampeanita
    (Cambon) Ric BA8862
GÁL, HANS (1890-   )
  Sonatina in G, Op. 71, No. 1
    Aug 7573a
  Sonatina in B flat, Op. 71, No. 2
    Aug 7573b
  Sonatina in F, Op. 71, No. 3
    Aug 7573c
  Suite
    Curwen
GALAJIKIAN, FLORENCE G. (1900-   )
  Girl with a Spanish Shawl
    CF B2385
GALAVERNI, ITALO
  Pezzi Facili, 10
    Carisch   2nd vln ad lib
GALINDO, BLAS (1910-   )
  Sonata
    EMM
  Suite
    EMM
GALLIARD, JOHANN ERNST (1687-1749)
  Sonate en mi mineur
    HL
  Sonata in sol
    (Salmon) Ric R356
GAMBURG, G.
  Reminiscence and Scherzo
    MZK
GANNE, LOUIS (1862-1923)
  Extase
    (Adler-Ambrosio) CF B3165
GANNE-ALDER
  Aubade fleurie
    Deiss
GARDNER, SAMUEL (1891-   )
  Babushka
    BMC
  Coquetterie
    GS
  From the canebrake, Op. 5, No. 1
    GS
    GS   simpl
  Journey Through the Forest
    BMC
  Little Waltz in D
    BMC
  Melancholy Flute
    BMC
  Miniatures, 5
    BMC

GARDNER, SAMUEL (cont.)
Night in the Rockies, Op. 8
CF B1245
Prelude in B, Op. 14, No. 1
CF B409
Prelude, Op. 14, No. 2
CF B410
Prelude in b, Op. 14, No. 3
CF B411
Prelude in g, Op. 14, No. 5
CF B413
Prelude No. 9, Op. 15, No. 4
GS
Romance, Op. 4, No. 1
CF B1207
Sketches, 4
BMC
Slovak, Op. 5, No. 2
CF B1244
Whimsical Whistler
CF B3326
GARRISON, E. RHEY
My Mother's Minuet
VL 143
GATTARI, ALFREDO
Parabole
Santis 533
GATTY, [NICHOLAS (1874-1946)]
Bagatelle
STB
GAUBERT, PHILIPPE (1879-1941)
Concerto
Heugel
GAUTIER, LÉONARD
Secret, Le,
CF B414
GAVINIÉS, PIERRE (1728-1800)
Sonatas, 6
(Englebert-Gallon) Senart 5345A,B   2V
GAY, NOEL
Windsor Melody
Mil
(GEHRKENS, VIRGINIA E.)
Dances, Vol 1: Mozart & Beethoven
BMC   for contents see title
GEIGER, OSKAR
Just for tonight
(Edwards) MK
GEMINIANI, FRANCESCO (1687-1762)
Chaconne, upon the sarabande theme from
Corelli's Violin Sonata, Op. 5, No. 7
Hin (Pet No. H1687)   vcl or gamba ad lib
Concerto No. 1
(Borrel) Senart 5348
Introduzione e Allegro
(Corti) Carisch
Minuets, 2
(Woof) JWL (Mil No. W1255)
Siciliènne
(Busch) BRH
(Herrmann) ESC
Sonata in A, Op. 1, No. 1
(Ruf) Baer HM173   vcl ad lib
Sonata in A
(Betti) GS L1761
Sonata in c
Carisch
Sonata in D, Op. 1, No. 4
Baer HM174   vcl ad lib
Sonata in d
(Betti) GS L1762
Sonata in G
(Salmon) Ric R744
Violin Pieces, 12
Kul   2V

GENZMER, HARALD (1909-   )
Concerto
SCH
Sonata No. 2
SCH
Sonata No. 3
Pet 5870
Sonatina
SCH
GERHARD, ROBERTO (1896-   )
Concerto
Mil-L 144
GERMAN, EDWARD (1862-1936)
Merrie England
Chap-L
Saltarelle
Aug
GERSCHEFSKI, EDWIN (1909-   )
Statement, Aria and Development
CFE
GERSHWIN, GEORGE (1898-1937)
Bess, You Is My Woman, from Porgy and
Bess
(Heifetz) Gersh
It Ain't Necessarily So, from Porgy and Bess
(Heifetz) Gersh
My Man's Gone Now, from Porgy and Bess
(Heifetz) Gersh
Short Story
(Dushkin) SCH
Summertime and A Woman is a Sometime
Thing, from Porgy and Bess
(Heifetz) Gersh
Tempo Di Blues, from Porgy and Bess
(Heifetz) Gersh
GHEDINI, GIORGIO FEDERICO (1892-   )
Bizzarria
UE 2175
Concentus Basiliensis, orig for vln and orch
Ric 128920
Concerto, "Il Belprato"
Ric 129010
Poemi, Due
UE 10641
GHYS, HENRI (1839-1908)
Amaryllis, Air du Louis XIII, Op. 10, No. 2
(Saenger) CF B2983
VL 39   2nd vln ad lib
Amaryllis; with Country Gardens
(Harris) Lud S-1577
GIARDINI, FELICE DE' (1716-1796)
Concerto in A
(Bonelli) ZA
GIBB, ROBERT W.
In Melody Land
Big 3
GIBBS, CECIL ARMSTRONG (1889-1960)
Lyric Sonata
Curwen
GIBBS, JOSEPH (1699-1788)
Sonata No. 1 in d
(Salter) Aug
Sonata in d
(Moffat) Nov
Sonata No. 5 in E
(Salter) Aug
GIDEON, MIRIAM (1906-   )
Air
CFE
Three Biblical Masks
CFE
GIL
Sonatina
Ric BA10066

GILARDI, [GILARDO (1889-   )]
  Aire de baguala
    (Pessina) Ric BA10267
  Aire de chamamé
    (Pessina) Ric BA9407
  Aire de vidala
    (Pessina) Ric BA9408
  Aires pampeanos
    (Pessina) Ric BA10266
GILLET, ERNEST (1856-1940)
  Au Moulin
    (Moses-Tobani) CF B2995
  Babillage
    (Moses-Tobani) CF B2997
  Loin du Bal. Waltz Movement and Entr'acte
      Gavotte
    (Moses-Tobani-Ambrosio) CF B3016
  Passe-Pied
    (Rosey) MK
GILLIS, DON (1912-   )
  Retrospection
    Mil
GILMORE, JOYCE
  Dancing Sailor Boys
    CF B2255   includes 2nd vln part for
      teacher
GINASTERA, ALBERTO (1916-   )
  Pampeana No. 1
    Barry
GINASTERA, [ALBERTO]
  Milonga
    (Tonini) Ric BA10389
(GINGOLD)
  Solos for the Violin Player
    GS   for contents see title
GIORNOVICHI, GIOVANNI MANE (c.1735-1804)
  Concerto in A
    (Lebermann) SCH
GIULIANI, MAURO (1781-1828)
  Minuetto
    (Cherry) CF B2349
GLAGOLEV, Y.
  Sonata
    MZK
GLASS, LOUIS (1864-1936)
  Sonata No. 2, Op. 29
    WH 1207
GLAZUNOV, ALEXANDER (1865-1936)
  Album Leaf
    MZK
  Concerto in a, Op. 82
    (Auer) CF 03440
    (Auer) Int
    Belaieff
    MZK
  Entr'acte, from Raymonda
    MZK
  Grand Adagio, from Raymonda
    MZK
  Méditation, Op. 32
    (Heifetz) CF B2442
    (Saenger) CF B2644
    BH
    MZK
  Sonatina in a
    (Levy-Zeitlin) Leeds
  Waltz, Op. 42, No. 3
    MZK
  Waltz, from Raymonda
    MZK
GLENDALE WALTZ
  (Harvey) VL 30   2nd vln ad lib
GLIÈRE, REINHOLD M. (1875-1956)
  Album of Pieces
    MZK

  Andante, from Bronze Horseman
    MZK
  Aria; Pastorale; Humoresque
    MZK
  Dances, 2, from Taras Bulba
    MZK
  Easy Pieces, 8, Op. 45
    MZK
  Equisse, Op. 54, No. 3
    (Hartmann) Leeds
  Folk Song; with Spinning Song by
      Rubinstein
    MZK
  Instructional Pieces, 7, Op. 54
    MZK
  Prelude; Waltz
    MZK
  Romance, Op. 3
    Int
    MZK
  Romance
    (Hartmann) AMP
  Romance; At the Brook
    MZK
  Romance; with Improvisation by
      Kabalevsky
    MZK
  Russian Folk Song
    (Levy-Zeitlin) Leeds
GLINKA, MIKHAIL I. (1804-1857)
  Album Leaf
    MZK
  Feeling, Simplicity; with Waltz by
      Verstovsky
    MZK
  Lark; Polka; Dance from Ivan Sussanin
    MZK
  Mazurka
    (Hartmann) AMP
  Mazurka
    MZK
  Nocturne
    MZK
  Persian song
    (Zimbalist) GS
  Remembrances of a Mazurka; with Serenade
      by Borodin and Romance by Rubinstein
    MZK
  Song of Ilininshna; with Waltz by Griboyedov
      and Waltz by Kozlovsky
    MZK
  Waltz; Mazurkas, 2
    MZK
GLUCK, CHRISTOPH WILLIBALD (1714-1787)
  Andante, from Orpheus
    VL 68   2nd vln ad lib
  Andantino, Ballet Music from Orpheus
    (Ries-Riles-Winn) CF B3241
  Concerto in G, orig for flute
    (Scherchen) Hug (Pet No. A18)
  Dance of the Blessed Spirits, from Orpheus
    (Abbado) Carisch
    (Flies) SCH
  Gavotte, from Iphigenia in Aulis
    (Klengel) Pet 4163
  Melodie, from Dance of the Blessed Spirits
    (Kreisler) Fol 1143
  Melody, from Dance of the Blessed Spirits
    (Sgambati-Wilhelmj-Saenger) CF B2743
  Musette, from Armide
    (Malkin) CF B418
  Sonata
    (Heifetz) CF B2653

GNESSIN, MIKHAIL (1883-1957)
  Suite
    MZK
GNESSIN, [MIKHAIL]
  Song of the Wandering Knight, Op. 34
    (Szigeti) UE 9911
GODARD, BENJAMIN (1849-1895)
  Adagio non troppo
    Sal
  Adagio Pathétique, Op. 128, No. 3
    (Saenger) CF B421
    GS
  Berceuse, from Jocelyn
    (Ambrosio) CF B2539   simpl
    (Eisenberg) MK
    (Mittell) GS   transcribed by the composer
    (Saenger) CF S3097
    (Trinkaus) Fill
    SCH
    VL 118
  Concerto Romantique, Op. 35
    (Winn) CF 03487
  Sonate No. 1 en ut mineur, Op. 1
    Dur
  Sonate No. 2 en la mineur, Op. 2
    Dur
  Sonate No. 3 en sol mineur, Op. 9
    Dur
GODOWSKY, LEOPOLD (1870-1938)
  Alt Wien
    (Heifetz) CF B2257
    (Press) GS
  Avowal, Poem No. 2
    (Godowsky, Jr.) CF B2176
  Élégie, No. 7 of 12 Impressions
    (Kreisler) CF B429
  Larghetto lamentoso, No. 1 of
    12 Impressions
    (Kreisler) CF B423
  Légende, No. 3 of 12 Impressions
    (Kreisler) CF B425
  Nocturnal Tangier, from Triakontameron
    (Kreisler) CF B2174
  Orientale, No. 10 of 12 Impressions
    (Kreisler) CF B432
  Perpetuum Mobile, No. 6 of 12 Impressions
    (Kreisler) CF B428
  Poème, No. 5 of 12 Impressions
    (Kreisler) CF B427
  Tyrolean, No. 4 of 12 Impressions
    (Kreisler) CF B426
  Valse, No. 8 of 12 Impressions
    (Kreisler) CF B430
  Valse Macabre, No. 9 of 12 Impressions
    (Kreisler) CF B431
  Viennese, No. 12 of 12 Impressions
    (Kreisler) CF B434
  Waltz Poem No. 1
    (Godowsky, Jr.) CF B2173
  Waltz Poem No. 2
    (Godowsky, Jr.) CF B2172
GODOWSKY, LOUIS
  Allegro Appasionata
    Chap-L
  Dusk
    JWL (Mil No. W1228)
  Melody
    Chap-L
  Tango
    JWL (Mil No. W1227)
GODOWSKY
  Fandango
    Leng (Mil No. L1104)
  Song without words
    Leng (Mil No. L1114)

GOEB, ROGER (1914-   )
  Variations
    CFE
GOEDICKE, ALEXANDER (1877-1957)
  Easy Pieces, 3
    MZK
  Pieces in the First Position, 10, Op. 80
    MZK
  Sonata, Op. 10
    MZK
GOENS, DANIEL VAN
  Romance Sans Paroles, Op. 12, No. 1
    (Saenger) CF B2627
    (Mittell) GS
  Scherzo, Op. 12, No. 2
    CF S3420
GOEYENS, [FERNANDO (1892-   )]
  English Melody
    Brogneaux
  Song of Love
    Brogneaux
GOLD, ERNEST (1921-   )
  Exodus, Main Theme
    (Noeltner) Chap
GOLDBERG, JOHANN GOTTLIEB (1727-1756)
  Trio in g
    (Dürr) NAG   vcl ad lib
GOLDEN MARCH BOOK
    SCH
GOLDMARK, KARL (1830-1915)
  Air from Concerto, Op. 28
    (Saenger) CF B435
  Concerto, Op. 28
    (Auer) CF 03158
GOLDMARK, RUBIN (1872-1936)
  Call of the Plains
    CF B436
GOLESTAN, STAN (1872-1956)
  Concerto Roumain
    Sal
  Laoutar, Le
    Sal
GOLTERMANN
  Pieces, 2, Op. 13
    Pet 1996
GOLUBEV, E.
  Poem, Op. 3
    MZK
  Sonata, Op. 37
    MZK
GOMEZ CARRILLO
  Aires santiagueños: Canción y Danza
    Ric BA11308
  Canción criolla
    Ric BA10885
  Danzas y Cantos regionales del Norte
    argentino. 1⁰ Album
    Ric BA8905
  Siete de Abril
    (Zamba) Ric 10886
GOODENOUGH, FORREST (1918-   )
  Reminiscence
    CFE
  Romanza
    CFE
GOOSSENS, EUGÈNE (1893-1962)
  Lyric Poem, Op. 35
    Ches
  Phantasy Concerto, Op. 63
    Ches
  Romance, from Don Juan de Mañara
    Ches   transcribed by composer
  Sonata No. 1, Op. 21
    Ches

GOOSSENS, EUGÈNE (cont.)
Sonata No. 2
Ches
GORINI, GINO (1914-   )
Concerto
SZ
GOSSEC, FRANÇOIS-JOSEPH (1734-1829)
Gavotte
(Ambrosio) CF B2564   simpl
(Burmester) GS
(Napolitano) Ric BA11439
CF S3218
SCH
VL 105   2nd vln ad lib
Tambourine
(Saenger) CF B2714
GOTTSCHALK, LOUIS MOREAU (1829-1869)
Last Hope
(Moses-Tobani) CF B3129
See also Mason: Nearer, My God,
to Thee, under vln unacc
GOULD, MORTON (1913-   )
Suite
G & C
GOUNOD, CHARLES (1818-1893)
Ave Maria. Meditation on the first
prelude of J.S. Bach
(Ambrosio) CF B2550   simpl
(Del Maglio) Ric 127672
(Eisenberg) MK
(Halle) Bel 698
(Mittell) GS "Meditation"
Paxton (Mil No. P525) "Meditation"
(Ritter) SCH
(Saenger) CF S3060   organ ad lib
VL 92
Faust. Fantaisie, see Alard, Sarasate,
Wieniawski
Faust. Transcription
(Ambrosio) CF B3302
Garden Scene, from Faust
CF B3025
Vision de Jeanne d'Arc
CF B3093
Waltz, Op. 33, No. 7
(Wichtl) CF S3206
Waltz, from Faust
(Wichtl-Mittell) GS
CF S3207
GRADED PIECES
ABRS (Mil No. 268-274)   7V
GRAENER, [PAUL (1872-1944)]
Concerto, Op. 104
SCH
GRAFF, JOHANN
Sonata, see vln and harpsichord
GRAINGER, PERCY (1882-1961)
Harvest hymn
GS
Molly on the shore
GS
Sussex mummers' Christmas carol
GS
GRAM, PEDER (1881-   )
Konzert in d, Op. 20
WH
GRANADOS, ENRIQUE (1867-1916)
Danse Espagnole[25]
(Thibaud) CF B1208
Intermezzo, from Goyescas
(Jacobsen) GS

Spanish Dance, No. 10[25]
UME
Spanish Dance[25]
(Kreisler) Fol 1187
GRAND, see Le Grand
GRANGER, J.
Doux songe
Gaudet
Jeunes virtuoses, Les. 6 morceaux
mélodiques et progressifs
Gaudet   published separately
Lycée musical, Le. 15 morceaux mélodiques
et progressifs
Gaudet   published separately
Soirée d'Automne
Gaudet
Souvenir de Printemps
Gaudet
Sur l'Onde
Gaudet
GRANVILLE, NORMAN
Aubade
VL
GRASSI, ANTONIO DE
Berceuse
MK
SCH
GRASSO & WILSON
Chanson du Violon
Mil
GRATTON, HECTOR (1900-   )
Chanson Ecossaise
CL
Danse Canadiènne No. 4
CL
GRAUN, JOHANN GOTTLIEB (1703-1771)
Sonatas, 6, for vln and Bc
Sik 395a-e   published separately
GRAZIOLLI
Adagio; with Minuet by Haydn
MZK
GREEN, PHIL
Romance, on a theme by Paganini,
from film "The Magic Bow"
Chap-L
GREEN, RAY (1909-   )
Duo Concertante
AME
GREENE, EDWIN
Sing Me to Sleep
(Hollas) BMC
GREENE, W.
Playful Rondo
(Teres-Ambrosio) CF B2731
(GREENWOOD, NEVA GARNER)
Violinist's Introduction to Bach
Willis
GRENZ, ARTUR (1909-   )
Concerto, Op. 7
Sik 196
GRETCHANINOV, ALEXANDER T. (1864-1956)
Berceuse, Op. 1, No. 5
Belaieff   arr by composer
Chant d'Automne
(Hartmann) AMP
Early Morn, Op. 126a
(Willms) SCH
Morning Stroll and The Joker
(Robjohns) SCH
On a Winter's Eve and Burlesque Waltz
(Robjohns) SCH
Slumber Song
(Hartmann) AMP

---

[25] No doubt from the 12 Spanish Dances, originally for piano.

GRETRY, ANDRÉ ERNEST MODESTE
  (1741-1813)
  Air de Ballet
    (Franko) RE (Pet No. RE4)
  Andantino, from Le Huron
    (Pochon) CF B1783
GRIBOYEDOV
  Waltz, see Glinka: Song of Ilininshna
GRIEG, EDVARD (1843-1907)
  Album Leaf, Op. 12, No. 7, orig for pno
    VL 94
  Anitra's Dance, from Peer Gynt Suite
    No. 1, Op. 46
    (Saenger) CF B2698
    (Seidel) CF B1286
  Erotikon, Op. 43, No. 5, orig for pno
    (Sitt) Pet 2425b
  Lyric Pieces, orig for pno
    (Sitt) Pet 2664, 2665   2V
    Vol 1: from op. 38
      Berceuse
      Elegy
      Folk Song
      Melody
      Norwegian Dance
      Waltz
    Vol 2: from Op. 43 and Op. 47
      Erotikon
      Melancholy
      Melody
      Halling
      Solitary Traveller
      To Spring
  Miniatures, Op. 61
    (Carse) Aug AS.77
  Norwegian Bridal Procession, Op. 19, No. 2,
    orig for pno
    Pet 2546
  Norwegian Dances, Op. 35, orig for orch
    (Sitt) Pet 2547
  Norwegian Dance, Op. 35, No. 2
    (Flesch) Pet 4170
    (Sitt) CF B3330
  Notturno, Op. 54, No. 4, orig for pno
    (Elman) CF B1304
  Peer Gynt Suite No. 1, Op. 46, orig for orch
    (Sitt) GS L924
    Pet 2493
  Peer Gynt Suite No. 2, Op. 55
    Pet 3517A
  Scherzo Impromptu, Op. 73, No. 2, orig
    for pno
    (Achron) CF B2001
  Solvejg's Song, from Peer Gynt Suite
    No. 2
    (Hubay) CF B1834
    (Sauret) CF B2712
    (Sauret) Pet 2176D
  Sonata No. 1 in F, Op. 8
    (Lichtenberg) GS L980
    (Spiering-Ganz) CF L271
    Pet 1340
  Sonata No. 2 in G, Op. 13
    (Auer-Ganz) CF 03699
    GS L524
    Pet 2279
  Sonata No. 3 in c, Op. 45
    (Spiering-Ganz) CF L786
    GS L981
    Pet 2414
  Sonata in a, Op. 36, orig for vcl and pno
    (Petri) Pet 2210
  Songs, 5
    (Sauret) Pet 2176b

  To Spring, Op. 43, No. 6, orig for pno
    (Forbes) Oxf 20.111
    (Sitt) Pet 2422b
    CF S3045
  Wedding Day at Troldhaugen, Op. 65, No. 6,
    orig for pno
    Pet 3099
GRIFFES, CHARLES T. (1884-1920)
  Poem, orig for fl and orch
    (Barrère-Kortschak) GS
GRIFFIS, ELLIOT (1893-   )
  Sonata in G
    CP
GRØNDAHL, LAUNY (1886-   )
  Concerto
    Dansk 93
GROSS, ROBERT
  Sonata, Op. 15
    CFE
GROVLEZ, GABRIEL (1879-1944)
  Sonate
    Dur
GRUBER, EDWARD L.
  Caissons go rolling along
    (Applebaum) Bel SI15
GRUBER, FRANZ
  Silent Night, Holy Night. Fantasia
    see Kron-Saenger, Schultze, Wohlfahrt
GRUEN, RUDOLPH
  Taj Majal, Op. 43
    CFE
GUARNIERI, CAMARGO (1907-   )
  Cantiga de Ninar
    AMP
  Cantiga là de Longe
    AMP
  Canto No. 1
    AMP
  Encantamento
    AMP
  Sonata No. 4
    Ric BA11508
GUARNINO, M.
  Concerto
    Carisch
GUASTAVINO, [CARLOS (1914-   )]
  Llanura
    Ric BA10307
GUBITOSI, E.
  Allegro appassionato
    Curci
GUERINI
  Allegro con brio
    (Salmon) Ric R81
GUERRINI, [GUIDO (1890-   )]
  Egloga
    Carisch
GUIGNON, JEAN-PIERRE (1702-1774)
  Sonate en sol majeur
    HL
GUILLARD, see Le Guillard
GUILLEMAIN, [GABRIEL (1705-1770)]
  Allegro
    (Pincherle) Senart 5378
GUION, DAVID W. (1895-   )
  Harmonica player, from Alley tunes
    GS
  Turkey in the Straw
    (MacMillen) GS
GUSIKOFF, MICHAEL & MACHAN, BENJAMIN
  American Concerto
    GS
GUSTAVE OF SWEDEN
  Where Roses Fair
    (Lehmann) CF B453

GYLDMARK
  Green Violin
    (Edwards) Mil
GYPSY FIDDLE
    (Russ-Bovelino) Bel EL508
    (Russ-Bovelino) SCH
GYULAI, G.
  Tarantella
    Kul
HAAS, JOSEPH (1879-1960)
  Capriccio
    Schultheiss
  Sonata in b, Op. 21
    SIM
HADLEY, HENRY (1871-1937)
  Air Plaintif, No. 3 of Suite Ancienne, Op. 101
    CF B2009
  Gigue, No. 4 of Suite Ancienne, Op. 101
    CF B2010
  Marguerites
    CF B1933
  Minuetto, No. 2 of Suite Ancienne, Op. 101
    CF B2008
  October Twilight
    CF B1832
  Prelude, No. 1 of Suite Ancienne, Op. 101
    CF B2007
HAESCHE, WILLIAM EDWIN (1867-1929)
  Gavotte Rococo
    BMC
  Hungarian dance in d
    GS
HAESSLER, see Hässler
HAHN, REYNALDO (1875-1947)
  Concerto
    Heugel
  Romance in A
    Heugel
  Sonata in C
    Heugel
HAIEFF, ALEXEI (1914-   )
  Air
    AMP
  Polka
    AMP
  Ritornel
    AMP
HAIGH, T.
  Sonata
    Paxton (Mil No. P501)
HALE, A.M.
  Moto Perpetuo
    STB
(HALE, A.M.)
  Pieces from the 18th century, 6
    STB
HALÉVY, JACQUES-FRANCOIS (1799-1862)
  Call Me Thine Own, from L'Eclair
    (Saenger) CF B3001
HALFFTER, ERNESTO (1905-   )
  Dance of the Gypsy, from Sonatina Ballet
    (Heifetz) CF B2249 "Danza de la Gitana"
    ESC
  Dance of the Shepherdess, from Sonatina
      Ballet
    ESC
HALFFTER, RODOLFO (1900-   )
  Pastorale
    Peer
HALKIN, N.
  Serenade
    MZK
HALL, JOHN T.
  Wedding of the Winds
    (Applebaum) Bel SI33

HALVORSEN, JOHAN (1864-1935)
  Danses Norwégiennes
    WH 3164
  Serenader, 2
    Norsk
HAMANN, ERICH (1898-   )
  Adagio, Op. 29
    DOB
  Sonata in a, Op. 16
    DOB
  Sonata, Op. 18
    DOB
  Sonata, Op. 20
    DOB
  Sonatine, Op. 23
    DOB
HAMBLEN, BERNARD
  Smile Through Your Tears
    Chap
HAMILTON, ADELE MCNAIR
  Little solos for beginners, 10
    GS
HANDEL, GEORG FRIEDRICH (1685-1759)
  Adagio in b, from Occasional Oratorio
    ABRS (Mil No. A224)
  Adagio and Allegro
    MZK
  Air and Gigue
    (Brown) Aug
  Airs de Ballet, 15
    Hug (Pet No. A29)
  Andante in D, from Flute Sonata No. 9
    (Klengel) Pet 4164
  Andante and Allegro
    MZK
  Andante larghetto, from Berenice
    ABRS (Mil No. A225)
  Aria. He shall feed His flock, from Messiah
    (Flesch) CF B2058
  Aria. Oh had I Jubal's lyre, from Joshua
    (Flesch) CF B2057
  Bourree, from Sonata No. 5
    ABRS (Mil No. A242)
  Bouree
    (Slatter) STB
  Concerto in b, orig for vla and orch
    (Casadesus) ESC
  Concerto in B flat, Sonata a 5
    (David) SCH
  Entr'acte, from Semele
    (Gordon) Shapiro, Bernstein
  Gavotte in B flat
    Wagenaar
  Hornpipe, from Water Music
    ABRS (Mil No. A226)
  Hornpipe in F
    (Harty) SCH
  Lamento. Who calls my parting soul, from
      Esther
    (Flesch) CF B2056
  Larghetto, from flute sonata in G
    (Hubay) GS
  Larghetto in b
    (Hubay) ZM (Pet No. ZM216)
  Larghetto; with Bouree by Bach
    MZK
  Largo, from Xerxes
    (Ambrosio) CF B2548   simpl
    (Mittell) GS
    (Palaschko) SCH
    (Perlman) CF S3266
    (Polo) Ric 127972
    VL 43   simpl

HANDEL, GEORG FRIEDRICH (cont.)
  Marcia. There the brisk sparkling nectar
    drain, from Choice of Hercules
    (Flesch) CF B2059
  Menuet, from Concerto Grosso No. 5
    (Applebaum) Mil
  Menuett in F
    (Burmester) GS
  Minuet, from Samson
    ABRS (Mil No. A240)
  Minuet; with Rondo by Mozart
    MZK
  Minuet and Allegretto
    (Hanson) Lud S-15A14
  Pastoral Symphony, from Messiah
    (Haddack-Saenger) CF B2723
  Pastorale. Beneath the vine, from Solomon
    (Flesch) CF B2055
  Prayer. Vouchsafe O Lord, from Te Deum
    (Flesch) CF B2054
  Sarabande, from Harpsichord Suite No. 4
    (Klengel) Pet 4165
  Sonatas, 10, orig for fl
    Pet 4554, 4553, 4552 3V vcl ad lib
      Vol 1: Sonatas in a,e,b
      Vol 2: Sonatas in e,G,b
      Vol 3: Sonatas in g,a,C,F
  *Sonatas, 6, Op. 1[26]
    No. 3 in A; No. 10 in g; No. 12 in F;
      No. 13 in D; No. 14 in A; No. 15 in E
    (Auer-Friedberg) CF L846
    (Betti) GS L1545
    (Davisson-Ramin) Pet 4157A,b 2V
      vcl ad lib
    (Doflein) SCH 2V vcl ad lib
    (Francescatti) Int 2V realization by
      K.H. Fuessl
    (Gevaert-Colyns) BRH 2V
    (Grüters-Busch) SIM
    (Hinnenthal) Baer 4004 vcl ad lib
    (Jacobsen) Pet 2475C,D 2V
    (Maglioni) Ric ER2449
    (Sitt) Pet 2475A,b 2V
    (Vidal-Heymann) Senart 5262, 5271 2V
    Aug 8668 2V
    Nov 2V
  Sonatas, 4, Op. 1
    (Hillemann) SCH vcl ad lib
  Sonatas, 2, orig for fl
    (Jensen) Aug 7385
  Sonata in A, Op. 1, No. 3[27]
    (Auer-Friedberg) CF B3280 "No. 1"
    (Hermann) Aug 7376
    (Jensen) Aug 7422
    (Wessely) JWL (Mil No. W1219) "No. 1"
  Sonata in g, Op. 1, No. 10
    (Jensen) Aug 7426
    (Seiffert) BRH vcl ad lib
      "Chamber Sonata No. 11"
    (Wessely) JWL (Mil No. W1219) "No. 2"
  Sonata in F, Op. 1, No. 12
    (Riemann) Aug 7502
    (Wessely) JWL (Mil No. W1219) "No. 3"
    BRH vcl ad lib
      "Chamber Sonata No. 13"

  Sonata in D, Op. 1, No. 13
    (Auer-Friedberg) CF B2703 "No. 4"
    (Jensen) Aug 7427
    (Wessley) JWL (Mil No. W1219) "No. 4"
    BRH vcl ad lib
      "Chamber Sonata No. 14"
  Sonata in A, Op. 1, No. 14
    (Seiffert) BRH vcl ad lib
      "Chamber Sonata No. 15"
    (Wessely) JWL (Mil No. W1219) "No. 5"
  Sonata in E, Op. 1, No. 15
    (Auer-Friedberg) CF B3325 "No. 6"
    (Gibson) Aug 7377
    (Wessely) JWL (Mil No. W1219) "No. 6"
    BRH vcl ad lib
      "Chamber Sonata No. 16"
  Sonata in A
    (Doflein) SCH
  Sonata in A
    (Schradieck) GS L416 realization by
      F. David
  Sonata in D
    (Doflein) SCH
  Sonata in F
    (Doflein) SCH
  Variations
    MZK
HANDEL ALBUMS, Bks. 1-5, 7
  (Lang) Aug 9501-5, 9507 6V
HANESYAN, H.
  Andantino
    ESC
HANSEN, J.
  Largo
    Senart
HAQUINIUS, ALGOT (1886-   )
  Svit
    Gehrmans
HARDELOT, GUY D' (1858-1936)
  Because
    Chap-L
HARMER, D.J.
  Evening, from Prairie Sketches
    CL
  Morning, from Prairie Sketches
    CL
  On a Summer's Day, from Prairie Sketches
    CL
HARRIS, ARTHUR E.
  Blue bells of Scotland. Fantasy
    CF B464
  Home sweet home. Fantasy
    CF B482
  Lullaby. Byl-lo Baby
    CF B462
HARRIS, A.E., see Brayley-Stein-Harris
HARRIS, DONALD
  Fantaisie, orig for vln and orch
    Jobert for rent
HARRIS, F.O.
  Gay Minuet
    Lud S-1565
HARRIS, ROY (1898-   )
  Four Charming Little Pieces
    Mil
  Sonata in 4 movements
    Mil each movement published separately
      1. Fantasy
      2. Dance of Spring
      3. Melody
      4. Toccata
HARRISON, JULIUS (1885-   )
  Bredon Hill. Rhapsody, orig for vln and orch
    BH

---

[26] Numbers are those given to the violin sonatas in Vol. XXVII
of the Handel-Gesellschaft. Op. 1 contains 15 sonatas for a
solo instrument and basso continuo: 6 for violin; 3 for
traversa (flute); 4 for flauto (recorder); 2 for oboe.
[27] Identification of individual sonatas by Handel is compli-
cated by the use of two numbering systems. Some publishers
use the numbers found in the Handel-Gesellschaft; some
simply number the violin sonatas 1 to 6. It is assumed that
the sonatas are in the same order in each system, No. 1
being the same as No. 3 in the Gesellschaft, etc.

HARRISON, JULIUS (cont.)
  Sonnet
    BMC
HARRISON, LOU (1917-   )
  Concerto, see vln and orch
HARSÁNYI, TIBOR (1898-1954)
  Concerto
    Sal
HARSANYI, [TIBOR]
  Chant sans paroles
    Deiss
HARTMANN, [ARTHUR (1881-1956)]
  Matouska Goloboushka
    AMP
  Negro Croon
    AMP
  Prayer
    AMP
HARTMANN, JOHAN PEDER EMILIUS
        (1805-1900)
  Fantasie-Allegro
    WH 770
  Sonate, Op. 8
    WH 172
  Sonate, Op. 39
    WH 173
  Sonate in g, Op. 83, No. 3
    WH 903
HARTMANN, KARL AMADEUS (1905-   )
  Concerto funebre
    SCH
HARTMANN, [THOMAS DE (1885-1956)]
  Menuet Fantastique du Concerto, Op. 66
    Belaieff
  Sonata, Op. 51
    BH
HARTY, [HAMILTON (1879-1941)]
  Concerto in D
    EKN
HARVEY, ALBERT
  Goldenrod
    VL 86   2nd vln ad lib
HASSE, JOHANN ADOLPH (1699-1783)
  Sonata in e
    Hof
HÄSSLER, JOHANN WILHELM (1747-1822)
  Sonatas, 2, in D and G, orig for flute
    MT (Pet No. MV1035)
  Sonatas, 2
    NAG
HATIKWOH
    (Ambrosio) CF B2594   simpl.
HAUBIEL, CHARLES (1892-   )
  Asymmetry, from Epochs
    CP
  En Saga, from Epochs
    CP
  Fear, from Nuances
    CP
  Gentle, from Nuances
    CP
  Gothic Variations
    CP
  Jocose, from Nuances
    CP
  Lullaby
    CP
  Madonna
    CP
  Nocturne, from Epochs
    CP
  Plaintive, from Nuances
    CP

Shadows
  CP
Still, from Nuances
  CP
Sonata in d
  CP
Symmetry, from Epochs
  CP
HAUDEBERT, [LUCIEN (1877-   )]
  Une Légende au vieux Chateäu
    Senart
HAUPTMANN, MORITZ (1792-1868)
  Sonatinas, 3, Op. 10
    (Herrmann) GS L512
    Pet 2948
HAUSER, MISKA (1822-1887)
  À la Hongroise, Op. 50, No. 4
    (Saenger) CF S3027
  Cradle Song in A, Op. 11, No. 2
    (Ambrosio) CF B2536   simpl
    CF S3155
    VL 116   2nd vln ad lib
  Hungarian Rhapsody, Op. 43
    (Saenger) CF 03695
    Pet 2567
  Reverie, Op. 39, No. 3; with Nocturne,
      Op. 39, No. 4
    (Saenger) CF B3190
  Songs without Words, 15
    (Sitt) Pet 1493
HAVE, WILLIAM TEN, see Ten Have
HAVEMANN, G.
  Concerto, Op. 3
    BB
HAWTHORNE, ALICE (1827-1902)
  Mocking bird, see Ambrosio; Berton
  Whispering Hope
    (Applebaum) Bel SI24
HAYDN, JOSEPH (1732-1809)
  Adagio, from String Quartet, Op. 20
    (Forbes) Oxf 20.106
  Adagio
    (Pochon) CF B1253
  Adagio and Presto, from String Quartet,
      Op. 54, No. 2
    (Heifetz) CF B2507
  Bull's Minuet, see Pergolesi: Aria
  Concerto No. 1 in C
    (Davisson-Klengel) BRH
    (Flesch) Pet 4322   with cadenzas
  Concerto No. 2 in G
    (Davisson-Scharwenka) BRH
    (Kuechler) Pet 4182   with cadenzas
    (Spiller) Ric BA11571
  Concerto in A
    (Melk-Heiller) UE   with cadenzas
  Divertimento in B flat
    (Weismann) LEU   vcl ad lib
  Divertimento in F
    (Weismann) LEU   vcl ad lib
  Divertimento in G
    (Weismann) Pet 4964
  Double Concerto in F, orig for vln, pno
      and orch
    (Borman) BH   orch reduction for 2nd pno
  Gypsy Rondo
    (Dietrich-Seredy) CF B3144
  Hungarian Rondo
    (Kreisler) Fol 1198
  Menuet, from "Military" Symphony
    (Nagy) Lud S-1524
  Menuetto
    (Godowsky) Bosw

HAYDN, JOSEPH (cont.)
  Minuet, see Graziolli: Adagio
  Moto Pérpetuo from String Quartet,
      Op. 64, No. 5
      (Applebaum) GS
  Serenade, from String Quartet, Op. 3, No. 5
      (Palaschko) SCH
  Serenade
      (Becker) CF B3284
  Sonatas, 9
      (Betti) GS L1541
      No. 1 in G; No. 2 in D; No. 3 in E flat;
      No. 4 in A; No. 5 in G; No. 6 in C; No. 7
      in D; No. 8 in G, transcription of Quartet,
      Op. 77, No. 1; No. 9 in F, transcription
      of Quartet, Op. 77, No. 2.
  Sonatas, 8
      (David) Aug 8672
  Sonatas, 8
      Pet 190
  Sonata in A, orig for vln and vla
      (Zatschek) DOB
  Sonata in B flat, orig for vln and vla
      (Zatschek) DOB
  Sonata in F, orig for vln and vla
      (Zatschek) DOB
  Symphonies, 3, Nos. 99, 103, 104, arr for
      vln and pno
      Pet 1331A
HAYDN, MICHAEL (1737-1806)
  Concerto in B flat
      (Angerer) DOB
HAZELETT, FRITZI
  Habanera
      Mil
  Tears for Vienna
      CF B3272
HECKER, BERTA JOSEPHINE
  Spanish Dance
      CF B2754
HEGER, [ROBERT (1886-   )]
  Concerto, Op. 16
      UE 5302
HEIDEN, BERNHARD (1910-   )
  Sonata
      AMP
  Sonatina
      AMP
HEIDENROSLEIN
      (Sladek) VL
HEIFETZ, EMANUEL R.
  Gypsy Smoke Dreams
      Mil
  Little Dutch Dolls
      CF B2474   2nd vln ad lib
  Procession
      Mil
(HEIFETZ, JASCHA)
  New Favorite Encore Folio
      CF 02137   for contents see title
HELLMESBERGER, J.
  Ball-Szene
      (Lutz) SCH
HELM, EVERETT (1913-   )
  Sonata
      SCH
HELM, HEINRICH
  Summer Scenes
      (Hintze) BMC
  Sylvan Sketches
      (Stoessel) BMC
HELSTED, GUSTAV (1857-1924)
  Concerto
      Dansk 94

HELTMAN, FRED
  Mary Jane Waltz
      VL 45   2nd vln ad lib
  Merry Christmas March
      VL 100   2nd vln ad lib
  Hansel and Gretel Waltz
      VL 151   2nd vln ad lib
  Her Kiss Valse
      VL 47
HELYER, MARJORIE
  Midsummer's Day; Gay Dance; Morning
      Song; Dainty Measures; Off to Sea
      Aug
  My First Violin Solos
      Aug
  Sketches, 7
      Aug
HEMEL, OSCAR VAN (1892-   )
  Sonata No. 2
      DN (Pet No. D226)
HENRIQUES, FINI (1867-1940)
  Sonate, Op. 10
      WH 3310
  Wiegenlied
      WH 2489
HENRY, J. HAROLD
  Cavatina
      Bosw
  Dans un reve
      Bosw
HENZE, HANS WERNER (1926-   )
  Concerto
      SCH
  Sonata
      SCH
HERBERT, M.
  Enchanted April
      STB
  Giboulee
      STB
HERBERT, VICTOR (1859-1924)
  A la valse
      GS
  Kiss me again
      Bel
  Pensée amoureuse
      GS
  Petite valse
      GS
  Romance
      GS
  Serenade, from Suite, Op. 3
      (Ambrosio) CF B2559
      CF S3431
(HERFURTH, C. PAUL)
  Christmas Carols
      BMC   for contents see title
  Classical Album of Early Grade Pieces
      by Famous Composers
      BMC   for contents see title
  see also Ellert-Herfurth
(HERFURTH-STRIETEL)
  Violin music the whole world loves
      Willis
HERMAN, A.
  Heure de loisir
      Gaudet
  Pièces, 6
      Gaudet
  Reverie
      Gaudet
HERMAN, AD
  Kathleen Mavourneen. Fantaisie,
      Op. 155, No. 5
      CF B3036

HERMAN, AD (cont.)
　Souvenir des Alpes, Op. 91, No. 1
　　CF B3086
HERMANN
　Short Recital Pieces, 15
　　Pet 2247
(HERMANN)
　Classic Pieces
　　Pet 1413A,b,C,D　4V
　　　for contents see title
HÉROLD, LOUIS J.F. (1791-1833)
　Overture, from Zampa
　　(Weiss-Ambrosio) CF
HERRANDO, JOSE
　Affectuese, L'
　　(Nin) ESC
　Aira Mistica
　　(Nin) ESC
　Allègre, L'
　　(Nin) ESC
　Gaillarde, La
　　(Nin) ESC
　Galante, La.
　　(Nin) ESC
　Minuet
　　(Nin) ESC
　Mouvement Perpétuel
　　(Nin) ESC
　Pastorale
　　(Nin) ESC
　Scherzetto
　　(Nin) ESC
　Souveraine, La.
　　(Nin) ESC
HERRMANN, HUGO (1896-　)
　Sonata
　　Sik 534
HERRMANN, TH
　Mignonne gavotte in D, Op. 61
　　CF B3097
　Serenade in F, Op. 50
　　CF B3233
(HERRMANN)
　Easy Sonatas of Old-French Masters
　　SCH　vcl ad lib
　　　Sonatas by Aubert, Dandrieu, and Senaillé
HESELTINE, PHILIP, see Warlock, Peter
HESSENBERG, [KURT (1908-　)]
　Sonata in F, Op. 25
　　SCH
HEUBERGER, RICHARD (1850-1914)
　Midnight Bells, from Opera Ball
　　(Kreisler) Fol 1142
HEYKENS, J.
　Célèbre Sérénade
　　Sal
HIDAS, FRIGYES (1928-　)
　Concertino
　　Kul
HIER, ETHEL GLENN (1889-　)
　Rhapsody
　　CFE
HIGH SCHOOL OF VIOLIN PLAYING
　(David) Pet 3076A,b　2V
　　　Vol 1: Sonatas by Biber, Leclair, Nardini,
　　　　Porpora, Vivaldi; Folies d'Espagne by
　　　　Corelli
　　　Vol 2: Sonatas by J.S. Bach, Geminiani,
　　　　Handel, Locatelli, Tartini, Veracini;
　　　　Ciaconna by Vitali
HILL, ALFRED (1870-　)
　Black Baby
　　Chap-L

HILTON-TURVEY, T.
　Cavatina pathetique
　　STB
HINDEMITH, PAUL (1895-1963)
　Concerto
　　SCH
　Kammermusik No. 4, Op. 36, No. 3, Concerto
　　SCH
　Meditation from Nobilissima Visione
　　SCH
　Music of Mourning, orig for str orch
　　SCH
　Sonata in C
　　SCH
　Sonata in D, Op. 11, No. 2
　　SCH
　Sonata in E
　　SCH
　Sonata in E flat, Op. 11, No. 1
　　SCH
HIRAO, [KISHIO (1907-　)]
　Sonate
　　Leduc
HIVELY, WELLS
　Credo
　　CFE
　Weary Gleaner
　　CFE　score only
HOCHSTEIN, DAVID
　Minuet
　　CF B514
HODGSON
　Supplementary Pieces, see vln study
HOELLER, see Höller
HOLBROOKE, JOSEPH (1878-　)
　Danse Moderne
　　Paxton (Mil No. P502)
HOLLAENDER, GUSTAV (1855-1915)
　Canzonetta
　　VL 117　2nd vln ad lib
HOLLAENDER, VIKTOR (1866-1940)
　Canzonetta in G
　　CF S3122
HOLLANDER, RALPH
　Gitane
　　CF B3324
HÖLLER, KARL (1907-　)
　Musik, Op. 27
　　LEU
　Sonata No. 2 in g, Op. 33
　　Pet 5030
HOLLINS, A.
　Song of Sunshine
　　STB
HOLMBOE, VAGN (1909-　)
　Sonata
　　Dansk 95
HOLMES, MARKWOOD
　Romanza
　　CF B3267
　Tune Town
　　CF 03448
HOLT, PATRICIA BLOMFIELD
　Suite No. 2
　　CL
HOLTON, ALBERT
　Masquerade Party
　　CF B2291　includes 2nd vln part for
　　　teacher
HOME ON THE RANGE
　　(Buchtel) Kjos S-5013
　　(Eckstein) CF M308
　　(Harvey) VL 149　2nd vln ad lib

HONEGGER, ARTHUR (1892-1955)
  Sonate No. 1
    Sal
  Sonate No. 2
    Sal
HOOK, JAMES (1746-1827)
  Little Princess
    (Applebaum) Bel SI28
  Sonata in G, Op. 99
    (Bergmann) SCH
HOSKINS, WILLIAM
  Berceuse
    CFE
  Rondo
    CFE   score only
  Tarantella
    CFE   score only
HOUSE CONCERT
  (Schmidtner) Sik 171-2 2V
    Vol 1
      Bach: Air
      Beethoven: Menuett
      Beethoven: Sechs Deutsche
      Beethoven: Sonatine
      Corelli: Sarabande
      Dittersdorf: Tempo di minuetto
      Händel: Adagio
      Haydn: Serenade
      Mozart: Andante con variazioni
      Pugnani: Andantino amoroso
      Rameau: Gavotte
      Schubert: Polonaise
      Weber: Romanze
    Vol 2
      Brahms: Walzer, Op. 39
      Chopin: Notturno
      Fibich: Poème
      Martini: Plaisir d'amour
      Paganini: Romanze
      Poliakin: Le canari
      Raff: Cavatine
      Tchaikovsky; Walzer, from Serenade
      Wieniawski: Legende
HOVHANESS, ALAN (1911-   )
  Duet, see vln and harpsichord
  Khirgiz Suite, Op. 73, No. 3
    Pet 6547
  Oror, Op. 1
    Pet 6473
  Saris, Op. 67
    Pet 6575
  Shatakh
    Peer
  Three Visions of Saint Mesrob, Op. 198
    Pet 6603
HOWE, MARY (1882-   )
  Sonata in D
    Pet 6469
HOWELL, D.
  Pieces, 2
    SCH
HOWELLS, HERBERT (1892-   )
  "Chosen" Tune
    STB
  Luchinushka
    STB
  Pastorale
    STB
  Sonata in E
    BH
HUBAY, JENÖ (1858-1937)
  Concerto dramatique
    HL
  Concerto No. 24
    Haml

Hejre Kati, Op. 32. Scènes de la
  Csárda No. 4
  (Ambrosio) CF B2554   simpl
  (Mittell) GS
  (Saenger) CF S3159
  Bosw
Hullamzo Balaton, Op. 33. Scènes
  de la Csárda No. 5
  Bosw
Hungarian Gypsy Song, Op. 57, No. 6
  (Schermann) CF B3114
Poèmes Hongrois, Op. 76
  Haml
Rozsa Csardas
  Bosw
Scènes de la Csárda, Nos. 3 and 10
  Haml
Scènes de la Csárda, see also Hejre
  Kati and Hullamzo Balaton
Sonate Romantique
  Haml
Variations on a Hungarian Theme, Op. 72
  SIM
Violin Solo, from Violin Maker of Cremona
  CF B3027
Zephyr, Op. 30, No. 5
  Bosw
  CF B2824
HUBEAU, JEAN (1917-   )
  Concerto en do majeur
    Dur
  Sonate en ut mineur
    Dur
HUBER, ADOLF
  Concertino in d, Op. 5
    Eul (Pet No. Z182)
  Concertino No. 2 in G, Op. 6
    CF B2682
  Concertino in F, Op. 7
    Eul (Pet No. Z169)
  Concertino No. 4 in G, Op. 8
    (Ambrosio) CF S3469
    GS
  Concertino in G, Op. 36
    Eul (Pet No. Z168)
HÜE, GEORGES-ADOLPHE (1858-1948)
  Fantaisie, orig for vln and orch
    Leduc
  Romance
    RL
HUERTER, CHARLES
  Mélodie
    BMC
  Told at Twilight
    BMC
HUGON, [GEORGES (1904-   )]
  Impromptu
    Sal
HUGUET, R.
  Humoresque
    Sal
HUMMEL, JOHANN NEPOMUK (1778-1837)
  Rondo in E flat, orig for pno
    (Heifetz) CF B2250
  Sonata in B flat, Op. 5, No. 1
    (Samohyl) DOB
  Waltz
    BMC
HUMPHRIES, FREDERICK
  Idyll
    JWL (Mil No. W1269)
HUMPHRIES, JOHN
  Sonate en ut mineur
    HL

HUNGARIAN AIRS NO. 1
  (Bagos) VL 138   2nd vln ad lib
HUNGERFORD, EVE
  First Position Violin Pieces for Begin-
      ners, 10
    BMC
HUNT, H.W.
  Short Pieces, 4
    SCH
HURE, JEAN (1877-1930)
  Mélodie
    Mathot
  Petite Chanson
    Mathot
  Sonate en ut mineur
    Mathot
  Sonatine
    Mathot
HURLSTONE, WILLIAM Y. (1876-1906)
  Caprice, from 4 English Sketches
    JWL (Mil No. W1257)
  Pastoral, from 4 English Sketches
    JWL (Mil No. W1256)
  Revelry, from 4 English Sketches
    JWL (Mil No. W1259)
  Romance, from 4 English Sketches
    JWL (Mil No. W1258)
HUSITSKA
  (Harvey) VL 97   2nd vln ad lib
HUYBRECHTS, ALBERT (1899-1938)
  Sonata
    CBDM
I WONDER AS I WANDER
  (Niles-Wright) GS
  (Niles-Wright) GS   simpl
IDLE, HARRY
  Berceuse
    JWL (Mil No. W1242)
  Blarney Stone
    JWL (Mil No. W1226)
  Couronne d'or, La
    JWL (Mil No. W1244)
IGLESIAS VILLOUD
  Cholo
    (Pessina) Ric BA9089
  Criolla
    (Pessina) Ric BA9088
I'LL TAKE YOU HOME AGAIN KATHLEEN
  (Eckstein) CF M310
ILYNSKI, [ALEXANDER (1859-1919)]
  Mazurka
    (Hartmann) AMP
IMBRIE, ANDREW (1921-   )
  Impromptu
    Malcolm
IMMORTAL WALTZES
    SCH   3V
d'INDY, VINCENT (1851-1931)
  Karadec. Chanson
    (Samazeuilh) Heugel
  Sonate en ut, Op. 59
    Dur
INFANTE, [MANUEL (1883-   )]
  Chanson Gitané
    Mathot
INGHELBRECHT, DÉSIRÉ ÉMILE (1880-   )
  Iberiana
    Mathot
  Nocturne
    Mathot
  Sonate
    Sal
INGRAM, J.
  To a Child
    AMP

IORDAN
  Top, see Kirkor: Tadjik Song
IPPOLITOV-IVANOV, MIKHAIL (1859-1935)
  Melody; with Spinning Song by Yanishkov
    MZK
IRELAND, JOHN (1879-1962)
  Bagatelle
    Nov
  Berceuse
    Aug
  Holy Boy
    BH   arr by composer
  Sonata in d
    Aug
  Sonata No. 2 in a
    BH
(ISAAC, MERLE)
  Album of Favorite Violin Solos
    Cole 218   for contents see title
  Melody Book for Strings
    CF 03828A,B
ISAMITT, CARLOS (1887-   )
  Pastorales, Tres
    ECIC
IVANNIKOV, V.
  Poem on Polish Themes
    MZK
IVANOVICI, J. (1848-1905)
  Waves of the Danube
    (Edwards) Mil
    (Halle) Bel 658
    (Marchisio) SCH
    (Tocaben) CF B3156
    VL 71   2nd vln ad lib
IVES, CHARLES E. (1874-1954)
  Sonata No. 1
    Peer
  Sonata No. 2
    GS
  Sonata No. 3
    Pr
  Sonata No. 4, "Children's Day at the Camp
      Meeting"
    AMP
JACHINO, CARLO (1890-   )
  Pastorale di Natale, orig for orch
    Ric 123190
JACKNO, RALPH JOHN
  Fantasia
    CF B3291
JACOB, GORDON (1895-   )
  Concerto
    JWL (Mil No. W1223)   arr for vln and
      pno by composer
  Little Dancer
    JWL (Mil No. W1249)
  Village Dance
    ABRS (Mil No. A253)
JACOBI, FREDERICK (1891-1952)
  Ballade
    (Persinger) CF B2624
  Con movimento dolce, from 3 Preludes
    (Kneisel) CF B2748
  Concerto
    Leeds
  Furioso, from 3 Preludes
    (Kneisel) CF B2747
  Impressions from the Odyssey
    Val
JACOBSON, MAURICE (1896-   )
  Margaret's Minuet
    Leng (Mil No. L1107)
(JACOBSON, MAURICE)
  Pieces, 8, by Old Masters
    Nov

JACOBY, HANOCH (1909-   )
  King David's Lyre
    IMP
JANÁČEK, LEOŠ (1854-1928)
  Romance
    Artia
  Sonata
    Artia
  Sonata, Op. 21
    Artia
JANSA, LEOPOLD (1795-1875)
  Concertino in D, Op. 54
    Eul (Pet No. Z117
JAQUES-DALCROZE, EMILE (1865-1950)
  Berceuse
    RL
  Canzonetta
    RL
  Chant mélancolique
    RL
  Danses frivoles, 4
    Senart
  Romance
    RL
JÁRDÁNYI, PÁL (1920-   )
  Arietta
    Kul
  Concertino
    Kul
  Hungarian Dance
    Kul
  Sonata
    Kul
JARNACH, PHILIPP (1892-   )
  Sonate en mi majeur, Op. 9
    Dur
JÄRNEFELT, ARMAS (1869-1958)
  Berceuse
    (Saenger) CF B3336
JEANJEAN, FAUSTIN & MAURICE
  Balançôire
    Sal
  Danse des Violons, La
    (Dambrosy) Sal
  Violons s'amusent, Les
    Sal
JELINEK, HANNS (1901-   )
  Zehn zahme Xenien
    EDW
JEMNITZ, S.
  Arioso-Intermezzo
    Kul
JENKINSON, EZRA
  Elves Dance
    Bosw
JENSEN, A.
  Serenade
    (Powell) AMP
JERVIS-READ, HAROLD V. (1883-1954)
  Legend
    ABRS (Mil No. A248)
JESSEL, LEON
  Parade of the Wooden Soldiers
    MK
JINGLE BELLS MARCH
    (Harvey) VL 63   2nd vln ad lib
JOHANSEN, DAVID MONRAD (1888-   )
  Sonata in A, Op. 3
    Musikk-Huset
JONES, CHARLES (1910-   )
  Sonatina
    Pet 6019
JONES, RICHARD
  Minuet in G, No. 1 of Six Suites of Lessons
    ABRS (Mil No. A227)

JONES, THOMAS H.
  Memories of Wales
    VL
JONES
  Sonata in D
    (Moffat) Nov
JONGEN, JOSEPH (1873-1953)
  Concerto en si mineur, Op. 17
    Dur
  Légende naive, Op. 59, No. 1, from
    2 Aquarelles
    Ches
  Sonata in D, Op. 27
    Ches
  Sonata No. 2 in E, Op. 34
    Dur
  Valse libre, Op. 59, No. 2, from
    2 Aquarelles
    Ches
JORDAN, [SVERRE (1889-   )]
  Poème Lyrique, Op. 36
    LY (Pet No. LY5)
JOSTEN, WERNER (1885-   )
  Sonata
    AME
  Sonatina
    AME
JOUBERT, JOHN (1927-   )
  Concerto, Op. 13
    Nov
JUON, PAUL (1872-1940)
  Bagatelles, 3, Op. 19
    LN (Pet No. R60)
  Élégie, Op. 72, No. 2
    CF B1763
  Konzert in a, Op. 88
    Birnbach
  Sonate in b, Op. 86
    Birnbach
KABALEVSKY, DMITRI (1904-   )
  Concerto, Op. 48
    Leeds
    Pet 4618
  Improvisation, Op. 21, No. 1
    (Szigeti) Leeds
  Improvisation, see Gliere: Romance
KAFKA, JOHANN (1819-1886)
  Tyrolean Sounds from Home, Op. 118
    CF B3091
KAHN, ERICH ITOR (1905-1956)
  Concerto a Due
    CFE   score only
  Paganini Caprices, 3
    CFE   score only
  Suite
    CFE   score only
KALINNIKOV, VASSILI (1866-1901)
  Chanson Triste
    (Sibrawa-Centano) CF S3698
    MZK
KALMAN, EMMERICH (1882-1953)
  Love's Own Sweet Song, from Sari
    (Grunes) MK
KANITZ, ERNEST (1894-   )
  Suite
    AMP
KAPP, EUGEN (1908-   )
  Estonian Dances, 5
    MZK
  Sonata
    MZK
KAPP & SAPOZHNIN
  Estonian Dance
    MZK

KARAGITCHEFF, B.W.
 Exaltation
  (Hartmann) AMP
KARAYEV
 Lullaby; with Scherzo by Gadzhiev
  MZK
KARGANOFF, G.
 Mazurka
  (Hartmann) AMP
KARGANOFF
 Scherzino
  (Graves) Francis Day & Hunter
KARJINSKY, N.
 Berceuse
  RL
 Capriccio, from 5 Pieces
  ESC
 Dialogue, from 5 Pieces
  ESC
 Guitare, from 5 Pieces
  ESC
 Orientale, from 5 Pieces
  ESC
 Skazka
  ESC
 Sous la fenêtre, from 5 Pieces
  ESC
 Trepak No. 2
  ESC
KARLOWICZ, MIECZYSLAW (1876-1909)
 Concerto, Op. 8
  MZK
KAUFMAN, L.
 Oh, Fairest Varmland
  Pr
KAY, ULYSSES (1917-   )
 Partita in A
  Leeds   in preparation
 Sonatina
  CFE
KAZACSAY, T.
 Little Suite, Op. 111
  Kul
KÉLER-BÉLA (1820-1882)
 Lustspiel Overture
  (Ambrosio) CF
  (Lechner) SCH "Comedy Overture"
 Son of the Plains, Op. 134, No. 2
  CF S3376
  GS "Son of the Puszta"
KELLEY, JOHN CRAIG
 Hey, Diddle, Diddle
  CF B2189
KELLY, BRYAN
 Pieces, 3
  Nov
KELLY, ROBERT (1916-   )
 Sonata
  CFE
KELSEY
 Fiddle de Dum
  Mil
KELTERBORN, RUDOLF (1931-   )
 Essays, 5
  EDW
KENNAWAY, LAMONT
 Exuberance
  STB
KENNEDY, JAMES PAUL
 Lyric Episode
  CP
KERBY, PAUL
 Viennese Memories
  (Elman) CF B2382

KERN
 Etta Waltz
  Willis
 Hispania
  Willis
KERNOCHAN, M.
 Molto cantabile
  Galx
KERR, HARRISON (1897-   )
 Sonata
  CFE
KERSTERS, W.
 Partita, Op. 9
  CBDM
KESNAR
 In the Land of the Czardas
  Pr
 Once Upon a Time
  Pr
KETELBEY, ALBERT W. (1885-1959)
 In a Chinese Temple Garden
  Bosw
 In a Persian Market
  Bosw
KHACHATURIAN, ARAM (1903-   )
 Chante Poem
  (Szigeti) Leeds
 Concerto
  (Oistrakh) Int
  MZK
  Pet 4701
  cadenza published separately, see under
   vln unacc: Oistrakh
 Dance in B flat
  (Persinger) Leeds
 Dance of Ayshe, from Gayne Ballet
  (Heifetz) Leeds
 Lullaby; with Etude by Mostras
  MZK
 Nocturne, from Masquerade Suite
  (Persinger) Leeds
 Sabre Dance, from Gayne Ballet
  (Heifetz) Leeds
 Waltz, from Masquerade
  (Fichtenholz) Pet 4700
KHANDOSHKIN, [IVAN (1747-1804)]
 Canzona; with Etude No. 24 by Lvov
  MZK
 Sonatas, 3, and Aria
  MZK
KIALLMARK
 Old Oaken Bucket
  (Franz) VL 74
KILPATRICK, JACK
 Concertino in g
  CFE
 Forked Deer River. Fantasia on an Ozark
   Folk Tune, Op. 1
  CFE
KILWORTH, CLAUDE
 Tone Poem, Op. 33
  MK
KING GANAM'S CANADIAN FIDDLE TUNES
  CL
KINKEL, CHARLES
 Mountain Bell Schottische
  VL 84   2nd vln ad lib
 Whisperings of Love
  VL 132
KINSEY, HERBERT
 Pastorale
  ABRS (Mil No. A235)
 Serenade
  ABRS (Mil No. A228)

KINSEY, H.H.
Barcarolle
Aug
Canzonetta
Aug
Country Dance, from 3 Contrasted Pieces
Aug
Elegy
Aug
Fisherman's Tale, from 3 Contrasted Pieces
Aug
Greenwood Glades, from 3 Contrasted
Pieces
Aug
Little Fairy Pictures, 4
Aug
KIRCHHOFF, G.
Sonatas, 12
(Serauky) SCH   2V   vcl ad lib
KIRCHNER, LEON (1919-   )
Duo
Mercury
Sonata Concertante
Mercury
KIRKOR, [GUEORGI (1910-   )]
Tadjik Song, Dance; with Top by Iordan
MZK
KJERULF, HALFDAN (1815-1868)
Bridal Party in Hardanger
VL 128   2nd vln ad lib
KLAUSS, N.
Summer Sunset
CP
KLEBANOV, see Shtogarenko & Klebanov
KLEBE, GISELHER (1925-   )
Sonata, Op. 14
SCH
KLEINSINGER, GEORGE (1914-   )
Concerto
Chap
Scherzo
Chap
(KLENGEL)
Classic Pieces. New Series
Pet 3855   for contents see title
KLEVEN, ARVID (1899-1929)
Canzonetta
Musikk-Huset
KLINGSOR, T.
Berceuse de Sylvie
Senart
Sonatine
Senart
KLIUZNER, B.
Concerto
MZK
KNEASS, NELSON
Ben Bolt, see Ambrosio
KNIGHT, MORRIS (1933-   )
Prelude
Tritone   manuscript reproduction
Romance
Tritone   manuscript reproduction
Sonata
Tritone   manuscript reproduction
KNIPPER, LEV (1898-   )
Meadowlands, Cavalry of the Steppes
(Eckstein) CF M306
KNUDSEN, GUNNAR
Noveletta
CP
KOCH, FREDERICK
Three Pictures
Tritone   manuscript reproduction

KOCH, HOWARD LEE
Folk Tunes in Fiddle Finger Forms
BMC   2V
KOCHUROV, Y.
Melody; On the Lake
MZK
KODÁLY, ZOLTÁN (1882-   )
Adagio
Kul
Intermezzo, from Háry Janos
(Szigeti) UE 12147
Valsette
(Telmanyi) Kul
KOECHLIN, CHARLES (1867-1950)
Sonate
Senart
KOEHLER, EMIL
Sonatina
CFE
KOEHLER & ARLEN
Stormy Weather
Sal
KOHS, ELLIS (1916-   )
Sonatina
Mercury
KOKAI, REZSO (1906-   )
Concerto
Kul
Recruiting Rhapsody
Kul
KOLLERITSCH, JOSEF (1897-   )
Sonate, Op. 9
Krenn
KOMAROVSKY, [ANATOLI (1907-   )]
Concerto in G
MZK
Concerto No. 3 in D
MZK
Variations in g
MZK
KOMPANEYETZ, Z.
Ballade; Scherzo
MZK
Bashkir Song and Dance
MZK
KORCHMAREV, K.
Pieces, 3, on Turkmenian Themes
MZK
KORDA
Jura-Jura
(Bakony) Mil
KORNAUTH, EGON (1891-1959)
Sonata in e, Op. 9
DOB
Sonata in D, Op. 15
DOB
Sonatina, Op. 46a
DOB
KORNGOLD, ERICH WOLFGANG (1897-1957)
Pieces, 4, from Much Ado About Nothing
SCH
KOSA, [GYÖRGY (1897-   )]
Violin Pieces, 4
Kul
KOSENKO, V.
Pieces, 2, Op. 4
MZK
Sonata
MZK
KOUGUELL, A.
Berceuse in b
ESC
Danse Orientale, Op. 60
ESC

KOUGUELL, A.(cont.)
Poème
ESC
KOUNADIS, ARGHYRIS (1924-   )
Duo, for fl or vln and pno
EDW
Moments musicaux
EDW
KOUTZEN, BORIS (1901-   )
Nocturne
Leeds
KOVÁCS, CHARLES
Hungarian Rhapsody No. 1, Op. 84
CF B2137
Little Valse
CF B1947
Pizzicato Gavotte, Op. 79
CF B1816
Souvenir Russe, Op. 78
CF B1817
KOZLOVSKY
Adagio; with 3 Waltzes by Zhilin
MZK
Piece; with Dance by Aliabev
MZK
Waltz, see Glinka: Song of Ilininshna
KRAEHENBUEHL, D.
Diptych
AMP
KRAKAUER
Paradise
(Kreisler) Fol 1162
KRAMER, A. WALTER (1890-   )
Eclogue
EMM
Elegy in g, Op. 32, No. 3
BMC
Entr'acte, Op. 46, No. 2
CF B1830
In Elizabethan Days, Op. 32, No. 2
CF B540
Like a Cradle Song, Op. 46, No. 3
CF B1886
Scherzo, Op. 46, No. 5
CF B1888
Symphonic Rhapsody in f, Op. 35
CF 0627
Tango, Op. 46, No. 4
CF B1887
KRANZ, JULIUS
Begin with pieces
Willis
KRANZ
Jolly Juniors
Pr
Wonderland Waltz
Pr
KRAUS, J.
Concerto in C
(Lebermann) BRH
KREBS, L.
Chamber Sonatas, 6
Pet 9024A,B   2V; for fl or vln and
keyboard
KREIN, ALEXANDER (1883-1951)
Dance No. 4
(Heifetz) CF B2702
KREIN, [GRIGORY (1880-   )]
Concert Fantasy
MZK
Pieces, 2, on Yakut Themes
MZK
KREISLER, FRITZ (1875-1962)
Allegretto, in the style of Boccherini
Fol 1006

Allegretto in g, in the style of Porpora
Fol 1002
Andantino, in the style of Martini
Fol 1003
Aubade Provencale, in the style of
Couperin
Fol 1008
Berceuse Romantique
Fol 1009
Caprice Viennois
Fol 1014
Cavatina
Fol 1016
Chanson Louis XIII and Pavane, in the
style of Couperin
Fol 1017
Chasse, La, in the style of Cartier
Fol
Concerto in C, in the style of Vivaldi
Fol 1018
SCH
Gitana, La
Fol 1029
Gypsy Caprice
Fol
Liebesfreud
Fol 1031
Fol 1032   simpl
Liebesleid
Fol 1033
Malaguena
Fol 1037
Menuet, in the style of Porpora
Fol 1038
Old Refrain
Fol 1065
Praeludium and Allegro, in the style of
Pugnani
Fol 1042
Precieuse, La, in the style of Couperin
Fol 1030
Preghiera, in the style of Martini
Fol 1043
Retrospection, from String Quartet in a
Fol 1112
Romance
Fol 1047
Rondino on a theme of Beethoven
Fol 1048
Scherzo, from String Quartet in a
Fol 1174
Scherzo, in the style of Dittersdorf
Fol 1054
Schön Rosmarin
Fol 1055
Sicilienne and Rigaudon, in the style of
Francoeur
Fol 1057
Tambourin Chinois
Fol 1063
Tempo di minuetto, in the style of Pugnani
Fol 1064
Toy Soldiers March
Fol 1066
Viennese Rhapsodic Fantasietta
Fol 1114
KREISLER ASSEMBLED EDITIONS, VOLS.
1 AND 3
Fol 3502, 3504
Vol 1
Beethoven: Rondino, simpl
Dvorak: Negro Spiritual Melody
Foster: Old folks at home
Kreisler: Aucassin and Nicolette

KREISLER ASSEMBLED EDITIONS (cont.)
  Fol 3502, 3504 (cont.)
    Vol 1 (cont.)
      Kreisler: Caprice Viennois, simpl
      Kreisler: Miniature Viennese March
      Kreisler: Syncopation
      Kreisler: Toy Soldiers March
    Vol 3
      Chopin: Mazurka, Op. 67, No. 4
      Couperin: La Precieuse
      Glazounoff: Serenade Espagnole
      Kreisler: Polichinelle
      Kreisler: Shepherd's Madrigal
      Leclair: Tambourin
      Mendelssohn: May breeze, Op. 62,
        No. 1
      Porpora: Allegretto
      Schubert: Ballet music, from
        Rosamunde
      Weber: Larghetto
KREISLER FAVORITE ENCORE FOLIO
  (Kreisler) CF 01290
    Bach-Kreisler: Gavotte in E
    Bizet-Godard: Adagietto, from
      L'Arlesienne
    Brahms-Hochstein: Waltz in A
    Grasse: Song without words in G
    Mendelssohn-Kreisler: Song without
      words
    Millocker-Winternitz: Blue lagoon
    Rameau-Kreisler: Tambourin
    Schuett-Friedberg: Slavonic lament
    Townsend-Saenger: Berceuse
    Valdez: Serenade du tsigane
    White: Nobody knows the trouble I've
      seen, from Bandanna Sketches
    Willeke: Chant sans paroles
(KREITNER)
  Concert Pieces, 6
    MZK
KRENEK, ERNST (1900-   )
  Marginal Sounds, see vln and orch
  Sonata
    UE 11839
(KRENTZLIN)
  Operas and Operettas
    SCH   2V
KREUTZER, RODOLPHE (1766-1831)
  Concerto No. 13 in D
    (Brun-Kaiser) Senart 5084
    (Davisson) Pet 1091A   with cadenzas
    CF 03480
  Concerto No. 14 in A
    (Hermann) Pet 1091b   with cadenzas
  Concerto No. 18 in e
    (Brun-Kaiser) Senart 5085
    (Hermann) Pet 1091D   with cadenzas
  Concerto No. 19 in d
    (Auer) CF 03386
    (Davisson) Pet 1091D   with cadenzas
  Perpetuum mobile
    (Linz) SCH
  Sonate No. 1, from 3 Sonates faciles.
    (Kaiser-Hardy) Senart 5243
  Sonate No. 2, from 3 Sonates faciles.
    (Kaiser-Hardy) Senart 5244
  Sonate No. 3, from 3 Sonates faciles.
    (Kaiser-Hardy) Senart 5245
KRIUKOV, [VLADIMIR (1902-   )]
  Romance; Elegy
    MZK
  Sonata
    MZK

KROGMANN, C.W.
  Robin's lullaby from Zephyrs from
    melodyland, Op. 15
    GS
  Zephyrs from melodyland, Op. 15
    GS
KROL, BERNHARD (1920-   )
  Sonata, Op. 8
    SIM
KROLL, LOUIS
  Perpetual Motion
    (Heifetz) CF B2484
KROLL, WILLIAM (1901-   )
  Banjo and fiddle
    GS
  Caprice
    GS
  Contra Dance
    GS   2nd vln ad lib
  Donkey Doodle
    GS   2nd vln ad lib
  Happy-go-lucky
    GS
  Pantomime
    GS
  Peter Rabbit
    GS   2nd vln ad lib
  Polka
    GS   2nd vln ad lib
KRON, LOUIS & SAENGER, GUSTAV
  Ach, wie ist's möglich dann. Fantasia
    CF B3167
  Adeste Fideles. Fantasia
    CF B3217
  Carnival of Venice. Fantasia
    CF B3004
  Home sweet home. Fantasia
    CF B3031
  Nearer, my God to Thee. Fantasia
    CF B3056
  O Sanctissima. Fantasia
    CF B3153
  Old folks at home. Fantasia
    CF B3061
  Stille nacht, heilige nacht. Fantasia
    CF B3238
KRUMPHOLTZ, JOHANN BAPTIST (1742-1790)
  Sonata in F
    (Zingel) NAG
KRYUKOV, see Kriukov
KUBIK, GÁIL (1914-   )
  Concerto in D
    Chap
  Soliloquy and Dance
    SMP
KÜCHLER, F.
  Concertino in G, Op. 11
    Bosw (Bel No. 9)
  Concertino in D, Op. 12
    Bosw (Bel No. 10)
  Concertino in D, Op. 14
    Hug (Pet No. A44)
  Concertino in D, Op. 15
    Bosw (Bel No. 21)
KUHLAU, FRIEDRICH (1786-1832)
  Duos Brillants, 3, Op. 110
    Lit (Pet No. L562)
KULLMANN, ALFRED
  Sonate
    Senart
KUNTNER, LEOPOLD
  Sonatina in D
    OBV

KVELVE, RUDOLPH
  Birds in Springtime
    VL 120   2nd vln ad lib
  Boy Scouts March
    VL 113   2nd vln ad lib
  Norwegian Lullaby
    VL 109   2nd vln ad lib
  Pitter-Patter
    VL 124   2nd vln ad lib
  Tick Tock
    VL 108   2nd vln ad lib
  Winnebago Suite
    VL,
L'ABBÉ, [JOSEPH (1727-1803)]
  Sonate en ré majeur
    HL
LABEY, MARCEL (1875-   )
  Sonate
    RL
LABROCA, [MARIO (1896-   )]
  Sonatina
    SZ
LACK, [THÉODORE (1864-1921)]
  Arietta
    (Hartmann) AMP
  Gavotte et Musette
    Benoit
  Menuet alsacien
    Benoit
LACOMBE, PAUL (1837-1927)
  Sonate en la mineur
    Haml
  Sonate No. 2
    Haml
  Sonate No. 3
    Haml
LADMIRAULT, PAUL (1877-1944)
  Sonate en Sol majeur
    Heugel
LAJTAI, L.
  Valse Caprice
    SZ
LAJTHA, LÁSZLÓ (1891-1963)
  Sonatine, Op. 13
    Leduc
  Sonate No. 2, Op. 28
    Leduc
LAKE, HAROLD C.
  Pieces, 3
    Oxf 23.003
LALO, EDOUARD (1823-1892)
  Allegro maestoso
    Billaudot
  Aubade, from Le Roi d'Ys
    (Szigeti) CF B2447   Concert and simpl
      versions
  Chants Russes, from Concerto, Op. 29
    Senart 5383
  Concerto in f, Op. 20
    Dur
    Pet 3796
  Concerto Russe, Op. 29
    (Hermann) Pet 3798
  Fantaisie Norvégienne, orig for vln
      and orch
    Haml
  Fantaisie originale, Op. 1
    Billaudot
  Guitare
    Haml
  Pastorale, Op. 8
    Billaudot
  Sonate, Op. 12
    Dur

  Symphonie Espagnole, Op. 21, orig for
      vln and orch
    (Francescatti) Int
    (Lichtenberg) GS L1236
    (Menuhin) Pet 3797A
    (Pessina) Ric BA9125
    BRH
    CF 03422
    Dur
LAMBERT, CECILY
  Acrobats
    BMC
  Cuban Spell
    BMC
  Rhumba Rhythm
    BMC
LAMBERT, LOUIS
  When Johnny Comes Marching Home
    (Eckstein) CF M319
LANDAU, VICTOR
  Scherzo
    CFE
LANG, [CRAIG SELLAR (1891-   )]
  Miniature Suite, Op. 10
    Aug AS.90
(LANG, C.S.)
  Handel Albums, Bks. 1-5, 7
    Aug 9501-5, 9507   6V
LANGE, GUSTAV (1830-1899)
  Flower Song, Op. 39
    (Ambrosio) CF B2535   simpl
    VL 15
LANGER, G.
  Grossmütterchen, Op. 20
    (Palaschko) SCH   2nd vln ad lib
LANTIER, P.
  Ménétrier, Le. Mouvement concertante
    ESC
LAPIS, SANTO
  Easy Sonatas, 3, Op. 1
    (Ruf) SCH   vcl or gamba ad lib
LA PRESLE, JACQUES DE (1888-   )
  Chanson Intime
    RL
  Sonate
    RL
LARA, AGUSTIN
  Granada
    SMP
LARGHETTO
    (D'Ambrosio) Ric 129413
LARSSON, LARS-ERIK (1908-   )
  Concertino, Op. 45, No. 8
    Gehrmans
LATANN, C.
  Frei weg, March
    (Lechner) SCH
LATES
  Sonata in G
    (Moffat) Nov
LAUB, [FERDINAND (1832-1875)]
  Polonaise in G, Op. 8
    Pet 1093
LAURENT, LÉON
  Menuet en ré
    RL
  Rondeau Mignon
    RL
LAURICELLA, [REMO (1912-   )]
  African Interlude
    BH
LAUWERYNS, GEORGES
  Sonate
    Senart

LAVIOLETTE, [WESLEY (1894-   )]
  Sonata
    AMP
LAVRY, MARC (1903-   )
  Hora, from 3 Jewish Dances
    IMP
  Sher, from 3 Jewish Dances
    IMP
  Yemenite Wedding Dance, from 3 Jewish
    Dances
    IMP
LAZZARI, SYLVIO (1857-1944)
  Rapsodie, orig for vln and orch
    Heugel
  Sonate, Op. 24
    Dur
LEACH, ROWLAND (1885-   )
  Impromptu
    CF B1861
LE BLANC
  Sonate en mi bemol majeur
    HL
LEBORNE, FERNAND (1862-1929)
  Sonate, Op. 29
    Haml
LE BOULCH
  Lamento
    Ricard
(LECHNER)
  Easy March Book
    SCH
LECLAIR, JEAN-MARIE (1697-1764)
  Adagio, from Concerto No. 2 in D
    (Cellier) Senart 5473
  Concerto in d, Op. 7, No. 1
    Pet 2967A
  Concerto No. 2
    (Borrel) Senart 5381
  Gigue
    (Barrère) GS
  Musette
    (Barrère) GS
  Pieces, 7
    Kul
  Sarabande and Tambourin
    (Tolhurst) Paxton (Mil No. P512)
  Sonata in A, Op. 1, No. 5[28]
    (Ruf) Baer 3411   vcl ad lib
  Sonata in A, Op. 9, No. 1
    (Polnauer) CF B3347
  Sonata in A, Op. 9, No. 4
    (Polnauer) CF B3348
  Sonata No. 5 in A
    ESC
  Sonata No. 9 in A
    ESC
  Sonata in a, Op. 5, No. 7
    (Ruf) Baer 3415   vcl ad lib
  Sonata No. 1 in a
    ESC
  Sonata in b, Op. 5, No. 5
    (Ruf) Baer 3414   vcl ad lib
  Sonata in b
    (Ruf) Ric SY501
  Sonata in b
    (Reyes) CF B2974
  Sonata No. 12 in b
    ESC
  Sonata No. 3 in B flat
    ESC

Sonata No. 11 in B flat
    ESC
  Sonata in C, Op. 11, No. 3
    (Ruf) Ric SY500
  Sonata No. 2 in C
    ESC
  Sonata in c, "Le Tombeau"
    (David) Int
    (Jacobsen) Pet 4369
  Sonata in D, Op. 9, No. 6
    (Polnauer) CF B3349
  Sonata No. 3 in D
    (Lichtenberg) GS L722
  Sonata in D
    (Moffat) SIM
  Sonata No. 4, in D
    ESC
  Sonata No. 10 in D
    ESC
  Sonata No. 6 in e
    ESC
  Sonata in e
    (Bouillard) ESC
  Sonata in F, Op. 2, No. 2
    (Ruf) Baer 3412   vcl ad lib
  Sonata No. 7 in F
    ESC
  Sonata in G, Op. 2, No. 5
    (Ruf) Baer 3413   vcl ad lib
  Sonata No. 8 in G
    ESC
  Sonata in G
    SCH
  Suite de 3 Pièces
    (Reuchsel) Senart 5256
LECUONA, ERNESTO (1896-1963)
  Andalucia, from Andalucia Suite
    (Stone) MK
  Malaguena, from Andalucia Suite
    (Stone) MK
LE DUC, SIMON (1748-1777)
  Sonatas, 4
    (Doflein) SCH   2V
LEE, E. MARKHAM (1874-1956)
  Easy Pieces, 4
    Leng
LEE, NOEL (1924-   )
  Dialogues
    Pr
LEEMANS, P.
  Croquis Chinois
    Cranz
LEEUW, TON DE (1924-   )
  Sonata
    DN (Pet No. D228)
LEFFLOTH, MATTHIAS (? -1733)
  Concerto in D
    (Ruf) NAG
LE FLEM, PAUL (1881-   )
  Sonate en sol mineur
    HL
LE FLEMING, CHRISTOPHER (1908-   )
  Air and Dance
    Ches
LEGLEY, VICTOR (1915-   )
  Burlesque
    CBDM
  Sonata, Op. 12
    CBDM
  Summer Poem No. 1, Op. 51
    CBDM
LE GRAND, R.
  Fantaisie en La majeur
    RL

---

[28] The Leclair sonatas are arranged by key because there
is no system of identification by opus numbers, or other
numbers, in general use.

LE GRAND, R.(cont.)
Sicilienne
CH (Pet No. C363)
LEGRIS, P
Mélodie sur une petite étude de
Schumann, Op. 68
Gaudet
Pastorale
Gaudet
LE GUILLARD, [ALBERT (1887-   )]
Andantino
Gaudet
Sonate
Gaudet
LEHAR, FRANZ (1870-1948)
Frasquita Serenade
(Kreisler) Fol 1105
(Kun) MK
Gold and Silver Waltz
(Garrison) MK
Merry Widow Waltz
(Ambrosio) CF B2596   simpl
(Applebaum) Mil
(Eckstein) CF M316
(Halle) Bel 668
VL 58   2nd vln ad lib
Vilia, from The Merry Widow
(Klein) Chap
LEHMAN, A
Concerto
MZK
(LEHMANN, GEORGE)
Pieces, 25, in the first position
GS for contents see title
LEHMBERG, E.
Zapateado
UME
LEIBOWITZ, [RENÉ (1913-   )]
Rapsodie Concertante, Op. 36
BMP   blueprint
LEICHTE HAUSMUSIK
(Doflein) SCH
6 easy little suites from an old collec-
tion, ca. 1740
LEIGHTON, KENNETH (1929-   )
Concerto, Op. 12
Nov
Nocturne
Nov
Sonata
Leng (Mil No. L1119)
Sonata No. 2
Leng (Mil No. L1132)
LEKEU, GUILLAUME (1870-1894)
Sonate en sol
RL
LEMAIRE, G
Gavotte des Mathurins
Gilles
LEMARE, EDWIN H. (1865-1934)
Andantino
(Saenger) CF B3343
VL 135
Andantino; with Élégie by Massenet
(Trinkaus) Fill
(LENZEWSKI)
Sonatinas and Pieces
SCH   2V
Works by Beethoven, Fischer, Handel,
Haydn, Purcell, Telemann and others
LÉONARD, HUBERT (1819-1890)
Ane et le meunier, L', Op. 61, No. 4, from
Scènes humoristiques
Billaudot

Au fond des bois, Op. 61, No. 2, from
Scènes humoristiques
Billaudot
Chatte et souris, Op. 61, No. 3, from
Scènes humoristiques
Billaudot
Concerto No. 1, Op. 10
Billaudot
Concerto No. 2, Op. 14
Billaudot
Concerto No. 3, Op. 16
Billaudot
Coq et poules, Op. 61, No. 1, from
Scènes humoristiques
Billaudot
Sérénade du lapin belliqueux, Op. 61,
No. 5, from Scènes humoristiques
Billaudot
Solos, 6, Op. 41
(Schill) GS L912
Solos progressifs, 6, Op. 62
Billaudot   published separately
Progressive solo, in B flat, Op. 62
GS
LEONCAVALLO, RUGGIERO (1858-1919)
Pagliacci: Selection
(Saenger) CF
Vesti la giubba, from Pagliacci
(Halle) Bel 676
LERPERGER, KURT (1921-   )
Allegretto
OBV
Andante
OBV
LESSARD, JOHN (1920-   )
Duo Sonata in 5 Movements
CFE   score only
LET US HAVE MUSIC FOR VIOLIN
(Perlman) CF 03206-7   2V
Vol 1
Adams: Holy City
Bland: Carry me back to old
Virginny
Brahms: Famous Waltz
Brahms: Hungarian Dance No. 5
Cucaracha, La
Dark Eyes
Foster: Jeanie with the light
brown hair
Foster: Old black Joe
Gounod: Waltz, from Faust
Home on the range
Humperdinck: Evening prayer
Humperdinck: Theme from Hansel
and Gretel
Kol Nidrei
Liliuokalani: Aloha Oe
Liszt: Liebestraume
Londonderry Air
Meacham: American patrol
Mendelssohn: On wings of song
Pergolesi: Tre giorni, from Nina
Ponce: Estrellita
Rossini: Fanfare, from William Tell
Saint-Saens: Excerpt from Danse
Macabre
Schubert: Ave Maria
Schubert: Theme from ''Unfinished''
Symphony
Simonetti: Madrigale
Song of the Volga boatmen
Star-Spangled Banner
Strauss: Blue Danube Waltz
Strauss: Tales from the Vienna Woods

LET US HAVE MUSIC FOR VIOLIN (cont.)
  (Perlman) CF 03206-7 2V (cont.)
    Vol 1 (cont.)
      Sullivan: Lost chord
      Swing low, sweet chariot
      Tchaikovsky: Theme from Romeo and
        Juliet
      Turkey in the straw
      Two guitars
    Vol 2
      All through the night
      Auld lang syne
      Ay, Ay, Ay
      Beethoven: Turkish March
      Believe me if all those endearing
        young charms
      Bishop: Home sweet home
      Bull: Nordic song
      Carnival of Venice
      Cui: Orientale
      Denza: Love song
      Drigo: Valse bluette
      Drink to me only with thine eyes
      Handel: Largo
      Hatikwoh:
      Hummel: Waltz
      Lemare: Andantino
      Massenet: Last dream of the Virgin
      Mlynarski: Mazurka
      Mozart: Minuet, from Don Giovanni
      Nobody knows the trouble I've seen
      Rimsky-Korsakov: Excerpt from
        Scheherazade
      Rubinstein: Melody in F
      Sarasate: Gypsy air
      Schubert: Ballet music, from Rosamunde
      Schubert: Serenade
      Schumann: Happy farmer
      Schumann: Traumeri
      Scott: Annie Laurie
      Sibelius: Theme from Finlandia
      Steal away
      Tchaikovsky: None but the lonely heart
      Tchaikovsky: Theme from Piano
        Concerto No. 1
      Vieuxtemps: Ballade
      Wieniawski: Themes from Souvenir de
        Moscou
LEVINE, M.
  Chanson Triste, Op. 6
    MZK
  Elegy, Op. 13
    MZK
LEVITIN, [YURI (1912-   )]
  Sonata
    MZK
LEVY, ELLIS
  Cariole
    CF B1204
  Coronado
    CF B2297
  Ghost Dance
    CF B1205
  Gypsy
    CF B2296
LÉVY, HENIOT (1879-1946)
  Passacaglia
    (Sametini) CF B1311
LEWANDO, RALPH
  Minuet
    CF B2123
LEWIS, GEORGE
  Boston Beauty March
    VL 31   2nd vln ad lib

LEWIS
  Lovely Day
    Pr
LIADOV, ANATOL K. (1855-1914)
  Musical Snuff Box, orig for pno
    MZK
  Prelude; Little Waltz
    MZK
(LIADOV)
  Russian Folk Songs, 10
    MZK
LICHNER, H.
  Along the Brook
    (Applebaum) Bel SI25
  Gypsy Dance
    (Applebaum) Bel SI19
  Lily, Op. 160, No. 8
    (Applebaum) Bel SI20
  Tulip, Op. 111, No. 4
    (Applebaum) Bel SI32
LIDDICOAT, J.G.
  Director's Choice March
    VL 32   2nd vln ad lib
  Morenas, Las
    VL 104   2nd vln ad lib
  Our Institute March
    VL 10   2nd vln ad lib
LIE, SIGURD (1871-1904)
  Snow
    (Szigeti) CF B2404
    (Szigeti) CF B2405   simpl
LIEBMAN, HERMAN
  March of the Wooden Soldier
    CF B2228
LIEDERLAND
  (Cockburn) BH
    7 songs by Brahms & Schubert
(LIEPMANN)
  Songs and Marches by Famous Composers
    GS   for contents see title
LILIUOKALANI
  Aloha Oe
    (Eckstein) CF M317
    (Kreisler) Fol
  Aloha Oe; with Like no a like
    (Ambrosio) CF B3239
LILY OF THE VALLEY
  (Maresh) VL 89   2nd vln ad lib
LINCKE, PAUL (1866-1946)
  Gavotte des vers luisants
    Deiss
  Glow-Worm
    MK
LINDE, BO (1933-   )
  Concerto, Op. 18
    Gehrmans
LINK, JOACHIM DIETRICH (1925-   )
  Sonata in b
    BRH
LINZ, M.
  Alte Spielmannsweise
    SCH
  Dialogo
    SCH
  Spanish Serenade
    SCH
LIONCOURT, GUY DE (1885-   )
  Petite Suite dans le style ancien
    Senart
LIPINSKY, CARL (1790-1861)
  Capriccios, 4
    MZK
  Concerto Militare in D, Op. 21
    Pet 2642

LIPKIN, MALCOLM
Sonata
Ches
LISZT, FRANZ (1811-1886)
Au Lac de Wallenstadt
(Mitnitzky) AMP
Duo
SMP
Hungarian Rhapsody No. 2, orig for pno
(Falk) Kul
(Sitt) CF 03303
(Windsperger) SCH
Liebesträume, Nocturne No. 3, orig for pno
(Halle) Bel 697 "Dreams of Love"
(Larsen) SCH
(Saenger) CF S3572 "Dreams of Love"
(Such) GS "Love's Dream"
Ric 128089 "Sogni d'amore"
LITEN EKORN
(Kvelve) VL 139
LIVIABELLA, [LINO (1902-   )]
Sonata in un tempo
Ric 124666
LLOYD, NORMAN (1919-   )
Pieces, 3
AMP
LLOYD
Morning Song, from 4 Miniatures
JWL (Mil No. W1277)
LOBKOVSKY, A.
Suite
MZK
LOCATELLI, PIETRO (1695-1764)
Largo in F, from Sonata, Op. 8, No. 1
Pet 4227
Sonata in D
HL
Sonata in f, "Le Tombeau"
(Ysaye) SF (Pet No. SCH27)
Sonata in f
(Powell) GS L1096   realization by
L.A. Zellner
Sonata in G
(Moffat-Mlynarczyk) SIM
Sonata in g
Carisch
LOEILLET, JEAN-BAPTISTE (1680-1730)
Sonata in A
HL
Sonata in a
(Salmon) Ric R364
Sonata in B flat
HL
Sonata in D
(Moffat-Mlynarczyk) SIM
Sonata in D
(Salmon) Ric R737
Sonata in D
HL
Sonata in G
(Salmon) Ric R365
Sonata in G
(Salmon) Ric R738
Sonata in g
HL
LOEWE, FREDERICK (1904-   )
My Fair Lady. Selections
Chap
LOKSHIN, A.
Hungarian Fantasy
MZK
LOLLI, [ANTONIO (c.1730-1802)]
Sonate, 6, Op. 1
(Gatti) Ric ER664

LONDONDERRY AIR
(Ambrosio-Perlman) CF B2589
(Eckstein) CF M318
(Edward) MK
(Kreisler) Fol 1131
(Kvelve) VL 136
(Spalding) VL
BMC
LONGAS, [FEDERICO (1895-   )]
Malaguena, from 2 Petites Pièces
Espagnoles
Senart
Sevillana, from 2 Petites Pièces
Espagnoles
Senart
LONGO, ACHILLE (1900-1954)
Sonatina
Curci
LONQUE, G.
Estrella
CBDM
Poem of the sea, Op. 19
CBDM
LOPATNIKOFF, NIKOLAI (1903-   )
Concerto Op. 26
AMP
Sonata No. 2, Op. 32
Leeds
LÓPEZ BUCHARDO, CARLOS (1881-1948)
Campera
(Napolitano) Ric BA11311
LORJE, M.
Dans un Rêve
Gaudet
LOUEL, JEAN (1914-   )
Concerto
CBDM
Sonata
CBDM
Tema con Variazioni
CBDM
LOVELL, J.
Bartholomew Fair
STB
LOVELL, JOAN & REEKS, GERTRUDE
Tuning Up
Oxf 23.108
LOVELOCK, WILLIAM (1899-   )
Easy Miniatures, 4
Chap-L
LUCAS, LEIGHTON (1903-   )
Concert Champêtre
Ches
Soliloquy
JWL (Mil No. W1268)
LUCK, ANDREW
Menuet
VL 78   2nd vln ad lib
LUDWIG, CARL
Christmas Night
Lud S-1550
LUENING, OTTO (1900-   )
Andante and Variations
CFE
Legend
CFE
Short Fantasy
CFE
Sonata
CFE
LUIGINI, ALEXANDRE (1850-1906)
Air de ballet No. 1, from Ballet Egyptien
(Saenger) CF B3187

LULLY, JEAN-BAPTISTE (1632-1687)
Air tendre
(Zighéra) ESC
Aria e Corrente
(Corti) Carisch
Ballet des Muses. Entrée d'Orphée
(Pincherle) Senart 5390
Gavotte
(Winn) CF S3220
Gavotte, see Deplan: Entrada
Melody
(Spalding) CF B1222
Pieces, 20
Hug (Pet No. A27)
(LUTZ)
My Violin Book
SCH   2nd vln and vcl ad lib
11 melodies by Gossec, Mozart, Handel,
Mendelssohn, Tschaikovsky and others
Unterhaltungs-Konzert
SCH   2V
A collection of semi-classical selections
by Braga, Lortzing, Strecker, Strauss
and others
LUZZATTI
Humoresque
Ric BA11247
LVOV, [ALEXEY F. (1798-1870)]
Etudes, 2
MZK
Etude No. 24, see Khandoshkin: Canzona
MACALISTER
Irish Suite
Pigott (Mil No. PT407)
MACBETH, ALLAN (1856-1910)
Forget Me Not, Op. 22
CF B3139
VL 81
Love In Idleness
(Ambrosio) CF B35   simpl
(Hofmann-Saenger) CF B700
MCBRIDE, ROBERT (1911-   )
Fine Thought
CFE   score only
Prelude
CFE
Quietude
CFE
Stuff
CFE   score only
Variety Day, orig for vln and orch
CFE
MACCANN
Little Tunes. A simple suite
JWL (Mil No. W1281)
Tunes from the Countryside
JWL (Mil No. W1282)
MACCOLL, HUGH F.
Suite in A
Templ
MACCOY, WILLIAM J. (1854-1926)
Sonate
Senart
MACDOWELL, EDWARD (1861-1908)
Midsummer Lullaby, Op. 47, orig for voice
(Hartmann) AMP
Robin sings in the apple tree, Op. 47, orig
for voice
AMP
To a wild rose, orig for pno
(Applebaum) Bel SI23
(Isaac) CF B3319
MACHAN, BENJAMIN, see Gusikoff & Machan

MACHAVARIANI, A.
Concerto
MZK
MACKAY, NEIL
Four Modern Dance Tunes
Aug
MACKAY, NEIL & TATE, PHYLLIS
Melodies, 22, from Position Changing for
the Violin
Oxf
MACKLEAN, CHARLES
Sonata No. 9
(Bullock) Oxf 74.106
MACKLIN, CHARLES B.
Cradle Song, No. 3 of Cavalier Series
CF B1980
Jig, No. 1 of Cavalier Series
CF B1978
Minuet, No. 2 of Cavalier Series
CF B1979
MACMURRAY, FREDERICK
Souvenir, Op. 12
CF B2500
MAGAZINE, SAMUEL
Doubt, No. 1 of Human Adventure
CF B3269
Hope, No. 2 of Human Adventure
CF B3270
Triumph, No. 3 of Human Adventure
CF B3271
MAGHINI, RUGGERO
Canzone. Song for a Winter Evening
(Pierangeli) SZ
MAGIC FIDDLE, Vol. 6
(Seybold) SIM
(MAGLIONI)
Antologia violinistica
Ric ER2651
MAGNARD, ALBÉRIC (1865-1914)
Sonate, Op. 13
RL
MAGNIFICO
Serenata
Ric BA10747
(MAGYARY, I.)
Play Up Gypsy
Kul
MAHLER, GUSTAV (1860-1911)
Adagietto, from Symphony No. 5
Pet 3497
MAHY, A.
Almeria
Cranz
MAIKAPAR, S.
Bagatelles
MZK
MAINARDI, ENRICO (1897-   )
Sonata
SCH
Sonatina
SZ
MALIPIERO, GIAN FRANCESCO (1882-   )
Arménia
Senart
Concerto
Carisch
MALIPIERO, RICCARDO (1914-   )
Concerto
SZ
Sonata
SZ
MALOTTE, ALBERT HAY (1895-   )
Lord's prayer
(Kroll) GS

MALTESE, FRANCESCO
  Mazurka Militaire, Op. 25, No. 1
    CF B1319
MAMEDOV, I.
  Symphonic Variations
    MZK
MAMLOK, URSULA
  Designs, 1962
    CFE   score only
MANÉN, [JOAN (1883-   )
  Caleseras, from 5 Spanish Melodies
    UE 10984
  Caprice No. 3
    Mil
MANGEAN
  Sonate en fa majeur
    HL
MANHIRE, WILSON
  Fiddle Fancies
    Leng (Mil No. L1105)
  Impromptu
    STB
  Rowing Song in A
    STB
MANOILOVITCH-MILOIEVITCH
  Danses, 2
    RL
MANZONI, GIACOMO (1932-   )
  Little Suite No. 2
    SZ
MARAIS, MARIN (1656-1728)
  Old French Dances, 5
    (Aldis-Rowe) Ches
MARC
  Suite en Ré
    (Reuchsel) Senart 5255
MARCELLO, BENEDETTO (1686-1739)
  Concerto in D
    (Nachèz) SCH
  Pavane in g
    (Franko) RE (Pet No. RE7)
  Scherzando; with Round Dance by Porpora,
      Gigue by dall'Abaco, Minuet by
      Boccherini
    MZK
  Sonata in a
    (Ermeler) Noet (Pet No. N3278)   vcl ad lib
  Sonata in B flat
    (Ermeler) Noet (Pet No. N3277)   vcl ad lib
  Sonata in B flat
    (Pearson) Oxf 70.710
  Sonata in e
    (Salmon) Ric R367
  Sonata in G
    (Ermeler) Noet (Pet No. N3279)   vcl ad lib
  Sonata in G
    (Salmon) Ric R368
  Sonata in G
    (Salmon) Ric R369
  Sonata in g
    (Salmon) Ric R370
MARCH OF THE MEN OF HARLECH
  (Kvelve) VL 77   2nd vln ad lib
MARCHAND, JOSEPH
  Suite Sonate
    HL
MARCHETTI, F.D.
  Fascination
    (Sandler) Liber-S
MARCKHL, ERICH (1902-   )
  Plomberger Dances
    OBV
  Sonata in D
    DOB

MAREO, E.
  Chansonnette
    EKN
MARGOLA, FRANCO (1908-   )
  Sonata Breve No. 3
    SZ
MARIE, GABRIEL (1852-1928)
  Cinquantaine, La
    (Ambrosio) CF B2597   simpl
    (Halle) Bel 653
    (Mittell) GS
    CF S3148
    VL 101   2nd vln ad lib
  Sérénade Badine
    CF B3290
    VL 14
MARINES' HYMN
  (Eckstein) CF M303
MARINI, BIAGIO (c.1595-1665)
  Romanesca, La, see Solo Violin Music
      of the Earliest Period
MARJANCE, NA. BOHEMIAN MARCH
  (Maresh) VL 7   2nd vln ad lib
MARSHALL, LOIS
  May morning
    CP
  Winds in the pines
    CP
MARSICANI, M.
  Souvenir of the Volga, Op. 35
    MZK
MARTELLI, [HENRI (1895-   )]
  Concertino No. 2, Op. 84
    ESC
  Sonata
    ESC
  Three Short Movements, Op. 53
    ESC
(MARTIN, DOROTHY)
  Christmas Carols
    Aug
MARTIN, E.
  Evensong
    BH
MARTIN, FRANK (1890-   )
  Concerto
    UE 11678
  Sonata, Op. 1
    Hug (Pet No. A53)
  Sonata
    UE 12874
MARTINI, GIAMBATTISTA (1706-1784)
  Arietta
    (Corti) Carisch
  Gavotte
    (Winn) CF B3285
    ABRS (Mil No. A243)
    Kjos S-5014
  Minuet
    (Corti) CF B2155 "Minuetto"
    BMC
  Sonata No. 1 in D
    (Endicott-Spalding) CF B2744
  Sonata No. 2 in E
    (Endicott-Spalding) CF B2745
MARTINI, JEAN PAUL EGIDE (1741-1816)
  Plaisir d'Amour
    (Danbé) SCH
    (Powell) AMP
MARTINON, JEAN (1910-   )
  Concerto giocoso, Op. 18
    Billaudot
  Concerto No. 2, Op. 51
    SCH

MARTINON, JEAN (cont.)
  Duo, Op. 47
    SCH
  Sonatine No. 2, Op. 19, No. 2
    Billaudot
  Suite nocture, Op. 34
    Billaudot
MARTINU, BOHUSLAV (1890-1959)
  Arabesques, 7
    Deiss
  Concerto
    Artia pno reduction by Solc
  Impromptu
    Artia
  Intermezzo
    Artia
  Madrigal Stanzas, 5
    AMP
  Pièces brèves, 5
    Leduc
  Rapsodie Tcheque
    ESC
  Sonata No. 1
    Leduc
  Sonata
    Deiss
  Sonata No. 3
    AMP
  Sonatina
    Artia
  Suite Concertante
    (Dushkin) SCH
MARX, [JOSEPH (1882-   )]
  Spring Sonata
    UE 11688
MARX, KARL (1897-   )
  Concerto in C, Op. 24
    BRH
  Musik in drei Sätzen, Op. 53, No. 1
    Baer 2688
  Sonatine in G, Op. 48, No. 2
    Baer 2077
MARYLAND MY MARYLAND
  (Franz) VL 24
MASCAGNI, PIETRO (1863-1945)
  Cavalleria Rusticana. Transcription
    (Ambrosio) CF B3316
  Intermezzo, from L'Amico Fritz
    (Farinelli) SON
  Intermezzo sinfonico, from
    Cavalleria Rusticana
    (Ambrosio) CF B2528 simpl
    (Farinelli) SON
    (Franko) GS
    (Halle) Bel 693
    (Saenger) CF S3130
    (Saenger) CF S3132 transposed to D
  Prelude and Sicilienne, from Cavalleria
    Rusticana
    (Wilhemj) CF B3246
  Sogno di Ratcliff, Il, from Guglielmo
    Ratcliff
    (Farinelli) SON
MASCITTI, MICHELE (1664-1760)
  Chamber Sonatas, Op. 2, Nos. 1-3
    WM (Pet No. WM44)
MASCITTI, [MICHELE]
  Psyché. Divertissement, Op. 5, No. 12
    (Noske) SCH vcl or gamba ad lib
MA-SI-TZUN
  Concerto
    MZK
MASON, JOHN
  Bright Interlude
    CP

MASON, LOWELL
  Nearer, my God, to Thee. Fantasia
    see Kron & Saenger
MASSENET, JULES (1842-1912)
  Crépuscule
    (Hubay) CF B3009
  Elegie, from Les Erynnies, Op. 10
    (Ambrosio) CF B2573 simpl
    (Halle) Bel 655
    CF S3186
    VL 76
    see also Lemare: Andantino
  Méditation, from Thais
    (Marsick) CF B2642
    BMC
    Heugel
MASSIS, AMABLE (1893-   )
  Sonatine
    Dur
MASSON & KICK
  En relisant vos lettres
    Gaudet
MASTER MELODIES FROM THE CLASSICS
  (Beer) Bel 3V
MASTERPIECES, 52
  Bel
MASTERS FOR THE YOUNG
  Pet 2725-7, 4159 4V
    Vol 1: 16 Pieces by Haydn & Mozart
    Vol 2: 14 Pieces by Beethoven & Schubert
    Vol 3: 16 Pieces by Mendelssohn &
      Schumann
    Vol 4: 12 Pieces by Brahms &
      Tchaikovsky
MASTERWORKS FOR THE YOUNG VIOLINIST
  (Applebaum-Steiner) GS
    Bach, J.S.: Bourree, from Chamber
      Suite No. 1
    Beethoven: Scherzo, from String
      Quartet, Op. 18, No. 4
    Handel: Gigue, from Concerto Grosso
      No. 9
    Haydn: Minuet, from String Quartet,
      Op. 76, No. 2
    Haydn: Rondo, from String Quartet,
      Op. 33, No. 3
    Mendelssohn: Romance, from Piano
      Trio in d, Op. 49
    Mozart: Minuet, from Serenade in
      B flat, K. 361
    Schubert: The Brook, from Die Schöne
      Müllerin
    Schubert: Minuet, from String Quartet,
      Op. 168
    Schubert: My sweet repose
    Tchaikovsky: Mazurka, from Piano
      Trio, Op. 50
    Telemann: Les Plaisirs, from Suite in a
MATHIAS, WILLIAM (1934-   )
  Sonata
    Oxf
MATHIEU, TH.
  Au lendemain des tumultes
    Sal
  Prelude en mi majeur
    Sal
MATRAS, MAUDE
  Ballade, Op. 8, orig for vln and orch
    Aug 7534
MATSUTIN, K.
  Dances, 2, on Adigei Themes
    MZK
  Pieces, 3, on Adigei Themes
    MZK

MATTHESON, [JOHANN (1681-1764)]
  Air in e
    SCH
  Sicilienne
    (Francescatti) Mil
MATYAS
  Old Scottish Air
    (Seiber) Mil
MAURAT, EDMOND
  Oblation, from Le Troisième Livre
    des Jeux
    ESC
  Obsessions, from Le Troisième Livre
    des Jeux
    ESC
  Premier Livre des Jeux, Le
    ESC   3V
      Vol 1: Entrée, Arabesque, Récit
      Vol 2: Méandres, Incantation
      Vol 3: Caprices
  Songes, from Le Troisième Livre des Jeux
    ESC
MAYWOOD, FRANK E.
  Keepsakes of Old
    Fill
  Love's Ideal
    Fill
  Romance of Eden
    Fill
  Unforgotten Thoughts
    Fill
MAZAS, JACQUES-FÉRÉOL (1782-1849)
  Little Duets, 12, Op. 38, Bk. 1
    CF 03471   for 1 or 2 vln and pno
  Little Duets, 12, Op. 38, Bk. 2
    CF 04264   for 1 or 2 vln and pno;
      in preparation
MAZELLIER, [JULES (1879-1959)]
  Berceuse
    ESC
  Poème romantique
    Billaudot
  Saltarella
    Ric R1586
MAZZACURATI
  Minuetto all'antica
    Ric 125786
  Ninna-nanna, Op. 5
    Ric 125760
MEDTNER, A.
  Barcarolle
    MZK
MEDTNER, NIKOLAI (1880-1951)
  Canzona and Dance, Op. 43, No. 1
    ZM (Pet No. ZM98)
  Canzona and Dance, Op. 43, No. 2
    ZM (Pet No. ZM99)
  Fairy Tale, Op. 20, No. 1, orig for pno
    (Heifetz) CF B3254
  Fairy Tale, Op. 51, No. 3, orig for pno
    ZM (Pet No. ZM185)
  Nocturne in d, Op. 16, No. 1
    Belaieff
  Nocturne in g, Op. 16, No. 2
    Belaieff
  Nocturne in c, Op. 16, No. 3
    Belaieff
    MZK
  Sonata No. 1 in b, Op. 21
    Belaieff
    MZK
  Sonata No. 2 in G, Op. 44
    ZM (Pet No. ZM31)
  Sonata Epica
    Nov

MEIN HEIMATLAND
  (Andersen) SCH
MELIKIAN, R.
  Suite
    MZK
MELODIES IN FIRST POSITION
  (Whistler) Ru   2nd vln ad lib
MELODIES ITALIENNES, 12
  (Beriot-Sitt) Pet 2991
MELODY BOOK FOR STRINGS
  (Isaac) CF 03828A,B
    Abaca-Isaac: Rondino
    Adams: Valse melodique
    d'Archet: Sans souci
    Chiang: T sin hsu
    Isaac: Barcarolle
    Isaac: From the Northland
    Isaac: Romanza
    Isaac: Strummin'
    Kroma: Autumn leaves
    Leland: All in step
    Monroe: In the garden
MENASCE, JACQUES DE (1905-   )
  Lullaby
    GS
  Rhapsody
    GS
  Sonata No. 1
    MK
MENDELSON, J.
  Sonata
    ESC
MENDELSSOHN, FELIX (1809-1847)
  Andante, from Concerto, Op. 64
    (Heim) Aug 11550
  Capriccietto
    (Burmester) CF B247
  Concerto in d
    (Menuhin) Pet 6070
  Concerto in e, Op. 64
    (Auer) CF L794
    (Flesch) Int
    (Flesch) Pet 1731A
    (Jacobsen) UE 311
    (Joachim-Dessauer) CF 03153
    (Joachim-Schnirlin) SIM
    (Polo) Ric ER2207
    (Sauret) Aug 7955
    (Sauret) SCH
    (Schradieck) GS L235
  Gondolier's Song, Op. 19, No. 2
    (Hauser) CF S3837
  Marches, 2, orig for orch
    Pet 1786
      Wedding March; March of the Priests
  March. War March of the Priests, from
    Athalia
    (Saenger) CF B2994
  March. Wedding March, from Midsum-
    mer Night's Dream
    (Del Maglio) Ric 125605 "Marcia nuziale"
    SCH
  Nocturno; with Valse Triste by Sibelius
    (Trinkaus) Fill
  On Wings of Song, Op. 34, No. 2, orig
    for voice and pno
    (Achron-Heifetz) CF B2435
    (Achron-Saenger) CF B729
    (Ambrosio-Perlman) CF B2576   simpl
    (Edwards) MK
    (Trinkaus) Fill
    VL 140
  Overtures, 5
    Pet 1736

MENDELSSOHN, FELIX (cont.)
Overture to Midsummer Night's Dream,
Op. 21, orig for orch
(Weiss-Ambrosio) CF
Rondo Capriccioso, Op. 14, orig for pno
(Applebaum) CF B2693
Scherzo, from Midsummer Night's Dream
(Heifetz) CF B2612
Scherzo, from Piano Trio
(Heifetz) CF B2626
Sonata in f, Op. 4
Pet 1732
Sonata in F
(Menuhin) Pet 6075
Songs without Words, orig for pno
(Rauch) Lit (Pet No. L926)
Song Without Words, Op. 19, No. 1
(Chemet) CF B2070
(Heifetz) CF B3255 "Sweet Remembrance"
Spring Song, Op. 62, No. 6, orig for pno
(Del Maglio) Ric 125604
(Halle) Bel 695
(Palaschko) SCH
CF S3142
VL 28   2nd vln ad lib
Sweet Remembrance, see Song without words,
Op. 19, No. 1
War March of the Priests, see March
Wedding March, see March
MENDELSSOHN, LUDWIG
Student's Concerto in D, Op. 213
(Saenger) CF 02985
MENDELSSOHN
Mosquito Dance
Bosw
Petite Valse
Bosw
Polish
Bosw
Soldiers March
Bosw
MENNIN, PETER (1923-   )
Sonata Concertante
CF 04113
MENOTTI, GIAN CARLO (1911-   )
Concerto
GS
MERCANDANTE, SAVERIO
Variations on a theme of, see Dancla,
Charles: Air Varié, Op. 89, No. 6
MERKEL, GUSTAV (1827-1885)
Merry Hunter
VL 99   2nd vln ad lib
MERRILL & FORD
Blue Fantasy
Mil
MERULA, TARQUINIO (1600- ?)
Canzone, see Solo Violin Music of the
Earliest Period
MESSAGER, [ANDRÉ (1853-1929)]
Amour masqué, L'
Sal
MESSIAEN, OLIVIER (1908-   )
Thème et variations
Leduc
MEULEMANS, ARTHUR (1884-   )
Sonata No. 2
CBDM
MEYERBEER, GIACOMO (1791-1864)
Coronation March, from Le Prophète
(Trinkaus) Fill
(Weiss) CF
Shadow Dance, from Dinorah
(Saenger) CF B3197

MEYER-HELMUND, ERIK (1861-1932)
Rustic Dance, Op. 94, No. 13
(Saenger) CF B3199
MEYER-LUTZ
Pas de Quatre
Deiss
MIASKOVSKY, NIKOLAI (1881-1950)
Concerto
MZK
MICHEELSEN, HANS FRIEDRICH (1902-   )
Sonate
Baer 1444
MICHIELS
Monge-Czardas
Gaudet
MICHL, ARTUR (1897-   )
Sonatina, Op. 13
OBV
Stücke, 5, Op. 48, orig for vln and orch
Krenn
MIGNONE, FRANCISCO (1897-   )
Congada
Ric BR1997
MIGOT, GEORGES (1891-   )
Dialogue en 4 parties
Leduc
Dialogue No. 2
Leduc
Estampie, No. 2 of Le Premier Livre de
Divertissements Francais
Leduc
Sonate a danser
Leduc
Suite en 5 parties pour violon récitant,
orig for vln and orch
Leduc
MIHALOVICI, MARCEL (1898-   )
Sonata No. 2, Op. 45
Heugel
MIKESHINA, ARIADNA
Rhapsodie Russe, Op. 64
Paragon
MILANDRE
Minuetto
(D'Ambrosio) Ric 129412
MILES, PERCY H.
Rustic Dance
ABRS (Mil No. A234)
MILHAUD, DARIUS (1892-   )
Boeuf sur le Toit, Le, arr from ballet
ESC
Brazileira, from Scaramouche, orig for 2 pno
(Heifetz) Deiss
Concertino de printemps, orig for vln and
orch
Deiss
Concerto No. 1
Heugel
Concerto No. 2
AMP
Concert Royal, Concerto No. 3
ESC
Copacabana, from Saudades do Brazil, orig
for pno
(Levy) ESC
Corcovado, from Saudades do Brazil, orig
for pno
(Levy) ESC
Danses de Jacarémirim
Leeds
Farandoleurs, Les
Deiss
Ipanema, from Saudades do Brazil, orig for
pno
(Levy) ESC

MILHAUD, DARIUS (cont.)
  Leme, from Saudades do Brazil, orig for pno
    (Levy) ESC
  Modéré, from Scaramouche, orig for 2 pno
    (Heifetz) Deiss
  Printemps, Le
    Dur
  Sonata No. 1
    Dur
  Sonata No. 2
    Dur
  Sonata for vln and clavecin, or pno
    EV
  Suite, orig for vln and orch or harmonica
    BH
  Sumaré, from Saudades do Brazil, orig for
    pno
    (Levy) ESC
  Tijuca, from Saudades do Brazil, orig for pno
    (Levy) ESC
MILLER, CHARLES
  Yiskor
    EV
MILLER, E.J.
  Duo Concertante
    BB
MILLER, RUSSELL N.
  Danse Espagnol
    VL 96
MILLER
  Cubanaise
    Pr
MILLIES, HANS (1883-   )
  Concertino in D, in the style of Joseph Haydn
    Bosw (Bel 23)
  Concertino in D, in the style of Mozart
    Bosw (Bel No. 22)
MILLS, CHARLES (1914-   )
  Berceuse
    CFE score only
  Sonata No. 2
    CFE
  Sonata No. 3
    CFE score only
MILLS POPULAR STANDARD SOLOS
  Mil
MILLS SHOWCASE SPECTACULAR
  Mil
MILMAN, M.
  Concerto
    MZK
  Sonata No. 2, Op. 30
    MZK
MINIATURE MASTERPIECES
  (Ambrosio) CF 02647, 02638, 02648 3V
  Vol 1
    Bach-Gounod: Meditation
    Braga: Angel's serenade
    Brahms: Hungarian Dance No. 6
    Dvorak: Humoresque, Op. 101, No. 7
    Elgar: Salut d'amour, Op. 12
    Faure: Les Rameaux
    Godard: Berceuse, from Jocelyn
    Handel: Largo
    Hauser: Cradle song
    Lange: Flower song
    Mascagni: Intermezzo, from
      Cavalleria Rusticana
    Mendelssohn: Spring song
    Moszkowski: Serenata, Op. 15, No. 1
    Raff: Cavatina
    Rubinstein: Melody in F
    Schubert: Serenade

    Thomas: Gavotte, from Mignon
    Thomas: Valse, from Mignon
    Thomé: Simple aveu
    Verdi: Grand March, from Aida
    Vieuxtemps: Reverie, Op. 22, No. 3
    Wagner: Song to the evening star,
      from Tannhauser
    Wieniawski: Kuiawiak
    Wieniawski: Legende, Op. 17
  Vol 2
    Beethoven: Minuet in G
    Bohm: Cavatina
    Brahms: Hungarian Dance No. 5
    Chopin: Nocturne, Op. 9, No. 2
    Delibes: Pas des fleurs, from Naila
    Donizetti: Sextet, from Lucia
    Drdla: Serenade
    Drigo: Valse bluette
    Gossec: Gavotte
    Gutmann: Memories of home
    Herbert: Serenade, Op. 3
    Hubay: Hejre Kati
    Macbeth: Love in idleness
    Tobani: Hearts and flowers
    Verdi: Anvil Chorus, from Trovatore
    Vieuxtemps: Fantasie caprice, Op. 11
    Yradier: La Paloma
  Vol 3
    Beriot: Scene de ballet
    Brahms: Waltz
    Carnival of Venice
    Country gardens
    Dark eyes
    Drdla: Souvenir
    Drigo: Serenade
    Dvorak: Largo
    Dvorak: Songs my mother taught me
    Fernandez: Cielito lindo
    Fibich: Poem
    Londonderry air
    Mendelssohn: On wings of song
    Moszkowski: Spanish Dance,
      Op. 12, No. 1
    Offenbach: O belle nuit, from Tales
      of Hoffmann
    Old refrain
    Rimsky-Korsakov: Song of India
    Saint-Saens: The swan
    Schubert: Hark! Hark! the lark
    Two guitars
    Wagner: Grand March, from
      Tannhauser
MINUETS BY 18TH CENTURY COMPOSERS
  (Carse) Aug
    Compositions by Fränzl, Nicolay,
      Stamitz, Wanhal
MIQUEL, E.
  Méditatio
    Gaudet
  Reverie
    Gaudet
MISTOWSKI, A.
  Concerto in a
    Bosw
MITNITZKY, I.
  Danse Exentrique, Op. 19
    AMP
  Dear Irish Boy, Op. 18
    AMP
  Prière, Op. 17
    AMP
  Valse Mélancolique
    AMP

MITTELL'S POPULAR GRADED COURSE
GS L1152-3   2V
Vol 1
    Bloch, J.: Historiette
    Bloch, J.: Marche
    Bloch, J.: Romance
    Bloch, J.: Souvenir
    Bloch, J,: Valsette
    Dancla: Polka, Op. 123, No. 6
    Dancla: Valse, Op. 123, No. 2
    Dancla: Weber's last thought
    Eberhardt: Serenade, Op. 86, No. 4
    Ehrhardt: Andante, Op. 20, No. 1
    Eichhorn: Minuet, Op. 17, No. 6
    Faucheux: Rêverie
    Lagye: Premier sourire, Op. 34
    Lagye: Romance, Op. 20
    Moffat: Wedding-march
    Papini: Little drummer, Op. 83, No. 1
    Reinecke: Ländlicher Tanz
    Reinecke: Little suite, Op. 174a, No. 10
    Reinecke: Zur Guitarre, Op. 122a
    Schmidt: Cavatina, Op. 41
    Sitt: Gavotte, Op. 26, No. 4
    Sitt: Pastorale, Op. 26, No. 2
    Sitt: Tarantella, Op. 26, No. 12
    Tchaikovsky: Morning prayer,
      Op. 39, No. 1
    Tchaikovsky: New doll, Op. 39, No. 9
    Volkmann: Cuckoo and the wanderer,
      Op. 11, No. 5
    Volkmann: In the mill, Op. 11, No. 1
    Weiss: Variations on the Austrian
      hymn, Op. 38, No. 36
    Weiss: Variations on The red sarafan,
      Op. 38, No. 40
Vol 2
    Beriot: Air varié, No. 14
    Bloch, J.: Melodie, Op. 7, No. 2
    Bohm: Ländler, Op. 187, No. 6
    Bull: Alpine maid's Sunday
    Dancla: Barcarolle, Op. 187, No. 12
    Dancla: Minuet, Op. 187, No. 8
    Dancla: Plaisir d'amour,
      Op. 86, No. 12
    Dancla: Romance, Op. 187, No. 10
    Gounod: Méditation, Ave Maria
    Hauser: Boatman's song, Op. 16, No. 1
    Hauser: Village song, Op. 29, No. 5
    Huber, H.: Suave melody, Op. 99, No. 2
    Lagye: The angel's dream, Op. 18
    Massenet: Mélodie, Op. 10, No. 5
    Moszkowski: Mélodie, Op. 18, No. 1
    Moszkowski: Spanish dance,
      Op. 12, No. 1
    Neruda: Slavonic cradle-song, Op. 11
    Popper: Gavotte, Op. 23
    Reber: Berceuse
    Schumann: Träumerei
    Tchaikovsky: Song without words,
      Op. 2, No. 3
MITTELL'S VIOLIN CLASSICS
GS   5V
Vol 1
    Beethoven: Andante con moto, from
      Symphony No. 1
    Boccherini: Menuet
    Bohm: Cantilena
    Braga: Angel's serenade
    Danbé: Petite valse lente
    Field: Nocturne
    Gabriel-Marie: Cinquantaine, La
    Gillet: Loin du bal
    Gounod: Waltz from Faust

Grieg: Berceuse
Haydn: Serenade
Herbert: Canzonetta
Saint-Saëns: Swan
Tchetschulin: Alla zingaresca
Thomas: Entr'acte and gavotte from
  Mignon
Wagner: March and chorus from
  Tannhäuser
Wagner: Spinning-song from Der
  fliegender Holländer
Vol 2
    Bach, E.: Spring's awakening
    Bach, J.S.: Air and gavotte from
      Suite in D
    Becker: Romanza
    Bohm: Gavotte
    Brahms: Hungarian dance No. 6
    Fischer: Barcarole
    Godard: Canzonetta
    Hollaender: Spinning-song
    Paderewski: Melody
    Raff: Canzona
    Ries: Gondoliera
    Schubert, Francois: Bee
    Schumann: Slumber-song
Vol 3
    Becker: Gavotte
    Bohm: Cavatina
    Bruch: Kol Nidrei
    Godard: Berceuse from Jocelyn
    Handel: Largo from Xerxes
    Kéler-Béla: Son of the Pusztá
    Pierné: Sérénade
    Sarasate: Playera
    Schumann: Abendlied
    Simon: Berceuse
    Sitt: Barcarole
    Svendsen: Romance
    Wagner: Walther's prize-song from
      Meistersinger
    Wieniawski: Obertass
    Wieniawski: Romance from Concerto
      No. 2
Vol 4
    Bach: Air on the G string
    Brahms: Hungarian dance No. 5
    Bull: Nocturne
    Gluck: Largo, O del mio dolce ardor
      from Paride ed Elena
    Hauser: Ungarischer
    Mendelssohn: Consolation
    Mendelssohn: Spring song
    Ries: Adagio, Suite, Op. 34
    Ries: Perpetuum mobile, from Suite,
      Op. 34
    Simonetti: Madrigale
    Sinding: Romance
    Tchaikovsky: Canzonetta from Con-
      certo, Op. 35
    Van Goens: Romance sans paroles
    Vieuxtemps: Regrets
    Wagner: Romanze, Albumblatt
    Wagner: Träume
    Wieniawski: Souvenir de Posen
    Wilhelmj: Romanza
Vol 5
    Galkine: Serenade
    Hauser: An die Heimat
    Hubay: Hejre Kati
    Huber, H.: Consecration, 2nd mvt.,
      Sonata, Op. 18
    Nachez: Abendlied
    Ries: Romance, Suite, Op. 27

MITTELL'S VIOLIN CLASSICS (cont.)
  GS 5V (cont.)
    Vol. 5 (cont.)
      Sarasate: Zigeunerweisen
      Tchaikovsky: Sérénade mélancolique
      Vieuxtemps: Aria and gavotte, Suite
        Op. 43
      Wagner-Wilhelmj: Parsifal, para-
        phrase
      Zarzycki: Mazurka
(MLYNARCZYK)
  Classical and Modern
    BRH
MLYNARSKI, EMIL (1870-1935)
  Mazurka in G
    (Schill) GS
    BMC
    CF S3301
MODERN VIOLIN MOODS
  (Nero) CF 03404
MODERN VIOLIN SOLOIST
  (Perlman) CF 02940
    Ambrosio: Ben Bolt
    Beethoven: Minuet in G
    Beriot: Air Varie No. 14
    Bohm: Air gavotte, Op. 378, No. 4
    Bohm: Sarabande
    Danbe: Carnival of Venice, Op. 22, No. 3
    Drigo: Serenade
    Gillet: Passepied
    Gillis: Reverie, Op. 50, No. 1
    Ghys: Amaryllis, Op. 10, No. 2
    Hollaender: Canzonetta
    Hubay: Hungarian poem, Op. 76, No. 4
    Marie, Gabriel: La Cinquantaine
    Neruda: Berceuse Slave
    Rieding: Hungarian folk song,
      Op. 4, No. 2
    Rimsky-Korsakov: Song of India
    Saint-Saens: Swan
    Singelee: Fantaisie melodique
    Tchaikovsky: Andante cantabile, from
      String Quartet Op. 11
MOERAN, ERNEST JOHN (1894-1950)
  Concerto
    Nov
  Sonata in e
    Ches
MOESCHINGER, ALBERT (1897-   )
  Konzert, Op. 40
    Baer 2481
MOFFAT, ALFRED (1866-1950)
  Easy Original Pieces, 12
    SCH
  Easy Pieces, 6
    SCH
  Gavotte
    Aug
  Holly Bush, Northumbrian Country Dance
    SCH
  Jepthas' Daughter, from 3 Old Hebrew
    Melodies
    Leng (Mil No. L1129)
  Mist on the Mountain, from 3 Old
    Hebrew Melodies
    Leng (Mil No. L1127)
  Mr. Shield's Giocoso in 5/4 time
    Aug
  Retrospects
    Aug AS.78
  Song of Sleep, from 3 Old Hebrew Melodies
    Leng (Mil No. L1128)
  Tambourin de la Reine, Le
    (Robjohns) SCH

(MOFFAT, ALFRED)
  Classical Pieces, 12
    Aug 7526a,b 2V
  Classical Pieces
    SCH 2V
      12 Pieces by Bach, Handel, Veracini,
      Corelli, Boyce and others
  English Classical Album
    Aug 7523
  English Masters (17th and 18th Centuries)
    Aug 7537
  Old Fiddle Pieces
    SCH
      Pieces by Rameau, Beethoven, Couperin,
      Corelli, Sammartini, Pepusch and others
  Old-French Melodies
    SCH
  Old Masters For Young Players
    SCH 3V
  Old-Russian Melodies
    SCH
MOKRY, J.
  Concertino in G
    Bosw (Bel No. 20)
MOLLENHAUER, EDWARD (1827-1914)
  Boy Paganini, Fantasia
    CF B747
  Infant Paganini, Fantasia
    CF B746
MOLLIER, G.
  Badinage, from 3 Pieces caractéristiques
    Gaudet
  Ballade, from Les Virtuoses du Lycée
    Gaudet
  Barcarolle, from Les Virtuoses du Lycée
    Gaudet
  Brindisi, from 3 Pieces caractéristiques
    Gaudet
  Chanson d'autrefois, from Les Virtuoses
    du Lycée
    Gaudet
  Chanson Vénitienne, from Esquisses
    Mélodiques
    Gaudet
  Choeur des Gondoliers, from Esquisses
    Mélodiques
    Gaudet
  Fanfare de Chasse, from Les Virtuoses
    du Lycée
    Gaudet
  Farandole, from Esquisses Mélodiques
    Gaudet
  Menuet, from Les Virtuoses du Lycée
    Gaudet
  Mosaique du Collégien. 4 récréations
    Gaudet published separately
  Polonaise, from Les Virtuoses du Lycée
    Gaudet
  Ronde de Nuit, from Les Virtuoses du
    Lycée
    Gaudet
  Ronde Villageoise, from Les Virtuoses
    du Lycée
    Gaudet
  Ruisseau, Le, et le Torrent, from 3 Pieces
    caractéristiques
    Gaudet
  Scherzo, from Les Virtuoses du Lycée
    Gaudet
  Solo de Concerto No. 1
    Gaudet
  Solo de Concerto No. 2
    Gaudet
  Tarentelle, from Les Virtuoses du Lycée
    Gaudet

MOLLOY, JAMES LYMAN (1837-1909)
  Kerry Dance
    (Eckstein) CF M312
  Love's Old Sweet Song
    (Eckstein) CF M311
    VL 42   2nd vln ad lib
MOLLY ON THE SHORE
  (Grainger-Kreisler) CF B1924
MOLNÁR, [ANTAL (1890-   )]
  Easy Small Violin Pieces, 5
    Kul
  Fantasie Hongroise
    Kul
  Suite
    Kul
MOMPOU, FRÉDÉRIC (1893-   )
  Jeunes Filles au Jardin, from Scènes
    d'enfants
    (Szigeti) CF B2408
MONASTERIO, JESÚS DE (1836-1903)
  Sierra Morena
    CF S3864
MONDONVILLE, C.C.
  Sonate en fa mineur
    HL
MONDONVILLE, JEAN-JOSEPH DE (1711-1772)
  Allegro et aria
    (Pincherle) Senart 5389
  Sonata in F
    Noet (Pet No. N6057)
MONFRED, A.
  Petites Pièces, 4
    Sal
  Valse
    Sal
MONSIGNY, PIERRE-ALEXANDRE (1729-1817)
  Rigaudon
    (Franko) GS
MONTI, VITTORIO
  Aubade d'amour
    Ric 119004
  Czárdás No. 1
    Ric 102595
  Csárdás
    (Czerwonky) CF B1678
    (Herfurth) BMC
MONTSALVATGE, XAVIER (1912-   )
  Poema Concertante, orig for vln and orch
    SMP
  Variacones sobre La Spagnoletta de
    Giles Farnaby
    SMP
MOORE, DOUGLAS (1893-   )
  Down East Suite
    CF 03412
MOORE, JOHN
  Scottish Song, "Turn ye to me"
    Oxf 20.110
MOORE, M.
  Country Tune
    STB
MORENO GANS, J. (1897-   )
  Zapateado. Homenaje a Pablo Sarasate
    UME
MOREY, FLORENCE
  Boatman's Song
    CP
  Tanglefoot's mad chase
    CP
MORRIS, H.
  Celtic Lament
    STB
  Moto Perpetuo, from 2 Characteristic
    Pieces
    STB

Spanish Dance, from 2 Characteristic
  Pieces
  STB
MORRIS, S.E.
  Jolly Santa Claus
    Lud S-1520
MORTELMANS, [LODEWIJK (1868-1952)]
  Regrets
    Metr
  Romanza
    Metr
MORTENSEN
  Cock-A-Doodle Dandy
    Mil
MOSS, LAWRENCE
  Sonata
    CFE
MOSTRAS
  Etude, see Khachaturian: Lullaby
  March, see Saliman-Vladimirov: Impromptu
  Oriental Dance, see Rakov: Vocalise
(MOSTRAS)
  Easy Pieces by Russian Composers
    MZK
MOSZKOWSKI, MORITZ (1854-1925)
  Ballade in g, Op. 16, No. 1, orig for vln and
    orch
    Aug 7528
  Guitarre, Op. 45, No. 2, orig for pno
    (Sarasate) Pet 2529
    (Sarasate-Heifetz) CF B2445
  Melody, Op. 82, No. 3 and Humoresque,
    Op. 82, No. 4
    Pet 3250b
  Polish Dances, Op. 55
    (Sitt) Pet 2905
  Serenata, Op. 15, No. 1, orig for pno
    (Ambrosio) CF B2545   simpl
    (Rehfeld) CF S3433
  Spanish Dances, 5, Op. 12, orig for
    pno duet
    (Scharwenka) Pet 2167
    (Scharwenka-Saenger) CF   2V
    (Scharwenka-Spiering) GS L1089
  Spanish Dance, Op. 12, No. 1
    (Ambrosio) CF B2561   simpl
    (Applebaum) Bel SI31
    (Scharwenka-Saenger) CF
    VL 115
  Spanish Dance No. 2
    VL 134
  Valse in E, Op. 34, No. 1, orig for pno
    Bosw
MOTTU, A.
  Sonatine No. 1
    Senart
  Sonatine No. 2
    Senart
MOUQUET, JULES (1867-1946)
  Sonate en la majeur
    HL
MOUSSORGSKY, see Mussorgsky
MOYA
  Song of Songs
    (Langey) Chap-L
MOZART, LEOPOLD (1719-1787)
  Little Pieces, 12, from Notebook for
    Wolfgang Amadeus
    (Todt) BRH
    Noet (Pet No. N3004)
MOZART, WOLFGANG AMADEUS (1756-1791)
  Adagio in E, K.261, orig for vln and orch
    (Francescatti) Int
    (Hermann) BRH

MOZART, WOLFGANG AMADEUS (cont.)
  Adagio in E, K.261 (cont.)
    (Rostal) SCH
    Pet 3827   with cadenzas; published with
      Rondo, K.373 and Rondo Concertante,
      K.269
  Adagio, from Les petits riens
    (Hartmann) AMP
  Adagio, from String Quartet, K.172
    (Klengel) Pet 4166
  Allegro
    (Hanson) Lud S-15A16
  Allegro molto, from String Quartet
    in C, K.465
    (Heifetz) CF B2739
  Andante
    (Seiffert) Wagenaar
  Andante and Gavotte gracieuse, from Les
    petits riens
    (Hartmann) AMP
  Andantino molto grazioso, from Les petits
    riens
    (Hartmann) AMP
  Ave Verum Corpus
    CF B2996
  Cantabile
    (Slatter) STB
  Cherubino, from Marriage of Figaro, see
    Castelnuovo-Tedesco
  Concerto No. 1 in B flat, K. 207
    (Jacobsen) Pet 2193E   with cadenzas
    (Waldersee) BRH
    Paragon   cadenzas by Bacevicius
  Concerto No. 2 in D, K.211
    (Auer-Strasser) CF 03393   with cadenza
      by Auer
    (Kuechler) Pet 2193F   with cadenzas
    (Waldersee) BRH
    UE 794
  Concerto No. 3 in G, K.216
    (Auer-Strasser) CF 03458   with
      cadenza by Auer
    (Flesch) Pet 2193L   with cadenzas
    (Francescatti) Int   with cadenzas by
      Eugene Ysaÿe
    (Franko) GS L1580   with cadenzas
    (Waldersee) BRH
    cadenzas published separately, see under
      vln unacc: Arrieu, Badura-Skoda,
      Kreisler, Mackerras, Quiroga, Szigeti,
      Ysaÿe
  Concerto No. 4 in D, K.218
    (Auer-Strasser) CF 03394   with
      cadenza by Auer
    (Herrmann) GS L890   with cadenza
    (Joachim) Int   with cadenzas
    (Joachim) SIM
    (Marteau) Pet 2193C   with cadenzas
    (Sauret) Aug 7957
    (Sauret) SCH
    (Spiller) Ric BA11506   with cadenzas
      by Joachim
    (Waldersee) BRH
    cadenzas published separately, see under
      vln unacc: Badura-Skoda, Heifetz,
      Kreisler, Menuhin, Quiroga, Spalding
  Concerto No. 5 in A, K.219
    (Anzoletti) Ric ER834
    (Auer-Strasser) CF 03392   with
      cadenza by Auer
    (Franko) GS L1276   with cadenzas
    (Hess) Baer 4712a
    (Joachim) Int   with cadenzas
    (Joachim) SIM

    (Marteau) Pet 2193A   with cadenzas
    (Rostal) SCH
    (Sauret) Aug 7958
    (Sauret) SCH
    (Sitt) BRH
    UE 797
    cadenzas published separately, see under
      vln unacc: Badura-Skoda, Kreisler,
      Quiroga
  Concerto No. 6 in E flat, K.268[29]
    (Auer) GS L1391 "No. 7"
    (Marteau) Pet 2193b   with cadenzas
    (Sauret) Aug 7956
    (Spiering) CF 03883
    (Waldersee) BRH
    cadenzas published separately, see
      under vln unacc: Kreisler, Quiroga
  Concerto No. 7 in D, K.271a[29]
    (Sitt-Taubmann) BRH
    cadenzas published separately, see under
      vln unacc: Enesco, Quiroga
  Concerto in D, "Adelaide"[29]
    (Casadesus) SCH
  Cradle Song, see Wiegenlied
  Eine Kleine Nachtmusik, K.525, orig
    for str quintet
    (Carse) Aug 8684 "Serenade in G"
    (Larssen) SCH
    (Stoessel) CF AS6 "Serenade"
    BRH
    Pet 4325
  Gavotte in F
    (Hartmann) AMP
    (Robjohns) SCH
  Gavotte
    (Auer) BMC
  Gavotte
    (Ries) CF B1851
  German Dances, 6
    (Dushkin) SCH
  German Dance, K. 509, No. 1, orig for orch
    (Burmester) SCH
  German Dance in B flat
    (Burmester) SCH
  Ländler, after K.606, orig for orch
    (Ries) RE (Pet No. RE8)
  Ländler
    (Ries) CF B1854
  Ländler
    (Yost) VL
  Larghetto, from Clarinet Quintet, K.581
    SCH
  Larghetto, from Quintet in A
    (Dal Maglio) Ric 125606
  Little Concerto in F, after K.185
    Pet 4696
  Marches, 5
    Aug 8694
  Marcia turca, dalla Sonata in la
    (Del Maglio) Ric 125607
  Minuet, from Divertimento in D, K. 334
    (Bender) SCH
    ABRS (Mil No. A239) "Minuet and Trio"
    Aug 5237a
  Minuet in D, from Divertimento in D
    (Polo) Ric 128441 "Minuetto"
  Minuet, from Divertimento in D
    JWL (Mil No. W1280)
  Minuet, from String Quartet in B flat, K.458
    (Heifetz) CF B2740   "Menuetto"
  Minuet in A, from Viennese Sonatinas
    (Ross) BMC

----

[29] Authenticity doubtful.

MOZART, WOLFGANG AMADEUS (cont.)
Minuet in C, from Viennese Sonatinas
(Ross) BMC
Minuet in C
(Forbes) SCH
Minuet No. 1 in D
(Burmester) GS "Menuett"
Minuet and Trio in D
(Winn) CF S3525
Minuet
(Barrère) GS "Menuetto"
Minuet
(Heifetz) CF B2434 "Menuet"
Minuet
(Heifetz) CF B2738 "Menuetto"
Overtures by Beethoven, Mozart, Weber
Pet 3299A
Pantomine
(Hartmann) AMP
Rondo Concertante, K.269, orig for vln and
orch
Pet 3827   with cadenzas; published with
Adagio, K.261 and Rondo, K.373
Rondo in C, K. 373, orig for vln and orch
(Hermann) Int
(Rostal) Nov
BRH
Pet 3827   with cadenzas; published with
Adagio, K.261 and Rondo Concertante,
K.269
Rondo
(Kreisler) Fol 1169
Rondo, see Handel: Minuet
Rondo alla turca, from Piano Sonata, K. 331
(Danbé) SCH
Serenade
Kjos S-5004
Serenade
see also Eine kleine Nachtmusik
Sonatas and Variations
(Röntgen) BRH   7V
Sonatas, 21
(Schmid-Lampe-Röhrig) Henle   2V
Vol 1: K. 301-6, 296, 376-80
Vol 2: K. 454, 481, 526, 547, 359, 360,
403, 402, 570
Sonatas, 20
BRH   2V
Sonatas, 19
(Flesch-Schnabel) Int
(Flesch-Schnabel) Pet 3315
Sonatas, 19
(Nachèz) Aug 8669a,b   2V
Sonatas, 18
(Principe-Vitali) Ric ER59-60   2V
Sonatas, 18
(Schradieck) GS L836
Sonatas, 6, K.55-60, "Romantic"[29]
(Gärtner) BRH
Pet 3329
Sonatas, 6, K.301-6, "Mannheim"
Pet 4619
Sonata in C, K. 296
GS "No. 8"
Sonata in e, K. 304
(Kehr-Schröter) SCH
GS "No. 4"
Sonata in A, K. 305
(Kehr-Schröter) SCH
Sonata in B flat, K. 454
(Kehr-Schröter) SCH
Sonata No. 1 in A
(Dyke) JWL (Mil No. W1235)
Sonatinas, 6 Viennese
(Lenzewski) SCH

Sonatinas, 2, after K. 439b
Pet 4555
Variations, see Sonatas and Variations
Variations on "Se vuol ballare", see
Beethoven
Wiegenlied[30]
(Flies) SCH "Cradle Song"
.. VL 127   2nd vln ad lib
(MÜLLER, HERMANN)
Airs and Graces
BH   for contents see title
MÜLLER, J. FREDERICK
At the Ballet
Kjos S5029
On the Beach
Kjos S5032
Sleigh Ride Party
Kjos S5030
Summertime
Kjos S5031
MURAT, RONALD
March
CF B2792
Valse
CF B2793
MURRAY, ALAN
I'll Walk Beside You
(Lucas) Chap-L
MURRAY, ELEANOR
Still More Tunes for My Violin
BH
MURRAY, ELEANOR & TATE, PHYLLIS
Dance Suite
Oxf 23.109
More Tunes for My Violin
BH   2nd vln ad lib
Playing Together
Oxf 23.110
Tunes for My Violin
BH
MUS, A.
Cancion de Cuna No. 1
RL
Legenda Mora No. 2
RL
MUSCARO, MARTIN
Negro Spiritual
Mil
MUSCAT, H.
Concerto in D, Op. 11
Bosw
MUSGRAVE, THEA (1928-   )
Colloquy
Ches
MUSHEL, G.
Suite No. 2
MZK
MUSIC
(Ellert-Herfurth) Willis
MUSIC FOR LEISURE HOURS
(Agarkov) MZK
MUSIC FOR MILLIONS SERIES, see Standard
Violin Pieces and Standard Easy
Violin Pieces
MUSICA HUNGARICA
Kul
Bartok (Gertler): Sonatina
Borzo (Orszagh): Csardas
Dohnanyi: Ruralia Hungarica No. 1
Kodaly: Adagio
Kodaly (Telmanyi): Valsette
Liszt: Romance Oubliee

---

[30] Probably Wiegenlied, K.350, actually written by Bernard
Flies.

MUSICA HUNGARICA (cont.)
  Kul (cont.)
    Vecsey: Caprice
    Vecsey: Cascade
    Weiner: Hungarian Wedding Dance
    Weiner: Hungarian Dance
MUSIN, OVIDE (1854-1929)
  Caprice in D, extract from Fiorillo
    Caprices
    MK
  Extase, Op. 22
    MK
  Funeral March, extract from Fiorillo
    Caprices
    MK
  Mazurka de Bravoure No. 2, Op. 14
    MK
  Mazurka de concert
    (Perlman) CF B2648
  Mexicana, Op. 33
    MK
  Nightingale, Op. 24
    MK
MUSSORGSKY, MODEST P. (1839-1881)
  Hopak
    (Dushkin) SCH
    (Rachmaninoff) CF B2014
    (Rachmaninoff) Fol 1111
  Tears; with Bagpipes by Cui and
    Characteristic Dance by Rebikov
    MZK
  Troubadour, from Pictures at an Exposition
    (Mitnitzky) AMP
MY LORD WHAT A MOURNIN'
  see Ray, Ruth
MY VIOLIN BOOK
  (Lutz) SCH 2nd vln and vcl ad lib
    11 melodies by Gossec, Mozart,
    Handel, Mendelssohn, Tchaikovsky
    and others
MYDDLETON, WILLIAM H.
  Down South
    MK
MYERS, SHERMAN
  Fiddler in the Barn
    Liber-S
NABOKOV, NICOLAS (1903-   )
  Canzone
    (Milstein) AMP
  Introduction and Allego
    (Milstein) AMP
NACHEZ, TIVADAR (1859-1930)
  Danses Tziganes, Op. 14
    (Saenger) CF B2768
NAGY, FERENZ
  Zigany
    Lud S-15A27
NAPOLITANO
  Gato. Al estilo popular
    (Cambón) Ric BA10264
  Triste. De Fiesta pampeana
    Ric BA10265
NAPRAVNIK, [EDUARD (1839-1916)]
  Melancholia, Op. 48, No. 3
    MZK
NARDINI, PIETRO (1722-1793)
  Concerto in A
    (Nachèz) SCH
  Concerto in e
    (Hauser) CF L598
    (Hauser-Franko) GS L934
    (Hauser-Sitt) LEU
  Concerto in e
    (Pente) SCH

Concerto in e
  (Polo) Ric ER786
Concerto in e
  (Ridgway) Nov
Concerto in e
  (Sauret) Aug 7952
Sonata in D
  (David-Spiering) CF 03197
Sonata in D
  (Flesch) Pet 4167
Sonata in D
  (Moffat) SIM
Sonata in D
  Carisch
NATIONAL HYMNS
  CF
    God Save the King
    Marseillaise, La
    Star-Spangled Banner
(NEAGO)
  With My Violin Round the World, Bk. 1
    SIM
NELSON
  Lovely Marianne
    Mil
NEMEROVSKY, [ALEXANDRE]
  Alla Mazurka
    (Hartmann) AMP
  Meditation, Op. 8
    (Winn) CF B3198
NEMIROFF, [ISAAC (1912-   )]
  Sonata No. 2
    Pr
NERI, MASSIMILIANO (1622- ?)
  Sonata, see Solo Violin Music of the
    Earliest Period
NERINI, ÉMILE (1882-   )
  Feux Follets
    Gilles
  Rêverie Mauresque
    Gilles
  Romance en ut majeur
    Gilles
  Romance sans paroles
    Gilles
  Sonate en mi mineur
    Gilles
  Sur l'eau
    Gilles
NERO, PAUL
  Cat and His Fiddle
    CF B2710
  Concerto for Hot Fiddle
    CF 03388
  Eight Bells and All's Jumpin'
    CF B2707
  Whistler's Father
    Mil
(NERO, PAUL)
  Modern Violin Moods
    CF 03404
NERUDA, FRANZ (1843-1915)
  Berceuse Slave, Op. 2
    (Gilman) CF B1781
    CF S3099
  Slavonian Cradle Song, Op. 11
    (Seybold) SIM
NEUWIRTH, G.
  Sonata Brevis
    DOB
NEVIN, ETHELBERT (1862-1901)
  Narcissus, Op. 13, No. 4, orig for pno
    (Edwards) Mil
    (Moffat) BMC simpl
    (Strube) BMC

NEVIN, ETHELBERT (cont.)
 Rosary, orig for voice and pno
  (Kreisler) BMC
  (Lutz) SCH
  (Miersch) BMC   simpl
  (Strube) BMC
NEW FAVORITE ENCORE FOLIO
  (Heifetz) CF 02137
   Achron: Hebrew melody
   Brahms-Joachim: Hungarian Dance No. 7
   Drigo: Valse bluette
   Elgar: La Capricieuse
   Glazounoff: Meditation
   Mendelssohn-Achron: On wings of song
   Moszkowski-Sarasate: Guitarre
   Mozart: Minuet
   Popper: Fileuse
   Rameau: Rigaudon
   Saenger: Intermezzo scherzoso
   Sarasate: Malaguena
   Sarasate: Zapateado
   Schubert-Wilhelmj: Ave Maria
   Schumann: Prophetic bird
NICODE, JEAN-LOUIS (1853-1919)
 Romance, Op. 14, orig for vln and orch
  Aug
NICOLAYEVA, see Nikolayeva
NIELSEN, CARL (1865-1931)
 Konzert, Op. 33
  WH 1928
 Romance, Op. 2
  (Sitt) WH 3311
 Sonate in A, Op. 9
  (Telmányi) WH 1618
 Sonate No. 2, Op. 35
  WH 1982
NIELSEN, RICCARDO (1908-   )
 Musica a 2
  SZ
NIKOLAYEV, [LEONID (1878-1942)]
 Sonata, Op. 11
  MZK
NIKOLAYEVA, TATIANA (1924-   )
 Sonatina
  MZK
NILES, ALICE
 Evening Song
  CF B2266   includes 2nd vln part for
   teacher
NIN, JOAQUIN (1879-1949)
 Cantilena Asturiana
  ESC
 Chants d'Espagne
  (Kochanski) ESC
 Commentaries, 5
  ESC
 In the Lindaraja Garden, Dialogue
  ESC
 Rapsodie Ibérienne
  ESC
 Suite Espagnole
  ESC
NOELS. OLD FRENCH CHRISTMAS DANCES
  (Frotscher) Noet (Pet No. N3228,
   N3234)   2V   vcl or gamba ad lib
NÖLCK, AUGUST
 Butterfly
  (Simon) CF B2105
 Etude Mélodique
  BMC
NORDEN, HUGO
 Viking Lullaby
  Templ

NORDIO, CESARE (1891-   )
 Poema, orig for vln and orch
  Ric 123944
NOVÁČEK, OTTOKAR (1866-1900)
 Perpetuum Mobile
  CF B2668
  Pet 2786
NOVY
 Hora Fantastic
  Mil
NOWAK, LIONEL (1911-   )
 Sonatina
  CFE
NYSTEDT, KNUT (1915-   )
 Sonata, Op. 10
  Musikk-Huset
O BLAME NOT THE BARD
  (Moffat) Aug
OBER
 Presto, see Pergolesi: Aria
O'BRAONIAN, CATHAOIR
 Cavatina
  Pigott (Mil No. PT408)
O'CONNOR-MORRIS, [GEOFFREY (1886-   )]
 Boyne Water, Op. 59, No. 5
  Kuhl (Mil No. K101)
 Draherin O'Machree, Op. 59, No. 4
  Kuhl (Mil No. K100)
 Nora O'Neill, Op. 59, No. 6
  Kuhl (Mil No. K102)
OEHMLER, LEO
 Gipsy street-violinist, from Little melodies,
   Op. 229
  GS
OERTZEN, R.
 Symphonischer Dialog, Op. 34
  SIM
OFFENBACH, JACQUES (1819-1880)
 O Belle Nuit. Barcarolle, from Les Contes
   d'Hoffmann
  (Ambrosio) CF B2558   simpl
  (Kaiser) SCH "Barcarole-Waltz"
  (Woltag) CF B3279
  VL 69   2nd vln ad lib
 Orpheus in the Underworld. Overture
  (Lechner) SCH
O'HARA, GEOFFREY (1904-   )
 Perfect Melody
  (Langey) Chap-L
OLD AIRS
  (Burmester) SCH   4V
OLD ENGLISH VIOLIN ALBUM
  (Carse) Aug A.S.83
OLD FIDDLE PIECES
  (Moffat) SCH
   Pieces by Rameau, Beethoven, Couperin,
    Corelli, Sammartini, Pepusch and others
OLD-FRENCH MELODIES
  (Moffat) SCH
OLD IRISH AIR
  (Tertis) GS
OLD IRISH DANCE, based on Norah O'Neill
   and Foggy Dew
  (Spalding) CF B2219
OLD MCDONALD IN THE DELL
  (Buchtel) Kjos S-5003
OLD MASTERS FOR THE VIOLIN
  Pet 3226
   13 Pieces by Benda, Birckenstock,
    Corelli, Locatelli, Pisendel, Porpora,
    Rebel, Tartini, Tremais, Vachon,
    Veracini, Vivaldi, Walther
OLD MASTERS FOR YOUNG PLAYERS
  (Moffat) SCH   3V

OLD REFRAIN
  (Ambrosio) CF B2590   simpl
  (Kreisler) Fol 1065
OLD-RUSSIAN MELODIES
  (Moffat) SCH
OLD TREASURES, VOL I
  (Brayley-Stein-Harris) CF
OLD VIENNESE MELODY
  (Herfurth) BMC
d'OLLONE, MAX (1875-1959)
  Romanichels, orig for vln and orch
    Heugel
O'MALLEY, E.
  Jig, from Irish Airs
    STB
  Lament, from Irish Airs
    STB
  Romance, from Irish Airs
    STB
ONDŘIČEK, FRANZ (1859-1922)
  Rhapsodie Bohème, Op. 21
    BRH
OPERAS AND OPERETTAS
  (Krentzlin) SCH   2V
ORBAN, MARCEL (1884-1958)
  Pièces faciles, 4
    RL
  Sonate
    Senart
ØRBECK, ANNE-MARIE (1911-   )
  Melodi
    Musikk-Huset
ORE
  Sonatina in C, Op. 22
    Paxton (Mil No. P527)
ORNSTEIN, [LEO (1895-   )]
  Russian Festival, Op. 61, No. 3
    (Hartmann) AMP
ORR, ROBIN (1909-   )
  Sonatina
    Oxf 23.023
ORSZAGH, T.
  Short Violin Pieces, 5
    Kul
ORTMANS, RENÉ
  Concertino No. 1 in a, Op. 12
    CF B2715
  Concertino No. 2 in D, Op. 14
    CF B2825
OTEY, WENDALL
  Kentucky Suite
    Pr
OUR FAVORITES
  (Palaschko) SCH
OVERTURES BY BEETHOVEN, MOZART &
    WEBER
    Pet 3299A
OVERTURES BY BELLINI & ROSSINI
    Pet 494
PABST, LOUIS (1846-1903)
  Cradle Song
    VL 17   2nd vln ad lib
  Danza, I1
    VL 27
  Gavotte
    VL 19   2nd vln ad lib
  Minuet
    VL 20   2nd vln ad lib
  Reverie
    VL 38   2nd vln ad lib
  Romance
    VL 33
  Serenade
    VL 18   2nd vln ad lib

PACHULSKI
  Prelude
    (Moffat) JWL (Mil No. W1237)
PACINI
  Variations on a theme of, see Dancla,
    Charles; Air Varié, Op. 89, No. 1
PADEREWSKI, IGNACE JAN (1860-1941)
  Melody, Op. 16, No. 2
    (Kreisler) Fol 1144
  Menuet, Op. 14, No. 1, orig for pno
    (Centano) CF B3289
    (Halle) Bel 673
    (Kreisler) Fol 1145
    (Trinkaus) Fill
PAGANETTI
  Au Luxembourg
    Deiss
  Dimanche soir au Village
    Deiss
  Papillons
    Deiss
  Sommeil d'Ange
    Deiss
PAGANI WALTZ
  (Harvey) VL 59   2nd vln ad lib
PAGANINI, NICCOLÒ (1782-1840)
  Adagio, from Concerto No. 2 in b, Op. 7
    (Kortschak) GS
  Adagio amoroso e tamburino, from
    Sonatas Op. 3, Nos. 4 and 5, orig
    for vln and guitar
    (Abbado) Ric ER2074
  Bell, see Rondo à la clochette
  Campanella, see Rondo à la clochette
  Caprices, 24, Op. 1, orig for vln unacc
    (Abbado) SZ
    GS L1663
  Caprices, 24, Op. 1, pno part only
    Pet 4497A,b   2V; pno accomp by
    Schumann
  Caprices, 3, see Kahn
  Caprice No. 13
    (Kreisler) Fol 1088
  Caprice No. 17 in E flat
    (Busch) BRH
  Caprice No. 20
    (Kreisler) Fol 1089
    (Rostal) Nov
  Caprice No. 24
    (Auer) CF B76
    (Elman) CF 03531
    (Kreisler) Fol 1090
    (Yost) VL
  Carnival of Venice, Op. 10
    (Campanini) Ric 127729
    7 selected variations
    (Halle) Bel 682[31]
    (Samethini) CF S3129   Introduction,
      Theme, 10 Variations and Finale
    see also Paganini Album
  Clochette, see Rondo à la clochette
  Concerto No. 1 in D, Op. 6
    (De Guarnieri) Ric ER126
    (Flesch) Int   with cadenza
    (Flesch) Pet 1991
    (Francescatti) Mil
    (Sauret) SCH
    (Wilhelmj) CF L605   freely transcribed
    (Wilhelmj) Paragon
    (Wilhelmj) SIM
    cadenzas published separately, see
      under vln unacc: Friedman, Quiroga,
      Sauret, Winkler

_____
[31] Probably theme only.

PAGANINI, NICCOLO (cont.)
Concerto in one movement, from Concerto
No. 1 in D, Op. 6
(Kreisler) Fol 1092
Concerto No. 1, in D, first movement
(Wilhelmj-Zimbalist) GS L1460
Concerto No. 2 in b, Op. 7
(Wilhelmj) SCH
Carisch
cadenza published separately, see
under vln unacc: Baller
Concerto No. 2 in b, second movement,
see Rondo à la clochette
Duetti Fiorentini, 6
(Kergl) SCH 2V
Duetto amoroso
(Kergl) SCH
I Palpiti. Variations, Op. 13
(Kreisler) Eul (Pet No. Z243)
(Kreisler) Fol 1121
(Kreisler) Ric ER2249
(Lichtenberg) GS
(Maglioni) Ric ER534
see also Paganini Album
Moses-Fantasy, see Variations on the
G string
Moto Perpetuo, Op. 11
(Kreisler) Eul (Pet No. Z241)
(Kreisler) Fol 1147
(Kreisler) Int
(Kreisler) Ric 128646
(Lichtenberg) GS L521
(Mittel) CF L88
(Polo) SZ
(Tagliacozzo) Ric 128063
ZA 3626
see also Paganini Album
Napoleone, see Sonata on the G string
Non più mesta. Variations, Op. 12
(Kreisler) Eul (Pet No. Z242)
(Kreisler) Fol 1155
(Kreisler) Ric ER2248
Perpetual Motion, see Moto Perpetuo
Primavera, La. Polacca and Variations
(Kergl) SCH
Romance, from The Magic Bow, see
Green, Phil
Rondo à la clochette, from Concerto
No. 2 in b, Op. 7, "La Campanella"
(Kreisler) Eul (Pet No. Z239)
"La Clochette"
(Kreisler) Fol 1125 "La Clochette"
(Kreisler) Int "La Campanella"
(Kreisler) Ric 128706 "La Campanella"
(Liszt-Kochanski) CF B1824
"Campanella"
(Wilhelmj) SCH "La Campanella"
SCH "La Campanella"
Sonatas, 6, Op. 2, orig for vln and guitar
Paragon
see also vln and guitar
Sonatas 6, Op. 3, orig for vln and guitar
Paragon
see also vln and guitar
Sonata in A
(Sontag) Fox
Sonata No. 12 in e, from Op. 3, orig for
vln and guitar
(Alard) Ric 36588
(Alard-Meyer) SCH
(Bonelli) ZA 3624
(David) Int
(Prihoda) BH
(Spalding) VL

Sonata on the G string. Napoleone
(Abbado) Ric ER2073
Sonatina in E, orig for vln and guitar
(Polo) SZ
Streghe, Le, Op. 8
(Kreisler) Eul (Pet No. Z240)
(Kreisler) Fol 1129
(Kreisler) Ric ER2243
(Tagliacozzo) Ric ER81
see also Paganini Album
Variations on the G string, on a theme
from Mosè by Rossini
(Wilhelmj) SCH "Moses-Fantasy"
Carisch "Mosè"
Int
Ric ER1984 "Variazioni di bravura"
Variations, Op. 8, see Streghe
Variations, Op. 12, see Non più mesta
Variations, Op. 13, see I Palpiti
Variations, see also Ysaye
Witches Dance, see Streghe, Le
PAGANINI ALBUM
(Becker) Pet 1990
Le Streghe, Op. 8
Carnival of Venice, Op. 10
Moto Perpetuo, Op. 11
I Palpiti, Op. 13
PAGIN
Sonate en ré majeur
HL
PAHISSA, [JAIME (1880-   )]
Nocturno
Ric BA9653
PALASCHKO
Bilderbuch. 10 Pezzi facili, Op. 63
Ric ER393
(PALASCHKO)
Classical Violin
SCH
Our Favorites
SCH
PALMER, EDWINA & BEST, AGNES
Melodic Pieces, 8
Oxf 23.115
More Tunes for Beginners, 20
Oxf 23.321
Tunes for Technique, 12
Oxf 29.001-2 2V
PALMGREN, SELIM (1878-1951)
Preghiera, Op. 78, No. 7
CF B2816
Prelude, Op. 78, No. 1
CF B2814
PANIZZA, ETTORE (1875-   )
Rêverie
Ric BA8227
Sonata in a
SZ
PAPINI, GUIDO
Hope March
CF B3260
Marche Nuptiale
CF B3046
Theme and Variations, Op. 57, No. 1
CF B3328
PARADIES, PIETRO DOMENICO (1707-1791)
Toccata
(Forbes) Oxf 20.107
(Heifetz) CF B2455
PARADIS, MARIA THERESIA (1759-1824)
Sicilienne
(Dushkin) SCH
PARAY, PAUL (1886-   )
Sonate en ut mineur
Jobert

PARKER, ALBERT
Dancing Sunbeams
CF B2293   includes 2nd vln part for
teacher
Hay-Makers Festival
CF B2274   includes 2nd vln part for
teacher
PARKER, CLIFTON (1905-   )
Iquique
Chap-L
PARRIS, ROBERT (1924-   )
Sonata for vln and harpsichord, or pno
CFE
PARRY, CHARLES HUBERT (1848-1918)
Partita in d
Bosw
PARSADANIAN, B.
Concerto
MZK
PARTOS, ÖDÖN (1907-   )
Yiskor, orig for vla and orch
Leeds
PASCAL, A.
Concertino, orig for vln and orch
Dur
Fontainebleau
Dur
1. Le Palais - Cour du Cheval blanc
2. Ciel et forêt
3. Les Bellifontaines
4. Marche des Bellifontains
PASCAL, CLAUDE (1921-   )
Sonate
Dur
Sonatine
Dur
PASQUALI, [NICOLÒ (? -1757)]
Sonata[32]
(Ysaÿe) SF
PASSANI, EMILE (1905-   )
Menuet
Chant du Monde
PATRIOTIC AIRS
(Harvey) VL 1   2nd vln ad lib
PEDROLLO, ARRIGO (1878-   )
Sonata in b
ZA 4083
PEERY, ROB ROY
June Waltz
CF B2149
PEETERS, FLOR (1903-   )
Aria[33]
Heuwek
PEIKO, [NIKOLAI (1916-   )]
Concert Fantasy
MZK
(PENSEL)
Sonatinas and Pieces
Pet 4690A,b   2V   for contents see title
PENTLAND, B.
Vista
CL
PEPUSCH, JOHN CHRISTOPHER (1667-1752)
Chamber Sonatas, 6
(Kolneder) SCH   vcl ad lib
Sonatas, 6
SCH   vcl ad lib
PEQUENO VIOLINISTA, EL
(Spiller) Ric BA8650

PERAGALLO, L.A.
Venetian Serenade
VL 123
PERAGALLO, [MARIO (1910-   )]
Concerto
UE 12299
PEREDIAZ
Piezas españolas, 3
Ric BA10397
PERGAMENT, B.
Serenade
(Ludwig) Lud S-15A2
PERGOLESI, GIOVANNI BATTISTA (1710-1736)
Aria; with Presto by Ober and Bull's
Minuet by Haydn
MZK
Concertino in B flat
(Dushkin) SCH
Concerto
Carisch
Se tu m'ami
(Elkan) H Elkan
Sonatas, 12
(Longo-Giarda) Ric ER660
Sonata No. 12 in E
(Longo) Int
Sonata in G
(Oboussier) SCH   vcl ad lib
Tre giorni, from Nina[34]
(Perlman) CF B2769
PERLMAN, GEORGE
Clown's Greeting To a Dummy
CF B2485
Dance of the Rebbitzen, from Suite Hébraique
CF B2204
Hebrew Chant and Dance, No. 3 of Ghetto
Sketches
CF B2263
Indian Concertino
CF B3286
Little Sleepy Head
CF B2346
Parade of the Colored Puppets
CF B2343
(PERLMAN, GEORGE)
Let Us Have Music for Violin
CF 03206-7   2V   for contents see title
Modern Violin Soloist
CF 02940   for contents see title
Violinist's Contest Album
CF 02779   for contents see title
Violinists' First Solo Album
CF 02663-4   2V   for contents see title
Violinists' Program Builder
CF 02930   for contents see title
PERRAULT, M.
Solitude
CL
PERRY, HAROLD
Concertino
BH
PESCETTI, GIOVANNI BATTISTA
Allegro
(Spalding) VL
PESENTI, MARTINO (1600-1647)
Lamento e Corrente, see Solo Violin
Music of the Earliest Period
Tänze aus Op. 15
(Cerha) DOB
PESSARD, ÉMILE (1843-1917)
Andalouse, Op. 20
CF B3096

---

[32] This publication is not listed in current U.S. catalogues.
Information was received from Fondation Eugène Ysaÿe.
[33] In the U.S.A. this publication can be obtained through
Elkan-Vogel.

---

[34] Attributed to Pergolesi.

PESSARD, EMILE (cont.)
  Méditation
    Gaudet
PESTALOZZA, ALBERTO
  Ciribiribin
    (Eckstein) CF M314
PETER, H.A.
  Bagatelle
    OBV
  Pastorale
    OBV
PETER LEE OF PUTNEY
  Rigaudon
    (Applebaum) Bel SI22
PETERKIN, NORMAN (1886-   )
  Twilight Tune
    Oxf 20.105
PETIT, A.S.
  Doux Réve
    Gaudet
PETRASSI, GOFFREDO (1904-   )
  Introduzione e allegro
    Ric 122923
PETRASSI, [GOFFREDO]
  Canto per Addormentare Una Bambina
    (Corti) Carisch
PETRI, W
  Short Waves Tunes
    Wagenaar
PETZOLD, RUDOLF (1908-   )
  Sonate, Op. 19
    Gerig
PFEIFFER, [GEORGES-JEAN (1835-1908)]
  Musette
    (Gregh) RL
PFEIFFER, JOHANN (1697-1761)
  Sonata in D
    (Schäffler) NAG
PFITZNER, HANS (1869-1949)
  Concerto in b, Op. 34
    BH
  Sonata in e, Op. 27
    Pet 3620
PHILIPPART-GONZALEZ, R.
  Petites Piéces, 3
    Senart
PIASTRO, JOSEPH, see Borissoff, Josef
PICK-MANGIAGALLI, RICCARDO (1882-1949)
  A Coralline
    Carisch
PIECES, 7
    MZK
      Compositions by Ernesaks, Eller, Kapp,
      Auster, Arro
PIECES, 5
    (Zakharina) MZK
PIECES, 8, BY OLD MASTERS
    (Jacobsen) Nov
PIECES, 8, BY RUSSIAN COMPOSERS
    (Utkin) MZK
PIECES, 6, BY RUSSIAN COMPOSERS
    (Utkin) MZK
PIECES, 6, BY RUSSIAN AND SOVIET COM-
      POSERS
    (Agarkov) MZK
PIECES, 7, BY SOVIET COMPOSERS
    (Fortunatov) MZK
PIECES, 7, BY SOVIET COMPOSERS
    (Utkin) MZK
PIECES FROM THE 18TH CENTURY, 6
    (Hale) STB
PIECES, 25, IN THE FIRST POSITION
    (Lehmann) GS
      Beriot: Rondo
      Bloch, F.: Lullaby

Cursch-Bühren: Melody
Dancla, C.: Air varié, Op. 123, No. 7
Dancla, C.: Mazurka, Op. 123, No. 11
Dancla, L.: Petite valse, Op. 48, No. 4
Dancla, L.: Serenade, Op. 48, No. 13
Eichberg: Album leaf
Eichhorn: Cradle-song
Eulenstein: Serenade
Gilis: Réverie
Grünwald: Theme with variations
Hauser: Dorflied, Village song
Jacoby: Polonaise
Klassert: Melody
Klassert: Scherzo
Köhler: Cradle-song
Köhler: Gypsy melody
Lagye: Farewell song
Papini: Theme with variations
Reinecke: Cavatina
Rieding: Polonaise
Sitt: Romance
Sitt: Waltz
Thomas: Rustic dance
(PIECHLER)
  Auserlesene Melodien
    SCH   for vln and pno or organ
    for contents see title
PIERNÉ, GABRIEL (1863-1937)
  Sérénade in A
    (Mittell) GS
    (Saenger) CF B3323
  Sonate, Op. 36
    Dur
PIJPER, WILLEM (1894-1947)
  Sonata No. 1
    Ches
  Sonata No. 2
    DN (Pet No. D230
PILATI, MARIO (1903-1938)
  Caccia
    Carisch
  Pezzi, Due
    Curci
  Preludio, Aria e Tarantella Sopra
      Vecchi Motivi Populari Napoletani
    Carisch
PILLOIS, [JACQUES (1877-1935)]
  Chanson triste
    Senart
PISENDEL, JOHANN GEORG (1687-1755)
  Sonata in e
    (Hausswald) SCH
PISK, PAUL (1893-   )
  Eclogue, Op. 86, No. 1
    CFE
  Shanty-Boy
    AMP
PISTON, WALTER (1894-   )
  Concerto
    BH
  Concerto No. 2
    AMP
  Sonata
    AMP
  Sonatina, for vln and harpsichord or pno
    BH
PIZZETTI, ILDEBRANDO (1880-   )
  Aria
    Curci
  Canti, 3
    Ric 119894
  Concerto in A
    SZ
  Sonata in A
    Ches

PLANTATION MEDLEY
  (Harvey) VL 29   2nd vln ad lib
PLATTI, [GIOVANNI (1690-1763)]
  Sonata in A
    (Jarnach) SCH
  Sonata in e
    (Jarnach) SCH
PLAY UP GYPSY
  (Magyary) Kul
PLEYEL, IGNAZ (1757-1831)
  Duets, 6, Op. 8, orig for 2 vln
    (Herrmann) GS L832   2nd vln ad lib
    Aug 7545
    CF L147-A
    Pet 2970A   2nd vln ad lib
  Duets, 6, Op. 23
    CF 03481-A
  Duets, 3, Op. 44
    Aug 7544
  Duets, 6, Op. 48
    (Herrmann) GS L833   2nd vln ad lib
    Aug 7546 "Sonatinas"
    CF L157-A
    Pet 2970b   2nd vln ad lib
PLOTÉNYI, F.
  Gioja, La
    (Hartmann) AMP
POCHON, ALFRED (1878-1959)
  Forlana, after Aubert
    CF B1836
  Spirit of the 18th Century, after Martini
    CF B1255
POLDINI, EDUARD (1869-1957)
  Poupée Valsante
    (Ambrosio) CF B2599   simpl
    (Hartmann) AMP
    (Kreisler) Fol 1097
    (Moses-Tobani-Saenger) CF B2690
    (Sandler) Ric LD287
POLDINI
  General Boom Boom
    (Applebaum) Mil
POLIAKIN, F.
  Canary
    (Hero) Paragon
    Sal
POLIAKOV, V.
  Concerto
    MZK
POLLET
  Farolito de mi barrio. Tango
    Ric BA11538
PONCE, MANUEL MARÍA (1882-1948)
  Cancion de Otono
    Peer
  Estrellita
    (Halle) Bel 680
    (Heifetz) CF B2141
    (Ludlow) CF B2094
    (Simon) CF B2606   simpl
    AMP
    VL 131   2nd vln ad lib
PONCHIELLI, AMILCARE (1834-1886)
  Dance of the Hours, from La Gioconda
    (Centano) CF B2629
    (Centano) CF B3712   simpl
    (Morlacchi) Ric 126836
POOT, MARCEL (1901-   )
  Ballade
    ESC
  Duo
    ESC
POP GOES THE WEASEL
  (Harvey) VL 142   2nd vln ad lib

POPPER, DAVID (1843-1913)
  Elfentanz, Op. 39, orig for vcl and orch
    (Sauret) CF B3018
  Fond Recollections, Op. 64, No. 1, orig
    for vcl and pno
    (Willeke) CF B1843
  Gavotte No. 2, Op. 23, orig for vcl and orch
    (Auer-Saenger) CF B2684
  Spinning Song, Op. 55, No. 1, orig for
    vcl and pno
    (Heifetz) CF B2438
POPULAR VIOLIN ALBUM
  Aug AS.81
    Goltermann: Le Reve
    Gounod-Bach: Meditation
    Gounod: Serenade
    Raff: Cavatina
    Reber: Berceuse
    Rubinstein: Melodie
    Schumann: Slumber Song
POPY, F.
  Valse poudrée
    Gaudet
PORPORA, NICOLA ANTONIO (1686-1768)
  Allegro giocoso
    (Klengel) Pet 4168
  Aria
    (Corti) Carisch
  Minuet, see Deplan: Entrada
  Minuetto
    (Corti) Carisch
  Presto
    (D'Ambrosio) Ric 129411
  Round Dance, see Marcello: Scherzando
  Sonata in F
    (Salmon) Ric R372
  Sonata in G
    (David) Curci
  Sonata in G
    Carisch
  Sonata in g
    (Jacobsen-Toni) Ric ER1785
  Sonata in g
    (Moffat) SIM
PORTER, QUINCY (1897-   )
  Improvisation
    CFE
  Pieces, 4
    Mercury
  Sonata No. 2
    Pet 6670
PORTNOFF, LEO
  Concertino in e, Op. 13
    Bosw (Bel No. 1)
  Concertino in a, Op. 14
    Bosw (Bel No. 2)
  Concertino in D, Op. 92
    Noet (Pet No. N837)
  Concertino in D, Op. 94
    Noet (Pet No. N838)
  Concertino in d, Op. 95
    Noet (Pet No. N839)
  Concertino in d, Op. 96
    Noet (Pet No. N840)
  Concertino in G, Op. 97
    Noet (Pet No. N841)
POTSTOCK, WILLIAM H.
  Souvenir de Sarasate, Op. 15
    CF B813
POULENC, FRANCIS (1899-1963)
  Bagatelle No. 1
    RL
  Mouvements Perpetuels, orig for pno
    (Heifetz) CF B2242

POULENC, FRANCIS (cont.)
  Presto in B flat
    (Heifetz) CF B2513
  Sonata
    ESC
POWELL, JOHN (1882-   )
  From a loved past, Op. 23a
    GS
  Natchez-on-the-Hill
    GS
  Sonata Virginianesque, Op. 7
    GS
PRACHT, ROBERT
  Easy Pieces, 12, Op. 12
    BMC
PREDIERI, LUCA ANTONIO (1688-1767)
  Concerto in b
    Hug (Pet No. A50)
PRESLE, see La Presle
PRESS, JACQUES
  Wedding Dance
    Weintraub
PRESTON, STANLEY
  Song of the Canoe
    CF B2268   includes 2nd vln part for
      teacher
PRINCIPE
  El Campielo
    Ric 122901
  Nei boschi del Renon
    Ric 122902
PROCTOR, CHARLES (1906-   )
  Sonata in a
    Leng (Mil No. L1111)
PROKOFIEV, SERGEY (1891-1953)
  Concerto No. 1 in D, Op. 19
    (Persinger) Leeds
    BH
    Int
  Concerto No. 2 in g, Op. 63
    (Francescatti) Int
    (Persinger) Leeds
    BH
  Fairy Winter, from Cinderella
    (Rostal) Nov
  Gavotta, Op. 32, orig for pno
    (Heifetz) CF B2431
  Gavotte, from Classical Symphony
    (Grunes) Omega
    see also Alexandrov: Aria
  Larghetto and Gavotta, from Classical
    Symphony, Op. 25
    (Heifetz) CF B2481
  March, from Love for Three Oranges
    (Heifetz) CF B2480
  March, Op. 12, No. 1, orig for pno
    (Heifetz) CF B2651
  March; with March by Vlasov
    MZK
  Marchand amoreux, Le, from Chout
    (Heifetz) CF B3351
  Masks, from Romeo and Juliette
    (Heifetz) CF B2616
  Melodies, 5, Op. 35 bis
    (Persinger) Leeds
    BH
  Pieces, 3, from Music for children,
    Op. 65, orig for pno
    (Liepmann) GS
  Pieces, 3, from Romeo and Juliet
    (Grunes) Omega
  Sonata No. 1 in f, Op. 80
    (Oistrakh) Int
    (Oistrakh) Pet 4718
    (Szigeti) Leeds

  Sonata No. 2 in D, Op. 94a
    (Oistrakh) Int
    (Szigeti) Leeds
  Theme and Processional, from Peter and
    the Wolf
    (Grunes) Omega
PROSSE, ANGELO DE
  Petite Bourree
    (Saenger) CF B826
PUGNANI, GAETANO (1731-1798)
  Allegro entusiastico
    (Moffat) CF B736
  Amoroso in E, from Sonata, Op. 6, No. 4
    (Jacobsen) Pet 4228
  Gavotta Variata
    Carisch
  Largo; with Allegro by Fiocco
    MZK
  Sonata No. 3
    (Arrieu) Ric R1554
  Sonata in E, see Solo Violin Music of the
    Earliest Period
PURCELL, DANIEL (c.1660-1717)
  Hornpipes, 2
    (Moffat) Aug
PURCELL, HENRY (c.1659-1695)
  Airs, 2
    (Mangeot) Aug
  Air
    (Reed) Aug
  Pieces, 14
    (Dolmetsch) Nov
  Pieces, 6
    Pet 4156A
  Pieces, 3
    (Reed) Aug
  Pieces for Violin
    (Brodszky) Kul 2V
  Purcell Suite
    (Goldsbrough) Oxf 23.107
  Slow Air, from The Virtuous Wife
    (Bridgewater) BH
  Slow Air and Hornpipe, from The Married
    Beau
    (Harrison) Aug
  Sonata in g
    (Ferguson) Hin (Pet No. H574A)
  Sonata in g
    (Goldsbrough) Oxf 23.031
  Sonata in g
    (Moffat) SIM
  Sonata in g
    (Schroeder) BRH vcl ad lib
PÜRINGER, ANTON
  Sonatina
    OBV
QUARATINO
  El flechazo. Canción argentina
    Ric BA9893
  Vidala del plenilunio
    (Cambón) Ric BA11066
QUENTIN
  Sonata in D
    (Soëtens) SCH
QUILTER, ROGER (1877-1953)
  Slumber Song, from Where the Rainbow Ends
    EKN
QUINET, FERDNAND (1898-   )
  Sonata in d
    Bosw
QUINET, MARCEL (1915-   )
  Sonatina
    CBDM

QUIROGA, [MANUEL (1890-   )]
  Danza Argentina
    Sal
  Rondalla
    Sal
RACHMANINOFF, SERGEY (1873-1943)
  Daisies, Op. 38, No. 3, orig for voice
    (Heifetz) CF B2819
    (Kreisler) Fol 1139
  Danse Hongroise
    BH
  Danses Tziganes
    (Dushkin) SCH
  Elegie, Op. 3, No. 1, orig for pno
    (Schuster) MK
    MZK
  Etude.Tableau No. 2, orig for pno
    (Heifetz) CF B2800
  Italian Polka
    (Kreisler) Fol 1034
    MZK
  Marguerites, see Daisies
  Melodia, Op. 3, No. 3, orig for pno
    (D'Ambrosio) Ric 119233
  Melody, Op. 21, No. 9, orig for voice
    (Heifetz) CF B3341
  Melody
    (Altschuler) CP
  Oriental Sketch, orig for pno
    (Heifetz) CF B2820
  Preghiera, from Concerto No. 2 for pno
    (Kreisler) Fol
  Prelude, Op. 23, No. 4, orig for pno
    MZK
  Prelude No. 5, orig for pno
    (Heifetz) CF B2801
  Prelude in e flat, orig for pno
    (Heifetz) CF B2423
  Prelude in g, orig for pno
    (Kreisler) Fol 1028
  Romance, Op. 4, No. 5, orig for voice
    (Orszagh) Kul
  Romance, Op. 6, No. 1
    MZK
  Romance
    (Persinger) Leeds
  Serenade, Op. 3, No. 5, orig for pno
    (D'Ambrosio) Ric 119234
    (Narsaroff) BH
  Serenade
    (Elman) CF B362
  Variation 18 from Rhapsody on a Theme of
    Paganini, orig for pno and orch
    (Kreisler) Fol 1170
  Vocalise, Op. 34, No. 14, orig for voice
    (Press-Gingold) Int
    BMC
    MZK
RADIO CITY ALBUM
  MK
    Brahms: Waltz in G
    Chaminade: Scarf Dance
    Dark Eyes
    Geiger: Just for tonight
    Jessel: Parade of the Wooden Soldiers
    Lehar: Frasquita Serenade
    Lincke: Glow-Worm
    Londonderry Air
    Mendelssohn: On wings of song
    Rubinstein: Romance
    Saint-Saens: Swan
    Schubert: Ave Maria
    Schubert: March Militaire

    Schubert: Moment Musical
    Strauss: On the beautiful blue Danube
    Two Guitars
RADIO COLLECTION OF MODERN GEMS
  Ru
RADIO COLLECTION OF NATIONAL SONGS
  AND HYMNS
  Ru
RADIO COLLECTION OF SWING SOLOS
  Ru
(RADMALL, PEGGY)
  Chesterian Series of Graded Violin Music
  Ches   8V
RAFF, JOSEPH JOACHIM (1822-1882)
  Cavatina, Op. 85, No. 3
    (Palaschko) SCH
    (Perlman) CF S3135
    (Schradieck) GS
    Ric 128628
    VL 75
  Declaration of Love, from String Quartet,
    Op. 192, No. 2
    (Saenger) CF
RAFTER, LEONARD (1911-   )
  Pieces, 5
    Bosw
RAKES OF MALLOW
  (Moffat) Aug
RAKOV, [NICOLAI (1908-   )]
  Concerto
    MZK
  Improvisation; Scherzino; Poem
    MZK
  Poem
    MZK
  Scherzino
    (Hartmann) MZK
  Sonata
    MZK
  Vocalise; with Oriental Dance by Mostras
    MZK
RALSTON, F.M.
  Sonate Spirituelle
    AMP
RAMEAU, JEAN-PHILIPPE (1683-1764)
  Aria
    (Slatter) STB
  Dances from the Operas and Ballets
    (Ross) BMC
  Gavotta
    (Salmon) Ric R82
  Gavotte
    (Burmester) GS
  Minuet in E
    (Franko) RE (Pet No. RE9)
  Minuetto
    (Salmon) Ric R83
  Passepied, from Castor and Pollux
    (Szigeti) CF B2426
  Rigaudon
    (Heifetz) CF B2185
  Tambourin
    (Achron-Heifetz) GS
  Tambourin in E
    (Franko) RE (Pet No. RE10)
  Tambourin
    (Kigyosi) Kul
  Tambourin
    (Kreisler) Fol 1191
RANGSTRÖM, TURE (1884-1947)
  Partita
    UE 10289
  Suite, in modo antico
    WH 1640

RANKI, [GYÖRGY (1907-   )]
  Aristophanes Suite
    Kul
  Serenata all'antiqua
    Kul
  Sword Dance
    Kul
RAPHAEL, GÜNTER (1903-1960)
  Jabonah, Op. 66a. Ballet Suite
    BRH
  Sonata in E, Op. 12, No. 1
    BRH
  Sonata in G, Op. 12, No. 2
    BRH
RASBACH, OSCAR (1888-   )
  Trees
    (Hartmann) GS
RATCLIFFE, DESMOND
  Sonata
    Nov
RATEZ, [ÉMILE-PIERRE (1851-1934)]
  Sonate Dorienne
    Senart
RATHAUS, KAROL (1895-1954)
  Sonata No. 1, Op. 14
    UE 8639
  Suite, Op. 27
    UE 9977
RAVEL, MAURICE (1875-1937)
  Berceuse, sur le nom de Fauré
    Dur
  Bolero, orig for orch
    Dur
  Forlane, from Le Tombeau de Couperin,
      orig for pno
    (Heifetz) CF B2611
  Habanera, from Rapsodie espagnole, orig
      for orch
    (Kreisler) CF B2133
  Jeux d'eau, orig for pno
    (Castelnuovo-Tedesco & Szigeti) CF B2766
  Kaddisch, orig for voice
    (Garban) Dur
  Pavane pour une Infante défunte, orig for pno
    (Fleury) ESC
    (Kochanski) ESC
  Piece en forme de Habanera, orig for voice
    Leduc
  Sonate
    Dur
  Tzigane[35]
    Dur
  Valses Nobles et Sentimentales, Nos. 6 and 7,
      orig for pno
    (Heifetz) CF B2613
RAWSTHORNE, ALAN (1905-   )
  Concerto No. 1
    Oxf 23.013
  Concerto No. 2
    Oxf 23.030
  Sonata
    Oxf 23.101
RAY, RUTH
  Midland Tune
    CF B2788
  My Lord, what a mournin'
    CF B2787
READ, GARDNER (1913-   )
  Intimate Moods, 6, Op. 35
    CF 03435
REBEL, JEAN-FÉRY (c.1661-1747)
  Sonate en ré mineur
    HL

REBEL, [JEAN-FÉRY]
  Iris, L'. Sonata No. 3
    Transatlantiques
REBIKOV, VLADIMIR I. (1866-1920)
  Characteristic Dance, see Mussorgsky:
    Tears
  Song Without Words; Tarantella
    MZK
  Waltz, from The Christmas Tree
      (Grunes) Omega
    MZK
  Without Thee
    (Simon) CF B2107
REDMAN, REGINALD (1892-   )
  Barcarolle
    Aug
  Pieces, 5
    Aug AS.91
  Short Pieces, 9
    Aug AS.87
REED, WILLIAM HENRY (1876-1942)
  Alla Marcia, from Suite of 4 Pieces
    JWL (Mil No. W1272)
  Concerto in a
    Aug
  Minuet in G, from Suite of 4 Pieces
    JWL (Mil No. W1270)
  Pastorale, from Suite of 4 Pieces
    JWL (Mil No. W1271)
  Roundelay
    ABRS (Mil No. A229)
  Sailor's Song
    ABRS (Mil No. A252)
  Spinning Song, from Suite of 4 Pieces
    JWL (Mil No. W1273)
REEKS, GERTRUDE, see Lovell & Reeks
REGER, MAX (1873-1916)
  Aria, from Suite in a
    (Strub) BB
  Concerto in A, Op. 101
    Pet 3112
  Fugue, from Suite im alten Stil, Op. 93
    (Strub) BB
  Largo, from Sonata, Op. 139
    (Flesch) Pet 4171
  Largo, from Suite im alten Stil, Op. 93
    (Strub) BB
  Pieces, 3, Op. 79d
    Sik 358
  Prelude, from Suite im alten Stil, Op. 93
    (Strub) BB
  Sonata No. 1 in d, from 2 Little Sonatas,
      Op. 103b
    BB
  Sonata No. 2 in A, from 2 Little Sonatas,
      Op. 103b
    BB
  Sonata in c, Op. 139
    Pet 3985
  Sonata in B flat, Op. 107, orig for clar
    BB
  Suite im alten Stil, Op. 93
    (Strub) BB
  Suite in a, Op. 103a
    (Strub) BB
  Valse d'amour, Op. 130, No. 5, from Ballet
      Suite
    Pet 4259
  Virgin's Slumber Song, Op. 76, No. 52,
      orig for voice
    (Vecsey) BB
REHFELD, FABIAN
  Prayer
    (Sylvain) BMC

---

[35] Also for violin and orchestra.

REHFELD, FABIAN (cont.)
Spanish Dance, Op. 47, No. 5
CF S3514
GS
Spanish Dance, Op. 48, No. 1
CF S3464
REINHOLD, OTTO (1899-   )
Konzert
Baer 2028a
Sonate
Baer 1989
REITER, [ALBERT (1905-   )]
Little Pieces, 4
SIM
Sonatina
OBV
REIZENSTEIN, FRANZ (1911-   )
Concerto in G
Leng (Mil No. L1125)
Fantasia Concertante
Leng (Mil No. L1134)
Pieces, 3
BH
Prologue, Variations and Finale
BH
Sonata in G sharp
Leng (Mil No. L1113)
RELIGIOUS MEDITATIONS
(Ambrosio) CF 02585
Batiste: Pilgrim of love
Bizet: Intermezzo
Bohm: Calm as the night
Bott: Adagio religioso, Op. 6
Bull: Saeterjentens sondag
Chaine: Romanza, Op. 43, No. 10
Gillet: Andante religioso
Gounod: Communion
Gounod: Hymne à Sainte Cecile
Gounod: Nazareth
Grieg: Hail, Star of heaven
Handel: Pastoral symphony, from
Messiah
Mackenzie: Benedictus, Op. 37
Massenet: Last dream of the Virgin
Peron: Meditation religieuse
Peron: Offertoire
Schubert: Prayer, Adagio from Octet
Thomé: Andante religioso, Op. 70
REMEMBER THEE & ST. PATRICK WAS A
GENTLEMAN
(Moffat) Aug
RENARD, FÉLIX
Berceuse No. 2, Op. 20
CF S3092
RESPIGHI, OTTORINO (1879-1936)
Concerto Gregoriano
UE 7050
Poema Autunnale, orig for vln and orch
BB
Sonata in si min.
Ric 117619
REUCHSEL, MAURICE (1880-   )
Rhapsodie Franc-Comtoise
HL
Sonate No. 2
HL
REUTER, [FLORIZEL VON (1890-   )]
Old American Negro Songs
UE 2740
REUTER, FRITZ
Dance Fantasy in D, Op. 36, No. 1
MT (Pet No. MV1203)
Little Sonata in C, Op. 37
MT (Pet No. MV1211)

Sonata in e, "Lausitzer"
MT (Pet No. MV1212)
REUTER, F.
Concerto
BRH
REVUELTAS, SILVESTRE (1899-1940)
Pieces, 3
SMP
REVUTZKY
Little Song; with Lullaby by Shaporin
MZK
REZNICEK, EMIL NIKOLAUS VON (1860-1945)
Konzert in e
Birnbach
Nachtstück, orig for vcl, harp, 4 horns and
str quartet
Birnbach
RIBÁRI, ANTAL
Sonata No. 1
Kul
RICHARDS, H.W.
Melody in G
ABRS (Mil No. A230)
RICHARDSON, ALAN (1904-   )
Sonnet
JWL (Mil No. W1276)
RICHTER, FRANZ XAVER (1709-1789)
Sonata da Camera in A
(Riemann) BRH   vcl ad lib
RIECKEN, GUSTAV
Souvenir de Lubeck, Op. 3
(Lehmann) CF B2794
RIEDING, OSCAR
Air Varié
CF B3127
Concertino in D, Op. 5
CF 03486
Kul
Concertino in e, Op. 7
Bosw (Bel No. 17)
Concertino in a, Op. 21
Bosw (Bel No. 3)
Concertino in G, Op. 24
Bosw (Bel No. 4)
Concertino in D, Op. 25
Bosw (Bel No. 5)
Concertino in G, Op. 34
Bosw (Bel No. 6)
Concertino in b, Op. 35
Bosw (Bel No. 7)
Concertino in D, Op. 36
Bosw (Bel No. 8)
Impromptu
CF B3135
Pastorale, Op. 23, No. 1
Bosw
Polonaise de Concert, Op. 10
Kul
Polonaise
CF B3068
Rondo, Op. 22, No. 3
Bosw
Slumber Song, Op. 22, No. 1
Bosw
RIEGGER, WALLINGFORD (1885-1961)
Sonatina, Op. 39
MK
Variations, Op. 71, orig for orch
AMP
Whimsy, Op. 2, orig for vcl and pno
AMP
RIES, FRANZ (1846-1932)
Adagio, from Suite No. 3, Op. 34, No. 3
(Saenger) CF B2716

RIES, FRANZ (cont.)
  Capricciosa, La
    CF B2175
  Perpetuum Mobile, from Suite No. 3,
    Op. 34, No. 5
    (Saenger) CF S3362
  Suite No. 3, in G, Op. 34
    (Schradieck) GS L418
RIESCO, CARLOS
  Canzona e Rondo
    Peer
RIETI, VITTORIO (1898-   )
  Rondo Variato
    (Dushkin) AMP
  Serenata
    Deiss
  Variations on a Chinese Theme
    UE 7393
RIISAGER, KNUDAGE (1897-   )
  Lullaby
    LY (Pet LY7)
  Sonate
    WH 2456
RIMSKY-KORSAKOV, NIKOLAY (1844-1908)
  Chanson Arabe, from Scheherazade
    (Kreisler) Fol 1091
  Dance of the Gold and Silver Fishes, from
    Sadko
    (Bolotone) MZK
  Dance of the Rivers and Brooks, from Sadko
    MZK
  Fantaisie de concert sur des thèmes
    russes, Op. 33, orig for vln and orch
    (Kreisler) Fol 1104
    Belaieff
  Fantasy on a theme from Coq d'or
    MZK
  Flight of the Bumblebee, from Tsar Saltan
    (Heifetz) CF B2258
    (Kun) MK
    MZK
  Hymn to the Sun, from Le Coq d'or
    (Kreisler) Fol 1124
  Mazurka on 3 Polish Folk Themes
    MZK
  Oriental Romance
    (Hartmann) AMP
  Russian Folk Songs, 2
    MZK
  Snowmaiden's Arietta
    MZK
  Song of India, from Sadko
    (Ambrosio) CF B2592   simpl
    (Eisenberg) MK "Chanson Indoue"
    (Kreisler) Fol 1182
    (Orszagh) Kul   simpl "Hindu Song"
    (Powell) AMP
    (Sammons) Belaieff "Hindu Song"
    (Sandby) CF B942
    BMC
    VL 34
RIVIER, [JEAN (1896-   )]
  Burlesque, orig for vln and orch
    Senart
  Concerto
    Sal
ROBAUDI, VINCENZO
  Alla Stella Confidente
    CF B2985
ROBEL, BERNHARDT
  Kitty's Waltz
    VL 107   2nd vln ad lib
  Polish Medley
    VL 106   2nd vln ad lib

ROBERT, C.
  Petite Maison, La
    Gaudet
ROBYN, ALFRED GEORGE (1860-1935)
  Manzanillo
    (Saenger) CF B2700
ROCHE
  Fantasia on Irish Airs
    Pigott (Mil No. PT410)
RODE, PIERRE (1774-1830)
  Concerto No. 1 in d
    (Auer) CF 03152
    (Hermann) Pet 1095F
    (Quesnot) Senart 5169
  Concerto No. 4 in A
    (Davisson) Pet 1095A   with cadenzas
    (Quesnot) Senart 5168
  Concerto No. 6 in B flat
    (Davisson) Pet 1095b   with cadenzas
      by Klengel
    (Franko) CF 03304   with cadenzas
    (Sauret) Aug 7959
  Concerto No. 7 in a, Op. 9
    (David-Ambrosio) CF L382
    (David-Schradieck) GS L514
    (Davisson) Pet 1095C
    (Gingold) Int   with cadenzas by
      Wieniawski
    (Quesnot) Senart 5170
    (Sauret) Aug 7960
  Concerto No. 8 in e, Op. 13
    (Davisson) Pet 1095D
    (Herrmann) GS L648
    (Sauret) Aug 7961
  Concerto No. 11 in D
    (Davisson) Pet 1095E
RODNEY, PAUL
  Calvary
    (Saenger) CF B3002
RODRIGO, [JOAQUIN (1902-   )]
  Amoureuse au bord de la petite fontaine,
    from 2 Esquisses
    RL
  Petite Ronde, from 2 Esquisses
    RL
RODRIGUEZ, G.H.
  Cumparsita, La
    (Goehr) MK
RODRIGUEZ
  Nocturno melanconico
    Ric BA11517
ROGERS, [BERNARD (1893-   )]
  Portrait, orig for vln and orch
    Pr
ROGERS, H.
  Farmer in the dell; Baa Baa black sheep;
    Mary had a little lamb; Rock-a-bye
    baby
    (Halle) Bel 690
  Swanee river; Home sweet home; My old
    Kentucky home
    (Halle) Bel 688
ROGERS
  Cantilena
    Mil
  Tarantella
    Mil
  Zingaresca
    Mil
ROHOZINSKY, F.
  Pièces, 3
    Senart
ROLLA, [ALESSANDRO (1757-1841)]
  Concerto in A
    (Abbado) SZ

ROLLAND, PAUL & FLETCHER, STANLEY
Perpetual Motion No. 1
  Mil
ROMAN, JOHAN HELMICH (1694-1758)
Concerto in d
  (Rosenberg) Nordiska
Concerto in f
  (Rosenberg) Gehrmans
Sonata in b
  MT (Pet No. MV1196) vcl ad lib
Sonata in c
  (Vretblad) Nordiska
ROPARTZ, J. GUY (1864-1955)
Adagio
  RL
Lamento
  RL
Sonate No. 1 en ré mineur
  Dur
Sonate No. 2 en mi majeur
  Dur
Sonate No. 3 en la majeur
  Dur
ROREM, NED (1923-   )
Mountain Song
  SMP
Sonata
  Pet 6211
ROSAS, JUVENTINO
Over the Waves Waltz
  (Ambrosio) CF B3249
  (Del Maglio) Ric 125608 "Sulle onde"
  (Halle) Bel 662
  VL 48
ROSENBERG, HILDING (1892-   )
Concerto No. 2
  Nordiska
Sonata
  Nordiska
Sonata No. 2
  Nordiska
Suite in D
  Nordiska
ROSEY, GEORGE
Military Tactics
  MK
ROSLAVETZ
Dances, 3
  UE 7344
ROSNER, HENRY
Valse Polonaise
  MK
ROSSELLINI, [RENZO (1908-   )]
Aria dell'800
  Curci
Fontana malata, La
  Ric 122016
ROSSI, M.
Andantino
  (Corti) CF B2157
ROSSINI, GIOACCHINO (1792-1868)
Barber of Seville. Transcription
  (Ambrosio) CF B3294
Figaro, see Castelnuovo-Tedesco
La Gazza Ladra. Overture
  (Lechner) SCH
Moses-Fantasy, see Paganini
Overtures by Bellini and Rossini
  Pet 494
Rosina, see Castelnuovo-Tedesco
Variations on a theme, see Dancla, Charles:
  Air Varié, Op. 89, No. 2
William Tell. Fantasia, see Singelée

William Tell. Overture
  (Weiss-Ambrosio) CF
William Tell. Transcription
  (Ambrosio) CF S3497
ROTA, [NINO (1911-   )]
Sonata
  Ric 124373
ROUSSEL, ALBERT (1869-1937)
Sonate en ré mineur
  RL
Sonate No. 2, Op. 28
  Dur
ROWLEY, ALEC (1892-1958)
Canzona
  EKN
Easy Pieces, 10, Op. 45
  Pet 4384
First Pieces for Violin and Piano, Bk. 4[36]
  GT
Miniature Suite
  JWL (Mil No. W1241)
Pastoral, from 4 Contrasted Pieces
  JWL (Mil No. 1216B)
Pastoral Elegie
  JWL (Mil No. W1216E)
Plaint, from 3 Characteristic Pieces
  Paxton (Mil No. P504)
Poem, from 3 Characteristic Pieces
  Paxton (Mil No. P505)
Rant, from 3 Characteristic Pieces
  Paxton (Mil No. P506)
Romance, from 4 Contrasted Pieces
  JWL (Mil No. W1216C)
Short Lyric Sonata, Op. 48
  Pet 4388
Slumber Song, from 4 Contrasted Pieces
  JWL (Mil No. W1216A)
Tarantella, from 4 Contrasted Pieces
  , JWL (Mil No. W1216D)
RÓZSA, MIKLÓS (1907-   )
Concerto, Op. 24
  BRH
Variations on a Hungarian Peasant Song,
    Op. 4
  BRH
RUBBRA, EDMUND (1901-   )
Concerto, Op. 103
  Leng (Mil No. L1145)
Improvisation, orig for vln and orch
  (Reizenstein) Leng (Mil No. L1133)
Pieces, 4, Op. 29
  Leng (Mil No. L1124)
Sonata No. 2
  Oxf 23.410
RUBINOFF, DAVE
Banjo Eyes
  CF B2398
Dance of the Russian Peasant
  CF B2396
Danse Russe
  CF B2395
Gypsy Fantasy
  Mil
Romance
  CF B2409
Russian Hearts
  DeSylva Brown & Henderson
Slavonic Fantasy
  CF B2410
Souvenir
  DeSylva Brown & Henderson
Tango Tzigane
  Mil

---

[36] In the U.S.A. this publication can be obtained through Mills.

RUBINSTEIN, ANTON (1829-1894)
  Barcarolle in f, orig for pno
    (Ornstein) AMP
  Concerto, Op. 46
    MZK
    Pet 1339
  Melody in F, Op. 3, No. 1, orig for pno
    (Ambrosio-Perlman) CF B2556   simpl
    (Auer-Saenger) CF B3332
    (Palaschko) SCH
    ABRS (Mil No. A237)
    VL 67
  Rêve Angélique, from Kamennoi Ostrow,
    Op. 10, No. 22, orig for pno
    CF S3257
    VL 79 "Kamennoi Ostrow"
  Romance, Op. 44, No. 1, orig for pno
    MZK
  Romance
    (Cheyette) Fox
  Romance
    (Rosey) MK
  Romance, see Glinka: Remembrances of a
    Mazurka
  Spinning Song, see Gliere: Folk Song
RUDHYAR, DANE (1895-   )
  Poems, 3, No. 1
    CFE
RUEGGER, CHARLOTTE
  Concertante in G
    CF B1975
RUMANIAN VIOLIN SOLI, 3
  (Csoka) DOB
RUMEAU, G.
  Pieces, 3
    ESC
(RUSS-BOVELINO)
  Gypsy Fiddle
    Bel EL508
    SCH
RUSSELL, HENRY (1812-1900)
  Life on the Ocean Wave
    Kjos S-5011
RUSSELL, LESLIE
  Easy Pieces for Strings, 3
    Oxf 20.006-32
RUSSIAN FOLK SONGS, 10
  (Liadov) MZK
RUSSIAN FOLK SONGS, 2
  (Fortunatov) MZK
RUSSIAN GYPSY FANTASY
  (Kvelve) VL 158
RUSSOW, L
  First Steps
    BMC
RYELANDT, [JOSEPH (1870-   )]
  Sonatina No. 6, Op. 85
    CBDM
RZAYEV, A
  Concerto
    MZK
SABATINI, GUGLIELMO
  Elegia
    Cor ST4
SABITOV, N
  Concerto
    MZK
(SACHSE)
  Climax Album No. 14
    Paxton (Mil No. P516)   2nd and 3rd
    vlns, vcl ad lib
SADUN, I.
  Romanza
    Gaudet

SAENGER, GUSTAV (1865-1935)
  Bichette, No. 1 of Concert Miniatures,
    Op. 130
    CF B925
  Fantasias, see Korn & Saenger
  Intermezzo Scherzoso
    (Heifetz) CF B1914
  Little Highland Maid, No. 2 of Suite of
    Melodious Solos, Op. 131
    CF B929
  Scotch Pastorale, No. 2 of Concert Minia-
    tures, Op. 130
    CF B1758
  Soldier Song, No. 3 of Concert Miniatures,
    Op. 130
    CF B927
  Springtime, No. 3 of Suite of Melodious
    Solos, Op. 131
    CF B930
SAEVERUD, HARALD (1897-   )
  Romanza, Op. 23
    Musikk-Huset
SAEYS, E
  Concertino No. 1
    Metr
SAGGIONE, GIOSEPPE FEDELI
  Sonate en mi majeur
    HL
SAINT AMANS, LOUIS
  Ninette at court
    (Applebaum) Bel SI21
SAINTON, PHILIP (1891-   )
  Departure of the Pequod
    Leeds
SAINT-SAENS, CAMILLE (1835-1921)
  Caprice andalou, Op. 122[37]
    Dur
  Caprice d'apres l'Etude en forme de
    valse, Op. 52, No. 6
    (Ysaÿe) Dur
    (Ysaÿe) Int "Caprice, Op. 52"
    MZK "Etude in the form of a waltz"
  Concerto No. 1 in A, Op. 20
    (Loeffler) GS L1540   with cadenza
    Haml
    LEU "Konzertstück in A, Op. 20"
  Concerto No. 2 in C, Op. 58
    Dur
  Concerto No. 3 in b, Op. 61
    (Francescatti) Int
    (Sauret) L860
    (Schradieck) CF L372
    Dur
  Danse de la Gypsy, from Henry VIII
    (Saenger) CF B3203
  Danse Macabre, Op. 40, orig for orch
    Dur
  Deluge, Le, Op. 45
    (Saenger) CF S3169
  Havanaise, Op. 83[37]
    (Francescatti) Int
    (Loeffler) BMC
    (Spiering) CF B2664
    Dur
  Introduction and Rondo Capriccioso, Op. 28[37]
    (Francescatti) Int
    (Schradieck) GS L224
    CF L84
    Dur
  Jota Aragonese, Op. 64
    Dur

---

[37] Also for violin and orchestra.

SAINT-SAENS, CAMILLE (cont.)
Melody
(Tertis) GS
Mon coeur s'ouvre à ta voix, from Samson
et Dalila
(Papin-Skalmer) CF B2826
Romance, Op. 37
CF B3074
Sonate No. 1 in d, Op. 75
Dur
Sonate No. 2, Op. 102
Dur
Swan, from Carnival of the Animals, orig
for orch
(Ambrosio) CF B2574 simpl
(Eisenberg) MK
(Godowsky) CF B2177
(Heifetz) CF B2798
(Mittell) GS
(Trinkaus) Fill
CF S3158
VL 119
Willis
SALABERT, [FRANCIS (1884-1946)]
Rêverie exotique
Sal
Un Lac sous la pluie
Sal
SALIMAN-VLADIMIROV, D.
Impromptu; with March by Mostras
MZK
Pieces, 2, on Chinese Themes
MZK
SALMANOV, V.
Lyrical Pages
MZK
SALTA
Nostalgic Serenade
Mil
SAMAZEUILH, GUSTAVE (1877-   )
Sonate
Dur
SAMINSKY, LAZARE (1882-1959)
Chasidic Dance, No. 1 of Chasidic Suite,
Op. 24
CF B2368
Hamavdil, No. 3 of Chasidic Suite, Op. 24
CF B2415
Meditation, No. 2 of Chasidic Suite, Op. 24
CF B2424
Troubadour Song
CF B2370
SAMINSKY, [LAZARE]
Rhapsody
UE 8403
SAMMARTINI, GIOVANNI BATTISTA
(1701-1775)
Canto Amoroso
(Elman) SCH
Canzonetta
(Corti) Carisch
Danses de ballet, Deux
(Moffat) JWL (Mil No. W1234)
Passacaglia
(Nachèz) SCH
Sonata in e
(Moffat) SIM
Sonata in G
(Salmon) Ric R76
Sonata in g
(Salmon) Ric R743
SAMUEL-ROUSSEAU, MARCEL (1882-1955)
Chanson pour Bercer
RL

SANCAN, P.
Concerto, 1st movement
Dur
SANDBERGER, ADOLF (1864-1943)
Sonata, Op. 10
Lit (Pet No. L2869)
SANDI, LUIS (1905-   )
Aire Antiguo
EMM
SANDOR, FRIGYES
Fiddler's Compendium
Kul
SANTA-CRUZ, DOMINGO (1899-   )
Pieces, 3
Pr
SANTA LUCIA
(Harvey) VL 154 2nd vln ad lib
(Herfurth-Strietel) Willis
SAPHIR, SEVERIN
Dream
CP
SAPOZHNIN, see Kapp & Sapozhnin
SARAI, T.
Capriccio
Kul
Lassu and Friss
Kul
SARASATE, PABLO DE (1844-1908)
Adieux, Les, Op. 9
CF B3345
Ballade, Op. 31
Dur
Caprice Basque, Op. 24
(Jacobsen) SIM
(Zimbalist) GS L1485
CF L644
Carmen. Fantaisie de concert, Op. 25
(Saenger) CF 03714
(Zimbalist) GS
Danse Espagnole, Op. 37
(Lutz) SCH
Faust. Fantaisie
CF S3203
Gypsy Airs, see Zigeunerweisen
Habanera, see Spanish Dance No. 2
Introduction et Tarentelle, Op. 43[38]
CF B1256
Jota Aragonesa, Op. 27
(Jacobsen) SIM
Jota Navarra, see Spanish Dance No. 4
Malaguena, see Spanish Dance No. 1
Playera, see Spanish Dance No. 5
Romanza Andaluza, see Spanish Dance No. 3
Serenata Andaluza
(Jacobsen) SIM
Spanish Dances Nos. 1 and 2, Op. 21.
Malaguena and Habanera
CF S3826
SIM
Spanish Dance No. 1, Op. 21, Malaguena
(Heifetz) CF B2441
CF S3824
Spanish Dance No. 2, Op. 21. Habanera
(Butéra) GS
CF B3329
Spanish Dances Nos. 3 and 4, Op. 22
Romanza Andaluza and Jota Navarra
SIM
Spanish Dance No. 3, Op. 22.
Romanza Andaluza
(Pintér) GS
CF S3795

---

[38] Also for violin and orchestra.

SARASATE, PABLO DE (cont.)
  Spanish Dances Nos. 5 and 6, Op. 23.
      Playera and Zapateado
      CF B2778
      SIM
  Spanish Dance No. 5, Op. 23. Playera
      CF B3282
  Spanish Dance No. 6, Op. 23. Zapateado
      (Heifetz) CF B2440
  Spanish Dances Nos. 7 and 8, Op. 26
      SIM
  Spanish Dance, Op. 37, see Danse
      Espagnole
  Zapateado, see Spanish Dance No. 6
  Zigeunerweisen, Op. 20, orig for vln
      and orch
      (Lechner) SCH "Gypsy Airs"
      (Mittell) GS L1064
      (Saenger) CF S3165
      (Wilhelmj) SIM "Gypsy Airs"
      Pet 4990
SÁS, ANDRÉS (1900-   )
  Cantos del Peru
      SMP
SATIE, ERIK (1866-1925)
  Choses vues à droite et à gauche
      RL
  Gymnopédie, orig for pno
      (Stoessel) CF B1116
SAUGUET, HENRI (1901-   )
  Concerto d'Orphée
      Heugel
  Sonatine
      RL
SAUVERPLAINE, HENRY (1892-   )
  Habanera
      Chant du Monde
SAUVREZIS, [ALICE (1866-1946)]
  Chant sans Paroles
      Senart
  Sonate
      Senart
SAVELIEV, B.
  Tarantella
      MZK
  Waltz
      MZK
SAYGUN, A. ADNAN (1907-   )
  Sonata, Op. 20
      SMP
SCARLATESCU, J.
  Bagatelle
      SCH
SCARLATTI, ALESSANDRO (1660-1725)
  Minuet
      (Hartmann) AMP
  Sonatas, 2, in G, F
      (Ewerhart) WM (Pet No. WM29)
      vcl ad lib
SCARLATTI, DOMENICO (1685-1757)
  Caprice
      (Herrmann) ESC
  Pastorale
      (Herrmann) ESC
  Pieces, 12 Selected
      (Heifetz) CF 03222, 03297 2V
  Sonatas, 8
      (Salter) Aug   published separately
  Sonatina
      (Heifetz) CF B2316
SCARLATTI
  Gigue
      (Godowsky) Bosw

SCARMOLIN, A. LOUIS (1890-   )
  One fingered waltz
      Lud S-15A22
  Violinist on parade
      Lud S-15A21
SCARMOLIN, [A. LOUIS]
  Dancing Fireflies
      Pr
  First Finger Pieces, 3
      Pr
SCASSOLA, A.
  Méditation
      Sal
  Sérénade Romantique
      Sal
SCELZI, GIACINTO (1905-   )
  Sonata
      Santis 724
SCHAEFER
  Invocation
      Leng (Mil No. L1140)
  Springtime
      Leng (Mil No. L1144)
SCHARRES, C.
  Sonatina in C
      Brogneaux
SCHELLING, ERNEST (1876-1939)
  Concerto
      (Kreisler) LEU
  Irlandaise
      (Kreisler) CF B2122
(SCHERMANN, L.)
  Album Hongrois
      CF 04
SCHERS
  Sonatas, 4, orig for fl and pno
      RH (Pet Nos. ER9-10) 2V
SCHIAVO DE GREGORIO, M.
  Suite
      Carisch
SCHIFF, [HELMUT (1918-   )]
  Variationen
      DOB
SCHISKE, KARL (1916-   )
  Sonata, Op. 18
      DOB
SCHMELZER, JOHANN HEINRICH
      (c.1623-1680)
  Sonatae unarum fidium, 6, per violino e
      basso continuo
      (Cerha) UE 13301-2 2V
  Suite in D
      Noet (Pet No. N3245)
SCHMID, HEINRICH KASPAR (1874-1953)
  Allegretto, Op. 34, No. 2
      SCH
SCHMIDT, ERNST
  Alla turca, No. 8 of Easy and Instructive
      Pieces, Op. 19
      (Centano) CF B986
  Idylle, No. 6 of Easy and Instructive
      Pieces, Op. 19
      (Centano) CF B984
  Romance, No. 2 of Easy and Instructive
      Pieces, Op. 19
      (Centano) CF B980
SCHMIDT, OSCAR
  Cavatine, Op. 41
      (Ambrosio) CF S3137
(SCHMIDTNER, FRANZ)
  House Concert
      Sik 171-2 2V for contents see title
SCHMITT, FLORENT (1870-1958)
  Barcarolle
      HL

SCHMITT, FLORENT (cont.)
Chant du soir
  RL
Habeyssée, Op. 110, orig for vln and orch
  Dur
Lied
  HL
Nocturne
  HL
Scherzo vif, orig for vln and orch
  Mathot
Sérénade
  HL
Sonate libre en deux parties enchaînées
  Dur
SCHNABEL, A.
Sonata
  BH
SCHNEIDT, HANNS-MARTIN (1930-   )
Kleine Stücke, 5
  Baer 2683
SCHOBERT, JOHANN (c.1720-1767)
Sonata in A, Op. 9, No. 2
  (Kramolisch) NAG
Sonata, see vln and harpsichord
SCHOENBERG, ARNOLD (1874-1951)
Concerto, Op. 36
  GS
 *Phantasy, Op. 47
  Pet 6060
Sonata, after Quintet for wind instruments,
  Op. 26
  (Greissle) UE 8375
SCHOLLUM, ROBERT (1913-   )
Concerto, Op. 65
  DOB
Sonata, Op. 42, No. 3
  DOB
Sonatina, Op. 55, No. 1
  DOB
SCHRAMMEL, J.
Wien bleibt Wien, March
  SCH
SCHRÖDER, H
Musical Reflections, Op. 29, 10 Pieces
  CF
SCHROEDER, H.
Duo, Op. 28
  SCH
Pieces, 5
  SCH
SCHUBERT, FRANCOIS (1808-1878)
Abeille, L', Op. 13, No. 9
  (Mittell) GS
  (Saenger) CF S3001
  (Spiller) Ric BA11723
  (Wilhelmj) SCH "Die Biene"
  see also Benda: Caprice
SCHUBERT, FRANZ (1797-1828)
Adagio, from Arpeggione Sonata
  (Spiro) BRH
Ave Maria, Op. 52, No. 6, orig for voice
  (Ambrosio) CF B2582 simpl
  (Del Maglio) Ric 124694
  (Edward) MK
  (Hauser) CF S3062
  (Hauser-Mittell) GS
  (Palaschko) SCH
  (Wilhelmj) GS
  (Wilhelmj-Heifetz) CF B2433
  (Wilhelmj-Perlman) CF S3064
Ballet Music from Rosamunde
  (Kreisler) Fol 1186
  (Lechner) SCH "Ballet Music No. 2"

Concert Piece, see Konzertstück
Cradle Song, see Wiegenlied
*Duos
  (David) Pet 156b
    Rondeau brillant in b, Op. 70
    Fantaisie in C, Op. 159
    Introduction and Variations in e,
     Op. 160
    Duo Sonata in A, Op. 162
Duo Sonata in A, Op. 162, D.574[39]
  Int
  MZK
  Pet 156bb
  see also Duos
Entr'acte, from Rosamunde
  ABRS (Mil No. A231)
Fantasia in C, Op. 159, D.934[39]
  Int
  see also Duos
German Dances, Op. 33, orig for pno duet
  (Sitt) Pet 2471
Hark! Hark! the Lark, orig for voice
  (Ambrosio) CF B2578 simpl
Impromptu in G, Op. 90, No. 3, orig for pno
  (Barmas) Leng (Mil No. L1109)
  (Heifetz) CF B2317
Introduction and Variations in e, Op. 160,
  D.802, orig for fl and pno
  see Duos
Konzertstück in D, D.345,[39] orig for vln
  and orch
  (Hermann) BRH
  (Jacobsen) Hin (Pet No. H206)
Marche Militaire, Op. 51, No. 1, orig for
  pno duet
  (Ambrosio) CF B2600 simpl
  (Applebaum) Bel SI29
  (Lutz) SCH
  (Rosey) MK
  (Weiss) CF
  VL 50
Minuets, 2 Easy
  (Ross) BMC
Moment Musical, Op. 94, No. 3, orig for pno
  (Kreisler) Fol 1146
  (Moffat) SCH
Moment Musical
  (Rosey) MK
Overture, from Rosamunde
  (Lechner) SCH
Reverie
  (Forbes) Oxf
Rondo in A, D.438,[39] orig for vln and str
  quartet
  (Jacobsen) Hin (Pet No. H207)
Rondo brillant in b, Op. 70, D.895[39]
  BRH
  Int
  see also Duos
Rondo, Op. 53, orig for pno
  (Friedberg-Kreisler) CF B400
Serenade, orig for voice
  (Alard) Ric 43336
  (Ambrosio) CF B2557 simpl
  (Elman) GS
  (Halle) Bel 670
  (Moffat) SCH
  (Reményi) CF S3440
  (Reményi) GS
  CF S3437

---

[39] D. number refers to the Schubert Thematic Catalogue by
Otto Erich Deutsch, in collaboration with Donald R. Wakeling.
London, 1951.

SCHUBERT, FRANZ (cont.)
  Sonata in A, Op. 162, see Duo Sonata
  *Sonatinas, 3, Op. 137, D.384, 385, 408[39]
    (David) GS L921
    (Henle-Röhrig) Henle
    (Hermann) Pet 156A
    (Kehr-Schröter) SCH
    (Pessina) Ric BA11060
    Aug 7571
    BRH
  Sonatina in D, Op. 137, No. 1, D.384
    (Jacobsen) Pet 156A
    (Kehr-Schröter) SCH
    JWL (Mil No. W1274)
  Sonatina in a, Op. 137, No. 2, D.385
    (Jacobsen) Pet 156A
  Sonatina in g, Op. 137, No. 3, D.408
    JWL (Mil No. W1275)
    Pet 156A
  Songs, 12 Selected
    (Sitt) Pet 2267
  Songs, 2. Ave Maria and Am Meer
    (Wilhelmj) SCH
  Ständchen, see Serenade
  Symphony No. 8 in b, "Unfinished"
    Pet 2275
  Valse, see Waltz
  Variations on a theme of, see Sinigaglia
  Viennese Dances, 30
    (Hoffmann) SCH
  Waltzes, 3
    (Applebaum) GS
  Waltz in a, from Deutsche Tänze,
    Op. 33, No. 10, orig for pno duet
    (Achron) CF B2238
  Waltz in A, from Valses sentimentales,
    Op. 50, No. 5, orig for pno
    (Achron) CF B2236
  Waltz
    (Kigyosi) Kul "Valse"
  Wiegenlied, Op. 98, No. 2, orig for voice
    (Kvelve) VL 161   2nd vln ad lib
    "Cradle Song"
    Ric 127836 "Ninna-nanna"
SCHUETTE, FLORENCE
  Mother's Memory
    (Chemet) CF B2126
SCHULTZE, M.
  Christmas Songs. Fantasia
    (Ambrosio) CF B1008
      O Sanctissima; Tomorrow will be
      Christmas; O come little children;
      O faithful pine; Silent night
SCHULZ, JOHANN ABRAHAM PETER
    (1747-1800)
  Sonata in D
    (Hillemann) Noet (Pet No. N3258)
SCHUMAN, WILLIAM (1910-   )
  Concerto
    Pr
SCHUMANN, ROBERT (1810-1856)
  Abendlied, Op. 85, No. 12, orig for pno duet
    (Singer) BMC
  Adagio and Allegro, Op. 70, orig for horn
    and pno
    BRH
    Pet 2386
  Childish Pranks
    (Applebaum) Mil
  Concerto in d
    SCH
  F-A-E Sonata, see Brahms-Dietrich-
    Schumann
  Fairy Tales, see Märchenbilder

Fantasiestücke, Op. 73, orig for clar and pno
  (Schradieck) GS L412
  Pet 2366b
Fantasy, Op. 131, orig for vln and orch
  (Davisson) Pet 2368A
  (Kreisler) Fol 1103
  (Parent) Senart 5322
Garden Melody
  Leng (Mil No. L1141)
Intermezzo
  (Rostal) Nov
Märchenbilder, Op. 113, orig for vla
  and pno
  (Schradieck) GS L415
    "Pictures from Fairyland"
  BRH
  Pet 2372 "Fairy Tales"
Mélodie sur une petite étude, Op. 68,
  see Legris
Rêverie, see Träumerei
Romances, 3, Op. 94, orig for ob and pno
  (Schradieck) GS L413
  BRH
  Pet 2387
Romance in A
  (Kreisler) Fol 1168
Slumber Song, Op. 124, No. 16, orig for pno
  ABRS (Mil No. A241)
Soldier's March, orig for pno
  Kjos S-5012
Sonatas, 2, Op. 105 and Op. 121
  (Hermann) Int
  Aug 7585
  Pet 2367
Sonata No. 1 in a, Op. 105
  (Bauer) GS L1696
  MZK
Sonata No. 2 in d, Op. 121
  (Bauer) GS L1699
  BRH
Sonata No. 3 in a[40]
  SCH
Songs, 15 Selected
  Pet 2371
Träumerei, Op. 15, No. 7, orig for pno
  (Del Maglio) Ric 125609 "Rêverie"
  (Eisenberg) MK
  (Halle) Bel 696
  (Palaschko) SCH
  (Perlman) CF S3003
  (Singer) BMC
  (Singer) CF S3384
  (Tonini) Ric BA10872 "Rêverie"
  FR (Pet No. F42)
  VL 72 "Träumerei and Nocturne"
Vogel als Prophet, from Waldscenen,
  Op. 82, No. 7, orig for pno
  (Heifetz) CF B2436
  (Saenger) CF B1009
SCHWARTZ, LEON
  Bar-Mitzvah Nigun
    Bel 659
SCHWARTZ, PAUL
  Allegro Ostinato
    CFE
  Sonata, Op. 12
    CFE
SCIOSTAKOVIC, see Shostakovitch
SCOTT, CYRIL (1879-   )
  Aubade
    SCH

---

[40] In <u>Kammermusik-Katalog</u> compiled by J. F. Richter
(Leipzig, 1960) this is identified as the F-A-E Sonata.

SCOTT, CYRIL (cont.)
  Cherry Ripe, orig for pno
    SCH
  Danse Negre, Op. 58, No. 5, orig for pno
    (Kramer) EKN
  Fantasie Orientale
    EKN
  Gentle Maiden
    SCH
  Intermezzo
    (Lange) EKN
  Lotus Land, orig for pno
    (Kreisler) EKN
  Lullaby, Op. 57, No. 2, orig for voice
    (Barns) EKN
  Sonata Melodica
    EKN
SCRIABIN, ALEXANDER (1872-1915)[41]
  Etude, Op. 2, No. 1
    (Krane) GS
  Etude in Thirds, Op. 8, No. 10
    (Szigeti) CF B2446
  Etude, Op. 8, No. 11
    MZK
  Impromptu a la Mazur, Op. 7, No. 1
    MZK
  Mazurka, Op. 3, No. 3
    MZK
  Mazurka, Op. 3, No. 5
    MZK
  Mazurka, Op. 3, No. 8
    MZK
  Nocturne, Op. 5, No. 1
    MZK
  Nocturne in F
    MZK
  Prelude, Op. 2, No. 2
    MZK
  Waltz, Op. 1
    MZK
SCULL, HAROLD (1898-   )
  Portrait, Op. 122, No. 3
    Mil
SEGESDY
  Hortensia. Czardas húngara
    Ric BA11348
SEIBER, MÁTYÁS (1905-1960)
  Concert Piece
    SCH
  Easy Dances, Vol. I
    SCH
  Fantasia concertante, orig for vln and orch
    SCH
  Sonata
    SCH
SEITZ, FRIEDRICH
  Concerto in D, Op. 7
    (Mittell) GS L947 "No. 1"
    Bosw (Bel No. 24)
    CF L590 "No. 1"
    Noet (Pet No. N283) "No. 5"
  Concerto in g, Op. 12
    (Mittell) GS L948 "No. 3"
    Bosw (Bel No. 25)
    CF L592 "No. 3"
    Noet (Pet No. N282) "No. 3"
  Concerto in G, Op. 13
    Bosw (Bel No. 26)
    CF L591 "No. 2"
    GS L945 "No. 2"
    Noet (Pet No. N238) "No. 1"

Concerto in D, Op. 15
  (Mittell) GS L949 "No. 4"
  Bosw (Bel No. 27)
  CF L593 "No. 4"
  Noet (Pet No. N239) "No. 4"
Concerto in D, Op. 22
  (Mittell) GS L950 "No. 5"
  Bosw (Bel No. 28)
  CF L594 "No. 5"
  Noet (Pet No. N240) "No. 2"
Concerto No. 5 in D, Op. 22, first movement
  (Klotman) Mil
Gypsies are coming, Op. 16, No. 4
  BMC
(SEITZ, FRIEDRICH)
  Album of Classical Sonatinas
    BMC for contents see title
SELECTED CLASSICAL SONATAS, VOL. I
  (Twarz) Cranz
SENAILLÉ, JEAN BAPTISTE (1687-1730)
  Allegro spiritoso
    (Salmon) Ric R80
  Little French Boy
    (Applebaum) Bel SI27
  Polichinelles, Les
    (Moffat) SCH
  Sarabanda e allemanda
    (Salmon) Ric R376
  Sonata in c
    HL
  Sonata in d
    (Parkinson) Oxf
  Sonata in E
    HL
  Sonata in G, Op. 5
    (Jensen) Aug 7405
  Sonata in G
    (Moffat) SIM
  Sonata in G
    (Salmon) Ric R753
  Sonata in g
    (Salmon) Ric 754
  Sonata, see Easy Sonatas of Old-French
    Masters
(SEREDY, JULIUS S.)
  Themelodies for Violin
    CF 03259
      Themes and melodies from famous
      compositions
SERENADE
  (Kempf) BMC; Italian Folk Melody
SERMON, E.
  Little Piece, Op. 10
    Brogneaux
SERRADELL, NARCISO
  Golondrina, La
    (Heilbron) CF B3244
    VL 122 2nd vln ad lib
ŠEVČIK, OTAKAR (1852-1934)
  Holka Modrooká. Bohemian Dances and
    Songs, Bk. 1, Op. 10
    CF B1017
SÉVERAC, [DÉODAT DE (1873-1921)]
  Lied romantique
    RL
  Minyoneta
    RL
  Souvenirs de Céret
    RL
SEVERN, EDMUND (1862-1942)
  Brunette, La
    CF B1020
  Dancing Master
    CF B1846

---

[41] All compositions listed were originally written for piano solo.

SEVERN, EDMUND (cont.)
  Fileuse, La
    CF B1022
  Gavotte in G
    CF B1024
  Gavotte Moderne in D
    CF B1023
  In Picture Land
    CF 0489
  Juggler
    CF B1037
  Perpetuum Mobile
    CF B1044
  Polish Dance
    CF B1045
  Russian Dance No. 1
    CF B1896
  Russian Dance No. 2
    CF B1897
  Swan Boats, from In Central Park
    CF B1026
(SEVERN, EDMUND)
  Big notes for little violinists
    Willis
SEYBOLD, ARTHUR (1868-1948)
  Polonaise, Op. 86
    BMC
(SEYBOLD)
  Magic Fiddle   Vol. 6
    SIM
SHANAHAN, LEONARD
  Irish Fantasy
    Pigott (Mil No. PT409)
SHAPERO, HAROLD (1920-   )
  Sonata
    SMP
SHAPEY, RALPH (1921-   )
  Five for violin and piano
    CFE
  Sonata
    CFE
SHAPORIN
  Lullaby, see Revutzky: Little Song
SHATIRIAN, S.
  Fantasy
    MZK
SHAVERZASHVILI, [ALEXANDER (1919-   )]
  Sonata
    MZK
SHAW, CHRISTOPHER
  Sonata
    Nov
SHAW
  Gaelic Moods
    Mozart Allan (Mil No. MA61)
SHEBALIN, VISSARION Y. (1902-   )
  Concertino
    MZK
  Sonata, Op. 51, No. 1
    MZK
SHEINKMAN
  Sonata
    Pet 5851
SHEPHERD, ARTHUR (1880-1958)
  Sonate
    Senart
SHER, V.
  Tarantella; Toccata
    MZK
SHIELD, WILLIAM (1748-1829)
  Tempo di Minuetto
    (Anderson) Oxf
SHLONSKY, V.
  Hora
    Senart

SHORE, BERNARD (1896-   )
  Fairy Ring
    Aug AS.89
  Impressions, 6
    JWL (Mil No. W1263)
SHORT'NIN' BREAD
  (Eckstein) CF M301
SHOSTAKOVITCH, DMITRI (1906-   )
  Concerto, Op. 99
    (Oistrakh) Int
    (Oistrakh) Leeds
    Pet 4728
    Ric 129372
  Fantastic Dances, 3, Op. 1, orig for pno
    (Glickman) Leeds
  Polka, from Golden Age Ballet, Op. 22
    (Glickman) Leeds
    (Grunes) Omega
  Preludes, 4, from Op. 34, orig for pno
    (Tziganov) MZK
SHTOGARENKO & KLEBANOV
  Song
    MZK
SIBELIUS, JEAN (1865-1957)
  Berceuse, Op. 79, No. 6
    WH 2214
  Concerto in D, Op. 47
    (Francescatti) Int
  Danse characteristique, Op. 79, No. 3
    WH 2211
  Danses Champêtres, 5, Op. 106
    WH 3132-6   published separately
  Humoresque No. 1, Op. 87, No. 1, orig
    for vln and orch
    WH 2340
  Humoresque No. 2, Op. 87, No. 2, orig
    for vln and orch
    WH 2342
  Humoresque No. 3, Op. 89, No. 1, orig
    for vln and orch
    WH 2295
  Humoresque No. 4, Op. 89, No. 2, orig
    for vln and orch
    WH 2241
  Humoresque No. 6, Op. 89, No. 4, orig
    for vln and orch
    WH 2294
  Impromptu, Op. 78, No. 1
    WH 2341
  Laetare anima mea, Op. 77, No. 1, orig
    for vln or vcl and orch
    WH 2173
  Musette, from King Christian II
    (Powell) AMP
  Novellette, Op. 102, No. 1
    WH 2262
  Religioso, Op. 78, No. 3
    WH 2202
  Rigaudon, Op. 78, No. 4
    WH 2339
  Romance, Op. 24, No. 9[42]
    (Herfurth) BMC
  Romance in F, Op. 78, No. 2
    BMC
    WH 2201
  Serenade, Op. 79, No. 4
    WH 2212
  Sonatine, Op. 80
    WH 2143
  Souvenir, Op. 79, No. 1
    WH 2209
  Tanz-Idylle, Op. 79, No. 5
    WH 2213

---

[42] Transcription, perhaps originally for orchestra.

SIBELIUS, JEAN (cont.)
Tempo di menuetto, Op. 79, No. 2
WH 2210
Valse Triste, Op. 44, orig for orch
(Franko) AMP
(Hermann) BRH
(Saenger-Perlman) CF B2742
see also Mendelssohn: Nocturno
SIEGL, OTTO (1896-   )
Albumblatt, from 8 Pieces, Op. 148
OBV
Allegretto, from 8 Pieces, Op. 148
OBV
Andante Cantabile, from 8 Pieces, Op. 148
OBV
Canon, from 8 Pieces, Op. 148
OBV
Capriccio, from 8 Pieces, Op. 148
OBV
Galanterie, from 8 Pieces, Op. 148
OBV
Geigenbüchlein, Das
DOB
Ländler, from 8 Pieces, Op. 148
OBV
Psalm, from 8 Pieces, Op. 148
OBV
Sonata No. 1, Op. 39
DOB
Sonata No. 2 in c, Op. 117
DOB
SIEM, KARE
Skorgelaten
Musikk-Huset
SILENT NIGHT
(Harvey) VL 46   2nd vln ad lib
SILESU, LAO
Peu D'Amour, Un
(Langey) Chap-L
SIMONDS, BRUCE (1895-   )
Habanera
Oxf 92.301
SIMONETTI, ACHILLE (1857-1928)
Madrigale
CF S3289
GS
Kjos S-5016
Ric 54914
SINANIAN, G
Allegro appasionato
Marcotte
Chant élégiaque
Marcotte
Feuille d'album
Fèret
Habanera
Marcotte
Impression
Marcotte
Mouvement perpétuel
Marcotte
SINDING, CHRISTIAN (1856-1941)
Ballade, Op. 43, No. 2
WH 288
Berceuse, Op. 43, No. 3
WH 289
Cantus doloris, Variations, Op. 78
Pet 3134
Konzert in A, Op. 45
WH 407
Legende, Op. 46, orig for vln and orch
WH 637
Prélude, Op. 43, No. 1
WH 287

Romance, Op. 9
WH 577
Sonata in C, Op. 12
WH 5
Sonata in E, Op. 27
Pet 2826
Suite in a, Op. 10
(Flesch) Pet 2477A
(Svecenski) GS L1446
MZK
Suite in F, Op. 14
WH 222
SINFONIAS, 3
(Kölz) DOB   vcl or gamba ad lib
18th century, composer unknown
SINGELEE, JEAN-BAPTISTE (1812-1875)
Favorita, La. Fantasia
CF B3154
Mandolinata. Fantasia
CF B1076
Rigoletto. Fantasia
(Pollitzer) CF B2656
Trovatore, Il. Fantasia
CF B3346
William Tell. Fantasia
CF B2734
SINIGAGLIA, LEONE (1868-1944)
Variations, 12, on a Schubert theme, Op. 19
BRH
SIOHAN, [ROBERT (1894-   )]
Concert
Sal
SISATO, NA
(Maresh) VL 103   2nd vln ad lib
SITT, HANS (1850-1922)
Concertino in e, Op. 31
(Saenger) CF L628
Eul (Pet No. Z165)
GS L1074
Concertino in d, Op. 65
Eul (Pet No. Z167)
Concertino in a, Op. 70
Bosw (Bel No. 12)
Concertino in a, Op. 93
Eul (Pet No. Z133)
Concertino in C, Op. 104
(Centano) CF B2828 "No. 1"
Concertino in a, Op. 108
(Centano) CF B2727 "No. 2"
Concertino in d, Op. 110
(Centano) CF B2827 "No. 3"
Sonatina in C, Op. 62, No. 1
Pet 2747A
Sonatina in a, Op. 62, No. 2
Pet 2747b
Sonatina in D, Op. 62, No. 3
Pet 2747C
Sonatina in C, Op. 109, No. 1
Aug 7558a
Sonatina in G, Op. 109, No. 2
Aug 7558b
Tarantella, Op. 26, No. 12
(Saenger) CF S3836
SITT
Song without words
Bosw
SJÖGREN, EMIL (1853-1918)
Sonata in g, Op. 19
Pet 2215
Sonata No. 4, Op. 47
BRH
SKERJANC, LUCIJAN MARIJA (1900-   )
Dithyrambic Pieces, 4
Ches

SKORULSKY, M.
  Largo
    MZK
SKORZENY, [FRITZ (1900-   )]
  Fantasie-Sonate
    DOB
SLADEK, PAUL
  Berceuse
    Mil
  Caprice Villageois
    VL
  Elegy
    VL
  Gavotte Coquette
    Mil
  Isle of Mists
    VL
  Mazurka
    Mil
  Menuet Pompadour
    CP
  Old Clock
    CP
  Poeme d'Amour
    VL
SLONIMSKY, NICOLAS (1894-   )
  Moto Perpetuo
    Templ
SMETANA, BEDŘICH (1824-1884)
  Aus der Heimat, Nos. 1 and 2
    Pet 2634
  Aus der Heimat, No. 1
    (Sitt-Saenger) CF B1101
  Bohemian Dance, from The Bartered Bride
    (Ondřícek) SIM
  Fantasy on a Czech Folk Song "Sil jsem
      prose"
    Artia
  From the Home Land
    Artia
SMITH, DAVID STANLEY (1877-1949)
  Sonata
    SPAM
SMITH, HALE (1925-   )
  Duo
    CFE
  Epicedial Variations
    CFE
SMITH, LELAND
  Sonata Movement
    CFE
  Sonatina
    CFE   score only
SMITH, SYDNEY (1839-1889)
  Chanson Russe, Op. 31
    (Barres) CF B3005
    (Halle) Bel 679
SOKOLOFF, NOEL (1923-   )
  Epithalamium
    Peer
SOLIS, SOLITO DE
  Reverie
    Mil
SOLO VIOLIN MUSIC OF THE EARLIEST
      PERIOD
    (Zimbalist) Pr
    Bassani: Balletto
    Biber: Passacaglia, for vln unacc
    Farina: Capriccio stravagante, for
        vln unacc
    Geminiani: Adagio e Allegro, for
        vln unacc
    Marini: La Romanesca

    Merula: Canzone
    Neri: Sonata
    Pesenti: Lamento e Corrente
    Pugnani: Sonata in E
    Torelli: Preludio e Allegro
    Uccellini: Aria
    Veracini, A: Grave e Allegro
    Vitali: Due Capricci
    Vivaldi: Sonata in C
SOLOS FOR STRINGS
    (Whistler) Ru
SOLOS FOR THE VIOLIN PLAYER
    (Gingold) GS
    Bach, J.S.: Siciliano, from Sonata No. 4
    Brahms-Klengel: Hungarian Dance
        No. 2
    Faure: Berceuse, Op. 16
    Grieg: Album Leaf, from Lyric Pieces,
        Op. 12
    Grieg: Waltz, from Lyric Pieces, Op. 12
    Mondonville: Tambourin
    Mozart: Rondo in D
    Paganini: Sonata No. 12
    Prokofiev: Aria, from Alexander Nevsky
    Rebel: The Bells
    Schubert: Allegro, excerpt from
        Concertpiece
    Schumann: Abendlied, Op. 85, No. 12
    Senallié: Allegro spiritoso
    Sinding: Adagio, from Suite in a, Op. 10
    Tchaikovsky-Kleinecke: Valse
        Scherzo No. 2
SOMERVELL, ARTHUR (1863-1937)
  Allemande
    Aug
  Barcarolle
    Aug
  Concertstück, orig for vln and orch
    Aug
  Miniature Pieces
    JWL   2V
  School of Melody
    Aug
  Suite of 4 Pieces
    JWL
  What You Will
    Aug
SOMIS, GIOVANNI BATTISTA (1686-1763)
  Sonata in G
    HL
SOMIS, [GIOVANNI BATTISTA]
  Sonata in G
    (Salmon) Ric R378
SONATINAS AND PIECES
    (Lenzewski) SCH   2V
    Works by Beethoven, Fischer, Handel,
        Haydn, Purcell, Telemann and others
SONATINAS AND PIECES
    (Pensel) Pet 4690A,b   2V
    Vol 1: 16 pieces by J.C. Bach, J.S. Bach,
        Beethoven, Dussek, Dvorak, Genzmer,
        Glière, Handel, Hauptmann, Kuhlau,
        Martini, Nardini, Purcell, Telemann,
        Veracini
    Vol 2: 14 pieces by Corelli, Dvorak,
        Grieg, Haydn, Mozart, Reger, Rowley,
        Schubert, Smetana, Thilman, Vieux-
        temps, Viotti, Weber, Weyrauch
SONG OF VERMLAND
    (Kvelve) VL 129
SONGS AND MARCHES BY FAMOUS COM-
      POSERS
    (Liepmann) GS
    Beethoven: March from Fidelio
    Beethoven: Theme from Symphony No. 7

SONGS AND MARCHES BY FAMOUS COM-
POSERS (cont.)
(Liepmann) GS (cont.)
Beethoven: Theme from Violin Sonata
No. 1
Mozart: Aria from Bastien and Bas-
tienne
Mozart: Cavatina from The Marriage
of Figaro
Mozart: March from The Marriage of
Figaro
Schubert: Hedge-Rose
Schubert: Linden Tree
Schubert: Trout
Schumann: Gypsies' Song
Schumann: Little Owl
Schumann: Song of the Bride
SONGS OF SCOTLAND
(Harvey) VL 4   2nd vln ad lib
SONTAG, WESLEY
Set of Four
Fox
(SONTAG, WESLEY)
Folk- and master-melodies for the young
violinist
GS   3V
SORANTIN, ERICH
Rondo in G, Op. 3
CF B2243
SORESINA, [ALBERTO (1911-   )]
Sonatina serena
Curci
SOULAGE, M.
En Première
Sal
SOURIS, [ANDRE (1899-   )]
Fatrasie
CBDM   for vln and pno or harp
SOWERBY, LEO (1895-   )
Suite
BMC
SPALDING, ALBERT (1888-1953)
Castles in Spain, Op. 7, No. 4
CF B1221
Etchings, Op. 5
CF 03428
From the Cottonfields, Op. 7, No. 3
CF B1220
Gavotte Caprice, Op. 7, No. 1
CF B1218
Gavotte Pompadour
CF B2763
Lettre de Chopin, Op. 7, No. 2
CF B1219
Menuet Watteau
CF B2760
Pond Lily
CF B2761
Prelude, from Suite
CF B2019
Wind in the Pines
CF B2366
Ye Olde Troubadour Song
CF B2762
SPEAKS, OLEY (1874-1948)
Sylvia
(Hartmann) GS
SPIELBUCH FÜR DIE GEIGE, see Sonatinas
and Pieces (Pensel)
SPILLER, A.
Fly Swallow   "Repulj fecskem"
Kul
(SPILLER)
Pequeno violinista, El
Ric BA8650

SPOHR, LUDWIG (1784-1859)
Barcarolle
CF B2998
Concerto No. 2 in d, Op. 2
(Auer) CF 03945
(David-Svecenski) GS L363
(Davisson) Pet 1098A
Concerto No. 6 in g, Op. 28
(Auer) CF L901
(Remy) Senart 5286
Pet 1098B
Concerto No. 7 in e, Op. 38
(Auer) CF L709
(David) Pet 1098C
Concerto No. 8 in a, Op. 47, in modo d'una
scena cantante
(Auer) 03718
(Carri) CF L461
(Davisson) Pet 1098D
(Remy) Senart 5283
(Schradieck) GS L389
(Wessely) SCH
Concerto No. 9 in d, Op. 55
(Davisson) Pet 1098E
(Remy) Senart 5285
(Schradieck) GS L360
Concerto No. 11 in G, Op. 70
(Auer) CF 03717
(Davisson) Pet 1098F
(Remy) Senart 5284
(Svecenski) GS L1481
Concerto No. 12 in A, Op. 79
(Seeger) Pet 1098G
Concerto in A
(Göthel) Baer 2309a
Grande Polonaise in a, Op. 40
Lit (Pet No. L1922)
Sonata in c, see vln and harp
SPOLIANSKY, M.
Tango-Habanera
Senart
SQUEO, ALFREDO
Capriccio a Fantasia, Op. 6
CF B2619
Étude Caprice, Op. 5, No. 5
CF B2660
Little Marching Soldiers
CF B2660
Petite Berceuse, Op. 5, No. 4
CF B2198
Rondino, Op. 5, No. 2
CF B2196
SQUIRE, WILLIAM HENRY (1871-   )
Meditation
BH
STADLMAIR, [HANS (1929-   )]
Concerto
BRH
STAFFELLI, A
Sonata in La
Curci
STAHLBERG, FRITZ (1877-1937)
Petite Gavotte, Op. 27, No. 3
CF B1108
STAMIC, J
Sonata in G, Op. 6a
Artia
STAMITZ, JOHANN (1717-1757)
Concerto in G
(Lebermann) SCH
STAMITZ, KARL (1745-1801)
Sonata in B flat, for vla or vln and pno
VW (Pet No. V49)

STANDARD EASY VIOLIN PIECES
  CF 03628
STANDARD VIOLIN PIECES
  CF 03624
STANFORD, CHARLES VILLIERS (1852-1924)
  Ace and Deuce, from 6 Irish Dances
    STB
  Arietta con variazioni, from 6 Sketches,
    Op. 155
    JWL
  Bourrée, from 6 Sketches, Op. 155
    JWL (Mil No. W1248)
  Father Quinn, from Irish Airs
    STB
  Gavotte, from 6 Sketches, Op. 155
    JWL
  Gobby O, from 6 Irish Dances
    STB
  Green Woods of Truigha, from Irish Airs
    STB
  Groves, from Irish Airs
    STB
  Humours of Bandon, from 6 Irish Dances
    STB
  Jig, from 6 Irish Dances
    STB
  Leprechaun's Dance, from 4 Irish Dances
    STB
  Long Dance, from 6 Irish Dances
    STB
  March-Jig, from 4 Irish Dances
    STB
  Minuet in G, from 6 Sketches, Op. 155
    JWL
  Morris Dance, from 6 Sketches, Op. 155
    JWL (Mil No. W1246)
  Reel, from 4 Irish Dances
    STB
  Rocky Road, from 6 Irish Dances
    STB
  Scherzino, from 6 Sketches, Op. 155
    JWL (Mil No. W1247)
  Slow-Dance, from 4 Irish Dances
    STB
STANLEY, [JOHN (1713-1786)]
  Sonata in g
    (Moffat) Nov
STAR SPANGLED BANNER AND DIXIE
  (Halle) Bel 674
STARER, ROBERT (1924-   )
  Introduction and Hora
    Peer
STAROKADOMSKY, [MIKHAIL (1901-1954)]
  Concerto, Op. 20
    MZK
STEIN, C. see Brayley-Stein-Harris
STEIN, E.
  Elegy
    Metr
STEIN, LEON (1910-   )
  Introduction and Dance Chassidic
    CFE
  Prelude No. 1, Duet
    CFE
  Prelude No. 2, Air
    CFE
  Prelude No. 3, March
    CFE
  Prelude No. 4
    CFE
  Prelude No. 5, Cornstack Fiddle
    CFE
  Prelude No. 6, Eidolons
    CFE

  Prelude No. 7, Badinage
    CFE
  Prelude No. 8, Canto Funebre
    CFE
  Prelude No. 9, Punchinello
    CFE
  Prelude No. 10, Toccata
    CFE
  Prelude No. 11, Chant
    CFE
  Prelude No. 12, Barialoge
    CFE
  Sonata
    CFE
STEINBERG, [MAXIMILIAN (1883-1946)]
  Concerto
    MZK
STEINER, see Applebaum & Steiner
STEKEL, ERIC-PAUL (1898-   )
  Concerto, Op. 6
    Paterson 2718
STEKL, KONRAD (1901-   )
  Sonatine, Op. 55b
    Krenn
STEPANIAN, [RUBEN (1902-   )]
  Sonata
    MZK
STERN, MARCEL
  Fantasie Tzigane
    Mil
STEVENS, BERNARD (1916-   )
  Concerto
    Leng (Mil No. L1102)
  Fantasia on a theme of Dowland, Op. 23
    Leng (Mil No. L1131)
  Sonata
    Oxf 23.800
STEVENS, HALSEY (1908-   )
  Elegy
    CFE
  Sonata No. 1
    CFE
  Sonatina No. 11
    CFE
STILL, WILLIAM GRANT (1895-   )
  Suite
    Leeds
STINE, MAURICE
  Small Fry Melodies
    (Isaac) CF 03734B,H
STÖCKIGT, SIEGFRIED
  Sonata
    BRH
STOESSEL, ALBERT (1894-1943)
  Lullaby, Op. 8, No. 1
    BMC
  Miniatures, 5
    BMC
STONE, DAVID
  Pieces in third position, 8
    Nov
STONE, GREGORY
  Doina
    (Seidel) GS
  Hora in suoni armonici
    (Seidel) GS
STONE, HAROLD
  Let's Play the Violin
    BH
STOUT, ALAN (1932-   )
  Sonata, Op. 45
    CFE
STRADELLA, ALESSANDRO (1642-1682)
  Pietà, Signore
    (Hofmann) CF B3158

STRAUS, OSCAR (1870-1954)
  Love's Roundelay, from Waltz Dream
    (Grunes) MK
  Waltz Dream
    (Harris) Lud S-1568
STRAUSS, JOHANN (1825-1899)
  Blue Danube Waltz, Op. 314
    (Ambrosio) CF B2527 simpl
    (Ernst-Ambrosio) CF B3335
    (Rosey) MK
    Bel
    SCH
    VL 2 2nd vln ad lib simpl
  Fledermaus, Die. Overture
    (Lutz) SCH
  Perpetuum Mobile, Op. 257
    (Persinger) CF B2625
  Rosen aus dem Süden, Op. 388
    SCH
  Tales from the Vienna Woods, Op. 325
    (Godowsky) Leng (Mil No. L1115)
    SCH
  Waltzes
    Amsco 61; for contents see Viennese
      Waltzes
  Wiener Blut, Op. 354
    (Spalding) VL
STRAUSS, RICHARD (1864-1949)
  Concerto in d, Op. 8
    UE 1012
  Rosenkavalier Waltz
    (Prihoda) BH
  Sonata in E flat, Op. 18
    UE 1047
STRAVINSKY, IGOR (1882-   )
  Airs de Rossignol et Marche Chinoise,
      from Rossignol
    BH
  Ballad, from Le Baiser de la fée
    (Gautier) BH
  Berceuse, from Firebird
    (Dushkin) SCH
    SCH
  Chanson Russe, from Mavra
    BH arr by composer and Dushkin
  Circus Polka, orig for orch
    (Babitz) SCH
  Concerto in D
    SCH
  Danse Russe, from Petrouchka
    BH arr by composer and Dushkin
  Divertimento, from Le Baiser de la fée
    BH
  Duo Concertant
    BH
  Pastorale
    (Dushkin) SCH
  Prelude and Ronde des princesses, from
      Firebird
    SCH
  Scherzo, from Firebird
    (Dushkin) SCH
  Suite after Pergolesi
    BH orig version; each part published
      separately
      1. Introduzione
      2. Serenata
      3. Tarantella
      4. Gavotta con due variazioni
      5. Minuetto e Finale
  Suite Italienne
    BH revised version of Suite after
      Pergolesi

Supplications, from Firebird
  (Grunes) Omega
Variations d'Apollon
  (Szigeti) BH
STRIMER, [JOSEPH (1881-   )]
  Pièces Mélodiques, 5
    RL
STRINGFIELD, LAMAR (1897-   )
  Doll's Lullaby
    CF B2384
STRUNGK, NICOLAUS ADAM (1640-1700)
  Airs, 2, and Suites, 2
    Pet 4565 vcl ad lib
STUDER, HANS (1911-   )
  Suite innocente
    Baer 2689
STYRIAN PEASANT DANCE
  (Moffat) JWL (Mil No. W1238)
SUCHON, [EUGEN (1908-   )]
  Sonatina, Op. 11
    UE 11459
SUGÁR, RESZO (1919-   )
  Concertino
    Kul
  Sonata
    Kul
  Variations for Youth
    Kul
SUITE IN F
  (Bouvet) ESC vcl ad lib
    1668, composer unknown
SUK, JOSEPH (1874-1935)
  Burlesca, from 4 Pieces, Op. 17
    (Gingold) Int
  Fantasy, Op. 24
    (Jiránek) SIM
  Introduction to the Fairy Tale "Raduz and
      Mahulena"
    Artia
  Love Melody
    Artia
  Love Song
    (Kocian) Artia
    Artia simpl
  Melody
    Artia
  Minuet
    (Engel) GS
  Pieces, 4, Op. 17
    SIM 2V
  Village Serenade
    Artia
SULIMOV
  Etude-March; with Etude Staccato by
      Baklanova
    MZK
SULLIVAN, ARTHUR S. (1842-1900)
  Lost Chord. Paraphrase
    (Saenger) CF B3042
  Mikado. Transcription
    (Ambrosio) CF B3306
SULYOK, IMRE
  Easy Pieces, 4
    Kul
  Introduction and Rondo
    Kul
  Variations on a Hungarian Folk Song
    Kul
SUPPÉ, FRANZ VON (1820-1895)
  Light Cavalry Overture
    (Ambrosio) CF
    (Lechner) SCH
  Poet and Peasant Overture
    Ric 127071
    SCH

SUTCLIFFE
  Melody
    Leng (Mil No. L1139)
SVENDSEN, JOHAN S. (1840-1911)
  Romance, Op. 26, orig for vln and orch
    (Hollaender) BMC   simpl
    (Kreisler) BMC
    (Mittell) GS
    (Saenger) CF B3344
    Aug 7587
    Pet 9016   pno reduction by composer
    SCH
SWAIN, FREDA (1902-   )
  Irish Lullaby, from 3 Pleasant Pieces
    JWL (Mil No. W1225-2)
  Kitchen Clock, from 3 Pleasant Pieces
    JWL (Mil No. W1225-1)
  Running Dance, from 3 Pleasant Pieces
    JWL (Mil No. W1225-3)
SWANSON, HOWARD (1909-   )
  Nocturne
    Weintraub
SWEETING, E.T.
  Moods
    STB
  Summer Idyll
    STB
SWIFT, RICHARD
  Stravaganza 1, Op. 10
    CFE
SWING, R.G.
  Fantasia, Quasi una Sonata
    BMI
SWINSTEAD, FELIX
  Cradle Song
    ABRS (Mil No. A249)
  Good Cheer
    ABRS (Mil No. A251)
  Valse-Intermezzo
    ABRS (Mil No. A250)
SZABO, FERENC (1902-   )
  Air
    Kul
SZELENYI, [ISTVAN (1904-   )]
  Easy Little Concert Pieces, 24
    Kul   2V
  Improvisations
    Kul
SZERVÁNSZKY, ENDRE (1912-   )
  Easy Pieces, 10
    Kul
SZONYI, E.
  Air
    Kul
  Serenade - Dance at Dawn
    Kul
SZYMANOWSKI, KAROL (1882-1937)
  Berceuse, Op. 52
    UE 8432
  Chanson Polonaise
    (Kochanski) UE 5298
  Chant de Roxane, from King Roger
    (Kochanski) UE 8694
  Concerto, Op. 35
    UE 6624
  Concerto No. 2, Op. 61
    ESC
  Dryades et Pan, Op. 30, No. 3, from
      Mythes
    UE 6838
  Fontaine d'Arethuse, Op. 30, No. 1,
      from Mythes
    UE 6836

Narcisse, Op. 30, No. 2 from Mythes
    UE 6837
  Nocturne and Tarantella, Op. 28
    UE 6626
  Peasant Dance, from Harnaise
    UE 1511
  Romance in D, Op. 23
    UE 3866
  Sonata, Op. 9
    UE 3858
TAILLEFERRE, GERMAINE (1892-   )
  Pastorale
    EV
  Sonate
    Dur
  Sonate No. 2
    Dur
TAJČEVIČ, M.
  Kolo Romana
    (Herzog) CF B2776
  Macedonian Courting Dance
    (Herzog) CF B2775
TAKÁCS, JENÖ (1902-   )
  Goumbri. Rhapsodie, Op. 20
    DOB
  Little Pieces, 8, Op. 50
    OBV   published separately
  Rhapsody. Op. 49 "Hungarian airs"
    DOB
  Sonata Concertante, Op. 65
    DOB
TAL, JOSEPH (1910-   )
  Sonata
    IMP
TALIAN, V.
  Sonata
    MZK
TAMBOURIN, LE
    (Moffat) SCH   18th century, composer
      unknown
TANENBAUM, ELIAS (1924-   )
  Fantasia
    CFE
TANEYEV, SERGEY (1856-1915)
  Suite de Concert, Op. 28, orig for vln and
      orch
    Belaieff; published separately for vln
      and pno
      1. Prelude
      2. Gavotte
      3. Conte
      4. Theme and Variations
      5. Tarantelle
    MZK
TANSMAN, ALEXANDER (1897-   )
  Air Obstiné, from Nous jouons pour Maman
    ESC
  Cavatine, from Nous jouons pour Maman
    ESC
  Little Easy Pieces, 6
    ESC
  Méditation, from Nous jouons pour Maman
    ESC
  Petit Air Populaire, from Nous jouons pour
      Maman
    ESC
  Petite Marche, from Nous jouons pour Maman
      Maman
    ESC
  Pieces, 5
    ESC
  Sicilienne, from Nous jouons pour Maman
    ESC

TANSMAN, ALEXANDER (cont.)
  Sonata quasi una fantasia
    Senart
  Sonata No. 2
    ESC
  Sonatine, orig for fl and pno
    Senart
TAPIA COLMAN, SIMON
  Sonata "El Afilador"
    EMM
  Suite Espanola
    EMM
TARDI, FRANCESCO
  Sonata in G
    (Bonelli) ZA 3312
TARP, SVEND ERIK (1908-   )
  Concertino
    WH 3334
TARTINI, GIUSEPPE (1692-1770)
  Adagio
    (Corti) Carisch
  Andante cantabile
    (Ticciati) Oxf 23.112
  Andante and Presto
    (Bridgewater) SCH
  Aria
    (Nadaud-Vidal) Senart 5207
  Concerto in D
    (Corti) Ric ER622
  Concerto in D
    (Ross) GS L1765   with cadenzas;
      pno reduction by Ross Lee Finney
  Concerto in d
    (Baumgartner) Hug (Pet No. A23)
  Concerto in d
    (Pente) SIM
  Concerto in d
    (Szigeti) CF 03256   with cadenzas
  Concerto in E
    (Scherchen) Hug (Pet No. A13)
  Concerto in G
    (Pente) SCH
  Concerto in g
    (Rostal) Nov
  Concerto
    (Chaumont) Senart 5413
  Devil's Trill, see Sonata in g
  Fugue in A
    (Kreisler) Fol 1106
  Lento serioso
    (Corti) Carisch
  Sonatas, 7
    Pet 1099A,b,C   3V
      Vol 1: No. 2 in F; No. 4 in G;
        No. 5 in e
      Vol 2: No. 10 in g; Devil's Trill
      Vol 3: No. 6 in D; Sonata in C
  Sonatas, 6, Op. 5
    (Bonelli) ZA3829
  Sonatas, 6
    (Polo) Ric ER177
  Sonatas, 3
    Kul
  Sonatas, 2, in e and G, from Op. 1
    (Lichtenberg) GS L725
  Sonata No. 18 in A
    (Nadaud-Kaiser) Senart 5266
  Sonata No. 23 in A
    (Nadaud-Kaiser) Senart 5268
  Sonata No. 21 in b
    (Nadaud-Kaiser) Senart 5267
  Sonata No. 13 in B flat
    (Nadaud-Kaiser) Senart 5265

  Sonata in D
    Carisch
  Sonata No. 25 in D
    (Nadaud-Kaiser) Senart 5269
  Sonata in E
    (Nadaud-Vidal) Senart 5208
  Sonata No. 11 in F
    (Nadaud-Kaiser) Senart 5264
  Sonata in G
    (Corti) Carisch
  Sonata in g, Op. 1, No. 10, Didone
      abbandonata
    (Polo) Ric 128856
  Sonata in g, "Devil's Trill"
    (Auer) CF B2695
    (Hubay) Bosw
    (Joachim) SIM
    (Kreisler) Eul (Pet No. Z100)
    (Kreisler) Fol 1193
    (Kreisler) Int
    (Kreisler) Ric ER2244
    (Lichtenberg-Volkmann) GS L522
    (Nachèz) SCH
    (Nadaud-Kaiser) Senart 5259
    (Polo) Ric ER178   secondo l'edizione
      integra Cartier, Parigi 1798
  Sonata in g
    (Auer) CF B2665
  Sonata in g
    Ric R429
  Tartiniana, see Dallapiccola
  Trillo del diavolo, see Sonata in g,
      "Devil's Trill"
  Variations on a theme of Corelli
    (Corti) Carisch
    (Francescatti) Mil
    (Kreisler) Fol 1196
TATE, PHYLLIS (1912-   )
  Irish Song
    Oxf 23.028
  Triptych
    Oxf 23.029
  see also Mackay & Tate
  see also Murray & Tate
TAUBER, RICHARD (1892-1948)
  Romanze
    Chap-L
TAYLOR, COLIN
  Greeting, from 3 Short Fiddle Tunes
    Aug
  Mischief, from 3 Short Fiddle Tunes
    Aug
  Remembrance, from 3 Short Fiddle Tunes
    Aug
  Sea Shanty
    Aug
TAYLOR, LOUIS
  Connemarra, from 6 Pieces, Op. 109
    JWL (Mil No. W1215D)
  Gavotte in D, from 6 Pieces, Op. 109
    JWL (Mil No. W1215F)
  Havanaise, from 6 Pieces, Op. 109
    JWL (Mil No. W1215B)
  Morris Dance, from 6 Pieces, Op. 109
    JWL (Mil No. W1215C)
  Pierrot, from 6 Pieces, Op. 109
    JWL (Mil No. W1215A)
  Serbia, from 6 Pieces, Op. 109
    JWL (Mil No. W1215E)
TCHAIKOVSKY, PIOTR ILYITCH (1840-1893)
  Adagio lamentoso, from Symphony No. 6
    FR (Pet No. F47)
  Allegro con grazia, from Symphony No. 6
    FR (Pet No. F46)

TCHAIKOVSKY, PIOTR ILYITCH (cont.)
Andante, from Symphony No. 5
  (Ambrosio) CF B1939   simpl
Andante cantabile, from String Quartet,
  Op. 11
  (Auer) CF B50
  (Del Maglio) Ric 125610
  (Kreisler) Fol 1078
  (Sauret-Saenger) CF S3042
Autumn Song, Op. 37, No. 10, orig for pno
  MZK
Autumn Song; Song Without Words
  MZK
Barcarolle, Op. 43, No. 1, orig for orch
  (Ornstein) AMP
Canzonetta, from Concerto, Op. 35
  (Del Maglio) Ric 125612
  (Polo) SZ
  (Winn) CF B3331
  Lit (Pet No. L7825)
  MZK
Chanson Triste, Op. 40, No. 2, orig for pno
  (Palaschko) SCH
  (Saenger) CF S3139
  VL 133
Chant sans paroles, Op. 2, No. 3, orig
  for pno
  (Del Maglio) Ric 125611 "Canzona senza
    parole"
  (Kreisler) Fol 1185 "Song without words"
  (Mittell) GS
  (Ritter) SCH
  (Rosey) MK "Chanson sans paroles"
  (Trinkaus) Fill
  MZK "Song without words"; with
    Scherzetto by Cui
Christmas
  (Hartmann) AMP
Concerto in D, Op. 35
  (Auer) CF 03655
  (Davisson) BRH
  (Flesch) Pet 3019A with cadenzas
  (Kreisler) Fol 1093 with cadenza
  (Mittell) GS L1185
  (Oistrakh) Int includes Auer's version
  Aug 7967
  MZK
Declaration of Love
  MZK
Entr'acte, from Sleeping Beauty
  MZK
Humoresque, orig for pno
  (Hartmann) AMP
Lullaby in the Storm; The Organ Grinder
  Sings; A Game at Horses
  MZK
Marche Slave, orig for orch
  (Halle) Bel 675
Mazurka de salon, Op. 9, No. 3, orig for pno
  (Saenger) CF S3303
Méditation, Op. 42, No. 1
  (Schuster) Pet 4172C
Mélodie, Op. 42, No. 3
  (Auer) CF S3315
  (Flesch) Pet 4172b
  (Herrmann) GS
  MZK
Nocturne
  (Harrison) Leng (Mil No. L1120)
None but the lonely heart, Op. 6, No. 6,
  orig for voice
  (Eckstein) CF M304
  (Saenger) CF S3506

BMC
Mil
VL 159
Romance, Op. 5, orig for pno
  (Orszagh) Kul
  (Perlman) CF B3339
Scherzo, Op. 42, No. 2
  (Flesch) Pet 4172A
  (Hartmann) MZK
  (Kreisler) Fol 1171
Sérénade mélancolique, Op. 26, orig for
  vln and orch
  (Mittell) GS
  (Wilhelmj) SCH
  CF S3802
  Pet 4333
Song without words, see Chant sans paroles
Swan Lake. 2nd vln solo
  MZK
Valse, Op. 40, No. 8, orig for pno
  CF B3210
Valse, from the Serenade for Strings, Op. 48
  (Auer-Saenger) CF B934
Valse-Scherzo, Op. 34
  (Gingold) Int
  (Orszagh) Kul
  (Schmidtner) Sik 520 "Valse-caprice"
Valse sentimentale, Op. 51, No. 6, orig
  for pno
  (Grunes) Omega
  (Press) CF B2399
TCHEGODAEVA, IRENA
Gitana
  BMC
TCHEREPNINE, ALEXANDRE (1899-   )
Allegretto, from 5 Arabesques, orig for pno
  Heugel
Elégie
  Dur
Mouvement perpétuel
  Dur
Sonata in F
  Dur
TELEMANN, GEORG PHILIPP (1681-1767)
Concerto in a
  (Füssl) Baer 3718
Concerto in a
  Cor ST11
Concerto in c
  (Schlövogt) SCH
Heldenmusik, 12 Marches
  LN (Pet No. R21)
Little Chamber Music, see Suites
Minuets, 15, from Seven times seven and
  one minuet
  LN (Pet No. R16) vcl or gamba ad lib
Partiten, 6
  (Woehl) Baer HM47 vcl ad lib
  see also Suites
Solo in A. Tafelmusik II
  (Hinnenthal) Baer 3542 vcl ad lib
Sonatas, 12
  (Seiffert) Baer 2951 vcl ad lib
    "Methodische Sonaten"
Sonatas, 6
  (Friedrich) SCH vcl ad lib
Sonatas, 6
  (Kaufman) Pr
Sonatinas, 6
  (Kauffman) BH
Sonatinas, 6
  (Schweickert-Lenzewski) SCH vcl ad lib
Sonatas, 2, in d and C, from Essercizii
  Musici
  Pet 4551 vcl ad lib

TELEMANN, GEORG PHILIPP (cont.)
Sonata No. 4 in C
    MT (Pet No. MV1073) vcl ad lib
Sonata in C, from Getreuer Musikmeister
    Pet 4550 vcl ad lib
Sonata in c
    (Hinnenthal) BRH vcl ad lib
Sonata No. 1 in D
    MT (Pet No. MV1070) vcl ad lib
Sonata in d
    Broe (Pet No. B557) vcl ad lib
Sonata in F
    Broe (Pet No. B560) vcl ad lib
Sonata No. 2 in G
    MT (Pet No. MV1071) vcl ad lib
Sonata in G
    SCH
Sonata No. 3 in g
    MT (Pet No. MV1072) vcl ad lib
Suites, 6, see Partiten
Suites, 3, "Little Chamber Music"
    FR (Pet No. F34) vcl or gamba ad lib
        orig text plus suggested ornamentation
        in the style of the period
Wedding Divertissement
    (Bergmann) SCH
TELMA, MAURICE
Adoration
    BMC
TEMPLETON, ALEC (1909-   )
Siciliano
    Leeds
TENAGLIA
Air
    ABRS (Mil No. A236)
Aria in f
    RE (Pet No. RE11)
Aria in g
    JWL (Mil No. W1278)
Aria
    (Polo) Ric 128877
TEN HAVE, WILLIAM
Allegro Brilliant, Op. 19
    (Perlman) CF S3560
    (Tadema) GS
Concerto in D, Op. 30
    Bosw
TER-GEVONDIAN, A.
Fantasy
    MZK
TERRY, FRANCES (1884-   )
Sonata
    SPAM
TERTIS, LIONEL (1876-   )
Blackbirds
    Aug
TESSARINI, CARLO (1690-c.1765)
Sonate en ré majeur
    HL
TESTI, FLAVIO (1923-   )
Musica da concerto No. 1, orig for vln
    and orch
    Ric 129863
THÄRICHEN, W.
Concerto, Op. 36
    BB
THEMELODIES FOR VIOLIN
    (Seredy) CF 03259
        Themes and melodies from famous
        compositions
THERE IS A TAVERN IN THE TOWN
    (Eckstein) CF M313
THILMAN, JOHANNES PAUL (1906-   )
Concerto, Op. 59
    (Neubauer) BRH

Sonata, Op. 80
    BRH
THIMAN, ERIC H. (1900-   )
Cradle Song
    Aug
London Pride
    Aug
Marjoram
    Aug
THIRIET, [MAURICE (1906-   )]
Pièces, 4
    Sal 2V
        Vol 1: Grave; Berceuse
        Vol 2: Aria en forme de blues;
        Saltarello
THOMAS, ALEX
Pièces, 4
    Sal
THOMAS, AMBROISE (1811-1896)
Entr'acte Gavotte, from Mignon
    (Ambrosio) CF B2524 simpl
Raymond, Overture
    (Ambrosio) CF
Romance, from Raymond Overture
    (Halle) Bel 703
Romance and Gavotte, from Mignon
    (Sarasate-Saenger) CF B3247
THOMÉ, FRANCIS (1850-1909)
Andante Religioso, Op. 70
    (Saenger) CF B3283
Simple Aveu, Op. 25
    (Ambrosio) CF B2546 simpl
    (Eisenberg) MK
    (Schenkman) GS
    CF S3409
Under the Leaves
    (Rosey) MK
THOMSON, MILLARD S.
Epitaph
    CF B3322
THOMSON, VIRGIL (1896-   )
Sonata No. 1
    BH
Three Portraits
    Mercury
THUILLE, LUDWIG (1861-1907)
Gavot
    (Engel) GS
TIESSEN, HEINZ (1887-   )
Duo-Sonata, Op. 35
    BB
TITL, ANTON EMIL (1809-1882)
Serenade
    CF S3441
TOBANI, THEO.
Hearts and Flowers, Op. 245
    (Ambrosio) CF B34 simpl
    CF B1134
TOCH, ERNST (1887-   )
Sonata, Op. 4
    SCH
TOLDRÁ, [EDUARDO (1895-   )]
Sonetos, 6, Vol. 1
    UME
TOLHURST
Cavatina
    Bosw
Twilight Musings
    Bosw
TOMASI, [HENRI (1901-   )]
Capriccio, orig for vln and orch
    HL
Tristesse d'Antar, La
    Sal

TOP OF CORK ROAD AND BY THE FEAL'S
    WAVE BENIGHTED
    (Moffat) Aug
TORELLI, GIUSEPPE (1658-1709)
    Concerto in e, Op. 8, No. 9
      (Abbado) Ric 130155
      (Baumgartner) Hug (Pet No. A6)
    Concerto
      (Pincherle) Senart 5377
    Preludio e Allegro, see Solo Violin Music
      of the Earliest Period
TOSATTI, VIERI (1920-   )
    Piccola sonata
      Ric 128880
TOSELLI, ENRICO (1883-1926)
    Serenade, Op. 6
      (Fradkin) BMC
      (Simon) BMC simpl
      BMC
TOWNSEND, MADAME LAWRENCE
    Berceuse
      (Saenger) CF B3163
TRACK, E.
    Serenade im Park
      DOB
TRADITIONAL SONGS AND DANCES
    (Twinn) JWL (Mil Nos. W1291-2) 2V
TRANSCRIPTIONS OF MUSIC OF WESTERN
    COMPOSERS, VOL. II
    (Zakharina) MZK
TREMAIS (18th century)
    Sarabande and Minuet, from Sonatas,
      Op. 1, Nos. 9 and 10
      (Jacobsen) Pet 4226
TRIGGS, HAROLD (1900-   )
    Danza Braziliana
      (Kaufman) CF B2785
TRINKAUS, GEORGE J.
    Lament
    Fill
(TRINKAUS, GEORGE J.)
    World's Best-known Pieces
      CF
TROEMEL, A.
    Aunt Sally in Switzerland
      Omega
TROIANI, GAETANO (1873-1942)
    Escondido, de Motivos de la sierra y la
      llanura
      (Gil) Ric BA7805
    Estilo, de Motivos de la sierra y la llanura
      (Gil) Ric BA7807
    Evocaciones. Serenata
      (Gil) Ric BA7806
TROOSTWYK, ARTHUR
    Dance of the Elves, Op. 14
      CF B1138
TROTT, JOSEPHINE
    Puppet-show, Op. 5, No. 1
      GS
TSCHAIKOWSKY, see Tchaikovsky
TSCHETSCHULIN, AGNES
    Alla Zingaresca
      CF B2986
TUNES FROM EVERYWHERE
    (Anrold) Willis
TURINA, JOAQUIN (1882-1949)
    Andante, from Sevilla
      MZK
    Euterpe, from Las Musas de Andalucia
      UME
    Homenaje a Navarra, Op. 102, from Ciclo
      Plateresco
      UME

Oración del Torero, orig for str quartet
    (Heifetz) CF B2618
Poema de una sanluqueña, El
    UME
Sonate No. 1 en Ré, Op. 51
    RL
Sonate No. 2, Op. 82 "Sonata Espagnola"
    RL
Variaciones clásicas
    UME
TURKEY IN THE STRAW
    (MacMillen) GS
TURNER, CHARLES (1921-   )
    Serenade for Icarus
      GS
(TWARZ, W.)
    Selected Classical Sonatas, Vol. I
      Cranz
    Violine and Klavier
      SIM
    Young Fiddler's Companion
      SIM 2V for contents see title
TWINKLING STARS
    (Harvey) VL 52 2nd vln ad lib
TWINN, SYDNEY
    Czardas
      Leng (Mil No. L1103A)
    First Term Violin Pieces, 3
      Mil
    Pastoral Dance
      Leng (Mil No. L1137)
    Romance
      Leng (Mil No. L1138)
(TWINN, SYDNEY)
    Traditional Songs and Dances
      JWL (Mil Nos. W1291-2) 2V
TWO GUITARS
    (Ambrosio-Perlman) CF B2588 simpl
    (Horlick-Ludlow) CF B2217 concert and
      simpl versions
    (Sandler) Liber-S
UCCELLINI, MARCO (c.1610- ?)
    Aria, see Solo Violin Music of the Earliest
      Period
UHE, A.E.
    A la Mazur, from Characteristic Impressions
      AMP
    Au Memoire
      AMP
    Characteristic Impressions
      AMP
    Mirage, Le
      AMP
    Pantomime, from Characteristic Impres-
      sions
      AMP
    Plaisanterie
      AMP
    Poème
      AMP
    Scotch Paragraph
      AMP
    Soliloquy, from Characteristic Impressions
      AMP
    Whims
      AMP
UNTERHALTUNGS-KONZERT
    (Lutz) SCH 2V
      A collection of semi-classical selections
      by Braga, Strecker, Strauss, and others
URAY, ERNST LUDWIG (1906-   )
    Suite in A
      DOB
    Variations in f
      DOB

(UTKIN)
Easy Violin Pieces, 11
MZK
Pieces, 8, by Russian Composers
MZK
Pieces, 6, by Russian Composers
MZK
Pieces, 7, by Soviet Composers
MZK
VACATION MEDLEY
(Harvey) VL 3   2nd vln ad lib
VADON, J
Menuet
Senart
VAINBERG, MOYSEY (1919-   )
Moravian Rhapsody
MZK
Sonata No. 5
MZK
Sonatina
MZK
VAINUNAS, S.
Rhapsody on Lithuanian Themes, Op. 20
MZK
VALDEZ, CHARLES ROBERT
Sérénade du Tsigane
CF B1309
VALE, F.
Ao pé da fogueira
(Heifetz) CF B2609
Folguedo Campestre
(Francescatti) Mil
VALEN, FARTEIN (1887-1952)
Sonata, Op. 3
Norsk
VALENTINE, ROBERT (18th century)
Sonatas, 3
LN (Pet No. R103)   vcl or gamba ad lib
VALENTINI, GIUSEPPE (c.1681-c.1740)
Sonata in sol
(Respighi) Ric ER270
VAN BEVEREN, A.
Elegie. Meditation
Metr
VAN DE VELDE, E.
Romance
Gaudet
VAN DOREN, T.
Concertino Romantique, Op. 11
Metr
VAN GOENS, see Goens
VANHALL, JOHANN BAPTIST (1739-1813)
Rondo in B flat, from Trois Duos pour
Deux Violons
ABRS (Mil No. A232)
VAN HEMEL, O.
Concerto
Metr
VARDI, EMANUEL (1915-   )
Suite on American Folk-songs
GS
VARLAMOV, ALEXANDER
Red Sarafan, see Aliabev: Nightingale
VASSILENKO, SERGEY (1872-1956)
Easy Pieces, 5
MZK
Toccata, from Suite, Op. 69
(Hartmann) MZK
VASZY, V.
Preludio e Allegro
Kul
VAUGHAN WILLIAMS, RALPH (1872-1958)
Concerto in d, "Accademico"
Oxf 23.801

Fantasia on Greensleeves
(Mullinar) Oxf 23.014
Galop, from Suite for Viola
(Persinger) Oxf 23.001
Lark Ascending, orig for vln and orch
Oxf 23.411
Pieces, 2: Romance and Pastorale
Curwen
Sonata in a
Oxf 23.100
Studies in English Folk-Song, 6, orig for
vcl and pno
STB
VECSEY, [FRANZ VON (1893-1935)]
Caprice No. 1, Le Vent
Kul
Cascade
Kul
Conte Passione
Kul
Preludio e Fuga
Kul
Valse Triste
Kul
SZ
VERACINI, ANTONIO (1660- ?)
Grave e Allegro, see Solo Violin Music of
the Earliest Period
Pastorale
(Szante) Kul
Sonata No. 1
(Paumgartner) BH
Sonata No. 2
(Paumgartner) BH
VERACINI, FRANCESCO MARIA (1690-c.1750)
Concerto in D
(Vogt) Baer 3716
Largo
(Corti) Carisch
Largo
(Corti) Int
Largo and Allegro
MZK
Menuetto
(Ludwig) Lud S-1523
Pezzi, 16, dalle Sonate accademiche a
violino solo e basso
(Tagliacozzo-Boghen) Ric ER128
Sonatas, 12, Op. 1
(Kolneder) Pet 4937A,b,C,D   4V
vcl or gamba ad lib
Sonatas, 12, after Corelli, Op. 5
(Kolneder) SCH   4V   vcl ad lib
Sonatas, 12, for rec or vln and pno
(Kolneder) Pet 4965A,b,C,D   4V
vcl or gamba ad lib
Sonata accademica in D, Op. 2, No. 1
(Bär) Baer 316   vcl ad lib
Pet 9011A   vcl ad lib
Sonata accademica in B flat, Op. 2, No. 2
(Bär) Baer 317   vcl ad lib
Sonata accademica in C, Op. 2, No. 3
(Bär) Baer 318   vcl ad lib
Sonata accademica in d, Op. 2, No. 12
Pet 9011M   vcl ad lib
Sonata in a
(Salmon) Ric R726
Sonata in d
(Moffat-Winn) CF B2726
Sonata No. 6 in d
(Respighi) Ric ER278
Sonata in d
(Salmon) Ric R724

VERACINI, FRANCESCO MARIA (cont.)
  Sonata in e
    (David) Int
  Sonata in e
    (Salmon) Ric R727
  Sonata in e
    Carisch
  Sonata in e, "Concert Sonata"
    Pet 4345
  Sonata in g
    (Salmon) Ric R725
  Sonata No. 8
    (Respighi) Ric ER279
VERDI, GIUSEPPE (1813-1901)
  Ah! I have sighed to rest me
    (Halle) Bel 672
  Celeste Aida, from Aida
    (Saenger) CF B3236
  Donna e mobile, from Rigoletto
    VL 137   2nd vln ad lib
  Prelude to Act I of La Traviata
    Ric 25574
  Quartet, from Rigoletto
    (Saenger) CF
    VL 37
  Rigoletto. Fantasia, see Singelée
  Traviata. Transcription
    CF B3313
  Triumphal March, from Aida
    VL 110
  Trovatore. Fantasia
    (Ambrosio) CF B3314
    see also Singelée
  Violetta, from Traviata, see Castelnuovo-
    Tedesco
VERESS, SÁNDOR (1907-   )
  Concerto
    SZ
  Sonata No. 2
    SZ
  Sonatina
    SZ
VERETTI, ANTONIO (1900-   )
  Sonata
    SZ
VERSTOVSKY
  Waltz, see Glinka: Feeling
VIARDOT, [PAUL (1857-1941)]
  Sonate No. 3
    Senart
VIENNESE WALTZES
  Amsco 61
    Strauss: Artist's Life
    Strauss: Beautiful Blue Danube
    Strauss: Kiss Waltz
    Strauss: Roses from the South
    Strauss: Tales from the Vienna Woods
    Strauss: Vienna Life
    Strauss: Voices of Spring
    Waldteufel: Dolores
    Waldteufel: Estudiantina
    Waldteufel: Skaters
VIEUXTEMPS, HENRI (1820-1881)
  Air Varié in D, Op. 22, No. 2
    (Centano) CF B2520
  Ballade and Polonaise, Op. 38, orig for
    vln and orch
    (Arbós) Pet 2581
    (Schradieck) GS L356
    CF L86
  Bohémienne, Op. 40, No. 3
    Aug 11759
  Canto d'Amore
    (Polo) SZ

Concert Study
  (Radmall) Ches
Concerto No. 1 in E, Op. 10
  (Quesnot) Senart 5310
  (Schradieck) GS L716
  Pet 3324
Concerto No. 2 in f sharp, Op. 19
  (Arbós) Pet 2574   with cadenzas
  (Auer) CF 03521
Concerto No. 3, Op. 25
  Dur
Concerto No. 4 in d, Op. 31
  (Arbós) Pet 3322   with cadenzas
  (Spiering) GS L1428
  (Wilhelmj) CF L387
  Carisch
Concerto No. 5 in a, Op. 37
  (Arbós) Pet 3323   with cadenzas
  (Quesnot) Senart 5291
  (Schradieck) GS L225
  (Spiering) CF L805
Fantaisie, Op. 21
  Aug 11750
Fantaisie-Caprice, Op. 11, orig for
  vln and orch
  (Ambrosio) CF B2543   simpl
  (Arbós) Pet 3320
  (Schradieck) GS L218
Fantasia appassionata, Op. 35, orig for
  vln and orch
  (Arbós) Pet 2580
  (Lichtenberg) GS L982
  (Quesnot) Senart 5165
Regrets, Op. 40, No. 2
  Aug
Rêverie, Op. 22, No. 3
  (Ambrosio) CF B2542   simpl
  (Hermann) SCH
  (Quesnot) Senart 5167
  (Saenger) CF S3005
Romance, Op. 40, No. 1
  (Wessely) Aug
  CF B3287
  SCH
Rondino, Op. 32, No. 2
  (Centano) CF S3581
Suite, Op. 43
  (Arbós) Pet 2582
VILLA-LOBOS, HEITOR (1887-1959)
  Alma Convulsa, from Fantasia de Movimentos
    Mixtos
    SMP
  Contentamente, from Fantasia de Movimentos
    Mixtos
    SMP
  Fantasia de Movimentos Mixtos, orig for
    vln and orch
    AMP
  Serenidade, from Fantasia de Movimentos
    Mixtos
    SMP
  Sonata-Fantasy No. 1
    ESC
  Sonata-Fantasy No. 2
    ESC
  Sonata No. 3
    ESC
  Song of the Black Swan
    MK
VINCENT, T.
  Sonata in D
    (Dawes) SCH
VIOLIN CLASSICS IN THE FIRST POSITION
  (Zimmer) Pr

VIOLIN CONCERTOS, THE SLOW MOVEMENTS
  (Forbes-Johnson) Pet 561
    Bruch, Mendelssohn, Tchaikovsky
VIOLIN MUSIC THE WHOLE WORLD LOVES
  (Herfurth-Strietel) Willis
VIOLIN OF BYGONE DAYS
  BH
    Albrechtsberger: Minuetto
    Bach, C.P.: Allegro
    Bach, J.S.: Polacca
    Bach, J.S.: Rondeau
    Beethoven: German Dance
    Corelli: Allegro
    Fux: Aria
    Gluck: Andante
    Handel: Allegretto
    Handel: Gavotte
    Haydn: Minuetto
    Haydn: Tema con variazioni
    Mozart: Gavotte
    Mozart: German Dance
    Muffat: Bourree
    Peuerl: Intrada
    Peuerl: Padouan
    Tartini: Minuetto
    Vivaldi: Largo
VIOLIN PIECES YOU LIKE TO PLAY, 37
  GS
    Ambrosio: Canzonetta
    Bach, J.S.: Air on the G string
    Boccherini: Menuet
    Braga: Serenata
    Brahms: Cradle-song
    Bruch: Kol Nidrei
    Debussy: Beau soir
    Drdla: Souvenir
    Drigo: Valse-bluette
    Fauré: Aurora
    Friml: Chanson
    Gillet: Loin du bal
    Godard: Berceuse, from Jocelyn
    Handel: Largo
    Haydn: Serenade
    Herbert: Canzonetta
    Hubay: Hejre Kati
    Kéler-Béla: Son of the Pusztá
    Marie, Gabriel: Cinquantaine
    Mlynarski: Mazurka
    Moszkowski: Serenata
    Offenbach: Barcarolle, from Tales
      of Hoffmann
    Paderewski: Melody
    Pierné: Sérénade
    Rehfeld: Spanish dance
    Saint-Saëns: Swan
    Schubert, Francois: Bee
    Schubert, Franz: Ave Maria
    Schubert, Franz: Serenade
    Simonetti: Madrigale
    Svendsen: Romance
    Tchaikovsky: Canzonetta from violin
      concerto
    Vieuxtemps: Rêverie
    Wagner: Träume
    Wagner: Walther's prize-song, from
      Die Meistersinger
    Wieniawski: Obertass
    Wieniawski: Romance from concerto
      No. 2
VIOLIN PLAYER'S PASTIME FOLIO
  CF 02658
VIOLIN SINGS
  (Bornoff-Wilson) CF 03615
    De Koven: O Promise Me
    From the Great Plains

Godard: Florian's Song
Home on the Range
Marines' Hymn
Nevin: Narcissus
Offenbach: Orpheus
Red River Valley
Sailors' Hornpipe
Skip to my Lou
Tchaikovsky: Argentina
Tchaikovsky: Finale, from Serenade
  for Strings, Op. 48
Tchaikovsky: Theme, from Piano
  Concerto No. 1
Tchaikovsky: Waltz, Op. 39, No. 9
There is a tavern in the town
Ward: Band played on
White Cockade
Wilson: Curtain Music
Wilson: Down Gypsy Trail
Wilson: This is what you ought to do
VIOLIN SOLOS
  Amsco 66
    Adam: Cantique de Noel
    Adeste Fidelis
    America
    Annie Laurie
    Arkansas Traveler
    Arne: Lass with a Delicate Air
    Auld Lang Syne
    Believe Me If All Those Endearing
      Young Charms
    Blue Bells of Scotland
    Brahms: Hungarian Dance No. 4
    Campbells Are Coming
    Carnival of Venice
    Dark Eyes
    Eili, Eili
    Farmer's Song
    Foster: Beautiful Dreamer
    Foster: Jeannie With the Light Brown
      Hair
    Foster: My Old Kentucky Home
    Garry Owen
    Glazer: Palestinian Dance
    Glazer: Sarabande
    Gruber: Silent Night
    Handel: Come Unto Him, from Messiah
    Hoffmann: Berceuse
    Hoffmann: Poor Punchinello
    Hoffmann: Prayer
    Hoffmann: Song Without Words
    Home On the Range
    Imber: Hatikvoh
    Irish Washerwoman
    Ivanovici: Waves of the Danube
    Last Rose of Summer
    Lavallee: O Canada
    Liszt: Liebestraum
    Marseillaise, La
    Mozart: Ave Verum Corpus
    Muir: Maple Leaf Forever
    Paddy Whack
    Parris: Prelude
    Pop Goes the Weasel
    Rameau: Rigaudon
    Santa Lucia
    Schubert: Who Is Sylvia
    Schumann: Thou Art Like a Flower
    Serradell: Golondrina, La
    Silcher: Lorelei
    Sousa: Washington Post March
    Star Spangled Banner
    Strauss: Tales From the Vienna Woods

VIOLIN SOLOS (cont.)
  Amsco 66 (cont.)
    Tschaikowsky: Andante Cantabile
    Verdi: Anvil Chorus, from Il Trovatore
    Verdi: Celeste Aida, from Aida
    Verdi: Duel, from Il Trovatore
    Verdi: In My Heart, from Rigoletto
    Verdi: Pity, Kind Heaven, from Aida
    Verdi: Woman is Fickle, from Rigoletto
    Wagner: Walter's Prize Song, from
      Die Meistersinger
    Yankee Doodle
VIOLIN SOLOS, 107
  Bel
VIOLINE AND KLAVIER
  (Twarz) SIM
    Pieces by Maasz, Schäfer, Heiss
    and others
VIOLINIST'S BOOKS OF CAROLS
  (Benoy) Oxf 23.113-32; 23.114-32   2V
VIOLINIST'S CONTEST ALBUM
  (Perlman) CF 02779
    Bohm: Perpetual Motion
    Bull: Saeterjentens sondag
    Capua: O sole mio
    Carleton: Russian fantasie
    Durand: Chaconne
    Farmer: Blue bells of Scotland
    Gossec: Tambourine
    Gounod: Waltz, from Faust
    Kedlitz: Lolita
    Schmidt: Holiday waltz
    Severn: Juggler
    Singelee: Mandolinata
    Sullivan: Lost chord
    Wachs: Air de ballet
VIOLINISTS' FIRST SOLO ALBUM
  (Perlman) CF 02663-4   2V
    Vol 1
      Ambrosio: Kol Nidre
      America
      Andre: Cantilena
      Bloch: Melody, Op. 48, No. 1
      Bloch: Romance, Op. 48, No. 6
      Bloch: Valsette, Op. 48, No. 7
      Bohm: Canzonetta
      Conte: Romance sans paroles
      Dancla: Polka, Op. 123, No. 6
      Dancla: Weber's last thought,
        Op. 86, No. 6
      Eberhardt: Harlequin, Op. 85, No. 2
      Eberhardt: Song without words,
        Op. 98, No. 1
      Green: Playful rondo
      Harris: Bilo baby
      Harris: Haste thee, winter
      Harris: Lovely May
      Kelly: Baa, baa, black sheep
      Klassert: Melodie, Op. 32, No. 1
      Le Jeune: Evening song
      Le Jeune: Melody
      Mendelssohn: Consolation
      Oehmler: Little Bugler, Op. 117, No. 2
      Oehmler: Morning greeting,
        Op. 117, No. 1
      Rieding: Tempo di valse
      Schmidt: Alla Turca, Op. 19, No. 8
      Schmidt: Cavatine
      Simon: Melody
      Sitt: Waltz, Op. 26, No. 6
      Spies: Minuetto, Op. 45, No. 5
    Vol 2
      Aletter: Melodie
      Bloch: Confidences, Op. 48, No. 5

    Bohm: Intermezzo
    Bohm: Moto perpetuo from Suite 3,
      No. 6
    Danbe: Petite gavotte, Op. 20, No. 3
    Dancla: Petit air varie, Op. 123
    Dancla: Petite valse, Op. 48, No. 4
    Donizetti: Sextet, from Lucia
    Harris: Lullaby, fantasie
    Lachmund: Trembling leaves,
      Op. 12, No. 1
    Losey: Alita
    Marie, Gabriel: La Cinquantaine
    Papini: Theme and variations,
      Op. 57, No. 1
    Poldini: Poupee valsante
    Prosse, de: Petite bourree
    Rieding: Air varie
    Schmidt: Perpetual motion,
      Op. 19, No. 12
    Schmidt: Serenade, Op. 19, No. 7
    Silcher-Harris: Loreley, fantaisie
    Sitt: Tarantella, Op. 26, No. 12
    Wolfermann: Romanze, Op. 3, No. 1
VIOLINIST'S INTRODUCTION TO BACH
  (Greenwood) Willis
VIOLINISTS' PROGRAM BUILDER
  (Perlman) CF 02930
    Aiqouni: May-pole dance
    Aletter: Chanson populaire
    Barnett: Flower garden
    Behr: Snowdrops
    Bohm: Italian romance
    Chesney: Twilight
    Dallam: Fiddlin' Jim
    Grieg: Sailor's song
    Henkel: Gavotte
    Kohler: Gypsy's frolic
    Komzak: Folk song
    Kovacs: Berceuse
    Macklin: Gallants all
    Oehmler: Rustic dance
    Saenger: Berceuse
    Saenger: Capriccio
    Saenger: Spring time
    Schubert: Military march
    Severn: Donkey ride
    Sitt: March
    Sitt: Pastorale
    Tchaikovsky: Andante, from
      Symphony No. 5
    Wolfermann: First fantasia
VIOTTI, GIOVANNI BATTISTA (1755-1824)
  Concerto No. 14
    Billaudot
  Concerto No. 17 in d, 1st movement
    (Lichtenberg) GS L761   with cadenza by
    H. Wieniawski
  Concerto No. 18 in e
    (Abbado) Ric ER1916
  Concerto No. 19
    (Quesnot) Senart 5308
  Concerto No. 20 in D
    (Corti) Carisch
    (Fusella) Ric ER271
    Pet 2823A   with cadenzas
  Concerto No. 22 in a
    (David-Schradieck) GS L443
    (Fusella) Ric ER272
    (Joachim) SIM
    (Musin) CF 03805
    (Quesnot) Senart 5303
    (Sauret) Aug 7970
    Pet 1100A   with cadenzas
    cadenzas published separately, see under
    vln unacc; Ysaÿe, Winkler

VIOTTI, GIOVANNI BATTISTA (cont.)
Concerto No. 22 in a, 1st movement
(Lichtenberg) GS L762   with cadenza
by H. Wieniawski
Concerto No. 23 in G
(David) CF L406
(David-Schradieck) GS L444
(Gingold) Int
(Jacobsen) Aug 7971
(Quesnot) Senart 5343
Pet 1100b   with cadenzas
Concerto No. 24 in b
(Quesnot) Senart 5302
Pet 2823b   with cadenzas
cadenza published separately, see under
vln unacc: Dancla
Concerto No. 28 in a
(David-Petri-Scharwenka) BRH
(Quesnot) Senart 5301
Pet 1100C   with cadenzas
Concerto No. 29 in e
(Auer) CF 03522
(David-Petri-Scharwenka) BRH
(Quesnot) Senart 5304
Pet 1100D   with cadenzas
Minuetto
(Corti) Carisch
Tempo di danza
(Corti) Carisch
VIOZZI, GIULIO (1912-   )
Concerto
Ric 130136
VISKI, [JANOS (1906-   )]
Concerto
Kul
VITALI, GIOVANNI BATTISTA (c.1644-1692)
Capricci, Due, see Solo Violin Music of
the Earliest Period
VITALI, TOMMASO ANTONIO (c.1665- ?)
Ciaccona in g
(Charlier) BRH
(Charlier-David-Auer) CF 03917
(David-Petri) CF L767
(David-Schradieck) GS L417
(Jacobsen) Pet 4346
(Maglioni) Ric ER2450
Carisch
VIVALDI, ANTONIO (c.1669-1741)
Adagio
(Corti) Carisch
Andante, from Organ Concerto
(Bach-Pochon) CF B1835
Berger sommeille, Le, from Concerto
"Le Printemps", F.I no. 22
(Pente) SCH
Chasse, La, from Concerto "L'Automne",
F.I no. 24
(Pente) SCH
Concerto in A, F.I no. 104[43]
(Bellezza) Ric 129660
Concerto in A
(Guarnieri) Ric ER1983
Concerto in A. Pisendel
(Landshoff) Pet 4207   with cadenza
by Vivaldi

[43] F. number refers to the classification system devised by
Antonio Fanna and used by the Instituto Italiano Antonio
Vivaldi, under whose sponsorship the complete works of
Vivaldi are being published. In most cases the publications
identified with Fanna numbers are not the same as the ear-
lier ones, Op. 1-13. However, duplications undoubtedly
exist in the listing presented here, particularly in the case
of works without any identifying numbers. Concerti are
arranged by key in order to make the search for a partic-
ular edition as convenient as possible.

Concerto in A
(Nachèz) SCH
Concerto in a, Op. 3, No. 6
(Abbado) Ric 130164
(Borrel) Senart 5347
(Galamian) Int
(Kuechler) Pet 3794
(Nachèz) SCH
(Perlman) CF B2631
Concerto in B flat, Op. 4, No. 1
(Frenkel) RE (Pet No. RE14)
Concerto in B flat
(Nachèz) SCH
Concerto in C, "Per la S.S. Assunzione
di Maria Vergine", F.I no. 13
(Bellezza) Ric 129590
Concerto in c, "Il Sospetto", F.I no. 2
(Glenn) Ric 129156
Concerto in c, Op. 11, No. 5
(Abbado) Ric 130165
Concerto in c
(Casella) UE 10999
Concerto in c
(Moffat) SCH
Concerto in D, F.I no. 45
(Bellezza) Ric 129591
Concerto in D, "Per la S.S. Assunzione
di Maria Vergine", F.I no. 62
(Bellezza) Ric 129592
Concerto in D, F.I no. 116
(Bellezza) Ric 129773
Concerto in D, Op. 3, No. 9
(Dandelot) ESC
Concerto in d, F.I no. 28
(Malipiero) Ric 129381
Concerto in d
(Nachèz) SCH
Concerto in E, F.I no. 7
(Ephrikian) Ric 129298
Concerto in E, "La Primavera" F.I no. 22
(Soresina) Ric 128888
Concerto in E, Op. 3, No. 12
(Borrel) Senart 5319
(Kuechler) Pet 4379
Concerto in e, Op. 4, No. 2
(Füssl) Baer 3714
Concerto in E flat, "Il Ritiro"
(Ephrikian) Kul
Concerto in F, "L'Autunno", F.I no. 24
(Soresina) Ric 128890
Concerto in f, "L'Inverno", F.I no. 25
(Soresina) Ric 128891
Concerto in G
(Dandelot) ESC
(Nachèz) SCH
Concerto in G
(Kuechler-Hermann) Hug (Pet No. A21)
Concerto in G
(Orszagh) Kul
Concerto in g, F.I no. 16
(Malipiero) Ric 129380
Concerto in g, "L'Estate", F.I no. 23
(Soresina) Ric 128889
Concerto in g, Op. 4, No. 6
(Franko) RE (Pet No. RE2)
Concerto in g, Op. 12, No. 1
(Lenzewski) SCH
(Nachèz) SCH
Concerto in g
Kul
Larghetto, from Concerto Grosso in d
(Franko) GS "Intermezzo"
(Heifetz) CF B2186

VIVALDI, ANTONIO (cont.)
  Largo in d
    (Chiarappa) ZA3083
  Moment Paisible. Largo, from Concerto
      "L'Hiver", F.I no. 25
    (Pente) SCH
  Repos troublé, Le, from Concerto "L'Été",
      F.I no. 23
    (Pente) SCH
  Seasons, see
    Concerto in E, "La Primavera"
    Concerto in g, "L'Estate"
    Concerto in F, "L'Autunno"
    Concerto in f, "L'Inverno"
  Siciliano
    (Szabolcsi-Zathureczky) Kul
  Sonatas, 12, Op. 2
    (Hillemann) SCH   2V vcl ad lib
    Ric   score only
  Sonatas, 4, Op. 5
    (Upmeyer) NAG vcl ad lib
  Sonatas, 3 Chamber
    (Hillemann) BRH vcl ad lib
  Sonatas, 2, in F and d
    WM (Pet No. WM24) vcl or gamba ad lib
  Sonata in A
    (Francescatti) Int
  Sonata in C, see Solo Violin Music of the
      Earliest Period
  Sonata in c, Op. 2, No. 7
    (Mompellio) ZA3751
  Sonata in c
    (Salmon) Ric R732
  Sonata in c
    (Schlövogt) SCH vcl ad lib
  Sonata in D, Pincherle, Dresden National
      Library Cx, 1103
    (Respighi) Ric 128437
  Sonata in e
    (Salmon) Ric R733
  Sonata in F
    Broe (Pet No. B517)
  Sonata in g, Op. 2, No. 1
    (Moffat) SIM
  Sonata in g
    (Moffat) Int
  Sonata in g, Op. 13a, No. 6
    (Fussan) SCH vcl or gamba ad lib
    (Marx-Bodky) MM
  Sonata in g, F.XIII no. 5, for vln and Bc
    (Malipiero) Ric PR1006 score only
  Sonata in D, F. XIII no. 6, for vln and Bc
    (Malipiero) Ric PR1014 score only
  Sonata in d, F. XIII no. 7, for vln and Bc
    (Malipiero) Ric PR1015 score only
  Sonata in C, F. XIII no. 8, for vln and Bc
    (Malipiero) Ric PR1016 score only
  Sonata in d, F. XIII no. 9, for vln and Bc
    (Malipiero) Ric PR1017 score only
  Sonata in c, F. XIII no. 10, for vln and Bc
    (Malipiero) Ric PR1018 score only
  Sonata in C, F. XIII no. 11, for vln and Bc
    (Malipiero) Ric PR1019 score only
  Sonata in A, F. XIII no. 12, for vln and Bc
    (Malipiero) Ric PR1020 score only
  Sonata in G, F. XIII no. 13, for vln and Bc
    (Malipiero) Ric PR1021 score only
  Sonata in c, F. XIII no. 14, for vln and Bc
    (Malipiero) Ric PR1022 score only
  Sonata in g, F. XIII no. 15, for vln and Bc
    (Malipiero) Ric PR1023 score only
  Sonata in B flat, F. XIII no. 16, for vln and Bc
    (Malipiero) Ric PR1024 score only
  Sonata in g, F. XIII no. 29, for vln and Bc
    (Malipiero) Ric PR1069 score only

Sonata in A, F. XIII no. 30, for vln and Bc
    (Malipiero) Ric PR1070 score only
  Sonata in d, F. XIII no. 31, for vln and Bc
    (Malipiero) Ric PR1071 score only
  Sonata in F, F. XIII no. 32, for vln and Bc
    (Malipiero) Ric PR1072 score only
  Sonata in b, F. XIII no. 33, for vln and Bc
    (Malipiero) Ric PR1073 score only
  Sonata in C, F. XIII no. 34, for vln and Bc
    (Malipiero) Ric PR1074 score only
  Sonata in c, F. XIII no. 35, for vln and Bc
    (Malipiero) Ric PR1075 score only
  Suite in A
    (Busch) BRH
VIVASNO, J.B.
  Tuyo Siempre Waltz
    VL 13
VLADIGEROV, see Wladigeroff
VLASOV, V.
  Kirghiz March, see Aivazian: Song
  March, see Prokofiev: March
  Slovakian Rhapsody
    MZK
VOLGA BOATMEN SONG
    (Ambrosio) CF E102
    (Edward) MK
    (Harvey) VL 83 2nd vln ad lib
VOLOSHINOV, V.
  Sonata
    MZK
VOLPATTI, F.
  Réverie
    Gaudet
  Romance No. 1
    Gaudet
VON BLON, FRANZ (1861-1945)
  Meditation
    (Ambrosio) CF
  Serenade d'Amour
    (Rosey) MK
    CF B3237
VOORMOLEN, ALEXANDER (1895-   )
  Gavotte
    Wagenaar
  Sicilienne et Rigaudon
    RL
  Sonate
    RL
VORISEK, [JAN (1791-1825)]
  Sonata, Op. 5
    Artia
VOSS, FRIEDRICH
  Concerto
    BRH
VOULTSOS, PERICLES
  Only with you
    (Halle) Bel 686
VRANICKY, ANTONIN (1761-1820)
  Concerto in B flat
    Artia
VREULS, VICTOR (1876-1944)
  Sonata No. 1 in B
    Bosw
  Sonata No. 2 in G
    Bosw
WACHS, [PAUL (1851-1915)]
  Ce que dansait Grand'Mere
    Deiss
  Chanson de Marinette
    Deiss
  Quand l'oiseau chante
    Deiss
  Soixantaine, La
    Deiss

WAGNER, JOSEPH (1900-   )
Sonata No. 2
Mil
WAGNER, RICHARD (1813-1883)
Adagio, orig for clar and str quintet
(Schmeisser) BRH
Bridal March, from Lohengrin
(Centano) CF S3523
(Meyer) SCH
VL 36   2nd vln ad lib
Dreams, orig for voice and pno
(Auer) CF B1295
Entrance of the Black Swans
(Polo) SZ
Entrance of the Guests, from Tannhäuser
(Ambrosio) CF B2565   simpl
"Grand March"
(Thomas-Meyer) SCH
Overtures and Preludes, 6
Pet 3440
Pilgrims' Chorus, from Tannhäuser
(Thomas) SCH
Prelude, from Lohengrin
(Saenger) CF
Song to the Evening Star, from Tannhäuser
(Ambrosio) CF B2534
(Halle) Bel 699
(Trinkaus) Fill
Tannhäuser. Transcription
(Ambrosio) CF B3312
Walther's Prize Song, from Meistersinger
(Trinkaus) Fill
(Wilhelmj) CF S3493
(Wilhelmj) SCH
WALDTEUFEL, EMIL (1837-1915)
Tres Jolie and Skaters Waltz
Kjos S-5006
WALKER, ERNEST (1870-1949)
Sonata in a
JWL
WALLACE, WILLIAM (1812-1865)
Maritana. Transcription
(Ambrosio) CF B3304
WALLINGTON
Morning Dew
(Edwards) Mil
WALSH, MARY E.
Black Hawk Waltz
VL 145   2nd vln ad lib
WALTERS, JEFFERSON
Mazurka Champetre, Op. 34
MK
WALTHER, JOHANN JAKOB (1650- ?)
Scherzi. 12 Sonaten
(Beckmann) Baer   vcl ad lib
Sonata in G
(Bethan) NAG   vcl ad lib
Sonata No. 3
MM   Photolith reproduction
Sonate mit Suite, for vln and Bc
KS   vcl ad lib
WALTHEW, RICHARD HENRY (1872-1951)
Cheerful, from Impressions
STB
Pensive, from Impressions
STB
Regretful, from Impressions
STB
WALTON, WILLIAM (1902-   )
Concerto
Oxf 23.007
Pieces, 2: Canzonetta and Scherzetto
Oxf 23.016

Sonata
Oxf 23.005
WARD, ROBERT (1917-   )
Sonata No. 1
Peer
WARD
Devotion
Pr
WARLOCK, PETER (1894-1930)
Pieces, 3, from Capriol Suite, orig for orch
(Szigeti) CF B2483
Basse-Danse; Mattachins; Pavane
Pieds-en-l'air, from Capriol Suite
(Szigeti) CF B2483
WARREN, DAVID
Sonatina
Lud S-15A23
WATERS, CHARLES F. (1895-   )
Suite of Three Tunes
STB
WEBBER, LLOYD
Minuet
Mil
WEBBER, RUSSELL
Fiddle Fun for the Young Soloist
Bel EL247
Little march
GS
WEBBER
Romany Caprice
Pr
WEBER, ALAIN (1930-   )
Thème et variations
Leduc
WEBER, BEN (1916-   )
Sonata No. 1, Op. 5
CFE
Sonata da camera
BH
WEBER, CARL MARIA VON (1786-1826)
Air Russe and Rondo, from Sonata No. 3
(Szigeti) CF B2373
Country Dance
BMC
Dernière Pensée de Weber, see Dancla C.
Freischütz, Der. Fantasia, see Dancla, C.
Grand Duo Concertant, Op. 48, orig for
clar and pno
Pet 3317
Invitation to the Dance, Op. 65, orig for pno
(Danbé-Saenger) CF B2639
(Scarmolin) Lud S-15A20
(Weiss-Saenger) CF
Oberon. Fantaisie, see Danbé
Overtures by Beethoven, Mozart, Weber
Pet 3299A
Rondo, from Sonata No. 3
(Heifetz) CF B2314
Sonatas, 6, Op. 10
Pet 191
Waltz No. 1
BMC
WEBER, H.
Composition No. 2
BRH
WEBERN, ANTON VON (1883-1945)
Pieces, 4, Op. 7
UE 6642
WECKER, KARL
Dream Waltz, from Echoes from Melody
Land, Op. 8
(Simpkinson) CF B1899
Echoes from Melody Land, 12, Op. 8
(Simpkinson) CF 0564

WECKER, KARL (cont.)
  Happy Gondolier, from Echoes from Melody
    Land, Op. 8
    (Simpkinson) CF B1902
  In a Red Rose Garden, from Echoes from
    Melody Land, Op. 8
    (Simpkinson) CF B1904
  Little Lost Sunbeam, from Echoes from
    Melody Land, Op. 8
    (Simpkinson) CF B1906
  Marche Militaire, from Echoes from
    Melody Land, Op. 8
    (Simpkinson) CF B1905
  Visit in Poland, from Echoes from Melody
    Land, Op. 8
    (Simpkinson) CF B1903
WEIGL, KARL (1881-1949)
  Pictures From Childhood
    CFE   score only
  Pieces, 2
    CFE
  Sonata No. 2 in G
    CFE
WEIGL
  Variations on a theme of, see Dancla,
    Charles: Air Varié, Op. 89, No. 5
(WEIL, HEINITZ)
  Album clásico del joven violinista
    Ric BA10442, 10892   2V
WEINBERGER, JAROMIR (1896-   )
  Polka, from Shvanda the Bagpiper
    (Wladigeroff) AMP
WEINBERT, JACOB
  Cabalist, Op. 31, No. 1
    (Piastro) MK
  Speed Ahead, Op. 31, No. 2
    (Piastro) MK
WEINER, LEO (1885-1960)
  Hungarian Wedding Dance, Op. 21b
    Kul
  Pereg: Recruiting Dance
    Kul
  Sonata, Op. 9
    Kul
  Sonata, Op. 11
    Kul
WEINZWEIG, JOHN JACOB (1913-   )
  Sonata
    Oxf 23.806
WEISS, ADOLPH (1891-   )
  Fantasies, based on Sukehiro Shiba's
    transcriptions of Gagaku
    CFE
  Sonata
    CFE
WEISS
  Raccolta di fiori, Op. 38
    (Anzoletti-Polo) Ric ER1072
WELSH AIRS
  (Brown) JWL (Mil No. W1801A,B)   2V
WERNER, FRITZ
  Sonata, Op. 41
    BRH
WESLY, E.
  Confidences
    Gaudet
  Fincailles
    Gaudet
  Heure du réve, L'
    Gaudet
  Hyménée
    Gaudet
  Réverie d'Automne
    Gaudet

Songes roses
  Gaudet
WESSELY, H.
  Bolero
    JWL (Mil No. W1208)
  Caprice
    JWL (Mil No. W1211)
  Feu Follet
    JWL (Mil No. W1213)
  Little Waltz
    JWL (Mil No. W1212)
  Mazurka No. 1
    JWL (Mil No. W1209)
  Mazurka No. 2
    JWL (Mil No. W1210)
  Spring Message
    JWL (Mil No. W1214)
WESTERMAN, GERHART VON
  Sonata in G, Op. 14
    BB
WEYBRIGHT
  Hungarian Dance
    Willis
WHEAR, PAUL (1925-   )
  Soliloquy, from Concerto
    Interlochen Press
WHEN JOHNNY COMES MARCHING HOME
  (Eckstein) CF M319
WHEN LOVE IS KIND
  (Buchtel) Kjos S-5005
WHILE STROLLING THROUGH THE PARK
  ONE DAY
  (Applebaum) Bel SI34
(WHISTLER, HARVEY S.)
  Christmas Time
    Ru
  First Solo Album
    Ru
  Melodies in First Position
    Ru   2nd vln ad lib
  Solos for Strings
    Ru
WHITE, CECIL
  Suite for Violin on Open Strings
    JWL (Mil No. W1222)
WHITE, CLARENCE CAMERON (1880-   )
  Cabin Song, From the Cotton Fields,
    Op. 18
    CF B1199
  Chant. Nobody knows de trouble I've see,
    from Bandanna Sketches, Op. 12
    CF B1171
  Cradle Song, Op. 10, No. 1
    BMC
  Lament. I'm troubled in mind, from Ban-
    danna Sketches, Op. 12
    CF B1172
  Levee Dance, based on "Go Down Moses",
    Op. 27
    CF B2061
  Pilgrim Song, based on "Somebody's Knock-
    ing at Your Door", Op. 27
    CF B2348
  Plantation Song, based on "Swing Low, Sweet
    Chariot", Op. 27
    CF B2347
  Slave Song. Many thousand gone, from Ban-
    danna Sketches, Op. 12
    CF B1173
  Spiritual. From the Cotton Fields, Op. 18
    CF B1201
  Twilight, Op. 17, No. 1
    CF B1791

WHITE, CLARENCE CAMERON (cont.)
Valse Coquette, Op. 17, No. 4
CF B1794
WHITE, [PAUL (1895-   )]
Sonata
EV
WHITELEY, HARRY E.
Brancaster Pictures
Leng (Mil No. L1101)
WHITHORNE, EMERSON (1884-1958)
Blue Dusk, Op. 47, No. 1
CF B2142
WIDOR, CHARLES-MARIE (1844-1937)
Serenade in A
(Schneider) CF B3149
Sonate
Haml
WIEN, WIEN, NUR DU ALLEIN
SCH
WIENIAWSKI, HENRI (1835-1880)
Adagio Elégiaque, Op. 5, see Polonaises, 2
Airs Russes, see Souvenir de Moscou
Caprices, 2
(Francescatti) Int
Caprice in a
(Kreisler) Fol 1086
Caprice in E flat, "Alla Saltarella"
(Kreisler) Fol 1087
Caprice
(Heifetz) CF B2505
Capriccio-Valse, Op. 7
(Auer) CF B3277
(Lichtenberg) GS L610
Carnaval Russe, Op. 11
Pet 5509
Concerto No. 1 in f sharp, Op. 14
(Auer) CF 03318
(De Guarnieri) Ric ER219
(Quesnot) Senart 5163
Pet 5504
Concerto No. 2 in d, Op. 22
(Galamian) Int
(Lichtenberg) GS L951
(Quesnot) Senart 5293
(Wilhelmj) SCH
CF L373
Pet 3296
Dudziarz. Mazurka, Op. 19, No. 2
CF B3137
Fantaisie Orientale; with Gigue, Op. 23
Lit (Pet No. L2464)
Fantasy on Gounod's "Faust"
MZK
Fantasy
(Ondricek) AMP
Gigue, see Fantaisie Orientale
Kuyawiak. Mazurka No. 2
(Ambrosio) CF B2537   simpl
(Lichtenberg) GS
(Quesnot) Senart 5162
(Rosey) MK
(Saenger) CF S3261
(Wilhelmj) SCH
Kjos S-5019
Pet 3297
Ric BA6629
Légende, Op. 17, orig for vln and orch
(De Guarnieri) Ric 127771
(Quesnot) Senart 5161
(Saenger) CF B3334
(Schradieck) GS L1067
(Wilhelmj) SCH
see also Mazurkas, Op. 12
Mazurkas, Selected
MZK

Mazurkas, 2, Op. 12
Sielanka; Chanson polonaise
(Marteau) Pet 3291
(Schradieck) GS L366; with Légende
Mazurkas, 2, Op. 19
(Quesnot) Senart 5287
(Wilhelmj) SCH
Pet 3294
Mazurka, Op. 19, No. 1, see Obertass
Mazurka, Op. 19, No. 2, see Dudziarz
Mazurka, No. 2, see Kuyawiak
Obertass. Mazurka, Op. 19, No. 1
(Pollitzer) CF S3610
(Wilhelmj) SCH
Polish Song, see Fibich: Poem
Polonaises, 2, Op. 4 and Op. 21; with
Adagio Elégiaque, Op. 5
Pet 5500
Polonaise brillante No. 1 in D, Op. 4
(Lichtenberg) GS L607
(Napolitano) Ric BA10859
(Quesnot) Senart 5164
MZK
Polonaise brillante No. 2 in A, Op. 21
(Lichtenberg) GS L944
(Napolitano) Ric BA10865
(Pollitzer) CF L581
(Quesnot) Senart 5315
MZK
Romance, from Concerto No. 2, Op. 22
(Mittell) GS
(Tonini) Ric BA9383
CF S3405
Romance sans paroles and Rondo élégant,
Op. 9
(Lichtenberg) GS L611
Lit (Pet No. L2456)
Sautillé, Le
(Rostal) Nov
Scherzo-Tarantelle, Op. 16, orig for
vln and orch
(Marteau) Pet 3292
(Napolitano) Ric BA10689
(Sitt) Eul (Pet No. Z237)
(Spiering) CF L806
GS L613
MZK
Souvenir de Moscou, Op. 6, orig for
vln and orch
(Kreisler) Fol 1076 "Airs Russes"
(Lichtenberg) GS L609
(Pessina) Ric BA10316
(Quesnot) Senart 5316 "Airs Russes"
CF B2735
MZK
Pet 3296
WILLAN, HEALEY (1880-   )
Sonata No. 1 in e
CL
Sonata No. 2
Bosw
WILLIAMS
Dream of Olwen
(Edwards) Mil
WILLNER, [ARTHUR (1881-1959)
Sonatine
Senart
WILSON
Little Tunes with Cartoons
Bel EL677
WILSON, see Grasso & Wilson
WINN, EDITH LYNWOOD
Playtime Pieces for Little Violinists, 5
CF B856

WINNER, SEPTIMUS, see Hawthorne, Alice
WINTERNITZ, FELIX
  Dance of the Marionette
    CF B2062
  Once Upon a Time
    CF B2013
  Troika
    Fol 1195
WIREN, DAG (1905-   )
  Concerto, Op. 23
    Gehrmans
  Sonatin, Op. 15
    Nordiska
WISHART, PETER (1921-   )
  Pieces, 4
    Oxf 23.002
WISSMER, PIERRE (1915-   )
  Sonatine
    Amphion 128
WITH MY VIOLIN ROUND THE WORLD, BK. I
  (Neago) SIM
WITKOWSKY, GEORGES-MARTIN (1867-1943)
  Introduction et Danses
    Senart
  Sonate
    Dur
WLADIGEROFF, PANTCHO (1899-   )
  Chant, Op. 21, No. 2
    UE 9725
  Concerto in f, Op. 11
    UE 7138
  Folk-tune, Op. 7, No. 2, from 2 Impro-
      visations
    UE 9979
  Poème érotique, Op. 7, No. 1, from
      2 Improvisations
    UE 9978
  Song, from Bulgarian Suite[44]
    MZK
  Vardar. Bulgarian Rhapsody, Op. 16
    UE 6561
WOELBER, FRANK
  Student's Concerto
    CF B2179
WOHLFAHRT, FRANZ
  Easy Fantasia on 2 Christmas songs:
      Silent Night and O Sanctissima, Op. 83
    (Saenger) CF B3126
WOLFERMANN, ALBERT
  Fantasia No. 1, Op. 3, No. 2
    CF B3020
  Fantasia No. 2, Op. 3, No. 3
    (Centano) CF B3021
WOLFF, CHRISTIAN (1934-   )
  Duo for Violinist and Pianist
    Pet 6494
WOLF-FERRARI, ERMANNO (1876-1948)
  Concerto in D, Op. 26
    (Bustabo) SON
  Sonata in a, Op. 10
    SIM
WOLFSTAHL
  Recuerdos
    BH
WOLPE, STEFAN (1902-   )
  Sonata
    MM
WOOD, C.
  Jig
    STB
  Melody
    STB

Planxty
  STB
WOOD, HAYDN (1882-1959)
  Concerto
    BH
  Little Pieces, 2
    STB
  Pieces, 2
    STB
  Roses of Picardy
    Chap-L
WOOD, JOSEPH
  Sonata
    CFE   score only
WOOF, ROWSBY
  Hornpipe
    ABRS (Mil No. A233)
  Valse Capriccio
    JWL (Mil No. W1207)
WOOLLETT, HENRI (1864-1936)
  Sonate No. 2 en mi majeur
    Haml
  Sonate No. 5
    Senart
WORDSWORTH, WILLIAM (1908-   )
  Sonata in b
    Leng (Mil No. L1112)
WORLD'S BEST-KNOWN PIECES
  (Trinkaus) CF
WORLD'S VIOLIN
  SIM
WORŽISCHEK, see Vorisek
WUORINEN, CHARLES
  Eight Variations, see vln and harpsichord
WYMAN, ADDISON P. (1832-1872)
  Woodland Echoes, Op. 34
    (Ambrosio) CF
YANSHINOV, A.
  Concertino, Op. 35
    MZK
  Spinning Song, see Ippolitov-Ivanov: Melody
YATSEVICH, Y.
  Concerto No. 2
    MZK
  Musical Pictures, 4
    MZK
  Sonata
    MZK
YOST, GAYLORD (1888-1958)
  Arlette
    VL
  Contrition
    VL
  Dawn Greets the Rose
    VL
  Eclogue
    VL
  Funny Clown
    VL
  Leaves are falling
    VL
  Merry Elves
    VL
  Sleeping Princess
    VL
  Song and Dance
    CF B2752
  Tango
    VL
  Viennese
    VL
YOUNG, VICTOR (1889-   )
  Nocturne
    Victor Young

---

[44] Under Vladigerov in the Leeds catalogue.

YOUNG, VICTOR (cont.)
  Stringin' Along
    Victor Young
YOUNG FIDDLER'S COMPANION
    (Twarz) SIM   2V
      20 easy pieces by Praetorius, Dowland,
      Bach, Marpurg, Farnaby, Mozart,
      Rameau, Handel and others
YRADIER, SEBASTIÁN (1809-1865)
  Paloma, La
    (Ambrosio) CF B2563   simpl
    (Halle) Bel 689
    VL 70   2nd vln ad lib
YSAŸE, EUGÈNE (1858-1931)
  Berceuse de l'Enfant pauvre[45]
    SF
  Chant d'Hiver[45]
    ENO
  Concerto d'après deux poèmes[45]
    (J. Ysaÿe) SF
  Divertimento[45]
    SF
  Etude Poème
    Cinedisc
  Extase,[45] orig for vln and orch
    SF
  Fantaisie,[45] orig for vln and orch
    SF
  Lointain Passé in b, Op. 11
    BRH
    (Dounis) Mil "Mazurka No. 3"
  Mazurka No. 1 in G
    (Dounis) Mil
  Mazurka No. 2 in a
    (Dounis) Mil
  Mazurka No. 3, see Lointain Passé
  Neiges d'Antan[45]
    SF
  Paganini Variations, orig for vln and orch
    (J. Ysaÿe) BH
  Poème Elégiaque, orig for vln and orch
    Cinedisc
  Rêve d'Enfant[45]
    ENO
  Rouet, Le[45]
    SF
YULETIDE MELODIES
    (Harvey) VL 130
ZABACH, FLORIAN
  Funny Fiddle
    (Haring) Shapiro, Bernstein
ZACHARIAS, HELMUT
  Fantasy on 3 themes
    Mil
ZAKHARINA, T.
  First Steps
    MZK
(ZAKHARINA, T.)
  Pieces, 5
    MZK
  Transcriptions of Music of Western Com-
      posers, Vol. II
    MZK
ZANDONAI, RICCARDO (1883-1944)
  Concerto romantico
    Ric 118239
ZANI, ANDREA (18th century)
  Sonata No. 7
    (Cortot-Pochon) Ric 128797
ZBINDEN, JULIEN-FRANCOIS (1917-   )
  Rhapsody, Op. 25
    BRH

Sonata, Op. 15
    SZ
ZECCHI, ADONE (1904-   )
  Sonata in F
    Carisch
ZEISL, ERIC (1905-   )
  Menuhim's Song, from Job
    Mil
  Sonata
    (Baker) DOB
ZEITZ, F.
  Concerto No. 2, Op. 22
ZELENKA, I.
  Little Duets, 11
    UE 13119
ZHILIN
  Waltzes, 3, see Kozlovsky: Adagio
ZHUK, O.
  Poem
    MZK
ZIMBALIST, EFREM (1889-   )
  Improvisation on a Japanese tune
    GS
  Sonata in g
    GS
  Suite in alter Form
    SCH
(ZIMBALIST, EFREM)
  Solo Violin Music of the Earliest Period
    Pr   for contents see title
(ZIMMER)
  Violin Classics in the First Position
    Pr
ZIMMERMANN, BERND ALOIS (1918-   )
  Sonata
    SCH
ZOLOTAREV, B.
  Elegy, Op. 11, No. 1
    MZK
ZUCCOLI, GASTONE DE
  Elevation
    ZA 2320

Duos: Violin, Harpsichord[46]

GRAFF, JOHANN
  Sonata in D, Op. 1, No. 3
    KS   vcl ad lib
HOVHANESS, ALAN (1911-   )
  Duet for violin and harpsichord
    Pet 6439
MILHAUD, DARIUS (1892-   )
  Sonata for vln and clavecin
    EV
MONDONVILLE, JEAN-JOSEPH DE (1711-1772)
  Sonata in F
    Noet (Pet No. N6057)
PARRIS, ROBERT (1924-   )
  Sonata
    CFE
PISTON, WALTER (1894-   )
  Sonatina
    BH
SCHOBERT, JOHANN (c.1720-1767)
  Sonata
    Aug 11698
WUORINEN, CHARLES (1938-   )
  Eight Variations
    CFE

---

[45] This publication is not listed in current U.S. catalogues. Information was received from Fondation Eugène Ysaÿe.

[46] Many compositions listed for violin and piano are suitable for violin and harpsichord. This section includes only those titles specifically designated for harpsichord by the publisher.

Duos: Violin, Organ

ALBUM FOR VIOLIN AND ORGAN
  Pet 2450
    Compositions by Bach, Beethoven,
    Corelli, Handel, Mozart, Nardini,
    Tartini
AUSERLESENE MELODIEN
  (Piechler) SCH   for contents see title
    under vln, pno
BACH, JOHANN SEBASTIAN (1685-1750)
  Air on the G String
    (Wilhelmj-Perlman) CF S3019
  Andante in G, from Sonata No. 5 for fl
    Pet 3183
  Ave Maria, see Gounod
BADINGS, HENK (1907-   )
  Intermezzo
    DN (Pet No. D154)
ERDLEN, HERMANN (1893-   )
  Chaconne
    Pet 4187
FELDERHOF, [JAN (1907-   )]
  Aria
    DN (Pet No. D153)
FOURVIÈRES, PAUL
  Méditation Religieuse
    (Ambrosio) CF S3649
FUCHS, FRANZ
  Praeludium, Op. 58 and Fantasie, Op. 56
    Krenn
GOLDMARK, KARL (1830-1915)
  Air, from Violin Concerto, Op. 28
    (Ries) BMC
GOTTSCHALK, LOUIS MOREAU (1829-1869)
  Last Hope
    (Moses-Tobani) CF B3129
GOUNOD, CHARLES FRANCOIS (1818-1893)
  Ave Maria. Meditation on the first
      prelude of J.S. Bach
    (Barnes) GS
  Vision de Jeanne d'Arc
    CF B3093
HOELLER, KARL (1907-   )
  Fantasy, Op. 49
    Pet 5868
NOYON, J.
  Arioso
    Procure Générale du Clergé
RELIGIOUS MEDITATIONS
  (Ambrosio) CF 02585   for contents see
    title under vln and pno
TCHAIKOVSKY, PIOTR ILYITCH (1840-1893)
  Chanson Triste, Op. 40, No. 2, orig for pno
    (Saenger) CF S3139

Duos: Violin, Guitar

ALBERT
  Sonatina in old style
    LN (Pet No. R91)
BLOCH, W.
  Neuberger Tänze
    DOB
  Sonate
    DOB
CARULLI, FERDINANDO (1770-1841)
  Sonata in A, Op. 21, No. 1
    ZM (Pet No. ZM244)
  Sonata in D, Op. 21, No. 2
    ZM (Pet No. ZM245)
CORELLI, ARCANGELO (1653-1713)
  Sonata in d, Op. 5, No. 7
    (Scheit) DOB

GIULIANI, MAURO (1781-1828)
  Grand Sonata in e, Op. 25
    ZM (Pet No. ZM116)
GRAGNANI
  Sonata in D, Op. 8, No. 1
    ZM (Pet No. ZM46)
  Sonata in C, Op. 8, No. 2
    ZM (Pet No. ZM47)
  Sonata in A, Op. 8, No. 3
    ZM (Pet No. ZM48)
KUEFFNER, JOSEPH (1776-1856)
  Serenade in A, Op. 68
    Noet (Pet No. N3099)
LOCATELLI, PIETRO (1695-1764)
  Sinfonia
    (Scheit) DOB
  Sonata in D
    (Scheit) DOB
PAGANINI, NICCOLÒ (1782-1840)
  Cantabile
    ZM (Pet No. ZM190)
  Centone di Sonate
    ZM (Pet No. ZM119)
  Sonatas, 6, Op. 2
    ZM (Pet No. ZM193)
  Sonatas, 6, Op. 3
    Paragon
    Ric 543
    ZM (Pet No. ZM194)
  Sonata Concertata in A
    ZM (Pet No. ZM49)
  Tarantella
    ZM (Pet No. ZM195)
  Variazioni di Bravura
    ZM (Pet No. ZM197)
PEPUSCH, JOHN CHRISTOPHER (1667-1752)
  Sonata in G
    (Scheit) DOB
REITER, [ALBERT (1905-   )]
  Sonatina
    (Scheit) DOB
RUST, FRIEDRICH WILHELM (1739-1796)
  Sonata in d
    VW (Pet No. V19)
  Sonata in G
    VW (Pet No. V20)
SIEGL, OTTO (1896-   )
  Sonatine in d
    DOB
VIVALDI, ANTONIO (c.1669-1741)
  Sonata in c
    (Scheit) DOB
  Sonata in d
    (Scheit) DOB

Duos: Violin, Harp

ALBERSTOETTER
  Romance, Op. 7
    ZM (Pet No. ZM705)
BADINGS, HENK (1907-   )
  Cavatina
    DN (Pet No. D78)
BUESSER, HENRI-PAUL (1872-   )
  Sommeil de l'enfant Jésus
    CH (Pet No. C99)
GILLMANN
  Poem
    ZM (Pet No. ZM699)
MARTELLI, HENRI (1895-   )
  Duos, 7, Op. 66
    Dur

NATRA, S.
 Music for violin and harp
  IMI
RENIÉ, HENRIETTE (1875-1956)
 Scherzo-Fantaisie
  Leduc
ROSSINI, GIOACCHINO (1792-1868)
 Andante e Variazioni
  MM   Photolith reproduction
SAINT-SAENS, CAMILLE (1835-1921)
 Fantaisie, Op. 124
  Dur
SCHWARTZ, PAUL
 Little Suite, Op. 23B
  CFE
SOURIS, [ANDRE (1899-   )]
 Fatrasie
  CBDM
SPOHR, LUDWIG (1784-1859)
 Sonata in c
  (Zingel) Baer 2307
  ZM (Pet No. ZM145)
STAHL
 Romance in F, Op. 69
  ZM (Pet No. ZM700)
TEDESCHI, L.M.
 Elegia, Op. 22
  ZA 3217
 Fantasia, Op. 48
  ZA 3218
 Serenade, Op. 28
  ZM (Pet No. ZM725)
TOURNIER, MARCEL (1879-1951)
 Préludes romantiques, 2, Op. 17
  Dur
VERDALLE
 Cantilene, Op. 26
  ZM (Pet No. ZM704)
 Chant d'Amour, Op. 29
  ZM (Pet No. ZM701)
 Larghetto, Op. 20
  ZM (Pet No. ZM702)
 Melancolie, Op. 30
  ZM (Pet No. ZM706)
 Pleurs et Reves, Op. 32
  ZM (Pet No. ZM707)
 Reverie, Op. 24
  ZM (Pet No. ZM703)

Duos: Viola, Piano

ACCOLAY, J.B.
 Concerto No. 1, orig for vln
  (Doty) GS L1785
ADOLPHUS, MILTON
 Improvisations, Op. 61
  CFE
AGUIRRE, JULIÁN (1868-1924)
 Huella, orig for pno
  (Heifetz-Primrose) CF B2672
ALBENIZ, ISAAC (1860-1909)
 Tango in D, orig for pno
  (Forbes) Oxf
ALBUM, CLASSICAL
 (Moffat-Laubach) Aug 5566
ALBUM OF CELEBRATED PIECES, BK. 1
 (Stehling) Aug 7625a
ALBUM OF SIX PIECES
 (Conus-Katims-Borissovsky) Int
ALBUM OF 24 CLASSICAL PIECES
 (Klengel) Int   3V
ALETTER, W.
 Mélodie
  CF B2319

 Petite Gavotte
  CF B2353
AMES, WILLIAM (1901-   )
 Sonata
  CFE   score only
AMRAM, DAVID (1930-   )
 Wind and the Rain
  Pet 6692
ANDERSON, KENNETH (1903-   )
 Diversions, 3
  Bosw
ANGERER, PAUL (1927-   )
 Concerto, 1962
  DOB
ANTUFEYEV, B.
 Concerto
  MZK
 Dramatic Fragments, 2, Op. 40
  MZK
ARIOSTI, ATTILIO (1666-c.1740)
 Sonatas 1 and 2, from 6 Sonatas for
  vla d'amore
  (Sabatini Renzo) Santis 981
 Sonata
  MZK
ARNE, THOMAS (1710-1778)
 Sonata in B flat
  (Craxton) Oxf 20.007
ARNOLD, MALCOLM (1921-   )
 Sonata
  Leng (Mil No. L2003)
ASAFIEV
 Gavotte, see Rakov: Tale
ASHTON, A.T.L.
 Landler
  STB
 Tarantella
  STB
AVSHALOMOFF, JACOB (1919-   )
 Sonatine
  Mercury
BABBITT, MILTON (1916-   )
 Composition
  BMP   blueprint
BACH, C.P.E., see Bach, K.P.E.
BACH, JOHANN CHRISTIAN (1735-1782)
 Concerto en Ut mineur
  (Casadesus) Sal
BACH, JOHANN CHRISTOPH (1642-1703)
 Lament
  Ed M
BACH, JOHANN SEBASTIAN (1685-1750)
 Adagio, from Organ Concerto No. 3, after
  Vivaldi
  (Borissovsky) Int
 Adagio, from Toccata in C for organ
  (Siloti-Tertis) CF B1950
 Air, "Celebrated", from Orchestral
  Suite in D
  (Wilhelmj-Pagels) CF B2468
 Air and Gavottes, from Suite in D
  (Tolhurst) JWL (Mil No. W1409)
 Air and Gavotte
  (Ries) SCH
 All glory be to God on high
  (Forbes-Richardson) Oxf 22.020
 Andante, from Italian Concerto, orig
  for clavier
  (Ronchini) ESC
 Arioso, from Cantata No. 156
  (Isaac) CF B2496
 Bourree, from Cello Suite in E flat
  (Browne) JWL (Mil No. W1406)
 Bourree, see Hasse; Bouree

BACH, JOHANN SEBASTIAN (cont.)
Come, Redeemer of our race
(Forbes-Richardson) Oxf 22.102
Gavotte in A
(Forbes) Oxf 22.330
Jesu, joy of man's desiring
(Forbes) Oxf 22.100
Komm', süsser Tod
(Tertis) GS
Largo, dalla Cantata, "Gottes Zeit ist die
allerbeste Zeit"
(Janigro) Ric 127917
Lord Jesus Christ, be present now
(Forbes-Richardson) Oxf 22.021
Pieces, 3, from Sonata No. 1 for
unacc vcl
(Johnson) Leng (Mil No. L2006)
Praeludium
(Shore) BH
Prelude in A
(Forbes) Oxf 22.320
Prelude and Gigue
(Cooley) Leeds
Sheep may safely graze
(Forbes) Oxf 23.416
Sonatas, 6, S. 1014-19,[47] orig for vln
and clavier
(David-Hermann) Int 2V
Sonatas, 3, S.1027-29,[47] orig for gamba
and clavier
(Consolini) Ric ER116
(Forbes) Pet 4286A
(Naumann) BRH
(Naumann) Int
Sonata in F, orig for vln and clavier
(Forbes) Pet 4460A
see also Select Teaching Pieces
BACH, KARL PHILIPP EMANUEL (1714-1788)
Concerto in B flat[48]
(Klengel) BRH
Solfeggieto
(Primrose) CF B2683
Sonata in g
(Primrose) Int
BACH, WILHELM FRIEDEMANN (1710-1784)
Sonata in c, for vla and harpsichord or pno
(Pessl) Oxf
BACICH, ANTHONY P.
Tone Poems
Willis
BACON, ERNST (1898-   )
Koschatiana
Leeds
BADINGS, HENK (1907-   )
Cavatina
DN (Pet No. D7)
Sonata
DN (Pet No. D3)
BAERVOETS, R
Rhapsody
Metr
BAEYENS, AUGUST (1895-   )
Concerto
Metr
BANTOCK, GRANVILLE (1868-1946)
Sonata in F
Ches

BARATI, GEORGE (1913-   )
Cantabile e Ritmico
Peer
BARNETT, DAVID
Ballade, Op. 16
(Primrose) Oxf 92.201
BARTOK, BELA (1881-1945)
Concerto
BH   prepared by Serly
Evening in the Village
(Vaczy) Kul
Rhapsody on Folk Songs, see Serly
BASSETT, LESLIE (1923-   )
Sonata
CFE
BAUER, MARION (1887-1955)
Sonata
SPAM
BAX, ARNOLD (1883-1953)
Phantasy, orig for vla and orch
Chap
Sonata
Chap
BEALE, JAMES (1924-   )
Ballade, Op. 23
CFE
BECK, CONRAD (1901-   )
Concerto
SCH
BEETHOVEN, LUDWIG VAN (1770-1827)
Alla polacca
(Forbes) Oxf 22.033
Country Dances, orig for orch
(Forbes-Richardson) Oxf 22.004
Mozart Variations, 7. Bei Maennern,
welche Liebe fuehlen, from
Magic Flute, orig for vcl and pno
Pet 7049
Notturno, Op. 42
(Beck) GS
(Primrose) SCH
Romances, 2: in G, Op. 40; in F, Op. 50;
orig for vln and orch
(Hermann) Pet 2413
Int
Rondo, orig for vln and pno
(Forbes) SCH
Sonata in g, Op. 5, No. 2, orig for vcl and pno
(Tertis) Aug
Int
Sonata, Op. 17, orig for horn and pno
Int
Sonata in F, Op. 24, "Spring", orig for
vln and pno
(Forbes) Pet 4066b
Sonata in A, Op. 69, orig for vcl and pno
Int
Sonatina, Minuet, see Hasse: Bouree
see also Select Teaching Pieces
BEN-HAIM, PAUL (1897-   )
Songs Without Words, 3
IMP
BENJAMIN, ARTHUR (1893-1960)
Sonata or Concerto. Elegy, Waltz and
Toccata
BH
Tombeau de Ravel, Le
BH
BERGSMA, WILLIAM (1921-   )
Fantastic Variations
Galx
BERIOT, CHARLES DE (1802-1870)
Serenade
Bel

---

[47] S. number is from the thematic catalogue by W. Schmieder;
Thematisch-systematisch Verzeichnis der musikalischen
Werke von Johann Sebastian Bach. Leipzig, 1950.
[48] Probably originally for gamba or cello.

BERKELEY, LENNOX (1903-   )
  Sonata in d
  Ches
BERLIOZ, HECTOR (1803-1869)
  Harold in Italy orig for vla and orch
  (Liszt-Riley) Uni Music Press
BEZRUKOV, G.
  Easy Pieces, 3
  MZK
BIGOT, E.
  Thême et variations
  Dur
BIZET, GEORGES (1838-1875)
  Adagietto, from L'Arlésienne
  (Primrose) SCH
  Aria, from L'Arlésienne
  CH (Pet No. C259)
BLACHER, BORIS (1903-   )
  Concerto, Op. 48
  BB
BLACKWOOD, EASLEY (1933-   )
  Sonata
  EV
BLISS, ARTHUR (1891-   )
  Sonata
  Oxf 22.405
BLOCH, ERNEST (1880-1959)
  Meditation and Processional
  GS
  Suite
  GS
  Suite Hebraique, orig for vla and orch
  GS
      Rapsodie, Processional, Affirmation
BOCCHERINI, LUIGI (1743-1805)
  Concerto No. 3 in G, orig for vcl and orch
  (Ross) GS L1726   with cadenzas
  Sonata No. 3 in G, orig for vcl and pno
  (Alard-Meyer) Int
  Sonata No. 6 in A, orig for vcl and pno
  (Katims) Int
  Sonata in c[49]
  Carisch
(BOETJE, JOSEPH)
  Viola Music for Concert and Church
  BMC
BOHM, CARL
  Perpetual Motion, from Third Suite,
      No. 6, orig for vln and pno
  (Isaac-Lewis) CF B1383
BOISDEFFRE, RENÉ DE (1838-1906)
  Pièces, 3
  Haml
BONI, P.
  Largo and Allegro
  MZK
BORISSOVSKY, VADIM, see Conus, Katims &
      Borissovsky
BORNOFF'S FIDDLER'S HOLIDAY
  (Bornoff-Wilson) CF 04246, 4248
(BORNOFF, GEORGE)
  Fun for Fiddle Fingers
  Gordon V. Thompson
BORODIN, ALEXANDER (1833-1887)
  Nocturne
  (Primrose) Oxf 22.031
  Scherzo
  (Primrose) Oxf 22.032
BORRIS, SIEGFRIED (1906-   )
  Kleine Suite
  Sirius   in preparation
  Sonate, Op. 51
  Sirius

---

[49] This may have been for violin originally.

BOTTJE, WILL GAY (1925-   )
  Fantasy Sonata
  CFE
BOURNONVILLE, ARMAND
  Appassionata
  Billaudot
BOWEN, YORK (1884-1961)
  Sonata No. 1 in c
  (Tertis) SCH
BOYCE, WILLIAM (1710-1779)
  Tempo di gavotta
  (Craxton-Forbes) Oxf 20.108
BOZZA, EUGENE (1905-   )
  Concertino
  Ricard
BRAEIN, EDVARD (1887-1957)
  Serenade, orig for vla and orch
  LY (Pet No. LY4)
BRAHMS, JOHANNES (1833-1897)
  Hungarian Dances Nos. 1 and 3, orig
      for pno duet
  (Forbes) Hin (Pet No. H699)
  Sonatas, 2, Op. 120, for clar, or vla, and pno
  Pet 3896C
  Sonata in f, Op. 120, No. 1
  (Katims) Int
  Aug
  BRH
  SIM
  Sonata in E flat, Op. 120, No. 2
  (Katims) Int
  Aug
  SIM
  Sonata in e, Op. 38, orig for vcl and pno
  (Tertis) Aug
  Int
  Sonatensatz. Scherzo, orig for vln and pno
  (Katims) Int
  Waltz, Op. 39, No. 2, orig for pno duet
  (Grunes) Omega
  Wie Melodien zieht es mir, Op. 105, No. 1,
      orig for voice and pno
  ,(Primrose) CF B2680
BREVILLE, PIERRE DE (1861-1949)
  Prière
  RL
  Sonata
  ESC
BRITTEN, BENJAMIN (1913-   )
  Lachrymae, Op. 48. Reflections on a song
      of Dowland
  BH
BROWN, CH
  Caprice
  Sal
BROWN, JAMES
  Air and English Jig
  STB
  Burletta
  STB
  Chauve Souris
  STB
  Fling
  STB
  Pedlar
  STB
  Promenade
  STB
  Revellers
  STB
  Rondeau en Musette
  STB
  Sprigged Muslin
  STB

BROWN, JAMES (cont.)
Tea-Time
STB
BRUCH, MAX (1838-1920)
Kol Nidrei, orig for vcl and orch
(Lehmann) CF B1385
Romance, Op. 85, orig for vla and orch
SCH
BUCHTEL, FORREST L.
Ambition Waltz
Kjos S-5100
Happy Days
Kjos S-5103
Jolly Fellows
Kjos S-5104
BULAKOV, P
Barcarolle
MZK
BUNIN, R
Concerto
MZK
Sonata
MZK
BURKHARD, WILLY (1900-1955)
Konzert
Baer 2786a
BURTON, ELDIN
Sonata
CF 04174
BUSH, ALAN (1900-   )
Dance Melody, from 2 Melodies, Op. 47
JWL (Mil No. W1421)
Song Melody, from 2 Melodies, Op. 47
JWL (Mil No. W1420)
BUTTERWORTH, NEIL
French Pieces, 2
Chap
CAIX D'HERVELOIS, LOUIS DE (c.1670-c.1760)
Chambor, La. Allemande
(Marchet) Int
CALDARA, [ANTONIO (1670-1736)]
Canto
(Rostal) Ches
CAMPAGNOLI, [BARTOLOMMEO (1751-1827)]
Divertissements
(Ginot) Jobert
CAPITANIO, I
Leggenda in a
SZ
CARSE, ADAM (1878-1958)
Breezy Story
Aug
Calm Reflections
Aug
Heartache
Aug
Thoughtfulness
Aug
CARTER, ELLIOTT (1908-   )
Pastoral
Pr
CAZDEN, NORMAN (1914-   )
Recitations, 3, Op. 24
CFE
CELLIER, ALESANDRE (1883-   )
Sonate en Sol
Senart
CHAILLEY, JACQUES (1910-   )
Sonate
Leduc
CHALLAN, HENRI (1910-   )
Diptyque
Leduc

CHAUSSON, ERNEST (1855-1899)
Pièce
RL
CHOPIN, FRÉDÉRIC (1810-1849)
Nocturne in E flat, Op. 9, No. 2, orig for pno
(Sarasate-Rehfeld) CF B1386
CIRRI
Arioso
Ed M
CLARKE, HENRY L. (1907-   )
Nocturne
CFE
CLARKE, REBECCA (1886-   )
Passacaglia on an old English tune
GS
Sonata
Ches
CLASSIC PIECES
(Klengel) Pet 3853A,b,C   3V
Vol 1: 8 pieces by Bach, Corelli, Handel,
Locatelli, Tartini
Vol 2: 8 pieces by Bach, Galeotti, Han-
del, Leclair, Mozart, Tartini, Vivaldi
Vol 3: 9 pieces by Bach, Gluck, Handel,
Lully, Martini, Mozart, Rameau,
Schubert
CLASSICAL ALBUM
(Herfurth) BMC
CLASSICAL PIECES, BOOK I
(Forbes) Oxf 22.013
Bach: Sinfonia, from Cantata 156
Couperin: Menuet, from Concerts
Royaux and Bourree, from Les
Nations.
Handel: Prelude, from Harpsichord
Suite No. 14
Haydn: Andante, from Trumpet
Concerto
Mendelssohn: Song without words,
Op. 62, No. 1
CLASSICAL PIECES, BOOK II
(Forbes) Oxf 22.035
Beethoven: Sonatina, orig for mandoline
and pno
Brahms: Chorale Prelude, Es ist ein'
Ros'
Greene: Allemanda, from A favourite
Lesson for the Harpsichord
Handel: Bourree, from Organ Concerto
Op. 4, No. 6
Mozart: Adagio, K. 356
CLASSICAL SOLO COMPOSITIONS
(Simon) Ed M
COLLET, HENRI (1885-1951)
Rhapsodie Castillane, orig for vla and orch
Senart
CONCERT ALBUM
(Simon) Ed M
CONCERT AND CONTEST ALBUM
(Whistler & Hummel) Ru
(CONUS, KATIMS & BORISSOVSKY)
Album of 6 Pieces
Int
COOLEY, C
Concertino
H Elkan
Song and Dance
Senart
COOLS, EUGÈNE (1877-1936)
Andante serio
ESC
Berceuse, Op. 86
ESC
Poème, Op. 74, orig for vla and orch
ESC

CORELLI, ARCANGELO (1653-1713)
  Prelude and Allemande
    (Akon) Mil
  Sonata in d, Op. 5, No. 12, "La Folia",
      orig for vln and Bc
    (Alard-Dessauer) SCH
    (David-Hermann) Int
  Sonata in d
    (Katims) Int
  Sonata da camera
    (Forbes-Richardson) Oxf 22.400
COWELL, HENRY (1897-   )
  Hymn and Fuguing Tune No. 7
    Peer
CRESTON, PAUL (1906-   )
  Homage
    GS
  Suite, Op. 13
    Templ
CRUFT, ADRIAN (1921-   )
  Impromtu in B flat, Op. 22
    JWL (Mil No. W1413)
  Romance, Op. 13
    JWL (Mil No. W1414)
CUI, CESAR (1835-1918)
  Orientale, from Kaleidoscope, Op. 50, No. 9
    (Gottlieb-Saenger) CF B1387
  Perpetual Motion, see Kalinnikov: Sad Song
  Scherzetto, see Spendiarov: Lullaby
  Scherzo, see Tchaikovsky: Sweet Daydream
DAHL, INGOLF (1912-   )
  Divertimento
    SPAM
DARE, MARIE
  Lac, Le
    Ches
DARGOMIZHSKY, [ALEXANDER (1813-1869)]
  Elegy
    MZK
DAVID, GYULA (1913-   )
  Concerto
    Kul
DAVID, JOHANN NEPOMUK (1895-   )
  Melancholia, Op. 53, orig for vla and orch
    BRH
DAVID
  Concertino
    Billaudot
DAVID OF THE WHITE ROCK
    (Browne) JWL (Mil No. W1407)
DAVIDOV, [KARL (1838-1889)]
  Romance; with Waltz by Titov
    MZK
DEBUSSY, CLAUDE (1862-1918)
  Beau Soir, orig for voice and pno
    (Katims) Int
  Clair de Lune, orig for pno
    (Cazden) Jack Spratt
  Il pleure dans mon coeur, orig for voice
      and pno
    (Hartmann) Ed M
  Romance, orig for voice and pno
    (Katims) Int
DECADT, J.
  Nocturne
    Metr
DE JONG, MARINUS (1891-   )
  Concerto, Op. 111
    CBDM
DELDEN, LEX VAN (1919-   )
  Suite, Op. 4
    DN (Pet No. D224)
DELIUS, FREDERICK (1862-1934)
  Serenade, from Hassan
    (Tertis) BH

Sonata No. 2, orig for vln and pno
  (Tertis) BH
Sonata No. 3, orig for vln and pno
  (Tertis) BH
DI BIASE, EDOARDO
  Reverie
    CF B2978
D'INDY, see Indy, d'
DINICU
  Hora Staccato
    (Heifetz-Primrose) CF B2671
DITTERSDORF, KARL DITTERS VON
    (1739-1799)
  Andantino
    (Primrose) Int
  Concerto in F
    (Lebermann) SCH
    cadenzas published separately, see under
      vla unacc: Hanesyan
  Sonata in E flat
    (Mlynarczyk-Lürmann) Hof
  Sonata in E flat
    (Vieland) Int
DODGSON, STEPHEN
  Four Fancies
    Chap-L
(DOKTOR, PAUL)
  Solos for the Viola Player
    GS for contents see title
DRIESSLER, JOHANNES (1921-   )
  Stücke, 5, Op. 24/3b
    Baer 2698
DRIGO, RICHARD (1846-1930)
  Serenade
    (Schloming-Ambrosio) CF B1389
DRUSCHETZKY, GEORG
  Concerto in D
    (Schwamberger) SIM
DUBOIS, P. M.
  Suite de danses, orig for vla and orch
    Leduc
DUKE, JOHN (1899-   )
  Melody in E flat
    EV
DUNHILL, THOMAS F. (1877-1946)
  Alla Sarabande
    JWL (Mil No. W1410)
  In Courtly Company
    JWL (Mil No. W1411)
  Meditation, on a study by Schumann
    JWL (Mil No. W1405)
  Triptych, orig for vla and orch
    Oxf
  Willow Brook
    JWL (Mil No. W1404)
DUVERNOY, VICTOR-ALPHONSE (1842-1907)
  Lied
    Haml
DVARIONAS, B.
  Theme and Variations
    MZK
DVORAK, ANTONIN (1841-1904)
  Bagatelle, Op. 47, No. 3, orig for 2 vln,
      vcl, harmonium
    (Forbes) Hin (Pet No. H626b)
  Concerto, Op. 104, orig for vcl and orch
    (Vieland) Int
  Humoreske, Op. 101, No. 7
    (Saenger-Himmel-Schloming) CF B1390
DYER, JOHN
  In Cheerful Mood, from 3 Pieces
    JWL (Mil No. W1412-3)
  In Quiet Mood, from 3 Pieces
    JWL (Mil No. W1412-1)

DYER, JOHN (cont.)
  In the Row, from Riding in Hyde Park
    ABRS (Mil No. A320)
  In Whimsical Mood, from 3 Pieces
    JWL (Mil No. W1412-2)
  Mantilla
    Aug
  Meditation
    Aug
  Old Redcoat
    ABRS (Mil No. A321)
  On the Serpentine
    ABRS (Mil No. A322)
  Tempo di Gavotta
    ABRS (Mil No. A323)
  Woodland Serenade
    Aug
DYSON, GEORGE (1883-   )
  Prelude, Fantasy and Chaconne, orig for
    vcl and orch
    Nov
ECCLES, HENRY (c.1652-c.1742)
  Sonata in g
    (Katims) Int
  Sonata in g
    (Klengel) Pet 4326
EDELSON
  Night Song
    Ed M
EDER, HELMUT (1916-   )
  Sonatina, Op. 34, No. 2
    DOB
EDMUNDS, CHRISTOPHER (1899-   )
  Sonata in D
    Nov
EDMUNDS
  Pieces, 4
    Leng (Mil No. L2001)
  Windmill
    Leng (Mil No. L2008)
ELGAR, EDWARD (1857-1934)
  Canto Popolare, orig for orch
    Nov
  Concerto, orig for vcl and orch
    (Tertis) Nov
  Pomp and Circumstance. Theme, orig for
    orch
    (Akers) CF
  Very Easy Pieces, 6, Op. 22
    Bosw
ENESCO, GEORGES (1881-1955)
  Concertpiece
    Int
ETLER, A.
  Sonata, see vla and harpsichord
FARKAS, FERENC (1905-   )
  Arioso
    Kul
FAURÉ, GABRIEL (1845-1924)
  Après un rêve, orig for voice and pno
    (Katims) Int
  Elegy, Op. 24, orig for vcl and pno
    (Katims) Int
  Lamento[50]
    (Katims) Int
  Sicilienne. Op. 78, orig for vcl and pno
    (Katims) Int
FERGUSON, HOWARD (1908-   )
  Short Pieces, 4
    BH

FIBICH, ZDENKO (1850-1900)
  Poem, orig for pno
    (Ambrosio-Isaac-Lewis) CF B2375
FINKE, FIDELIO FRITZ (1891-   )
  Sonata
    BRH
FIRST YEAR CLASSICAL ALBUM
  (Forbes) Oxf 22.809
    Bach: Choral
    Beethoven: Ecossaise in D
    Brahms: The Blacksmith, Op. 19, No. 4
    Couperin: Le Petit Rien
    Handel: Chaconne in F
    Handel: March, from Flavius
    Haydn: Romance, from Symphony
      No. 85, "La Reine"
    Lully: Air, from Amadis
    Mozart: Waltz in C
    Purcell: Minuet in G
    Schubert: Lullaby, Op. 98, No. 2
    Schumann: In der fremde, from Scenes
      of Childhood, Op. 15, No. 1
    Schumann: Melody, Op. 68, No. 1, from
      Album for the Young
FITELBERG, JERZY (1903-1951)
  Serenade
    SMP
FITZENHAGEN, W., see Select Teaching Pieces
FLACKTON, WILLIAM (1709-1798)
  Sonata in C, Op. 2, No. 4
    (Bergmann) SCH
    (Sabatini) DOB   vcl ad lib
  Sonata in D, Op. 2, No. 5
    (Sabatini) DOB   vcl ad lib
  Sonata in G, Op. 2, No. 6
    (Sabatini) DOB   vcl ad lib
    SCH
  Sonata in c
    (Cullen) Leng (Mil No. L2010)
FLETCHER, see Rolland & Fletcher
FORBES, WATSON (1909-   )
  Scottish Tunes, 2
    (Richardson) Oxf 22.806
(FORBES, WATSON)
  Classical Pieces, Books I and II
    Oxf 22.013; 22.035   for contents see title
  First Year Classical Album
    Oxf 22.809   for contents see title
  Second Year Classical Album
    Oxf 22.038   for contents see title
FORST, RUDOLF (1900-   )
  Homage to Ravel
    Ed M
FORSYTH, CECIL (1870-1941)
  Concerto in g
    SCH
FORTINO, MARIO
  Prelude and Rondo
    Tritone   manuscript reproduction
FOSTER, STEPHEN (1826-1864)
  Jeanie with the Light Brown Hair
    (Heifetz-Primrose) CF B2674
FRANCK, CÉSAR (1822-1890)
  Sonata in A, orig for vln and pno
    (Vieland) Int
FRANCK, MAURICE (1892-   )
  Theme et Variations
    Dur
FRANCOEUR, FRANCOIS (1698-1787)
  Sonata No. 4 in E
    (Alard-Dessauer) Int
FRANKLIN, HOWARD
  Moonlight On the River
    CF B2320

---

[50] Probably Chanson du Pêcheur, originally for voice and piano.

FREED, ISADORE (1900-   )
Rhapsody
CF B2706
FRICKER, PETER RACINE (1920-   )
Concerto, Op. 20
SCH
FRISKIN, JAMES (1886-   )
Elegy
STB
FULEIHAN, ANIS (1900-   )
Recitative and Sicilienne
GS
FULTON, NORMAN (1909-   )
Sonata da Camera
Ches
FUN FOR FIDDLE FINGERS
(Bornoff-Cooper) Gordon V. Thompson
FÜRST, PAUL WALTER (1926-   )
Sonata, Op. 33
DOB
GADZHIBEKOV, [UZEIR (1885-1948)]
Azerbaijan Folk Song; with Georgian Folk
Song by Paliashvili and Lyric Song,
Humorous Song by Taktakishvili
MZK
GALUPPI, [BALDASSARE (1706-1785)]
Aria amorosa
(Tertis) Aug
GARDNER, SAMUEL (1891-   )
From the Canebrake, Op. 5, No. 1
GS
GAUBERT, PHILIPPE (1879-1941)
Ballade
ESC
GAULDIN, ROBERT
Sonata Serioso
Tritone   manuscript reproduction
GEISSLER, FRITZ (1921-   )
Sonatina
BRH
GENZMER, HARALD (1909-   )
Sonata in D
RE (Pet No. RE32)
Sonate No. 2
Baer 3223
GERSTER, OTTMAR (1897-   )
Sonate
Hof
GIAMPIERI, ALAMIRO
Fantasia
Ric ER2038
GIDEON, MIRIAM (1906-   )
Sonata
CFE
GIFFORD, ALEXANDER M.
Madrigal
Aug
(GIFFORD)
Irish Airs, 12
SCH
GIPPS, RUTH (1921-   )
Lyric Fantasy
Fox
GLANVILLE-HICKS, PEGGY (1912-   )
Concerto Romantico
CFE
GLAZUNOV, ALEXANDER (1865-1936)
Elegie, Op. 44
Belaieff
Int
Serenade Espagnole
(Ginot) Jobert
GLIÈRE, REINHOLD (1875-1956)
Prelude; Romance; Rondo
MZK

GLINKA, MIKHAIL I. (1804-1857)
Barcarolle
MZK
Children's Polka
MZK
Mazurka
MZK
Sentiment, Mazurka; with Tear by
Mussorgsky
MZK
Sonata in d, see more than 1 instrumental
combination
Waltz, see Lvov: Folk Melody
GLUCK, CHRISTOPH WILLIBALD (1714-1787)
O del mio dolce ardor
(Elkan) H Elkan
see also Select Teaching Pieces
GLUCK, M.
Pieces, 4
MZK
GODARD, BENJAMIN (1849-1895)
Berceuse, from Jocelyn
(Isaac-Lewis) CF B2428
GOEB, ROGER (1914-   )
Concertant No. 3 in C
CFE
GOEDICKE, ALEXANDER (1877-1957)
Prelude; with Andantino by Khachaturian
and Etude by Kabalevsky
MZK
GOLESTAN, STAN (1872-1956)
Arioso et Allegro de Concert
Sal
GOLTERMANN, GEORG (1824-1898)
Andante, from Concerto, Op. 14, for vcl
(Roth-Isaac-Lewis) CF B2362
Grand Duo, Op. 15
(Such) Aug 7680b
see also Select Teaching Pieces
GOSSEC, FRANÇOIS-JOSEPH (1734-1829)
Gavotte
(Isaac-Lewis) CF B2377
GOW, DAVID (1924-   )
Nocturne and Capriccio
Aug
GRANADOS, ENRIQUE (1867-1916)
Orientale. Spanish Dance No. 2
(Katims) Int
GRAUN, JOHANN GOTTLIEB (1703-1771)
Sonata No. 1 in B flat
(Wolff) BRH   vcl ad lib
Sonata No. 2 in F
(Wolff) BRH   vcl ad lib
GRAZIOLI, GIOVANNI BATTISTA
(c.1750-c.1820)
Sonata in F
(Marchet) Aug 5569
GREEN, RAY (1909-   )
Concertante
AME
GRENZ, ARTUR (1909-   )
Fantasy, Op. 12
Sik 191
GRIEG, EDVARD (1843-1907)
Sonata in a, Op. 36, orig for vcl and pno
(Platz) Pet 2157A
Int
To the Spring, orig for pno
(Forbes) Oxf
GUERRINI, GUIDO (1890-   )
Arcadica, orig for ob and pno
Curci
GURLITT, C., see Select Teaching Pieces

HAERTEL
  Evening Serenade
    (Tobani) CF B1394
HAMANN, ERICH (1898-   )
  Sonata, Op. 33
    DOB
HAMBLEN, B.
  Reverie
    BH
HAMILTON, IAIN (1922-   )
  Sonata, Op. 9
    SCH
HAMMER, XAVER
  Sonata in D
    Ed M
  see also Old Masters of the Viola
HANDEL, GEORG FRIEDRICH (1685-1759)
  Concerto in b
    (Casadesus) ESC
    cadenzas published separately, see under
      vla unacc: Hanesyan
  Concerto
    (Barbirolli) Oxf 22.012
  Preludium
    (Sontag) Shapiro, Bernstein
  Sonata in C, orig for gamba and Bc
    (Jensen) Int
    SCH
    see also vla and harpsichord
  Sonata in g, orig for gamba and Bc
    (Dart) SCH
    (Katims) Int
  Sonata No. 3, orig for vln and Bc
    (Shore) JWL
  Sonata No. 4, orig for vln and Bc
    (D'Ambrosio) Ric ER2106
    (Shore) JWL (Mil No. W1400)
  Sonata No. 6, orig for vln and Bc
    (Shore) JWL (Mil No. W1401)
    MZK
  Sonata in A
    (David-Hermann) Int
  Sonata in A
    (Forbes-Richardson) Oxf 22.007
  see also Select Teaching Pieces
HANDOSHKIN, IVAN (1747-1804)
  Concerto
    Int
HANESYAN, [HARUTYUN]
  Andantino
    ESC
  Prelude and Capriccio
    ESC
  Romance
    ESC
HARRIS, ROY (1898-   )
  Soliloquy and Dance
    GS
HARRIS, WILLIAM H. (1883-   )
  Suite
    Oxf 22.407
HARRISON, JULIUS (1885-   )
  Sonata in c
    Leng (Mil No. L2005)
HARSANYI, TIBOR (1898-1954)
  Sonata
    Heugel
(HARVEY)
  Viola Players Repertory
    Pr
HASSE
  Bouree and Minuet; with Bouree by Bach
    and Sonatina, Minuet by Beethoven
    MZK

HAUBIEL, CHARLES (1892-   )
  Lullaby
    CP
HAUSER, MISKA (1822-1887)
  Berceuse
    (Ambrosio-Isaac-Lewis) CF B2376
HAYDN, JOSEPH (1732-1809)
  Adagio, from String Quartet, Op. 20
    (Forbes) Oxf 20.106
  Concerto in D, orig for vcl and orch
    (Gevaert) BRH
    (Spitzner) Int
  Concerto, orig for ob and orch
    MZK
  Divertimento
    (Piatigorsky-Elkan) EV
  see also Select Teaching Pieces
HENNESSY, SWAN (1866-1929)
  Sonata Celtique, Op. 62
    ESC
(HERFURTH, C. PAUL)
  Classical Album
    BMC
(HERFURTH-DEVERTITCH)
  Viola and Piano
    Willis
HINDEMITH, PAUL (1895-1963)
  Kammermusik No. 5. Concerto,
    Op. 36, No. 4
    SCH
  Konzertmusik, orig for vla and orch
    SCH
  Meditation, from Nobilissima Visione
    SCH
  Music of Mourning, orig for str orch
    SCH
  Schwanendreher, Der. Concerto on old
    folksongs
    SCH
  Sonata, 1939
    SCH
  Sonata, Op. 11, No. 4
    SCH
HIVELY, WELLS
  Psalmody
    CFE
HODDINOTT, ALUN (1929-   )
  Concertino
    Oxf 22.409
HOEFFER, PAUL (1895-1949)
  Viola Music
    MT (Pet No. MV1025)
HOFFMEISTER, FRANZ ANTON (1754-1812)
  Concerto in D
    (Doktor) Int
    GR (Pet No. GR9)   with cadenzas
  Concerto
    (Vieux) ESC
HOLLAND, [THEODORE (1878-1947)]
  Suite in D
    BH
HOLLAND
  Ellingham Marshes
    Hin (Pet No. H340)
HOLST, IMOGEN (1907-   )
  Easy Pieces, 4
    Aug
HOLT, PATRICIA BLOMFIELD
  Suite No. 2
    CL
HOME ON THE RANGE
    (Buchtel) Kjos S-5106
HONEGGER, ARTHUR (1892-1955)
  Sonata
    ESC

HONNORÉ, LEON
  Morceau de Concert
    Gilles
HOVHANESS, ALAN (1911-   )
  Talin. Concerto, Op. 93
    AMP
HOWARD
  Still Waters
    Ed M
HÜE, GEORGES (1858-1948)
  Theme Varié, orig for vla and orch
    Heugel
HUMMEL, HERMAN A., see Whistler & Hummel
HUMMEL, JOHANN NEPOMUK (1778-1837)
  Sonata in E flat, Op. 5, No. 3
    (Doktor) DOB
  Sonata
    (Rood) MM
HURÉ, JEAN (1877-1930)
  Petite Chanson
    Mathot
HUSA, KAREL (1921-   )
  Poem, orig for vla and orch
    SCH
IBERT, JACQUES (1890-1962)
  Aria
    Leduc
d'INDY, VINCENT (1851-1931)
  Lied, Op. 19
    Int
  Sonate en Ré[51]
    RL
INGHELBRECHT, DÉSIRÉ ÉMILE (1880-   )
  Impromptu
    Leduc
  Nocturne
    Mathot
  Prélude et Saltarelle
    Mathot
IPPOLITOV-IVANOV, MIKHAIL (1859-1935)
  Piece; with Spinning Wheel by Yanshinov
    MZK
IRELAND, JOHN (1879-1962)
  Sonata
    (Tertis) Aug
IRISH AIRS, 12
    (Gifford) SCH
(ISAAC, MERLE J.)
  Melody Book for Strings
    CF 03828A,C for contents see title
      under vln, pno
IVANOV-RADKÉVICH, NIKOLAY (1904-   )
  Sonata-Poem
    MZK
JACOB, GORDON (1895-   )
  Air and Dance
    Oxf 22.408
  Pieces, 3
    Curwen
  Sonatina
    Nov
JACOBI, FREDERICK (1891-1952)
  Fantasy
    CF B2622
JACOBI, WOLFGANG (1894-   )
  Sonata
    Sik 387
JACOBSON, MAURICE (1896-   )
  Berceuse
    Oxf 22.023
  Humoreske
    Leng (Mil No. L2002)

JACOBY, HANOCH (1909-   )
  King David's Lyre
    IMP
JÄRNEFELT, ARMAS (1869-   )
  Berceuse
    (Deery) CF B2351
JOACHIM, JOSEPH (1831-1907)
  Hebrew Melodies, Op. 9
    Aug 7630
JONGEN, JOSEPH (1873-1953)
  Allegro appassionato
    Leduc
  Suite, orig for vla and orch
    HL
JONGEN, LÉON (1885-   )
  Pastorale and Gigue
    Brogneaux
JOUBERT, JOHN (1927-   )
  Sonata, Op. 6
    Nov
JULLIEN, R.
  Lied, Op. 36
    ESC
JUON, PAUL (1872-1940)
  Sonata in D, Op. 15
    (Katims) Int
    LN (Pet No. R31)
KABALEVSKY, DMITRI (1904-   )
  Etude, see Goedicke: Prelude
  Improvisation, Op. 21, No. 1
    (Kievman) Leeds
KABALIN, FEDOR
  Poem and Rhymes
    Tritone manuscript reproduction
KALAS, JULIUS (1902-   )
  Concerto
    BH
KALINNIKOV, VASSILI (1866-1901)
  Chanson Triste
    Ed M
    MZK "Sad Song"; with Perpetual Motion
      by Cui
KALLIWODA, JOHANN WENZEL (1801-1866)
  Nocturnes, 6, Op. 186
    Pet 2104
  Nocturnes, 3, Op. 186
    Int
KATIMS, MILTON, see Conus, Katims &
    Borissovsky
KELLER, HOMER
  Sonata
    CFE
KELLY, ROBERT (1916-   )
  Sonata
    CFE
KHACHATURIAN, ARAM (1903-   )
  Andantino, see Goedicke: Prelude
KHANDOSHKIN, IVAN (1747-1804)
  Concerto
    MZK
  Variations on a Russian Song
    MZK
KITTLER, RICHARD (1924-   )
  Sonatina
    DOB
KJERULF, H., see Select Teaching Pieces
(KLENGEL, PAUL)
  Album of 24 Classical Pieces
    Int 3V
  Classic Pieces
    Pet 3853A,b,C 3V for contents see title
  Viola Album of Classical Pieces
    Pet 7074

---

[51] This is a transcription. It is probably the cello sonata.

KODALY, ZOLTAN (1882-   )
  Adagio
    Kul
KOECHLIN, CHARLES (1867-1950)
  Sonate
    Senart
KORNAUTH, EGON (1891-1959)
  Pieces, 3, Op. 47
    DOB
  Sonata in c sharp, Op. 3
    DOB
  Sonatina, Op. 46a
    DOB
KRANCHER, W.
  Rhapsody
    Metr
KRENEK, ERNST (1900-   )
  Sonata
    Mil
KREUTZER, RODOLPHE (1766-1831)
  Concerto No. 9, 1st solo, orig for vln
    (Ginot) Jobert
  Concerto No. 13, 1st solo, orig for vln
    (Ginot) Jobert
KREUZ, EMIL (1867-1932)
  Concerto in C, Op. 20
    Aug 5571
  see also Select Teaching Pieces
KRIUKOV, [VLADIMIR (1902-   )]
  Sonata
    MZK
KROL, BERNHARD (1920-   )
  Konzertante Musik, Op. 6, orig for vla and
      woodwind octet
    BRH
  Lassus-Variationen, Op. 33, for vla and
      harpsichord or pno
    SIM
KUBIZEK, AUGUSTIN (1918-   )
  Sonatina, Op. 5a
    DOB
KURTAG, GYÖRGY
  Concerto
    Kul
LABROCA, MARIO (1896-   )
  Suite
    SZ
LALO, EDOUARD (1823-1892)
  Concerto in d, orig for vcl and orch
    (Casadesus) Int
  Sonata, orig for vcl and pno
    (Casadesus) Heugel
LARSSON, LARS-ERIK (1908-   )
  Concertino, Op. 45, No. 9
    Gehrmans
LAUBACH, see Moffat & Laubach
LECLAIR, JEAN MARIE (1697-1764)
  Sonata, "Le Tombeau", orig for vln and Bc
    (David-Hermann) Int
LEGLEY, VICTOR (1915-   )
  Elegiac Lied, Op. 7
    CBDM
  Sonata, Op. 13
    CBDM
  Spring Poem No. 2, Op. 51
    CBDM
LEIGHTON, KENNETH (1929-   )
  Fantasia on the name BACH
    Nov
LIADOV, ANATOL K. (1855-1914)
  Prelude, Op. 11, No. 1
    MZK
LISZT, FRANZ (1811-1886)
  Liebesträum, Notturno No. 3, orig for pno
    (Tertis) Aug

LOCATELLI, PIETRO (1695-1764)
  Sonata in g, Op. 6, No. 12
    (Doktor) Int
  Sonata in g
    (David-Hermann) Int
LOEILLET, JEAN-BAPTISTE (1680-1730)
  Sonata in B flat
    Int
  Sonata in f sharp
    Int
LOHSE, FRED (1908-   )
  Sonata
    Metr
LOLIVREL, L.
  Sérénade de Printemps
    ESC
LONDONDERRY AIR
    (Ambrosio-Isaac-Lewis) CF B2374
    (Spalding) VL
LOPEZ BUCHARDO, CARLOS (1881-1948)
  Piezas, 2
    (Bandini) Ric BA6216
LOVELL, JOAN
  Easy Tunes, 44
    Oxf 22.810
LUNDÉN, LENNART (1914-   )
  Suite
    Nordiska
LUTYENS, ELIZABETH (1906-   )
  Concerto, Op. 15
    Leng (Mil No. L2000)
LVOV, [ALEXEY F. (1798-1870)]
  Folk Melody, Caprice; with Waltz by Glinka
    MZK
MAASZ, GERHARD (1906-   )
  Musik
    Baer 2236
MACDOWELL, EDWARD (1861-1908)
  To a Wild Rose, orig for pno
    (Isaac) CF B3321
    Bel
MAES, JEF (1905-   )
  Concerto
    CBDM
MAGANINI, QUINTO (1897-   )
  Ancient Greek Melody
    Ed M
  Night Piece
    Ed M
  Song of a Chinese Fisherman
    Ed M
MALIGE, FRED (1895-   )
  Concerto
    BRH
MARAIS, MARIN (1656-1728)
  Fantaisie
    (Boulay) Leduc
  Old French Dances, 5
    (Aldis-Rowe) Ches
  Suite in D
    (Dalton) Pet 6461
MARCELLO, BENEDETTO (1686-1739)
  Scherzando, see Tartini: Sarabande
  Sonatas, 2, in F and g
    (Katims) Int
  Sonatas, 2, in G and C
    (Vieland) Int
  Sonata in e
    (Marchet) Int
  Sonata in G
    (Gibson) SCH
  Sonata in g, Op. 11, No. 4
    (Piatti-d'Ambrosio) Ric 125328

MARTEAU, HENRI (1874-1934)
  Chaconne, Op. 8
    SIM
MARTINI, GIAMBATTISTA (1706-1784)
  Celebrated Gavotte
    Kjos S-5107
MARTINU, BOHUSLAV (1890-1959)
  Sonata No. 1
    (Fuchs) AMP
MARTUCCI, GIUSEPPE (1856-1909)
  Canto d'amore, Op. 38, No. 3
    (Quaranta-d'Ambrosio) Ric 125327
MASCAGNI, PIETRO (1863-1945)
  Siciliana, from Cavalleria Rusticana
    CF B2355
MASSENET, JULES (1842-1912)
  Elégie, from Les Erynnies, Op. 10
    (Deery) CF B2354
MASSIS, A.
  Poème
    Billaudot
MATZ, ARNOLD (1904-   )
  Mixolydian Sonatina
    Pet 4608
  Theme and Variations
    (Baer) BRH
MAZELIER, J.
  Nocturne et rondeau
    Billaudot
MEDTNER, NIKOLAI (1880-1951)
  Fairy Tale, Op. 51, No. 3, orig for pno
    ZM (Pet No. ZM247)
MELLERS, WILFRID (1914-   )
  Sonata
    Leng (Mil No. L2004)
MELODY BOOK FOR STRINGS
    (Isaac) CF 03828A,C   for contents see
    title under vln, pno
MÉNASCE, JACQUES DE (1905-   )
  Sonate en un mouvement
    Dur
MENDELSSOHN, FELIX (1809-1847)
  Song without words, Op. 109, orig for vcl
    and pno
    (Katims) Int
  see also Select Teaching Pieces
MEULEMANS, ARTHUR (1884-   )
  Concerto
    CBDM
  Sonata
    CBDM
MEYERBEER, G., see Select Teaching Pieces
MIGOT, GEORGES (1891-   )
  Estampie, No. 4 of Le Premier Livre de
    Divertissements Francais
    Leduc
MIHALOVICI, MARCEL (1898-   )
  Sonata, Op. 47
    Heugel
MIHALY, ADAM
  Rhapsody
    Kul
MILFORD, ROBIN (1903-1959)
  Air
    Oxf 22.027
MILHAUD, DARIUS (1892-   )
  Bruxelloise, La
    Heugel
  Californienne, La
    Heugel
  Concerto
    UE 3718
  Concerto No. 2
    Heugel

Parisienne, La
  Heugel
Sonata No. 1
  Heugel
Sonata No. 2
  Heugel
Wisconsonian
  Heugel
(MOFFAT)
  Old Masters for Young Players
    (Palaschko) SCH   for contents see title
(MOFFAT & LAUBACH)
  Album, Classical
    Aug 5566
MOHLER, PHILIPP (1908-   )
  Konzertante Sonata, Op. 31
    SCH
MONTEUX, [PIERRE (1875-1964)]
  Arabesque
    Gilles
  Mélodie
    Gilles
MOÓR, EMANUEL (1863-1931)
  Prelude, Op. 123
    (Katims) Int
MOORE, JOHN
  Scottish Song, "Turn ye to me"
    Oxf 20.110
MOULE-EVANS, DAVID (1905-   )
  Moto perpetuo
    JWL (Mil No. W1402)
MOURANT, WALTER (1910-   )
  Fantasy
    CFE
MOZART, WOLFGANG AMADEUS (1756-1791)
  Adagio and Rondo
    (Forbes-Richardson) Oxf 22.037
  Concerto in A, K.622, orig for clar and orch
    Int
  Concerto No. 3, orig for horn and orch
    MZK
  Divertimento in C
    (Piatigorsky-Elkan) EV
  Divertimento in F
    (Courte) Uni Music Press
  Magic Flute, variations, see Beethoven:
    Mozart Variations
  Minuet in C
    (Forbes) SCH
  Sonata in e, K.304, orig for vln and pno
    (Ritter) Int
    Pet 7089
  Sonata in E flat
    (Courte) Uni Music Press
  Sonatina in C
    (Piatigorsky-Elkan) EV
MÜLLER, J. FREDERICK
  At the Ballet
    Kjos S5119
  On the Beach
    Kjos S5122
  Sleigh Ride Party
    Kjos S5120
  Summertime
    Kjos S5121
MÜLLER-ZÜRICH, PAUL (1898-   )
  Concerto, Op. 24
    SCH
MURRAY, ELEANOR & TATE, PHYLLIS
  New Viola Books
    Oxf   3V
  Tunes Old and New
    Oxf 22.811
      Cradle Song
      Drink to me only

MURRAY, ELEANOR & TATE, PHYLLIS (cont.)
Tunes Old and New (cont.)
Oxf 22.811 (cont.)
God rest you merry, gentleman
March
Moto perpetuo
O come, O come, Emmanuel
Past 3 o'clock
Scottish Air
MURRILL, [HERBERT (1909-1952)]
French Nursery Songs, 4
Ches
MUSSORGSKY, MODEST P. (1839-1881)
Tear, see Glinka: Sentiment
MYLIUS, HERMANN
Suite in c, Op. 30
BRH
NARDINI, PIETRO (1722-1793)
Sonata No. 1 in B flat
(Alard-Dessauer) Int
Sonata in D
(Katims) Int
Sonata in f
(Zellner) Int
NIGGELING, WILLY (1900-   )
Sonata
MT (Pet No. MV1057)
NOVACEK, OTTOKAR (1866-1900)
Mouvement perpétuel, orig for vln
(Ginot) Jobert
OLD MCDONALD IN THE DELL
(Buchtel) Kjos S-5101
OLD MASTERS FOR YOUNG PLAYERS
(Moffat-Palaschko) SCH
15 selected works by Purcell, Gluck,
Rameau, Handel, Lully, Bach, Beethoven,
Schumann and others
OLD MASTERS OF THE VIOLA
Pet 3816
Hammer: 3 Sonatas in D,G,G
Hammer: Sonata in D, for vla d'amore
and pno
Stamitz: Concerto in D
Unknown: Allegro in B flat
ONSLOW, GEORGES (1784-1853)
Sonata in A, Op. 16, No. 3
(Höckner) SIM
OVERTON, HALL (1920-   )
Sonata
CFE
PAGANINI, NICCOLÒ (1782-1840)
Campanella, La, from Concerto No. 2, orig
for vln and orch
(Primrose) SCH
Caprices, 2, Op. 1, Nos. 13 and 20, orig
for vln unacc
(Forbes-Richardson) Hin (Pet No. H1984A)
Caprice No. 9, orig for vln unacc
(Shimmin) Oxf 22.011
Caprice No. 24, orig for vln unacc
(Primrose) CF B2681
Moto Perpetuo, orig for vln and pno
(Forbes) Oxf 22.036
Int
Sonata No. 12, orig for vln and guitar
(Forbes-Richardson) Aug
PALIASHVILI
Georgian Folk Song, see Gadzhibekov:
Azerbaijan Folk Song
PALMER, ROBERT (1915-   )
Sonata
Peer
PANNAIN, [GUIDO (1891-   )]
Concerto
Curci

PARADIES, PIETRO DOMENICO (1707-1791)
Toccata
(Forbes) Oxf 20.107
Siciliana; with Bee by Schubert
MZK
PARRIS, ROBERT (1924-   )
Sonata
CFE
PARTOS, ÖDÖN (1907-   )
Oriental Ballad
IMP
Yiskor, orig for vla and orch
Leeds
PASCAL, ANDRE
Chant sans paroles
Dur
PASFIELD, WILLIAM REGINALD (1909-   )
Barcarolle, from 3 Simple Pieces
JWL (Mil No. W1425)
Chansonette, from 3 Simple Pieces
JWL (Mil No. W1423)
In Playful Mood, from 3 Simple Pieces
JWL (Mil No. W1424)
PAUL, ALAN (1905-   )
Sonata
Bosw
PEARSON
Carols, 2
Hin (Pet No. H319A)
PEPUSCH, JOHN CHRISTOPHER (1667-1752)
Largo and Allegro in d
Broe (Pet No. B9)
PERGOLESI, GIOVANNI BATTISTA (1710-1736)
Se tu m'ami
(Elkan) H Elkan
PERSICHETTI, VINCENT (1915-   )
Infanta Marina
EV
PETERKIN, NORMAN
Twilight Tune
Oxf 20.105
PIECES BY RUSSIAN AND SOVIET COM-
POSERS
(Strakhov) MZK   2V
PISK, PAUL (1893-   )
Movements, 3, Op. 36
CFE
PISTON, WALTER (1894-   )
Concerto
AMP
Interlude
BH
PLEYEL, IGNAZ (1757-1831)
Concerto in D, Op. 31
GR (Pet No. GR10)   with cadenzas
PODEST, LUDVIK (1921-   )
Suite
Artia
PONCE, MANUEL MARÍA (1882-1948)
Estrellita
(Simon-Isaac-Lewis) CF B2378
PORPORA, NICOLA ANTONIO (1686-1768)
Aria
(Tertis) Ches
Sonata No. 9 in E, orig for vln and clavier
(Alard-Dessauer) Int
Sonata in G, orig for vln and clavier
(David-Hermann) Int
PORTER, QUINCY (1897-   )
Concerto
AMP
Poem
Val
Speed Etude
Val

PROKOFIEV, SERGEY (1891-1953)
Kije's Wedding, from Lt. Kijé Suite
Ed M
March, see Rakov: Tale
Romance, from Lt. Kijé Suite
Ed M
Theme and Processional, from Peter and
the Wolf
(Grunes) Omega
PUGNANI, GAETANO (1731-1798)
Prelude et Allegro
(Jurgensen) Jobert
PURCELL, HENRY (c.1659-1695)
Air, Dance, Ground, from Dido & Aeneas
(Lutyens) Mil-L 147
Airs and Dances
(Vieland) Int
Aria
(Katims) Int
Bourrée and Hornpipe
(Forbes) Ches
Scotch Tune; with Dance
(Forbes) Ches
Sonata in g
(Forbes-Richardson) Oxf 22.802
QUINET, FERNAND (1898-   )
Sonate
Senart
RACHMANINOFF, SERGEY (1873-1943)
Melodia, Op. 3, No. 3, orig for pno
(D'Ambrosio) Ric 119233
Prelude, Op. 23, No. 4, orig for pno
MZK
Serenata, Op. 3, No. 5, orig for pno
(D'Ambrosio) Ric 119234
RAFF, JOACHIM (1822-1882)
Cavatina, orig for vln and pno
(Ritter-Schloming) CF B1392
RAINIER, PRIAULX (1903-   )
Sonata
SCH
RAKOV
Tale; with Gavotte by Asafiev and March
by Prokofiev
MZK
RAMEAU, JEAN-PHILIPPE (1683-1764)
Suite of 3 Dances
(Forbes-Richardson) Oxf 22.014
RAPHAEL, GÜNTHER (1903-   )
Sonata in E flat, Op. 13
BRH
Sonata No. 2, Op. 80
BRH
RAVEL, MAURICE (1875-1937)
Pavane pour une Infante défunte, orig for pno
(Kochanski) ESC
(Maganini) Ed M
Pièce en forme de Habanera, orig for voice
Leduc
RAWSTHORNE, ALAN (1905-   )
Sonata
Oxf 22.406
READ, GARDNER (1913-   )
Fantasy, Op. 38, orig for vla and orch
AMP
Poem, Op. 31a
CF B2675
REBIKOW, [VLADIMIR (1866-1920)]
Berceuse and Dance
(Forbes) Ches
REED, WILLIAM HENRY (1876-1942)
Rhapsody in D, orig for vla and orch
Aug

REGER, MAX (1873-1916)
Romance in G
(Sitt) BRH
Sonata in B flat, Op. 107, orig for clar
and pno
BB
REINHOLD, OTTO (1899-   )
Musik
Baer 1988
REITER, ALBERT (1905-   )
Sonata
DOB
RENDALL, HONOR
Island Lullaby, from 2 Pieces
JWL (Mil No. W1417)
Island Reel, from 2 Pieces
JWL (Mil No. W1418)
REUTTER, HERMANN (1900-   )
Musik
SCH
RIBOLLET
Suite, Op. 23
Leduc
RICHARDSON, ALAN (1904-   )
Autumn Sketches
Oxf 22.101
Sonata, Op. 21
Aug
RICHTER
Aria and Toccata
Mil
RIMSKY-KORSAKOV, NIKOLAY (1844-1908)
Dance of the Buffoons, from Snow Maiden
MZK
Song of India, from Sadko
(Deery) CF B2350
RIVIER, JEAN (1896-   )
Concertino, orig for vla and orch
Senart
RODE, PIERRE (1774-1830)
Concerto No. 7, 1st solo, orig for vln
(Ginot) Jobert
Concerto No. 7, 2nd solo, orig for vln
(Ginot) Jobert
Concerto No. 7, Andante et Final, orig for vln
(Ginot) Jobert
Concerto No. 8, 1st solo, orig for vln
(Ginot) Jobert
ROGER, K.G.
Irish Sonata, Op. 37
Francis Day & Hunter
ROGERS, WILLIAM KEITH (1921-   )
Sonatina
CL
ROLLAND & FLETCHER
First Perpetual Motion
Mil
ROPARTZ, J. GUY (1864-1955)
Adagio
RL
ROSSEAU, NORBERT (1907-   )
Sonatina, Op. 41
CBDM
RÖTSCHER, K.
Musik, Op. 27
BB
ROUGNON, PAUL
Concerto romantique
Haml
Fantaisie-Caprice
Leduc
ROWLEY, ALEC (1892-1958)
Aubade, from 4 Pieces
JWL (Mil No. W1403-1)

ROWLEY, ALEC (cont.)
 Farandole, from 4 Pieces
  JWL (Mil No. W1403-4)
 Reverie, from 4 Pieces
  JWL (Mil No. W1403-3)
 Scherzo, from 4 Pieces
  JWL (Mil No. W1403-2)
RUBBRA, EDMUND (1901-   )
 Concerto in A
  Leng (Mil No. L2009)
RUBINSTEIN, ANTON (1829-1894)
 Morceaux, 3
  Haml
 Romance
  (Cheyette) Fox
 Sonata in f, Op. 49
  BRH
RUSSELL, HENRY (1812-1900)
 Life on the Ocean Wave
  Kjos S-5105
RYELANDT, JOSEPH (1870-   )
 Sonata, Op. 73
  CBDM
SAINT-SAËNS, CAMILLE (1835-1921)
 Cygne, Le, from Le Carnaval des Animaux
  (Gottlieb) CF B1393
 Melody
  (Tertis) GS
SARAI, T.
 Humoresque
  Kul
SCHAEUBLE, HANS (1906-   )
 Musik, Op. 23, orig for vla and orch
  BB
SCHEBALIN, see Shebalin
SCHEER, L.
 Lament
  CP
SCHIFF, HELMUT (1918-   )
 Sonata
  DOB
SCHLEMÜLLER, HUGO
 Our Soldiers, Op. 12, No. 5
  CF B2323
 Prayer, Op. 12, No. 6
  CF B2324
 Song, Op. 12, No. 1
  CF B2322
SCHMITT, FLORENT (1870-1958)
 Légende, Op. 66, orig for vla and orch
  Dur
SCHOENDLINGER, ANTON (1919-   )
 Sonata
  BRH
SCHOLLUM, ROBERT (1913-   )
 Chaconne, Op. 54a
  DOB
 Sonata, Op. 42, No. 2
  DOB
 Sonatine, Op. 57, No. 2
  DOB
SCHUBERT, FRANCOIS (1808-1878)
 Bee, orig for vln and pno
  (Ginot) Jobert
 Bee, see Paradisi: Siciliana
SCHUBERT, FRANZ (1797-1828)
 Ave Maria, orig for voice and pno
  (Primrose) SCH
 Litany for All Souls Day, orig for voice
   and pno
  (Primrose) SCH
 Minuets, 3
  (Piatigorsky-Elkan) EV
 Reverie
  (Forbes) Oxf

 Sonata in a, orig for arpeggione and pno
  (Katims) Int
  (Platz) DOB
 Sonatinas, 3, Op. 137, orig for vln and pno
  (Forbes) Aug 7571a
 Sonatina in D, Op. 137, No. 1
  (Ritter) Int
 see also Select Teaching Pieces
SCHUMANN, ROBERT (1810-1856)
 Adagio and Allegro, Op. 70, orig for horn
   and pno
  (Vieland) Int
  Pet 2386
 Märchenbilder, Op. 113
  (Schradieck) GS L415
  BRH
  Pet 2372 "Fairy Tales"
 Meditation, see Dunhill
 Romance in F, Op. 28, No. 2, orig for pno
  (Tertis) Aug
 Träumerei, Op. 15, No. 7, orig for pno
  (Davidoff-Isaac-Lewis) CF B2363
 see also Select Teaching Pieces
SCHWARTZ, MAXIMILIAN (1899-   )
 Theme and Variations
  BRH
SCRIABIN, ALEXANDER (1872-1915)
 Etude, Op. 2, No. 1, orig for pno
  (Krane) GS
 Prelude, Op. 9, orig for pno
  (Borissovsky) Int
SECOND YEAR CLASSICAL ALBUM
 (Forbes) Oxf 22.038
  Bach: Two Minuets, in G and g
  Beethoven: Sonatina in G
  Boyce: Gentle Shepherd, from the
    Serenata "Solomon"
  Brahms: Waltz, Op. 39, No. 15
  Gossec: Gavotte, from Rosine
  Handel: Tempo di gavotta, from
    Op. 1, No. 2
  Haydn: Innocence, from Op. 53, No. 1
  Mozart: Larghetto, from Divertimento
    No. 2, KVA 229
  Schubert: Serenade, "An den mond"
  Schumann: Merry Peasant
  Wolf: Wiegenlied
SEIBER, MÁTYÁS (1905-1960)
 Elegy, orig for vla and orch
  (Banks) SCH
SEITZ, ALBERT
 Fantaisie de concert, Op. 31
  Leduc
SEITZ, FRIEDRICH
 Concerto No. 2, Op. 13, orig for vln
  (Lifschey) AMP
 Concerto No. 3, Op. 12, orig for vln
  (Lifschey) AMP
 Concerto No. 5 in D, Op. 22, first movement,
   orig for vln
  (Klotman) Mil
SELECT TEACHING PIECES
 Aug   all published separately
  First Series: 1st position
   Bach, J.S: Gavotte, from French
     Suite No. 6
   Beethoven: Sonatina and Romanze
   Fitzenhagen, W: Cavatina,
     Op. 39, No. 1
   Gluck: Air, from Orfeo
   Haydn, J: Air, from Seasons
   Kreuz, E: Gavotte, Op. 13b, No. 8
   Kreuz, E: Melody, Op. 25, No. 22
   Kreuz, E: Pensée fugitive, Op. 13d

SELECT TEACHING PIECES (cont.)
  Aug (cont.)
    First Series: 1st position (cont.)
      Kreuz, E: Romance, Op. 13c, No. 9
      Mendelssohn, F: Venetian Gondola
        Song, Op. 19, No. 6
      Schubert, F: Fishermaiden
      Schumann, R: Canon and Reaper's
        Song, Op. 68, Nos. 27 and 18
      Schumann, R: Humming Song and
        Hunting Song, Op. 68, Nos. 3 and 7
      Schumann, R: Melody and Soldiers'
        March, Op. 68, Nos. 1 and 2
      Schumann, R: Romance and Merry
        Peasant, Op. 68, Nos. 19 and 10
      Schumann, R: Siciliano, Op. 68
      Weber, C: Air, from Der Freischütz
    Second Series: 1st to 3rd position
      Gluck, C: Ballet, from Orfeo
      Gurlitt, C: Buds and Blossoms,
        Op. 107, No. 4
      Gurlitt, C: Slow Waltz, Op. 146, No. 1
      Handel, G.F: Largo
      Handel, G.F: Sonata
      Kjerulf, H: Longing
      Mendelssohn, F: Song without words,
        Op. 38, No. 2
      Mendelssohn, F: Song without words,
        Op. 53, No. 4
      Schubert, F: Serenade
      Schumann, R: Revery, Op. 15, No. 7
      Weber, C: Air, from der Freischütz
    Third Series: 1st-7th position
      Bach, J.S: Air, from Orchestral
        Suite in D
      Beethoven: Romance in F, Op. 50
      Goltermann, G: Romance, from
        Sonatina, Op. 114
      Kreuz, E; Liebesbilder, Op. 5, No. 2
      Kreuz, E: Spring fancies, Op. 9, No. 2
      Mendelssohn, F: Song without words,
        Op. 19, No. 1
      Meyerbeer, G: Air, from Les
        Huguenots
      Schubert, F: Romance
      Schumann, R: Evening song,
        Op. 35, No. 12
      Schumann, R: Little study,
        Op. 68, No. 14
      Schumann, R: Stück im Volkston,
        Op. 102, No. 2
      Squire, W.H: Gavotte humoristique,
        Op. 6
      Squire, W.H: Reverie, Op. 10
SENAILLE, JEAN BAPTISTE (1687-1730)
  Allegro spiritoso
    (Katims) Int
  Sonata No. 9, Op. 5
    (Morgan) Aug 7405a
SENDREY, ALBERT (1911-   )
  Sonata
    EV
SERLY, TIBOR (1900-   )
  Concerto
    Leeds
  Rhapsody, on folk songs harmonized by
    Bartok, orig for vla and orch
    SMP
SHAPEY, RALPH (1921-   )
  Duo
    CFE   score only
SHEBALIN, VISSARION Y. (1902-   )
  Sonata
    MZK

SHIELD, WILLIAM (1748-1829)
  Tempo di Minuetto
    (Anderson) Oxf
SHORE, BERNARD (1896-   )
  Scherzo
    Aug
SHULMAN, ALAN (1915-   )
  Homage to Erik Satie
    GS
  Theme and Variations, orig for vla and orch
    Chap
SIEGL, OTTO (1896-   )
  Sonata No. 1, Op. 41
    DOB
  Sonata No. 2 in E flat, Op. 103
    DOB
SIMON
  Lullaby for Johnny
    Ed M
(SIMON)
  Classical Solo Compositions
    Ed M
  Concert Album
    Ed M
SIMONETTI, ACHILLE (1857-1928)
  Allegretto romantico
    Ches
  Ballata
    Ches
SITT, HANS (1850-1922)
  Album Leaves, Op. 39
    Int
    Pet 2549
  Concert Piece in g, Op. 46, orig for vla
    and orch
    Eul (Pet No. Z129)
    Int
SKORZENY, FRITZ (1900-   )
  Sonate
    DOB
SKRYABIN, see Scriabin
SLADEK, PAUL
  Elegy
    VL
SMITH, LELAND
  Sonata
    CFE   score only; for heckelphon or
    vla and pno
SNOWY BREASTED PEARL
  (Browne) JWL (Mil No. W1408)
SOBANSKI, HANS JOACHIM (1906-   )
  Romantic Concerto
    UE 11135
SOLOS FOR STRINGS
  (Whistler) Ru
SOLOS FOR THE VIOLA PLAYER
  (Doktor) GS
    Bach, J.S.: Choral Prelude
    Bach, K.P.E.: Allegretto Grazioso
    Beethoven: March
    Boston Fancy
    D'Hervelois: Tambourin
    Dittersdorf: German Dance
    Handel: Menuetto
    I'm Just A-goin' Over Jordan
    Marais: Tema con Variazoni
    Mehul: Romance
    Mozart: Andante
    Schubert:Adagio
    Shenandoah
    Were You There?
    Wolf: Verborgenheit
SOMERVELL, ARTHUR (1863-1937)
  School of Melody
    (Mackinlay) Aug

SPENDIAROV, [ALEXANDER (1871-1928)]
  Lullaby; with Scherzetto by Cui
    MZK
SPIES, LEO (1899-   )
  Sommerbilder, 5
    BRH
SPRONGL, NORBERT (1892-   )
  Sonata, Op. 115
    DOB
SQUIRE, W.H., see Select Teaching Pieces
STAMITZ, JOHANN (1717-1757)
  Concerto in G
    (Laugg) Pet 5889
  Sonata
    MZK
STAMITZ, KARL (1745-1801)
  Concerto in D, Op. 1
    (Klengel) BRH
    (Meyer) Int
    (Polo) Ric ER1762
    Pet 3816A with cadenzas
    cadenzas published separately, see under
      vla unacc: Hanesyan
  Sonata in B flat
    (Lenzewski) VW (Pet No. V49)
    (Primrose) Int
  Sonata in e, Op. 6a
    (Borissovsky) Int
STANFORD, CHARLES VILLIERS (1852-1924)
  Sonata
    STB
STARER, ROBERT (1924-   )
  Concerto, orig for vla, strings and percussion
    Leeds
(STEHLING)
  Album of Celebrated Pieces, Bk. 1
    Aug 7625a
STEINER, GEORGE
  Rhapsodic Poem
    MZK
STEINER, HUGO
  Concerto in d, Op. 43
    Int
STEPANOV, [LEV (1908-   )]
  Miniatures, 3, from Children's Suite
    MZK
  Sonata
    MZK
STEPANOVA, V.
  Poem
    MZK
STEVENS, HALSEY (1908-   )
  Hungarian Folk Songs, 3
    CFE
  Sonata
    CFE
  Suite, for clar or vla and pno
    Pet 6031
STEVENS, JAMES (1927-   )
  Four Movements and a Coda
    EDW
STILL, ROBERT (1910-   )
  Sonata No. 2
    Ches
(STRAKHOV)
  Pieces by Russian and Soviet Composers
    MZK 2V
STRATTON, [GEORGE (1897-1954)]
  Pastorale Concerto
    Nov
STRAVINSKY, IGOR (1882-   )
  Berceuse, from Firebird
    Ed M
  Dance of the Princesses, from Firebird
    Ed M

STÜRMER, BRUNO (1892-1958)
  Kleine Hausmusik
    SCH
SUBOTNICK, MORTON
  Sonata
    MM
SUCHY, FRANTISEK (1891-   )
  Suite
    Artia
SWAIN, FREDA (1902-   )
  English Reel
    JWL (Mil No. W1415)
  Song at Evening
    JWL (Mil No. W1416)
SZABÓ, FERENC (1902-   )
  Air
    Kul
SZEKELY, E.
  Rhapsody No. 1
    Kul
TAKTAKISHVILI
  Lyric Song, Humorous Song, see
    Gadzhibekov: Azerbaijan Folk Song
TANEYEV, ALEXANDER (1850-1918)
  Album Leaves, Op. 33
    MZK
TANSMAN, ALEXANDER (1897-   )
  Concerto
    ESC
TARTINI, GIUSEPPE (1692-1770)
  Adagio and Fugue
    (Radmall) Ches
  Concerto in D
    (Vieux) ESC
  Sarabande; with Scherzando by Marcello
    and Largo and Allegro by Vivaldi
    MZK
  Sonata in c
    (Forbes-Richardson) Oxf 22.808
  Sonata in D
    (Hermann) Int
  Sonata No. 2 in F
    (Alard-Dessauer) Int
TATE, PHYLLIS, see Murray & Tate
TAUSINGER, J.
  Partita
    Artia
TCHAIKOVSKY, PIOTR ILYITCH (1840-1893)
  Autumn Song, Op. 37, orig for pno
    MZK
  By the Fireside, Op. 31, No. 1
    MZK
  Chanson Triste, Op. 40, No. 2, orig for pno
    (Isaac-Lewis) CF B2364
  Lullaby, from Mazeppa
    MZK
  Melody, Op. 42, No. 3, orig for vln and pno
    MZK
  Nocturne, Op. 19, No. 4, orig for pno
    (Borissovsky) Int
  Nocturne; Snowdrop
    MZK
  None But the Lonely Heart, Op. 6, No. 6,
    orig for voice
    (Hegner-Deery) CF B2352
    Mil
  Passionate Confession
    MZK
  Serenade
    Paxton (Mil No. P570)
  Song Without Words, Op. 2, No. 3, orig
    for pno
    MZK
  Sweet Day-dream; with Scherzo by Cui
    MZK

TCHAIKOVSKY, PIOTR ILYITCH (cont.)
Valse Sentimentale, Op. 51, No. 6, orig
for pno
(Grunes) Omega
MZK
White Nights, Op. 37, No. 5, orig for pno
MZK
TELEMANN, GEORG PHILIPP (1681-1767)
Concerto in G
(Füssl) Baer 3712
(Katims) Int
cadenzas published separately, see under
vla unacc: Hanesyan
Sonata in a, orig for gamba and clavier
(Dolmetsch) SCH
(Schulz-Vieland) Int
Sonata in D
Broe (Pet No. B8)
Sonata in D
Int
Suite in D
(Bergmann-Forbes) SCH
TERTIS, LIONEL (1876-   )
Blackbirds
Aug
Sunset
Ches
Tune
Aug
THOMAS, AMBROISE (1811-1896)
Gavotte, from Mignon
(Isaac-Lewis) CF B2380
TIESSEN, HEINZ (1887-   )
Serious Melodies, 2
RE (Pet No. RE12)
TINKER'S DANCE
(Sontag) Shapiro, Bernstein
TITOV
Waltz, see Davidov: Romance
TOMASI, HENRI (1901-   )
Concerto
Leduc
TORRANDELL, A.
Sonate, Op. 21
Deiss
TRANTOW, HERBERT (1903-   )
Duo
MT (Pet No. MV1023)
TREXLER, GEORG (1903-   )
Sonatina
BRH
TSELTER, K.
Concerto
MZK
TSINTSADZE, [SULKHAN (1925-   )]
Khorumi
MZK
TURINA, JOAQUIN (1882-1949)
Andante, from Sevilla
MZK
VALE
Ao pé da fogueira
(Heifetz-Primrose) CF B2673
VALENSIN, GEORGES
Minuet
(Katims) Int
VARDI, EMANUEL (1915-   )
Suite on American folk songs
GS
VASSILENKO, SERGEY (1872-1956)
Sonata, Op. 96
MZK
VAUGHAN WILLIAMS, RALPH (1872-1958)
Fantasia on Greensleeves
(Forbes) Oxf 20.001

Romance
Oxf
Studies in English Folk Song, 6, orig for
vcl and pno
STB
Suite, orig for vla and orch
Oxf 22.008-010
VERACINI, FRANCESCO MARIA (1690-c.1750)
Largo
(Katims) Int
Sonata in e
Int
VERSTOVSKY, [ALEXEY (1799-1862)]
Variations on 2 Themes
MZK
VIEUX, [MAURICE]
Étude de Concert No. 1 in C
ESC
Étude de Concert No. 2 in b
ESC
Étude de Concert No. 3 in G
ESC
Étude de Concert No. 4 in f
ESC
Étude de Concert No. 5 in c sharp
ESC
Étude de Concert No. 6 in f sharp
ESC
Scherzo
Leduc
VIEUXTEMPS, HENRI (1820-1881)
Concerto No. 2, 1st solo, orig for vln
(Ginot) Jobert
Concerto No. 4, 1st movement, orig for vln
(Ginot) Jobert
Concerto No. 5, 1st solo, orig for vln
(Ginot) Jobert
Elégie, Op. 30
(Scholz) Aug 7648
VILLA-LOBOS, HEITOR (1887-1959)
Aria, from Bachianas Brasileiras No. 5,
orig for voice and 4 vcl
(Primrose) AMP
VINKLER, see Winkler
VIOLA ALBUM OF CLASSICAL PIECES
(Klengel) Pet 7074
VIOLA AND PIANO
(Herfurth-DeVertitch) Willis
VIOLA MINIATURES
CF 04260
Compositions by Aletter, Franklin,
Kovacs, Mascagni, Massenet and
Schlemuller
VIOLA MUSIC FOR CONCERT AND CHURCH
(Boetje) BMC
VIOLA PLAYERS REPERTORY
(Harvey) Pr
VIOLA SOLOS, 34
Bel EL236
VIOTTI, GIOVANNI BATTISTA (1755-1824)
Concerto No. 22, 1st solo, orig for vln
(Ginot) Jobert
Concerto No. 29, 1st solo, orig for vln
(Ginot) Jobert
VITALI, TOMMASO ANTONIO (c.1665- ?   )
Ciaccona, orig for vln and Bc
(Bailly) GS
(Petri) BRH
VIVALDI, ANTONIO (c.1669-1741)
Adagio and Allegro
(Jacob) Nov
Concerto in e
(Primrose) Int

VIVALDI, ANTONIO (cont.)
  Concerto
    (Primrose) Mil
  Intermezzo, from Concerto Grosso in d
    (Franko) GS
  Largo and Allegro, see Tartini:
    Sarabande
  Sonatas, 6, orig for vcl and Bc
    (Primrose) Int; realization of figured
      bass by L. Dallapiccola
  Sonata in A
    (David-Hermann) Int
  Sonata in a
    (Primrose) Int
  Sonata in B flat
    (Primrose) Int
  Sonata in g
    (Katims) Int
VOORMOLEN, ALEXANDER (1895-   )
  Sonata
    DN (Pet No. D87)
VREULS, VICTOR (1876-1944)
  Poeme
    Bosw
WAGNER, RICHARD (1813-1883)
  Dreams, orig for voice and pno
    (Primrose) SCH
  Entrance of the Black Swans
    (Polo) SZ
  Song of the Evening Star, from Tannhäuser
    (Isaac-Lewis) CF B2381
WALKER, ERNEST (1870-1949)
  Romance, Op. 9
    JWL (Mil No. W1422)
  Variations on an original theme
    Nov
WALTHEW, H. W.[52]
  Serenade-Sonata in f
    JWL (Mil No. W1419)
WALTHEW, RICHARD HENRY (1872-1951)
  Regret and Conversation Galante
    BH
  Sonata in D
    STB
WALTON, WILLIAM (1902-   )
  Concerto
    Oxf 22.006
WALZEL, LEOPOLD MATTHIAS (1902-   )
  Sonata Ariosa, Op. 30
    DOB
WARD, ROBERT (1917-   )
  Arioso
    Highgate
  Tarantelle
    Highgate
WARREN, ELINOR REMICK (1905-   )
  Poem
    CF B2741
WEBBER, LLOYD
  Sonatina
    Aug
WEBER, CARL MARIA VON (1786-1826)
  Andante and Rondo ungarese, Op. 35
    (Primrose) Int
    SCH
  Serenata, Op. 3, No. 1
    (Forbes) SCH
  see also Select Teaching Pieces
WEINER, LEO (1885-1960)
  Sonata
    Kul

WESTERMANN, HELMUT (1895-   )
  Konzertante Musik, Op. 34, orig for vla
    and orch
    SIM
WHEN LOVE IS KIND
  (Buchtel) Kjos S-5102
(WHISTLER, HARVEY S.)
  Solos for Strings
    Ru
(WHISTLER, HARVEY S. & HUMMEL,
    HERMAN A.)
  Concert and Contest Album
    Ru
WHITTENBERG, CHARLES
  Set for 2
    CFE   score only
WIDDICOMBE, T,
  First Book of Viola Pieces
    Ches
WIENIAWSKI, HENRI (1835-1880)
  Caprices, 2, orig for vln
    (Forbes) Hin (Pet No. H3368A)
      Alla Saltarella, Op. 10, No. 5
      Alla Tarantella, Op. 18, No. 4
  Concerto No. 2, 1st solo, orig for vln
    (Ginot) Jobert
WIGGLESWORTH, FRANK (1918-   )
  Sound Piece
    CFE
WINKLER, ALEXANDER (1865-1935)
  Meditation Elegiaque, Op. 31, No. 1
    BH
  Sonata, Op. 10
    MZK
  Toupie, La, Op. 31, No. 2
    BH
WOLSTENHOLME, WILLIAM (1865-1931)
  Allegretto
    Nov
  Canzona
    (Tertis) Nov
  Romanza
    Nov
WOOD, H.
  Variations
    UE 12911
WOOD, JOSEPH
  Sonata
    CFE
WOOLLETT, HENRI (1864-1936)
  Sonate No. 5
    Senart
WORK, HENRY C. (1832-1884)
  Grandfather's Clock
    Bel
WUNDERER, ALEXANDER (1877-1955)
  Sonata, Op. 21
    DOB
YANSHINOV
  Spinning Wheel, see Ippolitov-Ivanov:
    Piece
ZAFRED, MARIO (1922-   )
  Concerto
    Ric 129165
ZEISL, ERIC (1905-   )
  Sonata in a
    (Reher) DOB
ZELTER, KARL FRIEDRICH (1758-1832)
  Concerto in E flat
    GR (Pet No. GR11)   with cadenzas
    cadenzas published separately, see
    under vla unacc: Hanesyan

---

[52] Although the publisher gives H.W. Walthew as the composer of this sonata, all other reference sources attribute it to Richard Henry Walthew.

Duos: Viola, Harpsichord or Organ

BACH, WILHELM FRIEDEMANN (1710-1784)
  Sonata in c, for vla and harpsichord
    (Pessl) Oxf
BORRIS, SIEGFRIED (1906-   )
  Canzona, Op. 11, No. 1, for vla and organ
    or cembalo
    Sirius in preparation
ETLER, [ALVIN (1913-   )]
  Sonata, for vla and harpsichord
    AMP blueprint set
HANDEL, GEORG FRIEDRICH (1685-1759)
  Sonata in C, orig for gamba and Bc,
    arr vla and harpsichord
    (Langin) Baer HM112
KROL, BERNHARD (1920-   )
  Lassus-Variationen, Op. 33, for vla and
    harpsichord
    SIM
MARAIS, MARIN (1656-1728)
  Suite in D, for vla and harpsichord
    (Dalton) Pet 6461
PORTER, QUINCY (1897-   )
  Duo for vla and harp or harpsichord
    AMP
SIEGL, OTTO (1896-   )
  Weihnachts-Sonate, Op. 137, for vla and
    organ
    DOB

Duos: Viola, Guitar or Harp or Percussion

BAX, ARNOLD (1883-1953)
  Fantasy-Sonata, for harp and vla
    Chap-L
BERGER, MELVIN
  14th Century Dances, 3, for vla and tambour
    Leeds
BORUP-JØRGENSEN, AXEL (1924-   )
  Music for Percussion and Viola, see
    vla and orch
MARCELLO, [BENEDETTO (1686-1739)]
  Sonata in G, orig for gamba, arranged for
    vla and guitar or lute
    (Azpiazu) ZM (Pet No. ZM363)
PORTER, QUINCY (1897-   )
  Duo, for vla and harp or harpsichord
    AMP
TELEMANN, GEORG PHILIPP (1681-1767)
  Sonata in a, orig for gamba, arranged
    for vla and guitar or lute
    (Azpiazu) ZM (Pet No. ZM362)

Duos: Viola d'Amore, Keyboard

ARIOSTI, ATTILIO (1666-c.1740)
  Sonatas 1 and 2, from 6 Sonatas for vla
    d'amore
    (Sabatini Renzo) Santis 980
BORRIS, SIEGFRIED (1906-   )
  Sonate, Op. 105, for vla d'amore and klavier
    Sirius
CASADESUS, HENRI (1879-1947)
  Préludes, 24, pour Viole d'Amour et Clavecin
    Sal
HAMMER
  Sonata in D, see Old Masters of the Viola
    under vla and pno

HINDEMITH, PAUL (1895-1963)
  Little Sonata, Op. 25, No. 2, for vla d'amore
    and pno
    SCH
MARTIN, FRANK (1890-   )
  Sonata da chiesa, for vla d'amore and organ
    UE 12118
TOESCHI, GIOVANNI (1727-1800)
  Sonata
    (Newlin-Stumpf) DOB
WAEFELGHEM, LOUIS VAN (1840-1908)
  Romance
    Dur
  Soir d'automne
    Dur

Duos: Cello, Piano

ABACO, EVARISTO FELICE DALL' (1675-1742)
  Passepied
    (Krane) Shapiro, Bernstein
  Sonata in C, "La Sampogna"
    (Moffat-Whitehouse) SIM
ABASOV, A.
  Poem
    MZK
ABEL, KARL FRIEDRICH (1723-1787)
  Romance
    (Moffat) Aug
ABSIL, JEAN (1893-   )
  Suite, Op. 51
    CBDM
ACCOLAY
  Concertino in a
    (Bazelaire) SF (Pet No. SCH26)
ACHRON, [JOSEPH (1886-1943)]
  Sicilenne in the Old Style
    (Kurtz) BH
ADAMIAN, G.
  Pieces, 2
    MZK
  Springtime; Lyrical Song; Reminiscences
    MZK
ADORIAN, ANDREW
  Serenade Basque
    Chap-L
AGAPIEV
  Gavotte, see Gurilev: Nocturne
d'AGREVES, E.
  Menuet
    Cranz
  Toccatelle
    Cranz
AGUIRRE, JULIÁN (1868-1924)
  Huella. Canzone argentina, Op. 49, orig
    for pno
    (Schiuma) Ric BA10854
AIVAZIAN, A.
  Armenian Dance, Op. 1, No. 1
    MZK
  Armenian Dance; with Lullaby, Impromptu
    by Arutunian
    MZK
  Canzonetta; Concert Etude
    MZK
  Concert Etude
    MZK
  Georgian Dance, see Arakishvili:
    Georgian Dance
AKHMEDOV, M.
  Song-Improvisation
    MZK

AKIMENKO, [FYODOR (1876-1945)]
  Mélodie Russe
  RL
ALBÉNIZ, ISAAC (1860-1909)
  Malaguena, Op. 165, No. 3, orig for pno
    (Stutschewsky) SCH
  Tango, Op. 165, No. 2, orig for pno
    (Bye) SCH
d'ALBERT, EUGÈNE (1864-1932)
  Concerto in C, Op. 20
    Int
    Pet 4405
ALBUM OF FAVORITE CELLO SOLOS
    (Isaac) Cole 216
    Annie Laurie
    Auld lang syne
    Ay, Ay, Ay
    Bach: Ave Maria
    Bach: Come, sweet death
    Balfe: Killarney
    Believe me, if all those endearing
      young charms
    Bizet: Agnus Dei
    Bland: Carry me back to old Virginny
    Bohm: Still as the night
    Capua: Beneath thy window
    Capua: Maria, mari
    Capua: O sole mio
    Carey: America
    Chiara: La Spagnola
    Cucaracha
    Debussy: Reverie
    Debussy: Romance
    Deep River
    Denza: Funiculi, Funicula
    Drink to me only with thine eyes
    Dvorak: Songs my mother taught me
    Dykes: Holy, Holy, Holy
    Eli, Eli
    Emmett: Dixie
    Fernandez: Cielto Lindo
    Flotow: Ah, so pure
    Foster: My old Kentucky home
    Foster: Oh, Susanna
    Foster: Old black Joe
    Foster: Old folks at home
    Godard: Berceuse, from Jocelyn
    Gounod: Ave Maria
    Grieg: I love thee
    Grieg: Solvejg's song
    Gruber: Silent Night
    Halevy: Call me thine own
    Handel: Largo
    Handel: Where'er you walk
    Home on the range
    How can I leave thee
    Humperdinck: Evening prayer
    Irish washerwoman
    Lehar: Merry Widow waltz
    Lehar: Vilia
    Little man
    Liszt: Liebestraum
    Loch Lomond
    Londonderry air
    Nessler: Young Werner's parting song
    Nobody knows the trouble I've seen
    Offenbach: Barcarolle
    Polly Wolly Doodle
    Reading: Adeste Fideles
    Reichardt: When the roses bloom
    Robin Adair
    Rossini: Cujus Animam
    Rubinstein: Melody in F

    Saint-Saens: My heart at thy sweet
      voice
    Schubert: By the sea
    Schubert: Cradle song
    Schubert: Serenade
    Schubert: Trout
    Schubert: Who is Sylvia
    Schumann: Traumerei
    Schumann: Two Grenadiers
    Seeing Nellie home
    Serradell: La Golondrina
    Steal away
    Sullivan: Lost Chord
    Sullivan: Onward, Christian soldiers
    Tchaikovsky: None but the lonely heart
    Verdi: Heavenly Aida
    Wagner: Evening Star
    Ward: America the beautiful
    Wearing of the green
    When love is kind
    Work: Marching through Georgia
ALDERIGHI, DANTE (1898-   )
  Suite
    Santis 495
ALETTER, WILLIAM
  Melodie
    (Buechner) CF B1403
  Petit Conte
    (Buechner) CF B1401
  Petite Gavotte
    (Buechner) CF B1399
ALEXANDER, A.
  Southward Bound
    SCH
ALEXANDROV, B.
  Sonata
    MZK
ALEXANDROV, JURLJ
  Sonata
    BRH
ALFANO, FRANCO (1876-1954)
  Giorno per Giorno. Arietta
    Carisch
ALFANO & SILVA
  Danses Roumaines, 4
    Deiss
ALLEGRETTO GRAZIOSO
    ZA 3187 unknown 18th century
      composer
ALLER
  Gavotte in G
    Ru
  March Petite
    Ru
  Slavonic Lullaby
    Ru
  Valse Mignonne
    Ru
ALPAERTS, [FLOR (1876-1954)]
  Serenata
    Metr
ALWYN, [WILLIAM (1905-   )]
  Mountain Scenes
    SCH
d'AMBROSIO, [ALFREDO (1871-1914)]
  Mélodie
    (Schroeder) BMC
(AMBROSIO)
  Cellist's Solo Album
    CF 0110 for contents see title
AMELLER, ANDRÉ (1912-   )
  Serenade
    ESC

AMES, WILLIAM (1901-   )
  Dust of snow
    CP
  Sonata
    CFE
  Suite
    CFE
AMFITEATROF, DANIELE (1901-   )
  Melodia
    Santis 214
AMIROV, [FIKRET (1922-   )]
  Elegy
    MZK
ANDANTE
    ZA 3190   unknown 18th century
      composer
ANDERSON, KENNETH (1903-   )
  Diversions, 3
    Bosw
ANDRIESSEN, [HENDRIK (1892-   )]
  Sonate
    Senart
ANGERER, PAUL (1927-   )
  Musica Exanimata
    DOB
(ANTHONY)
  Concert Encores for Cello
    Pr
ANTONIOTTI (1681-1767)
  Sonate No. 1 en Ré
    (Ruyssen) Delrieu
  Sonate No. 2 en Fa
    (Ruyssen) Delrieu
  Sonate No. 3 en Si bemol
    (Ruyssen) Delrieu
  Sonata in sol min.
    (Salmon) Ric R381
ANTONIOTTO, [GIORGIO (c.1692-c.1776)]
  Sonata in D, Op. 1, No. 1
    WM (Pet No. WM26)   2nd vcl ad lib
ANTUFEYEV, B.
  Concerto
    MZK
ARAKISHVILI, [DMITRI (1873-1953)]
  Georgian Song; with Lullaby by Tsintsadze
    and Georgian Dance by Aivazian
    MZK
ARDÉVOL, [JOSÉ (1911-   )]
  Sonatina
    Ric BA10927
ARENSKY, ANTON (1861-1906)
  Barcarolle; Sad Song
    MZK
  Little Ballade, Op. 12, No. 1
    MZK
  Lullaby; with Romance by Rachmaninoff
    and Barcarolle by Rubinstein
    MZK
ARIOSTI, ATTILIO (1666-c.1740)
  Sonate, 6
    Carisch
  Sonata in mi min.
    (Salmon) Ric R382
  Sonata in sol
    (Salmon) Ric R383
ARNE, THOMAS (1710-1778)
  Sonata in B flat
    (Craxton) Oxf 20.007
ARUTUNIAN
  Lullaby, Impromptu, see Aivazian:
    Armenian Dance
ASAFIEV, BORIS (1884-1949)
  Scene, from The Fountain of Bakhchisarai
    MZK

ASHTON, A.T.L.
  Cantilena
    STB
ASIOLI, BONIFAZIO (1769-1832)
  Sonata in C
    (Grützmacher) SIM
ATTERBERG, KURT (1887-   )
  Concerto, Op. 21
    BRH
AUBER, DANIEL-FRANCOIS-ESPRIT
    (1782-1871)
  Concerto in la min.
    (Salmon) Ric R718
  Tarentelle, see Garrat: Duo-Caprice
d'AUBERGE, ALFRED
  Malaguena
    CF B2634
AUBERT, PIERRE FRANCOIS OLIVIER
    (c.1763-c.1830)
  Sonate ancienne
    (Feuillard) Delrieu
AUSTIN, F.
  Captain Cockchafer
    (Withers) SCH
BABIN, VICTOR (1908-   )
  From an old notebook
    Aug
  Hebrew Slumber Song
    Aug
  Sonata-Fantasia
    Aug
  Variations on a theme of Purcell, 12
    AMP
BACH, C.P.E., see Bach, K.P.E.
BACH, JOHANN CHRISTIAN (1735-1782)
  Concerto en Ut mineur
    (Maréchal) Senart 5457C   realization
      by H. Casadesus
BACH, JOHANN CHRISTOPH FRIEDRICH
    (1732-1795)
  Sonate in A
    (Wenzinger) Baer 3970
  Sonate in G
    (Ruf) Baer 3745
BACH, JOHANN SEBASTIAN (1685-1750)
  Adagio from Sonata in G, orig for vln
    and harpsichord
    (Withers) SCH
  Adagio, from Toccata in C for organ
    (Siloti-Casals) CF B1946
    Pet 4214
  Adagio and Allegro, from Sonata No. 6 in A
    (Feuermann) CF B2771
  Air in D, from Suite No. 3, orig for orch
    (Rose) Int
    (Stutschevsky) Int
    (Wilhelmj-Rundnagel) CF B2708
      "Celebrated Air"
  Air in F, from Sonata No. 2 for vln
    (Ticciati) Oxf 21.013
  Air and Gavotte
    (Ries) SCH
  Andante, from Goldberg Variations, orig
    for clavier
    (Silva) ZA
  Andante, from Italian Concerto, orig
    for clavier
    (Ronchini) ESC
  Andante, from Sonata in a, orig for vln unacc
    (Siloti-Casals) CF B2031
  Arioso. Introduction to Cantata 156
    (Franko) GS
    (Isaac) CF B2497
  Ave Maria, see Gounod

BACH, JOHANN SEBASTIAN (cont.)
Bach for the 'cello
(Krane) GS
Choral Preludes, 3
(Kodály) BH
Choral Preludes, 3
(Kodály) UE 7756
Choral Prelude in f. Jesus, my Joy
(Siloti-Casals) CF B2032
Chorales, 6
(Fournier) Int
Chorale: O Jesu Christ, S. 639[53]
(Gendron) SCH
Concerto No. 1 in G, after Vivaldi
(Piatigorsky) Int
Concerto No. 1 in G, S.592[53]
(Piatigorsky) SCH
Concerto in g
GS L1609
Gavotte in c
(Schroeder) Aug
Gavotte in d
(Schroeder) Aug
Intermediate Bach for Cello
(Krane) Jack Spratt
Jesu, joy of man's desiring
(Grace) Oxf 20.004
Komm, süsser Tod
(Chiarappa) Ric 127920 "Aria religiosa"
(Tertis) GS
Largo
(Schroeder) Aug
Minuet, from Anna Magdalena's Notebook
Bel
Musette
(Pollain) Senart 5360
Now the sheep secure are grazing, from
Birthday Cantata
(Forbes) Oxf 23.416 "Sheep may safely
graze"
(La Forge) CF B2677
Pastorale
Int
Recitative in b, from Organ Concerto
after Vivaldi
(Silva) ZA 3117
Recitative
Int
Sarabandes, 2
(Henschel) Aug
Sheep may safely graze, see Now the
sheep secure are grazing
Slumber Song
(Squire) Aug
*Sonatas, 3, in G,D,g, S.1027-29,[53] orig for
gamba and clavier
(Gruetzmacher) Pet 239
(Klengel) BRH
(Klengel) Int
Sonata in C
(Schroeder) Aug 5520
Sonata in G
(Schroeder) Aug 5501
Suite in G, S.1007,[53] orig for vcl unacc
(Piatti-Rapp) SCH
see also Graded Teaching Pieces
BACH, KARL PHILIPP EMANUEL (1714-1788)
Concerto in a
(Grützmacher) BRH
Concerto in B flat
(Klengel) BRH

Concerto No. 3 in A
(Cassado) Int
(Pollain) Senart 5391
Sonata in C, orig for gamba and clavier
(Klengel) BRH
Sonata in D, orig for gamba and clavier
(Klengel) BRH
Sonata in D, orig for gamba and clavier
(Leyden) Pet 4287 2nd vcl ad lib
BACH, WILHELM FRIEDEMANN (1710-1784)
Grave
(Maréchal) ESC
BACICH, ANTHONY P.
Tone Poems
Willis
BACON, ERNST (1898-   )
Koschatiana
Leeds
BADINGS, HENK (1907-   )
Concert Pieces, 4
DN (Pet No. D22)
Sonata No. 2
AL (Pet No. AL1)
(BAECHI)
Unvergaengliche Melodien
Hug (Pet No. A36) for contents see title
BAKLANOVA
Etudes, 2; with Race by Komarovsky
MZK
Melody; Mazurka; Romance
MZK
BALAKIREV
Polka, see Rimsky-Korsakov: Lullaby
BALFE, MICHAEL WILLIAM (1808-1870)
Then You'll Remember Me, from Bohemian
Girl
(Buechner) CF B2868
BALLOU, ESTHER W.
Plaintive Note and a Cheerful Note
CFE
Suite
CFE
BANAITIS, K.
Sonata rapsodica
UE 10972
BANKS, D.
Studies, 3
SCH
BANNER, FILIPPO (18th century)
Sonata in g
(Upmeyer) NAG
BANTOCK, GRANVILLE (1868-1946)
Celtic Poem, orig for vcl and orch
Ches
Elegaic Poem[54]
JWL (Mil No. W1537)
Fantastic Poem
Ches
Hamabdil, for vcl and harp or pno
Ches
Pribroch, for vcl and harp or pno
Ches
Sonata in b
Ches
BARATI, GEORGE (1913-   )
Lamentoso, 1942
CFE   score only
BARBER, SAMUEL (1910-   )
Concerto, Op. 22
(Garbousova) GS
Sonata, Op. 6
GS

---

[53] S. number is from the thematic catalogue by W. Schmieder:
Thematisch-systematisch Verzeichnis der musikalischen
Werke von Johann Sebastian Bach. Leipzig, 1950.

[54] Also available for violoncello and orchestra.

BARBIROLLI, JOHN (1899-   )
  Airs, 6
    Oxf 20.003
BARDOS, [LAJOS (1899-   )]
  Evening Melody
    Kul
BARNS, ETHEL (1880-1948)
  Swing Song
    (Withers) SCH
BARRATT, E
  Coronach
    (Sharpe) EKN
BARRIÈRE, JEAN (18th century)
  Sonates, 12
    (Chaigneau & Morse-Rummel) Senart
    5246, 5394   2V
BARTOK, BELA (1881-1945)
  Concerto, orig for vla and orch
    (Serly) BH
  For Children
    (Liebner) Kul
  Rhapsody No. 1[55]
    BH   arr by composer
  Roumanian Folk Dances
    (Silva) BH
BASS, JOHN
  Contemplation, from Four Songs
      Without Words, Op. 11, No. 2
    MK
  Forgotten, from Four Songs Without Words,
      Op. 11, No. 4
    MK
  Longing, from Four Songs Without Words,
      Op. 11, No. 1
    MK
  Solitude, from Four Songs Without Words,
      Op. 11, No. 3
    MK
BASSETT, LESLIE (1923-   )
  Sonata
    CFE
BAUD, JEAN
  Petite suite dans le style ancien
    HL
BAUDIOT, CHARLES-NICOLAS (1773-1849)
  Concertino
    (Ruyssen) Delrieu
BAX, ARNOLD (1883-1953)
  Concerto
    Chap-L
  Folk-Tale
    Ches
  Legend-Sonata
    Chap-L
  Sonatina
    Chap-L
BAZELAIRE, PAUL (1886-1958)
  Cache-Cache
    Senart
  Concertino No. 1, Op. 126
    Dur
  Concertino No. 2, Op. 127
    Dur
  Funérailles, Op. 120
    Sal
  Images lointaines, 2, Op. 113
    Leduc
      1. Yamilé
      2. Danse nonchalante
  Suite Française
    SF (Pet No. SCH12)

Suite Italienne
  Consortium Musicale
Variations sur une chanson naive, Op. 125
  SF (Pet No. SCH28)
BAZELON, IRWIN
  Pieces, 5
    Weintraub
BECK, CONRAD (1901-   )
  Sonata No. 2
    SCH
BEETHOVEN, LUDWIG VAN (1770-1827)
  Adagio cantabile from Piano Sonata, Op. 13
    (Palaschko) SCH
  Minuet in G, orig for pno
    (Palaschko) SCH
    (Skalmer) CF B2921
    (Trinkaus) Fill
  Minuet
    (Schroeder) BMC
  Minuet, see Matteson: Aria
  Rondino on a theme of, see Kreisler
  *Sonatas, 5: Op. 5, Nos. 1, 2; Op. 69;
      Op. 102; Nos. 1, 2
    (Crepax-Lorenzoni) Ric ER2026
    (Schulz) GS L810
    (Tovey-Such) Aug 7660
    Pet 748
  Sonata in F, Op. 5, No. 1
    (Tovey-Such) Aug
  Sonata in g, Op. 5, No. 2
    (Rose) Int
    (Tovey-Such) Aug
  Sonata in A, Op. 69
    (Rose) Int
    (Tovey-Such) Aug
  Sonata in C, Op. 102, No. 1
    (Tovey-Such) Aug
  Sonata in D, Op. 102, No. 2
    (Tovey-Such) Aug
  Sonata in F, Op. 17, orig for horn and pno
    (Hermann) Pet 149
  Sonatina in d, orig for mandolin and cembalo
    Pet 4221
  Variations
    (Stutschewsky) Pet 748b
      12 variations on a theme of Handel
      12 variations on a theme of Mozart
      7 variations on a theme of Mozart
  Variations, 12, on a theme from Judas
      Maccabaeus by Handel
    (Such) Aug
  Variations, 12, on the theme "Ein Mädchen
      oder Weibchen" from Magic Flute by
      Mozart
    (Such) Aug
  Variations, 7, on Bei Männern, welche Liebe
      fühlen", from Magic Flute by Mozart
    (Stutschewsky) Pet 7048
    (Such) Aug
    Int
  Variationen
    (Münch-Holland & Henle) Henle
BELLA, DOMENICO DALLA (18th century)
  Sonata in C
    NAG
BEN-HAIM, PAUL (1897-   )
  Songs Without Words, 3
    IMP
BENJAMIN, ARTHUR (1893-1960)
  Negro Spirituals, 5
    BH
  Sonatina
    BH

---

[55] This is probably the first of the two rhapsodies written
originally for violin and piano.

(BENOY, A.W. & BURROWES, L.)
Cellists' Books of Carols
Oxf 21.019-20 2V for contents see title
BENSON
Sonatina
BH
BENTZON, NIELS VIGGO (1919-   )
Sonata
Dansk 97
BERGHOUT, JOHANN
Kinderstücke, Op. 26
Aug 7666
Sonatina, Op. 34
Aug 7668
BÉRIOT, CHARLES DE (1802-1870)
In the Swiss Alps
Bel
BERKELEY, LENNOX (1903-   )
Andantino
Ches
BERLINSKI, HERMAN (1910-   )
Suite No. 2
CFE
BERNARD, EMILE (1843-1902)
Sonate en sol, Op. 46
Dur
BERNARD, J.
Tarentelle
Senart
BERNARD, [ROBERT (1900-   )]
Sonate en do
Dur
BERTHET, F.
Andante
RL
Berceuse
RL
BERWALD, FRANZ (1796-1868)
Duo
Gehrmans
BINKERD, GORDON (1916-   )
Sonata
CFE
BIRKENSTOCK, JOHANN ADAM (1687-1733)
Sonata in e
(Moffat) SIM
(Salmon) Ric R384
BIRKENSTOCK
Sonata
MZK
BIZET, GEORGES (1838-1875)
Adagietto, from L'Arlésienne Suite No. 2
(Bernstein) AMP
Toreador Song, from Carmen
(Roberts) CF B2864
BLACKWOOD, EASLEY (1933-   )
Fantasy, Op. 8
GS
BLAINVILLE, CHARLES-HENRI (1711-1769)
Sonate ancienne
(Feuillard) Delrieu
BLAZEVICH
Etude No. 86
(Shuman) Jack Spratt
Etude No. 92
(Shuman) Jack Spratt
BLOCH, ERNEST (1880-1959)
From Jewish Life
see Prayer, Supplication, Jewish Song
Jewish Song
(Kindler) CF B1971
Méditation Hébraique
(Kindler) CF B1968

Nigun, from Baal Shem, orig for vln and pno
(Schuster) CF B2772
Prayer
(Kindler) CF B1969
Schelomo, orig for vcl and orch
GS arr for vcl and pno by composer
Supplication
(Kindler) CF B1970
Symphony for vcl or trombone and orch
Broude pno reduction by composer
Voice in the wilderness
GS composer's version for vcl and pno,
after the symphonic poem for orch and
vcl obligato
BLON, see Von Blon
(BLUMENTHAL & SAENGER)
Opera
CF 0802
BOCCHERINI, LUIGI (1743-1805)
Adagio in g, from Concerto No. 3
(Stutschewsky) Pet 4219
Adagio, from Sonata No. 6 in A
(Moffat-Whitehouse-Withers) SCH
Adagio and Allegro, from Sonata No. 6 in A
(Feuermann) CF B2771
Concerto No. 1 in C
(Papin) Leduc
Concerto No. 2 in D
(Papin) Leduc with cadenzas by
Rogister
(Pollain) Senart 5362
Concerto No. 3 in G
(Papin) Leduc
Concerto No. 4 in C
(Papin) Leduc
Concerto in B flat
(Grützmacher) BRH
(Grützmacher-Rose) Int
Concerto in B flat
(Sturzenegger) RH (Pet No. ER3)
Concerto
(Salmon) Ric R719
Largo and Allegro
(Mainardi) SCH
Minuet, "Celebrated", from Quintet,
Op. 13, No. 5
(Lamoury-Lutz) SCH
Minuetto, from Sonata in G
(Such) Aug
Minuetto
(Cassado) UE 8281
Rondo in C
(Schroeder) SCH
Int
Rondo; with Sonata in a by Marcello
(Schroeder) Aug 5510
Rondo
(Willeke) CF B1408
Sonatas, 6
(Piatti-Crepax) Ric ER2461
Sonata No. 1 in A
(Piatti) Ric ER1421
Sonata No. 2 in C
(Piatti) Int
(Piatti) Ric ER1422
Sonata No. 3 in G
(Piatti) Ric ER1423
(Schroeder) Aug 5506
(Schroeder-Rapp) SCH
Sonata No. 6 in A
(Piatti) Ric ER1426
(Piatti-Forino) Int
(Schroeder) Aug 5505
(Schroeder-Rapp) SCH

BOCCHERINI, LUIGI (cont.)
Sonata No. 7 in B flat
(Spiegl-Bergmann-Dickson) SCH
Sonata in A
(Moffat) SCH
Sonata in A
(Stutschewsky) Pet 4283
Sonata in C
(Crepax-Zanon) Ric ER362
BOËLLMANN, LÉON (1862-1897)
Sonate, Op. 40
Dur
Variations symphoniques, Op. 23, orig
for vcl and orch
(Marcelli) CF 03209
(Rose) Int
Dur
MZK
BOGDANOV-BEREZOVSKY, V.
Sonata, Op. 40
MZK
BOHM, CARL
Perpetual Motion No. 6, from Suite No. 3,
orig for vln and pno
(Isaac-Lewis) CF B2473
BOISMORTIER, JOSEPH BODIN DE
(c.1691-1755)
Sonata in D, Op. 50, No. 3
(Ruf) Baer 3963
Sonata in G
Delrieu
BOND, CARRIE JACOBS (1862-1946)
I Love You Truly
BMC
Perfect Day
BMC
BONI, P.G.
Sonata in C
(Moffat-Rapp) SCH
BONONCINI, GIOVANNI (1670-1747)
Sonata in la min.
(Salmon) Ric R386
BONPORTI, FRANCESCO ANTONIO (1672-1749)
Sonata in g, from 10 Inventions, Op. 10, orig
for vln and Bc
(Barblan) SZ
BORGHI, LUIGI (18th century)
Adagio
ZA 3185
Concerto
ZA 4387
(BORISYAK-DZGELENEK)
Pieces, 12, by Russian and Soviet Composers
MZK
BORNOFF'S FIDDLER'S HOLIDAY
(Bornoff-Wilson) CF 04246, 4249
(BORNOFF, GEORGE)
Fun for Fiddle Fingers
Gordon V. Thompson
BORNSCHEIN, FRANZ C. (1879-1948)
At the Lily Pond
CF B1410
BORODIN, ALEXANDER (1833-1887)
Chorus and Dance of the Polovetsian Maidens,
from Prince Igor
(Kozolupov) MZK
Serenata alla Spagnola
(Cassadó) SCH
Serenade
(Stutschewsky) Pet 4222
BORRIS, SIEGFRIED (1906-   )
Kleine Suite
Sirius
Sonate, Op. 53
Sirius

BORTNIANSKY, D.
Sonata: first movement
MZK
BOTTESINI, GIOVANNI (1821-1889)
Rêverie
CF B2941
BOTTJE, WILL GAY (1925-   )
Sonata
CFE
BOUKINIK, M.
Preludes, 10
MZK
BOULANGER, NADIA (1887-   )
Pieces, 3
Heugel   published separately
BOULNOIS, JOSEPH (1884-1918)
En Espagne
Senart
Hymne à Bacchus
Senart
Neige
Senart
Noël
Senart
Sarabande
Senart
Sonate
Senart
BOURGUIGNON, FRANCIS DE (1890-   )
Scherzo, Op. 56
CBDM
BOYCE, WILLIAM (1710-1779)
Tempo di gavotta
(Forbes-Craxton) Oxf 20.108
BOZZA, [EUGÈNE (1905-   )]
Concerto, Op. 57
Leduc
BRAGA, GAETANO (1829-1907)
Angel's Serenade
(Buechner) CF B2949
BRAHMS, JOHANNES (1833-1897)
Hangarian Dance No. 6 in C, orig for pno duet
(Piatti) SCH
Hungarian Dance in d, orig for pno duet
(Gendron) SCH
Intermezzo, Op. 116, No. 4, orig for pno
(Miersch) GS
Ninna-nanna, Op. 49, No. 4, orig for voice
and pno
(Chiarappa) Ric 127918
Sapphic Ode, orig for voice and pno
(Hegner) CF B2942
*Sonata in e, Op. 38
(Crepax-Lorenzoni) Ric ER2101
(Klengel) Pet 3897A
(Münch-Holland) Henle
(Rose) Int
(Schroeder) Aug 5116
(Van Vliet-Hughes) GS L1411
BRH
*Sonata in F, Op. 99
(Crepax-Lorenzoni) Ric ER2102
(Klengel) Pet 3897b
(Münch-Holland) Henle
(Rose) Int
Aug 7705
Valzer, Op. 39, No. 1, orig for pno duet
(Chiarappa) Ric 127919
see also Graded Teaching Pieces
BRANDUKOV, [ANATOL (1859-1930)]
Elegy; Song Without Words
MZK
BRANSON, [DAVID (1909-   )]
Rune
EKN

(BRECK, E.S.)
Christmas Joys
CF 03171   for contents see title
under vln and pno
BRERO, [GIULIO CESARE (1908-   )]
Variaciones sobre un tema popular
italiano
Ric BA11242
BRESGEN, [CESAR (1913-   )]
Sonata No. 2
Pet 5812
BREVAL, JEAN BAPTISTE (1756-1825)
Adagio, Rondo, see Mozart: Larghetto
Concertino No. 1 en Fa
(Feuillard) Delrieu
Concertino No. 2 en Ut
(Feuillard) Delrieu
Concertino No. 3 en La
(Feuillard) Delrieu
Concertino No. 4 en Ut
(Ruyssen) Delrieu
Concertino No. 5 en Ré
(Ruyssen) Delrieu
Concerto No. 1 en Sol
(Feuillard) Delrieu
Concerto No. 2 en Ré
(Feuillard) Delrieu
Sonata in C
(Schroeder) Aug 5502
(Schroeder-Rose) Int
Sonata in C
(Stutschevsky) SCH
Sonata in G
(Cahnbley) SCH
(Moffat) SIM
Sonata in G
(Cassado) Int
Sonata
MZK
Sonata
Ric R498
BREVILLE, PIERRE-ONFROY DE (1861-1949)
Fantaisie Appassionnata
Senart
Poème dramatique
RL
Prière
RL
Sonate en Ré mineur
RL
BRIDGE, FRANK (1879-1941)
Cradle Song
Aug
Elégie
Aug
Mélodie
Aug
Sonata
BH
see also Graded Teaching Pieces
BRIDGE
Berceuse
Kuhl (Mil No. K130)
BRIGHT, D.
Fischermädchen, Das
STB
Polka à la Strauss
STB
BRITTEN, BENJAMIN (1913-   )
Sonata, Op. 65
BH
(BROCKWAY, WILLIAM)
Traditional Tunes, 8
Oxf 21.026   for contents see title

(BRODSZKY, F.)
Old Music
Kul
BROECKX, J.
Preludium
Metr
BROWN, E.
Music
AMP
BROWN, JAMES
Blind Minstrel
STB
Burlesque
STB
Caprice
STB
Chattering Ditty
STB
Romance
STB
Romanesca
STB
Savoyards
STB
Solitude
STB
(BROWN)
Negro Folk Songs, 5
SCH
BRUCH, MAX (1838-1920)
Kol Nidrei
(Rose) Int
(Schroeder) BMC
(Schulz) GS
CF B2713
BUCHTEL, FORREST L.
Ambition Waltz
Kjos S-5200
Happy Days
Kjos S-5203
Jolly Fellows
Kjos S-5204
(BUECHNER)
Cellist's First Concert Album
CF 0107-108   2V
BUESSER, HENRI (1872-   )
Sommeil de l'enfant Jésus
CH (Pet No. C99)
BULL
Melody in D
(Schroeder) BMC
BUONONCINI, GIOVANNI BATTISTA
(1672-1764)
Aria
Pet 4213
Sonata in A; with Andante cantabile by
Stiasni
(Schroeder) Aug 5509
BURKHARD, WILLY (1900-1955)
Sonate
Baer 2685
Suite en miniature, orig for vln and pno
Baer 2107b
BURKHARD, [WILLY]
Concertino, Op. 60
UE 11574
BURROWES, L., see Benoy & Burrowes
BURROWS, BENJAMIN (1891-   )
Sonatina
Aug
BUSH, ALAN (1900-   )
Concert Suite, Op. 37, orig for vcl and orch
JWL (Mil No. W1518)
Fireside Story
JWL

BUSH, ALAN (cont.)
Song Across the Water
JWL
BUSONI, FERRUCCIO BENVENUTO
(1866-1924)
Kultaselle. Variations on a Finnish song
BRH
BUXTEHUDE, DIETRICH (c.1637-1707)
Sonata in D
(Längin) SCH
BYE, [FREDERICK (1901-   )]
Arioso
STB
Country Dance
STB
Menuet
STB
BYRD, WILLIAM (1543-1623)
Lachrymae Pavane
STB
CACCINI, GIULIO (c.1546-1618)
Amarilli
Pet 4210
CADMAN
Mad Empress Remembers
Mil
CAIX D'HERVELOIS, LOUIS DE (c.1670-c.1760)
Papillon
Pet 4217
Sonata in a
(Moffat) SIM
(Salmon) Ric R398
Suite No. 1 in A
(Schroeder-Rapp) SCH
Suite No. 2
(Feuillard) Delrieu
Suite No. 2 in D
(Schroeder-Rapp) SCH
CAMERINI, M.
Habañera
ESC
CAMINITI
Aria
Ric 122487
Giga
Ric 122488
CAPITANIO, I.
Leggenda in a
SZ
CAPLET, ANDRÉ (1878-1925)
Epiphanie, d'après une légende ethiopienne
Dur
CAPON, F.
Folk Fragments, 4
STB
CAPORALE, ANDREA (? -c.1756)
Sonata in d
(Salmon) Ric R387
Sonata in d
SCH
CAPUIS, MATILDE
Ballad
ZA 4372
Tema variata
ZA 4356
CARSE, ADAM (1878-1958)
Merry Dance
Aug
Serenata
Aug
Short Pieces, 3
Aug
Quiet tune; Lively tune; Martial tune

Short Pieces, 2
Aug
Little reverie; Valsette
CARTER, ELLIOTT (1908-   )
Sonata
AMP
CARWITHEN, DOREEN (1922-   )
Little Pieces, 6, Set 1
JWL (Mil No. W1520)
Little Pieces, 6, Set 2
JWL (Mil No. W1521)
CASADESUS, [ROBERT (1899-   )]
Sonate
Sal
CASELLA, ALFREDO (1883-1947)
Sonata in C
UE 9478
Sonata in C, 2nd mvt: Bourree
UE 9448
CASELLA
Notturno
(Silva) Ric 122233
Tarantella
(Silva) Ric 122234
CASINIERE, Y.
Sonatine
RL
CASSADO, GASPAR (1897-   )
Concerto
UE 8653
Concerto in a, see Schubert
Danse du Diable Vert
UE 8457
Serenade
UE 8131
Sonata nello stile antico spagnuolo
UE 7931
Sonate
Mathot
CASTELNUOVO-TEDESCO, MARIO (1895-   )
Figaro, from Barber of Seville by Rossini
(Piatigorsky) CF B2670
I nottambuli
UE 8992
CASTERA, RENÉ DE (1873-1955)
Lent et Grave
RL
CASTRO, JOSÉ MARÍA (1892-   )
Estudios, Tres
SMP
Piezas, Tres
SMP
CATURLA, ALEJANDRO GARCÍA (1906-1940)
Danza del Tambor
Senart
CAZDEN, NORMAN (1914-   )
American Suite, Op. 31
CFE
Three Recitations
CFE
CELLIER, [ALEXANDRE (1883-   )]
Sonate
Senart
CELLISTS' BOOKS OF CAROLS
(Benoy-Burrowes) Oxf 21.019-20   2V
Vol 1
Carol of Beauty
Coventry Carol
First Nowell
God rest you merry, gentlemen
Good King Wenceslas
Hark! the herald angels sing
Holly and the ivy
I saw three ships

CELLISTS' BOOKS OF CAROLS (cont.)
  (Benoy-Burrowes) Oxf 21.019-20 2V (cont.)
    Vol 1 (cont.)
      O come, all ye faithful
      Once in Royal David's City
      Unto us a boy is born
      While shepherds watched
    Vol 2
      Angels from the realms of glory
      As with gladness men of old
      Brightest and best of the sons of
        the morning
      Child this day is born
      Falan-tiding
      Gloucestershire Wassail
      Good Christian men rejoice
      O little town of Bethlehem
      Silent Night
      Song of the Crib
      Sussex Carol
      We three kings
CELLIST'S FAVORITE CONTEST ALBUM
  (Collier) CF 03220
    Bach-Isaac: Arioso, from Cantata,
      No. 156
    Beethoven: Minuet in G
    Bruch: Kol Nidre
    Massenet: Elegy
    Pergolese: Nina
    Ponce: Estrellita
    Saint-Saens: Allegro Appassionato
    Schubert: Ave Maria
    Tchaikovsky: Chant sans paroles
      and 6 other compositions
CELLIST'S FIRST CONCERT ALBUM
  (Buechner) CF 0107-8 2V
CELLIST'S FIRST SOLO REPERTOIRE
  (Hegner) CF 0109
    Becket: Red, White and Blue
    Charlie is My Darling
    Claribel: Come back to Erin
    Foster: Old Black Joe
    Foster: Old Folks at Home
    Listen to the Mocking Bird
    Lowry: Where Is My Boy Tonight?
    Robin Adair
    Woodworth: Old Oaken Bucket
CELLIST'S SOLO ALBUM
  (Ambrosio) CF 0110
    Bohm: Calm As the Night
    Cui: Orientale
    Elgar: Salut d'Amour
    Goltermann: Andante from Concerto
      in a
    Grieg: Solvejg's Song
    Handel: Largo
    Järnefelt: Berceuse
    Mascagni: Intermezzo Sinfonico
    Massenet: Mélodie
    Mendelssohn: On Wings of Song
    Popper: Autumn Flower
    Schumann: Träumerei
    Simonetti: Romanza
    Tchaikovsky: None But the Lonely
      Heart
    Wagner: Introduction and Song to
      the Evening Star
    Wagner: Walther's Prize Song
    8 additional compositions, not
      identified
CELLO SOLOS
  Amsco 40
CELLO SOLOS, 80
  Bel EL158

CERVETTO, GIACOMO (1747-1837)
  Sonatas, 2
    (Schroeder-Rapp) SCH
  Sonata in do
    (Salmon) Ric R95
  Sonata in sol
    (Salmon) Ric R388
CHABRIER, EMMANUEL (1841-1894)
  Larghetto, orig for horn and orch
    Sal
CHAMINADE, CÉCILE (1857-1944)
  Pièce romantique
    Dur
  Serenade
    Kjos S-5210
CHAMP, S.
  see Graded Teaching Pieces
CHAPUIS, AUGUSTE (1858-1933)
  Fantaisie concertante
    Dur
  Sonate en la mineur
    Dur
CHAUSSON, ERNEST (1855-1899)
  Interlude du Poème de l'Amour et de la
    Mer, orig for voice and orch
    RL
  Interlude
    (Ronchini) Int
  Pièce
    RL
CHERNOV, M.
  Canzona
    MZK
CHEVILLARD, CAMILLE (1859-1923)
  Petites pièces, 4, Op. 11
    Dur
  Sonate, Op. 15
    Dur
CHEVREUILLE, RAYMOND (1901-   )
  Burlesque, Op. 20
    CBDM
  Sonata, Op. 42
    CBDM
CHOPIN, FRÉDÉRIC (1810-1849)
  Etudes, 2: Op. 10, No. 6 and
    Op. 25, No. 1, orig for pno
    (Glazunov) Int
  Introduction et Polonaise brillante, Op. 3
    (Feuermann-Rose) Int
    (Gendron) SCH
    (Graudan) GS L1803
    Pet 1928 published with Sonata in g
  Lento
    (Schroeder) BMC
  Maiden's Wish, orig for voice and pno
    (Hegner) CF B2515
  Nocturnes, 4, orig for pno
    MZK
  Nocturne in c sharp, orig for pno
    (Piatigorsky) Int
    (Piatigorsky) SCH
  Nocturne in E flat, Op. 9, No. 2, orig for pno
    (Popper) Int
  Nocturne, Op. posth, orig for pno
    (York) GS
  Polonaise brillante, Op. 3, see Introduction
    et Polonaise brillante
  Prelude; with Evening, Spinner by Moniuszko
    MZK
  Sonata in g, Op. 65
    (Balakirev) Pet 1928; published with
      Polonaise brillante, Op. 3
    (Schulz) GS L64
  Theme Populaire
    (Hummel) Ru

CHOPIN, FRÉDÉRIC (cont.)
Valse Brillante, Op. 34, orig for pno
(Bernstein) AMP
Violoncello Album of 6 Pieces
(Sharpe) JWL (Mil No. W1500)
Waltzes, 2, orig for pno
MZK
Waltz, "Minute", orig for pno
(Cassado) Int
CHRÉTIEN, E.
Sérénade
RL
Vers l'Infini
RL
CHRISTMAS JOYS
(Breck) CF 03171   for contents see title
under vln and pno
CILÈA, FRANCESCO (1866-1950)
Canto, from Vocalizzo da concerto No. 2,
orig for voice and orch
(Martorana) Ric 130399
Pezzi, 3
Ric 127934
Sonata in D, Op. 38
Curci
CIRRI, GIAMBATTISTA
Concerto, Op. 14, No. 6
(Bonelli) ZA 4340
CLARKE, REBECCA (1886-   )
Passacaglia on an old English tune
GS
CLASSIC AND FOLK MELODIES
(Krane) Pr
CLASSIC PIECES
Pet 1418A,b,C,D   4V
Vol 1: 12 pieces by Bach, Beethoven,
Gluck, Handel, Hummel, Mozart,
Schubert, Tartini
Vol 2: 12 pieces by C.P.E. Bach,
Beethoven, Campagnoli, Haydn,
Martini, Mozart, Schubert, Schumann
Vol 3: 10 pieces by Beethoven
Vol 4: 9 pieces by J.S. Bach, Corelli,
Hasse, Leclair, Lotti, Nardini,
Tartini, Telemann
CLASSICAL ALBUM OF EARLY GRADE
PIECES
(Herfurth) BMC
CLASSICAL PIECES
(Schulz) SCH
for contents see title under gamba
and pno
COCKSHOTT, GERALD (1915-   )
Pastoral Interlude
Oxf 21.007
COLLET, HENRI (1885-1951)
Pena, La
Sal
(COLLIER)
Cellist's Favorite Contest Album
CF 03220   for contents see title
COME TO THE SEA
Bel
CONCERT ENCORES FOR CELLO
(Anthony) Pr
CONSTANTINESCU, [PAUL (1909-   )]
Variations on a Byzantine Melody
UE 11456
COOKE, ARNOLD (1906-   )
Sonata
Nov
COOKE
Sea Croon
JWL (Mil No. W1502)

COOLS, [EUGÈNE (1877-1936)]
Pliaska. Russian Dance
(Maréchal) ESC
Sérénade Toscane, Op. 83
ESC
COPLAND, AARON (1900-   )
Waltz and Celebration, from Billy the Kid
(Piatigorsky) BH
CORELLI, ARCANGELO (1653-1713)
Adagio, from Sonata, Op. 5, No. 1
Pet 4211
Adagio
(Schuster) BH
Adagio
(Setaccioli) Ric 127916
Gavotte in F
(Schroeder) Aug
Gavotte in G
(Schroeder) Aug
Sonata in d, Op. 5, No. 8[56]
(Lindner) Cranz
(Lindner) Int
Sonata, "La Follia", Op. 5, No. 12
(Salmon) Ric R679
MZK "Variations on a theme, Follia"
Sonata in d
(Salmon) Ric R389
Sonata in g
(Salmon) Ric R680
Sonata in g
(Salmon) Ric R681
Variations on a theme of, see Tartini
see also Graded Teaching Pieces
CORKER, M.
In Ireland
SCH
CORRETTE (1758- ?)
Sonate No. 6, "Les délices de la Solitude"
(Ruyssen) Delrieu
COSSMAN, [BERNHARD (1822-1910)]
Tarantelle
(Schroeder) BMC
COUPERIN, FRANCOIS (1668-1733)
Chérubins, Les
(Salmon) Ric R109
Pastorale
(Cassado) UE 8284
COWELL, HENRY (1897-   )
Four Declamations With Return
CFE   score only
Hymn and Fuguing Tune No. 9
AMP
CRAS, JEAN (1879-1932)
Légende, orig for vcl and orch
Senart
CRAWFORD, ROBERT (1899-   )
U.S. Air Force
(Kent) CF W1851
CRAXTON, HAROLD (1885-   )
Alman
Oxf 20.109
CRESCENZO, CONSTANTINO
Prima Carezza
(Cassado) Int
CRESTON, PAUL (1906-   )
Homage
GS
Suite, Op. 66
GS
CROSFIELD, A.H.
Reverie
STB

---

[56] The sonatas are all transcribed from Op. 5, originally for violin and Bc.

CUI, CÉSAR (1835-1918)
  Berceuse
    (Schroeder) BMC
  Orientale, from Kaléidoscope, Op. 50, No. 9,
    orig for vln and pno
    (Skalmer) CF B2925
D'AGREVES, see Agreves, d'
D'ALBERT, see Albert
DALL'ABACO, see Abaco
DALLA BELLA, see Bella
DALLAPICCOLA, LUIGI (1904-   )
  Dialoghi, orig for vcl and orch
    SZ
DAMASE, [JEAN-MICHEL (1928-   )]
  Aria
    Sal
DAMME, P. VAN
  Easy Pieces, 2: Melody
    ESC
DANBÉ, JULES (1840-1905)
  Mazurka de Salon
    CF B2977
DARE, M
  Serenade
    SCH
  Waltz in G
    SCH
D'AUBERGE, see Auberge
DAUTREMER, [MARCEL (1906-   )]
  Concertino
    Delrieu
DAVICO, [VINCENZO (1889-   )]
  Adagio Elegiaco
    RL
  Romance
    Ric R590
  Variations Carnavalesques, 10
    RL
DAVID, F
  Concertino, Op. 4
    SIM
DAVIDOV, KARL (1838-1889)
  At the Fountain, Op. 20, No. 2
    (Rose) Int
    (Withers) SCH
  Concert Allegro, Op. 11
    MZK
  Concerto No. 1
    (Gendron) Billaudot
  Concerto No. 2
    (Loeb) Billaudot
  Concerto No. 4
    (Loeb) Billaudot
  Romances, 2: Op. 22 and Op. 23
    MZK
  Romance Without Words, Op. 23
    MZK
  Waltz, Op. 41, No. 2
    MZK
DEÁK, STEPHEN (1897-   )
  Autumn Song, No. 1 of Juvenile Suite
    CF B2325
  Lullaby, No. 3 of Juvenile Suite
    CF B2327
  Norwegian Dance, No. 2 of Juvenile Suite
    CF B2326
  Waltz, No. 4 of Juvenile Suite
    CF B2328
DE BOURGUIGNON, see Bourguignon
DEBUSSY, CLAUDE (1862-1918)
  Beau Soir, orig for voice and pno
    (Piatigorsky) Int
  Bells
    (Schroeder) BMC

Clair de lune, from Suite Bergamasque,
    orig for pno
    (Ronchini) Jobert
Danse bohémienne, orig for pno
    (Stutschewsky) SCH
Fille aux cheveux de lin, from Douze
    Préludes, orig for pno
    (Feuillard) Dur
Little Shepherd, see Petit berger
Menuet, from Petite Suite, orig for pno duet
    (Gurt) Dur
    (Rose) Int
Petit berger, Le, from Children's Corner,
    orig for pno
    (Ronchini) Dur
Romance, orig for voice and pno
    (Piatigorsky) Int
Sonata in d
    Dur
DE FESCH, see Fesch
DELIUS, FREDERICK (1862-1934)
  Caprice
    BH
  Concerto
    BH
  Elegy
    BH
  Serenade, from Hassan
    (Tertis) BH
  Sonata
    BH
DELLO JOIO, NORMAN (1913-   )
  Duo Concertato
    GS
DELUNE, [LOUIS (1876-1940)]
  Ballades, 3
    Senart
  Berceuse de Noël
    Ricard
  Tableaux Espagnols, Nos. 1-3
    Ricard
  Tenerezza
    Ricard
DEPLAN
  Intrada; with Tambourine, Minuet by
    Rameau
    MZK
DÉRÉ, JEAN (1886-   )
  Chant Héroique
    Senart
(DERI, OTTO)
  Solos for the Cello Player
    GS for contents see title
DETHERIDGE, JOSEPH (1898-   )
  Impromptu in F
    Bosw
DEVEUX
  Andantino
    Gaudet
DEVREESE, [FREDERIC (1929-   )]
  Complaint
    Brogneaux
DIAMOND, DAVID (1915-   )
  Sonata
    Pr
DI BIASE, EDOARDO
  Reverie
    CF B2979
DIETERICH
  Gigue Jocose
    Ru
  Minuet and Trio
    Ru

DIETERICH (cont.)
Spinning Song
Ru
Valse Scherzo
Ru
DILLON, [HENRI (1912-   )]
Fantaisie
Haml
D'INDY, see Indy, d'
DINICU
Hora Staccato
(Heifetz) CF B2288
DITTERSDORF
German Dance, see Purcell: Aria
DOBOS, K.
Sonata
Kul
DOBROKHOTOV
Bagpipes, Cuckoo, see Melnikov:
Russian Song
DOHNÁNYI, ERNST VON (1877-1960)
Konzertstück in D, Op. 12, orig for vcl
and orch
DOB
Int
Ruralia Hungarica, Op. 32d
Kul
Sonata in B flat, Op. 8
Int
SCH
DONIZETTI, GAETANO (1797-1848)
Sextet, from Lucia di Lammermoor
(Saenger-Buechner) CF B2943
DOPPELBAUER, JOSEF FRIEDRICH
(1918-   )
Sonata No. 1
DOB
DORCINE, R.
Un Soir sur l'Estérel
Sal
DORET, [GUSTAVE (1866-1943)]
Air
RL
DRDLA, FRANZ (1868-1944)
Souvenir, orig for vln and pno
CF B2910
DRESDEN, SEM (1881-1957)
Sonate
Senart
DRIESSLER, JOHANNES (1921-   )
Fantasie, Op. 24, No. 2
Baer 2696
Kleine Stücke, 3
Baer 2534
Sonate
Baer 3968
DRIGO, RICHARD (1846-1930)
Serenade, from Les Millions d'Arlequin
(Wolff-Israel-Buechner) CF B1431
ZM (Pet No. ZM210)
DUBOIS, P.M.
Concerto
Leduc
DUCASSE, see Roger-Ducasse
DUKE, JOHN (1899-   )
Melody in E flat
EV
DUKELSKY, VLADIMIR (1903-   )
Concerto
CF 03305
DUMAS, [LOUIS (1877-1952)]
Berceuse
Senart
Rapsodie
Deiss

DUNHILL, THOMAS F. (1877-1946)
Intermezzo
JWL (Mil No. W1504)
Pieces, 2
STB
DUPONT, JACQUES (1910-   )
Navarrianas, orig for vcl and orch
Sal
DUPORT, JEAN-LOUIS (1749-1819)
Sonate No. 1
(Feuillard) Delrieu
Sonate No. 2
(Feuillard) Delrieu
DUPORT, JEAN PIERRE (1741-1818)
Romance
Jack Spratt
Sonate en La mineur
(Bazelaire) Senart 5353
DUPORT, J.P. & J.L.
Melodies, 2
(Benoy-Burrowes) Oxf
DUPUIS, [SYLVAIN (1856-1931)]
Invocation
Sal
DUPUITS, JEAN-BAPTISTE
Sonata in re
(Salmon) Ric R391
DUQUESNE, DE
Elegie
Brogneaux
DVARIONAS, [BALIS (1904-   )]
Theme and Variations
MZK
DVORAK, ANTONIN (1841-1904)
Concerto in A
(Raphael) BRH
Concerto in b, Op. 104
(Kletzki) BRH
(Mainardi-Degan) SCH
(Rose) Int
(Willeke) GS L1539
Artia
SIM
Indian Lament
(Cassado) Int
Lento, from String Quartet, Op. 96,
"American"
(Stutschewsky) Int
Restful Woods, Op. 68, No. 5
SIM
Romantic Piece, Op. 75, No. 4, orig for
vln and pno
(Fournier) Int
Rondo, Op. 94, orig for vcl and orch
(Rose) Int
Artia
SIM
Slavonic Dance No. 2 in e, Op. 72, orig for
orch
Int
Slavonic Dance No. 12, Op. 72, orig for
orch
(Bernstein) AMP
Songs my mother taught me, orig for
voice and pno
(Sandby) BMC
DYCK, V.
Pièces faciles, 10
Sal   2V
DYSON, GEORGE (1883-   )
Prelude, Fantasy and Chaconne, orig for
vcl and orch
Nov

DZEGELENEK, A.
  Concerto No. 2, Op. 24
    MZK
  see also Borisyak & Dzgelenek
EARNSHAW, ALFRED H
  Canzonetta, from 8 Recreations
    JWL (Mil No. W1522)
  Consolation, from Progressive Violoncellist
    JWL (Mil No. W1505-3)
  Contentment, from Progressive Violoncellist
    JWL (Mil No. W1505-6)
  Country Dance, from Progressive
      Violoncellist
    JWL (Mil No. W1505-5)
  Gavotte, from Progressive Violoncellist
    JWL (Mil No. W1505-1)
  Mazurka, from 8 Recreations
    JWL (Mil No. W1527)
  Melody, from Progressive Violoncellist
    JWL (Mil No. W1505-2)
  Menuet, from Progressive Violoncellist
    JWL (Mil No. W1505-7)
  Reverie, from 8 Recreations
    JWL (Mil No. W1529)
  Romance, from 8 Recreations
    JWL (Mil No. W1526)
  Rustic Song, from 8 Recreations
    JWL (Mil No. W1524)
  Serenade, from 8 Recreations
    JWL (Mil No. W1528)
  Swing Song, from 8 Recreations
    JWL (Mil No. W1525)
  Tarantelle, from Progressive Violoncellist
    JWL (Mil No. W1505-4)
  Valse, from 8 Recreations
    JWL (Mil No. W1523)
EASY CLASSICAL ALBUM
  (Moffat) SCH
    12 pieces by Handel, Weber, Schubert,
    Gluck, and others
EASY CLASSICAL PIECES
  (Such) SCH
    12 pieces by Mozart, Handel, Purcell,
    Schubert, Spohr, Telemann and others
EASY CLASSICS FOR THE CELLO
  (Forbes) Oxf 21.021
    Bach: Choral
    Beethoven: Ecossaise
    Brahms: Blacksmith, Op. 19, No. 4
    Couperin: A Trifle
    Handel: Chaconne in F
    Handel: March, from Flavius
    Haydn: Innocence, Op. 53, No. 1
    Mozart-Flies: Wiegenlied
    Purcell: Minuet in G
    Schubert: Serenade
    Schumann: A Distant Land, from
      Scenes of Childhood
    Schumann: Merry Peasant,
      Op. 68, No. 10
    Tchaikovsky: An Old French Song,
      Op. 39, No. 16
EASY PIECES, 5
  (Sapozhnikov) MZK
EASY PIECES, 5
  MZK
    Pieces by Miaskovsky, Alexandrov,
    Goedicke, Kabalevsky
EASY PIECES, 5
  MZK
    Pieces by Glinka, Cui, Kalinnikov,
    Rimsky-Korsakov
EASY PIECES FOR BEGINNERS
  (Utkin) MZK   2V

EASY VIOLONCELLO CLASSICS
  (Schroeder) BMC   2V
    Vol 1
      Gluck: Andante
      Grieg: Folk-Song
      Händel: Aria
      Mozart: Aria from Don Giovanni
      Mozart: Aria from Le Nozze di
        Figaro
      Reber: Berceuse
    Vol 2
      Grieg: Album-leaf
      Händel: Bourrée
      Meyerbeer: Aria from Les Huguenots
      Mozart: Canzona from Le Nozze di
        Figaro
      Tschaikowsky: Aria from Jeanne
        d'Arc
      Weber: Cavatina from Der
        Freischütz
ECCLES, HENRY (c.1652-c.1742)
  Prelude and Courante, from Sonata in g
    (Cahnbley) SCH
  Sonata in g
    (Cahnbley) SCH
    (Moffat) Int
    (Moffat) SIM
    (Salmon) Ric R92
  Sonata in g
    (Ticciati) Leng (Mil No. L3017)
  Sonata
    MZK
EGGEN, ARNE (1881-1955)
  Melodi fra Liti Kersti
    Norsk
EHRENBERG, [CARL (1878-   )]
  Concerto, Op. 46
    SIM
EIGES, K.
  Lullaby
    MZK
ELGAR, EDWARD (1857-1934)
  Canto Popolare
    Nov
  Carissima
    EKN
  Concerto in e, Op. 85
    Nov
  Pomp and Circumstance. Theme, orig for
      orch
    (Akers) CF
  Romance, Op. 62
    Nov
  Rosemary
    EKN
  Salut d'Amour, orig for orch
    (Buechner) CF B2950
    (Trinkaus) Fill
  Serenade, from Wand of Youth, Suite I
    Nov
EMBORG, JENS LAURSØN (1876-   )
  Nocturne, Op. 1
    WH
EMMANUEL, MAURICE (1862-1938)
  Sonate
    Senart
ENESCO, [GEORGES (1881-1955)]
  Sonate No. 2
    Sal
ENGEL, LEHMAN (1910-   )
  Sonata
    SPAM
ESIPOFF, S.
  see Graded Teaching Pieces

EVETT, ROBERT (1922-   )
　Sonata, for vcl and cembalo
　　CFE
EXAUDET, [JOSEPH]
　Minuet. Danse des Auvergnats
　　(Withers) SCH
FALLA, MANUEL DE (1876-1946)
　Danse de la Frayeur, from El Amor Brujo
　　(Piatigorsky) Ches
　Danse du meunier, from El Sombero de
　　Tres Picos
　　(Markovitz) Ches
　Danse Rituelle de Feu, from El Amor
　　Brujo
　　(Piatigorsky) Ches
　Spanish Dance No. 1, from La Vie Brève
　　(Gendron) ESC
　Suite Populaire Espagnole, orig Seven
　　Spanish Songs
　　(Maréchal) Ches
　　(Maréchal) ESC
FANTA, R.
　Concertante Sonata in A, Op. 10
　　DOB
FANTINI, ADOLFO
　Spinning Song
　　ZA 3656
FARKAS, FERENC (1905-   )
　Arioso
　　Kul
FASANO, RENATO (1902-   )
　Canti, 2
　　Ric 124852
　Il Signor Bonaventura, orig for vcl and orch
　　Ric 123888
　Sonatina in D
　　SZ
FASCH, JOHANN FRIEDRICH (1688-1758)
　Sonata
　　(Klitz-Seeber) MM
FASCH, [JOHANN FRIEDRICH]
　Sonata in C
　　Pet 5893   2nd vcl ad lib
FAUCONIER, B.C.
　Rêverie, Op. 114, No. 1
　　(Skalmer) CF B2944
FAURÉ, GABRIEL (1845-1924)
　Après un rêve, orig for voice and pno
　　(Casals) Int
　　Haml
　Berceuse, orig for vln and pno
　　GS
　Elégie, Op. 24
　　(Schroeder) BMC
　　Haml
　　Int
　Fileuse, Op. 80, No. 2, orig for orch
　　(Rose) Int
　Lamento[57]
　　(Schroeder) BMC
　　Int
　Nocturne No. 4, Op. 36, orig for pno
　　(Cassado) Int
　Papillon
　　Int
　Sicilienne, Op. 78
　　Haml
　　Int
　Sonata No. 1, Op. 109
　　Dur
　Sonata No. 2, Op. 117
　　Dur

---

[57] Probably Chanson du Pêcheur, originally for voice and piano.

FELDMAN, G.
　Elegy
　　MZK
　Serenade
　　MZK
FELDMAN, MORTON (1926-   )
　Durations II
　　Pet 6902
FERGUSON, HOWARD (1908-   )
　Irish Folktunes, 5
　　Oxf 21.300
FERRARI-TRECATE, LUIGI (1884-   )
　Il Canto dell'esule
　　Ric 123920
FERROUD, PIERRE-OCTAVE (1900-1936)
　Sonate en la
　　Dur
FESCH, WILLEM DE (1687-1761)
　Arietta, from Sonata in d
　　(Moffat-Whitehouse) SCH
　Sonatas, 6, Op. 8
　　(Schultz) Pet 4989   2nd vcl ad lib
　Sonata in d, Op. 8, No. 3
　　(Ruf) WM (Pet No. WM28)   2nd vcl ad lib
　Sonata in D, Op. 13, No. 1
　　(Koch-Weigart) SCH
　Sonata in d, Op. 13, No. 4
　　(Koch-Weigart) SCH
　　(Ruf) Baer 3962
　Sonata in D, Op. 13, No. 5
　　(Koch-Weigart) SCH
　Sonata in a, Op. 13, No. 6
　　(Koch-Weigart) SCH
　Sonata in d
　　(Moffat-Whitehouse-Rapp) SCH
　　(Salmon) Ric R88
　Sonata in F
　　(Moffat) SIM
　Sonata in G
　　(Salmon) Ric R85
(FEUILLARD, L.R.)
　Jeune Violoncelliste, Le
　　Delrieu 8V for contents see title
FÉVRIER, [HENRI (1875-1957)]
　Sonate
　　HL
FIBICH, ZDENKO (1850-1900)
　Poem, orig for pno
　　Artia
FIÉVET, C.
　Calme du Soir
　　Gaudet
FINE, VIVIAN (1913-   )
　Lyric Piece
　　CFE
FINNEY, ROSS LEE (1906-   )
　Sonata No. 2 in C
　　Val
FINZI, GERALD (1901-1956)
　Concerto
　　BH
FIOCCO, JOSEPH HEKTOR (1703-1741)
　Concerto in G
　　(Bazelaire) SF (Pet No. SCH20)
FIORE
　Sonata in E
　　(Ghedini) ZA910
FISCHER, IRWIN
　Lament
　　CFE
FITELBERG, [JERZY (1903-1951)]
　Concerto
　　UE 10395
FITZENHAGEN, W.
　see Graded Teaching Pieces

FLACKTON, [WILLIAM (1709-1798)]
Sonata No. 1 in C
(Sabatini) DOB
Sonata No. 2 in B flat
(Sabatini) DOB
Sonata No. 3 in F
(Sabatini) DOB
FLETCHER, see Rolland & Fletcher
FLOTOW, FRIEDRICH VON (1812-1883)
Last Rose of Summer, from Martha
(Buechner) CF B2927
FOGGY DEW
(Aller) Ru
FOLK MELODIES, BK. I
(Utkin) MZK
FOLK SONGS, 4
(Sapozhnikov) MZK
FOLK SONGS AND MELODIES, 10, BK. I
(Sapozhnikov) MZK
(FORBES, WATSON)
Easy Classics for the Cello
Oxf 21.021 for contents see title
FORDELL, J.
To the Mystic Rose
STB
FORINO, FERDINANDO
Canto religioso
Santis 313
FORTNER, WOLFGANG (1907-   )
Concerto
SCH
Sonata
SCH
FOSS, LUKAS (1922-   )
Capriccio
(Piatigorsky) GS
FOSTER, STEPHEN (1826-1864)
Old Black Joe
(Smith-Holmes) CF
FRANCAIX, JEAN (1912-   )
Berceuse
(Gendron) SCH
Fantasy, orig for vcl and orch
SCH
Mouvement perpétuel
(Gendron) SCH
Nocturne
(Gendron) SCH
Rondino-Staccato
(Gendron) SCH
Serenade
(Gendron) SCH
FRANCHOMME, [AUGUSTE-JOSEPH
(1808-1884)]
Concerto No. 1
HL
FRANCK, CÉSAR (1822-1890)
Panis Angelicus, arr for vcl and harp
or pno
BMC
Sonata in A, orig for vln and pno
(Delsart-Rose) Int
FRANCMESNIL, ROGER DE (1884-   )
Berceuse
Mathot
FRANCO, JOHAN (1908-   )
Fantasy, orig for vcl and orch
CFE
FRANCOEUR, FRANCOIS (1698-1787)
Gavotte in E
Pet 4216
Sonata in A, orig for vln and clavier
(Salmon) Ric R712
Sonata in E
(Trowell) SCH

FRANK
Concertino
Mil
FRANKEL, BENJAMIN (1906-   )
Elegie Juive
Aug
Inventions
Ches
Poems, 3, Op. 23
Aug
FRASER, [NORMAN (1904-   )]
En el tiempo de Chicha
Ches
FREDERICKSON, T.
Allegro
Pr
FRESCOBALDI, GIROLAMO (1583-1643)
Arietta
(Ronchini) ESC
Toccata
(Cassado) UE 8282
FRICKER, PETER RACINE (1920-   )
Sonata, Op. 28
SCH
FRIML, RUDOLF (1879-   )
Adieu
(Borch) BMC
Chanson, Mélodie
(Van Vliet) GS
FRISKIN, [JAMES (1886-   )]
Impromptu
STB
Romance
STB
Scherzo
STB
FROM FOUR CENTURIES
(Schulz) BRH
16 pieces by composers from Corelli to
Hindemith
FROMONT-DELUNE, J.
Ballade, La, from 6 Easy Pieces
ESC
Berceuse, La, from 6 Easy Pieces
ESC
Chasse, La, from 6 Easy Pieces
ESC
Fileuse, La, from 6 Easy Pieces
ESC
Ronde, La, from 6 Easy Pieces
ESC
Valse, La, from 6 Easy Pieces
ESC
FRUMERIE, GUNNAR DE (1908-   )
Elegisk Svit
Gehrmans
FUGA, SANDRO (1906-   )
Concerto
Ric 129183
FULEIHAN, ANIS (1900-   )
Epilogue
SMP
Interlude
SMP
Prologue
SMP
Rhapsody, orig for vcl and orch
CF 03479
FUN FOR FIDDLE FINGERS
(Bornoff-Cooper) Gordon V. Thompson
GABRIELI, DOMENICO (c.1650-1690)
Sonata in G
(Landshoff) SCH
Sonata in G
ZA4400

GABRIELI, DOMENICO (cont.)
Sonata No. 2 in A
(Landshoff) SCH
GAGNEBIN, HENRI (1886-   )
Sonate en la
Senart
GAILLARD, MARIUS FRANCOIS (1900-   )
Minutes du Monde
CH (Pet No. C255)
GALAJIKIAN, FLORENCE G. (1900-   )
Hill Billy's Dance
CF B2509
Lonely Dancer Waltzes
CF B2508
GALEOTTI, STEFANO (18th century)
Sonata No. 2 in G
(Rogister) ESC
GALINDO, BLAS (1910-   )
Sonata
EMM
GALLIARD, JOHANN ERNST (1687-1749)
Sonatas, 6
(Marx & Weiss-Mann) MM   2V
Sonata in a
(Moffat-Whitehouse) SIM
Sonata in e
(Salmon) Ric R393
Sonata in e
SCH
Sonata in G
(Ruf) Baer 3964
Sonata in G
(Salmon) Ric R392
GALLON, NOËL (1891-   )
Dolor
Billaudot
GALUPPI, BALDASSARE (1706-1785)
Sonata in D
(Schroeder) Aug 5531
GALUPPI, [BALDASSARE]
Aria amorosa
(Tertis) Aug
GARDONYI, Z.
Easy Rhapsodies, 2
Kul
GARRATT, PERCIVAL (1877-1953)
Duo-Caprice on Auber's Tarentelle,
from Masaniello
Paterson 2541
GARTENLAUB, [ODETTE (1922-   )]
Composition
Transatlantiques
GARTH, JOHN (1722-1810)
Concerto No. 2 in B flat
Hin (Pet No. H389G)
GASPARINO, [QUIRINO (? -1778)]
Sonata in d
(Schroeder) Aug 5515
GASSMAN, R.
Sonata
AMP
GEMINIANI, FRANCESCO (1687-1762)
Sonata in d, Op. 5, No. 2
(Merrick-James) SCH
Sonata in a, Op. 5, No. 6
(Merrick-James) SCH
GENISHTA, I.[58]
Sonata, Op. 7
MZK
GENZMER, HARALD (1909-   )
Concerto
SCH

[58] This may be the composer listed in Cobbett as Joseph
Genischta, 1810-c.1860.

Sonata No. 1
SCH
GERMAN, [EDWARD (1862-1936)]
Shepherd's Dance
(Bernstein) AMP
GERSCHEFSKI, EDWIN (1909-   )
King Lear Suite
CFE
Nocturne
CFE
GHEDINI, GIORGIO FEDERICO (1892-   )
Vocalizzo da concerto
Curci
GIARDINI, FELICE (1716-1795)
Rondo
ZA 3192
GIBBS, CECIL ARMSTRONG (1889-   )
Laughing Tune, Op. 121, No. 3, from
3 Pieces
Aug
Nocturne, Op. 121, No. 2, from 3 Pieces
Aug
She loves me not, Op. 121, No. 1, from
3 Pieces
Aug
Sonata in E
Oxf 21.301
GIDEON, MIRIAM (1906-   )
Fantasy on a Javanese Motive
CFE
Sonata
CFE
GIESEKING, WALTER (1895-1956)
Konzert-Sonatine
Oertel
GILIS, A.
Rêverie, Op. 50, No. 1
CF B2964
GILLESPIE
Pieces in Easy Style, 5
Leng (Mil No. L3001)
GILLET, ERNEST (1856-1940)
Passe-pied
CF B2947
GILLIS, [DON (1912-   )
From an Evening in Autumn
Mil
GILSON, [PAUL (1865-1942)]
Suite
Cranz
GINASTERA, ALBERTO (1916-   )
Pampeana No. 2
Barry
GINASTERA, [ALBERTO]
Triste
(Fournier) Ric BA10545
GIORDANI
Canzonetta
(Aller) Ru
GIRNATIS, WALTER (1894-   )
Sonatina
Sik 391
GLASS, LOUIS (1864-1936)
Frühlingslied, Op. 31, orig for vcl and orch
WH 891
GLAZUNOV, ALEXANDER (1865-1936)
Chant du Ménestrel, Op. 71, orig for vcl and
orch
Belaieff
Int
Elegie, Op. 17, "Une pensée à Liszt"
Belaieff
MZK

GLAZUNOV, ALEXANDER (cont.)
Melodie, Op. 20, No. 1, orig for vcl and orch
  Belaieff
Melodie Arabe
  Int
  MZK
Pieces, 2, Op. 71
  MZK
Romance Without Words
  MZK
Serenade Espagnole, Op. 20, No. 2, orig
    for vcl and orch
  (Rose) Int
  Belaieff
  CF B2843
GLIÈRE, REINHOLD M. (1875-1956)
Album Leaves, 6, Op. 51
  MZK
Ballade, Op. 4
  Hof
Concerto
  MZK
Rondo, see Rebikov: Song without words
Waltzes, 2: Op. 31, No. 6 and Op. 45
  MZK
Waltz, Op. 45
  MZK
GLINKA, MIKHAIL (1804-1857)
Nocturne, "Parting"
  MZK
Polka; Spanish Song
  MZK
Romance Melody
  Jack Spratt
Sentiment, Simplicity; with Tear by
    Mussorgsky
  MZK
GLINKA & KOCHUROV
Etudes, 5
  MZK
GNESSIN, MIKHAIL F. (1883-1957)
Pieces, 3, Op. 51
  MZK
Theme and Variations, Op. 67
  MZK
GODARD, BENJAMIN (1849-1895)
Berceuse, from Jocelyn
  (Moses-Buechner) CF B2919
  (Trinkaus) Fill
Sonate en ré mineur, Op. 104
  Dur
Sur le lac, Op. 36, No. 1
  CF B2952
GODOWSKY, LEOPOLD (1870-1938)
Elégie, from Impressions
  (Kindler) CF B1442
Orientale, from Impressions
  (Kindler) CF B1444
Valse Macabre
  (Kindler) CF B1445
GOEB, ROGER (1914-   )
Divertimento
  CFE
GOEDICKE, ALEXANDER (1877-1957)
Miniatures, 2, Op. 8
  MZK
Miniature; Waltz
  MZK
Pieces, 3, Op. 93
  MZK
Piece in Folk Style; Scherzo; Improvisation
  MZK
Sonata, Op. 88
  MZK

GOENS, DANIEL VAN
Concerto, Op. 7
  Haml
Scherzo, Op. 12, No. 2
  CF B2502
  GS
Tarentelle, Op. 24
  RL
Valse de Concert, Op. 23
  RL
GOEYENS, [FERNANDO (1892-   )]
Nocturne, Prelude and Polonaise
  Cranz
Song of Love
  Metr
GOLD, ERNEST (1921-   )
Exodus, theme
  (Noeltner) Chap
GOLDMARK, RUBIN (1872-1936)
Adon-Olam
  (Willeke) CF B1977
GOLESTAN, STAN (1872-1956)
Concerto moldave
  Dur   reduction by composer
GOLTERMANN, GEORG (1824-1898)
Alla Mazurka, Op. 113, No. 2, from
    6 Characteristic Pieces
  Aug
Andante, from Concerto in a, Op. 14
  (Roth-Buechner) CF B2931
Berceuse, Op. 113, No. 4, from 6
    Characteristic Pieces
  Aug
Cantilena
  Kjos S-5211
Canzone, Op. 113, No. 5, from 6 Charac-
    teristic Pieces
  Aug
Concerto No. 1 in a, Op. 14
  (Klengel) BRH
  (Rose) Int
  (Schulz) CF 03697
  Pet 4314
Concerto No. 2 in d, Op. 30
  (Hindemith) SCH
  (Willeke) CF 03687
Concerto No. 3 in b, Op. 51
  (Schulz) CF 03438
Concerto No. 4 in G, Op. 65
  (Rose) Int
  (Schulz) CF 04124
  (Van Vliet) GS L1412
  SCH
Concerto No. 5 in d, Op. 76
  (Schulz) CF 03375
  Pet 4328 "Concert Piece"
Duo, Grand, Op. 15
  (Such) Aug 7680a
Étude-Caprice, Op. 54, No. 4
  (Buechner) CF B2818
Étude-Caprice; Capriccio
  MZK
Foi, La, Op. 95, No. 1
  (Buechner) CF B2632
Gavotte, Op. 113, No. 3, from 6 Charac-
    teristic Pieces
  Aug
Gondoliera, Op. 113, No. 1, from 6
    Characteristic Pieces
  Aug
Grand Duo, see Duo
Intermezzo, Op. 113, No. 6, from 6
    Characteristic Pieces
  Aug

GOLTERMANN, GEORG (cont.)
Modern Suite, Op. 122
Aug 7691
Morceaux de Salon, 4, Op. 35
(Tabb) Aug 7695
Pieces, 2, Op. 13
Pet 1996
Sonatina No. 1 in A, Op. 36
(Such) Aug 7693
Tone-Pictures, 6, Op. 118
Aug 7690
Tone-Pictures, 6, Op. 129
Aug 7684
see also Graded Teaching Pieces
(GOLTERMANN)
Masters for the Young
Pet 2810-11   2V   for contents see title
GOLZ, W.
Romanza
CP
GOOSSENS, EUGÈNE (1893-1962)
Rhapsody, Op. 13
Ches
GORINI, GINO (1914-   )
Sonata
SZ
GOSSEC, FRANCOIS-JOSEPH (1734-1829)
Gavotte
(Skalmer) CF B2954
GOUNOD, CHARLES (1818-1893)
Ave Maria. Meditation on the first prelude
of J.S. Bach
(Buechner) CF
SCH
GRADED TEACHING PIECES, FIRST SERIES
Aug   all published separately
Grade 1: 1st position
1. Fitzenhagen, W: Russian Song
without words, Op. 22, No. 2
2. Fitzenhagen, W: Ave Maria,
Op. 38, No. 1
3. Champ, S: Cavatina
4. Champ, S: Serenade
5. Lebell, L: Meditation, Op. 10, No. 1
6. Goltermann, G: Contentment,
Op. 118, No. 5
7. Fitzenhagen, W; Mazurka,
Op. 38, No. 3
8. Champ, S: Spring Song
9. Lebell, L: Gavotte gracieuse,
Op. 10, No. 2
10. Squire, W.H: Le Plaisir,
Op. 16, No. 3
Grade 2
11. Squire, W.H: Joyeuse,
Op. 16, No. 2
12. Squire, W.H; Le Bonheur,
Op. 16, No. 4
13. Lebell, L: Chant, Op. 12, No. 1
14. Goltermann, G: Mourning,
Op. 118, No. 2
15. Nölck, A: Berceuse, Op. 92
16. Lebell, L: Menuet, Op. 10, No. 3
17. Squire, W.H: Romance, Op. 5, No. 1
18. Goltermann, G: Religioso,
Op. 129, No. 1
19. Goltermann, G: Merry Play,
Op. 129, No. 2
20. Squire, W.H: Gondoliera,
Op. 20, No. 2
Grade 3
21. Bach-Schroeder: Praeludium
22. Squire, W.H: Danse Rustique,
Op. 20, No. 5
23. Tchaikovsky: Chanson triste

24. Schumann-Samuel: Träumerei,
Op. 15, No. 7
25. Bridge, F: Meditation
26. Corelli: Giga
27. Rameau: Choeur de Castor et
Pollux
28. Zsolt, N: Elegie
29. Squire, W.H: Dreaming, Op. 7
30. Marcello: Sonata in e, 1st movement
GRADED TEACHING PIECES, SECOND
SERIES
Aug   all published separately
Grade 1
31. Fitzenhagen, W: Cavatine,
Op. 39, No. 1
32. Fitzenhagen, W: Tarantelle,
Op. 39, No. 3
33. Champ, S: Elegy
34. Champ, S: Hush song
35. Champ, S: Morning song
36. Lebell, L: Soirée de Vienne,
Op. 28, No. 4
37. Squire, W.H: Triste, Op. 16, No. 1
38. Fitzenhagen, W: Valse,
Op. 22, No. 3
39. Goltermann, G: Resignation,
Op. 118, No. 6
40. Lebell, L: Humoresque,
Op. 28, No. 3
Grade 2: pieces with extensions and
using 4 positions
41. Squire, W.H: Chant d'amour,
Op. 20, No. 1
42. Squire, W.H: L'Innocence,
Op. 16, No. 5
43. Goltermann, G: Evening song,
Op. 118, No. 1
44. Nölck, A: Danse de voile
45. Nölck, A: Berceuse
46. Esipoff, S: Berceuse d'enfant
47. Squire, W.H: Gavotte, Op. 5, No. 4
48. Goltermann, G: Dream,
Op. 129, No. 3
49. Lebell, L: Capriccio, Op. 28, No. 1
50. Squire, W.H: Minuet, Op. 19, No. 3
Grade 3: moderate difficulty, without
use of thumb position
51. Löw, J: Album-leaf
52. Squire, W.H: Humoresque, Op. 26
53. Pergolese, G: Tre giorni
54. Goltermann, G: Cantilena
55. Schumann, R: Stück im Volkston
56. Bach, J.S: Largo
57. Bridge, F: Spring song
58. Schubert, F: Wiegenlied
59. Brahms, J: Lied. Wie bist du
meine Königin
60. Nolck, A: Gavotte
GRAINGER, PERCY (1882-1961)
Sussex mummer's Christmas carol
GS
GRAINGER, [PERCY]
Norwegian Polka
(Withers) SCH
GRANADOS, ENRIQUE (1867-1916)
Intermezzo from Goyescas
(Cassadó) GS
Madrigal in a
(Rose) Int
Orientale[59]
(Piatigorsky) Int

---

[59] Probably from 12 Spanish Dances, originally for piano.

GRANADOS, ENRIQUE (cont.)
Playera, Op. 5, No. 5, from 12 Spanish
    Dances, orig for pno
    (Munzer) CF B2143
Tonadillas, 2[59]
    (Fournier) Int
GRANADOS, VICTOR
Madrigal Gallego
    MK
GRANT, J.
Nocturne Espagnol
    Senart
GRAZIOLI, GIOVANNI BATTISTA
    (c.1750-c.1820)
Sonata in F
    (Schroeder) SCH
    (Schroeder) Aug 5512; with Sonata in e
    by Marcello
Sonata in G
    (Salmon) Ric R395
GREENBERG, L.
Poem
    MZK
GREENE, EDWIN
Sing Me to Sleep
    (Hollas) BMC
GRETCHANINOV, ALEXANDER T. (1864-1956)
Early Morn, Op. 126b
    SCH
Sonata, Op. 113
    SCH
GRETRY, ANDRÉ E.M. (1741-1813)
Suite Rococo[60]
    (Bazelaire) SF (Pet No. SCH22)
GRIEG, EDVARD (1843-1907)
Air, from Holberg Suite, orig for orch
    (Forbes) Oxf 21.022
Berceuse, Op. 38, No. 1, orig for pno
    (Stutschewsky) Pet 4224
Butterfly, Op. 43, No. 1, orig for pno
    (Friedlander) CL
Chanson d'Amour
    (Hegner) CF B1449
Elegiac Melodies, Op. 34, orig for orch
    Pet 3304
Peer Gynt Suite No. 1, Op. 46, orig for orch
    (Goltermann) Pet 2830
Peer Gynt Suite No. 2, Op. 55, orig for orch
    (Sitt) Pet 3517b
Sonata in a, Op. 36
    (Rose) Int
    Pet 2157
To Spring, Op. 43, No. 6, orig for pno
    (Skalmer) CF B2958
GRONOWETTER, FREDA (1918-   )
In a Sacred Mood
    MK
GROVLEZ, M.
Sonate
    Senart
GRUENBERG, LOUIS (1884-1964)
Poème, Op. 19
    UE 7775
GUASTAVINO, [CARLOS (1914-   )]
Rosa y el Sauce, La
    Ric BA11115
GUERINI
Allegro con brio
    (Salmon) Ric R106
GUERRINI, [GUIDO (1890-   )]
Songs of the Ukraine, 3
    SZ

GURILEV, A.
Nocturne
    MZK
Nocturne; with Canzona by Khandoshkin and
    Gavotte by Agapiev
    MZK
HADLEY, HENRY (1871-1937)
Air Plaintif, No. 3 of Suite Ancienne,
    Op. 101
    CF B2005
Danse Ancienne, Op. 92, No. 13
    CF B1848
Gigue, No. 4 of Suite Ancienne, Op. 101
    CF B2006
October Twilight
    CF B1831
HAGEMAN, RICHARD (1882-   )
Recitative and Romance
    GS
HAHN, REYNALDO (1875-1947)
Airs Irlandais
    Heugel
Concerto inachevé, orig for vcl and orch
    Senart
HALFFTER, ERNESTO (1905-   )
Habañera
    (Gendron) ESC
Pregón
    (Gendron) ESC
Sérénade à Dulcinée
    (Gendron) ESC
HALFFTER, RODOLFO (1900-   )
Sonata
    EMM
HALL, RICHARD (1903-   )
Five Epigrams
    Hin (Pet No. H275)
HAMANN, ERICH (1898-   )
Sonata, Op. 22
    DOB
Suite, Op. 32
    DOB
HAMILTON, [IAIN (1922-   )]
Sonata
    SCH
HAMMER
Minuet
    (Stutschewsky) Pet 4218
HANDEL, GEORG FRIEDRICH (1685-1759)
Adagio and Allegretto in e, after violin
    sonata in g
    (Stutschewsky) Pet 4215
Adagio and Allegro, from Sonata in G,
    originally for ob and Bc
    (Moffat) SCH
Adagio and Pastorale, from Sonata No. 3
    in A, orig for vln and Bc
    (Withers) SCH
Arioso in F
    (Franke) SCH
Bourrée
    (Squire) BMC
Concerto in b, orig for vla and orch
    (Casadesus) ESC
Concerto in g, orig for ob and orch
    (Grümmer) UE 11172
Concerto in g
    (Squire) SCH
Larghetto
    (Schroeder) BMC
Largo, from Xerxes
    (Palaschko) SCH
    (Tobani-Buechner) CF B2790
Sarabande
    (Burmester-Moffat) SCH

---

[59]
[60] Also available for cello and string orchestra.

HANDEL, GEORG FRIEDRICH (cont.)
Sonata No. 3 in B flat[61]
(Lindner) BRH
(Lindner) Int
Sonata in C, orig for gamba and cembalo
(Jensen) Int
Pet 4903
Sonata in c
(Moffat) SCH
Sonata No. 4 in D, orig for vln and Bc
(D'Ambrosio) Ric ER2121
Sonata No. 2 in d
(Lindner) BRH
(Lindner) Int
Sonata in F
(Cahnbley) Int
Sonata No. 3 in F, orig for vln and Bc
Pet 3494
Sonata No. 1 in g
(Lindner) BRH
(Lindner) Int
Sonata in g
(Slatter) SCH
Variations on a theme of, see Beethoven
HANSEN, J.
Largo
Senart
HARRISON, JULIUS (1885-   )
Sonnet
BMC
HARRISON, PAMELA (1915-   )
Idle Dan, or Nothing to do
JWL (Mil No. W1533)
Pieces, 2
JWL (Mil No. W1534)
Sonnet
Chap-L
HARSÁNYI, TIBOR (1898-1954)
Aria, Cadence et Rondo
Deiss
Rhapsody
ESC
Sonata
ESC
HARTMANN, THOMAS DE (1885-1956)
Concerto, Op. 57
Belaieff
Concerto d'apres une cantate de Bach,
Op. 73
Belaieff
Sonata, Op. 63
Belaieff
HARTY, [HAMILTON (1879-1941)]
Romance and Scherzo, Op. 8
Aug 5553
Wistful Song
(Withers) SCH
HASSLER, J.
Stately Dance
Bel
HAUBIEL, CHARLES (1892-   )
A.D. 1865
CP
Lullaby
CP
Madonna
CP
Shadows
CP

Sonata in c
CP
HAUSER, MISKA (1822-1887)
Berceuse
(Stransky-Buechner) CF B2966
HAYDN, JOSEPH (1732-1809)
Adagio, from Concerto in D
(Withers) SCH
Andante, from Concerto
Jack Spratt
Concerto No. 1 in D, Op. 101[62]
(Cros Saint Ange) Senart 5153
(Gendron) SCH
(Gevaert) BRH
(Gevaert-Rose) Int   with cadenzas by
L. Rose
(Klengel) Pet 3049   with cadenzas
(Schulz) SCH
(Schulz-Moehn) SCH
(Stutschewsky) GS L1740
MZK
cadenzas published separately, see
under vcl unacc: Jullien, Schmidt,
Silwedel
Concerto No. 2 in D
(Grützmacher) BRH
(Trowell) Aug
Concerto in C, reconstructed by
Popper from a sketch
BH
RE (Pet No. RE6)
Concerto No. 3
cadenzas published separately, see
under vcl unacc: Pekker
Divertimento
(Piatigorsky) EV
Larghetto, from Sonata in D for vln
and pno
(Spalding) CF B2494
Minuet, from Sonata in C
(Piatti) Int
Minuet, see Matteson: Aria
Sonata in C, orig for vln and pno
(Piatti) Int
HECKER, BERTA JOSEPHINE
Spanish Dance
CF B2754
(HEGNER)
Cellist's First Solo Repertoire
CF 0109   for contents see title
Recreations for Young 'Cellists
CF 0263-265   3V   for contents see title
HELFER, WALTER (1896-   )
Soliloquy
CF B2650
HELM, [EVERETT (1913-   )]
Isomers, 7 pieces
BB
HENGARTNER
Notturno
Ric SY490
HENKEMANS, HANS (1913-   )
Sonata
DN (Pet No. D227)
HENZE, HANS WERNER (1926-   )
Ode an den Westwind, orig for vcl and orch
SCH
HERBERT, VICTOR (1859-1924)
Canzonetta, Op. 2, No. 4
CF B2849

---

[61] With the exception of the gamba sonata in C, the sonatas listed are probably from Op. 1, 15 sonatas for one instrument and continuo. 6 of these were written for violin; 3 for flute; 4 for recorder; 2 for oboe. Listing here is by key because there is no relationship between numbering systems.

[62] All publications titled simply "Concerto in D" have been listed as Op. 101. Only the Schott and Peters editions appear with opus number in the catalogues.

HERBERT, VICTOR (cont.)
  Concerto No. 2, Op. 30
    (Rose) Int
  Pensée amoureuse
    GS
  Petite valse
    GS
  Romance
    GS
  Serenade in D, from Suite, Op. 3
    (Ries) BMC
    CF B2956
(HERFURTH, C. PAUL)
  Classical Album of Early Grade Pieces
    BMC
HERVELOIS, see Caix d'Hervelois
HESSE, ERNST CHRISTIAN (1676-1762)
  Duo in D, for gamba or vcl and pno or
      lute or guitar
    MT (Pet No. MV1076)
HESSENBERG, [KURT (1908-   )]
  Sonata, Op. 23
    SCH
HINDEMITH, PAUL (1895-1963)
  Capriccio, Op. 8, No. 1
    BRH
  Concerto
    SCH
  Easy Pieces, 3
    SCH
  "A Frog He Went A-Courting". Variations
      on an Old-English Nursery Song
    SCH
  Kammermusik No. 3, Op. 36, No. 2.
      Concerto
    SCH
  Meditation, from Nobilissima Visione
    SCH
  Music of Mourning, orig for str orch
    SCH
  Phantasiestück, Op. 8, No. 2
    BRH
  Scherzo, Op. 8, No. 3
    BRH
  Sonata, Op. 11, No. 3
    SCH
  Sonata 1948
    SCH
HIVELY, WELLS
  Alba
    CFE
HOCHSTETTER, ARMIN C. (1899-   )
  Sonata
    Krenn
HOFFMAN, ADOLF G.
  Sarabande ed Allegro
    CF B3333
HOLLAENDER, GUSTAV (1855-1915)
  Easy Pieces, Op. 48
    (Rudinger) BMC
HOLMES, GUY E.
  Tyrolean Fantasia
    CF
HOLST, IMOGEN (1907-   )
  Scottish Airs, 2
    Nov
HOME ON THE RANGE
    (Buchtel) Kjos S-5206
HONEGGER, ARTHUR (1892-1955)
  Concerto
    Senart
  Sonata
    ESC

Sonatine, orig for clar and pno
    RL
HONNORE, L.
  Morceau de Concert, Op. 23
    (Ronchini) Sal
HOVHANESS, ALAN (1911-   )
  Suite, Op. 193
    Pet 6324
HÜE, [GEORGES-ADOLPHE (1858-1948)]
  Andante et Scherzo
    RL
HUGUET Y TAGELL, R.
  Complainte. Extraite de Guitarrerias
      pour Piano
    Sal
HUMMEL, HERMAN A.
  Evening Bells
    Ru
HURÉ, JEAN (1877-1930)
  Air
    (Rose) Int
  Petite Chanson
    Mathot
  Sonata in f sharp
    Int
    Mathot
  Sonata in F
    Mathot
  Sonata in F sharp
    Mathot
  Te Deum
    Mathot
HURLSTONE, WILLIAM YEATES (1876-1906)
  Sonata in D
    Curwen
HUYBRECHTS, ALBERT (1899-1938)
  Concertino
    CBDM
  Dirge
    CBDM
  Pastourelle
    CBDM
IBERT, JACQUES (1890-1962)
  Concerto, orig for vcl and wind instruments
    Heugel
ILLIASHENKO, A.
  Complaintes Russes, 3
    Senart
  Variations sur un Thème Russe
    Senart
INCH, HERBERT (1904-   )
  Sonata
    CF 03052
d'INDY, VINCENT (1851-1931)
  Lied, Op. 19
    Int
  Sonate en Ré, Op. 84
    RL
INGHELBRECHT, DÉSIRÉ ÉMILE (1880-   )
  Nocturne
    Mathot
IORDAN, I.
  Easy Pieces in the Form of Variations
    MZK
  Melody, Scherzo, see Kirkor: Melody
  Variations
    MZK
IRELAND, JOHN (1879-1962)
  Holy Boy
    BH   transcribed by composer
  Sonata
    Aug
IRISH MELODIES
    Pigott (Mil No. PT450-1)   2V

IRISH MELODIES, 3
    Pigott (Mil No. PT453)
(ISAAC, MERLE)
    Album of Favorite Cello Solos
        Cole 216   for contents see title
    Melody Book for Strings
        CF 03828A,D   for contents see title
        under vln, pno
JACOB, GORDON (1895-   )
    Concerto
        JWL (Mil No. W1517) arr for vcl and
            pno by composer
    Elegy
        JWL (Mil No. W1530)
    Rondino in modo classico
        Aug
    Sonata in d
        JWL (Mil No. W1519)
    Sonatina
        JWL
JACOBI, [FREDERICK (1891-1952)]
    Concerto
        UE 10481
JACOBSON, MAURICE (1896-   )
    Berceuse
        Oxf 22.023 and 21.014
    Humoreske
        Leng (Mil No. L3014)
JANÁČEK, LEOŠ (1854-1928)
    Fairy Tale
        Artia
    Fallen Leaf
        Artia
JAQUES-DALCROZE, EMILE (1865-1950)
    Chant Mélancolique
        RL
    Romance
        RL
    Rythmes délaissés
        Senart
JÁRDÁNYI, PÁL (1920-   )
    Melody
        Kul
JÄRNEFELT, ARMAS (1869-1958)
    Berceuse
        (Buechner) CF B2959
JEANJEAN, P.
    Carillon
        Gaudet
    Sommeil
        Gaudet
JENTSCH, WALTER (1900-   )
    Concerto, Op. 33
        Sik
JEUNE VIOLONCELLISTE, LE
    (Feuillard) Delrieu 8V; for vcl and
        pno, or 2 vcl, or 2 vcl and pno
        Vol 1A
            Caix d'Hervelois: Tendre plainte
            Chopin: Souvenir
            Exaudet: Menuet
            Haendel: Larghetto
            Haydn: Andante
            Lully: Ariette
            Mozart: Ave verum
            Schubert: Berceuse
            Schubert: L'Echo
            Schumann: Pays Lointain
            Schumann: Envoi
            Schumann: La Brise
        Vol 1B
            Brahms: Chant populaire
            Caix d'Hervelois: Sarabande
            Chant napolitain

            Couperin: Forlane
            Dalayrac: Andantino
            Dall'Abaco: Passepied
            Francoeur: Bourrée
            Gretry: Chanson
            Loeillet: Gavotte
            Monteclair: Menuet
            Rousseau: Rêverie
            Rowley-Bishop: Sweet Home
        Vol 2A
            Beethoven: Adagio
            Haendel: Largo
            Marais: Minuetto
            Martini: Plaisir d'amour
            Mendelssohn: Barcarolle
            Mendelssohn: Rêve
            Rameau: Air tendre
            Schubert: Ave Maria
            Schubert: Prière d'enfant
            Schumann: Chant du berceau
        Vol 2B
            Azais: Lourré
            Bach, J.S: Aria
            Caix d'Hervelois: Musette
            Couperin: Gavotte
            Eccles: Preludium
            Francoeur: Pavane
            Haendel: Arioso
            Lanzetti: Interlude
            Loeillet: Sicilienne
            Lully: Menuet Bourgeois Gentilhomme
            Mendelssohn: Minuetto
            Mozart: Andantino
        Vol 3A
            Caix d'Hervelois: Air gay
            Forqueray: Rigaudon
            Mendelssohn: Chant du Printemps
            Rameau: Menuet
            Schubert: Attente
            Schumann: Mélancolie
            Schumann: Rêverie
            Wagner: Maîtres Chanteurs
        Vol 3B
            Bach, J.S: Andantino
            Beethoven: Menuet
            Brahms: Berceuse
            Brahms: Sérénade inutile
            Butterne: Minuetto
            Caix d'Hervelois: Bourrée
            Fesch: Lento
            Haendel: Adagio
            Lotti: Aria
            Schenk: Gavotte
            Schubert: Chant élégiaque
            Schumann: Chant populaire
        Vol 4A
            Bach: Aria
            Chopin: Largo
            Corelli: Grave
            Forqueray: La Gaillarde
            Schubert: Moment Musical
            Schubert: Le ruisseau
            Schumann: Chant du soir
            Schumann: Fleur de lotus
        Vol 4B
            Bach, F: Largo
            Blainville: La chasse
            Boismortier: Le suppliant
            Couperin: Rigaudon
            Desplanes: Praeludium
            Duport: Romance
            Ferry-Rebel: Musette
            Fesch: Gavotte
            Francoeur: Pastourelle

JEUNE VIOLONCELLISTE, LE (cont.)
  (Feuillard) Delrieu 8V (cont.)
    Vol 4B (cont.)
      Marais: Air tendre
      Pergolese: Menuet
      Senaillé: Passepied
JOACHIM, OTTO (1910-   )
  Sonata
    CL
JONGEN, JOSEPH (1873-1953)
  Aria
    Senart
  Concerto, Op. 18
    Dur
  Dans la douceur des pins, Op. 51, No. 1
    Ches
  Habanera
    CBDM
  Moto perpétuo
    Senart
  Poem No. 1, Op. 16
    Ches
  Poem No. 2, Op. 46
    Ches
  Poeme
    Bosw
  Sonate, Op. 39
    Dur
JOSTEN, WERNER (1885-   )
  Sonata
    AME
JULLIEN, RENÉ (1878-   )
  Études de Concert, 6, Op. 35
    Sal
  Sonate
    Senart
JUON, [PAUL (1872-1940)]
  Mysterien, Op. 59, Tone Poem
    LEU
KABALEVSKY, DMITRI (1904-   )
  Concerto, Op. 49
    Leeds
  Etude, see Khachaturian: Andantino
  Improvisation, Op. 21, No. 1
    (Schuster) Leeds
  Sonata, Op. 22
    MZK
  Sonata, Op. 71
    (Rostropovich) Int
KABALIN, FEDOR
  Poem and Rhymes
    Tritone   manuscript reproduction
KADOSA, PÁL (1903-   )
  Improvisation on Three Rumanian Folk Songs
    Kul
KAHN, ERICH ITOR (1905-1956)
  Nenia
    CFE
KAHN, ROBERT (1865-1951)
  Sonate, Op. 37
    Birnbach
KÄHNEL, AUGUST
  Kammersonaten, 2, orig for gamba and Bc
    (Bennat) Birnbach
KALABIS, VIKTOR (1923-   )
  Concerto
    Artia
KALINNIKOV, VASSILI (1866-1901)
  Sad Song; with Barcarolle, Lullaby by
    Spendiarov
    MZK
KAPP, EUGEN (1908-   )
  Sonata
    MZK

KARJINSKY, N.
  Berceuse
    RL
  Capriccio, from 5 Pieces
    ESC
  Chanson Russe, from 6 Little Pieces
    ESC
  Dialogue, from 5 Pieces
    ESC
  Dimanche à Moscou, from 6 Little Pieces
    ESC
  Guitare, from 5 Pieces
    ESC
  Marche, from 6 Little Pieces
    ESC
  Melody, from 6 Little Pieces
    ESC
  Orientale
    (Piatigorsky) ESC
  Orientale, from 5 Pieces
    ESC
  Petite Histoire, from 6 Little Pieces
    ESC
  Ronde, from 6 Little Pieces
    ESC
  Skazka
    ESC
  Sous la Fenêtre. Serenade, from 5 Pieces
    ESC
KAUFMAN, L.
  Oh, Fairest Varmland
    Pr
KAUFMANN, ARMIN (1902-   )
  Kleine Vortragsstücke, 3, Op. 69
    DOB
  Pieces, 3
    OBV
KELKEL, MANFRED (1929-   )
  Concertino
    Ric R1440
KELLY, BRYAN
  Diversions, 3
    Chap-L
KELLY, ROBERT (1916-   )
  Sonata
    CFE
KENNAWAY
  Interrupted Serenade
    Hin (Pet No. H685)
KERNOCHAN, M.
  Molto cantabile
    Galx
KERR, HARRISON (1897-   )
  Overture, Arioso and Finale
    CFE
KEYS, IVOR (1919-   )
  Sonata
    Nov
KHACHATURIAN, ARAM (1903-   )
  Andantino; with Etude by Kabalevsky
    MZK
  Concerto
    (Kurtz) Leeds
  Sabre Dance, From Gayne Ballet
    Leeds
KHANDOSHKIN, [IVAN (1747-1804)]
  Canzona, orig for vln
    MZK
  Canzona, see Gurilev: Nocturne
KHUDOYAN, A.
  Adagio
    MZK
KILPINEN, YRIÖ (1892-   )
  Sonata, Op. 90
    BRH

KIRKOR, [GUEORGI V. (1910-   )]
  Melody; with Melody, Scherzo by Iordan
    MZK
  Sonata, Op. 7
    MZK
  Tadjik Song; with Waltz by Rakov
    MZK
KLEBE, [GISELHER (1925-   )]
  Concerto, Op. 29
    BB
KLENGEL, JULIUS (1859-1933)
  Concertino No. 1 in C, Op. 7
    (Rose) Int
    BRH
    GS 1826
  Concertino No. 3 in a, Op. 46
    BRH
  Concertpiece in d, Op. 10
    (Rose) Int
    BRH
  Scherzo, Op. 6
    Int
  Sonatina in c, Op. 48, No. 1
    Int
KLOCHKOV
  Evening Song, see Vlasov, A.: Melody
KLUGHARDT, AUGUST (1847-1902)
  Concerto in a, Op. 59
    Int
KNIGHT, MORRIS (1933-   )
  Sonata
    Tritone   manuscript reproduction
KOCHETOV
  Melody; with Arioso by Schwarz
    MZK
KOCHUROV, see Glinka & Kochurov
KODÁLY, ZOLTÁN (1882-   )
  Adagio
    Kul
  Sonata, Op. 4
    UE 7130
KOECHLIN, CHARLES (1867-1950)
  Chansons Bretonnes
    Senart   2V
  Sonate
    Senart
KÖGLER, HERMANN (1885-   )
  Sonata in F, Op. 34
    Pet 3756
KOKAI, REZSO (1906-   )
  Dances, 2
    Kul
KOLAR, HENRY
  Rhapsody
    Ybarra
KOMAROVSKY, [ANATOLI]
  Race, see Baklanova: Etudes
KONYOVITCH
  Morceaux, 2. Haidoutchka et Danse
    RL
KOPPES
  Valsette
    Willis
KORNAUTH, EGON (1891-1959)
  Pieces, 3, Op. 47
    DOB
  Sonata, Op. 28
    Pet 3771
KORNGOLD, ERICH WOLFGANG (1897-1957)
  Concerto in C, Op. 37
    SCH
KOSENKO
  Pastorale; with Dance, Etude by Vlasov
    MZK

Scherzino, see Sokalsky: Song
Sonata, Op. 10
  MZK
Waltz, Mazurka, see Lisenko: Elegy
KOUGUELL, A.
  Concertina No. 1
    Consortium Musicale
  Danse des Bedouins
    ESC
  Danse des Druses, Op. 56
    ESC
  Kaddisch and Hebraic Dance
    Consortium Musicale
  Suite in Ancient Style
    Consortium Musicale
KOWALSKY, A.
  Tableaux, 4, en forme de variations
    sur un Thème Russe
    Senart
KOZLOVSKY
  Old Dance, see Varlamov: Red Sarafan
  Romance
    MZK
KRAFT, ANTON (1752-1820)
  Concerto in C
    Artia
  Sonata, Op. 11, No. 2
    (Adam) MM
KRAMER, A. WALTER (1890-   )
  Elegy in g, Op. 32, No. 3
    BMC
(KRANE)
  Classic and Folk Melodies
    Pr
KREIN, [JULIAN (1913-   )]
  Sonata-Fantasy
    MZK
KREISLER, FRITZ (1875-1962)[63]
  Allegretto, in the style of Boccherini
    Fol 1303
  Andantino, in the style of Martini
    Fol 1304
  Chanson Louis XIII and Pavane, in the style
    of Couperin
    Fol 1307
  Liebesfreud
    Fol 1314
  Liebesleid
    Fol 1315
  Old Refrain
    Fol 1333
  Precieuse, La, in the style of Couperin
    Fol 1313
  Rondino on a theme of Beethoven
    Fol 1325
  Scherzo, in the style of Dittersdorf
    Fol 1328
  Schön Rosmarin
    Fol 1329
  Sicilienne and Rigaudon, in the style of
    Francoeur
    Fol 1330
KRENEK, ERNST (1900-   )
  Capriccio
    UE 12868
KUBIK, GAIL (1914-   )
  Serenade
    Chap
KUBIZEK, AUGUSTIN (1918-   )
  Concerto Breve, Op. 23
    DOB

---

[63] All the pieces by Kreisler were written originally for violin and piano.

KUBIZEK, AUGUSTIN (cont.)
Sonatina, Op. 5a
DOB
KÜHNEL, AUGUST (1645-c.1700)
Partita
Kul
Sonata No. 9 in D
(Döbereiner) SCH
KULLMANN, A.
Bagatelle
Senart
Nocturne
Senart
KUMMER, FRIEDRICH AUGUST (1797-1879)
Concertino
(Ruyssen) Delrieu
LACOMBE, PAUL (1837-1927)
Sonate, Op. 100
Haml
LAJTHA, LÁSZLÓ (1891-1963)
Concert
Leduc
Sonate, Op. 17
Leduc
LAKE, M.L.
Among the Roses
CF
Annie Laurie, Fantasia
CF
LAKS, S
Pièces de Concert, 3
Deiss
Sonate
HL
LALO, EDOUARD (1823-1892)
Chants Russe. Lento du Concerto,
Op. 29, orig for vln and orch
(Hegner) CF B1567
Senart 5386
Concerto in d
(Klengel) Pet 3799
(Rose) Int
(Trowell) Aug 7699
(Willeke) CF 01326
Senart 5382
Sonata
Heugel
LANGE, GUSTAV (1830-1889)
Flower Song, Op. 39
(Herrmann) CF B2961
LA PRESLE, JACQUES DE (1888-   )
Pièce de Concert
Senart
LARA, AGUSTIN
Granada
SMP
LARSSON, LARS-ERIK (1908-   )
Concertino, Op. 45, No. 10
Gehrmans
LAVAGNINO
Canto Bretone
(Cassado) Carisch
LEBELL, L.
Chant d'Amour, Op. 16
(Withers) SCH
Elementary Pieces in 1st position, 3
STB
see also Graded Teaching Pieces
LEBORNE, FERNAND (1862-1929)
Sonate, Op. 41
Haml
LEBRUN, E.
Shepherd's Song
Brogneaux

LECUONA, ERNESTO (1896-1963)
Andalucia, from Andalucia Suite
(Mendelssohn) MK
Malaguena, from Andalucia Suite
(Martinelli) MK
LEE, SEBASTIAN (1805-1887)
Gavotte, Op. 112
(Schulz) GS
LEFEBVRE, CHARLES (1843-1917)
Sonate, Op. 98
Dur
LE FLEMING, CHRISTOPHER (1908-   )
Air and Dance
Ches
LEGLEY, VICTOR (1915-   )
Sonata, Op. 20
CBDM
LE GUILLARD, [ALBERT (1887-   )]
Esquisse
Senart
LEIGHTON, [KENNETH (1929-   )]
Elegy
Leng (Mil No. L3006)
LEKEU, GUILLAUME (1870-1894)
Sonate en Fa
RL
Sonate en Sol, orig for vln and pno
RL
LEMAIRE, G.
Gavotte des Mathurins
Sal
LEMARE, EDWIN H. (1865-1934)
Andantino; with Elégie by Massenet
(Trinkaus) Fill
LENSEN, J.
Epitaphe
(Withers) SCH
Serenade
(Withers) SCH
LEO, LEONARDO (1694-1744)
Concerto in A
SCH
Concerto in D
(Cilèa-Viterbini) Ric ER193
Concerto
MZK
LEONCAVALLO, RUGGIERO (1858-1919)
Brise de mer. Impromptu
Birnbach
LIADOV, ANATOL K. (1855-1914)
Prelude, Op. 11, No. 1, orig for pno
MZK
see also Piatigorsky
LIE, SIGURD (1871-1904)
Snow
CF B2430
LIEGEOIS
Album du jeune violoncelliste
Billaudot   15 pieces published
separately
LISENKO
Elegy; with Waltz, Mazurka by Kosenko
MZK
LISZNYAI, G.
Autumn
Kul
LISZT, FRANZ (1811-1886)
Consolation No. 3 in D flat, orig for pno
(Fournier) Int
Liebesträum; Nocturne No. 3, orig
for pno
(Cassado) Int
(Maréchal) ESC
(Skalmer) CF B2848

LISZT, FRANZ (cont.)
Vergessener Walzer
(Busoni) BRH
LIVIABELLA, LINO (1902-   )
Sonata ciclica
Ric 124448
LOCATELLI, PIETRO (1695-1764)
Allegro
(Piatti) SCH
Sonata in D, orig for vln and Bc
(Piatti) Int
(Piatti) SCH
LOEILLET, JEAN BAPTISTE (1680-1730)
Sonata in a
(Salmon) Ric R400
Sonata in B flat
(Beon) Int
Sonata in f sharp
(Beon) Int
Sonata in G
(Salmon) Ric R401
Sonata in g
(Schroeder) Aug 5507
Sonata in g
(Schroeder) SCH
Suite in g
(Schroeder) Aug 5513
LOEWE, FREDERICK (1904-   )
My Fair Lady. Selection
Chap
LONDONDERRY AIR
BMC
LONGMIRE, JOHN (1902-   )
Sea Pieces, 3
Mil
LOPATNIKOV, NIKOLAI (1903-   )
Arabesque
Leeds
Variations and Epilogue, Op. 31
MK
LOST MELODIES
(Stutschewsky) UE 10627
12 compositions by Albrechtsberger,
Chiesa, Corelli, Handel, J. Haydn,
M. Haydn, Marcello, Philidor, Rubino,
and others
LOVELL, J. & PAGE, P.
4 Strings and a Bow
Bosw
LOVELL, KATHARINE
Summer Song, from 3 Summer Sketches
EKN
Swing, from 3 Summer Sketches
EKN
Train, from 3 Summer Sketches
EKN
LOW, J.
see Graded Teaching Pieces
LÖWLEIN, [HANS (1909-   )]
Musik, Op. 13, orig for vcl and orch
BRH
LUCAS, LEIGHTON (1903-   )
Meditation
Ches
Orientale
Ches
LUCKE, KATHERINE E.
Andante Cantabile
CF B2506
LUENING, OTTO (1900-   )
Aria
CFE
Suite
CFE

Variation on Bach's Choral Prelude,
Liebster Jesus wir sind hier
CFE
LULLY, JEAN-BAPTISTE (1632-1687)
Aria
(Withers) SCH
Courante
(Piatigorsky) SCH
Gavotte and Musette
(Moffat-Such) SCH
Melody
(Spalding) CF B1780
LUTYENS, ELIZABETH (1906-   )
Bagatelles, 9, Op. 10
Leng (Mil No. L3003)
LYONS, M.F.
Souvenir, El
AMP
Sur la Mer
AMP
MACBETH, ALLAN (1856-1910)
Love In Idleness
(Squire) CF B1506
MCBRIDE, ROBERT (1911-   )
Dance
CFE
MACDOWELL, EDWARD (1861-1908)
To a wild rose, orig for pno
(Aller) Ru
(Isaac) CF B3320
(MCGREGOR, RUTH & WAXMAN, DONALD)
Masterwork Cello Solos from the Chamber
Music Repertory
Galx
MACONCHY, ELIZABETH (1907-   )
Divertimento
Leng (Mil No. L3015)
MAGHINI, RUGGERO
Canzone: Song for a Winter Evening
(Mazzacurati) SZ
MAGNARD, ALBÉRIC (1865-1914)
Sonate, Op. 20
RL
MAIKAPAR, S
Melody, Op. 10, No. 1
MZK
MAINARDI, ENRICO (1897-   )
Concerto
(Rienzi) SZ
Japanese Folk Songs
SCH
Sonata
SCH
Sonatina
SCH
Suite
SZ
MALEINGREAU, PAUL DE (1887-1956)
Sonate
Dur
MALIPIERO, GIAN FRANCESCO (1882-   )
Concerto
SZ
Sonatina
SZ
MALIPIERO, RICCARDO (1914-   )
Concerto
SZ
MALTER, L
Pieces, 3
MZK
MARAIS, MARIN (1656-1728)
Chaconne
(Schultz) Pet 4993

MARAIS, MARIN (cont.)
  Folia, La.
    (Gendron) SCH
  Old French Dances, 5
    (Mukle) Ches
  Suite in A
    (de Bruyn) Senart 5359
  Suite in d
    (Döbereiner) SCH
  Suite No. 3
    (Feuillard) Delrieu
MARAIS, [ROLAND]
  Sonata in C
    (Schroeder) Aug 5525
MARCELLI, NINO (1890-   )
  Gavotte in G
    BMC
  Neapolitan Dance
    BMC
MARCELLO, BENEDETTO (1686-1739)
  Sonatas, 6[64] in F,e,a,g,C,G
    Pet 4647   2nd vcl ad lib
  Sonatas, 2, in C and G
    (Moffat) Int
    (Moffat-Whitehouse) SCH
  Sonatas, 2, in G and C
    (Schroeder) Aug 5511
  Sonatas, 2, in F and g
    (Piatti) Int
    (Schroeder) Aug 5503
  Sonatas, 2, in f and g
    (Moffat-Whitehouse) SCH
    (Piatti) SIM
  Sonata in A
    (Pollain) Senart 5370
  Sonata in a, see Boccherini: Rondo
  Sonata in C, Op. 2, No. 5
    ZA 4385
  Sonata in C
    (Ticciati) Leng (Mil No. L3018)
  Sonata in D
    (Moffat-Whitehouse) SCH
    (Salmon) Ric R98
  Sonata in e, Op. 2, No. 2
    ZA 4382
  Sonata No. 2 in e
    Ric SY644
  Sonata in e
    (Moffat-Whitehouse-Rapp) SCH
    (Salmon) Ric R403
    (Schroeder) Aug 5512; with Sonata
      in F by Grazioli
    (Schroeder) Int
    (Schroeder) SCH
  Sonata in F, Op. 2, No. 1
    ZA 4381
  Sonata No. 1
    (Cassado) Int
  Sonata in F
    ZA 4167
  Sonata in G, Op. 2, No. 6
    ZA 4386
  Sonata in G
    (Krane) Shapiro, Bernstein
  Sonata in G
    (Salmon) Ric R404
  Sonata in G
    (Ticciati) Leng (Mil No. L3020)
  Sonata in g, Op. 2, No. 4
    ZA 4384

Sonata No. 4
  (Cassado) Int
Sonata in g
  (Salmon) Ric R406
Sonata, Op. 2, No. 3
  ZA 4383
see also Graded Teaching Pieces
MARIE, GABRIEL (1852-1928)
  Cinquantaine, La
    (Buechner) CF B2732
    GS
    Kjos S-5208
  Lamento
    (Munzer) CF B2657
    (Schroeder) BMC
  Romance
    CF B2946
  Sérénade badine
    CF B2934
MAROS, REZSO (1917-   )
  Albanian Suite
    Kul
  March
    Kul
  Sunshine and Clouds
    Kul
MARSICK
  Improvisation et Final
    Mathot
MARTELLI, HENRI (1895-   )
  Scherzetto, Berceuse and Final, Op. 49
    ESC
  Sonatina, Op. 51
    ESC
MARTIN, E.
  Evensong
    BH
MARTIN, FRANCOIS
  Sonate en Mi mineur
    (Strauwen) Senart 5373
MARTIN, FRANK (1890-   )
  Ballade, orig for vcl and orch
    UE 12011
  Chaconne
    UE 12862
MARTINI, GIAMBATTISTA (1706-1784)
  Celebrated Gavotte
    Kjos S-5207
  Sonata in a, see Pasqualini: Sonata in A
MARTINI, JEAN PAUL EGIDE (1741-1816)
  Plaisir d'Amour
    (Sandby) AMP
MARTINU, BOHUSLAV (1890-1959)
  Arabesques, 7
    Deiss
  Concerto, original edition
    SCH
  Concerto, revised edition, 1956
    SCH
  Concerto No. 2
    AMP
  Nocturnes. 4 études
    Leduc
  Pastorales. 6 pièces
    Leduc
  Sonata No. 1
    Heugel
  Sonata No. 2
    (Kirsch) AMP
  Sonata No. 3
    Artia
  Suite miniature
    Leduc

---

[64] It appears that there are a number of editions of the same group of sonatas by Marcello. Single sonatas are listed here by key because only Zanibon gives opus numbers.

MARTINU, BOHUSLAV (cont.)
  Variationen über ein slowakisches Thema
    Baer 3969
  Variations on a Theme of Rossini
    BH
MARX, JOSEPH (1882-   )
  Pastorale
    UE 5499
MASCAGNI, PIETRO (1863-1945)
  Intermezzo Sinfonico, from Cavalleria
    Rusticana
    (Hegner) CF B2962
MASSENET, JULES (1842-1912)
  Elégie, from Les Érynnies, Op. 10
    (Buechner) CF B2839
    SCH
  Elégie, see Lemare: Andantino
  Meditation, from Thaïs
    Heugel
MASTERS FOR THE YOUNG
    (Goltermann) Pet 2810-11   2V
      Vol 1: 12 pieces by Haydn, Mozart
      Vol 2: 10 pieces by Beethoven, Schubert
MASTERWORK CELLO SOLOS FROM THE
    CHAMBER MUSIC REPERTORY
    (McGregor & Waxman) Galx
MATTESON, [JOHANN (1681-1764)]
  Aria; with Minuet by Haydn and Minuet
    by Beethoven
    MZK
MATTHAY, TOBIAS (1858-1945)
  Ballade, Op. 40
    JWL
MAURAT, EDMOND
  Impromptus and Cantilènes, Op. 23, No. 1
    ESC
MAZZACURATI, BENEDETTO
  Burlesca
    Carisch
  Studio
    Carisch
MAZZACURATI
  Minuetto all'antica
    Ric 125786
  Ninna-nanna, Op. 5
    Ric 125760
MELNIKOV
  Russian Song, Little Accordion; with Bag-
    pipes, Cuckoo by Dobrokhotov
    MZK
MELODY BOOK FOR STRINGS
    (Isaac) CF 03828A,D   for contents see
    title under vln, pno
MENDELSSOHN, [ARNOLD (1855-1933)]
  Concerto in g
    (Andrae) Pet 5892
MENDELSSOHN, FELIX (1809-1847)
  Nocturno; with Valse triste by Sibelius
    (Trinkaus) Fill
  On Wings of Song, orig for voice and pno
    (Hegner) CF B1514
    (Trinkaus) Fill
  Original Compositions
    Pet 1535
      Variations concertantes, Op. 17
      Sonata in B flat, Op. 45
      Sonata in D, Op. 58
      Song without words, Op. 109
  Sonata No. 1 in B flat, Op. 45
    (Such) Aug
  Sonata No. 2 in D, Op. 58
    (Such) Aug
  Song without words, Op. 109
    (Tabb) Aug "Lied ohne Worte"
    Int

Song without words
  (Krane) Fox
Song Without Words
  (Schuster) MK
Spinning Song, from Songs without words,
    orig for pno
  (Silva) ZA
Spring Song, from Songs without words,
    orig for pno
  (Goltermann) CF B2922
MENDELSSOHN, LUDWIG
  Student's Concerto in D, Op. 213
    (Buechner) CF 03121
MENNINI, LOUIS (1920-   )
  Sonatina
    BH
MERCI, LUIGI
  Sonata in g, Op. 3, No. 4
    (Bergmann) SCH
MESSAGER, [ANDRE (1853-1929)]
  Chant Birman
    Sal
MEULEMANS, ARTHUR (1884-   )
  Sonata
    CBDM
MEYERBEER, GIACOMO (1791-1864)
  Coronation March, from Prophète
    (Trinkaus) Fill
MIASKOVSKY, NIKOLAI (1881-1950)
  Concerto
    MZK
MIGOT, GEORGES (1891-   )
  Dialogue en 4 parties
    Leduc
  Dialogue No. 2
    Leduc
  Pieces, 3
    Leduc
MIHALY, ADAM
  Concerto
    Kul
  Suite
    Kul
MILFORD, [ROBIN (1903-1959)]
  Threne
    Curwen
MILHAUD, DARIUS (1892-   )
  Concerto
    Deiss
  Concerto No. 2
    AMP
  Corcovado, from Saudades do Brazil, orig
    for pno
    (Maréchal) ESC
  Elegie
    BH
  Sonate
    Sal
  Sorocaba, from Saudades do Brazil, orig
    for pno
    (Maréchal) ESC
  Suite Cisalpine, orig for vcl and orch
    ESC
  Tijuca, from Saudades do Brazil, orig
    for pno
    (Maréchal) ESC
MILLS, CHARLES (1914-   )
  Duo Fantasie, Op. 90
    CFE   score only
MILOIEVITCH, M.
  Légende de Yéphimia, Op. 25
    RL
MIROSHNIKOV, O
  Dance
    MZK

MIROSHNIKOV, O (cont.)
  Sad Tale; Toccatina
    MZK
MOAT, E.M.
  Nocturne
    STB
MOERAN, ERNEST JOHN (1894-1950)
  Concerto
    Nov
  Irish Lament
    Nov
  Prelude
    Nov
  Sonata
    Nov
MOESCHINGER, ALBERT (1897-   )
  Sonate
    Baer 2462
(MOFFAT)
  Easy Classical Album
    SCH   see title for contents
(MOFFAT-RAPP)
  Old Master Melodies For Young Cellists
    SCH   see title for contents
(MOFFAT-SUCH)
  Old Masters For Young Players
    SCH   see title for contents
MOHLER, PHILIPP (1908-   )
  Fantasiestück, orig for vcl and orch
    Gerig
MOLNAR, [ANTAL (1890-   )]
  Cradle Song
    Kul
MOMPOU, [FRÉDÉRIC (1893-   )]
  Chanson et Danse
    (Cassado) Sal
MONIUSZKO
  Evening, Spinner, see Chopin: Prelude
MONN, GEORG MATTHIAS (1717-1750)
  Concerto in g, orig for harpsichord,
        transcribed by A. Schoenberg
    GS
    UE 5351
MONNIKENDAM, [MARIUS (1896-   )]
  Sonate
    Senart
MONTANI
  Elegia
    Ric 125498
MONTI, VITTORIO
  Csárdás
    CF B2519
MOÓR, EMANUEL (1863-1931)
  Prelude, Op. 123
    Int
MOORE, JOHN
  Scottish Song, "Turn ye to me"
    Oxf 20.110
MOPPER, IRVING
  Short Pieces, 6
    BMC
MORTARI, VIRGILIO (1902-   )
  Sarabanda e Allegro
    Carisch
MOSZKOWSKI, MORITZ (1854-1925)
  Guitar, Op. 45, No. 2, orig for pno
    Pet 2224
  Intimité
    (Withers) SCH
  Scherzino
    (Bernstein) AMP
  Serenata, Op. 15, No. 1, orig for pno
    (Rehfeld-Skalmer) CF B2926

MOTTU, A.
  Sonatine
    Senart
  Suite Anglaise
    Senart
MOULAERT, RAYMOND (1875-   )
  Sonata Passacaglia
    CBDM
MOUQUET, JULES (1867-1946)
  Sonate, Op. 24
    HL
MOUSSORGSKY, see Mussorgsky
MOY, E.
  Berceuse & Valse-Caprice
    (Withers) SCH
MOZART, WOLFGANG AMADEUS
        (1756-1791)
  Adagio, K. 261, orig for vln and orch
    (Schuster) MK
    (Stutschewsky) Int
  Adagio, K.356, orig for glass harmonica
    (Isaacs) Aug
  Adagio, K.622, from Concerto for clar
        and orch
    (Squire) Aug
  Alla Turca
    (Cassado) Int
  Allegro. Monostato's Aria from Magic Flute
    (Withers) SCH
  Andante. Pamina's Aria from Magic Flute
    (Withers) SCH
  Andantino, K. Anh. 46
    (Schroeder) SCH
  Batti, Batti, from Don Giovanni, K.527
    (Squire) Aug
  Concerto in A, K.622, orig for clar and
        orch
    (Trowell) Aug
  Concerto No. 1 in B flat, Op. 96, K.191,
        orig for bsn and orch
    (Lévy) Senart 5128
    Pet 4347b
  Concerto No. 2 in B flat, orig for bsn
        and orch
    Pet 5883
  Concerto in D, K.314,[65] orig for fl and orch
    (Szell-Feuermann) GS L1591
  German Dance in G, K. 600, orig for orch
    (Withers-Rapp) SCH
  Laendler, after K. 606, orig for orch
    (Ries) RE (Pet No. RE8)
  Larghetto, from Clarinet Quintet, K.581
    (Withers) SCH
    SCH
  Larghetto. Tamino's Aria from Magic Flute
    (Withers) SCH
  Larghetto; with Adagio, Rondo by Breval
    MZK
  Larghetto et Rondo
    (Bazelaire) Sal
  Magic Flute Variations, see Beethoven
  Minuet in D, from Divertimento, K.334
    (Such) Aug
  Minuet, from Haffner Serenade
    (Stutschewsky) Pet 4220
  Sonata in B flat, K. 292, orig for bsn and vcl
    (Gruetzmacher) Pet 2170
    (Gruetzmacher) Int
  Sonata in F, K. 358, orig for pno duet
    (Cassado) SCH
  Sonatina in A
    (Piatigorsky) EV
  Variations on a theme, see Beethoven

[65] K.285d in Schirmer catalogue.

MULÈ, [GIUSEPPE (1885-1951)]
  Theme and Variations, orig for vcl and orch
    SZ
MÜLLER, J. FREDERICK
  Gulliver the Giant
    Kjos S5221
  King of the Deep
    Kjos S5220
  On the Riviera
    Kjos S5223
  One Summer Evening
    Kjos S5222
MURRILL, HERBERT (1909-1952)
  Capriccio: Alla marcia, Aria and Toccata
    Aug
  Concerto No. 2
    Oxf 21.012
  Sarabande
    Oxf 21.302
MUSHEL, G.
  Sonata
    MZK
MUSSORGSKY, MODEST P. (1839-1881)
  Chanson Russe. Une larme
    (Schroeder) BMC
  Tear, see Glinka: Sentiment
NAPRAVNIK
  Allegro, see Rubinstein: Melody
NARDINI, PIETRO (1722-1793)
  Adagio
    ZA 3186
  Arioso
    (Sametini) VL
  Sonata in do
    (Salmon) Ric R694
NECHAYEV, [VASSILY (1895-   )]
  Sonata, Op. 28
    MZK
NEGRO FOLK SONGS, 5
  (Brown) SCH
NERUDA, FRANZ (1843-1915)
  Concerto, Op. 59
    Artia
  Slavonian Cradle Song, Op. 11
    (Seybold) SIM
NEVIN, ETHELBERT (1862-1901)
  Narcissus, Op. 13, No. 4, orig for pno
    (Strube) BMC
  Rosary, orig for voice and pno
    (Strube) BMC
NIN, JOAQUIN (1879-1949)
  Chants d' Espagne
    ESC
  Commentaries, 4
    ESC
  Suite Espagnole
    ESC
NOËL-GALLON, see Gallon, Noël
NOETEL, KONRAD FRIEDRICH (1903-1947)
  Sonate
    Baer 1806
  Suite
    Sirius
NÖLCK, AUGUST
  Character Pieces, Op. 43, 6
    BMC
  Concerto, Op. 108
    Aug 7733
  Original Pieces, 10, Op. 116
    SCH
  Nocturne
    Kjos S-5209
  see also Graded Teaching Pieces

NOVÁK, JAN (1921-   )
  Capriccio
    Artia
NOWAK, LIONEL (1911-   )
  Sonata No. 1
    CFE
  Sonata No. 2
    CFE
  Sonata No. 3
    CFE
  Suite on Old Music
    CFE
NYSTROEM, GÖSTA (1890-   )
  Sinfonia Concertante, orig for vcl and orch
    Nordiska
OFFENBACH, JACQUES (1819-1880)
  O Belle Nuit. Barcarolle, from Les Contes
      d'Hoffmann
    (Woltag) CF B2783
  Pieces, 4
    (Stutschewsky) Pet 4904
OGANESIAN, E.
  Nocturne
    MZK
OLD MCDONALD IN THE DELL
  (Buchtel) Kjos S-5201
OLD MASTERS FOR YOUNG PLAYERS
  (Moffat-Such) SCH
      14 selected works by Purcell, Gluck,
        Rameau, Handel, Bach, Tartini and
        others
OLD MASTER MELODIES FOR YOUNG
    CELLISTS
  (Moffat-Rapp) SCH
      13 selected works by Corelli, Pepusch,
        Telemann, Weber, Sammartini, Mozart,
        and others
OLD MUSIC
  (Brodszky) Kul
OLD TUNES FOR YOUNG CELLISTS
  (Tabb) Aug
OPERA
  (Blumenthal-Saenger) CF 0802
ORBAN, [MARCEL (1884-1958)]
  Introduction, Theme and Variations
    ESC
  Pastorale et Ronde
    RL
ORE
  Sonatina, Op. 14
    Paxton (Mil No. P583)
OREFICE, [GIACOMO (1865-1922)]
  Tempio greco. Suite
    Ric 128313
ORREGO-SALAS, JUAN (1919-   )
  Duos Concertante
    Peer
ORTIZ, [DIEGO (c.1525- ?)]
  Recercada No. 2
    (Döbereiner) SCH
OSTRANSKY
  Meditation
    Mil
OVERTON, HALL (1920-   )
  Sonata, 1960
    CFE   score only
PADEREWSKI, IGNACE JAN (1860-1941)
  Minuet a l'Antique
    (Trinkaus) Fill
PAGANINI, CH.
  Au Luxembourg
    Deiss
  Dimanche soir au village
    Deiss

PAGANINI, CH. (cont.)
  Sommeil d'Ange
    Deiss
PAGANINI, NICCOLÒ (1782-1840)
  Moto Perpetuo, orig for vln
    (Klengel) Int
  Non più mesta. Variations on a theme by
    Rossini, orig for vln
    (Bockmuehl) Lit (Pet No. L812)
  Variations on a theme from Mosè by
    Rossini, orig for vln
    (Sametini) VL "Moses Fantasy"
    (Silva) ZA 3119 "Variazioni di Bravura"
  Variations on a theme of Rossini
    (Gendron) SCH
  Variations, see also Piatigorsky
PAGE, P., see Lovell & Page
PAHISSA, [JAIME (1880-   )]
  Notturno
    Ric BA9653
PALMGREN, SELIM (1878-1951)
  Dragonfly
    (Dann) CF B2770
PARADIS, MARIA THERESIA (1759-1824)
  Sicilienne
    (Dushkin) SCH
PARAY, PAUL (1886-   )
  Sonate en si majeur
    Jobert
PARRIS, ROBERT (1924-   )
  Cadenza, Caprice and Ricercare
    CFE
PARTOS, ÖDÖN (1907-   )
  Oriental Ballad
    IMP
  Yiskor, orig for vla and orch
    Leeds
PASCAL, CLAUDE (1921-   )
  Concerto
    Dur
PASCAL, FLORIAN (1827-1926)
  Sonata in g
    JWL
PASQUALINI
  Sonata in A; with Sonata in a by Martini
    (Schroeder) Aug 5508
PEETERS, FLOR (1903-   )
  Aria[66]
    Heuwek
PEIKO, [NIKOLAI (1916-   )]
  Bashkir Song
    MZK
PÉNAU, ROGER
  Pièces, 2
    Senart
PERGOLESI, GIOVANNI BATTISTA (1710-1736)
  Se tu m'ami
    (Elkan) H Elkan
  Sinfonia in F
    (Rapp) SCH
  Sinfonia
    Int
  Song; with Rigaudon by Rameau and
    Song by Weckerlen
    MZK
  Tre Giorni,[67]
    (Skalmer) CF B2724
  see also Graded Teaching Pieces
PERILHOU, ALBERT
  Marine Italienne
    Heugel

PERLE, GEORGE (1915-   )
  Lyric Piece, Op. 21A
    CFE
PERONI
  Al chiaro di luna. Serenata
    Ric
PERSICHETTI, VINCENT (1915-   )
  Vocalise, Op. 27
    EV
PETRASSI, GOFFREDO (1904-   )
  Preludio, aria e finale
    Ric 123140
PETRASSI, [GOFFREDO]
  Canto per Addormentare Una Bambina
    Carisch
PFEIFFER, [GEORGES-JEAN (1835-1908)]
  Musette
    (Gregh) RL
PFITZNER, HANS (1869-1949)
  Concerto in G, Op. 42
    SCH
  Concerto in a, Op. 52
    Oertel   pno reduction by Klussmann
  Sonata in f sharp, Op. 1
    BRH
PIANELLI, G.
  Sonata in sol
    (Salmon) Ric R407
  Sonata
    MZK
PIATIGORSKY, GREGOR (1903-   )
  Pliaska. Russian dance on a theme of
    Liadoff
    SCH
  Scherzo
    Ches
  Variations on a theme of Paganini
    EV
PIATTI, ALFREDO (1822-1901)
  Studienkonzert in d, Op. 26
    Hof
PICINETTI, FELICE MARIA (18th century)
  Sonata in C
    NAG
PIECES, 8
    (Stogorsky) MZK
PIECES, 6
    MZK
      Pieces by Miaskovsky, Shostakovich,
      Kabalevsky
PIECES, 5
    MZK
      Pieces by Goedicke, Gliere,
      Narimanidze
PIECES, 12, BY RUSSIAN AND SOVIET
    COMPOSERS
    (Borisyak-Dzgelenek) MZK
PIECES FOR CELLO, 13
    (Smoliansky) MZK
PIERNÉ, GABRIEL (1863-1937)
  Sérénade
    (Hegner) CF B1522
  Sonate en fa dièse mineur
    Dur
PIERNÉ, [PAUL (1874-1952)]
  Fantaisie
    Sal
  Masque de Comédie, No. 1
    Sal
  Masque de Comédie, No. 2
    Sal
PIJPER, WILLEM (1894-1947)
  Sonata No. 1
    Ches

---

[66] In the U.S.A. this publication can be obtained through Elkan-Vogel.
[67] Attributed to Pergolesi.

PILLOIS, [JACQUES (1877-1935)]
Chanson triste
  Senart
PINKHAM, DANIEL (1923-   )
Siciliana and Sailor's Dance, from ballet
    Narragansett Bay
  CFE
PITFIELD, THOMAS B. (1903-   )
Pavan
  Aug
Reel
  Aug
PIZZETTI, ILDEBRANDO (1880-   )
Canti, 3
  Ric 119895
Concerto in do
  Ric 123456
Sonata in fa
  Ric 119404
POLLAIN, F.
Première Étude, Les Bavardes
  Senart
PONCE, MANUEL MARÍA (1882-1948)
Estrellita
  (Cassado) Int
  (Simon) CF B2607
PONSE, LUCTOR (1914-   )
Sonata No. 2
  DN (Pet No. D229)
POPEJOY, E. KEITH
Singing Cello
  Bel EL507
POPOV, [GAVRIIL (1904-   )]
Melody, Op. 35
  MZK
POPPER, DAVID (1843-1913)
As once in happier days, Op. 64, No. 1
  (Willeke) CF B1530
    "Fond Recollections"
  SIM
Autumn Flower, Op. 50, No. 5
  (Buechner) CF B2916
Devotion, Op. 50, No. 2
  (Engel) SIM
Elfentanz, Op. 39, orig for vcl
    and orch
  (Cassado) Int "Dance of the Elves"
  CF B2938
Fond Recollections, see As once in
    happier days
Gavotte No. 2, Op. 23, orig for vcl
    and orch
  (Ries) BMC
  (Rose) Int
  CF B2709
Harlequin
  (Schroeder) BMC
Hungarian Rhapsody, Op. 68, orig for
    vcl and orch
  (Malkin) CF 03485
  (Rose) Int
Mazurka in g, Op. 11, No. 3
  Int
Papillon, Op. 3
  (Rose) Int
Romance in G
  Aug 7727
Romance
  Haml
Serenade, Op. 54, No. 2
  (Rose) Int
Spanish Dance, Op. 54, No. 5, see Vito
Spinning Song, Op. 55, No. 1
  Int

Studies, 4
  (Kordy) Nov
Suite in A, Op. 69
  Pet 2241
Tarantella, Op. 33, orig for vcl and orch
  (Rose) Int
  CF B2636
  SIM
Village Song, Op. 62, No. 2
  Int
Vito. Spanish Dance, Op. 54, No. 5
  (Neumann) SIM
  (Rose) Int
  CF B2929
POPPER, WILLIAM
Mazurka, Op. 3
  (Krane) Jack Spratt
PORPORA, NICOLA ANTONIO (1686-1768)
Aria
  (Zandonai) Ric 127921
Aria; with Song by Sammartini and
    Minuet by Valentini
  MZK
Concerto in G
  (Bächi) SCH
Sonata in F, orig for vln and Bc
  (Piatti-Rapp) SCH
  (Salmon) Ric R408
PORRINO, ENNIO (1910-1959)
Danza spagnola, dal balletto Mondo tondo
  Ric 127614
PORTER, QUINCY (1897-   )
Poem
  Val
POULENC, FRANCIS (1899-1963)
Serenade
  (Gendron) Heugel
Sonata No. 1
  Heugel
PRESLE, see La Presle
PRIETO, MARIA TERESA
Adagio y Fuga
  EMM
PROCTOR, CHARLES (1906-   )
Sonata in e
  Leng (Mil No. L3005)
PROKOFIEV, SERGEY (1891-1953)
Adagio, Op. 97 bis
  Leeds
Ballade
  Leeds
Concertino, Op. 132
  Leeds
Concerto in g, Op. 58
  BH
Concerto No. 2, see Symphonie Concertante
Gavotte from Classical Symphony, Op. 25
  (Mendelssohn) MK
  (Schuster) CF B2773
Pieces, 3, from Romeo and Juliet
  (Grunes) Omega
Sonata, Op. 119
  (Rostropovich) Int
  Leeds
  Pet 4710
Symphonie Concertante, Op. 125
  (Nelsova) Int
Waltz, Op. 65, orig for pno
  (Piatigorsky) Int
PUGNANI, GAETANO (1731-1798)
Adagio
  ZA 3191
PURCELL, HENRY (c.1659-1695)
Airs, 2
  (Mangeot) Aug

PURCELL, HENRY (cont.)
Air in d
(Moffat-Such) SCH
Aria
(Popper) Int
Aria; with German Dance by Dittersdorf
MZK
Dido's Lament
(Phillips) Oxf
Sarabanda and Gavotte
(Moffat) Aug
Slow Air, from Virtuous Wife
(Bridgewater) BH
Slow Air and Air
(Withers) SCH
PÜTZ, EDUARD
Sonatine
Gerig
RACHMANINOFF, SERGEY (1873-1943)
Dance Orientale, Op. 2, No. 2
(Rose) Int
BH
Elegie, Op. 3, No. 1, orig for pno
(Schuster) MK
MZK
Melodie, Op. 3, No. 3, orig for pno
Bosw
MZK
Melody
(Altschuler) CP
Pieces, 2, Op. 2
MZK
see also Prelude and Dance Orientale
Prelude, Op. 2, No. 1
(Rose) Int
Prelude, Op. 23, No. 4, orig for pno
MZK
Prelude, Op. 23, No. 10, see Scriabin: Etude,
Op. 2, No. 1
Romance, Op. 4, No. 3, orig for voice and pno
(Siloti-Casals) CF B2154
Romance
MZK
Romance, see Arensky: Lullaby
Sonata in g, Op. 19
(Nelsova) Int
BH
Vocalise, Op. 34, orig for voice
(Bernstein) AMP
(Rose) Int
RADIO COLLECTION OF MODERN GEMS
Ru
RADIO COLLECTION OF NATIONAL SONGS &
HYMNS
Ru
RAFF, JOSEPH JOACHIM (1822-1882)
Cavatina, Op. 85, No. 3, orig for vln and pno
(Buechner) CF B2957
(Palaschko) SCH
RAKOV, [NICOLAI (1908-   )]
Poem
MZK
Poem; Romance; Serenade
MZK
Romance; Serenade
MZK
Waltz; Canzonetta; Humoresque
MZK
Waltz, see Kirkor: Tadjik Song
RAMEAU, JEAN-PHILIPPE (1683-1764)
Gavotta
(Salmon) Ric R107
Rigaudon, see Pergolesi: Song

Tambourine, Minuet, see Deplan: Intrada
see also Graded Teaching Pieces
RANZATO, ATTILIO
Pezzi, Tre
Curci
RAPHAEL, GÜNTER (1903-1960)
Sonata in b, Op. 14
BRH
Stücke, 3, in c sharp
Baer 3746
RAPP, see Moffat-Rapp
RASSE, FRANCOIS (1873-1955)
Sonate
Senart
RAVEL, MAURICE (1875-1937)
Alborada del gracioso, orig for pno
(Castelnuovo-Tedesco) CF B3268
Pavane pour une Infante défunte, orig for pno
(Maréchal) ESC
Pièce en forme de Habanera, orig for voice
Leduc
Vallée des Cloches, La, orig for pno
(Castelnuovo-Tedesco) CF B2802
RAWSTHORNE, ALAN (1905-   )
Sonata
Oxf 21.006
REBEL, JEAN-FERY (c.1661-1747)
Rondo, "Les Cloches"
Pet 4212
REBIKOV, VLADIMIR I. (1866-1920)
Song without words; with Rondo by
Gliere
MZK
RECREATIONS FOR YOUNG 'CELLISTS
(Hegner) CF 0263-265   3V
Vol 1: Op. 30
Adeste Fideles
America
Home Sweet Home
Long, Long Ago
Nearer My God to Thee
Onward Christian Soldiers
Star-Spangled Banner
Stille Nacht, heilige Nacht
Tramp, Tramp, Tramp
Yankee Doodle
and 15 additional compositions
Vol 2: Op. 31
Auld Lang Syne
Carnival of Venice
Comin' through the Rye
Glory, Glory Hallelujah
Killarney
Last Rose of Summer
Maryland, My Maryland
Massa's in de Cold Ground
Rock of Ages
Rocked in the Cradle of the Deep
and 15 additional compositions
Vol 3: Op. 33
Beauty's Eyes
Flow gently, sweet Afton .
Girl I left behind me
Hail Columbia
Hail to the Chief
In einem kuhlen Grunde
Kerry Dance
Loch Lomond
My Old Kentucky Home
St. Patrick's Day
and 15 additional compositions
REED, H. OWEN (1910-   )
Concerto
CP

REGER, MAX (1873-1916)
Aria, from Suite in a, Op. 103a, orig for
vln and pno
BB
Pieces, 2, Op. 79e
Sik 362
Sonata in a, Op. 116
Pet 3283
REINHOLD, OTTO (1899-   )
Übungsmusik für Jugendliche
Hof
REINHOLD, [OTTO]
Sonata
BRH
REIZENSTEIN, FRANZ (1911-   )
Cantilene
Leng (Mil No. L3011)
Concerto in G
Leng (Mil No. L3000)
Elegy
Leng (Mil No. L3010)
Sonata in A
Leng (Mil No. L3004)
RENARD, FELIX
Berceuse No. 2, Op. 20
CF B2963
RESPIGHI, OTTORINO (1879-1936)
Notturno
(Mendelssohn) MK
REUCHSEL, MAURICE (1880-   )
Poème héroique, orig for vcl and orch
HL
Sonate
HL
REUTTER, HERMANN (1900-   )
Prozession. Dialogue, orig for vcl and
orch
SCH
REZAC, [IVAN (1924-   )]
Sonata
Artia
REZNICEK, EMIL NIKOLAUS VON (1860-1945)
Nachtstück, orig for vcl, harp, 4 horns
and str quartet
Birnbach
RHENÉ-BATON, (1879-1940)
Poème élégiaque, orig for vcl and orch
Dur
Sonate en ut
Dur
RIEGGER, WALLINGFORD (1885-1961)
Whimsy, Op. 2
AMP
Whimsy
GS
RIMSKY-KORSAKOV, NIKOLAY (1844-1908)
Flight of the Bumble-Bee, from Tsar Saltan
(Rose) Int
Lullaby, from Sadko; with Polka by
Balakirev
MZK
Serenade, Op. 37
Belaieff
Song of India, from Sadko
(Sandby) CF B1537
(Schroeder) BMC
Belaieff
Transcriptions from Tsar's Bride, see
Shirinsky
RIVIER, [JEAN (1896-   )]
Rhapsodie, orig for vcl and orch
Senart
ROBAUDI, VINCENZO
Alla Stella Confidente
CF B2923

ROGER-DUCASSE, JEAN (1873-1954)
Romance, orig for vcl and orch
Dur
ROGERS & SHREDNICK
Autumn Twilight
Mil
ROLLAND & FLETCHER
First Perpetual Motion
Mil
ROMBERG, BERNHARD (1767-1841)
Concert Pieces
Pet 2023b
Variations, Op. 50
Concertino, Op. 51
Variations, Op. 61
Concertino in e, Op. 38
(Ruyssen) Delrieu
Concertino, Op. 51
(Grützmacher-Malkin) CF B2617
(Rose) Int
(Ruyssen) Delrieu
Concerto No. 1 in B flat, Op. 2
Pet 1343A
Concerto No. 2 in D, Op. 3
(Malkin) CF 03116
(Rose) Int
Pet 1343b
Concerto No. 3 in G, Op. 6
Pet 1343C
Concerto No. 4 in e, Op. 7
(Malkin) CF L810
(Rose) Int
Concerto No. 5 in f sharp, Op. 30
Billaudot
Concerto No. 6 in F, Op. 31
Billaudot
Concerto No. 7 in C, Op. 44
Billaudot
Concerto No. 8 in A, Op. 48
Billaudot
Concerto No. 9 in b, Op. 56
Billaudot
Concerto No. 10 in E, Op. posth.
Pet 1343K
Divertimenti, 3, on National Themes
(Stutschewsky) Pet 2023A
Swedish, Op. 42
Austrian, Op. 46
Westphalian, Op. 65
Divertimento, Op. 46, see also vcl and
guitar
Sonata in e, Op. 38, No. 1
Int
Sonata in G, Op. 38, No. 2
Int
Sonata in B flat, Op. 38, No. 3
Int
Sonata in B flat, Op. 43, No. 1
CF B3350
Int
Sonata in C, Op. 43, No. 2
Int
Sonata in G, Op. 43, No. 3
Int
Sonata; first movement
MZK
RONCHINI, F.
Andante religioso, from Miniatures, Suite 2
Billaudot
Appassionato, from Miniatures, Suite 2
Billaudot
Aria et Caprice Final
RL
Aveu, from Miniatures, Suite 1
Billaudot

RONCHINI, F. (cont.)
Barcarolle, from Miniatures, Suite 1
Billaudot
Berceuse, from Miniatures, Suite 1
Billaudot
Capriccioso, from Miniatures, Suite 2
Billaudot
Chanson vénitienne, from Esquisses
Billaudot
Chant de gloire, from Esquisses
Billaudot
Chant du pâtre, from Miniatures, Suite 2
Billaudot
Chant villageois, from Miniatures, Suite 1
Billaudot
Concerto da Camera No. 1
Billaudot
Conte
Senart
Danse vénitienne, from Esquisses
Billaudot
Elévation, from Miniatures, Suite 2
Billaudot
Fantaisie drôlatique, from Miniatures,
Suite 2
Billaudot
Forlana, from Esquisses
Billaudot
Gavotte, from Esquisses
Billaudot
Gavotte
RL
Lamento, from Esquisses
Billaudot
Mazurka, from Miniatures, Suite 1
Billaudot
Polonaise
Senart
Sérénade espagnole, from Miniatures,
Suite 1
Billaudot
Sérénade Vénitienne
Senart
ROPARTZ, J. GUY (1864-1955)
Adagio
RL
Rapsodie, orig for vcl and orch
Dur
Sonate No. 1 en sol mineur
Dur
Sonate No. 2 en la mineur
Dur
ROREM, NED (1923-   )
Mountain Song
SMP
ROSENBERG, HILDING (1892-   )
Concerto No. 2
Gehrmans
ROSSELLINI, [RENZO (1908-   )]
Fontana malata, La
Ric 122016
ROSSINI, GIOACCHINO (1792-1868)
Allegro agitato
MM   Photolith reproduction
Figaro, see Castelnuovo-Tedesco
Variations on a theme, see Martinu,
Paganini
RÖTTGER, [HEINZ (1909-   )]
Sonata
BRH
ROUSSEAU, SAMUEL-ALEXANDRE
(1853-1904)
Rondes et Blanches
RL

Sonate en la mineur
Dur
ROUSSEL, ALBERT (1869-1937)
Concertino, Op. 57, orig for vcl and orch
Dur
ROWLEY, ALEC (1892-1958)
Souvenance
STB
RUBBRA, EDMUND (1901-   )
Soliloquy, Op. 57, orig for vcl and orch
Leng (Mil No. L3009)
Sonata in g, Op. 60
Leng (Mil No. L3007)
RUBINSTEIN, ANTON (1829-1894)
Barcarolle, see Arensky: Lullaby
Melody in F, Op. 3, No. 1, orig for pno
(Palaschko) SCH
(Schulz) CF B2866
MZK
Melody; with Allegro by Napravnik
MZK
Romance
(Cheyette) Fox
Sonata, Op. 18
(Schulz) GS L63
RUBTZOV, F.
Scherzo on a Mordovian Theme
MZK
Song on a Mordovian Theme
MZK
RUSSELL, HENRY (1812-1900)
Life on the Ocean Wave
Kjos S-5205
RUSSIAN FOLK MELODIES, 10
(Sapozhnikov) MZK
RUYSSEN, PIERRE
Apprenti Celliste, L'
Delrieu
SADUN, I.
Romanza
Gaudet
SAENGER, see Blumenthal & Saenger
SAINT-SAENS, CAMILLE (1835-1921)
Allegro appassionato, Op. 43, orig for
vcl and orch
(Malkin) CF B2717
(Rose) Int
Aug 10020
Dur
Amour viens aider
(Whear) Lud S-2000
Concerto No. 1 in a, Op. 33
(Malkin) CF 03441
(Rose) Int
Dur
Concerto No. 2 in d, Op. 119
Dur
Cygne, Le, see Swan
Eléphant, L', du Carnaval des Animaux
(Garban) Dur
Melody
(Tertis) GS
Mon Coeur s' Ouvre à ta Voix, from Sam-
son et Dalila
(Papin-Skalmer) CF B2967
Romance, Op. 36
Int
Sonata No. 1, Op. 32
Dur
MZK
Sonata No. 2 in F, Op. 123
Dur
Suite in d, Op. 16
LEU

SAINT-SAENS, CAMILLE (cont.)
  Swan, from Carnival of the Animals
    (Buechner) CF B2789
    (Mittell) GS
    (Rose) Int
    (Schroeder) BMC
    (Trinkaus) Fill
SALMON, JOSEPH (1863-1943)
  Suite, Op. 7
    Dur
SAMINSKY, LAZARE (1882-1959)
  Chasidic Dance, No. 1 of Chasidic Suite,
    Op. 24
    CF B2369
  Hamavdil, No. 3 of Chasidic Suite, Op. 24
    CF B2416
  Meditation, No. 2 of Chasidic Suite, Op. 24
    CF B2425
  Troubadour Song, for vcl and pno or harp
    CF B2371
SAMMARTINI, GIOVANNI BATTISTA
    (1701-1775)
  Canto amoroso
    (Squire) SCH
  Sonata in G
    (Karjinsky) ESC
  Sonata in G
    (Moffat) SCH
  Sonata in G
    (Rose) Int
  Sonata in G
    (Salmon) Ric R101
  Sonata in G
    (Stutschewsky) Int
  Sonata in G
    Senart 5349
  Sonata in g
    (Salmon) Ric R703
  Song, see Porpora: Aria
SANDI, LUIS (1905-   )
  Hoja de Album
    EMM
(SAPOZHNIKOV)
  Easy Pieces, 5
    MZK
  Folk Songs, 4
    MZK
  Folk Songs and Melodies, 10, Bk. I
    MZK
  Russian Folk Melodies, 10
    MZK
  Songs, 8, of the U.S.S.R. Peoples, Bk. II
    MZK
SARASATE, PABLO DE (1844-1908)
  Zapateado, Op. 23, No. 2, orig for vln
    and pno
    (Rose) Int
SARTEL, H.
  Romance
    Gaudet
SAUVREZIS, ALICE (1866-1946)
  Poème
    Senart
SAYGUN, A. ADNAN (1907-   )
  Sonata, Op. 12
    SMP
SCARLATTI, DOMENICO (1685-1757)
  Suite, from the sonata for clavicembalo
    (Silva) ZA 3118
SCARMOLIN, A. LOUIS (1890-   )
  Introduction and Dance
    Lud S-1999
SCELZI, GIACINTO (1905-   )
  Ballata
    Santis 728

Dialogo
  Santis 750
SCHARWENKA, XAVER (1850-1924)
  Sonata in e, Op. 46
    Aug 9287
SCHELLSCHMIDT, A.H.
  Berceuse
    CF B1551
  Pensée
    CF B1552
SCHENK, [JOHANN (1753-1836)]
  Pieces, 12, from Scherzi Musicali
    Kul   2V
SCHIBLER, ARMIN (1920-   )
  Concertino, Op. 64
    Eul (Pet No. Z248)
SCHIFF, [HELMUT (1918-   )]
  Sonatine
    DOB
SCHLEMM, [GUSTAV ADOLF (1902-   )]
  Fantasiestück, orig for vcl and orch
    BRH
SCHLEMÜLLER, HUGO
  Cradle Song, from Easy Concert
    Pieces, Op. 12
    CF B2728
  Forward March, from Easy Solo Pieces,
    Op. 14
    (Buechner) CF B2630
  Gondola Song, from Easy Solo Pieces,
    Op. 14
    (Buechner) CF B2476
  Mélancolie, from Easy Solo Pieces, Op. 14
    (Buechner) CF B2933
  Menuet, from Easy Solo Pieces, Op. 14
    (Buechner) CF B2357
  Mountain Maiden, from Easy Concert Pieces,
    Op. 12
    CF B2871
  Our Soldiers, from Easy Concert Pieces,
    Op. 12
    CF B2796
  Prayer, from Easy Concert Pieces, Op. 12
    CF B2696
  Russian Song, from Easy Solo Pieces, Op. 14
    (Buechner) CF B2832
  Scherzo, from Easy Concert Pieces, Op. 12
    CF B2514
  Song, from Easy Concert Pieces, Op. 12
    CF B2621
  Waltz, from Easy Solo Pieces, Op. 14
    (Buechner) CF B2853
SCHLICK, JOHANN CONRAD (c.1759-1825)
  Sonate
    (Ladmirault-Laffra) Delrieu
SCHMID, HEINRICH KASPAR (1874-1953)
  Ode, Op. 34, No. 3
    SCH
SCHMIDT, ERNST
  Easy Pieces, 6, Op. 44
    BMC
SCHMIDT, OSCAR
  Cavatine, Op. 41
    (Buechner) CF B1560
SCHMITT, FLORENT (1870-1958)
  Chant élégiaque, Op. 24, orig for vcl
    and orch
    Dur
  Introit, récit et congé, Op. 113
    Dur
SCHOECK, OTHMAR (1886-1957)
  Sonata
    Baer 3960
  Sonata, Op. 41, orig for bass clar and pno
    (Hindermann) BRH

SCHOENBERG, ARNOLD (1874-1951)
 Concerto, see Monn
SCHOLLUM, ROBERT (1913-)
 Sonatina, Op. 57, No. 1
  DOB
(SCHROEDER, ALWIN)
 Easy Violoncello classics
  BMC 2V for contents see title
 Solo Concert Repertoire
  BMC 4V for contents see title
SCHUBERT, FRANCOIS (1808-1878)
 Bee
  (Casals) Int
  (Schroeder) BMC
SCHUBERT, FRANZ (1797-1828)
 Allegretto grazioso
  (Cassado) UE 8286
 Ave Maria, orig for voice and pno
  (Hauser-Ambrosio) CF B2701
  (Palaschko) SCH
 Berceuse
  (Krane) Shapiro, Bernstein
  see also Wiegenlied
 Concerto in a, after the Arpeggione Sonata
  (Cassadó) SCH
 Introduction, Theme and Variations,
   Op. 82, No. 2, orig for pno
  (Piatigorsky) EV
 Litanei, orig for voice and pno
  (Maréchal) ESC
 Moment Musical, Op. 94, No. 3, orig for pno
  (Moffat) SCH
 Reverie
  (Forbes) Oxf
 Serenade, orig for voice and pno
  (Moffat) SCH "Ständchen"
  CF B2917
 Sonata in a, orig for arpeggione and pno
  (Fournier) ESC
  (Mulder) BRH
  (Rose) Int
  Pet 4623
 Valses nobles, orig for pno
  (Silva) FC
 Wiegenlied
  (Becker) SCH
  see also Berceuse
  see also Graded Teaching Pieces
(SCHULZ)
 Classical Pieces
  SCH for contents see title under gamba
   and pno
 From Four Centuries
  BRH for contents see title
 Violoncello Classics
  GS 2V for contents see title
SCHUMAN, WILLIAM (1910-)
 Song of Orpheus
  Pr
SCHUMANN, ROBERT (1810-1856)
 Abendlied, Op. 85, No. 12, orig for pno duet
  (Lechner) SCH; with Träumerei,
   Op. 15, No. 7
  (Lee) SCH
 Adagio and Allegro, Op. 70, orig for horn
   and pno
  BRH
  Int
  Pet 2386
 Concerto in a, Op. 129
  (Feuermann) CF 03447
  (Klengel-Raphael) BRH
  (Rose) Int with cadenzas

  Pet 2374
  cadenzas published separately, see under
   vcl unacc: Selmi
 Fantasy Pieces, Op. 73, orig for clar and pno
  Int
 Original Compositions
  Pet 2373
   Adagio and Allegro in A flat, Op. 70
   Fantasy Pieces, Op. 73
   Pieces in Folk Style, Op. 102
 Pieces in Folk Style, Op. 102
  Int
 Romances, 3, Op. 94, orig for ob and pno
  Pet 2387
 Romances, 3
  (Gendron) SCH
 Romance
  (Krane) Fox
 Träumerei, Op. 15, No. 7, orig for pno
  (Davidoff-Buechner) CF B2845
  (Palaschko) SCH
  FR (Pet No. F42)
  see also Abendlied
  see also Graded Teaching Pieces
SCHWARZ
 Arioso, see Kochetov: Melody
SCIOSTAKOVIC, see Shostakovitch
SCOTT, CYRIL (1879-)
 Andante languido
  (Sharpe) EKN
 Ballade
  UE 10584
 Cherry Ripe, orig for pno
  (Withers) SCH
 Lullaby, Op. 57, No. 2, orig for voice
  (Evans) EKN
 Poem. The Melodist and the Nightingales
  SCH
 Vesperale
  (Hambourg) EKN
SCRIABIN, ALEXANDER (1872-1915)
 Etude, Op. 2, No. 1, orig for pno
  (Krane) GS
  MZK published with Prelude, Op. 23,
   No. 10 by Rachmaninoff
 Etude, Op. 8, No. 11, orig for pno
  (Piatigorsky) SCH
 Etude, Op. 8
  (Piatigorsky) Int
 Poem, Op. 32, No. 1, orig for pno
  (Piatigorsky) SCH
 Poem, Op. 32, No. 2, orig for pno
  (Piatigorsky) Int
SEIBER, MÁTYÁS (1905-1960)
 Pieces, 3
  SCH
 Sarabande and Gigue in Old Style
  SMP
SENAILLÉ, JEAN BAPTISTE (1687-1730)
 Allegro spiritoso
  (Salmon) Ric R105
  Int
 Minuetto
  (Salmon) Ric R411
 Sarabanda e allemanda
  (Salmon) Ric R412
 Sonata in sol, orig for vln and Bc
  (Salmon) Ric R713
 Sonata in sol min, orig for vln and Bc
  (Salmon) Ric R714
 Vivace in re min.
  (Salmon) Ric R413
SERENADE
 (Kempf) BMC

SERIEYX, [AUGUSTE (1865-1949)]
Sonate en fa mineur
HL
SERVAIS, FRANCOIS (1807-1866)
Concerto in b, Op. 5
(Gruetzmacher) Pet 2874
SÉVERAC, [DÉODAT DE (1873-1921)]
Lied Romantique
RL
SEVERN, EDMUND (1862-1942)
Cradle Song
CF B1570
SEYMOUR, JOHN L. (1893-   )
From the Far Off Hills
Leeds
Song on the Road
Leeds
SGAMBATI, GIOVANNI (1841-1914)
Serenata Napoletana, Op. 24
Int
SHAPORIN, [YURI (1889-   )]
Romances, 6
MZK
SHARPE, CEDRIC
Angelus
JWL (Mil No. W1514)
At the close of the day, from 5 Little Solos
JWL (Mil No. 1506-4)
Doll, from 5 Little Solos
JWL (Mil No. W1506-1)
Gavotte in g
JWL (Mil No. W1515)
Humoresque Rumbaesque
JWL (Mil No. W1513)
Pieces, 6
JWL
Sad Song, from 5 Little Solos
JWL (Mil No. W1506-2)
Sing Song, from 5 Little Solos
JWL (Mil No. W1506-5)
Sleepy Song, from 5 Little Solos
JWL (Mil No. W1506-3)
Soir, Le
JWL
SHIRINSKY, S.
Transcriptions, 2, from The Tsar's Bride
by Rimsky-Korsakov
MZK
SHOSTAKOVITCH, DMITRI (1906-   )
Concerto, Op. 107
(Rostropovich) Int
Leeds
Pet 4743
Ric 130139
Dance from Golden Age, Op. 22
(Schuster) MK
Pezzi, 2,[68] orig for vcl and orch
(Atovmian) Ric 129644
Pieces, 2: Adagio and Spring Waltz
(Atovmian) MZK
Pet 4767
Sonata, Op. 40
(Piatigorsky) Leeds
(Rose) Int
Pet 4748
SHREDNICK, see Rogers & Shrednick
SHUK, LAJOS
Csárdás
GS
SHULMAN, ALAN (1915-   )
Concerto
Chap

---

[68] These pieces may be Adagio and Spring Waltz.

Homage to Erik Satie
GS
Suite for the young cellist
Fox
SIBELIUS, JEAN (1865-1957)
Impromptu, Op. 78, No. 1
WH 2341
Laetare anima mea, Op. 77, No. 1, orig
for vln or vcl and orch
WH 2173
Malinconia, Op. 20
BRH
Religioso, Op. 78, No. 3
WH 2202
Rigaudon, Op. 78, No. 4
WH 2339
Romance, Op. 24, No. 9
(Schroeder) BMC
Romance in F, Op. 78, No. 2
BMC
WH 2201
Valse triste, see Mendelssohn: Nocturno
SIEGL, OTTO (1896-   )
Easy Pieces, 4
OBV
Little Variations on "Do You Know How
Many Stars Are Shining?"
OBV
Sonata No. 3, Op. 33
DOB
SIMPSON, CHRISTOPHER (c.1610-1669)
Variations
(Döbereiner) SCH
SIMS, EZRA (1930-   )
Sonata
CFE
SJÖGREN, EMIL (1853-1918)
Sonate, Op. 58
WH 1409
SKALKOTTAS, NIKOS (1904-1949)
Bolero
UE 12861
Sonatina
UE 12387
Tender Melody
UE 12429
SKORULSKY, M.
Classical Pieces, 2
MZK
SKORZENY, [FRITZ (1900-   )]
Fantasiestücke, 4
DOB
SKRYABIN, see Scriabin
SLADEK, PAUL
Elegy
VL
SMITH, CLAY
My Song of Songs
CF
Spirit of Joy
CF
SMITH, HALE (1925-   )
Sonata
CFE
SMITH, RUSSELL (1927-   )
Lyric Piece
CFE
(SMOLIANSKY)
Pieces for Cello, 13
MZK
SOKALSKY
Song; with Scherzino by Kosenko
MZK

SOLO CONCERT REPERTOIRE
  (Schroeder) BMC   4V
    Vol 1
      Bach: Prelude
      Bruch: Kol Nidrei
      Fauré: Lamento
      Glinka: Nocturne
      Händel: Sarabande
      Hill: Liebeslied
      Holter: Bagatelle
      Moussorgsky: Chanson Russe
      Popper: Vito
      Reinecke: Gavotte
      Schubert: Moment Musical
      Sitt: Serenade
    Vol 2
      Beethoven: Minuet
      Chopin: Lento
      Cossmann: Tarantelle
      Cui: Berceuse
      Fauré: Élégie
      Gluck: Mélodie
      Marie, Gabriel: Gavotte
      Offenbach: Musette
      Popper: Warum?
      Ropartz: Adagio
      Saint-Saëns: Swan
      Schubert: Bee
    Vol 3
      Ambrosio,d': Mélodie
      Bull: Melody in D
      Debussy: Bells
      Händel: Larghetto
      Holter: Hymmus
      Moussorgsky: Meditation
      Perrin: Gavotte
      Popper: Harlequin
      Rimsky-Korsakov: Song of India
      Schroeder: Neapolitan Dance
      Schumann: Romance
    Vol 4
      Dvořák: Waldesruhe
      Grieg: Air
      Grieg: Sarabande
      Händel: Minuet
      Lully: Gavotte
      Popper: Serenade, Op. 54
      Reinecke: Scherzo
      Saint-Saëns: Allegro Appassionato,
        Op. 43
SOLOS FOR STRINGS
  (Whistler) Ru
SOLOS FOR THE CELLO PLAYER
  (Deri) GS
    Bach, J.S.: Bouree 1 and 2, from
      Third Cello Suite
    Beethoven: Andante
    Brahms: Lullaby
    Debussy: Romance
    Faure: Sicilienne
    Gluck: Andante from Orfeo
    Handel: Allegro from Violin Sonata,
      Op. 1, No. 15
    Handel: Larghetto from Violin Sonata,
      Op. 1, No. 13
    Lotti, A.: Aria
    Marie, Gabriel: Cinquantaine, La
    Mozart: Menuet from Divertimento in
      D, K. 334
    Pergolesi: Nina
    Popper: Village Song
    Saint-Saens: Swan
    Schumann: Lento, from Five Pieces in
      Popular Mood

    Senallie: Allegro Spiritoso
    Weber: Country Dance
SOMERVELL, ARTHUR (1863-1937)
  Barcarolle, from 3 Original Pieces
    Aug
  Romance, from 3 Original Pieces
    Aug
  What you will
    Aug
  Whims, from 3 Original Pieces
    Aug
SOMIS, GIOVANNI BATTISTA (1686-1763)
  Allegretto
    (Silva) ZA 3189
SONGS, 8, OF THE U.S.S.R. PEOPLES, BK. II
  (Sapozhnikov) MZK
SONZOGNO, GIULIO CESARE (1906-   )
  Canzonetta
    SZ
SPENDIAROV
  Barcarolle, Lullaby, see Kalinnikov: Sad Song
SQUIRE, WILLIAM HENRY (1871-   )
  At Morn, from Petits Morceaux, Op. 16
    (Buechner) CF B2936
  At Twilight, from Petits Morceaux, Op. 16
    (Buechner) CF B2935
  Bourrée, Op. 24
    CF B2518
  Cradle Song, from Petits Morceaux, Op. 16
    (Buechner) CF B2711
  Danse Rustique, Op. 20, No. 5
    CF B2517
  Fairy Tales, from Petits Morceaux, Op. 16
    (Buechner) CF B2725
  In Dreamland, from Petits Morceaux, Op. 16
    (Buechner) CF B2733
  Meditation
    BH
  Tarantella, Op. 23
    CF B2691
  Violoncello Albums
    JWL (Mil Nos. 1508-11)   4V
  see also Graded Teaching Pieces
STAMITZ, KARL (1746-1801)
  Konzert No. 2 in A
    (Füssl) Baer 3711
STEHMAN, JACQUES (1912-   )
  Lamento
    CBDM
STEIN, LEON (1910-   )
  Air
    CFE
STEPAN, VACLAV (1889-1944)
  Poème
    RL
STEPANIAN, [RUBEN (1902-   )]
  Elegy
    MZK
  Sonata
    MZK
STEPANOVA, V.
  Poem
    MZK
STEPOVOI, Y.
  Cantabile
    MZK
STEVENS, HALSEY (1908-   )
  Hungarian Children's Songs
    Peer
  Intermezzo, Cadenza and Finale
    CFE
  Pieces, 3
    Pet 6029

STEVENS, HALSEY (cont.)
  Music for Christopher, Book 1
    CFE
  Sonatina Giocosa
    CFE
  Tunes from Olden Times
    CFE 2V
STIASNI
  Andante cantabile, see Buononcini:
      Sonata in A
STOCKHOFF, W.W.
  Variations
    BRH
STOGORSKY, A.
  Etudes-Variations
    MZK
(STOGORSKY)
  Pieces, 8
    MZK
STRADELLA, ALESSANDRO (1642-1682)
  Pietà, Signore
    (Hofmann) CF B2915
STRAUSS, RICHARD (1864-1949)
  Sonata in F, Op. 6
    (Rose) Int
    UE 1007
STRAVINSKY, IGOR (1882-   )
  Mavra: Russian Maiden's Song
    (Markevitch) BH
  Suite Italienne
    BH   transcribed by composer
STÜRMER, BRUNO (1892-1958)
  Sonate
    Baer 1911
  Kleine Hausmusik
    SCH
STUTSCHEWSKY, JOACHIM (1891-   )
  Israeli Melodies, 6
    Mil
  Jolly Dance, from Little Cellist
    Leeds
  Little Cellist
    Leeds
(STUTSCHEWSKY, J.)
  Lost Melodies
    UE 10627   for contents see title
(SUCH)
  Easy Classical Pieces
    SCH   for contents see title
  see also Moffat-Such
SUGAR, RESZO (1919-   )
  Capriccio
    Kul
  Theme with Variations
    Kul
  Violoncello Pieces, 2
    Kul
SUK, JOSEPH (1874-1935)
  Ballade and Serenade
    SIM
SUK
  Air
    Kul
SUTERMEISTER, [HEINRICH (1910-   )]
  Concerto
    SCH
SWANSON, HOWARD (1909-   )
  Suite
    Weintraub
SWEETING, E.T.
  Pieces, 3
    STB
SZELENYI, [ISTVAN (1904-   )]
  Air
    Kul

SZONYI, E.
  Play
    BH
TABB, R.V.
  Automne, L'
    STB
  Bourree
    STB
  By the Brook, from 4 Rhythmic Pieces
    JWL (Mil No. W1512-3)
  By the Sea, from 4 Rhythmic Pieces
    JWL (Mil No. W1512-2)
  By the Wayside, from 4 Rhythmic Pieces
    JWL (Mil No. W1512-1)
  Meadowsweet, from 4 Rhythmic Pieces
    JWL (Mil No. W1512-4)
  Menuet Piquante
    STB
  Poeme d'amour
    STB
  Printemps, Le
    STB
  Romance sans paroles
    STB
  Scherzo
    Aug
(TABB, R.V.)
  Old Tunes for Young Cellists
    Aug
TAKÁCS, JENÖ (1902-   )
  Rhapsody, Op. 49, "Hungarian Airs"
    DOB
TANSMAN, ALEXANDER (1897-   )
  Aria, from Nous jouons pour Maman
    ESC
  Danse Paysanne, from Nous jouons pour
      Maman
    ESC
  Elégie, from Nous jouons pour Maman
    ESC
  Fantaisie
    ESC
  Fête, from Nous jouons pour Maman
    ESC
  Matin, Le, from Nous jouons pour Maman
    ESC
  Pastorale, from Nous jouons pour Maman
    ESC
  Pieces, 2
    ESC
  Sonata
    ESC
TAPIA COLMAN, SIMON
  Sonata
    EMM
TARTANAC
  Canzone
    Sal
TARTINI, GIUSEPPE (1692-1770)
  Concerto in A
    (Ravanello-Silva) ZA 3168
  Concerto in D
    (Gruetzmacher) Int
  Concerto in D
    (Hindemith) SCH
  Concerto in D
    (Salmon) Ric R716
  Grave
    (Schuster) CF B2774
  Variations on a theme by Corelli, orig for vln
    Int
TAYLOR, COLIN
  As once she danced, from 3 Pieces
    Aug

TAYLOR, COLIN (cont.)
  Pantaloon, from 3 Pieces
    Aug
  Threnody, from 3 Pieces
    Aug
TCHAIKOVSKY, PIOTR ILYITCH (1840-1893)
  Album for the Young, Op. 39, orig for pno
    Pet 4714
  Barcarolle
    MZK
  Chanson Triste, Op. 40, No. 2, orig for pno
    (Palaschko) SCH
    (Popper) CF B2659
  Chanson Triste, from Piano Piece,
      Op. 96, No. 2
    (Withers) SCH
  Chant d'automne, Op. 37, No. 10, orig for pno
    (Stutschewsky) Pet 4223
    MZK "Autumn Song"
  Chant sans paroles, Op. 2, No. 3, orig
      for pno
    (Schulz) CF B1585
    (Trinkaus) Fill
  Concerto[69]
    (Cassadó) SCH
  Lullaby; Mazurka
    MZK
  Lullaby, from Mazeppa; Waltz
    MZK
  Meditation, Op. 72, No. 5
    MZK
  Nata-Waltz; Lullaby in a Storm
    MZK
  Neapolitan Song; Sad Song
    MZK
  Nocturne, Op. 19, No. 4, orig for pno
    MZK
  Nur wer die Sehnsucht Kennt, orig for voice
    BMC
  Pezzo capriccioso, Op. 62. Concertpiece,
      orig for vcl and orch
    Int
  Romance, Op. 51, No. 5
    MZK
  Valse Sentimentale, Op. 51, No. 6, orig
      for pno
    (Grunes) Omega
    (Press-Schuster) CF B2400
    (Rose) Int
    Cor ST13
  Variations on a Rococo Theme, Op. 33,
      orig for vcl and orch
    (Becker) SIM
    (Gruemmer) Pet 3776
    (Rose) Int
    Aug 7749
    CF 03519
    MZK
  see also Graded Teaching Pieces
TCHEREPNINE, ALEXANDRE (1899-   )
  Ode
    (Hekking) Dur
  Rapsodie géorgienne, orig for vcl and orch
    (Hekking) Dur
  Sonata in D
    (Hekking) Dur
  Songs and Dances, Op. 84
    Belaieff
  Violoncelle bien tempéré, Op. 38
    (Fournier) Dur
TELEMANN, GEORG PHILIPP (1681-1767)
  Sonata in a
    (Ruyssen) Delrieu

Sonata in D
  (Degen) Baer HM13
Sonata in D
  (Upmeyer) Int
see also sonatas for gamba and keyboard
TEMPLETON, ALEC (1909-   )
  Elegie
    Leeds
TENAGLIA
  Aria in f
    RE (Pet No. RE 11)
TERTIS, LIONEL (1876-   )
  Sunset
    Ches
TESSARINI, [CARLO (1690-c.1765)]
  Sonata in F
    (Trowell) SCH
THIMAN, ERIC H. (1900-   )
  Sarabande and Almayne
    (Withers) SCH
THOMÉ, FRANCIS (1850-1909)
  Simple Aveu, Op. 25
    (Buechner) CF B2863
    (Schenkman) GS
THOMPSON, ROY
  Ballad, from 6 Easy Pieces
    Aug
  Bumpkins' Dance
    Aug
  Dance, from 6 Easy Pieces
    Aug
  Harlequins' Serenade
    Aug
  Mazurka, from 6 Easy Pieces
    Aug
  Rondel, from 6 Easy Pieces
    Aug
  Scherzo, from 6 Easy Pieces
    Aug
  Serenade, from 6 Easy Pieces
    Aug
  Waltz
    Aug
THOMSON, VIRGIL (1896-   )
  Concerto
    FC
TICCIATI, NISO (1924-   )
  Sonata in G
    Oxf
  Young Cellist
    Oxf 21.016-18   3V
TOMASI, [HENRI (1901-   )]
  Obsessions, sur un rythme de habanera,
      orig for vcl and orch
    HL
TOMMASINI, VINCENZO (1878-1950)
  Macchiette, 2
    SZ
  Scherzo
    ZA 3202
TORELLI, GIUSEPPE (1658-1709)
  Sonata in G
    (Giegling) Baer HM69
TORRANDELL, A
  Serenata Espanola
    Deiss
  Sonate, Op. 21
    Deiss
TORTELIER, [PAUL (1914-   )]
  Sonate en ré mineur
    Dur
  Spirales
    Dur

---

[69] The publisher gives no information about the source of
this listing. It may be Pezzo capriccioso, Op. 62, or an
arrangement of a concerto for another instrument.

TOSELLI, ENRICO (1883-1926)
  Serenade, Op. 6
    (Schulz) BMC
    (Simon) BMC simpl
TOSTI, FRANCESCO PAOLO (1846-1916)
  Good-Bye!
    (Hegner) CF B2932
TOVEY, DONALD F. (1875-1940)
  Concerto in C
    Oxf 21.304
TRADITIONAL TUNES, 8
  (Brockway) Oxf 21.026
    Annie Laurie
    Barbara Allen
    First Nowell
    Good King Wenceslas
    Heart of Oak
    Meeting of the waters
    Old air
    Small folk's song
TREXLER, GEORG (1903-   )
  Concerto
    BRH
  Sonata
    (Eichhorn) BRH
TREW, A.
  Alla Polka, from 4 Contrasts
    Ches
  Foundation Pieces for Cello
    Ches
  Meditation, from 4 Contrasts
    Ches
  Promenade, from 4 Contrasts
    Ches
  Serenade in the Dark, from 4 Contrasts
    Ches
TRICKLIR, J.B. (1745-1813)
  Sonata in sol
    (Salmon) Ric R415
TRIMBLE, J.
  Coolin'
    BH
TRINKAUS, GEORGE J.
  Lament
    Fill
TROWBRIDGE, L.
  Chromatico
    CP
TROWELL, A.
  Easy Pieces, 12, Op. 4
    SCH 4V
  Rigaudon, Op. 15, No. 6
    (Withers) SCH
TSCHAIKOWSKY, see Tchaikovsky
TSINTSADZE, [SULKHAN (1925-   )]
  Lullaby, see Arakishvili: Georgian Song
  Pieces, 5
    MZK
TURINA, JOAQUIN (1882-1949)
  Jeudi Saint a Minuit, from Sevilla
    ESC
  Polimnia, Op. 93, No. 4, from Las Musas
    de Andalucia
    UME
TWEEDY, DONALD (1890-1948)
  Sonata
    Leeds
UHE, A.E.
  Poême
    AMP
UNVERGAENGLICHE MELODIEN
  (Baechi) Hug (Pet No. A36)
    8 pieces by Bach, Bach-Gounod,
    Handel, Mozart, Schubert, Schumann

URAY, ERNST LUDWIG (1906-   )
  Sonata in f
    DOB
(UTKIN)
  Easy Pieces for Beginners
    MZK 2V
  Folk Melodies, Bk. I
    MZK
VAINBERG, MOYSEY (1919-   )
  Concerto, Op. 43
    MZK
  Fantasy, Op. 52
    MZK
VALENSIN, GEORGES
  Minuet
    Int
VALENTINI, GIUSEPPE (c.1681-c.1740)
  Grave and Allegro, from Sonata in E
    (Piatti) SCH
  Minuet, see Porpora: Aria
  Sonata in A flat
    (Moffat) SIM
  Sonata in B flat
    (Salmon) Ric R416
  Sonata in E
    (Piatti) Int
    (Piatti-Rapp) SCH
    (Salmon) Ric R699
VAN DE VELDE, E.
  Romance
    Gaudet
VANDINI, A.
  Sonatas, 2
    (Stutschevky-Rapp) SCH
VAN GOENS, see Goens
VARLAMOV, ALEXANDER (1801-1848)
  Red Sarafan; with Old Dance by
    Kozlovsky
    MZK
VASSILENKO, [SERGEY (1872-1956)]
  Pieces, 4
    MZK
VAUGHAN WILLIAMS, RALPH (1872-1958)
  Fantasia on Greensleeves
    Oxf 20.001
  Studies in English Folk-Song, 6
    STB
VEGA, AURELIO DE LA (1925-   )
  Leyenda del Ariel Criollo
    Pan American Union
VELGORSKY, A.
  Theme and Variations
    (Ginsburg) MZK
VERACINI, FRANCESCO MARIA (1690-c.1750)
  Sonata in d, orig for vln and Bc
    (Piatti-Rapp) SCH
    (Salmon) Ric R686
  Sonata in g, orig for vln and Bc
    (Salmon) Ric R684
VERDI, GIUSEPPE (1813-1901)
  Miserere, from Il Trovatore
    (Saenger-Buechner) CF B2920
VERESS, SÁNDOR (1907-   )
  Sonatina
    SZ
VERMEULEN, MATTHIJS (1888-   )
  Sonate No. 1
    Senart
VERRALL, JOHN (1908-   )
  Appalachian Folk Song
    CFE
VERZHBILOVICH, A.
  Etude
    MZK

VILLA-LOBOS, HEITOR (1887-1959)
Aria, from Bachianas Brasileiras No. 5, orig
for voice and 8 vcl
(Barab) AMP
Fantasia, orig for vcl and orch
AMP
Grand Concerto
ESC
Sonata No. 2
ESC
Song of the Black Swan
MK
VIOLONCELLO CLASSICS
(Schulz) GS 2V
Vol 1
Bargiel: Adagio
Davidoff: Romance sans paroles
Godard: Berceuse from Jocelyn
Goltermann: Cantilena
Marie: Sérénade badine
Massenet: Melodie
Matys: Romance
Offenbach: Musette
Popper, D: Widmung
Saint-Saëns: Romance
Schubert: Moment musical
Schumann: Adagio, Concerto
Tchaikovsky: Andante cantabile
Van Goens: Scherzo
Wagner: To the evening star from
Tannhäuser
Zelenski: Berceuse
Vol 2
Bruch: Kol Nidrei
Fischer: Romance
Gluck: Andante from Orfeo
Godard: Sur le lac
Goltermann: Romance
Goltermann: Saltarello
Lee: Gavotte
Marie: Cinquantaine, La
Nölck: Wiegenlied
Popper, D: Herbstblume
Popper, D: Sarabande and Gavotte
Romberg: Andante, from Concerto
No. 2
Scharwenka: Mazurek
Thome: Andante religioso
Triebel: Ein Albumblatt
Van Goens: Romance sans paroles
VISKI, JANOS (1906-)
Concerto
Kul
VITALI, TOMMASO ANTONIO (c.1665- ?)
Chaconne, orig for vln
(Kurtz) AMP
(Silva) ZA 3116
VIVALDI, ANTONIO (c.1669-1741)
Concerto in a
(Schulz) Pet 4961
(Sturzenegger) RH (Pet No. ER6)
Concerto in c, F.III no. 1
(Ephrikian) Ric 129536
Concerto in D, Op. 3, No. 9, orig for vln
(Dandelot-Tzipine) ESC
Concerto in D
SCH
Concerto in e
see Sonata No. 5 in e
Concerto in G, Op. 3, No. 3, orig for vln
(Dandelot) ESC
Largo in d
(Chiarappa) ZA3083
Recitative in b, see Bach, J.S.

Sonatas, 6
(Chaigneau) Senart 5082 realization by
W. Morse-Rummel
(Graudan) GS L1794
(Hellmann) Pet 4938 2nd vcl ad lib
(Kolneder) SCH
(Rose) Int realization of figured bass by
L. Dallapiccola
Sonata No. 5 in e
(Rose) Int "Concerto in e"
(Ticciati) Hin (Pet No. H1442E)
Sonata No. 6 in B flat
(Ticciati) Hin (Pet No. H1442F)
Sonata in B flat
(Rose) Int
Sonata in a
(Rose) Int
VLASOV, A.
Melody
MZK
Melody; with Evening Song by Klochkov and
Uzbek Song and Dance by V. Vlasov
MZK
VLASOV
Dance, Etude, see Kosenko: Pastorale
VOGEL, [WLADIMIR (1896-)]
Concerto
SZ
VOLKMANN, ROBERT (1815-1883)
Concerto, Op. 33
(Klengel) BRH
(Mainardi) SCH
Pet 3465 with cadenzas
Waltz, from Serenade No. 2 for Strings,
Op. 63
(Withers) SCH
VOLPATTI, J.
Contemplation
Gaudet
Reverie
Gaudet
VON BLON, FRANZ (1861-1945)
Meditation
(Ambrosio) CF
VOORMOLEN, ALEXANDER (1895-)
Divertissement
RL
Romance
RL
Suite
RL
VREULS, VICTOR (1876-1944)
Poème
Bosw
Poème No. 2
Sal
Sonate
Senart
VUATAZ, [ROGER (1898-)]
Sonate
Senart
WAGENAAR, BERNARD (1894-)
Sonatina
(Benditzky) CF B2448
WAGENSEIL, GEORG CHRISTOPH (1715-1777)
Concerto in A
(Mainardi-Racek) DOB
Concerto in C
(Racek) DOB
Concerto in E flat
WM (Pet No. WM47)
WAGNER, RICHARD (1813-1883)
Adagio, orig for clar and str quintet
(Schmeisser) BRH

WAGNER, RICHARD (cont.)
  Entrance of the Black Swans
    (Polo) SZ
  Pilgrims' Chorus, from Tannhäuser
    (Thomas) SCH
  Selected Pieces, 5, from Meistersinger,
    Parsifal, Tristan, Walkuere
    Pet 3450
  Siegmund's Love Song, from Die Walküre
    (Wickede-Buechner) CF B2968
  Song to the Evening Star, from Tannhäuser
    (Kummer-Buechner) CF B2786
    (Trinkaus) Fill
  Walther's Prize Song, from Meistersinger
    (Trinkaus) Fill
WALKER, [ERNEST (1870-1949)]
  Adagio in E flat
    JWL (Mil No. W1503)
WALTON, WILLIAM (1902-   )
  Concerto
    Oxf 21.311
WALZEL, LEOPOLD MATTHIAS (1902-   )
  Sonatina Melodiosa, Op. 21, No. 3
    DOB
WARD, ROBERT (1917-   )
  Arioso
    Highgate
  Tarantelle
    Highgate
WAXMAN, DONALD, see McGregor & Waxman
WEBER, ALAIN (1930-   )
  Triptyque
    Leduc
WEBER, BEN (1916-   )
  Pieces, 5, Op. 13
    CFE   score only
  Sonata, Op. 17
    CFE
WEBER, CARL MARIA VON (1786-1826)
  Adagio and Rondo
    (Piatigorsky) Int
    (Piatigorsky) SCH
  Andante and Rondo Ungarese, Op. 35, orig
    for bsn and orch
    LN (Pet No. R25)
  Concerto in D, Op. 74, orig for clar
    (Cassadó) SCH
  Concerto in F, Op. 75, orig for bsn
    LN (Pet No. R13)
  Romance. Fatuna's Aria from Oberon
    (Moffat) SCH
  Sonata in A[70]
    (Piatigorsky) SCH
  Sonata in C[70]
    (Piatigorsky) SCH
  Waltz, No. 2
    (Burmester) BMC
WEBERN, ANTON VON (1883-1945)
  Little Pieces, 3, Op. 11
    UE 7577
WEBSTER, CARL
  Scherzo
    BMC
  Sethney Waltz
    BMC
WECKERLEN
  Song, see Pergolesi: Song
WEIGL, [KARL (1881-1949)]
  Pieces, 2
    BH

---

[70] This may be an arrangement of a sonata for piano and violin.

WEIGL, VALLY
  Old Time Burlesque
    CFE
WEINER
  Chanson Hebraique
    Mil
WERBA, [ERIK (1918-   )]
  Slawisches Lied
    DOB
WERNER, [FRITZ (1898-   )]
  Sonate en ut majeur, Op. 20
    Dur
WERNER, GREGOR JOSEPH (1695-1766)
  Concerto per la Camera à 4
    (Moder) SIM
WESLY, E.
  Rêverie d'Automne
    Gaudet
WESTERMAN, GERHART VON
  Sonata in F, Op. 15
    (Dorner) BB
WEYBRIGHT
  Indian Drums
    Willis
  Jumbo's Good-night
    Willis
  Spanish Dance
    Willis
WHEN LOVE IS KIND
  (Buchtel) Kjos S-5202
WHISTLER, HARVEY S.
  Autumn Nocturne
    (Aller) Ru
  Starlight Waltz
    (Aller) Ru
(WHISTLER, HARVEY S.)
  Solos for Strings
    Ru
WHITEHOUSE, WILLIAM EDWARD (1859-1935)
  Easy Solos, 6
    JWL (Mil No. W1535-6)   2V
WHITTENBERG, CHARLES
  Sonata
    CFE   score only
WIDOR, CHARLES-MARIE (1844-1937)
  Concerto
    Haml
  Sérénade
    (Schneider)   CF B2940
  Sonate, Op. 80
    Heugel
WIENIAWSKI, JOSEPH (1837-1912)
  Sonate, Op. 26
    Dur
WILKINSON, MARC (1929-   )
  Pieces, 3
    Pr
WINKLER, ALEXANDER (1865-1935)
  Dernier Printemps, Op. 24
    BH
  Sonata, Op. 19
    BH
WIREN, DAG (1905-   )
  Concerto, Op. 10
    Gehrmans
  Sonatin, Op. 1
    Gehrmans
  Suite Miniature
    Gehrmans
WOLF, [HUGO (1860-1903)]
  Wiegenlied
    (Withers-Wunderlich) SCH

WÖLFL, JOSEPH (1773-1812)
Sonate in d
(Längin) Baer HM111
WOOD, HAYDN (1882-1959)
Philharmonic Variations, orig for vcl
and orch
BH
Little Pieces, 2
STB
WOOLLETT, HENRI (1864-1936)
Sonate
Leduc
WORDSWORTH, WILLIAM (1908-)
Nocturne, Op. 29
Leng (Mil No. L3013)
Scherzo, Op. 42
Leng (Mil No. L3016)
Sonata in e
Leng (Mil No. L3008)
WUORINEN, CHARLES (1938-)
Chamber Concerto, see vcl and orch
Duuiensela
MM
YRADIER, SEBASTIÁN (1809-1865)
Paloma, La
(Buechner) CF B2960
YSAŸE, EUGÈNE (1858-1931)
Méditation[71]
SF
Sérénade[71]
SF
ZANDONAI, RICCARDO (1883-1944)
Concerto andaluso
Ric 123800
ZAREMBA, S.
Romance; Polonaise
MZK
ZBINDEN, JULIEN-FRANCOIS (1917-)
Divertissement, Op. 10, orig for vcl and orch
SCH
ZEISL, ERIC (1905-)
Sonata
DOB
ZNOSKO-BOROVSKY, O.
Romance, Op. 20
MZK
ZOCARINI, MATTEO
Concertini, 6
(Kolneder) SCH   2V
Concertino No. 1
(Chaigneau & Morse-Rummel) Senart 5247
ZSOLT, N.
See Graded Teaching Pieces
ZUMSTEEG, JOHANN RUDOLF (1760-1802)
Sonata in B flat
Pet 4823

Duos: Cello, Organ

NOYON, J.
Arioso
Procure Générale du Clergé

---

[71] This publication is not listed in current U.S. catalogues.
Information was received from Fondation Eugène Ysaÿe.

STOUT, ALAN (1932-   )
Serenity
Pet 6886
UNVERGAENGLICHE MELODIEN
(Baechi) Hug (Pet No. A36)
for contents see title under vcl and pno

Duos: Cello, Guitar or Harp or Percussion

BANTOCK, GRANVILLE (1868-1946)
Hamabdil, for vcl and harp
Ches
Pibroch, for vcl and harp
Ches
BOURGUIGNON, FRANCIS DE (1890-   )
Prelude and Danse, for vcl and harp
CBDM
BUESSER, HENRI (1872-   )
Sommeil de l'enfant Jesus, for vcl and harp
CH (Pet No. C99)
FINE, VIVIAN (1913-   )
Divertimento, for vcl and percussion
CFE   score only
GILLMANN
Poem, for vcl and harp
ZM (Pet No. ZM699)
FRANCK, CÉSAR (1822-1890)
Panis Angelicus, arr for vcl and harp
BMC
HARRISON, LOU (1917-   )
Suite, for vcl and harp
Peer
HESSE, ERNST CHRISTIAN (1676-1762)
Duo in D, for gamba or vcl and lute or guitar
MT (Pet No. MV1076)
HOPF, H.
Album Leaf, Op. 2, No. 1, for vcl and harp
ZM (Pet No. ZM708)
Gavotte in a, Op. 2, No. 2, for vcl and harp
ZM (Pet No. ZM709)
HUBER, W.
Fantasy, Op. 13, for vcl and harp
ZM (Pet No. ZM710)
ROMBERG, BERNHARD (1767-1841)
Divertimento, Op. 46, for vcl and guitar
SIM
SAMINSKY, LAZARE (1882-1959)
Troubadour Song, for vcl and harp
CF B2371
SLUZER, [JULIUS (1834-1891)]
Idyl in Thuringian folk style, Op. 26, for
vcl and harp
ZM (Pet No. ZM711)
TEDESCHI, L.M.
Elegia, Op. 22, for vcl and harp
ZA 3217
Fantasia, Op. 48, for vcl and harp
ZA 3218
Impromptu Dramatique, Op. 33, for vcl and
harp
ZM (Pet No. ZM712)
VERDALLE
Meditation, Op. 18, for vcl and harp
ZM (Pet No. ZM713)

Duos: Gamba, Keyboard[72]

ABEL, KARL FRIEDRICH (1723-1787)
  Sonatas, 6, for gamba and Bc
    (Bacher-Woehl) Baer HM39-40   2V
    Vol 1: Sonatas No. 3 in e, No. 4 in
      D, No. 6 in G
    Vol 2: Sonatas No. 1 in G, No. 2 in A,
      No. 5 in A
BACH, JOHANN SEBASTIAN (1685-1750)
  *Sonatas, 3, in G,D,g
    (Leyden) Pet 4286
BACH, KARL PHILIPP EMANUEL (1714-1788)
  Sonata in D
    (Leyden) Pet 4287   2nd vcl ad lib
BUXTEHUDE, DIETRICH (c.1637-1707)
  Sonata in D, for gamba and harpsichord
    (Längin) SCH
CAIX D'HERVELOIS, LOUIS (c.1670-c.1760)
  Piéces de viole avec clavecin
    (Chapuis) Dur   2V
CLASSICAL PIECES
    (Schultz) SCH
    Caix d'Hervelois: Altfranzosisches
      Weihnachtslied
    Marais, M: Idylle
    Marais, M: La Polonaise
    Martini, G.B: Gavotte des moutons
    Rameau, J.P: Gavotte
    Tenaglia, A.F: Aria
HANDEL, GEORG FRIEDRICH (1685-1759)
  Sonata in C, for gamba and cembalo
    (Längin) Baer HM112
  Sonata in C
    Pet 4903
  Sonata, for gamba and cembalo
    (Jensen) Aug 5551
HESSE, ERNST CHRISTIAN (1676-1762)
  Duo in D, for gamba and pno or lute
    or guitar
    MT (Pet No. MV1076)
KÜHNEL, A
  Sonata No. 8 in A
    (Döbereiner) SCH
  Sonata No. 9 in D
    (Döbereiner) SCH
LEICHTE SPIELMUSIK
    (Bacher-Woehl) Baer HM123
    Marais: 4 Pieces
    Schenk: Suite in a, from Scherzi
      musicali
MARAIS, MARIN (1656-1728)
  Chaconne
    (Schultz) Pet 4993
  see also vcl and pno
PFEIFFER, JOHANN (1697-1761)
  Sonata in D
    (Schäffler) NAG
TELEMANN, GEORG PHILIPP (1681-1767)
  Sonata in a, for gamba and harpsichord
    (Dolmetsch) SCH
  Sonata in a
    (Rubardt) MT (Pet No. MV1079)
    Pet 4625
  Sonata in e, from "Essercizii Musici"
    Pet 5631
  Sonata in G, for gamba and harpsichord
    WM (Pet No. WM62)
WORDSWORTH, WILLIAM (1908-   )
  Nocturne, Op. 29, for gamba and harpsichord
    Leng (Mil No. L3013)

Duos: Double-Bass, Piano

ALPERT, HERMAN
  Trigger Fantasy
    Mutual
AMELLER, ANDRÉ (1912-   )
  Concertino
    Int
  Sonate No. 1, Op. 39
    Dur
ANDERSEN, ARTHUR OLAF (1880-   )
  Sonatina
    CF B2494
ANGERER, PAUL (1927-   )
  Gloriatio, orig for d-b and orch
    DOB
ARDÉVOL, JOSÉ (1911-   )
  Duet
    SMP
BACH, JOHANN SEBASTIAN (1685-1750)
  Adagio, from Organ Toccata in C
    Int
  Aria in D, from Suite No. 3
    Int
  Gavotte
    (Zimmermann) CF B2465
  Gigue, from Sonata No. 4
    (Delmas-Boussagol) Leduc
  Menuet in G
    (Zimmermann) CF B2464
  Sonata No. 2 in D
    (Sankey) Int
  Suite No. 1, orig for vcl unacc: Allemande;
    Courante; Sarabande; Menuet; Gigue
    (Nanny) Leduc; published separately
  Suite No. 2, orig for vcl unacc: Prelude;
    Courante; Sarabande
    (Nanny) Leduc; published separately
  Suite No. 3, orig for vcl unacc: Allemande;
    Courante; Bourrée
    (Nanny) Leduc; published separately
  Suite No. 4, orig for vcl unacc: Allemande,
    Courante; Bourrée
    (Nanny) Leduc; published separately
  Suite No. 5, orig for vcl unacc: Prelude
    (Delmas-Boussagol) Leduc
  Suite No. 6, orig for vcl unacc: Allemande;
    Gavotte; Courante
    (Nanny) Leduc; published separately
BEAUCAMP
  Cortège
    Leduc
BEETHOVEN, LUDWIG VAN (1770-1827)
  Menuets, 3
    (Sterling) Pet 238E
  Sonata, orig for horn and pno
    (Khomenko) MZK
BELLINI, VINCENZO, see Dancla
BEYER, FRANZ
  Bass Fiddle Waltz
    Bel
BIGOT
  Capriccio
    Leduc
BIRKENSTOCK, [JOHANN ADAM (1687-1733)]
  Sonate
    (Delmas-Boussagol) Leduc
BOCCHERINI, LUIGI (1743-1805)
  Adagio
    (Capon) Leduc
  Sonata No. 6 in A
    (Sankey) Int
BORNOFF'S FIDDLER'S HOLIDAY
    (Bornoff-Wilson) CF 04246, 4250

---

[72] The music in this section was specifically listed for gamba
in the publishers' catalogs. Many other compositions originally written for gamba will be found under cello and piano.

(BORNOFF, GEORGE)
  Fun for Fiddle Fingers
    Gordon V. Thompson
BOTTESINI, GIOVANNI (1821-1889)
  Capriccio Bravura
    DOB
  Concerto
    (Nanny-Sankey) Int
  Elegia in ré
    (Caimmi) Ric ER636
  Fantaisie sur la Somnambule
    Billaudot
  Introduction et variations sur le Carnaval
      de Venise
    Billaudot
  Rêverie
    (Buschmann) CF B1612
    Int
  Tarentella
    (Flechsig) Billaudot
    (Zimmermann) Int
BOZZA, EUGÈNE (1905-   )
  Allegro et Finale
    Leduc
  Pièce sur le nom d'Édouard Nanny
    Leduc
  Prélude et Allegro
    Leduc
BRENNAND
  Bass-Faddle
    (Thompson) Uni Music Press
BUCHTEL, FORREST L.
  Ambition Waltz
    Kjos S-5300
  Happy Days
    Kjos S-5303
  Jolly Fellows
    Kjos S-5304
BUSSER, [HENRI-PAUL (1872-   )]
  Concertino, Op. 80
    Leduc
  Pièce en ut, Op. 45
    Leduc
CAIMMI
  Pezzi, 2. Barcarola & Gavotta
    Ric 127922
CAIX D'HERVELOIS, LOUIS (c.1670-c.1760)
  Gavotte
    (Capon) Leduc
CAPUZZI, [G.A. (1735-1818)]
  Concerto
    (Baynes) BH
CARROLL, IDA
  Simple Pieces, 5
    Aug
CHAPUIS, AUGUSTE (1858-1933)
  Fantaisie concertante
    Dur
CHAPUIS, [AUGUSTE]
  Choral
    Leduc
CHARPENTIER, J.
  Prélude et Allegro
    Leduc
CHAYNES, CHARLES
  Lied, Scherzando et Final
    Leduc
CHOPIN, FRÉDÉRIC (1810-1849)
  Maiden's Wish, orig for voice and pno
    (Zimmermann) CF B2458
CLÉRISSE
  Pièce lyrique
    Leduc

Voce nobile
    Leduc
CORELLI, ARCANGELO (1653-1713)[73]
  Adagio, from Sonata No. 1
    (Sterling) Aug
  Adagio, from Sonata No. 5
    (Sterling) Aug
  Prelude, from Sonata No. 8
    (Sterling) Aug
  Sarabande
    (Zimmermann) CF B2459
  Sonata, Op. 4, No. 8, orig for 2 vln and Bc
    (Dragonetti-Turetzky) MM
  Sonata in d
    Int
COUNTRY GARDENS
    (Isaac-Lewis) CF B2469
DALLIER, HENRI
  Duo No. 1
    (Delmas-Boussagol) Leduc
DAMAIS, ÉMILE (1906-   )
  Appassionato
    ESC
DANCLA, CHARLES (1817-1907)
  Air Varié on theme from I Montecchi e
      Capuleti, orig for vln and pno
    (Southland) CF B1613
DE CAPUA, G.
  Romanza senza parole
    Curci
DESENCLOS, [ALFRED (1912-   )]
  Aria et Rondo
    Leduc
DILLMANN, KL
  Introduktion und Allegro
    Hof
  Sonate in e
    Hof
DITTERSDORF, KARL DITTERS VON
      (1739-1799)
  Concerto in E
    (Jaeger) SCH
  Concerto in E flat
    (Jaeger) SCH
DRAGONETTI, DOMENICO (1763-1846)
  Concerto in A
    (Nanny-Sankey) Int
  Studienkonzert
    (Siebach) Hof
  Variations brillante
    (Malarić) DOB
DUBOIS, P.M.
  Cornemuse
    Leduc
DULAURENS
  Morceau de concert
    Leduc
DVORAK, ANTONIN (1841-1904)
  Songs my mother taught me, orig for
      voice and pno
    CF B2460
ECCLES, HENRY (c.1652-c.1742)
  Sonata in g
    Int
EIGHTEENTH CENTURY PIECES, 2
    (Sterling) Aug
      Giordani: Larghetto
      Rameau: Tambourin
EISENGRÄBER, J.
  Variations on a favorite Styrian Folk-Song
    CF B2457

---

[73] It is probable that the music by Corelli listed here has
been arranged from either the violin sonatas or the trio
sonatas.

ELGAR, EDWARD (1857-1934)
Theme from Pomp and Circumstance,
orig for orch
Bel
FARKAS, FERENC (1905-   )
Sonatina, based on Hungarian folk songs
Kul
FAURÉ, GABRIEL (1845-1924)
After a Dream, orig for voice and pno
Int
Sicilienne, Op. 78, orig for vcl and pno
Int
FESCH, WILLEM DE (1687-1761)
Übungssonate
(Siebach) Hof
FUCHS, ROBERT (1847-1927)
Sonata, Op. 97
MM
FUN FOR FIDDLE FINGERS
(Bornoff-Cooper) Gordon V. Thompson
GABAYE, [PIERRE (1930-   )]
Tubabillage
Leduc
GALLIARD, JOHN ERNEST (1687-1749)
Sonata in F
Int
GEIER, O.
Konzert in E, Op. 11
Hof
GLIÈRE, REINHOLD (1875-1956)
Intermezzo
Int
Prelude
Int
Scherzo
Int
GOSSEC, FRANCOIS-JOSEPH (1734-1829)
Gavotte
(Isaac-Lewis-Skalmer) CF B2470
GOUFFE
Concertino
Billaudot
HALAHAN, GUY
Bagatelles
Chap-L
HANDEL, GEORG FRIEDRICH (1685-1759)
Allegro
(Thompson) Uni Music Press
Largo
(Zimmermann) CF B2461
Sonata in g
Int
HEGNER, LUDVIG
Cavatine, from 3 Morceaux
WH 1272
Fantasie russe, from 3 Morceaux
WH 1274
Menuet d'Orphée, from 3 Morceaux
WH 1273
HERTL, [FRANTISEK (1906-   )]
Concerto
Artia
Sonata
Artia
HIGUET
Fantaisie
Leduc
HINDEMITH, PAUL (1895-1963)
Sonata
SCH
HOME ON THE RANGE
(Buchtel) Kjos S-5306
ISAAC, MERLE J. & LEWIS, RALPH
Jolly Dutchman
CF B2490

Nautical Medley
CF B2471
JOHNSON, HAROLD M.
Lento and Zapateado, Op. 12-A
Fill
JONGEN, JOSEPH (1873-1953)
Prelude, Habanera and Allegro, Op. 106
CBDM
JULLIEN
Allegro de concert
Leduc
KELEMEN, MILKO (1924-   )
Concertino
Pet 5876
(KHOMENKO, V.)
Repertoire for String Bass, Vol. II
MZK   for contents see title
KLOSE, [OSKAR]
Concert in A, Op. 18
DOB
Mazurka di Bravura, Op. 315
DOB
Serenade, Op. 13
DOB
KOUSSEVITZKY, SERGEY (1874-1951)
Chanson Triste, Op. 2
Int
Concerto, Op. 3
FR (Pet No. F24)
Int
Humoresque, Op. 4
Int
Valse Miniature, Op. 1, No. 2
Int
LALO, EDOUARD (1823-1892)
Chants russes[74]
(Capon) Leduc
LARSSON, LARS-ERIK (1908-   )
Concertino, Op. 45, No. 11
Gehrmans
LEMAIRE
Danses, 3
Leduc
LEWIS, RALPH, see Isaac & Lewis
LORENZITI
Gavotte
(Nanny) Leduc
LUENING, OTTO (1900-   )
Suite
CFE
LULLY, JEAN-BAPTISTE (1632-1687)
Menuet, from Le Bourgeois gentilhomme
(Nanny) Leduc
MANIET, RENÉ
Piece in C
Brogneaux
Poco Allegro
Brogneaux
MARCELLO, BENEDETTO (1686-1739)
Sonata in a
Int
Sonata in e
Int
Sonata in F
Int
Sonata in g
Int
Sonata in g
Int
MARTIN, CARROLL
Pompola
CF B2489

---

[74] Chants russes is probably an arrangement of the second
movement of the Concerto, Op. 29, originally for violin and
orchestra.

MARTINI, GIAMBATTISTA (1706-1784)
Celebrated Gavotte
Kjos S-5307
MASSENET, JULES (1842-1912)
Mélodie. Elégie, from Les Érynnies, Op. 10
(Zimmermann) CF B2462
MERLE, JOHN
Caballero
CF B2466
Demetrius
CF B2488
Mummers
CF B2467
MIGOT, GEORGES (1891-   )
Prélude
Leduc
MISEK, ADOLF
Sonate in A, Op. 5
Hof
Sonate in e, Op. 6
Hof
(MONTAG, L.)
Works by Hungarian Composers
Kul   2V
MORBIDUCCI, ANGELO
Concerto in re min.
Santis 488
MOZART, WOLFGANG AMADEUS (1756-1791)
Air de la Flûte enchantée
(Delmas-Boussagol) Leduc
Concerto, K.191, orig for bsn
(Sankey) Int
Minuet, K.334, from Divertimento in D
Int
MÜLLER, J. FREDERICK
Gulliver the Giant
Kjos S5314
King of the Deep
Kjos S5313
MUNOT
Concerto No. 1
Leduc
NANNY
Airs russes
Leduc
Berceuse
Leduc
Caprices, 3
Leduc
Concerto en mi mineur, orig for d-b and
orch
Leduc
Tarentelle
Leduc
OLD DANCES FOR YOUNG BASSES
(Turetzky) MM
OLD MCDONALD IN THE DELL
(Buchtel) Kjos S-5301
PASCAL, [CLAUDE (1921-   )]
Air varié
Dur
PERGOLESI, GIOVANNI BATTISTA (1710-1736)
Tre Giorni[75]
(Zimmermann) CF B2463
PETIT, [PIERRE (1922-   )]
Grave
Leduc
PHILIDOR
Rondeau
(Capon) Leduc
PORTER, QUINCY (1897-   )
Lyric Piece
CFE

PRESSER, WILLIAM (1916-   )
Sonatina
Tritone   printed with musicwriter
PURCELL, HENRY (c.1659-1695)
Aria
Int
RATEZ
Arabesque, from 6 Pièces caractéristiques
Billaudot
Cantabile, from 6 Pièces caractéristiques
Billaudot
Menuet varié, from 6 Pièces caractéristiques
Billaudot
Novelette, from 6 Pièces caractéristiques
Billaudot
Parade, from 6 Pièces caractéristiques
Billaudot
Scherzo, from 6 Pièces caractéristiques
Billaudot
RATIGLIA, LUIGI
Canto della sera
Curci
REPERTOIRE FOR STRING BASS, VOL. II
(Khomenko) MZK
Russian Folk Songs
RIVIER, [JEAN (1896-   )]
Pièce en ré
Leduc
RUSSELL, HENRY (1812-1900)
Life on the Ocean Wave
Kjos S-5305
SAFRANSKI, EDDIE
Concerto
Mutual
SAINT-SAENS, CAMILLE (1835-1921)
Eléphant, L', du Carnaval des Animaux
(Garban) Dur
SCARMOLIN, A. LOUIS (1890-   )
Introduction and Dance
Lud S-1899
SCHLEMÜLLER, HUGO
Cradle Song
CF B2337
Menuet
CF B2341
Mountain Maiden
CF B2340
Our Soldiers
CF B2342
Prayer
CF B2338
Song
CF B2339
SCHMID-SEKYT, H.
Sonata im antiken Stil, Op. 93
DOB
SCHMITT, A.
Morceau de concours
Leduc
SCHUBERT, FRANZ (1797-1828)
Sonata in a, orig for arpeggione and pno
(Sankey) Int
SCHUMANN, [ROBERT (1810-1856)]
Chant du soir
(Capon) Leduc
Danse rustique
Leduc
Reverie
(Nanny) Leduc
SERVENTI
Largo et Scherzando
Leduc
SIMANDL, FRANZ (1840-1912)
Concert Study, Op. 66
Int

---

[75] Attributed to Pergolesi.

SIMANDL, FRANZ (cont.)
Larghetto. Etude No. 23
CF B3352 pno accomp by Durkee
Sarabande and Gavotte, Op. 74
Int
Scherzo Capriccioso, Op. 72
Int
Tarantella, Op. 73
Int
Tempo di Polacca, Etude No. 17
CF B3353 pno accomp by Durkee
SKORZENY, FRITZ (1900-)
Sonatina No. 1
DOB
Sonatina No. 2
DOB
SOLOS FOR STRINGS
(Whistler) Ru
SOMMER, MAX
Albumblatt
Birnbach
Andante
Birnbach
Konzert in E
Birnbach
Romanze
Birnbach
Valse caprice
Birnbach
SOUDERE, VALÉRIE
Suite
Billaudot
SPRONGL, NORBERT (1892-)
Sonata
UE 11683
STAMITZ, KARL (1745-1801)
Concerto in D, Op. 1
(Gianelli) DOB
STEIN, E.D. [(1818-1864)]
Concertpiece
Int
(STERLING, H. SAMUEL)
Eighteenth Century Pieces, 2
Aug for contents see title
STEVENS, HALSEY (1908-)
Arioso and Etude
AME
Sonatina Giocosa
CFE
STIRZ, HANS
Konzertstück zum Probespiel
Birnbach
STOUT, ALAN (1932-)
Pieces, 3, Op. 63
CFE score only
STRING BASS SOLOS, 34
Bel EL237
TARTINI, GIUSEPPE (1692-1770)
Adagio
(Capon) Leduc
TCHAIKOVSKY, PIOTR ILYITCH (1840-1893)
Andante cantabile, Op. 11, orig for str
quartet
Int
Barcarolle, Op. 37a, orig for pno
Int
TÉNAGLIA
Aria
(Nanny) Leduc
(TURETZKY, BERTRAM)
Old Dances for Young Basses
MM

VANHAL, JOHANN BAPTIST (1739-1813)
Konzert in E
(Hermann) Hof
VIVALDI, ANTONIO (c.1669-1741)
Concerto in a, Op. 3, No. 6, orig for vln
Int
Intermezzo, from the concerto in d
(Zimmerman) GS
Sonata No. 3 in a[76]
Int
Sonata No. 4 in B flat
Int
Sonata No. 5 in e
Int
Sonata No. 6 in B flat
Int
WAGNER, RICHARD (1813-1883)
Meistersinger
(Isaac) CF B2623
To the evening star, from Tannhäuser
(Zimmerman) GS
WALLNER, K.
Konzert
Hof
WALZEL, LEOPOLD MATTHIAS (1902-)
Sonata Burlesca, Op. 37
DOB
WARREN, DAVID
Mantis Dance
Lud S-1896
WEILLER
Concerto No. 1 en sol mineur
Jobert
Fantaisie concertante
Billaudot
Morceau de Concours No. 2
Jobert
Morceau de Concours No. 3
Jobert
Pièces classiques, 2
Billaudot published separately
Polonaise de concert
Billaudot
Solo de Concert
Jobert
WHEN LOVE IS KIND
(Buchtel) Kjos S-5302
(WHISTLER, HARVEY S.)
Solos for Strings
Ru
WORKS BY HUNGARIAN COMPOSERS
(Montag) Kul 2V
ZBINDEN, JULIEN-FRANCOIS (1917-)
Divertissement, Op. 10, orig for d-b and
orch
SCH

Duos: Unspecified Instruments

BICINIEN
(Zirnbauer) SCH score only; for 2
melody instruments
12 duets by 16th century composers
CAGE, JOHN (1912-)
Sonata for two voices
Pet 6754 any 2 or more instruments
encompassing the following ranges
1: c' to c'''; 2: c to c''
GENZMER, HARALD (1909-)
Sonata in f sharp, for 2 melody instruments
SCH

---

[76] These sonatas are undoubtedly transcriptions of the cello
sonatas.

HANSCHKE, H.G.
    Variations on a Children's Song, for
       1 melody instrument and pno
      SCH
HESSENBERG, KURT (1908-   )
    Der Tag, der ist so freudenreich, for
       1 melody instrument and pno
      SCH

KRAEHENBUEHL, D.
    Variations for Two
      AMP for woodwinds or strings or
       keyboard in any combination
STEVENS, HALSEY (1908-   )
    Canons, 6, for 2 equal instruments
      CFE score only

MUSIC FOR
THREE INSTRUMENTS

Trios: 3 Violins

(ARMA)
   Little Old-French Airs
   SCH
BECK, FREDERICK
   Triads on Parade
   CP
(BERLINSKI, HERMAN)
   Three and Four Part Canons and Rounds
   Mercury
BIEDERMANN-KLIMESCH & REITER
   Fröhlicher Anfang
   DOB
BODON, PÁL
   Little Pictures, 5
   Kul   score included
BORRIS, SIEGFRIED (1906-   )
   Partita, Op. 23
   Sirius
BRADLEY, VINCENT
   Three-Part Tunes for Violin Classes
   Oxf 23.802-3   2V
BURLINGAME
   Violin Voices, for 3 and 4 vln
   Ru
CARSE, ADAM (1878-1958)
   King Cole's Fiddle Book
   Aug   2V   score included
CHAPUIS, AUGUSTE (1858-1933)
   Marche des petits violons
   Dur
CHASSMAN, JOACHIM
   Salute to Kreutzer
   Ru   pno ad lib; score included
CHORALES FOR STRINGS, see more than 1
   instrumental combination
COBURN
   Trio Album for Three Violins
   Bel
DANCLA, CHARLES (1817-1907)
   Easy Little Trios, Op. 99, Nos. 1-3
   SCH
DELAMATER
   All Grades for Violins
   Ru   for 3 and 4 vln
DESDERI, ETTORE (1892-   )
   *Divertimento
   Schwann
DOFLEIN, ERICH & ELMA
   Doflein Method
   SCH   3V
      Vol 1: Studies
      Vol 2 and Vol 3: Progressive Pieces
DONINGTON, [ROBERT (1907-   )]
   Suite No. 1
   EKN

DVORAK, ANTONIN (1841-1904)
   Gavotte; with Miniatures, Op. 75A, for 2
   vln, vla
   Artia
ENSEMBLE TRIO ALBUM
   (Elkan) H Elkan
   Compositions by Delibes, Gounod,
   Haydn, Mozart, Offenbach, Rossini,
   Verdi
FIDDLE SESSIONS
   (Gearhart & Green) Shawnee; for contents
   see title under 2 vln
FIDDLERS THREE
   (Wehrmann) GS   score included
      Boieldieu: Andantino
      Corelli: Pastorale, from Christmas
         concerto
      Godard: Andantino
      Handel: Pastorale, Christmas section
         of Messiah
      Hänsel: Allegretto
      Hänsel: Andante
      Mozart: Andante
      Paradies: Andante
      Pergolesi: Siciliana
      Rameau: Menuet
FIRST PRACTICE IN ENSEMBLE PLAYING
   (Hermann) Aug 5291   2V
FIRST TRIO ALBUM
   (Whistler & Hummel) Ru
FREDERICK THE GREAT (1712-1786)
   Andante in d, from Symphony No. 3
   VW (Pet No. V35)
FUX, JOHANN JOSEPH (1660-1741)
   Sonata a 3
   SCH
GAY DANCES OF OLD MASTERS
   (Hoffmann) SCH   for contents see title
      under 2 vln
(GEARHART, LIVINGSTON & GREEN, ELIZA-
      BETH)
   Fiddle Sessions
   Shawnee   for contents see title under 2 vln
GENZMER, HARALD (1909-   )
   Spielmusik
   SCH
GERSTER, OTTMAR (1897-   )
   Little Festival Music
   SCH
GIESEKING, WALTER (1895-1956)
   Kleine Musik
   Oertel
GRAUPNER, CHRISTOPH (1683-1760)
   Suite in F. Ouverture à trois chalumeaux
   Pet 4564
GREEN, ELIZABETH, see Gearhart & Green
HAAGER, MAX (1905-   )
   *Music for 3 Instruments, Op. 6a
   OBV

HANDEL, GEORG FRIEDRICH (1685-1759)
Sonata in C
NAG   score only
HERMANN, FRIEDRICH
Burlesque, Op. 9
Int
(HERMANN)
First Practice in Ensemble Playing
Aug 5291   2V
HINDEMITH, PAUL (1895-1963)
Canons, 8, Op. 44, No. 2
SCH   score only
(HOFFMANN)
Gay Dances of Old Masters
SCH   for contents see title under 2 vln
HOOK, JAMES (1746-1827)
Sonata in G, Op. 83, No. 4
BH
HUMMEL, HERMAN A., see Whistler &
Hummel
JACOBSON
Three Visions for Violins
Mil
JEANNERET, A.
Suite Pittoresque
HL
Suite No. 2
HL
*Trios, 4
Senart
KREUTZER, RODOLPHE
Caprice No. 2, see Chassman: Salute to
Kreutzer
LACHNER, IGNAZ (1807-1895)
Sonatina in G, Op. 90, No. 1
Hof
Sonatina in D, Op. 90, No. 2
Hof
Sonatina in A, Op. 90, No. 3
Hof
LITTLE OLD-FRENCH AIRS
(Arma) SCH
MALER, WILHELM (1902-   )
Trio
SCH
MANN, ALFRED
Kleine Schulmusik
Moeck 1203
MICHEELSEN, HANS FRIEDRICH (1902-   )
Variationen und Fuge über "Es sungen
drei Engel"
Baer 2234
MORITZ, EDVARD
Divertimento
Mercury
MOZART, WOLFGANG AMADEUS (1756-1791)
Adagio, K.356, orig for glass harmonica;
with Menuet and Rondo from K.S.229a,
orig for 2 clar, bsn
Pet 4508
Laendlerische Taenze, 6, for 2 or 3 vln
Noet (Pet No. N200)   pno ad lib
Larghetto, see Dancla: 3 Pieces, Op. 178
under 4 vln
Minuets, 4
Noet (Pet No. N3216)
QUANTZ, JOHANN JOACHIM (1697-1773)
Sonata in D
NAG
REIN, WALTER (1893-1955)
Spielbuch
SCH
REITER, see Biedermann-Klimesch & Reiter

(ROSENTHAL)
Trios, 18th Century
MK   for contents see title
Trios, from Corelli to Beethoven
MK   for contents see title
Trios, Russian Composers
MK   for contents see title
SCHAFFRATH, CHRISTOPH (1709-1763)
Trio in C
(Neemann) BRH   score included
SCHALK, CARL
Ricerare on an old English melody
Concordia
(SCHEUMANN)
Tanz Mägdlein Tanz
SCH   for 2 or 3 vln
SCHMICORER, J.A.
Dances, 9, from Zodiaci Musici
(Tiedemann) BRH   score only
SIDERITS, JOSEPH
Little Pieces, 12
OBV   score only
(STONE, DAVID)
Rounds for Violins, for 3 or 4 vln
Oxf 23.807
STÜRMER, BRUNO (1892-1958)
Präludium, Passacaglia und Fuge
Baer 1912
Suiten, 2
Tonger
TANZ MÄGDLEIN TANZ
(Scheumann) SCH   for 2 or 3 vln
TELEMANN, GEORG PHILIPP (1681-1767)
Little Suite, from Musique de Table
Noet (Pet No. N3220)   for 3 vln or
2 vln, vcl
Little Suite
Int
THREE AND FOUR PART CANONS AND
ROUNDS
(Berlinski) Mercury
TITTEL, ERNST (1910-   )
Sonata, Op. 30
OBV   score included
TOCH, ERNST (1887-   )
Serenade
Mil
TRIOS, 18TH CENTURY
(Rosenthal) MK   for 3 clar or 3 vln
Bach: Air, from Cantata No. 128
Bach: Anglaise, from French Suite No. 3
Corelli: Allegro, from Sonata a tre,
Op. 1, No. 1
Couperin: Gigue "La Babet", from
Pièces de Clavecin, Bk. 1
Couperin: Gavotte "Les Moissonneurs",
from Pièces de Clavecin, Bk. 2
Handel: Alla breve, from Sonata a
tre No. 6 for 2 ob and bsn
Handel: Menuetto, from Concerto
Grosso No. 5
Rameau: Rigaudon, from Nouvelles
Suites de Pièces de Clavecin, Bk. 2
Rameau: Menuet, from Nouvelles Suites
de Pièces de Clavecin, Bk. 3
Scarlatti: Sonata No. 55 for Clavi-
cembalo
TRIOS, FROM CORELLI TO BEETHOVEN
(Rosenthal) MK   for 3 clar or 3 vln
Beethoven: Contre Dances
Corelli: 5 movements from Concerto
Grosso No. 8, Christmas Concerto
Couperin: Rigaudon, from Nouvelles
Suites de Pièces de Clavecin, Bk. 1

TRIOS, FROM CORELLI TO BEETHOVEN (cont.)
  (Rosenthal) MK (cont.)
    Gluck: Gavotte, from Iphigenie en
      Aulide
    Haydn: Minuet and Trio, from str
      quartet, Op. 3, No. 5
    Mozart: German Dance, from K. 605
    Purcell: 2 movements, from 12 Sonatas
    Rameau: Rondeau, from Nouvelles
      Suites de Pièces de Clavecin, Bk. 2
TRIOS, RUSSIAN COMPOSERS
  (Rosenthal) MK for 3 clar or 3 vln
    Gliere: Scherzo, from 24 Pièces
      Characteristiques, Op. 34
    Gnessin: Fairy Tale, from Miniatures
      for Piano
    Liadov: Mazurka, Op. 15, No. 1
    Maikapar: Scherzino, from
      Bagatelles, Op. 28
    Moussorgsky: Meditation
    Prokofiev: March, from Musique
      d'Enfants, Op. 65
    Rachmaninoff: Lilac, from 12 songs,
      Op. 21
    Rimsky-Korsakov: Novelette,
      Op. 11, No. 2
    Shostakovich: Prelude, from 24
      Preludes, Op. 34
    Tchaikovsky: Folk Song, from Album
      for the Young, Op. 39
    Tchaikovsky: Polka, from Album for
      the Young, Op. 39
VALE, C.
  Hatfield Suite. Suite of 16th century dances
    STB
WEELKES
  Gay Tune
    Ed M
(WEHRMANN)
  Fiddlers Three
    G3 for contents see title
(WHISTLER, HARVEY S. & HUMMEL,
    HERMAN A.)
  First Trio Album
    Ru

Trios: 3 Violas

JACOBSON
  Three Varieties for Violas
    Mil

Trios: 3 Cellos

(ARNOLD-ALSHIN)
  Easy Ensembles, for 2-4 vcl
    AMP
BACH, JOHANN SEBASTIAN (1685-1750)
  Canons, 8, from Goldberg Variations
    Hin (Pet No. H381)
  Sonata in G, S.1027, orig for gamba
    and clavier
    (Ronchini) ESC
BANTOCK, [GRANVILLE (1868-1946)]
  Witches Frolic[77]
    GT
BASS CLEF SESSIONS
  (Gearhart, Cassel & Hornibrook) Shawnee
    for contents see title under 2 vcl

[77] In the U.S.A. this publication can be obtained through Mills.

(BENOY, A.W. & SUTTON, L.)
  Trios, 20, for Young Cellists
    Oxf 21.015 for contents see title
BYE, [FREDERICK (1901-   )]
  Diversions, 6
    BH
DAVID, JOHANN NEPOMUK (1895-   )
  Sonata for 3 celli, Op. 57
    BRH score included
EASY ENSEMBLES
  (Arnold-Alshin) AMP for 2-4 vcl
(GEARHART, CASSEL & HORNIBROOK)
  Bass Clef Sessions
    Shawnee for contents see title under
      2 vcl
HANDEL, GEORG FRIEDRICH (1685-1759)
  Grave and Fugue
    Int
JACOBSON
  Three Conversations for Cellos
    Mil
LA TOMBELLE, FERNAND DE (1854-1928)
  *Suite
    Senart
MARCELLO, BENEDETTO (1686-1739)
  Adagio et Allegro
    (Bazelaire) Senart
STRADELLA, ALESSANDRO (1642-1682)
  Aria di Chiesa
    (Bazelaire) Senart
TREW, ARTHUR
  Duets and Trios for Unaccompanied Cellos
    Oxf 21.005
TRIOS FOR YOUNG CELLISTS, 20
  (Benoy & Sutton) Oxf 21.015
    Annie Laurie
    Arne: Rule, Britannia
    Auld lang syne
    Away in a manger
    Brahms: Slumber Song
    British National Anthem
    Drink to me only
    Early one morning
    First Nowell
    Hanover
    Here's a health unto his Majesty
    Highland lad
    Highland lullaby
    Holy night
    Loch Lomond
    Londonderry Air
    Mendelssohn: On wings of song
    Old 100th
    Once in Royal David's city
    Tallis's Ordinal

Trios: 3 Double-Basses

JACOBSON
  Three Burlesques for Basses
    Mil
PORADOWSKI, STEFAN BOLESLAW (1902-   )
  Trio, Op. 56
    Hof score included

Trios: 3 Viols

(ARNOLD-ALSHIN)
  Easy Ensembles, for 2-4 viols
    AMP
(BACHER)
  Leichte Fantasien
    Baer HM64 for contents see title

BASSANO, GIOVANNI (c.1657-1716)
  Trios, 7
    (Kiwi) Baer HM16
COPERARIO, GIOVANNI
  Fantasia, see vln, vla, vcl
DRAKEFORD, R.
  Fantasia, for treble, tenor, bass viols
    SCH   score only
EAST, MICHAEL (c.1580-c.1648)
  Fancies, 3, for 2 soprano viols and
    tenor viol
    (N. Dolmetsch) SCH
  My Lovely Phillis and 2 other Fancies,
    for 2 treble and tenor or bass viols
    (N. Dolmetsch) SCH   score included
EASY ENSEMBLES
  (Arnold-Alshin) AMP   for 2-4 viols
*ENGLISCHE FANTASIEN AUS DEM 17
    JAHRHUNDERT
    (Meyer) Baer HM14
GIBBONS, ORLANDO
  Fantasies
    see 2 vln, vcl
    see vln, vla, vcl
(GIESBERT)
  Old-English Viol Music
    NAG   2V   for contents see title
JENKINS, JOHN (1592-1678)
  Fantasien, 7
    (Dolmetsch) Baer HM149   score included
LEICHTE FANTASIEN
    (Bacher) Baer HM64
      Fantasies by Bassano, Lupo and Morley
LOCKE, MATTHEW (c.1630-1677)
  Suiten, 6
    (Dolmetsch) Baer HM180
  Suites, see also
    2 vln, vcl
    vln, vla, vcl
LUPO, THOMAS (17th century)
  Almains, 2, for 2 treble viols and bass viol;
    with 2 Pavans for treble, tenor and
    bass viols
    (Donington) SCH   score included
(MEYER)
  Englische Fantasien aus dem 17 Jahrhundert
    Baer HM14
MOCHENI, F.
  Trinitas in Unitate, see vln, vla, vcl
OLD-ENGLISH VIOL MUSIC
  (Giesbert) NAG   2V   score included
    Vol 1: 8 Fantasies by Gibbons,
      Coperario, Lupo
    Vol 2: 13 Fantasies by Gibbons and Lupo
PURCELL, HENRY (c.1659-1695)
  Fantasies, see more than one instrumental
    combination
TOMKINS, THOMAS (1572-1656)
  Fantasias a 3, 2, for 2 treble viols and
    bass viol
    (Rose) SCH
  Fantasy, see vln, vla, vcl
  In Nomine a 3. Fantasia on plainsong tune,
    "Gloria tibi Trinitatis", for 2 treble
    viols and bass viol
    Hin (Pet No. H558A)   score included
  In Nomine, see vln, vla, vcl
WILLAERT, ADRIAN (c.1490-1562)
  Ricercari, see vln, vla, vcl

Trios: 2 Violins, Viola

BACH, JOHANN CHRISTIAN (1735-1782)
  Trios, 3, in B flat, E flat, D
    (Möbius) Moeck 1055
  Trio, see also String Quartet Starts
    Rehearsing, under more than 1
    instrumental combination
BACH, JOHANN SEBASTIAN (1685-1750)
  Terzetti, 15
    (David) Int
BEETHOVEN, LUDWIG VAN (1770-1827)
  German Dances, 12
    Int
  Serenade, Op. 25, see fl, vln, vla
  Trio, Op. 87, orig for 2 ob, English horn
    BRH
    Int
    OBV
(BETTIN)
  Preludes of Old Masters, 16
    NAG   for contents see title
BOATWRIGHT, HOWARD (1918-   )
  Trio
    Val
BORDIER D'ANGERS, JULES (1846-1896)
  Ménétriers du Diable, Les, Op. 33
    RL
BORRIS, SIEGFRIED (1906-   )
  Sonatina per tre, Op. 45, No. 1
    Sirius
CHASSMAN, JOACHIM
  Salute to Kreutzer
    Ru   pno ad lib; score included
CHORALES FOR STRINGS, see more than 1
    instrumental combination
CRÉMONT, PIERRE (1784-1846)
  Easy Trios, 3, Op. 13
    (Herrmann) Lit (Pet No. L2022)
DE LAMARTER, [ERIC (1880-1953)]
  Triolet
    Mil
DONOVAN, RICHARD (1891-   )
  Terzetto
    Val   score included
DVORAK, ANTONIN (1841-1904)
  *Miniatures, Op. 75A; with Gavotte for 3 vln
    Artia
    SIM "Trio, Op. 75a"
  *Terzetto in C, Op. 74
    Artia
    Int
    SIM
EAST, MICHAEL (c.1580-c.1648)
  Fancies, 3
    (Dolmetsch) SCH
  My Lovely Phillis and 2 other Fancies
    (Dolmetsch) SCH   score included
GASSMANN, FLORIAN (1729-1774)
  Trios, see fl, vln, vla
HAMANN, ERICH (1898-   )
  Trio, Op. 37
    DOB
HANDEL, GEORG FRIEDRICH (1685-1759)
  Overture in D
    (Haas) SCH   score included
HAYDN, JOSEPH (1732-1809)
  Easy Trios, 12
    Int   2V

HAYDN, JOSEPH (cont.)
  Theme and Variations
    (Elkan) H Elkan
HINDEMITH, PAUL (1895-1963)
  Canons, 8, Op. 44, No. 2
    SCH
HOESL, ALBERT
  Serenade
    Cor ST9
  Suite
    Cor ST6   score included
KODÁLY, ZOLTÁN (1882-   )
  *Serenade, Op. 12
    UE 6655
KOSA, [GYÖRGY (1897-   )]
  Trio
    Kul
KREUTZER, RODOLPHE
  Caprice No. 2, see Chassman: Salute to
    Kreutzer
LERICH, RUDOLF (1903-   )
  Trio in C
    LN (Pet No. R65)   score included
MALER, WILHELM (1902-   )
  Trio
    SCH
MARTELLI
  Terzetto
    Leng (Mil No. L4006)
MARTINU, BOHUSLAV (1890-1959)
  *Serenade No. 2
    Artia
MOZART, WOLFGANG AMADEUS (1756-1791)
  Divertimento No. 3 in C, K. Anh.229, orig
    for 2 basset horns and bsn
    (Klengel) BRH
NAUMANN, JOHANN GOTTLIEB (1741-1801)
  Trio in E flat
    (Bormann) Sik 272
NOWAK, LIONEL (1911-   )
  Diptych
    Val
PORTER, QUINCY (1897-   )
  Divertimento
    Val   score included
PRELUDES OF OLD MASTERS, 16
    (Bettin) NAG   for 2 vln and vla or vcl;
    score only
      Short pieces by Fischer, Froberger,
      Hammerschmidt, Krieger, Kuhnau,
      Pachelbel, Schmikerer, Weckmann
RACEK, FRITZ (1911-   )
  Eine Kleine Hausmusik: Rondino
    DOB   score included
REGER, MAX (1873-1916)
  Serenade No. 2 in G, Op. 141a
    Pet 3453A
SCHROEDER, [HERMANN (1843-1909)]
  Trio, Op. 14, No. 2
    SCH
SIEGL, OTTO (1896-   )
  Trio No. 1, Op. 134a
    OBV
SIGTENHORST-MEYER, BERNHARD
    (1888-1953)
  Trio, Op. 49
    AL (Pet No. AL2)
SUGÁR, REZSO (1919-   )
  *Serenade
    Kyl
SZABO, FERENC (1902-   )
  Trio
    Kul   score only

TANEYEV, SERGEY IVANOVITCH (1856-1915)
  *Trio in D, Op. 21
    FR (Pet No. F32)
    Int
    MZK
TARTINI, GIUSEPPE (1692-1770)
  Trio Sonatas, 2, orig for 2 vln and Bc
    Ed M
TOCH, ERNST (1887-   )
  *Serenade, Op. 25
    Leeds
TWO VIOLINS PLUS ONE
    (Zimmerman) GS   for 2 vln and vla
    or vcl
      Bach, J.C.: Allegretto
      Bach, J.S: Presto
      Bartok: Dance tune
      Beethoven: Menuetto III
      Cambini: La chasse
      Chopin: Prelude in A
      Gibbons: Fantasy No. 1
      Glinka: Kamarinskaya
      Gluck: Gavotte
      Gretchaninov: Tale
      Grieg: National song
      Handel: March
      Haydn: String trio
      Jenkins: Fantasia for three instruments
      King Henry VIII: Dance tune for three
        instruments
      Martini: Gavotte
      Mendelssohn: Consolation
      Mozart: Allegro
      Prokofiev: Vision fugitive
      Purcell: Cebell
      Rameau: Tambourin
      Ravel: Pavane
      Schubert: Ballet music
      Stamitz: Rondo
      Tartini: Presto in g
      Tchaikovsky: Chanson triste
VERRALL, JOHN (1908-   )
  Trio
    Val   score included

Trios: 2 Violins, Cello

ALBUM OF 10 CLASSICAL COMPOSITIONS
    (Elkan) H Elkan   for contents see title
    under vln, vla, vcl
ALIABEV, [ALEXANDER (1787-1851)]
  Variations on "In the Garden"
    MZK   score included
ANTES, JOHN (1740-1811)
  Trios, 3, Op. 3
    (Johnson-McCorkle) BH   score included
ASTORGA, DOM OLIVER (18th century)
  Trio
    Senart 5368
BACH, JOHANN CHRISTIAN (1735-1782)
  Trios, 6 easy, Op. 4
    Noet (Pet No. N6017)
BACH, JOHANN SEBASTIAN (1685-1750)
  Terzetti, 15, after 3-part Inventions,
    orig for clavier
    (Hofmann) Int   2V
BACH
  Trio Album
    (Berlinski) Mercury
BAILLOT, P.-M.-FR DE SALES (1771-1842)
  Air varié
    (Expert) Senart 5352

BAUERNFEIND, HANS (1908-   )
  Gay Play
    OBV   score included
BEETHOVEN, LUDWIG VAN (1770-1827)
  Bagatelle, Op. 33, No. 2, orig for pno
    (Elkan) H Elkan
  Country Dances, 6, orig for orch
    Int   score included
  Fugue
    Ed M
  Gesellschafts-Menuette, 6, for 2 vln and
      vcl or d-b
    SCH   score included
  Ländlerische Tänze, 6
    BRH
  Prelude and Fugue in e
    (Hess) NAG   score included
BENDA, FRANZ
  Trio, see String Quartet Starts Rehearsing,
      under more than 1 instrumental combi-
      nation
(BETTIN)
  Preludes of Old Masters, 16
    NAG   for contents see title under
    2 vln, vla
BOCCHERINI, LUIGI (1743-1805)
  Divertimento in A, Op. 2, No. 3
    (Pulkert) LEU
  Trios, 6, Op. 9
    Int
  Trios, 6, Op. 35
    SCH   2V
  Trios, 2
    Mercury "Terzetti"
  Trio, Op. 54, No. 3
    (Upmeyer) Int "Terzetto"
BRESCIANELLO, GIOVANNI ANTONIO
    (c.1690-1757)
  Concerti a tre, 6
    (Damerini) Baer HM66-8   3V; score
    included
BUONAMENTE, GIOVANNI BATTISTA
    (? -1643)
  Sonata, "La Monteverde"
    (Stevens-Menuhin) Hin (Pet No. H680)
    pno ad lib
CLEMENTI, [MUZIO (1752-1832)]
  Sonatina, Op. 36, No. 3
    (Elkan) H Elkan
CORELLI, ARCANGELO
  see Trio Sonatas
COUPERIN
  Bacchanales, Les
    (Elkan) H Elkan
CRÉMONT, PIERRE (1784-1846)
  Trios, 3 easy, Op. 13
    (Herrmann) Lit (Pet No. L2022)
DU CAURROY, FRANCOIS-EUSTACHE
    (1549-1609)
  Fantaisie No. 1
    (Expert) Senart 2645   avec réduction du
    trio au clavier
  Fantaisie No. 2
    (Expert) Senart 2648
DUSSEK
  Canzonetta
    (Elkan) H Elkan
DVORAK, ANTONIN (1841-1904)
  Humoreske, Op. 101, No. 7, orig for pno
    (Saenger) CF
(ELKAN, H.)
  Album of 10 Classical Compositions
    H Elkan   for contents see title under
    vln, vla, vcl

FUX, JOHANN JOSEPH (1660-1741)
  Church Sonata in d, for 2 vln and vcl or d-b
    VW (Pet No. V109)   score included
GÁL, HANS (1890-   )
  Little Suite, Op. 49a
    OBV   pno ad lib; score included
GIBBONS, ORLANDO (1583-1625)
  Fantasies, 9
    STB   2V
  Fantasies, 5
    Mercury
  Fantasies V and VI, for 2 vln and vcl or d-b
    VW (Pet No. V36)   score included
GOSSEC, FRANCOIS JOSEPH (1734-1829)
  Trio No. 1 in E flat, Op. 9
    (Riemann) Int
GRIEG, EDVARD (1843-1907)
  Rigaudon
    (Elkan) H Elkan
HAMANN, ERICH (1898-   )
  Sizilianische Suite, Op. 36
    DOB
HANDEL, GEORG FRIEDRICH (1685-1759)
  Fire Work Suite, orig for orch
    (Elkan) H Elkan
  Fugue, from Cello Sonata No. 2
    (Elkan) H Elkan
  Movements for Strings
    Hin (Pet No. H276E)   for contents see
    2 vln, pno
  Music for Strings
    SCH   3V   score included
  Sonata Quinta in g
    (Pochon) CF 01694
  Suites, 2
    (Jensen) Aug
HAYDN, JOSEPH (1732-1809)
  Divertimento in G, Hob. XI/89,[78] orig
      Baryton Trio
    Noet (Pet No. N997)   score included
  Divertimento in C, Hob. XI/90, orig
      Baryton Trio
    Noet (Pet No. N998)   score included
  Divertimento in D, Hob. XI/91, orig
      Baryton Trio
    Noet (Pet No. N999)   score included
  German Dances, 12
    (Giesbert) SCH   pno ad lib
  Trios, 6, for 2 vln and vcl or d-b
    (Marguerre) SCH
  Trios, 5, Eisenstädter
    (Hoffman) BRH
  Trios, 3, "London"
    (Koehler) Pet 4972   score included
  Trio in G
    (Hinnenthal) BRH
  Trios, see also 2 fl, vcl and Trio Sonatas
  Wiener Hofball-Menuette
    SCH   pno ad lib
HEISS, HERMANN (1897-   )
  Trio
    WH
HEROLD, [RUDOLF]
  Suite, Op. 70
    Pet 5165   score included
HOFFMEISTER, FRANZ ANTON (1754-1812)
  Terzetto Scholastico
    Int
    Noet (Pet No. N319)
JÁRDÁNYI, PÁL (1920-   )
  Variations
    Kul

---

[78] Hob. number refers to the thematic index by Anthony
van Hoboken.

KREUTZER, RODOLPHE (1766-1831)
  Trios brillants, Op. 15
    Lit (Pet No. L2023)
LOCKE, MATTHEW (c.1630-1677)
  Broken Consort. 6 Suites
    Noet (Pet No. N994A,b)   2V
  Suite in C
    (Warlock) Aug
      Fantazia; Courante; Ayre and Sarabande
MASTERS OF THE BAROQUE
  Pet 4539   pno ad lib; for contents see
    trio sonata
MAYR, ANTON
  Little Suite
    OBV   score included
MOZART, LEOPOLD (1719-1787)
  Divertimenti, 3
    KS
  Divertimenti, 3, in G,C,D
    VW (Pet No. V42)   score included
MOZART, WOLFGANG AMADEUS (1756-1791)
  Adagio, from Sonatina No. 5
    (Elkan) H Elkan
  Allegretto, from Sonata No. 6 for vln and pno
    (Trinkaus) MPH   score included
  Alleluja
    (Elkan) H Elkan
  Contredanses, 6, K.462, orig for orch, arr
    for 2 vln and vcl or d-b
    OBV
  Divertimento No. 1 in B flat, K. Anh. 229,
    orig for 2 basset horns and bsn
    (Kolneder) SCH   score included
  Divertimento No. 2 in B flat, K. Anh. 229
    orig for 2 basset horns and bsn
    (Klengel) BRH
  Ländler, 6, K.606, orig for orch, arr for 2
    vln and vcl or d-b
    BRH   score included
    OBV
  Little Pieces, 18
    (Giesbert) SCH   score included
  Minuets, 12, for 2 vln and vcl or d-b
    SCH
  Minuets with Trios, 8, K.585, orig for orch
    (Rohm) OBV
  Minuets with Trios, 7, K.65a, for 2 vln and
    vcl or d-b
    OBV
  Minuets, 6, K.61h, orig for orch, arr for
    2 vln and vcl or d-b
    Hug (Pet No. A9)   score included;
      vla ad lib
  Trios, 3 Easy
    Int
  Trio in B flat, K.266
    BRH
    Int
    OBV
    VW (Pet No. V45)   score included
NOWAK, LIONEL (1911-   )
  Diptych
    Val
PESCETTI
  Presto
    (Elkan) H Elkan
PRELUDES OF OLD MASTERS, 16
  (Bettin) NAG   for contents see title
    under 2 vln, vla
REINHOLD, O
  Instruktive Spielmusik
    Hof
SCHUBERT, FRANZ (1797-1828)
  Trio, D.471, see vln, vla, vcl

SHOSTAKOVITCH, DMITRI (1906-   )
  Preludes
    Ed M
SIEGL, OTTO (1896-   )
  Kleine Kammersuite
    DOB   score included
STAMITZ, JOHANN
  see Trio Sonatas
STAMITZ, KARL (1745-1801)
  Sonata in F
    VW (Pet No. V50)   score included
STEINBAUER, O.
  Die Ros' is ohn' Warum. Tricinium
    OBV   score only
TARTINI, GIUSEPPE (1692-1770)
  Sonatas, 2[79]
    (Pente) Int   score included
  Trio Sonatas, 2
    Ed M
TCHAIKOVSKY, PIOTR ILYITCH (1840-1893)
  Pieces, 12, from Children's Album
    (Mogilevsky) MZK
TELEMANN, GEORG PHILIPP (1681-1767)
  Little Suite, from Musique de Table
    Noet (Pet No. N3220)   for 3 vln or
      2 vln, vcl
TOMKINS, THOMAS (1572-1656)
  Fantasias a 3, 2
    (Rose) SCH
  In Nomine a 3. Fantasia on plainsong
    tune, "Gloria tibi Trinitatis"
    Hin (Pet No. H558A)   score included
(TRINKAUS, GEORGE J.)
  Trinkaus Trios
    Fill
TWINN, SYDNEY
  Old English Tunes, 12
    Oxf
TWO VIOLINS PLUS ONE
  (Zimmerman) GS   for contents see
    title under 2 vln and vla
VANHAL, see Wanhal
VIOTTI, GIOVANNI BATTISTA (1755-1824)
  Trio in B flat, Op. 19, No. 1
    Noet (Pet No. N6019)
WANHAL, JOHANN BAPTIST (1739-1813)
  Easy Trios
    Artia   with alternate combinations
  Easy Trios, 15
    Aug 5360
ZACH, JOHANN (1699-1773)
  Trio Sonata
    Artia
  see also Trio Sonata section
ZACHOW, FRIEDRICH WILHELM (1663-1712)
  Pieces, 2
    VW (Pet No. V56)   score included
      Prelude and Fugue
      Chorale Variations
(ZIMMERMAN, RUTH L.)
  Two Violins Plus One
    GS   for contents see title under 2 vln, vla

Trios: 2 Violas, Cello

HUMMEL, JOHANN NEPOMUK (1778-1837)
  Trio in E flat
    Pet 4862A
  Trio in G
    Pet 4862b

---

[79] These are undoubtedly trio sonatas, originally for
2 violins and Bc.

Trios: Violin, Viola, Cello

ABSIL, JEAN (1893-   )
Trio No. 1, Op. 17
CBDM   score included
*Trio No. 2, Op. 39
Ches
ACHLEITNER, WALTER (1925-   )
Trio
Krenn
ALBUM OF 10 CLASSICAL COMPOSITIONS
(Elkan) H Elkan   score included
Beethoven: Bagatelle, Op. 33, No. 2
Clementi: Sonatina, Op. 36, No. 3
Couperin: Les Bacchanales
Dussek: Canzonetta
Grieg: Rigaudon
Handel: Fire Work Suite
Handel: Fugue, from Cello Sonata No. 2
Mozart: Adagio, from Sonatina No. 5
Mozart: Alleluja
Pescetti: Presto
BACH, JOHANN SEBASTIAN (1685-1750)
Adagio, from Goldberg Variations
(Brearley) Hin (Pet No. H284)
Art of Fugue: Contrapunctus VIII, XIII
(Forbes) Pet 218C
Preludes and Fugues, see Mozart, K.404a
Terzetti, 15, after 3-part Inventions, orig
for clavier
(Hofmann) Int   2V
Trio Sonata No. 2 in c, orig for organ
(Forbes) Hin (Pet No. H56)
BACH, WILHELM FRIEDEMANN (1710-1784)
see Mozart: Preludes and Fugues, K.404a
BASSANO, GIOVANNI (c.1657-1716)
Trios, see 3 viols
BAUERNFEIND, HANS (1908-   )
Gay Play
OBV   score included
Heitere Musik
DOB   score included
BECK, CONRAD (1901-   )
Trio
ESC
BEETHOVEN, LUDWIG VAN (1770-1827)
Bagatelle, Op. 33, No. 2, orig for pno
(Elkan) H Elkan
*Serenade in D, Op. 8
BRH
Int
Pet 194b
*Trios, 6
Pet 194
Trio in E flat, Op. 3
Serenade in D, Op. 8
Trios, Op. 9, Nos. 1-3
Serenade in D, Op. 25, for fl, vln, vla
Trio in E flat, Op. 3
BRH
Int
Trio in G, Op. 9, No. 1
Int
Trio in D, Op. 9, No. 2
Int
Trio in c, Op. 9, No. 3
Int
BERKELEY, LENNOX (1903-   )
*Trio
Ches
BEZANSON, PHILIP (1916-   )
Trio
CFE   score included

BOCCHERINI, LUIGI (1743-1805)
Trios, 6, Op. 14
(Bonelli) ZA 4126
Trios, 3, Op. 14
(Bormann) Sik 299
Trios, 3, Op. 38
Int
BORRIS, SIEGFRIED (1906-   )
Trio No. 2 in G, Op. 52
Sirius
BOUCHERIT-LE-FAURÉ
Impressions
Sal
BOURGUIGNON, FRANCIS DE (1890-   )
Trio, Op. 49
CBDM   score included
BRUGK, HANS MELCHIOR
Trio, Op. 11
SIM
BRUNNER, ADOLF (1901-   )
*Streichtrio
Baer 2091
BURKHARD, WILLY (1900-1955)
*Divertimento
Baer 1596
CLEMENTI, [MUZIO (1752-1832)]
Sonatina, Op. 36, No. 3
(Elkan) H Elkan
COOKE, ARNOLD (1906-   )
*Trio
Nov
COPERARIO, GIOVANNI (c.1575-1626)
Fantasia a 3
STB
COUPERIN
Bacchanales, Les
(Elkan) H Elkan
COWELL, HENRY (1897-   )
Paragraphs, 6
CFE   score only
CRAS, JEAN (1879-1932)
*Trio
Senart
DAVID, JOHANN NEPOMUK (1895-   )
Trio, Op. 33, No. 1
BRH
Trio, Op. 33, No. 2
BRH
Trio, Op. 33, No. 3
BRH
Trio, Op. 33, No. 4
BRH
Trio in G
BRH
DE BOURGUIGNON, see Bourguignon
DE LAMARTER, [ERIC (1880-1953)]
Apple Tree
Mil   score included
Serenade. Flourish and Dances
Mil   score included
DELVAUX, A
Trio No. 1
CBDM   score included
DIERCKS, JOHN (1927-   )
Lyric Suite
Tritone   manuscript reproduction
DITTERSDORF, KARL DITTERS VON
(1739-1799)
Divertimento
(Pasquier Trio) Int
DOHNANYI, ERNST VON (1877-1960)
*Serenade, Op. 10
DOB
Int

DRIESSLER, JOHANNES (1921-   )
 *Streichtrio, Op. 1, No. 2
   Baer 2699
DUSSEK
 Canzonetta
  (Elkan) H Elkan
DVORAK, ANTONIN (1841-1904)
 Humoreske, Op. 101, No. 7, orig for pno
  (Saenger) CF
EHRENBERG, CARL (1878-   )
 Trio in D, Op. 44
   SIM
(ELKAN, H.)
 Album of 10 Classical Compositions
  H Elkan   for contents see title
ENDRES, O.P.
 Dirge
   Frangelo Press
FANCY
 STB
FINE, IRVING (1914-1962)
 *Fantasia
   Mil
FINE, VIVIAN (1913-   )
 Trio
   CFE   score included
FINZI, GERALD (1901-1956)
 *Prelude and Fugue
   BH
FORTNER, WOLFGANG (1907-   )
 Madrigals, 6
   SCH   score only
 Trio
   SCH
FRANCAIX, JEAN (1912-   )
 Trio
   SCH
FRANKEL, BENJAMIN (1906-   )
 *Trio, Op. 3
   Aug
 *Trio No. 2, Op. 34
   Ches
GAMBURG, G.
 Trio
   MZK   score only
GIARDINI, FELICE (1716-1795)
 Trios, 7, Op. 20
  (Bonelli) ZA 3697
GIBBONS, ORLANDO (1583-1625)
 Fantasies, 9
   STB   2V
GODARD, BENJAMIN (1849-1895)
 Morceaux, 4, Op. 5
   Dur
GOEB, ROGER (1914-   )
 Trio
   CFE   score included
GRIEG, EDVARD (1843-1907)
 Rigaudon
  (Elkan) H Elkan
GROSS, ROBERT
 Trio
   CFE   score included
GROSSMANN, FERDINAND (1887-   )
 *Trio
   DOB
HAMANN, ERICH (1898-   )
 Trio, Op. 28
   DOB
 Trio, Op. 30
   DOB   score included
HANDEL, GEORG FRIEDRICH (1685-1759)
 Fire Work Suite, orig for orch
  (Elkan) H Elkan

Fugue from Cello Sonata No. 2
  (Elkan) H Elkan
 Movements for Strings
   Hin (Pet No. H276E)   for contents see
    2 vln, pno
HARRISON, LOU (1917-   )
 *Trio
   Pet 6428
HAUBENSTOCK-RAMATI, ROMAN (1919-   )
 *Ricercare
   Leeds
HAUBIEL, CHARLES (1892-   )
 Trio in d
   H Elkan   score included
HAYDN, JOSEPH (1732-1809)
 *Divertimenti, 6
  (Gardonyi) Kul
 Divertimenti, 3
   Int
 Divertimento No. 109 in C
   SCH
 Divertimento No. 113 in D
   SCH
 Divertimento, for vln, vla or vla d'amore,
    and vcl
  (Meyer) NAG   score included
 Trios, 3, Op. 32
  (Pasquier Trio) Int
   Lit (Pet No. L2791)
 Trios, 3, Op. 53
   Int
HENNESSY, SWAN (1866-1929)
 Petit Trio Celtique, Op. 52
   ESC
HESSENBERG, KURT (1908-   )
 Trio, Op. 48
   SCH
HIER, ETHEL GLENN (1889-   )
 Poems For Remembrance
   CFE   score included
HINDEMITH, PAUL (1895-1963)
 Trio No. 1, Op. 34
   SCH
 Trio No. 2
   SCH
HIVELY, WELLS
 Trio
   CFE   score included
(HÖCKNER-MLYNARCZÝK)
 String Trio
   SIM   2V   for contents see title
HOFFMEISTER, FRANZ ANTON (1754-1812)
 Terzetto Scholastico
   Int
HOVHANESS, ALAN (1911-   )
 Trio, Op. 201
   Pet 6649
HUMMEL, JOHANN NEPOMUK (1778-1837)
 Trio in E flat, orig for 2 vla, vcl
  (Stein) Pet 4862A
 Trio in G, orig for 2 vla, vcl
  (Stein) Pet 4862b
HUYBRECHTS, ALBERT (1899-1938)
 Trio
   CBDM   score included
JACOB, GORDON (1895-   )
 *Shakespearian Sketches, 6
   Nov
JAUBERT, MAURICE (1900-1940)
 Sarabande
 Chant du Monde
JELINEK, HANNS (1901-   )
 *Trio. Twelve-Note-Music, Op. 15, No. 9
   UE 12027

JEMNITZ, ALEXANDER (1890-   )
  *Serenade, Op. 26
    UE 9541
JENNI, DONALD
  Terzetto
    CFE   score included
JIRÁK, KAREL BOLESLAV (1891-   )
  Divertimento, Op. 28
    UE 8701
JONGEN, JOSEPH (1873-1953)
  Trio, Op. 135
    CBDM   score included
JOUBERT, JOHN (1927-   )
  *Trio
    Nov
KAHN, ERICH ITOR (1905-1956)
  Leichte Nachtmusik
    CFE   score only
KNIGHT, MORRIS (1933-   )
  Glimpses
    Tritone   manuscript reproduction
  Trio in one movement
    Tritone   manuscript reproduction
KOFFLER, JOSEF (1896-1943)
  *Trio, Op. 10
    UE 9771
KOKAI, REZSO (1906-   )
  Serenade
    Kul   score only
KRAFT, KARL (1903-   )
  *Partita in d
    Schwann   2nd vln may be substituted
      for vla
KUBIZEK, AUGUSTIN (1918-   )
  Pieces, 4
    BRH   score included
LAJTHA, LÁSZLÓ (1891-1963)
  *Trio No. 2, Op. 18
    Leduc
  *Trio No. 3, Op. 41
    UE 11838
LESSARD, JOHN (1920-   )
  Trio
    CFE   score only
LIDHOLM, INGVAR (1921-   )
  Liten Straktrio
    Gehrmans   score only
LILBURN, DOUGLAS (1915-   )
  Trio in G
    Hin (Pet No. H142)
LOCKE, MATTHEW (c.1630-1677)
  Suite
    STB
LOTHAR, FRIEDRICH WILHELM (1885-   )
  *Trio, Op. 65
    Baer 2092
LUENING, OTTO (1900-   )
  Fantasia Brevis
    CFE   score included
LUPO, THOMAS (17th century)
  Almains, 2, and 2 Pavans
    (Donington) SCH   score included
LUTYENS, ELIZABETH (1906-   )
  Trio, Op. 5, No. 6
    Leng (Mil No. L4000)
MAASZ, GERHARD (1906-   )
  Miniatrio
    SCH
MAROS, REZSO (1917-   )
  *Divertimento
    Kul
MARTINU, BOHUSLAV (1890-1959)
  *Trio
    Heugel

MELLERS, WILFRID (1914-   )
  *Trio
    Leng (Mil No. L4001)
MENDELSSOHN, FELIX (1809-1847)
  Wedding March, from Midsummer Night's
    Dream
    (Weiss) CF
MICHL, ARTUR (1897-   )
  Streichtrio, Op. 52
    Krenn
MILHAUD, DARIUS (1892-   )
  *Trio No. 1
    Heugel
MLYNARCZYK, see Höckner-Mlynarczyk
MOCHENI, F.
  Trinitas in Unitate. Canon
    STB
MOERAN, ERNEST JOHN (1894-1950)
  *Trio in G
    Aug
MOULAERT, RAYMOND (1875-   )
  Divertimento
    CBDM   score included
MOZART, WOLFGANG AMADEUS (1756-1791)
  Adagio, from Sonatina No. 5
    (Elkan) H Elkan
  Adagio, K.404a, and Allegro, K.A.66
    (Tilmouth) Oxf
  Alleluja
    (Elkan) H Elkan
  Divertimenti, 3. K.439b, orig for 2 clar
    and bsn
    Int
  *Divertimento in E flat, K.563
    (Doflein) Baer 2670
    BRH
    Int
    Pet 1419
  Divertimento No. 1 in B flat, K. Anh. 229
    orig for 2 basset horns and bsn
    (Klengel) BRH
  Divertimento No. 4 in B flat, K. Anh. 229
    orig for 2 basset horns and bsn
    (Klengel) BRH
  Preludes and Fugues, K.404a[80]
    (Landshoff) GS L1749
    "4 Preludes and Fugues"
    (Pasquier Trio) Int   2V
    "6 Preludes and Fugues"
    BRH "6 Slow Movements and Three-Part
      Fugues, K.404a"
NEDBAL, M.
  Little Trio
    DOB   score included
NOE, ARTUR
  Streichtrio, Op. 81b
    Krenn
OTTE, HANS (1926-   )
  *Trio
    SMP
OVERTON, HALL (1920-   )
  Trio No. 1
    CFE   score included
PARRIS, ROBERT (1924-   )
  Trio
    CFE   score included
  Trio No. 2, Lament for Joseph
    CFE   score included
PARRY, CHARLES HUBERT (1848-1918)
  Intermezzi, 2
    Curwen

[80] Mozart arranged five fugues by J.S. Bach and one by
W.F. Bach, and provided preludes in slow tempo for four
of them. For the other two he used movements from Bach's
organ sonatas. The four preludes composed by Mozart
are K.404a.

PESCETTI
  Presto
    (Elkan) H Elkan
PETRASSI, GOFFREDO (1904-   )
  Trio
    SZ
PETYREK, FELIX (1892-1951)
  *Variations on Folk Songs
    DOB
PISK, PAUL (1893-   )
  Trio
    CFE   score included
PONCE, MANUEL MARÍA (1882-1948)
  *Petite Suite dans le style ancien
    Peer
  Trio
    EMM   score only
PURCELL, HENRY (c.1659-1695)
  Fantasies, see more than one
    instrumental combination
QUINET, MARCEL (1915-   )
  Trio
    CBDM   score included
RAASTED, NIELS OTTO (1888-   )
  *Primavera. Trio, Op. 96
    Dansk 224
REGER, MAX (1873-1916)
  *Trio in a, Op. 77b
    BB
  Trio No. 2 in d, Op. 141b
    Pet 3453b
RIVIER, JEAN (1896-   )
  *Trio
    Senart
ROGERS, BERNARD (1893-   )
  *Trio
    SMP
ROLAND-MANUEL (1891-   )
  *Trio
    Senart
ROPARTZ, J. GUY (1864-1955)
  *Trio en la mineur
    Dur
ROUSSEL, ALBERT (1869-1937)
  *Trio
    Dur
RÓZSA, MIKLÓS (1907-   )
  Trio, Op. 1. Serenade
    BRH
SAMAZEUILH, GUSTAVE (1877-   )
  *Suite en Trio
    Dur
SCHISKE, KARL (1916-   )
  *Triosonate, Op. 41
    DOB
SCHMIDEK, KURT
  *Trio, Op. 39
    DOB
SCHMITT, FLORENT (1870-1958)
  *Trio, Op. 105
    Dur
SCHNABEL
  Trio, Op. 30
    BH
SCHOENBERG, ARNOLD (1874-1951)
  *Trio, Op. 45
    BMP
SCHROEDER, [HERMANN (1843-1909)]
  Trio in e, Op. 14, No. 1
    SCH
SCHUBERT, FRANZ (1797-1828)
  Marche Militaire, Op. 51, No. 1, orig
    for pno duet
    (Weiss) CF

Trio No. 1 in B flat, D.471,[81] in one move -
    ment
    BRH
    Hin (Pet No. H734)   2nd vln may be
      substituted for vla
    Int
  Trio No. 2 in B flat, D.581[81]
    BRH
    Int
    UE 8478
SIEGL, OTTO (1896-   )
  Trio in B flat, Op. 130
    OBV
SKORZENY, FRITZ (1900-   )
  Trio
    DOB   score only
STRING TRIO
    (Höckner-Mlynarczyk) SIM   2V
      Vol. I: 15 easy movements by Abel,
        Stamitz, Mozart, Bruni, Weber,
        Haydn and others
      Vol. II: 5 trios by Kirmayr, J.C. Bach,
        Zappa, Schmitt and Sammartini
SWIFT, RICHARD
  Trio, Op. 6
    CFE   score only
TANEYEV, SERGEY (1856-1915)
  Trio in b
    MZK   score only
  Trio in D
    MZK   score only
  Trio in E flat, Op. 31
    Int
TANSMAN, ALEXANDER (1897-   )
  Serenade No. 2
    ESC   score included
TOCH, ERNST (1887-   )
  Trio, Op. 63
    AMP
TOMKINS, THOMAS (1572-1656)
  Fantasias a 3, 2
    (Rose) SCH
  Fantasy
    STB
  In Nomine
    STB
TOMMASINI, VINCENZO (1878-1950)
  *Trio
    Senart
VERESS, SÁNDOR (1907-   )
  Trio
    SZ
VILLA-LOBOS, HEITOR (1887-1959)
  Trio
    ESC
WAGNER-RÉGENY, RUDOLF (1903-   )
  Introduction et communication a mon
    angegardien
    UE 11671   score included
WALTHEW, RICHARD HENRY (1872-1951)
  Diversions, 5
    STB
WEBER, BEN (1916-   )
  Trio, Op. 19
    CFE   score included
WEBERN, ANTON VON (1883-1945)
  *Trio, Op. 20
    UE 8999
WILDGANS, FRIEDRICH (1913-   )
  Little Pieces, 3
    DOB   score included

---

[81] D. number refers to the Schubert Thematic Catalogue by
Otto Erich Deutsch, in collaboration with Donald R. Wakeling. London, 1951.

WILLAERT, ADRIAN (c.1490-1562)
*Ricercari, 9
(Zenck) SCH
WIRTH, HELMUT (1912-   )
*Trio
Sik 397
WORDSWORTH, WILLIAM (1908-   )
*Trio in g, Op. 25
Leng (Mil No. L4002)
YSAŸE, EUGÈNE (1858-1931)
Trio de Concert
Cinedisc

Trios: Double-Bass, 2 other String Instruments

BEETHOVEN, LUDWIG VAN (1770-1827)
Gesellschafts-Menuette, 6, for 2 vln and
vcl or d-b
SCH   score included
FUX, JOHANN JOSEPH (1660-1741)
Church Sonata in d, for 2 vln and vcl or d-b
VW (Pet No. V109)   score included
GIBBONS, ORLANDO (1583-1625)
Fantasies V and VI, for 2 vln and vcl or d-b
VW (Pet No. V36)   score included
HAYDN, JOSEPH (1732-1809)
Trios, 6, for 2 vln and vcl or d-b
(Marguerre) SCH
HAYDN, MICHAEL (1737-1806)
Divertimento in C, for vln, vcl, d-b
SCH   vla and 2nd vcl ad lib
MOZART, WOLFGANG AMADEUS (1756-1791)
Contredanses, 6, K.462, orig for orch, arr
for 2 vln and vcl or d-b
OBV
Ländler, 6, K.606, orig for orch, arr for
2 vln and vcl or
BRH   score included
OBV
Minuets, 12, for 2 vln and vcl or d-b
SCH
Minuets with Trios, 7, K.65a, for 2 vln and
vcl or d-b
OBV
Minuets, 6, K.61h, orig for orch, arr for
2 vln and vcl or d-b
Hug (Pet No. A9)   score included; vla
ad lib
Trio in B flat, K.266, for 2 vln and vcl or d-b
BRH
OBV
ROMBERG, BERNHARD (1767-1841)
Trios, 3, for vla, vcl, d-b
MM   published separately
SKORZENY, FRITZ (1900-   )
Suite No. 1, for vln, vla, d-b
DOB
Suite No. 2, for vln, vla, d-b
DOB
STAMITZ, JOHANN
see Trio Sonatas

Trios: String-Wind

AGERSNAP, HARALD (1899-   )
*Interludium, for fl, vln, vcl
Dansk 81
AHLGRIMM, HANS (1904-   )
Divertimento, for fl, vln, vla
LN (Pet No. R34)   score included

AMBROSIUS, HERMANN (1897-   )
Preludes and Fugues, 3, for fl, 2 vln
Pet 5502
ANDERSEN, KARL (1903-   )
*Trio, for fl, clar, vcl
Norsk
ARDÉVOL, JOSÉ (1911-   )
*Sonatas a Tres, Dos
ECIC
1. Sonata for ob, clar, vcl
2. Sonata for 2 fl, vla
AULICH, BRUNO (1902-   )
Divertimento, for alto rec, vln, vla
Moeck 1501
BACH, JOHANN CHRISTIAN (1735-1782)
Sonata in F, for fl, vln, vcl
(Marguerre) Moeck 1063
BEALE, JAMES (1924-   )
Miniatures, 3, Op. 3, for ob, clar, vla
CFE   score included
BEETHOVEN, LUDWIG VAN (1770-1827)
*Serenade in D, Op. 25, for fl, vln, vla
BRH
Int
Pet 194A
Trio in C, Op. 87, orig for 2 ob and
English horn; arr for 2 vln and
English horn, or 2 ob and vla
BRH
BINKERD, GORDON (1916-   )
Trio, for clar, vla, vcl
CFE   score included
BJERRE, JENS (1903-   )
*Mosaique musicale, for fl, vln, vcl
Dansk 82
BORRIS, SIEGFRIED (1906-   )
Villanellen, Op. 97, for fl, vln, vcl
Sirius
DAHL, INGOLF (1912-   )
Concerto a tre, for vln, vcl, clar
BH
DANZI, FRANZ (1763-1826)
*Trio in F, Op. 24, for vln, horn, bsn
(Wojciechowski) SIM
Trio in G, Op. 71, No. 1 for fl, vln, vcl
Noet (Pet No. N3249)
Trio in e, Op. 71, No. 2, for fl, vln, vcl
WM (Pet No. WM42)
DAVID, JOHANN NEPOMUK (1895-   )
Trio, Op. 30, for fl, vln, vla
BRH
DAVID, THOMAS CHRISTIAN (1925-   )
Trio, Op. 1, No. 1, for fl, vln, vla
BRH
DEVIENNE, FRANCOIS (1759-1803)
Trio in g, Op. 66, No. 2, for fl, vln, vcl
KN (Pet No. K19)
DIERCKS, JOHN (1927-   )
Lyric Suite, for clar or vla, vln, vcl
Tritone   manuscript reproduction
ETLER, ALVIN (1913-   ))
Sonata, for ob, clar, vla
Val   score included
FERE, see Vlasov & Fere
FREDERICK THE GREAT (1712-1786)
Andante in d, from Symphony No. 3,
for 2 fl, vln
VW (Pet No. V35)
GASSMANN, FLORIAN (1729-1774)
*Trio in A, for fl, vln, vla
KS
*Trio in B flat, for fl, vln, vla
KS
*Trio in C, for fl, vln, vla
KS

GASSMANN, FLORIAN (cont.)
*Trio in D, for fl, vln, vla
KS
Trio in E flat, for fl, vln, vla
KS score included
*Trio in G, for fl, vln, vla
KS
GILSE, JAN VAN (1880-1944)
*Trio, for fl, vln, vla
AL (Pet No. AL3)
GRAF, FRIEDRICH (1727-1795)
Trio in D, for fl, vln, vcl
Noet (Pet No. N6016)
GROFÉ, FERDE (1892-   )
Table d'Hote, for fl, vln, vla
Kjos G2000
HAYDN, JOSEPH (1732-1809)
Divertimenti, 3, for fl, vln, vcl
VW (Pet No. V37) score included
Divertimento in E flat, Hob. IV/5,
for horn, vln, vcl
(Landon) DOB score included
Theme and Variations, arr for fl, vln,
clar; or fl, vln, vla; or fl, ob, vln
(Elkan) H Elkan
Trios, 6, Op. 100, for fl, vln, vcl
ZM (Pet No. ZM15-16) 2V
Trios, 4, "London", for 2 fl, vcl
Int
NAG
Trios, 3, for 2 fl, vcl
VW (Pet V38) score included
HOLST, GUSTAV (1874-1934)
*Terzetto, for fl, ob, vla
Ches
HONEGGER, ARTHUR (1892-1955)
Choral à 3 voix, from Trois Contre-
points,[82] for vln, vcl, English horn
WH 2693
JETTEL, RUDOLF (1903-   )
Trio, for clar, vln, vla
DOB score included
JUON, PAUL (1872-1940)
*Divertimento, Op. 34, for clar, 2 vla
LN (Pet No. R112)
KANITZ, ERNEST (1894-   )
Notturno, for fl, vln, vla
Val score included
KATZ, E.
Trio, for 2 fl and vln or vla
Omega score included
KOERPPEN, ALFRED (1926-   )
Serenade in F, for fl, vln, vla
BRH
KOPPEL, HERMAN D. (1908-   )
*Divertimento pastorale, Op. 61, for ob,
vla, vcl
Dansk 83
KORN, PETER J. (1922-   )
Aloysia Serenade, Op. 19, for fl, vla, vcl
BH
KOUTZEN, BORIS (1901-   )
Music, for alto sax, bsn, vcl
BMI
KROMMER, FRANZ (1759-1831)
Treize Pieces, Op. 47, for 2 clar, vla
KN (Pet No. K35)
LEGLEY, VICTOR (1915-   )
Serenade, Op. 44, No. 3, for fl, vln, vcl
CBDM score included

LERICH, RUDOLF (1903-   )
Trio in C, for rec and 2 vln or vln, vla
LN (Pet No. R65) score included
MARTEAU, HENRI (1874-1934)
Terzetto, Op. 32, for fl, vln, vla
SIM
MILLS, CHARLES (1914-   )
Music, for rec, sax, d-b
CFE score only
MOZART, WOLFGANG AMADEUS (1756-1791)
Adagio in C, K.356, orig for glass harmonica;
arr for fl, ob, vla or fl, vln, vla
ZM (Pet No. ZM178)
MYSLIVECEK, JOSEF (1737-1781)
Trio, Op. 1, No. 4, for fl, vln, vcl
(Riemann) Int pno ad lib
NEDBAL, M.
Little Trio, for clar, bsn, vcl
DOB score included
NEMIROFF, ISAAC (1912-   )
Variations to a Theme, for fl, ob, vcl
or bsn
MM
NEUBAUR, FRANZ CHRISTOPH (1760-1795)
Trio in C, Op. 3, No. 3, for fl, vln, vla
(Bormann) Sik 289
NOWAK, LIONEL (1911-   )
Trio, for clar, vln, vcl
CFE score included
PIKET, [FREDERICK (1903-   )]
Trio, for fl, clar, vcl or bsn
Omega score included
PORTER, QUINCY (1897-   )
Little Trio, for fl, vln, vla
Val score included
PRESSER, WILLIAM (1916-   )
Rhapsody on a Peaceful Theme, for horn,
vln, vcl
Tritone printed with Musicwriter
RAPHAEL, GÜNTER (1903-1960)
Sonatina, Op. 65, No. 4, for vln, horn, bsn
BRH
REGER, MAX (1873-1916)
Serenade No. 1, Op. 77a, for fl, vln, vla
(Schnirlin) BB
Serenade No. 2 in G, Op. 141a, for fl,
vln, vla
Pet 3453A
ROUSSEL, ALBERT (1869-1937)
*Trio, Op. 40, for fl, vla, vcl
Dur
SCHISKE, KARL (1916-   )
*Music for clar, trumpet, vla, Op. 27
UE for rent
SCHWEIZER, KLAUS (1939-   )
Zwei Sätze über bewegliche Zeitmasse,
for fl, vln, vla
EDW
SENSTIUS, KAI (1889-   )
*Serenade, Op. 36, for ob, vla, bsn
Dansk 85
SIEGL, OTTO (1896-   )
Trifolium, Op. 145, for fl, ob, vla
Hof
SIGTENHORST-MEYER, BERNHARD VAN DEN
(1888-1953)
Trio, Op. 49, for fl, vln, vla
AL (Pet No. AL2)
SONGS, 12, OF THE SOVIET NATIONALITIES
(Vlasov-Fere) MZK for clar, vln, vcl
score only
SYDEMAN, WILLIAM (1928-   )
Trio, for fl, vln, d-b
MM

---

[82] Trois Contrepoints: 1. Prélude à 2 voix, for ob and vcl;
2. Choral à 3 voix; 3. Canon sur bass obstinée à 4 voix, for
vln, vcl, piccolo, English horn.

SZERVÁNSZKY, ENDRE (1912-   )
*Trio, for fl, vln, vla
  Kul
TANENBAUM, ELIAS (1924-   )
Trio, for fl, vcl, d-b
  CFE   score included
TOMASI, HENRI (1901-   )
*Pastorale Inca, for fl, 2 vln
  Leduc
TURCHI, GUIDO (1916-   )
Trio, for fl, clar, vla
  SZ   score only
(VLASOV & FERE)
Songs, 12, of the Soviet Nationalities
  MZK   for clar, vln, vcl; score only
WAGNER, JOSEPH (1900-   )
*Serenade, for ob or fl or clar, vln, vcl
  SMP
WEBER, BEN (1916-   )
Concertino, Op. 11B, for vln, clar, vcl
  CFE   score only
WEISGARBER, ELLIOT
Divertimento for clar, vln, vla
  Cor WS4   score included
WEISS, ADOLPH (1891-   )
Trio, for clar, vla, vcl
  CFE   score included
WILDGANS, FRIEDRICH (1913-   )
Kleine Haus-und Spielmusik, for fl, vln, vcl
  DOB
WOLFF, CHRISTIAN (1934-   )
Trio I, for fl, trumpet, vcl
  Pet 6502   score included
WUORINEN, CHARLES (1938-   )
Turetzky Pieces, for fl, clar, d-b
  CFE   score only
ZENDER, HANS
Serenade, for fl, vln, vcl
  BRH

Trios: 2 Violins, Piano

ABACO, EVARISTO FELICE DALL'
see Trio Sonatas
ADAM, ADOLPHE (1803-1856)
Cantique de Noel
  Ru
ADAMS, STEPHEN
Nancy Lee
  (Saenger) CF B2879
ADESTE FIDELES
  (DeLamater) Ru
ALARD, JEAN-DELPHIN (1815-1888)
Symphonie No. 1, Op. 31
  HL
Symphonie No. 2, Op. 33
  HL
Symphonie No. 3, Op. 34
  HL
ALBICASTRO, see Trio Sonatas
ALBINONI, TOMASO (1671-1750)
Balletti, 3, Op. 3, Nos. 1-3
  (Kolneder) SCH
see also Trio Sonatas
AMALIE, PRINCESS OF PRUSSIA
see Trio Sonatas
AMBROSIO, W.F.
Song of the Volga Boatmen
  CF
(AMBROSIO)
Best Selected Album
  CF 069   for contents see title

ANDRÉ, LUDWIG
Alpine Violets
  (Ambrosio) CF W1205
APOLLO ALBUM
  (Whistler & Hummel) Ru
(APPLEBAUM)
Classical Pieces
  GS   2V
ARNE, THOMAS AUGUSTINE
see Trio Sonatas
ASPELMAYR, FRANZ
see Trio Sonatas
AUBERT, JACQUES (1689-1753)
Suite, "Ma Pinte et Ma Mie au Gay"
  HL
AVISON, CHARLES
see Trio Sonatas
BACH, JOHANN SEBASTIAN (1685-1750)
Ave Maria, see Gounod
Chorales, 3
  (Cope) BH
Concerto in d, S.1043,[83] orig for 2 vln and
    orch
  (Galamian) Int
  (Hauerkampf-Davisson) BRH
  (Joachim) SIM
  (Sauret) Aug 7942
  (Spiering) CF L787
  (Spiro) BRH
  (Weingand) Ric ER860
  (Wilhelmj) SCH
  GS L899
  Pet 231
Concerto in c, S.1060,[83] orig for ob and vln,
    or 2 vln, and orch
  (Berner) SCH
  (Seiffert) Int
  Pet 3722
Concerto in d, orig for 2 pno and orch
  (Schneider) BRH
Easter Concerto. Kommet, eilet und laufet
  Pet 263
see also Trio Sonatas
BACH, KARL PHILIPP EMANUEL (1714-1788)
Little Pieces, 12, Wotquenne No. 81[84]
  6 pieces for 2 fl or 2 vln
  6 pieces for 2 fl or 2 vln and pno
  MT (Pet No. MV1205)
  VW (Pet No. V28)   score included
  ZM (Pet No. ZM126)
see also Trio Sonatas
BACH, WILHELM FRIEDEMANN
see Trio Sonatas
BADARZEWSKA, THEKLA (1838-1861)
Maiden's Prayer
  CF B2881
BADINGS, HENK (1907-   )
Concerto, orig for 2 vln and orch
  DN (Pet No. D89A)
BALFE, MICHAEL WILLIAM (1908-1870)
I Dreamt I Dwelt in Marble Halls, from
    Bohemian Girl
  (Saenger) CF B2882
BARNBY, JOSEPH (1838-1896)
Sweet and Low
  CF B2883
BASSANI, GIOVANNI BATTISTA
see Trio Sonatas
BEAUMONT, PAUL
Mazurka
  (Saenger) CF B2851

---

[83] S. number is from the thematic catalogue by W. Schmieder:
Thematisch-systematisch Verzeichnis der musikalischen
Werke von Johann Sebastian Bach. Leipzig, 1950.
[84] Thematic catalogue by A. Wotquenne. Leipzig, 1905.

BEAUMONT, PAUL (cont.)
  Serenade
    (Saenger) CF B2884
BECKERATH, ALFRED VON (1901-   )
  Sonatine
    Moeck 1018
BEETHOVEN, LUDWIG VAN (1770-1827)
  Farewell to the Piano
    (Saenger) CF B2842
  Minuet No. 2 in G, orig for pno
    CF B2878
BENDA
  see Trio Sonatas
BERTOUILLE, GERARD (1898-   )
  Trio
    CBDM
BEST, AGNES, see Palmer & Best
BEST SELECTED ALBUM
    (Ambrosio) CF 069
      Bizet: Entr'acte, from Carmen
      Chaminade: Flatterer
      Chopin: Polonaise Militaire
      Donizetti: Sextet, from Lucia
      Elgar: Salut d'Amour
      Faure: Palms
      Godard: Berceuse, from Jocelyn
      Handel: Largo
      Haydn: Emperor Variations
      Mascagni: Intermezzo, from Cavalleria
        Rusticana
      Mendelssohn: Spring Song
      Meyerbeer: Coronation March, from
        Prophet
      Morse: By the River
      Moszkowski: Spanish Dance,
        Op. 12, No. 1
      Pache: Pizzicato Gavotte
      Schubert: Moment Musical, Op. 94, No. 3
      Schubert: Serenade
      Schumann: Träumerei
BIZET, GEORGES (1838-1875)
  Adagietto, from L'Arlésienne
    Ed M
  Aragonaise, from Carmen
    Ed M
BLON, see Von Blon
BOCCHERINI, LUIGI
  see Trio Sonatas
BOHM, KARL
  Zingara, La
    (Saenger) CF
BOISMORTIER, JOSEPH BODIN DE
  see Trio Sonatas
BOND, CARRIE JACOBS (1862-1946)
  Perfect Day
    BMC
BONONCINI, GIOVANNI MARIA
  see Trio Sonatas
BONPORTI, FRANCESCO ANTONIO
  see Trio Sonatas
BORODIN, ALEXANDER (1833-1887)
  Solicitude
    Ed M
BOYCE, WILLIAM
  see Trio Sonatas
BRAGA, GAETANO (1829-1907)
  Serenata, La, orig for vcl
    (Ritter-Saenger) CF B2663
BRAHMS, JOHANNES (1833-1897)
  Cradle Song
    (Herfurth) BMC
  Hungarian Dance No. 8, orig for pno duet
    (Kvelve) VL
  Waltz in A, Op. 39, No. 15, orig for pno duet
    (Kuechler) Hin (Pet No. H30)

BRASOLINI, DOMENICO
  see Trio Sonatas
(BRAYLEY-STEIN-HARRIS)
  Old Treasures, Vol I
    CF
(BRECK, E.S.)
  Christmas Joys
    CF 03171 for contents see title under
    vln and pno
BROWN, JAMES
  Bavarian Dance; See-Saw
    STB
  Frolic; Honeysuckle Waltz; Happy March
    STB
  Habanera; Quick March
    STB
  Kiss in the ring; La Varsovienne
    STB
  Quiet Life; Gypsy Camp
    STB
  Redowa; Tom and Jack
    STB
  Shepherd Prince; At the Pictures
    STB
  Swedish Country Dance; Cinderella's
    Minuet
    STB
BUNS, BENEDICTUS
  see Trio Sonatas
BUONAMENTE, GIOVANNI BATTISTA
  see Trio Sonatas
CALDARA, ANTONIO
  see Trio Sonatas
CAMERLOHER, PLACIDUS VON
  see Trio Sonatas
CAPUA, see Di Capua
CAROL TUNES FOR BEGINNERS
    (Widdicombe) Chap-L
      Child This Day is Born
      God Rest Ye Merry, Gentlemen
      Good King Wenceslas
      Here is Joy for Every Age
      Jacob's Ladder
      On This Day
      Past Three O'Clock
      This New Christmas Carol
      Unto Us a Boy is Born
      What New, Shepherdess?
CARSE, ADAM (1878-1958)
  In double harness. Waltz in D, from
    3 Easy Duets
    Aug
  Mimic. Canon in G, from 3 Easy Duets
    Aug
  Scenes Afloat
    Aug
  Two abreast. March in C, from 3 Easy
    Duets
    Aug
CAZZATI, MAURITO
  see Trio Sonatas
CHAMINADE, CÉCILE (1857-1944)
  Callirhoë
    CF B2287
  Lisonjera, La
    (Klugescheid) CF B2888
CHRISTMAS JOYS
    (Breck) CF 03171 for contents see
    title under vln and pno
CLASSIC PIECES
    Pet 2954A,b,C   3V
      Vol 1: 12 pieces by Bach, Beethoven,
        Gluck, Handel, Mozart, Schubert,
        Schumann, Tartini

CLASSIC PIECES (cont.)
  Pet 2954A,b,C   3V (cont.)
    Vol 2: 12 pieces by C.P.E. Bach,
      Beethoven, Campagnoli, Field,
      Hummel, Mozart, Schubert, Weber
    Vol 3: 12 pieces by Beethoven
CLASSICAL PIECES
  (Applebaum) GS   2V
CLASSICAL VIOLIN
  (Palaschko) SCH
CLERAMBAULT, NICOLAS
  see Trio Sonatas
COLISTA, LELIO
  see Trio Sonatas
CORBETT, WILLIAM
  see Trio Sonatas
CORELLI, ARCANGELO (1653-1713)
  Gavotte and Gigue
    Ed M
  Gigue
    Ed M
  Sonata, Op. 5, No. 12, "La Folia",
    orig for vln and Bc
    (Leonard-Marteau) SCH
  see also Trio Sonatas
COUNTRY GARDENS
  (Ranger) CF
  Lud
COUPERIN, FRANCOIS
  see Trio Sonatas
CRESTON, PAUL (1906-   )
  Partita, for fl, vln or 2 vln, and pno
    Leeds
CZIBULKA, ALPHONSE (1842-1894)
  Love's Dream After the Ball, Op. 356
    CF B2889
DANCLA, CHARLES (1817-1907)
  Symphonie Concertante No. 4 in G, Op. 98
    CF B2601
  Symphonies, 3 Little, Op. 109
    (Saenger) CF 03384
  Symphony in D, Op. 109, No. 1
    (Saenger) CF B2821
  Symphony in G, Op. 109, No. 2
    (Saenger) CF B2822
DANDRIEU, JEAN FRANCOIS
  see Trio Sonatas
DEBUSSY, CLAUDE (1862-1918)
  Mandoline, orig for voice and pno
    Ed M
DELBRÜCK, G.
  Berceuse
    CF B2890
DENZA, LUIGI (1846-1922)
  Funiculi-Funicula
    (Saenger) CF B2891
DEROSIER, NICOLAS
  see Trio Sonatas
DI CAPUA, EDUARDO (1864-1917)
  O Sole Mio
    CF B2855
DICHLER, JOSEF (1912-   )
  Musik
    DOB
DISTLER, HUGO (1908-1942)
  Sonate, Op. 15a, über alte deutsche
    Volkslieder
    Baer 1091
DONATH, G.
  Trio in the Old Style
    OBV
DONIZETTI, GAETANO (1797-1848)
  Sextet, from Lucia di Lammermoor
    CF

DRDLA, FRANZ (1868-1944)
  Souvenir
    (Severn) CF B2082
DRIGO, RICHARD (1846-1930)
  Serenade, from Les Millions d'Arlequin
    (Borch) CF
DVORÁK, ANTONIN (1841-1904)
  Humoreske, Op. 101, No. 7, orig for pno
    (Saenger) CF B2872
EASY VIOLIN PIECES
  Consolidated 6; for contents see title
    under vln, pno
EASY VIOLIN SOLOS
  Consolidated 38; for contents see title
    under vln, pno
ELGAR, EDWARD (1857-1934)
  Salut d'Amour, Op. 12, orig for orch
    (Klugescheid) CF B2833
    (Saenger) CF B2873
ERBACH, FRIEDRICH KARL
  see Trio Sonatas
ERLEBACH, PHILIPP HEINRICH
  see Trio Sonatas
FASCH, JOHANN FRIEDRICH
  see Trio Sonatas
FAURÉ, GABRIEL (1845-1924)
  En Priere, orig for voice and pno
    Ed M
FAURE, JEAN-BAPTISTE (1830-1914)
  Rameaux, Les, orig for voice and pno
    (Klugescheid) CF B2893
FESCH, WILLEM DE
  see Trio Sonatas
FONTANA, GIOVANNI BATTISTA
  see Trio Sonatas
FORST, RUDOLF (1900-   )
  Homage to Ravel
    Ed M
FÖRSTER, CHRISTOPH
  see Trio Sonatas
FOSTER
  Village Festival
    Ed M
FRASER, [NORMAN (1904-   )]
  Cueca
    Ches
FRESCOBALDI, GIROLAMO
  see Trio Sonatas
FUX, JOHANN JOSEPH
  see Trio Sonatas
GABRIELLI, DOMENICO
  see Trio Sonatas
GAGNEBIN, HENRI (1886-   )
  Trio in D, for fl, vln and pno, or 2 vln, pno
    Curci
GANNE, LOUIS GASTON (1862-1923)
  Extase
    (Tobani) CF   harp and organ ad lib
GANZ, WILHELM (1833-1914)
  Sing, Sweet Bird
    CF B2869
GASSMANN, FLORIAN
  see Trio Sonatas
GHYS, HENRI (1839-1908)
  Amaryllis; with Country Gardens
    (Harris) Lud D-20077
GILLET, ERNEST (1856-1940)
  Passe-Pied
    (Saenger) CF B2894
GLUCK, CHRISTOPH WILLIBALD (1714-1787)
  Ballet Music, from Orpheus
    (Saenger) CF B2895
  see also Trio Sonatas

GODARD, BENJAMIN (1849-1895)
Character Pieces, 6, Op. 18
Pet 3795
Duets, 6
GS L1272
GOLDBERG, JOHANN GOTTLIEB
see Trio Sonatas
GORDON, PHILIP
Easy Two-Voice Canons, 4
Hans
GOSSEC, FRANCOIS-JOSEPH (1734-1829)
Gavotte
(Ambrosio) CF B2795
GOUNOD, CHARLES (1818-1893)
Angélus, L' and Les Pifferari
(Saenger) CF B2914
Ave Maria. Meditation on the first
prelude of J.S. Bach
(Saenger) CF
Serenade
(Ritter-Saenger) CF B2860
GRANGER, J.
Saisons, Les
Gaudet
GRAUN, JOHANN GOTTLIEB
see Trio Sonatas
GRAY, HAMILTON
Dream of Paradise
CF B2896
GRIEG, EDVARD (1843-1907)
Last Spring, Op. 34, No. 2, orig for orch
(Saenger) CF B2897
Peer Gynt Suite No. 1, Op. 46, orig
for orch
(Sitt) Pet 3307
To Spring, Op. 43, No. 6, orig for pno
(Klugescheid) CF B2836
GRONEMAN, A.
Sonata No. 2, Op. 2
Wagenaar   vcl ad lib
GRUBER, FRANZ
Silent Night, Holy Night. Fantasia,
see Kron
GUNGL, JOSEF
Sounds from Home, Op. 361
(Tobani-Saenger) CF B2850
HAAS, JOSEPH (1879-1960)
Chamber Trio, Op. 38
SCH
HACQUART, CHARLES
see Trio Sonatas
HANDEL, GEORG FRIEDRICH (1685-1759)
Movements for Strings, 4
Hin (Pet No. H276)   2 vln or vln, vla and
pno; or 2 vln, vla and pno; vcl or d-b
ad lib
2 Dances, from Alcides
Ouverture, from Esther
Largo, from Saul
Overture, from Messiah
(Stoessel) CF
Studies, 20, based on Concerti Grossi, Op. 6
(Jacobsen) Bosw
Suite in C
(Murdoch) SCH
Suite of Airs and Dances
Hin (Pet No. H383)   2 vln or vln, vla
and pno; vcl or d-b ad lib
Air, from Serse
Gavotte, from Semele
March, from Ariodante
Menuetto, from Berenice
Sarabande, from Theodora
see also Trio Sonatas

HARRIS, A.E., see Brayley-Stein-Harris
HARSÁNYI, TIBOR (1898-1954)
Divertimento No. 1, orig for 2 vln and
orch
Sal
HASSE, JOHANN ADOLPH
see Trio Sonatas
HAUBIEL, CHARLES (1892-   )
Cradle Song
CP
Plaint
CP
HAYDN, JOSEPH (1732-1809)
Emperor Variations, from String Quartet,
Op. 76
(Stoessel) CF
see also Trio Sonatas
HEIFETZ, EMANUEL R
Little Dutch Dolls
CF B2474
HELYER, MARJORIE
Little Suite
Aug
(HERFURTH, C. PAUL)
Violin Duet Book
Willis
HESSENBERG, KURT (1908-   )
Trio in G, Op. 26
Pet 4533
HÖCKH, KARL
see Trio Sonatas
HOFFMANN, LEOPOLD
see Trio Sonatas
(HOFMANN)
Masters for the Young
Pet 3364   for contents see title
HOLST, GUSTAV (1874-1934)
Concerto
Curwen   for rent
Fugal Concerto
Nov
HOLZBAUER, IGNAZ
see Trio Sonatas
HUBER
Concertino in g, Op. 11
Eul (Pet No, Z170)
HUMMEL, HERMAN A., see Whistler &
Hummel
JACCHINI
see Trio Sonatas
JUNGMANN, ALBERT (1824-1892)
Longing for Home, Op. 117
(Ambrosio) CF
(André-Saenger) CF B2875
JUON, PAUL (1872-1940)
Kleine Tondichtungen, 7, Op. 81
LEU
KALINNIKOV, VASSILI (1866-1901)
Chanson Triste
Ed M
KAMINSKI, HEINRICH (1886-1946)
Music for 2 vln and cembalo
Pet 4183
KEATES, RONALD
Sunday Afternoon
Chap-L
KETELBEY
In a Monastery Garden
(MacLean) MPH 304
KOVÁCS, CHARLES
Hungarian Rhapsody No. 1, Op. 84
CF B2140
KREBS, JOHANN LUDWIG
see Trio Sonatas

KREISLER, FRITZ (1875-1962)
  Old Refrain
    (Biederman) Fol 1457
KRIEGER, JOHANN PHILIPP
  see Trio Sonatas
KRON, LOUIS
  O Sanctissima. Fantasia, Op. 88, No. 1
    CF B2971
  Stille nacht, heilige nacht. Fantasia,
    Op. 88, No. 2
    (Saenger) CF B2898
LABITZKY, AUGUST (1832-1903)
  Alp-maid's Dream, Op. 45
    (Ambrosio) CF B2852
    GS
LANGER, G.
  Grossmütterchen, Op. 20
    (Palaschko) SCH
LECLAIR, JEAN MARIE
  see Trio Sonatas
LEGLEY, VICTOR (1915-   )
  Serenade No. 1, Op. 44
    CBDM
LEGRENZI, GIOVANNI (1626-1690)
  Concerto Bernardi, arr from Sonata a tre,
    Op. 4, No. 1
    (Sontag) Skidmore
  see also Trio Sonatas
LEONCAVALLO, RUGGIERO (1858-1919)
  I Pagliacci. Selection
    (Saenger) CF
LINICKE, JOHANN GEORG
  see Trio Sonatas
LOCATELLI, PIETRO (1693-1764)
  Aria
    Ed M
  see also Trio Sonatas
LOEILLET, JEAN-BAPTISTE (1680-1730)
  Courante
    Ed M
  see also Trio Sonatas
LOSEY, F. H.
  Alita
    (Ambrosio) CF
LUDWIG, CARL
  Christmas Night
    Lud D-20050
(LUTZ)
  My Violin Book
    SCH for contents see title
  Unterhaltungs Konzert
    SCH
LYRIC ALBUM
  (Whistler & Hummel) Ru
MACBETH, ALLAN (1856-1910)
  Love In Idleness
    CF
MAGANINI
  Album for Strings
    Ed M
MANFREDINI, FRANCESCO (1688-1748)
  Concerto in g, Op. 3, No. 10
    Hug (Pet No. A1)
MARIE, GABRIEL (1852-1928)
  Cinquantaine, La
    (Saenger) CF B2658
MARTINU, BOHUSLAV (1890-1959)
  Sonate
    Deiss
  Sonatine
    Leduc
MASCAGNI, PIETRO (1863-1945)
  Intermezzo Sinfonico, from Cavalleria
    Rusticana
    (Saenger) CF

MASSENET, JULES (1842-1912)
  Last Dream of the Virgin
    (Klugescheid) CF B2846
MASTERS FOR THE YOUNG
  (Hofmann) Pet 3364
    14 pieces by Beethoven and Schubert
MASTERS OF THE BAROQUE, see under
    trio sonata
MATTEI, TITO (1841-1914)
  Non è Ver!
    CF B2876
MAZAS, JACQUES-FÉRÉOL (1782-1849)
  Little Duets, 12, Op. 38, Bk. 1
    CF 03471 for 1 or 2 vln and pno
  Little Duets, 12, Op. 38, Bk. 2
    CF 04264 for 1 or 2 vln and pno; in
      preparation
MAZZAFERRATA, GIOVANNI BATTISTA
  see Trio Sonatas
MENDELSSOHN, FELIX (1809-1847)
  I would that my love, Op. 63, No. 1, orig
    for voice and pno
    (Saenger) CF B1361
  On Wings of Song, orig for voice and pno
    (Trinkaus) Fill
  Spring Song, Op. 62, No. 6, orig for pno
    (Klugescheid) CF B2903
  Wedding March, from A Midsummer Night's
    Dream
    (Weiss) CF
MEULEMANS, ARTHUR (1884-   )
  Sonata
    CBDM
MEYERBEER, GIACOMO (1791-1864)
  Coronation March, from Le Prophète
    (Weiss) CF
MIGALI, PIETRO
  see Trio Sonatas
MILHAUD, DARIUS (1892-   )
  Sonata
    Dur
MOFFAT, ALFRED (1866-1950)
  Edina. Fantasia on Scottish airs
    Paterson 192 vcl ad lib
  Thistle of Scotland. Fantasia on Gaelic airs
    Paterson 193 vcl ad lib
MONDONVILLE, JEAN-JOSEPH
  see Trio Sonatas
MORET, V.
  Petite Symphonie, Op. 74
    CF B2666
MORRIS, REGINALD OWEN (1886-1948)
  Concerto Piccolo
    Oxf 26.106
MORRIS, S.E.
  Jolly Santa Claus
    Lud D-20020
MOSZKOWSKI, MORITZ (1854-1925)
  Hungary, Op. 23, No. 6, orig for pno duet
    (Saenger) CF B2877
  Spanish Dances, Op. 12, orig for pno duet
    (Scharwenka-Saenger) CF 2V
  Spanish Dance in C, Op. 12, No. 1
    (Saenger) CF
  Suite, Op. 71
    Int
MOZART, LEOPOLD
  see Trio Sonatas
MOZART, WOLFGANG AMADEUS (1756-1791)
  Ave Verum Corpus
    (Saenger) CF
  Concertante in D, after Sonata for 2 pno,
    K.448
    (David) CF 01461
    Pet 3234 with cadenza

MOZART, WOLFGANG AMADEUS (cont.)
  Concertone in C, K.190
    (David) Int
    (Hermann) BRH
  German Dance
    Hin (Pet No. H143)   vcl ad lib
  Serenade, K.525, orig for str quintet
    (Stoessel) CF AS 6
MUFFAT
  Gigue
    Ed M
MY VIOLIN BOOK
    (Lutz) SCH
      11 melodies by Gossec, Mozart, Handel,
      Tchaikovsky, Brahms, Dvorak and others
NEVIN, ETHELBERT (1862-1901)
  Transcriptions, 6
    (Schneider) BMC   vcl ad lib
      Au Printemps
      Au Soir
      Gavotte
      Pastorale
      Slumber Song
      Vieille Chanson
OFFENBACH, JACQUES (1819-1880)
  Barcarolle, from Tales of Hoffman
    (Woltag-Ambrosio) CF B1368
OLD TREASURES, VOL I
    (Brayley-Stein-Harris) CF
OUR FAVORITES
    (Palaschko) SCH
PACHELBEL, JOHANN
    see Trio Sonatas
(PALASCHKO)
  Classical Violin
    SCH
  Our Favorites
    SCH
PALMER, EDWINA & BEST, AGNES
  Rhymes and Rhythms, for 2 or 3 vln, pno
    Oxf 23.111
PAPINI, GUIDO
  Cinderella
    CF B2847
  Home, Sweet Home
    CF B1206
  Hope March
    (Saenger) CF B2840
PARK, STEPHEN (1911-   )
  Gigue, from First Dance Suite
    CP
  Gymnopedie, from First Dance Suite
    CP
  Pavane, from First Dance Suite
    CP
PASCAL, A.
  Sonatine, 3 scènes enfantines
    Dur
PEPUSCH, JOHN CHRISTOPHER
    see Trio Sonatas
PERGOLESI, GIOVANNI BATTISTA (1710-1736)
  Sicilian Air
    Ed M
    see also Trio Sonatas
PFEIFFER, [JOHANN (1697-1761)]
  Concerto
    (Steglich) NAG   vcl ad lib
PLEYEL, IGNAZ (1757-1831)
  Duets, 6, Op. 8, orig for 2 vln unacc
    Aug 7308 "Trios"
    CF L147
    GS L832
    Pet 2970A

Duets, 6, Op. 23
  CF 03481
Duets, 6, Op. 48, orig for 2 vln unacc
  Aug 5336 "Sonatinas"
  CF L157
  GS L833
  Pet 2970b
Trios, 3, Op. 44
  Aug 5334
POLDINI, EDUARD (1869-1957)
  Poupée Valsante
    CF
PONCE, MANUEL MARÍA (1882-1948)
  Estrellita
    (Simon) CF B2510
PORPORA, NICOLA ANTONIO
    see Trio Sonatas
PUGNANI, GAETANO
    see Trio Sonatas
PURCELL, DANIEL
    see Trio Sonatas
PURCELL, HENRY
    see Trio Sonatas
QUANTZ, JOHANN JOACHIM
    see Trio Sonatas
RACHMANINOFF, SERGEY (1873-1943)
  Polka Italienne
    Ed M
  Vocalise
    Ed M
RAMEAU, JEAN-PHILIPPE (1683-1764)
  Pièces de clavecin en concerts, for vln or
    fl, gamba or 2nd vln, clavecin
    (Jacobi) Baer 3803
      5 Concerts in c,G,A,B flat, d;
      also published separately
  Pièces en concert
    (Saint-Saens) Dur
  Rigodon de Dardanus
    Ed M
RAPHLING, SAM (1910-   )
  Square Dance
    Ed M
RAVENSCROFT, JOHN
    see Trio Sonatas
RIMSKY-KORSAKOV, NIKOLAY (1844-1908)
  Flight of the Bumble Bee
    (Applebaum) CF B3253
ROMAN, JOHAN HELMICH
    see Trio Sonatas
ROSENMÜLLER, JOHANN
    see Trio Sonatas
ROSENTHAL, MANUEL (1904-   )
  Sonatine
    Heugel
RUBBRA, EDMUND (1901-   )
  Phantasy, Op. 16
    Leng (Mil No. L1117)
RUBINSTEIN, ANTON (1829-1894)
  Melody in F, Op. 3, orig for pno
    (Klugescheid) CF B2867
RUGGIERI, G.M.
    see Trio Sonatas
RUSSELL, LESLIE
  Easy Pieces, 3
    Oxf 20.006-32
SACCHINI, ANTONIO
    see Trio Sonatas
SAENGER, GUSTAV (1865-1935)
  Adeste Fideles, Fantasia
    CF B2972
SAINT-GEORGE
  Petite Suite No. 1
    Aug

SAINT-GEORGE (cont.)
Petite Suite No. 2, Op. 60
Aug
SAMMARTINI, GIOVANNI BATTISTA
see Trio Sonatas
SAMMARTINI, GIUSEPPE
see Trio Sonatas
SARASATE, PABLO DE (1844-1908)
Navarra, Op. 33
Int
SIM
SCARMOLIN, A. LOUIS (1890-   )
One fingered waltz
Lud D-200A22
SCHEIDT, SAMUEL
see Trio Sonatas
SCHRÖDER, HERMANN
Musical Reflections Op. 29
CF
SCHUBERT, FRANZ (1797-1828)
Ave Maria, orig for voice and pno
(Borch) CF
Marche Militaire, Op. 51, No. 1, orig
for pno duet
(Stoessel) CF
(Weiss) CF
SCHUMANN, ROBERT (1810-1856)
Evening Song, Op. 85, No. 12, orig for
pno duet
(Klugescheid) CF B2858
SEVERN, EDMUND (1862-1942)
Wings and Motors
CF
SHERARD, JAMES
see Trio Sonatas
SILVESTRI, JOSEPH
In Days of Knighthood
(Centano) CF B2856
SINDING, CHRISTIAN (1856-1941)
Serenade in A, Op. 92
Pet 3139
SMITH, EM
Dance Pantomime, from 3 Tunes in
3 Rhythms
CF
Romance, from 3 Tunes in 3 Rhythms
CF
Valse Capriccietto, from 3 Tunes in
3 Rhythms
CF
SONNLEITHNER, CHRISTOPH VON
see Trio Sonatas
SONTAG, WESLEY
Five Tunes for Two Fiddles
Fox
STAMITZ, JOHANN
see Trio Sonatas
STAMITZ, KARL (1745-1801)
Sinfonia Concertante in D, orig for 2 vln
and orch
(Schroeder) Sik 504
STAMITZ
Andantino
Ed M
STEIN, C., see Brayley-Stein-Harris
STEVENS, BERNARD (1916-   )
Fantasia
Leng (Mil No. L1126)
STOESSEL, ALBERT (1894-1943)
Suite Antique
SPAM
STÖLZEL, GOTTFRIED HEINRICH
see Trio Sonatas
STRADELLA, ALESSANDRO
see Trio Sonatas

STRINGS IN SERVICE
Hin (Pet No. H170A)
12 hymn tunes for pno or organ with
unison, 2-part or descant vlns
STRUNGK, NIKOLAUS ADAM
see Trio Sonatas
SUK, JOSEPH (1874-1935)
Bagatelle
Artia
TARTINI, GIUSEPPE
see Trio Sonatas
TELEMANN, GEORG PHILIPP
see Trio Sonatas
TENAGLIA
Aria Antica
Ed M
THOMÉ, FRANCIS (1850-1909)
Simple Aveu
(Ambrosio) CF
Under Sheltering Leaves, Op. 29
(Klugescheid) CF B2857
TITL, ANTON EMIL (1809-1882)
Serenade
(Moses) CF
TORELLI, GIUSEPPE (1658-1709)
Concerto in a, Op. 8, No. 2
(Paumgartner) SCH
Concerto in G, Op. 8
(Jensen) Int
TOSELLI, ENRICO (1883-1926)
Serenade, Op. 6
BMC
TOSTI, FRANCESCO PAOLO (1846-1916)
Good-bye
CF B2911
TUMA, FRANZ
see Trio Sonatas
TURINI, FRANCESCO
see Trio Sonatas
UCCELLINI, MARCO
see Trio Sonatas
UNTERHALTUNGS KONZERT
(Lutz) SCH
VERACINI, ANTONIO
see Trio Sonatas
VERDI, GIUSEPPE (1813-1901)
Miserere, from Il Trovatore
(Saenger) CF B2912
Quartet, from Rigoletto
(Saenger) CF
VIERDANCK, JOHANN
see Trio Sonatas
VIOLIN DUET BOOK
(Herfurth) Willis
VITALI, GIOVANNI BATTISTA
see Trio Sonatas
VITALI
Concerto in d
(Sontag) Fox
VIVALDI, ANTONIO (c.1669-1741)
Concerto in A, Op. 3, No. 5
(Füssl) Baer 3713
Concerto in a, Op. 3, No. 8
(Galamian) Int
(Vené) FC 2071
Concerto in d, Op. 3, No. 11
(Dandelot) ESC
(Galamian) Int   pno reduction by
K.H. Fuessl
Pet 4327
Concerto in c, Op. 21, No. 4
Int
Concerto in D, Op. 21, No. 7
Int

VIVALDI, ANTONIO (cont.)
    Concerto in g, Op. 27, No. 2
        Int
    Concerto in d, Op. 27, No. 3
        Int
    Concerto in a
        (Nachèz) SCH
    see also Trio Sonatas
VON BLON, FRANZ (1861-1945)
    Sérénade d'Amour
        CF B2870
    Vision Characteristic
        CF B2885
    Whispering Flowers
        CF
WAGENSEIL, GEORG CHRISTOPH
    see Trio Sonatas
WARLOCK, PETER (1894-1930)
    Pieces, 3, from the Capriol Suite
        (Szigeti) CF B2422
WEBER, CARL MARIA VON (1786-1826)
    Invitation to the Dance, Op. 65, orig for pno
        (Weiss-Saenger) CF
WERNER, GREGOR JOSEPH
    see Trio Sonatas
(WHISTLER, HARVEY S. & HUMMEL,
        HERMAN A.)
    Apollo Album
        Ru
    Lyric Album
        Ru
WHITE
    Jeunesse
        Gilles
(WIDDICOMBE, TREVOR)
    Carol Tunes for Beginners
        Chap-L   for contents see title
WYMAN, ADDISON P. (1832-1872)
    Woodland Echoes, Op. 34
        (Ambrosio) CF
YRADIER, SEBASTIAN (1809-1865)
    Paloma, La
        (Ambrosio) CF
        (Saenger) CF B2913
YSAŸE, EUGÈNE (1858-1931)
    Amitié[85]
        SF
ZACH, JOHANN
    see Trio Sonatas
ZILCHER, PAUL
    Country Dance, Op. 227, No. 5, from
        5 Easy Duets
        Aug
    Gavotte and Serenata, Op. 227, Nos. 3 and
        4, from 5 Easy Duets
        Aug
    On the march and Waltz, Op. 227, Nos. 1
        and 2, from 5 Easy Duets
        Aug

Trios: 2 Violas, Piano

BACH, JOHANN SEBASTIAN (1685-1750)
    Brandenburg Concerto No. 6, orig for
        str orch
        Hin (Pet No. H670)
BACH, KARL PHILIPP EMANUEL
    Trio in F, see Trio Sonatas
FUX, JOHANN JOSEPH
    see Trio Sonatas
GORDON, PHILIP
    Easy Two-Voice Canons, 4
        Hans

---

[85] This publication is not listed in current U.S. catalogues.
Information was received from Fondation Eugène Ysaÿe. It
is also available for 2 violins and orchestra.

WRANITZKI, ANTON (1761-1820)
    Concerto in C, orig for 2 vla and orch
        Hof

Trios: 2 Cellos, Piano

A DEUX VIOLONCELLES
    (Feuillard-Ruyssen) Delrieu 8V
        contents same as Le Jeune
        Violoncelliste for vcl and pno
ANTONIOTTO
    see vcl, pno
DELUNE, [LOUIS (1876-1940)]
    Fileuse
        Sal
FASCH, JOHANN FRIEDRICH
    see vcl, pno
FESCH, WILLEM DE
    see vcl, pno
(FEUILLARD & RUYSSEN)
    A Deux Violoncelles
        Delrieu 8V; contents same as Le Jeune
        Violoncelliste for vcl and pno
FOSTER, STEPHEN
    Old black Joe, see Smith & Holmes
GODARD, BENJAMIN (1849-1895)
    Duettini, 6, Op. 18
        WH 887
GOUNOD, CHARLES (1818-1893)
    Ave Maria. Meditation sur le premier
        prélude de J.S. Bach
        (Buechner) CF
GRIMM, CARL
    Adagio in G
        Int
HANDEL, GEORG FRIEDRICH (1685-1759)
    Double Concerto in C
        (Ronchini) ESC
    Sonata in g, Op. 2, No. 8, orig for
        2 vln and Bc
        (Beyer) Int
        (Beyer) Pet 6082
HARGITT
    Confidences, Les
        JWL (Mil No. W1516)
HOLMES, GUY E.
    Tyrolean Fantasia
        CF
    see also Smith & Holmes
KLENGEL, JULIUS (1859-1933)
    Concerto in e, Op. 45
        Int
LAKE, MAYHEW L.
    Annie Laurie, Fantasia
        CF
LOVELL, K.
    Duets, 2
        STB
MARCELLO, BENEDETTO (1686-1739)
    Sonatas, 2, for 2 vcl and Bc
        (Glode) Moeck 1056
    see also vcl, pno
MÜNTZING, ARNE (1903-   )
    Serenade
        DOB
ROMBERG, BERNHARD (1767-1841)
    Concertino No. 2 in G
        UME
    Concertino No. 3 in B flat
        UME
RUYSSEN, PIERRE
    Concerto
        Delrieu
    see also Feuillard & Ruyssen

SOMIS, GIOVANNI BATTISTA (1686-1763)
Tambourin
(Bazelaire) Senart
SMITH, CLAY
My Song of Songs
CF
Spirit of Joy
CF
SMITH, CLAY & HOLMES, GUY E.
Old black Joe. Air varié
CF
TARTINI, GIUSEPPE (1692-1770)
Sonate
(Bazelaire) Leduc
VIVALDI, ANTONIO (c.1669-1741)
Concerto in g
(Ghedini) Int
Sonatas, 6
Pet 4938

Trios: 2 Double-Basses, Piano

MCKAY, GEORGE FREDERICK (1899-)
Suite
(Turetzky) MM

Trios: Violin, Viola, Piano

BACH, KARL PHILIPP EMANUEL (1714-1788)
Trio No. 1 in D[86]
Int
Trio No. 2 in a
Int
Trio No. 3 in G
Int
BAX, ARNOLD (1883-1953)
Trio in one movement
Ches
BEETHOVEN, LUDWIG VAN (1770-1827)
Trios, 6 Celebrated, orig for vln, vcl, pno
Int   viola part only, to replace vcl
Trios, Op. 1, Nos. 1-3, orig for vln, vcl, pno
BRH   viola part only, to replace vcl;
published separately
BENJAMIN, ARTHUR (1893-)
Romantic Fantasy, orig for vln, vla, and
orch
BH
BIZET, GEORGES (1838-1875)
Adagietto, from L'Arlésienne
Ed M
BORODIN, ALEXANDER (1833-1887)
Solicitude
Ed M
BRAHMS, JOHANNES (1833-1897)
Concerto in a, Op. 102, orig for vln, vcl
and orch
Int   viola part only, to replace vcl
Trio in E flat, Op. 40, for pno, vln, horn
or vla or vcl
Aug 5117
BRH
Int
Pet 3899b
CAPET, LUCIEN (1873-1928)
Aria
Mathot
DEBUSSY, CLAUDE (1862-1918)
Il pleure dans mon coeur, orig for voice
and pno
Ed M

Mandoline, orig for voice and pno
Ed M
DIERCKS, JOHN (1927-)
Diversion
Tritone   manuscript reproduction
DONIZETTI, GAETANO (1797-1848)
Sextet, from Lucia di Lammermoor
(Saenger) CF
DVORAK, ANTONIN (1841-1904)
Trio in e, Op. 90, "Dumky", orig for vln,
vcl, pno
(Martin) BRH
SIM
Int   viola part only, to replace vcl
ERLEBACH, PHILIPP HEINRICH
see Trio Sonatas
FASCH, JOHANN FRIEDRICH
see Trio Sonatas
FORST, RUDOLF (1900-)
Homage to Ravel
Ed M
HANDEL, GEORG FRIEDRICH (1685-1759)
Movements for Strings, 4
Hin (Pet No. H276)   for contents see
2 vln, pno
Overture, from Messiah
(Stoessel) CF
Sonata in F, Op. 2, No. 3, orig for
2 vln and Bc
(Vieland) Int
Sonata in g, Op. 2, No. 8, orig for
2 vln and Bc
(Vieland) Int
Suite of Airs and Dances
Hin (Pet No. H383)   for contents see
2 vln, pno
HEINICHEN, JOHANN DAVID
see Trio Sonatas
(HOFMANN)
Masters For The Young
Pet 3364   for contents see title
JARECKI, TADEUSZ (1888-)
Trio
Ches
JENKINS, JOHN
see Trio Sonatas
JONGEN, JOSEPH (1873-1953)
Trio. Prélude, Variations et Final, Op. 30
Dur
JUON, PAUL (1872-1940)
Trio Miniatures, for vln, vcl or vla, pno
LN (Pet No. R17)
KALINNIKOV, VASSILI (1866-1901)
Chanson Triste
Ed M
KAUDER, HUGO (1888-)
Trio, for ob or vln, vla, pno
UE 7587
KHACHATURIAN, ARAM (1903-)
Trio, orig for clar, vln, pno
Int
KOPPEL, HERMAN D. (1908-)
Concerto, Op. 43, orig for vln, vla and orch
WH 3834
KORNAUTH, EGON (1891-1959)
Trio-Suite, Op. 45, for vln, vcl or vla, pno
DOB
LACHNER, J.
Trio in B flat, Op. 37
Hof
Trio in D, Op. 58
Hof
Trio, Op. 89
Hof

---

[86] These are probably the sonatas written for flute, viola
and piano.

LECLAIR, JEAN MARIE (1697-1764)
Sonata in D
(David) Int
see also Trio Sonatas
LOCATELLI, PIETRO (1695-1764)
Aria
Ed M
LOEILLET, JEAN-BAPTISTE (1680-1730)
Courante
Ed M
Sonata in D, orig for 2 vln, Bc
(Beon-Vieland) Int
Sonata in G, orig for 2 vln, Bc
(Beon-Vieland) Int
LOTTI, ANTONIO
see Trio Sonatas
MACDOWELL, EDWARD (1861-1908)
To a Wild Rose, orig for pno
(Isaac) CF B3318
MAGANINI
Album for Strings
Ed M
Moonlight on the Painted Desert
Ed M
MASSENET, JULES (1842-1912)
Under the Linden Trees
Ed M
MASTERS FOR THE YOUNG
(Hofmann) Pet 3364   for 2 vln and pno;
or vln, vla, pno
14 pieces by Beethoven and Schubert
MENDELSSOHN, FELIX (1809-1847)
Wedding March, from Midsummer
Night's Dream
(Weiss) CF
MEYERBEER, GIACOMO (1791-1864)
Coronation March, from Le Prophète
(Weiss) CF
MIGOT, GEORGES (1891-   )
Trio
Leduc
MOZART, WOLFGANG AMADEUS (1756-1791)
Serenade, K.525, orig for str quintet
(Stoessel) CF AS6
Sinfonia Concertante in E flat, K.364,
orig for vln, vla and orch
(Tertis) Aug 7269   with cadenza
(Tillmetz) BRH
GS L1590
Int   with cadenzas by Mozart and
Hellmesberger
Pet 2206   with cadenza
Trio in E flat, K.498, for clar or vln,
vla, pno
(Adamowski) GS L1403
Aug 7268g
BRH
LN (Pet No. R40)
MUFFAT
Gigue
Ed M
NARDINI
Shepherd's Pipes
Ed M
OSTRČIL, OTAKAR (1879-1935)
Sonata, Op. 22
UE 9000
PEPUSCH, JOHN CHRISTOPHER
see Trio Sonatas
PERGOLESI, GIOVANNI BATTISTA (1710-1736)
Sicilian Air
Ed M
PISTON, WALTER (1894-   )
Partita, for vln, vla, organ
AMP

PLEYEL, IGNAZ (1757-1831)
Trios, 3, Op. 44
(Hermann) Aug 5280
PURCELL, HENRY (c.1659-1695)
Golden Sonata, orig for 2 vln and Bc
Int
RACHMANINOFF, SERGEY (1873-1943)
Vocalise
Ed M
RAVEL, MAURICE (1875-1937)
Pavane
Ed M
ROHOZINSKY, LADISLAV (1886-1938)
Suite Brève, for fl, vla, harp; or vln,
vla, pno
Senart
SCHUBERT, FRANZ (1797-1828)
Marche Militaire, Op. 51, No. 1, orig
for pno duet
(Weiss) CF
Nocturne in E, Op. 148, orig for vln,
vcl, pno
Int
Trio in E flat, Op. 100, orig for vln, vcl, pno
(Altmann) BRH
SCHUMANN, ROBERT (1810-1856)
Marchenerzählungen, Op. 132, for clar or
vln, vla, pno
BRH
Int "Fairy Tales"
SMITH, EM
Dance Pantomime, from 3 Tunes in
3 Rhythms
CF
Romance, from 3 Tunes in 3 Rhythms
CF
Valse Capriccietto, from 3 Tunes in
3 Rhythms
CF
STAMITZ, KARL (1745-1801)
Symphonie Concertante, orig for vln,
vla and orch
KN (Pet No. K21)
STAMITZ
Andantino
Ed M
STRAVINSKY, IGOR (1882-   )
Dance of the Princesses, from Firebird
Ed M
TELEMANN, GEORG PHILIPP
see Trio Sonatas
TENAGLIA
Aria Antica
Ed M
VERDI, GIUSEPPE (1813-1901)
Quartet, from Rigoletto
(Saenger) CF
WEBER, CARL MARIA VON (1786-1826)
Invitation to the Dance, Op. 65, orig for pno
(Weiss-Saenger) CF
YOUNG, WILLIAM
see Trio Sonatas

Trios: Violin, Cello, Piano

ABSIL, JEAN (1893-   )
Trio, Op. 7
CBDM
ALBINONI, [TOMASO (1671-1750)]
Sonatas, 3: Op. 6, Nos. 4, 5, 7
(Reinhart) Hug (Pet No. A26)
(ALDER)
Fantaisies, 12, en Trio sur des Opéras
célèbres
Deiss

ALFANO, FRANCO (1876-1954)
  Concerto in a
    SZ
ALIABEV, [ALEXANDER (1787-1851)]
  Trio No. 1
    MZK
  Trio. Unfinished
    MZK
ALTMAN, ARTHUR, see Deutsch & Altman
AMBROSIO, W.F.
  Song of the Volga Boatmen. Paraphrase
    CF
(AMBROSIO)
  Encore Trio Album
    CF 02661
  Modern Trio Album
    CF 0379 for contents see title
AMRAM, DAVID (1930-   )
  Dirge and Variations
    Pet 6680
ANDERSON, LEROY (1908-   )
  Belle of the Ball
    Mil
  Blue Tango
    Mil
  Fiddle-Faddle
    Mil
  Jazz Legato
    Mil
  Jazz Pizzicato
    Mil
  Promenade
    (Edwards) Mil
  Saraband
    Mil
  Serenata
    (Edwards) Mil
  Syncopated Clock
    Mil
  Waltzing Cat
    Mil
ARENSKY, ANTON (1861-1906)
  Trio No. 1 in d, Op. 32
    Aug 7241
    Int
    MZK
    Pet 4315
  Trio No. 2, Op. 73
    MZK
ARNOLD, MALCOLM (1921-   )
  Trio, Op. 54
    Paterson 2714
ARRIEU, CLAUDE (1903-   )
  Trio
    Amphion 176
AUSTIN, ERNEST (1874-1947)
  Trio No. 4
    STB
BABAYEV, ANDRE (1923-   )
  Trio
    MZK
BACH, JOHANN CHRISTIAN (1735-1782)
  Trio in D
    (Riemann) Int
BACH, JOHANN CHRISTOPH FRIEDRICH
    (1732-1795)
  Sonata in D, for vln or fl, vcl and keyboard
    (Ruf) NAG
BACH, JOHANN SEBASTIAN (1685-1750)
  Ave Maria, see Gounod
  Sheep may safely graze
    (Grace) Oxf 26.500
BALLOU, ESTHER W.
  Trio
    CFE

BARGIEL
  Trio en ré mineur
    Haml
  Trio No. 2
    Haml
  Trio No. 3
    Haml
(BARJANSKY)
  Classical Masters
    GS 2V for contents see title
(BARON)
  New Trio Album
    BMI
BASSMAN, GEORGE (1914-   )
  I'm getting sentimental over you
    (Sopkin) Mil
BAX, ARNOLD (1883-1953)
  Trio in B flat
    Chap-L
BEACH, H.
  Trio, Op. 150
    CP
BEALE, JAMES (1924-   )
  Trio
    CFE
BEETHOVEN, LUDWIG VAN (1770-1827)
  Adagio cantabile, from Septet, Op. 20
    (Saenger) CF
  Allegretto in E flat
    (Werner) EKN
  Andante
    (Kreisler) Fol 1408
  Concerto, Op. 56, orig for vln, vcl, pno and
    orch
    (Oistrakh-Rose) Int 3 solo parts and
      orch reduction for 2nd pno
  Rondo in D
    (Werner) Chap-L
  Symphony No. 2 in D, Op. 36
    (Burchard) BRH; for pno 4 hands, vln, vcl
  Symphony No. 3 in E flat, Op. 55, "Eroica"
    (Burchard) BRH; for pno 4 hands, vln, vcl
  Symphony No. 4 in B flat, Op. 60
    (Burchard) BRH; for pno 4 hands, vln, vcl
  Symphony No. 5 in c, Op. 67
    (Burchard) BRH; for pno 4 hands, vln, vcl
  Symphony No. 6 in F, Op. 68, "Pastoral"
    (Burchard) BRH; for pno 4 hands, vln, vcl
  Symphony No. 7 in A, Op. 92
    (Burchard) BRH; for pno 4 hands, vln, vcl
  Symphony No. 8 in F, Op. 93
    (Burchard) BRH; for pno 4 hands, vln, vcl
  Symphony No. 9 in d, Op. 125
    (Burchard) BRH; for pno 4 hands, vln, vcl
  Trios, 13
    Pet 166 3V
      Vol 1
        Op. 1, Nos. 1, 2, 3
        Op. 11, for clar or vln, vcl, pno
        Op. 70, Nos. 1, 2
      Vol 2
        Op. 44
        Op. 97, "Archduke"
        Op. 121a, "Kakadu" Variations
        Op. posth., 2, in B flat and in E flat
      Vol 3
        Op. 36, after Symphony No. 2
        Op. 38, after Septet, for clar or vln,
         vcl, pno
  *Trios, 8
    (Raphael-Lampe) Henle 2V
      Vol 1
        Op. 1, Nos. 1, 2, 3
        Op. 11

BEETHOVEN, LUDWIG VAN (cont.)
  *Trios, 8 (cont.)
    (Raphael-Lampe) Henle   2V (cont.)
      Vol 2
        Op. 70, Nos. 1, 2
        Op. 97
        Op. 121a
  *Trios, 6 Celebrated
    Int
      Op. 1, Nos. 1 and 3
      Op. 11
      Op. 70, No. 1
      Op. 97
      Op. 121a. 10 Variations, "Kakadu"
    Trios, 2, in B flat and E flat, Op. posth.
      Aug 7250h
    Trio in E flat, Op. 1, No. 1
      (Adamowski) GS L1421
      Aug 7250a
      BRH
    Trio in G, Op. 1, No. 2
      (Adamowski) GS L1422
      Aug 7250b
      BRH
    Trio in c, Op. 1, No. 3
      (Adamowski) GS L1423
      Aug 7250c
      BRH
    Trio in B flat, Op. 11, for clar or vln,
      vcl, pno
      (Adamowski) GS L1424
      Aug 7250d
      BRH
    Trio in D, Op. 70, No. 1
      (Adamowski) GS L1425
      Aug 7250e
      BRH
    Trio in E flat, Op. 70, No. 2
      (Adamowski) GS L1426
      Aug 7250f
      BRH
    Trio in B flat, Op. 97, "Archduke"
      (Adamowski) GS L1427
      Aug 7250g
      BRH
    Variations, Op. 121a, "Ich bin der Schneider
      Kakadu"
      BRH
BENNETT, STERNDALE (1816-1875)
  Allegro Fermato
    Paxton (Mil No. P550)
  Serenade
    Paxton (Mil No. P551)
BERNARD, ROBERT (1900-   )
  Trio en fa dieze
    Dur
BERWALD, FRANZ (1796-1868)
  Trio No. 1 in E flat
    Gehrmans
  Trio No. 2 in f
    Gehrmans
  Trio No. 3 in d
    Gehrmans
  Trio No. 4 in C
    Gehrmans
BEZANSON, PHILIP (1916-   )
  Trio
    CFE
(BIEDERMAN)
  Trio Album
    GS   for contents see title
BIXIO
  Serenade in the night
    (Leaman) Mil

BIZET, GEORGES (1838-1875)
  Adagietto
    Ed M
  Intermezzo, from L'Arlésienne Suite No. 2
    (Kreisler) Fol 1414
BLAKE, HOWARD
  Fantasy Allegro
    Chap-L
BLANCHET, G.
  Boîte à Musique, La, from 3 Very Easy
    Little Trios
    ESC
  Tempo di Minuetto, from 3 Very Easy Little
    Trios
    ESC
  Vieille Chanson, from 3 Very Easy Little
    Trios
    ESC
BLOCH, ERNEST (1880-1959)
  Nocturnes, 3
    CF 01319
BLON, see Von Blon
BOELLMANN, LÉON (1862-1897)
  Trio, Op. 19
    Haml
BOHM, CARL
  Zingara, La, Op. 102
    CF
BOIELDIEU, ADRIEN LOUIS VICTOR
    (1815-1883)
  Trio, Op. 5
    (de Saint-Foix) Senart 5379
BOISMORTIER, JOSEPH BODIN DE
    see Trio Sonatas
BOLDIREV, [IGOR (1912-   )]
  Trio
    MZK
BOND, CARRIE JACOBS (1862-1946)
  Perfect Day
    BMC
(BORCH)
  Favorite Trio Album
    CF 0199   for contents see title
BORODIN, ALEXANDER (1833-1887)
  Solicitude
    Ed M
  Trio. Unfinished
    MZK
BORRIS, SIEGFRIED (1906-   )
  Trio, Op. 90, No. 1
    Sirius
BOSTON MUSIC COMPANY TRIO ALBUM
  BMC   5V
    Vol 1
      Albeniz: Tango in D
      Beethoven: Minuet
      Boisdeffre: By the Brook
      Cui: Prelude in A flat
      Délibes: Passepied
      Herbert: Serenade
      Huerter: Told at Twilight
      Nevin: Valzer gentile
      Rimsky-Korsakov: Interlude oriental
      Shuk: Elegy
    Vol 2
      Blockx: Serenade
      Brahms: Hungarian Dance
      Clough-Leighter: My Lady Chlo'
      Ganne: Ecstasy
      Hellmesberger: Entr'acte-Valse
      Lacome: Scène espagnole
      Leclair: Gavot
      Ocki-Alibi: In the Woodland
      Pache: At Evening
      Sibelius: Romance

BOSTON MUSIC COMPANY TRIO ALBUM (cont.)
  BMC   5V (cont.)
    Vol 3
      Cui: Farniente, Op. 40, No. 2
      Dancla: Andante Mélodique, Op. 214
      Fernandez-Abrós: Bolero, Op. 1, No. 1
      Glinka: Doubt, Romance
      Godard: Vivace from Trio, Op. 72
      Liebe: Serenade, Op. 86
      Moszkowski: Spanish Dance,
        Op. 12, No. 1
      Nevin: Narcissus, Op. 13, No. 4
      Pache: Ständchen
      Tschaikowsky: Waltz, Op. 66, No. 6
    Vol 4
      Arensky: Elégie from Trio in d
      Beethoven: Adagio from Sonate
        pathétique, Op. 13
      Dvorák: Slavic Dance No. 16
      Fauré: Melody in D, Cantique de
        Racine
      Gounod: Serenade from "Quand tu
        chantes"
      Martini: Gavotte, Les Deux moutons
      Moszkowski; Spanish Dance,
        Op. 12, No. 2
      Nevin: Rosary
      Rasch: Moorish Nightsong
      Thomé: Andante Religioso
    Vol 5
      Bargiel: Andante sostenuto from
        Trio in F, Op. 6
      Chaminade: Lento from Trio
        No. 11, Op. 34
      Debussy: Bells
      Goens: Romance sans paroles
      Lassen: Epithalame
      Moszkowski: Bolero, Op. 12, No. 5
      Offenbach: Barcarolle from The Tales
        of Hoffmann
      Pierné: Serenade
      Strauss: Waltz-Scherzo
      Tschaikowsky: Canzonetta, June
BOULNOIS, JOSEPH (1884-1918)
  Trio
    Senart
BRAGA, GAETANO (1829-1907)
  Angel's Serenade
    (Ritter-Saenger-Buechner) CF B1642
BRAHMS, JOHANNES (1833-1897)
  Concerto in a, Op. 102, orig for vln, vcl,
    and orch
    BRH
    Int
    Pet 3902
  Hungarian Dance No. 1 in g
    (Borch) CF B1643
  Hungarian Dance No. 2 in d
    (Borch) CF B1644
  Hungarian Dance No. 3 in F
    (Borch) CF B1645
  Hungarian Dance No. 5 in g
    (Borch) CF B1646
  Hungarian Dance No. 6 in D
    (Borch) CF B1647
  *Trio in B, Op. 8
    BRH
    GS L1514
    Pet 3899A
  *Trio in E flat, Op. 40, for pno, vln, horn
    or vla or vcl
    Aug 5117
    BRH
    Int
    Pet 3899b

*Trio in C, Op. 87
  Aug 9301
  BRH
  GS L1768
  Int
  Pet 3899C
*Trio in c, Op. 101
  (Adamowski) GS L1510
  (Trieste Trio) Int
  Aug 9302
  BRH
  Pet 3899D
*Trio in a, Op. 114, for clar or vln or vla,
  vcl, pno
  BRH
  Int
  Pet 3899E
  Trio in A
  (Bücken-Hasse) BRH
(BRECK, E.S.)
  Christmas Joys
    CF 03171   for contents see title under
      vln and pno
BRETÓN, TOMAS (1850-1923)
  Spanish Pieces, 4
    ESC   also published separately
    1. Danse Orientale
    2. Boléro
    3. Polo Gitano
    4. Scherzo Andalou
BRIDGE, FRANK (1879-1941)
  Miniatures, Set 1
    Aug
      Minuet; Gavotte; Allegretto
  Miniatures, Set 2
    Aug
      Romance; Intermezzo; Saltarello
  Miniatures, Set 3
    Aug
      Valse Russe; Hornpipe; Marche
        Militaire
  Phantasie in c. Trio No. 1
    Aug
  Trio No. 2
    Aug
BRUCH, MAX (1838-1920)
  Pieces, 8, Op. 83, orig for clar, vla, pno
    SIM   published separately
  Trio, Op. 5
    Haml
BUXTEHUDE, DIETRICH
  see Trio Sonatas
CALLAERTS, [JOSEPH (1838-1901)]
  Trio, Op. 16
    Haml
CARMICHAEL, HOAGY (1899-   )
  One morning in May
    (Sopkin) Mil
  Star Dust
    (Leaman) Mil
CARSE, ADAM (1878-1958)
  Duetto
    Aug
  Follow your leader
    Aug
  Minuet
    Aug
  Rondino
    Aug
  Serenade
    Aug
(CARSE, ADAM)
  Trio Album
    Aug   2V   for contents see title

CASTÉRA, RENÉ DE (1873-1955)
  Trio en Ré
    RL
CASTILLON, ALEXIS DE (1838-1873)
  Trio, Op. 4
    Dur
  Trio No. 2 in d
    Heugel
CHAPUIS, [AUGUSTE (1858-1933)]
  Trio en sol
    Dur
CHAUSSON, ERNEST (1855-1899)
  Trio en Sol mineur, Op. 3
    RL
CHEVILLARD, [CAMILLE (1859-1923)]
  Trio en fa, Op. 3
    Dur
CHEVREUILLE, RAYMOND (1901-   )
  Trio, Op. 8
    CBDM
CHOPIN, FRÉDÉRIC (1810-1849)
  Trio in g, Op. 8
    (Balakirev) Pet 1919
CHRISTMAS ALBUM
    Pet 2800A
CHRISTMAS JOYS
    (Breck) CF 03171   for contents see title
      under vln and pno
CLAPP, CHARLES (1899-   )
  Girl of my dreams
    (Sopkin) Mil
CLASSIC PIECES
    Pet 3339A,b,C   3V
      Vol. 1: 12 Pieces by Bach, Beethoven,
        Gluck, Handel, Mozart, Schubert,
        Schumann, Tartini
      Vol. 2: 12 Pieces by C.P.E. Bach,
        Beethoven, Campagnoli, Field, Hum-
        mel, Mozart, Schubert, Weber
      Vol. 3: 12 Pieces by Beethoven
CLASSIC TRIOS, 6
    (Norfleet) CF 01493
      Beethoven: Adagio, from Trio, Op. 11
      Haydn: Trio in G
      Mendelssohn: Andante, from Trio,
        Op. 49
      Mozart: Trio in G, K.564
      Rameau: Menuets, 2
      Schubert: Scherzo, from Trio, Op. 100
CLASSICAL MASTERS
    (Barjansky) GS   2V
      Vol 1
        Bach: Air
        Bach: Little prelude
        Couperin: Lugubre, La
        Gluck: Dance of the sylphs from Orfeo
        Grétry: Gavotte
        Krebs: Bourrée
        Mattheson: Air
        Mendelssohn: Theme
        Mozart: Andante, Sonata in C, K. 545
        Schubert: Theme, Impromptu in B flat
        Schumann: Andante con espressione
        Weber: Waltz
      Vol 2
        Beethoven: Country dances, 2
        Chopin: Prelude in b
        Grieg: Grandmother's minuet
        Handel: Chaconne
        Handel: Sarabande
        Haydn: Minuet in C
        Mozart: Theme, Sonata in A, K. 331
        Rameau: Rigaudon
        Schumann: Merry farmer
        Tchaikovsky: Old French song

Tchaikovsky: Russian dance, Kamarin-
  skaia
CLASSICAL VIOLIN
    (Palaschko) SCH
CONTET & DURAND
  Habanera
    (Edwards) Mil
COPERARIO, GIOVANNI (c.1575-1626)
  Suites, 2
    STB
COPLAND, AARON (1900-   )
  Vitebsk. Study on a Jewish Theme
    BH
COUNTRY GARDENS
    (Ranger) CF
COUPERIN, LOUIS
  see Trio Sonatas
CRAS, [JEAN (1879-1932)]
  Trio en ut
    Dur
DANDELOT, [GEORGES (1895-   )]
  Trio en forme de suite
    HL
DANEAU, [NICOLAS (1866-1944)]
  Trio
    Cranz
DARK EYES
    (Kun) MK
DEBUSSY, CLAUDE (1862-1918)
  Il pleure dans mon coeur, orig for voice
    and pno
    Ed M
DELACHI, PAOLO
  Trio
    SZ
DELIUS, FREDERICK (1862-1934)
  Concerto, orig for vln, vcl and orch
    Aug   pno reduction by Heseltine
DE MARTINO, ALADINO
  Adagio e Allegro
    Santis 866
DEUTSCH, EMERY & ALTMAN, ARTHUR
  Play Fiddle Play
    (Deutsch) MK
DIAMOND, DAVID (1915-   )
  Trio
    SMP
DIERCKS, JOHN (1927-   )
  Serenade
    Tritone   manuscript reproduction
D'INDY, see Indy, d'
DONIZETTI, GAETANO (1797-1848)
  Sextet, from Lucia di Lammermoor
    (Saenger) CF
DONOVAN, RICHARD (1891-   )
  Trio
    BH
DORIAN ALBUM
    (Whistler & Hummel) Ru
DRDLA, FRANZ (1868-1944)
  Souvenir, orig for vln and pno
    (Borch) CF B1755
DRIGO, RICHARD (1846-1930)
  Serenade, from Les Millions d'Arlequin
    (Borch) CF
DURAND
  Song of the rain
    Mil
DURAND, see Contet & Durand
DVORAK, ANTONIN (1841-1904)
  Humoreske, Op. 101, No. 7, orig for pno
    (Saenger) CF
  *Trio in B flat, Op. 21
    (Adamowski) GS L1524
    Artia
    LN (Pet No. R37)

DVORAK, ANTONIN (cont.)
*Trio in g, Op. 26
Artia
Int
*Trio in f, Op. 65
Artia
Int
SIM
*Trio in e, Op. 90, "Dumky"
Artia
Int
Mercury
SIM
ELDERS, JOOP
Spanish Coquette
(Edwards) Mil
ELGAR, EDWARD (1857-1934)
Carissima
EKN
ELKIN, R
Menuet Antique
EKN
ELLINGTON, EDWARD K. (1899-   )
Solitude
(Sopkin) Mil
Sophisticated Lady
(Leaman) Mil
ENCORE TRIO ALBUM
(Ambrosio) CF 02661
ENESCO, GEORGES (1881-1955)
Rumanian Rhapsody No. 1, orig for orch
SMP
ERBSE, HEIMO (1924-   )
Trio, Op. 8
BB
ERLEBACH, PHILIPP HEINRICH
see Trio Sonatas
FANTAISIES, 12, EN TRIO SUR DES OPÉRAS
CÉLÈBRES
(Alder) Deiss
FAURÉ, GABRIEL (1845-1924)
En Prière, orig for voice and pno
Ed M
Trio, Op. 120
Dur
FAVORITE TRIO ALBUM
(Borch) CF 0199
Chaminade: Pierrette
Drdla: Serenade
Glazounow: Autumn and Winter from
Seasons
Iljinsky: Berceuse, from Noure and
Anitra Suite
Massenet: Prelude to Act IV of
Hérodiade
Rachmaninoff: Prelude, Op. 3, No. 2
Roze: Extase d'Amour, Op. 28
Rubinstein: Rêve Angélique, from
Kamennoi Ostrow
Tchaikovsky: Mélodie, from Souvenir
d'un lieu cher, Op. 42, No. 3
Tchaikovsky: Waltz, from Serenade
for String Orchestra, Op. 48
Wagner: Quintet, from Die Meister-
singer
FELIX
Trio, Op. 5
Artia
FERNANDEZ, OSCAR LORENZO (1897-1948)
Trio brasiliano, Op. 32
Ric BA6113
FINKE, [FIDELIO (1891-   )]
Trio
UE 10321

FINNEY, ROSS LEE (1906-   )
Trio No. 2
CF 04104
FOLK-TUNE TRIOS
(Kinscella) CF 02425
All Thro' the Night
An Old Round
Believe Me, If All Those Endearing
Young Charms
Brother John, French Folk Song
Evening Song, Portuguese Folk Air
How Can I leave Thee?
It Was a Shepherdess, Old French
Rondo
Little Valse, German Melody
Looby Loo! English Singing Game
O Sanctissima, Sicilian Folk Song
FORST, RUDOLF (1900-   )
Homage to Ravel
Ed M
FRANCK, CESAR (1822-1890)
Trio Op. 1, No. 1
Pet 3745
Trio, Op. 1, No. 2
Haml
Trio No. 2 d'ap. 1'O Salutaris[87]
Haml
Trio No. 4, Op. 2
Haml
FRANCKENSTEIN, CLEMENS VON (1875-1942)
Arabesques, Op. 36
UE 5380
FRIML, RUDOLF (1879-   )
Adieu
(Borch) BMC
FRISKIN, JAMES (1886-   )
Phantasie in e
Nov
FRÜHLING, CARL (1868-1937)
Trio in a, Op. 40, for vln or clar, vcl, pno
LEU
FRUMERIE, GUNNAR DE (1908-   )
Trio No. 2
Nordiska
FUGA, SANDRO (1906-   )
Trio
SZ
GADZHIBEKOV, [UZEIR (1885-1948)]
Trio. "Ashug"
MZK
GÁL, HANS (1890-   )
Trio, Op. 49b
OBV
Variations on a Viennese Popular Tune, Op. 9
SIM
GALININ, G
Trio
MZK
GANNE, LOUIS GASTON (1862-1923)
Extase
(Tobani) CF   organ and harp ad lib
GENZMER, HARALD (1909-   )
Trio in F
Pet 5025
GERHARD, ROBERTO (1896-   )
Trio
Senart
GERSCHEFSKI, EDWIN (1909-   )
Rhapsody, Op. 46
CFE

[87] The reference is not clear. According to Cobbett (Cyclopedic Survey of Chamber Music) the first three trios were
dedicated to Leopold I of Belgium. Perhaps this is the
reason for the title. This may be the trio Cobbett labels
Op. 1, No. 3.

GHEDINI, GIORGIO FEDERICO (1892-)
Ricercari, 7
SZ
GIBBS, CECIL ARMSTRONG (1889-1960)
Country Magic
Curwen for rent
Yorkshire Dales
Curwen for rent
GILLIS, [DON (1912-)]
Silhouettes
Mil
GLUCK, CHRISTOPH WILLIBALD (1714-1787)
Iphigenia in Aulis, Overture
(Weiss-Ambrosio-Skalmer) CF
GNESSIN, MIKHAIL (1883-1957)
Trio, Op. 63
MZK
GODARD, BENJAMIN (1849-1895)
Trio No. 1
Heugel
Trio No. 2 in F, Op. 72
Dur
GOLDENWEISER, [ALEXANDER (1875-)]
Trio, Op. 31
MZK
GOSSEC, FRANCOIS-JOSEPH (1734-1829)
Gavotte
(Saenger) CF
GOUNOD, CHARLES (1818-1893)
Ave Maria, Méditation sur le premier
prélude de J.S. Bach
(Saenger-Buechner) CF
GRAINGER, PERCY (1882-1961)
Harvest hymn
GS
GREENE, EDWIN
Sing Me to Sleep
(Hollas) BMC
GRETCHANINOV, ALEXANDER (1864-1956)
Trio No. 1 in c, Op. 38
Belaieff
GRIEG, EDVARD (1843-1907)
Peer Gynt Suite No. 1, Op. 46, orig for orch
(Sitt) Pet 2799
GRÜNER-HEGGE, ODD (1899-)
Trio, Op. 4
WH 2288
GYRING, ELIZABETH
Trio Fantasy
CFE
GYROWETZ, ADALBERT (1763-1850)
Divertissement, Op. 50
KS
HAHN, REYNALDO (1875-1947)
Ah! Si vous étiez Nicolas!
Sal d-b ad lib
HAMANN, ERICH (1898-)
Trio, Op. 27
DOB
HAMILTON, IAIN (1922-)
Trio, Op. 25
SCH
HANDEL, GEORG FRIEDRICH (1685-1759)
Duo cantabile. Largo from Sonata in g
for 2 vln
(Kopsch) DOB
Largo
(Saenger) CF
Messiah, Overture
(Stoessel) CF
HARRIS, ROY (1898-)
Trio
Pr

HARSÁNYI, TIBOR (1898-1954)
Trio
Heugel
HAUBIEL, CHARLES (1892-)
Mother Goose Ensemble Book
CP
Romanza
CP
HAYDN, JOSEPH (1732-1809)
Divertimento in B flat
Artia
Divertimento in E, Hob. XV:34[88]
(Landon) DOB
Emperor Variations, from Quartet, Op. 76
(Stoessel) CF
Sonata in F, Hob. VI:1, orig for vln and vla
(Zatschek) DOB
Sonata in A, Hob. VI:2, orig for vln and vla
(Zatschek) DOB
Sonata in B flat, Hob. VI:3, orig for vln and
vla
(Zatschek) DOB
*Trios, 31
Pet 192A,b,C 3V
Vol 1: 12 celebrated trios
Vol 2: 10 trios
Vol 3: 9 trios, including 3 for fl, vcl, pno
Trios, 12[89]
Aug 7265a-f 6V
Vol 1: No. 1 in G; No. 2 in f sharp
Vol 2: No. 3 in C; No. 4 in E
Vol 3: No. 5 in E flat; No. 6 in D
Vol 4: No. 7 in e; No. 8 in E flat
Vol 5: No. 9 in B flat; No. 10 in D
Vol 6: No. 11 in A flat; No. 12 in C
Trios, 5 Celebrated
Int
Trio No. 1 in G
BMC
BRH
Trio No. 2 in f sharp
(Tovey) Oxf 20.013
Trio No. 4 in E
(David) BRH
Trio No. 5 in E flat
(David) BRH
Trio No. 6 in D
(David) BRH
Trio No. 7 in A
(David) BRH
Trio No. 18 in C
(David) BRH
Trio No. 26 in C
(David) BRH
Trio No. 27 in F
(David) BRH
Trio No. 28 in G
(David) BRH
Trio No. 29 in F
(David) BRH
Trio No. 30 in D
(David) BRH
Trio No. 31 in G
BRH
Trio in F, Hob, XV:40
(Heussner) DOB
HEIDEN, BERNHARD (1910-)
Trio
AMP

---

[88] Hob. refers to the thematic catalogue by Anthony van Hoboken.

[89] There are two numbering systems for the Haydn Trios. Augener uses one and Breitkopf & Härtel the other. However, they agree on the first six.

HEILMAN, WILLIAM CLIFFORD (1877-1946)
  Trio, Op. 7
    SPAM
HESSENBERG, KURT (1908-   )
  Trio, Op. 53
    WH
HODKINSON, SYDNEY
  Stanzas
    Tritone   manuscript reproduction
HÖFFER, PAUL (1895-1949)
  Trio
    MT (Pet No. MV1029)
HÖLLER, KARL (1907-   )
  Trio in c, Op. 34
    Pet 5027
HOVHANESS, ALAN (1911-   )
  Trio in e, Op. 3
    Pet 6475
HUGUET Y. TAGELL
  Aveux
    Sal   d-b ad lib
  Prière Paienne
    Sal   d-b ad lib
  Wang. Rêverie Chinoise
    Sal   d-b ad lib
HUMMEL, HERMAN A., see Whistler &
    Hummel
HURÉ, JEAN (1877-1930)
  Suite sur des Chants Bretons
    Mathot
ILJINSKY, ALEXANDER (1859-1919)
  Berceuse, from Noure and Anitra Suite,
    Op. 13
    (Borch) CF B1686
IMBRIE, ANDREW (1921-   )
  Birthday Greeting
    Malcolm   for rent
  Trio
    Malcolm   for rent
d'INDY, VINCENT (1851-1931)
  Trio, Op. 29, orig for pno, clar, vcl
    Int
  Trio No. 2, en forme de suite
    RL
IPPOLITOV-IVANOV, MIKHAIL (1859-1935)
  Variations, 12
    MZK
IRELAND, JOHN (1879-1962)
  Phantasie in a
    Aug
  Trio No. 2 in E
    Aug
  Trio No. 3 in E
    BH
IVES, CHARLES E. (1874-1954)
  Trio
    Peer
JACOB, GORDON (1895-   )
  Trio
    JWL (Mil No. W2303)
JACOBSON, MAURICE (1896-   )
  Shanty Fantasia
    Curwen   for rent
JAQUES-DALCROZE, EMILE (1865-1950)
  Échos du Dancing
    Senart
JELINEK, [JOSEPH (1758-1825)]
  Trio, Op. 10
    Artia
JENKINS, JOHN (1592-1678)
  Aria, for vln, gamba or vcl, pno
    Hin (Pet No. H559A)
  Fantasy Suite No. 4 in G
    STB

Sonata a 2 in d, for vln, gamba or vcl, pno
    Hin (Pet No. H559b)   2nd vcl ad lib
  see also Trio Sonatas
JERAL, WILHELM
  Serenade
    (Winternitz-Willeke) CF B1809
  Serenade Viennois, Op. 18
    UE 6815
JONES, DOUGLAS
  Ayton Airs
    Chap-L
JONES, HENRY
  Trio for Young Players
    Oxf
JONGEN, JOSEPH (1873-1953)
  Pieces, 2, Op. 95
    CBDM
JUON, PAUL (1872-1940)
  Legende, Op. 83
    Birnbach
  Litaniae, Op. 70, Tone Poem
    LEU
  Suite, Op. 89
    Birnbach
  Trio Miniatures
    LN (Pet No. R17)
KADOSA, PAL (1903-   )
  Trio, Op. 49d
    Kul
KALINNIKOV, VASSILI (1866-1901)
  Chanson Triste
    Ed M
KALOMIRIS, [MANOLIS (1883-   )]
  Trio
    Senart
KAUFMANN, [ARMIN (1902-   )]
  Trio, Op. 57, No. 2
    DOB
KERR, HARRISON (1897-   )
  Trio
    CFE   score only
KETELBEY
  Bells Across the Meadows
    (Sopkin) Mil
(KINSCELLA)
  Folk-Tune Trios
    CF 02425   for contents see title
KIRCHNER, LEON (1919-   )
  Trio
    AMP
KLEBE, GISELHER (1925-   )
  Elegia appassionata, Op. 22
    BB
KLENGEL, JULIUS (1859-1933)
  Children's Trio, Op. 35, No. 2
    BRH
  Children's Trio, Op. 39, No. 2
    BRH
  Concerto, Op. 61, orig for vln, vcl and orch
    (Davisson) BRH
  Trio, Op. 25
    BRH
KLIUZNER, B.
  Trio
    MZK
KNIGHT, MORRIS (1933-   )
  Trio
    Tritone   manuscript reproduction
KONDOR, ERNO
  Old Gypsy
    (Kun) MK
KORNAUTH, EGON (1891-1959)
  Trio-Suite, Op. 45, for vln, vcl or vla, pno
    DOB

KORNGOLD, ERICH WOLFGANG (1897-1957)
    Trio, Op. 1
    UE 2996   score only
KOUGUELL, ARCADIE
    Melodie and Danse Hebraique
    Mercury
KOZELUCH, LEOPOLD ANTON (1752-1818)
    Trio, Op. 12, No. 1
    KS
    Trio, Op. 12, No. 2
    KS
    Trio, Op. 12, No. 3
    KS
KRAMER, A. WALTER (1890-   )
    In Elizabethan Days, Op. 32, No. 2
    CF B1688
KRAUS, [JOSEPH (1756-1792)]
    Trio in D
    (Lebermann) BRH
KREISLER, FRITZ (1875-1962)
    Caprice Viennois
    (Biederman) Fol 1410
    Miniature Viennese March
    Fol 1419
    Old Refrain
    (Biederman) Fol 1430
KRIEGER, JOHANN PHILIPP
    see Trio Sonatas
KUULA, TOIVO (1883-1918)
    Trio, Op. 7
    WH 2479
LABEY, MARCEL (1875-   )
    Trio
    Senart
LABROCA, [MARIO (1896-   )]
    Trio
    UE 8613
LACOMBE, PAUL (1838-1927)
    Trio, Op. 12
    Haml
    Trio No. 3, Op. 134
    Haml
LALO, EDOUARD (1823-1892)
    Trio No. 3 en la mineur, Op. 26
    Dur
LALOUX, FERNAND
    Trio in D
    Curwen   for rent
LAWES, WILLIAM (1602-1645)
    Fantasy Suite No. 5 in d
    STB
LECLAIR, JEAN MARIE
    see Trio Sonatas
LECUONA, ERNESTO (1896-1963)
    African Lament
    (Kun) MK
LEHAR, FRANZ (1870-1948)
    Frasquita Serenade
    (Kun) MK
LEKEU, GUILLAUME (1870-1894)
    Trio
    RL
LEMARE, EDWIN H (1865-1934)
    Andantino
    (Severn) CF B2081
LINCKE, PAUL (1866-1946)
    Glow-Worm
    (Kun) MK
LOCATELLI, PIETRO (1695-1764)
    Aria
    Ed M
LOEILLET, JEAN BAPTISTE (1680-1730)
    Sonata in b
    (Beon) Int
    HL

Sonata in G
    (Beon) Int
    HL
LOHSE, FRED (1908-   )
    Variations on a theme of Mozart
    BRH
LONDONDERRY AIR
    (Kreisler) Fol 1416
LOTTI, ANTONIO
    see Trio Sonatas
LOVELL
    Birdcage Walk (St. James's Park), from
        Green London
    Hin (Pet No. H712)
    Lake Scene (Regent's Park), from
        Green London
    Hin (Pet No. H711)
    Rotten Row (Hyde Park), from Green
        London
    Hin (Pet No. H713)
LUENING, OTTO (1900-   )
    Trio
    CFE
(LUTZ)
    My Violin Book
    SCH
    Unterhaltungs Konzert
    SCH
LYDIAN ALBUM
    (Whistler & Hummel) Ru
MACBETH, ALLAN (1856-1910)
    Love in Idleness
    (Saenger) CF
MCDONALD, HARL (1899-   )
    Trio in g
    EV
MACDOWELL, EDWARD (1861-1908)
    To a Wild Rose, orig for pno
    (Isaac) CF B3318
MAGANINI
    Album for Strings
    Ed M
MAGNARD, ALBÉRIC (1865-1914)
    Trio, Op. 18
    RL
MAINARDI, ENRICO (1897-   )
    Notturno
    SZ
    Trio, 1939
    SZ
    Trio, 1954
    SCH
MAIZEL, B
    Trio, Op. 26
    MZK
MALIPIERO, GIAN FRANCESCO (1882-   )
    Concerto a tre, orig for vln, vcl, pno
        and orch
    SZ   orch reduction for 2nd pno
    Sonata a tre
    UE 9515
MALLING, OTTO (1848-1915)
    Trio, Op. 36
    WH 934
MANZIARLY, MARCELLE DE (1899-   )
    Trio
    Senart
MARGOLA, FRANCO (1908-   )
    Trio No. 2
    ZA 3712
MARIE, GABRIEL (1852-1928)
    Cinquantaine, La
    (Arnold) CF B1666

MARINI, BIAGIO
  see Trio Sonatas
MARTIN, FRANK (1890-   )
  Trio on Irish Folk Songs
    Hug (Pet No. A47)
MARTINI, JEAN PAUL EGIDE (1741-1816)
  Plaisir d'Amour
    (Sandby) AMP
MARTINU, BOHUSLAV (1890-1959)
  Bergerettes
    SMP
  Trio in d
    ESC
  Trio, 1930
    SCH
  Trio No. 3 in C
    ESC
MASCAGNI, PIETRO (1863-1945)
  Intermezzo Sinfonico, from Cavalleria
    Rusticana
    (Werner-Saenger) CF
MASCITI, MICHEL (? -1750)
  Sonate en Sol mineur
    (Peyrot-Rebuffat) Senart 2643
MASSENET, JULES (1842-1912)
  Elegy, Op. 10, from Les Érynnies
    (Borch) CF B1744
  Under the Linden Trees
    Ed M
MASSON, FERNAND (1882-1942)
  Trio
    Senart
MATHIAS, GEORGES (1826-1910)
  Trio No. 3, Op. 33
    Haml
  Trio No. 6 en si bemol
    Dur
MENDELSSOHN, FELIX (1809-1847)
  On Wings of Song, orig for voice and pno
    (Biederman) CF B2201
    (Trinkaus) Fill
  Spring Song, Op. 62, No. 6, orig for pno
    (Klugescheid) CF B1698
  *Trios, 2: Op. 49 in d; Op. 66 in c
    Pet 1740
  Trio in d, Op. 49
    (Adamowski) GS L1458
    Aug 7267a
  Trio in c, Op. 66
    (Adamowski) GS L1459
  Wedding March, from A Midsummer Night's
    Dream
    (Weiss) CF
MESSAGER, [ANDRÉ (1853-1929)]
  Chant Birman
    Sal d-b ad lib
  Romance
    Sal d-b ad lib
MEYER & SALABERT
  Bajadère, La
    Sal d-b ad lib
  Causerie d'Amour
    Sal d-b ad lib
  Madame Récamier
    Sal d-b ad lib
  Pastorale Rococo
    Sal d-b ad lib
  Petite Valse
    Sal d-b ad lib
MEYERBEER, GIACOMO (1791-1864)
  Coronation March, from Le Prophète
    (Weiss) CF
MICHAELIS, AUGUST HENRICH
  Sonaten, 3
    (Schafer) Gerig

MIGOT, GEORGES (1891-   )
  Trio ou Suite a Trois
    Leduc
MIRON
  Cradle Song
    Mil
(MLYNARCZYK)
  Piano Trio, Vol. I
    SIM
MODERN TRIO ALBUM
  (Ambrosio) CF 0379
    Atherton: Elégie and Consolation
    Brahms: Hungarian Dance No. 5 in g
    Dvorak: Humoreske
    Ghys: Gavotte Louis XIII, Amaryllis
    Herbert: Serenade, from Op. 3
    Liszt: Liebesträume
    Marie, Gabriel: Cinquantaine, La
    Offenbach: O Belle Nuit, Barcarolle,
      from Les Contes d'Hoffmann
    Reissiger: Celebrated Andante
    Saint-Saëns: My Heart At Thy Sweet
      Voice, from Samson et Dalila
    Sinding: Mélodie Mignonne
    Strauss: Vienna Life
    Tchaikovsky: Autumn Song
    Tchaikovsky: Chant Sans Paroles
    Wagner: Song to the Evening Star,
      from Tannhäuser
MONFRED, A.
  Humoresque interrompue
    Sal
MOORE, DOUGLAS (1893-   )
  Trio
    Galx
MORRIS, HAROLD (1890-   )
  Trio No. 2
    SPAM
MOSZKOWSKI, MORITZ (1854-1925)
  Spanish Dances, Op. 12, Nos. 1-5, orig for
    pno duet
    (Scharwenka-Saenger) CF 2V
  Spanish Dance in C, Op. 12, No. 1
    (Scharwenka-Saenger) CF
MOZART, WOLFGANG AMADEUS (1756-1791)
  Ave, Verum Corpus
    (Moses-Tobani-Saenger) CF
  Serenade, K.525, orig for str quintet
    (Stoessel) CF AS6
  *Trios, 7
    (David) Int
  *Trios, 7
    Pet 193
      K. 254, 496, 502, 542, 548, 564,
      K. 498 for clar or vln, vla, pno
  Trio No. 1 in G, K. 496
    (Adamowski) GS L1602
    Aug 7268a
    BRH
  Trio No. 2 in B flat, K. 502
    (Adamowski) GS L1603
    Aug 7268b
    BRH
  Trio No. 3 in E, K. 542
    (Adamowski) GS L1604
    Aug 7268c
    BRH
  Trio No. 4 in C, K. 548
    (Adamowski) GS L1605
    Aug 7268d
    BRH
  Trio No. 5 in G, K. 564
    (Adamowski) GS L1606
    Aug 7268e
    BRH

MOZART, WOLFGANG AMADEUS (cont.)
  Trio No. 6 in B flat, K. 254
    (Adamowski) GS L1607
    Aug 7268f
    BRH
  Trio No. 7 in E flat, K.498, orig for pno,
    clar, vla
    (Adamowski) GS L1403
  Trio No. 8 in d, K. 442
    (Adamowski) GS L1608
    BRH
  Trio in E flat after Quintet, K.407, orig
    for horn, vln, 2 vla, vcl
    BRH
  Variations on a theme of, see Lohse
MÜNTZING, ARNE (1903-   )
  Serenade
    DOB
MURRAY-JACOBY, H.
  Moon Over the Caribbean
    Leeds
MUSIN, OVIDE (1854-1929)
  Mexicana
    (Roberts) MK
MY VIOLIN BOOK
    (Lutz) SCH
      11 melodies by Gossec, Mozart, Handel,
      Mendelssohn, Tchaikovsky, Brahms,
      and others
MYDDLETON, WILLIAM H.
  Down South
    (Kun) MK
NEVIN, ETHELBERT (1862-1901)
  Rosary
    (Riesenfeld) BMC
NEW TRIO ALBUM
    (Baron) BMI
      12 pieces by Albeniz, Debussy, Faure,
      Rossini, Shostakovich, and others
NEWLIN, DIKA (1923-   )
  Trio, Op. 2
    CFE   score only
NORFLEET, HELEN
  Little Trios, 8
    CF 01322
(NORFLEET, HELEN)
  Classic Trios, 6
    CF 01493   for contents see title
NØRHOLM, IB (1931-   )
  Trio, Op. 22
    Dansk 223
NOWAK, LIONEL (1911-   )
  Trio
    CFE
OFFENBACH, JACQUES (1819-1880)
  Barcarolle, from Tales of Hoffmann
    (Sylvain) BMC
    (Woltag-Ambrosio) CF B1702
    "O Belle Nuit"
d'OLLONE, MAX (1875-1959)
  Trio en la mineur
    Dur
OUR FAVORITES
    (Palaschko) SCH
PACHE, JOHANNES
  Barcarolle
    (Saenger) CF B1704
(PALASCHKO)
  Classical Violin
    SCH
  Our Favorites
    SCH
PEETERS, [FLOR (1903-   )]
  Larghetto
    SF (Pet No. SCH85)

PERGOLESI, GIOVANNI BATTISTA (1710-1736)
  Sicilian Air
    Ed M
  Tre Giorni
    (Kreisler) Fol 1421
PERSICHETTI, VINCENT (1915-   )
  Serenade No. 3
    SMP
PFITZNER, HANS (1869-1949)
  Trio, Op. 8
    SIM
PIANO TRIO, VOL. I
    (Mlynarczyk) SIM
PIERNÉ, [GABRIEL (1863-1937)]
  Trio, Op. 45
    Dur
PIETRI, G.
  Pietriana. Fantasia No. 1
    (Fabor) SON   2nd vln and d-b ad lib
  Serenata Elbana in G
    SZ
PISTON, WALTER (1894-   )
  Trio
    AMP
PLANCHET, DOMINIQUE-CHARLES
    (1857-1946)
  Trio
    Haml
POLDINI, EDUARD (1869-1957)
  Poupée Valsante
    (Saenger) CF
POLLINI, CESARE (1858-1912)
  Suite
    ZA 534
PONCE, MANUEL MARÍA (1882-1948)
  Estrellita
    (Simon) CF B2109
PROGRAM ALBUM
    (Whistler & Hummel) Ru
RACHMANINOFF, SERGEY (1873-1943)
  Trio Elegiaque, Op. 9
    BH
    Int
    MZK
  Variation 18, from Rapsodie on a theme of
    Paganini, orig for pno and orch
    Fol 1431
  Vocalise No. 14, Op. 38, orig for voice
    (Cornus) BH
    Ed M
RAFF, JOSEF JOACHIM (1822-1882)
  Allegretto
    Paxton (Mil No. P554)
  Trio No. 3, Op. 155
    Haml
  Trio No. 4, Op. 158
    Haml
  Vivace
    Paxton (Mil No. P555)
RAMEAU, JEAN-PHILIPPE (1683-1764)
  Concert No. 1
    (Peyrot-Rebuffat) Senart 2683
  Concert No. 2
    (Peyrot-Rebuffat) Senart 2634
  Concert No. 3
    (Peyrot-Rebuffat) Senart 2719
  Concert No. 4
    (Peyrot-Rebuffat) Senart 2916
  Concert No. 5
    (Peyrot-Rebuffat) Senart 2917
  Pièces en concert
    (Saint-Saens) Dur
RAVEL, MAURICE (1875-1937)
  Pavane
    Ed M

RAVEL, MAURICE (cont.)
*Trio in a
  Dur
RAWSTHORNE, ALAN (1905-   )
  Trio
  Oxf
REGER, MAX (1873-1916)
  Trio in e, Op. 102
  BB
REINECKE, CARL (1824-1910)
  Trio in a, Op. 188, orig for ob, horn, pno
  BRH
  Trio No. 2, Op. 230
  BRH
REISSIGER, CARL (1798-1859)
  Andante
    Paxton (Mil No. P552)
  Romance
    Paxton (Mil No. P553)
REIZENSTEIN, FRANZ (1911-   )
  Trio in one movement, Op. 34
  Leng (Mil No. L602)
REUCHSEL, AMÉDÉE (1875-   )
  Trio en mi bemol
  HL
RHENÉ-BATON (1879-1940)
  Trio
  Dur
RIDKY, J.
  Trio, Op. 44
  Artia
RIEGGER, WALLINGFORD (1885-1961)
  Trio
  AMP
RIMSKY-KORSAKOV, NIKOLAY (1844-1908)
  Song of India, from Sadko
    (Severn) CF B2084
ROPARTZ, J. GUY (1864-1955)
  Trio en la mineur
  Dur
ROSENMÜLLER, JOHANN
  see Trio Sonatas
ROUSSEL, ALBERT (1869-1937)
  Trio
  RL
ROWLEY, ALEC (1892-1958)
  Four Contrasts
  JWL
  Pastel Portraits[90]
  GT
  Puppet Show
  JWL
  Short Suite
  JWL
  Short Trios on English Tunes, Op. 46a
    Pet 4385A
  Short Trios on French Tunes, Op. 46b
    Pet 4385b
  Short Trios on Irish Tunes, Op. 46c
    Pet 4385C
RUBBRA, EDMUND (1901-   )
  Trio in one movement
  Leng (Mil No. L4003)
RUBINSTEIN, ANTON (1829-1894)
  Rêve Angélique, Op. 10, No. 12
    (Borch) CF B1713
  Trio No. 2, Op. 15, No. 2
  Haml
  Trio No. 3, Op. 52
  Haml
  Trio No. 4, Op. 85
  Haml

Trio No. 5, Op. 108
  Haml
SAINT-SAENS, CAMILLE (1835-1921)
  Trio, Op. 19
  Haml
  Trio No. 2 en mi mineur, Op. 92
  Dur
SALABERT, F, see Meyer & Salabert
SALMANOV, V.
  Trio No. 2
  MZK
SAMMARTINI, GIOVANNI BATTISTA
    (1701-1775)
  Sonata in four movements, selected from
    the "Sonate notturne", Op. 7
    (Casella) GS L1577
SANDBY, HERMAN (1881-   )
  Danish Folk Dance
  CF B2215
SAPP, ALLEN (1922-   )
  Trio No. 1
  CFE
SCASSOLA, A.
  Nuit d'Amour
    Sal d-b ad lib
  Sérénade Romantique
    Sal
SCELZI, GIACINTO (1905-   )
  Trio
  Santis 727
SCHISKE, KARL (1916-   )
  Sonatine, Op. 34
  DOB
SCHOBERT, [JOHANN (c.1720-1767)]
  Trio in E flat, Op. 6, No. 1
    (Karsch) NAG
SCHOENBERG, ARNOLD (1874-1951)
  Serenade, Op. 24, orig for 7 instruments
    and voice; arr for vln, vcl, pno
  WH
SCHROEDER, HERMANN (1843-1909)
  Trio, Op. 33
  SCH
SCHRÖTER, HEINZ (1907-   )
  Trio in C, Op. 2
  BB
SCHUBERT, FRANZ (1797-1828)
  Ave Maria, orig for voice and pno
    (Borch) CF
  Entr'acte from Rosamunde
    Paxton (Mil No. P556)
  Marche Militaire, Op. 51, No. 1, orig
    for pno duet
    (Weiss) CF
  *Nocturne in E flat, Op. 148
  BRH
  Int
  Sonata for pno, vln, vcl
  UE 11472
  *Trios, 2: Op. 99 and Op. 100
  Pet 167
  Trio No. 1 in B flat, Op. 99
    (Adamowski) GS L1471
  Aug 7277
  BRH
  UE 4851
  Trio No. 2 in E flat, Op. 100
    (Adamowski) GS L1472
  Aug 7278
  BRH
SCHUMANN, ROBERT (1810-1856)
  Phantasiestücke, Op. 88
  BRH
  Int
  Pet 2378

---

[90] In the U.S.A. this publication can be obtained through Mills.

SCHUMANN, ROBERT (cont.)
  Träumerei and Romance, Op. 15, No. 7,
    orig for pno
    (Klugescheid) CF B1722
  *Trios, 3: Op. 63, Op. 80, Op. 110
    Pet 2377
  Trio No. 1 in d, Op. 63
    (Adamowski) GS L1476
  Trio No. 2 in F, Op. 80
    (Adamowski) GS L1477
  Trio No. 3 in g, Op. 110
    (Adamowski) GS L1478
SCHWARTZ, PAUL
  Trio, Op. 10
    CFE
SCOTT, CYRIL (1879-   )
  Trio No. 2
    SCH
  Vesperale
    EKN
  Waltz No. 1
    EKN
SHAPEY, RALPH (1921-   )
  Trio
    CFE
SHEBALIN, VISSARION (1902-   )
  Trio, Op. 39
    MZK
SHOSTAKOVICH, DMITRI (1906-   )
  Trio, Op. 67
    Int
    MZK
    Pet 4744
SIBELIUS, JEAN (1865-1957)
  Musette, from King Christian II
    (Powell) AMP
SINDING, CHRISTIAN (1856-1941)
  Trio in C, Op. 87
    Pet 3136
(SITT)
  Trio Album
    Pet 2738A,b   2V   for contents see title
SIXT, JOHANN ABRAHAM (1757-1797)
  Trio No. 1 in D
    (Fischer) BB
  Trio No. 2 in G
    (Fischer) BB
  Trio No. 3 in E flat
    (Fischer) BB
SKALKOTTAS, NIKOS (1904-1949)
  Variations, 8, on a Greek Folk Song
    UE 12735
SKORZENY, FRITZ (1900-   )
  Trio in A
    DOB
SMETANA, BEDŘICH (1824-1884)
  *Trio in g, Op. 15
    Artia
    Int
    Pet 4238
SMITH, EM
  Dance Pantomime, from 3 Tunes in
    3 Rhythms
    CF
  Romance, from 3 Tunes in 3 Rhythms
    CF
  Valse Capriccietto, from 3 Tunes in
    3 Rhythms
    CF
SMITH, LELAND
  Trio
    CFE
SOHY, CHARLOTTE (1887-1955)
  Petite Suite
    Senart

SOUBEYRAN
  Fête Provencale
    RL
  Joyeux forestiers, Les
    RL
STEIN, LEON (1910-   )
  Adagio and Dance
    CFE
STEINERT, [ALEXANDER (1900-   )]
  Trio
    UE 5307
STEVENS, BERNARD (1916-   )
  Trio
    Leng (Mil No. L4004)
STEVENS, HALSEY (1908-   )
  Trio No. 3
    CFE
STRADELLA, ALESSANDRO (1642-1682)
  Sinfonia, for vln, vcl, and continuo
    (Grützbach) Sik 348
STRAUSS, JOHANN (1825-1899)
  Blue Danube Waltz, Op. 214
    (Ambrosio-Perlman) CF B2498   simpl
STRAVINSKY, IGOR (1882-   )
  Berceuse, from Firebird
    Ed M
  Dance of the Princesses from Firebird
    Ed M
STRINGFIELD, LAMAR (1897-   )
  In a Log Cabin, from Mountain Sketches,
    Op. 19, No. 4
    CF B2397
STRINGFIELD
  Morning
    Ed M
SUGÁR, REZSO (1919-   )
  Little Suite
    Kul
TALIAN, V.
  Trio
    MZK
TANEYEV, SERGEY IVANOVITCH (1856-1915)
  Trio in D, Op. 22
    SIM
TANSMAN, ALEXANDER (1897-   )
  Air Champêtre, from Nous jouons pour
    Maman
    ESC
  Bateau, Le, from Nous Jouons pour Maman
    ESC
  Chanson Nègre, from Nous jouons pour
    Maman
    ESC
  Danse Slave, from Nous jouons pour Maman
    ESC
  Gavotte, from Nous jouons pour Maman
    ESC
  Orientale, from Nous jouons pour Maman
    ESC
  Serenade
    Leduc
  Trio No. 2
    ESC
TCHAIKOVSKY, PIOTR ILYITCH (1840-1893)
  *Trio in a, Op. 50
    Aug 7285
    Int
    MZK
    Pet 3777
TCHEREPNINE, ALEXANDER (1899-   )
  Trio
    Dur
TELEMANN, GEORG PHILIPP (1681-1767)
  Concerto in E, for vln, gamba or vcl, pno
    (Doebereiner) Pet 3875   2nd vcl ad lib

TELEMANN, GEORG PHILIPP (cont.)
Concerto No. 1 in F
(Ruyssen) Delrieu
Concerto No. 2 in g
(Ruyssen) Delrieu
TENAGLIA
Aria Antica
Ed,M
THOMÉ, FRANCIS (1850-1909)
Simple Aveu, Op. 25
CF B1730
TOBANI, THEO M.
Hearts and Flowers
CF B1732
TORELLI, GIUSEPPE
see Trio Sonatas
TOSELLI, ENRICO (1883-1926)
Serenade, Op. 6
(Schulz) BMC
TRIO ALBUM
(Biederman) GS
Edwards: By the bend of the river
Friml: Russian dance
Gilbert: Dresden shepherdess
Grever: Jurame
Irish Folk-Tune: Londonderry air
Levitzki: Valse
Padwa: Electric
Rasbach: Trees
Speaks: Sylvia
Strickland: Mah Lindy Lou
TRIO ALBUM
(Carse) Aug   2V
Vol 1
Coleridge-Taylor: Three-fours,
Valse, Op. 71, No. 6
Lind, G: Once upon a time
Moszkowski: Melodie, Op. 18, No. 1
Scharwenka: Polish Dance,
Op. 3, No. 1
Vol 2
Adam, L: Liselotte
Ilynski, A: Berceuse
Schubert, F: Entr'acte II, from
Rosamond
Shield-Moffat: Countess of
Westmoreland's Delight
TRIO ALBUM
(Sitt) Pet 2738A,b   2V
Vol. 1: 10 Pieces by Beethoven, Haydn,
Mendelssohn, Mozart, Schubert,
Schumann, Weber
Vol. 2: 8 Pieces by Beethoven, Chopin,
Grieg, Haydn, Mendelssohn, Mozart,
Schubert, Schumann
TRIOS FOR VIOLIN, PIANO AND CELLO
Amsco 53
TURINA, JOAQUIN (1882-1949)
Circulo, Op. 91, Fantasia
UME
Trio No. 1, Op. 35
RL
Trio No. 2, Op. 76
RL
TWINN, SYDNEY
Old Scottish Tunes
JWL (Mil No. W2400)
UNTERHALTUNGS KONZERT
(Lutz) SCH
VALENCIA, ANTONIO MARIA (1902-1952)
Emociones Caucanas
Pan American Union
VAN HULSE, C.
Elegy
CP

VASSILENKO, [SERGEY (1872-1956)]
Trio
MZK
VERETTI, ANTONIO (1900-   )
Trio in Do
Santis 529
VILLA-LOBOS, HEITOR (1887-1959)
Trio No. 1
ESC
Trio No. 2
ESC
Trio No. 3
ESC
VITALI, GIOVANNI BATTISTA (c.1644-1692)
Sonata, Op. 4, No. 9
(Hinnenthal) Int
VIVALDI, ANTONIO (c.1669-1741)
Concerto in B flat, orig for vln, vcl and
orch
Int
Pastorale, Op. 13, No. 4
(Upmeyer) Int
NAG
Sonata in c
(Ghedini) Int
see also Trio Sonatas
VOLKMANN, ROBERT (1815-1883)
Trio, Op. 3
Haml
Trio, Op. 5
Haml
VON BLON, FRANZ (1861-1945)
Meditation
(Ambrosio) CF
Whispering Flowers
(Borch) CF
VOORMOLEN, ALEX (1895-   )
Trio
RL
VOSS, FRIEDRICH (1930-   )
Trio
BRH
VRANICKY, [PAVEL (1756-1808)]
Trio
Artia
VREULS, VICTOR (1876-1944)
Trio in d
Bosw
WAGNER, RICHARD (1813-1883)
Bridal Chorus, from Lohengrin
(Saenger) CF
Vorspiel, from Lohengrin
(Saenger) CF
WALLACE, CATHERINE
Play Together Tunes
MK
WALLINGTON
Morning Dew
(Edwards) Mil
WEBER, CARL MARIA VON (1786-1826)
Invitation to the Dance, Op. 65, orig for pno
(Weiss-Saenger-Buechner) CF
Trio in g, Op. 63, orig for fl, vcl, pno
Int
Pet 1473
WEIGL, KARL (1881-1949)
Trio
CFE
(WHISTLER, HARVEY S. & HUMMEL,
HERMAN A.)
Dorian Album
Ru
Lydian Album
Ru

(WHISTLER, HARVEY S. & HUMMEL,
HERMAN A.) (cont.)
Program Album
Ru
WIDOR, CHARLES-MARIE (1844-1937)
Serenade
Heugel
SCH
WILLIAMS, GERRARD (1888-1947)
Traditional Tunes, 4
Oxf 77.014-32
WILLIAMS
Dream of Olwen
(Edwards) Mil
WILLIAMS
Theme, from The Apartment
Mil
WIRÉN, DAG (1905-   )
Trio No. 1, Op. 6
Gehrmans
Trio No. 2, Op. 36
Gehrmans
WOHLFAHRT, FRANZ
Easy Trio in e, Op. 66, No. 5
CF B1749
WOLF-FERRARI, ERMANNO (1876-1948)
Trio No. 1 in D, Op. 5
LEU
WOOLLEN, RUSSELL (1923-   )
Trio
CFE
WORDSWORTH, WILLIAM (1908-   )
Trio in A
Leng (Mil No. L4005)
WRANITZKY, see Vranicky
WYMAN, ADDISON P. (1832-1872)
Woodland Echoes, Op. 34
CF
YSAŸE, EUGÈNE (1858-1931)
Poème Nocturne,[91] orig for vln, vcl, orch
SF
ZAFRED, MARIO (1922-   )
Trio No. 3
Ric 129607   score included
ZANDONAI, RICCARDO (1883-1944)
Trio Serenata
Curci

Trios: Viola, Cello, Piano

BACH, KARL PHILIPP EMANUEL (1714-1788)
Sonatas, 6
Int
Trio in F
Int
BRAHMS, JOHANNES (1833-1897)
Trio in a, Op. 114, for clar or vln or
vla, vcl, pno
BRH
Int
Pet 3899E
FIFTEENTH CENTURY FOLK SONG
(Tertis) Bosw
MÜNTZING, ARNE (1903-   )
Serenade
DOB

---

[91] This publication is not listed in current U.S. catalogues.
Information was received from Fondation Eugène Ysaÿe.

Trios: Viola, Double-Bass, Piano

DITTERSDORF, KARL DITTERS VON
(1739-1799)
Symphonie Concertante in D, orig for
vla, d-b and orch
Int

Trios: Violin, Organ, Piano

BEETHOVEN, LUDWIG VAN (1770-1827)
Adagio Cantabile, from Septet, Op. 20
CF
Menuet No. 2 in G, orig for pno
(Saenger) CF
BOHM, CARL
Zingara, La, Op. 102
CF
BUESSER, HENRI-PAUL (1872-   )
Sommeil de l'enfant Jésus
CH (Pet No. C55)
DVORAK, ANTONIN (1841-1904)
Humoreske, Op. 101, No. 7, orig for pno
(Saenger) CF
GOUNOD, CHARLES (1818-1893)
Ave Maria. Méditation sur le premier
prélude de J. S. Bach
(Saenger) CF S3060
HANDEL, GEORG FRIEDRICH (1685-1759)
Largo
(Saenger) CF
MASCAGNI, PIETRO (1863-1945)
Intermezzo Sinfonico, from Cavalleria
Rusticana
(Saenger-Moses) CF
MIETZKE, GEORGE A.
Meditation
GS
MOSZKOWSKI, MORITZ (1854-1925)
Spanish Dance in C, Op. 12, No. 1, orig
for pno duet
(Scharwenka-Saenger) CF
MOZART, WOLFGANG AMADEUS (1756-1791)
Ave, Verum Corpus
(Saenger-Moses-Tobani) CF
POLDINI, EDUARD (1869-1957)
Poupée Valsante
CF
WAGNER, RICHARD (1813-1883)
Bridal Chorus, from Lohengrin
CF
Vorspiel. Prelude to Lohengrin
CF

Trios: String-Wind-Keyboard

ABEL, KARL FRIEDRICH
see Trio Sonatas
ANDRÉ, LUDWIG
Alpine Violets, Op. 100, for fl, vln, pno
(Saenger-Ambrosio) CF W1205
ANDRIESSEN, HENDRIK (1892-   )
Pastorale, for fl, vln, pno
DN (Pet No. D45)
BACH, JOHANN CHRISTOPH FRIEDRICH
see Trio Sonatas

BACH, JOHANN SEBASTIAN (1685-1750)
Ave Maria, see Gounod
Canonic Trio, for ob, vln, pno
(Marx) MM realization of figured bass
by Weiss-Mann
Concerto in c, S.1060, orig for ob, vln and
orch; arr for ob, vln, pno
(Berner) SCH
(Seiffert) Int
Pet 3722
Concerto in d, orig for 2 pno and str orch;
arr for vln, ob or 2 vln and pno
(Schneider) BRH
see also Trio Sonatas
BACH, KARL PHILIPP EMANUEL (1714-1788)
Spring's awakening, for cornet, vln, pno
(Ambrosio) CF
Spring's Awakening, for fl, vln, pno
(Ambrosio) CF
Trio No. 1 in D, for fl, vla, pno
Int
Trio No. 2 in a, for fl, vla, pno
Int
Trio No. 3 in G, for fl, vla, pno
Int
Trio in F, for vla, bsn, pno
Int
see also Trio Sonatas
BACH, WILHELM FRIEDEMANN
see Trio Sonatas
BARTÓK, BÉLA (1881-1945)
*Contrasts, for pno, vln, clar
BH
BASSETT, LESLIE (1923-)
Trio, for clar, vla, pno
CFE
BAUER, MARION (1887-1955)
Trio Sonata No. 1, for fl, vcl, pno
CFE
BEAN, MABEL
Bubble Dance, for vln, saxaphone, pno
CF
BECERRA-SCHMIDT, GUSTAVO
Trio, for fl, vln, pno
Pan American Union score included
BEETHOVEN, LUDWIG VAN (1770-1827)
Trio in B flat, Op. 11, for clar, vcl, pno
(Adamowski) GS L1424
Aug 7250d
BRH
Int
Pet 7064
Trio in E flat, Op. 38, for clar or vln,
vcl, pno
Int arr by composer from Septet, Op. 20
BERKELEY, LENNOX (1903-)
Trio, for horn, vln, pno
Ches
BLOCH, ERNEST (1880-1959)
Concertino, for fl, vla or clar, pno
GS for rent
BLOMDAHL, KARL-BIRGER (1916-)
Trio, for clar, vcl, pno
SCH
BÖDDECKER, PHILIPP FRIEDRICH
(1615-1683)
Sonate sopra "La Monica", for vln, bsn,
cembalo
KS
BODINUS, see Trio Sonatas
BOISMORTIER, JOSEPH BODIN DE
see Trio Sonatas
BRAGA, GAETANO (1829-1907)
Angel's Serenade, for clar, vln, pno
(De Ville) CF

Angel's Serenade, for cornet, vln, pno
(De Ville) CF
Angel's Serenade, for fl, vln, pno
(De Ville) CF
BRAHMS, JOHANNES (1833-1897)
*Trio in E flat, Op. 40, for horn, vln, pno
Aug 5117
BRH
Int
Pet 3899b
*Trio in a, Op. 114, for clar, vcl, pno
BRH
Int
Pet 3899E
BRUCH, MAX (1838-1920)
Pieces, 8, Op. 83, for clar in A, vla, pno
SIM published separately
CHRISTIANSEN, [F. MELIUS (1871-1955)]
Caprice, for clar, vln, pno
Kjos D2803
COUPERIN, LOUIS
see Trio Sonatas
CRESTON, PAUL (1906-)
Partita, for fl or vln, vln, pno
Leeds
CZIBULKA, ALPHONSE (1842-1894)
Stephanie, for clar, vln, pno
(Ambrosio) CF
Stephanie, for cornet, vln, pno
(Ernst) CF W1219
DELLO JOIO, NORMAN (1913-)
Trio, for fl, vcl, pno
CF 03536
D'INDY, see Indy, d'
DRIESSLER, JOHANNES (1921-)
Serenata a tre, Op. 34, No. 2, for fl,
gamba and cembalo
Baer 3302
DURUFLE, MAURICE (1902-)
Prélude récitatif et variations, Op. 3, for
fl, vla, pno
Dur
DVOŘÁK, ANTONIN (1841-1904)
Humoreske, Op. 101, No. 7, for clar, vln,
pno
(Ambrosio) CF
Humoreske, Op. 101, No. 7, for cornet,
vln, pno
(Ambrosio) CF
Humoreske, Op. 101, No. 7, for fl, vln, pno
(Saenger) CF
EL-DABH, HALIM (1921-)
Thulathiya, for ob, vla, pno
Pet 6189
ELGAR, EDWARD (1857-1934)
Salut d'Amour, Op. 12, for fl, vln, pno
(Klugescheid-Saenger) CF W1187
ERBSE, HEIMO (1924-)
Aphorisms, 12, Op. 13, for fl, vln, pno
Pet 5844
FAURE, JEAN-BAPTISTE (1830-1914)
Palms, for fl, vln, pno
(De Ville) CF
FELDMAN, MORTON (1926-)
Durations III, for vln, tuba, pno
Pet 6903
FOLK TUNE TRIOS
(Kinscella) CF 02425; for fl, vcl, pno;
for contents see title under vln, vcl,
pno
FRANCAIX, JEAN (1912-)
Musique de Cour, orig for fl, vln, and orch;
arr for fl, vln, pno
SCH

FRANKEL, BENJAMIN (1906-   )
Trio, Op. 10, for clar, vcl, pno
Aug
FRÜHLING, CARL (1868-1937)
Trio in a, Op. 40, for vln or clar, vcl, pno
LEU
GAGNEBIN, HENRI (1886-   )
Trio in D, for fl or vln, vln, pno
Curci
GANNE, LOUIS GASTON (1862-1923)
Extase, for cornet, vln, pno
(Tobani) CF   organ and harp ad lib
Extase, for fl, vln, pno
(Tobani) CF   organ and harp ad lib
Extase, for fl, vcl, pno
(Tobani) CF   organ and harp ad lib
GERSHWIN, GEORGE (1898-1937)
Ballad, from Porgy and Bess, for vln, clar,
pno
(Bennett) Gersh
GOEYVAERTS, [KARL (1923-   )]
Piece for Three, for fl, vln, pno
CBDM
GOOSSENS, EUGÈNE (1893-1962)
Five Impressions of a Holiday, Op. 7, for
pno, fl, vcl
Ches
Sketches, 4, for fl, vln, pno
Ches   2V
GOUNOD, CHARLES (1818-1893)
Ave Maria. Méditation sur le premier pré-
lude de J.S. Bach, for fl, vcl, pno
(Saenger) CF
Flower Song, from Faust, for clar, vln, pno
(De Ville) CF
Flower Song, from Faust, for cornet, vln
pno
(De Ville) CF
GRAUN, JOHANN GOTTLIEB
see Trio Sonatas
HALÉVY, JACQUES FRANCOIS (1799-1862)
Romance from L'Eclair, for clar, vln, pno
(De Ville) CF
(Saenger-Laurendeau) CF W1168
HANDEL, GEORG FRIEDRICH (1685-1759)
Largo, for fl, vln, pno
(Saenger) CF W1191
Nightingale Scene, from Il Pensieroso for
fl, vln, pno
CF
see also Trio Sonatas
HAUBIEL, CHARLES (1892-   )
In the French Manner, for fl, vcl, pno
CP
HAYDN, JOSEPH (1732-1809)
Trio in F, Op. 11, No. 4, for fl, vln, pno
(Bergmann) SCH   vcl ad lib
HEINICHEN, JOHANN DAVID
see Trio Sonatas
HIER, ETHEL GLENN (1889-   )
Scherzo, for fl, vcl, pno
CFE
HINDEMITH, PAUL (1895-1963)
Trio, Op. 47, for vla, Heckelphone or tenor
sax, pno
SCH
IBERT, JACQUES (1890-1962)
Interludes, 2, for fl, vln, harpsichord
or harp
Leduc
IMBRIE, ANDREW (1921-   )
Serenade, for fl, vla, pno
Malcolm   for rent

d'INDY, VINCENT (1851-1931)
Trio, Op. 29, for clar, vcl, pno
Int
IVES, CHARLES E. (1874-1954)
Largo, for clar, vln, pno
SMP
JUNGMANN, ALBERT (1824-1892)
Longing for Home, Op. 117, for clar,
vln, pno
(Ambrosio) CF
Longing for Home, Op. 117, for cornet,
vln, pno
(Ambrosio) CF
Longing for Home, Op. 117, for fl, vln, pno
(Ambrosio) CF
(André-Saenger) CF B2875
JUON, PAUL (1872-1940)
Trio Miniatures, for clar, vcl, pno
LN (Pet No. R18)
KAHN, ERICH ITOR (1905-1956)
Divertimento, for fl, vln, harpsichord
CFE
KAUDER, HUGO (1888-   )
Trio, for horn, vln, pno
BH
Trio, for ob, vla, pno
UE 7587
KEISER, REINHARD
see Trio Sonatas
KELLY, ROBERT (1916-   )
Introduction and Dialogue, for horn
vcl, pno
CFE
KELTERBORN, RUDOLF (1931-   )
Kammermusik, for fl, vln, pno
EDW
KERR, HARRISON (1899-   )
Trio, for clar, vcl, pno
Pr
KHACHATURIAN, ARAM (1903-   )
Trio, for clar, vln, pno
Int
Trio, for clar, vla, pno
MZK   score included
(KINSCELLA)
Folk Tune Trios, for fl, vcl, pno
CF 02425   for contents see title under
vln, vcl, pno
KLUGHARDT, AUGUST (1847-1902)
Schilflieder, for ob, vla, pno
MM
KRENEK, ERNST (1900-   )
Trio, for clar, vln, pno
AMP
LANGER, G.
Grandma, Op. 20, for clar, vln, pno
(Laurendeau-Centano-Ambrosio) CF
W1170
LECLAIR, JEAN MARIE
see Trio Sonatas
LEFÈVRE, CHARLES (1843-1917)
Ballade, for fl, vcl, pno
RL
LEONCAVALLO, RUGGIERO (1858-1919)
I Pagliacci. Selection, for fl, vln, pno
(Saenger) CF
LESSARD, JOHN (1920-   )
Trio, for fl, vln, pno
CFE
LOEILLET, JEAN BAPTISTE
see Trio Sonatas
LOSEY, F.H.
Alita, for clar, vln, pno
(Ambrosio) CF

LOSEY, F. H. (cont.)
Alita, for cornet, vln, pno
(Ambrosio) CF
Alita, for fl, vln, pno
(Ambrosio) CF
LOTTI, ANTONIO
see Trio Sonatas
LUENING, OTTO (1900-   )
Trio, for fl, vln, pno
CFE
Trio No. 2, for fl, vcl, pno
CFE   score only
MACBETH, ALLEN (1856-1910)
Love in Idleness, for fl, vln, pno
(Saenger) CF
MARTINU, BOHUSLAV (1890-1959)
Madrigal Sonata, for fl, vln, pno
AMP
Trio, for fl, vcl or vla, pno
AMP
MASCAGNI, PIETRO (1863-1945)
Intermezzo Sinfonico, from Cavalleria
Rusticana, for fl, vln, pno
(Werner-Anderssen-Saenger) CF
MASON
Pastorale, for vln, clar or vla, pno
Mathot
MENZEL, F.
Sweet Longing, for fl, vcl, pno
(Moses) CF
MILHAUD, DARIUS (1892-   )
Concerto, orig for fl, vln and orch,
arr for fl, vln, and pno
Sal
Suite, for vln, clar, pno
Deiss
MOZART, WOLFGANG AMADEUS (1756-1791)
Sonatinas, 2, after K.439b, orig for 2 clar,
bsn; arr for rec, vln, pno
Pet 4555
*Trio in E flat, K.498, for clar, vla, pno
(Adamowski) GS L1403
Aug 7268g
BRH
Int
LN (Pet No. R40)
Trio in E flat, K.498, arr for clar, vcl, pno
(Seiber) Aug 7268h
NAGEL, ROBERT
Trio Concerto, for fl, vcl, pno
CFE   score only
NIKOLAYEVA, TATIANA (1924-   )
Trio, Op. 18, for pno, fl, vla
MZK
NOWAK, LIONEL (1911-   )
Suite, for clar, vcl, pno
CFE
PARRIS, ROBERT (1924-   )
Trio, for clar, vcl, pno
CFE
PIERNÉ, [GABRIEL (1863-1937)]
Sonata da Camera, Op. 48, for fl, vcl, pno
Dur
PISK, PAUL (1893-   )
Moresca Figures, for vln, clar, pno
CFE
PLEYEL, IGNAZ (1757-1831)
Sonate, Op. 16, No. 1, for fl or vln,
vcl, pno
KS
Sonate, Op. 16, No. 2, for fl or vln,
vcl, pno
KS

Sonate, Op. 16, No. 5, for fl or vln,
vcl, pno
KS
PRESSER, WILLIAM (1916-   )
Rhapsody on a Peaceful Theme, for horn,
vln, pno
Tritone   printed with Musicwriter
QUANTZ, JOHANN JOACHIM
see Trio Sonatas
RAMEAU, JEAN-PHILIPPE (1683-1764)
Pièces de clavecin en concerts, for fl,
gamba or vln, clavecin
(Jacobi) Baer 3803
5 Concerts in c,G,A,B flat, d;
also published separately
RAPHAEL, GÜNTHER (1903-   )
Trio, Op. 70, for clar, vcl, pno
BRH
RIETHMÜLLER, HELMUT (1912-   )
Trio, for clar, vln, pno
Sik 508
ROREM, NED (1923-   )
Trio, for fl, vcl, pno
Pet 6430
SCHUBERT, FRANZ (1797-1828)
Barcarole, for clar, vln, pno
(De Ville) CF
Serenade, for clar, vln, pno
(De Ville) CF
Serenade, for cornet, vln, pno
(De Ville) CF
Serenade, for fl, vln, pno
(De Ville) CF
SCHUMANN, ROBERT (1810-1856)
Märchenerzählungen, Op. 132, for clar,
vla, pno
BRH
Int "Fairy Tales"
SCHWERTSIK, KURT (1935-   )
Trio, for vln, horn, pno
EDW
SMIT, LEO (1900-1944)
Trio, for clar, vla, pno
DN (Pet No. D289)
SMYTH, ETHEL (1858-1944)
Trio, for pno, vln, horn
Curwen
STAMITZ, KARL
see Trio Sonatas
STÖLZEL, GOTTFRIED HEINRICH
see Trio Sonatas
STRAVINSKY, IGOR (1882-   )
Suite, from L'Histoire du Soldat, for
clar, vln, pno
Ches
Int   arr by composer
SUK, JOSEPH (1874-1935)
Bagatelle, for fl, vln, pno
Artia
SWIFT, RICHARD
Trio, Op. 14, for clar, vcl, pno
CFE   score only
TATE, PHYLLIS (1911-   )
Air and Variations, for clar, vln, pno
Oxf 07.011
TELEMANN, GEORG PHILIPP (1681-1767)
Concerto in a, for alto rec, gamba and pno
(Haendler) Moeck 1064
see also Trio Sonatas
THOMÉ, FRANCIS (1850-1909)
Simple Aveu, for clar, vln, pno
(Ambrosio) CF
Simple Aveu, for cornet, vln, pno
(Ambrosio) CF

THOMÉ, FRANCIS (cont.)
Simple Aveu, for fl, vln, pno
(Ambrosio) CF
TITL, ANTON EMIL (1809-1882)
Serenade, for cornet, vln, pno
(De Ville) CF
Serenade, for fl, vln, pno
(De Ville) CF
UHL, ALFRED (1909-   )
Kleines Konzert, for clar, vla, pno
DOB
VALENTINE, ROBERT
see Trio Sonatas
VERDI, GIUSEPPE (1813-1901)
Miserere, from Il Trovatore, for clar,
vln, pno
(De Ville) CF
Miserere, from Il Trovatore, for clar,
vcl, pno
(De Ville) CF
Miserere, from Il Trovatore, for cornet,
vln, pno
(De Ville) CF
Miserere, from Il Trovatore, for fl, vln,
pno
(De Ville) CF
VIVALDI, ANTONIO (c.1669-1741)
Pastorale, Op. 13, No. 4, for fl or vln,
vcl, pno
(Upmeyer) Int
WEBER, [BEN (1916-   )]
Nocturne, for fl, vcl, celeste
Pr
WEBER, CARL MARIA VON (1786-1826)
Trio, Op. 63, for fl, vcl, pno
Int
Pet 1473
WEIGL, VALLY
New England Suite, for clar or fl, vcl, pno
CFE
WEISGARBER, ELLIOT
Divertimento for horn, vla, pno
Cor WSP1
WEISS, ADOLPH (1891-   )
Trio, for fl, vln, pno
CFE
WERNER, FRITZ
Concertino, for fl, vcl, pno
Dur
WUORINEN, CHARLES (1938-   )
Trio Concertant, for ob, vln, pno
CFE   score only
WYMAN, ADDISON P. (1832-1872)
Woodland Echoes, Op. 34, for fl, vln, pno
(Ambrosio) CF
YRADIER, SEBASTIAN (1809-1865)
Paloma, La, for clar, vln, pno
(Ambrosio) CF
Paloma, La, for cornet, vln, pno
(Ambrosio) CF
Paloma, La, for fl, vln, pno
(Ambrosio) CF
ZELENKA, ISTVAN (1936-   )
Trio, for horn, vln, pno
EDW

Trios Including Guitar

BADINGS, HENK (1907-   )
Trio No. 9, for fl, vla, guitar
DN   score only

CALL, LEONHARD VON (c.1768-1815)
Notturno in A, Op. 85, for fl or vln, vla,
guitar or lute
VW (Pet No. V7)
Notturno in a, Op. 89, for fl or vln, vla,
guitar or lute
VW (Pet No. V8)
Notturno in D, Op. 93, for fl or vln, vla,
guitar or lute
VW (Pet No. V9)
Trio in E flat, Op. 134, for fl or vln, vla,
guitar or lute
ZM (Pet No. ZM45)
CARULLI, [FERDINAND (1770-1841)]
Notturno in a, for fl, vln, guitar or lute
VW (Pet No. V3)
Notturno in C, for fl, vln, guitar
VW (Pet No. V4)
CORELLI, ARCANGELO (1653-1713)
Sonata da Camera, Op. 2, No. 2, for
2 vln and guitar
(Scheit) DOB
Sonata da Chiesa in F, Op. 3, No. 1, for
2 vln and guitar
ZM (Pet No. ZM306)
DAVID, JOHANN NEPOMUK (1895-   )
Sonata, Op. 26, for fl, vla, guitar
BRH
HANDEL, GEORG FRIEDRICH (1685-1759)
Sonata in c, for vln, alto rec or vln, guitar
(Scheit) DOB
HAYDN, JOSEPH (1732-1809)
Cassation in C, for vln, vcl, guitar
(Scheit) DOB
Cassation in C, for vln, vcl, guitar
or lute
VW (Pet No. V12)
Divertimento in F, for vln, vcl, guitar
(Scheit) DOB
KUEFFNER, JOSEPH (1776-1856)
Notturno, Op. 110, for vln, vla, guitar
or lute
VW (Pet No. V14)
Serenade in a, Op. 4, for fl, vln, guitar or
or lute
VW (Pet No. V15)
Serenade in A, Op. 21, for clar or vln, vla,
guitar or lute
VW (Pet No. V16)
Serenade in A, for vln, vla, guitar or lute
VW (Pet No. V17)
LEGLEY, VICTOR (1915-   )
Trio, Op. 55, for fl, vla, guitar
CBDM   score included
LOTTI, ANTONIO (c.1667-1740)
Sonata, for fl, vcl, guitar
(Behrend) BB   score included
MATIEGKA, WENZL (1773-1830)
Notturno in G, Op. 21, for fl, vla, guitar
ZM (Pet No. ZM299)
see also Schubert: Quartet for fl, vla,
vcl, guitar
Trio in C, Op. 26, for fl or vln, vla,
guitar
ZM (Pet No. ZM97)
MOLINO, FRANCESCO (1775-1847)
Trio in D, Op. 45, for fl or vln, vla,
guitar
ZM (Pet No. ZM155)
PAGANINI, NICCOLÒ (1782-1840)
Terzetto in D, for vln, vcl, guitar
ZM (Pet No. ZM30)
Terzetto Concertante in D, for vla,
vcl, guitar
ZM (Pet No. ZM123)

PERONI, G.
  Concerto a tre, for 2 vln, guitar
    (Scheit) DOB
SCHRAMM, WERNER (1903-   )
  Chamber Trio, for vln, vla, guitar
    BRH score included
SKORZENY, FRITZ (1900-   )
  Trio, for fl, vla, guitar
    DOB
TELEMANN, GEORG PHILIPP (1681-1767)
  Sonata in a, for alto rec, vln, guitar
    (Scheit) DOB
WEBER, CARL MARIA VON (1786-1826)
  Minuet, from Donna Diana, for fl, vla,
    guitar
    (Behrend) BB
  Minuet, for fl, vla or vln, guitar
    (Scheit) DOB

Trios Including Harp

BAX, ARNOLD (1883-1953)
  Elegiac Trio, for fl, vla, harp
    Ches
BERNIER, [RENÉ (1905-   )]
  Trio, for fl, vcl, harp
    CBDM score included
DAMASE, JEAN-MICHEL (1928-   )
  Trio, for fl, harp, vcl
    HL
DEBUSSY, CLAUDE (1862-1918)
  *Sonata, for fl, vla, harp
    Dur
DUPIN, PAUL (1865-1949)
  Pièces dialoguées, for fl, vcl, harp
    Dur
FROMMER
  Serenade, Op. 47, for vln, vcl, harp
    ZM (Pet No. ZM147)
GENZMER, HARALD (1909-   )
  Trio, for fl, vla, harp
    Pet 5859
GOOSSENS, EUGÈNE (1893-1962)
  Suite, Op. 6, for fl, vln, harp
    Ches
IBERT, JACQUES (1890-1962)
  Interludes, 2, for fl, vln, harp or
    harpsichord
    Leduc
  Trio, for vln, vcl, harp
    Leduc
JONGEN, JOSEPH (1873-1953)
  Pièces en trio, 2, Op. 80, for fl, vcl, harp
    CBDM score included
KLUGHARDT, [AUGUST (1847-1902)]
  Prayer, Op. 75, for vcl, harp, organ
    ZM (Pet No. ZM719)
LAJTHA, LÁSZLÓ (1891-1963)
  Trio, Op. 22, for fl, vcl, harp
    Leduc
  Trio No. 2, Op. 47, for fl, vcl, harp
    Leduc
MEULEMANS, ARTHUR (1884-   )
  Sonata, for fl, vla, harp
    CBDM score included
MIGOT, GEORGES (1891-   )
  Concert, for fl, vcl, harp
    Leduc
MOSTLER
  Harp Serenade, Op. 20, for vln, vcl, harp
    ZM (Pet No. ZM714)
OELSCHLEGEL, A.
  Serenade, for vln, vcl, harp
    Cranz

To the Madonna, Op. 144, for vln, vcl, harp
    ZM (Pet No. ZM715)
OSORIO-SWAAB
  Trio No. 4, for clar, vcl, harp
    DN (Pet No. D250)
PILLNEY, KARL HERMANN (1896-   )
  Minuet, Op. 14, No. 2, for vln, vcl, harp
    ZM (Pet No. ZM148)
  Notturno, Op. 14, No. 1, for vln, vcl, harp
    ZM (Pet No. ZM162)
RAPHAEL, GÜNTER (1903-1960)
  Sonatina, Op. 65, No. 1, for fl, vla, harp
    BRH score included
RENIÉ, HENRIETTE (1875-1956)
  Trio, for harp, vln, vcl
    Leduc
ROHOZINSKY, LADISLAV (1886-1938)
  Suite Brève, for fl, vla and harp
    Senart
SMIT, LEO (1900-1944)
  Trio, for fl, vla, harp
    Senart
SNOER, [JOHANNES (1868-1936)]
  Preghiera, Op. 35, for vln, vcl, harp
    ZM (Pet No. ZM149)
STRAUSS, JOHANN (1825-1899)
  Hochzeitspraeludium, Op. 469, for vln,
    organ, harp
    (Racek) DOB
TEDESCHI
  Suite, Op. 46, for vln, vcl, harp
    ZM (Pet No. ZM141)
TRNEČEK, HANUŠ (1858-1914)
  Nocturno, Op. 29, for vln, vcl, harp
    ZM (Pet No. ZM151)
WACHTMEISTER, AXEL (1865-1947)
  Trio, for vln, harp, pno
    Heugel
WEBER, BEN (1916-   )
  Aubade, for fl, vcl, harp
    CFE score included
WEBER
  Dream, for vln, vcl, harp
    ZM (Pet No. ZM717)
  Farewell, for vln, vcl, harp
    ZM (Pet No. ZM716)
ZAGWIJN, HENRI (1878-1955)
  Introduction and Scherzetto, for fl, vla, harp
    DN (Pet No. D77)
ZIEMS, HARRY
  Elegy, for vla, harp, pno, orig for vla, harp
    and strings
    BB

Trios Including Percussion

COWELL, HENRY (1897-   )
  Set of Five, for pno, vln, percussion
    CFE score included
FELDMAN, MORTON (1926-   )
  Durations IV, for vln, vcl, vibraphone
    Pet 6904
GAILLARD, [MARIUS FRANCOIS (1900-   )]
  Para Alejo, for vln, vcl, percussion
    ESC
GLANVILLE-HICKS, PEGGY (1912-   )
  Scary Time, for vln, clar, percussion
    CFE score only
HOVHANESS, ALAN (1911-   )
  *Suite, Op. 99, for vln, pno, percussion
    Pet 6047
NAGELE, ALBERT
  Sonata à tre, for ob, vln, percussion
    Krenn

PARTOS, ÖDÖN (1907-   )
  Agada, for vla, pno, percussion
    IMI
WUORINEN, CHARLES (1938-   )
  Triptych, for vln, vla, percussion
    CFE   score included

Trios: Unspecified Instruments

BACH, JOHANN SEBASTIAN (1685-1750)
  Musical Offering, see more than 1
    instrumental combination
  Selected Pieces, 21, for 2 melody
    instruments and bass
    SCH   score included
BERGER, JEAN (1909-   )
  *Divertimento for 3 treble instruments
    Broude; for various combinations of
    flutes, oboes, clarinets, violins
BOISMORTIER, JOSEPH BODIN DE (1691-1755)
  Sonatas, 6, Op. 7, for 3 melody instruments
    (Doflein) SCH   2V
CAGE, JOHN (1912-   )
  Composition for 3 voices
    Pet 6704   any 3 or more instruments
    encompassing the following ranges:
    1: d' to d'''; 2: a to a''; 3: d to d''
HAAGER, M.
  Music for 3 Instruments, Op. 6a
    OBV   score only

HARRIS, ARTHUR (1927-   )
  *Four Pieces for Three Instruments
    Rongwen   for various combinations of
    flute, oboes, English horn, clarinets,
    violins, viola
HOLYOKE, SAMUEL (1762-1820)
  Instrumental Assistant
    (Carpenter-Luckenbill) EV
    3 part pieces for soprano, alto and
    bass instruments; score included
HONNEGER, ARTHUR (1892-1955)
  Petite Suite, for 2 instruments in C and pno
    Chant du Monde
MANN, ALFRED
  Kleine Schulmusik, for 3 equal string in-
    struments; with Sätze, for 3 equal string
    instruments by Bauer
    Moeck 1203
MUSIC OF THE EARLY BAROQUE
  (Mönkemeyer) SCH   score included; for
    3 melody instruments
    Compositions by Demantius, Franck,
    Frescobaldi, Monteverdi and others
NAGAN, ZVI
  Israeli Miniatures, for 3 melody instruments
    IMP
TRITONE FOLIO
  (Maddy, Giddings, Roberts and Stringham)
    CF   3-part music for string or wind
    instruments
WILLAERT, ADRIAN (c.1490-1562)
  *Ricercari, 9, for 3 woodwinds or strings
    (Zenck) SCH

Section IV

MUSIC FOR
FOUR INSTRUMENTS

Quartets: 4 Violins

ALTVATER, H.
Portraits, 3
AMP
(AUER, LEOPOLD)
Graded Course of Ensemble Playing
CF 01420-1445   6V   for contents see
title under more than 1 instrumental
combination
BEETHOVEN, LUDWIG VAN (1770-1827)
Allegro, from Symphony No. 7
(Clemens) Conco   score included
BRAHMS, JOHANNES (1833-1897)
Allegretto grazioso, from Symphony No. 2
(Clemens) Conco   score included
BURLINGAME
Violin Voices, for 3 and 4 vln
Ru
CLARK, SCOTSON
Gavotte
CF
COBURN
Quartet Album for Four Violins
Bel
DANCLA, CHARLES (1817-1907)
Air varié, Op. 89, No. 5
(Weigl) CF   score included
Pieces, 3, Op. 178; with Larghetto by
Mozart arr for 3 or 4 vln, and
Träumerei by Schumann
(Saenger) CF
DELAMATER
All Grades for Violins, for 3 and 4 vln
Ru
DONT, JAKOB (1815-1888)
Larghetto
CF
(FAEL, V.)
Musiche Antiche
ZA 3358-9   2V   for contents see title
FARMER, G.
Four Violins at Play
BH
FIDDLE SESSIONS
(Gearhart & Green) Shawnee   for contents
see title under 2 vln
FOR-4-VIOLINS
(Kuhn) Bel EL1188-89   2V
GAY DANCES OF OLD MASTERS
(Hoffmann) SCH   for contents see title
under 2 vln
(GEARHART, LIVINGSTON & GREEN,
ELIZABETH)
Fiddle Sessions
Shawnee   for contents see title under
2 vln

(GORDON)
Melodious Pieces, 4
BMI   score included
GRADED COURSE OF ENSEMBLE PLAYING
(Auer-Saenger) CF 01420-1445   6V
for contents see title under more
than 1 instrumental combination
GRANGER, J.
Doux Souvenir, Op. 58
Gaudet
Marche des Lycéens, Op. 80
Gaudet
Veillée, La, Op. 81
Gaudet
GREEN, ELIZABETH, see Gearhart & Green
(HOFFMANN)
Gay Dances of Old Masters
SCH   for contents see title under 2 vln
KERN, F.
Vier Geigerlein, Die, Op. 73
DOB   score included
(KUHN, WOLFGANG)
For-4-Violins
Bel EL1188-89   2V
MCKAY, GEORGE FREDERICK (1899-   )
American Panorama. 7 Pieces in the
American Folk Idiom
CF W1898
Fiesta Mejicana, Songs of the Mexican
children
CF W2272
MASTER MELODIES AND FOLK SONGS
(Weston-Persinger) Conco
score included
MAYER, RUDOLF (1893-   )
Little Pieces
OBV
Little Quartet
OBV
MELODIOUS PIECES, 4
(Gordon) BMI   score included
MOZART, WOLFGANG AMADEUS (1756-1791)
Allegro vivace, from "Jupiter" Symphony
(Clemens) Conco   score included
Alleluia
Ed M
Larghetto, see Dancla: 3 Pieces, Op. 178
MUSICHE ANTICHE
(Fael) ZA   2V
Vol 1: Compositions by Corelli, Handel,
Vivaldi
Vol 2: Compositions by Corelli, Handel,
Telemann
NERO, PAUL
Frantic Fantasy for four fiddles
CF B2767   score included

QUARTETTES, 18TH CENTURY
  (Rosenthal) MK for 4 clar or 4 vln
    Bach: Menuetto, from Brandenburg
      Concerto No. 1
    Bach: Bourrée, from Suite for
      Orchestra No. 2
    Beethoven: Menuetto, from Piano
      Sonata, Op. 2, No. 1
    Beethoven: Scherzo, from Piano
      Sonata, Op. 2, No. 3
    Couperin: Gavotte, from Pièces
      de Clavecin
    Handel: Air, from Piano Suite No. 5
    Handel: Largo, from Concerto
      Grosso No. 2
    Haydn: Scherzo, from str quartet,
      Op. 33, No. 6
    Haydn: Theme, from str quartet,
      Op. 20, No. 4
    Mozart: Andante, from Piano
      Sonata, K. 331
    Mozart: Presto, from Divertimento
      for 2 ob, 2 horn, 2 bsn, K. 252
    Mozart: Presto, from Divertimento
      for 2 ob, 2 horn, 2 bsn, K. 270
    Mozart: Menuetto, from Symphony
      No. 40
    Rameau: Rondeau "La Timide", from
      Concert de Clavecin No. 3
    Scarlatti: Grave, from Sonata
      No. 271 for Clavicembalo
    Telemann: Les Plaisirs, from Suite
      for flute and strings
REIN, WALTER (1893-   )
  Spielbuch
    SCH
RIMSKY-KORSAKOV, NIKOLAY (1844-1908)
  Scheherezade, 3rd movement
    (Herbert) Conco vcl ad lib
    score included
(ROSENTHAL)
  Quartettes, 18th Century
    MK for contents see title
SALIERI, ANTONIO (1750-1825)
  Danse from Tarare
    Ed M
SCHUMANN, ROBERT
  Träumerei, see Dancla: 3 Pieces, Op. 178
(STONE, DAVID)
  Rounds for Violins, for 3 or 4 vln
    Oxf 23.807
SWIFT
  Farmer in the dell and Mulberry bush
    Pro Art 28
TELEMANN, GEORG PHILIPP (1681-1767)
  Concerto in A
    (Friedrich) SCH
  Concerto in C
    (Hausswald) Baer 2973
  Concerto in C
    Int score included
  Concerto in D HM
    (Engel) Baer HM20
  Concerto in D
    Int score included
  Concerto in D
    VW (Pet No. V52) score included
  Concerto in G
    (Hausswald) Baer 2974
  Concerto in G
    VW (Pet No. V51) score included
  Sonata a 4 in C
    (Friedrich) SCH

TRINKAUS, GEORGE J.
  Four Moods
    MPH score included; pno ad lib
WAGNER, RICHARD (1813-1883)
  Elsa before the court, from Lohengrin
    (Hermann) BRH
  Prelude to Act III, from Lohengrin
    (Hermann) BRH
(WESTON, P)
  Master Melodies and Folk Songs
    (Persinger) Conco score included
WETTLAUFER, J.M.
  Fiddlers Four
    BH 2V

Quartets: 4 Cellos

ABSIL, JEAN (1893-   )
  Fantasie Rhapsodique, Op. 21
    CBDM
  Quartet, Op. 28
    CBDM
AMELLER, [ANDRÉ-CHARLES (1912-   )]
  Chorale, for 4 trombones or 4 vcl
    Hin (Pet No. H718)
(ARNOLD-ALSHIN)
  Easy Ensembles
    AMP for 2-4 vcl
BASS CLEF SESSIONS
    (Gearhart, Cassel & Hornibrook) Shawnee
      for contents see title under 2 vcl
BOCCHERINI, LUIGI (1740-1805)
  Largo, from Sonata No. 3 in G, orig for
      vcl and pno
    (Bonelli) ZA 2476
CASSEL, DON, see Gearhart, Cassel &
      Hornibrook
DARE, M.
  Elegy
    Ches score included
EASY ENSEMBLES
    (Arnold-Alshin) AMP for 2-4 vcl
(GEARHART, CASSEL & HORNIBROOK)
  Bass Clef Sessions
    Shawnee for contents see title under
      2 vcl
GRIEG, EDVARD (1843-1907)
  Watchman's Song
    (Urban) Mil score included
HOLLAND, [THEODORE (1878-1947)]
  Cortège
    Hin (Pet No. H341) score included
HORNIBROOK, WALLACE, see Gearhart,
      Cassel & Hornibrook
JONGEN, JOSEPH (1873-1953)
  Pieces, 2, Op. 89
    CBDM
KLENGEL, JULIUS (1859-1933)
  Impromptu, Op. 30
    Int
  Pieces, 2, Op. 5
    Int
  Theme and Variations, Op. 28
    Int
  Variations, Op. 15
    Int
KREIN, ALEXANDER (1883-1951)
  Lyrical Fragment, Op. 1a
    Int score included
LEVY, F.
  *Ricercari
    Cor ST3

METZLER, FRIEDRICH
Quartet
LN (Pet No. R61)   score included
MEULEMANS, ARTHUR (1884-   )
Suite
CBDM
MOULAERT, RAYMOND (1875-   )
Choral Varie
CBDM
PIERRE-PETIT
*Suite
Heugel
RIEGGER, WALLINGFORD (1885-1961)
Introduction and Fugue, Op. 69
AMP   score included
SCHMITT, FLORENT (1870-1958)
Andante Religioso, Op. 109, orig for
4 trombones
Dur   transcribed by composer
SCHUBERT, FRANZ (1797-1828)
Andantino, from Rosamunde
(Dare) Hin (Pet No. H704)
score included
TANSMAN, ALEXANDER (1897-   )
Mouvements, 2
ESC   score included

Quartets: 4 Double-Basses

ALT, BERNHARD (1903-   )
Suite
Hof   score included

Quartets: 4 Viols

(ARNOLD-ALSHIN)
Easy Ensembles
AMP   for 2-4 viols
BACH, JOHANN SEBASTIAN (1685-1750)
*Kunst der Fuge, Die
(Diener) Baer 2599
BAINES, FRANCIS (1917-   )
Pavan
SCH   score included
(BECK, SYDNEY)
English Instrumental Music, 16th and
17th Centuries
Pet   2V; for contents see title under
2 vln, vla, vcl
(BRENNECKE)
Carmina germanica et gallica
Baer HM137-8   2V; for contents see
title
BYRD, WILLIAM (1543-1623)
Fantasy Quartet No. 4, for 4 viols or
vln, 2 vla, vcl
STB
Fantasy Quartet No. 5, for 4 viols or
vln, 2 vla, vcl
STB
CARMINA GERMANICA ET GALLICA
(Brennecke) Baer HM137-8   2V
score included
32 pieces from the 16th century
for 4 viols or 2 vln, vla, vcl
DOWLAND, JOHN
Pavan, see 2 vln, vla, vcl, pno
EASY ENSEMBLES
(Arnold-Alshin) AMP   for 2-4 viols

ENGLISH INSTRUMENTAL MUSIC, 16TH AND
17TH CENTURIES
(Beck) Pet   2V; for contents see 2 vln,
vla, vcl
FERRABOSCO, ALPHONSO
Fantasia, see 2 vln, vla, vcl
GALILEI, [VINCENZO (c.1520-1591)]
Ricercari, 12, for soprano, alto, tenor,
bass viols
(Giesbert) SCH   score only
GIBBONS, ORLANDO
Fantazias, see 2 vln, vla, vcl
(GIESBERT)
Instrumental Fantasies, 8
NAG   for contents see title
IN NOMINE. ALTENGLISCHE KAMMERMUSIK
(Stevens) Baer HM134   for 4 or 5 viols;
score included
INSTRUMENTAL FANTASIES, 8
(Giesbert) NAG   score included
Colin: Fantasy, for soprano or
alto viol
Modena: Fantasies, Nos. 1-4, for
soprano, 2 tenor, bass viols
Willaert: Fantasies, Nos. 1-3, for
alto, 2 tenor, bass viols
IVES, SIMON (1600-1662)
Fantasy in D
(Dolmetsch-Ward) SCH
JENKINS, JOHN (1592-1678)
Ayres, 2, for 2 treble, tenor, bass viols
(C. Dolmetsch) SCH   score only
LOCKE, MATTHEW
Consort of 4 parts, see 2 vln, vla, vcl
LUPO, THOMAS
Fantasia, see 2 vln, vla, vcl
MERULO, CLAUDIO
Canzoni da sonar, see 2 vln, vla, vcl
Fantasy, see 2 vln, vla, vcl
MICO, RICHARD (17th century)
Fancy No. 3, for 2 treble, tenor, bass viols
(Grubb) SCH   score included
Fancy No. 9, for 2 treble, tenor, bass viols
(Grubb) SCH   score included
Fancy No. 13, for 2 treble, tenor, bass
viols
(Grubb) SCH   score included
PURCELL, HENRY
Fantasies, see more than one instrumental
combination
Spielmusik zum Sommernachtstraum,
see 2 vln, vla, vcl, pno
SIMPSON, T.
Bonny Sweet Robin, see 2 vln, vla, vcl, pno
Dances, see 2 vln, vla, vcl, pno
(STEVENS)
In Nomine. Altenglische Kammermusik
Baer HM143   for 4 or 5 viols; score
included
TOMKINS, THOMAS
Alman, see 2 vln, vla, vcl
WARD, JOHN
Fancy, see 2 vln, vla, vcl
Fantasia, see 2 vln, vla, vcl

Quartets: 3 Violins, Viola

DE LAMARTER, [ERIC (1880-1953)]
Foursome
Mil   score included
ITALIAN QUARTETS, 13, FROM THE 16TH
CENTURY
(Arx) Noet (Pet No. N3233)

Quartets: 3 Violins, Cello

BACH, JOHANN SEBASTIAN (1685-1750)
Choral, from Christmas Oratorio
(Springer) MPH score included
Gavottes, 2
(Finney) MPH score included
DITTERSDORF, KARL DITTERS VON
(1739-1799)
Andante, from Quartet in B flat
(Lockhart) MPH score included
GRIEG, EDVARD (1843-1907)
Gavotte, Op. 40, No. 3, orig for pno
(Springer) MPH score included
HANDEL, GEORG FRIEDRICH (1685-1759)
Music for Strings, Vol. IV, for solo vln,
2 vln, vcl
SCH score included
JÁRDÁNYI, PÁL (1920-   )
Quartettino
Kul
KLUSSMANN, ERNST GERNOT (1901-   )
*Spielmusik No. 1. 5 Variations on a
Folksong
Sik 405
NOWAK, LIONEL (1911-   )
Sonatina
CFE score included
(PIJPER, WILLEM)
*Pezzi Antichi, 4
DN (Pet No. D132)
PURCELL, HENRY (c.1659-1695)
Pavane and Chaconne
SCH score included
ROSENMÜLLER, JOHANN
see more than 1 instrumental combination
THILMAN, JOHANN PAUL (1906-   )
Music for Strings
BRH
WOLL, ERNA
Spielmusik in A
Gerig rec and tambourin ad lib

Quartets: 2 Violins, Viola, Cello

ABENDROTH, WALTER (1896-   )
*Quartet, Op. 33
Sik 321
ABSIL, JEAN (1893-   )
Quartet No. 2, Op. 13
CBDM score included
Quartet No. 3, Op. 19
CBDM score included
Quartet No. 4, Op. 47
CBDM score included
ACADEMIC STRING QUARTET ALBUM
(Pochon) CF 02919
Bach: Sarabande
Bach, J.C.F.: Andante, from
Quartet No. 3, Op. 1
Dall'Abaco: Grave, Allegro
Handel-Pochon: Gavotte
Haydn: Minuet
Haydn: Presto
Haydn, M.: Menuet
Mozart: Menuet
Pochon: Air
Pochon: Petite Etude
ADAMSON, HAROLD & DE ROSE, PETER
Moonlight Mood
Big 3

ADAMSON, HAROLD, see Grofe & Adamson
and McHugh & Adamson
ADESTE FIDELES
(Pochon) CF
ADOLPHUS, MILTON
Quartet No. 14, Op. 65
CFE score only
Quartet No. 20, Op. 80
CFE score only
Quartet No. 21 in ancient style
CFE score only
Quartet No. 23, Op. 91
CFE score included
AIVAZIAN, A.
Quartet No. 2
MZK min score only
ALBRECHTSBERGER, JOHANN GEORG
(1736-1809)
Quartet in A, Op. 21, No. 1
Noet (Pet No. N6020)
ALEXANDROV, ANATOLY (1888-   )
Quartet No. 3, Op. 55
MZK min score only
Quartet No. 4, Op. 80
MZK min score only
ALEXANIAN, DIRAN (1881-1954)
Petite Suite Arménienne
Sal score included
ALFANO, FRANCO (1876-1954)
Quartet No. 2
UE 9402
Quartet No. 3 in G
SZ
ALFVÉN, HUGO (1872-1960)
*Elegi
Gehrmans
ALIABEV, [ALEXANDER (1787-1851)]
Quartet No. 1
MZK score only
Quartet No. 3
MZK score only
ALIX, RENÉ (1907-   )
*Quartet, Op. 13
CH (Pet No. C248)
ALPAERTS, FLOR (1876-1954)
Quartet No. 2
CBDM score included
ALWYN, WILLIAM (1905-   )
*Quartet in d
Leng (Mil No. L4076)
AMES, WILLIAM (1901-   )
Quartet No. 1, 1931
CFE score included
Quartet No. 2
CFE score included
Quartet No. 3. Declamation, Poem
CFE score included
Quartet No. 5
CFE score included
Rhapsody
CFE score included
AMRAM, DAVID (1930-   )
*Quartet
Pet 6688
ANGERER, PAUL (1927-   )
"Ei du feiner Reiter". 7 variations on
the folksong
DOB score only
ANGOT-BRACQUEMOND, M.
*Pieces, 3
Senart
ANSORGE, CONRAD (1862-1930)
*Quartet, Op. 13
Birnbach

APOSTEL, HANS ERICH (1901-   )
*Quartet, Op. 7
UE   for rent
*Quartet No. 2, Op. 26
UE 12746   for rent
ARDÉVOL, JOSÉ (1911-   )
*Quartet No. 2
SMP
ARMA, PAUL (1904-   )
Petite Suite[92]
GT
ARMSTRONG, W.D. (1868-1936)
Evening Prayer
CF
ARNOLD, MALCOLM (1921-   )
*Quartet No. 1
Leng (Mil No. L4067)
ARRIAGA, JUAN CRISÓSTOMO (1806-1826)
Quartets, 3
Int
UME
Quartet No. 1 in d
Noet (Pet No. N6021)
Quartet No. 2 in A
Noet (Pet No. N6022)
Quartet No. 3 in E flat
Noet (Pet No. N6023)
ASAFIEV, [BORIS (1884-1949)]
Quartet
MZK   score only
ATTERBERG, [KURT (1887-   )]
*Suite No. 7, Op. 29
BRH
AVIDOM, MENAHEM (1908-   )
*Quartet No. 2, from Wisdom of the Fathers
Mil
AVSHALOMOV, AARON (1894-   )
Quartet in e, 1954
CFE   score included
BAAREN, KEES VAN (1906-   )
Quartet No. 2
DN   score only
BACH, JOHANN CHRISTIAN (1735-1782)
Quartet in F, Op. 8, No. 4
(Hillemann) NAG
BACH, JOHANN CHRISTOPH FRIEDRICH
      (1732-1795)
Quatuors, 6
(Duttenhofer) Senart 5355-56   2V
BACH, JOHANN SEBASTIAN (1685-1750)
*Art of the Fugue
(Diener) Baer 2600
(Harris-Herter Norton) GS
score included
Come, Sweet Death
EV
Fugues, 14, from Well-Tempered Clavier
(Hofmann) Int   2V
Inventions, 4, orig for clavier
(Palmer-Best) Oxf 27.910
Jesu, joy of man's desiring
(Tate) Oxf 25.505   for rent
Kommt, Seelen, dieser Tag and Jesu,
      meines Glaubens Zier
Hin (Pet No. H644)
March
(Wolpert) Noet (Pet No. N771)
score included
Menuet
(Wolpert) Noet (Pet No. N770)
score included

Musette
(Wolpert) Noet (Pet No. N769)
score included
*Organ Choral Preludes
(Hodge) Paterson 253-4   2V
Vol 1
Ertödt' uns durch dein' Güte
Ich ruf' zu dir
Schmücke dich, O liebe Seele
Vol 2
Gott, durch deine Güte
Meine Seele, erhebt den Herrn
Nun komm' der Heiden Heiland
Sarabandes and other Movements
(Sturm) VW (Pet No. V97-8)   2V
score included
Vol 1: From the English Suites, 7
Vol 2: From the French Suites, 8
BACH, KARL PHILIPP EMANUEL (1714-1788)
*Suite, orig concerto for viols
(Casadesus) GS   d-b ad lib
BACH FOR STRINGS
(Clarke) GS   score included
BAEYENS, AUGUST (1895-   )
Quartet No. 4
CBDM   score included
BAINES, FRANCIS (1917-   )
Quartet, in the first position
JWL (Mil No. W2309)   score included
BALAZS, FREDERIC (1920-   )
Divertimento
CFE   score included
Quartet No. 3
CFE   score included
BALLOU, ESTHER W.
Divertimento
CFE   score included
BALOGH, ERNO (1897-   )
Pieces, 2
CF   for rent
BALSIS, E.
Quartet in g
MZK   score only
BANTOCK, GRANVILLE (1868-1946)
*In a Chinese Mirror
Ches
BARATI, GEORGE (1913-   )
Quartet, 1944
CFE   score only
Quartet No. 2
CFE   score included
BARBER, SAMUEL (1910-   )
*Quartet, Op. 11
GS
*Serenade, Op. 1
GS
BARBIER, RENÉ (1890-   )
Quartet, Op. 65
CBDM   score included
BARRAUD, HENRY (1900-   )
*Quatuor
Amphion 131
BARTÓK, BÉLA (1881-1945)
*Pieces, 5, from Mikrokosmos, orig for pno
(Serly) BH
*Quartet No. 1, Op. 7
BH
*Quartet No. 2, Op. 17
BH
*Quartet No. 3
BH
*Quartet No. 4
BH

---

[92] In the U.S.A. this publication can be obtained through Mills.

BARTÓK, BÉLA (cont.)
*Quartet No. 5
  BH
*Quartet No. 6
  BH
BASNER, V.
*Quartet No. 2
  MZK
BASSETT, LESLIE (1923-   )
*Pieces, 5
  Highgate
Quartet No. 2
  CFE   score included
BATE, STANLEY RICHARD (1911-1959)
*Quartet No. 2
  Leng (Mil No. L4068)
BAUER, MARION (1887-1955)
Five Pieces
  CFE   score included
BAX, ARNOLD (1883-1953)
Quartet in G
  Chap-L
Quartet No. 2
  Chap-L
Quartet No. 3 in F
  Chap-L
BEACH, JOHN (1877-1953)
*Poem
  Ches
BEALE, JAMES (1924-   )
Quartet No. 2, Op. 30
  CFE   score included
BECK, CONRAD (1901-   )
Quartet No. 4
  SCH
(BECK, SYDNEY)
English Instrumental Music, 16th and 17th
    Centuries
  Pet   2V   for contents see title
BEETHOVEN, LUDWIG VAN (1770-1827)
Adagio Cantabile, from Septet, Op. 20
  CF
Fugues, 3
  (Pochon) CF 01478
Grand Fugue, Op. 133
  BRH
  GS L1640; with Quartet, Op. 130
  see also Quartets, 17
Minuet No. 2 in G, orig for pno
  (Saenger) CF
  (Urban) Mil   score included
Prelude and Fugue in C
  (Hess) NAG   score included
Prelude and Fugue in F
  (Hess) NAG   score included
*Quartets, 17
  (Joachim-Moser) Pet 195A,b,C   3V
    Vol 1: Op. 18, Nos. 1-6
    Vol 2: Op. 59, Nos. 1-3; Op. 74; Op. 95
    Vol 3: Op. 127; Op. 130; Op. 131;
       Op. 132; Op. 133; Op. 135
Quartets, 6, Op. 18, Nos. 1-6
  GS L1808
Quartets, 3, Op. 18, Nos. 1-3
  UE 433
Quartets, 5: Op. 59, Nos. 1-3; Op. 74;
    Op. 95
  GS L1809
Quartets, Vol 3
  Kal
Quartet in F, Op. 18, No. 1
  (Withers) Aug 7201
  BRH

Quartet in G, Op. 18, No. 2
  (Withers) Aug 7202
  BRH
Quartet in D, Op. 18, No. 3
  (Withers) Aug 7203
  BRH
Quartet in c, Op. 18, No. 4
  (Withers) Aug 7204
  BRH
Quartet in A, Op. 18, No. 5
  (Withers) Aug 7205
  BRH
Quartet in B flat, Op. 18, No. 6
  (Withers) Aug 7206
  BRH
Quartet in F, Op. 59, No. 1
  (Withers) Aug 7194a
  BRH
Quartet in e, Op. 59, No. 2
  (Withers) Aug 7194b
  BRH
Quartet in C, Op. 59, No. 3
  (Withers) Aug 7194c
  BRH
Quartet in E flat, Op. 74
  BRH
Quartet in f, Op. 95
  BRH
Quartet in E flat, Op. 127
  BRH
  GS L1639
Quartet in B flat, Op. 130
  BRH
  GS L1640; with Grand Fugue, Op. 133
Quartet in c sharp, Op. 131
  BRH
  GS L1641
Quartet in a, Op. 132
  BRH
  GS L1642
Quartet, Op. 133, see Grand Fugue
Quartet in F, Op. 135
  BRH
  GS L1643
Quartet in F, after Piano Sonata,
    Op. 14, No. 1
  DOB
BENJAMIN, ARTHUR (1893-   )
*Quartet No. 2
  BH   for rent
BENOY, A.W.
*Violinist's Books of Carols
  Oxf 23.113-4   2V
BENTZON, JORGEN (1897-1951)
Quartet, Op. 15
  WH 3204a
BENTZON, NIELS VIGGO (1919-   )
*Quartet No. 3, Op. 72
  WH 3923a
BERG, ALBAN (1885-1935)
*Lyric Suite
  UE 8781
*Quartet, Op. 3
  UE 7538
BERGSMA, WILLIAM (1921-   )
*Quartet No. 3
  CF 03868
BERIO, LUCIANO (1925-   )
Quartet
  SZ
BERKELEY, LENNOX (1903-   )
*Quartet
  BH   for rent
*Quartet No. 2
  Ches   in preparation

BERLINSKI, HERMAN (1910-   )
  Quartet, 1953
    CFE   score included
BERNAL JIMÉNEZ, MIGUEL (1910-1956)
  Quartet. Cuarteto Virreinal
    EMM   score only
BERTHET, F.
  *Quatuor
    Senart
BERWALD, FRANZ (1796-1868)
  *Quartet in a
    Gehrmans
  *Quartet in E flat
    Gehrmans
  *Quartet in g
    Gehrmans
BEST, AGNES, see Palmer & Best
BEYER, FRANK MICHAEL (1928-   )
  Quartet
    Sirius   for rent
BEZANSON, PHILIP (1916-   )
  Quartet
    CFE   score included
BIGGS, RONALD (1893-   )
  Summer Landscape
    Curwen   for rent
BINKERD, GORDON (1916-   )
  Quartet No. 1
    CFE   score included
  Quartet No. 2
    CFE   score included
BIZET, GEORGES (1838-1875)
  Adagietto, from L'Arlésienne; with Au
    bord de la mer by Dunkler
    CF
BLACHER, BORIS (1903-   )
  Epitaph, Op. 41
    BB
  Quartet No. 2, Op. 16
    BB
  Quartet No. 3, Op. 32
    BB
BLACK IS THE COLOR OF MY TRUE LOVE'S
  HAIR
    (Niles-McCarty) GS   score included
BLACKWOOD, EASLEY (1933-   )
  Quartet No. 1
    SPAM   score included
  *Quartet No. 2, Op. 6
    GS
BLANC DE FONTBELLE, C.
  Quatuor
    Senart
BLISS, ARTHUR (1891-   )
  *Quartet No. 1
    Nov
  *Quartet No. 2
    Nov
BLOCH, ERNEST (1880-1959)
  In the Mountains
    CF 01411   score included
      Dusk
      Rustic Dance
  Night
    CF   score included
  Paysages
    CF 01320   score included
      Alpestre
      North
      Tongataboo
  *Pieces, Deux
    JWL (Mil No. W2300)
  Prélude
    CF   score included

*Quartet No. 1
  GS
*Quartet No. 2
  BH
*Quartet No. 3
  GS
*Quartet No. 4
  GS
*Quartet No. 5
  Broude
BOCCHERINI, LUIGI (1743-1805)
  Easy Dances, 5
    SCH
  Minuetto, from String Quintet in E
    (Pochon) CF
  Quartets, 9
    Int
      Op. 6, No. 6; Op. 8, No. 5;
      Op. 10, No. 2; Op. 10, No. 6;
      Op. 27, No. 2; Op. 32, No. 4;
      Op. 33, No. 5; Op. 33, No. 6;
      Op. 39, No. 1
  Quartets, 9
    Pet 3336   contents same as above
  Quartets, 8
    (Upmeyer) Baer 2676
      Op. 1, No. 1; Op. 24, No. 5;
      Op. 39; Op. 41 in c; Op. 41 in C;
      Op. 44, No. 4; Op. 48, No. 2;
      Op. 58, No. 2
  Quartets, 6, Op. 33
    (Höckner-Mlynarczyk) SIM   2V
  *Quartets, 6, Op. 58
    (Carmirelli) Ric 130187-92
    published separately
  Quartet in D, Op. 40, No. 3
    Noet (Pet No. N6024)
  Quartet No. 8 in B flat
    (Sitt) Int
BOHM, CARL
  Berceuse, Op. 151; with Love Song by
    Ehrlich
    CF
  Zingara, La, Op. 102
    (Saenger) CF
BONDON, JACQUES (1927-   )
  Quartet No. 1
    Transatlantiques
BONELLI, ETTORE (1900-   )
  *Quartet No. 2
    ZA 3146
BORODIN, ALEXANDER (1833-1887)
  Nocturne, from Quartet No. 2
    (Pochon) CF
  *Quartet No. 1 in A
    Belaieff
    BRH
    Int
  *Quartet No. 2 in D
    Belaieff
    BRH
    Int
BORODIN, GLAZUNOV, LIADOV & RIMSKY-
    KORSAKOV
  *Quartet on the name B-la-f[93]
    Belaieff
    Int
BØRRESEN, HAKON (1876-   )
  Quartet
    Dansk 70   score only

---

[93] The B-la-f quartet, written for Mitrofan Belaieff, consists
of four movements: 1. Sostenuto assai-Allegro by Rimsky-
Korsakov; 2. Scherzo by Liadov; 3. Serenata alla Spagnola
by Borodin; 4. Finale, Allegro by Glazunov.

BORRIS, SIEGFRIED (1906-   )
  *Quartet No. 2 in f sharp, Op. 28
    Sirius
  *Quartet No. 3, Op. 64
    Sirius
BOSMANS, A.
  Epigrammes, 3
    Metr
  Jakiana
    H Elkan   score included
  Sonatelle
    H Elkan   score included
BOSTON MUSIC COMPANY STRING QUARTET
    ALBUM
  BMC   2V
    Vol 1
      Bach: Air
      Boccherini: Minuet
      Cui: Perpetuum Mobile
      Délibes: Passepied
      Glazounow: Romance
      Grieg: Wedding-day at Troldhaugen
      Lalo: Serenade from Namouna
      Nedbal: Valse Noble
      Raff: Cavatina
      Sinigaglia: Hora Mystica
      Tschaikowsky: Andante Cantabile
    Vol 2
      Albeniz: Spanish Dance
      Antalffy: Aubade Hongroise
      Beethoven: Minuet
      Bizet: Adagietto
      Chaminade: Scarf-Dance
      Grieg: Anitra's Dance
      Herbert: Serenade
      Iljynsky: Berceuse
      Nevin: Song of the Brook
      Schubert: Moment Musical
      Tschaikowsky: Chant sans Paroles
BOTTJE, WILL GAY (1925-   )
  Quartet No. 2
    CFE   score included
BOZZA, EUGÈNE (1906-   )
  *Quatuor en la
    Leduc
BRAHMS, JOHANNES (1883-1897)
  Lullaby
    EV
  *Quartets, 3: Op. 51, Nos. 1, 2; Op. 67
    Pet 3903
  Quartet in c, Op. 51, No. 1
    BRH
    Int
  Quartet in a, Op. 51, No. 2
    BRH
    Int
  Quartet in B flat, Op. 67
    BRH
    Int
  Valse in A, Op. 39, orig for pno duet
    (Schwab) CF
BRANDTS-BUYS, JAN (1868-1933)
  Suite im alten Stil, Op. 23
    DOB
BRENNER, L.V.
  Slumber Song, Op. 61
    CF
BRETAGNE, S.
  *Quatuor
    RL
BREVAL, JEAN-BAPTISTE (1756-1825)
  Quartet, Op. 18, No. 1
    Noet (Pet No. N6036)
  Quartet in g
    STB

BRIDGE, FRANK (1879-1941)
  Phantasie
    Aug
  *Quartet No. 1 in e
    Aug
  *Quartet No. 2 in g
    Aug
  *Quartet No. 4
    Aug
BRITTEN, BENJAMIN (1913-   )
  *Quartet No. 1, Op. 25
    BH
  *Quartet No. 2, Op. 36
    BH
  Simple Symphony, orig for str orch
    Oxf 27.401
BRUCKNER, ANTON (1824-1896)
  Orchestral Studies from Symphonies
    Nos. 1-9
    (Schmalnauer) BRH   9V   score only
    d-b ad lib
  *Quartet in c
    Bruck (Pet No. BR25)
BRÜN, HERBERT (1918-   )
  Quartet
    IMP   score only
  *Quartet No. 3
    Tonos
BUCCHI, VALENTINO (1916-   )
  Quartet
    Carisch   score only
BÜCHTGER, FRITZ (1903-   )
  Quartet No. 2
    Baer 3227
BUESSER, HENRI (1872-   )
  *Divertissement, Op. 119
    Dur
BULL, JOHN (c.1562-1628)
  Fantasy, see English Instrumental Music,
    16th and 17th Centuries
BUNIN, R.
  Quartet No. 2, Op. 27
    MZK   min score only
BURKHARD, WILLY (1900-1955)
  *Quartett in einem Satz, Op. 68
    Baer 2230
BURT, FRANCIS (1926-   )
  Quartet, Op. 2
    BB
BUSH, ALAN (1900-   )
  *Dialectic
    BH
BUSTINI, ALESSANDRO (1876-   )
  Suite Scarlattiana
    Santis 538
BUSTINI, [ALESSANDRO]
  Quartet No. 2
    Ric PR675   score only
BYRD, WILLIAM (1543-1623)
  Fantasy, see English Instrumental Music,
    16th and 17th Centuries
  Fantasy Quartets, see 4 viols
  Queens Alman
    (Stevens) Oxf   in preparation
  see also Pieces from keyboard pieces
    of Farnaby and Byrd
CAGE, JOHN (1912-   )
  Quartet in Four Parts
    Pet 6757   score included
CAJA, ALFONSO (1889-   )
  Quartet
    Sal   score only
CAMBINI, GIOVANNI (1746-1825)
  Quartet in b, Op. 40, No. 3
    (Bonelli) ZA 4031

CAPET, LUCIEN (1873-1928)
*Quatuor No. 1
    Mathot
*Quatuor No. 2
    Senart
CARMINA GERMANICA ET GALLICA, see
    4 viols
CAROLS
    (Stanton) Oxf for rent; voices ad lib;
        published separately
        Joseph, dearest 27.512
        Rejoice and be merry 25.206
        Rocking 25.208
        Garden of Jesus 25.209
        Crown of Roses 27.500
        The Cradle 25.212
        O little one sweet 25.213
CARPENTER, JOHN ALDEN (1876-1951)
*Quartet
    GS
CARTER, ELLIOTT (1908-   )
*Elegy
    Peer
*Quartet No. 1
    AMP
*Quartet No. 2
    AMP
CASELLA, ALFREDO (1883-1947)
*Concerto
    UE 7583
    Pieces, 5
    UE 6880
CASTELNUOVO-TEDESCO, MARIO (1895-   )
*Quartet No. 2 in F, Op. 139
    Mil A.M.I. 4502
CASTILLON, ALEXIS DE (1838-1873)
*Quatuor, Op. 3
    Dur
CAZDEN, NORMAN (1914-   )
    Quartet, Op. 9
    CFE score included
CETTIER, PIERRE (1874-   )
    Quartet No. 2
    Sal score only
CHAGRIN, FRANCIS (1905-   )
    Elegy
    Mil-L 46 score included
CHAMBER MUSIC ALBUM
    (Pochon) CF 02699
        Agus-Pochon: Menuet
        Albrechtsberger: Scherzando
        Bach: Adagio in a
        Bach: Choral No. 241
        Boccherini: Rondeau
        Gluck-Pochon: Menuetto, from Iphi-
            genia in Aulis
        Handel: Overture from Oratorio
            Susanna
        Rameau-Pochon: Rigaudon
        Rousseau-Pochon: Allemande et Minuet
        Schubert: Rosamunde
CHASSMAN, JOACHIM
    Salute to Kreutzer
    Ru pno and d-b ad lib
        score included
CHAUSSON, ERNEST (1855-1899)
*Quartet in c, Op. 35. Unfinished
    Dur
    Int
CHEMBERDZHI, N.
    Quartet No. 3
    MZK min score only
CHERUBINI, LUIGI (1760-1842)
    Quartets, 3, in E flat, C, d
    Pet 1346

Quartet in C
    Noet (Pet No. N6041)
Quartet in E flat
    Int
Scherzo, from Quartet No. 1 in E flat
    (Pochon) CF
CHEVILLARD, [CAMILLE (1859-1923)]
*Quatuor en ré, Op. 16
    Dur
CHEVREUILLE, RAYMOND (1901-   )
    Quartet No. 4, Op. 13
    CBDM score included
    Quartet No. 5, Op. 23
    CBDM score included
CHILDS, BARNEY
    Quartet No. 4
    CFE score included
    Quartet No. 5
    CFE
CHORALES FOR STRINGS, see more than 1
    instrumental combination
CLAFIN, AVERY (1898-   )
    Laudate Dominum
    CFE
CLARKE, HENRY L. (1907-   )
    Quartet No. 2
    CFE score included
    Quartet No. 3
    CFE score included
(CLARKE, IRMA)
    Bach for Strings
    GS score included
    Introduction to String Quartets
    BMC 2V score included
        vln 3 may be substituted for vla
        for contents see title
    Short String Quartets from the Masters, 12
    GS score included, for contents see title
    String Music of the Baroque Era
    BMC score included
CLASSIC AND MODERN STRING QUARTET
    ALBUM
    (Strasser) CF AA24-25 2V
        Vol 1
            Arensky: Cuckoo
            Bungert: Canon
            Busoni: Contrapuntal Dance
            Chopin: Valse, Op. 35, No. 2
            Debussy: Mazurka
            Glazounov: Pastorale
            Liszt: Canzonetta del Salvator
                Rosa No. 3
        Vol 2
            Dvořák: Slavonic Dance, Op. 46
            Gade: Romance
            Granados: Jota
            Grieg: Gavotte, Op. 40, No. 3
            Karganoff: Reproach
            Tchaikovsky: Humoreske
            Yamada: Song of the Plovers
COLE, HUGO (1917-   )
*Miniature Quartet No. 1 in G
    Nov
*Miniature Quartet No. 2 in a
    Nov
COPLAND, AARON (1900-   )
*Pieces, 2
    BH
COWELL, HENRY (1897-   )
    Quartet No. 4, United Quartet
    Pet 6248 score included
*Quartet No. 5
    Pet 6118

CRAS, JEAN (1879-1932)
*Quatuor No. 1
　　RL
CRAWFORD, ROBERT (1925-　　)
*Quartet No. 1, Op. 4
　　Aug
*Quartet No. 2, Op. 8
　　Aug
CREMONA STRING ENSEMBLE FOLIO
　　(Johnson) CF 03839
　　Beethoven: March from Egmont
　　Brahms: Processional
　　Brahms: Waltz
　　Giordani: Aria
　　Gounod: Duet from Faust
　　Haydn: Allegro
　　Haydn: Exalted Chorus
　　Johnson: Whirlwind
　　Méhul: Music Box Gavotte
　　Mendelssohn: Auf Wiedersehn
　　Mozart: Country Dance
　　Mozart: Theme
　　Pleyel: String Quartet
　　Purcell: Air from Dido and Aeneas
　　Scarlatti: Consolation
　　Tchaikovsky: Cathedral
　　Vermeland, Swedish Folk Song
　　Western Folk Tune, Traditional
　　Will You Go, Spiritual
CRESTON, PAUL (1906-　　)
　　Quartet, Op. 8
　　Templ
CSERMAK, ANTON GEORG
*Quartet, "Die drohende Gefahr oder die
　　Vaterlandsliebe"
　　DOB
CUI, CÉSAR (1835-1918)
　　Orientale
　　(Schwab) CF
CUNDELL, EDRIC (1893-1961)
　　Quartet, Op. 18
　　Curwen　for rent
CUSTER, ARTHUR (1923-　　)
　　Coloquio Para Cuarteto de Cuerda
　　CFE　score included
DALAYRAC, NICOLAS (1753-1809)
　　Quatuor No. 3
　　(de la Laurencie) Senart 5350
　　Quatuor No. 5
　　(de la Laurencie) Senart 5351
DANCLA, [CHARLES (1817-1907)
　　Herald Quartet, from String Music for
　　　　Young People
　　(Klotman) Mil　score included
　　Rondo Caprice, from String Music for
　　　　Young People
　　(Klotman) Mil　score included
　　Serieux, from String Music for Young
　　　　People
　　(Klotman) Mil　score included
DAVID, THOMAS CHRISTIAN (1925-　　)
　　Quartet Op. 6, No. 1
　　BRH
　　Quartet, Op. 6, No. 2
　　BRH
　　Quartet, Op. 6, No. 3
　　BRH
DAVIES, EVAN THOMAS (1878-　　)
　　Eos Lais
　　STB
DAVIES, P.
　　Quartet
　　SCH　score only

DEBUSSY, CLAUDE (1862-1918)
*Quartet, Op. 10
　　Dur
　　Int
DEDIEU-PETERS, MADELEINE (1889-　　)
　　Pieces, 3
　　Sal　score only
　　Quartet No. 2
　　Sal　score only
DEFOSSEZ, RENÉ (1905-　　)
　　Quartet No. 2
　　CBDM　score included
DELAGE, [MAURICE (1879-　　)]
*Quartet in d
　　Dur
DELANNOY, MARCEL (1898-　　)
*Quatuor en mi majeur
　　Dur
DELDEN, LEX VAN (1919-　　)
*Quartet No. 1, Op. 43
　　DN (Pet No. D56)
DE LEMARTER, [ERIC (1880-1953)]
　　Quartette No. 2 in F
　　Mil　score included
DELIUS, FREDERICK (1862-1934)
*Quartet
　　Aug
DELVAUX, A.
　　Quartet No. 4
　　CBDM　score included
DELVINCOURT, CLAUDE (1888-1954)
*Quartet
　　Dur
DENNY, WILLIAM (1910-　　)
　　Quartet No. 2
　　BH　score included
DE ROSE, PETER, see Adamson & De Rose
　　and Gallop & De Rose
DESSAU, PAUL (1894-　　)
　　Quartettino, "Felsenstein". Quartet No. 5
　　BRH
DIAMOND, DAVID (1915-　　)
*Concerto
　　SMP
*Quartet No. 1
　　SMP
*Quartet No. 2
　　SMP
*Quartet No. 3
　　SMP
*Quartet No. 4
　　SMP
DIERCKS, JOHN (1927-　　)
　　Suite
　　Tritone　manuscript reproduction
　　　　vln 3 ad lib, substitute for vla
DIEREN, BERNARD VAN (1884-1936)
　　Quartet No. 2
　　Oxf 25.200
D'INDY, see Indy, d'
DITTERSDORF, KARL DITTERS VON
　　(1739-1799)
　　Andante, from Quartet in B flat
　　(Lockhart) MPH　score included
　　Andante, from Quartet in E flat
　　(Pochon) CF
　　Quartets, 6
　　(Müller) Oertel
　　Quartet in D
　　Noet (Pet No. N6033)
*Quartet in E flat
　　(Lauterbach) Int
　　(Lauterbach) Pet 2192

DITTERSDORF, KARL DITTERS VON (cont.)
  Quartet in G
    Int
DOHNÁNYI, ERNST VON (1877-1960)
  *Quartet in A, Op. 7
    DOB
  Quartet No. 2 in D flat, Op. 15
    SIM
  *Quartet No. 3 in a, Op. 33
    Kul
DONATO, ANTHONY (1909-   )
  Quartet in e
    SPAM   score included
DONATONI, FRANCO (1927-   )
  Quartet No. 2
    SZ
DORET, [GUSTAVE (1866-1943)]
  *Quatuor en Ré majeur
    RL
DRESDEN, SEM (1881-1957)
  *Quatuor No. 1
    Senart
DRIESSLER, JOHANNES (1921-   )
  Quartet, Op. 41, No. 1
    Baer 3229
DRINK TO ME ONLY WITH THINE EYES
    (Pochon) CF
DUCASSE, ROGER, see Roger-Ducasse
DU CAURROY, FRANÇOIS-EUSTACHE
    (1549-1609)
  Fantaisie, Neuviesme
    (Expert) Senart 2647
  Fantaisie, Vingtiesme
    (Expert) Senart 2649
  Fantaisie, Vingt-deuxiesme
    (Expert) Senart 2646
DUKE, VERNON (1903-   )
  Quartet in C
    FC 1885   score only
DUMLER, M.
  Cradle Song
    CP   score included
  Quartet
    CP   score included
DUNKLER, E.
  Au bord de la mer, see Bizet: Adagietto
DUPIN, PAUL (1865-1949)
  Poèmes
    Sal   score only
DU PLESSIS, see Plessis
DUPONT
  Quartet, Op. 27
    Sal   score only
DVOŘÁK, ANTONIN (1841-1904)
  Cypresses
    Artia   score only
  Humoreske, Op. 101, No. 7, orig for pno
    (Saenger) CF
  *Quartet in A, Op. 2
    Artia   score only
  *Quartet in a, Op. 16
    Artia
  *Quartet in d, Op. 34
    Artia
    LN (Pet No. R35)
  *Quartet in E flat, Op. 51
    Artia
    Int
    SIM
  *Quartet in C, Op. 61
    Artia
    Int
    SIM
  Quartet in E, Op. 80
    SIM

*Quartet in F, Op. 96, "American"
    Artia
    Int
    SIM
*Quartet in A flat, Op. 105
    Artia
    Int
    SIM
*Quartet in G, Op. 106
    Artia
    Int
    SIM
  Quartet in f
    (Raphael) BRH
  Quartet Fragment in F
    Artia   score only
  Serenade in E, Op. 22
    Artia   score only
EASY PIECES, 12, FOR STRING QUARTET OR
    STRING ORCHESTRA
    (Samford) GS   2V   d-b, pno ad lib
    score included
    Vol 1
      Bach: Break forth, O beauteous,
        heavenly light
      Bach: Commit thy ways, O pilgrim
      Brahms: Waltz
      Gluck: Gavotte, from Iphigenia in
        Aulis
      Grieg: Watchman's song
      Handel: Theme, from The Harmonious
        Blacksmith
    Vol 2
      Bach: Sarabande, from English suite
        in a
      Beethoven: Minuet, from Septet,
        Op. 20
      Grieg: Norwegian melody
      Handel: Little fugue
      Schubert: Andante, from Quartet
        in a, Op. 20
      Schumann: Morning promenade
EASY STRING QUARTET ALBUMS
    Kal   2V
EDMUNDS, CHRISTOPHER (1899-   )
  *Miniature Quartet
    Nov
EGENOLFF, CHRISTIAN (1502-1555)
  Gassenhawerlin und Reutterliedlin
    Noet (Pet No. N995)   voice ad lib
EHRENBERG, CARL (1878-   )
  Quartet No. 4 in E flat, Op. 43
    SIM
EHRLICH, A.
  Love Song, see Bohm: Berceuse
EKLUND, HANS (1927-   )
  Quartet No. 3
    Gehrmans
ELER, ANDREAS (1764-1821)
  *Quartet, Op. 2, No. 3
    KS
ELGAR, EDWARD (1857-1934)
  Quartet, Op. 83
    Nov
ELLER, H.
  Quartet No. 3
    MZK   min score only
EMMANUEL, [MAURICE (1862-1938)]
  *Quatuor en si bemol
    Dur
ENESCO, GEORGES (1881-1955)
  Quatuor No. 1
    Senart
  Quatuor No. 2
    Senart

*ENGLISH INSTRUMENTAL MUSIC, 16TH AND
   17TH CENTURIES
   (Beck) Pet 2V
      Vol 1: 4 Suites in 4 parts made from
         Consort Music by Matthew Locke
      Vol 2: 9 Fantasies in 4 parts by Byrd,
         Bull, Ferrabosco, Jenkins, Ives
ENSEMBLES FOR STRINGS
   (Whistler & Hummel) Ru pno ad lib
   score included
ERB, JOSEPH (1858-1944)
*Quatuor en fa maj.
   Senart
ERBSE, HEIMO (1924-   )
   Quartet No. 1, Op. 5
   BB
ERLANGER, P.D.
*Quatuor
   RL
ERÖD, IVAN (1936-   )
   Stücke, 4
   EDW
d'ESTRADE-GUERRA, O.
*Quatuor No. 3
   Jobert
EVANGELISTI, FRANCO (1926-   )
*Aleatorio
   Tonos
EXTON, JOHN
*Partita
   Ches in preparation
FARNABY, GILES (c.1560-1640)
   see Pieces, 8, from keyboard pieces of
      Farnaby and Byrd
FAURÉ, GABRIEL (1845-1924)
*Quartet, Op. 121
   Dur
FELDMAN, MORTON (1926-   )
   Pieces, 3
      Pet 6917 score only
   Structures
      Pet 6912 score only
FERRABOSCO, ALFONSO II (c.1575-1628)
   Fantasia a 4
      STB
   Fantasy, see English Instrumental Music,
      16th and 17th Centuries
FERRARI-TRECATE, LUIGI (1884-   )
   Quartetto in 3 tempi
      Curci score included
FERROUD, PIERRE-OCTAVE (1900-1936)
*Quatuor en ut
   Dur
FIBICH, ZDENKO (1850-1900)
   Quartet
      Artia
FILIPPENKO, ARKADY (1912-   )
   Quartet No. 2
      MZK min score only
FINE, IRVING (1914-1962)
   Quartet
      SPAM score included
FINE, VIVIAN (1913-   )
   Quartet
      CFE score included
FINNEY, ROSS LEE (1906-   )
*Quartet
      BH for rent
   Quartet No. 4
      SPAM score included
*Quartet No. 6 in E
      Pet 6458
   Quartets, 2, Nos. 7 and 8
      Val score included

FIRST NOËL
   (Pochon) CF
FIRST QUARTET ALBUM
   (Whistler & Hummel) Ru
FIRST STRING ENSEMBLE ALBUM
   (Johnson) CF 03540
      Alliance March
      Bach: Gavotte
      Bach: Morning Prayer
      Baulduin: Mimics
      Beethoven: Friendship
      Beethoven: Prelude
      Beethoven: Sonatina in G
      Diabelli: Andante in F
      Flower Girl of Florence
      Handel: Choral. Lord Remember David
      Haydn: Song of Praise
      Mehul: Romanza, from Joseph
      Morris Dance
      Mozart: Glockenspiel, from Magic Flute
      Mozart: Minuet
      Mozart: Minuet and Trio
      Mozart: Mocking Birds
      Mozart: Theme in C, from Andante
         with variations
      Pleyel: Harvest Hymn
      Purcell: Autumn
      Schubert: Melody
      Schumann: Toy Soldiers' March
      Serenade
      Tchaikovsky: Song Without Words
      Weber: Evening Hymn
FITELBERG, [JERZY (1903-1951)]
   Quartet No. 2
      UE 1147
FLONZALEY FAVORITE ENCORE ALBUM
   (Pochon) CF 0207, 1238, 1476, 1666 4V
      Vol 1
         Drink To Me Only With Thine Eyes
         Foster: Old Black Joe
         Gavotte
         Handel: Larghetto
         Haydn: Serenade
         Mendelssohn: Canzonetta, from String
            Quartet in E flat
         Raff: Mill, from String Quartet
         Schubert: All' ungherese
         Spirit of the 18th Century
         Stewart: Angel Gabriel
      Vol 2
         Boccherini: Larghetto from String
            Quartet
         Borodin: Nocturne, from String
            Quartet No. 2 in D
         Dittersdorf: Andante, from String
            Quartet in E flat
         Glazounov: Interludium in Modo
            Antico, from Five Novelettes
         Haydn: Andantino Grazioso, from
            String Quartet
         Irish Reel
         Mendelssohn: Scherzo, from String
            Quartet in e
         Mozart: Menuet, from String Quartet
            No. 2
         Osten-Sacken: Berceuse
         Song of the Volga Boatmen
      Vol 3
         Bach: Menuetto
         Deep River
         First Noel
         Go Down, Moses
         Grétry: Allegro grazioso, from Six
            Quartets
         Irish Cradle Song

FLONZALEY FAVORITE ENCORE
  ALBUM (cont.)
  (Pochon) CF 0207, 1238, 1476, 1666 4V (cont.)
    Vol 3 (cont.)
      Moussorgsky: Petite Suite, from
        Pictures at an Exhibition
      Mozart: Rondo, from String Quartet
        No. 6
      Rubinstein: Molto Lento, from Quartet
        Music of the Spheres
      Swing low, Sweet Chariot
    Vol 4
      Adeste Fidelis
      Balfe: Killarney
      Boccherini: Minuetto from the String
        Quartet in E
      Bonnie Banks o' Loch Lomond
      Cherubini: Scherzo, from String
        Quartet No. 1
      Drap O' Capie O!
      Hasse: Barberini's Minuet
      Haydn: Finale from Quartet in g
      Lily of the Vale
      Sally in our Alley
      Turkey in the Straw
FLOTHUIS, MARIUS (1914-   )
*Quartet, Op. 44
  DN (Pet No. D184)
FOGG, ERIC (1903-1939)
*Quartet in A flat
  STB
FOLK-SONG ALBUM
  (Pochon) CF 02531
    Air Chinois
    Cornish Air
    Danish Song
    Darling Nelly Gray
    Emigrants
    Highland Air
    Moreen
    Morris Dance
    Old Highland Cradle Song
    Parmi les gens on m'accuse
    Rose of Alabama
    Spanish Bolero
    'Tis Jordan's River
    Wedding Song
FÖRSTER, EMANUEL ALOYS (1748-1823)
  Quartet in C, Op. 21, No. 1
    (Angerer) DOB
FORTNER, WOLFGANG (1907-   )
  Quartet No. 3
    SCH
FOSS, LUKAS (1922-   )
  Quartet in G
    CF 04242 score included
FOSTER, STEPHEN COLLINS (1826-1864)
  From Foster Hall
    (Howard) CF 02696 score included
      Gentle Annie
      Hard times, come again no more
      Massa's in de cold ground
      O Susanna
      Ring de Banjo
FOURESTIER, [LOUIS (1892-   )]
  *Quatuor
    Dur
FRACKENPOHL, ARTHUR (1924-   )
  Suite for strings
    GS score included; d-b ad lib
FRANCAIX, JEAN (1912-   )
  Ode sur la naissance de Vénus
    Editions Francaises
  Quartet
    SCH

FRANCK, CÉSAR (1822-1890)
  *Quartet in D
    Haml
    Pet 3746
FRANCMESNIL, ROGER DE (1884-   )
  *Quatuor
    Mathot
FRANCO, JOHAN (1908-   )
  Pieces, 2, 1933
    CFE score included
  Prodigal, 6 Aphorisms
    CFE score included
  Quartet No. 3
    CFE score included
  Quartet No. 4
    CFE score included
  Quartet No. 5
    CFE score included
FRANKEL, BENJAMIN (1906-   )
  *Quartet No. 1, Op. 14
    Aug
  *Quartet No. 2, Op. 15
    Aug
  *Quartet No. 3, Op. 18
    Aug
  *Quartet No. 4, Op. 21
    Aug
FRESCOBALDI, GIROLAMO (1583-1643)
  Suite in D
    EV
FRICKER, PETER RACINE (1920-   )
  Quartet
    SCH
FRIED, G.
  Quartet No. 3, Op. 20
    MZK min score only
FRIML, RUDOLPH (1879-   )
  In a classical mood
    Big 3
FRISKIN, JAMES (1886-   )
  Phantasie Quartet
    Nov
FROBERGER, JOHANN JAKOB (1616-1667)
  Ricercare
    Hin (Pet No. H45) score included
FROMM, HERBERT (1905-   )
  Quartet
    BH score included
FUGA, SANDRO (1906-   )
  Quartet No. 2
    SZ
  Quartet No. 3 "Elegiaco"
    SZ
FULEIHAN, ANIS (1900-   )
  *Quartet No. 1
    SMP
  *Quartet No. 2
    SMP
FÜRST, PAUL WALTER (1926-   )
  Quartet, Op. 34
    DOB min score only
GABRIELI, GIOVANNI (c.1554-1612)
  Canzoni per Sonar a 4
    (Einstein) SCH organ or pno ad lib
  Ricercari, 3
    Mercury
GADZHIBEKOV, SULTAN (1919-   )
  Scherzo
    MZK score included
GAGNEBIN, HENRI (1886-   )
  Quatuor No. 2
    HL score included
  Quatuor No. 3
    HL score included

GAIGEROVA, V.
Quartet No. 2, Op. 17
MZK min score only
GAITO, CONSTANTINO (1878-1945)
*Quartetto No. 2, Op. 33
Ric BA6116
GALININ, G.
Quartet No. 1
MZK min score only
GALLOP, SAMMY & DE ROSE, PETER
Autumn Serenade
Big 3
GALUPPI, [BALDASSARE (1706-1785)]
*Concerto a quattro No. 1 in g
(Heussner) DOB
*Concerto a quattro No. 2 in G
(Heussner) DOB
GENZMER, HARALD (1909-   )
Quartet No. 1
SCH
GEORGE, EARL (1924-   )
Quartet
Oxf in preparation
GERHARD, ROBERTO (1896-   )
*Quartet
Kuhl for rent
GERSCHEFSKI, EDWIN (1909-   )
Fanfare, Fugato and Finale
CFE score only
Variations, 8, Op. 25
CFE score only
GERSTER, OTTMAR (1897-   )
*Quartet No. 2
Pet 4683
GERVAISE, CLAUDE (16th century)
Danses, 6, de la renaissance francaise
(Expert) Senart 3084
Old French Dances, 5
Hin (Pet No. H1550) score included
GHEDINI, GIORGIO FEDERICO (1892-   )
Quartet No. 1
SZ
GIANFERRARI
*Quartetto
Ric 121602
GIANNINI, VITTORIO (1903-   )
Quartet
AME
GIBBONS, ORLANDO (1583-1625)
Fantazia No. 1
STB
Fantazia No. 2
STB
Song 13, see Vaughan Williams: Hymn Tune
Prelude
GIBBS, CECIL ARMSTRONG (1889-1960)
Pastoral
Curwen for rent
Pieces, 3
Curwen
GIDEON, MIRIAM (1906-   )
Lyric Piece
CFE score only
Quartet
CFE score included
GINASTERA, ALBERTO (1916-   )
*Quartet No. 1
Belaieff
*Quartet No. 2
Belaieff for rent
GLASS, LOUIS (1864-1936)
Quartet No. 4 in f sharp, Op. 35
WH 1176 score included

GLAZUNOV, ALEXANDER (1865-1936)
Interludium in Modo Antico, from
5 Novelettes, Op. 15
(Pochon) CF
*Novelettes, 5, Op. 15
Belaieff
Int
*Quartet Slav in G, Op. 26
Belaieff
Quartet No. 5
MZK
Quartet on the name B-la-f
see Borodin, Glazunov, Liadov &
Rimsky-Korsakov
*Suite, Op. 35
Belaieff
GLAZUNOV, LIADOV & RIMSKY-KORSAKOV
Jour de Fête
Int "Festive Moods"
1. Carolers 2. Glory 3. Dancers
GLIÈRE, REINHOLD (1875-1956)
Quartets, 4
MZK score only
Quartets No. 1, Op. 2; No. 2, Op. 20;
No. 3, Op. 67; No. 4, Op. 83
Quartet in A, Op. 2
Int
GLINKA, MIKHAIL (1804-1857)
Quartets, see more than 1 instrumental
combination
GNESSIN, MIKHAIL (1883-1957)
Suite
MZK score only
GODARD, BENJAMIN (1849-1895)
Quatuor No. 1, Op. 33
Dur
Quatuor No. 3 en la, Op. 136
Dur
GODSKE-NIELSEN, SVEND
*Quartet, Op. 14
Dansk 71
GOEB, ROGER (1914-   )
Quartet No. 2
CFE score included
Quartet No. 3
CFE score included
Running Colors
CFE score included
GOEDICKE, [ALEXANDER (1877-1957)]
Quartet No. 2, Op. 75
MZK min score only
GOLD, ERNEST (1921-   )
Quartet No. 1
SPAM score included
GOLDSCHMIDT, BERTHOLD (1903-   )
*Quartet, Op. 8
UE 8693
GOLESTAN, STAN (1872-1956)
*Quartet No. 2
Dur
GOLOVKOV, A.
Quartet No. 2
MZK min score only
GOLUBEV, EVGENY (1910-   )
Quartet No. 2, Op. 31
MZK min score only
Quartet No. 3, Op. 38
MZK min score only
GOODENOUGH, FORREST (1918-   )
Quartet No. 3
CFE score included
Quartet No. 4
CFE score included
Sketches, 2
CFE score included

GOOSSENS, EUGÈNE (1893-1962)
  *Fantasy String Quartet, Op. 12
    Ches
  *Quartet, Op. 14
    Ches
  *Quartet No. 2, Op. 59
    BH
  *Sketches, 2, Op. 15
    Ches
GORDON, PHILIP
  Fiddling for fun
    GS   score included
(GORDON)
  Melodious Pieces, 4
    BMI   score included
GOSSEC, FRANÇOIS-JOSEPH (1734-1829)
  Gavotte
    (Saenger) CF
GOUNOD, CHARLES FRANCOIS (1818-1893)
  Quartet No. 3 in a, Op. posth.
    CH (Pet No. C200)
GOW, DOROTHY
  *Quartet in one movement
    Oxf 25.903
GRAF, FRIEDRICH (1727-1795)
  Quartet in C
    Noet (Pet No. N6025)
GRAM, PEDER (1881-1956)
  *Quartet No. 3, Op. 30
    Dansk 72
GRANDI, WALTER
  Fuga doppia
    Santis 829
GRANT, PARKS (1932-   )
  Quartet in c, Op. 27
    CFE   score included
  Quartet No. 2, Op. 56
    CFE   score included
GREEN, RAY (1909-   )
  *Epigrammatic Portraits, 5
    AME
GRENZ, ARTUR (1909-   )
  Quartet, Op. 8, No. 2
    Sik 341
GRETCHANINOV, ALEXANDER (1864-1956)
  Berceuse
    EV
GRIEG, EDVARD (1843-1907)
  Heart Wounds, Op. 34 and Last Spring
    CF AS1
  Quartets Nos. 1 and 2
    MZK   score included
  *Quartet in g, Op. 27
    Mercury
    Pet 2489
GRIFFES, CHARLES (1884-1920)
  *Sketches, 2, based on Indian themes
    (Betti) GS
GROFE, FERDE & ADAMSON, HAROLD
  Daybreak
    Big 3
GROSS, ROBERT
  Quartet No. 4
    CFE
  Quartet No. 5
    CFE   score included
GRUENBERG, LOUIS (1884-   )
  *Indiscretions, 4, Op. 20
    UE 7777
(GRUENBERG)
  String Quartet Album
    GS L263-4   2V   for contents see title
GUERRA-PEIXE, CÉSAR (1914-   )
  *Quartet No. 1
    ECIC

GUIDI, F.
  *Quatuor
    Senart
GUILLARD, ALBERT LE (1887-   )
  *Quatuor
    Senart
GÜRSCHING, ALBRECHT (1934-   )
  Quartet
    EDW
GUSIKOFF, MICHEL (1895-   )
  O Susanna Variations
    Mercury
GYRING, ELIZABETH
  Quartet
    CFE   score included
  Quartet No. 5
    CFE   score included
  Quartet No. 6
    CFE   score only
  Quartet No. 7
    CFE   score included
GYROWETZ, ADALBERT (1763-1850)
  Quartet in D
    OBV
HAAS, JOSEPH (1879-1960)
  Quartet, Op. 50
    SCH
HÁBA, ALOIS (1893-   )
  Quartet, Op. 7
    UE 6419
  Quartet No. 2, Op. 12
    UE 7589
HADLEY, HENRY (1871-1937)
  *Quartet, Op. 132
    GS
HAHN, REYNALDO (1875-1947)
  *Quartet No. 2 in a
    Heugel
HALFFTER, RODOLFO (1900-   )
  Quartet
    EMM   score only
HALLNÄS, HILDING (1903-   )
  *Quartet, Op. 32
    Gehrmans
HAMANN, ERICH (1898-   )
  Quartet, Op. 12
    DOB
  Quartet, Op. 14
    DOB
  Quartets, Op. 25, Nos. 1 and 2
    DOB
  Quartet, Op. 39
    DOB
HAMBOURG
  *Quartet No. 1 in D, from Introduction to
      Chamber Music
    Mil
  *Quartet No. 2 in F, from Introduction to
      Chamber Music
    Mil
HAMILTON, IAIN (1922-   )
  Quartet No. 1, Op. 5
    SCH
HANDEL, GEORG FRIEDRICH (1685-1759)
  Largo
    (Saenger) CF
  Messiah, Overture
    (Stoessel) CF
  Movements for Strings, 4
    Hin (Pet No. H276F)   for contents see
      2 vln, pno
HANNIVOORT, HENDRIK (1871-   )
  Quartet
    Sal   score only

HANSON, HOWARD (1896-   )
  *Quartet in one movement, Op. 23
    AME
HARRIS, ROY (1898-   )
  *Quartet No. 3
    Mil
  *Variations on a theme, 3
    GS
HARSÁNYI, TIBOR (1898-1954)
  Quartet
    ESC
HARUM, GÜNTHER
  Fugue in C, Op. 31
    OBV   score included
HAUBIEL, CHARLES (1892-   )
  Echi Classici
    H Elkan   score included
HAUDEBERT, [LUCIEN (1877-   )]
  Bienvenue à Claudie. Poème, Op. 9
    Sal   score only
HAUER, JOSEF MATTHIAS (1883-1959)
  Quartet No. 6, Op. 47
    UE 8687
HAUFRECHT, HERBERT (1909-   )
  Quartet No. 1
    CFE   score included
  Quartet No. 2
    CFE   score included
HAYDN, JOSEPH (1732-1809)
  Adagio, from Quartet, Op. 17, No. 1
    CF   score included
  Divertimento in D
    (Erdmann) NAG   d-b ad lib
  Divertimento in E flat
    SCH   score included
  Emperor Variations, from Quartet,
      Op. 76, No. 3
    (Finney) MPH   score included
    (Stoessel) CF
  Finale, from Quartet, Op. 54, No. 2
    CF   score included
  Largo assai, from Op. 74, No. 3
    EV   score included
  Largo Cantabile, from Quartet, Op. 9, No. 5
    CF   score included
  Lemberg Minuet and Trio
    (Moffat) Mil   score included
  Minuet, from String Quartet No. 10
    (Finney) MPH   score included
      3rd vln ad lib
  Minuet, from Op. 76, No. 4
    EV   score included
  *Quartets, 83
    (Moser-Dechert) Pet 289A,b,C,D   4V
      Vol 1: 14 Famous Quartets
        Op. 9, No. 2
        Op. 17, No. 5
        Op. 50, No. 6
        Op. 54, Nos. 1-3
        Op. 64, Nos. 2-4
        Op. 74, Nos. 1-3
        Op. 77, Nos. 1-2
      Vol 2: 16 Famous Quartets
        Op. 3, Nos. 3, 5
        Op. 20, Nos. 4-6
        Op. 33, Nos. 2, 3, 6
        Op. 64, Nos. 5, 6
        Op. 76, Nos. 1-6
      Vol 3: Remaining Quartets, Part I
        Op. 9, Nos. 1, 3-6
        Op. 17, Nos. 1-4, 6
        Op. 42
        Op. 50, Nos. 1-5
        Op. 55, Nos. 1-3
        Op. 64, No. 1

      Vol 4: Remaining Quartets, Part II
        Op. 1, Nos. 1-6
        Op. 2, Nos. 1-6
        Op. 3, Nos. 1, 2, 4, 6
        Op. 20, Nos. 1-3
        Op. 33, Nos. 1, 4, 5
        Op. 51. Seven Last Words
        Op. 71, Nos. 1-3
        Op. 103
  Quartets, 37 Famous, Vol I
    Kal
  Quartets, 30 Celebrated
    GS L1799-1800   2V
  Quartets, Op. 76, Nos. 1-6
    UE 1626-7   2V
  *Quartet in B flat, Op. 1, No. 1
    (Angerer) DOB
    (Scott) Oxf 25.400
  Quartet in E flat, Op. 1, No. 2
    (Angerer) DOB
  Quartet in F, Op. 3, No. 5
    (Angerer) DOB
    Aug 10250
  Quartet in D, Op. 20, No. 4
    Aug 10251
  Quartet in E flat, Op. 33, No. 2, "Russian"
    (David) BRH
    Aug 10252
  Quartet in C, Op. 33, No. 3, "Bird"
    Aug 10253
    BRH
  Quartet, Op. 51. Seven Last Words
    Pet 289E
  Quartet in G, Op. 54, No. 1
    Aug 10254
  Quartet in B flat, Op. 64, No. 3
    (David) BRH
    Aug 10255
  Quartet in G, Op. 64, No. 4
    Aug 10256
    BRH
  Quartet in D, Op. 64, No. 5
    Aug 10257
  Quartet in g, Op. 74, No. 3
    Aug 10258
    BRH
  Quartet in G, Op. 76, No. 1
    Aug 10259
    BRH
  Quartet in d, Op. 76, No. 2
    Aug 10260
    BRH
  Quartet in C, Op. 76, No. 3
    Aug 10261
  Quartet in B flat, Op. 76, No. 4
    Aug 10262
    BRH
  Quartet in D, Op. 76, No. 5
    Aug 10263
    BRH
  Quartet in G, Op. 77, No. 1
    Aug 10264
  Quartet in F, Op. 77, No. 2
    Aug 10265
  Quartet in E
    (Schmid) Baer HM98   score included
  Seven Last Words, see Quartet, Op. 51
  Variations, see Emperor Variations
HAYDN, MICHAEL (1737-1806)
  *Divertimento in D
    NAG
HAYDN
  Triomphe, Le
    (Moffat) Mil   score included

HELLER, JAMES G. (1892-   )
  Aquatints, 3
    SPAM   score included
HELY-HUTCHINSON, VICTOR (1901-1947)
  *Fugal Fancies, 3
    EKN
HENGARTNER, MAX
  *Petite Suite
    Eul (Pet No. Z101)
HENNESSY, SWAN (1866-1929)
  Quartet No. 3, Op. 61
    ESC
  Serenade, Op. 65
    ESC
HENRIQUES, FINI (1897-   )
  *Quartet in a
    WH 3336a
HENZE, HANS WERNER (1926-   )
  Quartet
    SCH
HERRMANN, HUGO (1896-   )
  *Quartet, Op. 101, No. 3, "Spring"
    Sik 354
  Short Pieces, Op. 50
    SIM   score included
HESSENBERG, KURT (1908-   )
  Quartet No. 3, Op. 33
    SCH
  Quartet No. 4, Op. 60
    SCH
HIER, ETHEL GLENN (1889-   )
  Carolina Christmas, Suite
    CFE   score only
HILL, ALFRED (1870-1960)
  Quartet in d
    Chap-L
HINDEMITH, PAUL (1895-1963)
  *Pieces, 8, Op. 44, No. 3
    SCH   d-b ad lib
  Quartet No. 1, Op. 10
    SCH
  Quartet No. 2, Op. 16
    SCH
  Quartet No. 3, Op. 22
    SCH
  Quartet No. 4, Op. 32
    SCH
  Quartet No. 5 in E flat
    SCH
  Quartet No. 6
    SCH
HIVELY, WELLS
  Quartet
    CFE   score included
(HÖCKNER)
  String Quartet
    SIM   3V   for contents see title
HOÉREE, ARTHUR (1897-   )
  *Pastorale et Danse
    Senart
HØFFDING, FINN (1899-   )
  *Quartet, Op. 6
    WH 3213a
HÖFFER, PAUL (1895-1949)
  Quartet No. 2, Op. 14
    MT (Pet No. MV2010)
HOFFSTETTER, [ROMANUS (1742-1815)]
  Quartet in F, Op. 2, No. 1
    Noet (Pet No. N6026)
HÖLLER, KARL (1907-   )
  *Quartet No. 6
    Sik 463
HONEGGER, ARTHUR (1892-1955)
  Quartet
    ESC

*Quatuor No. 2
  Senart
*Quatuor No. 3
  Senart
HORNEMAN, C.F.E.
  Quartet No. 1 in g
    Dansk 75   score only
HOROVITZ, JOSEPH (1926-   )
  *Quartet No. 4, Op. 16
    Mil-L 44
HORUSITZKY, [ZOLTAN (1903-   )]
  Quartet No. 4
    Kul   score only
HOSKINS, WILLIAM
  Quartet No. 1 in a
    CFE   score only
HOVHANESS, ALAN (1911-   )
  *Quartet No. 1 in d, Op. 8
    Pet   for rent
HOWELLS, HERBERT (1892-   )
  Fantasy
    Curwen   for rent
HUGON, [GEORGES (1904-   )]
  *Quatuor
    Dur
HUMMEL, HERMAN A., see Whistler &
    Hummel
HURÉ, JEAN (1877-1930)
  *Quatuor No. 1
    Mathot
  *Quatuor No. 2
    Senart
HURLSTONE, WILLIAM YEATES (1876-1906)
  *Phantasie Quartet
    Nov
HURUM, ALF (1882-   )
  Quartet, Op. 6
    Norsk
HUSA, KAREL (1921-   )
  Quartet No. 1, Op. 8
    SCH
HUTTEL, J.
  *Quatuor
    Senart
IBERT, JACQUES (1890-1962)
  *Quatuor
    Leduc
IMBRIE, ANDREW (1921-   )
  Quartet in B flat
    Malcolm   for rent
  Quartet No. 2
    Malcolm   for rent
  Quartet No. 3
    Malcolm   for rent
d'INDY, VINCENT (1851-1931)
  Quartet, Op. 35
    Haml
  *Quartet No. 2, Op. 45
    Dur
  *Quartet No. 3 in D flat, Op. 96
    Heugel
INGHELBRECHT, DÉSIRÉ ÉMILE (1880-   )
  *Quartet
    Dur
INTRODUCTION TO STRING QUARTET
    PLAYING
  (Sontag) Fox   score included
    Haydn: Presto, from Quartet in
      E flat, Op. 1, No. 2
    Haydn: Menuetto and Trio, from
      Quartet in D, Op. 1, No. 3
    Haydn: Finale, from Quartet in D,
      Op. 2, No. 5
    Haydn: Menuetto and Trio, from
      Quartet in G, Op. 3, No. 3

INTRODUCTION TO STRING QUARTET
    PLAYING (cont.)
    (Sontag) Fox   score included (cont.)
    Mozart: Allegretto, from Quartet
        No. 1 in G, K. 80
    Mozart: Rondo, from Quartet No. 1
        in G, K. 80
    Mozart: Molto allegro, from Quartet
        No. 2 in D, K. 155
    Mozart: Allegretto, from Quartet
        No. 13 in d, K. 173
INTRODUCTION TO STRING QUARTETS
    (Clarke) BMC   2V   score included;
    vln 3 may be subsitituted for vla
    Compositions by Beethoven, Corelli,
    Gretry, Handel, Haydn, Lully, Mozart,
    Rameau, Schubert
IORDAN, I.
    Quartet, Op. 10
    MZK   min score only
IPPOLITOV-IVANOV, MIKHAIL (1859-1935)
    Pieces, 4, on Armenian Folk Themes
    MZK   min score only
IRISH REEL
    (Pochon) CF
IVES, CHARLES EDWARD (1874-1954)
    *Quartet No. 1
    Peer
    *Quartet No. 2
    Peer
    *Scherzo
    Peer
IVES, SIMON (1600-1662)
    Fantasy in D
    (Dolmetsch-Ward) SCH
    Fantasy, see also English Instrumental
        Music, 16th and 17th Centuries
JACHINO, [CARLO (1889-   )]
    *Quatuor No. 2
    Senart
JACOB, GORDON (1895-   )
    Denbigh Suite, orig for str orch
    Oxf 25.104
JACOBI, FREDERICK (1891-1952)
    Quartet on Indian Themes
    SPAM   score included
    Quartet No. 2
    SPAM   score included
    *Quartet No. 3
    AME
JANÁČEK, LEOŠ (1854-1928)
    *Quartet No. 1
    Artia
    *Quartet No. 2, "Intimate Letters"
    Artia
JAQUES-DALCROZE, EMILE (1865-1950)
    *Dances, 7
    JWL   2V
    *Rythmes de Danse, Suites Nos. 1-3
    Heugel   published separately
JÁRDÁNYI, PÁL (1920-   )
    *Quartet No. 2
    Kul
JARNACH, PHILIPP (1892-   )
    Musik zum Gedächtnis der Einsamen
    SCH
JENKINS, JOHN (1592-1678)
    Ayres, 2
    (Dolmetsch) SCH   score only
    Fantasy, see English Instrumental Music,
        16th and 17th Centuries
JENTSCH, WALTER (1900-   )
    *Quartet, Op. 35
    Sik 342

JERSILD, JORGEN (1913-   )
    Quartetti Piccoli
    WH   score included
JESS MACFARLANE.
    (Pochon) CF
JETTEL, RUDOLF (1903-   )
    Quartet in C
    DOB
JOACHIM, O.
    Quartet
    CL
JOHANSON, SVEN-ERIC (1919-   )
    *Quartet No. 2
    Gehrmans
(JOHNSON, HAROLD M)
    Cremona String Ensemble Folio
    CF 03839   for contents see title
    First String Ensemble Album
    CF 03540   for contents see title
JOLIVET, ANDRÉ (1905-   )
    *Quartet No. 1
    Heugel
JONES, CHARLES
    Quartet No. 2
    Mercury
JONGEN, JOSEPH (1873-1953)
    *Quartet in A, Op. 50
    Ches
    *Quartet[94]
    Senart
    *Serenades, 2, Op. 61
    Ches
JORA, [MIHAIL (1891-   )]
    *Quatuor
    Sal
JOUBERT, JOHN (1927-   )
    *Miniature Quartet
    Nov
    *Quartet No. 1, Op. 1
    Nov
KADOSA, PAL (1903-   )
    *Quartet No. 2, Op. 25
    Kul
    *Quartet No. 3, Op. 52
    Kul
KAHN, ERICH ITOR (1905-1956)
    Quartet
    CFE   score included
KAHOWEZ, GUNTER
    Quartet No. 1
    DOB
KALLSTENIUS, EDVIN (1881-   )
    *Quartet in c, Op. 8
    Gehrmans
KAMINISKI, JOSEF (1903-   )
    *Quartet
    IMP
KARTZEV, [ALEXANDER (1883-   )]
    Quartet No. 2, Op. 14
    MZK   min score only
KATZ, E.
    Spielmusik
    SCH   score only
KAUDER, HUGO (1888-   )
    Quartet in c
    UE 6569
KAY, ULYSSES (1917-   )
    Quartet
    CFE   score included
    Quartet No. 2
    CFE   score included
    Serenade No. 3
    Leeds   in preparation

---

[94] This quartet is probably Op. 67.

KAZHLAYEV, M.
Quartet
MZK min score only
KELLY, ROBERT (1916-)
Quartet No. 1
CFE score included
Quartet No. 2
CFE score included
KELTERBORN, RUDOLF (1931-)
*Quartet No. 2
Baer 3228
*Quartet No. 3
Baer 3514
KERN, JEROME (1885-1945)
All the things you are
(Miller) T.B. Harms
Bill
(Miller) T.B. Harms
Once in a Blue Moon
(Miller) T.B. Harms
Smoke Gets In Your Eyes
(Miller) T.B. Harms
Song Is You
(Miller) T.B. Harms
Way You Look Tonight
(Miller) T.B. Harms
KERR, HARRISON (1897-)
*Quartet
BH
KERSTERS, W.
Quartet No. 1, Op. 23
CBDM score included
KIENZL, [WILHELM (1857-1941)]
*Quartet
UE
KILPATRICK, JACK
Little Pieces, 6, Op. 14
CFE score only
KING JAMES' PLEASURE
(Young) Hin (Pet No. H719)
score included
Suite of 17th century masque tunes
KIRCHNER, LEON (1919-)
Quartet
Mercury
*Quartet No. 2
AMP
KLATOVSKY, R.
*Impresiones Peruanas
UME
(KLAUSS, NOAH)
Miniatures for Strings
Pro Art for contents see title
Pieces for Pleasure
Pro Art for contents see title
KLEBE, GISELHER (1925-)
Quartet, Op. 9
BB
KNAB, ARMIN (1881-1951)
Festlicher Reigen
SCH d-b ad lib; score included
KOCHETOV, V.
Quartet, Op. 58
MZK min score only
KODÁLY, ZOLTÁN (1882-)
*Quartet No. 1, Op. 2
Kul
*Quartet No. 2, Op. 10
UE 6652
KOECHLIN, CHARLES (1867-1950)
*Quatuor No. 1
Senart
*Quatuor No. 3
Senart

KOEHLER, EMIL
Quartet No. 1
CFE score included
Quartet No. 2, Op. 8
CFE score included
KOENIG, GOTTFRIED MICHAEL (1926-)
*Quartet 1959
Tonos
KOHS, ELLIS B. (1916-)
Quartet
Mercury
Short Concert
CFE score included
KOMZAK, K.
Folk Tune and Fairy Tale
Cranz score included; harp ad lib
KOPPEL, HERMAN D. (1908-)
*Quartet No. 2, Op. 34
Dansk 76
*Quartet No. 3, Op. 38
WH 3918a
KORNAUTH, EGON (1891-1959)
*Quartet in g, Op. 26
DOB
KORNSAND, EMIL
Quartet No. 2
CF for rent
KOUNADIS, ARGHYRIS (1924-)
Quartet
EDW
KOUTZEN, BORIS (1901-)
Quartet No. 2
SPAM score included
KOZELUH, LEOPOLD ANTON (1752-1818)
Quartet No. 1, Op. 32
Artia
KRAMAR-KROMMER, FRANZ (1759-1831)
Quartet No. 1, Op. 5
Artia
KRAMER, A. WALTER (1890-)
Elegy in c sharp, Op. 30, No. 1
BMC
KRASNOV, G.
Quartet
MZK min score only
KREISLER, FRITZ (1875-1962)
Caprice Viennois, orig for vln and pno
(Leidzen) Fol 1461 score included
Liebesfreud, orig for vln and pno
(Leidzen) Fol 1462 score included
Liebeslied, orig for vln and pno
(Leidzen) Fol 1463 score included
Miniature Viennese March
(Leidzen) Fol 1465 score included
Quartet in a
Fol 1460
SCH
Schön Rosmarin, orig for vln and pno
(Leidzen) Fol 1464 score included
Tambourin Chinois, orig for vln and pno
(Leidzen) Fol 1466 score included
KRENEK, ERNST (1900-)
Quartet No. 1, Op. 6
UE 7080 score only
Quartet No. 3, Op. 20
UE 7529 score only
Quartet No. 5, Op. 65
UE 8209 score only
Quartet No. 6, Op. 78
UE 10896 score only
*Quartet No. 7, Op. 96
UE 11794
KREUSSER, [GEORG ANTON (1743-1810)]
Quartet in E flat, Op. 9, No. 5
Noet (Pet No. N6027)

KREUTZER, RODOLPHE (1766-1831)
  Caprice No. 2, see Chassman: Salute to
    Kreutzer
KRIENS, CHRISTIAAN (1881-1934)
  Nocturno, 3rd mvt of Quartet in B flat,
    Op. 74
    MPH
  Scherzo capriccioso, 2nd mvt of Quartet
    in B flat, Op. 74
    MPH
KROEGER, KARL (1932-   )
  Discussions, 5, 1957
    CFE   score only
KROLL, WILLIAM (1901-   )
  *Ancient, from 4 Characteristic Pieces
    GS
  *Cossack, from 4 Characteristic Pieces
    GS
  *Little march, from 4 Characteristic
    Pieces
    GS
  *Magyar, from 4 Characteristic Pieces
    GS
KROMMER, see Kramar-Krommer
KRUL, ELI (1926-   )
  *Quartet
    Pet 6362
LABEY, [MARCEL (1875-   )]
  *Quatuor, Op. 17
    Dur
LABROCA, MARIO (1896-   )
  Quartet No. 3
    SZ   score included
LAJTHA, LÁSZLÓ (1891-1963)
  *Etudes, 5, Op. 20
    Leduc
  Quartet No. 3, Op. 11
    UE 3763   score only
  *Quartet No. 7, Op. 49
    Leduc
  *Quartet No. 8, Op. 53
    Leduc
  *Quartet No. 9, Op. 57
    Leduc
  Quartet No. 10, Op. 58
    Leduc
LALO, EDOUARD (1823-1892)
  Quatuor, Op. 45
    Haml
LANDRÉ, GUILLAUME (1905-   )
  *Quartet No. 3
    DN (Pet No. D10b)
LANGGAARD, RUD (1893-1952)
  *Quartet No. 3
    Dansk 77
LA PRESLE, JACQUES DE (1888-   )
  *Suite en Sol
    Sal
LARSSON, LARS-ERIK (1908-   )
  *Intima Miniatyrer, Op. 20
    Gehrmans
  *Quartet No. 1, Op. 31
    Nordiska
  Quartetto alla Serenata, Op. 44
    Gehrmans
LAUDENSLAGER, HAROLD
  Quartet No. 3
    Cor ST7   score included
LAZARE-LÉVY
  *Quatuor
    Senart
LAZZARI, SYLVIO (1857-1944)
  *Quatuor
    RL

LEBORNE, FERNAND (1862-1929)
  Quatuor, Op. 23
    Haml
LEES, BENJAMIN (1924-   )
  Quartet No. 1
    BH   score included
  *Quartet No. 2
    BH   for rent
LEEUW, TON DE (1924-   )
  *Quartet
    DN (Pet No. D188)
LEFEBVRE, CHARLES EDOUARD (1843-1917)
  Suite, Op. 59
    Haml
LE FLEMING, [CHRISTOPHER (1908-   )]
  *Three Traditional Tunes
    Nov   d-b ad lib
LEGLEY, VICTOR (1915-   )
  Quartet No. 2, Op. 28
    CBDM   score included
  Quartet No. 3, Op. 50
    CBDM   score included
LE GUILLARD, see Guillard
LEIGH, WALTER (1905-1942)
  Drei Sätze für Streichquartett
    WH
LEIGHTON, [KENNETH (1929-   )]
  *Quartet No. 1, Op. 32
    Leng (Mil No. L4082)
LE JEUNE, CLAUDE (1528-1600)
  Fantaisie No. 2
    (Expert) Senart 2644
LEVITIN, YURI (1912-   )
  Quartet No. 6, Op. 37
    MZK   min score only
LÉVY, LAZARE, see Lazare-Lévy
LIADOV, ANATOL (1855-1914)
  Jour de Fête
    see Glazunov, Liadov & Rimsky-Korsakov
  Quartet on the name B-la-f
    see Borodin, Glazunov, Liadov &
      Rimsky-Korsakov
LIEBERSON, GODARD (1911-   )
  Quartet
    Oxf   in preparation
(LIEPMANN, KLAUS)
  Popular Dances from the 17th century
    BMC   score included
LINDBLAD, ADOLF FREDRIK (1801-1878)
  Quartet No. 4 in b
    Gehrmans
  Quartet No. 5 in E flat
    Gehrmans
  Quartet No. 6 in A
    Gehrmans
LIVIABELLA, LINO (1902-   )
  Quartet in f
    SZ   score included
LOCH LOMOND
  (Kriens) MPH   score included
LOCKE, MATTHEW (c.1630-1677)
  *Consort of 4 parts
    (Giesbert) SCH   2V
  *Quartets, 6
    (Warlock-Mangeot) Ches
  Suites, see English Instrumental Music,
    16th and 17th Centuries
LOCKWOOD, NORMAND (1906-   )
  Quartet No. 3
    SPAM   score included
  Serenades, 6
    Mercury
LOEFFLER, CHARLES MARTIN (1861-1935)
  Music for Four Stringed Instruments
    SPAM   score included

LONDONDERRY AIR
  (Elkan) EV
LONQUE, [GEORGES (1900-   )]
  Quartet, Op. 24
    CBDM   score included
LOSEY, F.H.
  Romance; with In Love by Ziehrer
    CF   pno ad lib for Romance
LUENING, OTTO (1900-   )
  Quartet No. 2
    CFE   score included
  Quartet No. 3
    CFE   score included
LUPO, THOMAS (17th century)
  Fantasia a 4
    STB
LUTYENS, ELIZABETH (1906-   )
  *Quartet No. 2, Op. 15, No. 5
    Leng (Mil No. L4056)
  *Quartet No. 3
    Leng (Mil No. L4071)
  *Quartet No. 6, Op. 25
    Leng (Mil No. L53)
MCBRIDE, ROBERT (1911-   )
  Foursome
    CFE   score included
  Prelude and Fugue.
    CFE   score included
MACDOWELL, EDWARD (1861-1908)
  To a Wild Rose, orig for pno
    (Isaac) CF B3317   score included
MCEWEN, JOHN BLACKWOOD (1868-1948)
  *Quartet in e
    BH   for rent
  *Threnody Quartet
    Oxf 25.100
MCHUGH, JIMMY & ADAMSON, HAROLD
  It's a most unusual day
    Big 3
MACMILLAN, ERNEST (1893-   )
  *Sketches, 2, on French Canadian Airs
    Oxf 92.501
MACONCHY, ELIZABETH (1907-   )
  *Quartet No. 1
    Leng (Mil No. L4080)
  *Quartet No. 2
    Leng (Mil No. L4083)
  *Quartet No. 3
    Leng (Mil No. L4084)
  *Quartet No. 4
    Leng (Mil No. L4057)
  *Quartet No. 5
    Leng (Mil No. L4058)
  *Quartet No. 6
    Leng (Mil No. L4066)
MADERNA, BRUNO (1920-   )
  Quartet
    SZ   score only
MADJERA, GOTTFRIED
  Quartet
    Pet 5074
MAGNANI
  Quartet
    Sal   score only
MAGNARD, ALBÉRIC (1865-1914)
  Quatuor, Op. 16
    RL
MALIPIERO, GIAN FRANCESCO (1882-   )
  *Quartet No. 1. Rispetti e Strambotti
    Ches
  *Quartet No. 2. Stornelli e ballate
    Ric 119321
  *Quartet No. 3. Cantari alla Madrigalesca
    Noet (Pet No. N3)

*Quartet No. 4
  WH 3337a
Quartet No. 5, from I Capricci di Callot
  SZ
*Quartet No. 6. L'Arca di Noè
  Ric 127825
*Quartet No. 7
  Ric 128235
MALIPIERO, RICCARDO (1914-   )
  Quartet No. 1
    SZ
  Quartet No. 2
    SZ
  Quartet No. 3
    SZ
MAMLOK, URSULA
  Quartet, 1962
    CFE   score only
MARTELLI, HENRI (1895-   )
  *Quartetto No. 2
    Ric R1364
MARTINET, JEAN-LOUIS (1916-   )
  *Variations
    Heugel
MARTINON, JEAN (1910-   )
  Quartet, Op. 43
    SCH
MARTINU, BOHUSLAV (1890-1959)
  Quartet No. 2
    UE 8706   score only
  *Quartet No. 3
    Leduc
  *Quartet No. 6
    BH
  *Quartet No. 7. Concerto da Camera
    SMP
MARUTAYEV, M.
  Quartet, Op. 5
    MZK   min score only
MARX, JOSEPH (1882-   )
  Quartet. In modo antico
    DOB
  Quartet. In modo classico
    DOB
  Quartetto Chromatico
    DOB
MARX, KARL (1897-   )
  Musik in 2 Sätzen, Op. 53, No. 2
    Baer 2490a
  *Partita über "Es ist ein Ros entsprungen"
    Baer 2687
  Variationen, 12, über "Nun laube, Lindlein,
    laube", Op. 53, No. 3
    Baer 2491a
MASCAGNI, PIETRO (1863-1945)
  Intermezzo Sinfonico from Cavalleria
    Rusticana
    (Saenger) CF
MASELLI, G.
  Movements, 4
    SZ   score only
MASON, DANIEL GREGORY (1873-1953)
  *Fanny Blair, Folk-song Fantasy, Op. 28
    Oxf 92.504
  Intermezzo
    Mercury
  Quartet on Negro Themes, Op. 19
    SPAM   score included
  Serenade
    SPAM   score included
  *Variations for String Quartet
    Oxf 92.502
MAYUZUMI, TOSHIRO (1929-   )
  *Prelude
    Pet 6525

MEDERITSCH, [JOHANN (1752-1835)]
  Quartet in F
    Noet (Pet No. N6028)
MELCHERS, HENRIK M. (1882-1961)
  *Quartet, Op. 17
    Gehrmans
MELODIOUS PIECES, 4
  (Gordon) BMI   score included
MENDELSON, JOACHIM
  Quartet No. 1
    ESC
MENDELSSOHN, FELIX (1809-1847)
  Quartets, 7
    Pet 1742
      Op. 12; Op. 13; Op. 44, Nos. 1-3;
      Op. 80; Op. 81
  *Quartets, 4 Celebrated
    Int
      Op. 12; Op. 44, Nos. 1-3
  Quartet in D, Op. 44, No. 1
    Aug 9249a
  Quartet in e, Op. 44, No. 2
    Aug 9249b
  Quartet in E flat, Op. 44, No. 3
    Aug 9249c
  Quartet in f, Op. 80
    Aug 9250
  Venetian Barcarolle
    EV
  Wedding March, from Midsummer Night's
    Dream
    (Weiss) CF
MENDOZA, VICENTE (1894-   )
  *Canto Funeral
    ECIC
MENNIN, PETER (1923-   )
  *Quartet No. 2
    CF 04002
MERULO, CLAUDIO (1533-1604)
  Canzoni da sonar a 4, 6
    (Disertori) SZ   score and pno reduction
  Fantasy
    STB
MEULEMANS, ARTHUR (1884-   )
  Quartet No. 5
    CBDM   score included
MEYEN, V.
  Quartet
    MZK   min score only
MEYER, ERNST HERMANN (1905-   )
  Quartet No. 2
    BRH
MEYER, M.
  Quartet
    ESC
MEYERBEER, GIACOMO (1791-1864)
  Coronation March, from Le Prophète
    (Weiss) CF
MIASKOVSKY, NIKOLAI (1881-1950)
  Quartets Nos. 1-13
    MZK   score only
  *Quartet No. 8, Op. 59
    BRH
    MZK
  *Quartet No. 11, Op. 67, No. 2
    MZK
  *Quartet No. 12, Op. 77
    MZK
MICA
  Quartet No. 2
    Artia
MICO, RICHARD (17th century)
  Fancy No. 3
    (Grubb) SCH   score included

Fancy No. 9
  (Grubb) SCH   score included
Fancy No. 13
  (Grubb) SCH   score included
MIGOT, GEORGES (1891-   )
  *5 Mouvements d'eau
    Leduc
MIHALOVICI, MARCEL (1898-   )
  Quartet No. 2, Op. 31
    ESC
  *Quartet No. 3, Op. 52
    Heugel
MILFORD, ROBIN (1903-1959)
  *Miniature Concerto. Miniature String
      Quartet in G
    Oxf 25.018
MILHAUD, DARIUS (1892-   )
  *Quartet No. 1
    Dur
  *Quartet No. 2
    Dur
  *Quartet No. 3, with voice
    Dur   words by Latil
  *Quartet No. 4
    Senart
  *Quartet No. 5
    Senart
  *Quartet No. 6
    UE 8141
  *Quartet No. 7
    UE 8496
  *Quartet No. 8
    Chant du Monde
  *Quartet No. 9
    Chant du Monde
  *Quartet No. 10
    Sal
  *Quartet No. 11
    Sal
  *Quartet No. 12
    Sal
  *Quartet No. 13
    Sal
  *Quartet No. 14[95]
    Heugel
  *Quartet No. 15[95]
    Heugel
  *Quartet No. 16
    Heugel
  *Quartet No. 17
    Heugel
  *Quartet No. 18
    Heugel
MILLER, GLEN, see Parish & Miller
MILLS, CHARLES (1914-   )
  Quartet No. 3
    CFE   score only
  Quartet No. 5
    CFE   score only
MILNER
  Miniature String Quartet
    Hin (Pet No. H1460)   score included
MINIATURES FOR STRINGS
  (Klauss) Pro Art 700-707
    America
    English Morris Dance
    For Christmas
    German Folk Song
    Haydn: Chorale
    Klauss: Dawn by the lake

---

[95] Quartets Nos. 14 and 15 were composed to be played separately or together as an Octet.

MINIATURES FOR STRINGS (cont.)
  (Klauss) Pro Art 700-707 (cont.)
    Klauss: Hymn Tune
    Klauss: Indian Echoes
    Klauss: Little Minuet
    Klauss: March of the Astronauts
    Klauss: Oriental Prelude
    Klauss: Short fugue
    Klauss: Sleigh Bells
    Klauss: Waltzing Scales
    Mountain Train
    Spilman: Flow gently, sweet Afton
    Tallis: Evening song
    Who made the sky so blue?
MIRZOYAN, E.
  Quartet
    MZK   min score only
MOERAN, ERNEST JOHN (1894-1950)
  *Quartet in a
    Ches
  *Quartet in E flat
    Nov
MOLLENHAUER, EDUARD (1827-1914)
  Chanson Sans Paroles
    CF
MOLNAR, [ANTAL (1890-   )]
  Quartet
    Kul
MOORE, DOUGLAS (1893-   )
  Quartet
    CF 04322   score included
MORTENSEN, OTTO (1907-   )
  *Quartet 1937
    Dansk 78
MOSS, LAWRENCE
  Quartet, 1957
    CFE   score included
MOSSOLOFF, ALEXANDER (1900-   )
  Quartet, Op. 24
    UE 8902
MOSZKOWSKI, MORITZ (1854-1925)
  Spanish Dance No. 1 in C, Op. 12
    (Saenger) CF
MOULINE, ETIENNE
  Fantaisies, 3
    (Cohen) CF 04278   score included
MOUQUET, JULES (1867-1946)
  Quatuor No. 1
    HL
MOURANT, WALTER (1910-   )
  Quartet No. 1
    CFE   score included
MOZART, WOLFGANG AMADEUS (1756-1791)
  Adagio and Fugue in c, K.546
    BRH
  Allegro Grazioso, Rondo from Quartet K. 159
    Pet 17D
  Andantino Grazioso, from Quartet K. 183
    Pet 17E
  Ave, Verum Corpus
    (Saenger) CF
  *Divertimenti, 3: K. 136, 137, 138
    Int
    Pet 4266
  Divertimento in D, K.136
    BRH
  Divertimento in F, K.138
    BRH
  *Eine Kleine Nachtmusik, K.525
    (Willms) SCH   d-b ad lib
    Aug 10311 "Quartet in G"
    CF AS6 "Serenade"
    Pet 3953 "Serenade in G"

Fantasy, K.608, orig for mechanical organ
  (Levi) BRH   score only
Quartets, 27
  (Moser-Becker) Pet 16-17   2V
    Vol 1: 10 Famous Quartets
    K. 387, 421, 428, 458, 464, 465,
    499, 575, 589, 590
    Vol 2: 17 Easy Quartets
    K. 155-160; 168-173;
    K. 285, orig for fl, vln, vla, vcl
    K. 298, orig for fl, vln, vla, vcl
    K. 370, orig for ob, vln, vla, vcl
    K. 525, Eine Kleine Nachtmusik
    K. 546, Adagio and Fugue
*Quartets, 10: K.387, 421, 428, 458, 464, 465,
  499, 575, 589, 590
  (Einstein) Nov
  (Finscher) Baer 4750
Quartets, Mailänder, K. Anh.210-213
  SCH   4V
Quartetti capricciosi, 6
  SCH   6V
Quartet in G, K. 80
  (Angerer) DOB
Quartet in F, K.168
  BRH
Quartet in A, K.169
  BRH
Quartet in C, K. 170
  BRH
Quartet in E flat, K.171
  BRH
Quartet in B flat, K.172
  Aug 10312
  BRH
Quartet in d, K.173
  BRH
*Quartet in G, K. 285a, orig for fl, vln, vla,
  vcl
  (Einstein) Hin (Pet No. H18)
Quartet in G, K.387
  Aug 10301
  BRH
Quartet in d, K.421
  Aug 10302
  BRH
Quartet in E flat, K. 428
  Aug 10303
  BRH
Quartet in B flat, K. 458
  Aug 10304
  BRH
Quartet in A, K. 464
  Aug 10305
Quartet in C, K. 465
  Aug 10306
Quartet in D, K. 499
  Aug 10307
Quartet in G, K.525, see Eine Kleine
  Nachtmusik
Quartet in D, K. 575
  Aug 10308
Quartet in B flat, K.589
  Aug 10309
Quartet in F, K. 590
  Aug 10310
Serenade in G, K. 525, see Eine Kleine
  Nachtmusik
MÜLLER VON KULM, WALTER (1899-   )
  *Quartetti, 3, Op. 56
    Ric SY336
MUSGRAVE, THEA (1928-   )
  *Quartet
    Ches

MYASKOVSKY, see Miaskovsky
NAPOLITANO
  Gato. Al estilo popular
    Ric BA10925 score included
  Vidalitay. Aire popular.
    Ric BA10926 score included
NARDINI, PIETRO (1722-1793)
  Quartets, 6
    BRH 3V
NARIMANIDZE, [NIKOLAI (1905-   )]
  *Quartet No. 3
    MZK
NEGRO SPIRITUALS
  (Pochon) CF
    Go down, Moses
    Swing low, sweet chariot
NELHYBEL, VACLAV (1919-   )
  *Quartet
    Eul (Pet No. Z245)
NEMIROFF, ISAAC (1912-   )
  Quartet
    MM score only
NERI, MASSIMILIANO (17th century)
  *Sonata for Quartet
    (Bonelli) ZA 3694
NIELSEN, CARL (1865-1931)
  Quartet in f, Op. 5
    WH 443 score included
  Quartet in g, Op. 13
    WH 638 score included
  Quartet in E flat, Op. 14
    WH 639 score included
  *Quartet in F, Op. 44
    Pet 3806
NIELSEN, JOHN (1927-   )
  *Otte aforismer for strygekvartet med
      sentenser fra H.C. Andersen's
      eventyr, Op. 1
    WH 3957a
NIKOLAYEV, [LEONID (1878-1942)]
  Quartet
    MZK min score only
NIVERD, LUCIEN (1879-   )
  *Quatuor
    Sal
NOETEL, KONRAD FRIEDRICH
  Kleine Musik
    SCH score included; vln 3 may be
      substituted for vla
  *Kleine Suite
    Sirius
NORMAN, LUDVIG (1831-1885)
  Quartet in E, Op. 20
    Gehrmans
  Quartet in A, Op. 65
    Gehrmans
NUSSIO, OTMAR (1902-   )
  *Quartet in D
    Oertel
ORBÓN, JULIÁN (1925-   )
  *Quartet No. 1
    SMP
ORREGO-SALAS, JUAN (1919-   )
  *Quartet No. 1
    Peer
OVERTON, HALL (1920-   )
  *Quartet No. 2
    Highgate
PAISIELLO, GIOVANNI (1740-1816)
  *Quartet No. 1 in A
    (Bonelli) ZA 3322
  *Quartet No. 2 in E flat
    (Bonelli) ZA 3325
  *Quartet No. 3 in E flat
    (Bonelli) ZA 3328

PALMER, EDWINA & BEST, AGNES
  Christmas Pieces for Strings, 2
    Oxf 27.907 pno ad lib
  Short Pieces, 6
    Oxf 27.100 pno ad lib
PARAY, PAUL (1886-   )
  *Quatuor
    Jobert
PARISH, MITCHELL, & MILLER, GLEN
  Moonlight Serenade
    Big 3
PARRIS, ROBERT (1924-   )
  Quartet No. 1
    CFE score included
  Quartet No. 2
    CFE score included
PARTOS, ÖDÖN (1907-   )
  *Concertino
    IMP
  Tehilim
    IMI score only
PASCAL, [ANDRE (1894-   )]
  *Quatuor
    Dur
PASCAL, CLAUDE (1921-   )
  *Quatuor
    Dur
PAUER, [JIRI (1919-   )]
  Quartet No. 1
    Artia score only
PERGAMENT, MOSES (1893-   )
  *Quartet No. 2
    Gehrmans
PERLE, GEORGE (1915-   )
  Quartet No. 5, Op. 42
    CFE score only
PETRASSI, GOFFREDO (1904-   )
  Quartet
    SZ
PETROVICS, E.
  *Quartet
    Artia
PFITZNER, HANS (1869-1949)
  *Quartet in c, Op. 50
    Oertel
PHILIDOR, FRANCOIS (1726-1795)
  Airs de Ballet du XVIIe siècle
    (Peyrot-Rebuffat) Senart 2722
PICHL, WENZEL (1741-1804)
  Quartet in e, Op. 2, No. 4
    Noet (Pet No. N6043)
PICK-MANGIAGALLI, RICCARDO (1882-1949)
  Fugues, 3
    SZ score only
PIECES FOR PLEASURE
  (Klauss) Pro Art 442-47
    Bayly: Long, long ago
    Beethoven: Themes from Symphony No. 7
    Drink to me only with thine eyes
    English country dance
    Haydn: Excerpt from Surprise
      Symphony
    Klauss: Ballet Music
    Klauss: Follow the leader
    Klauss: Jolly little string quartet
    Klauss: Now I lay me down to sleep
    Klauss: Prayer from Evangeline
    MacDowell: To a wild rose
    Turkey in the straw
PIECES, 8, FROM THE KEYBOARD PIECES
    OF FARNABY & BYRD
  (Russell) Oxf 25.014-5 2V; pno ad lib;
    Vol 1 for sale; Vol 2 for rent

PIERNÉ, GABRIEL (1863-1937)
  Adagietto
    Heugel
  Menuet du Roy
    Heugel
  Passepied
    Heugel
PIJPER, WILLEM (1894-1947)
  *Quartet No. 1
    Leng (Mil No. L4073)
  *Quartet No. 2
    Leng (Mil No. L4078)
  *Quartet No. 3
    Leng (Mil No. L4064)
  *Quartet No. 4
    Leng (Mil No. L4072)
  *Quartet No. 5, unfinished
    Leng (Mil No. L4062)
PISK, PAUL AMADEUS (1893-   )
  *Quartet No. 1, Op. 8
    UE 8182
PISTON, WALTER (1894-   )
  Quartet No. 1
    AMP
  *Quartet No. 2
    GS
  *Quartet No. 3
    BH
  Quartet No. 4
    AMP
  *Quartet No. 5
    AMP
PIZZETTI, ILDEBRANDO (1880-   )
  *Quartetto in re
    Ric 123152
PLESSIS, HUBERT DU (1922-   )
  *Quartet
    Nov
PLEYEL, IGNAZ (1757-1831)
  Quartet in E flat, Op. 1, No. 2
    WH
POCHON, ALFRED (1878-1959)
  Ballade
    CF
  Fantaisie Hébraique
    CF 02070   score included
  Indian Suite
    CF 01654
  Sketches, 2, for String Quartet
    CF
POCHON ENSEMBLE ALBUM
    CF 02532
      Chopin: Lullaby, Op. 74
      Gossec: Tambourin
      Grétry: Gavotte, from Andromaque
      Handel: Minuet d'Alcina
      Kozeluch: Andante and Allegro, from
        Quartet No. 2
      Mendelssohn: Scherzo, from Quartet
        in E flat, Op. 44, No. 3
      Pochon: Chanson de l'Hospodar
      Scriabin: Étude Op. 2, No. 1
      Tenaglia: Aria
      Valentini: Tarantella
(POCHON)
  Academic String Quartet Album
    CF 02919   for contents see title
  Chamber Music Album
    CF 02699   for contents see title
  Flonzaley Favorite Encore Album
    CF 0207, 1238, 1476, 1666   4V; for con-
      tents see title
  Folk-Song Album
    CF 02531   for contents see title

PODESVA, [JAROMIR (1927-   )]
  Quartet No. 4
    Artia   score only
POLDINI, EDUARD (1869-1957)
  Poupèe Valsante
    (Saenger) CF
POLOVINKIN, LEONID (1894-1949)
  Quartet No. 1
    MZK   min score only
PONCE, MANUEL MARIA (1882-1948)
  *Miniatures, 4
    Sal
  *Quartet
    Peer
POOT, MARCEL (1901-   )
  *Bagatelles, 5
    UE 11109
  Quartet
    ESC
POPOV, T.
  Quartet
    MZK   min score only
POPULAR DANCES FROM THE 17TH
    CENTURY
  (Liepmann) BMC   score included
PORTER, QUINCY (1897-   )
  Fugue
    CFE   score included
  *Quartet No. 3
    Pet 6671
  *Quartet No. 4
    BH
  Quartet No. 5
    CFE   score included
  *Quartet No. 6
    Pet 6672
  Quartet No. 7
    Val   score included
  Quartet No. 8
    Val   score included
POSER, HANS (1907-   )
  *Quartet No. 1, Op. 20
    Sik 279
  Quartet No. 2, Op. 38
    Sik 468
PRESLE, see La Presle
PRIETO, MARIA TERESA
  Quartet. Cuarteto Modal
    EMM   score only
PROCTOR, LELAND
  Quartet No. 2
    CFE   score included
PROKOFIEV, SERGEY (1891-1953)
  Pieces, 6, from Visions Fugitive and
    2 Pieces from Romeo and Juliet
    (Barshai) MZK   score only
  *Quartet No. 1 in b, Op. 50
    BH
    Int
  *Quartet No. 2 in F, Op. 92
    Int
    Leeds
PURCELL, HENRY (c.1659-1695)
  *Chacony in g
    Ches
    Int
  Fantaisies, see more than one instru-
    mental combination
  Golden Sonata, orig for 2 vln and Bc
    EV
PYLE, FRANCIS J.
  Frontier Sketches, orig for str orch
    Willis   d-b ad lib; score included

QUARTET ALBUM
  (Sitt) Pet 2739A,b 2V
    Vol 1: 11 short pieces and quartet
      movements by Bach, Beethoven,
      Boccherini, Cherubini, Handel,
      Hasse, Haydn, Mendelssohn,
      Mozart, Schumann
    Vol 2: 10 short pieces and quartet
      movements by Bach, Dittersdorf,
      Haydn, Mozart, Schubert, Schumann
QUEYLAR, DE
  Quartet in d
    Sal score only
QUINET, MARCEL (1915-   )
  Quartet
    CBDM score included
RADNAI, MIKLÓS (1892-1935)
  *Divertimento, Op. 7
    UE 9847
RAFF, JOACHIM (1822-1882)
  Mill, from Quartet, Op. 192, No. 2
    (Pochon) CF
RAINIER, PRIAULX (1903-   )
  Quartet
    SCH
RAMOUS, GIANNI
  *Quartet
    SZ
RANGSTRÖM, TURE (1884-1947)
  *Quartet
    Nordiska
RATEZ, EMILE-PIERRE (1851-1934)
  Quatuor, Op. 20
    Haml
RATHAUS, KAROL (1895-1954)
  Quartet No. 4
    SPAM score included
RAUCHVERGER, M.
  Quartet No. 1 on Kirghiz Themes
    MZK min score only
  Quartet No. 2
    MZK min score only
RAUTAVAARA, [EINO (1928-   )]
  Quartet No. 2, Op. 12
    BRH score only
RAVEL, MAURICE (1875-1937)
  *Quartet in F
    Dur
    Int
RAWSTHORNE, ALAN (1905-   )
  *Quartet No. 1, Theme and Variations
    Oxf 25.003
  *Quartet No. 2
    Oxf 25.901
RAXACH, ENRIQUE
  *Fases
    Tonos
RÉ, PETER
  *Quartet No. 1
    AMP
REGER, MAX (1873-1916)
  Quartet in g, Op. 54, No. 1
    UE 6936 score only
  Quartet in A, Op. 54, No. 2
    UE 6937 score only
  Quartet in d, Op. 74
    BB
  *Quartet in E flat, Op. 109
    BB
  *Quartet No. 5 in f sharp, Op. 121
    Pet 3284
  Quartet in d, Op. posth.
    (Stein) BRH

REISER, ALOIS (1887-   )
  Quartet, Op. 16
    SPAM score included
REITER, ALBERT
  Little Suite
    OBV score included
REIZENSTEIN, FRANZ (1911-   )
  *Divertimento
    Leng (Mil No. L4079)
RESPIGHI, OTTORINO (1879-1936)
  *Quartetto Dorico
    UE 8175
REUCHSEL, AMÉDÉE (1875-   )
  Quatuor No. 1 en ré mineur
    HL
REVUELTAS, SILVESTRE (1899-1940)
  *Quartet No. 1
    SMP
  *Quartet No. 2
    SMP
REYNOLDS, ROGER (1934-   )
  Quartet No. 2
    Pet 6623 score only
REZNICEK, EMIL NIKOLAUS VON
    (1860-1945)
  *Quartet No. 3 in d
    Birnbach
  *Quartet No. 4 in B flat
    Birnbach
RICHTER, FRANZ XAVER (1709-1789)
  Quartet in C, Op. 5, No. 1
    (Mies) BRH
RIEGGER, WALLINGFORD (1885-1961)
  Quartet No. 1, Op. 30
    AMP
  Quartet No. 2, Op. 43
    AMP
  Romanza, Op. 56a
    AMP score included
RIETI, VITTORIO (1898-   )
  *Quatuor en Fa
    Sal
RIISAGER, KNUDAGE (1897-   )
  *Quartet No. 3
    WH 2685a
RILEY, JOHN
  Quartet No. 2
    Val score included
RIMSKY-KORSAKOV, NIKOLAY (1844-1908)
  Jour de Fête
    see Glazunov, Liadov & Rimsky-
      Korsakov
  Quartet No. 1, Op. 12
    SCH
  Quartet on the name B-la-f
    see Borodin, Glazunov, Liadov and
      Rimsky-Korsakov
  see also more than 1 instrumental
    combination
RIVIER, JEAN (1896-   )
  Quartet No. 2
    Transatlantiques
ROCHBERG, GEORGE (1918-   )
  Quartet
    SPAM score included
ROGER-DUCASSE, JEAN (1873-1954)
  *Quartet in d
    Dur
  *Quartet No. 2 in D
    Dur
ROHWER, JENS (1914-   )
  *Heptameron, Suite in 4 parts
    BRH

RON, MARTIN DE (1789-1817)
*Quartet in f
    Gehrmans
ROPARTZ, JOSEPH GUY (1864-1955)
*Quatuor No. 1 en sol mineur
    RL
*Quatuor No. 2 en ré mineur
    Dur
*Quatuor No. 3 en sol majeur
    Dur
*Quatuor No. 4 en mi majeur
    Dur
*Quatuor No. 5 en ré majeur. Quasi
    una fantasia
    Dur
*Quatuor No. 6 en fa majeur
    Dur
*Sérénade
    RL
ROSEN, JEROME (1921-   )
    Quartet No. 1
    BH
ROSENBERG, HILDING (1892-   )
    Quartet No. 2
    Nordiska
*Quartet No. 4
    Gehrmans
*Quartet No. 5
    Nordiska
*Quartet No. 6
    Nordiska
    Quartet No. 7
    Nordiska
ROSENBERG, WOLF
*Quartet No. 3
    Tonos
ROSENMÜLLER, JOHANN
    see more than 1 instrumental combination
ROSSINI, GIOACCHINO (1792-1868)
    Quartet No. 1 in G
    (Bonelli) ZA 4032
    Quartet No. 2
    (Bonelli) ZA
    Quartet No. 3 in B flat
    (Bonelli) ZA 3648
    Quartet No. 5 in D
    (Bonelli) ZA 4021
ROUSSEAU, SAMUEL-ALEXANDER
    (1853-1904)
*Pièces, 2
    Dur
ROUSSEL, ALBERT (1869-1937)
*Quartet in D, Op. 45
    Dur
ROWLEY, ALEC (1892-1958)
*Miniature Quartet
    Nov
    Quartet in E, "Pastorale"[96]
    GT score included
ROYER, ÉTIENNE (1880-1928)
    Pour le temps de la Moisson
    Sal score only
RÓZSA, MIKLÓS (1907-   )
    Quartet, Op. 22
    AMP
RUBBRA, EDMUND (1901-   )
*Quartet No. 1 in f, Op. 35
    Leng (Mil No. L4061)
*Quartet No. 2 in E flat, Op. 73
    Leng (Mil No. L4069)
RUBINSTEIN, ANTON (1829-1894)
    Molto Lento, from Quartet Op. 17, No. 2
    (Pochon) CF

Quatuor, Op. 90, No. 1
    Haml
RUBINSTEIN, BERYL (1898-1952)
    Passe-pied
    CF
RUDHYAR, DANE (1895-   )
    Solitude, Tetragram No. 5
    CFE score only
RUEFF, JEANINE (1922-   )
*Quatuor, Op. 2
    Dur
RUSSELL, LESLIE
    Easy Pieces, 3
    Oxf 20.006 pno ad lib
(RUSSELL, LESLIE)
    Pieces, 8, from the Keyboard Pieces of
        Farnaby & Byrd
    Oxf 25.014-5 2V pno ad lib
        Vol 1 for sale; Vol 2 for rent
SABATINI, GUGLIELMO
    Leonesca. A Portrait
    Cor ST8 score included
SAINT-SAENS, CAMILLE (1835-1921)
*Quatuor No. 1, Op. 112
    Dur
*Quatuor No. 2 en sol majeur, Op. 153
    Dur
SALAZAR, ADOLFO (1890-1958)
    Rubaiyat
    ESC
SALLY IN OUR ALLEY
    (Pochon) CF
SALMHOFER, FRANZ (1900-   )
    Quartet No. 3, "The Lord's Year"
    OBV
SAMAZEUILH, GUSTAVE (1877-   )
*Cantabile et Capriccio
    Dur d-b ad lib
*Quatuor en ré
    Dur
(SAMFORD)
    Easy Pieces, 12, for String Quartet or
        String Orchestra
    GS 2V d-b ad lib; score
        included; for contents see title
SANDBY, HERMAN (1881-   )
    Song of Vermland
    CF d-b ad lib; score included
SANDI, LUIS (1905-   )
    Quartet
    EMM score only
SANTA CRUZ, DOMINGO (1899-   )
*Quartet No. 1
    Peer
*Quartet No. 2
    Peer
SAUGUET, HENRI (1901-   )
*Quartet No. 2 in A
    Heugel
SAUTEREAU, C.
*Quatuor
    Dur
SAUVEPLANE, HENRI (1892-1942)
    Quartet in f
    Sal score only
SAYGUN, AHMED ADNAN (1907-   )
*Quartet No. 1, Op. 27
    SMP
*Quartet No. 2
    SMP
SCARMOLIN, ANTHONY LOUIS (1890-   )
    Quartet
    CP score included

---

[96] In the U.S.A. this publication can be obtained through Mills.

SCHEIDT, SAMUEL (1587-1654)
Spielmusik
(Ochs) NAG   2V   pno ad lib
Vol. 1: 5 pieces from Tabulatura Nova
Vol. 2: Suite
SCHELLING, ERNEST (1876-1939)
Tarantella
CF B2237   score included
SCHISKE, KARL (1916-   )
Quartet No. 1, Op. 4
OBV
Quartet No. 2, Op. 21a
UE 11971
SCHLEMM, GUSTAV ADOLF (1902-   )
Quartet No. 2 in D
BRH
SCHMIDT, FRANZ (1874-1939)
Quartet No. 2 in G
DOB
SCHMITT, FLORENT (1870-1958)
*Quatuor, Op. 112
Dur
SCHNABEL, A.
Quartet No. 3
BH   score included
SCHOECK, OTHMAR (1886-1957)
Quartet, Op. 37
BRH
SCHOENBERG, ARNOLD (1874-1951)
*Quartet No. 1 in d, Op. 7
UE 3666
*Quartet No. 2 in f sharp, Op. 10, with
soprano
UE 2994
*Quartet No. 3, Op. 30
UE 8928
*Quartet No. 4, Op. 37
GS
SCHOLLUM, [ROBERT (1913-   )]
Variations on the folksong "Was wollen wir
singen und fangen an"
DOB   pno ad lib; score only
SCHOLZ, ARTHUR JOH.
Little Quartets, 6
OBV   2V
SCHROEDER, HERMANN
Quartet No. 2, Op. 32
SCH
SCHUBERT, FRANZ (1797-1828)
*German Dances, 5, and 7 Trios, D.90[97]
BRH
Int
German Dances, 5
Mercury
Marche Militaire, Op. 51, No. 1, orig for
pno duet
(Weiss) CF
Minuets, 5, and 6 Trios, D.89[97]
Int
Minuet in F
(Cafarella) MPH   score included
Moment Musical, orig for pno
(Pochon) CF
*Quartets, 9[97]
Pet 168A,b   2V
Vol 1
D.804, Op. 29
D.87, Op. 125, No. 1
D.353, Op. 125, No. 2
D.810, "Death and the Maiden"

Vol 2
D.887, Op. 161
D.112, Op. 168
D.173, Op. posth. in g
D.94, Op. posth. in D
D.703, Op. posth. in c
Quartet No. 2 in C
(Brown) BRH
Quartet No. 3 in B flat
BRH
Quartet No. 4 in C
BRH
Quartet No. 5 in B flat
BRH
Quartet No. 10 in E flat, Op. 125, No. 1, D.87
Aug 10324
BRH
Quartet No. 11 in E, Op. 125, No. 2, D.353
Aug 10325
BRH
Quartet No. 12 in c, D.703, "Quartett-Satz"
Aug 10323
BRH
Quartet No. 13 in a, Op. 29, D.804
Aug 10322
BRH
UE 88
Quartet No. 14 in d, D.810, "Death and the
Maiden"
Aug 10321
BRH
Quartet No. 15 in G, Op. 161, D.887
BRH
SCHULHOFF, ERWIN (1894-1942)
*Quartet No. 1
UE 8173
Quartet No. 2
UE 9670   score only
SCHULLER, [GUNTHER (1925-   )]
Quartet No. 1
UE 13002   score only
SCHULTZ, SV. S.
Quartet No. 4
Dansk 158   score included
SCHUMAN, WILLIAM (1910-   )
*Quartet No. 2
BH
*Quartet No. 3
Pr
*Quartet No. 4
GS
SCHUMANN, ROBERT (1810-1856)
*Quartets, 3, Op. 41
Int
Pet 2379
Quartet in a, Op. 41, No. 1
Aug 7224a
BRH
Quartet in F, Op. 41, No. 2
Aug 7224b
BRH
Quartet in A, Op. 41, No. 3
Aug 7224c
BRH
Rêverie and By the Fireside
CF
SCHWARTZ, PAUL
Chaconne and Fugue, Op. 17
CFE   score included
Quartet in 2 Movements, Op. 4
CFE   score included
SCHWARZ-SCHILLING, [REINHARD
(1904-   )]
*Quartet in f
Baer 3226

[97] D. number refers to the Schubert Thematic Catalogue by
Otto Erich Deutsch, in collaboration with Donald R. Wakeling. London, 1951.

SCHWERTSIK, KURT (1935-   )
  Quartet
    EDW
SCOTT, CYRIL (1879-   )
  *Quartet No. 1
    EKN
  *Quartet No. 2
    EKN
  *Quartet No. 3
    EKN
SEARCH, FREDERICK (1899-   )
  Quartet in A
    CFE   score included
  Quartet in e
    CP   score included
SEARLE, HUMPHREY (1915-   )
  Passacaglietta, Op. 16
    Leng (Mil No. L4053)   score included
SECHTER, SIMON (1788-1867)
  Four Temperaments
    SIM
  Quartet, see String Quartet Starts
    Rehearsing, under more than 1
    instrumental combination
SECUNDA, SHOLOM (1894-   )
  Quartet in c
    BMI
SEIBER, MÁTYÁS (1905-1960)
  Quartet No. 1
    SZ
  Quartet No. 2
    SZ
  Quartetto Lirico. Quartet No. 3
    SCH
SENSTIUS, KAI (1889-   )
  *Quartet in a
    Dansk 80
SESSIONS, ROGER (1896-   )
  *Quartet No. 1 in e
    MK
  *Quartet No. 2
    MK
SEVENTEENTH CENTURY SUITE
  (Young) Hin (Pet No. H204)
    score included
SHAPERO, HAROLD (1920-   )
  *Quartet No. 1
    SMP
SHAPEY, RALPH (1921-   )
  Quartet No. 1
    CFE   score included
  Quartet No. 2
    CFE   score included
  Quartet No. 3
    CFE   score included
  Quartet No. 4
    CFE   score included
SHCHERBACHEV, V.
  Suite
    MZK   score included
SHEBALIN, VISSARION (1902-   )
  Quartet No. 4, Op. 29
    MZK
  Quartet No. 6, Op. 34
    MZK   score only
  Quartet No. 7, Op. 41
    MZK   score only
SHEPHERD, ARTHUR (1880-1958)
  Quartet in e
    SPAM   score included
SHIFRIN, [SEYMOUR (1926-   )]
  Quartet
    BB

SHIRINSKY, [VASSILY (1901-   )]
  Pieces, 2
    MZK   score only
SHORT STRING QUARTETS FROM THE
    MASTERS, 12
  (Clarke) GS   score included
    Bach, J.S.: Air and Gavotte
    Beethoven: Deutscher Tanz, Menuet,
      Trinklied
    Boccherini: Menuet in A
    Dittersdorf: Minuet
    Gluck: Gavotte
    Lully: Marche du Regiment de
      Turenne
    Mozart: Gavotte, Pantomime
    Rameau: Tambourin
    Schubert: Deutscher Tanz
SHOSTAKOVITCH, DMITRI (1906-   )
  *Quartet No. 1, Op. 49
    Int
  *Quartet No. 3, Op. 73
    MZK
  *Quartet No. 4, Op. 83[98]
    MR
  *Quartet No. 5, Op. 92[98]
    MR
  *Quartet No. 6, Op. 101[98]
    MR
  *Quartet No. 7, Op. 108
    MR[98]
    MZK
  *Quartet No. 8, Op. 110
    MZK
SIBELIUS, JEAN (1865-1957)
  *Quartet, Op. 56, "Voces Intimae"
    Int
    LN (Pet No. R20)
SIDAY
  Fountain[99]
    GT   score included
SIMPSON, ROBERT (1921-   )
  *Quartet No. 1
    Leng (Mil No. L4074)
  *Quartet No. 2
    Leng (Mil No. L4077)
  *Quartet No. 3
    Leng (Mil No. L4081)
SIMPSON, THOMAS (17th century)
  Taffel Consort
    Noet (Pet No. N1009)   pno ad lib
SIMS, EZRA (1930-   )
  Quartet
    CFE   score included
SIOHAN, ROBERT (1894-   )
  *Quatuor No. 1
    Senart
(SITT)
  Quartet Album
    Pet 2739A,b   2V   for contents see title
SKALKOTTAS, NIKOS (1904-1949)
  *Greek Dances, 5
    UE 12344
  *Sketches, 10
    UE 12172
SMETANA, BEDŘICH (1824-1884)
  *Quartet No. 1 in e, "From my life"
    Artia
    Aug 10340b
    BRH
    Int
    Pet 2635

---

[98] In the U.S.A. this publication can be obtained through Presser.

[99] In the U.S.A. this publication can be obtained through Mills.

SMETANA, BEDŘICH (cont.)
*Quartet No. 2 in d
Artia
SMITH, DAVID STANLEY (1877-1949)
Quartet, Op. 46
SPAM   score included
*Quartet in E flat
Oxf 92.505
Quartet No. 6
SPAM   score included
SMITH, EM
Dance Pantomime, from 3 Tunes in
3 Rhythms
CF
Romance, from 3 Tunes in 3 Rhythms
CF
Valse Capricietto, from 3 Tunes in
3 Rhythms
CF
SMYTH, ETHEL (1858-1944)
Quartet in e
UE 5352   score only
SONG OF THE VOLGA BOATMEN
(Pochon) CF
(SONTAG, WESLEY)
Introduction to string quartet playing
Fox   score included; for contents
see title
SOWERBY, LEO (1895-   )
Serenade in G
SPAM   score included
SPALDING, [EVA RUTH]
Quartets, 2
Sal   scores only; published separately
SPELMAN, TIMOTHY (1891-   )
*Five Whimsical Serenades
Ches
SPOHR, LUDWIG (1784-1859)
*Quartets, 2, in E flat and D,
Op. 15, Nos. 1 and 2
(Leinert) Baer 2305
*Quartet in E flat, Op. 29, No. 1
(Leinert) Baer 2308
STAMITZ, KARL (1745-1801)
Quartet No. 1 in C
(Silzer) ZM (Pet No. ZM359)
Quartet in A, Op. 4, No. 6
(Ott) LEU   score included
Quartet in B flat, Op. 11
SIM
Quartet in C, Orchestral
(Mönkemeyer) SCH   score only
*Quartetto Concertante in G
(Mönkemeyer) SCH   vln 3 may be
substituted for vla
(STANTON, W.K.)
Carols
Oxf   for rent; for contents see title
STAR-SPANGLED BANNER
(Shulman) GS
STARER, ROBERT (1924-   )
Quartet
Mercury
STEIN, LEON (1910-   )
Quartet
CFE   score included
Quartet No. 2
CFE   score included
STENHAMMAR, WILHELM (1871-1927)
Quartet No. 3, Op. 18
WH
*Quartet No. 4 in a, Op. 25
WH 1351a
*Quartet No. 5 in C, "Serenad"
Gehrmans

*Quartet No. 6 in d, Op. 35
Nordiska
STERNBERG, ERICH (1898-   )
*Quartet No. 1, with mezzo-soprano
IMP   text in Hebrew and English
STEVENS, BERNARD (1916-   )
*Theme and Variations, Op. 11
Leng (Mil No. L4063)
STEVENS, HALSEY (1908-   )
Nepdalszvit. Magyar Folk Songs
CFE   score included
Quartet No. 3
CFE   score included
STILL, WILLIAM GRANT (1895-   )
*Danzas de Panama, based on Panamanian
Folk Themes collected by E. Waldo
SMP
STILLMAN, MITYA (1892-1936)
*Quartet No. 7
Leeds
STONE, DAVID
*Miniature Quartet No. 1 in a
Nov
*Miniature Quartet No. 2 in d
Nov
STOUT, ALAN (1932-   )
Quartet No. 1, Op. 1
CFE   score included
Quartet No. 2
CFE   score included
Quartet No. 3, Op. 18
CFE   score included
Quartet No. 4, Op. 21
CFE   score included
Quartet No. 5, Op. 43
CFE   score included
Quartet No. 6, Op. 51
CFE   score included
Quartet No. 7
CFE   score included
Quartet No. 8, Op. 60
CFE   score included
Quartet No. 9, Op. 62, No. 1
CFE   score included
Quartet No. 10
CFE   score only
(STRASSER)
Classic and Modern String Quartet Album
CF AA24-25   2V   for contents see title
STRAUSS, RICHARD (1864-1949)
Quartet in A, Op. 2
UE 1002
STRAVINSKY, IGOR (1882-   )
*Concertino
WH 2359a
Double Canon
BH   score only
*Pieces, 3
BH
STRING MUSIC OF THE BAROQUE ERA
(Clarke) BMC   score included
for str quartet or str orch
Bach, J.S.: Badinerie
Corelli: Corrente in C
Corelli: Corrente in F
Corelli: Menuetto
Handel: Air
Handel: Gigue
Handel: Passacaile
Handel: Rejouissance, La
Purcell: Hornpipe and Air
Purcell: Largo from "Golden" sonata
Rameau: Gavotte
Telemann: Gigue

STRING QUARTET
   (Höckner) SIM 3V
     Vol 1: 14 easy movements by Haydn,
      Abel, Stamitz, Boccherini and others
     Vol 2: 6 easy quartets by Boccherini,
      Gossec, Kraus, Lang, Stamitz
     Vol 3: 5 easy quartets by Boccherini,
      Gassmann, Schwindel, Distler
STRING QUARTET ALBUM
   (Gruenberg) GS L263-4 2V
     Vol 1
      Beethoven: Adagio sostenuto, from
       Sonata, Op. 27, No. 2
      Chopin: Prelude in e
      Gluck: Gavotte, from Paride ed
       Elena
      Hiller: Zur Guitarre
      Leclair: Sarabande et tambourin
      Mascagni: Intermezzo, from
       Cavalleria Rusticana
      Mozart: Alla turca, from Sonata in
       A, K. 331
      Paderewski: Menuet
      Reber: Berceuse
      Thomas: Entr'acte, from Mignon
     Vol 2
      Bach: Prelude in b, from Well-
       tempered clavichord
      Godard: Canzonetta, from Concert
       romantique, Op. 35
      Kassmayer: Ungarisch Nos. 1, 2
      Raff: Tarantella
      Schubert: The Erlking
      Schubert: Menuet, from Op. 78
STRING QUARTET ALBUM
   EV
STRING TIME
   (Whistler & Hummel) Ru; pno ad lib;
    vln III may be substituted for vla;
    score included
STRINGFIELD, LAMAR (1897-   )
  An Old Bridge
   Leeds score included; d-b ad lib
STRUBE, GUSTAV (1867-1953)
  Elegy and Serenade
   BMC d-b ad lib
SUK, JOSEF (1874-1935)
  Meditation on an old Bohemian choral
   Kal
SUTER, ROBERT (1919-   )
  Quartet No. 1
   EDW
SWEELINCK, JAN PIETER (1562-1621)
  *Chromatic Fantasy
   (Sigtenhorst-Meyer) DN (Pet No. D197)
SZABÓ, FERENC (1902-   )
  Quartet
   Kul score only
SZÁNTÓ, [THEODOR (1877-1934)]
  Quartet. Suite of 4 Choreographic
   Pieces
   Sal score only
SZERVÁNSZKY, ENDRE (1912-   )
  Quartet No. 2
   Kul score only
SZYMANOWSKI, KAROL (1882-1937)
  Quartet in C, Op. 37
   UE Ph248 score only
  Quartet No. 2, Op. 56
   UE 1058
TAILLEFERRE, [GERMAINE (1892-   )]
  *Quatuor
   Dur

TANENBAUM, ELIAS (1924-   )
  Quartet No. 1
   CFE score included
  Quartet No. 2
   CFE score included
TANEYEV, SERGEY IVANOVITCH (1856-1915)
  Quartets Nos. 1-9 and 3 Fragments
   MZK 4V; score included
  *Quartet No. 6 in B flat, Op. 19
   Belaieff
TANSMAN, ALEXANDER (1897-   )
  *Quartet No. 2
   Senart
  *Quartet No. 3
   UE 8885
  *Quartet No. 4
   ESC
  Quartet No. 6
   ESC
  *Triptych
   ESC
TARANOV, G.
  Quartet No. 2, Op. 19
   MZK score included
TARDOS, [BELA (1910-   )]
  *Quartet
   Kul
TARTINI, GIUSEPPE (1692-1770)
  Andante
   EV
  Quartet No. 1 in D
   (Pente) Int score included
TATE, PHYLLIS (1911-   )
  *Quartet in F
   Oxf 25.902
TCHAIKOVSKY, PIOTR ILYITCH (1840-1893)
  Andante Cantabile, from Quartet Op. 11
   (Jockisch) CF
  Chamber Music, Vol. 31
   MZK score included
    Quartet in B. Unfinished
    Quartet No. 1, Op. 11
    Quartet No. 2, Op. 22
    Quartet No. 3, Op. 30
  *Quartet No. 1 in D, Op. 11
   Aug 7227
   Int
   Pet 3172A
  *Quartet No. 2 in F, Op. 22
   Pet 3172b
  *Quartet No. 3 in e flat, Op. 30
   Pet 3172C
TCHEREPNINE, ALEXANDER (1899-   )
  *Quatuor No. 2
   Dur
TELEMANN, GEORG PHILIPP (1681-1767)
  Quartet in A
   (Wolff) Baer HM108
TEMPLETON, ALEC (1909-   )
  Quartette No. 1 in d
   Templ for rent
TER-TATEVOSIAN, J.
  Quartet
   MZK score only
THÄRICHEN, WERNER (1921-   )
  Quartet, Op. 31
   BB score only
THIMAN, ERIC (1900-   )
  *Folksong Suite
   Aug
THOMPSON, RANDALL (1899-   )
  *Quartet No. 1 in d
   CF 03565

THOMSON, VIRGIL (1896-   )
*Quartet No. 1
BH
*Quartet No. 2
BH
TICHY
Quartet in b flat
Sal   score only
TIPPETT, MICHAEL (1905-   )
Quartet No. 2 in F sharp
SCH
Quartet No. 3
SCH
TOCH, ERNST (1887-   )
Dedication
Mil   for str quartet or str orch;
d-b ad lib; score included
*Quartet, Op. 70
Leeds
TOLDRÁ, EDUARDO (1895-   )
*Vistas al mar
UME
TOMASINI, LUIGI (1741-1808)
Quartet No. 1 in A, Op. 8
(Bonelli) ZA 4125
TOMKINS, THOMAS (1572-1656)
Alman a 4; with Fantasia a 4 by Ward
STB
TOMMASINI, VINCENZO (1878-1950)
*Quatuor No. 2
Senart
TREMBLAY, GEORGE (1911-   )
Quartet, In Memoriam
CFE   score only
TREW, ARTHUR
*Miniature Quartet
Nov
TSINTSADZE, [SULKHAN (1925-   )]
Quartet No. 2
MZK   min score only
Quartet No. 4
MZK   min score only
TURCHI, GUIDO (1916-   )
Concerto Breve
SZ
TURINA, JOAQUÍN (1882-1949)
Oración del torero, La
UME
Quartet
ESC
Talía, from Las Musas de Andalucia
UME   score only
TURKEY IN THE STRAW
(Pochon) CF
TURNER, ROBERT (1920-   )
*Quartet No. 2
CL
UHL, ALFRED (1909-   )
*Jubiläums-Quartett
DOB
*Quartet No. 1
OBV
URBANNER, ERICH
Quartet No. 2
DOB   score included
USMANBAS, [ILKAN (1921-   )]
Quartet
(Wooldridge) BH
VACHON, PIERRE (1731-1802)
Quartet in D
(Brown) STB
VAINBERG, [MOYSEY (1919-   )]
Quartet No. 4, Op. 20
MZK   min score only

VALEN, FARTEIN (1887-1952)
*Quartet
WH 2246
*Quartet, Op. 13
Norsk
VAN BAAREN, see Baaren
VAN DELDEN, see Delden
VAN DIEREN, see Dieren
VANDOR, I.
Quartet
SZ   score only
VAN DURME, J.
Quartet No. 5
CBDM   score included
VARIATIONS ON A RUSSIAN FOLK SONG[100]
Int
VAUGHAN WILLIAMS, RALPH (1872-1958)
*Hymn Tune Prelude on Song 13 of Gibbons
Oxf 27.906
*Quartet in a
Oxf 25.004
Quartet in g
Curwen   for rent
*VENDREDIS, LES[101]
Belaieff   2V
Vol 1
1. Preludio e fuga by Glazunov
2. Serenade by Artsibo_uchev
3. Polka by Sokolov, Glazunov and Liadov
4. Minuet by Wihtol
5. Canon by Sokolov
6. Berceuse by Osten Sacken
7. Mazurka by Liadov
8. Sarabande by Blumenfeld
9. Scherzo by Sokolov
Vol 2
1. Allegro by Rimsky-Korsakov
2. Sarabande by Liadov
3. Scherzo by Borodin
4. Fuga by Liadov
5. Mazurka by Sokolov
6. Courante by Glazunov
7. Polka by Kopylov
VERDI, GIUSEPPE (1813-1901)
*Quartet in e
Int
Mercury
Pet 4255
Ric 44912
SCH
VERESS, SÁNDOR (1907-   )
Quartet No. 1
SZ
Quartet No. 2
SZ
VERRALL, JOHN (1908-   )
Quartet No. 2
Val   score included
*Quartet No. 3
Pr
*Quartet No. 4
Pr
Quartet No. 5
CFE   score included
Quartet No. 7
CFE   score included
VILLA-LOBOS, HEITOR (1887-1959)
*Quartet No. 1
SMP

---

[100] International lists this under Glazunov, Lyadov, Rimsky-Korsakov, Skryabin "and others." It is probably Les Vendredis.

[101] Two sets of pieces written for performance at musical parties.

VILLA-LOBOS, HEITOR (cont.)
Quartet No. 2, Op. 56
ESC
Quartet No. 3
ESC
Quartet No. 4
AMP
Quartet No. 5
AMP
Quartet No. 6
AMP
Quartet No. 7
AMP
*Quartet No. 8
Ric 127589
*Quartet No. 9
SMP
*Quartet No. 10
SMP
Quartet No. 12
AMP
Quartet No. 14
ESC
VINCENT, JOHN (1902-   )
*Quartet
Mil
VIOTTI, GIOVANNI BATTISTA (1755-1824)
Concert Quartets, 3
ZA 3828
VITALI, GIOVANNI BATTISTA (c.1644-1692)
*Capriccio
(Bonelli) ZA 3696
VIVALDI, ANTONIO (c.1669-1741)
Quartets, 3
(Ghedini) Int   d-b ad lib
1. Sinfonia "Al Santo Sepolcro"
2. Concerto Madrigalesco
3. Sonata "Al Santo Sepolcro"
VLASOV, [VLADIMIR (1903-   )]
Quartet
MZK   min score only
VOSS, FRIEDRICH (1930-   )
Quartet, 1960
BRH   score only
VREULS, VICTOR (1876-1944)
*Quartet in F
Bosw
WAGENAAR, BERNARD (1894-   )
*Quartet No. 2
BH
Quartet No. 3
SPAM   score included
WAGNER, RICHARD (1813-1883)
Bridal Chorus, from Lohengrin
(Saenger) CF
Quartet Movement
(Abraham) Oxf 25.404   for rent
Vorspiel, Prelude to Lohengrin
(Saenger) CF
WAILLY, PAUL DE (1854-1933)
*Poème
RL
WALKER, ERNEST (1870-1949)
*Fantasia in D
Nov
WALTON, WILLIAM (1902-   )
*Quartet in a
Oxf 25.005
WARD, JOHN (17th century)
Fancy
STB
Fantasia a 4
STB
Fantasia a 4, see Tomkins: Alman a 4

WARNER, HARRY WALDO (1874-1945)
Phantasie Quartet
Nov
WASHBURN, ROBERT (1928-   )
Quartet
Oxf   in preparation
Suite for Strings
Oxf 92.701   for str quartet or str orch
WEBER, BEN (1916-   )
Lyric Piece
CFE   score only
Quartet No. 2, Op. 35
CFE   score included
WEBER, CARL MARIA VON (1786-1826)
Invitation to the Dance, Op. 65, orig for pno
(Weiss-Saenger-Buechner) CF
WEBERN, ANTON VON (1883-1945)
*Bagatelles, 6, Op. 9
UE 7576
*Movements, 5, Op. 5
UE 5889
*Quartet, Op. 28
UE 12399
WEIGL, KARL (1881-1949)
Quartet in A, Op. 4
UE 2929   score only
Quartet No. 2, for 2 vln, vla d'amore, vcl
CFE   score only
Quartet in C, Op. 31
UE 10794   score only
Quartet No. 7 in f
CFE   score included
Quartet No. 8 in d
CFE   score included
WEIGL, VALLY
Adagio
CFE   score included
Andante
CFE   score included
WEILL, KURT (1900-1950)
*Quartet, Op. 8
UE 7700
WEINBERG, JACOB (1879-1956)
Quartet, Op. 55
CF 03724
WEINER, LEO (1885-1960)
*Quartet No. 2, Op. 13
Kul
*Quartet No. 3, Op. 26
Kul
WELLESZ, EGON (1885-   )
*Quartet No. 4, Op. 28
UE 6504
Quartet No. 5, Op. 60
SCH
*Quartet No. 6, Op. 64
Leng (Mil No. L4059)
*Quartet No. 7, Op. 66
Leng (Mil No. L4060)
Quartet No. 8
Sik 518
WERNER, GREGOR JOSEPH (1695-1766)
Fugues, 6
Noet (Pet No. N6044)
WESLEY, CHARLES (1757-1834)
*Quartet No. 1 in F
Hin (Pet No. H411)
*Quartet No. 2 in D
Hin (Pet No. H412)
*Quartet No. 5 in B flat
Hin (Pet No. H415)
WESSTROM, ANDERS (c.1720-1781)
*Quartet in E
Gehrmans

(WHISTLER, HARVEY S. & HUMMEL,
    HERMAN A.)
  Ensembles for Strings
    Ru   pno ad lib; score included
  First Quartet Album
    Ru
  String Time
    Ru   pno ad lib; vln III may be
      substituted for vla; score included
WHITHORNE, EMERSON (1884-1958)
  *Greek Impressions
    Senart
  *Quartet
    BH
WICKENS, DENNIS
  *Miniature Quartet
    Nov
WIDDICOMBE, TREVOR
  *Miniature Quartet
    Nov
  Quartets, 3
    Curwen
WILKINSON, PHILIP (1929-   )
  *Miniature Quartet
    Nov
WILLIAMS, GERRARD (1888-1947)
  Quartet No. 2
    Curwen
  Traditional Tunes, 4
    Oxf 77.014   pno ad lib
WILSON, GEORGE BALCH
  Quartet in G
    ŞPAM   score included
WIREN, DAG (1905-   )
  *Quartet No. 2, Op. 9
    Nordiska
  *Quartet No. 3, Op. 18
    Nordiska
  *Quartet No. 4, Op. 28
    Gehrmans
WITKOWSKI, GEORGES-MARTIN (1867-1943)
  *Quatuor
    Dur
WOLF, HUGO (1860-1903)
  *Italian Serenade
    BB
    Int
WOLFF, CHRISTIAN (1934-   )
  Summer
    Pet 6501
WOLF-FERRARI, ERMANNO (1876-1948)
  Quartet in e, Op. 23
    LEU
WOLPERT, FRANZ ALFONS (1917-   )
  Andante, Op. 8, No. 3. Trauermusik
    BRH
WOOD, JOSEPH
  Quartet, 1961
    CFE   score included
  Quartet No. 2
    CFE   score only
WOOLLETT, HENRI (1864-1936)
  *Quatuor
    Senart
WORDSWORTH, WILLIAM (1908-   )
  *Quartet No. 1 in D, Op. 16
    Leng (Mil No. L4055)
  *Quartet No. 2 in B flat, Op. 20
    Leng (Mil No. L4070)
  *Quartet No. 3 in A, Op. 30
    Leng (Mil No. L4065)
  *Quartet No. 4 in a
    Leng (Mil No. L4075)

WYK, ARNOLD VAN (1916-   )
  *Elegies, 5
    BH
WYLIE, R.
  Quartet No. 3, Op. 17
    Cor ST10   score included
YERZAKOVICH, V.
  Quartet No. 2
    MZK   min score only
(YOUNG, PERCY M.)
  King James' Pleasure, Suite of 17th
      Century masque tunes
    Hin (Pet No. H719)   score included
  17th Century Suite, after Elizabethan
      Theatre Music
    Hin (Pet No. H204)   score included
YUN, I.
  Quartet No. 3
    BB   score only
ZANETI, GASPARO (17th century)
  Danses à 4 parties
    (Peyrot-Rebuffat) Senart 3120
ZANGER, G.
  Quartets for Beginners, 12
    VL
ZECHLIN, R.
  Quartet
    BRH
ZEISL, ERIC (1905-1959)
  *Quartet No. 2 in d
    DOB
ZIEHRER, C.M.
  In Love, see Losey: Romance
ZILLIG, WINFRIED (1905-   )
  *Quartet No. 1
    Baer 3473
  *Quartet No. 2
    Baer 3474
ZIPP, FRIEDRICH (1914-   )
  Quartet in C, Op. 25
    Noet   score only
ZOLOTAREV, [VASSILY (1873-   )]
  Quartet No. 6
    MZK   min score only

Quartets: String-Wind

ABEL, KARL FRIEDRICH (1723-1787)
  Quartet in A, Op. 12, No. 2, for fl,
      vln, vla, vcl
    GS
  Quartet in G, for fl, vln, vla or
      gamba, vcl
    SCH
ABT VOGLER, see Vogler, Georg Joseph
BACH, JOHANN CHRISTIAN (1735-1782)
  Quartet in C, Op. 8, No. 1, for fl or
      ob, vln, vla, vcl
    (Dameck) BB
BALLOU, ESTHER W.
  Fantasia Brevis, for ob, vln, vla, vcl
    CFE   score included
BENEDICT
  Quartet in d, Op. 21, for fl, vln, vla, vcl
    Mil   score included
BOATWRIGHT, HOWARD (1918-   )
  *Quartet, for clar, vln, vla, vcl
    Oxf 90.701
BORRIS, SIEGFRIED (1906-   )
  *Oboenquartett, Op. 17, No. 1, for ob,
      vln, vla, vcl
    Sirius

BRITTEN, BENJAMIN (1913-   )
*Phantasy Quartet, Op. 2, for ob, vln,
    vla, vcl
    BH
CANNABICH, [CHRISTIAN (1731-1798)]
    Quartet in G, for fl, vln, vla, vcl
    Noet (Pet No. N3248)
CAZDEN, NORMAN (1914-   )
    Quartet, Op. 23, for clar, vln, vla, vcl
    CFE   score included
CHEVREUILLE, RAYMOND (1901-   )
    Salon Music, Op. 49, for fl, vln, vla, vcl
    CBDM   score included
COLE, HUGO (1917-   )
*Quartet, for ob, vln, vla, vcl
    Nov
COOKE, ARNOLD (1906-   )
*Quartet, for ob, vln, vla, vcl
    Nov
CRUFT, ADRIAN (1921-   )
    Fantasy, for ob, vln, vla, vcl
    JWL (Mil No. W2301)   score included
CRUSELL, BERNHARD (1775-1838)
    Quartet No. 2 in E flat, for clar, vln,
    vla, vcl
    KN (Pet No. K27)
DANZI, [FRANZ (1763-1826)]
    Quartet in d, Op. 56, No. 2, for fl, vln,
    vla, vcl
    Noet (Pet No. N6052)
DAVID, THOMAS CHRISTIAN (1925-   )
    Flötenquartett, for fl, vln, vla, vcl
    EDW
DEVIENNE, FRANCOIS (1759-1803)
    Quartet in G, Op. 11, No. 1, for fl, vln,
    vla, vcl
    GS
DONATO, ANTHONY (1909-   )
    Drag and Run, for clar, 2 vln, vcl
    CP   score included
EDER, [HELMUT (1916-   )]
    Divertimento, for alto rec, trumpet in C,
    vln, bass rec or vcl
    Noet (Pet No. N796)
ETLER, ALVIN (1913-   )
    Quartet, for ob, clar, vla, bsn
    Val   score included
FINE, VIVIAN (1913-   )
    Capriccio, for ob, vln, vla, vcl
    CFE   score included
FUCHS, F.
    Little Suite, for fl, 2 vln, vla
    OBV   score included
GIARDINI, FELICE DE (1716-1796)
    Quartet, Op. 25, No. 3, for ob, vln, vla, vcl
    BRH
GRIESBACH, KARL RUDI
    Musik, for fl, vln, vla, vcl
    BRH
GÜRSCHING, ALBRECHT (1934-   )
    Quartet, for ob, vln, vla, vcl
    EDW
GYRING, ELIZABETH
    Fugues Nos. 1, 2, 6, 7, 8, 9, 10, 11, 12, 13,
    14, 15, for clar, vln, vla, vcl
    CFE   score included; published separately
GYROWETZ, ADALBERT (1763-1850)
    Notturno, No. 3, Op. 26, for fl, vln, vla, vcl
    ZM (Pet No. ZM356)
    Quartet in C, for fl, vln, vla, vcl
    Noet (Pet No. N3259)
HANSCHKE, HANS GERHARD
    Variations on a Children's Song, for fl,
    vln, vla or vln, vcl
    SCH

HAYDN, JOSEPH (1732-1809)
    "Mann und Weib", oder Der Geburtstag,
    for fl, vln, vla, vcl
    Tonger   score included
    Quartet in D, Op. 5, No. 1, for fl, vln,
    vla, vcl
    GS
    Quartet in G, Op. 5, No. 2, for fl, vln,
    vla, vcl
    GS
HAYDN, MICHAEL (1737-1806)
    Quartet in D, for fl, vln, vla, vcl
    LN (Pet No. R106)   score included
HENNESSY, SWAN (1866-1929)
    Celtic Pieces, 4, Op. 59, for English horn,
    vln, vla, vcl
    ESC
    Variations on a Six-Note Theme, Op. 58,
    for fl, vln, vla, vcl
    ESC
HINDEMITH, PAUL (1895-1963)
*Abendkonzert No. 2, from Plöner
    Musiktag, for fl, 2 vln, vcl
    SCH
*Abendkonzert No. 4, from Plöner
    Musiktag, for clar, vln, vla, vcl
    SCH
(HÖCKNER & MLYNARCZYK)
    Original Quartets by Old Masters, for fl or
    rec, vln, vla, vcl
    SIM
HOFFMEISTER, FRANZ ANTON (1754-1812)
    Quartet in c, Op. 16, No. 2, for fl, vln,
    vla, vcl
    Noet (Pet No. N6093)
HONEGGER, ARTHUR (1892-1955)
    Canon sur basse obstinée à 4 voix, from
    Trois Contrepoints,[102] for vln, vcl,
    piccolo, English horn
    WH 2694
HOROVITZ, JOSEPH (1926-   )
*Quartet, for ob, vln, vla, vcl
    Mil-L 81
HUMMEL, JOHANN (1778-1837)
    Quartet in E flat, for clar, vln, vla, vcl
    GS
HYE-KNUDSEN, JOHAN (1896-   )
*Quartet, Op. 3, for fl, ob/English horn,
    vln, vcl
    WH 2688a
JACOB, GORDON (1895-   )
*Quartet, for ob, vln, vla, vcl
    Nov
KAHN, ERICH ITOR (1905-1956)
    Chansons Populaires de la Bretagne, Sept,
    for fl, vln, clar, bsn
    CFE   score only
MALIPIERO, GIAN FRANCESCO (1882-   )
*Epodi e Giambi, for vln, ob, vla, bsn
    WH 3303a
MARTINO, DONALD (1931-   )
    Quartet, for clar, vln, vla, vcl
    CFE   score included
MIEG, PETER (1906-   )
    Divertimento, for ob, vln, vla, vcl
    EDW
MILNER, ANTHONY (1925-   )
*Quartet, for ob, vln, vla, vcl
    Nov
MLYNARCZYK, see Höckner & Mlynarczyk

---

[102] Trois Contrepoints: 1. Prélude à 2 voix, for ob and vcl;
2. Choral à 3 voix, for vln, vcl, English horn; 3. Canon sur
basse obstinée à 4 voix.

MOERAN, ERNEST JOHN (1894-1950)
  *Fantasy Quartet, for ob, vln, vla, vcl
    Ches
MOJSISOVICS, RODERICH VON (1877-1953)
  Serenade, Op. 70, for fl, vln, vla, vcl
    Krenn
MOZART, WOLFGANG AMADEUS (1756-1791)
  Andante, K.616, orig for mechanical organ,
    arr for fl, ob, vla, vcl
    (Goehr) SCH
  *Quartets, 3: K. 285, 285b, 298, for fl, vln,
    vla, vcl
    Pet 17A
  Quartets, 3, for fl, vln, vla, vcl
    Int
  Quartet in D, K.285, for fl, vln, vla, vcl
    BRH
  *Quartet in G, K. 285a, for fl, vln, vla, vcl
    (Einstein) Hin (Pet No. H18)
  Quartet in A, K.298, for fl, vln, vla, vcl
    BRH
  *Quartet in F, K. 370, for ob, vln, vla, vcl
    BH
    BRH
    Int
    Pet 17b
NOWAK, LIONEL (1911-   )
  Quartet, for ob, vln, vla, vcl
    CFE score included
ORIGINAL QUARTETS BY OLD MASTERS
    (Höckner-Mlynarczyk) SIM
    for fl or rec, vln, vla, vcl
PARK, S.
  Pastorale, for fl, 2 vln, vcl
    CP score included
PINKHAM, DANIEL (1923-   )
  Prelude, for fl, vln, vla, vcl
    CFE score only
PISK, PAUL (1893-   )
  Music, for vln, clar, vcl, bsn
    CFE score included
PITTALUGA, GUSTAVO (1906-   )
  *Ricercare, for vln with accompaniment
    of clar, bsn, trumpet
    Leduc
PLEYEL, IGNAZ (1757-1831)
  *Quartet, Op. 20, No. 1, for fl, vln, vla, vcl
    KS
  *Quartet, Op. 20, No. 2, for fl, vln, vla, vcl
    KS
  *Quartet, Op. 20, No. 3, for fl, vln, vla, vcl
    KS
RAASTED, NIELS OTTO (1888-   )
  Serenade, Op. 40, for fl, ob, vla, vcl
    Dansk 87 score only
RAINIER, PRIAULX (1903-   )
  Quanta, for ob, vln, vla, vcl
    SCH score only
RAMEAU, JEAN PHILIPPE (1683-1764)
  Tambourin, arr for ob, vln, vla, vcl
    (Urban) Mil
RAWSTHORNE, ALAN (1905-   )
  *Quartet, for clar, vln, vla, vcl
    Oxf 07.200
RIISAGER, KNUDAGE (1897-   )
  *Sonata, for fl, vln, clar, vcl
    WH 3261a
RÖTSCHER, KONRAD
  Divertimento, Op. 22, for fl, clar, vln, vcl
    BB
SCHROEDER, HERMANN
  *Quartet, Op. 38, for ob, vln, vla, vcl
    SCH

SCHUBERT, FRANZ (1797-1828)
  Cradle Song, arr for fl, vln, vla, vcl
    (Urban) Mil score included
SCHWINDL, FRIEDRICH (1737-1786)
  Quartet in G, for fl, vln, vla, vcl
    VW (Pet No. V48) score included
SEARLE, HUMPHREY (1915-   )
  Quartet, Op. 12, for clar, bsn, vln, vla
    LY (Pet No. LY133) score included
SHIELD, WILLIAM (1748-1829)
  Quartet in F, Op. 3, No. 2, for ob, vln,
    vla, vcl
    SCH
STAMITZ, KARL (1745-1801)
  Quartets, 2, for fl or ob or clar, vln, vla, vcl
    (Marx-Zetlin) MM
  Quartet in E flat, Op. 8, No. 4, for clar or ob,
    vln, vla, vcl
    Int
SWIFT, RICHARD
  Quartet, for clar, bsn, vln, vcl
    CFE score included
TROWBRIDGE, L.
  Pensively, for clar, vln, vla, vcl
    CP score included
VOGEL, WLADIMIR (1896-   )
  Variétudes, 12, for fl, clar, vln, vcl
    SZ
VOGLER, GEORG JOSEPH (1749-1814)
  Quartet in B flat, for fl, vln, vla, vcl
    Sik 512
WAGNER, JOSEPH (1900-   )
  *Theme and Variations, for fl, clar, vln, vcl
    SMP
WAILLY, PAUL DE (1854-1933)
  *Serenade, for fl, vln, vla, vcl
    RL
WENDLING, JOHANN BAPTIST (c.1720-1797)
  Quartet in G, Op. 10, No. 4, for fl, vln,
    vla, vcl
    (Bopp) NAG
WILDBERGER, JACQUES (1922-   )
  Quartetto, for fl, clar, vln, vcl
    EDW
WOLF, ERNST WILHELM (1735-1792)
  Quartet in G, for fl, ob, bsn, vcl
    Noet (Pet No. N6029)
WOOLLEN, RUSSELL (1923-   )
  Quartet, for fl, vln, vla, vcl
    CFE score included
WORDSWORTH, WILLIAM (1908-   )
  *Quartet, Op. 44, for ob, vln, vla, vcl
    Leng (Mil No. L5054)
WYNER, YEHUDI (1929-   )
  Passover Offering, for fl, clar, vcl,
    trombone
    CFE score included
ZIELCHE, HANS HINRICH (1741-1796)
  Quartet in G, for fl, 2 vln, vcl
    Noet (Pet No. N6030)

Quartets: 3 Violins, Piano

ALL THROUGH THE NIGHT
    (Harvey) VL 61
AMBROSE, R.S.
  One Sweetly Solemn Thought
    VL 44
ASCHER, JOSEPH (1829-1869)
  Alice Where Art Thou
    VL 49

BACH, JOHANN SEBASTIAN (1685-1750)
  Concerto in D, arr from Concerto in C
    for 3 claviers and orch
    Hug (Pet No. A11)
  Kommt, Seelen, dieser Tag and Jesu,
    Meines Glaubens Zier
    Hin (Pet No. H644)
BAYLY, THOMAS (1797-1839)
  Long Long Ago
    (Gernert) VL 98
BELIEVE ME IF ALL THOSE ENDEARING
    YOUNG CHARMS
    (Harvey) VL 62
BENNARD, GEORGE
  Old Rugged Cross
    VL 152
BEST, AGNES, see Palmer & Best
(BORNSCHEIN, FRANZ C.)
  Easy Classics for Ensemble Players
    BMC vla, vcl ad lib; for contents
      see title
BRAHMS, JOHANNES (1833-1897)
  Cradle Song
    (Kvelve) VL 162
  Valse, Op. 39, No. 15, orig for pno duet
    VL 155
CORELLI, ARCANGELO (1653-1713)
  Gigue
    Ed M
CORRETTE, MICHEL
  Allure, L'. Concerto comique No. 2
    (Peyrot-Rebuffat) Senart 3114
      vcl ad lib
  Margoton. Concerto comique No. 3
    (Peyrot-Rebuffat) Senart 3115
      vcl ad lib
  Servante au bon tabac, La
    (Peyrot-Rebuffat) Senart 2919
      vcl ad lib
  V'la c'que c'est qu' d'aller au bois
    (Peyrot-Rebuffat) Senart 2915
      vcl ad lib
COUNTRY GARDENS
  Lud
DANCLA, CHARLES (1817-1907)
  Easy and Brilliant Trios, 3, Op. 99
    CF
DOMERC, J.
  Symphonie concertante
    HL
DONT, JACQUES
  Bon Vivant, Etude No. 24
    (Barnes) Lud T-21084
DRINK TO ME ONLY WITH THINE EYES
    (Harvey) VL 60
EASY CLASSICS FOR ENSEMBLE PLAYERS
    (Bornschein) BMC; vla, vcl ad lib
      Bach: Minuet
      Beethoven: Ecossaise
      Handel: Sarabande
      Haydn: Austrian Hymn
      Mozart: Minuet, from Notebook, 1764
      Schubert: Melody
      Schumann: Song of the Reapers
FAURE, JEAN-BAPTISTE (1830-1914)
  Palms, orig for voice and pno
    VL 53
FINGER, GOTTFRIED (1660-1723)
  Sonata ottava, for 3 vln and Bc
    (Stevens) Nov
FLOTOW, FRIEDRICH (1812-1883)
  Last Rose of Summer, from Martha
    VL 125

FOSTER, STEPHEN (1826-1864)
  Old Black Joe
    VL 88
GABRIELI, GIOVANNI (c.1554-1612)
  Sonata
    EN (Pet No. EN3) vcl ad lib
  Sonata
    Int vcl ad lib
(GARDNER, SAMUEL)
  Familiar Melodies, see title under more
    than 1 instrumental combination
GEMINIANI, FRANCESCO (1687-1762)
  Trio
    Int
GHYS, HENRI (1839-1908)
  Amaryllis; with Country Gardens
    (Harris) Lud T-21077
GLUCK, CHRISTOPH WILLIBALD (1714-1787)
  Andante, from Orpheus
    VL 68
HANDEL, GEORG FRIEDRICH (1685-1759)
  Overture, from Messiah
    (Stoessel) CF
HAYDN, JOSEPH (1732-1809)
  Andante, from Symphony No. 6
    (Papini) CF vcl and d-b ad lib
  Emperor Variations, from String Quartet,
    Op. 76
    (Stoessel) CF
HELLMESBERGER, JOSEPH
  Papillons
    Int
  Serenade
    Int
HENKEL, HENRI
  Marche, Op. 64
    CF vcl and d-b ad lib
HOLLYOAK
  Welsh Suite
    Hin (Pet No. H579A)
HORROCKS, HERBERT
  Tunes for Three Violins, 5
    Oxf 29.005 vla, vcl ad lib
HUSITSKA
    (Harvey) VL 97
KENNEDY
  Star of the East
    (Harris) Lud T-21063
LOCATELLI, PIETRO (1695-1764)
  Aria
    Ed M
MAGANINI
  Milady's Fan
    Ed M
MARCH OF THE MEN OF HARLECH
    (Kvelve) VL 77
MOLLENHAUER, EDUARD (1827-1914)
  Impromptu
    CF
MOLLOY, JAMES (1837-1909)
  Love's Old Sweet Song
    VL 42
MOZART, WOLFGANG AMADEUS (1756-1791)
  Serenade, K.525, orig for str quintet
    (Stoessel) CF AS6
  Turkish March, from Sonata No. 9 in A
    CF vcl, d-b ad lib
MUFFAT
  Gigue
    Ed M
PACHELBEL, JOHANN (1653-1706)
  Kanon und Gigue
    KS vcl ad lib

PALMER, EDWINA & BEST, AGNES
Rhymes and Rhythms, for 2 or 3 vln
and pno
Oxf 23.111
PAPINI, GUIDO
Ballata
CF   vcl and d-b ad lib
PONCE, MANUEL MARÍA (1882-1948)
Estrellita
VL 131
PURCELL, HENRY (c.1659-1695)
Fantasia in Three Parts upon a Ground
Hin (Pet No. H220)   vcl or gamba ad lib
ROSSINI, GIOACCHINI (1792-1868)
Barber of Seville
(Ambrosio) CF
RUEGGER, CHARLOTTE
Fun for 4 strings
EV
Junior Fiddlers Three
MPH
SANTA LUCIA
(Harvey) VL 154
SCARLATTI, ALESSANDRO (1660-1725)
Quartet in F, for rec, 2 vln, pno or
3 vln, pno
Pet 4558   vcl ad lib
Quartettino
Pet 4559
SCHUBERT, FRANZ (1797-1828)
Cradle Song
(Kvelve) VL 161
SCHUMANN, C.
Joyful Summertide, Op. 17, No. 1
(Saenger) CF
STINE, MAURICE
Small Fry Melodies
(Isaac) CF 03734
TELEMANN, GEORG PHILIPP (1681-1767)
Quartet in G, for rec, ob, vln, pno or
3 vln, pno
Pet 4562   vcl ad lib
TOSELLI, ENRICO (1883-1926)
Serenade, Op. 6
BMC
VIVALDI, ANTONIO (c.1669-1741)
Concerto in F
(Bonelli) ZA 3725
(Medefind) Int
VOLGA BOAT SONG
(Harvey) VL 83
WAGNER, RICHARD (1813-1883)
Bridal Chorus, from Lohengrin
VL 36
WOLFERMANN, ALBERT
Alla Marcia, Op. 13, No. 1
CF
YRADIER, SEBASTIAN (1809-1865)
Paloma, La
VL 70

Quartets: 3 Cellos, Piano

CREVECOEUR, L.
Ronde des Elphants
ESC
POPPER, DAVID (1843-1913)
Requiem, Op. 66
Int

Quartets: 2 Violins, Viola, Piano

BEETHOVEN, LUDWIG VAN (1770-1827)
Adagio Cantabile, from Septet Op. 20
(Saenger) CF
Menuet No. 2 in G, orig for pno
(Saenger) CF
BIZET, GEORGES (1838-1875)
Adagietto
Ed M
BOHM, CARL
Zingara, La, Op. 102
(Saenger) CF
CORELLI, ARCANGELO (1653-1713)
Gavotte and Gigue
Ed M
DONIZETTI, GAETANO (1797-1848)
Sextet, from Lucia di Lammermoor
CF
DVORAK, ANTONIN (1841-1904)
Humoreske, Op. 101, No. 1, orig for pno
(Saenger) CF
FASCH, JOHANN FRIEDRICH (1688-1758)
Sonata in d
(Ruf) SCH   score included
FUX, JOHANN JOSEPH (1660-1741)
Tänze
(Kuntner) Moeck 1050   vcl ad lib
GABRIELI, GIOVANNI (c.1554-1612)
Sonata
Int   vcl ad lib
GOSSEC, FRANÇOIS-JOSEPH (1734-1829)
Gavotte
(Saenger) CF
GUILLEMAIN, LOUIS GABRIEL (1705-1770)
Conversation galante et amusante,
Op. 12, No. 1, for fl or vln, vln, vcl,
or vla, pno
(Klengel) BRH
HANDEL, GEORG FRIEDRICH (1685-1759)
Largo
(Saenger) CF
Overture, from Messiah
(Stoessel) CF
Movements for Strings, 4
Hin (Pet No. H276)   for contents
see 2 vln, pno
HAYDN, JOSEPH (1732-1809)
Emperor Variations, from String Quartet,
Op. 76
(Stoessel) CF
Quartet in G, Op. 5, No. 4
NAG   vcl ad lib
LOCATELLI, PIETRO (1695-1764)
Aria
Ed M
MASCAGNI, PIETRO (1863-1945)
Intermezzo Sinfonico, from Cavalleria
Rusticana
(Werner-Saenger) CF
MENDELSSOHN, FELIX (1809-1847)
Wedding March, from A Midsummer Night's
Dream
(Weiss) CF
MEYERBEER, GIACOMO (1791-1864)
Coronation March, from Le Prophète
CF
MIGOT, GEORGES (1891-   )
Paravent de laque, Le
Leduc

MOSZKOWSKI, MORITZ (1854-1925)
  Spanish Dance in C, Op. 12, No. 1,
    orig for pno duet
    (Scharwenka-Saenger) CF
MOZART, WOLFGANG AMADEUS (1756-1791)
  Ave, Verum Corpus
    (Moses-Tobani-Saenger) CF
  Serenade, K.525, orig for str quintet
    (Stoessel) CF AS6
PERGOLESI, GIOVANNI BATTISTA (1710-1736)
  Sicilian Air
    Ed M
POLDINI, EDUARD (1869-1957)
  Poupée Valsante
    CF
RACHMANINOFF, SERGEY (1873-1943)
  Vocalise, orig for voice
    Ed M
SCHUBERT, FRANZ (1797-1828)
  Marche Militaire, Op. 51, No. 1, orig
    for pno duet
    (Weiss) CF
STAMITZ
  Andantino
    Ed M
VERDI, GIUSEPPE (1813-1901)
  Quartet, from Rigoletto
    (Saenger) CF
VIVALDI, ANTONIO (c.1669-1741)
  Sonata a Quattro in E flat, "Al S.
    Sepolcro", F.XVI no. 2, for 2 vln,
    vla and Bc
    (Ephrikian) Ric PR267   score only
WAGNER, RICHARD (1813-1883)
  Bridal Chorus, from Lohengrin
    (Saenger) CF
  Vorspiel, Prelude to Lohengrin
    CF
WEBER, CARL MARIA VON (1786-1826)
  Invitation to the Dance, Op. 65, orig for pno
    (Weiss-Saenger) CF

Quartets: 2 Violins, Cello, Piano

BACH, JOHANN SEBASTIAN
  Ave Maria, see Gounod
BEETHOVEN, LUDWIG VAN (1770-1827)
  Adagio Cantabile, from Septet, Op. 20
    CF
  Menuet No. 2 in G, orig for pno
    (Saenger) CF
BIZET, GEORGES (1838-1875)
  Adagietto
    Ed M
BLON, see Von Blon
BOHM, CARL
  Zingara, La, Op. 102
    CF
CLASSICAL VIOLIN
  (Palaschko) SCH
CONWAY
  Playing Together, Bk. 3
    Paxton (Mil No. P2204)
CORELLI, ARCANGELO (1653-1713)
  Gavotte and Gigue
    Ed M
COUNTRY GARDENS
  (Ranger) CF
DONIZETTI, GAETANO (1797-1848)
  Sextet, from Lucia di Lammermoor
    CF
DRIGO, RICCARDO (1846-1930)
  Sérénade, from Les Millions d'Arlequin
    (Borch) CF

DVORAK, ANTONIN (1841-1904)
  Bagatelles, Op. 47
    Artia
    Int
    SIM
  Humoreske, Op. 101, No. 7, orig for pno
    (Saenger) CF
GLUCK, CHRISTOPH WILLIBALD (1714-1787)
  Iphigenia in Aulis, Overture
    (Weiss-Ambrosio-Skalmer) CF
GOSSEC, FRANÇOIS-JOSEPH (1734-1829)
  Gavotte
    (Saenger) CF
GOUNOD, CHARLES (1818-1893)
  Ave Maria, Méditation sur le premier
    prélude de J.S. Bach
    (Saenger-Buechner) CF   organ ad lib
GREENSLEEVES
  (Johanson) Willis
GUILLEMAIN, LOUIS GABRIEL (1705-1770)
  Conversation galante et amusante,
    Op. 12, No. 1, for fl or vln, vln, vcl,
    or vla, pno
    (Klengel) BRH
HANDEL, GEORG FRIEDRICH (1685-1759)
  Concerto a 4 No. 1 in d, for fl or vln,
    vln, vcl, pno
    (Zobeley) SCH   2nd vcl or d-b ad lib
  Concerto a 4 No. 2 in D
    (Zobeley) SCH   2nd vcl or d-b ad lib
  Largo
    (Saenger) CF
  Overture, from Messiah
    (Stoessel) CF
HAYDN, JOSEPH (1732-1809)
  Concerto. Divertimento
    (Lassen) SCH
  Emperor Variations, from String Quartet
    Op. 76
    (Stoessel) CF
LOEHLEIN, GEORG SIMON
  Concerto No. 1 in F, Op. 7
    (Glasenapp) BRH
LOSEY, F.H.
  Alita
    (Ambrosio) CF   simplified
MAGANINI
  Album for Strings
    Ed M
MENDELSSOHN, FELIX (1809-1847)
  Wedding March, from Midsummer Night's
    Dream
    (Weiss) CF
MEYERBEER, GIACOMO (1791-1864)
  Coronation March, from Le Prophète
    CF
MOFFAT, [ALFRED (1866-1950)]
  Jephthas' Daughter
    Leng (Mil No. L5058)
MOSZKOWSKI, MORITZ (1854-1925)
  Spanish Dance In C, Op. 12, No. 1, orig
    for pno duet
    (Scharwenka-Saenger) CF
MOZART, WOLFGANG AMADEUS (1756-1791)
  Ave, Verum Corpus
    (Moses-Tobani-Saenger) CF
  Serenade, K.525, orig for str quintet
    (Stoessel) AS6 CF
  Sonatas, 9, for organ, 2 vln, vcl
    (Dounias) Baer 4731 "Kirchensonaten"
    K. 67, 68, 69, 144, 145, 212, 224,
    225, 241
  Sonatas, 5, for organ, 2 vln, vcl
    (Schleifer) Baer 402 "Kirchensonaten"
    K. 244, 245, 274, 328, 336

MOZART, WOLFGANG AMADEUS (cont.)
Sonata No. 1 in E flat, K.67, for organ
2 vln, vcl
BRH   score only
Sonata No. 11 in G, K.274, for organ,
2 vln, and vcl
(Hafert) BRH
(PALASCHKO)
Classical Violin
SCH
PERGOLESI, GIOVANNI BATTISTA (1710-1736)
Sicilian Air
Ed M
POLDINI, EDUARD (1869-1957)
Poupée Valsante
CF
PURCELL, HENRY (c.1659-1695)
Slow Movement from 5th Sonata of 3 parts
(Simkins) Aug
RACHMANINOFF, SERGEY (1873-1943)
Vocalise, orig for voice
Ed M
RAFF, JOACHIM (1822-1882)
Declaration of Love, from String Quartet
Op. 192, No. 2
(Saenger) CF
REINKEN, JAN ADAM
see Trio Sonatas
ROSENMULLER, JOHANN (c.1620-1684)
Sonata No. 4 in C
LN (Pet No. R45)   2nd vcl or d-b ad lib
Sonata No. 5 in g
LN (Pet No. R46)   2nd vcl or d-b ad lib
Sonata No. 6 in F
LN (Pet No. R47)   2nd vcl or d-b ad lib
RUBBRA, EDMUND (1901-   )
Lyric Movement, Op. 24
Leng (Mil No. L4052)
SCHUBERT, FRANZ (1797-1828)
Ave Maria
(Borch) CF
Marche Militaire, Op. 51, No. 1, orig
for pno duet
(Weiss) CF
SMITH, EM
Dance Pantomime, from 3 Tunes in
3 Rhythms
CF
Romance, from 3 Tunes in 3 Rhythms
CF
Valse Capricietto, from 3 Tunes in
3 Rhythms
CF
STAMITZ, JOHANN
see Trio Sonatas
STAMITZ
Andantino
Ed M
TELEMANN, GEORG PHILIPP (1681-1767)
Quartet in D, for fl or vln, vln, vcl, pno
ZM (Pet No. ZM96)
Quartet in g, for fl or vln, vln, vcl
or gamba, pno
ZM (Pet No. ZM117)
VERDI, GIUSEPPE (1813-1901)
Quartet, from Rigoletto
(Saenger) CF
VIVALDI, ANTONIO (c.1669-1741)
Sonata in g
(Ghedini) Int
VON BLON, FRANZ (1861-1945)
Whispering Flowers
(Borch) CF

WAGNER, RICHARD (1813-1883)
Bridal Chorus, from Lohengrin
(Saenger) CF
Vorspiel. Prelude to Lohengrin
CF
WEBER, CARL MARIA VON (1786-1826)
Invitation to the Dance, Op. 65, orig for pno
(Weiss-Saenger-Buechner) CF
WIDDICOMBE, TREVOR
Ebford Suite
Chap-L

Quartets: Violin, Viola, Cello, Piano

ABSIL, JEAN (1893-   )
Fantasy Quartet, Op. 40
CBDM
Quartet, Op. 33
CBDM
BACH, JOHANN CHRISTIAN (1735-1782)
Quartet in G
SCH
BAX, ARNOLD (1883-1953)
Quartet in One Movement
Chap-L
BEETHOVEN, LUDWIG VAN (1770-1827)
Adagio Cantabile, from Septet, Op. 20
CF
Menuet No. 2 in G, orig for pno
(Saenger) CF
*Quartet in E flat, Op. 16[103]
Aug 7198
BRH
GS L1623
Int
Pet 294
Quartet No. 2 in D, Op. posth
BRH
Quartet No. 3 in C, Op. posth
BRH
BERNARD, ÉMILE (1843-1902)
Quatuor en ut mineur, Op. 50
Dur
BOËLLMANN, LÉON (1862-1897)
Quatuor, Op. 10
Haml
BOHM, CARL
Zingara, La, Danse Hongroise, Op. 102
CF
BONIS, [MÉLANIE (1858-1937)]
Quatuor, Op. 72
Haml
BRAHMS, JOHANNES (1833-1897)
*Quartet in g, Op. 25
BRH
GS L1624
Pet 3939A
*Quartet in A, Op. 26
BRH
GS L1625
Pet 3939b
*Quartet in c, Op. 60
BRH
GS L1626
Pet 3939C

---

[103] Op. 16 is published as a quintet for piano, oboe, clarinet, bassoon, horn or a quartet for piano, violin, viola, violoncello.

CASTILLON, ALEXIS DE (1838-1873)
  Quatuor, Op. 7
    Haml
CHAUSSON, ERNEST (1855-1899)
  Quartet in A, Op. 30
    Int
    RL
CONWAY
  Playing Together, Bk. 3
    Paxton (Mil No. P2204)
COPLAND, AARON (1900-   )
  *Quartet
    BH
DANIEL-LESUR, see Lesur
DAWE, MARGERY
  Travel Tunes
    Cramer
D'INDY, see Indy, d'
DONIZETTI, GAETANO (1797-1848)
  Sextet, from Lucia di Lammermoor
    CF
DUBOIS, THÉODORE (1837-1924)
  Quartet in a
    Heugel
DUPUIS, ALBERT (1877-   )
  Quatuor
    Senart
DVORAK, ANTONIN (1841-1904)
  Humoreske, Op. 101, No. 7, orig for pno
    (Saenger) CF
  *Quartet in D, Op. 23
    Artia
    LN (Pet No. R36)
  *Quartet in E flat, Op. 87
    Artia
    Int
    SIM
EVETT, ROBERT (1922-   )
  Quartet
    CFE
FAURÉ, GABRIEL (1845-1924)
  *Quartet in c, Op. 15
    Haml
    Int
  *Quartet in g, Op. 45
    Haml
    Int
FRANKEL, [BENJAMIN (1906-   )]
  Quartet, Op. 26
    Nov
FREED, ISADORE (1900-   )
  Triptych
    SPAM
FRUMERIE, GUNNAR DE (1908-   )
  Quartet
    Nordiska
GLUCK, CHRISTOPH WILLIBALD (1714-1787)
  Iphigenia in Aulis, Overture
    (Weiss-Ambrosio-Skalmer) CF
GOSSEC, FRANÇOIS-JOSEPH (1734-1829)
  Gavotte
    (Saenger) CF
HAHN, REYNALDO (1875-1947)
  Quartet No. 3 in G
    Heugel
HAMANN, ERICH (1898-   )
  Quartet, Op. 31
    DOB
  Quartet, Op. 35
    DOB
HANDEL, GEORG FRIEDRICH (1685-1759)
  Largo
    (Saenger) CF
  Overture, from Messiah
    (Stoessel) CF

HAYDN, JOSEPH (1732-1809)
  Emperor Variations, from String Quartet
    Op. 76
    (Stoessel) CF
HURLSTONE, WILLIAM YEATES (1876-1906)
  Quartet in e
    Curwen for rent
d'INDY, VINCENT (1851-1931)
  Quartet in a, Op. 7
    Dur
JONGEN, JOSEPH (1873-1953)
  Quatuor en mi bemol, Op. 23
    Dur
JONGEN, [LÉON (1885-   )]
  Divertissement on a theme by Haydn
    CBDM
KAHN, ROBERT (1865-1951)
  Quartet, Op. 41
    Birnbach
KATTNIGG, RUDOLF (1895-1955)
  Quartet No. 2 in e, Op. 4
    UE 7620
KLEMPERER, [OTTO (1885-   )]
  Quatuor
    Senart
KULLMANN, ALFRED
  Quatuor
    Senart
LABEY, [MARCEL (1875-   )]
  Quatuor
    Dur
LACOMBE, PAUL (1838-1927)
  Quatuor, Op. 101
    Haml
LEFEBVRE, CHARLES (1843-1917)
  Quatuor, Op. 42
    Haml
LEKEU, GUILLAUME (1870-1894)
  Quartet, unfinished
    RL
LELEU, JEANNE (1898-   )
  Quartet
    Heugel
LESUR, DANIEL (1908-   )
  Suite
    Amphion 140
LOEILLET, JEAN BAPTISTE (1680-1730)
  Sonata in b
    HL
    (Beon) Int
LOTTI, ANTONIO
  see Trio Sonatas
(LUTZ)
  My Violin Book
    SCH
MAGANINI
  Album for Strings
    Ed M
MARTINU, BOHUSLAV (1890-1959)
  Quartet No. 1
    AMP
MASCAGNI, PIETRO (1863-1945)
  Intermezzo Sinfonico, from Cavalleria
    Rusticana
    (Saenger) CF
MENDELSSOHN, FELIX (1809-1847)
  Quartets, 3: Op. 1, Op. 2, Op. 3
    Pet 1741
  Wedding March, from Midsummer Night's
    Dream
    (Weiss) CF
MEYERBEER, GIACOMO (1791-1864)
  Coronation March, from Le Prophète
    CF

MOSZKOWSKI, MORITZ (1854-1925)
  Spanish Dance in C, Op. 12, orig for pno duet
    (Scharwenka-Saenger) CF
MOZART, WOLFGANG AMADEUS (1756-1791)
  Ave, Verum Corpus
    (Moses-Tobani-Saenger) CF
  *Quartets, 2: K.478, K.493
    BMC
    Pet 272
  Quartet No. 1 in g, K.478
    Aug 7190
    BRH
  Quartet No. 2 in E flat, K.493
    Aug 7191
    BRH
  Serenade, K.525, orig for str quintet
    (Stoessel) CF AS6
MY VIOLIN BOOK
  (Lutz) SCH
OUR FAVORITES
  (Palaschko) SCH
PAGANINI, NICCOLÒ
  see Quartets with guitar
PALMER, ROBERT (1915-   )
  Quartet
    SPAM
POLDINI, EDUARD (1869-1957)
  Poupée Valsante
    CF
POOT, MARCEL (1901-   )
  Quartet
    ESC
QUINET, MARCEL (1915-   )
  Quartet
    CBDM
REGER, MAX (1873-1916)
  Quartet in a, Op. 133
    Pet 3977
REUCHSEL, AMÉDÉE (1875-   )
  Quatuor
    HL
ROGER-DUCASSE, JEAN (1873-1954)
  Quatuor en sol mineur
    Dur
RUBINSTEIN, ANTON (1829-1894)
  Quatuor, Op. 55[104]
    Haml
  Quatuor, Op. 66
    Haml
SAINT-SAENS, CAMILLE (1835-1921)
  Quartet in B flat, Op. 41
    Dur
SCHMITT, FLORENT (1870-1958)
  A tour d'anches, Op. 97
    Dur
  Hasards, Op. 96
    Dur
SCHUBERT, FRANZ (1797-1828)
  Adagio and Rondo in F
    Int
    Pet 1347 "Quartet in F"
  Marche Militaire, Op. 51, No. 1, orig for
    pno duet
    (Weiss) CF
SCHUMANN, ROBERT (1810-1856)
  *Quartet in E flat, Op. 47
    (Bauer) GS L1711
    BRH
    Int
    Pet 2380

SJÖBERG, CARL LEOPOLD (1861-1900)
  Quartet
    Gehrmans
SMITH, EM
  Dance Pantomime, from 3 Tunes in
    3 Rhythms
    CF
  Romance, from 3 Tunes in 3 Rhythms
    CF
  Valse Capricietto, from 3 Tunes in
    3 Rhythms
    CF
SORESINA, ALBERTO (1911-   )
  Ciaccona a variazione
    Ric 127617-8
STAMITZ
  Andantino
    Ed M
STRAUSS, RICHARD (1864-1949)
  Quartet in c, Op. 13
    Int
SURINACH, CARLOS (1915-   )
  Quartet
    Peer
TANEYEV, SERGEY (1856-1915)
  Quartet
    MZK
TANSMAN, ALEXANDER (1897-   )
  Suite-Divertissement
    ESC
TURINA, JOAQUIN (1882-1949)
  Quatuor en La mineur, Op. 67
    RL
VERDI, GIUSEPPE (1813-1901)
  Quartet, from Rigoletto
    (Saenger) CF
WAGNER, RICHARD (1813-1883)
  Bridal Chorus, from Lohengrin
    (Saenger) CF
  Vorspiel. Prelude to Lohengrin
    CF
WEBER, CARL MARIA VON (1786-1826)
  Invitation to the Dance, Op. 65, orig for pno
    (Weiss-Saenger-Buechner) CF
  Quartet, Op. 8
    Int
    Pet 2177
WIDDICOMBE, TREVOR
  Ebford Suite
    Chap-L
WIDOR, CHARLES-MARIE (1844-1937)
  Quatuor en la mineur, Op. 66
    Dur
WORDSWORTH, WILLIAM (1908-   )
  Quartet in d, Op. 36
    Leng (Mil No. L8051)

Quartets: String-Wind-Keyboard

BENTZON, NIELS VIGGO (1919-   )
  Mosaique Musicale, Op. 54, for fl, vln,
    vcl, pno
    WH 3912
BERKELEY, LENNOX (1903-   )
  Concertino, for rec, vla, vcl and
    harpsichord
    Ches
CARTER, ELLIOTT (1908-   )
  Sonata, for fl, ob, vcl, harpsichord
    AMP
CASELLA, ALFREDO (1883-1947)
  Sinfonia, for pno, clar, trumpet, vcl
    Carisch

---

[104] Op. 55 is also published as a quintet for piano, flute,
clarinet, horn, bassoon.

CASTÉRA, RENÉ D'AVEZAC DE (1873-1955)
Concert, for pno, vcl, fl, clar
RL
CLAFLIN, AVERY (1898-   )
Recitativo, Aria and Stretta, for horn, vla,
vcl, pno
CFE
DESHEVOV, [VLADIMIR (1889-   )]
Exotic Suite, Op. 13, for pno, ob, vln, vcl
MZK
DVORAK, ANTONIN (1841-1904)
Humoreske, Op. 101, No. 7, arr for
fl, 2 vln, pno
(Saenger) CF
Humoreske, Op. 101, No. 7, arr for
fl, vln, vcl, pno
(Saenger-Buechner) CF
FELDMAN, MORTON (1926-   )
Durations I, for vln, vcl, alto fl, pno
Pet 6901
FORTNER, WOLFGANG (1907-   )
*New-Delhi-Musik, for fl, vln, vcl,
harpsichord
SCH   score only
GNESSIN, MIKHAIL (1883-1957)
Little Pieces, 3, Op. 60, for pno, clar,
vln, vcl
MZK
GREEN, RAY (1909-   )
*Holiday for Four, for vla, clar, bsn, pno
AME
GREENSLEEVES
(Johanson) Willis   for fl or vln,
vln, vcl, pno
GUILLEMAIN, LOUIS GABRIEL (1705-1770)
Conversation galante et amusante,
Op. 12, No. 1, for fl or vln, vln,
vcl or vla, pno
(Klengel) BRH
HAUBIEL, CHARLES (1892-   )
Masks, from In Praise of Dance, for ob,
vln, vcl, pno
H Elkan
Partita, from In Praise of Dance, for
ob, vln, vcl, pno
H Elkan
HAYDN, JOSEPH (1732-1809)
Quartet in G, Op. 5, No. 4, for fl, vln,
vla, pno
NAG   vcl ad lib
HINDEMITH, PAUL (1895-1963)
Quartet, for clar, vln, vcl, pno
SCH
HOVHANESS, ALAN (1911-   )
Quartet No. 1, Op. 97, for fl, ob, vcl,
harpsichord
Pet 6434
Quartet No. 2, Op. 112, for fl, ob, vcl, pno
Pet 6436
HURNIK, [ILJA (1922-   )]
Sonata da Camera, for fl, ob, vcl, pno
Artia
JANITSCH, JOHANN GOTTLIEB (1708-1763)
Chamber Sonata, Op. 8, "Echo", for fl, ob
or vln or fl, vla or gamba, keyboard
(Wolff) BRH   vcl ad lib
KAMINSKI, HEINRICH (1886-1946)
Quartet, Op. 1B, for clar, vla, vcl, pno
UE 8333
MACBETH, ALLAN (1856-1910)
Love in Idleness, for fl, 2 vln, pno
(Saenger) CF
Love in Idleness, for fl, vln, vcl, pno
(Saenger) CF

MARTINU, BOHUSLAV (1890-1959)
Quartet, for ob, vln, vcl, pno
ESC
MAYUZUMI, TOSHIRO (1929-   )
Metamusic, for pno, vln, saxophone
and conductor
Pet 6357
MESSIAEN, OLIVIER (1908-   )
Quatuor pour la fin du Temps, for vln,
clar, vcl, pno
Dur
MICHAEL, EDWARD
Petite Suite Antique, for fl, vln, vcl, pno
CH (Pet No. C365)
MILHAUD, DARIUS
Variations on a theme of, see Townsend
MORTENSEN, OTTO (1907-   )
Quatuor Concertant, for fl, vln, vcl, pno
WH 3850a
NAUMANN, JOHANN GOTTLIEB (1741-1801)
Quartet in E flat, Op. 1, No. 5, for fl,
vln, vcl, pno
Sik 275
SAMMARTINI
Sonata in D, for fl, 2 vln, pno
Noet (Pet No. N1000)   vcl ad lib
SCHMITT, FLORENT (1870-1958)
Pour presque tous les temps, Op. 134,
for vln, fl, vcl, pno
Dur
STARER, ROBERT (1924-   )
Concertino, for 2 voices or 2 instruments
(ob or trumpet; bsn or trombone),
vln, pno
IMP   score included
TELEMANN, GEORG PHILIPP (1681-1767)
Concerto in E, orig for fl, ob d'amore,
vla d'amore and orch; arr for fl,
ob d'amore, vla d'amore and pno
Pet 5885
Quartet in b, for fl, vln, vcl, pno
NAG   2nd vcl ad lib
Quartet in D, for fl, vln, vcl, pno
ZM (Pet No. ZM96)
Quartet in e, from Tafelmusik, for vln,
fl, vcl, keyboard
(Seiffert) BRH
Quartet in e, for fl, vln, vcl, pno
NAG
Quartet in G, for fl, ob, vln, Bc
(Töttcher-Grebe) Sik 473
Quartet in G, for rec, ob, vln, pno
Pet 4562   vcl ad lib
Quartet in g, for alto rec, vln, vla, Bc
(Moeck-Callenberg) Moeck 1042
Quartet in g, for fl, vln, vcl or gamba, pno
ZM (Pet No. ZM117)
TOWNSEND, DOUGLAS (1921-   )
8 x 8, Op. 3, No. 1. Variations on a theme
of Milhaud, for soprano rec or fl or
piccolo, trumpet or clar or ob, vcl or
bsn, pno
Pet 6094
VIVALDI, ANTONIO (c.1669-1741)
Concerto, for fl, 2 vln, keyboard
(Schröder) Moeck 1079   vcl ad lib
WEBER, BEN (1916-   )
Serenade, Op. 39, for fl, vln, vcl, pno
CFE
Variations, Op. 11a, for pno, clar, vln, vcl
CFE
WEBERN, ANTON (1883-1945)
Quartet, Op. 22, for vln, clar, sax, pno
UE 10050   score only

Trio Sonatas:[105] 2 Violins, Keyboard, Cello ad lib

ABACO, EVARISTO FELICE DALL' (1675-1742)
Suite in g
Aug 5390
Trio Sonata in F, Op. 3, No. 2
VW (Pet No. V34)
ABEL, KARL FRIEDRICH (1723-1787)
Trio Sonata in C, for fl, vln, Bc
(Möbius) Moeck 1054
ALBICASTRO, [D.B.H. (1680-1750)]
Sonata in b, Op. 1, No. 3
VW (Pet No. V27)
ALBINONI, TOMASO (1671-1750)
Trio Sonatas, 3, Op. 1, Nos. 10-12
(Kolneder) SCH
Trio Sonata in a, Op. 1, No. 3
(Upmeyer) NAG
Trio Sonata in a, Op. 1, No. 6
OBV
Trio Sonata in g, Op. 8, No. 4a
(Schenk) OBV "Sonata da Chiesa"
Trio Sonata in B flat, Op. 8, No. 4b
(Schenk) OBV "Sonata da Camera"
AMALIE, PRINCESS OF PRUSSIA (1723-1787)
Trio in D
VW (Pet No. V96)
ANDRIEU, see D'Andrieu
ARNE, THOMAS AUGUSTINE (1710-1778)
Trio Sonata in A, Op. 3, No. 1
(Langley-Seiffert) BRH
Trio Sonata in G, Op. 3, No. 2
Hin (Pet No. H64)
Trio Sonata in E flat, Op. 3, No. 3
Hin (Pet No. H78)
Trio Sonata in f, Op. 3, No. 4
Hin (Pet No. H624)
Trio Sonata in D, Op. 3, No. 5
Hin (Pet No. H625)
Trio Sonata in e, Op. 3, No. 7
Hin (Pet No. H627)
Trio Sonata in e
Nov
ASPELMAYR, FRANZ (1728-1786)
Trio in D, Op. 1, No. 4
(Schenk) OBV
AVISON, CHARLES (1709-1770)
Sonata a tre in e
(Moffat) SIM
BACH, JOHANN CHRISTOPH FRIEDRICH
(1732-1795)
Sonata, for fl, vln, Bc
(Frotscher) Sik 366
BACH, JOHANN SEBASTIAN (1685-1750)[106]
Trio Sonatas, 4
(Landshoff) Pet 4203A,b 2V
Vol 1: No. 1 in C; No. 2 in G
Vol 2: No. 3 in G; No. 4 in c,
from Musical Offering
Trio Sonatas, 3: in C; in G; in c, from
Musical Offering
Pet 237   no separate bass part

Trio Sonatas, 2, S.1037, 1038
(David) BRH
Trio Sonata in d, S.1036
NAG
(Seiffert) Int
Trio Sonata in C, S.1037
SCH
(David) Int   no separate bass part
Trio Sonata in G
(Hermann) Int   no separate bass part
Trio Sonata in G, for fl, vln, Bc
Int   no separate bass part
Trio Sonata in B flat, orig in G for
2 fl and Bc
Pet 4563
Trio in c, from Musical Offering, for
fl, vln, Bc
(David) GS
(Seiffert) BRH
Int   no separate bass part
see also more than 1 instrumental
combination
Trio Sonata in g, for ob or vln, vla, Bc
(Hindermann) Hug (Pet No. A35)
BACH, KARL PHILIPP EMANUEL
(1714-1788)[107]
Trio Sonatas in F, 2
Pet 4288
Trio Sonata in A, for fl, vln, Bc
(Dürr) Moeck 1073
Trio Sonata in a, for fl, vln, Bc
(Dürr) Moeck 1072
Trio Sonata in B flat
(Schumann) LEU
Trio Sonata in B flat
Int
Trio Sonata in B flat
Pet 4237
Trio Sonata in b
ZM (Pet No. ZM118)
Trio Sonata in d, for fl, vln, Bc
(Dürr) Moeck 1074
Trio Sonata in E
ZM (Pet No. ZM154)   no separate
bass part
Trio Sonata in F, for 2 vla, Bc
(Brandts-Buys) SCH
Trio Sonata in G
(Franko-Riemann) GS L3
Trio Sonata in G
(Hinze-Reinhold) LEU
(Riemann) BRH
Trio Sonata in G, for fl, vln, Bc
Broe (Pet No. B645)
Trio Sonata in G
Int
see also Trios for fl, vla, pno
BACH, WILHELM FRIEDEMANN (1710-1784)
Sonata in B flat, for fl, vln, Bc
(Seiffert) Int
Sonata in B flat, for fl, vln, Bc
BRH
Sonata in D
ZM (Pet No. ZM94)   no separate bass part
Sonata in F
Broe (Pet No. B1)
BASSANI, GIOVANNI BATTISTA (c.1657-1716)
Sonata a tre in d, Op. 5, No. 2
ZA 4440

---

[105] Most of the music in this section can be played by 2 violins and a keyboard instrument, with cello or gamba ad lib. If any other combination is required the instrumentation is given immediately after the title. For additional information on the trio sonatas, see HOW TO USE THIS BOOK.

[106] Trio Sonatas listed in the thematic catalogue by W. Schmieder are:
S.1036, in d, for 2 vln and Bc
S.1037, in C, for 2 vln and Bc
S.1038, in G, for fl, vln and Bc
S.1039, in G, for 2 fl and Bc
S.1079, Musical Offering; No. 8 is a
Trio in c, for fl, vln and Bc

[107] K.P.E. Bach wrote trio sonatas for 2 violins and Bc, and for flute, violin and Bc. Without identifying numbers it is not possible to tell how many duplications are listed here. Most publishers consider the trios for flute and violin suitable for two violins also.

BASSANI, GIOVANNI BATTISTA (cont.)
Sonata a tre in A, Op. 5, No. 7
ZA 4441
Sonata a tre, Op. 5, No. 9
(Schenk) OBV
BENDA, [JIRI (1715-1752)]
Trio Sonata
Artia   no separate bass part
BOCCHERINI, LUIGI (1743-1805)
Sonata a 3 in c
(Moffat) SIM
BODINUS
Sonata in E flat, for 2 ob or fl, vln and Bc
VW (Pet No. V33)
BOISMORTIER, JOSEPH BODIN DE (1691-1755)
Gentillesses, 6
(Walter) Senart 5249-54
published separately
Sonata in e, Op. 37, No. 2, for fl or ob or vln,
gamba, Bc
(Ruf) Baer HM160
Trio in D, Op. 50, No. 6, for vln, vcl, Bc
(Ruyssen) NAG
BONONCINI, GIOVANNI MARIA (1642-1678)
Sonata a tre in d, Op. 1, No. 6
(Schenk) OBV
Sonata a tre, Op. 6, No. 9
MM   Photolith reproduction
BONPORTI, FRANCESCO ANTONIO
(1672-1749)
Sonata a tre in b, Op. 4, No. 2
(Schenk) OBV
Sonata a tre, Op. 4, No. 9
MM   Photolith reproduction
Sonata a tre in C
(Moffat) SIM
BOYCE, WILLIAM (1710-1779)
Trio Sonata No. 2 in F
Hin (Pet No. H55)
Trio Sonata No. 3 in A
(Jensen) Aug 7432
Trio Sonata No. 6 in B flat
Hin (Pet No. H733)
Trio Sonata No. 8 in E flat
Hin (Pet No. H641)
Trio Sonata No. 9 in C
Hin (Pet No. H642
Trio Sonata No. 11 in c
(Moffat) SIM
Trio Sonata No. 12 in G
Hin (Pet No. H643)
BRASOLINI, DOMENICO (18th century)
Sonata da Camera in G
WM (Pet No. WM33)
BUNS, BENEDICTUS (1642-1716)
Sonata in d, Op. 8, No. 3
Heuwek (Pet No. EH803)
BUONAMENTE, GIOVANNI BATTISTA
(? -1643)
Sonata, "La Monteverde"
(Stevens-Menuhin) Hin (Pet No. H680)
BUXTEHUDE, DIETRICH (c.1637-1707)
Trio Sonata in F, Op. 1, No. 1, for vln,
gamba or vcl, Bc
(Grusnick-Wenzinger) Baer 1151
(Peyrot-Rebuffat) Senart 2721
Trio Sonata in G, Op. 1, No. 2, for vln,
gamba or vcl, Bc
(Grusnick-Wenzinger) Baer 1152
(Peyrot-Rebuffat) Senart 2918
Trio Sonata in a, Op. 1, No. 3, for vln,
gamba or vcl, Bc
(Grusnick-Wenzinger) Baer 1153
SCH

Trio Sonata in B flat, Op. 1, No. 4, for
vln, gamba or vcl, Bc
(Grusnick-Wenzinger) Baer 1154
Trio Sonata in e, Op. 1, No. 7, for vln,
gamba or vcl, Bc
Int
KS
Trio Sonata in D, Op. 2, No. 2, for vln,
gamba or vcl, Bc
Int
KS
Trio Sonata in E, Op. 2, No. 6, for vln,
gamba or vcl, Bc
Int
NAG
Trio Sonata in D, for vln, gamba or vcl, Bc
(Döbereiner) BRH
CALDARA, ANTONIO (1670-1736)
Sonata a tre in B flat, Op. 1, No. 4
(Upmeyer) NAG
Sonata a tre in e, Op. 1, No. 5
(Schenk) OBV
Sonata a tre in c, Op. 1, No. 6
(Upmeyer) NAG
Sonata a tre, Op. 1, No. 7
MM   Photolith reproduction
Sonata a tre in b, Op. 1, No. 9
(Schenk) OBV
Sonata da Chiesa in b
VW (Pet No. V99)   no separate bass part
CAMERLOHER, PLACIDUS VON (1718-1782)
Sonatas, 4
SCH   2V
CAZZATI, MAURITO (c.1620-1677)
Capriccio a 3 in A, Op. 50, No. 29
"Il Guastavilani"
(Schenk) OBV
Trio Sonata in d, Op. 18, No. 9
(Danckert) Baer HM34
CLÉRAMBAULT, NICOLAS (1676-1749)
Sonate No. 7 en Mi mineur
(Peyrot-Rebuffat) Senart 266
Sonate en sol majeur
HL
COLISTA, LELIO (1629-1680)
Trio Sonata in A
(Wessely-Kropik) Baer HM172
Trio Sonata in D
(Kropik) OBV
CORBETT, WILLIAM (c.1669-1748)
Sonatas, 3, in G, C, d
Pet 4507
CORELLI, ARCANGELO (1653-1713)
Sonatas, 48, Op. 1-4
(Woehl) Baer 701-716   16V
Vol. 1-4: 12 Sonate da camera, Op. 2
Vol. 5-8: 12 Sonate da chiesa, Op. 3
Vol. 9-12: 12 Sonate da camera, Op. 4
Vol. 13-16: 12 Sonate da chiesa, Op. 1
Sonatas, 12, Op. 1
Int   4V
Sonatas, 2, from Op. 1
SCH
Sonatas, 12, Op. 2
Int   3V
Sonatas, 6, from Op. 1 and Op. 2
(Dolmetsch) Nov   2V "Trios"
Sonatas 3: Op. 2, Nos. 1, 5, 7
Pet 4567
Sonatas, 12, Op. 3
(Kolneder) SCH   4V
Sonata da Chiesa in b, Op. 3, No. 4
(Seiffert) Int

CORELLI, ARCANGELO (cont.)
Sonata da Chiesa, Op. 3, No. 5
(Erdlen) Sik 212
Sonata da Chiesa in e, Op. 3, No. 7
(Klengel) BRH
Sonatas, 12, Op. 4
(Kolneder) SCH   2V
Sonatas, 6, Op. 4, Nos. 1-6
(Jensen) Aug
Pet 3531
Sonatas, 6, from Op. 4
(Jensen) SCH
Sonatas, 6, from Op. 4
(Sitt) Int   no separate bass part
Sonatas da chiesa in g, Op. 1, No. 10 and
in d, Op. 3, No. 5
Pet 3876A
Sonata da chiesa in b, Op. 1, No. 6 and
Sonata da camera in d, Op. 2, No. 2
Pet 3876C
Sonatas da camera in e, Op. 2, No. 4 and
in B flat, Op. 4, No. 9
Pet 3876b
Sonata in b
(Peyrot-Rebuffat) Senart 2912
Sonata in B flat
(Peyrot-Rebuffat) Senart 2716
Sonata in C
(Moffat-Mlynarczyk) SIM
Sonata in D
(Peyrot-Rebuffat) Senart 2642
Sonata in d
(Moffat) SIM
Sonata in d
(Peyrot-Rebuffat) Senart 3117
Sonata in F
(Peyrot-Rebuffat) Senart 2658
COUPERIN, FRANCOIS (1668-1733)
Apothéose de Corelli
Int   no separate bass part
Apothéose de Lulli
(Marty) Dur
Astree, L'. Sonate en Sol mineur
(Peyrot-Rebuffat) Senart 2718
Impériale, L'. Sonata
Transatlantiques
Pucelle, La. Sonate en Mi mineur
(Peyrot-Rebuffat) Senart 265
Steinkerque, La. Sonate en Si bemol
(Peyrot-Rebuffat) Senart 2914
Visionnaire, La. Sonate en Ut mineur
(Peyrot-Rebuffat) Senart 2641
COUPERIN, LOUIS (c.1626-1661)
Symphonies, 2, for fl or vln or vla
d'amore, vcl or gamba, Bc
(Bouvet) ESC
DALL' ABACO, see Abaco
DANDRIEU, JEAN FRANCOIS (1682-1738)
Sonata No. 1 in d
Noet (Pet No. N1045)
Sonata, Op. 1, No. 6
(Schenk) OBV
Sonata, in e
HL
DEROSIER, NICOLAS (17th century)
Fuite du Roy d'Angleterre, La
(Dart) Oxf 70.735
ERBACH, FRIEDRICH KARL (1680-1731)
Divertissement melodieux in D
KS
ERLEBACH, PHILIPP HEINRICH (1657-1741)
Sonata No. 1 in D, for 2 vln, Bc; or vln,
gamba or vla, Bc
(Zobeley) Baer HM117

Sonata No. 3 in A, for 2 vln, Bc; or vln,
gamba or vla, Bc
(Zobeley) Baer HM118
Sonata in e, for vln, gamba or vcl, Bc
KS
FASCH, JOHANN FRIEDRICH (1688-1758)
Sonata a 3, Canon a 2
(Kranz) LEU
Trio in a
(Riemann) BRH
Trio in D
(Hausswald) NAG
Trio in D, for vln, vla, Bc
(Riemann) BRH
Trio in F
(Riemann) BRH
Trio in G
(Riemann) BRH
Trio in G
MT (Pet No. MV1228)
FESCH, WILLEM DE (1687-1761)
Sonatas, 3, Op. 12, Nos. 1-3
Heuwek (Pet No. EH802)
FONTANA, GIOVANNI BATTISTA
Sonata a 3 in e
(Schenk) OBV
FÖRSTER, CHRISTOPH (1693-1745)
Trio in B flat
KS
FRESCOBALDI, GIROLAMO (1583-1643)
Canzoni per Sonar, 5
(David) SCH
FUX, JOHANN JOSEPH (1660-1741)
Partiten, 2, in G and F
(Liess) Baer HM51
Partita a 3 in g
(Schenk) OBV
Sinfonia a 3
(Schenk) OBV
Sonata. Kanon, for 2 gamba or 2 vla, Bc
(Wolff) Baer HM30
Sonata a tre in d
Noet (Pet No. N3257)
Sonata pastorale a 3 in F
(Schenk) OBV
GABRIELLI, DOMENICO (c.1650-1690)
Balletto a 3 in A, Op. 1, No. 9
(Schenk) OBV
GASSMANN, FLORIAN (1729-1774)
Divertimento a 3 in C
(Schenk) OBV
GLUCK, CHRISTOPH WILLIBALD (1714-1787)
Trio No. 1 in C
(Beckmann) BRH
Trio No. 2 in g
(Beckmann) BRH
Int
Trio No. 3 in A
(Beckmann) BRH
Trio No. 4 in B flat
(Beckmann) BRH
Trio No. 5 in E flat
(Beckmann) BRH
Trio No. 6 in F
(Beckmann) BRH
VW (Pet No. V119)
Trio No. 7 in E
(Beckmann) BRH
Trio Sonata in F
(Moffatt) SIM
Trio Sonata in g
(Bouvet) ESC "Sonata in g"
Trio Sonata in g
(Möbius) NAG

GOLDBERG, JOHANN GOTTLIEB (1727-1756)
Trio in a
(Dürr) NAG
Trio in g
(Dürr) NAG
GRAUN, JOHANN GOTTLIEB (1703-1771)
Trio in c
(Riemann) BRH
Trio in F
(Riemann) BRH
Trio in F
ZM (Pet No. ZM347)
Trio in G
(Riemann) BRH
HACQUART, CHARLES (1640-1730)
Sonatas, 3, from Harmonia Parnassia
Broe (Pet No. B35)
HANDEL, GEORG FRIEDRICH (1685-1759)
Trio Sonata in c, Op. 2, No. 1
(Kolneder) SCH
Int   no separate bass part
Trio Sonata in g, Op. 2, No. 2
(Lenzewski) SCH
Int
Trio Sonata in F, Op. 2, No. 3
(Lenzewski) SCH
Int   no separate bass part
Pet 3951A   no separate bass part
Trio Sonata in B flat, Op. 2, No. 4
(Kolneder) SCH
Int   no separate bass part
Pet 3119b   no separate bass part
Trio Sonata in F, Op. 2, No. 5
(Krause) SCH
Int
Trio Sonata in g, Op. 2, No. 6
(Seiffert) BRH
(Willms) SCH
Int   no separate bass part
Pet 3119C   no separate bass part
Trio Sonata in g, Op. 2, No. 7
(Willms) SCH
Int   no separate bass part
Pet 3119A   no separate bass part
Trio Sonata in g, Op. 2, No. 8
(Barth) Int   no separate bass part
(Willms) SCH
Pet 3578   no separate bass part
Trio Sonata in E, Op. 2, No. 9
(Kolneder) SCH
Int   no separate bass part
Pet 3119D   no separate bass part
Trio Sonatas, 7, Op. 5
Pet 4630A,b,C   3V
Vol 1: Nos. 1-2 in A,D
Vol 2: Nos. 3-4 in e,G
Vol 3: Nos. 5-7 in g,F, B flat
Trio Sonata in A, Op. 5, No. 1
(Moffat) SIM
Int   no separate bass part
Trio Sonata in D, Op. 5, No. 2
(Moffat) SIM
Int   no separate bass part
Trio Sonata in e, Op. 5, No. 3
Int   no separate bass part
Trio Sonata in G, Op. 5, No. 4
Int   no separate bass part
Trio Sonata in g, Op. 5, No. 5
Int   no separate bass part
Trio Sonata in F, Op. 5, No. 6
(Roth) SCH
Int   no separate bass part

Trio Sonata in B flat, Op. 5, No. 7
(Moffat) SIM
Int   no separate bass part
Trio No. 7 in c, for fl, vln, Bc
(Seiffert) BRH[108]
Trio No. 8 in g
(Seiffert) BRH
Trio No. 9 in F
(Seiffert) BRH
Trio No. 14 in g
BRH
Trio No. 19 in G
(Seiffert) BRH
Trio Sonata in A
(Peyrot-Rebuffat) Senart 292
Trio Sonata in C
(Peyrot-Rebuffat) Senart 2724
Trio Sonata in D
(Peyrot-Rebuffat) Senart 3116
Trio Sonata in D
Int   no separate bass part
Trio Sonata in d
Int   no separate bass part
Trio Sonata in E flat
Int
Trio Sonata in F, for vln, alto rec, Bc
(Rodemann) NAG
Trio Sonata in g
(Peyrot-Rebuffat) Senart 2723
HASSE, JOHANN ADOLPH (1699-1783)
Trio Sonata in D
NAG
HAYDN, JOSEPH (1732-1809)
Sonatas, 6, Op. 8
Pet 4376A,b
Vol 1: Nos. 1-3 in E flat, G,b
Vol 2: Nos. 4-6 in E flat, G,A
HEINICHEN, JOHANN DAVID (1683-1729)
Trio Sonata in c, for ob or vln, gamba
or vla, Bc
MT (Pet No. MV1074)
HÖCKH, KARL (1707-1772)
Partita a 3 in B flat
(Schenk))OBV
HOFFMANN, LEOPOLD
Divertimento a 3 in C
(Schenk) OBV
HOLZBAUER, IGNAZ (1711-1783)
Sinfonia a 3
SCH
JACCHINI
Trio Sonata in G, Op. 5, No. 3
VW (Pet No. V40)
JENKINS, JOHN (1592-1678)
Fantasia in d, for vln, gamba or vla or
vcl, Bc
(Evans) SCH
Fantasy Suite No. 5 in C
STB
KEISER, REINHARD (1674-1739)
Trio Sonata No. 1 in D, for fl, vln, Bc
(Schenk) NAG
Trio Sonata No. 2 in G, for fl, vln, Bc
(Schenk) NAG
Trio Sonata No. 3 in D, for fl, vln, Bc
(Schenk) NAG
KREBS, JOHANN LUDWIG (1713-1780)
Trio in D
(Riemann) BRH

---

[108] All editions published by BRH are listed in catalogues
as "Chamber Trios."

KRIEGER, JOHANN PHILIPP (1649-1725)
  Trio Sonata in a, for vln, gamba, Bc
    NAG
  Trio Sonata in F, Op. 1, No. 3
    KS
  Trio Sonata in d, Op. 2, No. 2, for vln,
    gamba or vcl, cembalo
    KS
LAWES, WILLIAM (1602-1645)
  Fantasy Suite No. 5 in d
    STB
LECLAIR, JEAN MARIE (1697-1764)
  Trio Sonata in B flat
    (Moffat) SIM
  Trio Sonata in D, Op. 2, No. 8, for fl
    or vln, gamba or vcl, Bc
    (Bouvet) ESC
    (Döbereiner) SCH
  Trio Sonata in D, Op. 2, No. 8, for fl
    or vln, vla, Bc
    (Döbereiner) SCH
  Trio Sonata in D, Op. 2, No. 8, for fl
    or vln, vla or vcl, Bc
    (Eitner) BRH
  Trio Sonata No. 8, for flauto dolce, vcl
    or gamba, Bc
    (Höffer-v.Winterfeld) Sik 350
  Trio Sonata in d
    (Moffat) SIM
LEGRENZI, GIOVANNI (1626-1690)
  Trio Sonata in a, Op. 2, No. 13
    ZA 4442
  Trio Sonata in D, Op. 4, No. 1
    "La Bernarda"
    (Schenk) OBV
  Trio Sonata in D, Op. 10, No. 5
    WM (Pet No. WM34)
  Trio Sonata in d
    EN (Pet No. EN2)
LINICKE, JOHANN GEORG (c.1680-1730)
  Overture in C
    VW (Pet No. V41)
  Suites, 2
    MT (Pet No. MV1224)
LOCATELLI, PIETRO (1695-1764)
  Trio Sonata in G, Op. 3, No. 1
    (Riemann) BRH
    Int
  Trio Sonata in G, Op. 5, No. 1
    KS
  Trio Sonata in C, Op. 5, No. 4
    KS
  Trio Sonata in d, Op. 5, No. 5
    KS
  Trio Sonata in d
    (Moffat-Mlynarczyk) SIM
  Trio Sonata in G
    (Moffat-Mlynarczyk) SIM
LOEILLET, JEAN BAPTISTE (1680-1730)
  Sonata, Op. 2, No. 2, for rec or fl, ob
    or fl or vln, Bc
    Noet (Pet No. N1016)
  Sonata in D
    (Beon) Int   no separate bass part
    HL
  Sonata in G
    (Beon) Int   no separate bass part
    HL
LOTTI, ANTONIO (c.1667-1740)
  Sonata in G, for fl or vln, vcl or vla, Bc
    Int
  Sonata in G, for fl or vln, gamba or vcl, Bc
    ZM (Pet No. ZM130)

MARINI, BIAGIO (c.1595-1665)
  Trio Sonata in d, for vln, gamba or vcl, Bc
    (Danckert) Baer HM129
MASTERS OF THE BAROQUE
    Pet 4539
    5 pieces and trio sonatas by
    Becker, Buxtehude, Foerster,
    Reinken, Schop
MAZZAFERRATA, GIOVANNI BATTISTA
  Sonata a 3 in F, Op. 5, No. 6
    (Schenk) OBV
MIGALI, PIETRO (17th century)
  Trio Sonata in d, Op. 1, No. 4
    WM (Pet No. WM32)
MONDONVILLE, JEAN-JOSEPH (1711-1772)
  Sonate en Sol
    (Peyrot-Rebuffat) Senart 2657
MOZART, LEOPOLD (1719-1787)
  Sonata a 3 No. 4 in G
    (Schenk) OBV
MOZART, WOLFGANG AMADEUS
  Sonatas da Chiesa, see organ, 2 vln, vcl
PACHELBEL, JOHANN (1653-1706)
  Suites, 2, in F and c
    Int
PEPUSCH, JOHN CHRISTOPHER (1667-1752)
  Trio Sonatas, 6
    (Hoffmann-Erbrecht) BRH   2V
  Trio Sonata in a, for vln, gamba or vla, Bc
    (Hoffmann-Erbrecht) NAG
  Trio Sonata in C
    (Hausswald) SCH
  Trio Sonata in D
    KS
  Trio Sonata in F
    KS
  Trio Sonata in G
    KS
  Trio Sonata in g
    Pet 4556
PERGOLESI, GIOVANNI BATTISTA (1710-1736)
  Trio Sonatas, 2
    (Werner) NAG
  Trio Sonata No. 1 in G
    (Riemann) BRH
  Trio Sonata No. 3 in G
    Pet 4888A
  Trio Sonata No. 4 in B flat
    Pet 4888b
  Trio Sonata in C
    Pet 4557
  Trio Sonata in d
    (Schenk) OBV
PORPORA, NICOLA ANTONIO (1686-1768)
  Sinfonie da Camera, 4
    (Laccetti) Curci
  Sinfonia da Camera. Concerto,
    Op. 2, No. 4
    (Riemann) BRH
  Sinfonia da Camera in B flat, Op. 2, No. 6
    (Schenk) OBV
  Sinfonia da Camera in C
    SIM
PUGNANI, GAETANO (1731-1798)
  Sonata a tre in C, Op. 1, No. 3
    (Schenk) OBV
  Sonata a tre, Op. 1, No. 4
    MM   Photolith reproduction
PURCELL, DANIEL (c.1660-1717)
  Trio Sonata in d
    (Ruf) SCH
PURCELL, HENRY (c.1659-1695)
  Trio Sonatas Nos. 1 and 2, in g and B flat
    Pet 4649A

PURCELL, HENRY (cont.)
  Trio Sonatas Nos. 3 and 4, in a and in g,
    Chaconne
    Pet 4649b
  Trio Sonatas, 2, in E flat and in F, the
    Golden Sonata
    Pet 4242A
  Trio Sonatas, 2, in D and d
    Pet 4242B
  Trio Sonatas, 2
    (David) SCH "Sonnata's of 3 Parts"
  Trio Sonata No. 10 in A
    STB
  Trio Sonata in a
    Aug
  Trio Sonata in b
    Aug
  Trio Sonata in C
    Aug
  Trio Sonata in F, Golden Sonata
    BH realized by B. Britten
    (Jensen-Carse) Aug
    (Tippett-Bergmann) SCH
    Int no separate bass part
  Trio Sonata in G
    VW (Pet No. V46)
  Trio Sonata No. 1 in g
    (Dart) STB
  Triostücke
    (Just) SCH
QUANTZ, JOHANN JOACHIM (1697-1773)
  Trio Sonata in C, for alto rec or fl, vln
    or ob or tenor rec, Bc
    (Bergmann-Lefkovitch) SCH
  Trio Sonata in c
    ZM (Pet No. ZM95) no separate bass part
  Trio Sonata in D
    (Schroeder) BRH
  Trio Sonata in D
    FR (Pet No. F1) no separate bass part
  Trio Sonata in F, for vla d'amore or vln,
    fl or vln, Bc
    ZM (Pet No. ZM88)
RAVENSCROFT, JOHN (? -c.1708)
  Trio da Chiesa, Op. 1, No. 2
    (Riemann) BRH
REINKEN, JAN ADAM (1623-1722)
  Sonata No. 6 in A, from Hortus Musicus,
    for 2 vln, gamba or vla or vcl, Bc
    BRH
    KS "Triosuite"
ROMAN, JOHAN HELMICH (1694-1758)
  Trio Sonatas, 7
    (Vretblad) Gehrmans
  Trio Sonatas, 6
    (Vretblad) Gehrmans
ROSENMÜLLER, JOHANN (c.1620-1684)
  Sonata No. 1 in g
    LN (Pet No. R42)
    NAG
  Sonata No. 2 in e
    LN (Pet No. R43)
    (Saffe) NAG
  Sonata No. 3 in d, for vln, vcl or gamba, Bc
    LN (Pet No. R44)
RUGGIERI, G.M.
  Sonata da Chiesa in e, Op. 3, No. 1
    OBV
  Sonata da Chiesa in b, Op. 3, No. 2
    OBV
  Sonata da Chiesa in B flat, Op. 3, No. 3
    OBV
  Sonata da Chiesa in F, Op. 3, No. 4
    OBV

Sonata da Chiesa in g, Op. 3, No. 5
  OBV
Sonata da Chiesa in A, Op. 3, No. 6
  OBV
Sonata da Chiesa in a, Op. 3, No. 7
  OBV
Sonata da Chiesa in G, Op. 3, No. 8
  OBV
Sonata da Chiesa in d, Op. 3, No. 9
  OBV
Sonata da Chiesa in D, Op. 3, No. 10
  OBV
SACCHINI, ANTONIO (1730-1786)
  Trio Sonata in G, Op. 1
    (Riemann) BRH
SALZBURGER TRIOSONATA (c.1700)
  (Schenk) OBV
SAMMARTINI, GIOVANNI BATTISTA
    (1701-1775)
  Sonata in E flat, Op. 1, No. 3
    (Riemann) Int
SAMMARTINI, [GIUSEPPE (c.1693-c.1770)]
  Sonata a 3 in g
    (Moffat) SIM
SCHEIDT, SAMUEL (1587-1654)
  Symphonies, 15
    (Keller) SCH
SHERARD, JAMES
  Trio Sonata in c, Op. 2, No. 4
    (Tilmouth) STB
SONNLEITHNER, CHRISTOPH VON
    (1734-1786)
  Divertimento in E flat
    OBV
STAMITZ, JOHANN WENZEL ANTON
    (1717-1757)
  Orchestral Trio in C, Op. 1, No. 1, for
    2 vln, vcl, pno
    BRH
  Orchestral Trio in C, Op. 1, No. 1, for
    2 vln, vcl or d-b
    SCH pno and vla ad lib
  Orchestral Trio in A, Op. 1, No. 2
    (Riemann) BRH
  Orchestral Trio in F, Op. 1, No. 3
    (Riemann) BRH
  Orchestral Trio in D, Op. 1, No. 4
    (Riemann) BRH
  Orchestral Trio in B flat, Op. 1, No. 5 for
    2 vln, vcl or d-b
    SCH pno and vla ad lib
  Orchestral Trio in E, Op. 5, No. 3
    (Riemann) BRH
  Orchestral Trio No. 10 in C, Op. 9, No. 6
    (Riemann) BRH
  Sonata a 3 in G
    (Moffat) SIM
STAMITZ, KARL (1745-1801)
  Trio, Op. 14, No. 1, for fl, vln, Bc
    Int
    NAG
STÖLZEL, GOTTFRIED HEINRICH (1690-1749)
  Trio Sonata No. 2 in B flat
    (Bachmair) BRH
  Trio Sonata No. 5 in D
    (Bachmair) BRH
  Trio Sonata in e
    (Frotscher) BRH
  Trio Sonata in f
    (Osthoff) NAG
  Trio Sonata in G, for fl, vln, Bc
    WM (Pet No. WM31) no separate bass
    part
  Trio Sonata, for fl, vln, Bc
    (Frotscher) Sik 367

STÖLZEL, GOTTFRIED HEINRICH (cont.)
Trio Sonata, for fl, vln, Bc
(Hausswald) BRH
STRADELLA, ALESSANDRO (1642-1682)
Sinfonia a 3
(Kolneder) SCH
STRUNGK, NIKOLAUS ADAM (1640-1700)
Triosonate in d
KS
TARTINI, GIUSEPPE (1692-1770)
Trios, 3, in G, D and E
(Pente) Int   no separate bass part
Trios, 2, in F and D
(Pente) Int   no separate bass part
Trio Sonata in D, Op. 8, No. 6
(Schenk) OBV
Trio Sonata in D
(Dameck) BB
Trio Sonata in D
(Dameck) Int
TELEMANN, GEORG PHILIPP (1681-1767)
Concerto or Sonata, see vln, vcl, pno
Sonata Polonese No. 1, for vln, vla, Bc
NAG
Sonata Polonese No. 2
NAG
Trietti metodichi, 3, and 3 Scherzi
(Schneider) BRH   3V
Trio Sonatas, 6
(Kolneder) SCH   2V
Trio Sonata in A, for vln, vla, Bc
Int
Trio Sonata in A, for ob d'amore, vln, Bc
Sik 319
Trio Sonata in a, from Essercizii Musici
Pet 4560
Trio Sonata in a
Int
Trio Sonata in b, for fl or vln, vla and Bc
(Ruf) SCH
Trio Sonata in C, for rec, vln or rec, Bc
(Hoffmann) BRH
Trio Sonata in c, from Essercizii Musici
Pet 4561
Trio Sonata in c
Int
Trio Sonata in D
WM (Pet No. WM30)   no separate bass
part
Trio Sonata in E, for fl, vln, Bc
(Ermeler-Pasler) NAG
Trio Sonata in e
(Moffat) SIM
Trio in E flat, aus Tafelmusik I
(Hinnenthal) Baer 3536
Trio in E flat
(Riemann) BRH
Trio in E flat
Int
Trio in F, for fl or alto rec, vcl or vla or
gamba, Bc
(Upmeyer) NAG
Trio Sonata in g
(Ruf) SCH
TORELLI, GIUSEPPE (1658-1709)
Sonata a tre in D, for vln, vcl, Bc
(Bonelli) ZA
TUMA, FRANZ (1704-1774)
Partita a 3 in A
(Schenk) OBV
TURINI, FRANCESCO (1595-1656)
Sonata a tre
MM   Photolith reproduction

UCCELLINI, MARCO (c.1610- ?)
Sinfonia a 3, Op. 9, No. 7
(Schenk) OBV
Trio Sonata in c, Op. 4, No. 17
ZA 4443
Wedding of the Hen and the Cuckoo
VW (Pet No. V53)   no separate bass part
VALENTINE, ROBERT (c.1670-1730)
Trio Sonatas, 3, for 2 rec or fl, vln, Bc
LN (Pet No. R101)
VERACINI, ANTONIO
Sonata in c, Op. 1
(Jensen) Aug 7415
(Jensen) Int   no separate bass part
VIERDANCK, JOHANN (c.1610- ?)
Triosuite
KS
VITALI, GIOVANNI BATTISTA (c.1644-1692)
Sonata a 3 in d, Op. 2, No. 6
(Schenk) OBV
see also vln, vcl, pno
VIVALDI, ANTONIO (c.1669-1741)
Sonate da camera, 12, Op. 1
(Upmeyer) Baer 351-2   2V
Sonate en Sol mineur, Op. 1, No. 1
(Peyrot-Rebuffat) Senart 2717
Sonate en Mi mineur, Op. 1, No. 2
(Peyrot-Rebuffat) Senart 2720
Sonate en Ut mineur, Op. 1, No. 3
(Peyrot-Rebuffat) Senart 2913
Sonate en Mi majeur, Op. 1, No. 4
(Peyrot-Rebuffat) Senart 3118
Sonatas, 2, Op. 5, Nos. 5 and 6
(Upmeyer) NAG
Sonata in d
(Moffat) SIM
Sonata in e
(Moffat) SIM
Sonata in e
(Schenk) NAG
Sonata in F
(Ghedini) Int
Sonata in g
OBV
Sonata in G, F.XIII no. 1
(Olivieri) Ric PR273   score only
Sonata in B flat, F.XIII no. 2
(Malipiero) Ric PR268   score only
Sonata in F, F.XIII no. 3
(Malipiero) Ric PR344   score only
Sonata in F, F.XIII no. 4
(Malipiero) Ric PR345   score only
Sonata in g, F.XIII no. 17
(Malipiero) Ric PR1057   score only
Sonata in e, F.XIII no. 18
(Malipiero) Ric PR1058   score only
Sonata in C, F.XIII no. 19
(Malipiero) Ric PR1059   score only
Sonata in E, F.XIII no. 20
(Malipiero) Ric PR1060   score only
Sonata in F, F.XIII no. 21
(Malipiero) Ric PR1061   score only
Sonata in D, F.XIII no. 22
(Malipiero) Ric PR1062   score only
Sonata in E flat, F.XIII no. 23
(Malipiero) Ric PR1063   score only
Sonata in d, F.XIII no. 24
(Malipiero) Ric PR1064   score only
Sonata in A, F.XIII no. 25
(Malipiero) Ric PR1065   score only
Sonata in B flat, F.XIII no. 26
(Malipiero) Ric PR1066   score only

VIVALDI, ANTONIO (cont.)
  Sonata in b, F.XIII no. 27
    (Malipiero) Ric PR1067   score only
  Sonata in d, F.XIII no. 28, "La Follia"
    (Malipiero) Ric PR1068   score only
  Sonata in c, F.XVI no. 1, for vln, vcl,
    and Bc
    (Olivieri) Ric PR269   score only
WAGENSEIL, GEORG CHRISTOPH (1715-1777)
  Sonata a 3 in B flat, Op. 1, No. 3
    (Schenk) OBV
WERNER, GREGOR JOSEPH (1695-1766)
  December, from Musical Calendar
    VW (Pet No. V55)
  May, from Instrumental Calendar
    OBV
  October, from Musical Calendar
    VW (Pet No. V54)
YOUNG, WILLIAM (? -1671)
  Trio Sonata in D, for vln, gamba, Bc
    (Evans) SCH
  Trio Sonata in D, for vln, vla, Bc
    (Evans) SCH
ZACH, JOHANN (1699-1773)
  Sinfonien, 2
    (Gottron) Baer HM145
  see also 2 vln, vcl

Quartets Including Guitar

ALBERT, R
*Quartet in D, for vln, vla, vcl, guitar
  UME
HAYDN, JOSEPH (1732-1809)
  Quartet in D, for vln, vla, vcl, guitar
    (Behrend) BB
  Quartet in D, for vln, vla, vcl, guitar
    (Scheit) DOB   score included
  Quartet in G, Op. 5, No. 4, for fl or vln,
    vln, vla, guitar
    (Scheit) DOB   vcl ad lib; score included
PAGANINI, NICCOLO (1782-1840)
  Quartet in D, for vln, vla, vcl, guitar or
    keyboard
    (Mangeot) SCH
  Quartet No. 7 in E, for vln, vla, vcl,
    guitar
    ZM (Pet No. ZM191)
SCHUBERT, FRANZ (1797-1828)
  Quartet, after Notturno, Op. 21, by
    Matiegka, for fl, vla, vcl, guitar
    (Behrend) BB
    Pet 6078
VIVALDI, ANTONIO (c.1669-1741)
  Concerto in A, for vln, vla, vcl, guitar
    (Pujol) ESC   score included

Quartets Including Harp

HEINISCH
  Elegy, for vln, vcl, harp, harmonium
    ZM (Pet No. ZM718)

HOVHANESS, ALAN (1911-   )
*Upon enchanted ground, Op. 90, No. 1,
    for fl, vcl, harp, tam tam
    Pet 6046
KEMPTER, LOTHAR
  Romance, Op. 43, for vln, vla, vcl, harp
    ZM (Pet No. ZM152)
MACONCHY, ELIZABETH (1907-   )
*Reflections, for ob, clar, vln, harp
    Oxf 07.016
MIGOT, GEORGES (1891-   )
  Quatuor, for fl, vln, clar, harp
    Leduc
MULDER, ERNEST WILLEM (1898-   )
*Quartet, for ob, bsn, vcl, harp
    DN (Pet No. D54)
PROSPERI, [CARLO (1921-   )]
  Inventions, 4, for clar, vln, vla, harp
    SZ   score only
STAHL, ERNST
  Nocturne, Op. 66, for fl, vln, vcl, harp
    ZM (Pet No. ZM150)

Quartets: Unspecified Instruments

ALTE LIEDSÄTZE
  (Gerhardt) NAG   score included; for
    4 melody instruments; voice ad lib;
    12 old song settings from the
    Liederbuch of Peter Schöffer. 1513
BOISMORTIER, JOSEPH BODIN DE (1691-1755)
  Sonata in a, for 3 melody instruments and
    continuo
    (Ruf) SCH
  Sonata in e, for 3 melody instruments and
    continuo
    (Ruf) SCH
DEMANTIUS, J.C.
  Nürnberger Tanzbuch, for 4 or 5 instruments
    (Mönkemeyer) SCH   score only
MADDY, J.E. & GIDDINGS, T.P.
  Foursomes
    Willis; quartets for any combination of
    strings, woodwinds or brass
OLD-GERMAN DANCE MOVEMENTS, 22
  (Steglich) NAG   score included; for
    4 parts, with keyboard reduction
ROHWER, JENS (1914-   )
*Heptameron. Suite in 4 parts
    BRH
SCHEIDT, SAMUEL (1587-1654)
  Paduanen, 2, for 3 melody instruments and
    continuo
    NAG
VENEZIANISCHE CANZONEN (1608)
  (Mönkemeyer) SCH   score only; for
    any four part combination

MUSIC FOR
FIVE INSTRUMENTS

Quintets: 5 Viols

BRADE, WILLIAM
  see 2 vln, 2 vla, vcl
COPERARIO, GIOVANNI (c.1575-1626)
  Fantasy, "Chi Pue Mirarvi"
    (Dolmetsch-Ring) Hin (Pet No. H578A)
    pno or harpsichord or organ ad lib;
    score included
  Fantasy, see also 2 vln, 2 vla, vcl
DOWLAND, JOHN (1562-1626)
  Lachrimae
    (Giesbert) NAG score included
    see also 2 vln, vla, 2 vcl
  *Stücke, 5, für Streichmusik zu 5
    Stimmen
    (Pudelko) Baer 75
EAST, MICHAEL (c.1580-c.1648)
  Desperavi. Fancy in 5 parts, for
    2 soprano, alto or tenor, tenor,
    bass viols
    (N. Dolmetsch) SCH
FARRANT, DANIEL
  Four-Note Pavan, see 2 vln, 2 vla, vcl
FERRABOSCO, ALFONSO (1543-1588)
  Fantasy, "Vias Tuas"
    (Dolmetsch-Ring) Hin (Pet No. H578b)
    score included
  Fantasy on "In nomine"
    (Dolmetsch) SCH
  Four-Note Pavan, see 2 vln, 2 vla, vcl
GIBBONS, ORLANDO
  In Nomine, see 2 vln, 2 vla, vcl
IN NOMINE. ALTENGLISCHE KAMMERMUSIK
  (Stevens) Baer HM143 for 4 or 5 viols;
    score included
SCHEIDT, SAMUEL (1587-1654)
  *Canzon, "Bergamasca"
    (Garff) Baer HM96
  *Canzon super Intradam Aechiopicam
    (Garff) Baer HM140
  Suite in C
    (Ochs) NAG score included
SHORT ELIZABETHAN DANCE TUNES, see
  2 vln, 2 vla, vcl
STOLTZER, THOMAS (c.1475-1526)
  Octo tonorum Melodiae. Fantasies in
    5 parts
    (Gombosi) SCH score included
TOMKINS, THOMAS (1572-1656)
  Pavan a 5
    Hin (Pet No. H558b) score included

Quintets: 4 Violins, Cello

HANDEL, GEORG FRIEDRICH (1685-1759)
  Music for Strings, Vol. V, for 2 solo
    vln, 2 vln, vcl
    SCH score included

SCHEIDT, SAMUEL (1587-1654)
  Suite in C, for 3 vln, vla, vcl or 4 vln, vcl
    (Ochs) NAG score included; pno ad lib
WIDMANN
  Canzonas, Intradas and Gagliarda, for
    4 vln and vcl
    Noet (Pet No. N1023)

Quintets: 3 Violins, Viola, Cello

ALBRECHTSBERGER, JOHANN GEORG
    (1736-1809)
  Quintet in C
    Noet (Pet No. N6031)
DITTERSDORF, KARL DITTERS VON
    (1739-1799)
  Partitas, 3
    (Rhau) BRH
LOEFFLER, CHARLES MARTIN (1861-1935)
  *Quintet
    GS
REBEL, [JEAN FERRY (1661-1747)]
  Iris, L'. Sonata No. 3, for vln and str
    quartet
  Transatlantiques
SCHEIDT, SAMUEL (1587-1654)
  Suite in C, for 3 vln, vla, vcl or 4 vln, vcl
    (Ochs) NAG score included; pno ad lib
TOMKINS, THOMAS (1572-1656)
  Pavan a 5
    Hin (Pet No. H558b) score included

Quintets: 2 Violins, 2 Violas, Cello

AST, M.
  Quintet
    UE 1345
BAX, ARNOLD (1883-1953)
  Lyrical Interlude
    Chap-L
BEETHOVEN, LUDWIG VAN (1770-1827)
  *Quintets, 4
    Pet 599
      Op. 4 in E flat, after Octet,
        Op. 103 for 2 ob, 2 clar,
        2 horn, 2 bsn
      Op. 29 in C
      Op. 104 in c, after Trio, Op. 1, No. 3
        for pno, vln, vcl
      Op. 137 Fugue in D
  Quintet in E flat, Op. 4
    Int

BEETHOVEN, LUDWIG VAN (cont.)
  Quintet in C, Op. 29
    BRH
    Int
BOCCHERINI, LUIGI (1743-1805)
  Quintet in C, Op. 60, No. 1
    (Sabatini) DOB
  Quintet in B flat, Op. 60, No. 2
    (Sabatini) DOB
  Quintet in A, Op. 60, No. 3
    (Sabatini) DOB
  Quintet in G, Op. 60, No. 5
    (Sabatini) DOB
BRADE, WILLIAM (c.1560-1630)
  Paduanes, Galliardes, Canzones, Allemandes
    and Courantes
    Noet (Pet No. N1010)
BRAHMS, JOHANNES (1833-1897)
  *Quintet in F, Op. 88
    Int
    Pet 3905A
  *Quintet in G, Op. 111
    Int
    Pet 3905b
  *Quintet in b, Op. 115, for clar or vla, 2 vln,
    vla, vcl
    BRH
    Int
    Pet 3905C
BROWN, HAROLD
  Quintet
    CFE   score only
BRUCKNER, ANTON (1824-1896)
  Intermezzo, Op. posth.
    Int
  *Quintet in F
    BRH
    Int
    Pet 3842
COPERARIO, GIOVANNI (c.1570-1627)
  Fantasia a 5
    STB
DVORAK, ANTONIN (1841-1904)
  *Quintet in E flat, Op. 97
    Artia
    Int
    SIM
EAST, MICHAEL (c.1580-c.1648)
  Desperavi. Fancy in 5 parts
    (Dolmetsch) SCH
FARRANT, DANIEL
  Four-Note Pavan a 5; with Four-Note
    Pavan a 5 by Ferrabosco
    STB
(FELLOWES, E.)
  Short Elizabethan Dance Tunes, 8
    STB
FRIBOULET
  Suite sans fin, pour quintette à cordes
    Editions Francaises
GARDINER, [H. BALFOUR (1877-1950)]
  *Movement in c
    (Grainger) SCH
GIBBONS, ORLANDO (1583-1625)
  In Nomine a 5
    STB
GRANT, PARKS (1932-   )
  Poem, Op. 18
    CFE   score included
HAYDN, MICHAEL (1737-1806)
  Quintet in C, Op. 88
    Int
  *Quintet in C
    KS

*Quintet in F
  KS
*Quintet in G
  KS
KAMINSKI, HEINRICH (1886-1946)
  Quintet in f sharp
    UE 8942
MALZAT, JOHANN MICHAEL
  Quintet No. 5 in E flat
    (Senn) OBV   d-b ad lib
MARTINET, JEAN-LOUIS (1916-   )
  Leçon d'Anatomie, La, pour quintette
    à cordes
    Editions Francaises
MARTINU, BOHUSLAV (1890-1959)
  Quintet
    ESC
MENDELSSOHN, FELIX (1809-1847)
  Quintets, 2: Op. 18 and Op. 87
    Pet 1743
MILHAUD, DARIUS (1892-   )
  *Quintet No. 3
    Heugel
MOZART, WOLFGANG AMADEUS (1756-1791)
  Quintets, 10
    Pet 18-19   2V
    Vol 1
      K. 406, 515, 516, 593, 614
    Vol 2
      K. 46, 174, K.S.179
      K. 407 for horn, vln, 2 vla, vcl
      K. 581 for clar or vla, 2 vln
        vla, vcl
  *Quintet in c, K.406
    (Schmid) Baer 4721
  *Quintet in C, K.515
    (Schmid) Baer 4720
    BRH
  *Quintet in g, K. 516
    BRH
  *Quintet in A, K. 581, orig for clar, 2 vln,
    vla, vcl
    (Katims) Int
  *Quintet in D, K.593
    (Schmid) Baer 4706
    BRH
  *Quintet in E flat, K.614
    (Schmid) Baer 4707
    BRH
MYSLIVECEK, [JOSEPH (1737-1781)]
  Quintetto d'archi
    Artia   score included
NIGG, SERGE (1924-   )
  Musique Funèbre, pour quintette à
    cordes
    Editions Francaises
  Thème et Variations, pour quintette
    à cordes
    Editions Francaises
PETER, JOHN FREDERICK (1746-1813)
  *Quintets, 6
    (David) Pet 6098
REGER, MAX (1873-1916)
  Quintet in A, Op. 146, for clar or vla,
    2 vln, vla, vcl
    Pet 3997
ROSENMULLER, JOHANN
  see more than 1 instrumental combination
SCHILLINGS, MAX VON (1868-1933)
  *Quintet in E flat, Op. 32
    UE 5686
SESSIONS, ROGER (1896-   )
  *Quintet
    MK

SHORT ELIZABETHAN DANCE TUNES, 8
  (Fellowes) STB
SIEGL, OTTO (1896-   )
  Quintet in G
    DOB
STOLTZER, THOMAS (c.1475-1526)
  Octo tonorum Melodiae. Fantasies in 5 parts
    (Gombosi) SCH   score included
TIESSEN, HEINZ (1887-   )
  Quintet, Op. 32
    UE 8456
VAUGHAN WILLIAMS, RALPH (1872-1958)
  Phantasy Quintet
    STB
WINDING, AUGUST (1835-1899)
  *Quintet, Op. 23
    WH
YSAŸE, EUGÈNE (1858-1931)
  Quintet
    Cinedisc

Quintets: 2 Violins, Viola, 2 Cellos

BOCCHERINI, LUIGI (1743-1805)
  *Quintets, 6
    (Polo) Ric ER2171, 2173, 2175 3V
      Vol 1: No. 1 in E, Op. 13, No. 5
             No. 2 in d, Op. 20, No. 4
      Vol 2: No. 3 in C, Op. 37, No. 1
             No. 4 in D, Op. 37, No. 2
      Vol 3: No. 5 in a, Op. 47, No. 1
             No. 6 in E flat, Op. 47, No. 2
  Quintet in C
    (Lauterbach) Int
  Quintet in C
    (Lauterbach) Pet 2231
  Quintet in D, "Bird Sanctuary"
    Int
  Quintet in E flat, Op. 12, No. 2
    Int
  Quintettino in C. Procession of the military
    night watch in Madrid
    VW (Pet No. V32)   score included
CAZDEN, NORMAN (1914-   )
  Quintet
    CFE   score included
COPERARIO, GIOVANNI (c.1575-1626)
  Fantasy, "Chi Pue Mirarvi"
    (Dolmetsch-Ring) Hin (Pet No. H578A)
    pno or harpsichord or organ ad lib;
    score included
COUPERIN, FRANCOIS (1668-1733)
  *Pièces en concert, for vcl solo and 2 vln,
    vla, vcl
    (Bazelaire) Leduc
DITTERSDORF, KARL DITTERS VON
    (1739-1799)
  Quintet No. 6 in G
    Int   score included
DOWLAND, JOHN (1562-1626)
  *Lachrimae, or Seven Teares
    (Warlock) Oxf 27.002
    lute or keyboard ad lib
GLAZUNOV, ALEXANDER (1865-1936)
  Quintet in A, Op. 39
    Belaieff
HAMANN, ERICH (1898-   )
  Quintett
    DOB
MILHAUD, DARIUS (1892-   )
  *Quintet No. 4
    Heugel

MOURANT, WALTER (1910-   )
  Quintet
    CFE   score included
POSER, HANS (1907-   )
  Music for Five Strings, Op. 5
    Sik   for rent
SCHUBERT, FRANZ (1797-1828)
  *Quintet in C, Op. 163
    Int
    Pet 775
TANEYEV, SERGEY IVANOVITCH (1856-1915)
  *Quintet in G, Op. 14
    Belaieff
VIVALDI, ANTONIO (c.1669-1741)
  Sonates en Concert, 6, for vcl solo and
    2 vln, vla, vcl
    (d'Indy) Senart; published separately
WALDSTEIN, WILHELM (1897-   )
  Variations on a Theme of Mozart, Op. 11
    OBV
WINKLER, ALEXANDER (1865-1935)
  Quintet, Op. 29
    BH

Quintets: 2 Violins, Viola, Cello, Double-Bass

BASSETT, LESLIE (1923-   )
  Quintet
    CFE   score included
DVORAK, ANTONIN (1841-1904)
  *Quintet in G, Op. 77
    Artia
    Int
    SIM
JANÁČEK, LEOŠ (1854-1928)
  *Idyll
    Artia
LANCEN, S.
  Concerto, for d-b solo and 2 vln, vla, vcl
    Editions Francaises
MILHAUD, DARIUS (1892-   )
  *Quintet No. 2
    Heugel
MOZART, LEOPOLD (1719-1787)
  Little Symphony for Music Lovers
    Noet (Pet No. N6032)
MOZART, WOLFGANG AMADEUS
  Eine Kleine Nachtmusik. Serenade, K.525,
    see 2 vln, vla, vcl
REGER, MAX (1873-1916)
  *Lyrisches Andante
    Tonger
SIGNORINI
  Pezzi Poetici, 3
    Carisch   score included

Quintets: String-Wind

ADOLPHUS, MILTON
  Elegy, Op. 81, for clar, horn, vln, vla, vcl
    CFE   score only
AMES, WILLIAM (1901-   )
  Quintet, for clar in A, 2 vln, vla, vcl
    CFE   score included
BALLOU, ESTHER W.
  Fantasia Brevis II, for ob, 2 vln, vla, vcl
    CFE   score included
BARATI, GEORGE (1913-   )
  Quintet, for ob, 2 vln, vla, vcl
    CFE   score included

BENTZON, JORGEN (1897-1951)
*Variazioni interrotti, Op. 12, for clar,
    bsn, vln, vla, vcl
    WH 2748a
BLACKWOOD, EASLEY (1933-   )
*Concertino for five instruments, Op. 5, for
    fl, ob, vln, vla, vcl
    GS
BLISS, ARTHUR (1891-   )
Conversations, for vln, vla, vcl, fl, ob
    Curwen for rent
*Quintet, for clar, 2 vln, vla, vcl
    Nov
*Quintet, for ob, 2 vln, vla, vcl
    Oxf 07.002
BOCCHERINI, LUIGI (1743-1805)
*Quintet in E flat, Op. 21, No. 6, for fl,
    2 vln, vla, vcl
    (Haas) Nov
    Santis 957 score only
Quintets, 3, Op. 45, Nos. 4, 5, 6, for ob,
    2 vln, vla, vcl
    (Giegling) Sik 503
BOURGUIGNON, FRANCIS DE (1890-   )
Quintet, Op. 100, for ob, 2 vln, vla, vcl
    CBDM score included
BRAHMS, JOHANNES (1833-1897)
*Quintet in b, Op. 115, for clar, 2 vln,
    vla, vcl
    BH
    BRH
    Int
    .. Pet 3905C
BRÄUTIGAM, H.
*Fröhliche Musik, for fl, ob, 3 vln
    BRH
Tänzerische Spielmusik, for 2 fl or rec,
    2 vln, vcl
    (Wagner) SCH score included; d-b ad lib
BUTTERFIELD
Romanza, for horn, 2 vln, vla, vcl
    Hin (Pet No. H447b) d-b ad lib;
    score included
CASELLA, ALFREDO (1883-1947)
*Serenata, for clar, bsn, trumpet, vln, vcl
    UE 8823
CAZDEN, NORMAN (1914-   )
Quintet, Op. 74, for ob, 2 vln, vla, vcl
    CFE score included
COOKE, ARNOLD (1906-   )
Quintet, for clar, 2 vln, vla, vcl
    Oxf
DE BOURGUIGNON, see Bourguignon
DIAMOND, DAVID (1915-   )
*Quintet, for clar, 2 vla, 2 vcl
    SMP
DORATI, ANTAL (1906-   )
Notturno and Capriccio, for ob, 2 vln, vla,
    vcl
    Mil score included
DUSHKIN, DOROTHY (1903-   )
Quintet for Amanda, for ob, 2 vln, vla, vcl
    Val
FARNABY, GILES (c.1565-1640)
Variations, for fl, ob, clar, vla, vcl
    (Foster) Oxf 70.709
FELDMAN, MORTON (1926-   )
Pieces, 2, for clar, 2 vln, vla, vcl
    Pet 6920 score only
FINZI, GERALD (1901-1956)
*Interlude, for ob, 2 vln, vla, vcl
    BH
FRANCO, JOHAN (1908-   )
Divertimento, for fl, 2 vln, vla, vcl
    CFE score included

FRANKEL, BENJAMIN (1906-   )
*Quintet, for clar, 2 vln, vla, vcl
    Ches
FROMM-MICHAELS, ILSE (1888-   )
*Musica Larga, for clar, 2 vln, vla, vcl
    Sik 517
GINASTERA, ALBERTO (1916-   )
*Impresiones de la Puna, for fl, 2 vln, vla, vcl
    SMP
GOEB, ROGER (1914-   )
Quintet, for trombone, 2 vln, vla, vcl
    CFE score included
GOLDBERG, THEO (1921-   )
Quintet, Op. 7, for clar, 2 vln, vla, vcl
    BB
GOLZ, W.
For Flute and Muted Strings, for fl, 2 vln,
    vla, vcl
    CP score included
HAUFRECHT, HERBERT (1909-   )
Caprice, for clar, 2 vln, vla, vcl
    CFE score included
HAYDN, MICHAEL (1737-1806)
*Divertimento in B flat, for ob, bsn,
    vln, vla and bass
    (Strassl) DOB
*Divertimento in G, for fl, horn, vln vla,
    and bass
    (Strassl) DOB
*Quintetto, for vln, vla, clar, post horn, bsn
    Kul
HAYDN
Quintet, for vln, vla, vcl or d-b, 2 horns
    (Faulx) Brogneaux
HEIDEN, BERNHARD (1910-   )
Quintet, for horn, 2 vln, vla, vcl
    AMP
HEMEL, OSCAR VAN (1892-   )
*Quintet, for clar, 2 vln, vla, vcl
    DN (Pet No. D199)
HINDEMITH, PAUL (1895-1963)
Quintet, Op. 30, for clar, 2 vln, vla, vcl
    SCH
HOFFMEISTER, FRANZ ANTON (1754-1812)
Quintet in E flat, for horn, 2 vln, vla, vcl
    (Steinbeck) DOB
HÖLLER, KARL (1907-   )
Quintet, Op. 46, for clar, 2 vln, vla, vcl
    WM (Pet No. WM43)
JACOB, GORDON (1895-   )
*Quintet, for clar, 2 vln, vla, vcl
    Nov
KAY, ULYSSES (1917-   )
Quintet, for fl, 2 vln, vla, vcl
    CFE score included
KORNAUTH, EGON (1891-1959)
Quintet, Op. 33, for clar, 2 vln, vla, vcl
    DOB
KRAUS, J.
Quintet in D, for fl, 2 vln, vla, vcl
    (Lebermann) BRH
KUHLAU, FRIEDRICH (1786-1832)
*Quintet, Op. 51, No. 1, for fl, vln, 2 vla, vcl
    (Winkel) Dansk 221
LEUKAUF, ROBERT (1902-   )
Quintet, Op. 32a, for fl, ob, vln, vla, vcl
    DOB
LOKSHIN, A.
Quintet, for clar, 2 vln, vla, vcl
    MZK min score only
LOURIÉ, A.
Pastorale de la Volga, for ob, bsn, 2 vla, vcl
    ESC score only

MAASZ, GERHARD (1906-   )
  Divertimento, for fl or ob, 2 vln, vla, vcl
    Sik 407   score included
MCBRIDE, ROBERT (1911-   )
  Comfortable Flight, for English horn, 2 vln,
    vla, vcl
    CFE   score included
  *Quintet, for ob, 2 vln, vla, vcl
    GS
MACONCHY, ELIZABETH (1907-   )
  Quintet, for clar, 2 vln, vla, vcl
    Oxf   in preparation
MARTINU, BOHUSLAV (1890-1959)
  Serenade, for 2 clar, vln, vla, vcl
    ESC
MILHAUD, DARIUS (1892-   )
  *Rêves de Jacob, Les, for ob, vln, vla,
    vcl, d-b
    Heugel
MILLS, CHARLES (1914-   )
  Piece, for fl, rec, vln, vla, vcl
    CFE   score only
MOORE, DOUGLAS (1893-   )
  Quintet, for clar, 2 vln, vla, vcl
    CF 04210
MOZART, WOLFGANG AMADEUS (1756-1791)
  Adagio and Allegro, K.594, orig for mechan-
    ical organ; arr for 2 fl or 2 ob, vln,
    vla, vcl
    (Spiegl) Oxf 70.707   score included
  *Quintet in E flat, K. 407, for vln, 2 vla,
    horn, vcl
    Baer 4708
    BRH
    Int
    Pet 19D
  Quintet, K.516 Anh.91. Fragment for clar,
    2 vln, vla, vcl
    MM   Photolith reproduction
  *Quintet in A, K.581, for clar, 2 vln, vla, vcl
    Baer 4711
    BH
    BRH
    Int
    Kal
    Pet 19A
MÜLLER, SIGFRID WALTHER (1905-1946)
  Divertimento, Op. 13, for clar, 2 vln, vla, vcl
    BRH
PARRIS, ROBERT (1924-   )
  Quintet, for fl, ob, bsn, vln, vcl
    CFE   score included
PISTON, WALTER (1894-   )
  Quintet, for fl, 2 vln, vla, vcl
    AMP
PONSE, LUCTOR (1914-   )
  *Quintet, Op. 25, for fl, ob, vln, vla, vcl
    DN (Pet No. D193)
PORTER, QUINCY (1897-   )
  Quintet, for clar, 2 vln, vla, vcl
    CFE   score included
  Quintet, for fl, 2 vln, vla, vcl
    CFE   score included
PRESSER, W.
  Passacaglia, for clar, horn, vln, vla, vcl
    CP   score included
PROKOFIEV, SERGEY (1891-1953)
  *Quintet in g, Op. 39, for ob, clar, vln,
    vla, d-b
    BH
    Int
RAPHAEL, GÜNTER (1903-1960)
  Quintet, Op. 4. Serenade, for clar, 2 vln,
    vla, vcl
    SIM

REGER, MAX (1873-1916)
  *Quintet in A, Op. 146, for clar, 2 vln,
    vla, vcl
    Pet 3997
REICHA, ANTON (1770-1836)
  Quintet, Op. 107, for ob, 2 vln, vla, vcl
    MM   Xerox reproduction
REIZENSTEIN, FRANZ (1911-   )
  *Theme, Variations and Fugue, for clar,
    2 vln, vla, vcl
    Leng (Mil No. L5059)
RUBBRA, EDMUND (1901-   )
  *Buddha Suite, Op. 64, for fl, ob, vln,
    vla, vcl
    Leng (Mil No. L5050)
SMITH, JOHN SHAFFER
  Quintet, for ob or clar, 2 vln, vla, vcl
    CF W2238   score included
STEIN, LEON (1910-   )
  Quintet, for sax, 2 vln, vla, vcl
    CFE   score included
STOUT, ALAN (1932-   )
  Quintet, Op. 12, for clar, 2 vln, vla, vcl
    CFE   score included
STRATEGIER, HERMAN (1912-   )
  *Pieces, 3, for ob, 2 vln, vla, vcl
    DN (Pet No. D14b)
STRAUSS, RICHARD (1864-1949)
  Till Eulenspiegel einmal anders, arr for
    clar, bsn, horn, vln, d-b
    (Hasenoehrl) Pet 3191
STRAVINSKY, IGOR (1882-   )
  Pastorale. Chant sans paroles, for vln,
    ob, clar in A, English horn, bsn
    (Dushkin) SCH
SÜSSMAYR, FRANZ XAVER (1766-1803)
  Quintet, for fl, ob, vln, vla, vcl
    (Steinbeck) DOB
TARP, SVEND ERIK (1908-   )
  *Serenade, for fl, clar, vln, vla, vcl
    Dansk 91
THOMSON, VIRGIL (1896-   )
  Sonata da Chiesa, for clar in E flat,
    trumpet, vla, horn, trombone
    BH
TOSATTI, VIERI (1920-   )
  *Divertimento, for clar, bsn, vln, vla, vcl
    Ric   for rent
VAN VACTOR, DAVID (1906-   )
  Quintet, for fl, 2 vln, vla, vcl
    SPAM   score included
VAUGHAN WILLIAMS, RALPH (1872-1958)
  *Preludes, 3. Household Music for horn,
    2 vln, vla, vcl
    Oxf 25.001
WEBER, CARL MARIA VON (1786-1826)
  Introduction, Theme and Variations,
    for clar, 2 vln, vla, vcl
    (Kohl) BB
  Quintet in B flat, Op. 34, for clar, 2 vln,
    vla, vcl
    BRH
    Int
    LN (Pet No. R41)
WELLESZ, EGON (1885-   )
  Quintet, Op. 81, for clar, 2 vln, vla, vcl
    Noet   score only
WHITNEY, M.
  Adagio and Fugue, for fl, clar, vln,
    vla, vcl
    CP   score included
WORDSWORTH, WILLIAM (1908-   )
  Quintet, Op. 50, for clar, 2 vln, vla, vcl
    Leng (Mil No. L5056)

Quintets: 4 Violins, Piano

ALBENIZ, ISAAC (1860-1909)
Tango
(Ambrosio) CF vcl ad lib
ALESSIO, CAMILLO D'
Childhood Days
MK
Dance of the Little Clowns
CF
Flirtation
MK
Serenade to the Moon
CF
ALL THROUGH THE NIGHT
(Harvey) VL 61
BARNES, ETHEL (1880-1948)
Swing Song
(Ambrosio) CF vcl ad lib
BEETHOVEN, LUDWIG VAN (1770-1827)
Adagio Cantabile, from Septet, Op. 20
CF
Minuet No. 2 in G, orig for pno
(Saenger) CF
BELIEVE ME IF ALL THOSE ENDEARING
YOUNG CHARMS
(Harvey) VL 62
BENNARD, GEORGE
Old Rugged Cross
VL 152
BOHM, CARL
Zingara, La, Op. 102
CF
BOOK OF VIOLIN QUARTETS
(Watters & Pyle) Mil score included
BRAHMS, JOHANNES (1833-1897)
Cradle Song
VL 162
Famous Waltz
(Ambrosio) CF simpl
Valse, Op. 39, No. 15, orig for pno duet
VL 155
DRINK TO ME ONLY WITH THINE EYES
(Harvey) VL 60
DVOŘÁK, ANTONIN (1841-1904)
Humoreske, Op. 101, No. 7, orig for pno
(Saenger) CF
Largo, from the New World Symphony
(Ambrosio) CF simpl
EICHBERG, JULIUS (1824-1893)
Andante
BMC
Nocturne
CF
Rondo
CF
FOLK SONGS AND DANCES FOR VIOLIN
QUARTET
(Sontag) Fox
Adeste Fideles, Portuguese melody
Doctor Ironbeard, German song
French folk songs, 2
Fun game, Swedish folk dance
Go down Moses, Negro spiritual
John Anderson, Scottish song
Jolly young waterman, sailor song
Little Gardener, Bohemian dance
Lullaby, Chilean song
Noel, Spanish Christmas song
Norwegian dances, 2
Trip to town, Swedish folk dance
FOLK-SONGS AND FOLK-DANCES, 10
(Sontag) GS vcl ad lib
score included

(GARDNER, SAMUEL)
Familiar Melodies, see title under more
than 1 instru comb
GHYS, HENRI (1839-1908)
Amaryllis
(Ambrosio) CF simpl
GLUCK, CHRISTOPH WILLIBALD (1714-1787)
Andante from Orpheus
VL 68
GOSSEC, FRANCOIS-JOSEPH (1734-1829)
Gavotte
(Saenger) CF
GRIEG, EDVARD (1843-1907)
Norwegian Dance, Op. 35, No. 2
(Ambrosio) CF vcl ad lib
HANDEL, GEORG FRIEDRICH (1685-1759)
Largo
(Saenger) CF
HAYDN, JOSEPH (1732-1809)
Menuetto, from Military Symphony
(Simonis) MK
HAWTHORNE, ALICE (1827-1902)
Whispering Hope
(Stock) VL
HELLMESBERGER, JOSEPH
Romance, Op. 43, No. 2
Int
Tarantella, Op. 43, No. 1
Int
HUSITSKA
(Harvey) VL 97
KETELBEY
In a Monastery Garden
(MacLean) MPH
LACHMUND, CARL VALENTINE (1857-1928)
Lullaby, Op. 10, No. 1
CF
LEGRENZI, GIOVANNI (1626-1690)
Sonata, Op. 10, No. 1
(Fellerer) Baer HM83 vcl ad lib
LEMARE, EDWIN HENRY (1865-1934)
Andantino
(Ambrosio) CF simpl
LEO, LEONARDO (1694-1744)
Concerto in D
VW (Pet No. V62) vcl or d-b ad lib
LEVY, ELLIS
Marche Triomphale, Op. 21
CF
LOSEY, F.H.
Alita
(Ambrosio) CF vcl ad lib
MCCOY, EARL E.
Lights Out
CF
Mountain Sunset
CF
MARCH OF THE MEN OF HARLECH
(Kvelve) VL 77
MASCAGNI, PIETRO (1863-1945)
Intermezzo Sinfonico, from Cavalleria
Rusticana
(Saenger) CF
MAURER, LOUIS WILHELM (1789-1878)
Concertante in A, Op. 55
Pet 2908
MOSZKOWSKI, MORITZ (1854-1925)
Spanish Dance in C, Op. 12, No. 1,
orig for pno duet
CF
MOZART, WOLFGANG AMADEUS (1756-1791)
Ave, Verum Corpus
(Moses-Tobani) CF
Serenade in G, K.525, orig for str quintet
Aug 7074

PAPINI, GUIDO
  Hope March
    CF   vcl and d-b ad lib
POLDINI, EDUARD (1869-1957)
  Poupée Valsante
    CF
PYLE, see Watters & Pyle
ROSSINI, GIOACCHINO (1792-1868)
  Introduction to Semiramide; with Mermaid's
    Song and Hunters' Chorus by Weber
    (Harris) CF
RUEGGER, CHARLOTTE
  Concert Pieces, 6
    MPH   score included
SCHUBERT, FRANZ (1797-1828)
  By the Sea
    (Kvelve) VL
  Cradle Song
    VL 161
SEVERN, EDMUND (1862-1942)
  Blacksmith
    CF
  Brunette, La
    CF
  Carousel, from In Central Park
    CF
  Dancing Master
    CF
  Donkey Ride, from In Central Park
    CF
  Fun on the Mall, from In Central Park
    CF
  Gavotte Moderne
    CF
  Gypsy Prince
    CF
  May Pole Dance, from In Central Park
    CF
  Swan Boats, from In Central Park
    CF
  Tennis Players, from In Central Park
    CF
  Wings and Motors
    CF   vla and vcl ad lib
SMITH, EM
  Dance Pantomime, from 3 Tunes in 3
    Rhythms
    CF
  Romance, from 3 Tunes in 3 Rhythms
    CF
  Valse Capriccietto, from 3 Tunes in
    3 Rhythms
    CF
(SONTAG, WESLEY)
  Folk Songs and Dances for Violin Quartet
    Fox   for contents see title
  Folk-songs and Folk-dances, 10
    GS   vcl ad lib, score included
TCHAIKOVSKY, PIOTR ILYITCH (1840-1893)
  Adagio lamentoso, from Pathetique
    Symphony
    (Simonis) MK
  Andante, from Symphony No. 5
    (Ambrosio) CF   simpl
TELEMANN, GEORG PHILIPP (1681-1767)
  Concerto in G
    (Dameck) Int
TOSELLI, ENRICO (1883-1926)
  Serenade, Op. 6
    BMC   vcl ad lib
VIVALDI, ANTONIO (c.1669-1741)
  Concerto in b, Op. 3, No. 10
    (Bonelli) ZA 3698
    (Bouvet) ESC

Concerto
  (Bouvet-Gingold) Int
VOLGA BOAT SONG
  (Harvey) VL 83
WAGNER, RICHARD (1813-1883)
  Bridal Chorus, from Lohengrin
    CF
    VL 36
  Prelude to Lohengrin
    CF
(WATTERS & PYLE)
  Book of Violin Quartets
    Mil   score included
WEBER, CARL MARIA VON
  Hunters' Chorus from Der Freischütz, see
    Rossini: Introduction to Semiramide
  Mermaid's Song, from Oberon, see
    Rossini: Introduction to Semiramide
WHITE
  Jeunesse, for 2 or 4 vln and pno
    Gilles
YRADIER, SEBASTIAN (1809-1865)
  Paloma, La
    VL 70

Quintets: 3 Violins, Cello, Piano

AIRS IN PAIRS
  (Nicholls) STB   3V
STRING PLAYERS' VERY FIRST ENSEMBLE
  (Clarke) BMC
TOSELLI, ENRICO (1883-1926)
  Serenade, Op. 6
    BMC

Quintets: 2 Violins, Viola, Cello, Piano

AGAFONNIKOV, N.
  Quintet in D
    MZK   min score only
ALADOV, [NIKOLAI (1890-   )]
  Quintet, Op. 15
    MZK
ALESSIO, CAMILLO D'
  Serenade to the Moon
    CF
ALFANO, FRANCO (1876-1954)
  Quintet in A flat
    SZ
ALIABEV, [ALEXANDER (1787-1851)]
  Quintet
    MZK
BEETHOVEN, LUDWIG VAN (1770-1827)
  Adagio Cantabile, from Septet, Op. 20
    CF
  Menuet No. 2 in G, orig for pno
    (Saenger) CF
  Quintet in E flat, Op. 16, orig for pno, ob,
    clar, bsn, horn
    (Naumann) BRH
    Int
    see also vln, vla, vcl, pno
  Rondeau in B flat, Op. posth.
    Hin (Pet No. H596)
BENDA, J.
  Concerto
    Artia
BERWALD, FRANZ (1796-1868)
  Quintet No. 1 in c
    Gehrmans

BERWALD, FRANZ (cont.)
 Quintet No. 2 in A
  Gehrmans
BLOCH, ERNEST (1880-1959)
 Quintet
  GS
 Quintet No. 2
  Broude
BLOCKX, JAN (1851-1912)
 Quintet
  Heugel
BOCCHERINI, LUIGI (1743-1805)
 Quintet in B flat, Op. 57, No. 2
  GS
 Quintet, Op. 57, No. 6. Military Night
  Watch in Madrid
  Int
BOHM, CARL
 Zingara, La, Op. 102
  CF
BORODIN, ALEXANDER (1833-1887)
 Quintet in c
  BRH
BRAHMS, JOHANNES (1833-1897)
 *Quintet in f, Op. 34
  BRH
  GS L1646
  Pet 3660
BRIDGE, FRANK (1879-1941)
 Quintet
  Aug
BUTTERFIELD, J. & M.
 Easy Studies
  AMP
CAESAR, J.M.
 Ballet Suite
  (Schmid) NAG   d-b ad lib
CAPLET, ANDRÉ (1878-1925)
 Conte fantastique, for harp or pno, 2 vln,
  vla, vcl
  Dur   d-b ad lib
CARPENTER, JOHN ALDEN (1876-1951)
 Quintet
  GS
CASTILLON, ALEXIS DE (1838-1873)
 Quintette, Op. 1
  Dur
CELLIER, ALEXANDRE (1883-   )
 Quintette No. 2
  Senart
CHEVILLARD, [CAMILLE (1859-1923)]
 Quintette
  Dur
COLE, ULRIC (1905-   )
 Quintet
  SPAM
CRAS, [JEAN (1879-1932)]
 Quintette
  Senart
DIAMOND, DAVID (1915-   )
 Night Music, for accordion, 2 vln, vla,
  vcl
  SMP   score included
D'INDY, see Indy, d'
DOHNÁNYI, ERNST VON (1877-1960)
 Quintet in c, Op. 1
  DOB
  Int
 *Quintet in e flat, Op. 26
  SIM
DONIZETTI, GAETANO (1797-1848)
 Sextet, from Lucia di Lammermoor
  CF

DOWLAND, JOHN (1562-1626)
 Pavan; with Bonny Sweet Robin by
  Simpson
  STB
DUPONT, GABRIEL (1878-1914)
 Poème
  Heugel
DVORÁK, ANTONIN (1841-1904)
 Humoreske, Op. 101, No. 7, orig for pno
  (Saenger) CF
 Quintet in A, Op. 5
  Artia
 *Quintet in A, Op. 81
  Artia
  GS L1627
  Int
  SIM
ELGAR, EDWARD (1857-1934)
 Quintet in a, Op. 84
  Nov
EVETT, ROBERT (1922-   )
 Quintet
  CFE
FAURÉ, GABRIEL (1845-1924)
 Quintet in d, Op. 89
  GS
 Quintet No. 2, Op. 115
  Dur
FINNEY, ROSS LEE (1906-   )
 Quintet
  Pet 6457
FRANCK, CÉSAR (1822-1890)
 *Quintet in f
  BMC
  Haml
  Int
  Pet 3743
FRISKIN, JAMES (1886-   )
 Phantasy in f
  STB
 Quintet in c
  STB
GARGIULO, T.
 Quintetto
  Curci
GOEB, ROGER (1914-   )
 Quintet
  CFE
GOLUBEV, EVGENY (1910-   )
 Quintet, Op. 20
  MZK   score only
GOOSSENS, EUGÈNE (1893-1962)
 Quintet, Op. 23
  Ches
GOSSEC, FRANCOIS-JOSEPH (1734-1829)
 Gavotte
  (Saenger) CF
GRAINGER, PERCY (1882-1961)
 Harvest hymn
  GS
HAHN, REYNALDO (1875-1947)
 Quintet
  Heugel
HANDEL, GEORG FRIEDRICH (1685-1759)
 Largo
  (Saenger) CF
 Overture, from Messiah
  (Stoessel) CF
HARRIS, ROY (1898-   )
 Quintet
  GS
HARSÁNYI, TIBOR (1898-1954)
 Concertino
  Deiss

HAYDN, JOSEPH (1732-1809)
Emperor Variations, from String Quartet,
Op. 76
(Stoessel) CF
HOVHANESS, ALAN (1911-   )
Quintet, Op. 9
Pet 6568
HURÉ, JEAN (1877-1930)
Quintette
Mathot
d'INDY, VINCENT (1851-1931)
Quintette
Senart
IVES, CHARLES EDWARD (1874-1954)
Hallowe'en
BMP
Largo Risoluto No. 1
Peer
Largo Risoluto No. 2
Peer
JACOBI, FREDERICK (1891-1952)
*Hagiographa
AME for rent
KENNAN, KENT (1913-   )
Quintet
GS
KLEBANOV, [DMITRI (1907-   )]
Quintet
MZK
KORNAUTH, EGON (1891-1959)
Quintet, Op. 35a
DOB
KORNGOLD, ERICH WOLFGANG (1897-1957)
Quintet in E, Op. 15
SCH
LEFEBVRE, CHARLES EDOUARD (1843-1917)
Quintette, Op. 50
Haml
LE FLEM, PAUL (1881-   )
Quintette en mi mineur
HL
LEIGHTON, KENNETH (1929-   )
Quintet, Op. 34
Nov
MAGNARD, ALBÉRIC (1865-1914)
Quintette
RL
MALIPIERO, RICCARDO (1914-   )
Quintet
SZ
MANDL, RICHARD (1859-1918)
Quintet in G
UE 3350
MANÉN, JOAN (1883-   )
Quintet, Op. 18
UE 10764
MARSICK, [ARMAND (1877-1959)]
Stele "In Memoriam"
CBDM
MARTINU, BOHUSLAV (1890-1959)
Quintet
AMP
MASCAGNI, PIETRO (1863-1945)
Intermezzo Sinfonico, from Cavalleria
Rusticana
(Saenger) CF
MA-SZU-TS'UNG
Quintet
MZK
MEDTNER, NIKOLAI (1880-1951)
Quintet
ZM (Pet No. ZM6)

MENDELSSOHN, FELIX (1809-1847)
Wedding March, from Midsummer Night's
Dream
(Weiss) CF
MEYERBEER, GIACOMO (1791-1864)
Coronation March, from Le Prophète
CF
MIGOT, GEORGES (1891-   )
Quintette, Les Agrestides
Leduc
MILHAUD, DARIUS (1892-   )
Quintet No. 1
Heugel
MOSZKOWSKI, MORITZ (1854-1925)
Spanish Dance in C, Op. 12, No. 1, orig
for pno duet
(Schwarenka-Saenger) CF
MOZART, WOLFGANG AMADEUS (1756-1791)
Ave, Verum Corpus
(Moses-Tobani-Saenger) CF
Quintet in E flat, K.452, orig for ob, clar,
bsn, horn, pno
Int
Serenade, K.525, orig for str quintet
(Stoessel) CF AS6
Sinfonia Concertante, K.297b-Anh.9, orig
for ob, clar, horn, bsn, pno
Int
MUSHEL, G.
Suite
MZK
NIVERD, LUCIEN (1879-   )
Quintet
ESC
NOVÁK, VITEZSLAV (1870-1949)
Quintet, Op. 12
SIM
OGANESIAN, [EDGAR (1930-   )]
Quintet
MZK
PALMER, ROBERT (1915-   )
Quintet
Pet 6003
PERSICHETTI, VINCENT (1915-   )
Quintet
EV
PEZ, JOHANN CHRISTOPH (1664-1716)
Sonata a 4
(Schroeder) LEU d-b ad lib
PFITZNER, HANS (1869-1949)
Quintet in C, Op. 23
Pet 2923
PIERNÉ, GABRIEL (1863-1937)
Quintet, Op. 41
Haml
PILATI, [MARIO (1903-1938)]
Quintetto in re
Ric 121130
PISTON, WALTER (1894-   )
Quintet
AMP
POLDINI, EDUARD (1869-1957)
Poupée Valsante
CF
PURCELL, HENRY (c.1659-1695)
*Spielmusik zum Sommernachtstraum, for
4 viols and Bc or 2 vln, vla, vcl, pno
(Höckner) Baer HM50, 58 2V
REGER, MAX (1873-1916)
Quintet in c, Op. 64
Pet 3063
REIZENSTEIN, FRANZ (1911-   )
Quintet in D
Leng (Mil No. L8050)

RIEGGER, WALLINGFORD (1885-1961)
Quintet, Op. 47
AMP
ROBERTSON, LEROY (1896-   )
Quintet in a
SPAM
ROSENMÜLLER, JOHANN
see more than 1 instrumental combination
RÓZSA, MIKLÓS (1907-   )
Quintet, Op. 2
BRH
RUBINSTEIN, ANTON (1829-1894)
Quintette, Op. 99
Haml
SAINT-SAENS, CAMILLE (1835-1921)
Quintet, Op. 14
Haml
LEU
Wedding Cake. Caprice-valse, Op. 76
Dur
SCHMITT, FLORENT (1870-1958)
Andante et Scherzo, for 2 vln, vla, vcl,
harp or pno
Mathot
*Quintette
Mathot
SCHUBERT, FRANZ (1797-1828)
Marche Militaire, Op. 51, No. 1 orig
for pno duet
(Weiss) CF
SCHUMANN, ROBERT (1810-1856)
*Quintet in E flat, Op. 44
Aug 7166
BRH
GS L1648
Int
Pet 2381
SCOTT, CYRIL (1879-   )
Quintet
EKN
SHOSTAKOVITCH, DMITRI (1906-   )
Quintet, Op. 57
Int
Leeds
SIMIA, G.R. (1844-1924)
Quintette
RL
SIMPSON, THOMAS (17th century)
Bonny Sweet Robin, see Dowland: Pavan
Dances, 2
STB
SMITH, DAVID STANLEY (1877-1949)
Quintet
Oxf 92. 503
SMITH, EM
Dance Pantomime, from 3 Tunes in
3 Rhythms
CF
Romance, from 3 Tunes in 3 Rhythms
CF
Valse Capriccietto, from 3 Tunes in
3 Rhythms
CF
SONZOGNO, GIULIO CESARE (1906-   )
Pastorale, Allegro and Aria
SZ
SPRINGER, MAX (1877-1954)
Variations, 10, on a Swabish Folk Song
UE 7094
STEPAN, VACLAV (1889-1944)
Pruni Jara
RL

SZELL, GEORGE (1897-   )
Quintet in E, Op. 2
UE 3694
TCHEREPNIN, ALEXANDER (1899-   )
Quintet, Op. 44
UE 9722
THIMAN, ERIC (1900-   )
My Love's an Arbutus
Hin (Pet No. H269)   d-b ad lib
Sligo Dance Tune
Hin (Pet No. H270)   d-b ad lib
TOCH, ERNST (1887-   )
Quintet, Op. 64
Leeds
TORELLI, GIUSEPPE (1658-1709)
Concerto in d, Op. 6, No. 10
(Engel) NAG
TOUCHE, J. CL.
Quintette
Dur
TURINA, JOAQUÍN (1882-1949)
Caliope, from Las Musas de Andalucia
UME   score only
Quintette
RL
VAINUNAS, [STASIS (1909-   )]
Quintet
MZK
VERDI, GIUSEPPE (1813-1901)
Quartet, from Rigoletto
(Saenger) CF
VIERNE, LOUIS (1870-1937)
Quintette
Senart
VINCENT, JOHN (1902-   )
Consort
Mil
VIVALDI, ANTONIO
Sonata a Quattro, see 2 vln, vla, pno
VOLKONSKY, [ANDREI (1933-   )]
Quintet
MZK
WAGNER, RICHARD (1813-1883)
Bridal Chorus, from Lohengrin
CF
Vorspiel. Prelude to Lohengrin
CF
WAILLY, PAUL DE (1854-1933)
Quintette en Fa mineur
RL
WEBER, CARL MARIA VON (1786-1826)
Invitation to the Dance, Op. 65, orig for pno
(Weiss-Ambrosio-Skalmer) CF
WEBERN, ANTON VON (1883-1945)
*Quintet
BMP   blueprint
WERNER, GREGOR JOSEPH (1695-1766)
Hirtenmusik zur Weihnacht, for str
quartet and Bc
(Schmid) Baer 829
Kleine Hirtenmusik, for str quartet and Bc
(Schmid) Baer 1597
WHITHORNE, EMERSON (1884-1958)
Quintet, Op. 48
CF 01913
WIDOR, CHARLES-MARIE (1844-1937)
Quintette, Op. 7
Haml
YSAYE, THÉOPHILE (1865-1918)
Quintette
Senart

Quintets: 2 Violins, Cello, Double-Bass, Piano

BARRATT, E.
　Coronach
　　STB
ELGAR, EDWARD (1857-1934)
　Carissima
　　EKN
　Rosemary
　　EKN
ELKIN, [ROBERT (1896-　　)]
　Menuet Antique
　　EKN
HECTOR, C.
　Blue Sky
　　STB
QUILTER, ROGER (1877-1953)
　Moonlight on the lake
　　EKN
SATOW, K.
　Romance, from Über allen Zauber Liebe
　　BB
SCOTT, CYRIL (1879-　　)
　Intermezzo
　　EKN
　Passacaglia
　　EKN
　Three Little Waltzes, No. 1
　　EKN
　Three Little Waltzes, No. 2
　　EKN
　Vesperale
　　EKN

Quintets: Violin, Viola, Cello, Double-Bass, Piano

BORRIS, SIEGFRIED (1906-　　)
　Quintet, Op. 99, No. 3
　Sirius
HUMMEL, JOHANN NEPOMUK (1778-1837)
　Quintet, Op. 87
　　MM
SCHUBERT, FRANZ (1797-1828)
　*Quintet in A, Op. 114, "Trout"
　　BRH
　　Int
　　Mercury
　　Pet 169
WALTHEW, RICHARD HENRY (1872-1951)
　Phantasy Quintet in E
　　STB
WALZEL, LEOPOLD MATTHIAS (1902-　　)
　Quintet, Op. 27, "Parallelen-Quintett"
　　DOB

Quintets: String-Wind-Keyboard

AMRAM, DAVID
　see Quintets including percussion
BACH, JOHANN CHRISTIAN (1735-1782)
　Quintet in F, for ob, vln, vla or gamba,
　　vcl, pno
　　(Erhart) SCH
DVORAK, ANTONIN (1841-1904)
　Humoreske, Op. 101, No. 7, arr for fl,
　　2 vln, vcl, pno
　　(Saenger) CF

FELDMAN, MORTON (1926-　　)
　Projection II, for vln, vcl, fl, trumpet, pno
　　Pet 6940   score only
　see also Quintets including percussion
GERSCHEFSKI, EDWIN (1909-　　)
　Song without words, for fl, 2 vln, vla,
　　harp or pno
　　CFE   score only
HAYDN, JOSEPH (1732-1809)
　Divertissement, for ob, vln, vla, vcl,
　　keyboard
　　Oxf   for rent
　Sinfonie Concertante, Op. 84, orig for
　　vln, vcl, ob, bsn and orch; arr for
　　vln, vcl, ob, bsn, pno
　　(Sitt) BRH
　　(Sitt) Int
　Sonata in E flat, Op. 4, for 2 horns, vln, vcl,
　　pno
　　MT (Pet No. MV1208)
HINDEMITH, PAUL (1895-1963)
　Pieces, 3, for clar, trumpet, vln, d-b, pno
　　SCH
HOLZBAUER, IGNAZ (1711-1783)
　Quintet, for fl, vln, vla, vcl, keyboard
　　(Schroeder) BRH
MACBETH, ALLAN (1856-1910)
　Love in Idleness, for fl, 2 vln, vcl, pno
　　(Saenger) CF
MOZART, WOLFGANG AMADEUS (1756-1791)
　Adagio and Rondo in c, K.617, for
　　harmonica or pno, fl, ob, vla, vcl
　　Int
　Andante in Rondo Form, K.616, orig for
　　mechanical organ; arr for fl, 2 vln,
　　vla, cembalo
　　BRH
PEPUSCH, JOHN CHRISTOPHER (1667-1752)
　Quintet in F, for 2 rec, 2 vln, keyboard
　　(Dart) SCH   vcl ad lib
PETRASSI, GOFFREDO
　see Quintets including percussion
SAUGUET, HENRI (1901-　　)
　Près du bal, for vln, fl, clar, bsn, pno
　　RL
SCHOENBERG, ARNOLD (1874-1951)
　*Chamber Symphony, Op. 9, orig for 15
　　solo instruments; arr for fl, clar,
　　vln, vcl, pno
　　(Webern) UE   for rent
SHERMAN, ELNA
　St. Francis and the Birds, for 3 rec, vcl,
　　harpsichord
　　CFE   score only
SHIFRIN, SEYMOUR (1926-　　)
　Serenade, for ob, clar, horn, vla, pno
　　Pet 5853
SPITZMÜLLER, ALEXANDER (1894-　　)
　Divertimento Breve, Op. 6, for 2 vln, vla,
　　bsn, pno
　　UE 10445
STÖLZEL, GOTTFRIED HEINRICH (1690-1749)
　Sonata in F, for ob, horn, vln, vcl, pno
　　BRH
TANENBAUM, ELIAS
　see Quintets including percussion
VIVALDI, ANTONIO (c.1669-1741)
　Concerto in g, for fl, ob, vln, bsn, and pno
　　(Ghedini) Int   vcl and d-b ad lib
　Sonata in D, for fl, vln, bsn, vcl or d-b
　　and pno
　　(Ghedini) Int

Quintets: 2 Violins, Viola, Cello, Guitar

BAUMANN
Memento
ZM (Pet No. ZM369)   score included
BOCCHERINI, LUIGI (1743-1805)
Quintet No. 1 in D
ZM (Pet No. ZM44)
Quintet No. 2 in C, "La Ritarata di
Madrid"
ZM (Pet No. ZM153)
Quintet No. 3 in e
ZM (Pet No. ZM163)
CASTELNUOVO-TEDESCO, MARIO (1895-   )
Quintet, Op. 145
SCH
GIULIANI, [MAURO (1781-1828)]
Quintet, Op. 65
(Domandl) SIM
RÖVENSTRUNCK, BERNHARD (1920-   )
Serenade
EDW
SCHNABEL, JOSEPH (1767-1831)
Quintet
ZM (Pet No. ZM275)

Quintets Including Harp

ABSIL, JEAN (1893-   )
Concert a cinq, Op. 38, for fl, vln, vla,
vcl, harp
CBDM   score included
BADINGS, HENK (1907-   )
Capriccio, for fl, vln, vla, vcl, harp
DN (Pet No. D72)
CAPLET, ANDRÉ (1878-1925)
Conte fantastique, for harp, 2 vln, vla, vcl
Dur   d-b ad lib
CRAS, JEAN (1879-1932)
Quintette, for fl, vln, vla, vcl, harp
Senart
DESTENAY, ÉDOUARD (? -1924)
Quintette No. 2, Op. 12, for 2 vln, vla,
vcl, harp
Haml
GALLON, NOËL (1891-   )
*Quintette, for 2 vln, vla, vcl, harp
HL
GERSCHEFSKI, EDWIN (1909-   )
Song without words, for fl, 2 vln, vla,
harp or pno
CFE   score only
GLANVILLE-HICKS, PEGGY (1912-   )
Concertino Antico, for harp, 2 vln, vla, vcl
CFE   score only
HARRISON, JULIUS (1885-   )
Prelude Music, for 2 vln, vla, vcl, harp
Curwen   for rent
HOFFMANN, E.T.A. (1776-1822)
Quintet, for 2 vln, vla, vcl, harp
VW (Pet No. VP2)
INGHELBRECHT, DÉSIRÉ ÉMILE (1880-   )
Quintette en ut mineur, for 2 vln, vla,
vcl, harp
Leduc

LAJTHA, LÁSZLÓ (1891-1963)
Marionnettes, for fl, vln, vla, vcl, harp
Deiss
Quintette No. 2, Op. 46, for fl, vln, vla,
vcl, harp
Leduc   for rent
LEMBA
Berceuse, for 2 vln, vla, vcl, harp
ZM (Pet No. ZM721)
LESUR, DANIEL (1908-   )
*Suite médiévale, for fl, vln, vla, vcl, harp
Dur
MALIPIERO, GIAN FRANCESCO (1882-   )
*Sonata a cinque, for fl, vln, vla, vcl, harp
Ric 123629
PIERNÉ, GABRIEL (1863-1937)
*Variations Libres et Final, for fl, vln, vla,
vcl, harp
Sal
PILLOIS, JACQUES (1877-1935)
*Haï-Kaï, 5, for fl, vln, vla, vcl, harp
Dur
ROPARTZ, J. GUY (1864-1955)
*Prélude, Marine et chansons, for fl, vln,
vla, vcl, harp
Dur
ROUSSEL, ALBERT (1869-1937)
*Sérénade, Op. 30, for fl, vln, vla, vcl, harp
Dur
SCHMITT, FLORENT (1870-1958)
Andante et Scherzo, for 2 vln, vla, vcl, harp
Mathot
*Suite en rocaille, Op. 84, for fl, vln, vla,
vcl, harp
Dur
SMIT, LEO (1900-1944)
*Quintet, for fl, vln, vla, vcl, harp
DN (Pet No. D74)
TOURNIER, M.
Suite, for fl, vln, vla, vcl, harp or pno
HL
ZAGWIJN, HENRI (1878-1955)
Quintet, for fl, vln, vla, vcl, harp
DN (Pet No. D101)

Quintets Including Percussion

AMRAM, DAVID (1930-   )
Discussion, for fl, vcl, percussion
(2 players), pno
Pet 6681
FELDMAN, MORTON (1926-   )
de Kooning, for horn, percussion, pno,
vln, vcl
Pet 6951   score only
HARRISON, LOU (1917-   )
*Concerto in Slendro, for vln solo, celesta,
2 tackpianos, percussion
Pet 6610
PETRASSI, GOFFREDO (1904-   )
Serenata, for fl, vla, d-b, harpsichord,
percussion
SZ
TANENBAUM, ELIAS (1924-   )
Chamber Piece No. 1, for fl, clar, vcl, pno,
percussion
CFE   score included

MUSIC FOR
SIX INSTRUMENTS

Sextets: 6 Viols

BYRD, WILLIAM
Fantasia, see 2 vln, 2 vla, 2 vcl
Pavan & Galliard, see 3 vln, vla, 2 vcl
HASSLER, HANS LEO (1564-1616)
Intraden aus dem Lustgarten
(Höckner) Baer HM73   score included
PEERSON, MARTIN
see 2 vln, 2 vla, 2 vcl
TOMKINS, THOMAS
Fantasia, see 2 vln, 2 vla, 2 vcl

Sextets: 4 Violins, 2 Cellos

HAYDN, JOSEPH (1732-1809)
Echo
(Koschinsky) Noet (Pet No. N876)
(Schroeder) VW (Pet No. V100)   score
included

Sextets: 3 Violins, Viola, 2 Cellos

BYRD, WILLIAM (1543-1623)
Pavan and Galliard
STB
GOOSSENS, EUGÈNE (1893-1962)
*Sextet, Op. 37
Ches

Sextets: 2 Violins, 2 Violas, 2 Cellos

BACH, JOHANN SEBASTIAN (1685-1750)
Ricercare, from Musical Offering
VW (Pet No. V30)   d-b ad lib; score
included
see also more than 1 instrumental
combination
BEETHOVEN, LUDWIG VAN (1770-1827)
Sextet, Op. 81b, orig for 2 horns, 2 vln,
vla, vcl
Int
BRAHMS, JOHANNES (1833-1897)
*Sextet No. 1 in B flat, Op. 18
Int
Pet 3906A
*Sextet No. 2 in G, Op. 36
Int
Pet 3906b
BRIDGE, FRANK (1879-1941)
*Sextet
Aug

BYRD, WILLIAM (1543-1623)
Fantasia No. 1
STB
Fantasia No. 2
STB
DVORAK, ANTONIN (1841-1904)
*Sextet in A, Op. 48
Artia
Int
SIM
FULEIHAN, ANIS (1900-   )
*Divertimento
SMP
GLASS, LOUIS (1864-1936)
*Sextet, Op. 15
WH
d'INDY, VINCENT (1851-1931)
*Sextuor, Op. 92
Heugel
KORNAUTH, EGON (1891-1959)
Sextet, Op. 25
UE 8242
MARTINU, BOHUSLAV (1890-1959)
Sextet
AMP   d-b ad lib
MILHAUD, DARIUS (1892-   )
*Sextet
Heugel
MOSER, FRANZ JOSEF (1880-1939)
Sextet in F, Op. 23
UE 6214
PEERSON, MARTIN (c.1572-1650)
Fantasy and Almaine No. 1
SCH
Fantazia, "Beauty" and Almaine No. 2
SCH
Fantazia and Almaine No. 5
SCH
RIMSKY-KORSAKOV, NIKOLAY
Sextet, see more than 1 instrumental
combination
SCHOENBERG, ARNOLD (1874-1951)
*Verklärte Nacht, Op. 4
Birnbach
Int
SEARCH, FREDERICK (1899-   )
Sextet
SPAM   score included
SIEGL, OTTO (1896-   )
*Sextett in einem Satz, Op. 28
DOB
STEPAN, VACLAV (1889-1944)
*Sextet, Op. 11
RL
STRAUSS, RICHARD (1864-1949)
Overture, from Capriccio
BH

TCHAIKOVSKY, PIOTR ILYITCH (1840-1893)
Souvenir de Florence, Op. 70
Int
TOMKINS, THOMAS (1572-1656)
Fantasia
STB

Sextets: String-Wind

AMES, WILLIAM (1901-   )
Sextet, for ob, 2 vln, 2 vla, vcl
CFE   score included
ARDÉVOL, JOSÉ (1911-   )
Musica de Camera para seis instrumentos,
for fl, clar, bsn, trumpet in C, vln, vcl
Pan American Union; score only
BACH, JOHANN SEBASTIAN
Ricerar a 6, from Musical Offering, see
more than 1 instrumental combination
BACH, WILHELM FRIEDRICH ERNST
(1759-1845)
Sextet in E flat, for clar, 2 horns, vln, vla,
vcl
MT (Pet No. MV1207)   score included
BEETHOVEN, LUDWIG VAN (1770-1827)
*Sextet in E flat, Op. 81b, for 2 vln, vla,
vcl, 2 horns
BRH
Lit (Pet No. L192)
BERKELEY, LENNOX (1903-   )
*Sextet, for clar, horn, 2 vln, vla, vcl
Ches
BOCCHERINI, LUIGI (1743-1805)
Sextet, Op. 42, No. 1, for 2 vln, horn in E
flat, vla, 2 vcl
(Bormann) Sik 283
(Janetzky) BRH
Int
Sextet in E flat, Op. 42, No. 2, for ob or fl,
vln, vla, horn in E flat, bsn, d-b
(Bormann) Sik 343
Sextet in B flat, for ob, bsn, 2 vln, vla, vcl
(Janetzky) Hof   score included
FELDMAN, MORTON (1926-   )
Pieces, 2, for vln, vcl, fl, alto fl, horn,
trumpet
Pet 6930   score only
FLOTHUIS, MARIUS (1914-   )
*Divertimento, Op. 46, for clar, bsn, horn,
vln, vla, d-b
DN (Pet No. D12b)
GERHARDT, CARL (1900-   )
Sextet in G, for fl, English horn, bsn,
vln, vla, vcl
LN (Pet No. R56)   score included
GOEB, ROGER (1914-   )
Declarations, for vcl, fl, ob, clar, horn, bsn
CFE   score included
GYRING, ELIZABETH
Sextet-Fantasy, for fl, clar, horn, vln, vla,
vcl
CFE   score included
HAYDN, JOSEPH (1732-1809)
*Divertimento in D, orig str quartet,
Op. 2, No. 5; arr for 2 horns,
2 vln, vla, vcl
Pet 4878   d-b ad lib
HAYDN, MICHAEL (1737-1806)
Notturno in F, for 2 horns, 2 vln, vla
vcl or d-b
(Strassl) DOB
KILPATRICK, JACK
Sextet, for fl, horn and strings
CFE   score only

LEVY, F.
*Sextet for fl, clar, bsn, vln, vla, vcl
Cor WS1
LUENING, OTTO (1900-   )
Sextet, for fl, clar, horn, vln, vla, vcl
CFE   score included
MARTINU, BOHUSLAV (1890-1959)
*Serenade No. 1, for clar, horn, 3 vln, vla
Artia
MOZART, WOLFGANG AMADEUS (1756-1791)
*Divertimento No. 17 in D, K.334, for 2 vln,
vla, d-b or vcl, 2 horns
Int
*Musical Joke, "Village Musicians".
Sextet in F, K.522, for 2 vln, vla,
vcl, 2 horns
Int
LN (Pet R2)
QUINET, MARCEL (1915-   )
Ballade, for vln and woodwind quintet
CBDM   score included
ROSETTI, FRANCESCO ANTONIO (1746-1792)
*Notturno in D, for fl, 2 horns, vln, vla, vcl
.. Artia
RÖSSLER, F.A, see Rosetti
SCHAUB, HANS FERDINAND (1880-   )
Spielmusik, for fl, ob, clar in A, bsn,
vln, vla
SIM
SEIBER, MÁTYÁS (1905-1960)
Fantasia, for fl, horn, 2 vln, vla, vcl
SZ

Sextets: 5 String Instruments, Keyboard or Guitar

ALBINONI, TOMASO (1671-1750)
Sonata a 5 in g, Op. 2, No. 6, for 2 vln,
2 vla, vcl, keyboard
(Giegling) NAG   d-b ad lib
BACH, JOHANN CHRISTIAN (1735-1782)
Quintet in E flat, Op. 11, No. 4, for 3 vln
or fl, ob, vln; vla; vcl; keyboard
NAG
Quintet in D, Op. 11, No. 6, for 3 vln or fl,
ob, vln; vla; vcl; keyboard
NAG
BAZELAIRE, PAUL (1886-1958)
Ballade, Op. 91, for 2 vln, vla, 2 vcl, pno
Senart
CHAUSSON, ERNEST (1855-1899)
Concerto in D, Op. 21, for vln, pno and
str quartet
Int
RL
DEWANGER, A.
Sextuor, for 2 vln, 2 vla, vcl, pno
Dur
ENESCO, GEORGES (1881-1955)
Rumanian Rhapsody No. 1, orig for orch;
arr for 2 vln, vla, vcl, d-b, pno
SMP
FISCHER, JOHANN KASPAR FERDINAND
(c.1665-1746)
Suite No. 4 in d, for 2 vln, 2 vla, vcl,
keyboard
Pr
FURCHHEIM, [JOHANN WILHELM
(c.1635-1682)]
Sonata Quarta in G, for 2 vln, 2 vla, vcl, pno
MT (Pet No. MV1075)   d-b ad lib; 3rd
vln may be substituted for vla

GLINKA, MIKHAIL
Divertimento, see more than 1 instrumental
combination
Sextet, see more than 1 instrumental combi-
nation
HOLDEN, DAVID (1911-   )
Music, for 2 vln, vla, vcl, d-b, pno
SPAM
MENDELSSOHN, FELIX (1809-1847)
Sextet in D, Op. 110, for vln, 2 vla, vcl,
d-b, pno
Lit (Pet No. L636)
QUILTER, ROGER (1877-1953)
Moonlight on the lake, for 2 vln, vla, vcl,
d-b, pno
EKN
Water Nymph, for 2 vln, vla, vcl, d-b, pno
EKN
RIISAGER, KNUDAGE (1897-   )
Concertino, for 5 vln and pno
WH 3322a
ROSENMÜLLER, JOHANN (c.1620-1684)
Chamber Sonata in D, for 3 vln, vla, vcl, pno
VW (Pet No. V111)   score included
Sonatas Nos. 9, 10, 11, 12, see more than
1 instrumental combination
Studentenmusik. Suites Nos. 1 and 2,
for 2 vln, 2 vla, vcl, keyboard
NAG   3rd vln may be substituted for
2nd vla
TORELLI, GIUSEPPE (1658-1709)
Concerto, for vln solo, 2 vln, vla, vcl,
guitar
(Scheit) DOB
TURINA, JOAQUÍN (1882-1949)
Scène Andalouse, for vla solo and 2 vln,
vla, vcl, pno
Mathot
VIVALDI, ANTONIO (c.1669-1741)
Concerto in d, for vla d'amore, guitar,
2 vln, vla, vcl
ZM (Pet No. ZM320)

Sextets: String-Wind-Keyboard and/or Harp or Percussion

ACHRON, JOSEPH (1886-1943)
Childrens Suite, Op. 57, for clar, 2 vln,
vla, vcl, pno
UE 8879
BIBER, [HEINRICH IGNAZ FRANZ
(1644-1704)]
Sonata à 6, for trumpet, 2 vln, vla, vcl,
keyboard
GS
COPLAND, AARON (1900-   )
*Sextet, for clar, pno, 2 vln, vla, vcl
BH
DOHNÁNYI, ERNST VON (1877-1960)
Sextet in C, Op. 37, for clar, horn,
vln, vla, vcl, pno
Leng (Mil No. L5052)
DONOVAN, RICHARD (1891-   )
*Music for Six, for ob, clar, trumpet,
vln, vcl, pno
Pet 6666
ESCHER, RUDOLF (1912-   )
Tombeau de Ravel, Le, for fl, ob, vln,
vla, vcl, harpsichord
DN (Pet No. D23)

FELDMAN, MORTON (1926-   )
Durations V, for vln, vcl, horn,
vibraphone, harp, pno/celesta
Pet 6905   score only
FRID, GÉZA (1904-   )
*Nocturnes, for fl, harp, 2 vln, vla, vcl
DN (Pet No. D73)
GLANVILLE-HICKS, PEGGY (1912-   )
Masque of the Wild Man, for fl, percussion,
2 vln, vla, vcl
CFE   score included
GOEB, ROGER (1914-   )
Concertant IVb, for clar, 2 vln, vla,
vcl, pno
CFE
GOEHR, ALEXANDER (1932-   )
Suite, Op. 11, for fl, clar, horn, harp,
vln or vla, vcl
SCH   score only
HARRIS, ROY (1898-   )
*Concerto, Op. 2, for pno, clar, 2 vln,
vla, vcl
AMP   score only
HOVHANESS, ALAN (1911-   )
Sextet, Op. 164, for alto rec, 2 vln, vla,
vcl, harpsichord
Pet 6173   for rent
IVES, CHARLES EDWARD (1874-1954)
Allegretto Sombreoso, for fl, English
horn, 3 vln, pno
Peer   score included; trumpet or
basset horn may be substituted for
English horn
MASON, DANIEL GREGORY (1873-1953)
Pieces, 3, for fl, harp, 2 vln, vla, vcl
SPAM   score included
PFITZNER, HANS (1869-1949)
Sextet, Op. 55, for pno, vln, vla, vcl,
d-b, clar
Oertel
POWELL, MEL (1923-   )
Miniatures for Baroque Ensemble, Op. 8,
for fl, ob, vln, vla, vcl, harpsichord
GS 91   score only
PROKOFIEV, SERGEY (1891-1953)
*Overture on Hebrew Themes, Op. 34,
for clar, pno, 2 vln, vla, vcl
BH
Int
RUBBRA, EDMUND (1901-   )
Fantasia on a theme of Machaut, for rec,
2 vln, vla, vcl, harpsichord
Leng (Mil No. L5055)
SCHISKE, KARL (1916-   )
Sextet, for clar, 2 vln, vla, vcl, pno
UE 11209
SURINACH, CARLOS (1915-   )
Cantos Bereberes, Tres, for fl, ob,
clar, vla, vcl, harp
SMP   score included
TELEMANN, GEORG PHILIPP (1681-1767)
Konzertsuite, for alto rec, 2 vln, vla,
vcl, keyboard
(Hoffmann) NAG   3rd vln may be
substituted for vla
TIPPETT, MICHAEL (1905-   )
Prelude. Summer, from Crown of the Year,
for 2 rec or fl, trumpet or cornet, vln,
drum, pno
SCH
WOOLLEN, RUSSELL (1923-   )
Sextet, for clar, pno, 2 vln, vla, vcl
CFE   score only

MUSIC FOR
SEVEN INSTRUMENTS

Septets

BAAREN, KEES VAN (1906-   )
*Septet, for fl, ob, clar, bsn, horn, vln, d-b
   DN (Pet No. D17b)
BACH, KARL PHILIPP EMANUEL (1714-1788)
   Sonatina in C, for pno, 2 fl, 2 vln, vla, vcl
      (Dameck) BB
BEETHOVEN, LUDWIG VAN (1770-1827)
*Septet in E flat, Op. 20, for vln, vla,
      horn, clar, bsn, vcl, d-b
      BRH
      Int
      Pet 2446
BERWALD, FRANZ (1796-1868)
*Stor Septett, for clar, bsn, horn, vln, vla,
      vcl, d-b
      Gehrmans
BORRIS, SIEGFRIED (1906-   )
*Kleine Suite, Op. 31, No. 3, for fl, ob,
      clar, bsn, vln, vla, vcl
      Sirius   in preparation
BRUNSWICK, MARK (1902-   )
   Septet in 7 Movements, for fl, ob, clar,
      bsn, horn, vla, vcl
      CFE   score included
CAGE, JOHN (1912-   )
*Short Inventions, 6, for alto fl, clar in
      B flat, trumpet in B flat, vln, 2 vla, vcl
      Pet 6749
GENZMER, HARALD (1909-   )
*Septet, for harp, fl, clar, horn, vln, vla, vcl
      SCH
GLINKA, MIKHAIL
   Septet, see more than 1 instrumental
      combination
HODDINOTT, ALUN (1929-   )
*Variations, for fl, clar, harp, 2 vln, vla, vcl
      Oxf   for rent
HUMMEL, JOHANN N. (1778-1837)
*Septet in d, Op. 74, for fl, ob, horn, vla,
      vcl, d-b, pno
      Pet 1304
d'INDY, VINCENT (1851-1931)
   Suite en ré, for trumpet, 2 fl, 2 vln, vla, vcl
      Haml
JANÁČEK, LEOŠ (1854-1928)
*Concertino, for pno, 2 vln, vla, clar,
      horn, bsn
      Artia
MARTINU, BOHUSLAV (1890-1959)
*Rondi, for ob, clar, bsn, trumpet, 2 vln, pno
      Artia
*Serenade No. 3, for ob, clar, 4 vln, vcl
      Artia
MENGELBERG, KAREL (1902-   )
*Ballade, for fl, clar, 2 vln, vla, vcl, harp
      DN (Pet No. D75)
PERRY, JULIA (1927-   )
   Pastoral, for fl, 2 vln, 2 vla, 2 vcl
      SMP   score included

PIJPER, WILLEM (1894-1947)
   Septet, for fl/piccolo, ob/English horn,
      clar, horn, bsn, d-b, pno
      DN (Pet No. D2)
RAVEL, MAURICE (1875-1937)
*Introduction et Allegro, for harp, fl,
      clar, 2 vln, vla, vcl
      Dur
      Kal   for sale or rent
ROSSINI, GIOACCHINO (1792-1868)
   Serenata, for fl, ob, English horn, 2 vln,
      vla, vcl
      MM   Photolith reproduction
SAINT-SAENS, CAMILLE (1835-1921)
   Septet, Op. 65, for pno, trumpet, 2 vln,
      vla, vcl, d-b
      Dur
      Int
SCHAT, PETER (1935-   )
*Septet, for fl, ob, bass clar, horn, vcl,
      pno, percussion
      DN (Pet No. D195)
SCHOENBERG, ARNOLD (1874-1951)
   Serenade, Op. 24, see voice
      and instruments
*Suite, Op. 29, for clar in A, clar in B
      flat, bass clar, vln, vla, vcl, pno
      UE
SONTAG
   Folk Songs, 3, for 4 vln, vla, vcl, pno
      JWL (Mil No. W2350)   score included
STEVENS, HALSEY (1908-   )
   Septet, for clar, horn, bsn, 2 vla, 2 vcl
      CFE   score included
STRAVINSKY, IGOR (1882-   )
*Septet, for clar, bsn, horn, pno, vln,
      vla, vcl
      BH   for rent
TELEMANN, GEORG PHILIPP (1681-1767)
   Concerto in a, for 6 melody instruments
      and keyboard
      (Hechler) SCH   vcl or gamba ad lib;
      score included
   Concerto in B flat, for 3 ob, 3 vln, Bc
      (Töttcher) Sik 494
TIPPETT, MICHAEL (1905-   )
   Prelude. Autumn, from Crown of the Year,
      for ob, 2 vln, vla, vcl, handbells or
      chimebars, pno
      SCH   score included
VERRALL, JOHN (1908-   )
   Pastoral Elegy, for 2 fl, 2 vla, 3 vcl
      CFE   score included
WEBER, BEN (1916-   )
   Concertino, Op. 45, for fl, ob, clar, 2 vln,
      vla, vcl
      CFE   score included
WUORINEN, CHARLES (1938-   )
   Tiento Sobre Cabezon, for fl, ob, vln, vla,
      vcl, harpsichord, pno
      CFE

MUSIC FOR
EIGHT INSTRUMENTS

Octets

BACH, JOHANN SEBASTIAN (1685-1750)
Seven Part Canon in the unison on a
ground bass, for 8 vln
(Twinn) JWL (Mil No. W1825)
score included
BADINGS, HENK (1907-   )
*Octet, for clar, bsn, horn, 2 vln, vla,
vcl, d-b
DN (Pet No. D135)
BALAKIREV, MILY (1837-1910)
Octet, Op. 3, for pno, fl, ob, horn, vln, vla,
vcl, d-b
MZK   score included
BAX, ARNOLD (1883-1953)
Threnody and Scherzo, for bsn, harp,
2 vln, 2 vla, vcl, d-b
Chap   for rent
BORRIS, SIEGFRIED (1906-   )
*Oktett, Op. 99, No. 4, for clar, bsn, horn
and str quintet
Sirius
BURKHARD, WILLY (1900-1955)
*Serenade, Op. 77, for fl, clar, bsn, horn,
harp, vln, vla, d-b
BH
CAGE, JOHN (1912-   )
Dances, 16, for fl, trumpet, 4 percussion,
vln, vcl
Pet 6792   for rent
EDER, HELMUT (1916-   )
*Ottetto breve, Op. 33, for fl, ob, clar,
bsn, 2 vln, vla, vcl
DOB
FERGUSON, HOWARD (1908-   )
*Octet, for clar, bsn, horn, 2 vln, vla,
vcl, d-b
BH
GABRIELI, ANDREA (c.1510-1586)
Ricercar, for 4 vln, 2 vla, 2 vcl
(Bush) John Fields
GOOSSENS, EUGÈNE (1893-1962)
*Concertino for String Octet
Ches
HINDEMITH, PAUL (1895-1963)
Octet, for clar, bsn, horn, vln, 2 vla,
vcl, d-b
SCH
d'INDY, VINCENT (1851-1931)
*Suite in Olden Style, Op. 24, for trumpet,
2 fl, 2 vln, vla, vcl, bsn
Int
MENDELSSOHN, FELIX (1809-1847)
*Octet in E flat, Op. 20, for 4 vln,
2 vla, 2 vcl
Int
Pet 1782

MILHAUD, DARIUS (1892-   )
*Octet. Quartets Nos. 14 and 15[109]
Heugel
PEERSON, MARTIN (c.1572-1650)
Fantasy and Almaine No. 1, for 2 treble,
2 alto, 2 tenor, 2 bass viols
(A. & N. Dolmetsch) SCH
Fantazia, "Beauty" and Almaine No. 2, for
2 treble, 2 alto, 2 tenor, 2 bass viols
(Wailes) SCH
Fantazia and Almaine No. 5, for 2 treble,
2 alto, 2 tenor, 2 bass viols
(Wailes) SCH
PERAGALLO, MARIO (1910-   )
*Music for double quartet
UE 11979
SCHOLLUM, ROBERT (1913-   )
*Oktett in acht Skizzen, Op. 63, for fl, ob,
clar, bsn, vln, vla, vcl, d-b
DOB
SCHUBERT, FRANZ (1797-1828)
*Octet in F, Op. 166, for 2 vln, vla, vcl,
d-b, clar, horn, bsn
Int
Pet 1849
SHOSTAKOVICH, DMITRI (1906-   )
*Pieces, 2, Op. 11, for 4 vln, 2 vla, 2 vcl
Leeds   for rent
SHULMAN, ALAN (1915-   )
J.S. on the Rocks, for 2 vln, vla, vcl, d-b,
guitar, clar, harp
Templ   for rent
Suite Miniature, for 8 vcl
Templ
SIMS, EZRA (1930-   )
Sonate Concertante. Sonatine for ob, vln,
vcl, d-b, played simultaneously with
Sonate for 2 vln, vla, vcl
CFE   score included
SPOHR, LUDWIG (1784-1859)
*Doppelquartett in d, Op. 65
(Schmitz) Baer
*Octet, Op. 32, for clar, 2 horns, vln, 2 vla,
vcl, d-b
MM   Photolith reproduction
TIPPETT, MICHAEL (1905-   )
Prelude. Spring, from Crown of the Year,
for 2 rec or fl, clar, 2 vln, vla, vcl, pno
SCH
VILLA-LOBOS, HEITOR (1887-1959)
Bachianas Brasileiras No. 1, for 8 vcl
AMP
WELLESZ, EGON (1885-   )
*Octet, for clar, horn, bsn, 2 vln, vla, vcl, d-b
Leng   for rent

---

[109] Quartets Nos. 14 and 15 were composed to be played separately or together as an octet.

WHITTENBERG, CHARLES
    Chamber Concerto, for vln and 7 instru-
        mentalists: fl, percussion, clar,
        trumpet, trombone, vcl, d-b
        CFE   score only

WUORINEN, CHARLES (1938-   )
    *Octet, for ob, clar, horn, trombone, vln, vcl,
        d-b, pno
        MM   for rent

Section IX

MUSIC FOR NINE
OR TEN INSTRUMENTS

Nonets; Decets

CHEMIN-PETIT, HANS (1902-   )
*Suite, "Dr. Johannes Faust", for ob, clar,
     bsn, percussion, 2 vln, vla, vcl, d-b
   LN (Pet No. R4)
COPLAND, AARON (1900-   )
   Nonet, for 3 vln, 3 vla, 3 vcl
   BH
DIAMOND, DAVID (1915-   )
   Nonet, for 3 vln, 3 vla, 3 vcl
   SMP
DUBOIS, THÉODORE (1837-1924)
*Nonetto, for fl, ob, clar, bsn, 2 vln, vla,
     vcl, d-b
   Heugel
FELDMAN, MORTON (1926-   )
   Ixion, graph for 3 fl, clar, horn, trumpet,
     trombone, pno, vcl, d-b
   Pet 6926   score only
GILSE, JAN VAN (1880-1944)
*Nonet, for ob, clar, bsn, horn, 2 vln, vla,
     vcl, d-b
   DN (Pet No. D136)
HOVLAND, EGIL (1924-   )
   Music for 10 instruments, Op. 28, for fl,
     ob, clar, bsn, horn, 2 vln, vla, vcl, d-b
   Pet   for rent
KORNAUTH, EGON (1891-1959)
   Nonet, Op. 31,[110] for fl, ob, clar, horn, 2 vln,
     vla, vcl, d-b
   UE 8553   score only
KROL, BERNHARD (1920-   )
   Konzertante Musik, Op. 6, for vla solo, 2 ob,
     2 clar, 2 bsn, 2 horn
   BRH
LUTYENS, ELIZABETH (1906-   )
*Six Tempi for Ten Instruments, Op. 42, for

[110] This composition is listed in other catalogues as Kammermusik, Op. 31.   Three sources of information give three
different combinations of string and wind instruments. The
Universal catalogue listing is for fl, ob, clar, horn and str
quintet.

   fl, ob, clar, bsn, trumpet, horn, vln,
     vla, vcl, pno
   Leng (Mil No. L78)
MARTINU, BOHUSLAV (1890-1959)
*Serenade No. 4. Divertimento for vln solo,
     2 vln, vcl, vla solo, vla, 2 ob, pno
   Artia
MILLS, CHARLES (1914-   )
   Chamber Concerto for 10 instruments, for
     fl, ob, clar, bsn, 2 horns, 2 vln, vla, vcl
   CFE   score only
MOÓR, EMANUEL (1863-1931)
   Suite, Op. 103, for fl, ob, clar, horn, bsn,
     2 vln, vla, vcl, d-b
   Sal   score only
MOZART, WOLFGANG AMADEUS (1756-1791)
   Galimathias Musicum (Quodlibet) K. 32
     including K.S. 100a, for 2 ob, 2 horns,
     bsn, 2 vln, vla, vcl or d-b, pno
   (Einstein) Pet 6305
PISTON, WALTER (1894-   )
   Divertimento for 9 instruments, for fl,
     ob, clar, bsn, 2 vln, vla, vcl, d-b
   BMI   score included
RAWSTHORNE, ALAN (1905-   )
*Concerto for 10 Instruments, for fl,
     ob/English horn, clar, bsn, horn,
     2 vln, vla, vcl, d-b
   Oxf   for rent
SPOHR, LUDWIG (1784-1859)
*Nonet in F, Op. 31, for fl, ob, clar, bsn,
     horn, vln, vla, vcl, d-b
   Lit (Pet No. L1924)
TRIMBLE, LESTER (1923-   )
*Concerto for fl, ob, clar, bsn, 2 vln, vla,
     vcl, d-b
   Pet 6641   for rent
WEBER, BEN (1916-   )
   Chamber Fantasie, Op. 51, for solo vln,
     2 clar, bass clar, harp, 3 vcl, d-b
   CFE   score included
WOLFF, CHRISTIAN (1934-   )
   Nine, for fl, clar, horn, trumpet, trombone,
     2 vcl, celesta, pno
   Pet 6499   score included

Section X

MUSIC FOR MORE THAN ONE COMBINATION OF INSTRUMENTS

More Than One Instrumental Combination

ALBUM OF WALTZES
  CF 01009-10   for any combination of
  strings and winds with pno
(AUER, LEOPOLD)
  Graded Course of Ensemble Playing
  (Saenger) CF 01420-1445   6V
  for contents see title
AUS KLASSICHER ZEIT, see From Classical
  Times
BACH, JOHANN SEBASTIAN (1685-1750)
  *Musical offering
    (David) GS   for string and wind
    ensembles with keyboard instrument;
    parts for 2 vln, vla, vcl, fl, ob
    English horn, bsn
    I Ricercar a 3, for keyboard instrument
      or 3 strings, or 3 reeds
    II-VI Canons for 3 instruments
    VII Trio sonata for fl or vln, vln, vcl,
      pno or harpsichord
    VIII-XII Canons for 2-4 strings
    XIII Ricercar a 6 for keyboard
      instrument, or 6 strings, or
      3 reeds and 3 strings
  Spielstuecke
    Pet 4530   6 pieces for 1-3 vln; or vln, vla;
    or 2 vln, vla; all with pno and/or vcl
BACICH, ANTHONY P.
  Tone Poems
    Willis   solos for beginning or intermediate
    strings; pno accomp
BEETHOVEN, LUDWIG VAN (1770-1827)
  Minuet
    (Trinkaus) Fill; for 2 vln; vln and vcl; or
    vln and wind instrument; pno accomp
*CARMINA
  (Moser-Piersig) NAG   score only
  12 settings from the 16th century
  for groups of 2-5 strings
(CHEYETTE, IRVING & ROBERTS,
    CHARLES J.)
  Four-Tone Folios
    CF   3V   for contents see title
CHILDS, BARNEY
  Interbalances III
    Tritone   manuscript reproduction
    vcl and optional other instruments,
    up to 5
CHORALES FOR STRINGS
  (McLin) Pro Art   for 3 vln; or 2 vln, vla;
  or 2 vln, vla, vcl; or str orch
    Albert: God of earth

Bach, J.S.: Alas, my God
Bach, J.S.: Awake us Lord
Bach, J.S.: Child is born
Bach, J.S.: Draw us to Thee
Bach, J.S.: Eternity, tremendous word
Bach, J.S.: For as a tender father
Bach, J.S.: Glory be to God
Bach, J.S.: He brings the year
Bach, J.S.: Hence all fears
Bach, J.S.: Jesus bread of life
Bach, J.S.: Lord Jesus
Bach, J.S.: My God makes ready
Bach, J.S.: O Head, all bruised
Bach, J.S.: Praise to the Lord, the
  Almighty
Bach, J.S.: Puer Natus
Bach, J.S.: Storm wind o'er them
  passes
Bach, J.S.: Then pass forever now
Bach, J.S.: Wake, awake
Bach, J.S.: When all around
Cruger: Now thank we all our God
From Heaven above
Hassler: Lord hear my deepest
  longing
Jesus is my dwelling place
Let me from Thy wrath be free
Luther: Mighty fortress
Neumark: If thou but suffer
O Lamb of God
Palestrina: Adoramus Te
Praetorius: Lo, how a rose e'er
  blooming
CHRISTMAS MUSIC FOR EVERYONE
  Ru   for any solo instrument with pno
DALLEY, GRETCHEN
  Songs for Strings
    Kjos   for vln or vla or vcl solo with
    pno or ensemble accomp; or str duets,
    trios, quartets, with or without pno
    accomp; score included
ELGAR, EDWARD (1857-1934)
  Salut d'Amour
    (Trinkaus) Fill; for 2 vln; vln, vcl; or vln
    and wind instrument; pno accomp
FAMILIAR MELODIES, 6
  (Gardner) BMC   for 3 and 4 vln; vla, vcl,
    d-b, pno ad lib; score included
    Frere Jacques and his jolly friends:
      3 vln, pno
    Nearer, my God to Thee: 4 vln, pno
    Long, Long Ago: 4 vln, pno
    Silent Night, Holy Night: 4 vln, pno
    O Little Town of Bethlehem: 3 vln with
      ad lib instruments
    America: vln, vla, vcl, d-b, pno

FERRABOSCO, ALFONSO (1543-1588)
Fantasy, "Vias Tuas"
(Dolmetsch-Ring) Hin (Pet No. H578b)
for 5 viols; or vln, 2 vla, 2 vcl or
gambas; or 2 vln, vla, 2 vcl or
gambas; score included
Four note pavan
(Grainger-Cadek) GS from orig version
for viols by Dolmetsch, score for orig
instruments included. Parts for vln I,
vln II (substitute for vla I), vln III
(substitute for vla II), vla I, vla II, vla
III (substitute for vcl I), vcl I, vcl II,
d-b
FLETCHER, see Rolland & Fletcher
FOUR-TONE FOLIOS
(Cheyette & Roberts) CF 3V
quartets arr for all string and wind
instruments and playable by any
mixed ensemble; pno accomp ad lib
Vol 1
Bach: Passion Chorale
Ebeling: Evening and morning
Evanson: The log cabin
Gilman: The crusader
Gluck: Air de ballet, from Alceste
Go down Moses
Haydn: Days of wonder
March of the men of Harlech
Palestrina: Alleluia
Praetorius: Lo, how a rose e'er
blooming
Roberts: Old homestead
Sibelius: Finlandia, Introduction
to Overture
Wagner: Chorale, from Meistersinger
Vol 2
Arcadelt: Ave Maria
Bach: Choral for Sleepers Awake
Beethoven: Theme from Symphony
No. 9
Bizet: March, from L'Arlesienne
Brahms: Theme from Symphony No. 1
Deep River
Gluck: Aria, from Orpheus
Haydn: The spacious firmament
Mendelssohn: Song of farewell
Minstrel boy
Silcher: Loreley
Vol 3
Abt: Evening song
Abt: Sunday morning
Beethoven: The heavens resounding
Cherubini: Air, from Water Carriers
Flotow: Air, from Martha
Franz: Dedication
Mendelssohn: Whispering winds
Song of Thanksgiving
Spohr: Proudly as an eagle
Vulpius: Praise ye the Lord
Wagner: Choral, from Meister-
singer, Act III
FROM CLASSICAL TIMES
(Korda-Schnabel) OBV score included;
for various combinations of instruments;
15 pieces by M. Haydn, Gluck, Haydn,
Dittersdorf, Mozart and others
FROM THE ROMANTIC ERA
(Korda-Schnabel) OBV score included;
for various combinations of instruments;
compositions by Schubert, Hauptmann,
Weber, Schumann and Mendelssohn
(GARDNER, SAMUEL)
Familiar Melodies, 6
BMC for contents see title

(GEHRKENS, VIRGINIA E.)
Dances, Vol 1: Mozart & Beethoven
BMC for vln and pno; includes
several for 2, 3, 4 vln; for contents
see title under vln, pno
GLINKA, MIKHAIL (1804-1857)
Complete Works, Vols. 3 and 4
MZK score included
Vol 3
Septet, for ob, bsn, horn, 2 vln,
vcl, d-b
Quartet in D, for 2 vln, vla, vcl
Quartet in F, for 2 vln, vla, vcl
Vol 4
Sonata in d, for vla and pno
2 versions
Trio Pathetique, for pno, clar, bsn
Divertimento Brillante in A on themes
from La Sonnambula, for pno, 2 vln,
vla, vcl, d-b
Grand Sextet in E flat, for pno, 2 vln,
vla, vcl, d-b
2 versions
GODARD, BENJAMIN (1849-1895)
Berceuse, from Jocelyn
(Trinkaus) Fill; for 2 vln; vln and vcl; or
vln and wind instrument; pno accomp
GOUNOD, CHARLES (1818-1893)
Ave Maria. Meditation on the first prelude
of J.S. Bach
FR (Pet No. F45) for solo vln or vcl
and pno; fl or vln, vcl and pno; fl, vln,
vcl and pno
GRADED COURSE OF ENSEMBLE PLAYING
(Auer-Saenger) CF 01420-1445 6V
Vol 2 is for 2 vln; Vol 1, 3-6 are for
for 4 vln, with or without pno accomp;
playable in any string combination; vla,
vcl, d-b parts available
Vol 1: First Ensemble Folio
Ambrosio: Marching song
Auer: Polish folk-tune dance
Auer: Russian folk song
Bach: Musette
Berton, de: Processional March
Saenger: Little Senorita
Saenger: Little sleepy head
Saenger: Mazurka
Saenger: Mountain maid
Saenger: Old-time minuet
Vol 2: Fiddlers Two
96 duets for 2 vln
Vol 3: Old Time Songs and Dances
Bach: Minuet
Beethoven-Kreisler: Rondino
Dont: Will-o-the-wisp
Gluck: Musette
Mozart: Ave Verum
Saenger: Intermezzo Espagnol
Schumann: Hunter's Song
Tchaikovsky: Morning Prayers
Two French Folk Tunes
Two Old Christmas Songs
Vol 4: Romantic Concert Folio
Bach: Polonaise
Beethoven: Theme, from 1st move-
ment of Sonata No. 12 in A, Op. 26
Bohm: Sarabande
Dont: Intermezzo joyeux
Fiera de Mast'Andrea, La
Komzák: Fairy Tale
Kreisler: Caprice Viennois
Mendelssohn-Fritsche: Playtime
Memories

GRADED COURSE OF ENSEMBLE PLAY-
ING (cont.)
(Auer-Saenger) CF 01420-1445 6V (cont.)
Vol 4 (cont.)
Neury: Intermezzo Pizzicato
Tchaikovsky: March of the Wooden
Soldiers
Vol 5: Classic Repertoire
Blue Bells of Scotland
Dont: Caprice scherzando
Grieg: Watchman's Song
Haydn: Arietta
Karganoff: À la Gavotte
Moussorgsky: Hopak
Schubert: Moment Musical
Schubert: Scherzo
Slumber Song, Old German
Wagner: Song of the Sailors, from
The Flying Dutchman
Vol 6: Musical Masterpieces
Beethoven-Seiss: Contredanses
Beethoven: Minuet
Dont: Air mélodieux
Grieg: Morning Mood
Leoncavallo: Minuet and Gavotte,
from I Pagliacci
Schumann: Song of Spring
Two Finnish Folk Songs
Von Wilm: Gavotte and Musette
Wachs: Pavane and Choral
Weckerlin: Romance and Tambourine
HANDEL, GEORG FRIEDRICH (1685-1759)
Arrival of the Queen
Oxf for vln or vla and pno; 2 vln or
2 vla and pno; vln, vla, pno
Movements for Strings, 4
Hin (Pet No. H276)
2 vln, pno, vcl ad lib; or vln, vla, pno,
vcl ad lib; or 2 vln, vla, pno, vcl or d-b
ad lib; or 2 vln, vcl; or vln, vla, vcl; or
2 vln, vla, vcl
2 Dances, from Alcides
Largo, from Saul
Ouverture, from Esther
HARMONY SOLO, DUET AND TRIO ALBUM
(Roberts) CF for 1, 2 or 3 string or
wind instruments with either piano
accomp or ensemble accomp
Bizet: Serenade espagnole
Chenoweth: Dreams
Curtis: Come back to Sorrento
Dvorak: Largo, from New World
Symphony
Dvorak: Songs my mother taught me
Fernandez: Cielito lindo
Flégier: Stances
Holzel: Dreamland shadows
Kreisler: Old refrain
Londonderry air
Meyer-Helmund: Magic song
Nobody knows the trouble I've seen
Ponce: Estrellita
Yradier: La Paloma
(HÖCKNER)
String Quartet Starts Rehearsing
SIM for contents see title
(ISAAC, MERLE J.)
Melody Book for Strings
CF 03828 for contents see title
Sacred Music
CF 03952 for contents see title
JENKINS, JOHN (1592-1678)
Five-part fantasy No. 1
(Grainger-Cadek) GS from orig version
for viols by Dolmetsch, score for

orig instruments included. Parts for
vln I, vln II, vln III (substitute for vla I),
vla I, vla II, vcl I (substitute for vla II),
vcl II
JONES, DOUGLAS
Village
Chap-L; 5 pieces for unison violins,
2 for 2 vln, 1 for 3 vln; all with pno
accomp
KLEIN
Notebook I and II
Noet (Pet Nos. N606, 778) 2V
for recorders and violins
(KORDA)
Weg in Gegenwart, Der
OBV for contents see title
Wir Lernen Hausmusik
OBV for contents see title
(KORDA-SCHNABEL)
From Classical Times
OBV for contents see title
From the Romantic Era
OBV for contents see title
Musik im Jahreskreis
OBV for contents see title
Wir Spielen und Singen
OBV for contents see title
LAWES, WILLIAM (1602-1645)
Six-part fantasy and air No. 1
(Grainger-Cadek) GS from orig
version for viols by Dolmetsch,
score for orig instruments included.
Parts for vln I, vln II, vln III
(substitute for vla I), vla I, vla
II, vcl I, vcl II, d-b
LEMARE, EDWIN H. (1865-1934)
Andantino; with Elégie by Massenet
(Trinkaus) Fill; for 2 vln; vln and vcl;
or vln and wind instrument; pno accomp
(MCLIN, EDWARD M.)
Chorales for strings
Pro Art for contents see title
MASSENET, JULES (1842-1912)
Elegie, see Lemare: Andantino
MELODY BOOK FOR STRINGS
(Isaac) CF 03828 for 1 or more string
instruments with pno accomp, d-b
ad lib; for contents see title under
vln, pno
MENDELSSOHN, FELIX (1809-1847)
Nocturno; with Valse triste by Sibelius
(Trinkaus) Fill; for 2 vln; vln and vcl;
or vln and wind instrument; pno accomp
MEYERBEER, GIACOMO (1791-1864)
Coronation March, from Le Prophète
(Trinkaus) Fill; for 2 vln; vln and vcl; or
vln and wind instrument; pno accomp
(MOSER-PIERSIG)
Carmina
NAG for contents see title
MOZART, WOLFGANG AMADEUS (1756-1791)
Hausmusik Stunde
Pet 4521
9 pieces in 2-4 parts arr for various
combinations of recorders and violins;
with and without pno; vcl ad lib
MUSIK IM JAHRESKREIS
(Korda-Schnabel) OBV score only; for
various combinations of instruments
PADEREWSKI, IGNACE J. (1860-1941)
Minuet a l'Antique
(Trinkaus) Fill; for 2 vln; vln and vcl;
or vln and wind instrument; pno accomp

PURCELL, HENRY (c.1659-1695)
*Fantasies
(Just) NAG 2V
Vol 1: Fantasies for 3 and 4 viols
Vol 2: Fantasies for 4 to 7 viols
RIMSKY-KORSAKOV, NIKOLAY (1844-1908)
Chamber Music, Vol. 27
MZK score included
Sextet, for 2 vln, 2 vla, 2 vcl
Quartet in F, for 2 vln, vla, vcl
Quartet in G, for 2 vln, vla, vcl
Quartet in B-la-f, for 2 vln, vla, vcl
"Name-Day" Quartet, for 2 vln, vla, vcl
Fugue, "In a Monastery", for 2 vln, vla, vcl
4 Variations on a Russian Theme, for 2 vln, vla, vcl
Allegro, for 2 vln, vla, vcl
4 Variations and Chorale, for 2 vln, vla, vcl
Notturno, for 4 horns
2 Duets, for 2 horns
Canzonetta and Tarantella, for 2 clar
(ROBERTS, CHARLES J.)
Harmony Solo, Duet and Trio Album
CF for contents see title
see also Cheyette & Roberts
ROLLAND & FLETCHER
First Perpetual Motion
Mil for solo or unison vln, vla, vcl and pno; d-b ad lib
ROSENMÜLLER, JOHANN (c.1620-1684)
Sonatas Nos. 7 and 8
LN (Pet Nos. R48, 49) published separately; for 2 vln, vla, vcl; pno, 2nd vcl or d-b ad lib; 3rd vln may be substituted for vla
Sonatas Nos. 9, 10, 11, 12
LN (Pet Nos. R50-53) published separately; for 2 vln, 2 vla, vcl; pno, 2nd vcl or d-b ad lib; 3rd vln may be substituted for 2nd vla
see also 3 vln, vla, vcl, pno
SACRED MUSIC
(Isaac) CF 03952 solos or duets for string or wind instruments and pno
SAINT-SAËNS, CAMILLE (1835-1921)
Swan
(Trinkaus) Fill; for 2 vln; vln and vcl; or vln and wind instrument; pno accomp
(SCHAEFER, AUGUST H.)
Tri-form Folio for Soloists or Small Ensembles
CF for contents see title
Tri-form Operatic Immortals
CF for contents see title
SCHOENBERG, ARNOLD (1874-1951)
Kanons, 30, for 3 to 5 instruments
(Rufer) Baer 4340 score only.
SCOTTISH MUSIC
STB 12 Consorts for 3, 4 or 5 instruments
SIBELIUS, JEAN
Valse triste, see Mendelssohn: Nocturno
SOLOS FOR STRINGS
(Whistler) Ru vln or vla or vcl or d-b solo with pno accomp

(STOESSEL, ALBERT)
University String Orchestra Album
CF for contents see title
STRING QUARTET STARTS REHEARSING
(Höckner) SIM
J.C. Bach: Trio for 2 vln, vla
Beethoven: Duet for vla, vcl
Benda: Trio for 2 vln, vcl
Borghi: Duet for vln, vcl
Geminiani: Duet for 2 vln
Pichl: Duet for vln, vla
Schubert: Trio for vln, vla, vcl
Sechter: Quartet for 2 vln, vla, vcl
STÜCKE AUS DER ROMANTIK, see From the Romantic Era
TCHAIKOVSKY, PIOTR ILYITCH (1840-1893)
Chant sans paroles
(Trinkaus) Fill; for 2 vln; vln and vcl; or vln and wind instrument; pno accomp
TRI-FORM FOLIO FOR SOLOISTS OR SMALL ENSEMBLES
(Schaefer) CF for solo, duet or trio with or without pno accomp; various combinations of strings or strings and winds
TRI-FORM OPERATIC IMMORTALS
(Schaefer) CF for solo, duet or trio with or without pno accomp; various combinations of strings or strings and winds
(TRINKAUS, GEORGE J.)
World's Best-known Pieces
CF for contents see title
UNIVERSITY STRING ORCHESTRA ALBUM
(Stoessel) CF; for str orch or str quartet or other combinations including 2 vln, pno; 2 vln, vla, vcl, d-b; 3rd vln and pno ad lib
Compositions by Bach, Byrde, Gluck, Handel, Haydn, Rameau, Schubert, Tenaglia
WAGNER, RICHARD (1813-1883)
Song to the Evening Star, from Tannhäuser
(Trinkaus) Fill; for 2 vln; vln and vcl; or vln and wind instrument; pno accomp
Walther's Prize Song from Meistersinger
(Trinkaus) Fill; for 2 vln; vln and vcl; or vln and wind instrument; pno accomp
WATKINSON, G.
Musical Play Pieces, 4, for instruments and percussion
NAG score only
WEG IN DIE GEGENWART, DER
(Korda) OBV score included; for various combinations of instruments
(WHISTLER, HARVEY S.)
Solos for strings
Ru for contents see title
WIR LERNEN HAUSMUSIK
(Korda) OBV score only; for various combinations of instruments
WIR SPIELEN UND SINGEN
(Korda-Schnabel) OBV score only; for various combinations
WORLD'S BEST-KNOWN PIECES
(Trinkaus) CF for vln and pno
2nd parts for 8 different instruments available

MUSIC FOR
VOICE AND INSTRUMENTS

Voice and Instruments

ABBADO, MARCELLO (1926-   )
  Poesie T'Ang, 15, for mezzo soprano, fl,
    ob, vln, pno
    SZ   blueprints score
ARNE, THOMAS AUGUSTINE (1710-1778)
  Shakespeare Songs, 9, for voice, fl or rec,
    vln, vla or 2nd vln, vcl
    (Young) Chap-L   score included
BABBITT, MILTON (1916-   )
  Sonnets, 2, for baritone, clar, vla, vcl
    BMP   blueprints score
BACH, JOHANN SEBASTIAN (1685-1750)
  Selected Arias, for alto, obbligato instru-
    ment, keyboard
    (Mandyczewski) BRH   3V
  Selected Arias, 12, for bass, obbligato
    instrument, keyboard
    (Mandyczewski) BRH
  Selected Arias, for soprano, obbligato
    instrument, keyboard
    (Mandyczewski) BRH   4V
  Selected Arias, for tenor, obbligato instru-
    ment, keyboard
    (Mandyczewski) BRH   3V
  Stone, above all others treasured, from
    Cantata No. 152, for soprano,
    rec, vln or vla d'amore, keyboard
    (Hunt) SCH RMS26
BARBER, SAMUEL (1910-   )
  *Dover Beach, Op. 3, for medium voice,
    2 vln, vla, vcl
    GS   text by Matthew Arnold
BEETHOVEN, LUDWIG VAN (1770-1827)
  Neues Volksliederheft, for medium voice,
    vln, vcl, pno
    (Schünemann) BRH
BENTZON, JØRGEN (1897-1951)
  Mikrofoni No. 1, Op. 44, for baritone,
    fl, vln, vcl, pno
    Dansk 89
BERGER, [ARTHUR (1912-   )]
  Poems of Yeats, 3, for voice, fl, clar, vcl
    Pr   score only
BERIO, LUCIANO (1925-   )
  Chamber Music, for medium voice, clar,
    vcl, harp
    SZ   score included; text by J. Joyce
BIRTWISTLE, HARRISON (1934-   )
  Monody for Corpus Christi, for soprano,
    fl, vln, horn
    UE 12928   score only
BLACHER, BORIS (1903-   )
  Francesca da Rimini, Op. 47, for soprano
    and vln
    BB

BOTTO, CARLOS
  *Cantos al Amor y a la Muerte, for voice,
    2 vln, vla, vcl
    SMP   for rent; Spanish and English Text
BRAHMS, JOHANNES (1833-1897)
  Gestliches Wiegenlied, Op. 91, No. 2, for
    medium voice, vla, pno
    BRH
  Songs, 2, Op. 91, for alto, vla, pno
    SIM
    1. Gestillte Sehnsucht
    2. Geistliches Wiegenlied
BURKHARD, [WILLY (1900-1955)]
  Herbst, Op. 36.   Cantata for soprano,
    vln, vcl, pno
    (Morgenstern) SCH
CORTESE, [LUIGI (1899-   )]
  Psalm No. 8, Op. 21, for soprano, fl,
    vcl, pno
    SZ
DALLAPICCOLA, LUIGI (1904-   )
  *Canti, 5, for baritone, fl, alto fl, clar
    in A, bass clar, vla, vcl, harp, pno
    SZ
  *Liriche di Anacreonte, 2, for high voice,
    clar in E flat, clar in A, vla, pno
    SZ
EGENOLFF, CHRISTIAN
  see 2 vln, vla, vcl
EGK, WERNER (1901-   )
  Tentation de St. Antoine, for alto, 2 vln,
    vla, vcl
    SCH   score only
EICHENWALD, PHILIPP (1915-   )
  Suoni estremi, for woman speaker, 2 vln,
    vla, vcl
    EDW
EISLER, HANNS (1898-   )
  Palmström, Op. 5, for voice, fl, clar,
    vln, vcl
    UE 8322   score only
EL-DABH, HALIM (1921-   )
  Tahmeela, for soprano, vln, fl, ob, clar,
    bsn, horn
    Pet 6536   for rent
    1. Benighted is the Night
    2. Oh! Vista
    3. Pale in the Shadow
FELDMAN, MORTON (1926-   )
  For Franz Kline, for soprano, vln, vcl,
    horn, chimes, pno
    Pet 6948   score only
  Four Songs to e. e. cummings, for
    soprano, vcl, pno
    Pet 6936   score only
  Intervals, for bass-baritone, vcl, trombone,
    vibraphone, percussion
    Pet 6908   score only

FELDMAN, MORTON (cont.)
O'Hara Songs, for bass-baritone, vln, vla,
vcl, chimes, pno
Pet 6949   score only
Vertical Thoughts 5, for soprano, vln, tuba,
percussion, celesta
Pet 6956   score only
FORTNER, WOLFGANG (1907-   )
Berceuse royale, for soprano, vln, pno
SCH
FRICKER, PETER RACINE (1920-   )
Elegy. The Tomb of Saint Eulalia, Op. 25,
for counter-tenor or tenor or alto,
gamba or vcl, harpsichord
SCH
GINASTERA, [ALBERTO (1916-   )]
Cantos del Tucuman, for voice, fl, vln,
harp and 2 "cajas indigenas"
Ric BA11034   score included
GRAENER, PAUL (1872-1944)
Gedichte, 3, Op. 113, for voice and vcl
BB
HARRIS, ROY (1898-   )
Abraham Lincoln walks at midnight, for mezzo
soprano, vln, vcl, pno
AMP
HENZE, HANS WERNER (1926-   )
Being Beauteous. Cantata for soprano,
harp, 4 vcl
SCH   score only
Kammermusik 1958, for tenor, guitar or
harp, clar, horn, bsn, str quintet
(Hölderlin) SCH   score only
HESSENBERG, KURT (1908-   )
Lieder, 10, Op. 32, for mezzo soprano or
baritone, pno, vln, vla
(Storm) SCH
HINDEMITH, PAUL (1895-1963)
Junge Magd, Die, Op. 23, No. 2, for alto, fl,
clar, 2 vln, vla, vcl
SCH   score only
Martinslied, Op. 45, No. 5, for medium voice
and 3 melody instruments
SCH   score included
Serenaden, Die, Op. 35, for soprano, ob,
vla, vcl
SCH   score and pno reduction only
*Todes Tod, Des, Op. 23a, for mezzo
soprano, 2 vla, 2 vcl
SCH
HORVATH, JOSEPH MARIA (1931-   )
*Blinde, Die. Melodrama after Rilke, for
alto, 2 speaking voices, fl, trumpet,
vcl, pno
Pet
*Songs, 4, for soprano or tenor, fl, clar,
vla, vcl
Pet
JANÁČEK, LEOŠ (1854-1928)
*Children's Rhymes, for high voice, pno,
vla or vln
UE 9479
JELINEK, HANNS (1901-   )
Selbstbildnis des Mark Aurel, for speaker,
fl, vla, bass clar, pno
EDW
KAMINSKI, HEINRICH (1886-1946)
Sacred Songs, 3, for voice, vln, clar
UE 7569   score included
KAUDER, HUGO (1888-   )
Poems, 10, for soprano, alto, tenor, 2 vln,
vla, vcl
BH   score included; text is Chamber
Music by James Joyce

KNIGHT, MORRIS (1933-   )
Pansies, for baritone, vln, clar, horn,
vcl, d-b
Tritone   manuscript reproduction; text
by D.H. Lawrence
KÖBLER, R.
Wilhelm-Busch-Lieder, for soprano, vln,
pno
BRH
KOUNADIS, ARGHYRIS (1924-   )
Drei Nocturnes nach Sappho, for soprano,
fl, celesta, vibraphone, vln, vla, vcl
EDW
KRONSTEINER, J.
Rilke-Lieder, 4, for alto, vla, pno
OBV
LIEBERMANN, [ROLF (1910-   )]
Capriccio, for soprano, vln, pno
UE 13018
MILHAUD, DARIUS (1892-   )
*Cantate de l'enfant et de la mère, for
reciter, 2 vln, vla, vcl, pno
Heugel   for rent
Machines agricoles, for medium voice,
fl, clar, bsn, vln, vla, vcl, d-b
UE 8142   score only
*Quartet No. 3, for 2 vln, vla, vcl with
voice
Dur   words by Latil
NIN, JOAQUIN (1879-1949)
Chant du Veilleur, Le, for mezzo soprano,
vln, pno
ESC   score included
NIN-CULMELL, JOAQUIN (1908-   )
Poemas de Jorge Manrique, 2, for soprano,
2 vln, vla, vcl
ESC   score included
PETYREK, FELIX (1892-1951)
Late, for voice, pno, vln
UE 5886
PITTALUGA, GUSTAVO (1906-   )
Canciones del Teatro de Federico Garcia
Lorca
UME   for various voices and instruments
PIZZETTI, ILDEBRANDO (1880-   )
Songs, 3, for soprano, 2 vln, vla, vcl
Ric PR669   score only
POUSSEUR, H.
Chants Sacrés, 3, for soprano and str trio
SZ
POWELL, MEL (1923-   )
Two Prayer Settings, for high voice, ob, vln,
vla, vcl
GS   for rent
RAVEL, MAURICE (1875-1937)
Trois Poèmes de Mallarmé, for voice, pno,
2 vln, vla, vcl, 2 fl, 2 clar
Dur
RESPIGHI, OTTORINO (1879-1936)
*Il Tramonto, for mezzo soprano, 2 vln
vla, vcl
Ric 117088
REUTTER, HERMANN (1900-   )
Ein kleines Requiem, for bass, vcl, pno
SCH
ROETSCHER, KONRAD (1910-   )
Lieder nach schottischen Texten, 6,
Op. 25, for soprano, vla, pno
BB
ROREM, NED (1923-   )
Mourning Scene, from Samuel, for tenor,
2 vln, vla, vcl
Pet 6374   score included

RUBBRA, EDMUND (1901-   )
  Ave Maria Gratia Plena. 2 medieval
    songs for voice, 2 vln, vla, vcl
    Leng (Mil No. L937)   score included
  Sonnets, 2, Op. 87, for medium voice,
    vla, pno
    Leng (Mil No. L946)
SCHOECK, OTHMAR (1886-1957)
  *Notturno, Op. 47, for baritone, 2 vln,
    vla, vcl
    UE 10576
SCHOENBERG, ARNOLD (1874-1951)
  Ode to Napoleon Buonaparte, Op. 41,
    for reciter, 2 vln, vla, vcl, pno
    GS   score included; text by Byron
  Pierrot lunaire, Op. 21, for voice, pno,
    fl, clar, vln, vcl
    UE 5336   score only
  *Quartet No. 2 in f sharp, Op. 10, for
    2 vln, vla, vcl, with soprano
    UE 2994
  Serenade, Op. 24,[111]for clar, bass clar,
    mandolin, guitar, vln, vla, vcl and
    baritone
    WH
SEARLE, HUMPHREY (1915-   )
  *Owl and the Pussy-Cat, for speaker,
    fl or vln, vcl, guitar or pno
    Oxf   for rent
  *Two Practical Cats, for speaker,
    fl/piccolo, vcl, guitar
    Oxf   for rent
SEIBER, [MÁTYÁS (1905-1960)]
  Owl and the Pussy-Cat, for high voice,
    vln, guitar
    SCH
SHEPHERD, ARTHUR (1880-1958)
  Triptych, for high voice, 2 vln, vla, vcl
    SPAM   score included
SMIT, LEO (1921-   )
  Motets, 4, for medium voice, 2 fl, vln
    Broude   score only
SOURIS, ANDRÉ (1899-   )
  Autre Voix, L', for soprano, fl, clar, vla,
    vcl, pno
    CBDM
STARER, ROBERT (1924-   )
  Concertino, for 2 voices or 2 instruments,
    vln, pno
    IMP   score included
STERNBERG, ERICH (1898-   )
  *Quartet No. 1, for 2 vln, vla, vcl, with
    mezzo soprano
    IMP   text in Hebrew and English
STRAVINSKY, IGOR (1882-   )
  *In Memoriam Dylan Thomas. Dirge-
    Canons and Song, for tenor,
    4 trombones, 2 vln, vla, vcl
    BH   for rent
  Pribaoutki,[112] for voice, fl, ob, clar, bsn,
    vln, vla
    Ches   for rent
  *Songs from William Shakespeare, 3, for
    mezzo, fl, clar, vla
    BH
THOMSON, VIRGIL (1896-   )
  *Stabat Mater, for soprano, 2 vln, vla, vcl
    BH

TIPPETT, MICHAEL (1905-   )
  Summer has a heart of drums, from
    Crown of the Year, for 2 sopranos,
    vln, pno
    SCH   score included
  Victoria rules an autumn land, from
    Crown of the Year, for alto, clar,
    vcl, pno
    SCH   score included
TOCH, ERNST (1887-   )
  There is a season to everything, for mezzo
    soprano, fl, vln, clar, vcl
    Mil   score included
TURINA, JOAQUIN (1882-1949)
  Erato, from Las Musas de Andalucia,
    for high voice, 2 vln, vla, vcl
    UME   score only
ULMANN, HELLMUTH VON (1913-   )
  Songs of Farewell, for low voice and str trio
    Sik   for rent
VAUGHAN WILLIAMS, RALPH (1872-1958)
  Hymns, 4, for tenor, vla, pno
    BH
  *On Wenlock Edge, for tenor, pno, 2 vln,
    vla, vcl
    BH
VILLA-LOBOS, HEITOR (1887-1959)
  *Bachianas Brasileiras No. 5, for soprano
    and 8 vcl
    AMP
  Poêma da Criança e sua Mamã, for
    medium voice, fl, clar in A, vcl
    ESC   pno reduction included
  Suite, for medium voice and vln
    ESC
WALTON, WILLIAM (1902-   )
  *Facade Entertainment, for speaker, fl,
    clar, trumpet, sax, 1 or 2 vcl,
    percussion
    Oxf   for rent
WATKINSON, G.
  Processional and Evening Music
    NAG   score only; for voices, instruments,
    and percussion
WEBERN, ANTON (1883-1945)
  *Sacred Songs, 5, Op. 15, for soprano, vln,
    fl, clar, trumpet, harp
    UE 7630
  Songs, 6, Op. 14, for voice, clar, bass
    clar, vln, vcl
    UE 7578   score only
  *Traditional Rhymes, 3, Op. 17, for voice,
    vln and vla, clar, bass clar
    UE 12272   vla doubles vln
WEIGL, VALLY
  Echoes from Poems by Patricia Benton,
    for high or medium voice, vln, pno
    CFE
WEILL, KURT (1900-1950)
  Der neue Orpheus, Op. 15, for voice,
    vln, pno
    UE 8472
  Frauentanz, Op. 10, for soprano, fl,
    vla, clar, horn, bsn
    UE 7599   score only
WELLESZ, EGON (1885-   )
  *Leaden Echo and the Golden Echo, for
    soprano, vln, vcl, clar, pno
    SCH
  Sonnets of Elizabeth Browning, Op. 52,
    for soprano, 2 vln, vla, vcl
    UE 10281   for rent

---

[111] In 7 sections or movements. The fourth is a sonnet by
Petrarch, and requires "eine tiefe Männerstimme."
[112] In the U.S.A. this publication can be obtained through
G. Schirmer.

WILKINSON, MARC (1929-   )
  Voices, for voice, fl, clar, bass clar, vcl
    UE 12912   score only

ZILCHER, HERMANN (1881-1948)
  Marienlieder, Op. 52a, for high voice,
    2 vln, vla, vcl
    BRH
  *Rokoko-Suite, Op. 65, for high voice, vln,
    vcl, pno
    BRH

CHAMBER MUSIC SCORES

Chamber Music Scores

ABBADO, MARCELLO (1926-   )
Poesie T'Ang, 15, for mezzo soprano,
    fl, ob, vln, pno
  SZ
ABENDROTH, WALTER (1896-   )
Quartet, Op. 33, for 2 vln, vla, vcl
  Sik 321
ABSIL, JEAN (1893-   )
Concert a cinq, Op. 38, see fl, vln,
    vla, vcl, harp
Quartets Nos. 2, 3, 4, see 2 vln, vla, vcl
Trio No. 1, see vln, vla, vcl
Trio No. 2, Op. 39, for vln, vla, vcl
  Ches
ADOLPHUS, MILTON
Elegy, Op. 81, for clar, horn, vln,
    vla, vcl
  CFE
Quartet No. 14, Op. 65, for 2 vln, vla, vcl
  CFE
Quartet No. 20, Op. 80 for 2 vln, vla, vcl
  CFE
Quartet No. 21, in ancient style, for 2 vln,
    vla, vcl
  CFE
Quartet No. 23, see 2 vln, vla, vcl
AGAFONNIKOV, N.
Quintet in D, for pno, 2 vln, vla, vcl
  MZK
AGERSNAP, HARALD (1899-   )
Interludium, for fl, vln, vcl
  Dansk 81
AHLGRIMM, HANS
Divertimento, see fl, vln, vla
AIVAZIAN, A.
Quartet No. 2, for 2 vln, vla, vcl
  MZK
ALBERT, R.
Quartet in D, for vln, vla, vcl, guitar
  UME
ALEXANDROV, ANATOLY (1888-   )
Quartet No. 3, Op. 55, for 2 vln, vla, vcl
  MZK
Quartet No. 4, Op. 80, for 2 vln, vla, vcl
  MZK
ALEXANIAN, DIRAN
Petite Suite Arménienne, see 2 vln,
    vla, vcl
ALFVÉN, HUGO (1872-1960)
Elegi, for 2 vln, vla, vcl
  Gehrmans
ALIABEV, [ALEXANDER (1787-1851)]
Quartet No. 1, for 2 vln, vla, vcl
  MZK
Quartet No. 3, for 2 vln, vla, vcl
  MZK
Variations, see 2 vln, vcl

ALIX, RENÉ (1907-   )
Quartet, Op. 13, for 2 vln, vla, vcl
  CH (Pet No. C247)
ALPAERTS, FLOR
Quartet No. 2, see 2 vln, vla, vcl
ALWYN, WILLIAM (1905-   )
Quartet in d, for 2 vln, vla, vcl
  Leng
AMES, WILLIAM
Quartets, see 2 vln, vla, vcl
Quintet, see clar, 2 vln, vla, vcl
Sextet, see ob, 2 vln, 2 vla, vcl
AMRAM, DAVID (1930-   )
Quartet for 2 vln, vla, vcl
  Pet 6688a
ANDERSEN, KARL (1903-   )
Trio, for fl, clar, vcl
  Norsk
ANGERER, PAUL (1927-   )
"Ei du feiner Reiter". 7 variations on
    the folksong, for 2 vln, vla, vcl
  DOB
ANGOT-BRACQUEMOND, M.
Pieces, 3, for 2 vln, vla, vcl
  Senart
ANSORGE, CONRAD (1862-1930)
Quartet, Op. 13, for 2 vln, vla, vcl
  Birnbach
ANTES, JOHN
Trios, Op. 3, see 2 vln, vcl
APOSTEL, HANS ERICH (1901-   )
Quartet, Op. 7, for 2 vln, vla, vcl
  UE Ph387
Quartet No. 2, Op. 26, for 2 vln, vla, vcl
  UE 12745
ARDÉVOL, JOSÉ (1911-   )
Musica de Camera para seis instrumentos,
    for fl, clar, bsn, trumpet in C, vln, vcl
  Pan American Union
Quartet No. 2 for 2 vln, vla, vcl
  SMP
Sonatas a Tres, Dos
  ECIC
    1. Sonata for ob, clar, vcl
    2. Sonata for 2 fl, vla
ARNE, THOMAS
Shakespeare Songs, see voice and instru-
    ments
ARNOLD, MALCOLM (1921-   )
Quartet No. 1, for 2 vln, vla, vcl
  Leng
ASAFIEV, [BORIS (1884-1949)]
Quartet, for 2 vln, vla, vcl
  MZK
ATTERBERG, [KURT (1887-   )]
Suite No. 7, Op. 29, for 2 vln, vla, vcl
  BRH
AVIDOM, MENAHEM (1908-   )
Quartet No. 2, from Wisdom of the Fathers,
    for 2 vln, vla, vcl
  Mil

AVSHALOMOV, AARON
Quartet, see 2 vln, vla, vcl
BAAREN, KEES VAN (1906-   )
Quartet No. 2, for 2 vln, vla, vcl
DN
Septet, for fl, ob, clar, bsn, horn, vln, d-b
DN (Pet No. D17A)
BABBITT, MILTON (1916-   )
Sonnets, 2, for baritone, clar, vla, vcl
BMP
BACH, JOHANN SEBASTIAN (1685-1750)
Art of the Fugue
Baer TP26
Kal 180
Lea 73
Musical offering, for 2-6 string instru-
ments, with or without wind instru-
ments; with keyboard instrument
(David) GS
Musical Offering, 3 trio sonatas
Lea 26
Organ Choral Preludes, for 2 vln, vla, vcl
(Hodge) Paterson 251-2   2V
Sonatas, 6, for vln unacc; 6 Sonatas for
vcl unacc
Lea 2
Sonatas and Partitas, 6, for vln unacc
(Hausswald) Baer TP59
Sonatas, 6, for vln and clavier
Lea 4
Sonatas, 3, for gamba and clavier; with 7
sonatas for fl and clavier
Lea 10
BACH, KARL PHILIPP EMANUEL (1714-1788)
Suite for 2 vln, vla, vcl, orig concerto for
viols
(Casadesus) GS
BACH, WILHELM FRIEDRICH ERNST
Sextet, see clar, 2 horns, vln, vla, vcl
BADINGS, HENK (1907-   )
Octet, for clar, bsn, horn, 2 vln, vla, vcl, d-b
DN (Pet No. D135A)
Trio No. 9, for fl, vla, guitar
DN
BAEYENS, AUGUST
Quartet No. 4, see 2 vln, vla, vcl
BALAKIREV
Octet, Op. 3, see 8 instruments
BALAZS, FREDERIC
Quartets, see 2 vln, vla, vcl
BALLOU, ESTHER W.
Divertimento, see 2 vln, vla, vcl
Fantasia Brevis, see ob, vln, vla, vcl
Fantasia Brevis II, see ob, 2 vln, vla, vcl
BALSIS, E.
Quartet in g, for 2 vln, vla, vcl
MZK
BANTOCK, GRANVILLE (1868-1946)
In a Chinese Mirror, for 2 vln, vla, vcl
Ches
BARATI, GEORGE (1913-   )
Quartet, 1944, for 2 vln, vla, vcl
CFE
Quartet No. 2, see 2 vln, vla, vcl
Quintet, see ob, 2 vln, vla, vcl
BARBER, SAMUEL (1910-   )
Dover Beach, Op. 3, for medium voice,
2 vln, vla, vcl
GS 15
Quartet, Op. 11, for 2 vln, vla, vcl
GS 28
Serenade, Op. 1, for str quartet or str orch
GS

BARBIER, RENÉ
Quartet, see 2 vln, vla, vcl
BARRAUD, HENRY (1900-   )
Quatuor, for 2 vln, vla, vcl
Amphion 131
BARTÓK, BÉLA (1881-1945)
Contrasts, for pno, vln, clar
BH
Pieces, 5, from Mikrokosmos, for 2 vln,
vla, vcl
(Serly) BH
Quartets, 6, for 2 vln, vla, vcl
BH   with analysis
Quartets Nos. 1-6, for 2 vln, vla, vcl
BH   published separately
Quartet No. 1, for 2 vln, vla, vcl
Kal F253
BASNER, V.
Quartet No. 2, for 2 vln, vla, vcl
MZK
BASSETT, LESLIE (1923-   )
Pieces, 5, for 2 vln, vla, vcl
Highgate
Quartet No. 2, see 2 vln, vla, vcl
Quintet, see 2 vln, vla, vcl, d-b
BATE, STANLEY RICHARD (1911-1959)
Quartet No. 2, for 2 vln, vla, vcl
Leng
BAUER, MARION
Five Pieces, see 2 vln, vla, vcl
BAUERNFEIND, HANS
Gay Play, see vln, vla, vcl
Heitere Musik, see vln, vla, vcl
BEACH, JOHN (1877-1953)
Poem, for 2 vln, vla, vcl
Ches
BEALE, JAMES
Miniatures, Op. 3, see ob, clar, vla
Quartet No. 2, see 2 vln, vla, vcl
BEETHOVEN, LUDWIG VAN (1770-1827)
Prelude and Fugue in e, see 2 vln, vcl
Quartets, 17, for 2 vln, vla, vcl
EPS   published separately
Kal 128-130   3V
Vol 1: Op. 18, Nos. 1-6
Vol 2: Op. 59, Nos. 1-3; 74; 95
Vol 3: Op. 127; 130-33; 135
Lea 61-64   4V
Vol 1: Op. 18, Nos. 1-6
Vol 2: Op. 59, Nos. 1-3
Vol 3: Op. 74, 95, 127, 130
Vol 4: Op. 131, 132, 133, 135
Ric PR670   in one volume
Ric   published separately
Quartet, Op. 16, for vln, vla, vcl, pno
EPS (Pet No. E114)
Quintets, 4, for 2 vln, 2 vla, vcl
EPS   published separately
Op. 4; Op. 29; Op. 104; Op. 137
Septet in E flat, Op. 20, for clar, bsn,
horn, vln, vla, vcl, d-b
EPS (Pet No. E12)
Ric PR467
Serenade in D, Op. 8, for vln, vla, vcl
EPS (Pet No. E45)
Ric PR431
Serenade in D, Op. 25, for fl, vln, vla
EPS (Pet No. E103)
Ric PR615
Sextet in E flat, Op. 81b, for 2 horns, 2 vln,
vla, vcl
EPS (Pet No. E140)
Sonatas, 10, for vln and pno
Lea 3   2V

BEETHOVEN, LUDWIG VAN (cont.)
Sonatas, 5, for vcl and pno
Lea 18
Trios, 5, for vln, vla, vcl
Lea 99
Op. 3; Op. 9, Nos. 1-3; Op. 8
Trios, 4, for vln, vla, vcl
EPS (Pet Nos. E41-44)
published separately
Op. 3; Op. 9, Nos. 1-3
Trios, Op. 1, Nos. 1-3, for vln, vcl, pno
EPS (Pet Nos. E122-4)
published separately
Trio, Op. 11, for clar or vln, vcl, pno
EPS (Pet No. E223)
Trios, Op. 70, Nos. 1, 2, for vln, vcl, pno
EPS (Pet Nos. E82-3)
published separately
Trio, Op. 97, for vln, vcl, pno
EPS (Pet No. E79)
Trio, Op. 121a. Variations, for vln, vcl, pno
EPS (Pet No. E278)
BENEDICT
Quartet, Op. 21, see fl, vln, vla, vcl
BENJAMIN, ARTHUR (1893-   )
Quartet No. 2, for 2 vln, vla, vcl
BH
BENOY, A.W.
Violinist's Books of Carols, for 2 vln,
vla, vcl
Oxf 23.113-4   2V
BENTZON, JORGEN (1897-1951)
Variazioni interrotti, Op. 12, for clar,
bsn, vln, vla, vcl
WH
BENTZON, NIELS VIGGO (1919-   )
Quartet No. 3, Op. 72, for 2 vln, vla, vcl
WH
BERG, ALBAN (1885-1935)
Lyric Suite, for 2 vln, vla, vcl
UE Ph173
Quartet, Op. 3, for 2 vln, vla, vcl
UE 7537
BERGER, [ARTHUR (1912-   )]
Poems of Yeats, 3, for voice, fl, clar, vcl
Pr
BERGER, JEAN (1909-   )
Divertimento for 3 treble instruments
Broude
BERGSMA, WILLIAM (1921-   )
Quartet No. 3, for 2 vln, vla, vcl
CF 16
BERIO, LUCIANO
Chamber Music, see voice and instruments
BERKELEY, LENNOX (1903-   )
Quartet, for 2 vln, vla, vcl
BH
Quartet No. 2, for 2 vln, vla, vcl
Ches
Sextet, for clar, horn, 2 vln, vla, vcl
Ches
Trio, for vln, vla, vcl
Ches
BERLINSKI, HERMAN
Quartet, see 2 vln, vla, vcl
BERNAL JIMENEZ, MIGUEL (1910-1956)
Quartet. Cuarteto Virreinal, for 2 vln,
vla, vcl
EMM
BERNIER
Trio, see fl, vcl, harp
BERTHET, F.
Quatuor for 2 vln, vla, vcl
Senart

BERWALD, FRANZ (1796-1868)
Quartets, 3, for 2 vln, vla, vcl
Gehrmans   published separately
Stor Septett, for clar, bsn, horn, vln, vla,
vcl, d-b
Gehrmans
BEZANSON, PHILIP
Quartet, see 2 vln, vla, vcl
Trio, see vln, vla, vcl
BINKERD, GORDON
Quartets Nos. 1 and 2, see 2 vln, vla, vcl
Trio, see clar, vla, vcl
BIRTWISTLE, HARRISON (1934-   )
Monody for Corpus Christi, for soprano,
fl, vln, horn
UE 12928
BJERRE, JENS (1903-   )
Mosaique musicale, for fl, vln, vcl
Dansk 82
BLACKWOOD, EASLEY (1933-   )
Concertino, Op. 5, for fl, ob, vln, vla, vcl
GS 90
Quartet No. 1, see 2 vln, vla, vcl
Quartet No. 2, Op. 6, for 2 vln, vla, vcl
GS 88
BLISS, ARTHUR (1891-   )
Quartets Nos. 1 and 2, for 2 vln, vla, vcl
Nov   published separately
Quintet, for clar, 2 vln, vla, vcl
Nov
Quintet, for ob, 2 vln, vla, vcl
Oxf 07.002
BLOCH, ERNEST (1880-1959)
In the Mountains, see 2 vln, vla, vcl
Night, see 2 vln, vla, vcl
Paysages, see 2 vln, vla, vcl
Pieces, Deux, for 2 vln, vla, vcl
JWL (Mil No. W2300)
Prelude, see 2 vln, vla, vcl
Quartet No. 1, for 2 vln, vla, vcl
GS 1
Quartet No. 2, for 2 vln, vla, vcl
BH
Quartet No. 3, for 2 vln, vla, vcl
GS 63
Quartet No. 4, for 2 vln, vla, vcl
GS 72
Quartet No. 5, for 2 vln, vla, vcl
Broude
BOATWRIGHT, HOWARD (1918-   )
Quartet, for clar, vln, vla, vcl
Oxf 90.701
BOCCHERINI, LUIGI (1743-1805)
Quartets, 6, Op. 6, for 2 vln, vla, vcl
(Polo) Ric PR657-8   2V
Quartets, Op. 58, Nos. 1-6, for 2 vln, vla, vcl
(Carmirelli) Ric PR824
Quartets, 3, for 2 vln, vla, vcl
(Polo) Ric PR659
Op. 1, No. 1; Op. 10, No. 4;
Op. 27, No. 4
Quartets, 3, for 2 vln, vla, vcl
(Polo) Ric PR660
Op. 10, No. 1; Op. 33, No. 6;
Op. 27, No. 3
Quintets, 6, for 2 vln, vla, 2 vcl
(Polo) Ric ER2170, 2172, 2174   3V
for contents see 2 vln, vla, 2 vcl
Quintet in E flat, Op. 21, No. 6, for fl,
2 vln, vla, vcl
(Haas) Nov
Santis 957
BONELLI, ETTORE (1900-   )
Quartet No. 2, for 2 vln, vla, vcl
ZA 3145

BORODIN, ALEXANDER (1833-1887)
Quartet No. 1 in A, for 2 vln, vla, vcl
  Belaieff
Quartet No. 2 in D, for 2 vln, vla, vcl
  Belaieff
  EPS (Pet No. E201)
  Int
  Ric PR468
BORODIN, GLAZUNOV, LIADOV & RIMSKY-
  KORSAKOV
Quartet on the name B-la-f, for 2 vln,
  vla, vcl
  Belaieff
BØRRESEN, HAKON (1876-   )
Quartet, for 2 vln, vla, vcl
  Dansk 70
BORRIS, SIEGFRIED (1906-   )
Kleine Suite, Op. 31, No. 3, for fl, ob,
  clar, bsn, vln, vla, vcl
  Sirius in preparation
Oboenquartett, Op. 17, No. 1, for ob,
  vln, vla, vcl
  Sirius
Oktett, Op. 99, No. 4, for clar, bsn,
  horn and str quintet
  Sirius in preparation
Quartet No. 2 in f sharp, Op. 28, for
  2 vln, vla, vcl
  Sirius
Quartet No. 3, Op. 64, for 2 vln, vla, vcl
  Sirius
BOTTJE, WILL GAY
Quartet No. 2, see 2 vln, vla, vcl
BOTTO, CARLOS
Cantos al Amor y a la Muerte, for
  voice, 2 vln, vla, vcl
  SMP
BOURGUIGNON, FRANCIS DE
Quintet, Op. 100, see ob, 2 vln, vla, vcl
Trio, Op. 49, see vln, vla, vcl
BOZZA, EUGÉNE (1906-   )
Quatuor en la, for 2 vln, vla, vcl
  Leduc
BRAHMS, JOHANNES (1833-1897)
Chamber Music
  Pet 2V
    Vol 1
      Quartets Op. 51, Nos. 1, 2; Op. 67
      Quintets Op. 88, Op. 111, Op. 115
      Sextets Op. 18, Op. 36
    Vol 2
      Trios Op. 8, Op. 40, Op. 87,
        Op. 101, Op. 114
      Quartets Op. 25, Op. 26, Op. 60
      Quintet Op. 34
Quartets, 3, for 2 vln, vla, vcl
  Op. 51, Nos. 1, 2; Op. 67
  EPS (Pet No. E240-242)
  published separately
  Ric PR417-9 published separately
Quartets, 3, for vln, vla, vcl, pno
  EPS (Pet Nos. E243-5) published
    separately
  Op. 25, Op. 26, Op. 60
Quintets, 2, for 2 vln, 2 vla, vcl
  EPS (Pet Nos. E237-8)
  published separately
  Op. 88, Op. 111
Quintet, Op. 34, for 2 vln, vla, vcl, pno
  EPS (Pet No. E212)
  Ric PR483
Quintet, Op. 115, for clar, 2 vln, vla, vcl
  BH
  EPS (Pet No. E239)
  Ric PR482

Sextets, 2, for 2 vln, 2 vla, 2 vcl
  EPS (Pet Nos. E235-6)
  published separately
  Op. 18, Op. 36
Sonatas, 3, for vln and pno
  Lea 6
Sonatas, 2, for vcl and pno; with
  2 sonatas for clar and pno
  Lea 7
Trios, 3, for vln, vcl, pno
  EPS (Pet Nos. E246-8)
  published separately
  Op. 8, Op. 87, Op. 101
Trio, Op. 40, for horn, vln, pno
  EPS (Pet No. E249)
Trio, Op. 114, for clar, vcl, pno
  EPS (Pet No. E250)
BRÄUTIGAM, H.
Fröhliche Musik, for fl, ob, 3 vln
  BRH
BRESCIANELLO, GIOVANNI ANTONIO
Concerti a tre, see 2 vln, vcl
BRETAGNE, S.
Quatuor for 2 vln, vla, vcl
  RL
BRIDGE, FRANK (1879-1941)
Quartet No. 1 in e, for 2 vln, vla, vcl
  Aug
Quartet No. 2 in g, for 2 vln, vla, vcl
  Aug
Quartet No. 4, for 2 vln, vla, vcl
  Aug
Sextet, for 2 vln, 2 vla, 2 vcl
  Aug
BRITTEN, BENJAMIN (1913-   )
Phantasy Quartet, Op. 2, for ob, vln,
  vla, vcl
  BH
Quartet No. 1, Op. 25, for 2 vln, vla, vcl
  BH
Quartet No. 2, Op. 36, for 2 vln, vla, vcl
  BH
BROWN, HAROLD
Quintet, for 2 vln, 2 vla, vcl
  CFE
BRUCKNER, ANTON (1824-1896)
Quartet in c, for 2 vln, vla, vcl
  Bruck (Pet No. BR24)
Quintet in F, for 2 vln, 2 vla, vcl
  EPS (Pet No. E310)
BRÜN, HERBERT (1918-   )
Quartet, for 2 vln, vla, vcl
  IMP
Quartet No. 3, for 2 vln, vla, vcl
  Tonos
BRUNNER, ADOLF (1901-   )
Streichtrio, for vln, vla, vcl
  Baer
BRUNSWICK, MARK
Septet, see 7 instruments
BUCCHI, VALENTINO (1916-   )
Quartet, for 2 vln, vla, vcl
  Carisch
BUESSER, HENRI (1872-   )
Divertissement, Op. 119, for 2 vln, vla, vcl
  Dur
BUNIN, R.
Quartet No. 2, Op. 27, for 2 vln, vla, vcl
  MZK
BURKHARD, WILLY (1900-1955)
Divertimento, for vln, vla, vcl
  Baer TP25
Quartett in einem Satz, Op. 68, for 2 vln,
  vla, vcl
  Baer

BURKHARD, WILLY (cont.)
Serenade, Op. 77, for fl, clar, bsn, horn,
harp, vln, vla, d-b
BH
BUSH, ALAN (1900-   )
Dialectic, for 2 vln, vla, vcl
BH
BUSTINI, [ALESSANDRO (1876-   )]
Quartet No. 2, for 2 vln, vla, vcl
Ric PR675
CAGE, JOHN (1912-   )
Quartet, see 2 vln, vla, vcl
Short Inventions, 6, for alto fl, clar in B
flat, trumpet in B flat, vln, 2 vla, vcl
Pet 6749
CAJA, ALFONSO (1889-   )
Quartet, for 2 vln, vla, vcl
Sal
CAPET, LUCIEN (1873-1928)
Quatuor No. 1, for 2 vln, vla, vcl
Mathot
Quatuor No. 2 for 2 vln, vla, vcl
Senart
CARMINA
(Moser-Piersig) NAG
12 settings from the 16th century
for groups of 2-5 strings
CARMINA GERMANICA ET GALLICA, see
4 viols
CARPENTER, JOHN ALDEN (1876-1951)
Quartet, for 2 vln, vla, vcl
GS 2
CARTER, ELLIOTT (1908-   )
Elegy for 2 vln, vla, vcl
Peer
Quartet No. 1, for 2 vln, vla, vcl
AMP
Quartet No. 2, for 2 vln, vla, vcl
AMP
CASELLA, ALFREDO (1883-1947)
Concerto, for 2 vln, vla, vcl
UE Ph249
Serenata, for clar, bsn, trumpet, vln, vcl
UE Ph177
CASTELNUOVO-TEDESCO, MARIO (1895-   )
Quartet No. 2 in F, Op. 139, for 2 vln,
vla, vcl
Mil
CASTILLON, ALEXIS DE (1838-1873)
Quatuor, Op. 3, for 2 vln, vla, vcl
Dur
CAZDEN, NORMAN
Quartet, Op. 23, see clar, vln, vla, vcl
Quartet, see 2 vln, vla, vcl
Quintet, Op. 74, see ob, 2 vln, vla, vcl
Quintet, see 2 vln, vla, 2 vcl
CETTIER, PIERRE (1874-   )
Quartet No. 2, for 2 vln, vla, vcl
Sal
CHAGRIN, FRANCIS
Elegy, see 2 vln, vla, vcl
CHAUSSON, ERNEST (1855-1899)
Quatuor en ut mineur, Op. 35, for 2 vln,
vla, vcl
Dur
CHEMBERDZHI, N.
Quartet No. 3, for 2 vln, vla, vcl
MZK
CHEMIN-PETIT, HANS (1902-   )
Suite "Dr. Johannes Faust", for ob,
clar, bsn, percussion, 2 vln, vla,
vcl, d-b
LN (Pet No. R3)

CHEVILLARD, [CAMILLE (1859-1923)]
Quatuor en ré, Op. 16, for 2 vln, vla, vcl
Dur
CHEVREUILLE, RAYMOND
Quartets Nos. 4 and 5, see 2 vln, vla, vcl
Salon Music, Op. 49, see fl, vln, vla, vcl
CHILDS, BARNEY
Quartet No. 4, see 2 vln, vla, vcl
CLARKE, HENRY L.
Quartets Nos. 2 and 3, see 2 vln, vla, vcl
COLE, HUGO (1917-   )
Miniature Quartets Nos. 1 and 2, for
2 vln, vla, vcl
Nov   published separately
Quartet, for ob, vln, vla, vcl
Nov
COOKE, ARNOLD (1906-   )
Quartet, for ob, vln, vla, vcl
Nov
Trio, for vln, vla, vcl
Nov
COPLAND, AARON (1900-   )
Pieces, 2, for 2 vln, vla, vcl
BH
Quartet, for vln, vla, vcl, pno
BH
Sextet, for clar, pno, 2 vln, vla, vcl
BH
COUPERIN, FRANCOIS (1668-1733)
Pièces en concert, for vcl and string quartet
Leduc
COWELL, HENRY (1897-   )
Paragraphs, 6, for vln, vla, vcl
CFE
Quartet No. 4, see 2 vln, vla, vcl
Quartet No. 5, for 2 vln, vla, vcl
Pet 6117
Set of Five, see pno, vln, percussion
CRAS, JEAN (1879-1932)
Quatuor No. 1, for 2 vln, vla, vcl
RL
Trio, for vln, vla, vcl
Senart
CRAWFORD, ROBERT (1925-   )
Quartet No. 1, Op. 4, for 2 vln, vla, vcl
Aug
Quartet No. 2, Op. 8, for 2 vln, vla, vcl
Aug
CRUFT, ADRIAN
Fantasy, see ob, vln, vla, vcl
CSERMAK, ANTON GEORG
Quartet, for 2 vln, vla, vcl, "Die drohende
Gefahr oder die Vaterlandsliebe"
DOB
CUSTER, ARTHUR
Coloquio Para Cuarteto de Cuerda, see
2 vln, vla, vcl
DALLAPICCOLA, LUIGI (1904-   )
Canti, 5, for baritone, fl, alto fl, clar in A,
bass clar, vla, vcl, pno, harp
SZ
Liriche di Anacreonte, 2, for high voice,
clar in E flat, clar in A, vla, pno
SZ
DANZI, FRANZ (1763-1826)
Trio, Op. 24, for vln, horn, bsn
SIM
DAVIES, P.
Quartet, for 2 vln, vla, vcl
SCH
DEBUSSY, CLAUDE (1862-1918)
Quartet, Op. 10, for 2 vln, vla, vcl
Dur
Int
Kal 73

DEBUSSY, CLAUDE (cont.)
Sonata, for fl, vla, harp
Dur
DEDIEU-PETERS, MADELEINE (1889-   )
Pieces, 3, for 2 vln, vla, vcl
Sal
Quartet No. 2, for 2 vln, vla, vcl
Sal
DEFOSSEZ, RENÉ
Quartet No. 2, see 2 vln, vla, vcl
DELAGE, [MAURICE (1879-   )]
Quartet in d, for 2 vln, vla, vcl
Dur
DELANNOY, MARCEL (1898-   )
Quatuor en mi majeur, for 2 vln, vla, vcl
Dur
DELDEN, LEX VAN (1919-   )
Quartet No. 1, Op. 43, for 2 vln, vla, vcl
DN (Pet No. D56A)
DE LEMARTER
Quartet No. 2, see 2 vln, vla, vcl
DELIUS, FREDERICK (1862-1934)
Quartet, for 2 vln, vla, vcl
Aug
DELVAUX, A.
Quartet No. 4, see 2 vln, vla, vcl
Trio No. 1, see vln, vla, vcl
DELVINCOURT, CLAUDE (1888-1954)
Quartet, for 2 vln, vla, vcl
Dur
DEMANTIUS, J.C.
Nürnberger Tanzbuch, for 4 or 5
instruments
(Mönkemeyer) SCH
DENNY, WILLIAM
Quartet No. 2, see 2 vln, vla, vcl
DESDERI, ETTORE (1892-   )
Divertimento, for 3 vln
Schwann
DIAMOND, DAVID (1915-   )
Concerto, for 2 vln, vla, vcl
SMP
Nonet, for 3 vln, 3 vla, 3 vcl
SMP
Quartet No. 1, for 2 vln, vla, vcl
SMP
Quartet No. 2 for 2 vln, vla, vcl
SMP
Quartet No. 3 for 2 vln, vla, vcl
SMP
Quartet No. 4 for 2 vln, vla, vcl
SMP
Quintet for clar, 2 vla, 2 vcl
SMP
D'INDY, see Indy,d'
DITTERSDORF, KARL DITTERS VON
(1739-1799)
Quartet No. 5 in E flat, for 2 vln, vla, vcl
EPS (Pet No. E105)
Quintet No. 6, see 2 vln, vla, 2 vcl
DOHNÁNYI, ERNST VON (1877-1960)
Quartet in A, Op. 7, for 2 vln, vla, vcl
DOB
Quartet No. 3 in a, Op. 33, for 2 vln, vla, vcl
Kul
Quintet in e flat, Op. 26, for 2 vln, vla,
vcl, pno
EPS (Pet No. E343)
Serenade, Op. 10, for vln, vla, vcl
DOB
Int
DONATO, ANTHONY
Drag and Run, see clar, 2 vln, vcl
Quartet in e, see 2 vln, vla, vcl

DONOVAN, RICHARD (1891-   )
Music for Six, for ob, clar, trumpet,
vln, vcl, pno
Pet 6666A
Terzetto, see 2 vln, vla
DORATI, ANTAL
Notturno and Capriccio, see ob, 2 vln,
vla, vcl
DORET, [GUSTAVE (1866-1943)]
Quatuor en Ré majeur, for 2 vln, vla, vcl
RL
DOWLAND, JOHN (1562-1626)
Lachrimae, or Seven Teares, for 2 vln,
vla, 2 vcl
(Warlock) Oxf 27.002
Stücke, 5, für Streichmusik zu 5 Stimmen
Baer 75
DRAKEFORD, R.
Fantasia, for 3 viols
SCH
DRESDEN, SEM (1881-1957)
Quatuor No. 1, for 2 vln, vla, vcl
Senart
DRIESSLER, JOHANNES (1921-   )
Streichtrio, Op. 1, No. 2, for vln, vla, vcl
Baer
DUBOIS, THÉODORE (1837-1924)
Nonetto, for fl, ob, clar, bsn, 2 vln, vla,
vcl, d-b
Heugel
DUKE, VERNON (1903-   )
Quartet in C, for 2 vln, vla, vcl
FC 1885
DUMLER, M.
Quartet, see 2 vln, vla, vcl
DUPIN, PAUL (1865-1949)
Poèmes, for 2 vln, vla, vcl
Sal
DU PLESSIS, see Plessis
DUPONT
Quartet, Op. 27, for 2 vln, vla, vcl
Sal
DVORAK, ANTONIN (1841-1904)
Cypresses, for 2 vln, vla, vcl
Artia
Miniatures, Op. 75A, for 2 vln, vla; with
Gavotte for 3 vln
Artia
Quartets, 8, for 2 vln, vla, vcl
Artia   published separately
Op. 2; Op. 16; Op. 34; Op. 51
Op. 61; Op. 96; Op. 105; Op. 106
Quartets, 6, for 2 vln, vla, vcl
EPS (Pet Nos. E298-300; 302-4)
published separately
Op. 34, Op. 51, Op. 61, Op. 96,
Op. 105, Op. 106
Quartet No. 6 in F, Op. 96, "American",
for 2 vln, vla, vcl
Int
Quartet Fragment in F, for 2 vln, vla, vcl
Artia
Quartet, Op. 23, for vln, vla, vcl, pno
Artia
Quartet, Op. 87, for vln, vla, vcl, pno
Artia
EPS (Pet No. E330)
Quintet in G, Op. 77, for 2 vln, vla,
vcl, d-b
Artia
EPS (Pet No. E338)
Quintet in A, Op. 81, for 2 vln, vla, vcl, pno
Artia
EPS (Pet No. E305)

DVORAK, ANTONIN (cont.)
Quintet in E flat, Op. 97, for 2 vln,
2 vla, vcl
Artia
EPS (Pet No. E306)
Serenade in E, Op. 22, for 2 vln, vla, vcl
Artia
Kal 247
Sextet in A, Op. 48, for 2 vln, 2 vla, 2 vcl
Artia
EPS (Pet No. E337)
Terzetto in C, Op. 74, for 2 vln, vla
Artia
Int
Trio, Op. 21, for vln, vcl, pno
Artia
Trio, Op. 26, for vln, vcl, pno
Artia
Trio, Op. 65, for vln, vcl, pno
EPS (Pet No. E331)
Trio, Op. 90, "Dumky", for vln, vcl, pno
Artia
EPS (Pet No. E332)
EDER, HELMUT [(1916-   )]
Ottetto breve, Op. 33, for fl, ob, clar, bsn,
2 vln, vla, vcl
DOB
EDMUNDS, CHRISTOPHER (1899-   )
Miniature Quartet, for 2 vln, vla, vcl
Nov
EGK, WERNER (1901-   )
Tentation de St. Antoine, for alto, 2 vln,
vla, vcl
SCH
EISLER, HANNS (1898-   )
Palmström, Op. 5, for voice, fl, clar,
vln, vcl
UE 8322
ELER, ANDREAS (1764-1821)
Quartet, Op. 2, No. 3, for 2 vln, vla, vcl
KS
ELLER, H.
Quartet No. 3, for 2 vln, vla, vcl
MZK
EMMANUEL, [MAURICE (1862-1938)]
Quatuor en si bemol, for 2 vln, vla, vcl
Dur
ENGLISCHE FANTASIEN AUS DEM 17
JAHRHUNDERT
(Meyer) Baer HM14 for 3 viols
ENGLISH INSTRUMENTAL MUSIC, 16TH AND
17TH CENTURIES
(Beck) Pet 6174, 6176 2V; for 4 viols
or 2 vln, vla, vcl
ERB, JOSEPH (1858-1944)
Quatuor en fa maj. for 2 vln, vla, vcl
Senart
ERLANGER, P.D.
Quatuor for 2 vln, vla, vcl
RL
d'ESTRADE-GUERRA, O.
Quatuor No. 3, for 2 vln, vla, vcl
Jobert
ETLER, ALVIN
Quartet, see ob, clar, vla, bsn
Sonata, see ob, clar, vla
EVANGELISTI, FRANCO (1926-   )
Aleatorio, for 2 vln, vla, vcl
Tonos
EXTON, JOHN
Partita, for 2 vln, vla, vcl
Ches in preparation
FAURÉ, GABRIEL (1845-1924)
Quartet, Op. 15, for vln, vla, vcl, pno
Haml

Quartet, Op. 45, for vln, vla, vcl, pno
Haml
Quartet, Op. 121, for 2 vln, vla, vcl
Dur
FELDMAN, MORTON (1926-   )
de Kooning, for horn, percussion, pno,
vln, vcl
Pet 6951
Durations V, for vln, vcl, horn, vibraphone,
harp, pno/celesta
Pet 6905
For Franz Kline, for soprano, vln, vcl,
horn, chimes, pno
Pet 6948
Four Songs to e.e. cummings, for soprano,
vcl, pno
Pet 6936
Intervals, for bass-baritone voice, vcl,
trombone, vibraphone, percussion
Pet 6908
Ixion, graph for 3 fl, clar, horn, trumpet,
trombone, pno, vcl, d-b
Pet 6926
O'Hara Songs, for bass-baritone, vln, vla,
vcl, chimes, pno
Pet 6949
Pieces, 3, for 2 vln, vla, vcl
Pet 6917
Pieces, 2, for clar, 2 vln, vla, vcl
Pet 6920
Pieces, 2, for vln, vcl, fl, alto fl, horn,
trumpet
Pet 6930
Projection II, for vln, vcl, fl, trumpet, pno
Pet 6940
Structures, for 2 vln, vla, vcl
Pet 6912
Vertical Thoughts 5, for soprano, vln, tuba,
percussion, celesta
Pet 6956
FERGUSON, HOWARD (1908-   )
Octet, for clar, bsn, horn, 2 vln, vla, vcl, d-b
BH
FERRABOSCO, ALFONSO
Fantasy, see 5 viols
FERRARI-TRECATE, LUIGI
Quartet, see 2 vln, vla, vcl
FERROUD, PIERRE-OCTAVE (1900-1936)
Quatuor en ut, for 2 vln, vla, vcl
Dur
FILIPPENKO, ARKADY (1912-   )
Quartet No. 2, for 2 vln, vla, vcl
MZK
FINE, IRVING (1914-1962)
Fantasia, for vln, vla, vcl
Mil
Quartet, see 2 vln, vla, vcl
FINE, VIVIAN
Capriccio, see ob, vln, vla, vcl
Quartet, see 2 vln, vla, vcl
Trio, see vln, vla, vcl
FINNEY, ROSS LEE (1906-   )
Quartet, for 2 vln, vla, vcl
BH
Quartet No. 4, see 2 vln, vla, vcl
Quartet No. 6, for 2 vln, vla, vcl
Pet 6459
Quartets Nos. 7 and 8, see 2 vln, vla, vcl
FINZI, GERALD (1901-1956)
Interlude, for ob, 2 vln, vla, vcl
BH
Prelude and Fugue, for vln, vla, vcl
BH

FLOTHUIS, MARIUS (1914-   )
  Divertimento, Op. 46, for clar, bsn, horn,
    vln, vla, d-b
    DN (Pet No. D12A)
  Quartet, Op. 44, for 2 vln, vla, vcl
    DN (Pet No. D183)
FOGG, ERIC (1903-1939)
  Quartet in A flat, for 2 vln, vla, vcl
    STB
FORTNER, WOLFGANG (1907-   )
  Madrigals, 6, for vln, vla, vcl
    SCH
  New-Delhi-Musik, for fl, vln, vcl,
    harpsichord
    SCH
FOSS, LUKAS
  Quartet, see 2 vln, vla, vcl
FOURESTIER, [LOUIS (1892-   )]
  Quatuor, for 2 vln, vla, vcl
    Dur
FRACKENPOHL, ARTHUR
  Suite, see 2 vln, vla, vcl
FRANCK, CÉSAR (1822-1890)
  Quartet in D, for 2 vln, vla, vcl
    EPS (Pet No. E323)
    Int
  Quintet in f, for 2 vln, vla, vcl, pno
    EPS (Pet No. E329)
    Haml
FRANCMESNIL, ROGER DE (1884-   )
  Quatuor for 2 vln, vla, vcl
    Mathot
FRANCO, JOHAN
  Divertimento, see fl, 2 vln, vla, vcl
  Pieces, 2, see 2 vln, vla, vcl
  Prodigal, see 2 vln, vla, vcl
  Quartets Nos. 3, 4, 5, see 2 vln, vla, vcl
FRANKEL, BENJAMIN (1906-   )
  Quartet No. 1, Op. 14, for 2 vln, vla, vcl
    Aug
  Quartet No. 2, Op. 15, for 2 vln, vla, vcl
    Aug
  Quartet No. 3, Op. 18, for 2 vln, vla, vcl
    Aug
  Quartet No. 4, Op. 21, for 2 vln, vla, vcl
    Aug
  Quintet, for clar, 2 vln, vla, vcl
    Ches
  Trio, Op. 3, for vln, vla, vcl
    Aug
  Trio No. 2, Op. 34, for vln, vla, vcl
    Ches
FRID, GÉZA (1904-   )
  Nocturnes, Op. 24, for fl, harp, 2 vln,
    vla, vcl
    DN (Pet No. D73A)
FRIED, G.
  Quartet No. 3, Op. 20, for 2 vln, vla, vcl
    MZK
FROBERGER, JOHANN JAKOB
  Ricercare, see 2 vln, vla, vcl
FROMM, HERBERT
  Quartet, see 2 vln, vla, vcl
FROMM-MICHAELS, ILSE (1888-   )
  Musica Larga, for clar, 2 vln, vla, vcl
    Sik 517
FUCHS, F.
  Little Suite, see fl, 2 vln, vla
FULEIHAN, ANIS (1900-   )
  Divertimento for 2 vln, 2 vla, 2 vcl
    SMP
  Quartet No. 1 for 2 vln, vla, vcl
    SMP

Quartet No. 2 for 2 vln, vla, vcl
    SMP
FÜRST, PAUL WALTER (1926-   )
  Quartet, Op. 34, for 2 vln, vla, vcl
    DOB
GADZHIBEKOV, SULTAN
  Scherzo, see 2 vln, vla, vcl
GAGNEBIN, HENRI
  Quartets Nos. 2 and 3, see 2 vln, vla, vcl
GAIGEROVA, V.
  Quartet No. 2, Op. 17, for 2 vln, vla, vcl
    MZK
GAITO, CONSTANTINO (1878-1945)
  Quartetto No. 2, Op. 33, for 2 vln, vla, vcl
    Ric BA6115
GÁL, HANS
  Little Suite, see 2 vln, vcl
GALILEI, [VINCENZO (c.1520-1591)]
  Ricercari, 12, for 4 viols
    (Giesbert) SCH
GALININ, G.
  Quartet No. 1, for 2 vln, vla, vcl
    MZK
GALLON, NOËL (1891-   )
  Quintette, for 2 vln, vla, vcl, harp
    HL
GALUPPI, [BALDASSARE (1706-1785)]
  Concerto a quattro No. 1 in g, for
    2 vln, vla, vcl
    DOB
  Concerto a quattro No. 2 in G, for 2 vln,
    vla, vcl
    DOB
GAMBURG, G.
  Trio, for vln, vla, vcl
    MZK
GARDINER, [H. BALFOUR (1877-1950)]
  Movement in c, for 2 vln, 2 vla, vcl
    (Grainger) SCH
GASSMANN, FLORIAN (1729-1774)
  Trios, 5, in A, B flat, C, D, G, for
    fl, vln, vla
    KS   published separately
    see also fl, vln, vla
GENZMER, HARALD (1909-   )
  Septet, for harp, fl, clar, horn, vln, vla, vcl
    SCH
GERHARD, ROBERTO (1896-   )
  Quartet, for 2 vln, vla, vcl
    Kuhl (Mil No. K160)
GERHARDT, CARL
  Sextet in G, see fl, English horn, bsn,
    vln, vla, vcl
GERSCHEFSKI, EDWIN (1909-   )
  Fanfare, Fugato and Finale, for 2 vln, vla,
    vcl
    CFE
  Song without words, for fl, 2 vln, vla,
    harp or pno
    CFE
  Variations, 8, Op. 25 for 2 vln, vla, vcl
    CFE
GERSTER, OTTMAR (1897-   )
  Quartet No. 2, for 2 vln, vla, vcl
    Pet 4683A
GERVAISE, CLAUDE
  Old French Dances, see 2 vln, vla, vcl
GIANFERRARI
  Quartetto, for 2 vln, vla, vcl
    Ric PR365
GIDEON, MIRIAM (1906-   )
  Lyric Piece, for 2 vln, vla, vcl
    CFE
  Quartet, see 2 vln, vla, vcl

GILSE, JAN VAN (1880-1944)
Nonet, for ob, clar, bsn, horn, 2 vln, vla,
vcl, d-b
DN (Pet No. D136A)
Trio, for fl, vln, vla
AL (Pet No. AL5)
GINASTERA, ALBERTO (1916-   )
Impresiones de la Puna for fl, 2 vln, vla, vcl
SMP
Quartets Nos. 1 and 2, for 2 vln, vla, vcl
Belaieff   published separately
GINASTERA, [ALBERTO]
Cantos del Tucuman, see voice and
instruments
GLANVILLE-HICKS, PEGGY (1912-   )
Concertino Antico, for harp, 2 vln, vla, vcl
CFE
Scary Time, for vln, clar, percussion
CFE
GLASS, LOUIS (1864-1936)
Quartet No. 4, see 2 vln, vla, vcl
Sextet, Op. 15, for 2 vln, 2 vla, 2 vcl
WH
GLAZUNOV, ALEXANDER (1865-1936)
Works for String Quartet
MZK
5 Novelettes, Op. 15
Suite, Op. 35
7 Short Pieces
Novelettes, 5, Op. 115, for 2 vln, vla, vcl
Belaieff
Quatuor Slav in G, Op. 26, for 2 vln,
vla, vcl
Belaieff
GLIERE, REINHOLD (1875-1956)
Quartets, 4, for 2 vln, vla, vcl
MZK
Quartets No. 1, Op. 2; No. 2,
Op. 20; No. 3, Op. 67; No. 4, Op. 83
GLINKA, MIKHAIL
see more than 1 instrumental combination
GNESSIN, MIKHAIL (1883-1957)
Suite, for 2 vln, vla, vcl
MZK
GODSKE-NIELSEN, SVEND
Quartet, Op. 14, for 2 vln, vla, vcl
Dansk 71
GOEB, ROGER
Declarations, see vcl, fl, ob, clar, horn, bsn
Quartets Nos. 2 and 3, see 2 vln, vla, vcl
Quintet, see trombone, 2 vln, vla, vcl
Running Colors, see 2 vln, vla, vcl
Trio, see vln, vla, vcl
GOEDICKE, [ALEXANDER (1877-1957)]
Quartet No. 2, Op. 75, for 2 vln, vla, vcl
MZK
GOEHR, [ALEXANDER (1932-   )]
Suite, Op. 11, for fl, clar, horn, harp,
vln or vla, vcl
SCH
GOLD, ERNEST
Quartet No. 1, see 2 vln, vla, vcl
GOLDSCHMIDT, BERTHOLD (1903-   )
Quartet, Op. 8, for 2 vln, vla, vcl
UE 8692
GOLESTAN, STAN (1872-1956)
Quartet No. 2, for 2 vln, vla, vcl
Dur
GOLOVKOV, A.
Quartet No. 2, for 2 vln, vla, vcl
MZK
GOLUBEV, EVGENY (1910-   )
Quartet No. 2, Op. 31, for 2 vln, vla, vcl
MZK

Quartet No. 3, Op. 38, for 2 vln, vla, vcl
MZK
Quintet, Op. 20, for pno, 2 vln, vla, vcl
MZK
GOODENOUGH, FORREST
Quartets Nos. 3 and 4, see 2 vln, vla, vcl
Sketches, 2, see 2 vln, vla, vcl
GOOSSENS, EUGENE (1893-1962)
Concertino for String Octet
Ches
Fantasy String Quartet, Op. 12, for
2 vln, vla, vcl
Ches
Quartet, Op. 14, for 2 vln, vla, vcl
Ches
Quartet No. 2, Op. 59, for 2 vln, vla, vcl
BH
Sextet, Op. 37, for 3 vln, vla, 2 vcl
Ches
Sketches, 2, Op. 15, for 2 vln, vla, vcl
Ches
GOW, DOROTHY
Quartet in one movement, for 2 vln, vla, vcl
Oxf 25.903
GRAM, PEDER (1881-1956)
Quartet No. 3, Op. 30, for 2 vln, vla, vcl
Dansk 72
GRANT, PARKS
Poem, Op. 18, see 2 vln, 2 vla, vcl
Quartets, see 2 vln, vla, vcl
GREEN, RAY (1909-   )
Epigrammatic Portraits, 5, for 2 vln,
vla, vcl
AME
Holiday for Four, for vla, clar, bsn, pno
AME
GRIEG, EDVARD (1843-1907)
Quartet in g, Op. 27, for 2 vln, vla, vcl
EPS (Pet No. E276)
GRIFFES, CHARLES (1884-1920)
Sketches, 2, based on Indian themes, for
2 vln, vla, vcl
(Betti) GS 4
GROSS, ROBERT
Quartet No. 5, see 2 vln, vla, vcl
Trio, see vln, vla, vcl
GROSSMANN, FERDINAND (1887-   )
Trio, for vln, vla, vcl
DOB
GRUENBERG, LOUIS (1884-   )
Indiscretions, 4, Op. 20, for 2 vln, vla, vcl
UE 7776
GUERRA PEIXE, CÉSAR (1914-   )
Quartet No. 1 for 2 vln, vla, vcl
ECIC
GUIDI, F.
Quatuor, for 2 vln, vla, vcl
Senart
GUILLARD, ALBERT LE (1887-   )
Quatuor, for 2 vln, vla, vcl
Senart
GYRING, ELIZABETH
Fugues, see clar, vln, vla, vcl
Quartet No. 6, for 2 vln, vla, vcl
CFE
Quartets, see also 2 vln, vla, vcl
Sextet-Fantasy, see fl, clar, horn, vln,
vla, vcl
HAAGER, M.
Music for 3 Instruments, Op. 6a
OBV
HADLEY, HENRY (1871-1937)
Quartet, Op. 132, for 2 vln, vla, vcl
GS 26

HAHN, REYNALDO (1875-1947)
Quartet No. 2 in a, for 2 vln, vla, vcl
Heugel 153
HALFFTER, RODOLFO (1900-   )
Quartet for 2 vln, vla, vcl
EMM
HALLNÄS, HILDING (1903-   )
Quartet, Op. 32, for 2 vln, vla, vcl
Gehrmans
HAMANN, ERICH
Trio, Op. 30, see vln, vla, vcl
HAMBOURG
Quartets Nos. 1 and 2, from Introduction
to Chamber Music, for 2 vln, vla, vcl
Mil   published separately
HANDEL, GEORG FRIEDRICH (1685-1759)
Sonatas, 15, Op. 1; 3 early flute sonatas;
sonata for gamba
Lea 70
Sonata in C, for 3 vln
NAG
HANNIVOORT, HENDRIK (1871-   )
Quartet, for 2 vln, vla, vcl
Sal
HANSON, HOWARD (1896-   )
Quartet in one movement, Op. 23, for
2 vln, vla, vcl
AME
HARRIS, ARTHUR (1927-   )
Four Pieces for Three Treble Instruments
Rongwen
HARRIS, ROY (1898-   )
Concerto, Op. 2, for pno, clar, 2 vln,
vla, vcl
AMP
Quartet No. 3, for 2 vln, vla, vcl
Mil
Variations on a theme, 3, for 2 vln, vla, vcl
GS 17
HARRISON, LOU (1917-   )
Concerto in Slendro, for vln and celesta,
2 tackpianos, percussion
Pet 6610A
Trio, for vln, vla, vcl
Pet 6428p
HARUM, GÜNTHER
Fugue, see 2 vln, vla, vcl
HASSLER, HANS LEO
Intraden aus dem Lustgarten, see 6 viols
HAUBENSTOCK-RAMATI, ROMAN (1919-   )
Ricercare, for vln, vla, vcl
Leeds
HAUBIEL, CHARLES
Echi Classici, see 2 vln, vla, vcl
Trio in d, see vln, vla, vcl
HAUBRECHT, HERBERT
Quartets Nos. 1 and 2, see 2 vln, vla, vcl
HAUDEBERT, [LUCIEN (1877-   )]
Bienvenue à Claudie. Poème, Op. 9, for
2 vln, vla, vcl
Sal
HAUFRECHT, HERBERT
Caprice, see clar, 2 vln, vla, vcl
HAYDN, JOSEPH (1732-1809)
Divertimenti, 6, for vln, vla, vcl
(Gardonyi) Kul   2V
Divertimento in D, for 2 horns, 2 vln,
vla, vcl
Pet 4878A
Divertimenti, see also fl, vln, vcl
"Mann und Weib", from Der Geburtstag,
see fl, vln, vla, vcl

Quartets, 83, for 2 vln, vla, vcl
EPS   published separately
For opus numbers see Peters edition
under 2 vln, vla, vcl
Quartets, 12, for 2 vln, vla, vcl
Ric   published separately
Op. 17, No. 5; Op. 20, No. 6;
Op. 33, No. 3; Op. 54, No. 1;
Op. 64, No. 5; Op. 74, No. 3;
Op. 76, Nos. 1, 2, 3, 4, 5;
Op. 77, No. 1
Quartet, Op. 1, No. 1
(Scott) Oxf 25.400
Quartet in D, see vln, vla, vcl, guitar
Quartet in G, Op. 5, No. 4, see fl, vln,
vla, guitar
Trios, 31, for vln, vcl, pno
Lea 121-124   4V
Trio in G, for vln, vcl, pno
EPS (Pet No. E259)
HAYDN, MICHAEL (1737-1806)
Divertimento in B flat, for ob, bsn, vln,
vla, and bass
(Strassl) DOB
Divertimento in D for 2 vln, vla, vcl
NAG
Divertimento in G, for fl, horn, vln, vla,
and bass
(Strassl) DOB
Quartet in D, see fl, vln, vla, vcl
Quintets, 3, in C, F, G, for 2 vln, 2 vla, vcl
KS   published separately
Quintetto, for vln, vla, clar, post horn, bsn
Kul
HELLER, JAMES G.
Aquatints, 3, see 2 vln, vla, vcl
HELY-HUTCHINSON, VICTOR (1901-1947)
Fugal Fancies, 3, for 2 vln, vla, vcl
EKN
HEMEL, OSCAR VAN (1892-   )
Quintet, for clar, 2 vln, vla, vcl
DN (Pet No. D198)
HENGARTNER, MAX
Petite Suite, for 2 vln, vla, vcl
Eul (Pet No. Z244)
HENRIQUES, FINI (1897-   )
Quartet in a, for 2 vln, vla, vcl
WH
HENZE, HANS WERNER (1926-   )
Being Beauteous. Cantata for soprano,
harp, 4 vcl
SCH
Kammermusik 1958, for tenor, guitar or
harp, clar, horn, bsn, str quintet
(Hölderlin) SCH
HEROLD
Suite, see 2 vln, vcl
HERRMANN, HUGO (1896-   )
Quartet, Op. 101, for 2 vln, vla, vcl
Sik 354
HIER, ETHEL GLENN (1889-   )
Carolina Christmas. Suite, for 2 vln,
vla, vcl
CFE
Poems for Remembrance, see vln, vla, vcl
HINDEMITH, PAUL (1895-1963)
Abendkonzert No. 2, from Plöner
Musiktag, for fl, 2 vln, vcl
SCH
Abendkonzert No. 3, from Plöner
Musiktag, for vln and clar
SCH

HINDEMITH, PAUL (cont.)
  Abendkonzert No. 4, from Plöner
    Musiktag, for clar, vln, vla, vcl
    SCH
  Canons, 8, Op. 44, No. 2, for 3 vln
    SCH
  Junge Magd, Die, Op. 23, No. 2, for
    alto, fl, clar, str quartet
    SCH
  Martinslied, Op. 45, No. 5, see voice
    and instruments
  Pieces, 8, Op. 44, No. 3, for 2 vln, vla, vcl
    SCH
  Serenaden, Die, Op. 35, for soprano, ob,
    vla, vcl
    SCH
  Todes Tod, Des, Op. 23a, for mezzo
    soprano, 2 vla, 2 vcl
    SCH
HIVELY, WELLS
  Quartet, see 2 vln, vla, vcl
  Trio, see vln, vla, vcl
HODDINOTT, ALUN (1929-   )
  Variations, for fl, clar, harp, 2 vln,
    vla, vcl
    Oxf
HOÉREE, ARTHUR (1897-   )
  Pastorale et Danse for 2 vln, vla, vcl
    Senart
HOESL, ALBERT
  Suite, see 2 vln, vla
HØFFDING, FINN (1899-   )
  Quartet, Op. 6, for 2 vln, vla, vcl
    WH
HÖLLER, KARL (1907-   )
  Quartet No. 6, for 2 vln, vla, vcl
    Sik 463
HOLST, GUSTAV (1874-1934)
  Terzetto, for fl, ob, vla
    Ches
HONEGGER, ARTHUR (1892-1955)
  Quatuor No. 2, for 2 vln, vla, vcl
    Senart fac-simile du manuscrit
  Quatuor No. 3, for 2 vln, vla, vcl
    Senart fac-simile du manuscrit
HORNEMAN, C.F.E.
  Quartet No. 1 in g, for 2 vln, vla, vcl
    Dansk 75
HOROVITZ, JOSEPH (1926-   )
  Quartet No. 4, Op. 16, for 2 vln, vla, vcl
    Mil-L 43
  Quartet, for ob, vln, vla, vcl
    Mil-L 57
HORUSITZKY, [ZOLTAN (1903-   )]
  Quartet No. 4, for 2 vln, vla, vcl
    Kul
HORVATH, JOSEPH MARIA (1931-   )
  Blinde, Die. Melodrama after Rilke, for
    alto, 2 speaking voices, fl, trumpet,
    vcl, pno
    Pet 5824
  Songs, 4, for soprano or tenor, fl, clar,
    vla, vcl
    Pet 5823
HOSKINS, WILLIAM
  Quartet No. 1, in a, for 2 vln, vla, vcl
    CFE
HOVHANESS, ALAN (1911-   )
  Quartet No. 1, Op. 8, for 2 vln, vla, vcl
    Pet 6480
  Suite, Op. 99, for vln, pno, percussion
    Pet 6047p
  Upon enchanted ground, Op. 90, No. 1,
    for fl, vcl, harp, tam tam
    Pet 6046p

HUGON, [GEORGES (1904-   )]
  Quatuor, for 2 vln, vla, vcl
    Dur
HUMMEL, JOHANN N. (1778-1837)
  Septet, Op. 74, for fl, ob, horn, vla, vcl,
    d-b, pno
    Pet 1304A
HURÉ, JEAN (1877-1930)
  Quatuor No. 1 for 2 vln, vla, vcl
    Mathot
  Quatuor No. 2 for 2 vln, vla, vcl
    Senart
HURLSTONE, WILLIAM YEATES (1876-1906)
  Phantasie Quartet, for 2 vln, vla, vcl
    Nov
HUTTEL, J.
  Quatuor for 2 vln, vla, vcl
    Senart
HUYBRECHTS, ALBERT
  Trio, see vln, vla, vcl
HYE-KNUDSEN, JOHAN (1896-   )
  Quartet, Op. 3, for fl, ob/English horn,
    vln, vcl
    WH
IBERT, JACQUES (1890-1962)
  Quatuor, for 2 vln, vla, vcl
    Leduc
d'INDY, VINCENT (1851-1931)
  Quartet No. 2, Op. 45, for 2 vln, vla, vcl
    Dur
  Quartet No. 3 in D flat, Op. 96, for 2 vln,
    vla, vcl
    Heugel 155
  Sextuor, Op. 92, for 2 vln, 2 vla, 2 vcl
    Heugel 156
  Suite in Olden Style, Op. 24, for trumpet,
    2 fl, 2 vln, vla, vcl, bsn
    Int
INGHELBRECHT, DÉSIRÉ ÉMILE (1880-   )
  Quartet, for 2 vln, vla, vcl
    Dur
IORDAN, I.
  Quartet, Op. 10, for 2 vln, vla, vcl
    MZK
IPPOLITOV-IVANOV, MIKHAIL (1859-1935)
  Pieces, 4, on Armenian Folk Themes, for
    2 vln, vla, vcl
    MZK
IVES, CHARLES E. (1874-1954)
  Quartet No. 1 for 2 vln, vla, vcl
    Peer
  Quartet No. 2 for 2 vln, vla, vcl
    Peer
  Scherzo for 2 vln, vla, vcl
    Peer
JACHINO, [CARLO (1889-   )]
  Quatuor No. 2, for 2 vln, vla, vcl
    Senart
JACOB, GORDON (1895-   )
  Prelude, Passacaglia and Fugue, for vln
    and vla
    JWL (Mil No. W2100)
  Quartet, for ob, vln, vla, vcl
    Nov
  Quintet, for clar, 2 vln, vla, vcl
    Nov
  Shakespearian Sketches, 6, for vln, vla, vcl
    Nov
JACOBI, FREDERICK (1891-1952)
  Hagiographa, for 2 vln, vla, vcl, pno
    AME
  Quartet on Indian Themes, see 2 vln,
    vla, vcl

JACOBI, FREDERICK (cont.)
Quartet No. 2, see 2 vln, vla, vcl
Quartet No. 3, for 2 vln, vla, vcl
AME
JANÁČEK, LEOŠ (1854-1928)
Children's Rhymes, for high voice, pno,
vla or vln
UE 9479
Concertino, for pno, 2 vln, vla, clar,
horn, bsn
Artia
Idyll, for 2 vln, vla, vcl, d-b
Artia
Quartets Nos. 1 and 2, for 2 vln, vla, vcl
Artia   published separately
JAQUES-DALCROZE, EMILE (1865-1950)
Dances, 7, for 2 vln, vla, vcl
JWL
Rythmes de Danse, Suites Nos. 1-3, for
2 vln, vla, vcl
Heugel
JÁRDÁNYI, PÁL (1920-   )
Quartet No. 2, for 2 vln, vla, vcl
Kul
JEANNERET
Trios, 4, for 3 vln
Sal
JELINEK, HANNS (1901-   )
Trio. Twelve-Note-Music, Op. 15, No. 9,
for vln, vla, vcl
UE 12026
JEMNITZ, ALEXANDER (1890-   )
Serenade, Op. 24, for vln, vla, vcl
UE 9560
JENKINS, JOHN (1592-1678)
Ayres, 2, for 4 viols
(Dolmetsch) SCH
Fantasies, see 3 viols
JENNI, DONALD
Terzetto, see vln, vla, vcl
JENTSCH, WALTER (1900-   )
Quartet, Op. 35, for 2 vln, vla, vcl
Sik 342
JERSILD, JORGEN
Quartetti Piccoli, see 2 vln, vla, vcl
JETTEL, RUDOLF
Trio, see clar, vln, vla
JOHANSON, SVEN-ERIC (1919-   )
Quartet No. 2, for 2 vln, vla, vcl
Gehrmans
JOLIVET, ANDRÉ (1905-   )
Quartet No. 1, for 2 vln, vla, vcl
Heugel 164
JONGEN, JOSEPH (1873-1953)
Pieces en trio, Op. 80, see fl, vcl, harp
Quartet in A, Op. 50, for 2 vln, vla, vcl
Ches
Quartet, for 2 vln, vla, vcl
Senart
Serenades, 2, Op. 61, for 2 vln, vla, vcl
Ches
Trio, Op. 135, see vln, vla, vcl
JORA, [MIHAIL (1891-   )]
Quatuor for 2 vln, vla, vcl
Sal
JOUBERT, JOHN (1927-   )
Miniature Quartet, for 2 vln, vla, vcl
Nov
Quartet No. 1, Op. 1, for 2 vln, vla, vcl
Nov
Trio, for vln, vla, vcl
Nov
JUON, PAUL (1872-1940)
Divertimento, Op. 34, for clar, 2 vla
LN (Pet No. R111)

KADOSA, PÁL (1903-   )
Quartet No. 2, Op. 25, for 2 vln, vla, vcl
Kul
Quartet No. 3, Op. 52, for 2 vln, vla, vcl
Kul
KAHN, ERICH ITOR (1905-1956)
Chansons Populaires de la Bretagne, Sept,
for fl, vln, clar, bsn
CFE
Leichte Nachtmusik, for vln, vla, vcl
CFE
Quartet, see 2 vln, vla, vcl
KALLSTENIUS, EDVIN (1881-   )
Quartet in c, Op. 8, for 2 vln, vla, vcl
Gehrmans
KAMINSKI, HEINRICH
Sacred Songs, see voice and instruments
KAMINISKI, JOSEF (1903-   )
Quartet, for 2 vln, vla, vcl
IMP
KANITZ, ERNEST
Notturno, see fl, vln, vla
KARTZEV, [ALEXANDER (1883-   )]
Quartet No. 2, Op. 14, for 2 vln, vla, vcl
MZK
KATZ, E.
Spielmusik for 2 vln, vla, vcl
SCH
Trio, see 2 fl, vln
KAUDER, HUGO
Poems, see voice and instruments
KAY, ULYSSES
Quartets, 2, see 2 vln, vla, vcl
Quintet, see fl, 2 vln, vla, vcl
KAZHLAYEV, M.
Quartet, for 2 vln, vla, vcl
MZK
KELLY, ROBERT
Quartets, 2, see 2 vln, vla, vcl
KELTERBORN, RUDOLF (1931-   )
Quartet No. 2, for 2 vln, vla, vcl
Baer TP46
Quartet No. 3, for 2 vln, vla, vcl
Baer TP117
KERR, HARRISON (1897-   )
Quartet, for 2 vln, vla, vcl
BH
Trio, for vln, vcl, pno
CFE
KERSTERS, W.
Quartet No. 1, see 2 vln, vla, vcl
KIENZL, [WILHELM (1857-1941)]
Quartet, for 2 vln, vla, vcl
UE 11237
KILPATRICK, JACK
Little Pieces, 6, Op. 14, for 2 vln, vla, vcl
CFE
Sextet, for fl, horn and strings
CFE
KIRCHNER, LEON (1919-   )
Quartet No. 2, for 2 vln, vla, vcl
AMP
KLATOVSKY, R.
Impresiones Peruanas for 2 vln, vla, vcl
UME
KLENGEL, JULIUS (1859-1933)
Hymnus, Op. 57, for 12 vcl
BRH
KLUSSMANN, ERNST GERNOT (1901-   )
Spielmusik No. 1, for 3 vln, vcl
Sik 405
KOCHETOV, V.
Quartet, Op. 58, for 2 vln, vla, vcl
MZK

KODÁLY, ZOLTÁN (1882-   )
Quartet No. 1, Op. 2, for 2 vln, vla, vcl
Kul
Quartet No. 2, Op. 10, for 2 vln, vla, vcl
UE 6651
Serenade, Op. 12, for 2 vln, vla
UE 6654
KOECHLIN, CHARLES (1867-1950)
Quatuor No. 1, for 2 vln, vla, vcl
Senart
Quatuor No. 3, for 2 vln, vla, vcl
Senart
KOEHLER, EMIL
Quartets Nos. 1 and 2, see 2 vln, vla, vcl
KOENIG, GOTTFRIED MICHAEL (1926-   )
Quartet 1959, for 2 vln, vla, vcl
Tonos
KOFFLER, JOSEF (1896-1943)
Trio, Op. 10, for vln, vla, vcl
UE 9770
KOHS, ELLIS B.
Short Concert, see 2 vln, vla, vcl
KOKAI, REZSO (1906-   )
Serenade, for vln, vla, vcl
Kul
KOMZAK, K.
Folk Tune and Fairy Tale, see 2 vln, vla, vcl
KOPPEL, HERMAN D. (1908-   )
Divertimento pastorale, Op. 61, for ob,
vla, vcl
Dansk 83
Quartet No. 2, Op. 34, for 2 vln, vla, vcl
Dansk 76
Quartet No. 3, Op. 38, for 2 vln, vla, vcl
WH
KORNAUTH, EGON (1891-1959)
Nonet, Op. 31, for fl, ob, clar, horn,
2 vln, vla, vcl, d-b
UE 8553
Quartett in g, Op. 26, for 2 vln, vla, vcl
DOB
KOUTZEN, BORIS
Quartet No. 2, see 2 vln, vla, vcl
KRAFT, KARL (1903-   )
Partita in d, for vln, vla, vcl
Schwann
KRASNOV, G.
Quartet, for 2 vln, vla, vcl
MZK
KRENEK, ERNST (1900-   )
Quartet No. 1, Op. 6, for 2 vln, vla, vcl
UE 7080
Quartet No. 3, Op. 20, for 2 vln, vla, vcl
UE 7529
Quartet No. 5, Op. 65, for 2 vln, vla, vcl
UE 8209
Quartet No. 6, Op. 78, for 2 vln, vla, vcl
UE 10896
Quartet No. 7, Op. 96, for 2 vln, vla, vcl
UE Ph386
KROEGER, KARL (1932-   )
Discussions, 5, for 2 vln, vla, vcl
CFE
KROLL, WILLIAM (1901-   )
Characteristic Pieces, 4, for 2 vln, vla, vcl
GS 5
KRUL, ELI (1926-   )
Quartet, for 2 vln, vla, vcl
Pet 6362A
KUBIZEK, AUGUSTIN
Pieces, 4, see vln, vla, vcl
KUHLAU, FRIEDRICH (1786-1832)
Quintet, Op. 51, No. 1, for fl, vln, 2 vla, vcl
(Winkel) Dansk 221

LABEY, [MARCEL (1875-   )]
Quatuor, Op. 17, for 2 vln, vla, vcl
Dur
LABROCA, MARIO
Quartet No. 3, see 2 vln, vla, vcl
LAJTHA, LÁSZLO (1891-1963)
Etudes, 5, Op. 20, for 2 vln, vla, vcl
Leduc
Quartet No. 3, Op. 11, for 2 vln, vla, vcl
UE 3763
Quartets Nos. 7, 8, 9, for 2 vln, vla, vcl
Leduc   published separately
Trio No. 2, Op. 18, for vln, vla, vcl
Leduc
Trio No. 3, Op. 41, for vln, vla, vcl
UE Ph383
LANDRE, GUILLAUME (1905-   )
Quartet No. 3, for 2 vln, vla, vcl
DN (Pet No. D10A)
LANGGAARD, RUD (1893-1952)
Quartet No. 3, for 2 vln, vla, vcl
Dansk 77
LA PRESLE, JACQUES DE (1888-   )
Suite en Sol, for 2 vln, vla, vcl
Sal
LARSSON, LARS-ERIK (1908-   )
Intima Miniatyrer, Op. 20, for 2 vln, vla, vcl
Gehrmans
Quartet No. 1, Op. 31, for 2 vln, vla, vcl
Nordiska
LA TOMBELLE, FERNAND DE (1854-1928)
Suite, for 3 vcl
Senart
LAUDENSLAGER, HAROLD
Quartet No. 3, see 2 vln, vla, vcl
LAZARE-LÉVY
Quatuor for 2 vln, vla, vcl
Senart
LAZZARI, SYLVIO (1857-1944)
Quatuor for 2 vln, vla, vcl
RL
LEES, BENJAMIN (1924-   )
Quartet No. 1, see 2 vln, vla, vcl
Quartet No. 2, for 2 vln, vla, vcl
BH
LEEUW, TON DE (1924-   )
Quartet, for 2 vln, vla, vcl
DN (Pet No. D187)
LE FLEMING, [CHRISTOPHER (1908-   )]
Three Traditional Tunes, for 2 vln, vla, vcl
Nov
LEGLEY, VICTOR
Quartets Nos. 2 and 3, see 2 vln, vla, vcl
Serenade, Op. 44, No. 3, see fl, vln, vcl
Trio, Op. 55, see fl, vla, guitar
LEIGHTON, [KENNETH (1929-   )]
Quartet No. 1, Op. 32, for 2 vln, vla, vcl
Leng
LERICH, RUDOLF
Trio, see 2 vln, vla
LESSARD, JOHN (1920-   )
Trio, for vln, vla, vcl
CFE
LESUR, DANIEL (1908-   )
Suite médiévale, for fl, vln, vla, vcl, harp
Dur
LEVITIN, [YURI (1912-   )]
Quartet No. 6, Op. 37, for 2 vln, vla, vcl
MZK
LEVY, F.
Ricercar, for 4 vcl
Cor ST3
Sextet for fl, clar, bsn, vln, vla, vcl
Cor WS1

LEVY, LAZARE, see Lazare-Levy
LIDHOLM, INGVAR (1921-   )
  Liten Straktrio, for vln, vla, vcl
    Gehrmans
LIVIABELLA, LINO
  Quartet in f, see 2 vln, vla, vcl
LOCKE, MATTHEW (c.1630-1677)
  Consort of 4 Parts, for 2 vln, vla, vcl
    (Giesbert) SCH   2V
  Quartets, 6, for 2 vln, vla, vcl
    (Warlock-Mangeot) Ches
    published separately
LOCKWOOD, NORMAND
  Quartet No. 3, see 2 vln, vla, vcl
LOEFFLER, CHARLES MARTIN (1861-1935)
  Music for Four Stringed Instruments, see
    2 vln, vla, vcl
  Quintet, for 3 vln, vla, vcl
    GS 19
LOKSHIN, A.
  Quintet, for clar, 2 vln, vla, vcl
    MZK
LONQUE
  Quartet, Op. 24, see 2 vln, vla, vcl
LOTHAR, FRIEDRICH WILHELM (1885-   )
  Trio, Op. 65, for vln, vla, vcl
    Baer
LOTTI, ANTONIO
  Sonata, see fl, vcl, guitar
LOURIÉ, A.
  Pastorale de la Volga, for ob, bsn, 2 vla, vcl
    ESC
LUENING, OTTO (1900-   )
  Fantasia Brevis, see vln, vla, vcl
  Quartets Nos. 2 and 3, see 2 vln, vla, vcl
  Sextet, see fl, clar, horn, vln, vla, vcl
  Trio No. 2, for fl, vcl, pno
    CFE
LUPO, THOMAS
  Almains and Pavans, see 3 viols
LUTYENS, ELIZABETH (1906-   )
  Quartet No. 2, Op. 15, No. 5, for 2 vln,
    vla, vcl
    Leng
  Quartet No. 3, for 2 vln, vla, vcl
    Leng
  Quartet No. 6, Op. 25, for 2 vln, vla, vcl
    Leng
  Six Tempi for Ten Instruments, Op. 42, for
    fl, ob, clar, bsn, trumpet, horn, vln,
    vla, vcl, pno
    Leng
MAASZ, GERHARD
  Divertimento, see fl, 2 vln, vla, vcl
MCBRIDE, ROBERT (1911-   )
  Comfortable Flight, see English horn,
    2 vln, vla, vcl
  Foursome, see 2 vln, vla, vcl
  Prelude and Fugue, see 2 vln, vla, vcl
  Quintet, for ob, 2 vln, vla, vcl
    GS 40
MCEWEN, JOHN BLACKWOOD (1863-1948)
  Quartet in e, for 2 vln, vla, vcl
    BH
  Threnody Quartet, for 2 vln, vla, vcl
    Oxf 25.100
MACMILLAN, ERNEST (1893-   )
  Sketches, 2, on French Canadian Airs,
    for 2 vln, vla, vcl
    Oxf 92.501
MACONCHY, ELIZABETH (1907-   )
  Quartets Nos. 1-6, for 2 vln, vla, vcl
    Leng   published separately
  Reflections, for ob, clar, vln, harp
    Oxf 07.016

MADERNA, BRUNO (1920-   )
  Quartet, for 2 vln, vla, vcl
    SZ
MAGNANI
  Quartet, for 2 vln, vla, vcl
    Sal
MALIPIERO, GIAN FRANCESCO (1882-   )
  Epodi e Giambi, for vln, ob, vla, bsn
    WH
  Quartet No. 1. Rispetti e Strambotti, for
    2 vln, vla, vcl
    Ches
  Quartet No. 2. Stornelli e Ballate, for
    2 vln, vla, vcl
    Ric PR287
  Quartet No. 3. Cantari alla Madrigalesca,
    for 2 vln, vla, vcl
    Noet (Pet No. N4)
  Quartet No. 4, for 2 vln, vla, vcl
    WH
  Quartet No. 6. L'Arca di Noè, for 2 vln,
    vla, vcl
    Ric PR300
  Quartet No. 7, for 2 vln, vla, vcl
    Ric PR541
  Sonata a cinque, for fl, vln, vla, vcl, harp
    Ric PR288
MAMLOK, URSULA
  Quartet, 1962, for 2 vln, vla, vcl
    CFE
MAROS, REZSO
  Divertimento, for vln, vla, vcl
    Kul
MARTELLI, HENRI (1895-   )
  Quartetto No. 2, for 2 vln, vla, vcl
    Ric R1363
MARTINET, JEAN-LOUIS (1916-   )
  Variations, for 2 vln, vla, vcl
    Heugel 169
MARTINO, DONALD
  Quartet, see clar, vln, vla, vcl
MARTINU, BOHUSLAV (1890-1959)
  Quartet No. 2, for 2 vln, vla, vcl
    UE 8706
  Quartet No. 3, for 2 vln, vla, vcl
    Leduc
  Quartet No. 6, for 2 vln, vla, vcl
    BH
  Quartet No. 7. Concerto da Camera,
    for 2 vln, vla, vcl
    SMP
  Rondi, for ob, clar, bsn, trumpet, 2 vln, pno
    Artia
  Serenade No. 1, for clar, horn, 3 vln, vla
    Artia
  Serenade No. 2, for 2 vln, vla
    Artia
  Serenade No. 3, for ob, clar, 4 vln, vcl
    Artia
  Serenade No. 4. Divertimento for vln solo,
    2 vln, vcl, vla solo, vla, 2 ob, pno
    Artia
  Trio, for vln, vla, vcl
    Heugel 170
MARUTAYEV, M.
  Quartet, Op. 5, for 2 vln, vla, vcl
    MZK
MARX, KARL (1897-   )
  Partita über "Es ist ein Ros ent-
    sprungen", for 2 vln, vla, vcl
    Baer 2687
MASELLI, G.
  Movements, 4, for 2 vln, vla, vcl
    SZ

MASON, DANIEL GREGORY (1873-1953)
Fanny Blair, Folk-song Fantasy, Op. 28
for 2 vln, vla, vcl
Oxf 92.504
Quartet on Negro Themes, Op. 19, see
2 vln, vla, vcl
Serenade, see 2 vln, vla, vcl
Variations for String Quartet
Oxf 92.502
MAYR, ANTON
Little Suite, see 2 vln, vcl
MAYUZUMI, TOSHIRO (1929-   )
Prelude, for 2 vln, vla, vcl
Pet 6525p
MELCHERS, HENRIK M. (1882-1961)
Quartet, Op. 17, for 2 vln, vla, vcl
Gehrmans
MELLERS, WILFRID (1914-   )
Trio, for vln, vla, vcl
Leng
MENDELSSOHN, FELIX (1809-1847)
Octet, Op. 20, for 4 vln, 2 vla, 2 vcl
EPS (Pet No. E59)
Int
Quartets, 5, for 2 vln, vla, vcl
EPS   published separately
Op. 12; Op. 13; Op. 44, Nos. 1-3
Trio No. 1 in d, Op. 49, for vln, vcl, pno
EPS (Pet No. E80)
Trio No. 2 in c, Op. 66, for vln, vcl, pno
EPS (Pet No. E81)
MENDOZA, VICENTE (1894-   )
Canto Funeral for 2 vln, vla, vcl
ECIC
MENGELBERG, KAREL (1902-   )
Ballade, for fl, clar, 2 vln, vla, vcl, harp
DN (Pet No. D75A)
MENNIN, PETER (1923-   )
Quartet No. 2, for 2 vln, vla, vcl
CF 11
MERULO, CLAUDIO (1533-1604)
Canzoni da sonar a 4, 6, for 2 vln, vla, vcl
(Disertori) SZ
MEULEMANS, ARTHUR
Quartet No. 5, see 2 vln, vla, vcl
Sonata, see fl, vla, harp
MEYEN, V.
Quartet, for 2 vln, vla, vcl
MZK
MIASKOVSKY, NIKOLAI (1881-1950)
Chamber Music, Vol. 8. Quartets
Nos. 1-13, for 2 vln, vla, vcl
MZK
Quartet No. 6, Op. 43, for 2 vln, vla, vcl
MZK
Quartet No. 9, Op. 62, for 2 vln, vla, vcl
MZK
Quartet No. 10, Op. 67, No. 1, for 2 vln,
vla, vcl
MZK
Quartet No. 11, Op. 67, No. 2, for 2 vln,
vla, vcl
MZK
Quartet No. 12, Op. 77, for 2 vln, vla, vcl
MZK
Quartet No. 13, Op. 86, for 2 vln, vla, vcl
MZK
MICO, RICHARD
Fancies, see 4 viols
MIGOT, GEORGES (1891-   )
5 Mouvements d'eau, for 2 vln, vla, vcl
Leduc
MIHALOVICI, MARCEL (1898-   )
Quartet No. 3, Op. 52, for 2 vln, vla, vcl
Heugel 172

MILFORD, ROBIN (1903-1959)
Miniature Concerto. Miniature String
Quartet in G
Oxf 25.018
MILHAUD, DARIUS (1892-   )
Cantate de l'enfant et de la mère, for
reciter, 2 vln, vla, vcl, pno
Heugel 202
Machines agricoles, for medium voice, fl,
clar, bsn, vln, vla, vcl, d-b
UE 8142
Octet. Quartets Nos. 14 and 15, for 4 vln,
2 vla, 2 vcl
Heugel 178
Quartet No. 1, for 2 vln, vla, vcl
Dur
Quartet No. 2, for 2 vln, vla, vcl
Dur
Quartet No. 3, for 2 vln, vla, vcl
with voice
Dur
Quartet No. 4, for 2 vln, vla, vcl
Senart
Quartet No. 5, for 2 vln, vla, vcl
Senart
Quartet No. 6, for 2 vln, vla, vcl
UE 8140
Quartet No. 7, for 2 vln, vla, vcl
UE 8495
Quartet No. 8, for 2 vln, vla, vcl
Chant du Monde
Quartet No. 9, for 2 vln, vla, vcl
Chant du Monde
Quartet No. 10, for 2 vln, vla, vcl
Sal
Quartet No. 11, for 2 vln, vla, vcl
Sal
Quartet No. 12, for 2 vln, vla, vcl
Sal
Quartet No. 13, for 2 vln, vla, vcl
Sal
Quartets Nos. 14 and 15, see Octet
Quartet No. 16, for 2 vln, vla, vcl
Heugel 179
Quartet No. 17, for 2 vln, vla, vcl
Heugel 191
Quartet No. 18, for 2 vln, vla, vcl
Heugel 192
Quintet No. 2, for 2 vln, vla, vcl, d-b
Heugel 201
Quintet No. 3, for 2 vln, 2 vla, vcl
Heugel 212
Quintet No. 4, for 2 vln, vla, 2 vcl
Heugel 216
Rêves de Jacob, Les, for ob, vln, vla,
vcl, d-b
Heugel 204
Sextet, for 2 vln, 2 vla, 2 vcl
Heugel 228
Trio No. 1, for vln, vla, vcl
Heugel 180
MILLS, CHARLES (1914-   )
Chamber Concerto for 10 instruments, for
fl, ob, clar, bsn, 2 horns, 2 vln, vla, vcl
CFE
Music, for rec, sax, d-b
CFE
Piece, for fl, rec, vln, vla, vcl
CFE
Quartet No. 3, for 2 vln, vla, vcl
CFE
Quartet No. 5, for 2 vln, vla, vcl
CFE

MILNER, ANTHONY (1925-   )
Quartet, for ob, vln, vla, vcl
Nov
MILNER
Miniature String Quartet, see 2 vln, vla, vcl
MIRZOYAN, E.
Quartet, for 2 vln, vla, vcl
MZK
MOERAN, ERNEST JOHN (1894-1950)
Fantasy Quartet, for ob, vln, vla, vcl
Ches
Quartet in a, for 2 vln, vla, vcl
Ches
Quartet in E flat, for 2 vln, vla, vcl
Nov
Trio in G, for vln, vla, vcl
Aug
MOOR, EMANUEL (1863-1931)
Suite for double quintet, Op. 103, for
woodwind quintet and str quintet
Sal
MOORE, DOUGLAS (1893-   )
Quartet, see 2 vln, vla, vcl
Quintet, for clar, 2 vln, vla, vcl
CF 17
MORTENSEN, OTTO (1907-   )
Quartet 1937, for 2 vln, vla, vcl
Dansk 78
MOSS, LAWRENCE
Quartet, see 2 vln, vla, vcl
MOULAERT, RAYMOND
Divertimento, see vln, vla, vcl
MOURANT, WALTER
Quartet No. 1, see 2 vln, vla, vcl
Quintet, see 2 vln, vla, 2 vcl
MOZART LEOPOLD
Divertimenti, 3, see 2 vln, vcl
MOZART, WOLFGANG AMADEUS (1756-1791)
Divertimenti, 3, K. 136-8, for 2 vln, vla, vcl
Pet 4266A
Divertimento No. 7 in D, K. 205, for bsn,
2 horns, vln, vla, d-b
EPS (Pet No. E141)
Ric PR620
Divertimento No. 10 in F, K. 247, with
March, K. 248, for 2 horns, 2 vln,
vla, d-b
EPS (Pet No. E195)
Divertimento No. 11 in D, K. 251, for
ob, 2 horns, 2 vln, vla, d-b
EPS (Pet No. E349)
Ric PR621
Divertimento No. 15 in B flat, K. 287, for
2 horns, 2 vln, vla, d-b
EPS (Pet No. E73)
Divertimento No. 17 in D, K. 334, for
2 horns, 2 vln, vla, d-b
EPS (Pet No. E72)
Divertimento in E flat, K. 563, for vln,
vla, vcl
EPS (Pet No. E70)
Int
Eine Kleine Nachtmusik, K. 525
EPS (Pet No. E218)
Ric PR245 "Serenade"
Fantasy, K.608, orig for mechanical organ;
arr for 2 vln, vla, vcl
(Levi) BRH
Musical Joke. Sextet in F, K.522, for
2 vln, vla, vcl, 2 horns
Int
Quartets, 10, for 2 vln, vla, vcl
K.387, K.421, K.428, K.458, K.464,
K.465, K.499, K.575, K.589, K.590

Baer TP86-89, 140-6; published
separately
EPS   in 1 volume
EPS   published separately
Kal 228
Ric   published separately
Quartet in D, K. 285, for fl, vln, vla, vcl
EPS (Pet No. E192)
Quartet in G, K. 285a, for fl, vln, vla, vcl
(Einstein) Hin (Pet No. H140)
Quartet in A, K. 298, for fl, vln, vla, vcl
EPS (Pet No. E193)
Quartet in F, K. 370, for ob, vln, vla, vcl
BH
EPS (Pet No. E194)
Ric PR470
Quartets, 2, for vln, vla, vcl, pno
Lea 90
K. 478 in g; K. 493 in E flat; with
K. 452 for pno and winds
Quartet No. 1 in g, K. 478, for vln, vla,
vcl, pno
EPS (Pet No. E158)
Quartet No. 2 in E flat, K. 493, for vln,
vla, vcl, pno
EPS (Pet No. E159)
Quintets, 9
Lea 91-92   2V
Vol 1: K.174, K.406, K.407, K.515, K.516
Vol 2: K.581, K.593, K.614, K.525
Quintet in c, K.406, for 2 vln, 2 vla, vcl
Baer TP38
EPS (Pet No. E37)
Quintet in E flat, K.407, for vln, 2 vla,
horn, vcl
Baer TP13
EPS (Pet No. E347)
Quintet in C, K.515, for 2 vln, 2 vla, vcl
Baer TP15
EPS (Pet No. E38)
Quintet in g, K. 516, for 2 vln, 2 vla, vcl
EPS (Pet No. E13)
Ric PR469
Quintet in A, K.581, for clar, 2 vln,
vla, vcl
Baer TP14
BH
EPS (Pet No. E71)
Kal 214
Ric PR471
Quintet in D, K.593, for 2 vln, 2 vla, vcl
Baer TP11
EPS (Pet No. E50)
Quintet in E flat, K.614, for 2 vln, 2 vla, vcl
Baer TP12
EPS (Pet No. E51)
Serenades, 4, and 2 Divertimenti:
K.251, 334, 286, 361, 375, 388
Kal F306
Serenade, K.525, see Eine Kleine Nachtmusik
Sextet, K.522, see Musical Joke
Sonatas, for vln and pno
Lea 16   3V
Trios, 8, for vln, vcl, pno
Lea 49-50   2V
Trio in B flat, K.266, see 2 vln, vcl
Trio in E flat, K. 498, for clar, vla, pno
EPS (Pet No. E376)
MULDER, ERNEST (1898-   )
Quartet, for ob, bsn, vcl, harp
.. DN (Pet No. D54A)
MÜLLER VON KULM, WALTER (1899-   )
Quartetti, 3, Op. 56, for 2 vln, vla, vcl
Ric SY46

MUSGRAVE, THEA (1928-   )
Quartet, for 2 vln, vla, vcl
Ches
MYASKOVSKY, see Miaskovsky
MYSLIVECEK
Quintetto, see 2 vln, 2 vla, vcl
NAGEL, ROBERT
Trio Concerto, for fl, vcl, pno
CFE
NARIMANIDZE, [NIKOLAI (1905-   )]
Quartet No. 3, for 2 vln, vla, vcl
MZK
NEDBAL, M.
Little Trio, see vln, vla, vcl
NELHYBEL, VACLAV (1919-   )
Quartet, for 2 vln, vla, vcl
EPS (Pet No. E371)
NEMIROFF, ISAAC (1912-   )
Quartet, for 2 vln, vla, vcl
MM
NERI, MASSIMILIANO (17th century)
Sonata for Quartet, for 2 vln, vla, vcl
ZA 3693
NEWLIN, DIKA (1923-   )
Trio, Op. 2, for vln, vcl, pno
CFE
NIELSEN, CARL (1865-1931)
Quartets, Op. 5, Op. 13, Op. 14, see
2 vln, vla, vcl
Quartet in F, Op. 44, for 2 vln, vla, vcl
Pet 3807
NIELSEN, JOHN (1927-   )
Otte aforismer for strygekvartet med
sentenser fra H.C. Andersen's
eventyr, Op. 1
WH 3957a
NIKOLAYEV, [LEONID (1878-1942)]
Quartet, for 2 vln, vla, vcl
MZK
NIN-CULMELL, JOAQUIN
Poemas de Jorge Manrique, see voice
and instruments
NIVERD, LUCIEN (1879-   )
Quatuor, for 2 vln, vla, vcl
Sal
NOETEL, KONRAD FRIEDRICH
Kleine Musik, see 2 vln, vla, vcl
Kleine Suite, for 2 vln, vla, vcl
Sirius
NOWAK, LIONEL
Quartet, see ob, vln, vla, vcl
Sonatina, see 3 vln, vcl
Trio, see clar, vln, vcl
NUSSIO, OTMAR (1902-   )
Quartet in D, for 2 vln, vla, vcl
Oertel
ORBÓN, JULIÁN (1925-   )
Quartet No. 1 for 2 vln, vla, vcl
SMP
ORREGO-SALAS, JUAN (1919-   )
Quartet No. 1, for 2 vln, vla, vcl
Peer
OTTE, HANS (1926-   )
Trio, for vln, vla, vcl
SMP
OVERTON, HALL (1920-   )
Quartet No. 2, for 2 vln, vla, vcl
Highgate
Trio No. 1, see vln, vla, vcl
PAISIELLO, GIOVANNI (1740-1816)
Quartet No. 1 in A, for 2 vln, vla, vcl
ZA 3321
Quartet No. 2 in E flat, for 2 vln, vla, vcl
ZA 3324

Quartet No. 3 in E flat, for 2 vln, vla, vcl
ZA 3327
PARAY, PAUL (1886-   )
Quatuor, for 2 vln, vla, vcl
Jobert
PARK, S.
Pastorale, see fl, 2 vln, vcl
PARRIS, ROBERT
Quartets Nos. 1 and 2, see 2 vln, vla, vcl
Quintet, see fl, ob, bsn, vln, vcl
Trios, 2, see vln, vla, vcl
PARTOS, ÖDÖN (1907-   )
Concertino, for 2 vln, vla, vcl
IMP
Tehilim, for 2 vln, vla, vcl
IMI
PASCAL, [ANDRE (1894-   )]
Quatuor, for 2 vln, vla, vcl
Dur
PASCAL, CLAUDE (1921-   )
Quatuor, for 2 vln, vla, vcl
Dur
PAUER, [JIRI (1919-   )]
Quartet No. 1, for 2 vln, vla, vcl
Artia
PERAGALLO, MARIO (1910-   )
Music for double quartet
UE 11978
PERGAMENT, MOSES (1893-   )
Quartet No. 2
Gehrmans
PERLE, GEORGE (1915-   )
Quartet No. 5, Op. 42, for 2 vln, vla, vcl
CFE
PERRY, JULIA
Pastoral, see Septets
PETER, JOHN FREDERICK (1746-1813)
Quintets, 6, for 2 vln, 2 vla, vcl
Pet 6097
PETROVICS, E.
Quartet, for 2 vln, vla, vcl
Artia
PETYREK, FELIX (1892-1951)
Variations on Folk Songs, for vln, vla, vcl
DOB
PFITZNER, HANS (1869-1949)
Quartet in c, Op. 50, for 2 vln, vla, vcl
Oertel
PICK-MANGIAGALLI, RICCARDO (1882-1949)
Fugues, 3, for 2 vln, vla, vcl
SZ
PIERNÉ, GABRIEL (1863-1937)
Variations Libres et Final, for fl, vln, vla,
vcl, harp
Sal
PIERRE-PETIT
Suite, for 4 vcl
Heugel PH182
PIJPER, WILLEM (1894-1947)
Quartets Nos. 1-5, for 2 vln, vla, vcl
Leng   published separately
(PIJPER, WILLEM)
Pezzi Antichi, for 3 vln, vcl
DN (Pet No. D132A)
PIKET
Trio, see fl, clar, vcl
PILLOIS, JACQUES (1877-1935)
Haï-Kaï, 5, for fl, vln, vla, vcl, harp
Dur
PINKHAM, DANIEL (1923-   )
Prelude, for fl, vln, vla, vcl
CFE
PISK, PAUL (1893-   )
Music, see vln, clar, vcl, bsn

PISK, PAUL (cont.)
Quartet No. 1, Op. 8, for 2 vln, vla, vcl
UE 8181
Trio, see vln, vla, vcl
PISTON, WALTER (1894-   )
Divertimento, see Nonets
Quartet No. 2, for 2 vln, vla, vcl
GS 38
Quartet No. 3, for 2 vln, vla, vcl
BH
Quartet No. 5, for 2 vln, vla, vcl
AMP
PITTALUGA, GUSTAVO (1906-   )
Ricercare, for vln with accompaniment
of clar, bsn, trumpet
Leduc
PIZZETTI, ILDEBRANDO (1880-   )
Quartetto in ré, for 2 vln, vla, vcl
Ric 123151
Songs, 3, for soprano, 2 vln, vla, vcl
Ric PR669
PLESSIS, HUBERT DU (1922-   )
Quartet, for 2 vln, vla, vcl
Nov
PLEYEL, IGNAZ (1757-1831)
Quartets, Op. 20, Nos. 1-3, for fl, vln,
vla, vcl
KS   published separately
PODESVA, [JAROMIR (1927-   )]
Quartet No. 4, for 2 vln, vla, vcl
Artia
POLOVINKIN, LEONID (1894-1949)
Quartet No. 1, for 2 vln, vla, vcl
MZK
PONCE, MANUEL MARÍA (1882-1948)
Miniatures, 4, for 2 vln, vla, vcl
Sal
Petite Suite dans le style ancien for vln,
vla, vcl
Peer
Quartet for 2 vln, vla, vcl
Peer
Trio, for vln, vla, vcl
EMM
PONSE, LUCTOR (1914-   )
Quintet, Op. 25, for fl, ob, vln, vla, vcl
DN (Pet No. D192)
POOT, MARCEL (1901-   )
Bagatelles, 5, for 2 vln, vla, vcl
UE 11108
POPOV, T.
Quartet, for 2 vln, vla, vcl
MZK
PORTER, QUINCY (1897-   )
Divertimento, see 2 vln, vla
Fugue, see 2 vln, vla, vcl
Little Trio, see fl, vln, vla
Quartet No. 3 for 2 vln, vla, vcl
Pet 6671a
Quartet No. 4, for 2 vln, vla, vcl
BH
Quartet No. 5, see 2 vln, vla, vcl
Quartet No. 6 for 2 vln, vla, vcl
Pet 6672a
Quartet No. 7, for 2 vln, vla, vcl
Val
Quartet No. 8, for 2 vln, vla, vcl
Val
Quintet, see clar, 2 vln, vla, vcl
Quintet, see fl, 2 vln, vla, vcl
POSER, HANS (1907-   )
Quartet No. 1, Op. 20, for 2 vln, vla, vcl
Sik 279

POWELL, MEL (1923-   )
Miniatures for Baroque Ensemble, Op. 8,
for fl, ob, vln, vla, vcl, harpsichord
GS 91
PRESLE, see La Presle
PRESSER, W.
Passacaglia, see clar, horn, vln, vla, vcl
PRIETO, MARIA TERESA
Quartet. Cuarteto Modal, for 2 vln, vla, vcl
EMM
PROCTOR, LELAND
Quartet No. 2, see 2 vln, vla, vcl
PROKOFIEV, SERGEY (1891-1953)
Overture on Hebrew Themes, Op. 34, for
clar, 2 vln, vla, vcl, pno
Int
Pieces, 6, from Visions Fugitive and
2 Pieces from Romeo and Juliet, arr
for 2 vln, vla, vcl
(Barshai) MZK
Quartets Nos. 1 and 2, for 2 vln, vla, vcl
MZK
Quartet No. 1 in b, Op. 50, for 2 vln,
vla, vcl
BH
Int
Quartet No. 2 in F, Op. 92, for 2 vln, vla, vcl
Int
Quintet in g, Op. 39, for ob, clar, vln,
vla, d-b
BH
Int
PROSPERI, [CARLO (1921-   )]
Inventions, 4, for clar, vln, vla, harp
SZ
PURCELL, HENRY (c.1659-1695)
Chacony in g, for 2 vln, vla, vcl
Ches
Int
Fantasies, for 3 to 7 viols
NAG   2V
Spielmusik zum Sommernachtstraum, for
4 viols and Bc
(Höckner) Baer HM50, 58   2V
QUEYLAR, DE
Quartet in d, for 2 vln, vla, vcl
Sal
QUINET, MARCEL
Quartet, see 2 vln, vla, vcl
Trio, see vln, vla, vcl
RAASTED, NIELS OTTO (1888-   )
Primavera. Trio, Op. 96, for vln, vla, vcl
Dansk 224
Serenade, Op. 40, for fl, ob, vla, vcl,
Dansk 87
RACEK, FRITZ
Eine Kleine Hausmusik, see 2 vln, vla
RADNAI, MIKLÓS (1892-1935)
Divertimento, Op. 7, for 2 vln, vla, vcl
UE 9846
RAINIER, PRIAULX (1903-   )
Quanta, for ob, vln, vla, vcl
SCH
RAMOUS, GIANNI
Quartet, for 2 vln, vla, vcl
SZ
RANGSTRÖM, TURE (1884-1947)
Quartet, for 2 vln, vla, vcl
Nordiska
RAPHAEL, GÜNTER
Sonatina, Op. 65, No. 1, see fl, vla, harp
RATHAUS, KAROL
Quartet No. 4, see 2 vln, vla, vcl

RAUCHVERGER, M.
  Quartet No. 1 on Kirghiz Themes, for
    2 vln, vla, vcl
    MZK
  Quartet No. 2, for 2 vln, vla, vcl
    MZK
RAUTAVAARA, [EINO (1928-   )]
  Quartet No. 2, Op. 12, for 2 vln, vla, vcl
    BRH
RAVEL, MAURICE (1875-1937)
  Introduction et Allegro, for harp, fl,
    clar, 2 vln, vla, vcl
    Dur
    Int
  Quartet in F, for 2 vln, vla, vcl
    Dur
    Int
  Trio in a, for vln, vcl, pno
    Dur
RAWSTHORNE, ALAN (1905-   )
  Concerto for Ten instruments
    Oxf 07.015
  Quartet No. 1, Theme and Variations, for
    2 vln, vla, vcl
    Oxf 25.003
  Quartet No. 2, for 2 vln, vla, vcl
    Oxf 25.901
  Quartet, for clar, vln, vla, vcl
    Oxf 07.200
RAXACH, ENRIQUE
  Fases, for 2 vln, vla, vcl
    Tonos
RÉ, PETER
  Quartet No. 1, for 2 vln, vla, vcl
    AMP
REGER, MAX (1873-1916)
  Lyrisches Andante, for 2 vln, vla, vcl, d-b
    Tonger
  Quartet in g, Op. 54, No. 1, for 2 vln,
    vla, vcl
    UE 6936
  Quartet in A, Op. 54, No. 2, for 2 vln,
    vla, vcl
    UE 6937
  Quartet No. 4 in E flat, Op. 109, for
    2 vln, vla, vcl
    EPS (Pet No. E293)
  Quartet No. 5 in f sharp, Op. 121, for
    2 vln, vla, vcl
    EPS (Pet No. E314)
  Quintet, Op. 146, for clar, 2 vln, vla, vcl
    EPS (Pet No. E322)
  Trio in a, Op. 77b, for vln, vla, vcl
    EPS (Pet No. E288)
REISER, ALOIS
  Quartet, Op. 16, see 2 vln, vla, vcl
REITER, ALBERT
  Little Suite, see 2 vln, vla, vcl
REIZENSTEIN, FRANZ (1911-   )
  Divertimento, for 2 vln, vla, vcl
    Leng
  Theme, Variations and Fugue, for clar,
    2 vln, vla, vcl
    Leng
RESPIGHI, OTTORINO (1879-1936)
  Il Tramonto, for mezzo soprano, 2 vln,
    vla, vcl
    Ric 117087
  Quartetto Dorico, for 2 vln, vla, vcl
    UE Ph232
REVUELTAS, SILVESTRE (1899-1940)
  Quartet No. 1 for 2 vln, vla, vcl
    SMP

Quartet No. 2 for 2 vln, vla, vcl
    SMP
REYNOLDS, ROGER (1934-   )
  Quartet No. 2, for 2 vln, vla, vcl
    Pet 6623
REZNICEK, EMIL NIKOLAUS VON
    (1860-1945)
  Quartet No. 3 in d, for 2 vln, vla, vcl
    Birnbach
  Quartet No. 4 in B flat, for 2 vln, vla, vcl
    Birnbach
RIEGGER, WALLINGFORD
  Romanza, Op. 56a, see 2 vln, vla, vcl
RIETI, VITTORIO (1898-   )
  Quatuor en Fa for 2 vln, vla, vcl
    Sal
RIISAGER, KNUDAGE (1897-   )
  Quartet No. 3, for 2 vln, vla, vcl
    WH
  Sonata, for fl, vln, clar, vcl
    WH
RILEY, JOHN
  Quartet No. 2, for 2 vln, vla, vcl
    Val
RIMSKY-KORSAKOV, NIKOLAY
  see more than 1 instrumental combination
RIVIER, JEAN (1896-   )
  Trio, for vln, vla, vcl
    Senart   fac-similé du manuscrit
ROCHBERG, GEORGE
  Quartet, see 2 vln, vla, vcl
ROGER-DUCASSE, JEAN (1873-1954)
  Quartet in d, for 2 vln, vla, vcl
    Dur
  Quartet No. 2 in D, for 2 vln, vla, vcl
    Dur
ROGERS, BERNARD (1893-   )
  Trio, for vln, vla, vcl
    SMP
ROHWER, JENS (1914-   )
  Heptameron, for 4 instruments
    BRH
ROLAND-MANUEL (1891-   )
  Trio, for vln, vla, vcl
    Senart
RON, MARTIN DE (1789-1817)
  Quartet in f, for 2 vln, vla, vcl
    Gehrmans
ROPARTZ, J. GUY (1864-1955)
  Prélude, Marine et chansons, for fl, vln,
    vla, vcl, harp
    Dur
  Quartet No. 1 in g, for 2 vln, vla, vcl
    RL
  Quartets Nos. 2, 3, 4, 5, 6, for 2 vln,
    vla, vcl
    Dur   published separately
  Sérénade for 2 vlns, vla, vcl
    RL
  Trio en la mineur, for vln, vla, vcl
    Dur
ROREM, NED
  Mourning Scene from Samuel, see voice
    and instruments
ROSENBERG, HILDING (1892-   )
  Quartet No. 4, for 2 vln, vla, vcl
    Gehrmans
  Quartet No. 5, for 2 vln, vla, vcl
    Nordiska
  Quartet No. 6, for 2 vln, vla, vcl
    Nordiska
ROSENBERG, WOLF
  Quartet No. 3, for 2 vln, vla, vcl
    Tonos

ROSETTI, FRANCESCO ANTONIO (1746-1792)
Notturno in D, for fl, 2 horn, vln, vla, vcl
Artia
RÖSSLER, F.A., see Rosetti
ROUSSEAU, SAMUEL-ALEXANDER
(1853-1904)
Pièces, 2, for 2 vln, vla, vcl
Dur
ROUSSEL, ALBERT (1869-1937)
Quartet in D, Op. 45, for 2 vln, vla, vcl
Dur
Sérénade, Op. 30, for fl, vln, vla, vcl, harp
Dur
Trio, for vln, vla, vcl
Dur
Trio, Op. 40, for fl, vla, vcl
Dur
ROWLEY, ALEC (1892-1958)
Miniature Quartet, for 2 vln, vla, vcl
Nov
Quartet in E, see 2 vln, vla, vcl
ROYER, ÉTIENNE (1880-1928)
Pour le temps de la Moisson, for 2 vln,
vla, vcl
Sal
RUBBRA, EDMUND (1901-   )
Ave Maria Gratia Plena, see voice and
instruments
Buddha Suite, Op. 64, for fl, ob, vln,
vla, vcl
Leng
Quartets Nos. 1 and 2, for 2 vln, vla, vcl
Leng   published separately
RUDHYAR, DANE (1895-   )
Solitude, Tetragram No. 5, for 2 vln, vla, vcl
CFE
RUEFF, JEANINE (1922-   )
Quatuor, Op. 2, for 2 vln, vla, vcl
Dur
SAINT-SAENS, CAMILLE (1835-1921)
Quatuor No. 1, Op. 112, for 2 vln, vla, vcl
Dur
Quatuor No. 2, Op. 153, for 2 vln, vla, vcl
Dur
SAMAZEUILH, GUSTAVE (1877-   )
Cantabile et Capriccio, for 2 vln, vla, vcl
Dur
Quatuor en ré, for 2 vln, vla, vcl
Dur
Suite en Trio, for vln, vla, vcl
Dur
SANDI, LUIS (1905-   )
Quartet, for 2 vln, vla, vcl
EMM
SANTA CRUZ, DOMINGO (1899-   )
Quartet No. 1, for 2 vln, vla, vcl
Peer
Quartet No. 2, for 2 vln, vla, vcl
Peer
SAUGUET, HENRI (1901-   )
Quartet No. 2 in A, for 2 vln, vla, vcl
Heugel 185
SAUTEREAU, C.
Quatuor, for 2 vln, vla, vcl
Dur
SAUVEPLANE, HENRI (1892-1942)
Quartet in f, for 2 vln, vla, vcl
Sal
SAYGUN, A. ADNAN (1907-   )
Quartet No. 1, Op. 27, for 2 vln, vla, vcl
SMP
Quartet No. 2, for 2 vln, vla, vcl
SMP

SCARMOLIN, ANTHONY LOUIS
Quartet, see 2 vln, vla, vcl
SCHAT, PETER (1935-   )
Septet, for fl, ob, bass clar, horn, vcl,
percussion, pno
DN (Pet No. D194)
SCHEIDT, SAMUEL (1587-1654)
Canzon, "Bergamasca", for 5 viols
(Garff) Baer HM96
Canzon super Intradam Aechiopicam, for
5 viols
(Garff) Baer HM140
Suite in C, see 5 viols
SCHILLINGS, MAX VON (1868-1933)
Quintet in E flat, Op. 32, for 2 vln,
2 vla, vcl
UE 5685
SCHISKE, KARL (1916-   )
Music for clar, trumpet, vla, Op. 27
UE 11966
Triosonate, Op. 41, for vln, vla, vcl
DOB
SCHMICORER, J.A.
Dances, 9, from Zodiaci Musici, for 3 vln
(Tiedemann) BRH
SCHMIDEK, KURT
Trio, Op. 39, for vln, vla, vcl
DOB
SCHMITT, FLORENT (1870-1958)
Quatuor, Op. 112, for 2 vln, vla, vcl
Dur
Quintette, for 2 vln, vla, vcl, pno
Mathot
Suite en rocaille, Op. 84, for fl, vln, vla,
vcl, harp
Dur
Trio, Op. 105, for vln, vla, vcl
Dur
SCHNABEL, A.
Quartet No. 3, see 2 vln, vla, vcl
SCHOECK, OTHMAR (1886-1957)
Notturno, Op. 47, for baritone, 2 vln, vla, vcl
UE 10575
SCHOENBERG, ARNOLD (1874-1951)
Chamber Symphony, Op. 9, orig for 15
solo instruments; arr for fl, clar,
vln, vcl, pno
(Webern) UE Ph225
Kanons, 30, for 3 to 5 instruments
(Rufer) Baer 4340
Ode to Napoleon, Op. 41, see voice and
instruments
Phantasy, Op. 47, for vln and pno
Pet 6060A
Pierrot lunaire, Op. 21, for voice, pno,
fl, clar, vln, vcl
UE 5336
Quartet No. 1 in d, Op. 7, for 2 vln, vla, vcl
UE 3665
Birnbach
Quartet No. 2 in f sharp, Op. 10, for 2 vln,
vla, vcl, with soprano
UE Ph229
Quartet No. 3, Op. 30, for 2 vln, vla, vcl
UE Ph228
Quartet No. 4, Op. 37, for 2 vln, vla, vcl
GS 21
Suite, Op. 29, for pno, clar in A, clar in
B flat, bass clar, vln, vla, vcl
UE 8685
Trio, Op. 45, for vln, vla, vcl
BMP

SCHOENBERG, ARNOLD (cont.)
   Verklärte Nacht, Op. 4, for 2 vln,
      2 vla, 2 vcl
     Birnbach
     Int
SCHOLLUM, ROBERT (1913-   )
   Oktett in acht Skizzen, Op. 63, for fl, ob,
      clar, bsn, vln, vla, vcl, d-b
     DOB
   Variations on the folksong "Was wollen wir
      singen und fangen an", for 2 vln, vla, vcl
     DOB
SCHRAMM, WERNER
   Chamber Trio, see vln, vla, guitar
SCHROEDER, HERMANN
   Quartet, Op. 38, for ob, vln, vla, vcl
     SCH
SCHUBERT, FRANZ (1797-1828)
   German Dances, 5, and 7 Trios, for
      2 vln, vla, vcl
     BRH
   Notturno, Op. 148, D. 897, for vln, vcl, pno
     EPS (Pet No. E233)
   Octet, Op. 166, D. 803, for clar, bsn, horn,
      2 vln, vla, vcl, d-b
     EPS (Pet No. E60)
     Ric PR472
   Quartets, 9, for 2 vln, vla, vcl
     EPS published separately
      Op. 29, D. 804
      Op. 125, No. 1, D. 87
      Op. 125, No. 2, D. 353
      Op. 161, D. 887
      Op. 168, D. 112
      Op. posth: D. 173, 94, 703, 810
   Quartets for 2 vln, vla, vcl
     Lea 51-53 3V
   Quartets, 4, for 2 vln, vla, vcl
     Ric published separately
      No. 12 in c, Quartetsatz
      No. 13 in a, Op. 29
      No. 14 in d, "Death and the Maiden"
      No. 15 in G, Op. 161
   Quintets, 2
     Lea 111
      Op. 114 for vln, vla, vcl, d-b, pno
      Op. 163 for 2 vln, vla, 2 vcl
   Quintet, Op. 114, D. 667, "Trout", for
      vln, vla, vcl, d-b, pno
     EPS (Pet No. E118)
     Ric PR475
   Quintet, Op. 163, D. 956, for 2 vln,
      vla, 2 vcl
     EPS (Pet No. E15)
     Ric PR477
   Trios, for vln, vcl, pno
     Lea 110
      Op. 99; Op. 100; Op. 148, Nocturne
   Trio No. 1, Op. 99, D. 898, for vln,
      vcl, pno
     EPS (Pet No. E84)
     Ric PR474
   Trio No. 2, Op. 100, D. 929, for vln,
      vcl, pno
     EPS (Pet No. E85)
   Violin-Piano Works
     Lea 17
      Op. 70; Op. 137, Nos. 1-3;
      Op. 159; Op. 162
SCHULHOFF, ERWIN (1894-1942)
   Quartet No. 1, for 2 vln, vla, vcl
     UE 8172
   Quartet No. 2, for 2 vln, vla, vcl
     UE 9670

SCHULLER, [GUNTHER (1925-   )]
   Quartet No. 1, for 2 vln, vla, vcl
     UE 13002
SCHULTZ, SV.
   Quartet No. 4, see 2 vln, vla, vcl
SCHUMAN, WILLIAM (1910-   )
   Quartet No. 2, for 2 vln, vla, vcl
     BH
   Quartet No. 3, for 2 vln, vla, vcl
     Pr
   Quartet No. 4, for 2 vln, vla, vcl
     GS 62
SCHUMANN, ROBERT (1810-1856)
   Quartets, 3, Op. 41, for 2 vln, vla, vcl
     EPS (Pet No. E74-6)
      published separately
     Ric PR534, 535, 422; published separately
   Quartet, Op. 47, for vln, vla, vcl, pno
     EPS (Pet No. E77)
   Quintet, Op. 44, for 2 vln, vla, vcl, pno
     EPS (Pet No. E78)
     Ric PR463
   Trios, 3, for vln, vcl, pno
     EPS (Pet Nos. E86-88) published
     separately
     Op. 63; Op. 80; Op. 110
SCHWARTZ, PAUL
   Chaconne and Fugue, Op. 17, see 2 vln,
     vla, vcl
   Quartet, Op. 4, see 2 vln, vla, vcl
SCHWARZ-SCHILLING, [REINHARD
   (1904-   )]
   Quartet in f
     Baer TP118
SCHWINDL, FRIEDRICH
   Quartet in G, see fl, vln, vla, vcl
SCOTT, CYRIL (1879-   )
   Quartet No. 1, for 2 vln, vla, vcl
     EKN
   Quartet No. 2, for 2 vln, vla, vcl
     EKN
   Quartet No. 3, for 2 vln, vla, vcl
     EKN
SEARCH, FREDERICK
   Quartets in A and in e, see 2 vln, vla, vcl
   Sextet, see 2 vln, 2 vla, 2 vcl
SEARLE, HUMPHREY (1915-   )
   Owl and the Pussy-Cat, for speaker, fl
     or vln, vcl, guitar or pno
     Oxf 07.008
   Passacaglietta, Op. 16, see 2 vln, vla, vcl
   Quartet, Op. 12, see clar, bsn, vln, vla
   Two Practical Cats, for speaker, fl/piccolo,
     vcl, guitar
     Oxf 07.009
SENSTIUS, KAI (1889-   )
   Quartet in a, for 2 vln, vla, vcl
     Dansk 80
   Serenade, Op. 36, for ob, vla, bsn
     Dansk 85
SESSIONS, ROGER (1896-   )
   Quartet No. 1 in e, for 2 vln, vla, vcl
     MK
   Quartet No. 2, for 2 vln, vla, vcl
     MK
   Quintet, for 2 vln, 2 vla, vcl
     MK
SHAPERO, HAROLD (1920-   )
   Quartet No. 1, for 2 vln, vla, vcl
     SMP
SHAPEY, RALPH
   Quartets Nos. 1-4, see 2 vln, vla, vcl
SHCHERBACHEV, V.
   Suite, see 2 vln, vla, vcl

SHEBALIN, VISSARION (1902-   )
   Quartet No. 6, Op. 34, for 2 vln, vla, vcl
      MZK
   Quartet No. 7, Op. 41, for 2 vln, vla, vcl
      MZK
SHEPHERD, ARTHUR
   Quartet in e, see 2 vln, vla, vcl
   Triptych, see voice and instruments
SHERMAN, ELNA
   St. Francis and the Birds, for 3 rec,
      vcl, harpsichord
      CFE
SHIRINSKY, [VASSILY (1901-   )]
   Pieces, 2, for vln, vla, vcl
      MZK
SHOSTAKOVICH, DMITRI (1906-   )
   Pieces, 2, Op. 11, for 4 vln, 2 vla, 2 vcl
      Leeds
   Quartet No. 1, Op. 49, for 2 vln, vla, vcl
      Int
   Quartet No. 3, Op. 73, for 2 vln, vla, vcl
      MZK
   Quartet No. 4, Op. 83, for 2 vln, vla, vcl
      MR
      MZK
   Quartet No. 5, Op. 92, for 2 vln, vla, vcl
      MR
   Quartet No. 6, Op. 101, for 2 vln, vla, vcl
      MR
      MZK
   Quartet No. 7, Op. 108, for 2 vln, vla, vcl
      MR
      MZK
   Quartet No. 8, Op. 110, for 2 vln, vla, vcl
      MZK
SIBELIUS, JEAN (1865-1957)
   Quartet in d, Op. 56, for 2 vln, vla, vcl
      EPS (Pet No. E294)
SIEGL, OTTO (1896-   )
   Kleine Kammersuite, see 2 vln, vcl
   Sextett in einem Satz, Op. 28, for 2 vln,
      2 vla, 2 vcl
      DOB
SIMPSON, ROBERT (1921-   )
   Quartet Nos. 1-3, for 2 vln, vla, vcl
      Leng   published separately
SIMS, EZRA
   Quartet, see 2 vln, vla, vcl
   Sonate Concertante, see Octets
SIOHAN, ROBERT (1894-   )
   Quatuor No. 1, for 2 vln, vla, vcl
      Senart
SKALKOTTAS, NIKOS (1904-1949)
   Greek Dances, 5, for 2 vln, vla, vcl
      UE 12343
   Sketches, 10, for 2 vln, vla, vcl
      UE 12266
SKORZENY, FRITZ (1900-   )
   Trio, for vln, vla, vcl
      DOB
SMETANA, BEDRICH (1824-1884)
   Quartet No. 1 in e, for 2 vln, vla, vcl
      Artia
      Aug 10340a
      EPS (Pet No. E275)
      Ric PR433
   Quartet No. 2 in d, for 2 vln, vla, vcl
      Artia
   Trio in g, Op. 15, for vln, vcl, pno
      Artia
SMIT, LEO (1900-1944)
   Quintet, for fl, vln, vla, vcl, harp
      DN (Pet No. D74A)

SMIT, LEO (1921-   )
   Motets, 4, for 2 fl, medium voice, vln
      Broude
SMITH, DAVID STANLEY (1877-1949)
   Quartet in E flat, for 2 vln, vla, vcl
      Oxf 92.505
   Quartet, Op. 46, see 2 vln, vla, vcl
   Quartet No. 6, see 2 vln, vla, vcl
SMITH, JOHN SHAFFER
   Quintet, see ob, 2 vln, vla, vcl
SMYTH, ETHEL (1858-1944)
   Quartet in e, for 2 vln, vla, vcl
      UE 5352
SOWERBY, LEO
   Serenade in G, see 2 vln, vla, vcl
SPALDING, [EVA RUTH]
   Quartets, 2, for 2 vln, vla, vcl
      Sal   published separately
SPELMAN, TIMOTHY (1891-   )
   Five Whimsical Serenades, for 2 vln,
      vla, vcl
      Ches
SPOHR, LOUIS (1784-1859)
   Doppelquartett in d, Op. 65, for 4 vln,
      2 vla, 2 vcl
      Baer 2303
   Nonet, Op. 31, for fl, ob, clar, bsn,
      horn, vln, vla, vcl, d-b
      EPS (Pet No. E97)
      MM   Xerox reproduction
   Octet, Op. 32, for clar, 2 horns, vln,
      2 vla, vcl, d-b
      MM   Xerox reproduction
   Quartets, Op. 15, Nos. 1 and 2, for
      2 vln, vla, vcl
      Baer TP21
   Quartet in E flat, Op. 29, No. 1, for 2 vln,
      vla, vcl
      Baer TP22
STAMITZ, KARL (1745-1801)
   Orchestral Quartet in C for 2 vln, vla, vcl
      (Mönkemeyer) SCH
   Quartet, Op. 4, No. 6, see 2 vln, vla, vcl
   Quartetto Concertante in G, for 2 vln,
      vla, vcl
      SCH
STEIN, LEON
   Quartets, 2, see 2 vln, vla, vcl
   Quintet, see sax, 2 vln, vla, vcl
STEINBAUER, O.
   Die Ros' is ohn' Warum. Tricinium, for
      2 vln, vcl
      OBV
STENHAMMAR, WILHELM (1871-1927)
   Quartet No. 4 in a, Op. 25, for 2 vln,
      vla, vcl
      WH
   Quartet No. 5 in C, "Serenad", for 2 vln,
      vla, vcl
      Gehrmans
   Quartet No. 6 in d, Op. 35, for 2 vln, vla, vcl
      Nordiska
STEPAN, VACLAV (1889-1944)
   Sextet, Op. 11, for 2 vln, 2 vla, 2 vcl
      RL
STERNBERG, ERICH (1898-   )
   Quartet No. 1, for strings with mezzo-
      soprano
      IMP
STEVENS, BERNARD (1916-   )
   Theme and Variations, Op. 11, for 2 vln,
      vla, vcl
      Leng

STEVENS, HALSEY
  Nepdalszvit, see 2 vln, vla, vcl
  Quartet No. 3, see 2 vln, vla, vcl
  Septet, see 7 instruments
STILL, WILLIAM GRANT (1895-   )
  Danzas de Panama, for 2 vln, vla, vcl
  SMP
STILLMAN, MITYA (1892-1936)
  Quartet No. 7, for 2 vln, vla, vcl
  Leeds
STOLTZER, THOMAS
  Octo tonorum Melodiae, see 5 viols
STONE, DAVID
  Miniature Quartets Nos. 1 and 2, for 2 vln,
    vla, vcl
  Nov   published separately
STOUT, ALAN (1932-   )
  Quartets Nos. 1-9, see 2 vln, vla, vcl
  Quartet No. 10, for 2 vln, vla, vcl
  CFE
  Quintet, Op. 12, see clar, 2 vln, vla, vcl
STRATEGIER, HERMAN (1912-   )
  Pieces, 3, for ob, 2 vln, vla, vcl
  DN (Pet No. D14A)
STRAVINSKY, IGOR (1882-   )
  Concertino, for 2 vln, vla, vcl
  WH
  Double Canon, for 2 vln, vla, vcl
  BH
  In Memoriam Dylan Thomas, for tenor,
    4 trombones, 2 vln, vla, vcl
  BH
  Pieces, 3, for 2 vln, vla, vcl
  BH
  Septet, for clar, bsn, horn, pno, vln,
    vla, vcl
  BH
  Songs from William Shakespeare, 3, for
    mezzo, fl, clar, vla
  BH
SUGÁR, REZSO (1919-   )
  Serenade, for 2 vln, vla
  Kul
SWEELINCK, JAN PIETER (1562-1621)
  Chromatic Fantasy, for 2 vln, vla, vcl
  (Sigtenhorst-Meyer) DN (Pet No. D196)
SWIFT, RICHARD
  Quartet, see clar, bsn, vln, vcl
  Trio, Op. 6, for vln, vla, vcl
  CFE
  Trio, Op. 14, for clar, vcl, pno
  CFE
SZABÓ, FERENC (1902-   )
  Quartet, for 2 vln, vla, vcl
  Kul
  Trio, for 2 vln, vla
  Kul
SZÁNTÓ, [THEODOR (1877-1934)]
  Quartet. Suite of 4 Choreographic
    Pieces, for 2 vln, vla, vcl
  Sal
SZERVÁNSZKY, ENDRE (1912-   )
  Quartet No. 2, for 2 vln, vla, vcl
  Kul
  Trio, for fl, vln, vla
  Kul
SZYMANOWSKI, KAROL (1882-1937)
  Quartet in C, Op. 37, for 2 vln, vla, vcl
  UE Ph248
TAILLEFERRE, [GERMAINE (1892-   )]
  Quatuor, for 2 vln, vla, vcl
  Dur
TANENBAUM, ELIAS
  Chamber Piece No. 1, see fl, clar, vcl,
    pno, percussion

Quartets Nos. 1 and 2, see 2 vln, vla, vcl
Trio, see fl, vcl, d-b
TANEYEV, SERGEY (1856-1915)
  Quartets, for 2 vln, vla, vcl
  MZK   4V
    Vol 1: Nos. 1, 2, 3
    Vol 2: Nos. 4, 5, 6,
    Vol 3: Nos. 7, 8, 9
    Vol 4: 3 fragments
  Quartet No. 6 in B flat, Op. 19, for 2 vln,
    vla, vcl
  Belaieff
  Quintet in G, Op. 14, for 2 vln, vla, 2 vcl
  Belaieff
  Trio, Op. 21, for 2 vln, vla
  MZK
  Trio in b, for vln, vla, vcl
  MZK
  Trio in D, for vln, vla, vcl
  MZK
TANSMAN, ALEXANDER (1897-   )
  Quartet No. 2, for 2 vln, vla, vcl
  Senart
  Quartet No. 3, for 2 vln, vla, vcl
  UE 8884
  Quartet No. 4, for 2 vln, vla, vcl
  ESC
  Serenade No. 2, see vln, vla, vcl
  Triptych for 2 vln, vla, vcl
  ESC
TARANOV, G.
  Quartet No. 2, Op. 19, see 2 vln, vla, vcl
TARDOS, [BELA (1910-   )]
  Quartet, for 2 vln, vla, vcl
  Kul
TARP, SVEND ERIK (1908-   )
  Serenade, for fl, clar, vln, vla, vcl
  Dansk 91
TARTINI, GIUSEPPE
  Quartet in D, see 2 vln, vla, vcl
TATE, PHYLLIS (1911-   )
  Quartet in F, for 2 vln, vla, vcl
  Oxf 25.902
TCHAIKOVSKY, PIOTR ILYITCH (1840-1893)
  Quartets, 3, for 2 vln, vla, vcl
  EPS (Pet No. E161, E196-7)
    published separately
    Op. 11; Op. 22; Op. 30
  Quartets, for 2 vln, vla, vcl
  MZK
  Trio, Op. 50, for vln, vcl, pno
  EPS (Pet No. E251)
TCHEREPNINE, ALEXANDER (1899-   )
  Quatuor No. 2, for 2 vln, vla, vcl
  Dur
TER-TATEVOSIAN, J.
  Quartet, for 2 vln, vla, vcl
  MZK
THÄRICHEN, WERNER (1921-   )
  Quartet, Op. 31, for 2 vln, vla, vcl
  BB
THIMAN, ERIC H. (1900-   )
  Folksong Suite, for 2 vln, vla, vcl
  Aug
THOMPSON, RANDALL (1899-   )
  Quartet No. 1 in d, for 2 vln, vla, vcl
  CF 3
THOMSON, VIRGIL (1896-   )
  Quartets Nos. 1 and 2, for 2 vln, vla, vcl
  BH   published separately
  Stabat Mater, for soprano, 2 vln, vla, vcl
  BH
TICHY
  Quartet in b flat, for 2 vln, vla, vcl
  Sal

TOCH, ERNST (1887-   )
Quartet, Op. 70, for 2 vln, vla, vcl
Leeds
Quartet, Op. 74, for 2 vln, vla, vcl
Mil
Serenade, Op. 25, for 2 vln, vla
Leeds
There is a season to everything, see voice
and instruments
TOLDRÁ, EDUARDO (1895-   )
Vistas al mar, for 2 vln, vla, vcl
UME
TOMASI, HENRI (1901-   )
Pastorale Inca, for fl, 2 vln
Leduc
TOMKINS, THOMAS
Fantasia, see 3 viols
Pavan a 5, see 5 viols
TOMMASINI, VINCENZO (1878-1950)
Quatuor No. 2 for 2 vln, vla, vcl
Senart
Trio, for vln, vla, vcl
Senart
TOSATTI, VIERI (1920-   )
Divertimento, for clar, bsn, vln, vla, vcl
Ric 129759
TREMBLAY, GEORGE (1911-   )
Quartet, in Memoriam, for 2 vln, vla, vcl
CFE
TREW, ARTHUR
Miniature Quartet, for 2 vln, vla, vcl
Nov
TRIMBLE, LESTER (1923-   )
Concerto, for fl, ob, clar, bsn, 2 vln, vla,
vcl, d-b
Pet 6641
TROWBRIDGE, L.
Pensively, see clar, vln, vla, vcl
TSINTSADZE, [SULKHAN (1925-   )]
Quartet No. 2, for 2 vln, vla, vcl
MZK
Quartet No. 4, for 2 vln, vla, vcl
MZK
TURCHI, GUIDO (1916-   )
Trio, for fl, clar, vla
SZ
TURINA, JOAQUÍN (1882-1949)
Caliope, from Las Musas de Andalucia, for
2 vln, vla, vcl, pno
UME
Erato, from Las Musas de Andalucia, for
voice, 2 vln, vla, vcl
UME
Talía, from Las Musas de Andalucia for
2 vln, vla, vcl
UME
TURNER, ROBERT (1920-   )
Quartet No. 2, for 2 vln, vla, vcl
CL
UHL, ALFRED (1909-   )
Jubiläums-Quartett, for 2 vln, vla, vcl
DOB
Quartet No. 1, for 2 vln, vla, vcl
OBV
URBANNER, ERICH
Quartet No. 2, see 2 vln, vla, vcl
VAINBERG, [MOYSEY (1919-   )]
Quartet No. 4, Op. 20, for 2 vln, vla, vcl
MZK
VALEN, FARTEIN (1887-1952)
Quartet, for 2 vln, vla, vcl
WH
Quartet, Op. 13, for 2 vln, vla, vcl
Norsk

VAN BAAREN, see Baaren
VAN DELDEN, see Delden
VANDOR, I
Quartet, for 2 vln, vla, vcl
SZ
VAN DURME, J.
Quartet No. 5, see 2 vln, vla, vcl
VAN VACTOR, DAVID
Quintet, see fl, 2 vln, vla, vcl
VAUGHAN WILLIAMS, RALPH (1872-1958)
Hymn Tune Prelude on Song 13 of Gibbons,
for 2 vln, vla, vcl
Oxf 27.906
On Wenlock Edge, for tenor, pno, 2 vln,
vla, vcl
BH
Preludes, 3, "Household Music", for horn
and str quartet
Oxf 25.001
Quartet in a, for 2 vln, vla, vcl
Oxf 25.004
VENDREDIS, LES
Belaieff   2V   for 2 vln, vla, vcl
VENEZIANISCHE CANZONEN (1608)
(Mönkemeyer) SCH   for any four part
combination
VERDI, GIUSEPPE (1813-1901)
Quartet in e, for 2 vln, vla, vcl
EPS (Pet No. E207)
Ric PR538
VERRALL, JOHN (1908-   )
Pastoral Elegy, see Septets
Quartet No. 2, see 2 vln, vla, vcl
Quartet No. 3, for 2 vln, vla, vcl
Pr
Quartet No. 4, for 2 vln, vla, vcl
Pr
Quartets Nos. 5 and 7, see 2 vln,
vla, vcl
Trio, see 2 vln, vla
VILLA-LOBOS, HEITOR (1887-1959)
Bachianas Brasileiras No. 5, for
soprano and 8 vcl
AMP
Quartet No. 1, for 2 vln, vla, vcl
SMP
Quartet No. 8, for 2 vln, vla, vcl
Ric PR218
Quartet No. 9, for 2 vln, vla, vcl
SMP
Quartet No. 10, for 2 vln, vla, vcl
SMP
VINCENT, JOHN (1902-   )
Quartet, for 2 vln, vla, vcl
Mil
VITALI, GIOVANNI BATTISTA (c.1644-1692)
Capriccio, for 2 vln, vla, vcl
ZA 3695
VIVALDI, ANTONIO (c.1669-1741)
Concerto in A, see vln, vla, vcl, guitar
Sonatas, 19, for vln and Bc
Ric   published separately; for details
see listing under vln, pno
Sonatas, 16, for 2 vln and Bc
Ric   published separately; for details
see listing under trio sonatas
Sonata in c, F.XVI no. 1, for vln, vcl,
and Bc
(Olivieri) Ric PR269
Sonata a Quattro in E flat, "Al
S. Sepolcro", F.XVI no. 2, for
2 vln, vla and Bc
(Ephrikian) Ric PR267

VLASOV, [VLADIMIR (1903-   )]
  Quartet, for 2 vln, vla, vcl
    MZK
VOSS, FRIEDRICH (1930-   )
  Quartet, 1960, for 2 vln, vla, vcl
    BRH
VREULS, VICTOR (1876-1944)
  Quartet in F, for 2 vln, vla, vcl
    Bosw
WAGENAAR, BERNARD (1894-   )
  Quartet No. 2, for 2 vln, vla, vcl
    BH
  Quartet No. 3, see 2 vln, vla, vcl
WAGNER, JOSEPH (1900-   )
  Serenade, for ob, vln, vcl
    SMP
  Theme and Variations, for fl, clar,
    vln, vcl
    SMP
WAGNER-RÉGENY, RUDOLF
  Introduction et communication à mon
    angegardien, see vln, vla, vcl
WAILLY, PAUL DE (1854-1933)
  Poème for 2 vln, vla, vcl
    RL
  Serenade, for fl, vln, vla, vcl
    RL
WALKER, ERNEST (1870-1949)
  Fantasia in D, for 2 vln, vla, vcl
    Nov
WALTON, WILLIAM (1902-   )
  Facade Entertainment, for speaker, fl,
    clar, trumpet, saxophone, percussion,
    1 or 2 vcl
    Oxf 07.007
  Quartet in a, for 2 vln, vla, vcl
    Oxf 25.005
WEBER, BEN (1916-   )
  Aubade, see fl, vcl, harp
  Chamber Fantasie, Op. 51, see
    Nonets
  Concertino, Op. 11B, for vln, clar, vcl
    CFE
  Concertino, Op. 45, see Septets
  Lyric Piece, for 2 vln, vla, vcl
    CFE
  Quartet No. 2, Op. 35, see 2 vln, vla, vcl
  Trio, Op. 19, see vln, vla, vcl
WEBERN, ANTON VON (1883-1945)
  Bagatelles, 6, Op. 9, for 2 vln, vla, vcl
    UE 7575
  Movements, 5, Op. 5, for 2 vln, vla, vcl
    UE 5888
  Quartet, Op. 22, for vln, clar, sax, pno
    UE 10050
  Quartet, Op. 28, for 2 vln, vla, vcl
    UE 12398
  Quintet, for 2 vln, vla, vcl, pno
    BMP   blueprint
  Sacred Songs, 5, Op. 15, for soprano,
    vln, fl, clar, trumpet, harp
    UE 7629
  Songs, 6, Op. 14, for voice, clar, bass
    clar, vln, vcl
    UE 7578
  Traditional Rhymes, 3, Op. 17, for
    voice, vln and vla, clar, bass clar
    UE 12272
  Trio, Op. 20, for vln, vla, vcl
    UE Ph175
WEIGL, KARL (1881-1949)
  Quartet in A, Op. 4, for 2 vln, vla, vcl
    UE 2929

Quartet No. 2, for 2 vln, vla d'amore, vcl
    CFE
Quartet in C, Op. 31, for 2 vln, vla, vcl
    UE 10794
Quartets Nos. 7 and 8, see 2 vln, vla, vcl
WEILL, KURT (1900-1950)
  Frauentanz, Op. 10, for soprano, fl, vla,
    clar, horn, bsn
    UE 7599
  Quartet, Op. 8, for 2 vln, vla, vcl
    UE 7699
WEINER, LEO (1885-1960)
  Quartet No. 2, Op. 13, for 2 vln, vla, vcl
    Kul
  Quartet No. 3, Op. 26, for 2 vln, vla, vcl
    Kul
WEISGARBER, ELLIOT
  Divertimento, see clar, vln, vla
WEISS, ADOLPH
  Trio, see clar, vla, vcl
WELLESZ, EGON (1885-   )
  Leaden Echo and the Golden Echo, for
    soprano, vln, vcl, clar, pno
    SCH
  Octet, for clar, horn, bsn, 2 vln, vla,
    vcl, d-b
    Leng (Mil No. L5051)
  Quartet No. 4, Op. 28, for 2 vln, vla, vcl
    UE 6503
  Quartet No. 6, Op. 64, for 2 vln, vla, vcl
    Leng
  Quartet No. 7, Op. 66, for 2 vln, vla, vcl
    Leng
  Quintet, Op. 81, for clar, 2 vln, vla, vcl
    Noet
WESLEY, CHARLES (1757-1834)
  Quartets Nos. 1, 2, 5, for 2 vln, vla, vcl
    Hin (Pet Nos. H411E, 412E, 415E)
    published separately
WESSTRÖM, ANDERS (c.1720-1781)
  Quartet in E, for 2 vln, vla, vcl
    Gehrmans
WHITHORNE, EMERSON (1884-1958)
  Greek Impressions for 2 vln, vla, vcl
    Senart
  Quartet, for 2 vln, vla, vcl
    BH
WHITNEY, M.
  Adagio and Fugue, see fl, clar, vln, vla, vcl
WHITTENBERG, CHARLES
  Chamber Concerto, for vln and 7
    instrumentalists
    CFE
WICKENS, DENNIS
  Miniature Quartet, for 2 vln, vla, vcl
    Nov
WIDDICOMBE, TREVOR
  Miniature Quartet, for 2 vln, vla, vcl
    Nov
WILDGANS, FRIEDRICH
  Little Pieces, see vln, vla, vcl
WILKINSON, MARC (1929-   )
  Voices, for voice, fl, clar, bass clar, vcl
    UE 12912
WILKINSON, PHILIP (1929-   )
  Miniature Quartet, for 2 vln, vla, vcl
    Nov
WILLAERT, ADRIAN (c.1490-1562)
  Ricercari, 9, for 3 woodwinds or strings
    (Zenck) SCH
WILSON, GEORGE BALCH
  Quartet in G, see 2 vln, vla, vcl
WINDING, AUGUST (1835-1899)
  Quintet, Op. 23, for 2 vln, 2 vla, vcl
    WH

WIRÉN, DAG (1905-   )
  Quartet No. 2, Op. 9, for 2 vln, vla, vcl
    Nordiska
  Quartet No. 3, Op. 18, for 2 vln, vla, vcl
    Nordiska
  Quartet No. 4, Op. 28, for 2 vln, vla, vcl
    Gehrmans
WIRTH, HELMUT (1912-   )
  Trio, for vln, vla, vcl
    Sik 397
WITKOWSKI, GEORGES-MARTIN (1867-1943)
  Quatuor, for 2 vln, vla, vcl
    Dur
WOLF, HUGO (1860-1903)
  Italian Serenade, for 2 vln, vla, vcl
    EPS (Pet No. E286)
WOLFF, CHRISTIAN
  Nine, see Nonets
  Trio I, see fl, trumpet, vcl
WOOD, JOSEPH
  Quartet 1961, see 2 vln, vla, vcl
  Quartet No. 2, for 2 vln, vla, vcl
    CFE
WOOLLEN, RUSSELL (1923-   )
  Quartet, see fl, vln, vla, vcl
  Sextet, for clar, pno, 2 vln, vla, vcl
    CFE
WOOLLETT, HENRI (1864-1936)
  Quatuor for 2 vln, vla, vcl
    Senart
WORDSWORTH, WILLIAM (1908-   )
  Quartets Nos. 1-4, for 2 vln, vla, vcl
    Leng   published separately
  Quartet, Op. 44, for ob, vln, vla, vcl
    Leng
  Trio in g, Op. 25, for vln, vla, vcl
    Leng
WUORINEN, CHARLES (1938-   )
  Octet, for ob, clar, horn, trombone, vln,
    vcl, d-b, pno
    MM

Trio Concertante, for ob, vln, pno
    CFE
Triptych, see vln, vla, percussion
Turetzky Pieces, for fl, clar, d-b
    CFE
WYK, ARNOLD VAN (1916-   )
  Elegies, 5, for 2 vln, vla, vcl
    BH
WYLIE, R
  Quartet No. 3, Op. 17, see 2 vln, vla, vcl
WYNER, YEHUDI
  Passover Offering, see fl, clar, vcl,
    trombone
YERZAKOVICH, V
  Quartet No. 2, for 2 vln, vla, vcl
    MZK
YUN, I
  Quartet No. 3, for 2 vln, vla, vcl
    BB
ZACHOW, FRIEDRICH WILHELM
  Pieces, 2, see 2 vln, vcl
ZEISL, ERIC (1905-1959)
  Quartet No. 2 in d, for 2 vln, vla, vcl
    DOB
ZILCHER, HERMANN (1881-1948)
  Rokoko-Suite, Op. 65, for high voice,
    vln, vcl, pno
    BRH
ZILLIG, WINFRIED (1905-   )
  Quartet No. 1, for 2 vln, vla, vcl
    Baer TP50
  Quartet No. 2, for 2 vln, vla, vcl
    Baer TP131
ZIPP, FRIEDRICH (1914-   )
  Quartet in C, Op. 25, for 2 vln, vla, vcl
    Noet
ZOLOTAREV, [VASSILY (1873-   )]
  Quartet No. 6, for 2 vln, vla, vcl
    MZK

MUSIC FOR SOLO STRINGED INSTRUMENTS AND ORCHESTRA

Violin, Orchestra

ABENDROTH, WALTER (1896-   )
  Concerto, Op. 35
    Sik for rent
ACCOLAY, J.B.
  Concerto
    Kal for sale or rent
ALBERTI, GIUSEPPE MATTEO (1685-1750)
  Concerto in G, Op. 1, No. 3
    ZA 4062-3
  Concerto in e, Op. 1, No. 7
    ZA 4064-5
ALBINONI, TOMASO (1671-1750)
  Concerto in C
    VW
  Concerto in d, Op. 5, No. 7
    ZA 3721-2
  Concerto in F, Op. 9, No. 10
    (Giazotto) Ric 129464-5
AMES, WILLIAM (1901-   )
  Rhapsody
    CFE score only
ARENSKY, ANTON S. (1861-1906)
  Concerto in a, Op. 54
    GS for rent
ARNELL, RICHARD (1917-   )
  Concerto Capriccioso
    Hin for rent
ARRIEU, CLAUDE (1903-   )
  Concerto No. 2 in d
    Heugel for rent
BABIN, VICTOR (1908-   )
  Konzertstück
    Aug for rent
BACH, JOHANN CHRISTOPH (1642-1703)
  Lament
    (Maganini) Ed M
BACH, JOHANN SEBASTIAN (1685-1750)
  *Concerto No. 1 in a, S. 1041
    BRH
    CF for rent
    Kal for sale or rent
    Pet for rent
  *Concerto No. 2 in E, S. 1042
    BRH
    CF for rent
    GS for rent
    Kal for sale or rent
    Pet for rent
  Concerto in d[113]
    (Frotscher) Pet for rent
  Concerto in g[113]
    (Szigeti) Pet for rent

---
[113] For additional information see violin and piano.

BACH, KARL PHILIPP EMANUEL (1714-1788)
  Concerto
    (Casadesus) GS for rent
BÄCK, SVEN-ERIK (1919-   )
  Konzert
    WH
BARBER, SAMUEL (1910-   )
  *Concerto, Op. 14
    GS for rent
BARTOK, BELA (1881-1945)
  *Concerto No. 1
    BH for rent
  *Concerto No. 2
    BH for rent
  *Rhapsody No. 1
    BH for rent
  *Rhapsody No. 2
    BH for rent
BASTON, J
  Concertino in D (Concerto No. 6)
    (Dinn) AMP
BAX, ARNOLD (1883-1953)
  Concerto
    Chap for rent
BECKER, JOHN
  Concerto
    CFE score and solo part only
BEETHOVEN, LUDWIG VAN (1770-1827)
  *Concerto in D, Op. 61
    BRH
    Broude
    CF for rent
    GS for rent
    Kal for sale or rent
    Ric for rent
  Concerto in C. Fragment completed by
      Hellmesberger
    Kal for sale or rent
  *Romances, 2: in G, Op. 40 and in F,
      Op. 50
    BRH
    CF for rent
  Romance in G, Op. 40
    GS for rent
    Kal for sale or rent
    Ric for rent
  Romance in F, Op. 50
    GS for rent
    Kal for sale or rent
    Ric for rent
BENJAMIN, ARTHUR (1893-1960)
  Concerto
    BH for rent
BENOY, A.W.
  Violinist's Books of Carols
    Oxf 23.113-14 2V

BENTZON, NIELS VIGGO (1919-   )
  Konzert No. 1, Op. 70
    WH
  Konzert No. 2, Op. 136
    WH
BERIOT, CHARLES DE (1802-1870)
  Concerto No. 7 in G, Op. 76
    CF   for rent
    Kal   for sale or rent
  Concerto No. 9 in a, Op. 104
    Kal   for sale or rent
  Fantasy Ballet, Op. 100. Scène de Ballet
    Kal   for sale or rent
BERKELEY, LENNOX (1903-   )
  Concerto
    Ches   for rent
  Pieces, 5
    Ches
BERNSTEIN, LEONARD (1918-   )
  *Serenade
    GS   for rent
BIANCHI, GABRIELE (1901-   )
  Concerto
    Ric   for rent
BLOCH, ERNEST (1880-1959)
  Baal Shem
    CF   for rent
  Concerto
    BH   for rent
BOCCHERINI, LUIGI (1743-1805)
  Concerto in D
    (Dushkin) AMP
BONPORTI, FRANCESCO ANTONIO
    (1672-1749)
  Concerto in B flat, Op. 11, No. 3
    (Barblan) Ric 130069-70
  Concerto in B flat, Op. 11, No. 4
    (Barblan) Ric 129685-6
  Concerto in B flat
    Broude
  Concerto in F, Op. 11, No. 5
    Broude
BORCH, GASTON (1871-1926)
  Elegie, Op. 101
    Aug 7008b
BORGHI, LUIGI (18th century)
  Concerto
    Carisch
BØRRESEN, HAKON (1876-   )
  Konzert in G, Op. 11
    WH
BOSSI, RENZO (1883-   )
  Momenti agresti, Op. 35
    Ric   for rent
BRAHMS, JOHANNES (1833-1897)
  *Concerto in D, Op. 77
    BRH
    CF   for rent
    GS   for rent
    Kal   for sale or rent
BRITTEN, BENJAMIN (1913-   )
  Concerto, Op. 15
    BH   for rent
BRUCH, MAX (1838-1920)
  Adagio appassionato
    Kal   for sale or rent
  *Concerto No. 1 in g, Op. 26
    Broude
    CF   for rent
    GS   for rent
    Kal   for sale or rent
    Pet   for rent
  Concerto No. 2 in d, Op. 44
    CF   for rent
    GS   for rent

Concerto No. 3 in d, Op. 58
    GS   for rent
  Scottish Fantasy, Op. 46
    Kal   for sale or rent
BUESSER, HENRI (1872-   )
  Sommeil de l'enfant Jésus
    CH
BURLEIGH, CECIL (1885-   )
  Concerto No. 2, Op. 43
    CF   for rent
  Concerto No. 3, Op. 60
    CF   for rent
BUSH, ALAN (1900-   )
  Concerto
    JWL   for rent
CAMPAGNOLI, BARTOLOMMEO (1751-1827)
  Romance
    Kal   for sale or rent
CASTELNUOVO-TEDESCO, MARIO (1895-   )
  Concerto Italiano in g
    Ric   for rent
  Concerto No. 2, "I Profeti"
    Ric   for rent
CHAUSSON, ERNEST (1855-1899)
  Poème, Op. 25
    GS   for rent
CILEA, FRANCESCO (1866-1950)
  Suite in E
    Ric   for rent
CONUS, JULES (1869-1942)
  Concerto in e
    CF   for rent
    GS   for rent
    Kal   for sale or rent
CORELLI, ARCANGELO (1653-1713)
  Folia, La
    (David-Auer) CF   for rent
    (Leonard) GS   for rent
COWELL, HENRY (1897-   )
  Air
    CFE   score only
  Fiddler's Jig
    AMP
CRESTON, PAUL (1906-   )
  Concerto No. 1, Op. 65
    Ric   for rent
  Concerto No. 2, Op. 78
    Ric   for rent
CROSSE, GORDON
  Concerto da camera, for vln, 10 winds
      and 2 percussion
    Oxf
DARKE, HAROLD (1888-   )
  Meditation on Brother James's Air
    Oxf 74.103
DAVID, FERDINAND (1810-1873)
  Concerto No. 1
    Kal   for sale or rent
  Concerto No. 5
    Kal   for sale or rent
DAVID, THOMAS CHRISTIAN (1925-   )
  Konzert
    DOB   for rent
DELIUS, FREDERICK (1862-1934)
  *Concerto
    Aug   for rent
DINICU
  Hora staccato
    (Heifetz) CF   for rent
DOHNÁNYI, ERNST (1877-1960)
  Concerto, Op. 27
    Kul   for rent
  Ruralia Hungarica, Op. 32
    CF   for rent

D'OLLONE, see Ollone, d'
DRDLA, FRANZ (1868-1944)
  Serenade No. 1 in A
    CF for rent
DRIESCH, KURT (1904-   )
  Konzert in einem Satz, Op. 50
    Sirius for rent
DUBENSKI, LEONE (1915-   )
  Concerto in d
    Ric for rent
DUKELSKY, VLADIMIR (1903-   )
  Concerto
    CF for rent
DVORAK, ANTONIN (1841-1904)
  *Concerto in a, Op. 53
    Artia for rent
    Kal for sale or rent
EDER, HELMUT (1916-   )
  Konzert, Op. 32
    EDW
EGGE, KLAUS (1906-   )
  Concerto, Op. 26
    LY for rent
EK, GUNNAR (1900-   )
  Fantasi
    Gehrmans
ELIZALDE, FEDERICO (1907-   )
  Concerto
    Ches
ERDLEN, HERMANN (1893-   )
  Introduction and Chaconne
    Pet for rent
ERNST, HEINRICH WILHELM (1814-1865)
  Airs Hongroises, Op. 22
    Kal for sale or rent
  Concerto in f sharp, Op. 23
    Kal for sale or rent
FIEBIG, [KURT (1908-   )]
  Concertino
    BRH
FINNEY, ROSS LEE (1906-   )
  Concerto
    Pet 6668 for rent
FINZI, GERALD (1901-1956)
  Introit
    Oxf 23.004
FISCHER, IRWIN
  Idyll
    CFE score only
  Poem
    CFE score and solo part only
FITELBERG, JERZY (1903-1951)
  Concerto No. 1
    Omega for rent
FRANKEL, BENJAMIN (1906-   )
  *Concerto, Op. 24
    Aug for rent
GAUBERT, PHILIPPE (1879-1941)
  Concerto
    Heugel for rent
GERSCHEFSKI, EDWIN (1909-   )
  Concerto
    CFE score only
GHEDINI, GIORGIO FEDERICO (1892-   )
  Concentus basiliensis
    Ric for rent
  Concerto. "Il Belprato"
    Ric for rent
GIARDINI, FELICE (1716-1795)
  Concerto in A
    ZA
GIORNOVICHI, GIOVANNI (c.1735-1804)
  Concerto in A
    (Lebermann) SCH

GLAZUNOV, ALEXANDER (1865-1936)
  *Concerto in a, Op. 82
    Belaieff for rent
    Kal for sale or rent
  Meditation, Op. 32
    BH for rent
GLUCK, CHRISTOPH WILLIBALD (1714-1787)
  Concerto in G
    Hug
GODARD, BENJAMIN (1849-1895)
  Concerto Romantique, Op. 35
    CF for rent
GOLDMARK, KARL (1830-1915)
  Concerto, Op. 28
    Kal for sale or rent
GOLESTAN, STAN, see scores
GOOSSENS, EUGÈNE (1893-1962)
  Lyric Poem, Op. 35
    Ches
  Phantasy Concerto, Op. 63
    Ches
GRAM, PEDER (1881-   )
  Konzert in d, Op. 20
    WH
GRENZ, ARTUR (1909-   )
  Concerto
    Sik for rent
GUTCHE, GENE
  Concerto
    Highgate for rent
HAHN, REYNALDO (1875-1947)
  Concerto
    Heugel for rent
HALFFTER, RODOLFO (1900-   )
  Concerto
    EMM for rent
HANDEL, GEORG FRIEDRICH (1685-1759)
  Concerto in B flat. Sonata a 5
    (David) AMP
HARRIS, DONALD
  Fantaisie
    Jobert for rent
HARRISON, JULIUS (1885-   )
  Bredon Hill, Rhapsody
    BH for rent
HARRISON, LOU (1917-   )
  *Concerto, for vln and percussion ensemble
    Pet for rent
  Concerto in Slendro, see 4 instruments
    and percussion
HARTMANN, [THOMAS DE (1885-1956)]
  Menuet Fantastique du Concerto, Op. 66
    Belaieff for rent
HAUFRECHT, HERBERT (1909-   )
  Ballad and Country Dance
    CFE
HAUSER, MISCHKA (1822-1887)
  Hungarian Rhapsody No. 1 in d, Op. 43
    Pet for rent
HAYDN, JOSEPH (1732-1809)
  *Concerto No. 1 in C
    BRH
    Eul
    GS for rent
    Kal for sale or rent
  *Concerto No. 2 in G
    BRH
    Kal for sale or rent
HAYDN, MICHAEL (1737-1806)
  Concerto in B flat
    (Angerer) AMP
HEILNER, IRWIN
  Concerto in an Outmoded Idiom
    CFE score and solo part only

HENKEMANS, HANS (1913-   )
  *Concerto
    DN   for rent
HEUBERGER, RICHARD (1850-1914)
  Midnight Bells, from Opera Ball
    (Kreisler-Cornwell) Fol   for rent
HIDAS, FRIGYES (1928-   )
  *Concertino
    Kul   for rent
HINDEMITH, PAUL (1895-1963)
  Music of Mourning
    AMP
HODDINOTT, ALUN (1929-   )
  Concerto
    Oxf   for rent
HOFMANN, WOLFGANG (1922-   )
  Divertimento in A
    Sirius   for rent
  Konzert
    Sirius   for rent
HOHLFELD, C.
  Little Concerto in Classical Style
    BRH
HOLBROOKE, JOSEPH (1878-   )
  Concerto. "The Grasshopper"
    Ric   for rent
HOROVITZ, JOSEPH (1926-   )
  Concerto, Op. 11
    Mil-L 40   for rent
HOVHANESS, ALAN (1911-   )
  *Concerto No. 2, Op. 89a
    Pet   for rent
HUBAY, JENÖ (1858-1937)
  Hejre Kati, Op. 32
    GS   for rent
HUGGLER, JOHN
  Concerto, Op. 31
    Pet 6871   for rent
IMBRIE, ANDREW (1921-   )
  *Concerto
    Templ   for rent
JACHINO, CARLO (1890-   )
  Sonata drammatica
    Ric   for rent
JACOB, GORDON (1895-   )
  Concerto
    JWL   for rent
KAHN, ERICH ITOR (1905-1956)
  Concertante for vln and 26 instruments
    CFE
  Suite
    CFE   score only
KELLY, F.A.
  Serenade, Op. 7
    (d'Aranyi) Oxf   for rent
KERR, HARRISON (1897-   )
  Concerto
    CFE   score only
KILPATRICK, JACK
  Concertino in g, Op. 112A
    CFE
KING, REGINALD (1904-   )
  Autumn Sunshine
    Paxton (Mil No. P2104)
KLEINSINGER, GEORGE (1914-   )
  Concerto
    Chap   for rent
KOETSIER, JAN (1911-   )
  Barock-Suite in D
    Sirius   for rent
KOKAI, REZSO, see scores
KREISLER, FRITZ (1875-1962)
  Caprice Viennois
    Fol 3000   for sale or rent

Concerto in C, in the style of Vivaldi
    Fol   for rent
  Gitana, La
    Fol 3001   for sale or rent
  Liebesfreud
    Fol 3002   for sale or rent
  Liebeslied
    Fol 3003   for sale or rent
  Old Refrain
    (Cornwell) Fol   for rent
  Praeludium and Allegro, in the style of
      Pugnani
    (Piastro) Fol   for rent
  Rondino on a theme of Beethoven
    (Cornwell) Fol   for rent
  Schön Rosmarin
    Fol 3006   for sale or rent
  Stars in my eyes
    Fol   for rent
  Tambourin Chinois
    Fol   for rent
KRENEK, ERNST (1900-   )
  *Marginal Sounds, for percussion instruments
      with vln
    Rongwen   for rent
KUBIK, GAIL (1914-   )
  *Concerto in D
    Chap   for rent
LALO, EDOUARD (1823-1892)
  Concerto in f, Op. 20
    Dur
  *Symphonie Espagnole, Op. 21
    BRH
    Broude
    CF   for rent
    GS   for rent
    Kal   for sale or rent
LARSSON, LARS-ERIK (1908-   )
  Concertino, Op. 45, No. 8
    Gehrmans
LAZZARI, SYLVIO (1857-1944)
  Rapsodie
    Heugel   for rent
LECLAIR, JEAN-MARIE (1697-1764)
  Concerto in a, Op. 7, No. 5
    (Ruf) NAG
LEEUW, TON DE (1924-   )
  Concerto No. 2
    DN   for rent
LESSARD, JOHN (1920-   )
  Concerto
    CFE   score only
LINDE, BO (1933-   )
  Concerto, Op. 18
    Gehrmans
LOURIÉ, ARTHUR (1892-   )
  *Concerto da Camera
    Broude   for rent
LUCAS, LEIGHTON (1903-   )
  Concert Champêtre
    Ches
MCBRIDE, ROBERT (1911-   )
  Variety Day
    CFE
MACONCHY, ELIZABETH (1907-   )
  Serenata Concertante
    Oxf   in preparation
MALIPIERO, GIAN FRANCESCO (1882-   )
  *Fantasie concertanti: II
    Ric   for rent
MARCELLO, BENEDETTO (1686-1739)
  *Concerto in D
    Eul

MARTINI, GIAMBATTISTA (1706-1784)
Concerto per Violino Obbligato
ZA 4354-5
MARTINU, BOHUSLAV (1890-1959)
*Concerto
Artia   for rent
MASSENET, JULES (1842-1912)
Meditation, from Thaïs
Kal   for sale or rent
MATRAS, MAUDE
Ballade, Op. 8
Aug   for rent
MENDELSSOHN, FELIX (1809-1847)
*Concerto in e, Op. 64
BRH
Broude
CF   for rent
GS   for rent
GT
Kal   for sale or rent
Ric   for rent
Concerto in d
(Menuhin) Pet
MENOTTI, GIAN CARLO (1911-   )
Concerto
GS   for rent
MERLIN, VING
Open String Concerto
B.F. Wood
MIČA, JÁN ADAM FRANTIŠEK (18th century)
Concertino. Notturno
Artia
MILFORD, ROBIN (1903-   )
Darkling Thrush
Oxf   for rent
MILHAUD, DARIUS (1892-   )
Concertino de Printemps, see scores
Concerto No. 1
Heugel   for rent
Suite
BH   for rent
MONTSALVATGE, XAVIER (1912-   )
Poema Concertante
SMP   for rent
MOORE, DOUGLAS (1893-   )
Down East Suite
CF   for rent
MOSZKOWSKI, MORITZ (1854-1925)
Ballade in g, Op. 16, No. 1
Aug   for rent
MOZART, WOLFGANG AMADEUS (1756-1791)
*Concerto No. 1 in B flat, K. 207
BRH
GS   for rent
Kal   for sale or rent
*Concerto No. 2 in D, K. 211
BRH
CF   for rent
*Concerto No. 3 in G, K. 216
BRH
Broude
GS   for rent
GT
Kal   for sale or rent
*Concerto No. 4 in D, K. 218
BRH
Broude
GS   for rent
Kal   for sale or rent
Ric   for rent
*Concerto No. 5 in A, K. 219
BRH
Broude
GS   for rent
Kal   for sale or rent

*Concerto No. 6 in E flat, K. 268
CF   for rent
Kal   for sale or rent
*Concerto No. 7 in D, K. 271a
BRH
Concerto in D, "Adelaide"
(Casadesus) AMP
Rondo, K. 373
BRH
Kal   for sale or rent
NACHÈZ, TIVADAR (1859-1930)
Danses Tziganes, Op. 14
CF   for rent
NARDINI, PIETRO (1722-1793)
Adagio
(Jensen) Aug 7072
Concerto in e
(Ridgway) Nov
GS   for rent
NERO, PAUL
Concerto for Hot Fiddle
CF   for rent
NICODÉ, JEAN-LOUIS (1853-1919)
Romance, Op. 14
Aug   for rent
NIELSEN, CARL (1865-1931)
*Konzert, Op. 33[114]
WH
NIELSEN, RICCARDO (1908-   )
Concerto in D
Ric   for rent
NOGUEIRA, ASCENDINO THEODORO
Concerto
Ric   for rent
NORDIO, CESARE (1891-   )
Poema
Ric   for rent
NOVÁCEK, OTTOKAR (1866-1900)
Perpetuum Mobile
CF   for rent
Pet   for rent
d'OLLONE, MAX (1875-1959)
Romanichels
Heugel   for rent
OSWALD, ENRIQUE (1852-1931)
Concerto
Ric   for rent
PAGANINI, NICCOLÒ (1782-1840)
Concerto No. 1 in D, Op. 6
Kal   for sale or rent
Concerto in one movement, from Concerto
No. 1 in D, Op. 6
(Kreisler) Fol   for rent
Concerto No. 2 in b, Op. 7
Kal   for sale or rent
PARIBENI, GIULIO CESARE (1881-   )
Usignolo del Sassolungo, L'. Leggenda
Ric   for rent
PARRIS, ROBERT (1924-   )
Concerto
CFE   score only
PERGOLESI, GIOVANNI BATTISTA
(1710-1736)
Concerto in B flat
Broude
Concerto in B flat
Carisch
Concertino
(Kahn) AMP
PEROSI, LORENZO (1882-1956)
Concerto
Ric   for rent

---

[114] Can be obtained in the U.S.A. on rental from G. Schirmer.

PERRY, HAROLD
  Concertino
    BH
PETRASSI, GOFFREDO (1904-   )
  *Introduzione e Allegro, for vln and 11 instruments
    Ric   for rent
PFITZNER, HANS (1869-1949)
  Concerto in b, Op. 34
    BH   for rent
PINKHAM, DANIEL (1923-   )
  Concertante No. 2
    CFE
  Concerto
    CFE
PISENDEL, JOHANN GEORG (1687-1755)
  Concerto in E flat
    AMP
  Concerto in g
    Pet
PISK, PAUL A. (1893-   )
  Shanty Boy. Fantasy on an American
    ballad tune
    AMP
PISTON, WALTER (1894-   )
  Concerto
    BH   for rent
PROKOFIEV, SERGEY (1891-1953)
  *Concerto No. 1 in D, Op. 19
    BH   for rent
    Kal   for sale or rent
  Concerto No. 2 in g, Op. 63
    BH   for rent
RAVEL, MAURICE (1875-1937)
  *Tzigane
    Dur
RAWSTHORNE, ALAN (1905-   )
  Concerto No. 1
    Oxf 23.315   for rent
  Concerto No. 2
    Oxf   for rent
REED, WILLIAM HENRY (1876-1942)
  Concerto in a
    Aug   for rent
REGER, MAX (1873-1916)
  Concerto in A, Op. 101
    Pet   for rent
REICHARDT, JOHANN FRIEDRICH (1752-1814)
  Concerto in E flat
    AMP
REIZENSTEIN, FRANZ (1911-   )
  Prologue, Variations and Finale
    BH   for rent
RIETI, VITTORIO, see scores
RIISAGER, KNUDÅGE (1897-   )
  Rondo Giocoso
    Pet   for rent
RIMSKY-KORSAKOV, NIKOLAY (1844-1908)
  Fantasie de Concert, Op. 33
    Belaieff   for rent
    (Kreisler) Fol   for rent
    "Fantaisie on Russian Themes"
RIVIER, JEAN, see scores
ROBERTSON, LEROY (1896-   )
  Concerto
    Galx
ROGERS, [BERNARD (1893-   )]
  Portrait
    Pr   for rent
ROMAN, JOHAN HELMICH (1694-1758)
  Concerto in d
    Nordiska
  Concerto in f
    Gehrmans

ROWLEY, ALEC (1892-1958)
  Legend
    Hin
  Miniature Concerto
    Mil
  Miniature Suite
    JWL   for rent
RUBBRA, EDMUND (1901-   )
  Improvisation, Op. 89
    Leng   for rent
SABATINI, GUGLIELMO
  Elegia
    Cor ST4
SAINT-SAENS, CAMILLE (1835-1921)
  Caprice Andalouse, Op. 122
    Kal   for sale or rent
  Concerto No. 2 in C, Op. 58
    Kal   for sale or rent
  Concerto No. 3 in b, Op. 61
    CF   for rent
    Kal   for sale or rent
  Havanaise, Op. 83
    CF   for rent
    Kal   for sale or rent
  Introduction and Rondo Capriccioso, Op. 28
    CF   for rent
    GS   for rent
    Kal   for sale or rent
SAMMARTINI, GIOVANNI (1701-1775)
  *Concerto in C
    Eul
SARASATE, PABLO DE (1844-1908)
  Introduction et Tarentelle, Op. 43
    CF   for rent
  Zigeunerweisen, Op. 20
    Broude
    CF   for rent
    Kal   for sale or rent
SAUGUET, HENRI (1901-   )
  Concerto d'Orphée
    Heugel   for rent
SCHOENBERG, ARNOLD (1874-1951)
  *Concerto, Op. 36
    GS   for rent
SCHOLLUM, ROBERT (1913-   )
  Konzert, Op. 65
    DOB   for rent
SCHROEDER, HERMANN
  Konzert
    Gerig
SCHUBERT, FRANZ (1797-1828)
  Konzertstück in D
    BRH 'Concert Piece'
    Kal   for sale or rent
  Rondo in A
    BRH
SCHUMANN, ROBERT (1810-1856)
  Fantasy, Op. 131
    (Kreisler) Fol   for rent
SEITZ, FRIEDRICH
  Concerto No. 5 in D, Op. 22, first movement
    (Klotman) Mil
SESSIONS, ROGER (1896-   )
  Concerto
    MK
SHAPEY, RALPH (1921-   )
  Concerto
    CFE   score only
  Piece, for vln and instruments
    CFE
SIBELIUS, JEAN (1865-1957)
  *Concerto
    Kal   for sale or rent

SIBELIUS, JEAN (cont.)
Devotion, Op. 77, No. 2
WH
Humoresken, 6, Op. 87, Nos. 1, 2;
Op. 89, Nos. 1-4
WH published separately
Laetare anima mea, Op. 77, No. 1
WH
SINDING, CHRISTIAN (1856-1941)
Concerto in A, Op. 45
WH
Concerto No. 2 in D, Op. 60
Pet for rent
Suite in a, Op. 10
Pet for rent
SLADEK, PAUL
Isle of Mists
VL
SOMERVELL, ARTHUR (1863-1937)
Concertstück
Aug for rent
SPOHR, LUDWIG (1784-1859)
Concerto No. 7 in e, Op. 38
Kal for sale or rent
*Concerto No. 8 in a, Op. 47, in modo
d'una scena cantante
Kal for sale or rent
Pet for rent
Concerto, No. 9 in d, Op. 55
Kal for sale or rent
Concerto No. 15, Op. 128
Kal for sale or rent
STAMITZ, JOHANN (1717-1757)
Concerto in G
SCH
STAMITZ, KARL (1746-1801)
*Concerto in G
Eul
STEIN, LEON (1910-   )
Concerto in A
CFE score only
STOUT, ALAN (1932-   )
Eight Movements
CFE score and solo part only
SVENDSEN, JOHAN (1840-1911)
Concerto, Op. 6
Kal for sale or rent
Romance, Op. 26
CF for rent
TANEYEV, SERGEY (1856-1915)
Suite de Concert, Op. 28
Belaieff for rent
TARP, SVEND ERIK (1908-   )
Concertino
WH
TARTINI, GIUSEPPE (1692-1770)
Andante cantabile
(Ticciati) Oxf 23.117
Concerto in A
(Corti) Ric for rent
*Concerto in A
(Schroeder) Eul
Concerto in D
(Abbado) Ric for rent
Concerto No. 57 in D
(Bonelli) ZA 3979-80
Concerto in D
(Corti) Ric for rent
Concerto in d
Hug
Concerto in d
Kal for sale or rent
Concerto in E
Hug

Devil's Trill
(Kreisler) Fol for rent
(Zandonai) Ric for rent
"Sonata del diavolo"
Pastorale
(Respighi) Ric for rent
Variations on a theme of Corelli
(Kreisler) Fol for rent
TCHAIKOVSKY, PIOTR ILYITCH (1840-1893)
*Concerto in D, Op. 35
BRH
Broude
CF for rent
(Kreisler) Fol for rent
Kal for sale or rent
Mélodie, Op. 42, No. 3
CF for rent
Sérénade Mélancolique in b flat, Op. 26
CF for rent
TELEMANN, GEORG PHILIPP (1681-1767)
Concerto in a
Cor ST11
Concerto in c
(Schlövogt) AMP
*Concerto in G
(Schroeder) Eul
TESTI, FLAVIO (1923-   )
Musica da concerto No. 1
Ric for rent
THILMAN, [JOHANNES PAUL (1906-   )]
Lichtenberger Konzert
BRH
TORELLI, GIUSEPPE (c.1660-1708)
*Concerto in c, Op. 8, No. 8
Eul
Concerto in e, Op. 8, No. 9
Hug
VALEN, FARTEIN (1877-1952)
*Concerto in C, Op. 37
LY for rent
VAUGHAN WILLIAMS, RALPH (1872-1958)
*Concerto in d, "Accademico"
Oxf 23.012 for rent
*Lark Ascending
Oxf for rent
VERACINI, FRANCESCO (1690-1750)
Concerto Grande da Chiesa in D
ZA 4136-37
Largo
(Corti-Molinari) Carisch
VERRALL, JOHN (1908-   )
Concerto
CFE
VIEUXTEMPS, HENRI (1820-1881)
Ballade and Polonaise, Op. 38
CF for rent
Kal for sale or rent
Pet for rent
Concerto No. 1, Op. 10
Kal for sale or rent
Concerto No. 4, Op. 31
Kal for sale or rent
Concerto No. 5, Op. 37
CF for rent
Kal for sale or rent
Concerto, Op. 46
Kal for sale or rent
Concerto, Op. 50
Kal for sale or rent
Fantasia Appassionata, Op. 35
Fol for rent
Kal for sale or rent
Pet for rent

VILLA-LOBOS, HEITOR (1887-1959)
  Fantasia de Movimentos Mixtos
    SMP   for rent
VIOTTI, GIOVANNI BATTISTA (1755-1824)
  *Concerto No. 22 in a
    CF   for rent
    GS   for rent
    Kal   for sale or rent
  Concerto No. 23 in G
    CF   for rent
    Kal   for sale or rent
  Concerto No. 29 in e
    CF   for rent
VISKI, JANOS (1906-   )
  *Concerto
    Kul   for rent
VITALI, TOMMASO ANTONIO (c.1665- ?   )
  Ciaccona in g
    CF   for rent
VIVALDI, ANTONIO (c.1669-1741)
  Air and Country Dance, from Four Seasons
    (Kirk) Fox
  *Concerto in a, Op. 3, No. 6[115]
    (Nachèz) AMP
    Eul
  *Concerto in E, Op. 3, No. 12
    Eul
  Concerto in B flat, Op. 4, No. 1
    (Frenkel) RE
    Kal   for sale or rent
  Concerto in e, Op. 4, No. 2
    Kal   for sale or rent
  Concerto in G, Op. 4, No. 3
    Kal   for sale or rent
  Concerto in g, Op. 4, No. 6
    (Franko) RE
  *Concerto in g, Op. 6, No. 1
    (Gerheuser) AMP
    Eul
    Kal   for sale or rent
  *Concerto in D, Op. 7, No. 11
    (Schroeder) Eul
  *Concerto in D, Op. 7, No. 12
    (Schroeder) Eul
  *Concerti, Op. 8, Nos. 1-4. "Four Seasons"
    Broude   published separately
    Carisch   published separately
    Eul   published separately
    Kal   for sale or rent; published separately
    see also Concerti F.I nos. 22-25
  Concerto, Op. 9, No. 3
    (Casella) Carisch
  Concerto in b, Op. 9, No. 12
    (Carmirelli) ZA
  Concerto in g, Op. 12, No. 1
    (Kolneder) AMP
    (Nachèz) AMP
  Concerto in A, Pisendel
    Pet
  *Concerto in D, fatto per la Solennita della
      Lingua di San Antonio
    (Jenkins) Eul
  *Concerto in D
    (Schroeder) Eul
  Concerto in d
    (Nachèz) AMP
  *Concerto in E flat, "Il Ritiro"
    Kul   for rent

[115] The concerti of Vivaldi are listed in the following order:
1. Concerti with opus numbers 2. Concerti without opus
numbers, arranged by key 3. Concerti with Fanna numbers.
Scores are available for concerti with Fanna numbers.
For information on the Fanna system of classification see
note in violin and piano section.

Concerto in G
  (Kuechler-Herrmann) Hug
Concerto in G
  (Nachèz) AMP
Concerto in G
  (Orszagh) Kul   for rent
Concerto in g
  (Eller) BRH   Dresden version
Concerto in B flat, F.I no. 1
  (Ephrikian) Ric PR229   for rent
Concerto in c, "Il Sospetto", F.I no. 2
  (Ephrikian) Ric PR233   for rent
Concerto in C, F.I no. 3
  (Maderna) Ric PR249   for rent
Concerto in E, "Il Riposo", F.I no. 4
  (Fanna) Ric PR260   for rent
Concerto in A, F.I no. 5
  (Maderna) Ric PR261   for rent
Concerto in E, F.I no. 7
  (Ephrikian) Ric PR278   for rent
Concerto in D, F.I no. 8
  (Maderna) Ric PR289   for rent
Concerto in E flat, F.I no. 9
  (Ephrikian) Ric PR296   for rent
Concerto in D, "L'Inquietudine",
    F.I no. 10
  (Ephrikian) Ric PR295   for rent
Concerto in d, F.I no. 11
  (Malipiero) Ric PR310   for rent
Concerto in C, "Per la S.S. Assunzione di
    Maria Vergine", F.I no. 13
  (Maderna) Ric PR342   for rent
Concerto in B flat, F.I no. 15
  (Malipiero) Ric PR351   for rent
Concerto in g, F.I no. 16
  (Malipiero) Ric PR352   for rent
Concerto in F, F.I no. 17
  (Malipiero) Ric PR353   for rent
Concerto in D, F.I no. 18
  (Malipiero) Ric PR355   for rent
Concerto in D, F.I no. 19
  (Malipiero) Ric PR356   for rent
Concerto in F, "Per la Solennità di S.
    Lorenzo", F.I no. 20
  (Malipiero) Ric PR357   for rent
Concerto in d, F.I no. 21
  (Malipiero) Ric PR361   for rent
Concerto in E, "La Primavera", from
    Four Seasons, F.I no. 22
  (Malipiero) Ric PR434   for rent
Concerto in g, "L'Estate", from Four
    Seasons, F.I no. 23
  (Malipiero) Ric PR435   for rent
Concerto in F, "L'Autunno", from Four
    Seasons, F.I no. 24
  (Malipiero) Ric PR436   for rent
Concerto in f, "L'Inverno", from Four
    Seasons, F.I no. 25
  (Malipiero) Ric PR437   for rent
Concerto in E flat, "La Tempesta del
    mare", F.I no. 26
  (Malipiero) Ric PR442   on special
    order only
Concerto in C, "Il Piacere", F.I no. 27
  (Malipiero) Ric PR443   for rent
Concerto in d, F.I no. 28
  (Malipiero) Ric PR444   for rent
Concerto in B flat, "La Caccia", F.I no. 29
  (Malipiero) Ric PR445   for rent
Concerto in D, F.I no. 30
  (Malipiero) Ric PR446   for rent
Concerto in C, F.I no. 31
  (Malipiero) Ric PR447   for rent

VIVALDI, ANTONIO (cont.)
Concerto in B flat, F.I no. 32
  (Malipiero) Ric PR448   for rent
Concerto in F, F.I no. 33
  (Malipiero) Ric PR449   for rent
Concerto in g, F.I no. 36
  (Malipiero) Ric PR454   for rent
Concerto in e, F.I no. 37
  (Malipiero) Ric PR455   for rent
Concerto in b, F.I no. 38
  (Malipiero) Ric PR458   for rent
Concerto in A, F.I no. 39
  (Malipiero) Ric PR462   for rent
Concerto in D, F.I no. 45
  (Malipiero) Ric PR567   for rent
Concerto in C, F.I no. 46
  (Malipiero) Ric PR570   for rent
Concerto in C, F.I no. 47
  (Malipiero) Ric PR572   for rent
Concerto in E, F.I no. 48
  (Malipiero) Ric PR573   for rent
Concerto in G, F.I no. 49
  (Malipiero) Ric PR574   for rent
Concerto in b, F.I no. 50
  (Malipiero) Ric PR575   for rent
Concerto in A, F.I no. 51
  (Malipiero) Ric PR576   for rent
Concerto in g, F.I no. 52
  (Malipiero) Ric PR577   for rent
Concerto in a, F.I no. 53
  (Malipiero) Ric PR578   for rent
Concerto in A, F.I no. 54
  (Malipiero) Ric PR579   for rent
Concerto in B flat, F.I no. 55
  (Malipiero) Ric PR580   for rent
Concerto in d, F.I no. 56
  (Malipiero) Ric PR581   for rent
Concerto in c, F.I. no. 58
  (Malipiero) Ric PR583   for rent
Concerto in B flat, F.I no. 60
  (Malipiero) Ric PR586   for rent
Concerto in D, "Per la S.S. Assunzione
  di Maria Vergine", F.I no. 62, for
  vln, strings in 2 choirs and
  2 cembalos
  (Malipiero) Ric PR591   for rent
Concerto in G, F.I no. 64
  (Malipiero) Ric PR681   for rent
Concerto in B flat, F.I no. 65
  (Malipiero) Ric PR682   for rent
Concerto in F, F.I no. 66
  (Malipiero) Ric PR683   for rent
Concerto in C, F.I no. 67
  (Malipiero) Ric PR685   for rent
Concerto in C, F.I no. 68
  (Malipiero) Ric PR687   for rent
Concerto in B flat, F.I no. 69
  (Malipiero) Ric PR688   for rent
Concerto in e, F.I. no. 70
  (Malipiero) Ric PR689   for rent
Concerto in F, F.I no. 71
  (Malipiero) Ric PR690   for rent
Concerto in E, F.I no. 72
  (Malipiero) Ric PR691   for rent
Concerto in C, F.I no. 73
  (Malipiero) Ric PR692   for rent
Concerto in e, F.I no. 74
  (Malipiero) Ric PR693   for rent
Concerto in E flat, F.I no. 75
  (Malipiero) Ric PR694   for rent
Concerto in B flat, F.I no. 76
  (Malipiero) Ric PR695   for rent
Concerto in b, F.I no. 77
  (Malipiero) Ric PR696   for rent

Concerto in B flat, F.I no. 78
  (Malipiero) Ric PR697   for rent
Concerto in c, F.I no. 79
  (Malipiero) Ric PR698   for rent
Concerto in D, F.I no. 80
  (Malipiero) Ric PR699   for rent
Concerto in g, F.I no. 81
  (Malipiero) Ric PR700   for rent
Concerto in g, F.I no. 82
  (Malipiero) Ric PR703   for rent
Concerto in b, F.I no. 83
  (Malipiero) Ric PR704   for rent
Concerto in E, F.I no. 84
  (Malipiero) Ric PR705   for rent
Concerto in B flat, F.I no. 86
  (Malipiero) Ric PR708   for rent
Concerto in G, F.I no. 87
  (Malipiero) Ric PR711   for rent
Concerto in F, F.I no. 88
  (Malipiero) Ric PR712   for rent
Concerto in D, F.I no. 89
  (Malipiero) Ric PR713   for rent
Concerto in A, F.I no. 90
  (Malipiero) Ric PR716   for rent
Concerto in G, F.I no. 91
  (Malipiero) Ric PR717   for rent
Concerto in E flat, F.I no. 92
  (Malipiero) Ric PR718   for rent
Concerto in C, F.I no. 93
  (Malipiero) Ric PR719   for rent
Concerto in C, F.I no. 94
  (Malipiero) Ric PR720   for rent
Concerto in B flat, F.I no. 95
  (Malipiero) Ric PR724   for rent
Concerto in G, F.I no. 96
  (Malipiero) Ric PR752   for rent
Concerto in D, F.I no. 97
  (Malipiero) Ric PR753   for rent
Concerto in E flat, F.I no. 102
  (Malipiero) Ric PR827   for rent
Concerto in G, F.I no. 103
  (Malipiero) Ric PR828   for rent
Concerto in A, F.I no. 104
  (Malipiero) Ric PR829   for rent
Concerto in c, F.I no. 105
  (Malipiero) Ric PR830   for rent
Concerto in A, F.I no. 106
  (Malipiero) Ric PR845   for rent
Concerto in G, F.I no. 107
  (Malipiero) Ric PR847   for rent
Concerto in g, F.I no. 108
  (Malipiero) Ric PR878   for rent
Concerto in E flat, F.I no. 109
  (Malipiero) Ric PR879   for rent
Concerto in G, F.I no. 110
  (Malipiero) Ric PR880   for rent
Concerto in C, F.I no. 111
  (Malipiero) Ric PR881   for rent
Concerto in g, F.I no. 112
  (Malipiero) Ric PR882   for rent
Concerto in d, F.I no. 113
  (Malipiero) Ric PR883   for rent
Concerto in C, F.I no. 114
  (Malipiero) Ric PR884   for rent
Concerto in b, F.I no. 115
  (Malipiero) Ric PR885   for rent
Concerto in D, F.I no. 116
  (Malipiero) Ric PR886   for rent
Concerto in B flat, F.I no. 117
  (Malipiero) Ric PR887   for rent
Concerto in B flat, F.I no. 118
  (Malipiero) Ric PR934   for rent
Concerto in d, F.I no. 119
  (Malipiero) Ric PR935   for rent

VIVALDI, ANTONIO (cont.)
Concerto in D, F.I no. 120
(Malipiero) Ric PR936 for rent
Concerto in B flat, F.I no. 121
(Malipiero) Ric PR941 for rent
Concerto in g, F.I no. 122
(Malipiero) Ric PR942 for rent
Concerto in A, F.I no. 123
(Malipiero) Ric PR943 for rent
Concerto in D, F.I no. 124
(Malipiero) Ric PR944 for rent
Concerto in g, F.I no. 125
(Malipiero) Ric PR945 for rent
Concerto in d, F.I no. 126
(Malipiero) Ric PR946 for rent
Concerto in E, "L'Amoroso", F.I.no. 127
(Malipiero) Ric PR947 for rent
Concerto in F, F.I no. 128
(Malipiero) Ric PR951 for rent
Concerto in D, F.I no. 129
(Malipiero) Ric PR952 for rent
Concerto in F, F.I no. 130
(Malipiero) Ric PR953 for rent
Concerto in E flat, F.I no. 131
(Malipiero) Ric PR954 for rent
Concerto in D, F.I no. 132
(Malipiero) Ric PR955 for rent
Concerto in D, F.I no. 133
(Malipiero) Ric PR956 for rent
Concerto in D, F.I no. 134
(Malipiero) Ric PR957 for rent
Concerto in C, F.I no. 135
(Malipiero) Ric PR961 for rent
Concerto in D, F.I no. 136
(Malipiero) Ric PR962 for rent
Concerto in A, F.I no. 137
(Malipiero) Ric PR963 for rent
Concerto in D, F.I no. 138
(Malipiero) Ric PR964 for rent
Concerto in A, F.I no. 139, for vln,
3 solo vln in echo, and str orch
(Malipiero) Ric PR969 for rent
Concerto in C, F.I no. 140
(Malipiero) Ric PR972 for rent
Concerto in A, F.I no. 141
(Malipiero) Ric PR973 for rent
Concerto in d, F.I no. 142
(Malipiero) Ric PR974 for rent
Concerto in d, F.I no. 143
(Malipiero) Ric PR975 for rent
Concerto in b, F.I no. 144
(Malipiero) Ric PR976 for rent
Concerto in E, F.I no. 145
(Malipiero) Ric PR977 for rent
Concerto in C, F.I no. 146
(Malipiero) Ric PR978 for rent
Concerto in g, F.I no. 147
(Malipiero) Ric PR979 for rent
Concerto in A, F.I no. 148
(Malipiero) Ric PR980 for rent
Concerto in D, F.I no. 149
(Malipiero) Ric PR981 for rent
Concerto in B flat, F.I no. 150
(Malipiero) Ric PR982 for rent
Concerto in d, F.I no. 151
(Malipiero) Ric PR983 for rent
Concerto in g, F.I no. 152
(Malipiero) Ric PR984 for rent
Concerto in D, F.I no. 153
(Malipiero) Ric PR985 for rent
Concerto in d, F.I no. 154
(Malipiero) Ric PR986 for rent
Concerto in A, F.I no. 155
(Malipiero) Ric PR989 for rent

Concerto in E flat, F.I no. 156
(Malipiero) Ric PR990 for rent
Concerto in D, F.I no. 158
(Malipiero) Ric PR993 for rent
Concerto in D, F.I no. 160
(Malipiero) Ric PR995 for rent
Concerto in F, F.I, no. 161
(Malipiero) Ric PR996 for rent
Concerto in D, F.I no. 162
(Malipiero) Ric PR997 for rent
Concerto in B flat, "O Sia Il Corneto Da
Posta" F.I no. 163
(Malipiero) Ric PR998 for rent
Concerto in E flat, F.I no. 164
(Malipiero) Ric PR999 for rent
Concerto in g, F.I no. 165
(Malipiero) Ric PR1001 for rent
Concerto in E Flat, F.I no. 166
(Malipiero) Ric PR1002 for rent
Concerto in F, F.I no. 167
(Malipiero) Ric PR1007 for rent
Concerto in G, F.I no. 168
(Malipiero) Ric PR1008 for rent
Concerto in C, F.I no. 169
(Malipiero) Ric PR1051 for rent
Concerto in B flat, F.I no. 170
(Malipiero) Ric PR1052 for rent
Concerto in b, F.I no. 171
(Malipiero) Ric PR1053 for rent
Concerto in C, F.I no. 172
(Malipiero) Ric PR1054 for rent
VRANICKY, ANTONIN (1761-1820)
Concerto in B Flat
Artia for rent
WALTON, WILLIAM (1902-   )
Concerto
Oxf 23.415 for rent
WEBER, BEN (1916-   )
Chamber Fantasie, see Nonets
Concerto
CFE score and solo part only
WHITTENBERG, CHARLES
Chamber Concerto, see Octets
WIENIAWSKI, HENRI (1835-1880)
Concerto No. 1 in f sharp, Op. 14
CF for rent
Concerto No. 2 in d, Op. 22
AMP
CF for rent
GS for rent
Kal for sale or rent
Légende, Op. 17
CF for rent
GS for rent
Kal for sale or rent
Ric for rent
Polonaise brillante No. 2 in A, Op. 21
CF for rent
Scherzo-Tarentelle, Op. 16
CF for rent
Kal for sale or rent
Souvenir de Moscou, Op. 6
CF for rent
WIREN, DAG (1905-   )
Concerto, Op. 23
Gehrmans
WISHART, PETER (1921-   )
Concerto
Oxf for rent
WOESTYNE, DAVID VAN DE, see scores
WOOD, HAYDN (1882-1959)
Concerto
BH for rent

WOOD, JOSEPH
Concerto
CFE
WUORINEN, CHARLES (1938-   )
Concertante I
CFE   score only
Concertante II
ÇFE   score only
YSAYE, EUGENE (1858-1931)
Concerto d'après deux poèmes[116]
(J. Ysaÿe) SF   for rent
Extase[116]
SF   for rent
Fantaisie[116]
SF   for rent
Paganini Variations
Cinedisc   for rent
Poème Elégiaque
Cinedisc
ZACHARIAS, HELMUT
Fantasy on 3 themes
Mil   for rent
ZAFRED, MARIO (1922-   )
Concerto lirico
Ric   for rent
ZANDONAI, RICCARDO (1883-1944)
Concerto romantico
Ric   for rent

Viola, Orchestra

ANGERER, PAUL (1927-   )
Konzert
DOB   for rent
BACH, KARL PHILIPP EMANUEL (1714-1788)
Concerto, orig for vln and orch
(Casadesus) GS   for rent
BARTOK, BELA (1881-1945)
*Concerto
(Serly) BH   for rent
BAX, ARNOLD (1883-1953)
Phantasy
Chap-L   for rent
BENJAMIN, ARTHUR (1893-1960)
Sonata or Concerto. Elegy, Waltz and
Toccata
BH   for rent
BERLIOZ, HECTOR (1803-1869)
*Harold in Italy, Op. 16
GS   for rent
Kal   for sale or rent
BLOCH, ERNEST (1880-1959)
Suite
GS   for rent
*Suite Hebraique
GS   for rent
BORUP-JØRGENSEN, AXEL (1924-   )
*Music for Percussion and Viola, Op. 18
Dansk 218
BRAEIN, EDVARD (1887-1957)
Serenade
LY   for rent
CLARKE, HENRY LELAND (1907-   )
Encounters
CFE
DAVID, GYULA (1913-   )
*Concerto
Kul   for rent
DUNHILL, THOMAS F. (1877-1946)
Triptych
Oxf   for rent

GHEDINI, GIORGIO FEDERICO (1892-   )
*Musica da concerto, for vla or vla
d'amore and orch
Ric   for rent
GLANVILLE-HICKS, PEGGY (1912-   )
Concerto Romantico
CFE
GREEN, RAY (1909-   )
Concertante
AME   for rent
HANDEL, GEORG FRIEDRICH (1685-1759)
Concerto in b
(Casadesus) AMP
Concerto
(Barbirolli) Oxf 27.905
HENKEMANS, HANS (1913-   )
*Concerto
DN   for rent
HINDEMITH, PAUL (1895-1963)
Music of Mourning
AMP
HODDINOTT, ALUN (1929-   )
Concertino
Oxf   for rent
HOFFMEISTER, FRANZ ANTON (1754-1812)
Concerto in D
GR
HOLST, GUSTAV (1874-1934)
Lyric Movement
Oxf 77.412
HUGGLER, JOHN
Divertimento, Op. 32
Pet 6863   for rent
JACOB, GORDON (1895-   )
Concerto
Oxf   for rent
JOSEPHS, WILFRED (1927-   )
Meditatio de Beornmundo, Op. 30
Hin   for rent
KALAS, JULIUS (1902-   )
*Concerto
BH   for rent
KOETSIER, JAN (1911-   )
Concertino
Sirius   for rent
KREUZ, EMIL (1867-1932)
Concerto in C, Op. 20
Aug   for rent
KROL, BERNHARD (1920-   )
Konzertante Musik, see Nonets
KURTAG, GYÖRGY
*Concerto
Kul   for rent
LARSSON, LARS-ERIK (1908-   )
Concertino, Op. 45, No. 9
Gehrmans
MALIPIERO, GIAN FRANCESCO (1882-   )
*Dialoghi: V
Ric   for rent
MILFORD, ROBIN (1903-1959)
Elegiac Meditation
Oxf 22.030
MILHAUD, DARIUS (1892-   )
Concertino d'Eté
Heugel   for rent
Concerto No. 2
Heugel   for rent
PANNAIN, [GUIDO (1891-   )]
Concerto
Curci   for rent
PARRIS, ROBERT (1924-   )
Concerto
CFE

---

[116] This publication is not listed in current U.S. catalogues.
Information was received from Fondation Eugène Ysaÿe.

PARTOS, ÖDÖN (1907-   )
  Yiskor
  IMP
PLEYEL, IGNAZ (1757-1831)
  Concerto in D, Op. 31
  GR
READ, GARDNER (1913-   )
  Poem, Op. 31a
  CF for rent
REED, WILLIAM HENRY (1876-1942)
  Rhapsody in D
  Aug for rent
ROSENBERG, HILDING (1892-   )
  Concerto
  Nordiska
RUBBRA, EDMUND (1901-   )
  Concerto in A
  Leng for rent
SCHÄFER, KARL (1899-   )
  Divertimento über Thema von Conrad
      Paumann
  Gerig
SEITZ, FRIEDRICH
  Concerto No. 5 in D, Op. 22, first movement
      (Klotman) Mil
SERLY, TIBOR (1900-   )
  Rhapsody, on folk songs harmonized by
      Bartok
  SMP for rent
SHULMAN, ALAN (1915-   )
  Theme and Variations
  Chap for rent
STAMITZ, JOHANN (1717-1757)
  Concerto in G
  Pet
STAMITZ, KARL (1746-1801)
  Concerto in D, Op. 1
  Pet for rent
TELEMANN, GEORG PHILIPP (1681-1767)
  Concerto in G
  (Wolff) Baer
TURINA, JOAQUIN
  Scene Andalouse, see vla, pno and str quartet
VARDI, EMANUEL (1915-   )
  Suite on American Folk-Songs
  GS for rent
VAUGHAN WILLIAMS, RALPH (1872-1958)
  *Suite
  Oxf for rent
VELDEN, RENIER VAN DER, see scores
WALTON, WILLIAM (1902-   )
  *Concerto
  Oxf for rent
  Oxf for rent; 1962 version for
      smaller orch
WEBER, BEN (1916-   )
  Rapsodie Concertante
  CFE
ZAFRED, MARIO (1922-   )
  Concerto
  Ric for rent
ZELTER, KARL FRIEDRICH (1758-1832)
  Concerto in E flat
  GR
ZIMMERMANN, BERND ALOIS (1918-   )
  Antiphonen
  EDW

Cello, Orchestra

ADOLPHEUS, MILTON
  Interlude, Op. 96
  CFE score only

d'ALBERT, EUGÈNE (1864-1932)
  Concerto in C, Op. 20
  Pet for rent
BACH, JOHANN SEBASTIAN (1685-1750)
  Concerto in g
  GS for rent
BACH, KARL PHILIPP EMANUEL (1714-1788)
  *Concerto in a
  Eul
BALAZS, FREDERIC (1920-   )
  Concerto. In Memoriam
  CFE
BANTOCK, GRANVILLE (1868-1946)
  Celtic Poem
  Ches
  Elegiac Poem
  JWL (Mil No. W2801)
BARATI, GEORGE (1913-   )
  *Concerto
  Pet for rent
BARBER, SAMUEL (1910-   )
  *Concerto, Op. 22
  GS for rent
BAX, ARNOLD (1883-1953)
  Concerto
  Chap for rent
BEALE, JAMES (1924-   )
  Concerto, Op. 21
  CFE
BENTZON, NIELS VIGGO (1919-   )
  Konzert, Op. 106
  WH
BLOCH, ERNEST (1880-1959)
  *Schelomo
  GS for rent
  Symphony, see scores
  *Voice in the Wilderness. Symphonic
      Poem with vcl obligato
  GS for rent
BLUMER, THEODOR (1882-   )
  Burlesca
  Sik for rent
BOCCHERINI, LUIGI (1743-1805)
  *Concerto in B flat
  Eul
  Concerto in B flat
  Kal for sale or rent
  *Concerto in B flat
      (Grützmacher) BRH
      (Grützmacher) Kal for sale or rent
  Concerto in D, Op. 34
      (Silva) Ric for rent
  Concerto No. 2 in D
      (Silva) Ric for rent
BOELLMANN, LÉON (1862-1897)
  Variations Symphoniques, Op. 23
  CF for rent
  Kal for sale or rent
BORGHI, LUIGI (18th century)
  Concerto
  ZA 4388
BRIDGE, FRANK (1879-1941)
  Oration. Concerto Elegiaco
  Aug for rent
BRUCH, MAX (1838-1920)
  Kol Nidrei
  Kal for sale or rent
BUESSER, HENRI (1872-   )
  Sommeil de l'enfant Jésus
  CH
BUSH, ALAN (1900-   )
  Concert Suite, Op. 37
  JWL for rent

CASELLA, ALFREDO (1883-1947)
  Concerto, Op. 58
    Ric for rent
  Notturno e Tarantella
    Ric for rent
CASTELNUOVO-TEDESCO, MARIO (1895-   )
  Concerto in un tempo solo
    Ric for rent
CIRRI, GIOVANNI BATTISTA (1724-1808)
  Concerto in A, Op. 14, No. 1
    (Ghedini) Ric 129788-9
  Concerto, Op. 14, No. 6
    ZA 4341
COUPERIN
  Pièces en concert, see 2 vln, vla, 2 vcl
D'AMBROSI, DANTE (1902-   )
  Pezzi, 2, for orch with vcl obbligato
    Ric for rent
DAUTREMER, [MARCEL (1906-   )]
  Concertino
    Delrieu
DAVICO, VINCENZO (1889-   )
  Romanza
    Ric for rent
DEGEN, HELMUT (1911-   )
  Konzert
    Gerig
DELIUS, FREDERICK (1862-1934)
  Caprice
    BH
  Concerto
    BH for rent
  Elegy
    BH
DOHNÁNYI, ERNST VON (1877-1960)
  *Konzertstück, Op. 12
    DOB for rent
DUKELSKY, VLADIMIR (1903-   )
  Concerto
    CF for rent
DVORAK, ANTONIN (1841-1904)
  Concerto in A
    (Raphael) BRH
  *Concerto in b, Op. 104
    Artia for rent
    Kal for sale or rent
ERÖD, IVAN (1936-   )
  Sätze, 3
    EDW
FASANO, RENATO (1902-   )
  Il Signor Bonaventura
    Ric for rent
FAURÉ, GABRIEL (1845-1924)
  Elegy, Op. 24
    Kal for sale or rent
FERRO, PIETRO (1903-1960)
  Aria Italiana
    Ric for rent
FINZI, GERALD (1901-1956)
  Concerto
    BH for rent
FIOCCO, JOSEPH HEKTOR (1703-1741)
  Concerto in G
    (Bazelaire) SF
FISCHER, IRWIN
  Lament
    CFE score only
FIUME, ORAZIO (1908-   )
  Fantasia eroica
    Ric for rent
FRANCO, JOHAN (1908-   )
  Fantasy
    CFE

FUGA, SANDRO (1906-   )
  Concerto
    Ric for rent
FULEIHAN, ANIS (1900-   )
  Rhapsody
    CF for rent
GARTH, JOHN (1722-1810)
  Concerto No. 1 in D
    Hin for rent
  Concerto No. 2 in B flat
    Hin
  Concerto No. 3 in d
    Hin for rent
GAVAZZENI, GIANANDREA (1909-   )
  Concerto in A
    Ric for rent
GLASS, LOUIS (1864-1936)
  Frühlingslied, Op. 31
    WH
GLAZUNOV, ALEXANDER (1865-1936)
  Chant du Ménestrel, Op. 71
    Belaieff for rent
GOLTERMANN, GEORG (1824-1898)
  Concerto No. 1 in a, Op. 14
    CF for rent
    Kal for sale or rent
  Concerto No. 2 in d, Op. 30
    CF for rent
  Concerto No. 4 in G, Op. 65
    CF for rent
  Concerto No. 5 in d, Op. 76
    CF for rent
GRETRY, ANDRÉ E.M. (1741-1813)
  Suite Rococo
    (Bazelaire) SF
GUINAND, J.
  Pièces, 2
    Editions Francaises
HADLEY, HENRY K. (1871-1937)
  Concertstueck
    GS for rent
HARTMAN, THOMAS DE (1885-1956)
  Concerto, Op. 57
    Belaieff for rent
  Concerto d'apres une cantate de Bach,
      Op. 73
    Belaieff for rent
HAYDN, JOSEPH (1732-1809)
  *Concerto No. 1 in D, Op. 101
    (Gendron) AMP
    (Gevaert-Zilcher) BRH
    Broude
    Eul
    Kal for sale or rent
  Concerto No. 2 in D
    (Trowell) Aug for rent
HILLEMACHER, PAUL (1852-1933)
  Suite
    Ric for rent
HINDEMITH, PAUL (1895-1963)
  Music of Mourning
    AMP
HUYBRECHTS, ALBERT, see scores
IBERT, JACQUES (1890-1962)
  Concerto, for vcl and wind instruments
    Heugel for rent
JACOB, GORDON (1895-   )
  Concerto
    JWL for rent
JENTSCH, WALTER (1900-   )
  Concerto, Op. 33
    Sik for rent
KALABIS, VIKTOR (1923-   )
  Concerto
    Artia for rent

KELKEL, MANFRED (1929-   )
  Concertino
  Ric for rent
KOETSIER, JAN (1911-   )
  Barock-Suite in E, for vcl and 12
    woodwinds
  Sirius for rent
KUBIZEK, AUGUSTIN (1918-   )
  Concerto breve, Op. 23
  DOB for rent
LALO, EDOUARD (1823-1892)
  Concerto in d
  CF for rent
  Kal for sale or rent
LANDOWSKI, MARCEL (1915-   )
  Concerto
  CH for rent
LANGENDOEN, J.
  Burlesca
  H Elkan for rent
  Siciliana
  H Elkan for rent
LA ROSA PARODI, ARMANDO (1904-   )
  Poema
  Ric for rent
  Recitativo e Aria
  Ric for rent
LARSSON, LARS-ERIK (1908-   )
  Concertino, Op. 45, No. 10
  Gehrmans
LEO, LEONARDO (1694-1744)
  Concerto in A
  AMP
  *Concerto in D
  Eul
  Concerto in D
  (Cilea) Ric for rent
LOCATELLI, PIETRO ANTONIO (1695-1764)
  Adagio e Minuetto variato
  .. (Guerrini) Ric for rent
LÖWLEIN, [HANS (1909-   )]
  Musik, Op. 13
  BRH
MALIPIERO, GIAN FRANCESCO (1882-   )
  *Fantasie concertanti: III
  Ric for rent
MARCELLO, BENEDETTO (1686-1739)
  Sonata in F
  ZA 4165-6
MARGOLA, FRANCO (1908-   )
  Fantasia
  Ric for rent
MIHALY, ADAM
  *Concerto
  Kul for rent
MILHAUD, DARIUS, see scores
MOHLER, PHILIPP (1908-   )
  Fantasiestück
  Gerig
MONN, GEORG MATTHIAS (1717-1750)
  Concerto in g, orig for harpsichord,
    transcribed by A. Schoenberg
  GS for rent
MOZART, WOLFGANG AMADEUS (1756-1791)
  Concerto in B flat, orig for bsn and orch
  Pet
  Concerto in D, K.314,[117] orig for fl and orch
  (Szell) GS for rent
MURRILL, HERBERT (1909-1952)
  Concerto No. 1
  Oxf for rent
  Concerto No. 2
  Oxf for rent

NABOKOV, NICOLAS (1903-   )
  Hommages, Les. Concerto
  Ric for rent
NÖLCK, AUGUST
  Concerto, Op. 108
  Aug for rent
NYSTROEM, GÖSTA (1890-   )
  Sinfonia Concertante
  Nordiska
OSWALD, ENRIQUE (1852-1931)
  Elegia
  Ric for rent
PFITZNER, HANS (1869-1949)
  Konzert in a, Op. 52
  Oertel for rent
PIZZETTI, ILDEBRANDO (1880-   )
  Concerto in C
  Ric for rent
POPPER, DAVID (1843-1913)
  Concerto, Op. 18
  Kal for sale or rent
  Hungarian Rhapsody, Op. 68
  CF for rent
  Kal for sale or rent
  Tarentelle, Op. 33
  CF for rent
  Kal for sale or rent
PORPORA, NICOLA ANTONIO (1686-1766)
  Aria
  (Zandonai) Ric for rent
PORTER, QUINCY (1897-   )
  Fantasy
  CFE
POWELL, MEL (1923-   )
  Setting
  GS for rent
PROKOFIEV, SERGEY (1891-1953)
  Concerto in g, Op. 58
  BH for rent
REED, H. OWEN (1910-   )
  Concerto
  CP
RIETI, VITTORIO (1898-   )
  Concerto, for vcl and 12 instruments
  Ric for rent
  Concerto No. 2
  Ric for rent
RIVIER, JEAN, see scores
ROSENBERG, HILDING (1892-   )
  Concerto No. 2
  Gehrmans
RUBBRA, EDMUND (1901-   )
  Soliloquy
  Leng for rent
SAINT-SAENS, CAMILLE (1835-1921)
  Allegro appassionato, Op. 43
  Aug for rent
  CF for rent
  Kal for sale or rent
  Concerto No. 1 in a, Op. 33
  CF for rent
  GS for rent
  Kal for sale or rent
  Concerto No. 2 in d, Op. 119
  Kal for sale or rent
SALLUSTIO, GIACINTO (1879-1938)
  Il Canto della sposa rapita. Leggenda
  Ric for rent
SCHIBLER, ARMIN (1920-   )
  *Concertino, Op. 64
  Eul
SCHOENBERG, ARNOLD
  Concerto, see Monn

---

[117] K.285d in Schirmer catalogue.

SCHUMANN, GERHARD (1914-   )
  Kleine Suite
    Sirius   for rent
SCHUMANN, ROBERT (1810-1856)
  *Concerto in a, Op. 129
    BRH
    Kal   for sale or rent
SHULMAN, ALAN (1915-   )
  Concerto
    Chap   for rent
STAMITZ, KARL (1745-1801)
  Concerto No. 1 in G
    (Upmeyer) Baer
  Concerto No. 2 in A
    (Upmeyer) Baer
  Concerto No. 3 in C
    (Upmeyer) Baer
STRAUSS, RICHARD (1864-1949)
  *Don Quixote, Op. 35
    Kal   for sale or rent
    Pet   for rent
    vcl solo part only, see vcl unacc
TARTINI, GIUSEPPE (1692-1770)
  Concerto in A
    ZA 3167
  Concerto in D
    (Hindemith) AMP
TCHAIKOVSKY, PIOTR ILYITCH (1840-1893)
  *Variations on a Rococo Theme, Op. 33
    CF   for rent
    Kal   for sale or rent
TELEMANN, GEORG PHILIPP (1681-1767)
  Suite in D, for gamba or vcl and orch
    Pet 4526
THOMSON, VIRGIL (1896-   )
  Concerto
    Ric   for rent
TOMMASINI, VINCENZO (1878-1950)
  Scherzo
    ZA 3203B   for rent
TOVEY, DONALD F. (1875-1940)
  Concerto in C
    Oxf   for rent
  Intermezzo, from Concerto in C
    Oxf   for rent
VISKI, JANOS (1906-   )
  *Concerto
    Kul   for rent
VIVALDI, ANTONIO (c.1669-1741)
  Concerto in a
    (Upmeyer) AMP
  *Concerto in a
    RH
  Concerto in D
    (Rapp) AMP
  Concerto in D, Op. 3, No. 9, orig for
    vln and orch
    (Dandelot) AMP
  Concerto in c, F.III no. 1[118]
    (Ephrikian) Ric PR264   for rent
  Concerto in C, F.III no. 3
    (Malipiero) Ric PR754   for rent
  Concerto in a, F.III no. 4
    (Malipiero) Ric PR755   for rent
  Concerto in E flat, F.III no. 5
    (Malipiero) Ric PR756   for rent
  Concerto in C, F.III no. 6
    (Malipiero) Ric PR761   for rent
  Concerto in d, F.III no. 7
    (Malipiero) Ric PR762   for rent
  Concerto in C, F.III no. 8
    (Malipiero) Ric PR768   for rent

Concerto in b, F.III no. 9
  (Malipiero) Ric PR769   for rent
Concerto in a, F.III no. 10
  (Malipiero) Ric PR770   for rent
Concerto in F, F.III no. 11
  (Malipiero) Ric PR771   for rent
Concerto in G, F.III no. 12
  (Malipiero) Ric PR831   for rent
Concerto in a, F.III no. 13
  (Malipiero) Ric PR832   for rent
Concerto in F, F.III no. 14
  (Malipiero) Ric PR833   for rent
Concerto in g, F.III no. 15
  (Malipiero) Ric PR834   for rent
Concerto in D, F.III no. 16
  (Malipiero) Ric PR835   for rent
Concerto in F, F.III no. 17
  (Malipiero) Ric PR843   for rent
Concerto in a, F.III no. 18
  (Malipiero) Ric PR844   for rent
Concerto in G, F.III no. 19
  (Malipiero) Ric PR967   for rent
Sonates en concert, see 2 vln, vla, 2 vcl
WAGENSEIL, GEORG CHRISTOPH (1715-1777)
  Concerto in A
    DOB
  Concerto in C
    DOB
WALTON, WILLIAM (1902-   )
  Concerto
    Oxf 21.310   for rent
WASSIL, BRUNO (1920-   )
  Nenia
    Ric   for rent
WEBER, BEN (1916-   )
  Ballade
    CFE   score only
  Sinfonia
    CFE   score and solo part only
WIREN, DAG (1905-   )
  Concerto, Op. 10
    Gehrmans
WOOD, HAYDN (1882-   )
  Philharmonic Variations
    BH   for rent
WUORINEN, CHARLES (1938-   )
  *Chamber Concerto, for vcl and 10
    players
    MM   for rent
ZAFRED, MARIO (1922-   )
  Concerto
    Ric   for rent
ZANDONAI, RICCARDO (1883-1944)
  Concerto andaluso
    Ric   for rent
  Serenata medioevale
    Ric   for rent
  Spleen
    Ric   for rent

Double-Bass, Orchestra

ANGERER, PAUL (1927-   )
  Gloriatio
    DOB   for rent
CAPUZZI, [G.A. (1735-1818)]
  Concerto
    BH   for rent
DITTERSDORF, KARL DITTERS VON
    (1739-1799)
  Concerto in E
    (Jaeger) AMP

---

[118] Scores are available for concerti with Fanna numbers.
For information on this classification system, see Vivaldi
in violin and piano section.

DITTERSDORF, KARL DITTERS VON (cont.)
Concerto in E flat
(Jaeger) AMP
HERTL, [FRANTISEK (1906-   )]
*Concerto
Artia   for rent
KELEMEN, MILKO (1924-   )
*Concertino
Pet   for rent
KOUSSEVITZKY, SERGE (1874-1951)
Concerto, Op. 3
FR   for rent
LANCEN, S
Concerto, see 2 vln, vla, vcl, d-b
LARSSON, LARS-ERIK (1908-   )
Concertino, Op. 45, No. 11
Gehrmans

Viola d'Amore or Gamba, Orchestra

BORRIS, SIEGFRIED (1906-   )
Konzert, Op. 87, for gamba and orch
Sirius   for rent
GHEDINI, GIORGIO FEDERICO (1892-   )
*Musica da concerto, for vla or vla d'amore
and orch
Ric   for rent
LOEFFLER, CHARLES (1861-1935)
Mort de Tintagiles, La, for viole d'amore
and orch
GS   for rent
TELEMANN, GEORG PHILIPP (1681-1767)
Suite in D, for gamba and orch
Pet 4526
VIVALDI, ANTONIO (c.1669-1741)
*Concerto in A, F.II no. 1, for vla
d'amore and str orch
(Malipiero) Ric PR714   on special
order only
*Concerto in d, F.II no. 2, for vla
d'amore and str orch
(Malipiero) Ric PR721   for rent
*Concerto in d, F.II no. 3, for vla
d'amore and str orch
(Malipiero) Ric PR722   on special
order only
*Concerto in d, F.II no. 4, for vla
d'amore and str orch
(Malipiero) Ric PR723   on special
order only
*Concerto in D, F.II no. 5, for vla
d'amore and str orch
(Malipiero) Ric PR987   for rent
*Concerto in a, F.II no. 6, for vla
d'amore and str orch
(Malipiero) Ric PR991   for rent

Two or More Solo Instruments, Orchestra

BACH, JOHANN CHRISTIAN (1735-1782)
*Sinfonia Concertante in A, for vln, vcl
and orch
Eul
*Sinfonia Concertante in E flat, for 2 vln
and orch
Eul

BACH, JOHANN SEBASTIAN (1685-1750)
*Concerto in d, S.1043, for 2 vln and orch
BRH
Kal   for sale or rent
Pet   for rent
*Concerto in a, S.1044, for fl, vln, cembalo
and orch
BRH
Kal   for sale or rent
Pet   for rent
Concerto in c, S.1060, for ob, vln, and orch
BRH
Concerto in D, arr for 3 vln and orch
Pet
BADINGS, HENK (1907-   )
*Concerto, for 2 vln and orch
DN   for rent
BEETHOVEN, LUDWIG VAN (1770-1827)
*Concerto, Op. 56, for vln, vcl, pno and orch
BRH
GS   for rent
Kal   for sale or rent
for reduction of orch part, see vln, vcl, pno
BENJAMIN, ARTHUR (1893-   )
Romantic Fantasy, for vln, vla, and orch
BH   for rent
BENKER, [HEINZ (1921-   )]
Colloquium musicale for 2 vln, pno and orch
BRH
BENNETT, ROBERT RUSSELL (1894-   )
Concerto, for vln, pno and orch
Chap   for rent
BERGER, ARTHUR (1912-   )
*Serenade Concertante for fl, ob, clar, bsn,
vln and orch
Pet   for rent
BLOCH, ERNEST (1880-1959)
Concertino, for fl, vla and orch
GS   for rent
BRAHMS, JOHANNES (1833-1897)
*Concerto in a, Op. 102, for vln, vcl and orch
BRH
GS   for rent
Kal   for sale or rent
CAMBISSA, GIORGIO (1921-   )
Concerto per trio, for pno, vln, vcl and orch
Ric   for rent
CASELLA, ALFREDO (1883-1947)
*Concerto, Op. 56, for pno, vln, vcl and orch
Ric   for rent
CHAUSSON, ERNEST
Concerto, Op. 21, see vln, pno and str
quartet
CHEVREUILLE, RAYMOND (1901-   )
*Double Concerto, Op. 34, for vla, pno
and orch
CBDM   score only
COWELL, HENRY (1897-   )
Variations on Thirds, for 2 vla and orch
Pet   for rent
DELIUS, FREDERICK (1862-1934)
*Concerto, for vln, vcl and orch
Aug   for rent
Concerto, orig for vln, vcl and orch;
arr for vln, vla and orch
(Tertis) Aug   for rent
DIERCKS, JOHN (1927-   )
Diversion, for vln, vla and orch
Tritone   manuscript reproduction
GEISER, WALTER (1897-   )
Concerto da camera, Op. 50, for 2 vln,
clavicembalo and orch
Ric   for rent

GHEDINI, GIORGIO FEDERICO (1892-   )
*Concerto. "L'Alderina", for fl, vln
    and orch
    Ric   for rent
*Concerto. "L'Olmeneta", for 2 vcl and
    orch
    Ric   for rent
Pezzo concertante, for 2 vln, vla
    obbligato and orch
    Ric   for rent
GRAUN, JOHANN GOTTLIEB (1703-1771)
Concerto in c for vln, vla and orch
    (Janetzky) BRH
GRENZ, ARTUR (1909-   )
Concerto for 3 vln and orch, after Vivaldi
    Sik   for rent
HAINES, EDMUND (1914-   )
Concertino for fl, clar, horn, trumpet,
    vln, vla, vcl and orch
    AME   for rent
HARTMANN, KARL AMADEUS (1905-   )
Concerto, for vla, pno and orch
    SCH
HAYDN, JOSEPH (1732-1809)
Concerto in F, for vln, pno and orch
    BH
    Bruck   for rent; with cadenzas
    for reduction of orch part, see vln, pno
*Sinfonie concertante, Op. 84, for ob, bsn,
    vln, vcl and orch
    BRH
    Kal   for sale or rent
HOLST, GUSTAV (1874-1934)
Concerto, for 2 vln and orch
    Curwen
Fugal Concerto, for 2 vln and orch
    Nov
JOSEPHS, WILFRED (1927-   )
*Concerto da Camera, Op. 25, for vln,
    cembalo and orch
    Eul   for rent
KAHN, ERICH ITOR (1905-1956)
Triple Concerto
    CFE   score only
KIRCHNER, LEON (1919-   )
Concerto for vln, vcl, 10 winds and
    percussion
    AMP   score only
KOPPEL, HERMAN D. (1908-   )
Concerto, Op. 43, for vln, vla and orch
    WH
KOUTZEN, BORIS (1901-   )
Concerto for fl, clar, bsn, horn, vcl
    and orch
    AME   for rent
KREUTZER, RODOLPHE (1766-1831)
Symphony No. 3, for 2 vln and orch
    Kal   for sale or rent
KUBIK, GAIL (1914-   )
*Symphony Concertante, for trumpet, vla,
    pno and orch
    FC   for rent
LEGRENZI, GIOVANNI (1626-1690)
Concerto Bernardi, arr from Sonata a tre,
    Op. 4, No. 1, for 2 vln and orch
    (Sontag) Skidmore
LIER, BERTUS VAN (1906-   )
Concertante Music, for vln, ob and orch
    DN   for rent
MAURER, LOUIS WILHELM (1789-1878)
Concertante in A, Op. 55, for 4 vln and orch
    Pet

MORRIS, REGINALD OWEN (1886-1948)
Concerto Piccolo, for 2 vln and orch
    Oxf 26.101
MOZART, WOLFGANG AMADEUS (1756-1791)
*Sinfonia Concertante in E flat, K.364, for
    vln, vla, and orch
    Aug   for rent
    BRH
    Broude
    GS   for rent
    GT
    Kal   for sale or rent
NORDOFF, PAUL (1909-   )
Concerto for vln, pno and orch
    AME   for rent
PINKHAM, DANIEL (1923-   )
Serenade, for vln, harpsichord and orch
    CFE
RUYSSEN, PIERRE
Concerto, for 2 vcl and orch
    Delrieu   for rent
SCHIBLER, [ARMIN (1920-   )]
Elegische Musik, Op. 52, for fl, vcl and orch
    BRH
SCHOENBERG, ARNOLD (1874-1951)
Concerto for String Quartet and Orchestra,
    after Handel's Concerto Grosso,
    Op. 6, No. 7
    GS   for rent
SMYTH, ETHEL (1858-1944)
Concerto, for vln, horn and orch
    Curwen   for rent
SPOHR, LUDWIG (1784-1859)
Concerto, Op. 88, No. 2, for 2 vln and orch
    Kal   for sale or rent
Concerto, Op. 131, for 2 vln, vla, vcl
    and orch
    Kal   for sale or rent
STAMITZ, KARL (1746-1801)
Sinfonia Concertante in D, for vln, vla,
    and orch
    KN
STOUT, ALAN (1932-   )
Velut Umbra, Op. 35, for fl, vla, orch
    CFE
SURINACH, CARLOS (1915-   )
*Doppio Concertino, for vln, pno and
    chamber orch
    Broude   for rent
TOMMASINI, VINCENZO (1878-1950)
Concerto, for 2 vln, vla, vcl and orch
    Ric   for rent
UCCELLINI, MARCO (c.1610- ?)
Aria, for 2 vln and orch
    ZA
VIOTTI, GIOVANNI BATTISTA (1755-1824)
Sinfonia Concertante No. 2, for 2 vln
    and orch
    Carisch
WEINER, LEO (1885-1960)
Romance, for vcl, harp and orch
    Kul   score only
WUORINEN, CHARLES (1938-   )
Concertante IV, for vln, pno and orch
    CFE
YSAŸE, EUGÈNE (1858-1931)
Amitié,[119] for 2 vln and orch
    SF   for rent
Harmonies du Soir,[119] for 2 vln, vla, vcl
    and orch
    SF   for rent

---

[119] This publication is not listed in current U.S. catalogues.
Information was received from Fondation Eugène Ysaÿe.

YSAŸE, EUGÈNE (cont.)
 Poème Nocturne,[119] for vln, vcl and orch
  SF   for rent
ZAFRED, MARIO (1922-)
 Concerto, for vln, vcl, pno and orch
  Ric   for rent

ZENDER, H
 Divertimento, Op. 7b, for fl, vln, vcl
  and orch
 BRH

ORCHESTRAL
STUDY SCORES

Orchestral Study Scores

ADOLPHEUS, MILTON, see vcl and orch
AMES, WILLIAM, see vln and orch
BACH, JOHANN CHRISTIAN (1735-1782)
  Sinfonia Concertante in A, for vln, vcl
    and orch
    EPS (Pet No. E765)
  Sinfonia Concertante in E flat, for
    2 vln, orch
    EPS (Pet No. E768)
BACH, JOHANN SEBASTIAN (1685-1750)
  Violin Concerti Nos. 1 and 2; Double
    Concerto; Concerto Movement in D
    Lea 96
  Concerto No. 1 in a, S.1041, for vln
    and orch
    (Schering) EPS (Pet No. E711)
    Ric PR486
  Concerto No. 2 in E, S.1042, for vln
    and orch
    (Schering) EPS (Pet No. E712)
    Ric PR487
  Concerto in d, S.1043, for 2 vln and
    orch
    (Schering) EPS (Pet No. E727)
    Kal 143
  Concerto in a, S.1044, for fl, vln,
    cembalo and orch
    EPS (Pet No. E757)
BACH, KARL PHILIPP EMANUEL
  (1714-1788)
  Concerto in a, for vcl and orch
    EPS (Pet No. E781)
BADINGS, HENK (1907-)
  Concerto, for 2 vln and orch
    DN (Pet No. D89)
BARATI, GEORGE (1913-)
  Concerto for vcl and orch
    Pet 6602
BARBER, SAMUEL (1910-)
  Concerto, Op. 14, for vln and orch
    GS 75
  Concerto, Op. 22, for vcl and orch
    GS 61
BARTOK, BELA (1881-1945)
  Concerto No. 1, for vln and orch
    BH
  Concerto No. 2, for vln and orch
    BH
  Concerto, for vla and orch
    (Serly) BH
  Rhapsody No. 1, for vln and orch
    BH
  Rhapsody No. 2, for vln and orch
    BH
BECKER, JOHN, see vln and orch

BEETHOVEN, LUDWIG VAN (1770-1827)
  Concerto in C, Op. 56, for vln, vcl,
    pno and orch
    EPS (Pet No. E729)
  Concerto, Op. 61, for vln and orch
    BH
    EPS (Pet No. E701)
    Ric PR492
  Romances, 2, Op. 40 and Op. 50, for
    vln and orch
    EPS (Pet No. E803)
BERGER, ARTHUR (1912-   )
  Serenade Concertante, for vln, fl, ob,
    clar, bsn and orch
    Pet 6007
BERLIOZ, HECTOR (1803-1869)
  Harold in Italy, Op. 16, for vla and orch
    EPS (Pet No. E423)
    Int
BERSTEIN, LEONARD (1918-   )
  Serenade, for vln and orch
    GS 76
BLOCH, ERNEST (1880-1859)
  Schelomo, for vcl and orch
    GS 30
  Suite Hebraique, for vla or vln and orch
    GS 71
  Symphony, for vcl or trombone and orch
    Broude
  Voice in the Wilderness. Symphonic Poem
    with vcl obbligato
    GS 16
BOCCHERINI, LUIGI (1743-1805)
  Concerto in B flat, for vcl and orch
    EPS (Pet No. E780)
  Concerto in B flat, for vcl and orch
    (Grützmacher-Altman) EPS
    (Pet No. E780A)
BORUP-JØRGENSEN, AXEL (1924-)
  Music for Percussion and Viola, Op. 18
    Dansk 218
BRAHMS, JOHANNES (1833-1897)
  Concerto in D, Op. 77, for vln and orch
    EPS (Pet No. E716)
    Ric PR494
  Concerto in a, Op. 102, for vln, vcl
    and orch
    EPS (Pet No. E723)
    Int
BRUCH, MAX (1838-1920)
  Concerto No. 1 in g, Op. 26, for vln and orch
    Broude
    EPS (Pet No. E714)
    Kal 271
CASELLA, ALFREDO (1883-1947)
  Concerto, Op. 56, for pno, vln, vcl
    and orch
    Ric PR731

CHEVREUILLE, RAYMOND (1901-   )
　　Double Concerto, Op. 34, for vla, pno
　　　and orch
　　　CBDM
COWELL, HENRY, see vln and orch
DAVID, GYULA (1913-   )
　　Concerto, for vla and orch
　　　Kul
DELIUS, FREDERICK (1862-1934)
　　Concerto, for vln and orch
　　　Aug
　　Concerto, for vln, vcl, and orch
　　　Aug
DOHNÁNYI, ERNST VON (1877-1960)
　　Konzertstück in D, Op. 12, for vcl
　　　and orch
　　　DOB
DVORAK, ANTONIN (1841-1904)
　　Concerto in a, Op. 53, for vln and orch
　　　Artia
　　　EPS (Pet No. E751)
　　Concerto in b, Op. 104, for vcl and orch
　　　Artia
　　　EPS (Pet No. E785)
FAMOUS VIOLIN CONCERTOS, 4
　　　Kal F301
　　　Beethoven, Brahms, Mendelssohn,
　　　Tchaikovsky
FISCHER, IRWIN, see vln and orch; vcl
　　and orch
FRANKEL, BENJAMIN (1906-   )
　　Concerto, Op. 24, for vln and orch
　　　Aug
GERSCHEFSKI, EDWIN, see vln and orch
GHEDINI, GIORGIO FEDERICO (1892-   )
　　Concerto, "L'Alderina", for fl, vln,
　　　and orch
　　　Ric PR546
　　Concerto, "L'Olmeneta", for 2 vcl and
　　　orch
　　　Ric PR665
　　Musica da Concerto, for vla and orch
　　　Ric PR748
GLAZUNOV, ALEXANDER (1865-1936)
　　Concerto in a, Op. 82, for vln and orch
　　　Belaieff
　　　EPS (Pet No. E752)
GOLESTAN, STAN (1872-1956)
　　Concerto Roumain, for vln and orch
　　　Sal
HARRISON, LOU (1917-   )
　　Concerto, for vln and percussion ensemble
　　　Pet 6429
HAYDN, JOSEPH (1732-1809)
　　Concerto No. 1 in C, for vln and orch
　　　EPS (Pet No. E1202)
　　Concerto No. 2 in G, for vln and orch
　　　EPS (Pet No. E1228)
　　Concerto in D, Op. 101, for vcl and orch
　　　EPS (Pet No. E769)
　　　Broude
　　Sinfonie concertante, Op. 84, for ob, bsn,
　　　vln, vcl and orch
　　　EPS (Pet No. E790)
HEILNER, IRWIN, see vln and orch
HENKEMANS, HANS (1913-   )
　　Concerto, for vln and orch
　　　DN (Pet No. D142)
　　Concerto for vla and orch
　　　DN (Pet No. D94)
HERTL, [FRANTISEK (1906-   )]
　　Concerto, for d-b and orch
　　　Artia

HIDAS, FRIGYES (1928-   )
　　Concertino, for vln and orch
　　　Kul
HOVHANESS, ALAN (1911-   )
　　Concerto No. 2, Op. 89a, for vln and
　　　str orch
　　　Pet 6113
HUYBRECHTS, ALBERT (1899-   )
　　Dirge, for vcl and orch
　　　CBDM
IMBRIE, ANDREW (1921-   )
　　Concerto, for vln and orch
　　　Templ LC257
JOSEPHS, WILFRED (1927-   )
　　Concerto da Camera, Op. 25, for vln,
　　　cembalo and orch
　　　EPS (Pet No. E1235)
KAHN, ERICH ITOR, see vln and orch;
　　vln, vcl, pno and orch
KALAS, JULIUS (1902-   )
　　Concerto, for vla and orch
　　　Artia
KELEMEN, MILKO (1924-   )
　　Concertino, for double-bass and str orch
　　　Pet 5875
KERR, HARRISON, see vln and orch
KIRCHNER, LEON (1919-   )
　　Concerto for vln, vcl, 10 winds and
　　　percussion
　　　AMP
KOKAI, REZSO (1906-   )
　　Concerto, for vln and orch
　　　Kul
KRENEK, ERNST (1900-   )
　　Marginal Sounds, for percussion instru-
　　　ments with vln
　　　Rongwen
KUBIK, GAIL (1914-   )
　　Concerto in D for vln and orch
　　　Chap
　　Symphony Concertante, for trumpet, vla,
　　　pno and orch
　　　FC 1819
KURTAG, GYÖRGY
　　Concerto, for vla and orch
　　　Kul
LALO, EDOUARD (1823-1892)
　　Symphonie Espagnole, Op. 21, for vln
　　　and orch
　　　EPS (Pet No. E728)
　　　Kal 267
LEO, LEONARDO (1694-1744)
　　Concerto in D, for vcl and str orch
　　　EPS (Pet No. E1218)
LESSARD, JOHN, see vln and orch
LOURIÉ, ARTHUR (1892-   )
　　Concerto da Camera, for vln and str orch
　　　Rongwen
MALIPIERO, GIAN FRANCESCO (1882-   )
　　Dialoghi: V, for vla and orch
　　　Ric PR585
　　Fantasie concertanti, 4
　　　Ric PR800
MARCELLO, BENEDETTO (1686-1739)
　　Concerto in D, for vln and str orch
　　　EPS (Pet No. E1209)
MARTINU, BOHUSLAV (1890-1959)
　　Concerto, for vln and orch
　　　Artia
MENDELSSOHN, FELIX (1809-1847)
　　Concerto in e, Op. 64, for vln and orch
　　　EPS (Pet No. E702)
　　　Kal 145
　　　Ric PR508

MIHALY, ADAM
  Concerto, for vcl and orch
    Kul
MILHAUD, DARIUS (1892-   )
  Concertino de Printemps, for vln and
    orch
    Sal
  Concerto, for vcl and orch
    Sal
MOZART, WOLFGANG AMADEUS (1756-1791)
  Concertos, 3: K. 216, K. 218, K. 219, for
    vln and orch
    Kal F305
  Concerto No. 1 in B flat, K. 207, for vln
    and orch
    EPS (Pet No. E763)
  Concerto No. 2 in D, K. 211, for vln
    and orch
    EPS (Pet No. E764)
  Concerto No. 3 in G, K.216, for vln and orch
    Broude
    EPS (Pet No. E747)
    Ric PR514
  Concerto No. 4 in D, K. 218, for vln and orch
    EPS (Pet No. E748)
    Ric PR515
  Concerto No. 5 in A, K. 219, for vln and orch
    EPS (Pet No. E717)
    Ric PR516
  Concerto No. 6 in E flat, K. 268, for vln
    and orch
    EPS (Pet No. E718)
  Concerto No. 7 in D, K. 271a, for vln
    and orch
    EPS (Pet No. E766)
  Symphonie Concertante in E flat, K. 364,
    for vln, vla and orch
    EPS (Pet No. E734)
    Ric PR633
NIELSEN, CARL (1865-1931)
  Konzert, Op. 33, for vln and orch
    WH
PARRIS, ROBERT, see vln and orch
PETRASSI, GOFFREDO (1904-   )
  Introduzione e Allegro, for vln and
    11 instruments
    Ric PR652
PROKOFIEV, SERGEY (1891-1953)
  Concerto No. 1, Op. 19, for vln and orch
    Int
RAVEL, MAURICE (1875-1937)
  Tzigane, for vln and orch
    Dur
RIETI, VITTORIO (1898-   )
  Serenata, for vln and orch
    Sal
RIVIER, [JEAN (1896-   )]
  Burlesque, for vln and orch
    Sal
  Rapsodie, for vcl and orch
    Sal
SAMMARTINI, GIOVANNI (1701-1775)
  Concerto in C, for vln and orch
    EPS (Pet No. E1211)
SCHIBLER, ARMIN (1920-   )
  Concertino, Op. 64, for vcl and str orch
    EPS (Pet No. E1233)
SCHOENBERG, ARNOLD (1874-1951)
  Concerto, Op. 36, for vln and orch
    GS 80
SCHUMANN, ROBERT (1810-1856)
  Concerto in a, Op. 129, for vcl and orch
    Broude
    EPS (Pet No. E786)

SHAPEY, RALPH, see vln and orch
SIBELIUS, JEAN (1865-1957)
  Concerto in d, Op. 47, for vln and orch
    Broude
    EPS (Pet No. E770)
    Int
SPOHR, LUDWIG (1784-1859)
  Concerto No. 8 in a, Op. 47, for vln and orch
    EPS (Pet No. E703)
STAMITZ, KARL (1746-1801)
  Concerto in G, for vln and orch
    EPS (Pet No. E1210)
STEIN, LEON, see vln and orch
STOUT, ALAN, see vln and orch
STRAUSS, RICHARD (1864-1949)
  Don Quixote, Op. 35, for vcl and orch
    EPS (Pet No. E445)
    Kal 132
SURINACH, CARLOS (1915-   )
  Doppio Concertino, for vln, pno and
    chamber orch
    Rongwen
TARTINI, GIUSEPPE (1692-1770)
  Concerto in A, for vln and str orch
    (Schroeder) EPS (Pet No. E1231)
TCHAIKOVSKY, PIOTR ILYITCH (1840-1893)
  Concerto in D, Op. 35, for vln and orch
    EPS (Pet No. E708)
    Ric PR521
  Variations on a Rococo Theme, Op. 33, for
    vcl and orch
    EPS (Pet No. E788)
TELEMANN, GEORG PHILIPP (1681-1767)
  Concerto in G, for vln and str orch
    EPS (Pet No. E1242)
TORELLI, GIUSEPPE (c.1660-1708)
  Concerto in c, Op. 8, No. 8, for vln and
    str orch
    EPS (Pet No. E782)
VALEN, FARTEIN (1887-1952)
  Concerto, Op. 37, for vln and orch
    LY (Pet No. LY158)
VAUGHAN WILLIAMS, RALPH (1872-1958)
  Concerto in d, "Accademico", for vln
    and orch
    Oxf 23.350
  Lark Ascending, for vln and orch
    Oxf 23.340
  Suite, for vla and orch
    Oxf
VELDEN, RENIER VAN DER (1910-   )
  Chamber Music for vla and orch
    CBDM
VIOTTI, GIOVANNI BATTISTA (1753-1824)
  Concerto No. 22 in a, for vln and orch
    (Einstein) EPS (Pet No. E756)
VISKI, JANOS (1906-   )
  Concerto, for vln and orch
    Kul
  Concerto, for vcl and orch
    Kul
VIVALDI, ANTONIO (c.1669-1741)
  Concerti, 151, for vln and orch
    Ric   published separately
      for detailed listing see concerti
      with Fanna numbers under violin
      and orchestra
  Concerto in a, Op. 3, No. 6, for vln
    and orch
    EPS (Pet No. E753)
  Concerto in E, Op. 3, No. 12, for vln
    and orch
    EPS (Pet No. E787)

VIVALDI, ANTONIO (cont.)
Concerto in g, Op. 6, No. 1, for vln and orch
(Einstein) EPS (Pet No. E754)
Concerto in D, Op. 7, No. 11, for vln
and orch
EPS (Pet No. E1237)
Concerto in D, Op. 7, No. 12, for vln and
orch
EPS (Pet No. E1227)
Concerti, Op. 8, Nos. 1-4, "Four Seasons",
for vln and orch
EPS (Pet Nos. E1220-23)   in one vol or
published separately
Kal 305-308   published separately
Concerto in c, Op. 51, No. 3 "Il Sospetto",
for vln and orch
EPS (Pet No. E1245)
Concerto in D, fatto per la Solennita della
Lingua di San Antonio, for vln and orch
(Jenkins) EPS (Pet No. E1217)
Concerto in D, for vln and double str orch
EPS (Pet No. E1234)
Concerto in E flat, "Il Ritiro", for vln
and orch
Kul

Concerti, 6, F.II nos. 1-6, for vla
d'amore and orch
Ric   published separately
Concerti, 18, F.III nos. 1, 3-19, for
vcl and orch
Ric   published separately
Concerto in a, for vcl and orch
RH (Pet No. ER7)
WALTON, WILLIAM (1902-   )
Concerto, for vla and orch
Oxf
WEBER, BEN, see vln and orch; vcl and orch
WEINER, LEO (1885-1960)
Romance, for vcl, harp, and orch
Kul
WOESTYNE, DAVID VAN DE (1915-   )
Concerto, for vln and 12 instruments
CBDM
WUORINEN, CHARLES (1938-   )
Chamber Concerto, for vcl and 10 players
MM
see also vln and orch

STUDY MATERIAL

Study Material: Violin

ALARD, JEAN-DELPHIN (1815-1888)
Method
(Guarinoni-De Angelis-Franci) Ric 55412
CF 01-2   2V; English, French, German
text
Scuola del violino. Scale ed esercizi,
estratte dal Metodo
Ric ER2583
Studies
Etudes, 6, Op. 2
(Nadaud) Billaudot
Melodious and Progressive Studies,
Op. 10
(Abbado) Ric ER2484
(Wessely) Aug 5640
Etudes-Caprices, 24, Op. 41
(Lichtenberg) GS L1389
(Polo) Ric ER1766; Italian, French
and English text
Etudes-Caprices, Op. 41, Bk. 1
(Kross) SCH
Art moderne, L', Op. 53
HL   2V
Scale Studies in all keys
CF B1225
see also 2 vln
ALESSANDRI, GIUSEPPE
Perfetta indipendenza delle dita e
dell'arco sul violino
Ric ER2489
ALEXEYEV, V.
Scales and Arpeggios
MZK
ALSHIN, H.
Sing Out Strings
Universal Musical Instrument Co.
ANDERSON, KENNETH (1903-   )
Basic Exercises
Bosw   pno accomp
Modern Course for Violin
(Rokos) Bosw   6V   pno accomp
ANGUS, WALTER
Angus Approach to Orchestral Violin
Playing
CF 03879
Angus Approach to Violin Playing
CF 03879
From Third to First
CF 03733
APPLEBAUM, SAMUEL
Building Technic with Beautiful Music
Bel EL1057-60   4V; pno accomp for
Vols 1 and 2
see also 2 vln
AUER, LEOPOLD (1845-1930)
Characteristic Preludes, 12, in form of
melodic studies, Op. 8
CF 02583

Graded Course of Violin Playing
(Saenger) CF 01416, 01419, 01446-51   8V
see also more than 1 instrumental combi-
nation
AXÉN, GUNNAR
Fiolskola
Nordiska   3V
BABITZ, SOL, see literature
BACHMANN, A.
Études transcendantes, 6
Gaudet
BAILLOT, PIERRE (1771-1842)
Caprices, 12
(Heymann) Senart 5228
Etudes, 24
(Nadaud) Billaudot   3V
BAKER-LAGASSEY-SILVERSTEIN
Tune Tech Class Method for Violin
Kjos   2V
BANG, MAIA (1879-1940)
Gingham Books, Bk. 1
GS   pno accomp
Scale-tune Book
GS
Violin Course
GS   3V   pno accomp
Violin Method
CF 042, 02498, 044-47, 01410   7V
pno accomp; English, Spanish text
BARBAKOFF, SAMUEL
Fiddling by the Numbers
(Isaac) CF 03747   pno accomp
see also Rohner & Barbakoff
BARBAKOFF, SAM & HOLMES, MARKWOOD
My Second Book for Violin
CF 03254
BARBISON
Higher Technique for Violin
Carisch
BARMAS, ISSAYE (1872-1946)
Problems of Technique in Violin-Playing
Solved
BB   English, German, French text
BARNES & KUCZMARSKI
New School for Violin
Jack Spratt
BARTÓK, BÉLA, see Orchestral Studies
BARTOSCH, J.
Tonleiter und Akkordstudien
DOB   2V
BARTOSCH, J. & HUBER, F.
Ich bin ein Musikant
DOB   5V
BEAZLEY, J.C.
Early Stages
STB
BELOV, JOEL
White keys of the violin
GS
BERG, ALBAN, see Orchestral Studies
BERGER, THEODOR, see Orchestral Studies

BERIOT, CHARLES DE (1802-1870)
Brillant Studies, 6, Op. 17
Aug 5646
Concert Studies, 30, Op. 123
(Berkley) GS L1658
Concert Etudes, Vol. I
(Wessely) SCH
Études caractéristiques, 12, Op. 114
SCH
Method, Op. 102
(Jacobsen) Pet 2987A
(Lehmann) 2V
Method, Op. 102, Part I
(Anzoletti) Ric ER802
(Saenger) CF 01249; English and
French text
GS L1086; Spanish text
BERKLEY, HAROLD
Modern Technique of Violin Bowing
GS
Studies, 12, in modern violin bowing in
the 1st position
GS
BEROLD, WILLIAM
Primer and Modern Graded Course
Willis 4V
BERTHOUD, E.
Étude sur la 4ᵉ corde
Senart
Gammes, Les. Exercices Préparatoires
Senart
BEST, AGNES, see Palmer & Best
BIGNAMI, GIULIO
Tecnica del violino
Santis 669
BLOCH, ALEXANDER
Principles and Practice of Violin
Bowing
GS
BLOCH, J.
Finger Exercises, Op. 16
Kul
Scale Studies, Op. 5
Kul 3V; Hungarian and German text
School of Double-Stops, Op. 50
Kul 2V; Hungarian and German text
BLUMENSTENGEL, ALBRECHT
Exercises, 24, Op. 33
CF L621
GS L1032
Scale and Arpeggio Studies
CF L203-4 2V
GS L603-4 2V
BOEHMER, CARL
Studies in intonation, 75, Op. 54
(Schill) GS L1622
BOESEN, EJNAR
Den lille violinskole
WH
Violinskole
WH
BONELLI, ETTORE
Elementarstudien des Flageolett-Spiels,
Op. 39
ZA 4082
BORISSOFF, JOSEF (1889-   )
Foundation for Violin Technic
CF AA32
BORNOFF, GEORGE
Tonal Patterns in Melody
Gordon V. Thompson
BRADLEY, VINCENT
Famous Violin Tunes
Oxf 23.335-6 2V

Three-Part Tunes for Violin Classes
Oxf 23.802-3 2V
BRISSARD, A.
Gammes Majeures et Mineures
Gaudet
BROWN, HULLAH
First Position Melodic Studies, 21
JWL (Mil No. W1802)
New Fingerboard Dexterity for Young
Violinists
JWL (Mil No. W1803)
Peter Pan Violin Class Tutor
JWL (Mil No. W1805A,B,C,D) 4V
pno accomp for Vols. 1 and 2
Technique of the Fiddle Bow
JWL (Mil No. W1804)
BROWN, HULLAH & DYKE, SPENCER
Violin Method
JWL (Mil No. W1810)
Violin Method for Adults
JWL
BROWN, JAMES
Drills for Violin and Viola Players
STB
One Hundred Tunes for Violin
STB
Polychordia String Tutor, Steps 1-12
STB 12V
BROWN, see Wilhelmj & Brown
BURROWS, GRACE
Easy Exercises and Studies in the
3rd position
Aug
Reading by Interval in the 3rd position,
and simple exercises in double-
stopping
Aug pno accomp by B. Burrows
BUS
Modern Orchestral Studies, Vol 1
SCH for contents see title
BYTOVETSKI, PAVEL L.
Double Stopping for the Violin
CF 03055
Scale Technic
CF 03056
CAMPAGNOLI, BARTOLOMMEO (1751-1827)
Divertimenti, 7, Op. 18
(Polo) Ric ER189
(Quesnot) Senart 5146
CF 03391
Pet 3115
Fugues, see vln unacc
Metodo
(Polo) Ric ER625-6 2V; Italian and
Spanish text
see also 2 vln
CAPET, LUCIEN (1873-1928)
Technique supérieure de l'Archet
Senart
CARSE, ADAM (1878-1958)
New School of Violin
Aug 6V
Preliminary Exercises
Aug
Progressive Studies
Aug 4V
Scales and Arpeggios
Aug 3V
Sight-reading Exercises
Aug 2V
Violin Teacher
BMC 2V pno accomp

CASABONA, ALBERTO
  Tecnica del Violino, La
    Ric ER2671-6   6V; Italian and English
      text
CASORTI, AUGUST
  Technique of Bowing, Op. 50
    (Mittell) GS L932
    CF L345; English, German and French
      text
    Pet 2516
CATHERINE, G.
  Étude du mécanisme de l'archet
    Leduc
  Étude méthodique des gammes
    Leduc
  Gammes en sons harmoniques
    Leduc
CHAMP, S.
  Primary Studies, 40
    Aug
CHERNISHEV, V.
  Beginner's Etudes
    MZK
CLEAVE, MONTAGUE
  Coach and Horses, for vln class
    JWL (Mil No. W2305)   pno accomp
COBILOVICI, E.
  Tableaux synoptiques des sons
      harmoniques du violon
    HL
COHEN
  First Year Violin Method
    Paxton (Mil No. P529)   pno accomp
  Second Year Violin Method
    Paxton (Mil No. P530)   pno accomp
  Third Year Violin Method
    Paxton (Mil No. P531)   pno accomp
COLLINS, see Forbes & Collins
CONSOLINI
  Passi difficili e "a solo" di opere
      teatrali italiane
    Ric ER449
COURVOISIER, KARL (1846-1908)
  Violin School
    Aug 7600   3V
COUSIN & LE BOULCH
  École du Violon
    Ricard
      Collection complète des Premiers
      solos extraits des Concertos de:
      Rode, Kreutzer, Viotti, Habeneck,
      Baillot. 72 numéros.
      published separately
CRANE, A.
  Elementary Violin Tutor
    Aug
CRICKBOOM
  Masters of the Violin. Progressive
      studies
    SF (Pet No. SCH51-62)   12V
  Technique of the Violin
    SF (Pet No. SCH63-65)   3V
  Violin, Theory and Practice
    SF (Pet No. SCH66-70)   5V
CRISTALLI, LEONIDA
  Metodo preparatorio per lo studio
      del violino
    Santis 994
CURCI, A.
  Arco e le basi della sua tecnica, L'
    Curci
  Studi elementari, 24, in prima posizione
    Curci

Studi speciali, 20, nell'ambito della
      prima posizione
    Curci
  Studietti melodici e progressivi, 50
    Curci
  Tecnica fondamentale del violino
    Curci   5V; Italian, English and
      Spanish text
DANCLA, CHARLES (1817-1907)
  Method, Op. 52
    (De Angelis) Ric ER2212-5   4V
    (Lichtenberg) GS   2V
  Method, Op. 52, Part I
    CF 0148; English, French, German text
  School of Five Positions
    Vol 1: 20 easy exercises in first five
      positions, Op. 122
    Vol 2: 10 etudes, Op. 90
    Vol 3: 16 melodious studies, Op. 128,
      with 2nd vln in score
    CF 03369, L550, 04142   3V
    Ric ER1544-6   3V
  Scuola dell'arco, Libro II
    (Anzoletti) Ric ER630
  Studies
    Studies, 15, Op. 68, with 2nd vln part
      in score
    CF L330
    GS L602
    Pet 1078
  Etudes brillantes, 20, Op. 73
    GS L626
    Pet 1079; includes cadenza to Viotti
      Concerto No. 24
  School of Mechanism, Op. 74. 50
      exercises
    (Anzoletti) Ric ER431
    "Esercizi giornalieri";
      Italian and Spanish text
    (Lehmann) GS L219
    CF L129 "School of Velocity";
      English, German, French text
    Pet 1080
  Studi melodici e facilissimi, 36, Op. 84
    (Fael) Ric ER1543
  Easy Melodies, Op. 115, see vln and pno
  Melodious Studies, Op. 123, see
    20 Easy Pieces, Suite 1, under
    vln and pno
  Progrès, Le. 10 Études Mélodiques
    RL
  see also 2 vln
DANCLA-BERIOT
  Position Method, see McConnell
DANIELL, JENNIE
  Third Position Tunes for the Violin
    BMC
DAVID, FERDINAND (1810-1873)
  Etudes for beginners, 24, Op. 44,
      with 2nd vln part in score
    CF L771
  Violin harmonics and the pizzicato
    (Smith) GS L1410; English and Spanish
      text
  Violin School, Part I
    CF 0528; English and German text
DEPAS
  Agilité, L', Op. 127. 25 etudes
    (Catherine) Leduc
  Études préliminaires a la première
      position, Op. 122
    (Catherine) Leduc
  Méthode complete, Op. 28
    (Catherine) Leduc   2V

DEPAS (cont.)
Progrès, Le, Op. 124.   25 etudes
    (Catherine) Leduc
Progressive Studies, 24
    (Rodin) BMC
DETHERIDGE, JOSEPH (1898-   )
Violin School
    Bosw   4V
DOELL, W.
Gedächtnisstütze zum Violinkonzert,
    Op. 61, von Beethoven
    Hof
Intonations-Übungen für Violine
    Erdmann
DOFLEIN, ERICH & ELMA
Doflein Method
    SCH   5V; English text
Geigen-Schulwerk, Das
    SCH   5V; German text
DOMERC
Etude des cinq positions
    Billaudot
Guide du violoniste, Le
    HL
DONT, JAKOB (1815-1888)
Etudes and Caprices, 24, Op. 35
    (Flesch) Int
    (Flesch) SIM
    (Hendriks) Sik 187
    (Jacobsen) Pet 3705
    (Polo) Ric ER92; Italian, French and
        English text
    (Wessely) Aug 5653
    CF L306
    GS L1179
Exercises, 24, Op. 37, preparatory to the
    etudes of Kreutzer and Rode
    (Flesch) SIM
    (Garay) Kul
    (Hendriks) Sik 182
    (Polo) Ric ER93; Italian, French and
        English text
    (Svecenski) GS L328
    CF L276
    Pet 3706
Exercises, 30, Op. 38, with 2nd vln part
    in score
    (Rados) Kul   3V; Hungarian and
        German text
    GS L429
Exercises, 20, Op. 38a, with 2nd vln
    part in score
    (Wessely) Aug 7605
    CF L357
DORSON, CH.
Études Caprices, 6
    Deiss
DOUNIS, DEMETRIUS (1886-1954)
Absolute Independence of the Fingers,
    Op. 15
    CF 02900-01   2V
Advanced Studies, Op. 33
    Mil
Artist's Technic of Violin Playing, Op. 12
    CF 02695; English, German and
        French text
Change of Position Studies, Op. 36
    Mil
Development of Flexibility, Op. 35
    Mil
Essential Scale Studies, Op. 37
    Mil
Fundamental Trill Studies, Op. 18
    CF 02904

Higher Development of Thirds and
    Fingered Octaves, Op. 30
    CF 03378
Moto Perpetuo in fingered octaves, see
    Paganini under vln unacc
New Aids to the Technical Development
    of the Violinist, Op. 27
    CF 02906
Preparatory Studies in Thirds and
    Fingered Octaves, Op. 16
    CF 02902-03   2V
Staccato, Op. 21
    CF 02905
Studies in Chromatic Double-Stops,
    Op. 29
    CF 03012
DUE, HENRIK
Norwegian Violin School
    Musikk-Huset
DYKE, SPENCER
Progressive Studies
    JWL (Mil Nos. W1827-31)   5V
Scale Book
    JWL (Mil No. W1811)
see also Brown & Dyke
EBERHARDT, SIEGFRIED
Violin Vibrato
    CF 0184
see also literature
ELGAR, EDWARD (1857-1934)
Etudes caracteristiques, Op. 24
    Bosw
Very Easy Melodious Studies, Op. 22
    Bosw   pno accomp
ERET-HOVEY
Practical Violin Studies
    Bel EL142
ERNST, HEINRICH WILHELM (1814-1865)
Etudes for solo violin, 6, in 2 to 4 part
    harmony
    (Auer) GS L1470
Polyphonic Etudes, 6, and Der Erlkönig
    Sik 190
FECHNER, J.
Moderne Violintechnik
    SCH   2V
FEIGERL
Etudes, 24
    (Rados) Kul   2V; Hungarian and German
        text
FELDMAN, HARRY A.
Violin Takes a Bow
    Pro Art 108
FERRARA, [BERNARDO]
Studio del violino elementare e progressivo
    (De Angelis) Ric ER1311-5   5V
Study of the Violin, Part I
    (Chacon) CF 0200; English and Italian text
FINCH, see Marsh & Finch
FIORILLO, FEDERIGO (1755- ?)
Etudes or Caprices, 36
    (Capet) Senart 5005
    (Davisson) Pet 283A
    (Galamian) Int
    (Heim) Aug 5654
    (Hellmesberger) BRH
    (Kross) CF 03635; English and German
        text
    (Polo) Ric ER2206
    (Principe) Ric ER1449; Italian and
        Spanish text
    (Schmidtner) Sik 184
    (Schradieck) GS L228

FIORILLO, FEDERIGO (cont.)
Etudes or Caprices, 36 (cont.)
(Singer) CF L582
(Spohr) Pet 283B   2nd vln ad lib
UE 56
see also Winn under literature
FISCHER, BERNARD
Daily Violin Exercises
Bel EL486
Violin and Viola Calisthenics
Bel EL452
Violin Etudes in the Modern Style
Bel EL629-630   2V
FLESCH, CARL (1873-1944)
Basic Studies
CF 0205; English, German and French
text
Etüden-Sammlung für Violine
WH 2096-8   3V
Vol 1: 51 etudes by Corelli, Kayser,
Meerts, Kreutzer, David, Mazas,
Gravina, Lolli, Benda, Dont,
Fiorillo, Spohr
Vol 2: 47 etudes by Blumenthal,
Beriot, Campagnoli, Kreutzer,
Vieuxtemps, Gavinies, Rode,
Mayseder, Schubert
Vol 3: 44 etudes by Dont, Beriot,
Wieniawski, Baillot, Schubert,
Flesch, Paganini, Vieuxtemps,
Lipinsky
Problems of Tone Production in Violin
Playing
CF 02358
Scale System
CF 01509; English, German and French
text
see also literature
FLOOD, LEONA
Building up the Technique
Mil
FLOR, S.
Positions
H Elkan
FONTAINE, LEON J.
Graded Studies
Paxton (Mil Nos. P548-9)   2V
Short Melodious Studies, 30, in the First
Position
Paxton (Mil No. P541)
FORBES
Exercises for Violinists
ABRS (Mil No. A213-9)   5V
FORBES & COLLINS
Scales and Arpeggios for Violinists
ABRS (Mil Nos. A216-7)   2V
FORTUNATOV
Selected Etudes, 72
MZK
see also Garlitsky, Rodionov & Fortunatov
FRANK, PHILIP D.
My first violin scale book
GS
FRIEDEMANN, L.
Geigenschule für den Anfang
SCH
FRIEDEMANN
Studies, 8
Pet 5821
FRIEZ, A.
Pédagogie violonistique
ESC
GARDNER, SAMUEL (1891-   )
First Violin Book
BMC

School of Violin Study, based on harmonic
thinking
CF 02888-89   2V
GARLITSKY, RODIONOV & FORTUNATOV
Etudes, 66, in the First Position
MZK
GAUVREAU, GLADYS
Junior Violinist
BMC
Little Violinist
BMC
GAVINIES, PIERRE (1728-1800)
Etudes. 24 Matinées
(Abbado) Ric ER2481
(Capet) Senart 5008
(Davisson) Pet 1381
(Galamian) Int
(Lichtenberg) GS L929
(Schmidtner) Sik 186
MZK
see also Winn under literature
GEBAUER, MICHAEL
Scales for violin, and 12 methodic lessons
in the form of easy duos, Op. 10
see 2 vln
GEMINIANI, FRANCESCO (1687-1762)
Art of Violin Playing
(Boyden) Oxf 11.002   facsimile edition
GERLIER, F.
Études, 36
Gaudet
Études à la 1RE position dans les tons
majeurs et mineurs
Gaudet
Exercices de Perfectionnement, 100
Gaudet
Exercices de Perfectionnement, 50, sur
les 7 positions
Gaudet
Traité des Doubles-Cordes
Gaudet   2V
GINGOLD, JOSEF
Orchestral Excerpts from Classical and
Modern Works
Int   3V
GIRONI
Metodo pratico-elementare
Ric ER1220
GORDON, CARL
How to Play the Violin
Gord   2V
GRAHAM, JASPER
Very First Lessons on the Violin, Op. 11
BMC   pno accomp
JWL (Mil No. W1296)   pno accomp
GRIGORIAN, A.
Beginner's School
MZK
GRISSEN, CARL
Learn with Tunes
Willis   3V
GRUENBERG, EUGENE (1854-1928)
Elementary Violin Lessons
BMC
GRUENWALD, ADOLF
First exercises
(Svecenski) GS L1390
GRÜMMER, M.
Harmonisch neue tägliche Übungen
BB
GUHR, C.
Paganinis Kunst die Violine zu spielen
SCH

HAESCH, GEORG
New Practical Violin Method
Sik 123a,b 2V
HAIT
Caprices de concert, 5
Billaudot
Etudes d'artiste, 30
Billaudot 5V
HALIR, CARL
New Scale Studies
(Winn) CF 0252
HÄREN, YNGVE, see Sundquist & Hären
HARVEY, ALBERT
Progressive Course
VL 9V
HAUCHARD, MAURICE
Archet et Style
Leduc
Étude méthodique de la double corde
Leduc 2V
Étude méthodique des positions
Leduc 4V
Exercices de mécanisme
Leduc 2V
Gammes et arpèges
Leduc 2V; French, English and
Spanish text
Méthode élémentaire
Leduc 2V
HAYDN, JOSEPH, see Orchestral Studies
HAYDOU, I.
Octave System
CL
HEIM
Gradus ad Parnassum
Aug 5471-80 10V
HEIMANN, MOGENS (1915-   )
Intonation
WH 3856
Modern Violin Studies
WH 3475
Positions
WH 3855
Thirds and fingered octaves
WH 3857 "Tertser og fingersaetnings-
oktaver"
HENLEY, WILLIAM
Modern Violin School, Op. 51
JWL (Mil Nos. W1812-21) 10V
Vol 1: Initiatory course
Vol 2: First and second positions
Vol 3: Ground work of bowing
Vol 4: Elementary and double stopping
Vol 5: Art of shifting
Vol 6: Tone production and phrasing
Vol 7: Rapidity of fingering
Vol 8: Bravura and double stopping
Vol 9: Art of bowing
Vol 10: Chords and part playing
HENNING, CARL & THEODOR
Practical Violin School, Op. 15
CF 0273; English and German text
Practical Violin School, Op. 15, Part I
CF 0270; English and German text
HENROTTE, PIERRE
Daily Scale Technique of a Violinist
Mil
HERFURTH, C. PAUL
Scale Book
BMC
Tune a Day
BMC 3V pno accomp

HERMANN, FRIEDRICH
Studies, 100, Op. 20
(Mittell) GS L952-3 2V
Pet 2031A,B 2V
Violin School
CF 03298, 03301 2V; English and
German text
GS L742-743 2V
see also 2 vln
HERMANN
Special Studies, Op. 24
Aug 5659-61 3V
HERMANN
Second violin part for use with the 42 etudes
of Kreutzer
Pet 284a
HERSEY, L.E.
Modern Method
CF 02917-18 2V
HINDEMITH, PAUL (1895-1963)
Studies for Violinists
SCH
HODGSON, PERCIVAL (1882-   )
New Violin Method for Beginners
BH 4V
Supplementary Pieces
BH 4V pno accomp; 2nd vln ad lib
HOFMANN, RICHARD (1844-1918)
Double-Stop Studies for the Violin, Op. 96
(Ries) BMC
First Studies, Op. 25
GS L863-865 3V
First Studies, Op. 25, Bk. I
CF L200; English and German text
Melodic Studies, 80, Op. 90
SCH 2V
Studies, 40, Op. 91
Aug 5667 2V
HOHMANN, C.H.
Practical Method
(Ambrosio) CF 0286-90 5V
(Bostelmann) GS; published in
1 or 5 volumes;
English and Spanish text
Cole M420-425 5V
HOHMANN-WOHLFAHRT METHOD, see
Whistler
HOLLMANN, H.
Grundausbildung im Geigenspiel
DOB 2V
HOLMES, MARKWOOD & WEBBER, RUSSELL
Above First Position
CF 03807
HOLMES, MARKWOOD, see Barbakoff &
Holmes
HOLST, IMOGEN (1907-   )
Canons for Violin Classes, 6
Oxf 23.116
HRIMALY, JOHANN (1844-1915)
Scale Studies
(Jacobsen) Pet 3879
(Pelaia) Ric BA11390
CF L114
GS L842
HUBER, see Bartosch & Huber
HUMMEL, HERMAN A., see Whistler &
Hummel
IPOLYI, ISTVÁN
Kurs i dubbelgreppspel för violinister
Nordiska
Violinetuder for hőjre hånd
WH 3967
Violinetyder för höger hand
Nordiska

JACOBSEN, MAXIM
Daily 40 Minutes
Hin (Pet No. H214)
Daily Studies for the Violinist, 25
ZM (Pet No. ZM276-7) 2V
Preparatory Exercises, 24, to
Mendelssohn Violin Concerto, Op. 64
Pet 7052
Preparatory Studies to Mozart Concerto
No. 5, K.219
Pet 7053
Preparatory Studies to Wieniawski
Concerto No. 2, Op. 22
Pet 7054
Quartet Studies. 42 difficult passages from
Haydn string quartets
Pet 7050
Short Technical Paraphrases on Kayser
Etudes, 100
ZM (Pet No. ZM7-8) 2V
Technical Analysis of Bach Solo Sonatas
and Partitas
Pet 7081A,B,C 3V
Technical Paraphrases on Kreutzer Etudes
ZM (Pet No. ZM9-14) 6V
Violin Gymnastics
Bosw
JARDANYI, see Sandor, Jardanyi &
Szervanszky
JEANNERET, A.
Quarts d'Heure, 20, de lecture à vue
Senart
JOACHIM, JOSEPH & MOSER, ANDREAS
Violin School
(Jacobsen) SIM 7V; English, German,
French text
Vol I, Part 1: Instruction for beginners
Vol I, Part 2: Exercises in first,
second and third positions
Vol II, Part 1: Studies for developing
technique of changing positions
Vol II, Part 2: Progressive exercises
Vol III, Parts 1,2,3: Studies in
interpretation
KAUFMAN
Warming Up Scales and Arpeggios
Pr
KAYSER, HEINRICH ERNST (1815-1888)
Etudes, 36, Op. 20. Elementary and
Progressive Studies
(Anzoletti) Ric ER1053-5 3V; Italian,
French, English and Spanish text
(Heim) Aug 8662
(Hendriks) Sik 181
(Jacobsen) SCH
(Jacobsen) UE 6160
(Sandor) Kul 3V; Hungarian and German
text
(Stross) Sik 210
(Svecenski) GS L750
B.F. Wood 211
CF L115-117 3V
CF L118
GS L306-308 3V
Pet 3560
Study of the positions, Op. 67
GS L867
see also Jacobsen
KELOEBER
Elementary Scale and Chord Studies
Ru
KENDALL, JOHN
Listen and Play, based on the teaching of
Shinichi Suzuki

Summy-Birchard 2V; pno accomp
Vol 3 in preparation
KINSEY, HERBERT
Elementary Progressive Studies
ABRS (Mil No. A206-8) 3V
Preliminary Studies
ABRS (Mil No. A205)
KINSEY & REED
Violin Sight Reading Pieces
ABRS (Mil No. A211-212) 2V
KLEIN, MARKUS
Studies, 20, for 4th and 5th positions
VL
KNIGHT, VINCENT
Favourite Rounds and Catches, for vln class
JWL (Mil No. W1378)
KOCH, HOWARD LEE
Fiddle Finger Forms
BMC
KOMAROVSKY, A.
Etudes
MZK
KORGUYEV, S.
Exercises in double notes
MZK
KOTEK, J.
Practical Studies, 6, Op. 8
BB
KREUTZER, RODOLPHE (1766-1831)
Etudes or Caprices, 42
(Artok) Aug 5671
(Capet) Senart 5010
(Davisson) Pet 4310
(Flesch) Hug (Pet Nos. A7-8) 2V
(Galamian) Int
(Hendriks) Sik 183
(Hermann) Pet 284
(Jacobsen) UE 277
(Kross) CF 03520
(Principe) Ric ER1450; Italian and
Spanish text
(Saenger) CF L120
(Singer) GS L230
(Wessely) Aug 5670
see also Hermann
Studi, 40
(Polo) ER2209
Studi, 19
(Abbado) Ric ER2482
see also Jacobsen
KROSS, EMIL
Art of Bowing, Op. 40
CF 0626; English and German text
Systematic Scale Studies for the Violin,
Op. 18, Pt. I
BMC
KÜCHLER, F.
Elementary Etudes, 100, Op. 6
Hug (Pet Nos. A10, 19, 20) 3V
Praktische Violinschule, Op. 2
Erdmann 8V
Scales, Changing Position, Triads, Op. 7
SIM
KUCZMARSKI, see Barnes & Kuczmarski
KULA, K.
Neue Lagen-Wechsel auf der Violine, Der
Hof
KÜNZEL
Orchestral Studies for Violin I from the
works of Wagner
BRH
KVELVE, RUDOLPH
Violin Method
VL

MERRILL (cont.)
Swing Method
Mil
MERZ, OTTO
First Steps of the Young Violinist
Willis
METZ, LOUIS
Method for Beginners
Broe (Pet No. B650, 653, 670) 3V
MICHL, ARTUR
Technische Studien, Op. 53
Krenn
MODERN ORCHESTRAL STUDIES, Vol 1
(Bus) SCH
Britten: Variations on a theme of
Frank Bridge
Britten: Gloriana, Symphonic Suite
Debussy: Iberia
Debussy: La Mer
Egk: Orchester-Sonate
Egk: Französische Suite nach Rameau
Egk: Allegria
Hindemith: Concerto for Orchestra
Hindemith: Konzertmusik für Streich-
orchester und Blechbläser
Honegger: Symphonie Liturgique
Honegger: Symphonie No. 5
Liebermann: Furioso
Malipiero: Sesta Sinfonia
Petrassi: Partita
Ravel: Daphnis et Chloe
Ravel: La Valse
Reutter: Lyrisches Konzert
Stephan: Musik für Orchester
Stephan: Musik für sieben saiten-
instrumente
Stravinsky: Der Feuervogel
Stravinsky: Petrouchka
Stravinsky: Le sacre du printemps
MOLLIER, P.
École Chantante du Violon
Gaudet 3V
École du Second Violon
Gaudet
Grande Méthode
Gaudet
Traité des Doubles-Cordes
Gaudet
MORGAN, M., see Radmall & Morgan
MOSER, A., see Joachim & Moser
MOSTRAS, K.
Scales, Exercises and Arpeggios in the
Second Position
MZK
see also 2 vln
MOZART, W.A., see Orchestral Studies
MÜLLER, T.
Scales and Chord Studies
OBV 4V; English, German, French
text
MUSIN, OVIDE, see Léonard & Musin
NADAUD, EDOUARD
Études de concert, 12
Billaudot 2V
Gammes pratiques
Billaudot
NASTRI, GENE & VERRAL, JOHN
Starting from scratch
Willis pno accomp
NERO, PAUL
Etudes, 7, for violin in the modern idiom
CF 03476
Fiddler's Handbook
CF 03383

NOWINSKI, WILLIAM
Violinist's Guide to Orchestral Playing
CF 04080
ONDERET, MAURICE
Method
Bosw 4V
ONDRICEK
Artist's Studies, 15
(Schmidtner) Pet 3513
ORCHESTRAL EXCERPTS FROM CLASSICAL
AND MODERN WORKS
(Gingold) Int 3V
ORCHESTRAL SCHOOL FOR VIOLINISTS
(Schmalnauer) SCH 4V
Vol 1: Symphonic Works
Vol 2: Operas
Vol 3: Wagner Operas
Vol 4: "The Ring", by Wagner
ORCHESTRAL STUDIES
(Prill) Pet 4189A,b 2V; from the
works of Richard Strauss
ORCHESTRAL STUDIES
Int; from the 10 Symphonic Poems by
Richard Strauss
ORCHESTRAL STUDIES FOR THE FIRST
VIOLIN
(Künzel) BRH; from the works of
Richard Wagner
ORCHESTRAL STUDIES FOR THE FIRST
VIOLIN
Int 2V; from the works of Richard
Wagner
ORCHESTRAL STUDIES FOR THE VIOLIN
(Schmidtner) Sik 300-3 4V
Vol 1: from works of Haydn
Vol 2: from works of Mozart
Vol 3: from works of Tchaikovsky
Vol 4: from modern works by Bartok,
Berg, Berger, Martin, Schönberg,
Stravinsky
ORCHESTRAL STUDIES, see also
Bus, Consolini, Nowinski, Tromp
ORFF, CARL (1895-   )
Geigen-übung
SCH 2V
Vol 1: Little pieces for solo vln
Vol 2: Little pieces for 2 vln
ORSZAGH, T.
Rhythmical and Technical Studies, 15, Op. 15
Kul; Hungarian, German and French text
Violin Tutor I
Kul
PABST, HARRY
Bowing Studies, Op. 11
VL
Scale Studies, Op. 14
VL
PAGANINI, NICCOLO
Caprices, Op. 1; 60 Etudes, Op. 14
see vln unacc
PALASCHKO
Etudes melodiques, 25, sur la quatrième
corde, Op. 78
Leduc; French, English and German text
PALMER, EDWINA & BEST, AGNES
Easy Studies in the Third Position
Oxf 23.810
PAPINI, GUIDO
Elementary Studies, 24, Op. 68
Bosw 2V; pno accomp
Violin School, Op. 57
Bosw 2V
PARENT, ARMAND (1863-1934)
Exercices pour le Violon
RL

PASCAL, L.
A. B. C. of the Violin
ESC   2V
PASQUIER, J.
Exercises, 7
SCH
PAULSON, JOSEPH
Studies in the Positions
Pro Art 30-31   2V
PEERY
Third Position Violin Book
Pr
Very First Violin Book
Pr
PERLMAN, GEORGE
Fun with a Fiddle
CF 03727
POILLEUX
Etudes, 20
Billaudot
POLO
Primi esercizi per l'avviamento allo
studio
Ric ER1256; Italian, French and
English text
Progressive Studies, 25
SZ
Studi, 30, a doppie corde
Ric ER192; Italian, French and
English text
Studi di tecnica
Ric ER2184
Tecnica fondamentale delle scale e
degli arpeggi in tutti i toni
Ric ER1074
POTTER
Rubank Elementary Method
Ru
Rubank Intermediate Method
Ru
PRILL
Orchestra Studies from the works of
R. Strauss
Pet 4189A,b   2V
PRIMROSE, WILLIAM (1903-   )
Technique is Memory
Oxf 29.004
PRUME
.Etudes de concert, see vln unacc
PUSCHEL, J.
Elementar Violinschule
Hof   10V
RABA-MOSER
Fundamentale Violintechnik
Hieber   2V
RADMALL, P. & MORGAN, M.
And Studies Too
Ches
RAMOS MEJIA
Dinámica del violinista. Con la teoria
del "doigté"
Ric BA9799
RAPPOLDI, A.
Dresdener Etüden, 10
SIM
RATEZ
Etudes, 12, Op. 41
HL   2V   2nd vln ad lib
REED, W.H., see Kinsey & Reed
RICCI, VITTORIO
Art of Phrasing
JWL (Mil No. W1823A,B)   2V
RIEGGER, WALLINGFORD (1885-1961)
Begin with pieces
GS

Easy exercises for beginners
GS
RIES, HUBERT (1802-1886)
Elementary studies, 30, Op. 28
GS L449
Etudes, 15, Op. 26
Bosw
RITTER
Scale and Chord Exercises
(Stoessel) BMC
RODE, PIERRE (1774-1830)
Caprices, 24
(Anzoletti-Polo) Ric ER1464; Italian,
French, English and German text
(Berkley) GS L231
(Capet) Senart 5003
(Davisson) Pet 281A
(Galamian) Int
(Kross) CF 04035; English and German
text
(Principe) Ric ER1451; Italian and
Spanish text
(Schmidtner) Sik 185
(Singer) CF L583
(Wessely) Aug 5678
Etudes, 12
(Lichtenberg) GS L1433
Pet 2211A   2nd vln ad lib
RODIONOV, see Garlitsky, Rodionov &
Fortunatov
ROHNER, TRAUGOTT & BARBAKOFF, SAM
Carl Fischer Basic Method for the Violin
CF 02928
ROSTAL, MAX (1905-   )
Study in Fifths
Nov
Study in Fourths
Nov
ROVELLI, PIETRO (1793-1838)
Caprices, 12, Op. 3 and 5
(Lichtenberg) GS L759
(Polo) Ric ER91; Italian, French and
English text
(Singer) CF L595
Pet 3233
SACHSE, W.
Problems in Tone and Technique
Paxton (Mil No. P540)
SAINT-LUBIN, LÉON DE (1805-1850)
Caprices, 6, Op. 42
Int
SAMIE
Études mignonnes, Op. 31
(Catherine) Leduc
Études progressives, Op. 32
(Catherine) Leduc
Études mélodiques, Op. 33
(Catherine) Leduc
SAMMONS
Secret of Technique in Violin Playing
BH
Studies for the Violin
Aug   pno accomp
SANDOR, F.
Finger Exercises
(Kigyosi) Kul   2V; Hungarian and
German text
SANDOR, JARDANYI & SZERVANSZKY
Violin Tutor
Kul   6V; Hungarian and German text
SAUZAY, EUGENE (1809-1901)
Deux modes, Les. 24 exercices
Billaudot
Études harmoniques, Op. 14
(Catherine) Billaudot

SCHEER, LEO
  Violin Method, Bk. I
    Bel EL171
SCHILL, OTTO K.
  Scale Studies
    CF AA12
SCHLODER, JOSEF
  Geigenspiel, Das
    Heiber 6V
SCHMALNAUER
  Orchestral School for Violinists
    SCH 4V; for contents see title
SCHMIDTNER, FRANZ
  Orchestral Studies for the Violin
    Sik 300-3 4V for contents see title
  Technique of Fingering
    Sik 176a,b 2V
SCHOENBERG, ARNOLD, see Orchestral
    Studies
SCHRADIECK, HENRY (1846-1918)
  Chord studies
    (Svecenski) GS L1397
  First Position
    GS
  Scale Studies
    (Saenger) CF L641
    GS L364
  School of Violin Technics
      Vol 1: Exercises for promoting
        dexterity in different positions
      Vol 2: Exercises in double stops
      Vol 3: Exercises in bowing
    CF L177-9 3V; English and Spanish
      text
    GS L515-7 3V
SCHUBERT, FRANCOIS (1808-1878)
  Studies, 9, Op. 3
    Aug 5680
SCHUBERT, LOUIS (1828-1884)
  Method, Op. 50
    GS L396-7 2V
SCHWARTZENSTEIN, SIGMUND
  Modern Studies for Mastering the
    Violin Technique, Bk. 2
    Paragon
  Modern Technique of Violin Bowing, Bk. 3
    Paragon
  Technical Problems for Violin, Bk. 1
    Paragon
SEIBER, MÁTYÁS, see 2 vln
SELLERS-WHITE, D.
  Miniature Studies, 18
    STB 2nd vln accomp
SEVCIK, OTAKAR (1852-1934)
  Little Sevcik
    Bosw
  School of Violin Technic, Op. 1
      Vol 1: Exercises in first position
      Vol 2: Exercises in second to
        seventh position
      Vol 3: Exercises for change of
        position
      Vol 4: Exercises in double stops
    (Mittell) GS L844-7 4V
    Bosw 4V
    CF L282-5 4V; English, German and
      French text
  School of Violin Technic, Op. 1,
    Vols. 1, 2, 3
    BRH; English, German, French, Russian,
      Italian, Czech text
  School of Violin Technic, Op. 1a
    (Jacobsen) Bosw 4V; abridged

School of Bowing Technic, Op. 2
    Bosw 6V
    BRH 6V; German, French, Russian,
      Italian, English, Czech text
    CF L291-2 2V; English, German and
      French text
  School of Bowing Technic, Op. 2a
    (Jacobsen) Bosw 3V; abridged
  School of Bowing Technic, Op. 2, Part I
    (Mittell) GS L1182-3 2V; English
      and Spanish text
  School for Beginners, Op. 6
    Bosw 7V "Violin Method for Beginners"
    BRH 7V "Violinschule für Anfänger"
  Studies
    Variations, 40, Op. 3
      Bosw
    Preparatory Trill Studies, Op. 7
      (Brett) BRH 2V; English, Italian,
        German, French, Russian, Czech text
      (Svecenski) GS 2V; French, English
        and Spanish text
      Bosw 2V
      CF L637-8 2V; English, German and
        French text
    Studies Preparatory to the Shake and
        Development in Double Stopping, Op. 7a
      (Jacobsen) Bosw; abridged
    Changes of Position and Preparatory Scale
        Studies, Op. 8
      Bosw
      BRH "Lagenwechsel-und Tonleiter-
        Vorstudien"
      CF L140; English, German and French
        text
      GS L848
    Changes of Position and Preparatory Scale
        Studies, Op. 8a
      (Jacobsen) Bosw; abridged
    Preparatory Studies in Double Stopping,
        Op. 9
      Bosw
      BRH "Doppelgriff-Vorstudien"
      (Saenger) CF L750; English, German and
        French text
      GS L849
    Preparatory Studies in Double Stopping,
        Op. 9a
      (Jacobsen) Bosw; abridged
    Scales and Arpeggios
      Bosw
SEYBOLD, ARTUR (1868-1948)
  Easiest Studies for the Earliest Violin
    Teaching
    SCH 2V
SHAPIRO, H.M.
  Etudes-Caprices, 10
    Omega
  Modern Studies, 8
    Omega
SHER, V.
  Virtuoso Etudes, 12
    MZK
SILVERSTEIN, see Baker-LaGassey-
    Silverstein
SINGER, EDMUND (1830-1912)
  Daily Studies for Developing Flexibility and
    Independence in Fingering
    (Hofmann) CF 03882
SITT, HANS (1850-1922)
  Daily Exercises, 50, Op. 98
    Pet 3122
  Scale Studies
    (Mittell) GS L1084
    CF L346; English and German text

SITT, HANS (cont.)
Scale Studies in Double Stops, Op. 41
CF 04036
Eul (Pet No. Z 185)
Studies, 100, Op. 32
Vol 1: 20 studies in first position
Vol 2: 20 studies in 2nd to 5th
positions
Vol 3: 20 studies, change of position
Vol 4: 20 studies in 6th, 7th positions
and position changes
Vol 5: 20 studies in double stops
(Bassermann) Eul (Pet Nos. Z121-5)   5V
(Saenger) CF L110-2, L906, 04031   5V
Studies, Op. 32, Bks. 1-3
GS L871-3   3V
Studies, 24, Op. 80, Bk. I
CF L403
Studies, 20, Op. 90
Aug 5682
Technical Studies, Op. 92, Bk. 1
CF 03371
see also 2 vln
SIVORI, CAMILLO (1815-1894)
Study-Caprices, 12, Op. 25
(Polo) SZ
(Poltronieri) Ric ER2640
SOKOLOVSKY
Etudes, see 2 vln
SPINDLER, FR.
Violinetüden aus 3 Jahrhunderten in
progressiver Ordnung
Hof   4V
SPOHR, LUDWIG (1784-1859)
Études, 6, tirées de ses quatuors, Bk. 2
(Nadaud) Billaudot
Exercises, 45, from Violin School
(Wessely) JWL (Mil No. W1827)
Violin Method
Pet 2500   2nd vln ad lib
STOELZING, LEWIS J.
Basic Vibrato Studies
Bel EL422
STRAUSS, RICHARD, see Orchestral Studies
STRAVINSKY, IGOR, see Orchestral Studies
SUNDQUIST, RUDOLF & HAREN, YNGVE
Fiolspelets ABC
Nordiska   2V
SUZUKI, SHINICHI, see Kendall, John
SZERVANSZKY, see Sandor, Jardanyi &
Servanszky
TAJIRIAN
Violinist's Companion
Hin (Pet No. H846)
TARTINI, GIUSEPPE (1692-1770)
Art of Bowing. 50 variations on a gavotte
by Corelli
(David-Winn) CF L398
(Lichtenberg) GS L922
Deiss
TAYLOR, FREDERICK A.
Daily Scale Practice for Young Violinists
BMC
TCHAIKOVSKY, PIOTR, see Orchestral Studies
TELCS, ADAM
Minimax
Nordiska
TEMPORAL
Exercices journaliers
(Catherine) Leduc   6V
TOURS, BERTHOLD (1838-1897)
Violin
(Di Butéra) GS L1457; English and Spanish
text
(Reed) Nov

TROMP, SAM
New Approach to Orchestral Violin Playing
Broe (Pet No. B798)
TROTT, JOSEPHINE
Melodious double-stops
GS   2V
TWINN, SYDNEY
Violin Class. 3 Books of Tunes
JWL (Mil Nos. W1293-5)   3V
Violin Class Book of Scales and Arpeggios
JWL (Mil No. W1826)   pno accomp
TWINN
Study of Harmonics as an Aid to Technical
Mastery of the Violin
Hin (Pet No. H681)
UNIONE VIOLINISTICA ITALIANA
Tecnica del violino divisa in 5 parti.
Parte III.   Fasc. III: L'Arco
(De Guarnieri) Ric ER153
UNIVERSAL'S FUNDAMENTAL METHOD
Universal Musical Instrument Co.
VAN DEN BEEMT, H.
Scales and Arpeggios in the first 3 positions
H Elkan
VAN HOESEN, KARL D.
Violin Class Method
CF 02097, 02123, 02194   3V
VENUTI, JOE
Violin Rhythm
Big 3
VENZL, J.
School of the Positions, Op. 78
CF 03225
VERRAL, JOHN, see Nastri & Verral
VIARDOT, P.
Études Mélodiques et Progressives
RL   2V
VIEUXTEMPS, HENRI (1820-1881)
Concert Etudes, 6, Op. 16
(Arbós) Pet 2564
Int
Studies, 32, Op. 48
(Hubay) Kul   4V; Hungarian and
German text
VILLERS
Gammes
RL
VIOLINIST'S GUIDE TO ORCHESTRAL
PLAYING
(Nowinski) CF 04080
WAGNER, RICHARD, see Orchestral Studies
WEBBER, RUSSELL, see Holmes & Webber
WEINER, S.
Caprices, see vln unacc
WERY, N.
Exercices, 20
(Nadaud) Billaudot
Variations, 50, Op. 16
(Nadaud) Billaudot
WESSELY, [HANS]
Caprices d'artists, 7
Aug 5684
Practical Violin School
JWL (Mil No. W1822A,B,C,D)   4V
Scale Manual
Aug 5686
CF 02892
WHISTLER, HARVEY S.
Developing Double-Stops
Ru
Hohmann-Wohlfahrt Method
Ru   2V
Introducing the Positions
Ru   2V

WHISTLER, HARVEY S. (cont.)
Preparing for Kreutzer
Ru   2V
Scales in First Position
Ru
WHISTLER, HARVEY S. & HUMMEL,
HERMAN A.
First Etude Album
Ru
WHITE, GRACE
Studies, scales, and pieces in first position
GS
WIENIAWSKI, HENRI (1835-1880)
École Moderne, Op. 10. 10 Etudes-
Caprices
(Hendriks) Sik 188
(Polo) Ric ER1738; Italian, French and
English text
(Quesnot) Senart 5174
(Sitt) Pet 3368
Int
Etudes-Caprices, Op. 18, with 2nd vln part
in score
(Abbado) Ric ER2483
(Hubay) Kul   2V; Hungarian and German
text
(Lichtenberg) GS L1733
(Sitt) Int
(Sitt) Pet 3395
Etudes, 8
MZK
WILHELMJ & BROWN
Modern School for Violin
(Dressel) Nov   6V
WILSON, ELSIE S., see Lehman & Wilson
WOHLFAHRT, FRANZ
Easiest Beginning Elementary Method,
Op. 38
(Smith) GS L1404; English and Spanish text
CF L1061; English, German and French
text
Foundation Studies, from Op. 45, 54, 74
(Aiqouni) CF 02465-6   2V
Studies, 60, Op. 45
(Artok) Aug 7935a,b   2V
(Blay) GS L838-9   2V
(Sharp) CF L122-3   2V
(Sitt) Pet 3327
(Stross) UE 5969-70   2V
Studies, 40 Elementary, Op. 54
(Sitt) Pet 3328
(Sitt-Sharp) CF L553
GS L926
Studies, Op. 54, Bk. I
(Sitt-Sharp) CF L205
Studies, 50 Easy Melodic, Op. 74
(Artok) Aug 7937a,b   2V
(Sharp) CF L142-3   2V
GS L927-8   2V
Hohmann-Wohlfahrt, see Whistler
WOOF, ROWSBY
Elementary Studies, 50
ABRS (Mil No. A209)
Studies of Moderate Difficulty, 30
ABRS (Mil No. A210)
YANSHINOV, A. & N.
Etudes, 30
MZK
YOST, GAYLORD (1888-1958)
Bow and Finger Magic
VL
Exercises for Change of Position
VL

Key to the Mastery of Bowing
VL
Key to the Mastery of Double-Stopping
VL
Scale and Arpeggio Studies
VL
Studies in Finger Action and Position
Playing
VL
Studies in Pizzicato and Harmonics
VL
Violin Method
VL   3V
Yost System for Violin
BMC
YSAŸE, EUGÈNE (1858-1931)
Preludes, 10, Op. 35
SF (Pet No. SCH50)
Travail Journalier
(Szigeti) Cinedisc
ZACHARIAS, H.
Jazz-Violine, Die
SCH

Study Material: Viola

ALESSANDRI
Esercizi e letture ad uso dei candidati
all'esame di 8⁰ anno di violino
Ric ER1837
ANZOLETTI, MARCO
Studi, 12
Ric ER121
BERGER, MELVIN
Basic Viola Technique
Leeds
BLEIER, PAUL (1898-   )
Violaschule
Hieber
BLUMENSTENGEL, ALBRECHT
Studies, 24, Op. 33, orig for vln
(Wiemann) Int
BRAHMS, JOHANNES, see Orchestral Excerpts
BROWN, JAMES
Drills for Violin and Viola Players
STB
Polychordia String Tutor, Steps 1-12
STB   12V
BROWN, J. HULLAH
Bow-Craft Viola Tutor
JWL (Mil No. W1806)
BRUNI, ANTONIO BARTOLOMEO (1751-1821)
Method
(Consolini) Ric ER90; with 25 Studies;
Italian, French and English text
MZK "School for Viola"
SCH "Viola Schule"
Studies, 25
(Ambrosio) CF 03319
(Schulz) Int
CAMPAGNOLI, BARTOLOMMEO (1751-1827)
Caprices, 41, Op. 22
(Consolini) Ric ER114; Italian, French
and English text
(Kreuz) Aug 7651
(Lifschey) GS L1676
(Primrose) Int
Pet 2548
Caprices, 24, from Op. 22
(Schmidtner) Sik 317
CARSE, ADAM (1878-1958)
Viola School
Aug   5V

CASIMIR-NEY
Preludes, 24, in all keys
Ed M
CAVALLINI, EUGENIO
Guida per lo studio elementare e
progressivo
(Consolini) Ric ER122; Italian, French
and English text
COCCHIA, F.
Esercizi sulle doppie corde in prima
posizione
Curci
COOLEY, C.
Scales and Arpeggios
H Elkan
COPPERWHEAT
First-Year Viola Method
Paxton (Mil No. P572)
COURTE, ROBERT
Daily Technical Exercises
Uni Music Press
DANCLA, CHARLES (1817-1907)
School of Mechanism, Op. 74, orig for vln
(Vieland) Int
DONT, JAKOB (1815-1888)
Progressive exercises, 20, from Op. 38,
orig for vln
(Svecenski) GS L1493   with accomp for
2nd vla
Studies, Op. 35, orig for vln
(Spindler) Hof
Studies, Op. 37, orig for vln
(Spindler) Hof
DOUNIS, DEMETRIUS C. (1886-1954)
Specific Technical Exercises, Op. 23
CF B2605
FIORILLO, FEDERIGO (1755- ?)
Etüden-Capricen, 36, orig for vln
(Spindler) Hof
Selected Studies, 31, orig for vln
(Pagels) Int
FISCHER, BERNARD
Modern Viola Fundamentals
Willis
Selected Studies and Etudes
Bel EL487
Violin and Viola Calisthenics
Bel EL452
FLESCH, CARL (1873-1944)
Scale System, orig for vln
(Karman) CF 02921
FORBES, WATSON (1909-   )
Book of Daily Exercises
Oxf 22.005
Books of Scales and Arpeggios
Oxf 22.034; 22.812; 22.807   3V
Exercises for Viola Players, Vols 2-5
ABRS (Mil Nos. A302-5)   4V
FRANK, MARCO (1881-   )
Viola Etudes
OBV   3V
GARDNER, SAMUEL (1891-   )
Viola Method, Bk. 1
BMC
GAVINIES, PIERRE (1728-1800)
Matinées, 24, orig for vln
(Abbado) Ric ER2556
(Spitzner) Int "Studies"
GEBAUER, MICHEL JOSEPH
Méthode
HL
GIFFORD, ALEXANDER M.
Studies in the 1st, 2nd and 3rd positions, 12
Aug

GINOT, ETIENNE
New Method of Initiation to Viola
Jobert
GÖRING, LOUIS
Übungen, 6
Hof
HERFURTH, C. PAUL
Tune a Day
BMC   3V   pno accomp
HERMANN, FRIEDRICH
Concert Studies, 6, Op. 18
Int
Technical Studies, Op. 22
Int
HOFFMEISTER, FRANZ ANTON (1754-1812)
Etudes, 12
(Hermann) Int
(Schmidtner) Sik 329
Pet 1993
HOFMANN, RICHARD (1844-1918)
First Studies, Op. 86
Int
Pet 2732
Studies, 15, Op. 87
Int
IOTTI, RAOUL OSCAR
Practical Method, transcribed from
Method for vln by Laoureux
GS
KAYSER, HEINRICH ERNST (1815-1888)
Studies, Op. 20, orig for vln
(Lesinsky) CF 03824
(Vieland) Int
Studies, 36, Op. 43
Int
KINSEY, HERBERT
Easy Progressive Studies for Viola
ABRS (Mil No. A300-301)   2V
KREUTZER, RODOLPHE (1766-1831)
Studies, 42, orig for vln
(Blumenau) GS L1737
(Consolini) Ric ER117; Italian, French
and English text
(Pagels) Int
KREUZ, EMIL
Select Studies in progressive order
Aug   5V
LAFORGE, TH.
Gammes journalières et arpèges
Billaudot
LANGEY, OTTO (1851-1922)
Celebrated Tutor
CF 0735
LAOUREUX, NICOLAS
Method, see Iotti: Practical Method
LARSEN, HANS J.
Bratsch skole
WH
LAUBACH, ALFRED
Practical Viola School
Aug
LEWIS
Method
Cole A18
LIFSCHEY, SAMUEL
Daily Technical Studies
CF 03815
Double-stop studies
GS
Orchestral excerpts from the works of
Johannes Brahms
AMP
Scale and arpeggio studies
GS   2V

LUKACS, P.
Exercises in Change of Position
Kul; Hungarian, German and English
text
MACKAY, NEIL
Modern Viola Method
Oxf   in preparation
MARTINN, J.
Méthode d'Alto
(Laforge) Billaudot
MATZ, ARNOLD (1904-   )
Capricen, 25
Hof
Intonation Studies
BRH   5V
MAZAS, JACQUES-FÉRÉOL (1782-1849)
Études Spéciales, Op. 36, Bk. 1, orig
for vln
(Pagels) Int
Études Brillantes, Op. 36, Bk. 2, orig
for vln
(Pagels) Int
MICHELINI, BRUTO
Scuola della viola
Ric ER2466
MOLLIER
Nouvelle Méthode d'Alto
Gaudet   2V
MORAVEC, K.
Selected Studies
Artia   2V; Czech and German text
NAUMANN, GEORG
Volkstümliche Bratschenschule
Hof
ORCHESTRAL DIFFICULTIES FROM THE
WORKS OF TCHAIKOVSKY
(Strakhov) MZK
ORCHESTRAL EXCERPTS FROM CLASSICAL
AND MODERN WORKS
(Vieland) Int   3V
ORCHESTRAL EXCERPTS FROM THE WORKS
OF JOHANNES BRAHMS
(Lifschey) AMP
ORCHESTRAL STUDIES
(Steiner) Pet 4189C; from the works of
Richard Strauss
ORCHESTRAL STUDIES
Int; from the symphonic works of
Richard Strauss
ORCHESTRAL STUDIES
(Unkenstein) BRH; from the works of
Richard Wagner
ORCHESTRAL STUDIES
Int; from the works of Richard Wagner
ORCHESTRAL STUDIES, see also Vieux
ORSZAGH, TIVADAR
Viola Tutor
Kul; Hungarian and German text
PAGANINI, NICCOLÒ
Caprices, Op. 1, see vla unacc
PALASCHKO, JOHANNES
Concert Etudes, 10
MZK
Études mélodiques, 24, Op. 77
Leduc; French, English and German text
Studies, 20, Op. 36
Int
Studies, 12, Op. 62
Ric ER392
PASCAL, LÉON (1899-   )
Divertissements, 25
Heugel
Technique de l'Alto
ESC

POLO, ENRICO
Studi di tecnica, orig for vln
Ric ER2203
PRIMROSE, WILLIAM (1903-   )
Art and Practice of Scale Playing on the
Viola
Mil
Technique is Memory
Oxf 29.004
RODE, PIERRE (1774-1830)
Caprices, 24, orig for vln
(Blumenau) GS L1736
(Hoenisch) Pet 4861
(Pagels) Int
ROLLA, ALESSANDRO (1757-1841)
Esercizio ed Arpeggio
Ed M
ROVELLI, PIETRO (1793-1838)
Caprices, 12, Op. 3 and Op. 5, orig for vln
(Pagels) Int
SABATINI, RENZO
Metodo Practico per Viola
Carisch
SAUZAY, EUGÈNE (1809-1901)
Etudes harmoniques, orig for vln
(Laforge) Billaudot
SCHLOMING, HARRY
Studies, 24, Op. 15, Vol. I
SIM
SCHMIDTNER, FRANZ (1913-   )
Daily Studies
Sik 451
SCHRADIECK, HENRY (1846-1918)
School of Viola Technique, transcribed from
School of Violin Technique
(Pagels) Int   3V
Cranz   3V
School of Violin Technique, Bk. 1, tran-
scribed for vla
(Lifschey) GS L1750
SEVCIK, OTAKAR (1852-1934)
Changes of Position and Preparatory
Scale Studies, Op. 8, orig for vln
(Aronoff) EV
(Tertis) Bosw
School of Technic, Op. 1, orig for vln
(Tertis) Bosw   3V
School of Technic, Op. 1, Part 1.
Exercises in the first position
(Aronoff) EV
School of Bowing Technic, Op. 2, orig
for vln
(Tertis) Bosw   2V
Selected Studies in the first position, from
School of Violin Technics, Op. 1 and
School of Bowing Technics
(Lifschey) GS L1739)
SIMON
From Violin to Viola
Ed M
SITT, HANS (1850-1922)
Etudes, 15, Op. 116
Eul (Pet No. Z198)
Method
(Ambrosio) CF 0362
Int
Pet 2588   "Viola School"
SOPKIN, HENRY
Carl Fischer Basic Method
CF 02534
STEINER
Orchestra Studies, from the works of
Richard Strauss
Pet 4189C

STRAKHOV
Orchestral Difficulties from Tchaikovsky's
Works
MZK
STRAUSS, RICHARD, see Orchestral Studies
TCHAIKOVSKY, see Strakhov
TOURS, BERTHOLD (1838-1897)
Viola, The
(Shore) Nov
UNIVERSAL'S FUNDAMENTAL METHOD
Universal Musical Instrument Co.
UNKENSTEIN
Orchestral Studies, from the works of
Richard Wagner
BRH
VAKSMAN
Scales and Arpeggios
MZK
VIELAND, JOSEPH
Orchestral Excerpts from Classical and
Modern Works
Int 3V
VIEUX, MAURICE
Études, 20
Leduc
Études, 10, sur des traits d'orchestre
Leduc
Études, 10, sur les intervalles
Leduc
VOLMER, BERTA (1908-)
Bratschenschule
SCH 2V
Studies
SCH
WAGNER, RICHARD, see Orchestral Studies
WARD
Rubank Elementary Method
Ru
Rubank Intermediate Method
Ru
WESSELY, HANS
Practical Viola School
JWL (Mil No. W1824A,B) 2V
WHISTLER, HARVEY S.
Essential Exercises and Etudes
Ru
From Violin to Viola
Ru
Introducing the Positions
Ru 2V
WOHLFAHRT, FRANZ
Foundation Studies, orig for vln
(Isaac-Lewis) CF 02659-60 2V
Studies, 30, Op. 45, Vol 1, orig for vln
Int

Study Material: Cello

ALEXANIAN, DIRAN
Enseignement du Violoncelle, L'
Mathot; French and English text
ALVIN, JULIETTE
Cello Tutor for Beginners
Aug 2V
BACH, JOHANN SEBASTIAN
see Laenglin
BAST, H.
Scale and Arpeggio Manual
Aug 7768
BATTANCHON, [FÉLIX (1814-1893)]
Etudes, 3, Op. 1
Billaudot
Etudes, 24, Op. 4
Billaudot 2V

BAZELAIRE, PAUL (1886-1958)
Enseignement du Violoncelle en France, L'
Sal
Quelques notes sur différents points de la
Technique générale du Violoncelle
Senart
Scientific Instruction in the Violoncello
Dur translated by H. de Constant
Technique du violoncelle
Leduc 4V; French, English, Spanish and
Italian text
Vol 1: Gammes et arpèges
Vol 2: Exercice journalier
Vol 3: 10 études transcendantes
Vol 4: 12 études de vélocite
BECKER, HUGO (1863-1941)
Finger-und Bogen-Übungen
SCH; German and French text
Special Etüden, 6, Op. 13
WH 1999
BENEDETTI, U.
Exercices Techniques en Doubles Cordes
Delrieu
Traité Methodique Complet des Gammes
et Arpèges
Delrieu
BENOY & BURROWES
First-Year Violoncello Method
Paxton (Mil No. P581)
Second-Year Violoncello Method
Paxton (Mil No. P582)
BERKA, F.
Thumb Position Exercises
Artia
BLEIER, PAUL
Celloschule
Hieber
BOCCHERINI, LUIGI, see Ginsburg
BOCKMÜHL
Etudes
Billaudot 5V
BORISYAK, A.
School for Cello
MZK
BREVAL, see literature
BROCKWAY, WILLIAM
Oxford Cello Method
Oxf 21.024-25 2V
BROWN, HULLAH
Black Cat Violoncello Tutor
JWL (Mil No. W1807) pno accomp
BROWN, JAMES
Drills for Cello Players
STB
Polychordia String Tutor, Steps 1-12
STB 12V
BURROWES, see Benoy & Burrowes
CAMINITI
Tecnologia del violoncello
Ric ER1447
CASELLA, C.A.
Grandes Etudes, 6, see 2 vcl
COSSMAN, BERNHARD (1822-1910)
Cello Studies
SCH; English and French text
Concert Studies, Op. 10
Int
Studies for the development of agility
Int
CREPAX, G.
Passi difficili e "a solo" tolti da
importanti opere liriche e
sinfoniche italiane moderne
Ric ER2167

CUCCOLI
Divertimenti, 40
Carisch
Technique of the Bow
ZA61
DAVIDOV, [KARL (1838-1889)]
Violoncello School
MZK
Pet 2447 "Cello Method"; German text
Violoncello School Studies
(Berka) Artia; Czech and German text
DÉAK, STEPHEN (1897-   )
Modern Method for Violoncello
EV   2V
DEPAS
Méthode élémentaire
Leduc
DESWERT, see Swert, de
DOTZAUER, J.J. FRIEDRICH (1783-1860)
Method
(Klingenberg) CF 03674-5   2V
English, French and German text
(Klingenberg) Pet 5962A,b,C   3V
English, German and French text
Studies
Studies, 113, from Op. 47, 54, 120, 158,
160 and others
(Klingenberg) Int   4V
(Klingenberg) Pet 5956-59   4V
Exercises, 62
(Klingenberg-Girard) CF L455-6   2V
English, German and French text
Exercises
(Klingenberg) GS L1273-4   2V
Etudes, 60, from Op. 47, 54, 120, 158,
160 and others
(Schroeder) Pet 2531A,b   2V
Etudes, 12, Op. 54
Billaudot
Etudes, 12, Op. 70
Billaudot
Easy Studies, 12, Op. 107
(Gruetzmacher) Pet 2077   2nd vcl ad lib
Senart
Exercises, 18, Op. 120
(Hüllweck) BRH
(Schulz) GS L631
Senart
Méthode pour faire les sons harmoniques,
Op. 147
Billaudot
Hof "Violoncell-Flageolett-Schule"
Exercices, 6, Op. 148
Billaudot
Etudes, 6, Op. 168
Billaudot
Etudes, 7, Op. 175
Billaudot
Indépendance des doigts de la main
gauche, Op. 176
Billaudot
Etudes, 40
(Lee) Aug 7771
Daily Exercises, 24
(Brückner) Aug 7770
see also 2 vcl
DUPORT, JEAN-LOUIS (1749-1819)
Etudes, 21
(Crepax) Ric ER2619
(Gruetzmacher-Schulz) Pet 2508A
(Magrini) Ric ER52   2nd vcl ad lib
(Schulz) GS L637-638   2V
(Such) Aug 5543a
Senart

EARNSHAW, ALFRED H.
Elements of Cello Technique
JWL (Mil No. W3140)
EPPERSON, GORDON
Manual of Essential Cello Techniques
Fox
FEUILLARD, L.R.
Daily Exercises
SCH; English, German and French text
Études, 60, du Jeune Violoncelliste
Delrieu
Méthode du Jeune Violoncelliste
Delrieu
Technique du Violoncelle, La
Delrieu   8V
FIORILLO, FEDERIGO (1755- ?)
Studi, 36, orig for vln
(Mazzacurati) Ric ER2191
FITZENHAGEN, W., see Schulz: Technical
Studies
FORINO
Tecnica del violoncellista, La
Ric ER168-9   2V; Italian, French
and English text
FRANCESCONI, G.
Practical School for Violoncello
SZ   3V
FRANCHOMME, AUGUSTE-JOSEPH
(1808-1884)
Caprices, 12, Op. 7
(Becker) SCH   2nd vcl ad lib
(Klengel) Int
(Klengel) Pet 3469
Etudes, 12, Op. 35
(Becker) SCH; for 2 vcl
(Becker-Rose) Int
(Klengel) Pet 3470
FRANK, M.
Scales and Arpeggios
SCH; English, German and French text
FRISS, A.
Violoncello Tutor
Kul   2V; Hungarian, German and
English text
FUCHS, C.
Violoncello Method
SCH   3V
GINSBURG, L.
Bowing and Exercises to Boccherini's
Cello Sonata
MZK
see also Kozolupov & Ginsburg
GRUET
Ecole du mécanisme
Leduc; French, English and German text
GRÜMMER, PAUL (1879-   )
Daily Exercises for Advanced Cellists
SIM
Foundation of Classical and Virtuoso Cello
Technique. 40 studies after Wohlfahrt
UE 11229
Grundlage des Violoncellospiels, Die
BB
Harmonisch neue tägliche Übungen
BB
GRÜTZMACHER, FRIEDRICH (1832-1903)
Daily exercises, Op. 67
(Willecke) GS L954
Aug 7773
CF L273
Etudes, 12, Op. 72
Pet 2837A,b   2V   2nd vcl ad lib
Orchestral Studies. Excerpts from the
symphonic repertoire
BRH   2V

GRÜTZMACHER, FRIEDRICH (cont.)
Technology of Cello Playing, Op. 38.
  24 Studies
    (Klengel) Int 2V
    (Klengel) Pet 1417A,b 2V
    (Pais) Ric ER2530-31 2V; "24 Studi"
Technology of the Art of Playing the
    Violoncello, Op. 38, Bk. 1
    (Girard) CF 03433
GUERRERA
Method
  Cole A6
GUERRINI
Studi, 13
  (Silva) FC 1518
HAVIVI, MOSA
Caprices, 7
  CF B2429
HERFURTH, C. PAUL
Tune a Day
  BMC 2V pno accomp
HIRZEL, SUSANNE
Violoncello-Schule
  Baer 3741-4 4V
KABALEVSKY, D.
Major and Minor Etudes
  Leeds
KIESLING
Orchestral Studies, from the works of
    Richard Wagner
  BRH
KLENGEL, JULIUS (1859-1933)
Daily Exercises
  BRH 3V
Technical Studies
  (Rose) Int 2V
  BRH 4V
KLINGENBERG, see Dotzauer
KOZOLUPOV & GINSBURG
Collected Etudes
  MZK
KRANE
Method for Cello
  Jack Spratt
New School of Cello Studies
  Jack Spratt 2V
KREUTZER, RODOLPHE (1766-1831)
Studies, 42, orig for vln
  (Mazzacurati) Ric ER2136
  (Silva) ZA 3175-77 3V
Studies, 22 Selected
  (Dehn-Hüllweck) Int
KUMMER, FRIEDRICH AUGUST (1797-1879)
Grand Studies, 8, Op. 44
  (Brückner) Aug 5545 2nd vcl part
  Billaudot
Melodious Studies, 10, Op. 57
  (Pais) Ric ER2635
  (Stutschewsky) Pet 2248A
Method, Op. 60
  (Schulz) GS L1169
  Pet 3247 2nd vcl ad lib; German text
see also 2 vcl
KVARDA
Orchestra Studies, from works of R. Strauss
  Pet 4189D,E 2V
LAENGLIN
Studies for Violoncello. 12 solo passages
    from cantatas and orchestra works
  Pet 4808
LANGEY, OTTO (1851-1922)
Tutor
  CF 0736

LEBELL, LUDWIG
Studies and Exercises, 42
  JWL (Mil No. W1532, 1532a) 2V
Technique of the Lower Positions, Op. 22,
    Vol. I
  SCH
LEE, SEBASTIAN (1805-1887)
Method, Op. 30
  (Becker) SCH "Violoncello-Schule";
    German and French text
  CF 0335; includes Studies, Op. 31, Bk. 1
Studies
  Melodic Studies, 40, Op. 31
    (Becker-Rose) Int 2V
    (Krane) Jack Spratt
    (Schulz) L639-640 2V
    SCH 2V
  Melodic Studies, Op. 31, Bk. 1
    (Becker) CF L477
  Études de perfectionnement, 12, Op. 57
    Billaudot
  Easy Studies, 40, Op. 70
    (Becker) SCH
  First Steps, Op. 101
    Aug 5546 2nd vcl ad lib
  Melodic Studies, 12, Op. 113
    SCH
  Progressive Melodic Studies, 24
    Op. 131, see 2 vcl
  Daily Exercises, 40
    Aug 7775
see also 2 vcl
LEFEVRE
Études, 12, pour l'exercice, Op. 2
  Billaudot 2V
LIEGEOIS, C.
Art de se délier les doigts, L'
  HL
Étude complète du violoncelle
  HL 3V
Premiers Pas du Violoncelliste, Les
  HL
LOEB
Gammes et arpèges
  Billaudot
MAINARDI, ENRICO (1897-   )
Studi Trascendentali, 6
  SZ
Studies, 7; 2 Caprices and March
  SCH
Violoncello 1923-1953. Studies
  SCH
MALKIN, JOSEPH (1879-   )
Etudes, 24 Progressive
  CF AA23
Etudes, 10
  WH 1388
Fundamental Method
  CF 0356; English and German text
MARCELLI, NINO
Carl Fischer Basic Method
  CF 02644, 2755 2V
MARDEROVSKY, L.
Scales and Arpeggios
  MZK
Selected Etudes, 32
  MZK
MAZZACURATI, BENEDETTO
Scales and Arpeggios
  Carisch
MERK, JOSEPH (1795-1852)
Studies, 20, Op. 11
  (Klengel) Int
  (Pais) Ric ER2636

MERK, JOSEPH (cont.)
  Studies, 20, Op. 11 (cont.)
    (Schulz) GS L641
    (Stutschewsky) Pet 3288A
MOJA, L.
  Capricci Melodici, Op. 22
    (Crepax) SZ
  Exercises, 12, Op. 2
    (Francesconi) SZ
  Studies, 6, Op. 24
    (Buranello) SZ
OFFENBACH, J.
  Etudes, 12, Op. 78
    Billaudot   2V
  Petites Etudes, 20
    Billaudot
O'KELLY, H.
  Polyorgane. 160 Pièces pour les
    clés de fa
    Senart
ORCHESTRAL EXCERPTS FROM CLASSICAL
    AND MODERN WORKS
    (Rose) Int   3V
ORCHESTRAL STUDIES
    (Schulz) BMC   2V
    Vol 1: passages from works of
      Bach, Beethoven, Handel, Haydn,
      Mendelssohn, Mozart, Schubert
    Vol 2: passages from works of
      Auber, Berlioz, Cherubini, Dvorak,
      Gade, Goldmark, Liszt, Meyerbeer,
      Nicolai, Raff, Rossini, Schumann,
      Smetana, Thomas, Volkmann, Weber
ORCHESTRAL STUDIES. EXCERPTS FROM
    THE SYMPHONIC REPERTOIRE
    (Grützmacher) BRH   2V
ORCHESTRAL STUDIES
    (Kvarda) Pet 4189D,E   2V; from the
    works of Richard Strauss
ORCHESTRAL STUDIES
    Int   2V; from the works of Richard
    Strauss
ORCHESTRAL STUDIES
    (Kiesling) BRH; from the works of
    Richard Wagner
ORCHESTRAL STUDIES
    Int; from the works of Richard Wagner
ORCHESTRAL STUDIES, see also
    Crepax, Laenglin, Sharpe
OTIS, EDITH
  First book of study-pieces
    GS   pno accomp
PAGANINI, see vcl unacc
PAIS
  Studi, 20
    Ric ER2258
  Tecnica del violoncello, La
    Ric ER2148
PERSFELT, BROR
  Cellospelets ABC
    Nordiska   2V
PHILLIPS
  Exercises for Cellists
    ABRS (Mil Nos. A802-6)   5V
PIATTI, ALFREDO (1822-1901)
  Caprices, 12, Op. 25
    (Schroeder) CF 03944
    (Silva) Ric ER2014; Italian, English
      and German text
    (Stutschewsky) Pet 4260
    (Whitehouse) SIM
  Method
    (Whitehouse & Tabb) Aug 7774a,b,c   3V

POPEJOY, E. KEITH
  Melodious Studies
    Bel EL575, 575A   2V
POPPER, DAVID (1843-1913)
  High School of Cello Playing, Op. 73
    Int
  Studies, 25 Selected, from Op. 73
    MZK
  Studies, Op. 76. Preparatory for the High
    School of Cello Playing
    Int
  Studies, 15 Easy, Op. 76
    Int
POTTER, LOUIS, see literature
PREHN, HOLGER
  Violoncel-skole
    WH 2000
RABAUD
  Méthode complète, Op. 12
    Leduc
RAYNAL, A.
  Violoncelle, Le. Technique supérieurs
    des Arpèges
    Senart
ROMBERG, [BERNHARD (1767-1841)]
  Studies
    Hof   2V
ROSE, LEONARD
  Orchestral Excerpts from Classical and
    Modern Works
    Int   3V
SAKOM, J.
  School of Violoncello Etudes
    SIM   3V; English, German and French
    text
SALDARELLI, ANTONIO
  Scale e arpeggi
    Santis 627
SAPOZHNIKOV, R.
  School for Cello
    MZK
  Selected Studies, 53
    MZK
SCHRÖDER, ALWIN (1855-1928)
  Foundation Studies, 107
    CF 02469-71   3V
  Technical Exercises, 219
    LEU; English and German text
SCHRÖDER, KARL (1848-1935)
  First Exercises, 30, Op. 31
    Pet 1994
  Method
    (Ambrosio) CF 03315, 3483-4   3V;
      English and German text
  Short Studies, 12, without thumb positions,
    Op. 67
    Aug 7779
  Studies, 12, of medium difficulty, Op. 76
    Aug 7781
SCHULZ, LEO (1865-1944)
  Orchestral Studies
    BMC   2V   for contents see title
  Technical Studies; with 26 studies by
    W. Fitzenhagen
    GS
SCHULZ, W.
  Technical Studies for the Advanced Cellist
    SCH
  Violoncell-Schule
    Hof
SCHWAMBERGER, K.M.
  Etudes
    OBV   2V
  Tonleiter-Dreiklänge. Studies
    OBV

SELMI
  Nuovi esercizi giornalieri
    Ric ER2620
SERVAIS, ADRIEN-FRANCOIS (1807-1866)
  Caprices, 6, Op. 11
    (Becker) Int
    (Becker) SCH   2nd vcl ad lib
    (Silva) ZA3230
SEVCIK, OTAKAR (1852-1934)
  Changes of Position and Preparatory
      Scale Studies, Op. 8, orig for vln
    (Boyd) Bosw
    (Cole) EV
  School of Bowing Technic, Op. 2, orig
      for vln
    (Feuillard) Bosw   6V
  Thumb Placing Exercises, Op. 1, Part 1
    (Schulz) Bosw
  Variations, 40, Op. 3, orig for vln
    (Feuillard) Bosw; pno accomp
SHARPE, C.
  Book for the Principal Cellist. Solo
      passages from orchestral works
    Nov
SHULMAN, ALAN (1915-   )
  Duos, 5, for student and teacher
    Weintraub
SILVY, J.
  Pour Se Mettre en Doigts
    Delrieu
SOMLO, K.
  Studies
    Kul
SQUIRE, WILLIAM HENRY (1871-   )
  Easy Exercises, 12, Op. 18
    Aug 7780
STEWART, OLGA KRAUS
  Pathway for Young 'Cellists
    GS
STRAUSS, RICHARD, see Orchestral Studies
STUTSCHEVSKY, JOACHIM (1891-   )
  Art of Playing the Violoncello
    SCH   5V; German and English text
  New Collection of Studies
    SCH   4V
SUCH, [PERCY (1878-   )]
  New School of Studies
    Aug 7761a,b,c,d   4V
  Studies for the Left Hand
    SCH
SWERT, [JULES DE (1843-1891)]
  Violoncello, The
    (Sharpe) Nov
TABB, R.V.
  Position Studies, Op. 5 and 6
    Aug   2V
  Practical Studies, 10
    Aug
  see also Whitehouse & Tabb
TARTINI, GIUSEPPE (1692-1770)
  Variations, 50, sur un Thème de Corelli,
      orig for vln
    (Bazelaire) Senart
TICCIATI, NISO (1924-   )
  Studies in Style and Technique
    Oxf   3V   pno accomp
TREW, ARTHUR
  Primary Pieces for Cello Classes, Book 1
    Oxf 21.001   pno accomp
UNIVERSAL'S FUNDAMENTAL METHOD
  Universal Musical Instrument Co.
VAN DE VYVÈRE
  Études mélodiques 4, en forme de suite
    Leduc

Exercices et études, 64
  Leduc; French, English, German and
      Spanish text
VIOLONCELLO SIGHT READING PIECES
  ABRS (Mil Nos. A800-801)   2V
WAGNER, RICHARD, see Orchestral Studies
WARD
  Rubank Elementary Method
    Ru
  Rubank Intermediate Method
    Ru
WEILLER, E.
  Études de virtuosité, 12
    HL
WERNER, JOSEF (1837-1922)
  Practical Method, Op. 12 and Art of
      Bowing, Op. 43
    CF 0569
  Practical Method, Op. 12
    (Steiner) Sik 386
    CF 0567-8   2V; English, German and
        French text
  Studies, 40, Op. 46
    Aug 7764   2V
  Studies, 100 Easy, Op. 52
    Aug 7760   2V
WHISTLER, HARVEY S.
  Introducing the Positions
    Ru   2V
WHITEHOUSE, W.E. & TABB, R.V.
  Scale and Arpeggio Album
    SCH
WILLIE, G.
  Scale Studies
    SIM
YAMPOLSKY, M.
  Cello Technique
    MZK
ZELENKA, L.
  Leichte Etüden, 24
    (Schulz) Hof   2nd vcl ad lib
  Tägliche Übungen in der Daumenlage
    Hof
ZSAMBOKI, M.
  Arpeggio Studies
    Kul; Hungarian and German text

Study Material: Double-Bass

ABADIE, J.
  Méthode pour Contre-Basse à 3 et 4 cordes
    (Rousset) Gaudet
BENTZON, NIELS VIGGO (1919-   )
  Studie for kontrabas-solo
    WH 3424
BILLÈ, ISAIA
  Nuovo metodo per contrabbasso a 4 e
      5 corde
    Ric ER261-4, 303-5   7V; Italian, French
        and English text
  Piccoli studi melodici, 24, in tutti i toni
    Ric ER792
  Studi-capricci, 24
    Ric ER265; Italian, French and English
        text
  Studi caratteristici, 6
    Ric ER791
  Studi, 18, in tutti i toni per contrabbasso
      d'orchestra a 4 e 5 corde
    Ric ER266; Italian, French and English
        text
  Studies in different styles, 12
    EV

BLEIER, P.
  Einführung in das Kontrabass-Spiel
    SCH
BOTTESINI, GIOVANNI (1821-1889)
  Exercises, 24
    (Sterling) Aug 5696
  Méthode complète pour contrebasse à
    3 cordes
    HL   English text
  Metodo
    (Caimmi) Ric ER2479
BUTLER, H.J.
  Progressive Method
    CF 094-5   2V
CAIMMI
  Technica superiore del contrabbasso, La
    Ric ER415; Italian, French and English
    text
CRUFT, E.
  Excerpts from the orchestral repertoire
    Nov
CUNEO
  Esercizi e studi, 32, per lettura a prima
    vista, Op. 114
    Ric ER499; Italian, French, English and
    Spanish text
DRAGONETTI, DOMENICO (1763-1846)
  Studies, 5
    Carisch
DURIER, A.
  Méthode de Contre-Basse
    Ricard
FAHSBENDER
  String Bass Passages
    Bel EL231-2   2V
FINDEISEN, THEODORE A. (1881-1936)
  Technical Studies, 25
    Int   4V
FIORILLO, see Nanny
GAMBERINI, F.
  Scale e Arpeggi per contrabbasso a 4 e
    a 5 corde
    Curci
GASPARINI
  Gammes et arpèges pratiques
    Billaudot
GERTOVICH, I.
  Orchestral Difficulties from Operas by
    Russian Composers
    MZK
GOUFFE
  Etudes, 45
    Billaudot
GREGORA, F.
  Etüden
    Hof   pno accomp
GUERRERA
  Method
    Cole A8
GULLBRANDSSON, KNUT
  Grepptabell för kontrabas
    Nordiska
  Kontrabasskole
    Nordiska
HAGGART, BOB
  Bass Method
    Big 3
HAUSE, W.
  Etüden, 30, für tiefe Instrumente
    Hof
  Exercices progressifs, 90
    HL
  Méthode complète de contrebasse à 4 cordes
    HL

HEGNER, OSCAR
  Kontrabas-skole
    WH 3859
HERFURTH, C. PAUL
  Playing the String Bass
    BMC
  Tune a Day
    BMC   2V   pno accomp
HERMANN, H.
  Kontrabass-Spiel in unserer Zeit, Das
    Hof   2V
HRABÉ, JOSEPH
  Etudes, 86
    (Simandl) CF 02947-8   2V
    Int   2V
INGLESE, ANTONIO
  Skalenstudien fur Kontrabass
    ZA 1972
JACKSON
  4 Position System
    Cole SM26
JEDERBY, THORE
  Kontrabasskola
    WH
KAYSER, HEINRICH ERNST (1815-1888)
  Studies, 36, Op. 20, orig for vln
    (Malaric) DOB   2V
    (Winsel) Int
KHOMENKO, V.
  Etudes
    MZK
  New Fingering, Scales and Arpeggios
    Leeds
KMENT, J.
  Elementare Etüden
    Hof   2V
KREUTZER, RODOLPHE (1766-1831)
  Studies, 18[120]
    (Simandl-Zimmermann) Int
  see also Nanny
LANGEY, OTTO (1851-1922)
  Celebrated Tutor
    CF 0738
LÁSKA, GUSTAV (1847-1928)
  Kontrabass-Schule, Op. 50
    (Spitzbarth) BRH   2V
LEE, SEBASTIAN (1805-1887)
  Studies, Op. 31, orig for vcl
    (Zimmermann) Int
LOTTER, A.
  Practical Tutor. Hrabe's Method
    BH
MADENSKI, E.
  Double-Bass Studies
    UE 4992-3   2V
MADENSKY
  Orchestra Studies from the works of
    R. Strauss
    Pet 4189G
MALARIC, R.
  Grifftabelle in natürlicher Grosse
    DOB
MARCELLI, NINO (1890-   )
  Carl Fischer Basic Method
    CF 02576, 02646   2V
MAZAS
  Etüden, 12
    (Günther) Hof
MILUSHKIN, A.
  School
    MZK   2V; Russian text

---

[120] No doubt selected from studies for the violin.

MÖCHEL, K.B.
  Compendium for Double Bass Players
    SCH; English and German text
  Special Studies
    SCH   2V
MONTAG, L.
  Contrabass Tutor
    Kul   3V; Hungarian, German and
      English text
MONTANARI
  Studi, 14
    (Billè) Ric ER1407
NANNY
  Études caprices, 10
    Leduc
  Études de Kreutzer et de Fiorillo, précédées
    de 4 études préparatoires
    Leduc
  Études de virtuosité, 20
    Leduc
  Méthode
    Leduc   2V; French, English and German
      text
  Pièces, 24, en forme d'études sur des
    traits de symphonies
    Leduc
O'KELLY, H.
  Polyorgane. 160 Pièces pour les clés de fa
    Senart
ORCHESTRAL DIFFICULTIES FROM OPERAS
    BY RUSSIAN COMPOSERS
    (Gertovich) MZK
ORCHESTRAL EXCERPTS FROM CLASSICAL
    AND MODERN WORKS
    (Zimmermann) Int   3V
ORCHESTRAL PASSAGES FOR THE DOUBLE
    BASS
    BH
ORCHESTRAL STUDIES
    (Madensky) Pet 4189G; from the works of
      Richard Strauss
ORCHESTRAL STUDIES
    Int; from the works of Richard Strauss
ORCHESTRAL STUDIES
    Int; from the works of Richard Wagner
ORCHESTRAL STUDIES, VOL 2
    (Wolff-Siebach) BRH
ORCHESTRAL STUDIES, see also
    Cruft, Fahsbender, Nanny
RAKOV, L.
  Easy Etudes
    MZK
REINHOLD, O.
  Kontrabass-Studien
    Hof   pno accomp
SCHWABE, O.
  Scale Studies
    Int
SHMUKLOVSKY, DMITRY
  Scales, Triads and Exercises for the String
    Bass Beginner
    (Drew) CF 04401
SIMANDL, FRANZ (1840-1912)
  Etudes, 30
    CF 02941
  Etudes, 30, for the development of tone
    Int
  Gradus ad Parnassum. 24 studies
    (Zimmermann) Int   2V
  New Method
    CF 0492, 03567   2V; English and German
      text
    Int   2V

SLAMA, ANTON
  Studies in all keys, 66
    (Zimmermann) Int
    CF 0498
    Cranz
STARKE, A.
  Moderne technische Studien durch alle
    Tonarten
    Hof
STORCH-HRABE
  Studies, 57
    Int   2V
STRAUSS, RICHARD, see Orchestral Studies
STURM, WILHELM
  Studies, 110, Op. 20
    (Zimmermann) Int   2V
VANDE VELDE, L.
  Contest Studies and Scales and Arpeggios,
    Op. 24
    Metr
WAGNER, RICHARD, see Orchestral Studies
WARD
  Rubank Elementary Method
    Ru
WAUD
  Tutor
    Aug 5695
WEILLER, E
  Études de virtuosité, 12
    HL
  Études progressives, 6
    Billaudot
WHITE, A.C.
  Double Bass, The
    (Echlin) Nov
WITTER, C.
  Studien, 12
    Hof
WOLFF-SIEBACH
  Orchestral Studies, Vol. 2
    BRH
ZIMMERMAN, O.G.
  Elementary double-bass method
    GS
ZIMMERMANN, FREDERICK
  Orchestral Excerpts from Classical and
    Modern Works
    Int   3V

Study Material: Viols

CASADESUS, HENRI (1879-1947)
  Technique de la Viole d'Amour
    Sal
CORRAS, A.
  Méthode de Viole d'Amour
    Senart
DOLMETSCH, C.
  Supplement to 12 Lessons, for treble viol
    SCH
DOLMETSCH, N.
  12 Lessons on the Viola da Gamba
    SCH
  Supplement to 12 Lessons, for tenor viol
    SCH
MAJER, MARIANNE & WENZINGER, AUGUST
  Gambenfibel
    Baer 1666
MÖNKEMEYER, HELMUT
  Quintfidel, Die. Vols. 1, 2, 4
    Moeck 2045, 2046, 2048
      Vol 1: Spielanleitung für das Sopran-
        Alt-Instrument

MÖNKEMEYER, HELMUT (cont.)
Quintfidel, Die. Vols. 1, 2, 4 (cont.)
Moeck 2045, 2046, 2048 (cont.)
Vol 2: Spielanleitung für das Tenor-
Bass-Instrument
Vol 4: 10 Übungen für das Sopran-
Alt-Instrument
Schule für Soprangambe oder sechssaitige
Sopranfidel in Quart-Terz-Stimmung
Moeck 2042
Schule für Alt-Tenor-Gambe oder Fidel
Moeck 2043
Schule für Tenor-Bass-Gambe oder Fidel
Moeck 2044; German, English and
French text
MORLEY, THOMAS
First Book of Consort Lessons, see
literature
PLAYFORD, JOHN
Musick's Recreation on the Viol, see
literature
SHIRLEY
Study of the Viola d'Amore
Pet 6143   preface by Martens; English,
German and French text
STUMPF, K.
New School for Viola d'Amore
OBV; German, English, French text
WENZINGER, AUGUST (1905-   )
Gambenübung. Ein Lehrgang für chorisches
Gambenspiel
Baer 950, 1290   2V
see also Majer & Wenzinger
ZANOSKAR, H
Spiel auf der Altfidel, Das
SCH

String Class Methods

APPLEBAUM, SAMUEL
Building Technic with Beautiful Music
Bel   2V   pno accomp
Early Etudes for Strings
Bel   pno accomp
Scales for Strings
Bel   2V   pno accomp
String Builder
Bel   3V   pno accomp
BECKSTEAD, ROSS, see Gordon, Beckstead,
Stone
BENNETT, AILEEN, see Fischel & Bennett
BERGH, HARRIS
String Positions
Summy-Birchard
BORNOFF, GEORGE
Finger Patterns
Gordon V. Thompson
Patterns in Position
Gordon V. Thompson
CHEYETTE, IRVING & SALZMAN, EDWIN
Beginning String Musicianship
Bourne
Intermediate String Musicianship
Bourne
DASCH, GEORGE, see Jones, Dasch & Krone
DAWE, MARGERY
New Road to String Playing
Cramer   3V; for vln, vla, vcl; pno accomp
Travel Tunes, see vln, vla, vcl, pno
DILMORE, HERMON
Breeze-Easy Method for Strings
MPH   2V   pno accomp

FAY STRING METHOD
Paragon   pno accomp
FELDMAN, HARRY A.
Unison String Class Method
Pro Art 35-39
FISCHEL, MAX, & BENNETT, AILEEN
Gamble's Class Method for Strings
MPH   3V; English and Spanish text
GORDON, BECKSTEAD, STONE
Visual Method for Strings
Highland   pno accomp
GREEN, ELIZABETH
Hohmann for the String Class
CF 04137-41
HERFURTH, C. PAUL
Tune a Day
BMC   2V   pno accomp
HERMAN, HELEN
Bow and Strings
Bel   3V   pno accomp
HOHMANN, see Green, Elizabeth
HUMMEL, HERMAN A., see Whistler &
Hummel
ISAAC, MERLE
Method
Cole C30-39   2V   pno accomp
JOHNSON, HAROLD M.
Fillmore Beginning String Class
Fill   pno accomp
JONES, DASCH & KRONE
Strings from the Start, Part I
CF 02535-40
JONES, EDWIN
Strings from the Start, Part II
CF 03289-92
KELLER, MARJORIE & TAYLOR, MAURICE
Easy Steps to the Orchestra
Mil   2V   pno accomp
KLOTMAN, ROBERT
Action with Strings
Southern, Texas   pno accomp
KRONE, MAX T., see Jones, Dasch & Krone
MACKENZIE, CLEMEWELL
Play Right Away
Pro Art 261-65
MADDY, JOSEPH E.
Symphonic String Course
Kjos   pno accomp
MARTIN, PAULINE M.
Funway to Fiddletown
Seraphic Press   pno accomp
Runway to Fiddletown
Seraphic Press
MOEHLMANN, ROLAND & SKORNICKA,
JOSEPH
Boosey and Hawkes Instrumental Course
for Strings
BH   pno accomp
MÜLLER, J. FREDERICK
Etudes for Strings, 28
Bel
MÜLLER, J. FREDERICK & RUSCH,
HAROLD W.
String Method
Kjos   3V   pno accomp
NORD, ARTHUR C., see Whistler & Nord
PERKINS, NORMA L.
First Steps to Orchestra
Gord   pno accomp
PRESTON, HERBERT M.
Direct Approach to Higher Positions
Bel
REESE, WENDEL
Studies for Strings, 22
Bel

RUSCH, HAROLD W., see Müller & Rusch
SALZMAN, EDWIN, see Cheyette & Salzman
SKORNICKA, see Moelhmann & Skornicka
SMITH, JULIA, see Vashaw & Smith
STEPHENSON, LORAN D.
  Reading, Rhythm, and Rote
    Elementary Music Publ Co 2V
    pno accomp
TAYLOR, MAURICE D., see Keller & Taylor
TICCIATI, NISO
  Exercises, 10, for String Ensemble
    Oxf 29.003; vln, vla ad lib, vcl, pno
VASHAW, CECILE & SMITH, JULIA
  Work and Play String Method
    Pr pno accomp
WALLER, GILBERT
  String Class Method
    Kjos 2V
  Vibrato Method
    Kjos
WHISTLER, HARVEY S. & HUMMEL,
  HERMAN A.
  Elementary Scales and Bowings
    Ru pno accomp
  Intermediate Scales and Bowings
    Ru pno accomp
WHISTLER, HARVEY S. & NORD, ARTHUR C.
  Beginning Strings
    CF 02782-6 pno accomp
WIKSTROM, THOMAS
  Techniques for Strings
    CF 04325-30
WUNDERLICH, HELEN
  String Class Method
    Oxf in preparation
ZWISSLER, RUTH N.
  First Lessons for Beginning Strings
    Highland

Literature[121]

ALEXANIAN, DIRAN
  Enseignement du Violoncelle, L'
    Mathot; French and English text
APPLEBAUM, SADA & SAMUEL
  With the Artists
    Markert
AUER, LEOPOLD (1845-1930)
  Violin Playing as I Teach It
    Lippincott
BABITZ, SOL (1911-)
  Differences between 18th century and
    modern violin bowing
    ASTA
  Principles of extensions in violin playing
    Leeds
  Problem of rhythm in Baroque music; with
    Violin and its technique in the 18th
    century by Boyden
    ASTA
  Violin, Views and Reviews
    ASTA
BACH, JOHANN SEBASTIAN (1685-1750)
  Solo a Violino senza Basso accompagnato, 6
    Baer; Originalgetreuer Faksimile-
    Lichtdruck
  Sonatas, 6, for unacc vcl
    RH (Pet No. ER8) facsimile, in the hand-
    writing of Anna Magdalena Bach

  Sonatas and Partitas, 6, for unacc vln
    Pet facsimile
BACHMANN, WERNER
  Anfänge des Streichinstrumentenspiels
    BRH
BAZELAIRE, PAUL (1886-1958)
  Scientific instruction in the violoncello
    Dur; translated by H. de Constant
  see also vcl study material
BERKLEY, HAROLD
  Modern Technique of Violin Bowing
    GS
BOYDEN, DAVID
  Violin and its technique in the 18th century,
    see Babitz: Problem of rhythm in
    Baroque music
BREVAL
  Traité du Violoncelle
    Benoit
BYTOVETSKI, P.
  Technics for Violin
    Wehman
CHEEK, W.R.
  Treasure of Facts for the Violin
    Bel
COBBETT'S CYCLOPEDIC SURVEY OF
  CHAMBER MUSIC, 2nd edition
    Oxf 3V
COLLINS, GERTRUDE
  Violin Teaching in Class. Handbook for
    Teachers
    Oxf
COOK, CLIFFORD A.
  String teaching and some related topics
    ASTA
DOELL, W
  Müheloseste Geigenhaltung, Die
    Erdmann
DOLEJSI, ROBERT
  Modern Viola Technique
    ASTA
DONINGTON, ROBERT
  Interpretation of Early Music
    St Martin's Press
DUE, HENRIK
  What any violinist ought to know
    Musikk-Huset
EBERHARDT, SIEGFRIED (1883-)
  Absolute Treffsicherheit auf der Violine
    Oertel
  Lehre von der organischen Geigenhaltung
    Oertel
  Paganinis Geigenhaltung
    Oertel
  Violin Vibrato
    CF 0184
EISENBERG, MAURICE (1900-)
  Cello Playing of Today
    Strad
FLESCH, CARL (1873-1944)
  Alta scuola della diteggiatura violinistica
    Curci
  Art of Violin Playing
    CF 01317, 02046 2V
      Vol 1: Technique in General
      Vol 2: Artistic Realization and
      Instruction
  Problems of Tone Production in Violin
    Playing
    CF 02358
FRANK, ALAN, see Stratton & Frank
GALAMIAN, IVAN (1906-)
  Principles of Violin Playing and Teaching
    Prentice-Hall

---

[121] Not all of the listings in this section were obtained directly from the publishers. Other sources were used for information on books published by Columbia, Dover, Dufour, Lippincott, Markert and Wehman.

GEMINIANI, FRANCESCO (1687-1762)
Art of Violin Playing
(Boyden) Oxf 11.002; facsimile
GRUENBERG, EUGENE (1854-1928)
Violin Teaching and Violin Study
CF 0661
GRUPPE, PAULO M. (1891-   )
Reasonable and Practical Approach to the
Cello
ASTA
HAUCK, WERNER
Kleiner Katechismus für Geiger
Baer
HAVAS, KATO (1920-   )
New Approach to Violin Playing
Bosw
HEMANN, CHRISTINE
Intonation auf Streichinstrumenten
Baer
HERTER NORTON, M.D.
Art of String Quartet Playing
Simon & Schuster
HODGSON, PERCIVAL (1882-   )
Motion Study and Violin Bowing
ASTA
HUTTON, TRUMAN
Improving the School String Section
CF 04245
JAROSY, ALBERT
Nouvelle théorie du doigté (Paganini et
son secret)
ESC   French text
JOACHIM & MOSER
Violin School, see vln study material
KNOCKER, EDITHA
Violinist's Vade Mecum
Curwen
KOLNEDER, WALTER (1910-   )
Aufführungspraxis bei Vivaldi
BRH   German text
KROLICK, EDWARD
Basic Principles of Double Bass Playing.
String Instruction Program No. 8
MENC
KUHN, WOLFGANG
Principles of String Class Teaching
Bel
LELAND, VALBORG
Dounis Principles of Violin Playing
CF 03679
LÉNER, JENÖ (1894-1948)
Technique of String Quartet Playing
Ches; English, French and German text
LEVISTE, ROGER
Rational Technic of Vibrato
Bosw
LINDE, HANS-MARTIN
Kleine anleitung zum verzieren alter musik
SCH   German text
MANGEOT, ANDRE
Violin Technique
Dufour
MARLIAVE, JOSEPH DE
Beethoven's Quartets
Dover
MARTIN, PAULINE M.
Keyway Theory Book, for vln, vla, vcl, d-b
Seraphic Press
MASON, DANIEL GREGORY (1873-1953)
Chamber Music of Brahms
Pet
Quartets of Beethoven
Oxf

MATESKY, RALPH & RUSH, RALPH
Playing and Teaching Stringed Instruments
Prentice-Hall   2V
MORLEY, THOMAS (1557-c.1603)
First Book of Consort Lessons
(Beck) Pet 6100
MOZART, LEOPOLD (1719-1787)
Treatise on the Fundamental Principles
of Violin Playing
Oxf; translated by Knocker
PERNECKY, JACK
Basic Guide to Violin Playing
Cole
PLAYFORD, JOHN (1623-1686)
Musick's Recreation on the Viol, Lyra-Way
Hin (Pet No. H1682)   facsimile repro-
duction of 2nd edition of 1682
POTTER, LOUIS
Art of Cello Playing
Summy-Birchard
Basic Principles of Cello Playing. String
Instruction Program No. 9
MENC
RAY, JOHN M.
Elementary Theory and Harmony for the
Violinist
VL
ROLLAND, PAUL
Basic Principles of Violin Playing.
String Instruction Program No. 10
MENC
ROSENBERG, FRED
Violin. The technique of relaxation and
power
ASTA
RUSH, RALPH, see Matesky & Rush
SASS, A.L.
Secret of Acquiring a Beautiful Tone on
the Violin
Bel
Secrets of Violin Technic
Bel
SCHMITZ, HANS-PETER (1916-   )
Kunst der Verzierung im 18 Jahrhundert, Die
Baer
SHAPIRO, H.M.
Physical Approach to Violinistic Problems
Omega
SHIRLEY, PAUL
Right hand culture
CF 0687
SHIRLEY, [PAUL]
Study of the Viola d'Amore
Pet 6143; English, German, French text
SPIVAKOVSKY, TOSSY & YOST, GAYLORD
Spivakovsky Way of Bowing
VL
STOEVING, PAUL (1861-1948)
What Violinists Ought to Know
Bosw
STRATTON, GEORGE & FRANK, ALAN
Playing of Chamber Music
Dufour
STRING INSTRUCTION PROGRAM IN MUSIC
EDUCATION
MENC   Series of 10 reports by MENC
Committee on String Instruction in
the Schools
STUTSCHEVSKY, JOACHIM (1891-   )
Art of Playing the Violoncello
SCH   5V; German and English text

SZIGETI, JOSEPH (1892-   )
   Violinist's Notebook[122]
     Duckworth; English and German text
TARTINI, GIUSEPPE (1692-1770)
   Treatise on Ornaments in Music
     (Jacobi) Moeck; English, French,
     German, Italian text
TOVEY, DONALD FRANCIS (1875-1940)
   Essays in Musical Analysis; Chamber
     Music
     Oxf
TRZCINSKI, LOUIS C.
   Planning the School String Program
     Mil
ULRICH, HOMER (1906-   )
   Chamber Music
     Columbia

---

[122] In the U.S.A. this publication can be obtained through Boosey & Hawkes.

UNDERWOOD, REX
   Know your fingerboard. Violin fingerboard
     harmony work book
     ASTA
WADLER-WEBB
   Fun for Fiddlers. Theory papers
     BMC
WESSELY, H.
   Practical Guide to Violin Playing
     JWL (Mil No. W3137)
WINN, E.L.
   How to study Fiorillo
     CF 0702
   How to study Gavinies
     CF 0704
   Representative violin solos and how to
     play them
     CF 0705
YOST, GAYLORD (1888-1958)
   Basic Principles of Violin Playing
     VL

LIST OF PUBLISHERS

Agents marked with * do not have exclusive selling rights for all publications of the firm listed. This sign has been used for agents who have selling rights for part of a foreign catalogue, as well as for those who simply act as distributors. In most cases, the U.S. outlet has been listed at the suggestion of the foreign publisher concerned. No attempt has been made to include all of the importers who carry foreign music in stock.

		U.S. Agent
ABRS	Associated Board of the Royal Schools of Music	Mil
AL	G. Alsbach	Pet
	American Composers Alliance, see CFE	
AME	American Music Edition 258 East 7th Street New York 9, N.Y.	
AMP	Associated Music Publishers One West 47th Street New York 36, N.Y.	
Amphion	Editions Amphion	EV
Amsco	Amsco Music Publishing Company 240 West 55th Street New York 19, N.Y.	
Artia	Artia	BH
ASTA	American String Teachers Assoc. 1201 Sixteenth Street N.W. Washington, D.C.	
Aug	Augener, Ltd.	Galx
Avant	Avant Music 2859 Holt Avenue Los Angeles 34, California	
Baer	Bärenreiter-Verlag Heinrich-Schütz-Allee 29 35 Kassel-Wilhelmshöhe Germany	
Baron	M. Baron Company P.O. Box 149 Oyster Bay, N.Y.	
Barry	Barry & Cia.	BH
BB	Bote & Bock	AMP
Bel	Belwin, Inc. Rockville Centre, L.I., N.Y.	
Belaieff	M.P. Belaieff	BH
	Benjamin, see SIM	
Benoit	Benoit	FC
B.F. Wood	B.F. Wood Music Company, Inc.	Mil
BH	Boosey & Hawkes, Inc. Oceanside, N.Y.	
Big 3	Big 3 Music Corporation 1540 Broadway New York 36, N.Y.	

		U.S. Agent
Billaudot	Editions Billaudot, Editions Costallat, Editions Noel Paris, France	*Baron *CF *Southern, Texas
Birnbach	Richard Birnbach Dürerstrasse 28a 1 Berlin-Lichterfelde-West Germany	
BMC	Boston Music Company 116 Boylston Street Boston 16, Mass.	
BMI	Broadcast Music, Inc.	AMP
	BMI-Canada, see CL	
BMP	Bomart Music Publications	AMP
Bosw	Bosworth & Company, Ltd.	Bel
Bourne	Bourne Company 136 West 52nd Street New York 19, N.Y.	
BRH	Breitkopf & Härtel	AMP
Brodt	Brodt Music Company P.O. Box 1207 Charlotte, N.C.	
Broe	Broekmans & Van Poppel	Pet
Brogneaux	Editions Musicales Brogneaux	H Elkan
Broude	Broude Brothers 56 West 45th Street New York 36, N.Y.	
Brown	Robert B. Brown Music Company 1815 N. Kenmore Avenue Hollywood, California	
Bruck	Bruckner Verlag	Pet
Carisch	Carisch Milan, Italy	*Mil
CBDM	Belgian Centre of Music Documentation	H Elkan
CF	Carl Fischer, Inc. 56-62 Cooper Square New York 3, N.Y.	
CFE	Composers Facsimile Edition[1] American Composers Alliance 170 West 74th Street New York, N.Y. 10023	
CH	Choudens	Pet
Chant du Monde	Le Chant du Monde	Leeds
Chap	Chappell & Company, Inc. 609 Fifth Avenue New York 17, N.Y.	
Chap-L	Chappell & Company, Ltd. London, England	Chap
Ches	J. & W. Chester, Ltd. London, England	*Brodt *GS *MK
Cinedisc	Cinedisc Fondation Eugène Ysaÿe 39, rue de l'Escrime Brussels 19, Belgium	
CL	BMI-Canada, Ltd.	AMP

[1] Music printed to order.

U.S. Agent

Cole	M.M. Cole Publishing Company 823 S. Wabash Avenue Chicago, Illinois 60605	
	Colombo, Franco, see FC	
Columbia	Columbia University Press 2960 Broadway New York, N.Y.	
Conco	Concord Music Publishers	H Elkan
Concordia	Concordia Publishing House 3558 S. Jefferson Avenue St. Louis 18, Missouri	
Consolidated	Consolidated Music Publishers, Inc. 240 West 55th Street New York 19, N.Y.	
Consortium Musicale	Consortium Musicale	EV
Cor	Cor Publishing Company 67 Bell Place Massapequa, L.I., N.Y.	
	Costallat, see Billaudot	
CP	Composers Press, Inc.	Brown
Cramer	J.B. Cramer & Company, Ltd. London, England	*Brodt
Cranz	Editions A. Cranz	H Elkan
Curci	Edizioni Curci	Robbins
Curwen	J. Curwen & Sons, Ltd.	GS
Dansk	Samfundet til Udgivelse af dansk Musik Kronprinsessegade 26 Copenhagen K, Denmark	
Deiss	Deiss	FC
Delrieu	Georges Delrieu & Cie Nice, France	*Baron *EV
DeSylva, Brown, Henderson	DeSylva, Brown & Henderson, Inc.	Chap
DN	Donemus	Pet
DOB	Ludwig Doblinger Verlag	AMP
Dover	Dover Publications, Inc. 180 Varick Street New York, N.Y. 10014	
Duckworth	Gerald Duckworth & Co., Ltd. 3, Henrietta St., Covent Garden London, W.C.2, England	
Dufour	Dufour Editions Chester Springs, Pa.	
Dur	Durand & Cie	EV
Eastman	Eastman School of Music	CF
ECIC	Editorial Cooperativa Inter- americana de Compositores	SMP
E.C. Schirmer	E.C. Schirmer Music Company 600 Washington Street Boston 11, Mass.	
Ed M	Edition Musicus-N.Y., Inc. 333 West 52nd Street New York 19, N.Y.	
Editions Francaises	Editions Francaises de Musique 26, rue Beaujon Paris 8, France	

EDW	Edition Modern Musikverlag Hans Wewerka Franz-Josef-Strasse 2 Munich, Germany	
EKN	Elkin & Company, Ltd.	Galx
Elementary Music Co.	Elementary Music Publishing Co. P.O. Box 6325, Northwest Station Washington, D.C. 20015	
	Elkan, Henri, see H Elkan	
	Elkan-Vogel, see EV	
EMM	Ediciones Mexicanas de Musica	Peer
EN	Engstroem & Soedering	Pet
ENO	Enoch & Cie Paris, France	*AMP *Mil *SMP
EPS	Eulenburg Pocket Scores	Pet
Erdmann	Rudolf Erdmann Musikverlag Adolfsallee 34 Wiesbaden, Germany	
ESC	Editions Max Eschig	AMP
Eul	Edition Eulenburg	Pet
EV	Elkan-Vogel Company, Inc. 1712-16 Sansom Street Philadelphia 3, Pa.	
FC	Franco Colombo, Inc. 16 West 61st Street New York 23, N.Y.	
Fèret	Fèret	FC
Fill	Fillmore Music House	CF
	Fischer, Carl, see CF	
Fol	Charles Foley, Inc. 67 West 44th Street New York 36, N.Y.	
	Fondation Eugène Ysaÿe, see Cinedisc	
Fox	Sam Fox Publishing Company 1841 Broadway New York 23, N.Y.	
FR	Robert Forberg, Musikverlag	Pet
	Francaises, see Editions Francaises	
Francis Day & Hunter	Francis Day & Hunter, Ltd.	Robbins
Frangelo Press	Frangelo Press 4809 Regent Street Madison 1, Wisconsin	
G & C	G & C Music Corporation	Chap
Galx	Galaxy Music Corporation 2121 Broadway New York 23, N.Y.	
Gaudet	Gaudet	FC
Gehrmans	Carl Gehrmans Musikförlag Stockholm, Sweden	*BH *EV *Mil *SMP
Gerig	Musikverlag Hans Gerig Cologne, Germany	*Robbins
Gersh	Gershwin Publishing Corporation	Chap
Gilles	Gilles	FC

		U.S. Agent
Gord	Gordon Music Company 408 N. Rodeo Drive Beverly Hills, California	
Gordon V. Thompson	Gordon V. Thompson, Ltd.	Robbins
GR	H.L. Grahl, Taunus-Verlag	Pet
GS	G. Schirmer, Inc. 609 Fifth Avenue New York 17, N.Y.	
GT	Goodwin & Tabb, Ltd. London, England	*Mil *Pet
Haml	Hamelle & Cie	EV
Hans	Hansen Publications, Inc. 1842 West Avenue Miami Beach, Florida 33139	
	Hansen, Wilhelm, see WH	
	Harms, see T.B. Harms	
	Heinrichshofen's Verlag, see Noet	
H Elkan	Henri Elkan Music Publisher 1316 Walnut Street Philadelphia, Pa. 19107	
Henle	G. Henle Verlag Schongauer Strasse 24 Munich, Germany	
Heugel	Heugel & Cie	Pr
Heuwek	Edition Heuwekemeijer	*EV *Pet[2]
Hieber	Max Hieber Musikverlag Munich, Germany	*Pet
Highgate	Highgate Press	Galx
Highland	Highland Music Company 1311 N. Highland Avenue Hollywood 28, California	
Hin	Hinrichsen Edition, Ltd.	Pet
HL	Henry Lemoine & Cie	EV
Hof	Friedrich Hofmeister Frankfurt/Main, Germany	*Presto
Hug	Hug & Company	Pet
IMI	Israel Music Institute	BH
IMP	Israeli Music Publications	Leeds
Int	International Music Company 509 Fifth Avenue New York 17, N.Y.	
Interlochen Press	Interlochen Press National Music Camp Interlochen, Michigan	
Jack Spratt	Jack Spratt Music Company 77 West Broad Street Stamford, Conn.	
Jobert	Editions Jean Jobert	EV
John Fields	John Fields Music Co., Ltd.	Skidmore
JWL	Joseph Williams, Ltd.	Mil
Kal	Edwin F. Kalmus 1345 New York Avenue Huntington Station, L.I., N.Y.	

---

[2] Peters is agent for chamber music published by Heuwekemeijer.

		U.S. Agent
Kjos	Neil A. Kjos Music Company 525 Busse Park Ridge, Illinois	
KN	Kneusslin	Pet
Krenn	Musikverlag Ludwig Krenn Reindorfgasse 42 Vienna XV, Austria	
KS	Kistner & Siegel	Concordia[3]
Kuhl	Otto Kuhl Musikverlag	Mil
Kul	Kultura	BH
Lea	Lea Pocket Scores P.O. Box 138, Audubon Station New York, N.Y. 10032	Kal
Leduc	Alphonse Leduc & Cie Paris, France	*Baron *Brodt *MK
Leeds	Leeds Music Corporation 322 West 48th Street New York 36, N.Y.	
Leng	Alfred Lengnick & Co., Ltd.	Mil
LEU	F.E.C. Leuckart, Musikverlag	AMP
Liber-S	Liber-Southern, Ltd.	SMP
Lippincott	J.B. Lippincott Company East Washington Square Philadelphia, Pa.	
Lit	Collection Litolff	Pet
LN	Robert Lienau, Musikverlag	Pet
Lud	Ludwig Music Publishing Company 557-559 East 140th Street Cleveland 10, Ohio	
LY	Lyche	Pet
Magnamusic	Magnamusic Distributors, Inc. Sharon, Conn.	
Malcolm	Malcolm Music, Ltd.	Shawnee
Marcotte	Marcotte	FC
Markert	John Markert & Company 141 West 15th Street New York 11, N.Y.	
Mathot	Mathot	FC
MENC	Music Educators National Conference 1201 Sixteenth Street NW Washington, D.C. 20036	
Mercury	Mercury Music Corporation	Pr
Metr	Editions Metropolis	H Elkan
	Mexicanas, see EMM	
Mil	Mills Music, Inc. 1619 Broadway New York, N.Y.	
Mil-L	Mills Music, Ltd. London, England	Mil
MK	Edward B. Marks Music Corporation 136 West 52nd Street New York 19, N.Y.	
MM	McGinnis & Marx 408 Second Avenue New York 10, N.Y.	

---

[3] Concordia is agent for the organum series of Kistner & Siegel.

		U.S. Agent
Moeck	Hermann Moeck Verlag Celle, Germany	*E.C. Schirmer *Magnamusic
Mozart Allan	Mozart Allan	Mil
MPH	Music Publishers Holding Corporation 488 Madison Avenue New York 22, N.Y.	
MR	Musica Rara London, England	*Pr
MT	Mitteldeutscher Verlag	Pet
	Müller, Willy, see WM	
Musikk- Huset	Musikk-Huset A/S Karl Johansgt. 45 Oslo, Norway	
Mutual	Mutual Music Society, Inc.	Chap
MZK	Mezhdunarodnaya Kniga Music Publishers of the USSR	Leeds
NAG	Nagels Verlag	AMP
	Noel, see Billaudot	
Noet	Otto Heinrich Noetzel Heinrichshofen's Verlag	Pet
Nordiska	AB Nordiska Musikförlaget Fack 8 Stockholm Tull, Sweden	
Norsk	Norsk Musikforlag A/S Postboks 1499, Vika Oslo 1, Norway	
Nov	Novello & Company, Ltd. London, England	*Brodt *Mil
OBV	Oesterreichischer Bundesverlag	AMP
Oertel	Johannes Oertel Prinzregentenstrasse 64 Munich, Germany	
Omega	Omega Music Company 19 West 44th Street New York 36, N.Y.	
Oxf	Oxford University Press, Inc. 417 Fifth Avenue New York 16, N.Y.	
Pan American Union	Pan American Union	Peer
Paragon	Paragon Music Publishers 57 Third Avenue New York 3, N.Y.	
Paterson	Paterson's Publications, Ltd.	CF
Paxton	W. Paxton & Company, Ltd.	Mil
Peer	Peer International Corporation 1619 Broadway New York, N.Y. 10019	
Pet	C.F. Peters Corporation 373 Park Avenue South New York 16, N.Y.	
Pigott	Pigott & Company, Ltd.	Mil
Pr	Theodore Presser Company Presser Place Bryn Mawr, Pa.	
Prentice- Hall	Prentice-Hall, Inc. Englewood Cliffs, N.J.	

Presto	Presto Music Service Box 10704 Tampa, Florida	
Pro Art	Pro Art Publications, Inc. 469 Union Avenue Westbury, L.I., N.Y.	
Procure Gén- érale du Clergé	Procure Générale du Clergé	World Library of Sacred Music
	Rahter, see SIM	
RE	Ries & Erler, Musikverlag	Pet
RH	Reinhardt Verlag	Pet
Ric	G. Ricordi & Company	FC
Ricard	Ricard	FC
RL	Rouart-Lerolle et Cie	FC
Robbins	Robbins Music Corporation 1540 Broadway New York 36, N.Y.	
Rongwen	Rongwen Music, Inc.	Broude
Ru	Rubank, Inc. 5544 West Armstrong Avenue Chicago 46, Illinois	
Sal	Editions Salabert	FC
Santis	Edizioni de Santis	FC
	Schirmer, E.C., see E.C. Schirmer	
	Schirmer, G., see GS	
SCH	B. Schott's Söhne Schott & Company, Ltd.	AMP
	Schott Frères, see SF	
Schultheiss	C.L. Schultheiss Denzenbergstrasse 35 74 Tübingen, Germany	
Schwann	L. Schwann Musikverlag Düsseldorf, Germany	*World Library of Sacred Music
Senart	Maurice Senart	FC
Seraphic Press	Seraphic Press 1501 South Layton Blvd. Milwaukee 15, Wisconsin	
SF	Schott Frères	Pet
Shapiro, Bernstein	Shapiro, Bernstein & Co., Inc. 666 Fifth Avenue New York 19, N.Y.	
Shawnee	Shawnee Press, Inc. Delaware Water Gap, Pa.	
Sik	Hans Sikorski, Musikverlag	FC
SIM	N. Simrock, A. Benjamin, D. Rahter	AMP
Simon & Schuster	Simon & Schuster, Inc. 630 Fifth Avenue New York 20, N.Y.	
Sirius	Sirius-Verlag Berlin Wiclefstrasse 67 1 Berlin NW 21, Germany	
Skidmore	Skidmore Music Company, Inc. 666 Fifth Avenue New York 19, N.Y.	

		U.S. Agent
SMP	Southern Music Publishing Company 1619 Broadway New York, N.Y. 10019	
SON	Casa Musicale Sonzogno	AMP
Southern, Texas	Southern Music Company 1100 Broadway San Antonio 6, Texas	
SPAM	Society for the Publication of American Music, Inc.	Pr
St. Martin's Press	St. Martin's Press, Inc. 175 Fifth Avenue New York 10, N.Y.	
STB	Stainer & Bell, Ltd.	Galx
Steingräber	Steingräber Verlag Postfach 471 Wiesbaden, Germany	
Strad	The Strad 2, Duncan Terrace London, N.1, England	
Summy- Birchard	Summy-Birchard Publishing Co. 1834 Ridge Avenue Evanston, Illinois	
SZ	Edizioni Suvini Zerboni	AMP
	Taunus, see GR	
T.B. Harms	T.B. Harms Company	Chap
Templ	Templeton Publishing Co., Inc.	Shawnee
	Thompson, see Gordon V. Thompson	
Tonger	P.J. Tonger, Musikverlag Rodenkirchen/Rhein, Germany	*Pet
Tonos	Edition Tonos, Inc. c/o Mrs. J.E. Kambol 528 N. Douglas Street Bronson, Michigan	
Transat- lantiques	Editions Transatlantiques	Pr
Tritone	Tritone Press Box 158, Southern Station Hattiesburg, Miss.	
UE	Universal Edition	Pr
UME	Union Musical Espanola	AMP
Uni Music Press	University Music Press	Fox
Universal Musical In- strument Co.	Universal Musical Instrument Co. 732 Broadway New York 3, N.Y.	
Val	New Valley Music Press of Smith College Sage Hall 3 Northampton, Mass.	
Victor Young	Victor Young Publications, Inc.	Chap
VL	Volkwein Brothers, Inc. 632-34 Liberty Avenue Pittsburgh 22, Pa.	
VW	Chr. Friedrich Vieweg	Pet
Wagenaar	J.A.H. Wagenaar	H Elkan
Wehman	Wehman Brothers 156-158 Main Street Hackensack, N.J.	

		U.S. Agent
Weintraub	Weintraub Music Company 240 West 55th Street New York 19, N.Y.	
	Wewerka, Hans, see EDW	
WH	Wilhelm Hansen, Musik-Forlag	GS
	Williams, Joseph, see JWL	
Willis	Willis Music Company 440 Main Street Cincinnati, Ohio 45201	
WM	Willy Müller, Süddeutscher Musikverlag	Pet
	Wood, see B.F. Wood	

World Li-
  brary of
  Sacred
  Music
	World Library of Sacred Music
	1846 Westwood Avenue
	Cincinnati, Ohio	

Ybarra	Ybarra Music Box 665 Lemon Grove, California	

ZA	Zanibon Edition
	Padua, Italy
		*FC
		*Pet
		*World Library
		  of Sacred
		  Music

ZM	Wilhelm Zimmermann Musikverlag	Pet